THE OXFORD HANI

BANKING

Second Edition

Edited by

ALLEN N. BERGER

PHILIP MOLYNEUX

and

JOHN O. S. WILSON

OXFORD

UNIVERSITY PRESS

OXFORD

UNIVERSITY PRESS

Great Clarendon Street, Oxford, OX2 6DP,
United Kingdom

Oxford University Press is a department of the University of Oxford.
It furthers the University's objective of excellence in research, scholarship,
and education by publishing worldwide. Oxford is a registered trade mark of
Oxford University Press in the UK and in certain other countries

First Edition published in 2010
Second Edition published in 2015
First published in paperback 2017

Published in the United States of America by Oxford University Press
198 Madison Avenue, New York, NY 10016, United States of America

British Library Cataloguing in Publication Data
Data available

Library of Congress Cataloging in Publication Data
Data available

ISBN 978-0-19-968850-0 (Hbk.)
ISBN 978-0-19-880289-1 (Pbk.)

For Mindy (Allen N. Berger)
For Delyth, Alun, Gareth, Gethin, Catrin,
Lois, and Rhiannon (Philip Molyneux)
For Alison, Kathryn, Elizabeth, and Jean (John O. S. Wilson)

PREFACE TO THE PAPERBACK EDITION

The Oxford Handbook of Banking, Second Edition

Since the publication of the second edition of *The Oxford Handbook of Banking* in 2015, there are continued concerns regarding the stability and performance of the banking industry worldwide. At the same time, the pace at which new regulations are being implemented has slowed. In the US, for instance, only about 70% of the rules enshrined in the Dodd-Frank Wall Street Reform and Consumer Protection Act of 2010 have been implemented, and, as discussed below, the Trump Administration has promised to unwind part of it. Moreover, there is some evidence to suggest that the new legislation has done little to promote financial stability.[1] In Europe, the structural reforms proposed in the 2012 Liikanen Report were finalized by the ECOFIN Council in the summer of 2015 and are to be introduced in a phased manner. According to plan, a ban on proprietary trading will be in force, and by the start of 2018 national regulators will enforce the legal separation of high risk trading from core deposit-taking and lending (for 29 Global Systemically Important Banks). In the UK, the impending Brexit from the EU has raised uncertainty about the role of cross-border banking between Britain and the remaining EU members and the extent to which London will remain a dominant international banking center. A wide-ranging array of regulations relating to the new resolution regime covered in the Bank Recovery and Resolution Directive (BRRD) of 2015 have yet to be introduced fully in all 28 member states. There also remains discussion as to the way in which the new European deposit insurance arrangements as part of plans for a European Banking Union will be implemented. Banking sector problems throughout the region, and particularly in some of the more indebted states (such as Italy and Greece), continue to build. The implementation of Basel III continues, as major banks focus on increasing their risk-weighted capital-to-assets ratios. A number of proposals for change have emerged, dubbed by some commentators as 'Basel IV'. These proposals suggest revisions to the measurement and management of risk, restrictions on the use of banks' internal models to quantify risk, and more detailed disclosures of reserve positions.[2]

The new environment has compelled many banks, particularly those deemed systemically important, to reduce risks in order to meet more demanding capital and liquidity requirements, and pass stress tests undertaken by various regulatory agencies (such as the US Federal Reserve and the European Banking Authority). The trend has been for large

---

[1] Sarin, N and L. H. Summers, (2016) 'Have big banks gotten safer?' Brookings Papers on Economic Activity (BPEA) Conference Draft, September 15–16, 2016.

[2] The Economist (2016) 'Basel bust-up', 2 December.

banks to reduce exposure to higher risk (higher regulatory capital) areas of investment banking and securities trading toward lower risk-asset weighted areas such as retail banking and wealth management. Banks have also been forced to reduce their exposure to private equity and hedge funds, adversely affecting revenues. Compliance and restructuring costs have also increased. These pressures have led banks to reduce spending elsewhere.

Many of the aforementioned pressures are having a similar influence on banking business globally. The continued slowdown in growth, the low (and in some cases negative) interest rate environment, coupled with regulatory measures designed to improve safety and soundness, act as drags on bank performance. Low interest rates and relatively flat yield curves typically reduce bank margins as banks are reluctant to pass on very low rates onto their depositors and cannot earn significant net interest margins, reducing bank earnings and profits. Banks and regulators continue to grapple with the complexities of measuring and managing a host of risks. In particular there is significant interest in the measurement and management of credit, market, liquidity, systemic, and operational risks. Of particular recent interest has been the accounting treatment of credit risk indicators such as loan loss provisions and reserves, the fair valuation of financial instruments as well as issues related to the transparency of off-balance sheet activities. Bank financial reporting under International Financial Reporting Standards (IFRSs) has also changed. This includes the modification to IFRS 9 on valuing financial instruments and its alignment with new rules introduced under Basel III. There has also been a growing interest in using market indicators of credit risk (such as credit default swap spreads and credit ratings) as complements to accounting indicators (such as loan-loss provisioning).

An area of particular policy concern relates to the level of non-performing loans in some banking industries, and the (apparent) widespread forbearance by regulators and evergreening by banks. Italy and China stand out in this regard. By the middle of 2016, around 20% of Italian bank loans (70% of which are to SMEs) were non-performing and the banking system was teetering on collapse. The Bank of Italy has followed EU bank resolution rules (under BRRD), seeking capital injections via rights issues, the securitization and sale of bad (mainly SME) loans, and the use of bail-in bonds. However, banks have found it difficult to raise more capital, and attempts to make bank bonds bailinable have not been politically well-received. There are interesting parallels between Italy and China. Officially, non-performing loans in China stand at 1.75% of total loans. However, if so-called 'Special Mention Loans' that are overdue are included, estimates of non-performing loans increase to around 10% to 15% of total loans.

Other broad global trends are emerging. There has been no major industry consolidation. Some of the largest banks (such as Citi, RBS, HSBC, and Barclays) have reduced their international activities in order to focus on a smaller number of key markets. The major Swiss banks, UBS and Credit Suisse, have reduced their investment banking operations. Many banks in Europe and elsewhere are finding it difficult to generate returns greater than their cost of capital. These facts point to a possibility of significant restructuring and consolidation in the near future. Moreover, the nature of banking business is changing rapidly, as the so-called Fintech revolution forces banks to improve customer experience. In some cases, large and small banking organizations are joining with Fintech firms to maintain or increase market shares.

Uncertainty has heightened through 2016 with changes in the political order in the US and Europe with the success of anti-establishment candidates and parties in various national votes. In June, the UK voted to approve the Brexit referendum to leave the EU. This decision may shift the region's main financial centre, London, to Frankfurt or Paris, with implications for the UK and other banking systems. President Trump and his team have said that they will unwind Dodd-Frank and other onerous banking sector legislation, also adding to uncertainty. Prospects for banking business in other parts of the world also look volatile. All in all, it is an uncertain future world for banking.

Allen N. Berger,
Philip Molyneux
and John O. S. Wilson
January, 2017

Preface to the Hardback Edition

Since, the publication of the first edition of the *Oxford Handbook of Banking* in 2010, banking systems around the world have continued to be affected by the recent financial crisis which began in 2007. There have been wide-ranging regulatory reforms aimed at containing their risk-taking capabilities. Regulatory reform has been most marked in the US with the passing of the landmark Dodd–Frank Act of 2010, which aims to eliminate too-big-to-fail and the implicit taxpayer bailouts of major banks. The Act also seeks to reduce the risk-taking capacity of banks by limiting proprietary trading and other volatile business areas, embodied in the Volcker Rule. Similar major reforms are ongoing throughout the European Union following the Liikanen Report of 2012 and the Vickers Report of 2011, both of which aim to segregate or ring-fence banks' risky securities activities from less volatile retail banking operations. Coupled with this is the desire to bolster regulatory oversight as well as to force institutions to hold more capital and liquidity. The latter two are encapsulated by the Basel III reforms that national legislators are expected to put fully into place by 2019.

In addition to the turmoil associated with the recent financial crisis, Europe has also experienced a sovereign debt crisis, where weak banking systems and excessive government indebtedness have led to sovereign bailouts of Greece, Ireland, Spain, and Portugal (the so-called euro periphery countries). This has had implications for the credibility of the European single currency and policy conducted by the European Central Bank. It has also led to the recognition that bank and sovereign risks are inextricably linked.

The second edition is substantially updated and changed from the first edition, with at least 40% new material, reflecting the unprecedented changes that have occurred in global banking systems. This new edition provides the reader with a timely and comprehensive overview and analysis of many of these developments. The authors of the following 40 chapters comprise a collection of leading academics and policymakers in the field. These authors emanate from universities in North America, Europe, South America, and Asia; the US Federal Reserve System; the Office of the Comptroller of Currency; the Central Bank of Ireland, the European Central Bank; the World Bank; and the International Monetary Fund. The book strikes a balance among abstract theory, empirical research, practitioner analysis, and policy-related material. Chapters in the handbook have different emphases on these four ingredients. We hope that the contributions contained here set the stage for future research and policy debate for many years to come.

Allen N. Berger
Philip Molyneux
and John O. S. Wilson
October, 2014

Acknowledgments

First, and most important, we wish to thank the contributors to the handbook. We are delighted to have brought together such an outstanding set of research experts from academic and policy arenas across Europe, North America, South America, and Asia. These experts have shown a high level of commitment and perseverance to the project from beginning to end. Without their expertise, dedication, and efficiency in producing scholarly banking chapters, this handbook would never have been possible.

The production of this handbook has also relied heavily on the exceptional enthusiasm and commitment of Oxford University Press, most notably Adam Swallow, publisher for Economics and Finance, who was crucial in helping us kick-start the project. Oxford University Press delegates and a number of anonymous referees also played an important role in advising on the shape of the handbook. We would also like to especially thank and acknowledge the advice of Aimee Wright, who was always on hand to help and worked closely with us throughout the entire process. The team in New York also played a valuable role, and so we'd like to thank Michael De La Cruz and Lauren Konopko. The editors would particularly like to thank Elizabeth Stone, copy-editor, for doing an excellent job on the submitted manuscript. Carol Carnegie and Saipriya Kannan also played a crucial role toward the end of the project, and our proof reader, Denise Bannerman, provided invaluable service.

We would also like to acknowledge the support of our home institutions: the Moore School of Business at University of South Carolina, the Business School at Bangor University, and the Management School at University of St Andrews.

A number of individuals provided comments to us on the content and style on parts of the handbook, including Barbara Casu, Mark Flannery, Claudia Girardone, John Goddard, Dick Herring, Ed Kane, José Liñares-Zegarra, Donal McKillop, Joe Peek, and Larry White. A big thank you goes to them all.

Finally, we would like to thank our families and friends for their encouragement and patience over the last two years while we completed this handbook. Their support is much appreciated.

Contents

PART I THE THEORY OF BANKING

PART II BANK PERFORMANCE AND OPERATIONS

PART III REGULATORY AND POLICY PERSPECTIVES

PART IV MACROECONOMIC PERSPECTIVES

PART V BANKING SYSTEMS AROUND THE WORLD

LIST OF FIGURES

LIST OF TABLES

List of Abbreviations

ABCP	asset-backed commercial paper
ABS	asset-backed security
ACH	automated clearinghouse
AMA	advanced measurement approaches
AMLF	asset backed commercial paper money market mutual fund liquidity facility
AQR	Asset Quality Review
ARM	adjustable rate mortgage
ASF	available stable funding
ASRF	asymptotic-single-risk-factor
ATM	automated teller machine
AVC	asset-value correlation
BCBC	Basel Committttee on Banking Supervision
BHC	bank holding company
BIS	Bank for International Settlements
CAPM	Capital Asset Pricing Model
CB	central bank
CBC	commercial bank clearinghouse
CBOT	Chicago Board of Trade
CCF	credit conversion factor
CD	certificates of deposit
CDO	collateralized debt obligation
CDS	credit default swap
CEE	Central Eastern Europe
CFTC	Commodity Futures Trading Commission
CGR	credit guarantee corporations
CIPS	Clearinghouse Interbank Payments System
CLO	collateralized debt obligation
CLTV	combined loan-to-value
CME	Chicago Mercantile Exchange
CMO	collateralized mortgage obligation
CoVaR	Contagion Value at Risk
CP	commercial paper
CPFF	commercial paper funding facility
CRD IV	Fourth Capital Requirements Directive
CS	credit spread
CVA	credit valuation adjustments
EAD	exposure at default

EBA	European Banking Authority
ECB	European Central Bank
EL	expected loss
ELA	emergency liquidity assistance
EMH	efficient market hypothesis
ES	expected shortfall
EVT	extreme-value theory
FDIC	Federal Deposit Insurance Corporation
FDICIA	Federal Deposit Insurance Corporation Improvement Act
FHLMC	Federal Home Loan Mortgage Corporation (or Freddie Mac)
F-IRB	foundation internal ratings-based (approach)
FLS	Funding for Lending Scheme
FNMA	Federal National Mortgage Association (or Fannie Mae)
FSB	Financial Stability Board
FSLIC	Federal Savings and Loan Insurance Corporation
FSU	former Soviet Union
GLBA	Gramm–Leach–Bliley Act
GNMA	Government National Mortgage Association (also called Ginnie Mae)
G-SIBs	global systemically important banks
HELOC	home equity line of credit
HHI	Herfindahl–Hirschman indices
HQLA	high-quality liquid assets
IAIS	International Association of Insurance Supervisors
IASB	International Accounting Standards Board
IO	industrial organization
IOSCO	International Organization of Securities Commissions
IRB	internal-ratings-based (approach)
LCFI	large, complex financial institution
LCR	least cost resolution
LCR	liquidity coverage ratio
LGD	downturn loss-given-default
LIBOR	London Interbank Offered Rate
LMI	liquidity mismatch index
LTRO	long-term refinancing operations
M&A	mergers and acquisitions
MBS	mortgage-backed security
MERS	Mortgage Electronic Registration System
MES	marginal expected shortfall
MMF	money market fund
MMIFF	money market investment fund facility
MMMF	money market mutual fund
NCOF	net cash outflows
NEIO	new empirical industrial organization
NSFR	net stable funding ratio
OCC	Office of the Comptroller of the Currency
OLA	Orderly Liquidation Authority

OMO	open market operations
OTC	over-the-counter
OTD	originate-to-distribute
OTH	originate-to-hold
OTS	Office of Thrift Supervision
PCA	prompt corrective action
PD	probability of default
PDCF	Primary Dealer Credit Facility
RAROC	risk-adjusted return on capital
RBCR	risk-based capital ratio
RCTs	randomized controlled trials
REMICs	real estate mortgage investment conduits
RMBS	residential mortgage-backed security
ROA	return on assets
ROE	return on equity
RTGS	real-time gross settlement
RSF	required amount of stable funding
RWA	risk-weighted assets
SBCS	small business credit scoring
SCF	Survey of Consumer Finances
SCP	structure-conduct-performance
SEIR	structured early intervention and resolution
SES	systemic expected shortfall
SIB	systemically important bank
SIFI	systemically important financial institution
SIV	structured investment vehicle
SME	small and medium-size enterprises
SND	subordinated notes and/or bonds
SPV	special purpose vehicle
SSE	South Eastern Europe
SSM	Single Supervisory Mechanism
TAF	Term Auction Facility
TALF	Term Asset-Backed Securities Loan Facility
TARP	Troubled Asset Relief Program
TBTF	too-big-to-fail
TSLF	Term Securities Lending Facility
UL	unexpected loss
VaR	Value at Risk
VLTRO	very long term refinancing operations

LIST OF CONTRIBUTORS

Paola Morales Acevedo is a PhD student in Finance at Tilburg University. She is affiliated to the European Banking Center and the Central Bank of Colombia. Her research focuses on empirical banking. She has published in the *Journal of Risk Management in Financial Institutions* and the *China-USA Business Review*.

Tobias Adrian is a Vice President of the Federal Reserve Bank of New York and head of the Capital Markets Function of the Research and Statistics Group. His research covers asset pricing, financial intermediation, and macroeconomics, with a focus on the aggregate implications of capital market developments. He has contributed to the NY Fed's financial stability policy and to its monetary policy briefings. Adrian holds a PhD from the Massachusetts Institute of Technology (MIT) and an MSc from the London School of Economics (LSE). He has taught at MIT and Princeton University and has published in journals including *Journal of Finance, Journal of Financial Economics, Review of Financial Studies, Journal of Financial Intermediation, Journal of Empirical Finance, European Economic Review*.

Michel Aglietta is Professor at the University of Paris-X Nanterre, Scientific Advisor for the Research Center in International Economics, consultant at Groupama-am, and former member of the French Council of Economic Advisors attached to the prime minister. His most influential writings include *Régulation et crise du capitalisme, La Violence de la Monnaie* (with A. Orléan), and *Globalisation financière: l'aventure obligée* (with A. Brender and Virginie Coudert, 1990). Recent books include *Corporate Governance Adrift* (with A Rebérioux, 2005); *Désordres dans le capitalisme mondial* (with A. Berrebi, 2007); *La crise* (2008); and *Crise et rénovation de la finance* (2009).

Franklin Allen is the Executive Director of the Brevan Howard Centre and Professor of Finance and Economics at Imperial College London. He is on leave from the Wharton School of the University of Pennsylvania where he is the Nippon Life Professor of Finance and Professor of Economics. He was formerly the Nippon Life Professor of Finance and Professor of Economics at the Wharton School of the University of Pennsylvania. He has been on the faculty since 1980. Currently Co-Director of the Wharton Financial Institutions Center, he was formerly Vice Dean and Director of Wharton Doctoral Programs and Executive Editor of the Review of Financial Studies, and is currently Managing Editor of the Review of Finance. He is a past President of the American Finance Association, the Western Finance Association, the Society for Financial Studies, the Financial Intermediation Research Society, and the Financial Management Association and a Fellow of the Econometric Society. He received his doctorate from Oxford University. Allen's main areas of interest are corporate finance, asset pricing, financial innovation, comparative financial systems, and financial crises. He is a co-author with Richard Brealey and Stewart Myers of the eighth through eleventh editions of the textbook *Principles of Corporate Finance* (11th edition, 2013)

Linda Allen holds the William F. Aldinger Chair in Banking and Finance at Baruch College, City University of New York. Her broad areas of research are risk measurement and management focusing on systemic risk, credit risk and operational risk; the evolution of financial markets and bank regulation; and the organization of financial institutions. Professor Allen's latest book *Credit Risk Measurement In and Out of Crisis: New Approaches to Value at Risk and Other Paradigms* (3rd edition, with Anthony Saunders, 2010), describes her perspective on the global financial crisis that began in 2007, as well as deconstructs credit risk measurement models commonly used by bankers and other finance professionals. She is also the author of *Capital Markets and Institutions: A Global View* (1997) and co-author of *Understanding Market, Credit and Operational Risk* (2004). She is an associate editor of the *Journal of International Business Studies, Journal of Economics and Business, Multinational Finance Journal, Journal of Multinational Financial Management*, and *The Financier* and has published extensively in top academic journals in finance and economics. Along with her consulting in securities litigation, she has lectured and advised all over the world on topics of risk measurement and management, banking trends and financial market development.

Adam B. Ashcraft is a Senior Vice President at the Federal Reserve Bank of New York in the financial risk management area of the Credit and Payments Risk Group where he is head of the Structured Product Function. His research has focused on the effects of bank capital requirements, monetary policy and labor market issues. He joined the Bank in July 2001. Mr. Ashcraft received his PhD from MIT in June 2001 and has published in journals including the *Amercian Economic Review, Journal of Monetary Economics, Journal of Financial Intermediation, Journal of Money, Credit and Banking*, and *Journal of Financial Services Research*.

Olivier de Bandt holds a PhD from the Department of Economics of the University of Chicago. He is currently head of the Research Directorate at the Autorité de Contrôle Prudentiel et de Résolution, the French bank and insurance supervisor. He is an Associate Professor at the University of Paris Ouest. His research, published in various peer-reviewed academic journals, concentrates on stress testing methods and the economics of banking. He also serves as an associate editor of the *Journal of Financial Stability*.

James R. Barth is the Lowder Eminent Scholar in Finance at Auburn University and a senior fellow at the Milken Institute. His research focuses on financial institutions and capital markets, both domestic and global, with special emphasis on regulatory issues. He recently co-authored *Guardians of Finance: Making Regulators Work for Us* (2012) *and Fixing the Housing Market* (2012).

Thorsten Beck is Professor of Banking and Finance at Cass Business School in London. He was the founding chair of the European Banking Center at Tilburg University from 2008 to 2013. He is also a Research Fellow of the Centre for Economic Policy Research (CEPR). Previously he worked in the research department of the World Bank and has also worked as consultant for the International Monetary Fund, the European Commission, and the German Development Corporation. His research, academic publications, and operational work have focused on two major questions: What is the relationship between finance and economic development? What policies are needed to build a sound and effective financial system? Recently, he has concentrated on access to financial services, including SME finance, as well as on the design of regulatory and bank resolution frameworks. In addition to numerous academic publications in leading economics and finance journals, he has co-authored several policy reports on access to finance, financial systems in Africa and cross-border banking. His country experience, both in operational and research work, includes Bangladesh, Bolivia, Brazil, China, Colombia, Egypt, Mexico, Russia, and several countries in Sub-Saharan Africa. In addition to presentations at numerous academic conferences, including several keynote addresses, he is invited regularly to policy panels across Europe. He holds a PhD from the University of Virginia and an MA from the University of Tübingen in Germany.

Allen N. Berger is the H. Montague Osteen, Jr., Professor in Banking and Finance and Ph.D. coordinator of the Finance Department, Moore School of Business, and Carolina Distinguished Professor, University of South Carolina; Senior Fellow, Wharton Financial Institutions Center; and Fellow, European Banking Center. He also currently serves on the editorial boards of six professional finance journals. In addition, Professor Berger is past editor of the *Journal of Money, Credit, and Banking* from 1994–2001 and has co-edited six special issues of various professional journals and both editions of the *Oxford Handbook of Banking*. He was also Secretary/Treasurer, Financial Intermediation Research Society from 2008–2016. His research covers a variety of topics related to financial institutions. He is co-author of *Bank Liquidity Creation and Financial Crises* (Elsevier). He has published over 100 professional articles in refereed journals, including papers in top finance journals, *Journal of Finance, Journal of Financial Economics, Review of Financial Studies, Journal of Financial and Quantitative Analysis*, and *Review of Finance*; top economics journals, *Journal of Political Economy, American Economic Review, Review of Economics and Statistics*, and *Journal of Monetary Economics*; and other top professional business journals, *Managerial Science* and *Journal of Business*; and over 30 other non-refereed publications. Professor Berger was named Professor of the Year for 2015–2016 by the Darla Moore School of Business Doctoral Students Association. He was also Senior Economist from 1989 to 2008, and Economist from 1982–1989 at the Board of Governors of the Federal Reserve System. He received a Ph.D. in Economics from the University of California, Berkeley in 1983, and a B.A. in Economics from Northwestern University in 1976.

Robert R. Bliss is the F. M. Kirby Chair in Business Excellence at the Schools of Business at Wake Forest University, where he teaches courses in derivatives, financial engineering, and capital markets. Prior to returning to academia, Dr. Bliss served as a senior financial economist at the Federal Reserve Bank of Chicago and held research positions at the Bank of England and the Federal Reserve Bank of Atlanta. Previously, Dr. Bliss taught finance at Indiana University. Professor Bliss's research interests include fixed income securities and derivatives, structured finance, risk management, financial regulation, and the law and economics of insolvency. Professor Bliss earned his doctorate in finance from the University of Chicago.

John P. Bonin is Chester D. Hubbard Professor of Economics and Social Science at Wesleyan University in Middletown, Connecticut, where he has taught since 1970. Bonin was the Editor of the *Journal of Comparative Economics* from 1996 to 2006. He has served twice as President of the Association for Comparative Economic Studies, most recently in 2009. Bonin has published more than 65 articles in economic journals; he has co-authored three books, one of which is *Economics of Cooperation and the Labor Managed Economy* (with Louis Putterman, 2001), and co-translated with Hélène Bonin four French microeconomic theory books. Bonin has consulted for the World Bank, the United Nations, the US Treasury, the Institute for East–West Studies, and the 1990 Institute. He was an expert witness in an international banking case: Ceska Sporitelna a.s. v. Unisys Corporation. His recent papers focusing on banking and finance in transition and Asian countries are found in *Journal of Banking and Finance, Comparative Economic Studies*, and *Economic Systems*.

Arnoud W. A. Boot is Professor of Corporate Finance and Financial Markets at the University of Amsterdam, and research fellow at CEPR. He is the chairman of the Bank Council of the Dutch Central Bank and a member of the Advisory Scientific Committee of the European Systemic Risk Board in Frankfurt. His research focuses on corporate finance and financial institutions. Prior to his current positions, he was on the faculty of the J. L. Kellogg Graduate School of Management at Northwestern University.

Christa H. S. Bouwman is an Associate Professor of Finance at Texas A&M University. She holds a PhD in Finance from the University of Michigan. She is an associate editor of the *Review of Finance, Journal of Banking and Finance*, a Fellow of the Wharton Financial Institutions Center at the University of Pennsylvania, and a (part-time) Visiting Scholar at the Federal Reserve Banks of Boston and Cleveland. Bouwman's research has been published in the *Journal of Financial Economics*, the *Review of Financial Studies*, the *Journal of Banking and Finance* and the *MIT/Sloan Management Review*. Her research interests are in corporate finance and financial intermediation. In the area of intermediation, she co-developed measures that can be used to assess how effective commercial banks are at achieving one of their prime objectives: creating liquidity. She has studied how much liquidity banks create in the US, the determinants of bank liquidity creation (particularly the role of bank capital and monetary policy), and its behavior around financial crises. Because of her work on bank liquidity creation, she was invited and contracted by Elsevier to co-author a book on this topic. Prior to her current positions, she was an Associate Professor of Finanace and held the Lewis-Progressive Chair at Case Western University; she was a Visiting Assistant Professor of Finance at MIT's Sloan School of Management; held the Lewis-Progressive Chair at Case Western Reserve University; worked in Corporate Finance at ABN AMRO Bank; and was a litigative consultant for the US Department of Justice.

Christopher Brummer is a Professor of Law at Georgetown University, and a Senior Fellow at the Milken Institute. His research focuses on international financial regulation, with emphases on the banking and securities industries. He has taught at the University of Basel, the University of Heidelberg, and the London School of Economics. Prior to his academic career, he practiced law in the New York and London offices of Cravath, Swaine and Moore LLP. He holds a JD from Columbia Law School, and a PhD in Germanic Studies from the University of Chicago.

Claudia M. Buch is Deputy Governor of the Deutsche Bundesbank. Before being appointed to that position in March 2014, she led the Halle Institute for Economic Research and was Professor in Economics at Otto von Guericke University Magdeburg. From 2004 to 2013, she held the chair for International Macroeconomics and Finance at the University of Tuebingen, from 2005 to 2013 she was the Scientific Director of the Institute for Applied Economic Research (Institut für Angewandte Wirtschaftsforschung, Tuebingen). On March 1, 2012, she was appointed member of the German Council of Economic Experts ("Sachverstaendigenrat zur Begutachtung der gesamtwirtschaftlichen Entwicklung").

Charles W. Calomiris is the Henry Kaufman Professor of Financial Institutions at the Columbia University Graduate School of Business, a Professor at Columbia's School of International and Public Affairs, and a Research Associate of the NBER. Professor Calomiris is a member of the Advisory Scientific Committee of the European Systemic Risk Board, the Shadow Open Market Committee, and the Financial Economists Roundtable. He received a BA in Economics from Yale University in 1979 and a PhD in Economics from Stanford University in 1985.

Gerard Caprio Jr. is William Brough Professor of Economics at Williams College and Chair of the Center for Development Economics there. Previously he was the Director for Policy in the World Bank's Financial Sector Vice Presidency, and head of financial sector research. During his career there, he assembled a first-rate research team and worked in 30 countries in 18 years. His research included establishing the first databases on banking crises around the world and on bank regulation and supervision, and he has written widely on crises and regulatory issues. Earlier positions include: Vice President and Head of Global Economics at JP Morgan, and economist positions at the Federal Reserve Board and the IMF. He has taught at Trinity College Dublin, where he was a Fulbright Scholar, and at George Washington University. Jerry has authored numerous articles, and his latest book is *The Guardians of Finance: Making Regulators Work for Us* (with Jim Barth and Ross Levine, 2012). He is a co-editor of the *Journal of Financial Stability* and served as Editor-In-Chief of a three-volume handbook series on financial globalization for Elsevier (2012).

Elena Carletti is Professor of Finance at Bocconi University. Before that she was Professor of Economics at the European University Institute, where she held a joint chair in the Economics Department and the Robert Schuman Centre for Advanced Studies. She is also Research Fellow at CEPR, Extramural Fellow at Tilburg Law and Economics Center, Fellow at the Center for Financial Studies at CesIfo, and at the Wharton Financial Institutions Center. Her main areas of interest are financial intermediation, financial crises, financial regulation, corporate governance, industrial organization and competition policy. She has published numerous articles in leading economic journals, and has co-edited a book with Franklin Allen, Jan Pieter Krahnen and Marcel Tyrell on liquidity and crises. She has worked as consultant for the Organisation for Economic Co-operation and Development (OECD) and the World Bank and participates regularly in policy debates and roundtables at central banks and international organizations.

Jacopo Carmassi is Research Fellow at CASMEF, the Arcelli Center for Monetary and Financial Studies, University LUISS Guido Carli, and a Fellow of the Wharton Financial Institutions Center, University of Pennsylvania. He was formerly an economist at Assonime, the Association of Joint Stock Companies incorporated in Italy, a researcher at the Italian Banking Association and a Visiting Scholar at the Wharton Financial Institutions Center. His research and work activities have focused on banking regulation and supervision and financial crises, including the 2008 global financial crisis, bank capital rules, deposit insurance, the structure of financial supervision, derivatives, bank crisis management and resolution, bank recovery and resolution plans, corporate structures of Global Systemically Important Banks, and the EU banking union. He holds a PhD in Law and Economics from the University LUISS Guido Carli of Rome and a bachelor's degree in Economics from the University La Sapienza of Rome.

Fernando J. Cardim de Carvalho is Emeritus Professor of Economics at the Institute of Economics, Federal University of Rio de Janeiro (Brazil) and Director of the Money and Finance Study Group headquartered at the same university. A former chairman of the Brazilian Association of Graduate Schools in Economics, his research interests are Keynesian macroeconomics, international monetary economics, and financial systems.

Barbara Casu is currently the Director of the Centre for Banking Research at Cass Business School, City University London, where she is Associate Professor of Banking. Her research interests are banking, financial regulation, corporate governance, and industrial organization. She holds a BSc in Economics from the Catholic University of Milan (Italy) and PhD in Economics from Bangor Business School (UK).

Nicola Cetorelli is an Assistant Vice President in the Financial Intermediation Function at the Federal Reserve Bank of New York. His research has focused on the industrial organization and the corporate finance characteristics of the banking industry and the relationships with real economic activity. More recently he has worked on themes of international banking and on the evolution of financial intermediation. He represents the New York Fed on the Financial Stability Board's international working groups on shadow banking. He has published in a number of scholarly journals, among which are the *Journal of Finance, Journal of Economic Theory, and Journal of International Economics*. He has also written many articles in various policy journals and book chapters as well. He received his PhD in Economics from Brown University and a BA from the University of Rome, Italy.

Martin Čihák is an Advisor at the International Monetary Fund (IMF). In 2011–2013, he was on special assignment at the World Bank Group. In his work so far, he has focused on issues relating to financial sector regulation and supervision, financial stability, and financial system reforms. He has covered these topics in numerous World Bank/IMF missions and a range of publications. He was one of the co-editors of the *Bank-Fund Financial Sector Assessment Handbook*. Before joining the IMF in 2000, he was a chief analyst in a commercial bank, a university lecturer, and an advisor to a minister. He received a PhD in Economics from the Center for Economic Research and Graduate Education, Prague and has MAs both in Economics and in Law.

Ricardo Correa is Chief of the International Financial Stability section at the Board of Governors of the Federal Reserve System. His research fields include banking, empirical corporate finance, and financial foreign direct investment. He conducts policy analysis in the areas of cross-border bank exposures and financial stability. He received a PhD in Economics from Columbia University and a BA in Economics from the University of los Andes in Bogotá, Colombia. Prior to pursuing his PhD studies, he worked as a junior researcher at Fedesarrollo, the leading economic think tank in Colombia.

Robert Cull is a lead economist in the Finance and Private Sector Development Team of the Development Research Group of the World Bank. His most recent research is on the performance of microfinance institutions, African financial development, the effects of the global financial crisis on developing economies, and the design and use of household surveys to measure access to financial services. He has published more than 30 articles in peer-reviewed academic journals including the *Economic Journal, Journal of Development Economics, Journal of Economic Perspectives, Journal of Financial Economics, Journal of Law and Economics*, and the *Journal of Money, Credit, and Banking*. The author or editor of multiple books, his most recent co-edited book is *Banking the World: Empirical Foundations of Financial Inclusion* (2013). He is also co-editor of the *Interest Bearing Notes*, a bi-monthly newsletter reporting on financial and private sector research.

Hans Degryse is Professor of Finance at the Universities of Leuven and Tilburg and also a research fellow at the CEPR, CESIfo, European Banking Center, and TILEC. His research focuses on financial intermediation, including theoretical and empirical banking as well as market microstructure. He has published in many journals including the *American Economic Review, Journal of Finance, Journal of Financial Economics, Review of Financial Studies, Journal of Financial Intermediation*, and the *Economic Journal*, and has been presented in leading international conferences such as the *American Finance Association*, the *Western Finance Association*, the *European Finance Association*, and the *Financial Intermediation Research Society*. He co-authored, with Moshe Kim and Steven Ongena, the graduate textbook *Microeconometrics of Banking: Methods, Applications and Results* (2009).

Gayle L. DeLong is an Associate Professor in the Economics and Finance Department at Baruch College in the City University of New York. She received her Masters in International Business Studies from the University of South Carolina and her PhD in International Business and Finance from New York University. Her research interests include bank mergers, international finance, and public–private partnerships. She received research grants from the Zicklin School of Business, Wasserman Endowment, TransCoop Program of the Alexander Humboldt Foundation, and the Federal Deposit Insurance Corporation's Center for Financial Research. In 2012, she won the Abraham J. Briloff Prize in Ethics at Baruch College, New York

Asli Demirgüç-Kunt is the Director of Research in the World Bank. After joining the Bank in 1989 as a Young Economist, she has held different positions, including Director of Development Policy, Chief Economist of Financial and Private Sector Development Network, and Senior Research Manager, doing research and advising on financial sector and private sector development issues. She is the lead author of *World Bank Policy Research Report 2007, Finance for All? Policies and Pitfalls in Expanding Access* (2007). She has also created the World Bank's Global Financial Development Report and directed the issues entitled *Rethinking the Role of the State in Finance* (2013), and *Financial Inclusion* (2014). The author of over 100 publications, she has published widely in academic journals. Her research has focused on the links between financial development and firm performance and economic development. Banking crises, financial regulation, and access to financial services, including SME finance, are among her areas of research. Prior to coming to the Bank, she was an Economist at the Federal Reserve Bank of Cleveland. She holds a PhD and MA in Economics from the Ohio State University.

Robert DeYoung is Capitol Federal Distinguished Professor in Financial Institutions and Markets at the University of Kansas School of Business. He is also co-editor of the *Journal of Money, Credit and Banking* and a Senior Fellow at the Federal Deposit Insurance Corporation's Center for Financial Research.

Gregory Donadio is a Senior Research Assistant at the Office of Financial Stability at the Federal Reserve Board in Washington, DC. He is a graduate of Ithaca College and since joining the Fed has worked on the Comprehensive Capital Analysis and Review stress tests and other financial stability matters. His research focuses on banking, residential mortgages, and financial distress.

Thomas A. Durkin has specialized in the economics and regulation of consumer financial services in the federal government, academic, and private sectors. Before retiring in December, 2007, he was Senior Economist in the Division of Research and Statistics at the Federal Reserve Board where he has also been Visiting Professor. From 1988 to 1998 he was Regulatory Planning and Review Director in the Federal Reserve Office of the Secretary. Since retiring from the Federal Reserve position, he has been engaged in a variety of writing projects concerning consumer financial services. He has also been Assistant and Associate Professor of Finance at Penn State University and Chief Economist and Director of Research of the American Financial Services Association. In that position he frequently testified on financial matters before Congressional Committees, spoke to business groups, and appeared on radio and television interview programs. He holds an BA degree from Georgetown University and a PhD from Columbia University. He has published extensively in the field of financial institutions and especially consumer credit and is co-author of four books including *Truth in Lending: Theory, History, and a Way Forward* (2011) and *Consumer Credit and the American Economy* (2014).

Robert A. Eisenbeis is currently Vice-Chairman and Chief Monetary Economist of Cumberland Advisors. He retired as Executive Vice President and Director of Research at the Federal Reserve Bank of Atlanta. He previously had been Wachovia Professor of Banking and Associate Dean for Research at the Kenan-Flagler Business School at the University of North Carolina-Chapel Hill, and prior to that he held officer positions at the Federal Deposit Insurance Corporation and Federal Reserve Board of Governors. He presently is a member of the Shadow Financial Regulatory Committee and the Financial Economist Roundtable, and is a fellow at the Wharton Financial Institutions Center.

Gregory Elliehausen is Senior Economist in the Household and Real Estate Finance Section of the Division of Research and Statistics at the Board of Governors of the Federal Reserve System. His current research focuses on consumer financial behavior, regulation of financial markets and services, and markets for high-rate credit products. His research has been published in numerous professional journals. His *Truth in Lending: Theory, History, and a Way Forward* (with Thomas A. Durkin, 2011) is a guide to the purposes, strengths, and weaknesses of disclosures as consumer protections in financial transactions. Previously, he held research positions at George Washington University (2006– 2009), Georgetown University (1998–2005), and the Board of Governors of the Federal Reserve System (1981–1998). He has a PhD in business administration from the Pennsylvania State University.

W. Scott Frame is a financial economist and senior policy advisor at the Federal Reserve Bank of Atlanta. Prior to this, he was the Belk Distinguished Professor of Finance at the University of North Carolina at Charlotte, where he taught real estate finance and fixed income analysis. Frame has published in several leading academic journals, including the *Journal of Finance*, the *Journal of Financial Economics*, the *Journal of Business*, the *Journal of Money, Credit and Banking*, the *Journal of Economic Literature*, and the *Journal of Economic Perspectives*. He is also an associate editor of the *Journal of Money, Credit, and Banking* and the *Journal of Financial Services Research*. He is a member of the American Economic Association, the American Real Estate and Urban Economics Association, the Financial Management Association, the International Banking, Economics and Finance Association, and the Southern Finance Association.

Xavier Freixas is Chairman of the Department of Economics and Business and Professor at the Universitat Pompeu Fabra in Barcelona (Spain) after becoming full Professor at the Université de Toulouse. He is also Affiliated Professor at Barcelona Graduate School of Economics as well as Research Fellow at CEPR. He has previously been president of the European Finance Association, Deutsche Bank Professor of European Financial Integration at Oxford University, Houblon Norman Senior Fellow of the Bank of England and chairman of the Risk Based Regulation program of the Global Association of Risk Professionals. He has been a consultant for the European Investment Bank, the New York Fed, the European Central Bank, the World Bank, the Inter-American Development Bank and the European Investment Bank. He is associate editor of *Journal of Financial Intermediation* and of *Journal of Financial Services Research*. He is well known for his MIT Press book *Microeconomics of Banking* (with Jean-Charles Rochet, 2nd edition 2008) . His research focusses on banking and regulation, and has been published in top international journals. He gained a PhD from the University of Toulouse, France, in 1978.

John Goddard is Professor of Financial Economics at Bangor Business School, Bangor University, Wales. Before joining Bangor University in 2005, he was Professor of Economics at Swansea University. His research interests are in Industrial Organization, the Economics of Financial Institutions, and the Economics of Professional Sports. He has recent publications in *Journal of Money Credit and Banking, Journal of Banking and Finance, Journal of Forecasting, European Journal of Operational Research*, and *International Journal of Industrial Organization*.

Michael B. Gordy is a Senior Economist at the Federal Reserve Board. His current research focuses on credit risk pricing and on the estimation and computation of models of stochastic volatility. Michael is recipient of Risk's 2004 Quant of the Year and GARP's 2003 Financial Risk Manager of the Year, and currently serves as an associate editor of four journals. Michael received his PhD in Economics from MIT in 1994.

Xian Gu is currently a postdoctoral Research Fellow at the Wharton School of University of Pennsylvania. Previously she worked as a macroeconomist in the research department of CITIC Securities Co. in Beijing. She earned her PhD from Beijing Normal University in finance. Her main research interests are in the fields of financial intermediation, financial crisis, and China's economy.

Jens Hagendorff is the Martin Currie Professor in Finance and Investment at the University of Edinburgh. He previously worked at the Financial Stability Department of the Bank of Spain and as a lecturer at the University of Leeds. Jens held visiting positions in the US, Italy, and Spain, most recently as a visiting fellow at the Federal Reserve Bank of Atlanta and the Bank of Spain in Madrid. Hagendorff publishes and lectures on a range of topics in finance, banking, and investments, in particular the risk and return implications of corporate governance in the banking industry. His work has been published in leading international journals such as *Review of Finance, Journal of Corporate Finance, Journal of Banking and Finance, European Financial Management, Journal of Financial Services Research*, and *Journal of Business Ethics*. He is one of the authors of *Size, Risk and Governance in European Banking* (2013).

Philipp Hartmann is Deputy Director General Research and currently acting as Head of DG Research at the European Central Bank. He is also a chaired part-time professor for macrofinancial economics at Erasmus University Rotterdam and a Fellow of the Centre for Economic Policy Research. His work covers a wide set of issues in financial, monetary, and international affairs. His research is published in a range of peer-reviewed academic journals and several books. He also serves as an associate editor of the *Journal of Financial Stability*. His policy work has been discussed in fora such as the ECOFIN Council, the ECB Governing Council, European Commission fora, the Basel Committee on Banking Supervision, the United Nations Economic Commission for Europe and published in numerous reports.

Iftekhar Hasan is the E. Gerald Corrigan Professor of Finance at the Fordham University, New York, and concurrently serves as a Scientific Advisor to the Central Bank of Finland. A Fulbright Specialist Scholar, Hasan, has held visiting faculty positions at various European universities and has been a consultant or Visiting Scholar for numerous international organizations, including the World Bank, IMF, Banque de France, and the Italian Deposit Insurance Corporation. He is the managing editor of the *Journal of Financial Stability* and has served as an associate editor in several academic journals. He has over 275 publications in print, including 14 books and edited volumes, and over 165 journal articles in reputed finance, economics, management, and accounting journals.

Erik A. Heitfield is Chief of the Risk Analysis Section in the Federal Reserve Board's Research and Statistics Division. Heitfield manages a team of financial economists who conduct research and policy analysis on the risks arising from the trading and positioning of securities, loans, commodities, and derivative instruments. His own research focuses on the measurement and management of credit risk in complex financial institutions. During his 15 years as an economist at the Federal Reserve Board, he has participated in numerous domestic and international working groups tasked with developing risk-based bank regulatory capital standards and implementing derivatives market reforms. In 2006 and 2007 he served as a senior staff economist for the President's Council of Economic Advisors. He received his PhD in Economics from the University of California (Berkeley) in 1998.

Richard J. Herring is Jacob Safra Professor of International Banking and Professor of Finance at the Wharton School, University of Pennsylvania, where he is also founding director of the Wharton Financial Institutions Center. He is the author of more than 125 articles, monographs, and books on various topics in financial regulation, international banking, and international finance. At various times his research has been funded by grants from the National Science Foundation, the Ford Foundation, the Brookings Institution, the Sloan Foundation, the Council on Foreign Relations, and the Royal Swedish Commission on Productivity. Outside the university, he is co-chair of the US Shadow Financial Regulatory Committee and Executive Director of the Financial Economist's Roundtable, a member of the FDIC Systemic Resolution Advisory Committee, the Systemic Risk Council, and the Hoover Institution Working Group on Resolution Policy. Herring received his undergraduate degree from Oberlin College in 1968 and his PhD from Princeton University in 1973.

Patrick Honohan has been Governor of the Central Bank of Ireland since September 2009. Previously he was Professor of International Financial Economics and Development at Trinity College Dublin and before that a Senior Advisor in the World Bank working on financial sector policy. During the 1980s he was Economic Advisor to the Taoiseach (Irish Prime Minister) and he also spent several years at the Economic and Social Research Institute,

Dublin, at the International Monetary Fund and an earlier stint at the Central Bank of Ireland. He has taught economics at University College Dublin, at the University of California, San Diego, and at the London School of Economics, from which he received his PhD in 1978. His wide range of publications covers topics from financial development, banking crises, and exchange rate regimes, to cost–benefit analysis and statistical methodology.

Joseph P. Hughes is Professor of Economics at Rutgers University. His research has focused on incorporating endogenous risk-taking into the dual analysis of production to measure scale economies and efficiency in banking. He is currently investigating the tradeoff between the scale economies and global competitiveness of the largest financial institutions and their contribution to systemic risk. His research also examines the role of the too-big-to-fail policy in contributing to measured scale economies at the largest financial institutions. He has been a Visiting Scholar at the Federal Reserve Bank of Philadelphia, the Federal Reserve Bank of New York, and the Office of the Comptroller of the Currency. His research has been published in such journals as the *Atlantic Economic Journal*, the *American Economic Review*, the *Journal of Banking and Finance*, the *Journal of Economic Theory*, the *Journal of Financial Services Research*, the *Journal of Money, Credit, and Banking*, and the *Review of Economics and Statistics*. He received his PhD from the University of North Carolina at Chapel Hill.

David Humphrey is the F. W. Smith Eminent Scholar in Banking at Florida State University and is a Visiting Scholar at the Payments Cards Center at the Federal Reserve Bank of Philadelphia. He has taught at three universities and previously worked at the Federal Reserve for 16 years. His publications have focused on banking and payment system issues. He received his PhD from the University of California (Berkeley).

Edward J. Kane is Professor of Finance at Boston College. From 1972 to 1992 he held the Everett D. Reese Chair of Banking and Monetary Economics at Ohio State University. A founding member of the Shadow Financial Regulatory Committee, Kane rejoined the organization in 2005. He served for 12 years as a trustee and member of the finance committee of Teachers Insurance. Currently, he consults for the World Bank and is a Senior Fellow in the Federal Deposit Insurance Corporation's Center for Financial Research. Previously, Kane consulted for numerous agencies, including the IMF, components of the Federal Reserve System, and three foreign central banks. He consulted as well for the Congressional Budget Office, the Joint Economic Committee, and the Office of Technology Assessment of the US Congress. He is a past President and Fellow of the American Finance Association and a former Guggenheim Fellow. He also served as President of the International Atlantic Economic Society and the North American Economics and Finance Association. Kane is a longtime research associate of the NBER. Besides authoring three books, he has published widely in professional journals and currently serves on seven editorial boards. He received a BS from Georgetown University and a PhD from the Massachusetts Institute of Technology.

George G. Kaufman is the John F. Smith Professor of Economics and Finance at Loyola University Chicago and consultant to the Federal Reserve Banks of Chicago. Previously he was an economist at the Federal Reserve Bank of Chicago and the John Rogers Professor of Finance at the University of Oregon. Kaufman is co-editor of the *Journal of Financial Stability* and a founding editor of the *Journal of Financial Service Research*. He is former president of the Western Finance Association, the Midwest Finance Association, the Western Economics

Association, and the North American Economic and Finance Association. He serves as co-chair of the Shadow Financial Regulatory Committee. He holds a PhD in Economics from the University of Iowa.

Leora Klapper is a Lead Economist in the Finance and Private Sector Research Team of the Development Research Group at the World Bank. Her published work focuses on financial inclusion, entrepreneurship, access to finance, corporate governance, and risk management. She is founder of the Global Financial Inclusion (Global Findex) database, which measures how adults around the world save, borrow, make payments, and manage risk. Prior to coming to the Bank, she worked at the Board of Governors of the Federal Reserve System, the Bank of Israel, and Salomon Smith Barney. She holds a PhD in Financial Economics from New York University Stern School of Business.

Andreas Lehnert is Deputy Director of the Office of Financial Stability at the Federal Reserve Board in Washington, DC. He joined the Fed after earning his PhD in Economics from the University of Chicago. He worked in the household finance research group where he focused on a variety of topics in consumer and mortgage credit. During the financial crisis, he contributed to several projects including the Troubled Asset Relief Program, the 2009 bank stress tests and the Term Asset-Backed Securities Loan Facility. In November 2010 he moved to the Board's newly created financial stability group. His research focuses on banking, consumption, house prices, household credit choices and financial distress, including default, foreclosure, and bankruptcy.

Tong (Cindy) Li is a country manager and analyst at the Federal Reserve Bank of San Francisco. In that capacity, she conducts research on Asian financial sectors and monitors banking, regulatory, and economic developments in Emerging Asia. Li is also an adjunct fellow at the Milken Institute. Her research interests are in banking regulation and financial stability. Li received her PhD in Economics from the University of California (Riverside). She holds a BA in International Finance from Peking University in China.

Maria Soledad Martinez Peria is the Research Manager of the Finance and Private Sector Development Team of the Development Economics Research Group at the World Bank. Her published work has focused on currency and banking crises, depositor market discipline, foreign bank participation in developing countries, bank financing to SMEs, the impact of remittances on financial development, and the spread of the recent financial crisis. Prior to joining the World Bank, Sole worked at the Brookings Institution, the Central Bank of Argentina, the Federal Reserve Board, and the IMF. She holds a PhD in Economics from the University of California (Berkeley) and a BA from Stanford University.

Loretta J. Mester is President and Chief Executive Officer of the Federal Reserve Bank of Cleveland. In addition, she is an adjunct professor of finance at the Wharton School, University of Pennsylvania, and a fellow at the Wharton Financial Institutions Center. She is a co-editor of the *International Journal of Central Banking* and a co-editor of the *Journal of Financial Services Research*. In addition, she is an associate editor of several other academic journals and serves on the management committee of the *International Journal of Central Banking*. Her publications include research on the organizational structure and production efficiency of financial institutions, the theory and regulation of financial intermediation, agency problems in credit markets, credit card pricing and central bank governance journals. Her research has been published in the *Journal of Finance*, the *American Economic Review*, the *Review of Financial Studies*, and the *Review of Economics and Statistics*, among others. She received her PhD in Economics from Princeton University.

Benoit Mojon is Director of Monetary and Financial Studies at Banque de France and Professor at École Polytechnique. He previously worked in the research departments of the Federal Reserve Bank of Chicago (2007–2008) and the European Central Bank (1998–2006). He was Associate Professor at the University of Aix en Provence from 2004 to 2006. His research on monetary policy transmission and on inflation dynamics has been published in leading academic journals such as the *Journal of Monetary Economics*, the *Review of Economics and Statistics*, and the *NBER Macroannual*.

Philip Molyneux is Dean of the College of Business, Law, Education, and Social Sciences, and Professor of Banking and Finance at Bangor Business School, Bangor University, Wales. His main area of research is on the structure and efficiency of banking markets and he has published widely in this area; recent publications appear in the *Journal of Money, Credit and Banking, Journal of Banking and Finance*, and the *Review of Finance*. Previously he has acted as a consultant to the New York Federal Reserve Bank, World Bank, European Commission, UK Treasury, Citibank Private Bank, Barclays Wealth, McKinsey, Credit Suisse, and various other international banks and consulting firms.

Alan D. Morrison is Professor of Finance at the Saïd Business School of the University of Oxford, a Research Affiliate of the Centre for Economic Policy Research, and a Research Associate of the European Corporate Governance Institute. His research concerns the regulation and industrial organization of commercial and investment banks.

Daniel E. Nolle is a senior financial economist in the Economics Department at the Office of the Comptroller of the Currency. His fields of research and policy analysis include the structure of the US banking industry, foreign banking in the US, US and global financial regulatory system reform, cross-country comparisons of banking systems and financial regulation, technological innovation in banking and payments, and consumer financial protection. He holds a PhD in Economics from Johns Hopkins University, Maryland.

Steven Ongena is a Professor in Banking at the University of Zurich and the Swiss Finance Institute. He is a Research Fellow in financial economics of CEPR. He has published more than 35 papers in refereed academic journals, including in the *American Economic Review, Econometrica, Journal of Finance, Journal of Financial Economics, Journal of International Economics*, and *Review of Finance*, among other journals, and he has published more than 40 papers in books and other collections. He is currently a co-editor of the *Review of Finance*; and he serves as an associate editor for a number of other journals. He is a director of the *European Finance Association* and of the *Financial Intermediation Research Society*. In 2009 he received a Duisenberg Fellowship from the European Central Bank and in 2012 a Fordham-RPI-NYU Stern Rising Star in Finance Award.

Bruno M. Parigi is Professor of Economics at the University of Padua, Italy. He has been a consultant for the New York Fed, the European Central Bank, and he has held visiting positions at the University of Toulouse, the European University Institute, and the University of Munich. His research interests are in banking, central banking, and corporate goverance. He received his PhD in Economics from Rutgers University.

Luiz Fernando de Paula is Professor of Economics at the State University of Rio de Janeiro (Brazil) and CNPq Researcher. A former chairman of the Brazilian Keynesian Association, his research interests include banking efficiency, financial systems, Keynesian macroeconomics and economic policies related to emerging countries.

Joe Peek is a Vice President and Economist in the Research Department of the Federal Reserve Bank of Boston. He received a BS in Mathematics from Oklahoma State University, and a PhD in Economics from Northwestern University. His research topics include international banking, bank regulation, monetary policy, and credit availability.

José-Luis Peydró Alcalde is ICREA Professor of Economics at Universitat Pompeu Fabra, a Professor of Banking at Cass Business School in London, a Research Fellow of the CEPR, and an Advisor of Bank of Spain (Financial Stability Department). He has been consultant on macroprudential policy in 2012–13 of the Federal Reserve Board, the International Monetary Fund, the Bundesbank and the European Central Bank. His research and policy interests are in banking, macro/ microprudential policies, central bank policies including monetary policy, financial crises, financial innovation, law and finance, the euro, and international finance. He has published his research in *Econometrica, American Economic Review,* the *Review of Financial Studies* and *Journal of Finance,* among other journals. He holds a PhD in Finance from INSEAD.

Eric S. Rosengren is the President and Chief Executive Officer of the Federal Reserve Bank of Boston. In his research, Rosengren has written extensively on macroeconomics, international banking, bank supervision, and risk management. He holds a BA from Colby College and a PhD from the University of Wisconsin.

Horacio Sapriza is a Research Economist at the Board of Governors of the Federal Reserve System in the International Finance Division since 2009, and an Adjunct Professor at Georgetown University. Prior to working at the Board, he was a faculty member at Rutgers Business School in the Department of Finance and Economics. He has also been a consultant for the IMF. He conducts policy analysis in the area of sovereign debt markets. His research topics include sovereign credit risk, fiscal policy, and international banks. His work has been published in refereed journals such as the *Journal of Finance, International Economic Review; Journal of International Economics, Journal of Money, Credit and Banking, Review of Economic Dynamics, International Review of Economics and Finance,* and *Economic Quarterly.* He received a PhD in Economics from the University of Rochester and a BA in Economics from the Universidad de la Republica in Montevideo, Uruguay. Prior to pursuing his PhD he worked as a junior researcher at the Instituto de Estadistica de la Universidad de la Republica, a leading research institute in Uruguay.

Anna Sarkisyan is a Lecturer in Banking and Finance at Essex Business School, University of Essex (UK). She holds a PhD in Finance from Cass Business School, City University London. Her research focuses on securitization, risk, and performance in banking. In 2010 she was awarded a Lamfalussy Fellowship from the European Central Bank.

Anthony Saunders is the John M. Schiff Professor of Finance and former Chair of the Department of Finance at the Stern School of Business at New York University. Professor Saunders received his PhD from the London School of Economics and has taught both undergraduate and graduate-level courses at NYU since 1978. Throughout his academic career, his teaching and research have specialized in financial institutions and risk management. He has served as a Visiting Professor all over the world, including at INSEAD, the Stockholm School of Economics, and the University of Melbourne. He has held positions on the Board of Academic Consultants of the Federal Reserve Board of Governors as well as the Italian Bankers Association. In addition, Saunders has acted as a visiting scholar at the Comptroller of the Currency and at the Federal Reserve Banks of New York and Philadelphia. He also held a visiting position in the research department of the IMF. He is a former editor of the *Journal of Banking and Finance* and is the current editor of the *Journal of Financial Markets, Instruments and Institutions*, as well as the associate editor of eight other journals. His research has been published in all the major money and banking and finance journals and in several books, the most recent of which are: *Credit Risk Measurement: New Approaches to Value at Risk and Other Paradigms* (3rd edition, 2010), *Financial Institutions Management* (7th edition, 2010). In 2008 he was ranked the most published author in the seven top banking and finance journals over the last 50 years.

Kevin J. Stiroh is a senior vice president and co-head of the Markets Operations, Monitoring and Analysis Function in the Markets Group at the Federal Reserve Bank of New York. His academic research includes work on productivity and the sources of economic growth, the economic impact of information technology, and the efficiency and behavior of financial institutions. This research has been published in the *American Economic Review, Brookings Papers on Economic Activity, Journal of Banking and Finance, Journal of Economic Perspectives, Journal of Money, Credit and Banking, Review of Economics and Statistics* and other academic and business publications.

Anjan V. Thakor holds the John E. Simon Professorship of Finance and is Director of the Olin Business School's Doctoral program, and the Wells Fargo Associates Center for Finance and Accounting Research. He is also a Research Associate of the European Corporate Governance Institute. Until July 2003, he was the Edward J. Frey Professorship of Banking and Finance and Chairman of the Finance Group (2000–2003) at the University of Michigan Business School. Prior to joining the University of Michigan, he served as the NBD Professor of Finance and Chairman of the Finance Department at the School of Business at Indiana University. Anjan has also served on the faculties of Northwestern University and University of California (Los Angeles) as a Visiting Professor. He received his PhD in Finance from Northwestern University. His research, teaching, and consulting are in the areas of asymmetric information, corporate finance, banking, and corporate strategy. He has published research articles in leading economics and finance journals such as the *American Economic Review, Review of Economic Studies, RAND Journal of Economics, Economic Journal, Journal of Economic Theory, Journal of Finance, Journal of Financial Economics, Journal of Financial Intermediation*, and *Review of Financial Studies*. In 2008, he was identified as the fourth most prolific researcher in the world in finance over the past 50 years. He has also published eight books, and has served as managing editor of the *Journal of Financial Intermediation* and President of the Financial Intermediation Research Society.

Hirofumi Uchida is Professor of Banking and Finance at the Graduate School of Business Administration, Kobe University, Japan. His work has appeared in the *Journal of Financial Intermediation, Economica*, and *Journal of Banking and Finance*, among others. His main research interests focus on banking and financial institutions, and financial system architecture. He was a 2003 Fulbright Scholar, and is an associate editor of the *Journal of Money, Credit and Banking*.

Gregory F. Udell is the Chase Chair of Banking and Finance at the Kelley School of Business, Indiana University. He has been a visiting economist and consultant to the Board of Governors of the Federal Reserve System, a visiting scholar at the Bank of Japan, and a consultant to the Bank of Italy, the European Central Bank, the Federal Reserve Banks of Chicago and San Francisco, the International Finance Corporation, the OECD, the Riksbank, and the World Bank. Before joining the Kelley School of Business in 1998 he was Professor of Finance and Director of the William R. Berkley Center for Entrepreneurial Studies at the Stern School of Business at New York University. Prior to his academic career Udell was a commercial loan officer in Chicago. He has over 75 publications mostly focused on financial contracting, credit availability, and financial intermediation. He is the author of a textbook on asset-based lending, *Asset-Based Finance* (2004), *Principles of Money, Banking and Financial Markets* (12th edition, with L. Ritter and W. Silber, 2009), and is, or has been, an associate editor/editorial board member of seven journals including the *Journal of Money, Credit and Banking, Journal of Banking and Finance, Journal of Financial Services Research*, and *Small Business Economics*.

Paul Wachtel is a Professor of Economics at New York University Stern School of Business. He has been with Stern for over 40 years and has served as department chair and Vice Dean. He is currently the academic director for the BS in Business and Political Economy degree. He is the co-editor of *Comparative Economic Studies*. He received his BA from Queens College in 1966, his MA in Economics from the University of Rochester, and his DPhil from the University of Rochester in 1971. His primary areas of research include the relationship of financial development to economic growth, central banking in the post-crisis world, and financial sector reform in economies in transition. He has published widely in these areas.

Lawrence J. White is the Robert Kavesh Professor of Economics at the Stern School of Business, New York University, and Deputy Chair of Stern's Economics Department. He has taken leave from NYU to serve in the US Government three times: During 1986–1989 he was a Board Member on the Federal Home Loan Bank Board (and, in that capacity, also a board member for Freddie Mac); during 1982–1983 he was the Chief Economist of the Antitrust Division of the US Department of Justice; and in 1978–1979 he was a Senior Staff Economist on the President's Council of Economic Advisers. He is the General Editor of the *Review of Industrial Organization*. Among his publications are *The S & L Debacle: Public Policy Lessons for Bank and Thrift Regulation* (1991), and *Guaranteed to Fail: Fannie Mae, Freddie Mac, and the Debacle of Mortgage Finance* (with Viral Acharya, Matthew Richardson, and Stijn Van Nieuweburgh, 2011); and he is the co-editor (with John E. Kwoka, Jr.) of *The Antitrust Revolution: Economics, Competition, and Policy* (6th edition, 2014).

Jonathan Williams is a Professor in Banking and Finance at Bangor University, Wales, UK, where he is affiliated to the Center of Banking of Finance and Institute of European Finance. His research interests center on the effects that financial liberalization has had on the banking industry in both industrialized countries and emerging markets.

John O. S. Wilson is Professor of Banking and Finance and Director for the Centre for Responsible Banking and Finance at the University of St Andrews, Scotland. His research interests focus on the areas of industrial organization, banking, and credit unions. He is associate editor of the *British Accounting Review, European Journal of Finance*, and the *Journal of Money Credit and Banking* and sits on the editorial boards of a number of journals, including the *Journal of Business Finance and Accounting* and the *Journal of Financial Economic Policy*. In the period June 2011 to April 2012, he served as a full member of a Commission on Credit Unions established by the Irish Government.

Jason J. Wu is Chief of the Monetary Policy and Dealer Analysis Section at the Federal Reserve Board, where he studies the interaction between monetary policy, dealer-intermediated markets and financial institutions outside of the traditional banking system. Previously, he was a Senior Economist in the Division of Banking Supervision and Regulation at the Federal Reserve Board, and worked extensively on the formation and implementation of Basel capital regulations for banks' trading books. His current research interests are financial intermediation, banking and econometrics. Jason received his PhD in Economics from the University of Wisconsin-Madison in 2007.

Bilal Zia is a Senior Economist in the Finance and Private Sector Development Team of the Development Economics Research Group. He joined in July 2006 after completing his PhD in Economics from MIT. His research is focused on financial development at the household, firm and bank levels, and his work has appeared in top academic journals such as the *Journal of Finance, Journal of Financial Economics*, and the *Review of Financial Studies*. He uses both experimental and non-experimental methods and some of his recent work includes rigorous impact evaluations of financial literacy programs, testing innovative methods to improve financial access for households and firms, and applying insights from behavioral economics to development finance. He holds an MCP and a PhD in Economics from MIT, and a BSc (Hons) from the LSE.

CHAPTER 1

....

BANKING IN A POST-CRISIS WORLD

....

ALLEN N. BERGER, PHILIP MOLYNEUX,
AND JOHN O. S. WILSON

1.1 INTRODUCTION

....

BANKS play critical roles in the economy. They operate the payments system, act as a conduit for monetary policy, and are a major source of credit for households, corporations, and governments. Banks also act as a haven for depositors' funds. If intermediation is undertaken in an efficient manner, then deposit and credit demands can be met at low cost, leading to benefits for the parties concerned. Banks also create liquidity for the public on the balance sheet by transforming relatively illiquid assets such as loans into relatively liquid liabilities such as transactions deposits, and off the balance sheet through loan commitments and similar claims to liquid funds. Banks also reduce credit, interest rate, foreign exchange rate, and liquidity risk for the public through diversification and intermediation on the balance sheet and through derivatives activities off the balance sheet.

Evidence suggests that developed banking systems stimulate economic growth by increasing the funds available for investment and improving the quality of investments made (Levine, 2005).[1] However, the onset of the recent financial crisis has led researchers to reassess the relationship between financial development and economic growth (Cecchetti and Kharroubi, 2012).

In recent years, changes in the economic environment and regulation along with technological change and financial innovation have altered the banking industry. Barriers to entry in

---

[1] Numerous theories have sought to explain why banking is necessary. These theories primarily relate to: delegated monitoring; information production; liquidity transformation; consumption smoothing; and the role of banks as commitment mechanisms. Notable contributions include: Leland and Pyle (1977); Diamond and Dybvig (1983); Diamond (1984); Fama (1985); Boyd and Prescott (1986); Calomiris and Kahn (1991); Holmstrom and Tirole (1998); Diamond and Rajan (2001); and Kashyap, Rajan, and Stein (2002). Gorton and Winton (2003) provide a comprehensive discussion.

traditional and new product areas as well as geographic barriers have been reduced or removed. This has allowed for the creation of very large banking organizations and the adoption of the universal banking model in many countries. Some of the largest banks have transformed themselves into multi-product, multi-market, financial service conglomerates which offer retail banking, investment banking, brokerage, insurance, and wealth management services. Changes in technology have improved the processing, analysis, and transmission of financial data, as well as delivery and distribution systems. This has reduced bank costs and increased the capacity for lending and the quality and variety of banking services available to customers. Financial engineering, along with new derivatives markets, have transformed how banks manage risk.

There has also been an emergence of new funding sources. The securitization of residential mortgages, credit card receivables, and other loans as well as the outright sale of commercial loans has allowed banks to shift somewhat from an "originate-to-hold" model to an "originate-to-distribute" model and become less constrained by their respective deposit bases for lending. Structured investment vehicles (SIVs) have been created in order to enable large banks to collateralize assets funded by the issue of short-term paper, enabling the financing of funding gaps (loans minus deposits), although many of the assets in SIVs were brought back on the balance sheet during the recent financial crisis. Small and medium-sized banks have also participated actively in diversifying their product and funding features.

Many of the participants in asset securitization—which include investment banks, hedge funds, private equity firms, structured investment companies, and money market funds—operate in a less regulated, less supervised environment, which has become known as the shadow banking system. Investment banks and the securities arms of commercial banks also set up separately capitalized SIVs to conduct securitization activity off the balance sheet (Pozsar et al., 2012). The growth of shadow banking created opacity and complexity. The volume of transactions in the US shadow banking system grew dramatically after the year 2000 and was believed to be larger than $10 trillion by 2008, although some of the large investment banks became more regulated financial services holding companies during the crisis to gain access to steadier sources of liquidity.

Today, banks are sophisticated organizations that rely on scale and scope and a variety of risk management mechanisms to ensure that deposit withdrawals, loan supply, and off-balance-sheet obligations can be met. Such mechanisms are augmented by regulations such as deposit insurance, lender of last resort facilities, and liquidity and risk-based capital regulation. However, irrespective of what checks and balances are put in place, the specialness of banks means that any lack of confidence in an individual bank or group of banks can lead to contagion and signal potential disaster for the financial system and the economy.

1.2. THE RECENT FINANCIAL CRISIS AND ITS AFTERMATH

In the period leading up to late 2007, real estate prices declined in the US. Prime and subprime borrowers increasingly defaulted, which put downward pressure on the values of both securitized mortgage products and mortgages remaining on bank balance sheets.

Holders of investments backed by subprime mortgages did not know what they were worth, and banks became wary of lending to each other because they did not know the extent of losses held on balance sheets and in SIVs. This culminated in a liquidity freeze in interbank markets and a subsequent credit crunch (Brunnermeir, 2009). According to the Financial Crisis Inquiry Commission (2011), underlying factors contributing to the crisis include poor monetary policies; misaligned incentives for investors, banks, and credit rating agencies; limited financial disclosure; inadequate corporate governance and accounting rules; lax lending standards; loopholes in regulation and supervision; as well as fraud.

The recent financial crisis resulted in large losses and the failure and closure of many banks, while problems of market liquidity and capital losses drastically reduced lending and liquidity creation by banks and led to the intervention of both central banks and governments. Initial responses to the crisis included government purchase of troubled assets, additional programs and changes in existing programs to get financial institutions to borrow more from central banks, nationalization of or capital injections into financial institutions, and increased government guarantees of consumer deposits and other bank liabilities. The scale of intervention has been enormous. Estimates vary, but some put the net outlays of the US Treasury and Federal Reserve at $3.3 trillion and the value of the amount of guarantees provided at $16.9 trillion.[2]

It is very difficult to assess the effectiveness of individual government programs in restoring financial stability, market liquidity, and bank lending. Many programs occurred over a short period of time and affected many financial institutions simultaneously. However, some of the programs affected only a subset of banks and so as a consequence the effects of these programs on the risk and lending behavior of these banks can be measured and tested. For example, there are a number of studies of the effects on risk and lending of the Troubled Asset Relief Program (TARP) capital injections into US banks. Studies by Black and Hazelwood (2013) and Duchin and Sosyura (2014) suggest that large banks receiving TARP bailouts in the US increased their loan risk, presumably due to enhanced moral hazard incentives, although the former also finds that small recipient banks decreased their loan risk. The results of Black and Hazelwood (2013), and Li (2013) suggest that small TARP recipients increased their lending relative to non-TARP banks, although large bank lending was left unchanged or was reduced.[3] Berger, Black et al. (2013) find that US banks that borrowed from the Federal Reserve through the discount window and Term Auction Facility (TAF) increased their lending significantly relative to non-borrowing banks.

Governments have also responded in a number of ways to reduce the likelihood and severity of future crises, including: increased capital requirements; counter-cyclical capital requirements; enhanced regulation and supervision of liquidity; enhanced supervision of credit rating agencies; codes covering executive remuneration; improved arrangements for regulation of the activities of cross-border banks; reform of accounting disclosure rules; and the establishment of consumer protection agencies. Turning to some specifics, in 2010, global bank regulators agreed to Basel III, which greatly increased the amount of common

---

[2] Of these, the Federal Reserve Board asserted that it would also guarantee over $5 trillion in money market funds (Congressional Oversight Panel, 2009).

[3] Koetter and Noth (2012) and Berger and Roman (2014) also find that TARP distorted competition by giving the recipient banks comparative advantages.

equity capital that the world largest banks must hold, and the US regulators in 2012 decided to apply it to all US banks and to all bank holding companies with at least $500 million in assets. Also under Basel III, all banks will, under certain conditions, have to hold counter-cyclical capital buffers. In addition, they must also adhere to two new liquidity rules comprising: a liquidity coverage ratio, which requires banks to hold enough cash and liquid assets; and a net stable funding ratio that encourages banks to hold more long-term funding. Those banks deemed systemically important are required to hold even more capital.

In addition to these international developments, the US, UK, and European regulatory authorities have also engaged in their own reform process. The passing of the US Dodd–Frank Wall Street Reform and Consumer Protection Act in July 2010 is indicative of the type of measures that national governments have adopted. Other examples include the implementation of the September 2011 Independent Commission on Banking (Vickers Commission) into UK banking legislation; and recommendations made in October 2012 by the EU High-level Expert Group on Reforming the Structure of the EU Banking Sector chaired by Erkki Liikanen (Liikanen Report, 2012). However, the reform process at the time of writing (mid 2014) is still ongoing—for example, most of the provisions of Dodd-Frank have not been fleshed out by regulators.

In Europe, the banking system and economic recovery further stalled with the onset of the sovereign debt crisis that befell various economies (particularly Greece, Ireland, Portugal, Italy, and Spain) during 2010 and 2011. Government debt and deficits led to a crisis of confidence that resulted in widening bond yield spreads and risk insurance on credit default swaps between these countries and other EU members, most notably Germany (Lane, 2012). The Eurozone countries and the International Monetary Fund agreed on loans for Greece, Ireland, and Portugal, conditional on the implementation of tough austerity measures. The European Financial Stability Facility (comprising a broad rescue package amounting to $1 trillion) was established to ensure financial stability across the Eurozone. The aforementioned sovereign debt problems became inextricably linked to banking sector problems. In 2012, the European Council outlined proposals to establish a European banking union aimed at de-coupling sovereign risk from banking sector risk in order to enhance financial stability. The banking union will comprise three pillars. First, responsibility for bank supervision for the large banks will be at the European level. Second, common mechanisms will be established for the resolution of ailing banks. Finally, there will be a European deposit insurance fund. At the time of writing, however, the extent and pace of implementation remain uncertain, owing to disagreements over several key issues of principle.[4]

Many large banks have shifted in part away from riskier nontraditional activities, such as proprietary trading, to focus more on retail banking. The aim is to boost interest rate, fee, and commission related income from low risk activity. In many cases, a return to retail has occurred because retail business offers relatively stable returns that can help offset volatility in non-retail business. Large banks have also boosted their capital and liquidity to meet exacting national and Basel III requirements.

---

[4] These include questions around whether Eurozone banks should have different supervision, resolution, and deposit insurance rules relative to banks headquartered in EU countries that are not members of the Eurozone; the backstop for funding the single deposit insurance scheme and resolution fund resources run out; and how country-specific insolvency rules can be harmonized to deal with a uniform resolution regime.

While the banking business in the US and Europe has been dramatically reconfigured since the onset of the recent financial crisis, elsewhere the industry has been much less impacted, with many emerging markets experiencing rapid banking sector growth. In the context of these developments, we now outline various banking research themes that have emerged.

1.3. Emerging Research Themes and Unanswered Research Questions

There has been a theoretical and empirical renaissance in banking research. A number of key questions have emerged and promising avenues for future research developed. In this section we present a selective discussion.

1.3.1 Financial Development and Growth and the Role of the State

Up to the onset of the recent financial crisis, the academic and policy consensus was that financial institutions and markets aid long-run economic growth. Market frictions in the form of information and transaction costs necessitate the need for financial markets and intermediaries to mobilize savings, allocate resources, exert corporate control, facilitate risk management, and ease the exchange of goods and services. The level of financial development depends on a number of factors, including the degree of economic freedom, the protection of property rights, and the origin and quality of the legal system (La Porta et al., 1998). However, since the onset of the crisis, there have been some concerns that in many countries, the financial system is simply too large and in fact does not have a positive effect on economic growth. Arcand, Berkes, and Panizza (2012) explore whether there is a threshold above which financial development no longer has a positive effect on economic growth. The authors show that the effect of financial depth on output growth turns negative when credit to the private sector ranges between 80% and 100% of GDP. Cecchetti and Kharoubi (2012) utilize a large sample of developed and emerging economies to first show that there is a threshold beyond which financial development no longer enhances aggregate productivity growth. Furthermore, in the case of advanced countries, a fast-growing financial sector damages aggregate productivity growth. Beck et al. (2012) decompose overall bank aggregate lending to lending to households and lending to firms. The authors find that lending to firms stimulates economic growth, while lending to households does not.

The large-scale intervention by governments during the recent financial crisis has led academics and policy makers to reassess the role of the state within the financial system. Prior to the recent crisis, most evidence suggests that government ownership of banks leads to poor performance and retards financial development (La Porta, Lopez de Silanes, and Shleifer, 2002). However, more recent evidence suggests that lending by state-owned banks is less procyclical than that of private sector counterparts, and as such aids in smoothing macroeconomic volatility during crisis periods (Bertay, Demirgüç-Kunt, and Huizinga 2012).

1.3.2 Financial Innovation and Securitization

Competitive financial systems are characterized by widespread financial innovation. A key example of this before the crisis was the substantial growth in securitized products. In principle, trade in securitized assets and credit derivatives should improve the efficiency and stability of the financial system by facilitating the transfer of risk to those investors most willing or able to bear it, by spreading risk more widely throughout the system, and by transferring risk to non-bank purchasers of securitized assets (Gorton and Metrick, 2013). In practice, however, securitization contributed to the crisis by creating a lack of transparency in the valuation of credit risk and problems of adverse selection and moral hazard, and by creating disincentives for originating lenders to screen borrowers prior to lending and subsequently monitor their performance (Mian and Sufi, 2009; Keys et al., 2010; Dell'Ariccia, Igan, and Laeven, 2012).

Since securitization provides banks with additional liquidity, it might motivate them to shift their portfolios towards higher-risk, higher-expected return investments. Purnanandam (2011) provides evidence to show that banks use the proceeds from securitizations to issue loans with default risk that is higher than average. In particular, the author shows that US banks that had engaged in extensive securitization prior to the 2007 subprime crisis had significantly higher mortgage charge-offs after the crisis. However, the provision of either contractual or non-contractual arrangements to support the transactions' structure may imply that the risks inherent in the securitized assets are not transferred to investors and are, in effect, still held by the issuing bank, but off-balance sheet. Gorton and Pennacchi (1995) argue that originating banks that retain a portion of the loan on the balance sheet or offer an implicit guarantee on the value of the loan to reduce moral hazard problems have incentives to efficiently evaluate and monitor the borrower. Sarkisyan and Casu (2013) explore the relationship between the retained interests by banks in securitizations and insolvency risk. The authors find that the provision of credit enhancements and guarantees leads to an increase in bank insolvency risk. Recent research has been devoted to assessing how securitization affects overall bank performance. For example, Casu et al. (2013) use a propensity score matching technique to estimate the effects of securitization on a number of bank performance indicators, including the cost of funding, credit risk, and profitability. The authors find little evidence to suggest that securitization has an impact upon bank performance.

1.3.3 Why Do We Have Big Banks? Economies of Scale versus Too-Big-to-Fail

The recent financial crisis and the subsequent bailouts of banks and other large financial institutions highlight the implications for macroeconomic and financial market stability deriving from the increased size of banking firms. However, such concerns need to be set against the economies of scale benefits which large banks can bring. Recent research revisits the economies of scale issue. Wheelock and Wilson (2012) use a large panel of data on US banks between 1984 and 2006 and find that scale economies exist for banks of all sizes, while DeYoung (2013) and Hughes and Mester (2013) also find that scale economies are prevalent for the largest banks. However, part of the potential benefits which accrue to large banks may be from being considered too-big-to-fail (TBTF). For example, if private investors are confident that they will not incur losses if these TBTF banks perform badly, then the cost of capital held by these banks will be lower than their smaller counterparts. As a consequence, the economies of scale observed for large banks may arise in part or in whole from implicit subsidies arising from TBTF status (Laeven and Valencia, 2010; Carow, Kane, and Narayanan, 2011). Davies and Tracey (2014) use a sample of US and European banks to explore such a possibility by increasing the cost of bank funding upwards to a level that would prevail if these banks no longer enjoyed TBTF status. The authors find that large bank scale economies disappear. Thus, banks may increase scale not because of true economies, but because they are able to obtain higher credit ratings and lower funding costs related to superior access to government safety nets (Brewer and Jagtiani, 2013). The rapid growth in investment banking and the "originate-to-distribute" securitization model also encouraged banking sector consolidation as well as moral hazard resulting in excessive risk-taking (Blinder, 2010; Feldman and Stern, 2010). Also, as noted above, some of the large investment banks became or merged with financial services holding companies to gain access to steadier sources of liquidity, thereby becoming larger in the process.

1.3.4 Diversification

A large body of literature examines the determinants of corporate diversification and the subsequent impact of diversification on bank value and risk. Many academics and commentators have argued that refocusing on traditional domestic banking activities has been driven by the stability of revenue and profit from retail sources and the relative volatility of non-retail activities. In general, empirical research which has examined the performance and diversification of banks in North America generally concludes that expansion into less traditional financial activities is associated with increased risk and lower returns (DeYoung and Roland, 2001; Brunnemeier, Dong, and Palia, 2012). Similarly, international expansion by US banks appears to be associated with higher risk and lower returns (Berger, El Ghoul et al., 2014). DeYoung and Torna (2013) use a sample of US banks covering the recent financial crisis. Banks that diversify their activities to pure fee-based non-traditional activities such as securities brokerage and insurance sales enjoy stable revenue and as such have a lower likelihood of failure. However, large banks may also engage with asset-based non-traditional activities, which may increase the probability of bank failure. Hence, the overall impact of diversification on the hazard of failure is to some extent cancelled out.

Outside the US, a less uniform picture tends to emerge. In a study of Russian banks, Berger, Hasan, Korhonen, and Zhou (2014) find that a middle ground between complete focus and full diversification increases expected returns and decreases risk and the likelihood of failure. For cross-country studies of European banks, Lepetit et al. (2008) find that risk is negatively related to the extent of bank trading activities, while Mercieca, Schaeck, and Wolfe (2007) contend that small banks that have diversified into non-interest income activities are riskier than those that focus on traditional areas of business. Demirgüç-Kunt and

Huizinga (2010) examine the effects of diversification and funding strategies on bank risks and returns for a sample of banks from 101 countries covering the period 1999–2007. They find evidence that banks with high proportions of non-interest income, or those that rely on non-deposit funding, tend to be very risky. DeJonghe, Diepstraten, and Schepens (2014) examine the joint impact of bank size and non-interest income on the systemic risk exposures of listed banks around the world for the period 1997–2011. They find that a shift towards non-interest-income generating activities leads to increased exposure to systemic risk for small banks. They also find lower systemic risk when medium and large banks expand their non-interest generating activities. This disappears in countries where the banking industry is concentrated and where there is more asymmetric information and corruption.

1.3.5 Competition and Risk

There is a developed literature on the measurement of competition, and its implications for bank performance and economic welfare. However, it is only recently that researchers have sought to establish and understand links between competition and bank risk on the one hand, and financial stability on the other. One school of thought argues that less competitive banking systems are less fragile because the numerous lending opportunities, high profits, and charter values of incumbent banks provide disincentives for excessive risk-taking (competition-fragility view Keeley, 1990; Carletti, 2008). An alternative view argues that competition leads to less fragility. This is because the market power of banks results in higher interest rates, which exacerbate moral hazard and adverse selection problems for customers and makes it more difficult for them to repay loans. This increases the possibility of loan default and increases the risk of bank portfolios, and subsequently makes the financial system less stable (competition-stability view Boyd and De Nicolo, 2005). Berger, Klapper, and Turk Ariss (2009) use a variety of risk and competition measures derived from a dataset of banks from 23 countries. Their results provide limited support to both the competition-fragility view and competition-stability views—banks with more market power appear to have higher loan risk, but lower overall risk because they hold more capital to protect themselves. Martinez-Miera and Repullo (2010) suggest a non-linear relationship between bank competition and stability. They argue that heightened competition may reduce borrowers' probability of default (referred to as a risk-shifting effect), but it may also reduce the interest payments from performing loans, which serves as a buffer to cover loan losses (referred to as a margin effect). They postulate a U-shaped relationship between competition (measured by the number of banks) and bank stability. In highly concentrated markets, the risk-shifting effect dominates and more competition reduces bank risk, while in very competitive markets the margin effect dominates, and the increased competition erodes banks' franchise value and hence increases risk. Liu and Wilson (2013) investigate whether the relationship between competition and risk varies across different bank types for a sample of Japanese banks over the period 2000–09. The relationship between competition and risk varies by bank type and these variations can largely be explained by initial levels of bank risk. Banks with higher levels of risk (Regional, Tier 2 Regional, Shinkin and Credit Cooperative banks) take on more risks when facing increasing competition (which leads to a negative relationship between bank competition and risk). Those banks with lower risk (City banks) are more likely to avoid increasing risk so as to protect their franchise value when competition increases (which leads to an overall positive relationship between competition and risk). Trust banks exhibit a moderate level of risk and take on moderate risks when competition intensifies and hence results in no clear relationship between competition and risk. Beck, De Jonghe, and Schepens (2013) use a large cross-country dataset of banks to show that an increase in bank competition boosts financial fragility in countries with strict activity restrictions and low levels of concentration.

1.3.6 Liquidity Risk and Creation

The recent financial crisis highlighted the risks posed if liquidity disappears from markets as well as the important role liquidity creation has for the economy overall. During the recent crisis, investors withdrew funds from collective pools of cash by declining to roll over loans and other contractual agreements. These actions forced many banks to sell securities to meet the increased demand for liquidity (Cornett et al., 2011). The unexpected liquidity shock raised illiquidity. As a consequence, investors demanded higher expected returns on their assets, causing a rapid decline in asset prices and a subsequent liquidity spiral, amplifying the initial liquidity shock (Brunnermeier and Pedersen, 2009).[5] In order to offer an explanation of the severity of the decline in liquidity during the recent financial crisis, a recent strand of literature has emerged which investigates the interaction between market and funding liquidity. The results from this literature suggest that liquidity responds asymmetrically to changes in asset market values, declining more rapidly for negative shocks (Hameed, Kang, and Viswanathan 2010). Furthermore, asset shocks limit the ability of banks to roll over debt because of agency problems associated with high leverage. This leads to liquidity hoarding by banks and reduced lending. In extreme cases this can gridlock interbank markets. Adverse asset shocks during good times can lead to much greater deleveraging and more rapid drying up of market and funding liquidity (Acharya and Skeie, 2011; Acharya and Viswanathan, 2011).

Another development in the banking literature relates to empirical work on bank liquidity creation (Berger and Bouwman, 2009). Liquidity creation is measured by gauging the ability of banks to transform their relatively illiquid assets (such as commercial loans) into relatively liquid liabilities (such as transaction deposits) held outside the banking system. It also includes banks creating liquidity via off-balance-sheet instruments, such as loan commitments and other similar claims to liquid funds. Evidence suggests that the extent to which banks create liquidity differs by bank size, ownership structure, and the extent to which they are focused on retail banking activities. The amount of liquidity creation has been found to have a significant positive relationship with bank value (Berger and Bouwman, 2009).

Berger and Bouwman (2009) test recent theories of the relationship between capital and liquidity creation and find that the relationship is positive for large banks and negative for small banks. Hovath, Seidler, and Weill (2014) explore the relation between capital and liquidity creation for a sample dataset of Czech banks over the period 2000–2010. The authors find there is a negative, bi-causal relation between capital and liquidity creation. Specifically, capital is found to inhibit liquidity creation, especially for small banks.

---

[5] Under certain conditions, the interaction between market and funding liquidity leads to illiquidity spirals and finally to liquidity dry-ups (Acharya and Viswanathan, 2011).

The authors conclude that there is a tradeoff between the benefits induced by stronger capital requirements and the benefits of greater liquidity creation.

However, liquidity creation may not always provide benefits. Berger and Bouwman (2013) analyze financial crises over the last quarter century and find that high liquidity creation (relative to trend) helps predict future crises after controlling for other factors. This is presumably because such excess liquidity creation generates asset price bubbles that eventually burst and cause financial crises, consistent with arguments in Acharya and Naqvi (2012).

1.4. BOOK STRUCTURE AND CHAPTER SUMMARIES

1.4.1. The Theory of Banking

Part I of this *Handbook* comprises nine chapters and examines why banks exist, how they function, the risks to which they are exposed and how there are managed, and their legal, organizational, and governance structures. Particular emphasis is placed on the evolution of banks within the wider financial system. It is noted that the scale, scope, and complexity of banking business have increased as banks have diversified across product and geographic lines. This has led to changes in the techniques used to manage credit, liquidity, and other risks. New complex organizational structures have emerged, including systemically important financial institutions (SIFIs) that pose new challenges for regulation and supervision.

In Chapter 2, Franklin Allen, Elena Carletti, and Xian Gu examine the role of banks in ameliorating informational asymmetries that can arise between lenders and borrowers, providing intertemporal smoothing of risk, and contributing to economic growth. The authors note that banks play a crucial role as delegated monitors in order to ensure that firms make effective use of loans made to them. Furthermore, banks play a central role in diversification of risks and smoothing consumption. However, banks are by their very nature fragile, and small shocks can have a large effect on the financial system and the real economy.

Nations around the globe have very different degrees of development of their stock and bond markets, and therefore rely on their banks to a greater or lesser extent. In general, Eurozone countries have small but rapidly developing stock markets. Bank lending relative to GDP is substantial, and bond markets play an important role in the financial system. The UK has a large stock market and a large banking sector, but the UK bond market is relatively small. The US banking sector is small in relation to the size of the US economy, but both the stock market and the bond market are relatively large. Japan has a relatively large banking sector and highly developed capital markets.

Competition among banks, non-banking financial institutions, and financial markets has intensified in recent years. This competition has led to the transformation of banks, and the growing complementarities between banks and capital markets. In Chapter 3, Arnoud Boot and Anjan Thakor examine the implications of these changes for the recent evolution of financial institutions and markets, and for regulatory design. The authors illustrate how banks depend on the capital market for sources of revenue, for raising equity capital and for risk management, while capital market participants rely increasingly on banks' skills in financial innovation and portfolio management. The increased integration of banks with financial markets raises domestic and cross-border financial stability concerns, which in turn has implications for the design of domestic and international financial system regulation.

As commercial banks have diversified into investment banking, a number of large SIFIs have emerged. In Chapter 4, Richard Herring and Jacopo Carmassi examine the phenomenon of global systemically important banks (G-SIBs) and examine how their complexity has changed since the onset of the recent financial crisis. The authors note that taxation and regulation have increased corporate complexity, and this continues to hinder efforts to supervise G-SIBs. Some G-SIBs have simplified their organizational structures and reduced their sizes in recent years. However, many others have grown more complex and larger. Higher capital requirements, improved bank resolution schemes, and living wills may help in supervising G-SIBs, but there is an additional need for enhanced transparency and market discipline.

In universal banking, services of both commercial and investment banks are provided under one roof. Universal banks often offer traditional deposit taking, lending, and payments services, as well as asset management, brokerage, insurance, and securities underwriting services. In Chapter 5 Alan Morrison examines the evolution of universal banking across countries and over time. Universal banking has operated in Germany for many years, but was generally restricted in the US by the Glass–Steagall Act until Congress passed the 1999 Gramm–Leach–Bliley Act. Potential conflicts of interests, such as the cross-selling of inappropriate in-house insurance and investment services to bank customers, or the mis-pricing of internal capital transfers between different parts of financial service groups and so on, are key issues for the universal banking model which present significant challenges for regulators. The author concludes by explaining the emerging post-crisis regulatory consensus over universal banking.

In order to reflect differences in capital structure, opacity, and complexity as well as their importance to the wider economy, the corporate governance of banks should be different from that of non-financial firms. In Chapter 6, Jens Hagendorff focuses on aspects of corporate governance in which banks (should) differ from non-financial firms. He provides an extensive overview of literature related to executive compensation, board composition, ownership, and risk management. The main observation from his chapter is that bank governance structures geared to aligning the interests of shareholders and managers lead to higher risk-taking. The chapter posits various ways to address this problem and argues that the recent financial crisis has provided an opportunity for academics and policymakers alike to rethink the corporate governance of banks.

Banks are exposed to credit risk, liquidity risk, interest rate risk, market risk, and operational risk. For any bank, the measurement and management of these risks is of the utmost importance. In Chapter 7, Linda Allen and Anthony Saunders describe the widely used Value at Risk (VaR) method of risk measurement. Accurate risk measurement enables banks to develop a risk management strategy, using derivative instruments such as futures, forwards, options, and swaps. The recent financial crisis shows that we still have a lot to learn about risk measurement and risk management.

One of the key functions of the banking sector is to create liquidity. In Chapter 8, Christa Bouwman provides a review and synthesis of the theoretical and empirical literature on bank liquidity creation. The author provides a discussion of the impact on liquidity creation of new approaches which combine originate-to-hold with originate-to-distribute business models, and how this has implications for regulation and supervision. The analysis raises interesting research questions concerning the design of both liquidity and capital requirements for traditional and shadow banks. It is also important to investigate how liquidity and capital interact, as inefficient bank bailouts may occur because regulators cannot easily distinguish between insolvency and illiquidity.

Deregulation and technological innovation have permitted banking organizations such as financial services holding companies to capture an increasing share of their revenue from non-interest sources. The increase in non-interest income reflects in part diversification into investment banking, venture capital, insurance underwriting, and fee- and commission-paying services linked to traditional retail banking services. In Chapter 9, Kevin Stiroh examines the effects of diversification on the risk and return characteristics of financial institutions. In many cases, risk-adjusted returns have declined following diversification into non-interest earning activities. This phenomenon maybe due to the tendency to diversify revenue streams, rather than clients, with the effect that interest and non-interest income are increasingly exposed to the same shocks. Alternatively, managers may have been willing to sacrifice profits to achieve growth through diversification, or the adjustment costs associated with diversification may have been larger than anticipated.

1.4.2. Bank Performance and Operations

Part II of the book comprises eight chapters dealing with bank performance and operations. A number of issues are assessed, including efficiency, technological change, globalization, and the ability to deliver small business, consumer, and mortgage lending services. The crucial roles that banks play in operating the retail and wholesale payments systems are also discussed.

In Chapter 10, Joseph Hughes and Loretta Mester outline the different approaches used to examine the efficiency and overall performance of banks. Here the authors discuss various structural and non-structural approaches to efficiency measurement. The structural approach requires a choice of the underlying production features of banking (intermediation, production, value-added, or other) and the specification of cost, profit, or revenue functions, from which (using various optimization techniques) one can derive relative performance measures. The role of risk is important in banks' production features and therefore should be included in evaluations of bank performance. The authors show that research which does not incorporate risk reports little evidence of scale economies at very large banks, while the results of other studies that control for differing levels of risk across banks tend to find that there are scale economies at the largest banks.

Technological advances and financial innovation have led to fundamental changes in the nature of banking over the last 25 years. In Chapter 11, W. Scott Frame and Lawrence White focus on innovations in banking products (subprime mortgages, retail services including the growth of debit cards, online banking, and the use of prepaid cards) and processes (automated clearing houses, small businesses credit scoring, asset securitization, and risk management). In addition, various new organizational forms, such as internet-only banks and the establishment of Section 20 securities subsidiaries are discussed. Financial and technological innovations have affected bank performance and the wider economy. However, the authors note that there is still scant research on why financial innovations take place, and suggest that this is an area future research could focus on.

Banks are the single largest provider of external finance to small businesses. In lending to such firms, banks use a number of different lending technologies to overcome a lack of publicly available financial information. In Chapter 12, Allen Berger discusses bank small business lending. In particular, he covers how some of the technologies used to make lending decisions to small business have evolved over time from relationship-based models relying on qualitative soft information to more sophisticated models based on different combinations of quantitative hard and qualitative soft information. He also examines the effects of banking industry consolidation and technological progress on the use of the lending technologies and their effects on small business credit. He finds that consolidation and technological progress and their interactions appear to have resulted in banks placing a greater reliance on hard information to make lending decisions. This is reflected in greater distances between banks and their small business clients.

Consumer lending is an area of banking activity that attracts substantial political interest. Recent years have seen a substantial growth in consumer lending. In Chapter 13, Thomas Durkin and Gregory Elliehausen examine the key features and risks inherent in consumer lending, highlighting approaches to evaluating credit supply default risk, and the inextricable influence of adverse selection and asymmetric information in the consumer credit process. The authors note that the recent financial crisis reduced both the demand and supply of consumer credit beyond that associated with normal recessionary periods.

Mortgage lending is an important part of the banking industry. In Chapter 14, Gregory Donadio and Andreas Lehnert note that deregulation and process and product innovations allowed banks to separate origination, funding, and servicing functions. This allowed small-scale financial institutions to originate mortgages, and securitize them and sell securities backed by them to other financial institutions and investors. This unbundling process introduced tensions among borrowers, mortgage funders, investors, and regulators. Since the recent financial crisis, underwriting standards have increased. The chapter also assesses recent changes in regulation aimed at promoting financial stability in mortgage markets.

Securitization has transformed the business of banking, and the wider financial system and economy. The role of banks has been changed from "originate and hold" to "originate, repackage, and sell." Securitization has become an integral part of modern financial systems by alleviating credit constraints and allowing transfer of certain risks. However, since the recent financial crisis, securitization activities have diminished. In Chapter 15, Barbara Casu and Anna Sarkisyan provide an extensive review of the theoretical and empirical research that has been conducted to explain why banks securitize, and what the effects of such activities are on consumers, financial institutions, and the wider economy. The authors point to a number of imperfections, including misaligned incentives and opacity. Recent measures to tackle misaligned incentives and information asymmetries to improve the quality of the credit rating process are also discussed in detail.

In Chapter 16, Adam Ashcraft, Tobias Adrian, and Nicola Cettorelli note that the transformation of the credit intermediation process (from a single to multiple financial institutions) not only resulted in a reduction in the costs of intermediation, but also the growth of shadow banking activities which take place outside the confines of the traditional banking system. The authors explore the underlying causes for the emergence of the shadow banking industry, and how connections to the traditional financial system can increase systemic risk. Recent developments including: agency mortgage REITS; reinsurance; tri-party repos; money market mutual funds; and shadow banking in China are also discussed.

Payment systems were relatively unaffected during the recent financial crisis. In Chapter 17, David Humphrey analyzes the use of retail payments systems (cash, checks, debit cards, credit cards, automated clearing houses), and wholesale payment systems (wire transfer networks) across countries. The costs and benefits of different systems to the banking system are highlighted, and policy avenues are explored with respect to both retail (e.g., privacy issues, card interchange fees) and wholesale payment systems (integration of back-office systems and uses of large value payment systems, systemic risk).

1.4.3. Regulatory and Policy Perspectives

Part III of this *Handbook* comprises nine chapters that examine the various roles of central banks, regulatory and supervisory authorities, and other government agencies which impact directly on the banking industry. Central banks execute monetary policy, which operates to a large degree through the banking system; act as a lender of last resort; and perform various other functions such as operating parts of the payments system. The scale and scope of central bank activities has increased dramatically since the onset of the recent financial crisis. In order to prevent widespread or systemic bank failure, government agencies provide safety-net protection such as explicit or implicit deposit insurance, unconditional payment system guarantees, and takeovers of troubled institutions. In part to protect against systemic failure, and in part to offset some of the perverse incentive effects of government safety-net protection, government authorities also engage in prudential regulation and supervision, and set policies concerning bank closure. Competition policy aimed at preventing abuses of market power also directly affect the banking industry. So too does explicit or implicit government policy concerning foreign entry into domestic markets and foreign ownership of domestic industry.

The role of central banks within the modern financial system has been determined by successive monetary and financial crises. In Chapter 18, Michel Aglietta and Benoît Mojon examine issues related to central banking. Today, the major tasks of the central bank are the settlement of interbank payments, bank regulation and supervision, lender of last resort, and the execution of monetary policy. However, not all central banks perform all four tasks. In the US, responsibility for regulation and supervision is divided among several agencies, including the Office of the Comptroller of the Currency (OCC) and the Federal Deposit Insurance Corporation (FDIC), as well as the central bank (the Federal Reserve). Future challenges that will influence the further evolution of central banking include securitization, development of new electronic payments media, and asset price volatility.

In Chapter 19, Joe Peek and Eric Rosengren examine the role of central banks in executing monetary policy, and the broader role of the banking sector in monetary policy transmission. Monetary policy is believed to affect real expenditure through three channels: the traditional interest rate channel, whereby changes in interest rates affect the spending preferences of consumers; the broad credit channel, whereby interest rate changes influence investor behavior and the borrowing preferences of the corporate sector; and the bank lending channel, whereby monetary policy affects the supply of bank credit through its effect on depositor behavior or changes in the value of bank assets and liabilities. The authors note that the efficacy of the bank lending channel has received increased attention since the onset of the recent financial crisis. Research carried out in recent years has provided academics and policymakers with a better understanding of the role of banks in the transmission of monetary policy.

Central banks also play an important role as lender of last resort to banks experiencing liquidity problems. Lending of last resort provides insolvent banks with liquidity and allows them to escape market discipline. In Chapter 20, Xavier Freixas and Bruno Parigi examine this lender of last resort function and its relationship with bank closure policy. The difficulties in distinguishing liquidity and solvency shocks are highlighted. The lender of last resort function is usually handled by the central bank, while scrutiny of bank closure is commonly the responsibility of a separate agency, often a deposit insurer. The recent financial crisis highlights the complexity of the lender of last resort function, which encompasses issues relating to monetary policy, bank supervision and regulation, and the operation of the interbank market. The authors posit that the lender of last resort function should be an integral and interdependent part of an overall banking safety net, which encompasses a deposit insurance system, a system of capital regulation, and a set of legal procedures to bail out or liquidate troubled banks.

The design of regulatory arrangements for the banking industry can lead to conflicts of interest, with the potential to undermine the quality of supervision and enforcement. In Chapter 21, Edward Kane explains how, in extreme cases, conflicts of interest, combined with intense competition and technological and financial innovation, can give rise to inappropriate behavior on the part of bankers, increasing the probability of a banking crisis. Kane notes that recent technological change and regulatory competition have encouraged banks to securitize their loans in ways that mask credit risks, while supervisors have outsourced much of their responsibility to credit rating agencies.

Deposit insurance is intended to prevent "runs" on individual banks by depositors. It also limits losses to depositors in the event of bank failure, and reduces the risk that a run on one bank might undermine confidence in others through a contagion effect. The recent financial crisis illustrates that a flawed deposit insurance system might cause more harm than good, if moral hazard created by the insurance results in excessive risk-taking or recklessness on the part of banks. In Chapter 22, George Kaufman and Robert Eisenbeis describe a well-functioning and efficient deposit insurance guarantee system. This involves promptly closing struggling banks when leverage ratios decline to unacceptably low levels, assigning credit losses to uninsured bank claimants promptly, and reopening closed institutions as soon as possible to allow insured depositors and pre-existing borrowers full access to their funds and credit lines. Such a system, the authors argue, can be designed as part of an efficient financial safety net. However, the authors readily acknowledge that heterogeneity in deposit guarantee systems in different countries complicates resolution in cases where cross-border banks get into financial difficulty.

To reduce moral hazard and systemic risk, regulators require banks to hold capital in order to absorb unforeseen risks. Standards developed by the Basel Committee on Banking Supervision have gone some way to aligning such capital requirements with banks' risk profiles. In Chapter 23, Michael Gordy, Erik Heitfield, and Jason Wu examine the rationale for capital regulation, and describe the key features of the Basel Accords. The authors focus on the theoretical and empirical underpinnings of capital regulation, and the challenges in rating the riskiness of assets contained in bank portfolios. In the final parts of the chapter, the authors describe the development and implementation of Basel III and discuss ongoing Basel Committee initiatives.

As the banking business has become increasingly complex, the usefulness of the traditional tools of supervision in monitoring risk-taking by banks has been called into question. The efficient markets hypothesis suggests that private investors can identify the risks associated with investing in shares of banks and other complex financial institutions, and thus exert market discipline. However, the recent financial crisis led some commentators to assert that market participants failed to exert discipline. In Chapter 24, Robert Bliss defines the concept of market discipline and explains its importance. Particular attention is paid to the theory and practice of both direct and indirect channels of market discipline and especially the role of equity and bond markets. Since the recent financial crisis, regulators have sought to realign incentives in order to restore market discipline in the banking and financial sector. Bliss notes that proponents of market discipline still argue that sophisticated market participants are best placed to assess complex risks being undertaken by banks and other firms, and may provide the ultimate sanction against such firms taking on excessive risk. However, he argues that this traditional view is based on weak theoretical and empirical foundations and contends that behavioral factors influence market participants, particularly during crisis times, making market discipline substantially less effective.

Competition in banking is important, because any form of market failure or anti-competitive behavior on the part of banks has far-reaching implications for productive efficiency, consumer welfare, and economic growth. In Chapter 25, Hans DeGryse, Paolo Morales Acevedo, and Steven Ongena review the methods used by researchers and policy-makers to assess the form and intensity of competition in the banking industry. The relative merits of market structure and "non-market structure" indicators such as the Panzar-Rosse H-statistic, the Lerner index, and the Boone indicator are discussed. The authors also illustrate how regulation and information sharing between banks impacts on bank competition. The effects of competition on bank performance, credit availability, and risk are also examined.

As noted previously, the rise of SIFIs has posed particular challenges to policymakers since the recent financial crisis. In Chapter 26, James Barth, Daniel Nolle, Tong (Cindy) Li, and Christopher Brummer examine the regulation and supervision of systemically important banks (SIBs). The authors utilize a new dataset compiled at the World Bank to provide an overview of regulatory initiatives in 135 countries. In the latter part of the chapter, the authors identify a number of legal issues which continue to make the cross-border regulation of SIBs difficult.

1.4.4. Macroeconomic Perspectives

Part IV of the book comprises seven chapters discussing the interactions among banks, firms, and the macroeconomy. This part of the book includes a discussion of the determinants of bank failures and crises, and the impact on financial stability, institutional development, and economic growth.

In Chapter 27, Philipp Hartmann, Olivier DeBandt, and José-Luis Peydró-Alcalde present a comprehensive review of systemic risk in banking in order to understand how extreme financial crises cause severe negative effects to the macroeconomy. A clearer understanding of the causes and consequences of systemic risk also helps policymakers formulate better banking regulation, prudential supervision, and more effective crisis management tools. The first part of the chapter outlines key analytical elements of systemic risk and brings them together as a coherent working concept that can be used as a benchmark for policies ensuring the stability of financial systems. Three important sources of systemic risk are identified as contagion effects, aggregate shocks (exogenous to the financial system), and the endogenous build-up and unraveling of widespread financial imbalances. The authors then go on to discuss aspects of public policy designed to contain such risks—both from an ex ante (preventative) and ex post (crisis-management) perspective. Second, the chapter presents an extensive theoretical and empirical literature review on a wide range of issues relating to systemic risk that aims to identify fruitful areas for future research. In conclusion, the authors note that since the global banking crisis there has been substantial increase in interest in analyzing systemic risk and banking/financial crises, although they caution that much more work is needed on identifying the effects of macroprudential policies and the role of bank business models.

In Chapter 28, Gerard Caprio and Patrick Honohon chart the frequency and severity of banking crises. A combination of factors are attributed to causing banking crises including low real interest rates; unsound macroeconomic policies; the expansion of deposit insurance schemes; the accumulation of official foreign exchange reserves; and the over-expansion of derivatives and securitization. The authors point out that the recent financial crisis illustrates information problems in the financial system, which lead investors to take excessive risks on products they do not understand.

Sovereign debt crises have historically been associated with wars and commodity price fluctuations. However, in recent years and especially since the onset of the recent financial crisis, sovereign indebtedness has become linked to the health of the banking sector. In Chapter 29, Ricardo Correa and Horacio Sapriza explore the interconnections between banks and sovereigns, and show how these can lead to instability in the financial system and real economy. The chapter focuses on sovereign crises that result from a banking crisis and explains how stresses are transferred from the banking sector to the sovereign and vice versa. It is noted that regulators need to break the link between the banking sector and sovereign risk. It is widely recognized that this can be aided by having a more effective safety net that minimizes the cost to taxpayers from banking failures, especially of large banks.

In Chapter 30, Charles Calomiris reviews the theory and historical evidence related to the prevalence of bank failure, panics, and contagion. He argues that banking system panics are neither random events nor inherent to the function of banks or the structure of bank balance sheets, but are caused by temporary confusion about the incidence of shocks within the banking system. Drawing on empirical evidence, Calomiris argues that government safety nets have led to increased banking instability by lessening market discipline, in turn leading to excessive risk-taking by banks.

International bank mergers increased rapidly up to the onset of the recent financial crisis, but have since declined. In Chapter 31, Claudia Buch and Gayle DeLong examine the causes and effects of international bank mergers. The authors examine the determinants of and barriers to cross-border bank mergers, and their impact on the efficiency, competitiveness, and riskiness of financial institutions and financial systems. Bank mergers tend to take place mostly between institutions from large and developed countries, between banks based in countries in close regional proximity, and between banks from countries that share a common cultural background.

In Chapter 32, Asli Demirgüç-Kunt and Martin Čihák examine the role of the government in financial and economic development before and after the onset of the recent financial crisis. The authors argue that active state involvement in the financial sector can help maintain economic and financial stability during crisis periods, but that these effects are not long lasting. Nevertheless, state involvement in the form of regulation and supervision is important for stability, even in the long run. However, such regulation should aim to align private incentives with the wider public interest. Unfortunately, this is a far from straightforward task given the size and complexity of the modern financial system.

In Chapter 33, Nicola Cetorelli continues by examining the links between financial development and real economic activity, focusing on the specific mechanisms, such as competition, which link bank activity to the real economy. Evidence suggests that bank concentration is inversely related to economic growth due to lower credit availability, although this effect varies across industries. For instance, concentration allows for the development of long-lasting lending relationships and this seems to enhance growth in industries where young firms are more dependent on external finance.

1.4.5. Banking Systems around the World

Part V of the *Handbook* focuses on the features of banking systems in different parts of the world. Seven chapters highlight the main structural and institutional features of various systems. The chapters cover banking in the US, the EU15 countries, Japan, Africa, the developing nations of Asia, transition countries, and Latin America.

The US banking system has undergone dramatic changes in recent years. Following the removal of restrictive regulations pertaining to branching, product, and price competition, there has been a systematic decline in the number of banks via both mergers and acquisitions and bank failures. This has been accompanied by a significant increase in the number of new banks being chartered. Changes in regulation (notably the Gramm–Leach–Bliley Act of 1999) have allowed US banking organizations to establish financial services holding companies and engage in the full range of financial services. The move toward a universal banking model has led to changes in balance-sheet composition, strategy, and performance. In Chapter 34, Robert DeYoung discusses in detail the evolution of the US banking industry over the past 25 years. He examines how deregulation, technological change, and financial innovation have affected industry structure and the strategies banks pursue. He presents persuasive evidence that suggests that small and large banks can coexist and pursue very different strategies in long-run equilibrium. In such equilibrium, large banks use advantages afforded by scale to pursue a transaction-based banking business model, which is reliant on technology and hard information, while small banks maintain a geographically focused strategy to build and maintain long-term lending relationships. Large banks can thus produce high-volume standardized products at low cost, while small banks can produce lower volumes of more tailored products at a higher price. DeYoung notes that while this new equilibrium brought substantial benefits to the banking industry and the wider economy, it also brought instability evidenced by the losses and government bailouts during the recent financial crisis.

Banking in the European Union has experienced marked changes in recent years. In Chapter 35, John Goddard, Philip Molyneux, and John Wilson focus on the original EU15 countries and explain that the structural and conduct deregulation, which took place until the recent financial crisis, reduced or eliminated many of the lines of demarcation between banks and other financial service providers and helped to facilitate both domestic and cross-border competition. The recent financial crisis and European sovereign debt crisis have led to large losses and the failure and closure of many banks, and forced the intervention of both central banks and governments in domestic banking systems. This has necessitated regulatory change aimed at ensuring the stability of the financial system, including plans for a European Banking Union.

Japan has a banking system with a wide array of different types of private, cooperative, and public banks, all undertaking a range of banking business. The system has undergone dramatic changes over the past decades as a result of the major financial crisis that started in the early 1990s and then culminated in 1997–1998. This was caused to some extent by an asset price bubble in real estate which was amplified by excessive bank lending to the sector. This resulted in the failure of a number of banks and a massive build-up of non-performing loans in the banking system. The perilous state of the banking system in the late 1990s resulted in a wide range of reforms aimed at improving financial sector soundness and bank credit expansion including substantial industry restructuring as well as the widespread use of quantitative easing between 2001 and 2006. In Chapter 36, Hirofumi Uchida and Gregory Udell analyze the segmented nature of the Japanese banking system and market structure, competition, and bank efficiency. The authors also explore the Japanese main bank system and relationship banking.

Banking in Africa has experienced rapid development over the past 20 years. Globalization, technological change, and financial liberalization have led to more open, stable, and deeper financial systems. However, in most countries, there remains a lack of bank competition and relatively high levels of financial exclusion. In Chapter 37, Thorsten Beck and Robert Cull use a variety of data to illustrate the evolution of African banking systems. The authors discuss the usefulness of government policies aimed at financial deepening, and assess the effectiveness of various financial innovations in reaching out to segments of the populations which were previously financially excluded.

In Chapter 38, Leora Klapper, Maria Soledad Martinez Peria, and Bilal Zia examine banking in the developing nations of Asia. The authors examine the significant reforms and structural changes that have taken place in the aftermath of the financial crisis in East Asia in 1997. Reforms have included privatization and allowing greater foreign participation in the banking industry. The authors highlight variations across countries based on the extent to which they have been aggressive in the reform agenda. The chapter also discusses the impact of the crisis on the banking sectors in Asia and empirically analyzes the behavior of foreign bank lending in the region during the crisis.

In Chapter 39, John Bonin, Iftekhar Hasan, and Paul Wachtel examine banking in transition countries. They note that the centralized planning systems adopted by Soviet Bloc countries gave way to banking structures in transition countries that are for the most part populated by privately owned (mainly foreign) banks overseen by a set of regulations and supervision. These banks provide a wide range of services to firms and households. The authors note that the recent financial crisis tested the resilience of transition banking systems. For the most part, the transition banking systems turned out to be resilient.

Extensive deregulation has taken place in the banking systems of Latin America in recent years. In Chapter 40, Jonathan Williams, Fernando Carvalho, and Luiz de Paula, assess the extent to which interest rate deregulation, bank privatization, and the removal of barriers to foreign banking led to banking crises in Brazil, Chile, Argentina, and Mexico. The authors note that banking crises in the 1980s and 1990s did not lead to reversals in the financial liberalization process. Instead, most countries in the area invested in building regulatory and supervisory infrastructures to ensure the future stability of the banking system. Banking systems in Latin America were relatively unscathed by the recent financial crisis.

References

Acharya, V. V. and Skeie, D. (2011). A Model of Liquidity Hoarding and Term Premia in Inter-Bank Markets, *Journal of Monetary Economics* 58, 436–447.

Acharya, V. V. and Viswanathan, S. (2011). Leverage, Moral Hazard, and Liquidity, *Journal of Finance* 66, 99–138.

Arcand, J. L., Berkes, E., and Panizza, U. (2012). Too Much Finance? IMF Working Paper No. 12/161.

Beck, T., Buyukkarabacak, B., Rioja, F. K., and Valev, N. T. (2012). Who Gets the Credit? And Does it Matter? Household vs. Firm Lending across Countries, *B.E. Journal of Macroeconomics* 12, 1–44.

Beck, T., De Jonghe, O., and Schepens, G. (2013). Bank Competition and Stability: Cross-country Heterogeneity, *Journal of Financial Intermediation* 22, 218–244.

Berger, A. N., Black, L. K., Bouwman, C. H. S., and Dlugosz, J. L. (2014). The Federal Reserve's Discount Window and TAF Programs: Pushing on a String? University of South Carolina Working Paper.

Berger, A. N. and Bouwman, C. H. S. (2009). Bank Liquidity Creation, *Review of Financial Studies* 22, 3779–3837.

Berger, A. N. and Bouwman, C. H. S. (2013). Bank Liquidity Creation, Monetary Policy, and Financial Crises. University of South Carolina Working Paper.

Berger, A. N., El Ghoul, S., Guedhami, O., and Roman, R. A. (2014). Internationalization and Bank Risk. University of South Carolina Working Paper.

Berger, A. N., Hasan, I., Korhonen, I., and Zhou M. (2014). *Bank Portfolio Diversification, Performance, and Failures.* University of South Carolina Working Paper.

Berger, A. N., Klapper, L. F., and Turk-Ariss, R. (2009). Bank Competition and Financial Stability, *Journal of Financial Services Research* 35, 99–118.

Berger, A. N. and Roman, R. A. (2014). Did TARP Banks get Competitive Advantages? University of South Carolina Working Paper.

Bertay, A. C., Demirgüç Kunt, A., and Huizinga, H. (2012). Bank Ownership and Credit over the Business Cycle: Is Lending by State Banks less Pro-cyclical? Centre for Economic Policy Research Discussion Paper No. 9034.

Black, L. K. and Hazelwood, L. N. (2013). The Effect of TARP on Bank Risk-Taking, *Journal of Financial Stability* 9, 790–803.

Blinder, A. S. (2010). The Squam Lake Report: Fifteen Economists in Search of Financial Reform, *Journal of Monetary Economics* 57, 892–902.

Boyd, J. and De Nicolo, G. (2005). The Theory of Bank Risk Taking Revisited, *Journal of Finance* 60, 1329–1343.

Boyd, J. and Prescott, E. (1986). Financial Intermediary Coalitions, *Journal of Economic Theory* 38, 211–232.

Brewer, E. and Jagtiani, J. A. (2013). How Much did Banks Pay to Become Too-Big-To-Fail and to Become Systemically Important?, *Journal of Financial Services Research* 43, 1–35.

Brunnermeier, M. K. (2009). Deciphering the Liquidity and Credit Crunch 2007-08, *Journal of Economic Perspectives* 23, 77–100.

Brunnermeier, M. K., Dong, G., and Palia, D. (2012). Banks Non-Interest Income and Systemic Risk. Princeton University Unpublished Working Paper.

Brunnermeier, M. K. and Pedersen, L. (2009). Market Liquidity and Funding Liquidity, *Review of Financial Studies* 22, 2201–2238.

Calomiris, C.W. and Kahn, C. M. (1991). The Role of Demandable Debt in Structuring Optimal Banking Arrangements, *American Economic Review* 81, 497–513.

Carletti, E. (2008). Competition and Regulation in Banking. In: A. W. A. Boot and A. Thakor (Eds.), *Handbook of Financial Intermediation and Banking*, 449–482. Amsterdam: Elsevier.

Carow, K. A., Kane, E., and Narayanan, P. (2011). Safety-Net Losses from Abandoning Glass-Steagall Restrictions, *Journal of Money, Credit and Banking* 43, 1371–1398.

Casu, B., Clare, A., Sarkisyan, A., and Thomas, S. (2013). Securitization and Bank Performance, *Journal of Money, Credit and Banking* 45, 1617–1658.

Cecchetti, S. G. and Kharroubi, E. (2012). Reassessing the Impact of Finance on Growth. BIS Working Paper No. 381.

Congressional Oversight Panel (2009). *Guarantees and Continent Payments in TARP and Related Programs, November Oversight Report, Submitted under Section 125(b) (1) of Title 1 of the Emergency Economic Stabilization Act of 2008, Pub.* L. No. 110–343, November 6.

Cornett, M. M., Mcnutt, J. J., Strahan, P.E., and Tehranian, H. (2011). Liquidity Risk Management and Credit Supply in the Financial Crisis, *Journal of Financial Economics* 101, 297–312.

Davies, R. and Tracey, B. (2014). Too Big to be Efficient? The Impact of Too-big-to-fail Factors on Scale Economies for Banks, *Journal of Money, Credit, and Banking* 46, 219–253.

Dell'ariccia, G., Igan, D., and Laeven, L. (2012). Credit Booms and Lending Standards: Evidence from the Subprime Mortgage Market, *Journal of Money, Credit and Banking* 44, 367–384.

Demirgüç-Kunt, A. and Huizinga, H. (2010). Bank Activity and Funding Strategies: The Impact on Risk and Returns, *Journal of Financial Economics* 98, 626–650.

De Jonghe, O., Diepstraten, M., and Schepens, G. (2014). Banks' Size, Scope and Systemic Risk: What Role for Conflicts of Interest?, <http://papers.ssrn.com/sol3/papers.cfm?abstract_id=2394884.>.

DeYoung, R. (2013). Modelling Economies of Scale in Banking: Simple versus Complex models. In: F. Pasiouras (Ed.), *Efficiency and Productivity Growth: Modelling in the Financial Services Industry*, 49–94. Chichester: John Wiley & Sons.

DeYoung, R. and Roland, K. P. (2001). Product Mix and Earnings Volatility at Commercial Banks: Evidence from a Degree of Total Leverage Model, *Journal of Financial Intermediation* 10, 54–84.

DeYoung, R. and Torna, G. (2013). Nontraditional Banking Activities and Bank Failures during the Financial Crisis, *Journal of Financial Intermediation* 22, 397–421.

Diamond, D. W. (1984). Financial Intermediation and Delegated Monitoring, *Review of Economics Studies* 51, 393–414.

Diamond, D. W. and Dybvig, P. (1983). Bank Runs, Deposit Insurance, and Liquidity, *Journal of Political Economy* 91, 401–419.

Diamond, D. W. and Rajan, R. G. (2001). Liquidity Risk, Liquidity Creation, and Financial Fragility: A Theory of Banking, *Journal of Political Economy* 109, 287–327.

Duchin, R. and Sosyura, D. (2014). Safer Ratios, Riskier Portfolios: Banks' Response to Government Aid, *Journal of Financial Economics*, 113, 1–28.

Fama, E. F. (1985). What's Different about Banks?, *Journal of Monetary Economics* 15, 29–39.

Feldman, R. J. and Stern, G. H. (2010). The Squam Lake Report: Observations from Two Policy Professionals, *Journal of Monetary Economics* 57, 903–912.

Financial Crisis Inquiry Commission (2011). *The Financial Crisis Inquiry Report: Final Report of the National Commission on the Causes of the Financial and Economic Crisis in the United States*. Washington: US Government Printing Office.

Gorton, G. and Metrick, A. (2013). Securitization. In: G. Constantinides, M. Harris, and R. Stulz (Eds.), *Handbook of the Economics of Finance*. 2nd edition, 2–70. Amsterdam: Elsevier.

Gorton, G. and Pennacchi, G. (1995). Banks and Loan Sales: Marketing Non-Marketable Assets, *Journal of Monetary Economics* 35, 389–411.

Gorton, G. and Winton, A. (2003). Financial Intermediation. In: G. Constantinides, M. Harris, and R. Stulz (Eds.), *Handbook of the Economics of Finance*, 432–552. Amsterdam: Elsevier.

Hameed, A., Kang, W., and Viswanathan, S. (2010). Stock Market Declines and Liquidity, *Journal of Finance* 65, 257–293.

Holmstrom, B. and Tirole, J. (1998). Public and Private Supply of Liquidity, *Journal of Political Economy* 106, 1–40.

Horvath, R., Seidler, J., and Weill, L. (2014). Bank Capital and Liquidity Creation: Granger-Causality Evidence, *Journal of Financial Services Research* 45, 341–361.

Hughes, J. P. and Mester, L. J. (2013). Who said Large Banks don't Experience Scale Economies? Evidence from a Risk-Return-Driven Cost Function, *Journal of Financial Intermediation* 22, 559–585.

Kashyap, A. K., Rajan, R. G., and Stein, J. C. (2002). Banks as Liquidity Providers: An Explanation for the Coexistence of Lending and Deposit-Taking, *Journal of Finance* 57, 33–73.

Keys, B. J., Mukherjee, T., Seru, A., and Vig, V. (2010). Did Securitization Lead to Lax Screening? Evidence from Subprime Loans, *Quarterly Journal of Economics* 125, 307–362.

Koetter, M. and Noth, F. (2012). Competitive Distortions of Bank Bailouts, <http://papers.ssrn.com/sol3/papers.cfm?abstract_id=2190902>.

Laeven, L. and Valencia, F. (2010). Resolution of Banking Crises: The Good, the Bad, and the Ugly. International Monetary Fund Working Paper No. 10/146.

Lane, P. R. (2012). The European Sovereign Debt Crisis, *Journal of Economic Perspectives* 26, 49–68.

La Porta, R., Lopez De Silanes, F., Shleifer, A., and Vishny, R. (1998). Law and Finance, *Journal of Political Economy* 106, 1113–1155.

La Porta, R., Lopez De Silanes, F., and Shleifer, A. (2002). Government Ownership of Banks, *Journal of Finance* 57, 265–301.

Leland, H. and Pyle, D. E. (1977). Information Asymmetries, Financial Structure and Financial Intermediation, *Journal of Finance* 32, 371–387.

Lepetit, L., Nys, E., Rous, P., and Tarazi, A. (2008). Bank Income Structure and Risk: An Empirical Analysis of European Banks, *Journal of Banking & Finance* 32, 1452–1467.

Levine, R. (2005). Finance and Growth: Theory and Evidence. In: P. Aghion and S. Durlauf (Eds.), *Handbook of Economic Growth*, 836–964. Amsterdam: Elsevier.

Li, L. (2013). TARP Funds Distribution and Bank Loan Supply, *Journal of Banking & Finance* 37, 4777–4792.

Liikanen, E. (2012). *High-Level Expert Group on Reforming the Structure of the EU Banking Sector*. Brussels: European Commission.

Liu, H. and Wilson, J. O. S. (2013). Competition and Risk in Japanese Banking, *European Journal of Finance* 19, 1–18.

Martinez-Miera, D. and Repullo, R. (2010). Does Competition Reduce the Risk of Bank Failure? *Review of Financial Studies* 23, 3638–3664.

Mercieca, S., Schaeck, K., and Wolfe, S. (2007). Small European Banks: Benefits from Diversification?, *Journal of Banking & Finance* 31, 1975–1998.

Mian, A. R. and Sufi, A. (2009). The Consequences of Mortgage Credit Expansion: Evidence from the US Mortgage Default Crisis, *Quarterly Journal of Economics* 124, 1449–1496.

Pozsar, Z., Adrian, T., Ashcraft A., and Boesky, H. (2012). *Shadow Banking*, Federal Reserve Bank of New York Staff Reports No. 458.

Purnanandam, A. K. (2011). Originate-to-Distribute Model and the Sub-Prime Mortgage Crisis, *Review of Financial Studies* 24, 1881–1915.

Sarkisyan, A. and Casu, B. (2013). Retained Interests in Securitizations and Implications for Bank Solvency, European Central Bank Working Paper No. 1538.

Vickers, J. (2011). *Independent Commission on Banking, Final Report*. London: HMSO.

Wheelock, D. and Wilson, P. (2012). Do Large Banks have Lower Costs? New Estimates of Returns to Scale for US Banks, *Journal of Money, Credit, and Banking* 44, 171–199.

PART I

THE THEORY OF BANKING

CHAPTER 2

....

THE ROLES OF BANKS IN FINANCIAL SYSTEMS[*]

....

FRANKLIN ALLEN, ELENA CARLETTI, AND XIAN GU

2.1 INTRODUCTION

....

UNDERSTANDING the many roles that banks play in the financial system is one of the fundamental issues in theoretical economics and finance. The crisis that started in the summer of 2007 underlines just how important banks are to the economy. The efficiency of the process through which savings are channeled into productive activities is crucial for growth and general welfare. Banks are one part of this process. Figure 2.1 gives an overview of the functioning of a financial system. Lenders of funds are primarily households and firms. These lenders can supply funds to the ultimate borrowers, who are mainly firms, governments, and households, in two ways. The first is through financial markets, which consist of money markets, bond markets and equity markets. The second is through banks and other financial intermediaries such as money market funds, mutual funds, insurance companies, and pension funds.

Despite the trend of globalization in recent years, the importance of banks in different economies varies significantly. Figure 2.2 shows a comparison of the long-term financing structure of the Eurozone, the UK, the US, Japan, and non-Japan Asia in 2001 and 2012.[1] The figures are given as a percentage of GDP. Bank assets consist of domestic credit to the private sector. The figures in the stock market column are the total market capitalization. The bond market figures are divided into public and private sector bonds.

---

[*] We are grateful to the editors for their helpful comments.

[1] This includes Hong Kong, Indonesia, Korea, Malaysia, the Philippines, Singapore, Taiwan, and Thailand.

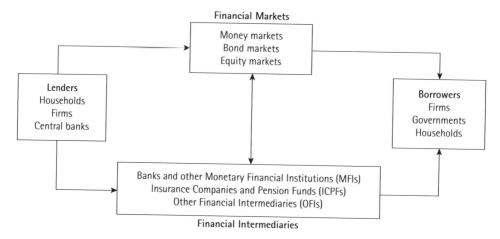

FIGURE 2.1 An overview of the financial system.

Source: Allen, Chui, and Maddaloni (2004) p. 491.

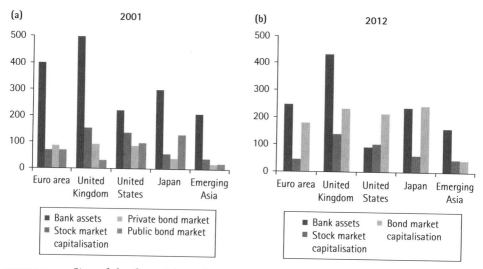

FIGURE 2.2 Size of the financial markets by country/region, percentage of GDP.

Source: IMF, Global Financial Stability Report.

It can be seen from Figure 2.2a that in 2001 the Eurozone had small stock markets but large bank loans and in that sense could be considered as bank-based. However, it also had a more significant bond market both in terms of public and private sector debt than stock market. The UK was significantly different with a large stock market and bank loans but a small bond market, particularly in terms of public sector debt.[2] In some sense it seems to be both

---

[2] The UK used to have a significant corporate bond market but this died during the 1970s when inflation was high. It has not revived in recent years despite the reduction in inflation.

market-based and bank-based. The main features of the US financial structure are a smaller amount of bank assets, a more significant stock market, and a much larger bond market than any of the other areas in relative terms. It is the most market-based economy. Japan has significant amounts of finance in all categories. It is very much a bank—and market-based—economy. Emerging Asia is more similar to the Eurozone: bank assets are important but the market is not.

Figure 2.2b shows the situation in 2012, several years after the 2008 global financial crisis. It can be seen that the structure is basically the same, while the bank assets shrank significantly. One interesting feature is that the financial structure in non-Japan Asia has not changed significantly despite the global financial crisis.

Figure 2.2 focuses on the claims that are issued by borrowers. Another way of considering the importance of banks is to look at household assets. These are shown in Figure 2.3a. This shows that all the economies are distinctly different. Households in the Eurozone own significantly fewer financial assets than in the other economies, with a total of 198% of GDP compared with 286%, 385%, and 289% for the UK, the US, and Japan respectively. In terms of the composition of assets there are also large differences. In the Eurozone, assets held in insurance and pension funds and banks are the most important two, with direct holdings of shares after that. One striking thing is that household portfolios in the UK are very similar to those in the Eurozone, with one significant difference: the investment in insurance and pension funds is dramatically higher. This is presumably a result of the difference in public sector pension schemes. In the UK the basic pension from the state is minimal, while in the Eurozone state pensions are usually generous. The US is an outlier in terms of the direct holdings of shares and other equity. Moreover, households have relatively few assets in banks. Meanwhile, Japan is an outlier in terms of the amount of assets held in banks, where households hold much more in this form than households in other countries. In fact the Japanese post office bank is the largest deposit-taker in the world. Japanese households

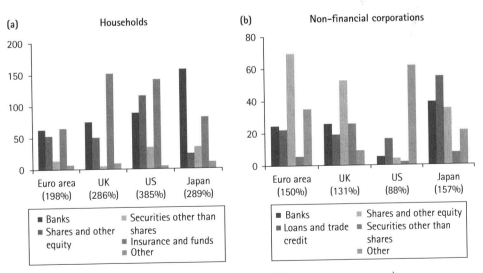

FIGURE 2.3 Portfolio allocation, percentage of GDP (average 1997–2012).

Source: Bank of Japan, ECB, EUROSTAT, Federal Reserve Board, Bank of England and the UK Office for National Statistics.

also have significant amounts in insurance and pension funds. This is to a large extent in insurance companies that offer debt-like contracts. Given the small holdings of shares and other equity, the Japanese bear significantly less financial risk than the households in the US and the UK. The US has somewhat less intermediation than the other economies, although the total amount of intermediation is significant in all economies.

Figure 2.3b shows the assets of non-financial corporations. These again underline significant differences across the economies. The Eurozone and the UK are quite similar except for the amount of shares and other equity held and the amount of securities, other than shares, held. The amount of shares and other equity held is larger in the Eurozone while the amount of securities other than shares held is larger in the UK. The US has much less investment than the other countries except for the "other" category. This includes holdings of other assets, which are not identified explicitly in the flow of funds data.[3] Japan is perhaps the most different. It has significantly more assets in banks and more trade credit than other countries.

The implication of Figures 2.2 and 2.3 is that the importance of banks and their roles are significantly different in different economies. We start by considering the basic rationales for the existence of banks. Section 2.2 considers the monitoring role of banks while Section 2.3 considers their risk-sharing role. The bearing of risks by banks can have important implications for financial stability. Section 2.4 considers banking crises and Section 2.5 the contagion between banks that can occur in a crisis. The role of banks in spurring growth is considered in Section 2.6. Section 2.7 is concerned with the corporate governance role of banks, Section 2.8 with relationship banking, and Section 2.9 contains concluding remarks.

2.2   Delegated Monitoring and Banks

An argument that is often put forward in favor of bank-based systems is that banks allow various informational problems to be solved. One important problem is if borrowers must take some action to make proper use of the funds they have borrowed. This action could be the level of effort or choice of project from among various different risky alternatives. The borrower can always claim that a low outcome is due to bad luck rather than from not taking the correct action. Lenders cannot observe the borrower's action unless they pay a fixed cost to monitor the borrower. In a financial market with many lenders, there is a free-rider problem. Each lender is small, so it is not worth paying the fixed cost. Everybody would like to free-ride, leaving it to someone else to bear the monitoring cost. As a result, no monitoring will be done.

A possible solution is to hire a single monitor to check what the borrower is doing. The problem then becomes one of monitoring the monitor, to make sure that he or she actually monitors the borrowers. Diamond (1984) develops a model of delegated monitoring to solve this problem. Intermediaries have a diversified portfolio of projects for which they provide

---

[3] The column representing "other" assets is unidentified miscellaneous assets. It is a residual item, arising after accounting for all asset or liability items reported by classified flow of funds sectors. In other words, accounting items that do not represent claims on another party are all classified as "other." One example would be the accounting value of goodwill after merger and acquisition (M&A) activities.

finance. They precommit to monitor borrowers by promising lenders a fixed return. If the intermediary does not monitor, then it will be unable to pay the promised return to lenders. Diamond's model thus illustrates how banks have an incentive to act as a delegated monitor and produce the information necessary for an efficient allocation of resources.

Boot and Thakor (1997) develop a model of financial system architecture that builds on this view of banks as delegated monitors. They assume there are three types of information problem. The first is that there is incomplete information about the future projects a firm has available to it. Outside investors can gather information about these possibilities. The second problem is that lenders cannot observe whether borrowers invest the funds in a risky or safe project. The third problem is the likelihood that borrowers will have the opportunity to invest in a risky project. Boot and Thakor are able to show that the first problem can best be solved by a financial market, and the second and third problems can best be solved by intermediaries. They argue that banks will predominate in an emerging financial system, while the informational advantages of markets may allow them to develop in a mature financial system.

2.3 THE RISK SHARING ROLE OF BANKS

One of the most important functions of the financial system is to share risk and it is often argued that financial markets are well suited to achieve this aim. As shown in Figure 2.3 and discussed in Section 2.1, if both direct holdings of equities and indirect holdings in insurance companies and mutual funds are taken account of, in the US and the UK a large amount of household assets is held in equity and only a small amount in banks. In both countries households are exposed to substantial amounts of risk through their holdings of equities. At the other extreme, households in Japan are shielded from risk because they ultimately hold a majority of their assets in banks and very little in equities. Households' asset holdings in the Eurozone, although not as safe as in Japan, are much safer than in the US and the UK.

Although the proportions of risky assets held by households in the US and the UK are much higher than in Japan, and the Eurozone, this does not necessarily mean that the absolute amount of risk borne by households is greater, because the amount invested in financial assets could be higher in the latter countries. However, it can be seen from Figure 2.2 that the Eurozone has a significantly lower amount of financial assets relative to GDP. Thus taking into account the amount of wealth held in financial assets increases the differences in the amount of risk borne by households in the different countries, rather than reducing it. Not only do households hold much higher proportions in risky securities in the US and the UK, they also hold more financial assets.

How can one explain these differences in the amount of risk households are apparently exposed to in different financial systems? Standard financial theory suggests that the main purpose of financial markets is to improve risk sharing. Financial markets in the US and the UK are more developed by most measures than in Japan and the Eurozone, so how can it be that households are exposed to much more risk in the US and the UK than in Japan and the Eurozone?

Allen and Gale (1997, 2000a, ch. 6) have provided a resolution to this paradox. They point out that traditional financial theory has little to say about hedging non-diversifiable risks.

It assumes that the set of assets is given and focuses on the efficient sharing of these risks through exchange. For example, the standard diversification argument requires individuals to exchange assets so that each investor holds a relatively small amount of any one risk. Risks will also be traded so that more risk-averse people bear less risk than people who are more risk tolerant. This kind of risk sharing is termed cross-sectional risk sharing, because it is achieved through exchanges of risk among individuals at a given point in time. However, importantly, these strategies do not eliminate macroeconomic shocks that affect all assets in a similar way.

Departing from the traditional approach, Allen and Gale focus on the intertemporal smoothing of risks that cannot be diversified at a given point in time. They argue that such risks can be averaged over time in a way that reduces their impact on individual welfare through intertemporal smoothing by banks. This involves banks building up reserves when the returns on the banks' assets are high and running them down when they are low. The banks can thus pay a relatively constant amount each period and do not impose very much risk on depositors. The authors show that the incentives for engaging in intertemporal smoothing are very different in market-based financial systems. Incomplete financial markets, on the one hand, may not allow effective intertemporal smoothing. The problem is that the long-lived asset "crowds out" the storage technology because it can be bought and sold for the same price and, in addition, it pays a dividend. Long-lived banks, on the other hand, can achieve intertemporal smoothing as explained above. However, for this result to hold, it is necessary that the banks are not subject to substantial competition from financial markets. In fact, competition from financial markets can lead to disintermediation and the unraveling of intertemporal smoothing provided by long-lived institutions.

2.4 BANKING CRISES

Banks perform an important role in terms of maturity transformation. They collect demandable deposits and raise funds in the short-term capital markets and invest them in long-term assets. This maturity mismatch allows them to offer risk sharing to depositors but also exposes them to the possibility that all depositors withdraw their money early. Runs can involve the withdrawal of funds by depositors (retail runs) or the drying up of liquidity in the short-term capital markets (wholesale runs). In the case of the run on Northern Rock in the UK in late 2007, both occurred.

There were traditionally two theories to explain the origins of banking crises. One line of argument maintains that they are undesirable events caused by random deposit withdrawals unrelated to changes in the real economy. In this case they occur spontaneously as a panic resulting from "mob psychology" or "mass hysteria" (e.g., Kindleberger, 1978). Alternatively they may arise from fundamental causes that are part of the business cycle (see Mitchell, 1941). Depositors use leading economic indicators to identify when the economy may be going into a recession where banks will be unable to meet their liabilities and they withdraw as a result.

The panic view suggests that crises are random events, unrelated to changes in the real economy. In the influential work of Bryant (1980) and Diamond and Dybvig (1983) bank runs are sunspot phenomena, as in Cass and Shell (1983). Given the assumption of first-come, first-served and costly liquidation of some assets there are multiple equilibria. If everybody believes that no panic will occur then only those with genuine liquidity needs will withdraw their funds and these demands can be met without costly liquidation of assets. However, if everybody believes a crisis will occur then it becomes a self-fulfilling prophecy as people rush to avoid being last in line. Which of these two equilibria occurs depends on extraneous variables or "sunspots." Although sunspots have no effect on the real data of the economy, they affect depositors' beliefs in a way that turns out to be self-fulfilling.

The second view is that banking crises are a natural outgrowth of the business cycle. An economic downturn will reduce the value of bank assets, raising the possibility that banks are unable to meet their commitments. Jacklin and Bhattacharya (1988) develop a theoretical model where, if depositors receive information about an impending downturn in the cycle, they will anticipate financial difficulties in the banking sector and try to withdraw their funds. This attempt will precipitate the crisis. According to this interpretation, crises are not random events but a response of depositors to the arrival of sufficiently negative information on the unfolding economic circumstances. Gorton (1988) provides evidence that in the US in the late nineteenth and early twentieth centuries, a leading economic indicator based on the liabilities of failed businesses could accurately predict the occurrence of banking crises. A number of authors have developed models of banking crises caused by aggregate risk. For example, Chari and Jagannathan (1988) focus on a signal extraction problem where part of the population observes a signal about future returns. Others must then try to deduce from observed withdrawals whether an unfavorable signal was received by this group or whether liquidity needs happen to be high. Chari and Jagannathan are able to show that crises occur not only when the outlook is poor but also when liquidity needs turn out to be high.

Building on the empirical work of Gorton (1988) that nineteenth-century banking crises were predicted by leading economic indicators, Allen and Gale (1998) develop a model that is consistent with the business-cycle view of the origins of banking crises. They assume that depositors can observe a leading economic indicator that provides public information about future bank asset returns. If there are high returns then depositors are quite willing to keep their funds in the bank. However, if the returns are sufficiently low they will withdraw their money in anticipation of low returns. There is thus a crisis.

Allen and Gale (2004) develop a general equilibrium framework for understanding the normative aspects of crises. This framework is used to investigate the welfare properties of financial systems and to discover conditions under which regulation might improve the allocation of resources. An interesting feature of the Allen–Gale framework is that it explicitly models the interaction of banks and markets. Financial institutions are the main players in financial markets, which allow banks and intermediaries to share risks and liquidity. Individuals do not have direct access to markets; instead, they access markets indirectly by investing in intermediaries. Financial intermediaries and markets play important but distinct roles in the model. Intermediaries provide consumers with insurance against idiosyncratic liquidity shocks. Markets allow financial intermediaries and their depositors to share risks from aggregate liquidity and asset return shocks.

Financial markets are said to be complete if it is possible for intermediaries to hedge all aggregate risks in the financial markets. This would be possible if securities contingent on all the possible combinations of aggregate liquidity and asset return shocks, or in other words all the states of nature, were available. Similarly, the risk-sharing contracts between intermediaries and consumers are said to be complete if the payoffs can be explicitly conditioned on all the possible combinations of aggregate liquidity and asset return shocks. An example of an incomplete contract would be something like debt, where the payoff on the contract does not depend explicitly on the aggregate state of liquidity demand and asset returns. Allen and Gale (2004) show that the laissez-faire allocation of resources is efficient provided markets are complete. This is the case even if contracts are incomplete. However, crises are inefficient if markets are incomplete. In this case financial fragility and contagion can occur.

While the multiple equilibria theory of bank runs explains how panics may occur, it is silent on which of the two equilibria will be selected. Depositors' beliefs are self-fulfilling and are coordinated by "sunspots." Sunspots are convenient pedagogically but they do not have much predictive power. Since there is no real account of what triggers a crisis, it is difficult to use the theory for any policy analysis. The business-cycle theory also has panic runs as well as fundamental runs. Again, there is no natural way to choose the equilbria.

Carlsson and van Damme (1993) showed how the introduction of a small amount of asymmetric information could eliminate the multiplicity of equilibria in coordination games. They called the games with asymmetric information about fundamentals "global games." Their work showed that the existence of multiple equilibria depends on the players having common knowledge about the fundamentals of the game. Introducing noise ensures that the fundamentals are no longer common knowledge and thus prevents the coordination that is essential to multiplicity. Morris and Shin (1998) applied this approach to models of currency crises. Rochet and Vives (2004), and Goldstein and Pauzner (2005), have applied the same technique to banking crises.

Using a global games approach to ensure the uniqueness of equilibrium is theoretically appealing. However, what is really needed in addition to logical consistency is empirical evidence that such an approach is valid. In an important contribution, Chen, Goldstein, and Jiang (2010) develop a global games model of mutual fund withdrawals. Using a detailed dataset they find evidence consistent with their model. This represents significant evidence supporting the global games approach.

A number of recent papers have contributed significantly to the banking crisis literature. One example is He and Xiong (2012). They depart from the static framework and develop a dynamic model of bank runs. The model highlights the dynamic coordination problem between creditors who make rollover decisions at different times. There exists a unique equilibrium in which preemptive debt runs occur through a "rat race" among the creditors based on the publicly observable time-varying firm fundamental.

Martin, Skeie, and von Thadden (2014) develop an infinite horizon model of shadow bank runs. The non-banks engage in maturity transformation that involves borrowing short term to invest in long-term assets. An important difference with standard banking models is that the long-term assets can be traded in a market. It is shown that net asset sales in the form of securitization weakens a borrower's balance sheet and makes the non-bank more fragile. It is also shown that if there is a shock to asset values that is sufficiently strong then a run on all the non-banks is possible as a self-fulfilling expectation.

Besides the theoretical literature, Reinhart and Rogoff (2009) provide a comprehensive empirical investigation of bank runs and bank failures in Europe from the Napoleonic Wars to the recent global financial crises that began with the US subprime crisis of 2007. They show that banking crises are an equal-opportunity menace affecting rich and poor countries alike and remain a recurring problem everywhere. The crisis that started in 2007 provides a dramatic example of how damaging banking crises can be. The complete causes for its occurrence are not fully understood yet, but many attribute them, at least partly, to the bad incentives in the origination of mortgages and their securitization, the provision of ratings for securitizations, and the risk management systems of investment firms. The large global impact of the crisis suggests, however, that the problems with subprime mortgages are a symptom rather than the cause. One main problem is that there was a bubble, first in stock prices and then in property prices, and the economic system is now suffering the fallout from the collapse of that bubble. The monetary policies of central banks, particularly the US Federal Reserve, appear to have been too loose and have focused too much on consumer price inflation and too little on asset price inflation. Moreover, the Asian crisis of 1997 and the policies of the IMF during that crisis led to a desire among Asian governments to hoard funds. This created important global imbalances that expanded the credit available and helped to fuel the bubble. Allen and Gale (2000b) show how such an expansion of credit can create a bubble.

Whatever the reasons behind the 1997 crisis, its effects certainly spread to the real economy. Most industrialized and non-industrialized countries experienced problems with many of their industries entering into recession. The problems were multiple. On the one hand, the difficulties of the financial sector induced intermediaries to tighten their credit standards, thus making it more difficult for firms to obtain credit and at good rates. On the other hand, the sharp fall in consumer demand decreased sales and future orders. As in the financial sector, the problems were not confined to single firms but affected whole industries. The car industry is one dramatic example, but also other manufacturing industries, construction, and many others were placed under considerable pressure. The aftermath of systemic banking crises also puts significant strains on government resources. As shown in Reinhart and Rogoff (2011), on average, government debt rises by 86% during the three years following a banking crisis due to the large scale of bank bailouts or the collapsing revenues. In some circumstances, if banks are overly exposed to government paper, banking crisis and debt crisis may also be more or less simultaneous.

2.5 BANKS AND CONTAGION

The prevalence of financial crises has led many to conclude that the financial sector is unusually susceptible to shocks. One theory is that small shocks can have a large impact. A shock that initially affects only a particular region or sector, or perhaps even a few institutions, can spread by contagion through interlinkages between banks and financial institutions to the rest of the financial sector and then infect the larger economy.

The theoretical literature on contagion takes two approaches. On the one hand, there are a number of papers that look for contagious effects via direct linkages. Allen and Gale (2000c) study how the banking system responds to contagion when banks are connected under different network structures. In a setting where consumers have the type of liquidity preferences as set out by Diamond and Dybvig (1983), banks perfectly insure against liquidity shocks by exchanging interbank deposits. The connections created by swapping deposits expose the system to contagion. The authors show that incomplete networks are more prone to contagion than complete structures. Better connected networks are more resilient to contagion since the proportion of the losses in one bank's portfolio is transferred to more banks through interbank agreements.

Other models capture well the network externalities created from an individual bank risk. Freixas, Parigi, and Rochet (2000) consider the case of banks that face liquidity needs in a situation such as that consumers are uncertain about the location where they are to consume. On their model, the connections between banks are realized through interbank credit lines that enable these institutions to hedge regional liquidity shocks. In the same way as in Allen and Gale (2000c), interbank connections enhance the resilience of the system to the insolvency of a particular bank. The drawback is that this weakens the incentives to close inefficient banks. Moreover, the authors find that the stability of the banking system depends crucially on whether many depositors choose to consume at the location of a bank that functions as a money center or not.

Dasgupta (2004) uses a global games approach to show how a unique equilibrium with contagion can arise when banks hold cross deposits. In the same spirit, Brusco and Castiglionesi (2007) show that there is a positive probability of bankruptcy and propagation of a crisis across regions when banks keep interbank deposits and may engage in excessive risk-taking if they are not well enough capitalized. Leitner (2005) develops a model of financial networks and demonstrates that agents may be willing to bail out other agents because of the threat of contagion. However, in some cases an agent may not have enough cash to make the necessary investment, thus the whole network may collapse.

A number of papers have linked the risk of contagion to financial innovation and the accounting system in use. The common feature in this analysis is the presence of incomplete markets where liquidity provision is achieved by selling assets in the market when required. Asset prices are determined by the available liquidity or, said differently, by the "cash in the market." It is necessary that people hold liquidity and stand ready to buy assets when they are sold. These suppliers of liquidity are no longer compensated for their opportunity cost of providing liquidity state by state. The cost must be made up on average across all states. This implies volatility in the asset prices that can, in turn, lead to costly and inefficient crises. In order for people to be willing to supply liquidity they must be able to make a profit in some states. In equilibrium, prices of assets will be such that the profit in the states where banks and intermediaries sell assets is sufficient to compensate the providers of liquidity for all the other states where they are not called upon to provide liquidity and simply bear the opportunity cost of holding it. In other words, asset prices are low in the states where banks and intermediaries need liquidity. But from an efficiency point of view this is exactly the wrong time for there to be a transfer from the banks and intermediaries who need liquidity to the providers of liquidity. This is because the banks' depositors who need liquidity will already have low income because they have to withdraw early.

Allen and Carletti (2006) rely on cash-in-the-market pricing to show how financial innovation in the form of credit risk transfer can create contagion across sectors and lower welfare relative to the autarky solution. They focus on the structure of liquidity shocks hitting the banking sector as the main mechanism determining contagion. When banks face a uniform demand for liquidity, they keep a sufficient amount of the short-term asset and do not need to raise additional liquidity in the market. In this case, credit risk transfer is beneficial as it improves risk sharing across sectors. Differently, when banks face idiosyncratic liquidity shocks, they invest also in the long risk-free asset and trade it in the market. The presence of credit risk transfer turns out now to be detrimental as it induces a higher need of liquidity in the market and consequently a greater variability in asset prices. This in turn affects banks' ability to face their liquidity shocks as it implies a severe reduction in the price of the long asset, which banks use to hedge their liquidity risk. The banks that are selling the long asset receive a lower amount and may be unable to pay their depositors.

The effect of introducing credit risk transfer depends crucially also on the accounting system in use, be it historical cost or mark-to-market accounting, as shown by Allen and Carletti (2008). The intuition is similar to that shown in Chapter 1. When banks need to liquidate a long-term asset on an illiquid market, it may not be desirable to value such assets according to market values as it reflects the price volatility needed to induce liquidity provision.

Another approach to modeling contagion focuses on indirect balance-sheet linkages. Lagunoff and Schreft (2001) construct a model where agents are linked in the sense that the return on an agent's portfolio depends on the portfolio allocations of other agents. On their model, agents who are subject to shocks reallocate their portfolios, thus breaking some linkages. Two related types of financial crisis can occur in response. One occurs gradually as losses spread, breaking more links. The other type occurs instantaneously when forward-looking agents preemptively shift to safer portfolios to avoid future losses from contagion. Similarly, de Vries (2005) shows that there is dependency between banks' portfolios, given the fat tail property of the underlying assets, and this carries the potential for systemic breakdown. Cifuentes, Ferrucci, and Shin (2005) present a model where financial institutions are connected via portfolio holdings. The network is complete as everyone holds the same asset. Although the authors incorporate in their model direct linkages through mutual credit exposures as well, contagion is mainly driven by changes in asset prices.

Complementary to the literature on network effects, Babus (2009) considers a model where banks form links with each other in order to reduce the risk of contagion. The network is formed endogenously and serves as an insurance mechanism. At the base of the link formation process lies the same intuition developed in Allen and Gale (2000c): better connected networks are more resilient to contagion. The model predicts a connectivity threshold above which contagion does not occur, and banks form links to reach this threshold. However, an implicit cost associated with being involved in a link prevents banks from forming connections more than required by the connectivity threshold. Banks manage to form networks where contagion rarely occurs. Castiglionesi and Navarro (2007) are also interested in whether banks manage to decentralize the network structure that a social planner finds optimal. In a setting where banks invest on behalf of depositors, and there are positive network externalities on the investment returns, fragility arises when banks that are not sufficiently capitalized gamble with depositors' money. When the probability of bankruptcy is low, the decentralized solution approximates the first best.

Allen, Babus, and Carletti (2012) develop a model of contagion based on the interaction of asset commonality between banks and the use of short-term debt. Banks swap assets to diversify their individual risk. Two asset structures arise. In a clustered structure, groups of banks hold common asset portfolios and default together. In an unclustered structure, defaults are more dispersed. Portfolio quality of individual banks is opaque but can be inferred by creditors from aggregate signals about bank solvency. When bank debt is short term, creditors do not roll over in response to adverse signals and all banks are inefficiently liquidated. This information contagion is more likely under clustered asset structures. In contrast, when bank debt is long term, welfare is the same under both asset structures.

Besides the theoretical investigations, there has been a substantial interest in looking for evidence of contagious failures of financial institutions resulting from the mutual claims they have on one another. Most of these papers use balance-sheet information to estimate bilateral credit relationships for different banking systems. Subsequently, the stability of the interbank market is tested by simulating the breakdown of a single bank. For example, Upper and Worms (2004) analyze the German banking system. They show that the failure of a single bank could lead to the breakdown of up to 15% of the banking sector in terms of assets. Cocco, Gomes, and Martins (2009) consider Portugal, Furfine (2003) the US, Boss et al. (2004) Austria, and Degryse and Nguyen (2007) Belgium. Iyer and Peydro-Alcalde (2011) conduct a case study of interbank linkages resulting from a large bank failure due to fraud. Jorion and Zhang (2009) provide evidence of credit contagion via direct counterparty effects. Upper (2010) contains a survey of this literature. The main conclusion of the literature is that contagion is usually not a serious risk provided there are not significant price movements in response to the turmoil. If there are, as in Cifuentes, Ferrucci, and Shin (2005), then contagion effects can be significant.

The current crisis in 2007–2009 illustrates the practical importance of contagion. The usual justification for intervention by central banks and governments to prevent the bankruptcy of systemic financial institutions is that this will prevent contagion. This was the argument used by the Federal Reserve for intervening to ensure Bear Sterns did not go bankrupt in March 2008, for example (see Bernanke, 2008). The bankruptcy of Lehman Brothers a few months later in September 2008 illustrated quite how damaging contagion can be. The process did not work in quite the way envisaged in the academic literature and occurred despite the judgment of the Federal Reserve and Treasury that Lehman should not be saved. The first spillover was to the money-market mutual fund sector. Reserve Capital "broke the buck" as it held a significant amount of paper issued by Lehman. This led to many withdrawals from other money-market mutual funds and, four days after Lehman announced bankruptcy, the US government was forced to announce guarantees for the entire sector. After seeing Lehman Brothers collapse, confidence in the creditworthiness of banks and other financial institutions and firms fell significantly and this is when the financial crisis started to spill over into the real economy and had such a damaging effect on it. Going forward, much more research is needed to understand the many channels of contagion in a crisis.

2.6 BANKS AND GROWTH

Another important role of banks is in spurring growth. There has been a debate on the relative effectiveness of banks compared to financial markets in doing this. This debate was originally conducted in the context of German and UK growth in the late nineteenth and early twentieth centuries. Gerschenkron (1962) argued that the bank-based system in Germany allowed a closer relationship between bankers providing the finance and industrial firms than was possible in the market-based system in the UK. Goldsmith (1969) pointed out that although manufacturing industry grew much faster in Germany than in the UK in the late nineteenth and early twentieth centuries the overall growth rates were fairly similar. More recently, Levine (2002) uses a broad database covering 48 countries over the period 1980–1995. He finds that the distinction between bank-based and market-based systems is not an interesting one for explaining the finance–growth nexus. Rather, elements of a country's legal environment and the quality of its financial services are most important for fostering general economic growth. In contrast, in a study of 36 countries from 1980 to 1985 Tadesse (2002) does find a difference between bank-based and market-based financial systems. For underdeveloped financial sectors, bank-based systems outperform market-based systems, while for developed financial sectors, market-based systems outperform bank-based systems. Levine and Zervos (1998) show that higher stock market liquidity or greater bank development lead to higher growth, irrespective of the development of the other. There is some evidence that financial markets and banks are complements rather than substitutes. Demirgüç-Kunt and Maksimovic (1998) show that more developed stock markets tend to be associated with increased use of bank finance in developing countries. More recent evidence in Beck and Demirgüç-Kunt (2009) shows that a general deepening of the financial sector over time is more pronounced in the high-income countries, and more significant for markets than for banks.

There is a large theoretical literature on the relative merits of bank-based and market-based systems for innovation and growth. Bhattacharya and Chiesa (1995) consider a model of research and development (R&D) incentives and financing. In a market system, lenders learn the value of each firm's R&D at the interim stage after R&D has been undertaken but before production takes place. The lenders can share the information among the firms and will do so if it is in their interest. Bhattacharya and Chiesa show that their incentives to do this correspond to maximizing the aggregate value of the firms' R&D projects. Also, a collusive agreement can be structured so that only one firm actually produces at the production stage. However, this collusion creates a free-rider problem and reduces incentives to undertake the R&D at the first stage. If this incentive problem is severe enough, bilateral financing may be preferable. Under this arrangement, each firm is financed by one bank and there is no scope for information sharing. As a result, each firm's R&D information remains proprietary.

Allen and Gale (1999, 2000a, ch. 13) ask whether financial markets or banks are better at providing finance for projects where there is diversity of opinion, as in the development of new technologies. Diversity of opinion arises from differences in prior beliefs, rather than differences in information. The advantage of financial markets is that they allow people with similar views to join together to finance projects. This will be optimal provided the costs necessary for each investor to form an opinion before investment decisions are made are sufficiently low. Finance can be provided by the market even when there is great diversity of opinion among investors. Intermediated finance involves delegating the financing decision to a manager who expends the cost necessary to form an opinion. There is an agency problem in that the manager may not have the same priority as the investor. This type of delegation turns out to be optimal when the costs of forming an opinion are high and there is likely to be considerable agreement in any case. The analysis suggests that market-based systems will lead to more innovation than bank-based systems.

2.7 THE CORPORATE GOVERNANCE ROLE OF BANKS

The importance of equity ownership by financial institutions in Japan and Germany, and the lack of a strong market for corporate control in these countries, have led to the suggestion that the agency problem in these countries is solved by banks acting as outside monitors for large corporations. In Japan, this system of monitoring is known as the main bank system. The characteristics of this system are the long-term relationship between a bank and its client firm, the holding of both debt and equity by the bank, and the active intervention of the bank should its client become financially distressed. It has been widely argued that this main bank relationship ensures that the bank acts as delegated monitor and helps to overcome the agency problem between managers and the firm. However, the empirical evidence on the effectiveness of the main bank system is mixed (see Hoshi, Kashyap, and Scharfstein, 1990, 1993; Aoki and Patrick, 1994; Hayashi, 2000). Overall, the main bank system appears important in times of financial distress, but less important when a firm is doing well.

In Germany the counterpart of the main bank system is the hausbank system. Banks tend to have very close ties with industry and form long-run relationships with firms not only because of the loans they make and the shares they directly own but also because of the proxies they are able to exercise. A number of studies have provided evidence on the effectiveness of the outside monitoring of German banks (see Gorton and Schmid, 2000).

In an important book, Edwards and Fischer (1994) have argued that in Germany the corporate governance role of banks has been overemphasized in the literature. They provide a variety of evidence that banks do not have the degree of influence as lenders, shareholders, or voters of proxies that is usually supposed. For example, they find that the number of votes controlled in a company is only weakly related to the number of representatives the bank has on the supervisory board. Hellwig (1991, 1994) also provides a number of theoretical arguments concerning the disadvantages of the banking system in Germany.

2.8 RELATIONSHIP BANKING

There is a growing literature that analyzes the advantages and disadvantages of relationships in banking (see, for reviews: Boot, 2000; Gorton and Winton, 2003; Degryse and Ongena, 2008). If on the one hand, close and durable relationships provide better access to firms and ameliorate some of the information problems characterizing lending relationships, on the other hand, they also involve inefficiencies related to the hold-up and the soft-budget-constraint problems. The hold-up problem refers to the possibility that a relationship bank uses the superior private information it possesses about the firm to extract rents, thus distorting entrepreneurial incentives and causing inefficient investment choices (Sharpe, 1990; Rajan, 1992; von Thadden, 1995). The soft-budget-constraint problem concerns the inability of a relationship lender to commit itself to a particular course of action in advance. Although it is optimal to threaten to terminate the availability of credit in advance, once the borrower has defaulted, the first loan becomes a "sunk cost." If the firm has another good project we should expect that the lender will continue to extend credit, even if the borrower defaults. Renegotiation thus creates a time-consistency problem. The threat to terminate credit creates good incentives for the borrower to avoid the risk of default. Termination of credit is not Pareto-efficient ex post, but the incentive effect makes both parties better off. However, if the borrower anticipates that the lender will not carry out the threat in practice, the incentive effect disappears. Although the lender's behavior is now ex post optimal, both parties may be worse off ex ante.

Multiple-bank relationships can help mitigate the drawbacks of single-bank relationships in terms of the hold-up and the soft-budget-constraint problems. As for the former, borrowing from multiple banks can restore competition among banks and, consequently, improve entrepreneurial incentives (Padilla and Pagano, 1997). As for the latter, Dewatripont and Maskin (1995) argue that, by complicating the refinancing process and making it less profitable, multiple-bank lending allows banks to commit not to extend further inefficient credit. Similarly, Bolton and Scharfstein (1996) show that multiple-bank lending reduces entrepreneurial incentives to default strategically because it complicates debt renegotiation.

The number of bank relationships also has important implications for banks' role as monitors. In a context where both firms and banks are subject to moral hazard problems, Carletti (2004) analyzes how the number of bank relationships influences banks' monitoring incentives, the level of loan rates, and a firm's choice between single- and multiple-bank relationships. Multiple-bank lending suffers from duplication of effort and free-riding but it benefits from diseconomies of scale in monitoring, thus involving a lower level of monitoring but not necessarily higher loan rates than single lending. Since banks choose their monitoring effort to maximize their expected profits, they may choose a level of monitoring that is excessive from the firms' perspective. When this is the case, the firm may choose multiple-bank relationships in order to reduce the overall level of monitoring. The attractiveness of such a choice increases with the cost of monitoring, the firm's private benefit, and expected profitability. In a similar framework, Carletti, Cerasi, and Daltung (2007) analyze the circumstances where banks with limited diversification opportunities find it profitable to enter into multiple-bank relationships. They show that sharing lending allows banks to better diversify their portfolios but still entails duplication of effort and free-riding. When the benefit of greater diversification dominates, multiple-bank lending leads to higher overall monitoring as a way to mitigate the agency problem between banks and depositors and achieve higher banks' expected profits. The attractiveness of multiple-bank lending now decreases with the level of banks' (inside) equity and firms' prior profitability, while it increases with the cost of monitoring.

Other rationales for multiple-bank relationships relate to firms' desire to reduce liquidity risk and disclose information through credit relationships. Detragiache, Garella, and Guiso (2000) show that, when relationship banks face internal liquidity problems, borrowing from multiple banks can avoid early liquidation of profitable projects. Yosha (1995) suggests that firms may prefer multiple-bank lending as a way to disclose confidential information about the quality of their projects and to avoid aggressive behavior by competitors.

As a final remark, note that there are ways other than multiple-bank relationships to solve the problem of lack of commitment affecting exclusive bank relationships. For example, financial institutions may develop a valuable reputation for maintaining commitments. In any one case, it is worth incurring the small cost of a suboptimal action in order to maintain the value of the reputation. Incomplete information about the borrower's type may lead to a similar outcome. If default causes the institution to believe it is more likely that the defaulter is a bad type, then it may be optimal to refuse to deal with a firm after it has defaulted. Institutional strategies such as delegating decisions to agents who are given no discretion to renegotiate may also be an effective commitment device. Several authors (Hart and Moore, 1988; Huberman and Kahn, 1988; Gale, 1991; Allen and Gale, 2000a, ch. 10) have argued that, under certain circumstances, renegotiation is welfare improving. In that case, the argument is reversed. Intermediaries that establish long-term relationships with clients may have an advantage over financial markets precisely because it is easier for them to renegotiate contracts.

2.9   CONCLUDING REMARKS

We have covered a number of roles of banks in the financial system in this chapter. Banks act as delegated monitors and ensure that firms use the resources allocated to them effectively. They also play an important role in sharing risk in the economy by diversifying and smoothing fluctuations over time. These are positive aspects of the roles banks play. However, the fixed nature of the claims they issue can cause fragility in the financial system. Banks are often at the center of financial crises as in the crisis that started in the summer of 2007. They can help spread crises if there is contagion and small shocks can have a large effect on the financial system and the economy. Banks play an important role in providing funds for firms and helping them and the economy to grow. They are also important for corporate governance, particularly in countries such as Germany, where bankers sit on boards and control a significant number of proxy votes. Finally, banks can help overcome asymmetric information problems by forming long-lived relationships with firms.

There are number of other roles that we have not covered as they are the subjects of other chapters of the book. These include the role of banks in underwriting securities (covered in Chapter 7) and the role of banks in payments systems (covered in Chapter 28).

There remain other roles that are important that are less well understood. Many of these involve the interaction of banks with financial markets of various kinds. The recent crisis has illustrated that securitization can lead to significant problems because bank incentives are fundamentally different when loans are sold rather than retained. The role that banks play in derivative markets is also not fully understood. If there is a chain of counterparties, how can that risk be fully assessed if the chain is opaque as it usually is? Finally, how can banks be prevented from taking risks if they retain the profits when there are good outcomes but are bailed out by the government in times of crisis? These are all important issues for future research.

REFERENCES

Allen, F., Babus, A., and Carletti, E. (2012). Asset Commonality, Debt Maturity and Systemic Risk, *Journal of Financial Economics* 104, 519–534.

Allen, F. and Carletti, E. (2006). Credit Risk Transfer and Contagion, *Journal of Monetary Economics* 53, 89–111.

Allen, F. and Carletti, E. (2008). Mark-to-Market Accounting and Liquidity Pricing, *Journal of Accounting and Economics* 46(2–3), 358–378.

Allen, F., Chui, M., and Maddaloni, A. (2004). Financial Systems in Europe, the USA, and Asia, *Oxford Review of Economic Policy* 20, 490–508.

Allen, F. and Gale, D. (1997). Financial Markets, Intermediaries, and Intertemporal Smoothing, *Journal of Political Economy* 105, 523–546.

Allen, F. and Gale, D. (1998). Optimal Financial Crises, *Journal of Finance* 53, 1245–1284.

Allen, F. and Gale, D. (1999). Diversity of Opinion and the Financing of New Technologies, *Journal of Financial Intermediation* 8, 68–89.

Allen, F. and Gale, D. (2000a). *Comparing Financial Systems*. Cambridge, MA: MIT Press.

Allen, F. and Gale, D. (2000b). Bubbles and Crises, *Economic Journal* 110, 236–255.

Allen, F. and Gale, D. (2000c). Financial Contagion, *Journal of Political Economy* 108, 1–33.

Allen, F. and Gale, D. (2004). Financial Intermediaries and Markets, *Econometrica* 72, 1023–1061.

Aoki, M. and Patrick, H. (Eds.) (1994). *The Japanese Main Bank System: Its Relevancy for Developing and Transforming Economies*. New York: Oxford University Press, 592–633.

Babus, A. (2009). The Formation of Financial Networks, Tinbergen Institute Discussion Paper No. 06-093.

Beck, T. and Demirgüç-Kunt, A. (2009). Financial Institutions and Markets across Countries and Over Time-Data and Analysis, World Bank Policy Research Working Paper No. 4943.

Bernanke, B. (2008). Reducing Systemic Risk. Federal Reserve Bank of Kansas City Opening Speech at the 2008 Jackson Hole Symposium.

Bhattacharya, S. and Chiesa, G. (1995). Financial Intermediation with Proprietary Information, *Journal of Financial Intermediation* 4, 328–357.

Bolton, P. and Scharfstein, D. (1996). Optimal Debt Structure and the Number of Creditors, *Journal of Political Economy* 104, 1–25.

Boot, A. (2000). Relationship Banking: What Do We Know?, *Journal of Financial Intermediation* 9, 7–25.

Boot, A. and Thakor, A. (1997). Financial System Architecture, *Review of Financial Studies* 10, 693–733.

Boss, M., Elsinger, H., Thurner, S., and Summer, M. (2004). Network Topology of the Interbank Market, *Quantitative Finance* 4, 1–8.

Brusco, S. and Castiglionesi, F. (2007). Liquidity Coinsurance, Moral Hazard and Financial Contagion, *Journal of Finance* 62, 2275–2302.

Bryant, J. (1980). A Model of Reserves, Bank Runs, and Deposit Insurance, *Journal of Banking and Finance* 4, 335–344.

Carletti, E. (2004). The Structure of Bank Relationships, Endogenous Monitoring and Loan Rates, *Journal of Financial Intermediation* 13, 58–86.

Carletti, E., Cerasi, V., and Daltung, S. (2007). Multiple-Bank Lending: Diversification and Free-Riding in Monitoring, *Journal of Financial Intermediation* 16, 425–451.

Carlsson, H. and van Damme, E. (1993). Global Games and Equilibrium Selection, *Econometrica* 61, 989–1018.

Cass, D. and Shell, K. (1983). Do Sunspots Matter?, *Journal of Political Economy* 91, 193–227.

Castiglionesi, F. and Navarro, N. (2007). Optimal Fragile Financial Networks, Tilburg University Center Discussion Paper No. 2007-100.

Chari, V. and Jagannathan, R. (1988). Banking Panics, Information, and Rational Expectations Equilibrium, *Journal of Finance* 43, 749–760.

Chen, Q., Goldstein, I., and Jiang, W. (2010). Payoff Complementarities and Financial Fragility: Evidence from Mutual Fund Flows, *Journal of Financial Economics* 97, 239–262.

Cifuentes, R., Ferrucci, G., and Shin, H. (2005). Liquidity Risk and Contagion, *Journal of European Economic Association* 3, 556–566.

Cocco, J., Gomes, F., and Martins, N. (2009). Lending Relationships in the Interbank Market, *Journal of Financial Intermediation* 18, 24–48.

Dasgupta, A. (2004). Financial Contagion through Capital Connections: A Model of the Origin and Spread of Bank Panics, *Journal of the European Economic Association* 6, 1049–1084.

Degryse, H. and Nguyen, G. (2007). Interbank Exposures: An Empirical Examination of Systemic Risk in the Belgian Banking System, *International Journal of Central Banking* 3(2), 123–171.

Degryse H. and Ongena, S. (2008). Competition and Regulation in the Banking Sector: A Review of the Empirical Evidence on the Sources of Bank Rents. In: A. Thakor and A. Boot (Eds.), *Handbook of Financial Intermediation and Banking*, 483–554. Amsterdam: Elsevier.

Demirgüç-Kunt, A. and Maksimovic, V. (1998). Law, Finance, and Firm Growth, *Journal of Finance* 53, 2107–2137.

Detragiache, E., Garella, P., and Guiso, L. (2000). Multiple vs. Single Banking Relationships: Theory and Evidence, *Journal of Finance* 55, 1133–1161.

Dewatripont, M. and Maskin, E. (1995). Credit and Efficiency in Centralized and Decentralized Economies, *Review of Economic Studies* 62, 541–555.

de Vries, C. (2005). The Simple Economics of Bank Fragility, *Journal of Banking and Finance* 29, 803–825.

Diamond, D. (1984). Financial Intermediation and Delegated Monitoring, *Review of Economic Studies* 51, 393–414.

Diamond, D. and Dybvig, P. (1983). Bank Runs, Deposit Insurance, and Liquidity, *Journal of Political Economy* 91, 401–419.

Edwards, J. and Fischer, K. (1994). *Banks, Finance and Investment in Germany*. Cambridge, UK: Cambridge University Press.

Freixas, X., Parigi, B., and Rochet, J. (2000). Systemic Risk, Interbank Relations and Liquidity Provision by the Central Bank, *Journal of Money, Credit and Banking* 32, 611–638.

Furfine, C. (2003). The Interbank Market during a Crisis, *Journal of Money, Credit and Banking* 35, 111–128.

Gale, D. (1991). Optimal Risk Sharing through Renegotiation of Simple Contracts, *Journal of Financial Intermediation* 1, 283–306.

Gerschenkron, A. (1962). *Economic Backwardness in Historical Perspective*. Cambridge, MA: Harvard University Press.

Goldsmith, R. (1969). *Financial Structure and Development*. New Haven, CT: Yale University Press.

Goldstein, I. and Pauzner, A. (2005). Demand-Deposit Contracts and the Probability of Bank Runs, *Journal of Finance* 60, 1293–1327.

Gorton, G. (1988). Banking Panics and Business Cycles, *Oxford Economic Papers* 40, 751–781.

Gorton, G. and Schmid, F. (2000). Universal Banking and the Performance of German Firms, *Journal of Financial Economics* 58, 29–80.

Gorton, G. and Winton, A. (2003). Financial Intermediation. In: G. Constantinides, M. Harris, and R. Stulz (Eds.), *Handbook of the Economics of Finance*, 431–552. Amsterdam: North-Holland.

Hart, O. and Moore, J. (1988). Incomplete Contracts and Renegotiation, *Econometrica* 56, 755–785.

Hayashi, F. (2000). The Main Bank System and Corporate Investment: An Empirical Reassessment. In: M. Aoki and G. Saxonhouse (Eds.), *Finance, Governance, and Competitiveness in Japan*, 81–97. Oxford and New York: Oxford University Press.

He, Z. and Xiong, W. (2012). Dynamic Debt Runs, *Review of Financial Studies* 25, 1799–1843.

Hellwig, M. (1991). Banking, Financial Intermediation and Corporate Finance. In: A. Giovannini and C. Mayer (Eds.), *European Financial Integration*, 35–63. New York: Cambridge University Press.

Hellwig, M. (1994). Liquidity Provision, Banking, and the Allocation of Interest Rate Risk, *European Economic Review* 38, 1363–1389.

Hoshi, T., Kashyap, A., and Scharfstein, D. (1990). The Role of Banks in Reducing the Costs of Financial Distress in Japan, *Journal of Financial Economics* 27, 67–68.

Hoshi, T., Kashyap, A., and Scharfstein, D. (1993). *The Choice between Public and Private Debt: An Analysis of Post-Deregulation Corporate Financing in Japan*, NBER Working Paper No. 4421.

Huberman, G. and Kahn, C. (1988). Limited Contract Enforcement and Strategic Renegotiation, *American Economic Review* 78, 471–484.

Iyer, R. and Peydro-Alcalde, J. L. (2011). Interbank Contagion at Work: Evidence from a Natural Experiment, *Review of Financial Studies* 24(4), 1337–1377.

Jacklin, C. J. and Bhattacharya, S. (1988). Distinguishing Panics and Information-based Bank Runs: Welfare and Policy Implications, *Journal of Political Economy* 96(3), 568–592.

Jorion, P. and Zhang, G. (2009). Credit Contagion from Counterparty Risk, *Journal of Finance* 64(5), 2053–2087.

Kindleberger, C. (1978). *Manias, Panics, and Crashes: A History of Financial Crises*. New York: Basic Books.

Lagunoff, R. and Schreft, S. (2001). A Model of Financial Fragility, *Journal of Economic Theory* 99, 220–264.

Leitner, Y. (2005). Financial Networks: Contagion, Commitment and Private Sector Bailout, *Journal of Finance* 60(6), 2925–2953.

Levine, R. (2002). Bank-Based or Market-Based Financial Systems: Which is Better?, *Journal of Financial Intermediation* 11, 398–428.

Levine, R. and Zervos, S. (1998). Stock Markets, Banks and Economic Growth, *American Economic Review* 88, 537–558.

Martin, A., Skeie, D., and von Thadden, E. (2014). The Fragility of Short-term Secured Funding Markets, *Journal of Economic Theory* 149, 15–42.

Mitchell, W. (1941). *Business Cycles and Their Causes*. Berkeley: University of California Press.

Morris, S. and Shin, H. (1998). Unique Equilibrium in a Model of Self-Fulfilling Currency Attacks, *American Economic Review* 88, 587–597.

Padilla, A. J. and Pagano, M. (1997). Endogenous Communication Among Lenders and Entrepreneurial Incentives, *Review of Financial Studies* 10, 205–236.

Rajan, R. (1992). Insiders and Outsiders: The Choice between Informed and Arm's-Length Debt, *Journal of Finance* 47, 1367–1400.

Reinhart, C. M. and Rogoff, K. S. (2009). *This Time Is Different: Eight Centuries of Financial Folly*. Princeton, NJ: Princeton University Press.

Reinhart, C. M. and Rogoff, K. S. (2011). From Financial Crash to Debt Crisis, *American Economic Review* 101(5), 1676–1706.

Rochet, J. and Vives, X. (2004). Coordination Failures and the Lender of Last Resort: Was Bagehot Right after All? *Journal of the European Economic Association* 2, 1116–1147.

Sharpe, S. (1990). Asymmetric Information, Bank Lending, and Implicit Contracts: A Stylized Model of Customer Relationships, *Journal of Finance* 45, 1069–1087.

Tadesse, S. (2002). Financial Architecture and Economic Performance: International Evidence, *Journal of Financial Intermediation* 11, 429–454.

Upper, C. (2010). Simulation Methods to Assess the Danger of Contagion in Interbank Markets, *Journal of Financial Stability* 7, 111–125,

Upper, C. and Worms, A. (2004). Estimating Bilateral Exposures in the German Interbank Market: Is There a Danger of Contagion? *European Economic Review* 48, 827–849.

von Thadden, E. (1995). Long-Term Contracts, Short-Term Investment and Monitoring, *Review of Economic Studies* 62, 557–575.

Yosha, O. (1995). Information Disclosure Costs and the Choice of Financing Source, *Journal of Financial Intermediation* 4, 3–20.

....

CHAPTER 3

COMMERCIAL BANKING AND SHADOW BANKING

The Accelerating Integration of Banks and Markets and its Implications for Regulation

....

ARNOUD W. A. BOOT AND ANJAN V. THAKOR

3.1 INTRODUCTION

....

THE financial sector has evolved rapidly over the last decade, with the impetus for change provided by deregulation and advances in information technology. Competition has become more intense. Interbank competition within domestic markets as well as across national borders and competition from financial markets have gained importance. Both the institutional structure of financial institutions and the boundary between financial institutions and financial markets have been transformed. At no stage has this blurring of boundaries been more evident than during the events leading up to the financial crisis that began in 2007, events that have highlighted how large the shadow banking sector has become.[1] Pozsar et al. (2010) estimate the size of the shadow banking system in the US at $16 trillion in 2010, but estimates (and measures) vary greatly (see Claessens et al., 2012). This chapter reviews the literature related to these developments and uses it to examine the importance of this

---

[1] Gorton and Metrick (2012) define the shadow banking system as one consisting of the following key components: (i) money-market mutual funds or other institutional (market-based) lenders who replace depositors as a primary funding source for shadow banks; (ii) securitization of bank-originated loans, which permits the creation of asset-backed securities that then serve as collateral for the bank's borrowing from mutual funds and other institutional lenders; and (iii) repurchase agreements (or repos), which represent the financial contract used by banks to raise funding from investors.

changing landscape for the structure of the financial services industry and the design and organization of regulation.

As we will argue, the increasingly intertwined nature of banks and financial markets is not without costs. In particular, as the financial crisis of 2007–2009 has illustrated, systemic risks may have become more prevalent. In this chapter, we seek to provide a fundamental analysis of the underlying forces that could explain the evolution of the banking industry. We begin by discussing the key insights from the financial intermediation literature, including the potential complementarities and conflicts of interest between intermediated relationship banking activities and financial market activities (underwriting, securitization, etc.). While debt contracts dominate the financial intermediation literature, the impressive growth of private equity firms has turned the spotlight on equity. In a sense, one could interpret private equity (PE) as intermediation driven from the equity side. Given their economic functions as debt and equity intermediaries, respectively, how do banks and PE firms interact?

Our discussion reveals that the interaction between banks and PE firms is only one aspect of an increasing integration of banks and markets. Banks have a growing dependence on the financial markets not only as source of funding but also for hedging purposes and off-loading risks via securitization, and possibly for engaging in proprietary trading. Financial market linkages often also imply that intra-financial sector linkages mushroom, for example, the asset-backed securities created by securitization can serve as collateral that financial institutions use to fund themselves in the shadow banking system. The multiple dimensions of bank dependence on markets generate both risk reduction and risk elevation possibilities for banks. For example, while hedging may reduce risk, proprietary trading, liquidity guarantees for securitized debt, and positions in credit default swaps can increase risk. This raises potential regulatory concerns. What do these developments imply for prudential regulation and supervision? Will the increasing interactions between banks and markets increase or decrease financial system fragility? The financial crisis of 2007–2009 suggests an increase in fragility, but how much can we generalize from this crisis? These questions have become particularly germane not only because of growing banks–markets integration, but also due to the (up to recently) growing cross-border footprint of financial institutions.

These developments have also focused attention on the role of "gatekeepers" (Coffee, 2002), like credit rating agencies. While the financial intermediation literature has acknowledged the role of credit rating agencies as information processors and sellers for some time now (e.g., Ramakrishnan and Thakor, 1984; Allen, 1990), the literature has not discussed how rating agencies may affect the fragility of the financial sector through the important role they play as "spiders in the web of institutions and markets." We take up this issue in our discussion.

The organization of the chapter is as follows. In Section 3.2, we focus on the economic role of financial intermediaries. The primary focus here is on the banks' role in lending and how this compares to non-intermediated finance directly from the financial market. We will also analyze the effects of competition on the banks' lending relationships. Does competition harm relationships and reduce their value and hence induce more transaction-oriented banking, or does competition augment the value of relationships? This discussion will summarize the key insights from the modern literature of financial intermediation. In Section 3.3 we discuss the increasingly interconnected nature of banks and financial markets, with a focus on securitization. This "technology" has been at the center of the 2007–2009 financial crisis. What are the future prospects for securitization? The proliferation of non-banking financial institutions, and particularly private equity firms, is discussed in Section 3.4. We will argue that much of this activity is complementary to the role of banks, rather than threatening their *raison d'être*. Subsequently, in Section 3.5 we focus on the role of credit rating agencies. These agencies have been indispensable for the explosive growth (and temporary demise) of securitization. How will their role develop? We then discuss in Section 3.6 regulatory implications. Here we link the role of banks in lending (as emphasized in our earlier discussions) to their role as providers of liquidity. This brings in the issue of fragility, which is at the heart of the current regulatory debate.

3.2 Understanding Banks as Information-Processing Intermediaries

In this section we discuss two issues: (1) what is the key role of banks vis-à-vis markets? and (2) how does competition impinge on this role?

3.2.1 The Economic Role of Banks

We first discuss the role of banks in qualitative asset transformation—i.e., the process by which banks absorb risk to transform both the liquidity and credit risk characteristics of assets (see Bhattacharya and Thakor, 1993). For example, banks invest in risky loans but finance them with riskless deposits (e.g., Diamond, 1984; Ramakrishnan and Thakor, 1984; Millon and Thakor, 1985). They also invest in illiquid loans and finance them with liquid demandable deposits (e.g., Diamond and Dybvig, 1983). The theory of financial intermediation has placed special emphasis on the role of banks in monitoring and screening borrowers in the process of lending. Bank lending is typically contrasted with direct funding from the financial markets. What are the comparative advantages of bank loans over public capital market-bond financing?

The most striking insight of the contemporary theory of financial intermediation is that banks are better than markets at resolving informational problems. The possession of better information about their borrowers allows banks to get closer to their borrowers. Interestingly, a feedback loop is generated, as this proximity between the financier and the borrowing firm in bank lending arrangements may also help mitigate the information asymmetries that typically plague arm's length arrangements in market transactions. This has several aspects. A borrower might be prepared to reveal proprietary information to its bank that it may have been reluctant to reveal to the financial markets (Bhattacharya and Chiesa, 1995). A bank might also have better incentives to invest in information acquisition. While costly, the substantial stake that it has in the funding of the borrower and the enduring nature of its relationship with the borrower—with the possibility of information reusability over time—increase the marginal benefit of information acquisition to the bank.[2] Boot and Thakor (2000) analyze the economic surplus that relationship banking can generate.

---

[2] Ramakrishnan and Thakor (1984) and Millon and Thakor (1985) focus on pre-contract information asymmetries to rationalize the value that financial intermediaries add relative to markets. Diamond

Such borrower–lender proximity may also have a dark side. An important one is the hold-up problem that stems from the information monopoly that the bank may develop due to the spontaneous generation of proprietary information on borrowers. Such an informational monopoly may permit the bank to charge higher loan interest rates ex post (see Sharpe, 1990; Rajan, 1992; Boot, 2000, for a review). The threat of being "locked in," or informationally captured by the bank, may dampen loan demand ex ante, causing a loss of potentially valuable investment opportunities. Alternatively, firms may opt for multiple-bank relationships (see Carletti, Cerasi, and Daltung, 2007). This may reduce the informational monopoly of any individual bank, but possibly at a cost. Ongena and Smith (2000) show that multiple-bank relationships indeed reduce the hold-up problem, but can worsen the availability of credit (see Thakor, 1996, for a theoretical rationale).

Another aspect is that relationship banking could accommodate an intertemporal smoothing of contract terms (see Boot and Thakor, 1994; Allen and Gale, 1995, 1997) that would entail losses for the bank in the short term that are recouped later in the relationship. Petersen and Rajan (1995) show that credit subsidies to young or "de novo" companies may reduce the moral hazard problem and informational frictions that banks face in lending to such borrowers. Banks may be willing to provide such subsidized funding if they can expect to offset the initial losses through the long-term rents generated by these borrowers. The point is that, without access to *subsidized* credit early in their lives, "de novo" borrowers would pose such serious adverse selection and moral hazard problems that *no* bank would lend to them. Relationship lending makes these loans feasible because the *proprietary* information generated during the relationship produces "competition-immune" rents for the bank later in the relationship and permits the early losses to be offset. The importance of intertemporal transfers in loan pricing is also present in Berlin and Mester (1999). They show that rate-insensitive core deposits allow for intertemporal smoothing in lending rates. This suggests a complementarity between deposit taking and lending. Moreover, the loan commitment literature has emphasized the importance of intertemporal tax subsidy schemes in pricing to resolve moral hazard (see Boot, Thakor, and Udell, 1991; Shockley and Thakor, 1997) and also the complementarity between deposit taking and *commitment* lending (see Kashyap, Rajan, and Stein, 2002).

The bank–borrower relationship also displays greater contractual flexibility than that normally encountered in the financial market. This flexibility inheres in the generation of hard and soft proprietary information during a banking relationship. This information gives the bank the ability to adjust contractual terms to the arrival of new information and hence encourages it to write "discretionary contracts" ex ante that leave room for such ex post adjustments. This is in line with the important ongoing discussion in economic theory on rules versus discretion, where discretion allows for decision making based on more

---

(1984) focuses on post-contract information asymmetries to rationalize intermediation. Coval and Thakor (2005) show that financial intermediaries can provide an institutional resolution of the problem of cognitive biases at the individual investor level, acting as a "belief's bridge" between pessimistic investors and optimistic entrepreneurs. James (1987), Lummer and McConnell (1989), and Gande and Saunders (2005) provide empirical evidence on the informational value of bank financing. See also the "stories" provided by Berlin (1996) supporting the special role of banks.

subtle—potentially non-contractible—information (see for example Simons, 1936; Boot, Greenbaum, and Thakor 1993).

The papers by Stein (2002), and Berger et al. (2005) highlight the value of "soft information" in lending. This could be an example of this more subtle and non-contractible information. On this issue, two dimensions can be identified. One dimension is related to the nature of the bank–borrower relationship, which is typically long term, with accompanying reinforcing incentives for both the bank and the borrower to enhance the durability of the relationship. This allows for *implicit*—non-enforceable—long-term contracting. An optimal information flow is crucial for sustaining these "contracts." Information asymmetries in the financial market, and the non-contractibility of various pieces of information, would rule out long-term alternative capital market funding sources as well as *explicit* long-term commitments by banks. Therefore, both the bank and the borrower may realize the added value of their relationship, and have an incentive to foster the relationship.[3]

The other dimension is related to the structure of the explicit contracts that banks can write. Because banks write more discretionary contracts, bank loans are generally easier to renegotiate than bond issues or other public capital market funding vehicles (see Berlin and Mester, 1992). Such renegotiability may be a mixed blessing because banks may suffer from a "soft-budget constraint" problem: borrowers may realize that they can renegotiate ex post, which could give them perverse ex ante incentives (see Dewatripont and Maskin, 1995; Bolton and Scharfstein, 1996). The soft-budget-constraint problem is related to the potential lack of toughness in enforcing contracts due to the ex post distribution of "bargaining power" linked with relationship banking proximity (see Boot, 2000). In practice, one way that banks can deal with this issue is through the priority structure of their loan contracts. If the bank has priority/seniority over other lenders, it could strengthen the bank's bargaining position and allow it to become tougher. These issues are examined in Diamond (1993), Berglöf and von Thadden (1994), and Gorton and Kahn (1993).

The bank could then credibly intervene in the decision process of the borrower when it believes that its long-term interests are in jeopardy. For example, the bank might believe that the firm's strategy is flawed, or a restructuring is long overdue. Could the bank push for the restructuring? If the bank has no priority, the borrower may choose to ignore the bank's wishes. The bank could threaten to call the loan, but such a threat may lack credibility because the benefits of liquidating the borrower's assets are larger for higher-priority lenders, and the costs from the termination of the borrower's business are higher for lower-priority lenders. When the bank loan has sufficiently high priority, the bank could *credibly* threaten to call back the loan, and this may offset the deleterious effect of the soft-budget constraint. This identifies a potential advantage of bank financing: *timely intervention*. Of course, one could ask whether bondholders could be given priority and allocated the task of timely intervention. Note that bondholders are subject to more severe information asymmetries and are generally more dispersed (i.e., have smaller stakes). Both characteristics make them ill-suited for an "early intervention" task.

---

[3] Mayer (1988) and Hellwig (1991) discuss the commitment nature of bank funding. Boot, Thakor, and Udell (1991) address the *credibility* of commitments.

3.2.2 Intermediation and Competition

Since relationship banking is an integral part of the economic services provided by banks and generates rents for banks, it also potentially invites multiple-bank entry, which then generates interbank competition. An interesting question this raises is how competition might affect the *incentives* for relationship banking. While this may ultimately be an empirical question, two diametrically opposite points of view have emerged theoretically. One is that competition among financiers encourages borrowers to switch to other banks or to the financial market. The consequent shortening of the expected "life span" of bank–borrower relationships may induce banks to reduce their relationship-specific investments, thereby inhibiting the reusability of information and diminishing the value of information (Chan, Greenbaum, and Thakor, 1986). Banks may then experience weaker incentives to acquire (costly) proprietary information, and relationships may suffer. There is empirical evidence that an increase in relationship length benefits the borrower. Brick and Palia (2007) document a 21-basis point reduction in the loan interest rate due to a one-standard deviation increase in relationship length.

Moreover, increased credit market competition could also hurt relationship lending by imposing tighter constraints on the ability of borrowers and lenders intertemporally to share surpluses (see Petersen and Rajan, 1995). In particular, it becomes more difficult for banks to "subsidize" borrowers in earlier periods in return for a share of the rents in the future. Thus, the funding role for banks that Petersen and Rajan (1995) see in the case of young corporations (as already discussed) may no longer be sustainable in the face of sufficiently high competition. This implies that interbank competition may have an ex post effect of diminishing bank lending.[4]

Another way in which competition can hurt relationship lending is through consolidation. An extensive empirical literature focuses on the effect of consolidation in the banking sector on small-business lending. This consolidation may in part be a response to competitive pressures. The effects on small-business lending, however, are not clear-cut. Sapienza (2002) finds that bank mergers involving at least one large bank result in a lower supply of loans to small borrowers by the merged entity. This could be linked to the difficulty that larger organizations have in using "soft information" (Stein, 2002; Berger, Miller et al., 2005). However, Berger et al. (1998) show that the actual supply of loans to small businesses may not go down after bank mergers, since they invite entry of "de novo" banks that specialize in small-business lending (see also Strahan, 2007).

The opposite point of view is that competition may actually *elevate* the importance of a relationship-orientation as a distinct competitive edge. The idea is that competition pressures profit margins on existing products and increases the importance of financier differentiation, and more intense relationship lending may be one way for the bank to achieve this. Boot and Thakor (2000) formalize this argument to show that a more competitive environment may encourage banks to become more client-driven and customize services, thus generating a *stronger* focus on relationship banking.[5] They distinguish

---

[4] Berlin and Mester (1999) provide a related, albeit different argument. Their analysis suggests that competition forces banks to pay market rates on deposits, which may impede their ability to engage in the potentially value-enhancing smoothing of lending rates.

[5] In related work, Hauswald and Marquez (2006) focus on a bank's incentives to acquire borrower-specific information in order to gain market share, and Dinç (2000) examines a bank's

between "passive" transaction lending and more intensive relationship lending by banks. Transaction lending competes head-on with funding in the financial market. Greater interbank competition results in banks engaging in more relationship lending, but each relationship loan has lower value to the borrower. By contrast, greater competition from the capital market leads to a lower volume of relationship lending, but each relationship loan has greater value. Berger et al. (2008) find empirically that bank ownership type (foreign, state-owned, or private domestic) affects the bank's choice between transaction and relationship lending.

Relationships may foster the exchange of information, but may simultaneously give lenders an information monopoly and undermine competitive pricing. As discussed above, the informational monopoly on the "inside" lender's side may be smaller if a borrower engages in multiple-banking relationships. This would mitigate the possibilities for rent extraction by informed lenders and induce more competitive pricing (see Sharpe, 1990; Petersen and Rajan, 1995). Transaction-oriented finance, however, may give banks little incentive to acquire information but is potentially subject to more competition. This suggests that markets for transaction-oriented finance may fail when problems of asymmetric information are insurmountable without explicit information acquisition and information-processing intervention by banks. This argument is used by some to highlight the virtues of (relationship-oriented) bank-dominated systems (e.g., Germany and Japan) vis-à-vis market-oriented systems. This is part of the literature on the design of financial systems (see Allen, 1993; Allen and Gale, 1995; Boot and Thakor, 1997). One objective of this literature is to evaluate the economic consequences of alternative types of financial system architecture.

What this discussion indicates is that the impact of competition on relationship banking is complex; several effects need to be disentangled. However, empirical evidence (see Degryse and Ongena, 2007) seems to support the Boot and Thakor (2000) prediction that the orientation of relationship banking *adapts* to increasing interbank competition, so higher competition does not drive out relationship lending. Despite this adaptation, there is also evidence that in recent years the geographic distance between borrowers and lenders has increased, and that this has been accompanied by higher loan defaults (see DeYoung, Glennon, and Nigro, 2008).

3.3 BANK LENDING, SECURITIZATION, AND CAPITAL MARKET FUNDING

Much of our focus in the previous section was on interbank competition. Nonetheless, banks also face competition from the capital market. The standard view is that banks and markets compete, so that growth in one is at the expense of the other (see Allen and Gale,

---

reputational incentives to honor commitments to finance higher-quality firms. Song and Thakor (2007) theoretically analyze the effect of competition on the mix between relationship and transaction lending, and focus on fragility issues in particular.

1995; Boot and Thakor, 1997). In this context, Deidda and Fattouh (2008) show theoretically that both bank and stock-market development have a positive effect on growth, but the growth impact of bank development is lower when there is a higher level of stock-market development. They also present supporting empirical evidence. What this shows is that dynamics of the interaction between banks and markets can have real effects. How banks and markets interact is therefore of great interest.

In contrast to the standard view that they compete, the observations in the previous section suggest that there are also potential complementarities between bank lending and capital market funding. We argued that prioritized bank debt may facilitate timely intervention. This feature of bank lending is valuable to the firm's bondholders as well. They might find it optimal to have bank debt take priority over their own claims, because this efficiently delegates the timely intervention task to the bank. The bondholders will obviously ask to be compensated for their subordinated status. This—ignoring the timely intervention effect— is a "wash." In other words, the priority (seniority) and subordination features can be priced. That is, as much as senior debt may *appear* to be "cheaper" (it is less risky), junior or subordinated debt will appear to be more expensive, and there should be no preference for bank seniority, other than through the timely bank-intervention channel. Consequently, the borrower may reduce its total funding cost by accessing both the bank-credit market and the financial market.[6]

Another manifestation of potential complementarities between bank lending and capital market activities is the increasing importance of securitization, this being an example of the unbundling of financial services. Securitization is a process whereby assets are removed from a bank's balance sheet, so banks no longer permanently fund assets when they are securitized; instead, the investors buying asset-backed securities provide the funding. Asset-backed securities rather than deposits thus end up funding dedicated pools of bank-originated assets. More specifically, the lending function can be decomposed into four more primal activities: origination, funding, servicing, and risk processing (Bhattacharya and Thakor, 1993). Origination subsumes screening prospective borrowers, and designing and pricing financial contracts. Funding relates to the provision of financial resources. Servicing involves the collection and remission of payments as well as the monitoring of credits. Risk processing alludes to hedging, diversification, and absorption of credit, interest rate, liquidity, and exchange-rate risks. Securitization decomposes the lending function such that banks no longer fully fund the assets, but continue to be involved in other primal

---

[6] This is directly related to the work on bargaining power and seniority; see the work of Gorton and Kahn (1993) and Berglöf and von Thadden (1994). The complementarity between bank lending and capital market funding is further highlighted in Diamond (1991), and Hoshi, Kashyap, and Scharfstein (1993). Diamond (1991) shows that a borrower may want to borrow first from banks in order to establish sufficient credibility *before* accessing the capital markets. Again, banks provide certification and monitoring. Once the borrower is "established," it switches to capital market funding. Hoshi, Kashyap, and Scharfstein (1993) show that bank lending exposes borrowers to monitoring, which may serve as a certification device that facilitates simultaneous capital market funding. In this explanation, there is a *sequential* complementarity between bank and capital market funding. In related theoretical work, Chammanur and Fulgheiri (1994) show that the quality of the bank is of critical importance for its certification role. This suggests a positive correlation between the value of relationship banking and the quality of the lender. See Petersen and Rajan (1994) and Houston and James (1996) for empirical evidence.

lending activities. One potential benefit of securitization is better risk sharing. The prolifera-tion of securitization may, however, also be induced by regulatory arbitrage—for example, as a vehicle to mitigate capital regulation (see Gorton and Pennacchi, 1995 for an economic rationale for bank loan sales and securitization). And a third benefit is highlighted by Boot and Thakor (1993), who show that the pooling of assets and tranching of claims in secu-ritization achieve both a diversification of idiosyncratic information and the creation of *information-sensitive* claims that increase the issuer's revenues from selling these securities.

Central to the extensive academic work on securitization is the idea that it is not effi-cient for originators to completely offload the risks in the originated assets. The originating bank needs to maintain an economic interest in the assets in order to alleviate moral haz-ard and induce sufficient effort on the originating bank's part in screening and monitoring. What this implies is that, even with securitization, banks do not become disengaged from the assets they originate. Banks still continue to provide the services involved in screen-ing and monitoring borrowers, designing and pricing financial claims, and providing risk-management and loan-servicing support. As such, securitization preserves those func-tions that are at the core of the *raison d'être* for banks. This militates against the notion that securitization effectively lessens the importance of banks.

Boyd and Gertler (1994) have argued that the substitution from on-balance-sheet to off-balance-sheet banking induced by securitization may have falsely suggested a shrink-ing role for banks. Indeed, by keeping banks involved in their primal activity of pre-lending borrower screening, securitization preserves much of the banks' value added on the asset side.

Up to the 2007–2009 financial crisis, securitization was rapidly gaining in importance. In fact, prior to the summer of 2007, securitization became prevalent for ever-wider types of credits, including business credits that were previously thought to be difficult to secu-ritize because of their information opaqueness. Also, a rather new market for securitization involving asset-backed commercial paper (ABCP) conduits emerged as a significant force. As the subprime crisis of 2007 has shown, these developments are not without problems. The structure of real-world securitization transactions appears to have taken a rather fragile form. In particular, it is important to note that much of the securitization leading up to the crisis involved the financing of long-term assets with short-term funding, which induced substantial liquidity risk. While this liquidity risk was sometimes mitigated by liquidity guarantees (e.g., stand-by letters of credit and refinancing commitments), the underwriting institutions often underestimated the risks involved and overstretched themselves.[7] Recent events may cast doubt on the optimality of such strategies. Also, because the originating institutions appeared to have retained minimal residual risk, monitoring incentives may have been compromised (see Mian and Sufi, 2009).[8] The eagerness of banks to securitize

---

[7] Most noteworthy are the bankruptcies among German Lander banks that were involved in providing liquidity guarantees.

[8] Securitization is facilitated in part by credit enhancement, including partial guarantees by the arranger of a securitization transaction (and/or he holds on to the most risky layer of the transaction). In the recent credit crisis, this disciplining mechanism broke down; residual risk with the arranger was minimal or framed as liquidity guarantees to off-balance-stheet vehicles without appropriately realizing the inherent risks. That is, banks have also been underwriting the liquidity risk in securitization transactions by, for example, guaranteeing the refinancing of commercial paper in ABCP transactions via stand-by letters of credit. Such guarantees have generated profits for banks, but also created risks, as

claims—and keep the repackaging "machine" rolling—may have also adversely impacted the quality of loans that were originated through a dilution of banks' screening incentives due to lower retained residual risks (e.g., subprime lending; see Keys et al., 2010).

The 2007–2009 financial crisis has brought securitization almost to a grinding halt. However, the risk diversification that securitization can accomplish appears to be of more than just ephemeral importance. Thus, we expect securitization to re-emerge, albeit possibly in a form that entails lower levels of liquidity risk, as well as lesser moral hazard in screening (loan underwriting standards) and monitoring. A caveat is that some of the activity in securitization may have been induced merely by capital arbitrage, in which case its social value may be rather limited.

Another effect of the interaction between banks and markets is that as markets evolve and entice bank borrowers away, banks have an incentive to create new products and services that combine services provided by markets with those provided by banks. This allows banks to follow their customers to the market rather than losing them. There are numerous examples. For instance, when a borrower goes to the market to issue commercial paper, its bank can provide a backup line of credit. Securitization of various sorts is another example in that banks not only originate the loans that are pooled and securitized, but they also buy various securitized tranches as investment securities. The impetus for such market-based activities grows stronger as interbank competition puts pressure on profit margins from traditional banking products, and the capital market provides access to greater liquidity and lower cost of capital for the bank's traditional borrowers. As a consequence, there is a natural propensity for banks to become increasingly *integrated* with markets, and a sort of unprecedented "co-dependence" emerges that makes banking and capital market risks become increasingly intertwined. A discussion of whether this is desirable and what the regulatory implications might be is given below.

3.4 BANKS, EQUITY, AND PRIVATE EQUITY FIRMS

The emergence of non-banking financial institutions such as PE firms is considered by some to be a (further) signal for the diminishing role of banks. However, we will argue that these developments are rather complementary to the role of banks. Let us first discuss the role that PE firms play.

The arguments above about the need for banks to have seniority suggest a natural economic inhibiting of investments by banks in the equity of corporations. Equity "softens" a bank's incentive to intervene for much the same reasons as does junior debt. So, while the emphasis of corporate finance theory on agency problems would suggest that it might be efficient for the bank to have both debt and equity claims on a corporation, this seems not to

---

illustrated by the losses incurred by banks in the recent subprime crisis. The marketability of securitized claims has also been facilitated by accreditation by credit rating agencies (see Boot, Milbourn, and Schmeits, 2006). However, even the role of rating agencies has been called into question during the subprime lending crisis.

be advisable from a timely intervention point of view. This might explain why equity inter-mediation has largely been in the hands of PE firms and/or bulge-bracket global investment banks that typically engage much less in relationship banking and focus more on transac-tions and the associated capital market activities.

Some more observations can be made about PE firms. Their activities could be viewed as intermediation driven from the equity side. That is, PE firms attract funding from a group of investors ("partners") and invest the funds as equity in businesses. They are exten-sively involved in monitoring and advising these businesses. How different is this from the role that banks play as debt intermediaries? To address this question, note first that banks do occasionally take equity positions in their role as venture capitalists, particularly for later-stage financing where there is a prospect for developing a valuable relationship on the lending side. Thus, banks participate in venture capital financing with higher probability if there is a greater likelihood of subsequent lucrative lending activity (Hellmann, Lindsey, and Puri, 2008). Banks may also have (participations in) PE subsidiaries that operate inde-pendently from the other businesses of the bank. However, this somewhat limited role as an equity financier does not mean that it would be efficient for the bank permanently to become an integrated provider of debt and equity finance, a "one-stop" financier of sorts (see our earlier discussion of the value of having senior claims). In particular, equity as a junior security may undermine a bank's bargaining power and thus compromise its role in timely intervention. Also, soft-budget constraint problems may then (re)emerge.

At a more general level, one could ask whether the monitoring role of PE firms substi-tutes for the lending-related monitoring of banks. It might. Note, however, that equity and debt are fundamentally different securities. The type of monitoring needed will differ sig-nificantly potentially across debt and equity. What will be true, however, is that the increas-ing involvement of PE investors induces banks to partner with these investors. In a sense, banks start building relationships with PE firms rather than the firms that the PE inves-tors take equity positions in. This is not without risks since it may affect the added value of banks in timely intervention vis-à-vis the (underlying) borrower and even the banks' incen-tives to be involved in this.[9] However, to the extent that PE firms are an integral part of the capital market, this development too makes the involvement of banks in the capital mar-ket deeper and more intricate. Such complexity is further exacerbated by the emergence of

---

[9] This suggests potential conflicts of interest. Much of the literature has focused on potential concerns related to banks combining lending and capital market activities, i.e., potential conflicts of interest in universal banking. This literature is motivated by the Glass–Steagall regulation in the US (see Kroszner and Rajan, 1994; Puri, 1996; Ramírez, 2002). In similar spirit, Drucker (2005) shows that junk-rated firms and companies in local lending relationships are more likely to select an integrated (universal) commercial investment bank when they expect to issue public debt in the future. This revealed preference for commercial investment bank relationships by firms that issue informationally sensitive securities suggests that there are benefits for banks to use private information from lending in investment banking. A similar rather positive picture emerges if one looks at US banking following the 1999 Financial Services Modernization Act. It appears that information collected through the banks' commercial lending businesses may have reduced the costs of underwriting debt and equity (see Drucker and Puri, 2005; Schenone, 2004). Gande (2007) concludes that commercial banks have distinct benefits in underwriting leading to lower issuer costs. He also concludes that "the value of banking relationships appears to be largest for non-investment grade, small and IPO firms for whom one would ex ante expect the benefit of bank monitoring to be the highest."

other intermediaries such as hedge funds, particularly because of the growing importance of hedge funds as direct lenders. See Brophy, Ouimet, and Sialm (2009), who point out that hedge funds have emerged as "lenders of last resort," providing finance to firms that banks do not typically lend to. This is part of the growing importance of the shadow banking sector as a source of financing.

3.5   ROLE OF CREDIT RATING AGENCIES

Credit ratings are a fascinating part of today's financial markets. Their importance is evident from the behavior of market participants. However, academic researchers have generally been skeptical about their incremental value, largely because of the absence of a theory of rating agencies. In the literature on financial intermediary existence, bank debt offers monitoring advantages that would not be available in the financial market. The typical argument for the lack of monitoring in the capital market is that free-rider problems among investors prevent effective monitoring. Boot, Milbourn, and Schmeits (2006) have shown that credit rating agencies (CRAs) add a monitoring-type element to the financial market, and thereby play a role as a "focal point" to resolve coordination failures among multiple dispersed investors (creditors). The CRA's ability to resolve such coordination failure arises from the effect of its actions—the assigned rating and the "credit watch" process—on firm behavior via the conditioning of investors' investment decisions on the assigned rating. Da Rin and Hellmann (2002) showed that banks could also resolve a multiple-equilibria problem among borrowers by helping coordinate the investment decisions of these borrowers. The role that Boot, Milbourn, and Schmeits (2006) give to CRAs has some similarity to this.

This role of CRAs in resolving coordination failures in the financial market qualifies the distinction between public debt and bank financing. The mechanism is, however, less "direct" than in the case of bank financing: the credit rating (and particularly the threat of a downgrade) *induces* good firm behavior rather than preventing bad behavior through direct intervention. Apart from bank loans, the non-bank private debt market also offers a potentially more direct alternative than credit rating agencies in the public debt market. In fact, private debtors often impose more discipline than banks and hence serve even riskier borrowers (Carey, Post, and Sharpe, 1998).

Another mechanism that links banks and CRAs is the certification role of bank loans. Datta, Iskandar-Datta, and Patel (1999) show that the monitoring associated with bank loans *facilitates* borrowers' access to the public debt market. This certification role of banks therefore complements what CRAs do. As rating agencies become more sophisticated and reliable, the certification role of banks diminishes in importance, causing bank borrowers to migrate to the capital market. In this sense, CRAs intensify the competition between banks and markets. But CRAs also pull banks into the capital market. For example, banks originate loans that they securitize, and then seek ratings for the securitized pools from CRAs. The ratings, in turn, facilitate the ability of banks to sell (securitized) asset-backed securities in the capital market.

This rather positive interpretation of CRAs is clouded somewhat by recent negative publicity. In the 2001 crisis surrounding Enron, CRAs were accused of being strategically sluggish in downgrading.[10] More recently, CRAs have been blamed (in part) for the sub-prime crisis in which they were allegedly too lenient in rating the senior tranches in securitization transactions. Allegations have been made about conflicts of interest for CRAs, arising from the fact that structured finance is a source of ever-increasing income for CRAs, which then corrupts their incentives for accurately rating the issuers involved in structured finance (Cantor, 2004). In this context, Coffee and Sale (2008) point out that it is naïve to think that reputation-building incentives alone would keep credit rating agencies in check.

Of particular concern are the so-called "rating triggers." For example, some debt contracts may dictate accelerated debt repayments when the rating falls. The consequences of such accelerated debt repayments might, however, be so severe as to cause rating agencies to become reluctant to lower the ratings of those borrowers in a timely manner. Complications also arise from the role played by the so-called "monoliners." These are insurers who traditionally guaranteed municipal bonds but now also guarantee the lowest-risk (best) tranches in securitization transactions. These insurers are virtually indispensable in the sense that the viability of many forms of securitization is predicated on this type of "reinsurance." However, the ability of the monoliners to issue credible guarantees (and hence their role in securitization) depends on these institutions themselves having AAA ratings. This potentially generates an indirect chain-reaction mechanism for CRAs. In rating (and monitoring) the monoliners, CRAs affect the viability of the securitization market. Thus, the impact of CRAs is both direct (rating securitization tranches) and indirect (rating the monoliners). The potential failure of such monoliners would have a significant effect on the value of various structured finance products and induce an additional chain reaction among players active in the structured finance market, including investors. This further underscores the increasing interlinkages in the financial markets. Other concerns are related to the oligopolistic nature of the industry, and the importance that ratings have due to regulation. The latter includes the exclusivity given to a few rating agencies via the "Nationally Recognized Statistical Rating Organization" (NRSRO) classification, weakened in the 2006 Credit Rating Agency Reform Act, but also the references to external ratings in the new Basel II capital regulation framework.

Under the Dodd–Frank Act 2010, the legal liability for CRAs has been elevated. Whether this will result in credit ratings that more accurately reflect credit risks is an open question. Others have examined the impact of the institutional features of the market for credit ratings on the structure of ratings (e.g., Sangiorgi, Sokobin, and Spatt, 2009).

---

[10] See, e.g., discussions in the US Senate: "On March 20, 2002, the Senate Committee held a hearing entitled 'Rating the Raters: Enron and the Credit Rating Agencies'... The hearing sought to elicit information on why the credit rating agencies continued to rate Enron a good credit risk until four days before the firm declared bankruptcy..." (US Senate Hearings, 2002). Similarly, US Senate Staff Report (2002): "in the case of Enron, credit rating agencies displayed a lack of diligence in their coverage and assessment of Enron." See also Cantor (2004) and Partnoy (1999).

3.6 Regulation and the Second *Raison D'être* for Banks: Liquidity Creation

In Section 3.2, we discussed the role of banks as information processors and delegated monitors. That information processing and monitoring referred to credit risk primarily. But banks also perform another important function, which is the provision of liquidity. That is, banks invest in illiquid assets (loans) but finance themselves largely with highly liquid demand deposits, and through this intermediation process create liquidity in the economy. However, in the process of creating liquidity, banks expose themselves to withdrawal risk and become fragile. Our discussion of this issue in this section will focus on "institution-driven fragility," manifested in the classic run on an individual bank, as well as "market-driven fragility," that refers to risks that come primarily via the financial market and interbank linkages, and appear to be more systemic. We will discuss how the increasing integration of banks into financial markets allows banks to shift some of their traditional risks to the markets, and what this implies for *financial system stability* and regulation. Issues related to the economics of bank regulation are covered in Bhattacharya, Boot, and Thakor (1998, 2004).

3.6.1 Fragile Banks as Liquidity Providers

In the classical interpretation, a financial crisis is directly linked to the notion of bank runs. In a fractional reserve system with long-term illiquid loans financed by (liquid) demandable deposits, runs may come about due to a coordination failure among depositors (Diamond and Dybvig, 1983). Even an adequately capitalized bank could be subject to a run if the deadweight liquidation costs of assets are substantial. Regulatory intervention via lender of last resort (LOLR) support, deposit insurance, and/or suspension of convertibility could all help, and perhaps even eliminate the inefficiency. In fact, such intervention can be justified because of its potential to expunge the negative social externalities arising from the possible contagion effects associated with an individual bank failure. While these implications arise theoretically in a rather simple and stylized setting, many have generalized this simple setting by allowing for asymmetric information and incomplete contracts; see Rochet (2004) for a review. The general conclusion is that fragility is real, and information-based runs are plausible. In particular, Gorton's (1988) empirical evidence suggests that bank runs are *not* sunspot phenomena (as in Diamond and Dybvig, 1983), but are triggered by adverse information about banks. More importantly, the banking crises stemming from such runs have *independent* negative real effects (see Dell'Ariccia, Detragiache, and Rajan, 2008). Also relevant in this context is the large literature that has now developed on banks and liquidity (see, e.g., Acharya and Schaefer, 2006; Acharya, Gromb, and Yorulmazer, 2007; Brunnemeier and Pedersen, 2009).

Given that bank runs are triggered by adverse information that depositors have about the financial health of banks, one might think that a simple solution would be to make banks safer by, for example, imposing higher capital requirements. Calomiris and Kahn (1991) first argued that the threat of bank runs may be a valuable disciplining device to keep bank managers honest, since a greater diversion of bank resources for personal consumption can increase the likelihood of a bank run. Building on this argument, Diamond and Rajan (2001) have suggested that financial fragility may play an important role in inducing banks to create liquidity, and thus a reduction in fragility through higher bank capital may lead to lower liquidity creation. Until recently, there has been no empirical work done on this issue, in part because of a paucity of empirical measures of liquidity creation. In recent work, Berger and Bouwman (2009) develop measures of liquidity creation and provide empirical evidence on the relationship between bank capital and liquidity creation. They show that higher capital leads to higher liquidity creation in the case of large banks (which create over 80% of the liquidity in the US economy), and lower liquidity creation in the case of small banks. Per dollar of capital, US banks created $4.56 of liquidity. Since capital requirements also affect the asset portfolios of banks through their lending decisions (see Thakor, 1996) and these requirements may be binding for some banks, this raises issues about the interaction of credit and liquidity risks that need to be explored. Nonetheless, Admati et al. (2011) argue against the relevance of these hypothesized costs of equity. Further, Coval and Thakor (2005) develop a theory of banking in which a bank needs a minimum capital level to be viable, and Mehran and Thakor (2011) show both theoretically and empirically that bank capital and value are positively related in the cross-section, pointing to the *private* benefits of higher capital for banks.

Complicating this issue further is that the liquidity provision function of banks is also affected by the financial markets. Two observations are germane in this regard. First, access to financial markets weakens the liquidity insurance feature of demand-deposit contracts. To see this, note that the root cause of the fragility in the Diamond and Dybvig (1983) world is the underlying demand-deposit contract. The rationale for this contract—as modeled by Diamond and Dybvig (1983)—is the desire for liquidity insurance on the part of risk-averse depositors with uncertainty about future liquidity needs. However, as shown by von Thadden (1998), the very presence of financial markets allows depositors to withdraw early and invest in the financial market, which puts a limit on the degree of liquidity insurance. In fact, when the market investment opportunity is completely reversible, deposit contracts cannot provide any liquidity insurance. This is related to the earlier work of Jacklin (1987), who shows that deposit contracts have beneficial liquidity insurance features, provided that restricted trading of deposit contracts can be enforced.[11] In any case, these arguments suggest that the proliferation of financial markets weakens the liquidity-provision rationale for demand deposits, which may help explain the market-based proliferation of close substitutes for deposits.

A second observation has to do with whether the development of financial markets leads to a diminished role for the Central Bank in providing liquidity via its LOLR function. In the Bagehot tradition, one could ask whether the LOLR has a role to play in providing liquidity to liquidity-constrained-yet-solvent institutions when capital markets and interbank

---

[11]   Actually, Jacklin (1987) shows that with the "extreme" Diamond-Dybvig preferences, a dividend-paying equity contract can achieve the same allocations without the possibility of bank runs. However, for basically all other preferences, a demand-deposit contract does better, provided that trading opportunities are limited.

markets are well developed. Goodfriend and King (1988) argue that solvent institutions then cannot be illiquid since informed parties in the repo and interbank market would step in to provide the needed liquidity. In this spirit, former European Central Bank (ECB) board member Tommaso Padoa-Schioppa suggested that the classical bank run may only happen in textbooks since the "width and depth of today's interbank market is such that other institutions would probably replace those which withdraw their funds" (as quoted in Rochet and Vives, 2004).

While these remarks correctly suggest that the development and deepening of financial markets could reduce the need for a LOLR in providing liquidity support, we believe that it would be hasty to conclude that there is no role for a LOLR, particularly when information asymmetries are considered. For example, Rochet and Vives (2004) show that a coordination failure in the interbank market may occur, particularly when fundamentals are weak, and that this may lead to a need for liquidity support by the LOLR for a solvent institution.[12] The 2007–2009 financial crisis gives ample reason to believe that coordination failures in interbank markets are real and that the role of a LOLR is still important.

This discussion suggests two somewhat tentative conclusions. First, the development of financial markets (including interbank markets) has improved the risk-sharing opportunities available to banks and has probably decreased the likelihood of a run on an individual bank. Whether the total insolvency risk of individual institutions has declined depends on the actual risk-taking and capitalization. Second, because these improved risk-sharing opportunities have arisen from a greater degree of integration between banks and markets, they may also have contributed to an *increase* in *systemic* risk. In other words, while the likelihood of an individual bank failing due to an idiosyncratic shock may have declined, there may be a concomitant increase in the probability that localized liquidity and solvency problems may propagate quickly through the financial system as a whole, leading to higher systemic risk. This raises thorny regulatory issues, which we turn to next.

3.6.2 Regulatory Implications

The preceding discussion has focused the spotlight on one fact: banks and markets are becoming increasingly integrated. This is happening in part because greater competition is inducing banks to follow their borrowers to the capital market and offer products that combine features of bank-based and market-based financing. It is also happening because banks themselves are using the financial market increasingly for their own risk management purposes. And the availability of market participants as purchasers of new bank products encourages financial innovations by banks. But, as Thakor (2012) shows, this can also increase the likelihood of financial crises. There is thus a multitude of factors that have contributed to an astonishingly rapid melding process.

An important implication of this integration is that it is becoming more and more difficult to isolate banking risks from financial market risks. A financial market crisis inevitably

---

[12]   Another line of research studies the impact of liquidity on asset pricing (e.g., Acharya and Pedersen, 2005) and the possible role of asset price bubbles as a source of fragility and contagion (see De Bandt and Hartmann, 2002; Allen, 2005, for surveys on contagion).

cascades through the banking system, and what happens in the banking system does not take long to reverberate through the financial market. So, if the main task of bank regulators is the safety and soundness of the banking system, they must now also worry about the financial market whose participants are outside the bank regulator's domain. Explicit recognition that these sorts of effects have created the specter of "endogenous systemic risk" has led to the creation of the Financial Stability Oversight Council (FSOC) in the US and the European Systemic Risk Board (ESRB) in the EU as parts of the post-subprime-crisis regulatory landscape.

Moreover, even though the explicit insurance guarantee applies only to bank deposits, the temptation for government regulators to bail out various uninsured participants—including investment banks and financial market investors—in the event of a crisis in the capital market seems difficult to resist on ex post efficiency grounds, particularly because of the implications for bank safety and systemic stability.[13] It will be interesting to examine the connotations of this for ex ante incentives and the magnitude of the implicit "soft" safety net provided by the government. What seems safe to conjecture is that a perception of a greater regulatory concern with ex post efficiency—and hence a greater desire to intervene—has elevated the importance of moral hazard. And this has happened in an environment in which regulatory issues are becoming increasingly international, both due to the cross-border proliferation of financial institutions and the increasing integration of banks with financial markets, which are typically international in scope.

3.6.3 Need for Cross-Border Coordination in Regulation and Supervision: The European Union Example

The regulatory task across national boundaries is rather complex. Consider the European Union as an example. The patchwork of national supervision and European-wide coordination in the European Union has so far produced mixed results.[14] As the 2007–2009 financial crisis has shown, in crisis situations important concerns can be raised about the adequacy of information sharing and cooperation between the various supervisors, the ECB, and the national central banks. In particular, in such situations the question about who will be in charge might become paramount. Potential tensions can easily be envisioned between

---

[13] The guarantee provided in 2008 to a collapsing Bear Stearns by the government to facilitate its sale to JPMorgan Chase is an example, as are the general measures to let investment banks qualify for a commercial banking license (and in doing so allow them access to deposits and let them qualify for deposit insurance).

[14] Several things did go wrong, most notably the non-coordinated actions surrounding deposit insurance. Some countries chose to offer blanket guarantees overnight (e.g., Ireland) and in doing so imposed severe externalities on other countries and also foreign banks in their own markets that were not covered. These foreign countries and banks faced an immediate erosion of their deposit base. In the subsequent euro crisis, a deadly embrace between weak domestic banks and governments became a central point of attention. It is generally perceived that governments are typically too lenient with their domestic banks, and this may in part be due to their interest in encouraging these banks to hold risky sovereign bonds of their home countries.

supervisory agencies, national central banks, and the ECB. Moreover, one could ask to what extent these arrangements accomplish the efficiency and effectiveness objectives that regulation and supervision should be subjected to.

Policymakers are aware of these issues. The question is how to coordinate these potentially diverse interests, particularly in crisis situations. The core message of the second Brouwer report (Economic and Finance Committee, 2001) was that no mechanism was in place to coordinate in case of a crisis.[15] For that reason, a Memorandum of Understanding between virtually all European national central banks and supervisors was formulated that specified principles and procedures for cooperation in crisis management situations (ECB, 2003). However, the fiscal side, in particular the budgetary obligations imposed on member states in the case of bailouts, also requires the approval of national finance ministries that have to incur the potential financial obligations associated with bailouts. In a follow-up Memorandum of Understanding, these finance ministries were also included (ECB, 2005). Several questions can be raised about the efficiency of the arrangements in general. The decentralized structure may give rise to potential conflicts of interest between the national authorities and "outsiders." For example, national authorities might be prone to "too-big-to-fail" (TBTF) rescues, and this worsens the moral hazard on the part of large institutions. Yet one could argue that the moral hazard engendered by TBTF policies could be attenuated somewhat by attaching to TBTF rescues specific provisions that would involve replacing management, wiping out the claims of shareholders and uninsured debtholders, etc. This is true in theory but does not appear to happen often in practice. One reason might be the possibility of capture of local regulators and supervisors due to the closeness of their relationships to the "national flagship" institutions (Boot and Thakor, 1993). There are also issues of "too many to fail" (see Acharya and Yorulmazer, 2007) or "too interconnected to fail" (Herring, 2008), which could also induce regulatory leniency toward these institutions. Alternatively, national authorities may not sufficiently internalize the disruptive consequences that a domestic bank failure could have in other countries. Efficiency might be hampered in other ways as well. For example, the national scope of supervision may help encourage the emergence of "national champions" among regulators, who may then seek to protect institutions in their countries. More fundamentally, the decentralized structure could give rise to an uneven playing field, regulatory arbitrage possibilities, and coordination failures in the resolution of financial distress in cross-border operating institutions.

Casual observation would seem to suggest that integration and further coordination (if not centralization of authority) of both regulation and supervision might yield substantial efficiency gains not only for the supervisory authorities but also, and perhaps more importantly, for the supervised financial institutions themselves. There are currently more than 35 supervisory authorities responsible for prudential supervision in the European Union, and a typical large financial institution might have to report to more than 20 supervisors (Pearson, 2003).

Yet, practical considerations suggest that a full integration of all regulatory and supervisory functions at the European level might not be easy to do in a way that guarantees effectiveness. While it is clear that regulatory and supervisory integration need to keep pace with the development of the size and the cross-border footprint of the covered banks, the heterogeneity of underlying supervisory systems and the implied costs of integration should not

---

[15] See Economic and Finance Committee, 2001 for further recommendations.

be underestimated. An interesting illustration is the evidence reported by Barth, Caprio, and Levine (2004) on the variation across the European Union (EU) countries in supervisory institutions and practices. Their conclusion is that supervisory arrangements within the EU are as diverse as in the rest of the world. Also, illustrating this point further, the EU countries are current or former standard bearers of all major legal origins. A vast literature now documents how legal origin matters for the shape and functioning of the financial system (see LaPorta et al., 1998). Bank regulation and supervisory practices also differ considerably between civil and common law countries, typically with a more flexible and responsive approach in the latter.

While common sense suggests that ultimately a more integrated regulatory and supervisory structure is desirable,[16] the way we should get there is far from clear. Indeed, practical considerations, including political concerns, suggest at least the short-run inevitability of a fragmented structure. A coordination layer will then need to be superimposed on this structure. A report by an EU committee chaired by Jacques de Larosière recommended in 2009 the introduction of pan-EU supervisory authorities. These recommendations have been implemented, and have led to, for example, the European Banking Authority. While in name it is an "authority," its powers are largely limited to facilitating coordination.[17]

This status quo has been challenged following the 2007–2009 credit crisis. The crisis may well lead to a situation in which central banks get a heavier role in supervision. While central banks always had a role in safeguarding the stability of the financial system, during the 2007–2009 crisis we have seen that both the Federal Reserve and the ECB became directly involved in rescuing depository as well as non-depository financial institutions. An important question in the current debate is whether this expanded role should be formalized. For example, in the EU, the euro crisis has led to a political drive to get to a banking union with (real) pan-European supervisory powers in the hands of the ECB. More specifically, decisions have been made such that the responsibility for the supervision of the largest banks will migrate to the ECB (the Single Supervisory Mechanism—SSM). This reflects a significant change in thinking. Prior to the crisis, the consensus appeared to be that caution was in order when it came to expanding the mandate of central banks, because an expanded mandate could compromise the pivotal function of central banks in conducting monetary policy.[18]

---

[16] Actually, some theoretical work suggests the potential value of competition between regulators. See, e.g., Kane (1988).

[17] An important distinction needs to be made between business conduct regulation and prudential regulation. We have focused on the latter. The former is closer to the functioning of financial markets and lends itself more readily for centralization at the European level. But even in context of these financial markets, the Lamfalussy report did not directly propose authority at the EU level, but introduced a collaboration model that ideally would induce regulatory and supervisory convergence. It stated that if its proposed approach is not successful, the creation of a single EU regulatory authority should be considered. The subsequent Larosière report—primarily focused on banks—was cast in the Lamfalussy spirit, emphasizing the need for coordination at the EU level. Note that the Larosière Report also introduced "authorities" for pension funds/insurers and financial market regulation and a systemic "authority"—the European Systemic Risk Board.

[18] The sustainability of the euro as common currency in the Eurozone is the key driving force behind the suggestions for a banking union. It is felt that weak domestic banks undermine their local governments, and via that channel the sustainability of the euro. Alternatively, governments might use their domestic banks as a source of financing, which might encourage irresponsible fiscal policies that are not compatible with having a common currency. See European Council (2012) and Véron and Wolff

3.6.4　Other Reform Suggestions

The struggle for better cross-border coordination in regulation and supervision should go hand in hand with more fundamental reforms in the regulatory structure. The first is that the scope of regulation and supervision needs to be clearly identified and, if possible, contained. Effective supervision and regulation—given the mushrooming cross-sector and cross-border footprint of financial institutions—requires a better delineation of safety and systemic risk concerns. The earlier discussion on the precise propagation mechanism as it relates to systemic risk is actually pointing at the same issue. The cross-sector integration of financial institutions and the increasingly more seamless integration of financial markets and institutions have considerably broadened the scope of regulation and the potential sources of systemic risk.

Another relevant question is whether market discipline could help in containing systemic risks, or whether market responses merely amplify such risks (see Flannery, 1998). Here the picture gets a bit murky. Basel II tries to encourage market discipline via its third pillar that is aimed at greater transparency. The idea is that market discipline could help supervisors in safeguarding the well-being of the financial sector. This has merit on the face of it and has support in the literature as well. The literature has viewed market discipline working in three ways: (1) by providing regulators with market-based signals of bank risk-taking through the yields on subordinated debt issued by banks; (2) by providing banks with disincentives to take excessive risk through the upward adjustments in sub-debt yields in response to greater bank risk; and (3) by choking off the supply of sub-debt when sufficiently high risk-taking by the bank is detected by the market, thereby providing additional encouragement to the bank to temper its risk-taking. Nonetheless, it has been shown both theoretically and empirically that market discipline can be effective only if the claims of uninsured investors (sub-debt and equity) are not protected via de facto ex post insurance in a government-sponsored rescue of a failing institution. For a theoretical treatment of these issues, see Decamps, Rochet, and Roger (2004), and for empirical analyses that support the risk-controlling role of market discipline, see Barth, Caprio, and Levine (2004), and Goyal (2005). However, despite all of the research support for the role of market discipline, our knowledge of whether market discipline facilitates or hinders the regulatory task of maintaining banking stability *during* a financial crisis is quite limited. In particular, when the financial sector is severely stressed, as during the 2007–2009 credit crisis, market discipline may induce herding behavior, as everybody "heads simultaneously for the exit," and this actually could be a source of instability. This suggests that regulation and supervision in "normal times" should perhaps be distinguished from that during crisis episodes. Market discipline, although valuable in normal times, may be very distortive in times of systemic stress. This may be one reason why, during crises, regulators have been inclined to provide more or less blanket guarantees to distressed institutions, ostensibly to counter the potentially adverse effects of market discipline. However, all of this notwithstanding, it would be dangerous to conclude that market

(2013). Acharya and Steffen (2013) argue that inducements provided to European banks to hold the sovereign debt of the countries (especially in the distressed countries) they are headquartered in may have contributed to a deepening of the crisis in Europe and the slow recovery of European banks from the crisis.

discipline, say via the use of market value accounting and other mechanisms, is something that should be relied upon in good times and eschewed in bad times. The key is to figure out the appropriate regulatory actions in *good* times—when banks have the flexibility to comply without compromising their viability—that would enable banks to be more capable of withstanding the stresses of market discipline during bad times. And it will also be important to remember that banks cannot be completely insured from the effects of market stress during bad times (e.g., through the use of blanket guarantees for *all* claimants), or else the ex ante effectiveness of market discipline is lost entirely (e.g., Decamps, Rochet, and Roger, 2004).

This brings up the issue of introducing firewalls in the financial sector. For example, does a subsidiary structure reduce systemic risk concerns? We do not think that an answer is readily available. More generally, what type of constraints, if any, should be put on the corporate structure of financial institutions? Until the 2007–2009 financial crisis, the general belief was that deregulation in the financial sector would continue further, possibly leading to even bigger and broader financial institutions. But now it is far from clear what the future will bring. Some have suggested reintroducing the Glass–Steagall Act to insulate local banking from the risks and fads that periodically afflict financial markets. Proposals that echo the Glass–Steagall Act include the Dodd–Frank Act in the US, the Vickers Report in the UK (Vickers, 2011), and the Liikanen Report (Liikanen, 2012) in the EU.[19] To what extent these are effective, and not overly costly, is open to debate. In any case, changes in the industrial structure of the financial sector are of paramount importance for the design and effectiveness of regulation and supervision.[20] If these issues cannot be satisfactorily addressed, we are not very optimistic about the possibilities for effective and efficient pan-European regulation, let alone globally coordinated regulation, even in the long run.

A second issue has to do with the evolution of capital regulation. Many believe that banks should operate with higher capital buffers (See Thakor (forthcoming)). This is somewhat at odds with the Basel II rules, which permit banks to fine-tune their required capital ratios based on their (certified) internal models. There are questions about whether these models induce procyclicality, and whether such model-dependency induces systemic risk by itself (e.g., institutions using the same models, and thus potentially being subject to the same shortcomings). There have also been concerns about the potential adverse consequences of the discretion that Basel II provides to banks.[21] Perhaps similar concerns led the FDIC

---

[19] All these proposals seek to protect core banking functions against risks originating from financial markets. In the case of the Dodd-Frank Act, restrictions particularly aim at containing risks coming from private equity, hedge fund investments and derivatives. Vickers and Liikanen focus on *internally* separating banking operations. See BIS (2013, ch. 5) for a discussion and comparison of the various proposals.

[20] A variety of other structural issues need to be considered. For example, earlier we referred to the concentration in the credit rating business and the importance of ratings for the markets for structured finance (securitization). It is interesting to ask what impact a meltdown of one of the main credit rating agencies would have on these markets, and what this in turn would imply for participants in these markets.

[21] This concern stems from the observation that individual banks are unlikely to sufficiently internalize the systemic-risk externalities of their actions. Consequently, the latitude that Basel II grants to banks in having them use their own internal risk assessment models to determine appropriate capital levels is misplaced. Banks appear to have powerful incentives to tweak these models in order to generate prescriptions to keep low levels of capital. Behn, Haselman and Vig (2014) provide evidence for German banks that validates this concern. The follow-up with Basel III tries to address these concerns.

to impose a minimum leverage ratio on banks in the Basel II environment. The FDIC has argued that requiring a minimum level of capital—regardless of risk—is essential for timely regulatory intervention in the event of problems. Such timely intervention seems particularly important in cross-border situations, given the complexities created by bank failures in such situations. In particular, timely regulatory intervention could help contain conflicts between local authorities in such cases (see Eisenbeis and Kaufman, 2005). This is one reason why new rules are proposed—commonly referred to as Basel III—that stipulate higher capital requirements, and indeed also a leverage ratio, although one could justifiably argue that the levels of even these higher requirements may be well short of adequate.[22]

A third issue is deposit insurance. The 2007–2009 financial crisis has made it clear that, when a real crisis hits, national authorities effectively feel compelled to fully guarantee the deposit bases of their financial institutions to eliminate the possibility of massive runs. This heavy dependence on insured deposits is an issue that needs a re-examination. Extant research (see Bhattacharya, Boot, and Thakor, 1998) has clearly shown the moral hazards that insured deposits entail. Moreover, Barth, Caprio, and Levine (2004) have shown that high levels of (de facto or de jure) deposit insurance impede the effectiveness of market discipline and increase the likelihood of a banking crisis. A question is whether strict regulatory limits should be put on the risks that institutions can expose these deposits to. Earlier research had at some point advocated narrow banking, which fully insulates insured deposits. But are there alternatives? And, more generally, can insured deposits be made less important as a funding vehicle for financial institutions?

A fourth issue is whether regulation and supervision sufficiently effectively address macro prudential issues, in particular systemic concerns. It appears that the majority of regulatory initiatives are focused on the well-being of individual financial institutions. That is, a micro prudential focus dominates (see Brunnemeier et al., 2009). This should be addressed to better reconcile regulation and supervision with the systemic concerns that are paramount.

The fifth issue is that very little is known about the efficiency and effectiveness of various regulatory and supervisory structures. As Barth et al. (2003) put it, "there is very little empirical evidence on how, or indeed whether, the structure, scope or independence of bank supervision affects the banking industry." Their own research suggests that the effect is at best marginal, but measurement problems are vexing. They conclude from this that we may thus choose to focus only on the effect that regulation has on systemic risk. But here, too, little is known about the regulatory structures that are most efficient in dealing with systemic risk. What this means is that we need considerable additional research to sharpen our identification of the costs and benefits of different regulatory and supervisory arrangements. Given the strikingly different national supervisory arrangements that exist today, our lack of knowledge on this issue is a significant barrier to progress toward a harmonized "superior model.[23]

---

[22] Berger and Bouwman (2013) provide empirical evidence that higher capital produces greater benefits for banks during financial crises, including a higher probability of survival for a bank with higher capital. This is consistent with Thakor's (2012) theory that higher capital weakens incentives for banks to introduce financial innovations that are associated with higher probabilities of financial crises.

[23] We have not focused on changes that might be needed in the internal incentive structure in banks. As has become clear in the current crisis, internal risk management showed substantial lapses (see Group of Thirty, 2009). Other issues abstained from in this chapter relate to procyclicality in Basel II and International Financial Reporting Standard (IFRS) accounting.

3.7 CONCLUSIONS

We have reviewed some of the literature on why banks exist, the risks they create, and how interbank competition as well as that from markets affects the economic roles served by banks as well as the attendant risks. One important development is that banks have become increasingly integrated with markets. This integration generates two effects that work in opposite directions. On the one hand, individual banks become better equipped to manage their own risks because it becomes easier and less costly to hedge these risks using the market. This could reduce the risk of an individual bank failing due to an idiosyncratic shock. On the other hand, there is an increase in the probability that a shock to a small subset of banks could generate systemic effects that ripple through the financial market, so that this banks–markets integration may be causing an elevation of systemic risk.

It is easy to see that this substantially complicates the task of prudential regulation of banks and raises the specter of a widening of the "implicit" governmental safety net as ex post efficiency concerns tempt the government to bail out even uninsured players. This is no longer a mere theoretical conjecture, as demonstrated by the bailouts of investment banks and insurance companies in 2008–2009. We believe that these are important issues that deserve greater theoretical and empirical attention. In particular, we need to have a better understanding of what the regulatory intervention should be in a crisis. Governmental initiatives such as those witnessed in the US during the 2007–2009 crisis—massive governmental injections of liquidity and capital into banks and other financial institutions without an adequate corporate control role for the government—are very costly and possibly ineffective due to daunting moral hazard and asymmetric information problems. Some key lessons might be learnt from previous financial crises—for example, the Swedish financial crisis of the 1990s (see Ingves and Lind, 1994; and Aghion, Bolton, and Fries, 1999).

To conclude, we believe the most important, yet only partially answered, research questions raised by our discussion are the following:

- What are the implications of the ever-increasing integration of banks and markets for *systemic* risk and fragility?
- What issues should we consider in the optimal design of regulation to respond to the (until recently, at least) growing cross-border footprints of major financial institutions and the increasing integration of banks and financial markets?
- What changes, if any, should be imposed on the structure of the financial services industry, and the banking sector in particular, to contain the "mushrooming" nature of systemic risk concerns (i.e., to contain the scope of regulation and supervision)?
- What role, if any, can market discipline play in helping safeguard the stability of the financial sector?
- How do banks and private equity firms (and other non-banking financial institutions) interact and what implications does this have for the regulation of banks and financial markets?

- What role do credit rating agencies play in financial markets, how does this affect banks, and what implications does this have for systemic risks that *bank* regulators care about?

These questions represent a rich agenda for future research.

REFERENCES

Acharya, V., Gromb, D., and Yorulmazer, T. (2007). Failure in the Market for Liquidity Transfers and the Origins of Central Banking. Working Paper.

Acharya, V., Gromb, D., and Yorulmazer, T. (2012). Imperfect Competition in the Inter-Bank Market for Liquidity. Working Paper.

Acharya, V. and Pedersen, L. (2005). Asset Pricing with Liquidity Risk, *Journal of Financial Economics* 77, 375–410.

Acharya, V. and Schaefer, S. (2006). Liquidity Risk and Correlation Risk: Implications for Risk Management. Working Paper.

Acharya, V. and Steffen, S. (2013). The Greatest Carry Trade Ever? Understanding the Eurozone Bank Risks. NYU Stern Working Paper.

Acharya, V. and Yorulmazer, T. (2007). Too Many to Fail—An Analysis Of Time-Inconsistency in Bank Closure Policies, *Journal of Financial Intermediation* 16, 515–554.

Admati, A. R., Demarzo, P. M., Hellwig, M. F., and Pfleiderer, P. C. (2011). Fallacies, Irrelevant Facts, and Myths in the Discussion of Capital Regulation: Why Bank Equity is Not Expensive. Stanford University Working Paper.

Aghion, P., Bolton, P., and Fries, S. (1999). Optimal Design of Bank Bailouts: The Case of Transition Economies, *Journal of Institutional and Theoretical Economics* 155, 51–70.

Allen, F. (1990). The Market for Information and the Origin of Financial Intermediation, *Journal of Financial Intermediation* 1, 3–30.

Allen, F. (1993). Stock Markets and Resource Allocation. In: C. Mayer and X. Vives (Eds.), *Capital Markets and Financial Intermediation*. Cambridge: Cambridge University Press, 81–108.

Allen, F. (2005). Modeling Financial Instability, *National Institute Economic Review* 192, 57–67.

Allen, F. and Gale, D. (1995). A Welfare Comparison of Intermediaries and Financial Markets in Germany and the US, *European Economic Review* 39, 179–209.

Allen, F. and Gale, D. (1997). Financial Markets, Intermediaries and Intertemporal Smoothing, *Journal of Political Economy* 105, 523–546.

Barth, J., Caprio, G., and Levine, R. (2004). Bank Regulation and Supervision: What Works Best?, *Journal of Financial Intermediation* 13, 205–248.

Barth, J. R., Nolle, D. E., Phumiwasana, T., and Yago, G. (2003). A Cross-Country Analysis of the Bank Supervisory Framework and Bank Performance, *Financial Markets, Institutions & Instruments* 12, 67–120.

Behn, M., Haselman, R., and Vig, V. (2014). The Limits of Model-Based Regulation. *Working Paper,* London Business School, 1–47.

Berger, A. and Bouwman, C. (2009). Bank Liquidity Creation, *Review of Financial Studies* 22, 3779–3837.

Berger, A. and Bouwman, C. (2013). How Does Bank Capital Affect Bank Performance During Financial Crises?, *Journal of Financial Economics* 109, 146–176.

Berger, A., Klappper, L. F., Martinez-Peria M. S., and Zaidi, R. (2008). Bank Ownership Type and Banking Relationships, *Journal of Financial Intermediation* 17, 37–62.

Berger, A., Miller, N., Petersen, M., Rajan, R., and Stein, J. (2005). Does Function Follow Organizational Form? Evidence from the Lending Practices of Large and Small Banks, *Journal of Financial Economics* 76, 237–269.

Berger, A., Saunders, A., Scalise, J., and Udell, G. (1998). The Effects of Bank Mergers and Acquisitions on Small Business Lending, *Journal of Financial Economics* 50, 187–229.

Berglöf, E. and von Thadden, E.-L. (1994). Short-Term Versus Long-Term Interests: Capital Structure with Multiple Investors, *Quarterly Journal of Economics* 109, 1055–1084.

Berlin, M. (1996). For Better and for Worse: Three Lending Relationships, *Business Review Federal Reserve Bank of Philadelphia* 3–12.

Berlin, M. and Mester, L. (1992). Debt Covenants and Renegotiation, *Journal of Financial Intermediation* 2, 95–133.

Berlin, M. and Mester, L. (1999). Deposits and Relationship Lending, *Review of Financial Studies* 12, 579–607.

Bhattacharya, S., Boot, A. W. A., and Thakor, A. V. (1998). The Economics of Bank Regulation, *Journal of Money, Credit and Banking* 30, 745–770.

Bhattacharya, S., Boot, A. W. A., and Thakor, A. V. (Eds.). (2004). *Credit Intermediation and the Macro Economy*. Oxford: Oxford University Press.

Bhattacharya, S. and Chiesa, G. (1995). Proprietary Information, Financial Intermediation, and Research Incentives, *Journal of Financial Intermediation* 4, 328–357.

Bhattacharya, S. and Thakor, A. V. (1993). Contemporary Banking Theory, *Journal of Financial Intermediation* 3, 2–50.

BIS (Bank for International Settlements) (2013). 83rd BIS Annual Report 2012/2013, June 23. BIS, Basel, Switzerland.

Bolton, P. and Scharfstein, D. (1996). Optimal Debt Structure and the Number of Creditors, *Journal of Political Economy* 104, 1–25.

Boot, A. W. A. (2000). Relationship Banking: What Do We Know?, *Journal of Financial Intermediation* 9, 7–25.

Boot, A. W. A., Greenbaum, S. G., and Thakor, A. V. (1993). Reputation and Discretion in Financial Contracting, *American Economic Review* 83, 1165–1183.

Boot, A. W. A., Milbourn, T., and Schmeits, A. (2006). Credit Ratings as Coordination Mechanisms, *Review of Financial Studies* 19, 81–118.

Boot, A. W. A. and Thakor, A. V. (1993). Self-Interested Bank Regulation, *American Economic Review* 83, 206–212.

Boot, A. W. A. and Thakor, A. V. (1994). Moral Hazard and Secured Lending in an Infinitely Repeated Credit Market Game, *International Economic Review* 35(3), 899–920.

Boot, A. W. A. and Thakor, A. V. (1997). Financial System Architecture, *Review of Financial Studies* 10, 693–733.

Boot, A. W. A. and Thakor, A. V. (2000). Can Relationship Banking Survive Competition?, *Journal of Finance* 55, 679–713.

Boot, A. W. A., Thakor, A. V., and Udell, G. (1991). Credible Commitments, Contract Enforcement Problems and Banks: Intermediation as Credibility Assurance, *Journal of Banking & Finance* 15, 605–632.

Boyd, J. H. and Gertler, M. (1994). Are Banks Dead, or Are the Reports Greatly Exaggerated?, *Federal Reserve Bank of Minneapolis Quarterly Review* 18, 2–23.

Brick, I. E. and Palia, D. (2007). Evidence of Jointness in the Terms of Relationship Lending, *Journal of Financial Intermediation* 16, 452–476.

Brophy, D., Ouimet, P. P., and Sialm, C. (2009). Hedge Funds as Investors of Last Resort?, *Review of Financial Studies* 22, 541–574.

Brunnemeier, M., Crockett, A., Goodhart, C., and Shin, H. (2009). *The Fundamental Principles of Financial Regulation, Preliminary Draft of Geneva Reports on the World Economy*, No. 11, International Center for Monetary and Banking Studies, Geneva.

Brunnemeier, M. and Pedersen, L. (2009). Market Liquidity and Funding Liquidity, *Review of Financial Studies* 22, 2201–2238.

Calomiris, C. and Kahn, C. (1991). The Role of Demandable Debt in Structuring Optimal Banking Arrangements, *American Economic Review* 81, 497–513.

Cantor, R. (2004). An Introduction to Recent Research on Credit Ratings, *Journal of Banking & Finance* 28, 2565–2573.

Carey, M., Post, M., and Sharpe, S. A. (1998). Does Corporate Lending by Banks and Finance Companies Differ? Evidence on Specialization in Private Debt Contracting, *Journal of Finance* 53, 845–878.

Carletti, E., Cerasi, V., and Daltung, S. (2007). Multiple Bank Lending: Diversification and Free-Riding in Monitoring, *Journal of Financial Intermediation* 16, 425–451.

Chan, Y. S., Greenbaum, S. G., and Thakor, A. V. (1986). Information Reusability, Competition and Bank Asset Quality, *Journal of Banking & Finance* 10, 243–253.

Chava, S., Ganduri, R., and Ornthanalai, C. (2012). Are Credit Ratings Still Relevant?. Working Paper, Georgia Tech, December, <http://ssrn.com/abstract=2023998>.

Chemmanur, T. J. and Fulghieri, P. (1994). Reputation, Renegotiation, and the Choice between Bank Loans and Publicly Traded Debt, *Review of Financial Studies* 7, 475–506.

Claessens, S., Pozsar, Z., Ratnovski, L., and Singh, M. (2012). *Shadow Banking: Economics and Policy*, IMF Staff Discussion Note No. SDN 12/12, December 4.

Coffee, J. C. (2002). Understanding Enron: It's about the Gatekeepers, Stupid, Columbia Center for Law and Economics Studies Working Paper No. 207.

Coffee, J. C. and Sale, H. A. (2008). Redesigning the SEC: Does the Treasury Have a Better Idea?, Columbia Center for Law and Economics Studies Working Paper No. 342.

Committee of Wise Men (2001). Final Report of the Committee of Wise Men on the Regulation of the European Securities Markets. Lamfalussy Report, Brussels.

Coval, J. and Thakor, A. V. (2005). Financial Intermediation as a Beliefs-Bridge between Optimists and Pessimists, *Journal of Financial Economics* 75, 535–570.

Da Rin, M. and Hellmann, T. (2002). Banks as Catalysts for Industrialization, *Journal of Financial Intermediation* 11, 366–397.

Datta, S., Iskandar-Datta, M., and Patel, A. (1999). Bank Monitoring and Pricing of Corporate Public Debt, *Journal of Financial Economics* 51, 435–449.

De Bandt, O. and Hartmann, P. (2002). Systemic Risk: A Survey. In: C. Goodhart and G. Illing (Eds.), *Financial Crises, Contagion and the Lender of Last Resort*. Oxford: Oxford University Press, 249–298.

Decamps, J., Rochet, J., and Roger, B. (2004). The Three Pillars of Basel II: Optimizing the Mix, *Journal of Financial Intermediation* 13, 132–155.

Degryse, H. and Ongena, S. (2007). The Impact of Competition on Bank Orientation, *Journal of Financial Intermediation* 16, 399–424.

Deidda, L. and Fattouh, B. (2008). Banks, Financial Markets and Growth, *Journal of Financial Intermediation* 17, 6–36.

Dell'Ariccia, G., Detragiache, E., and Rajan, R. (2008). The Real Effect of Banking Crises, *Journal of Financial Intermediation* 17, 89–112.

Dewatripont, M. and Maskin, E. (1995). Credit and Efficiency in Centralized and Decentralized Economies, *Review of Economic Studies* 62, 541–555.

DeYoung, R., Glennon, D., and Nigro, P. (2008). Evidence from Informational-Opaque Small Business Borrowers, *Journal of Financial Intermediation* 17, 113–143.

Diamond, D. (1984). Financial Intermediation and Delegated Monitoring, *Review of Economic Studies* 51, 393–414.

Diamond, D. (1991). Monitoring and Reputation: The Choice between Bank Loans and Directly Placed Debt, *Journal of Political Economy* 99, 689–721.

Diamond, D. (1993). Seniority and Maturity of Debt Contracts, *Journal of Financial Economics* 33, 341–368.

Diamond, D. and Dybvig, P. H. (1983). Bank Runs, Deposit Insurance and Liquidity, *Journal of Political Economy* 91, 401–419.

Diamond, D. and Rajan, R. G. (2001). Liquidity Risk, Liquidity Creation and Financial Fragility: A Theory of Banking, *Journal of Political Economy* 109, 287–327.

Dinç, I. S. (2000). Bank Reputation, Bank Commitment, and the Effects of Competition in Credit Markets, *Review of Financial Studies* 13, 781–812.

Drucker, S. (2005). Information Asymmetries and the Effects of Banking Mergers in Firm-Bank Relationships. Proceedings, Federal Reserve Bank of Chicago, 140–147.

Drucker, S. and Puri, M. (2005). On the Benefits of Concurrent Lending and Underwriting, *Journal of Finance* 60, 2763–2799.

ECB (European Central Bank) (2003). Memorandum of Understanding on High-Level Principles of Cooperation. ECB Press Release, March 10.

ECB (European Central Bank) (2005). Memorandum of Understanding on Cooperation between the Banking Supervisors, Central Banks and Finance Ministries of the European Union in Financial Crises Situations. ECB, May 10.

Economic and Finance Committee (2001). *Report on Financial Crisis Management*, Commission of the EC, Directorate-General for Economic and Financial Affairs European Economy Economic Papers No. 156.

EFC (2002). *Financial Regulation, Supervision and Stability*, Economic and Financial Committee Document No. EF76/ECOFIN 324.

Eisenbeis, R. A. and Kaufman, G. G. (2005). Bank Crises Resolution and Foreign-Owned Banks, *Federal Reserve Bank of Atlanta Economic Review* 90, 1–18.

European Council (2012). Towards a Genuine Economic and MonetaryUnion. Report by the President of the European Council, Herman Van Rompuy, June, <http://ec.europa.eu/economy_finance/focuson/crisis/documents/131201_en.pdf>.

Flannery, M. (1998). Using Market Information in Prudential Bank Supervision: A Review of the US Empirical Evidence, *Journal of Money, Credit and Banking* 30, 273–305.

Gande, A. (2007). Commercial Banks in Investment Banking. Vanderbilt University Working Paper.

Gande, A. and Saunders, A. (2005). Are Banks Still Special When There Is a Secondary Market for Loans? New York University Working Paper.

Goodfriend, M. and King, R. (1988). Financial Deregulation, Monetary Policy and Central Banking. In: W. Haraf and R. M. Kushmeider (Eds.), *Restructuring Banking and Financial Services in America*. American Enterprise Institute Studies 481, Lanham, MD: University Press of America.

Gorton, G. (1988). Banking Panics and Business Cycles, *Oxford Economic Papers* 40, 751–781.

Gorton, G. and Kahn, J. A. (1993). The Design of Bank Loan Contracts, Collateral, and Renegotiation, National Bureau of Economic Research Working Paper No. W4273.

Gorton, G. and Metrick, A. (2012). Securitized Banking and the Run on Repo, *Journal of Financial Economics* 104, 425–451.

Gorton, G. and Pennacchi, G. (1995). Banks and Loan Sales: Marketing Nonmarketable Assets, *Journal of Monetary Economics* 35, 389–411.

Goyal, V. (2005). Market Discipline of Bank Risk: Evidence from Subordinated Debt Contracts, *Journal of Financial Intermediation* 14, 318–350.

Group of Thirty (2009). Financial Reform: A Framework for Financial Stability. Report by the Working Group on Financial Reform, Washington, DC.

Hauswald, R. and Marquez, R. (2006). Competition and Strategic Information Acquisition in Credit Markets, *Review of Financial Studies* 19, 967–1000.

Hellmann, T., Lindsey, L., and Puri, M. (2008). Building Relationships Early: Banks in Venture Capital, *Review of Financial Studies* 21, 513–541.

Hellwig, M. (1991). Banking, Financial Intermediation and Corporate Finance. In: A. Giovanni and C. P. Mayer (Eds.), *European Financial Integration*, 35–63. New York: Cambridge University Press.

Herring, R. J. (2008). The US Subprime Crisis: Lessons for Regulators. Proceedings of the 44th Annual Conference on Bank Structure and Competition, Federal Reserve Bank of Chicago, 48–55.

Hoshi, T., Kashyap, A., and Scharfstein, D. (1993). *The Choice between Public and Private Debt: An Analysis of Post-Deregulation Corporate Financing in Japan*, National Bureau of Economic Research Working Paper No. 4421.

Houston, J. and James, C. (1996). Bank Information Monopolies and the Mix of Private and Public Debt Claims, *Journal of Finance* 51, 1863–1889.

Ingves, S. and Lind, G. (1994). The Management of the Bank Crisis: In Retrospect, *Sverigs Riksbank Quarterly Review* 1, 5–18.

Jacklin, C. J. (1987). Demand Deposits, Trading Restrictions and Risk Sharing. In: E. Prescott and N. Wallace (Eds.), *Financial Intermediation and Intertemporal Trade*. Minneapolis: University of Minnesota Press, 26–47.

James, C. (1987). Some Evidence on the Uniqueness of Bank Loans, *Journal of Financial Economics* 19, 217–235.

Kane, E. J. (1988). How Market Forces Influence the Structure of Financial Regulation. In: W. S. Haraf and R. M. Kushmeider (Eds.), *Restructuring Banking and Financial Services in America*, 343–382. Washington, DC: American Enterprise Institute Press.

Kashyap, A., Rajan, R., and Stein, J. (2002). Banks as Liquidity Providers: An Explanation for the Co-Existence of Lending and Deposit-Taking, *Journal of Finance* 57, 33–73.

Keys, B., Mukherjee, T., Seru, A., and Vig, V. (2010). Did Securitization Lead to Lax Screening: Evidence from Subprime Loans, *Quarterly Journal of Economics* 125, 307–362.

Kroszner, R. S. and Rajan, R. G. (1994). Is the Glass-Steagall Act Justified? A Study of the US Experience with Universal Banking before 1933, *American Economic Review* 84, 810–832.

LaPorta, R., Lopez-de-Silanes, L., Schleifer, A., and Vishny, R. W. (1998). Law and Finance, *Journal of Political Economy* 106, 1113–1155.

Liikanen, E. (2012). High-level Expert Group on Reforming the Structure of the EU Banking Sector, Brussels, October 2, <http://ec.europa.eu/internal_market/bank/docs/high-level_expert_group/report_en.pdf>.

Lummer, S. L. and McConnell, J. J. (1989). Further Evidence on the Bank Lending Process and the Reaction of the Capital Market to Bank Loan Agreements, *Journal of Financial Economics* 25, 99–122.

Mayer, C. (1988). New Issues in Corporate Finance, *European Economic Review* 32, 1167–1183.

Mehran, H. and Thakor, A. V. (2011). Bank Capital and Value in the Cross-Section, *Review of Financial Studies* 24(4), 1019–1067.

Mian, A. R. and Sufi, A. (2009). The Consequences of Mortgage Credit Expansion: Evidence from the 2007 Mortgage Default Crisis, *Quarterly Journal of Economics* 124, 1449–1496.

Millon, M. and Thakor, A. V. (1985). Moral Hazard and Information Sharing: A Model of Financial Information Gathering Agencies, *Journal of Finance* 40, 1403–1422.

Ongena, S. and Smith, D. C. (2000). What Determines the Number of Bank Relationships? Cross-Country Evidence, *Journal of Financial Intermediation* 9, 26–56.

Partnoy, F. (1999). The Siskel and Ebert of Financial Markets: Two Thumbs Down for the Credit Rating Agencies, *Washington University Law Quarterly* 77, 619–712.

Pearson, P. J. (2003). Comment. In: J. Kremer, D. Schoen-maker, and P. Wierts (Eds.), *Financial Supervision in Europe*, 51–57. Cheltenham: Edward Elgar.

Petersen, M. and Rajan, R. G. (1994). The Benefits of Lending Relationships: Evidence from Small Business Data, *Journal of Finance* 49, 1367–1400.

Petersen, M. and Rajan, R. (1995). The Effect of Credit Market Competition on Lending Relationships, *Quarterly Journal of Economics* 110, 407–443.

Pozsar, Z., Adrian, T., Ashcraft, A., and Boesky, H. (2010). *Shadow Banking*, Federal Reserve Bank of New York FRNBNY Staff Report No. 458.

Puri, M. (1996). Commercial Banks in Investment Banking: Conflict of Interest or Certification Role?, *Journal of Financial Economics* 40, 373–401.

Rajan, R. G. (1992). Insiders and Outsiders: The Choice between Informed and Arm's Length Debt, *Journal of Finance* 47, 1367–1400.

Ramakrishnan, R. and Thakor, A. V. (1984). Information Reliability and a Theory of Financial Intermediation, *Review of Economic Studies* 51, 415–432.

Ramírez, C. (2002). Did Banks' Security Affiliates Add Value? Evidence from the Commercial Banking Industry during the 1920s, *Journal of Money, Credit and Banking* 34, 391–411.

Rochet, J.-C. (2004). Bank Runs and Financial Crises: A Discussion. In: S. Bhattacharya, A. W. A. Boot, and A. V. Thakor (Eds.), *Credit Intermediation and the Macro Economy*. Oxford: Oxford University Press, 324–338.

Rochet, J.-C. and Vives, X. (2004). Coordination Failures and the Lender of Last Resort: Was Bagehot Right After All? *Journal of the European Economic Association* 2–6, 1116–1147.

Sangiorgi, F., Sokobin, J., and Spatt, C. (2009). Credit-rating Shopping, Selection and the Equilibrium Structure of Ratings. Carnegie Mellon University Working Paper.

Sapienza, P. (2002). The Effects of Banking Mergers on Loan Contracts, *Journal of Finance* 57, 329–367.

Schenone, C. (2004). The Effect of Banking Relationships on the Firm's Ipo Underpricing, *Journal of Finance* 59, 2903–3058.

Sharpe, S. A. (1990). Asymmetric Information, Bank Lending, and Implicit Contracts: A Stylized Model of Customer Relationships, *Journal of Finance* 45, 1069–1087.

Shockley, R. and Thakor, A. V. (1997). Bank Loan Commitment Contracts: Data, Theory and Tests, *Journal of Money, Credit and Banking* 29, 517–534.

Simons, H. C. (1936). Rules versus Authorities in Monetary Policy, *Journal of Political Economy* 44, 1–30.

Song, F. and Thakor, A. V. (2007). Relationship Banking, Fragility and the Asset-Liability Matching Problem, *Review of Financial Studies* 20, 2129–2177.

Stein, J. C. (2002). Information Production and Capital Allocation: Decentralized versus Hierarchical Firms, *Journal of Finance* 57, 1891–1921.

Strahan, P. E. (2007). Bank Structure and Lending: What We Do and Do Not Know. Boston College Working Paper.

Thakor, A. V. (1996). Capital Requirements, Monetary Policy and Aggregate Bank Lending: Theory and Empirical Evidence, *Journal of Finance* 51, 279–324.

Thakor, A. V. (2012). Incentives to Innovate and Financial Crisis, *Journal of Financial Economics* 103–1, 130–148.

Thakor, A. V. (Forthcoming). Bank Capital and Financial Stability: An Economic Tradeoff or a Faustian Bargain? *Annual Review of Financial Economics*.

US Senate Hearings (2002). Rating the Raters: Enron and the Credit Rating Agencies. Hearings before the Senate Committee on Governmental Affairs, Washington, DC.

US Senate Staff Report (2002). Financial Oversight of Enron: The SEC and Private-Sector Watchdogs. Report of the Staff to the Senate Committee on Governmental Affairs, Washington, DC.

Véron, N and Wolff, G. B. (2013). From Supervision to Resolution: Next Steps on the Road to European Banking Union. Bruegel Policy Contribution, Bruegel, Brussels, February 4.

Vickers, J. (2011). Independent Commission on Banking, Final Report, September 12, <http://webarchive.nationalarchives.gov.uk/+/bankingcommission.independent.gov.uk.>.

von Thadden, E.-L. (1998). Intermediated versus Direct Investment: Optimal Liquidity Provision and Dynamic Incentive Compatibility, *Journal of Financial Intermediation* 7, 177–197.

CHAPTER 4

....

COMPLEXITY AND SYSTEMIC RISK
*What's Changed Since the Crisis?**

....

RICHARD J. HERRING AND JACOPO CARMASSI

4.1 INTRODUCTION

....

MUCH has happened since the first version of this chapter was drafted in 2007. The issue of large, complex financial institutions (LCFIs) had just begun to catch the attention of some policymakers.[1] In general, however, officials appeared not to have anticipated the problems that would need to be addressed if one of these institutions should need to be resolved, much less considered whether the complex corporate structures of such institutions would impede or even prevent an orderly resolution.

During and after the financial crisis of 2008–2009, these issues surged to the top of the policy agenda. Events made clear that several institutions had become too-big-to-fail (TBTF).[2] One of the first actions of the G20 after the crisis was to transform the Financial Stability Forum into the Financial Stability Board (FSB) and give it the mandate to identify global systemically important banks (G-SIBs) and to ensure that each G-SIB filed a credible

* Support for this project was provided by the Systemic Risk Council, an independent and non-partisan council formed by CFA Institute and The Pew Charitable Trusts to monitor and encourage regulatory reform of US capital markets focused on systemic risk. The views expressed herein are those of the authors and do not necessarily reflect the views of the Systemic Risk Council, its members, or the supporting organizations.

[1] For example, both the Bank of England and the IMF had identified 16 LCFIs that were crucial to the functioning of the world economy. See Herring and Carmassi (2010) for a discussion of this classification approach. The 13 of the 16 LCFIs that survived the crisis are included in the sample of G-SIBs, which is the focus of this revised chapter.

[2] Although in common use, this term is regrettably inaccurate because size is one, but not the only attribute of such institutions. It should be interpreted as a proxy for institutions that are also too interconnected, too complex or too important to be resolved in an orderly fashion.

recovery and resolution plan. The principal accomplishment of the FSB has been to negoti-ate a set of key attributes of effective resolution regimes that each member country should implement (FSB 2011a, 2012a, 2013a, 2013b, 2013c). Moreover, it has set up a peer review sys-tem to monitor the progress of individual member countries in meeting these attributes (FSB, 2013d).

With the increased official scrutiny of G-SIBs, one might assume that more public data would be available to analyze their corporate structures. Alas, this is not the case. Despite the emphasis in official documents on greater market discipline, publicly available informa-tion remains fragmented and difficult to compare across institutions and sources because of differing definitions and reporting criteria and thresholds.[3]

Deregulation and technological innovation (Frame and White, 2014) have facilitated a remarkable degree of globalization among large financial institutions. These forces have transformed the scale, scope, and complexity of international banks over the past 25 years.[4] The result has been a larger and vastly more complicated financial system with much greater concentration of assets in the G-SIBs. From 1990 to 2007, the market share of the three larg-est US banks grew from 10% to 40% of total domestic deposits and the three largest banks in France, Germany, Switzerland, and the United Kingdom all control from two-thirds to three-quarters of total deposits in their home markets (Haldane, 2012). Not only are these institutions large, most are also conglomerates in the sense that they combine at least two of the three traditionally distinct functions of banks, securities firms, or insurance companies. The growth and increasing complexity of these G-SIBs have raised the question of whether these institutions have become TBTF. In effect, if one of the G-SIBs should falter, would the anticipated damage to the rest of the financial system be so great that the authorities feel obliged to put taxpayer funds at risk to prop up the G-SIB?

While excessive risk-taking and leverage may have caused the crisis, institutional com-plexity and opaque interconnections impeded effective oversight by the authorities ex ante and greatly complicated crisis management and the resolution of institutions ex post. The failure of Lehman Brothers provided clear evidence of the dangers inherent in complex, opaque legal structures that span multiple national borders and bear little relationship to how the business is managed. As Thomas Huertas (2009) has observed, "The Lehman bankruptcy demonstrates that financial institutions may be global in life, but they are national in death. They become a series of local legal entities when they become subject to administration and/ or liquidation." The challenges of coordinating, much less harmonizing, scores of legal pro-ceedings across multiple jurisdictions proved to be insuperable. Once the financial group has been dissolved into separate legal entities, information becomes so fragmented that it is vir-tually impossible to preserve any going concern value that the group may have had.

Despite the notable collapse of several major institutions during the crisis, the over-all trend toward bigger and more complex financial institutions has continued (often

---

[3] The US authorities missed an important opportunity to improve the transparency of the organizational structure of G-SIBs. Their guidance for the public section of living wills permitted banks to limit their disclosures to information that was already publicly available. And even these sparse disclosures were not required to employ common definitions and methodologies (Carmassi and Herring, 2013).

[4] On the rise of international banking see, for example, CGFS (2010a) and Claessens, Herring, and Schoenmaker (2010); on foreign banks' behavior and impact see, among others, Claessens and Van Horen (2012).

encouraged by publicly subsidized mergers). Although some firms have made some progress in rationalizing and simplifying their corporate structures, other firms have greatly increased their complexity so that, on average, the overall degree of complexity (as measured by the number of subsidiaries) has not decreased since the crisis.[5]

Our central premise is that the complexity of the corporate structures that most international financial conglomerates have developed is itself a significant source of systemic risk. In the event of bankruptcy, hundreds or even thousands of legal entities would need to be resolved. Since most of these firms are managed in an integrated fashion along lines of business with only minimal regard for legal entities, national borders, or functional regulatory domains, and with substantial and complex intragroup relationships, simply mapping an institution's business activities into its legal entities presents a formidable challenge. Moreover, these legal entities would be subject to numerous different national regulatory and bankruptcy procedures, many of which conflict.

We will begin with an overview of the G-SIBs that are the focus of our analysis. The current legal structures of G-SIBs are heavily influenced by tax and regulatory policies and so we first consider what degree of corporate complexity the G-SIBs would want in the absence of tax and regulatory distortions. Then we examine some of the (largely unintended) consequences for corporate structure of tax and regulatory policies. We analyze some of the challenges this corporate complexity poses to an orderly winding down of an international financial conglomerate and consider some of the policy reforms that have been implemented to deal with the problem. A brief comment on the challenges that remain concludes this chapter.

4.2 GLOBAL SYSTEMICALLY IMPORTANT BANKS AND COMPLEXITY

The 2008 financial crisis clearly indicated that some financial institutions may be regarded as TBTF because they perform services that are critical for the functioning of the financial system. Their failure would be expected to jeopardize the stability of the financial system and the real economy. After the crisis, policymakers have tried to identify the key factors that make these firms "systemic." They have agreed on criteria to identify "systemically important financial institutions" (SIFIs).[6] The Basel Committee on

---

[5] This is a very simplistic indicator of corporate complexity, but it remains the only indicator that can be measured with any degree of accuracy and even that is far from perfect. We have relied on Bankscope data because we used them in the first edition of this chapter and because they follow a clear methodology that is consistent across countries and across banks. Alternative sources such as SEC filings and the FED/National Information Center data follow different methodologies and provide different figures (which also differ from each other). However, the general trends in the data are usually highly correlated.

[6] Critics have charged that naming systemically important financial institutions might increase moral hazard rather than reduce it. The argument turns on whether the market believes that the authorities have the will and the means to resolve such institutions even when it requires imposing loss on some creditors. See Elliott and Litan (2011).

Banking Supervision (BCBS) has also agreed on a methodology to identify G-SIBs, the subset of SIFIs in which banking operations dominate. In July 2011 the BCBS published a consultative document outlining an indicator-based approach comprising five broad categories: size, interconnectedness, lack of readily available substitutes or financial institution infrastructure, global (cross-jurisdictional) activity, and complexity.[7] The analysis in this chapter focuses on the 28 G-SIBs identified by the FSB on the basis of these criteria in November 2012.

G-SIBs have developed a remarkable degree of corporate complexity. In what follows we focus on the number of majority-owned subsidiaries as an indicator of corporate complexity. Of course, this is a somewhat arbitrary, possibly misleading, and regrettably superficial measure of corporate complexity. Unfortunately, publicly available data do not permit us to distinguish shell corporations, transaction entities, or other inconsequential subsidiaries and so our data undoubtedly overstate the number of systemically important operations.[8] Moreover, it would be useful to supplement this simple quantitative measure with an indication of each entity's importance in the overall financial group, including the balance sheets and income statements, intra-affiliate transactions, cross-guarantees, the provision of key services to the rest of the group, and, more generally, the role of the entity in the overall business structure. Unfortunately, such information is not readily available to the public.[9] Nonetheless, the number of majority-owned subsidiaries is an indication of the magnitude of the legal challenge that would confront the authorities in taking a G-SIB through bankruptcy.

Table 4.1 presents an overview of the 28 G-SIBs, with data on subsidiaries, branches and the assets and income of the entire group.

The 28 G-SIBs are large, complex, and geographically diversified banking groups. Sixteen G-SIBs are headquartered in Europe, eight in the US, three in Japan, and one in China. The average size is about $1,600 billion in total assets. Shares of foreign assets and income tend to be large in many G-SIBs. Most earn more than 50% of their revenues/income from their foreign operations. On average, the number of majority-owned subsidiaries per bank is about 1,000, of which 60% reside in foreign countries.[10] And, on average, the G-SIBs

[7] Three indicators are used to measure complexity: notional amount of OTC derivatives; Level 3 assets and trading and available-for-sale securities. Each of the five indicators has a 20% weight in the calculation of an index of systemic importance. The final rules were published in November 2011 (BCBS, 2011, with an update in July 2013, BCBS, 2013). On the basis of the BCBS methodology, the FSB first identified 29 G-SIBs in November 2011 (FSB, 2011b). It then published an updated list comprising 28 G-SIBs in November 2012 (FSB, 2012b); the list is to be updated every year.

[8] However, it should be noted that the NIC/FED data on total subsidiaries often report much higher figures than the Bankscope majority-owned subsidiaries. For an analysis of corporate structures of US bank holding companies based on NIC/FED data see Avraham, Selvaggi, and Vickery (2012).

[9] Opencorporates is an organization focused on building an open database for every company in the world. The founders have noted that "[w]e've often heard company hierarchies and networks referred to as the Holy Grail of business information. That's not just a recognition of the value and importance of this data. It's also that it's really difficult to find. . . and to collect, and to make usable too." <http://blog.opencorporates.com/2013/07/11/open-corporate-network-data-not-just-good-but-better/>.

[10] These data are from Bankscope as of May 2013. Data reported by official bank documents confirm the magnitude of the numbers of subsidiaries, even though criteria for calculation may be different. For example, in its 2013 resolution plan submitted to the Federal Reserve and the FDIC Deutsche Bank, it states that "The DB Group consists of approximately 2,906 active legal entities" as of 31 December 2012 (Deutsche Bank, 2013: 20).

Table 4.1 Overview of Global Systemically Important Banks (ranked by 2012 total assets)

		Total assets 2012 (USD mln)	Total assets 2007 (USD mln)	% of foreign assets, 2012	% of foreign net revenues, 2012	Total subsidiaries (May 2013)	% of domestic subsidiaries (May 2013)	% of foreign subsidiaries (May 2013)	Number of countries (May 2013)	Subsidiaries in OFCs,[1] % (May 2013)	Branches, 2012	% of foreign branches, 2012
1	HSBC	2,692,538	2,354,266	65%	87%	1,565	21%	79%	69	27%	*	*
2	Deutsche Bank	2,655,138	2,833,804	73%	64%	2,124	24%	76%	61	27%	2,984	35%
3	Crédit Agricole	2,649,627	2,268,310	17%	19%	1,255	55%	45%	59	9%	11,300	20%
4	BNP Paribas	2,516,546	2,494,412	48%	68%	2,592	17%	83%	88	8%	*	*
5	Mitsubishi UFJ	2,407,111	1,824,397	31%	58%	112	46%	54%	21	4%	*	*
6	JPMorgan Chase	2,359,141	1,562,147	33%	12%	1,095	45%	55%	57	10%		
7	Barclays	2,351,777	2,459,149	66%	70%	1,739	37%	63%	58	21%	*	*
8	Bank of America	2,209,974	1,715,746	14%	13%	1,910	72%	28%	48	10%	*	*
9	Royal Bank of Scotland	2,070,846	3,807,892	31%	44%	799	40%	60%	36	13%	3,700	41%
10	Bank of China	2,016,124	820,198	8%	3%	116	72%	28%	16	15%	*	*
11	Citigroup	1,864,660	2,187,631	64%	58%	2,297	39%	61%	95	10%	*	*
12	Mizuho	1,839,477	1,495,285	25%	39%	103	62%	38%	16	7%	*	*
13	Santander	1,675,192	1,343,905	72%	85%	605	25%	75%	37	7%	14,392	68%
14	Société Générale	1,650,212	1,577,745	23%	57%	913	47%	53%	74	8%	*	*
15	Sumitomo Mitsui	1,578,522	1,124,788	15%	12%	165	59%	41%	20	18%	455	4%
16	ING Groep	1,541,934	1,932,151	58%	66%	764	32%	68%	44	4%	*	*
17	BPCE	1,514,080	n.a.	8%	16%	1,448	65%	35%	70	6%	*	*
18	Wells Fargo	1,422,968	575,442	5%	*	1,549	93%	7%	27	4%	*	*

(Continued)

Table 4.1 (Continued)

	Total assets 2012 (USD mln)	Total assets 2007 (USD mln)	% of foreign assets, 2012	% of foreign net revenues, 2012	Total subsidiaries (May 2013)	% of domestic subsidiaries (May 2013)	% of foreign subsidiaries (May 2013)	Number of countries (May 2013)	Subsidiaries in OFCs,[1] % (May 2013)	Branches, 2012	% of foreign branches, 2012
19 UBS	1,373,808	2,021,227	64%	57%	458	17%	83%	45	8%	*	*
20 Unicredit	1,222,889	1,504,134	54%	57%	2,216	41%	59%	67	3%	9,322	54%
21 Credit Suisse	1,008,379	1,208,956	78%	63%	242	10%	90%	37	21%	*	*
22 Goldman Sachs	938,555	1,119,796	35%	41%	420	29%	71%	24	11%	*	*
23 Nordea	893,665	572,728	79%	78%	220	5%	95%	19	4%	978	76%
24 BBVA	841,516	739,296	50%	70%	415	30%	70%	29	4%	7,978	56%
25 Morgan Stanley	780,960	1,045,409	25%	23%	1,311	41%	59%	45	20%	*	*
26 Standard Chartered	636,518	329,871	87%	94%	118	42%	58%	32	8%	*	*
27 Bank of New York Mellon	358,990	197,656	28%	36%	279	35%	65%	22	17%	*	*
28 State Street Corporation	222,582	142,543	25%	40%	155	26%	74%	14	28%	*	*
Average	1,617,633	1,528,107	42%	49%	964	40%	60%	44	12%	6,389	44%
Median	1,614,367	1,504,134	34%	57%	782	40%	61%	41	10%	5,839	48%
Range	2,469,956	3,665,349	82%	91%	2,489	88%	88%	81	25%	13,937	72%

[1] Offshore Financial Centers identified by the Financial Stability Forum (2000) and the International Monetary Fund (2000).

*We were unable to find sufficiently detailed data for these groups, to make consistent, meaningful comparisons. For six G-SIBs (Barclays, BNP Paribas, BPCE, Citigroup, JPMorgan Chase, and Société Générale) we could only find data on retail branches. Sources: Bankscope, SNL database, and annual reports for total assets; Bankscope for subsidiaries (majority-owned subsidiaries for which the G-SIB is the ultimate owner with a minimum control path of 50.01%); annual reports and other official bank documents for foreign assets and revenues and for branches. For additional details regarding the data please see the extended version of this chapter on the Wharton Financial Institutions Center website <http://fic.wharton.upenn.edu/fic/papers.html.>.

have subsidiaries in more than 40 countries, but the range extends from Citigroup with a presence in 95 countries to State Street, which operates in only 14 countries. Although information on branch networks is much less readily available, G-SIBs appear to have very large branch structures, ranging from about 450 to over 14,000 branches. It should be noted that for purposes of resolution planning, foreign branches should be taken into account. In the event of trouble, the host country may ring-fence the branch and treat it as if it were a subsidiary[11]. The lack of detailed and easily accessible data on global branch networks for many banking groups is a notable gap in disclosure policy. For these institutions, data on branches appear to be not available, or they are mingled with other figures related to the network of the group, which are not strictly branches but may include "offices," "stores," "agencies," "locations," "banking centers," and the like; thus, disentangling data on branches cannot be done from publicly available sources. Or, in some cases, data are available for retail branches, but not for wholesale branches, on which for systemic reasons the concern should be focused. Inconsistencies in the methodology used by different G-SIBs to report the information on their network can impede comparisons, unless the exact figures on branches and their locations are reported. For this reason, in Table 4.1 we have included data on branches only when we found numbers that explicitly refer to foreign and domestic branches. Collecting information on the size of branches appears even more arduous, if possible at all.

In the earlier version of this chapter (Chapter 8 of the first edition of this handbook) we focused on an ownership threshold of 50.01% to identify controlled subsidiaries. If we compare the number of controlled subsidiaries for the 13 banking groups that are in both our earlier analysis and the 2012 G-SIBs group,[12] we find that the number of subsidiaries has increased by an average of 23% since year end 2007, and the average number of subsidiaries per bank has risen from 1,088 to 1,343. Ten banking groups have increased their number of subsidiaries, while three have reduced their number of subsidiaries (see Figure 4.1). For BNP Paribas, the increase in the number of subsidiaries has been 122%; for Barclays the increase was 73%; Bank of America and JPMorgan Chase both had a 36% increase.[13] In terms of the number of subsidiaries, BNP Paribas experienced the largest increase (+1,422), followed by Barclays (+736), and Bank of America (+503). Most of these banks have all made significant acquisitions since 2008.[14] Some of the groups did manage to reduce their number of controlled subsidiaries. Citigroup, which had the highest number of subsidiaries in 2007, decreased the number by 6% and Credit Suisse achieved a reduction of 17%, but the most significant drop was for the UK government-owned Royal Bank of Scotland,

---

[11] For example, New York State ring-fenced the branch of BCCI when it collapsed (Herring, 1993).

[12] All LCFIs included in our 2007 sample are also in the November 2012 FSB list of G-SIBs, with three exceptions: Lehman Brothers, which collapsed in September 2008; ABN AMRO, which was first acquired in 2007 by a consortium of three banks: Royal Bank of Scotland, Santander, and Fortis—and after the collapse and bailout of Fortis the Dutch activities were taken over by the Dutch government; and Merrill Lynch, which was rescued and acquired by Bank of America in September 2008. The remaining 13 banking groups are currently in the G-SIBs list, together with 15 other institutions.

[13] Based on NIC/FED data, however, Bank of America and JPMorgan Chase have both significantly reduced the number of their subsidiaries relative to the post-2008 crisis peak.

[14] BNP Paribas acquired the banking business of the Belgian group Fortis; Bank of America acquired Merrill Lynch and Countrywide Financial. JPMorgan Chase acquired Bear Stearns and Washington Mutual.

with a 31% decline. These findings support one of the observations in the first version of this chapter (Herring and Carmassi, 2010): increased corporate complexity is often the result of acquisitions.

Despite the significant role played by acquisitions, an increase in the corporate legal complexity can also be observed in some groups that were not involved in significant acquisitions. If we eliminate from the overlap group of 13 the banks that engaged in the largest mergers, Bank of America, BNP Paribas, and JPMorgan Chase, the average number of majority-owned subsidiaries has still increased by 10% from 2007 to 2013; within this subset of ten G-SIBs Citigroup had the highest number of subsidiaries in both 2007 (2,435) and 2013 (2,297), while Credit Suisse had the lowest figure in both 2007 (290) and 2013 (242). Thus, although acquisitions play an important role in explaining the expanding number of subsidiaries, they are not the only factor.

Unfortunately we lack the data to make similar comparisons for the 16 G-SIBs that were not designated as LCFIs, since our chapter in the first edition of this handbook focused solely on the LCFIs. Nonetheless, we have been able to capture data for eight of these G-SIBs for April 2010. These data provide some indication of the trend over the last three years, the time during which policymakers were attempting to encourage G-SIBs to simplify and rationalize their corporate structures.

The comparison of data for 2010 with data for 2013 certainly does not show that the authorities have been overwhelmingly successful. Some banks significantly increased their number of subsidiaries while other banks achieved a significant decrease. On average, the number of their subsidiaries decreased by 16%, but there were significant variations. Unicredit increased its subsidiaries from 2010 to 2013 by 72% (to 2,216) and Sumitomo Mitsui by 15% (to 165). On the other hand, BBVA, Mitsubishi UFJ, Mizuho, Santander, ING Groep, and Standard Chartered all decreased their number of subsidiaries (respectively –16%, –23%, –26%, –33%, –55%, and –60%). However, some of the banks that have reduced the number of subsidiaries and tend to operate with a comparatively low number of subsidiaries overall rely on a very large network of branches: this is the case, for example, of BBVA and Santander, which have respectively about 400 and 600 subsidiaries (as of May 2013), but operate with 8,000 and 14,000 branches, of which more than half are located in foreign countries.

Complexity (as measured by the number of subsidiaries) has often increased as balance sheets increased: total assets for the entire sample of G-SIBs grew by an average of 23% from 2007 to 2012.[15] Nonetheless, for our sample of 13 G-SIBs size *decreased* on average by 5%, while the number of subsidiaries *increased* on average by 23%. For some banks the change in the number of subsidiaries mirrored the change in size; yet, for a number of banks (e.g., Barclays, Goldman Sachs, and Morgan Stanley), the number of subsidiaries increased despite a shrinking balance sheet (see Figure 4.1). And subsidiaries of BNP Paribas increased by 122% despite a 1% increase of total assets. Clearly balance sheet growth alone cannot explain the proliferations of subsidiaries.

To sum up, on average G-SIBs have not reduced the complexity of their corporate structures or the size of their balance sheets after the crisis. Several important caveats should be stressed. This analysis focuses on only one aspect of complexity, the number of subsidiaries, ignoring other relevant aspects of complexity such as the interactions of subsidiaries with

---

[15]   BPCE is not included since it was formed in 2009.

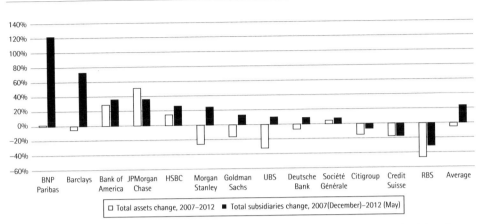

FIGURE 4.1 Evolution of size and complexity of 13 G-SIBs since 2007 (ranked by change in the number of subsidiaries).

Source: computations based on Bankscope data.

the rest of the group, interconnectedness with the financial system, and provision of critical services to the group. Moreover, this measure undoubtedly overstates the extent of corporate complexity because it includes transaction or shell subsidiaries that would pose no systemic threat in the event of the collapse of the group. But, it understates the extent of complexity given that significant foreign branches are not included, because in the event the group should falter, many of these branches would be ring-fenced and treated as if they were subsidiaries. Unfortunately, publicly available data do not permit a deeper analysis.

4.3 IF NOT CONSTRAINED BY REGULATIONS AND TAXES, WHAT DEGREE OF CORPORATE COMPLEXITY WOULD G-SIBS PREFER?

In the absence of tax and regulatory constraints, how much corporate complexity would G-SIBs choose to adopt? The formation of subsidiaries can be costly. In addition to the start-up costs of obtaining a charter and creating a governance structure, there are ongoing costs for accounting, financial reporting, and tax filings. Nonetheless, G-SIBs have adopted a considerable amount of corporate complexity even within some countries where they are under no regulatory obligation to do so. What are the perceived, compensating benefits that justify the formation of corporate subsidiaries?

In the frictionless world of Modigliani and Miller (1958), a firm's choice of capital structure and, by extension, its corporate structure, cannot affect its value. But financial institutions lack any rationale in such a world and so research on financial institutions generally begins with the assumption of imperfections such as asymmetric information, transactions costs, costs of financial distress, taxes, and regulation (Berger, Herring, and Szegö 1995). We will examine how each of these imperfections may influence a financial institution's choice of corporate structure.

4.3.1 Asymmetric Information and Transactions Costs

Asymmetric information problems appear to afflict financial institutions more seriously than many other kinds of firms.[16] Asymmetric information problems arise when one party to a transaction or relationship has information that the other does not, and it is too costly to write, monitor, and enforce a contract that would compensate adequately for the imbalance in information. When the firm's objectives differ from those of its creditors, counterparties or customers, firms incur agency costs to deal with concerns about adverse selection (the fear that the better-informed party will take advantage of the less-informed party by misrepresenting the quality of the product or service) or moral hazard (the fear that, once the transaction takes place, one party will covertly shift risk to the other's disadvantage). Financial firms have devised many different ways of mitigating these costs, including, sometimes, the creation of separate subsidiaries. The degree of asymmetric information exacerbates conflicts of interest, which may arise between shareholders and creditors, between shareholders and managers, and between the firm and its customers. We will consider each in turn.

4.3.2 Asymmetric Information: Shareholders vs. Creditors

The fundamental conflict of interest between shareholders and creditors springs from differences in their payoff functions. After debt-servicing costs have been paid, shareholders reap all the upside returns. They participate in the downside losses, however, only to the extent of their equity stake. In contrast, the upside return of creditors is limited to the promised return, while they may lose all that they have lent. Creditors will, thus, generally prefer safer investments than shareholders. With asymmetric information, creditors will be concerned that shareholders may engage in risk shifting after the terms of a loan have been set by substituting riskier assets for the safer assets. To safeguard against this possibility creditors may charge a higher premium and attempt to constrain the firm by insisting on a number of contractual clauses or, perhaps, even refusing to lend. Kahn and Winton (2004) have shown that the choice of a corporate structure can ease this problem. By forming a risky subsidiary, the firm provides a commitment that limits its incentive to engage in risk shifting. Placing safer assets in a separate subsidiary increases the safe subsidiary's net returns in bad states of the world and reduces its incentives to engage in risk shifting. It may also improve terms on which the safe subsidiary can obtain external financing. Although the firm may still have an incentive to engage in risk shifting in the riskier subsidiary, Kahn and Winton (2004) argue that this limits the amount of risk shifting that can take place within the conglomerate.[17]

---

[16] Morgan (2002) presents evidence that financial institutions are inherently more opaque than other firms based on disagreements among bond rating agencies.

[17] For an opposing view, see Merton and Perold (1993).

4.3.3 Asymmetric Information: Shareholders vs. Managers and Internal Agency Problems

International financial conglomerates generally have broadly dispersed shareholders with no one dominant owner. This separation of ownership from managerial control means that shareholders face an asymmetric information problem vis-à-vis the managers of a firm. This is a classic principal-agent problem in which managers may be tempted to pursue their own objectives, such as empire building or the enjoyment of lavish corporate perquisites, rather than serving the interests of shareholders. This may lead to several different kinds of resource misallocations that diminish share values. Managers may be excessively risk averse and seek to protect their entrenched positions by underinvesting in risky, positive net present value projects (Smith and Stulz, 1985). Or managers may take advantage of free cash flows to overinvest in value-destroying, negative net present value projects (Jensen, 1986). More broadly, managers may shirk.

Senior managers face similar issues with regard to managers lower down the corporate hierarchy. These internal agency costs include managerial entrenchment, misallocations of resources, and rent-seeking behavior (Fulghieri and Hodrick, 2005). Although a number of corporate governance mechanisms deal with these problems, the choice of organizational form can also be used as an instrument to control the behavior of multiple agents and better align the incentives of owners and managers. For example, if a particular line of business has compensation practices or a culture that is very different from other lines of business in the conglomerate, segregation of that line of business into a separate entity may facilitate oversight and control.

Despite massive investments in management information systems, integrated financial conglomerates may find it difficult to track and evaluate the performance of individual lines of business. Informal, internal capital markets sometimes contribute to the blurring of performance and result in unintended cross subsidies (Rajan, Servaes, and Zingales, 2000).[18] A degree of corporate separateness may be introduced to sharpen strategic focus and improve monitoring.

Occasionally a firm may take the additional step of partially spinning-off a subsidiary so that it has a separate listing and can be publicly traded. As Habib, Johnsen, and Naik (1997) observe, this enlists the help of capital markets in generating information that should improve the quality of investment decision. It may also reduce the uncertainty of uninformed investors regarding the value of the subsidiary. Both effects should increase the value of the firm.

Firms may achieve some of the incentive benefits by simply forming a separate entity even though the spin-off never actually occurs. Aron (1991, p. 505) notes that: "The possibility of a future spinoff induces the divisional manager to act as if he were being monitored and evaluated by the capital market, even though the capital market's evaluation is observed only if a spinoff actually occurs."

---

[18] Holod and Peek (2006), however, provide evidence that internal capital markets in multibank holding companies may enhance the efficiency of secondary loan markets. In particular, internal secondary loan markets avoid the asymmetric information problems faced by participants in the external secondary loan market and thus mitigate financial constraints faced by individual subsidiaries.

4.3.4 Information Asymmetry: Customer Concerns about Conflicts of Interest

Conflicts of interest are ubiquitous even in specialized financial institutions, but, as Walter (2003, p. 21) notes, "the broader the range of clients and products, the more numerous are the potential conflicts of interest and the more difficult is the task of keeping them under control—and avoiding even larger franchise losses." Customers fear that a firm may use its informational advantage to their detriment. Firms invest substantial resources to reassure clients and potential customers that they will not be disadvantaged vis-à-vis the firm or other clients. Such efforts include the erection of "Chinese walls" restricting the flow of information across lines of business, the adoption of codes of conduct reinforced with compliance audits, and disclosures of potential conflicts.[19] Sometimes firms take the additional step of segregating activities into separate subsidiaries. For example, investment advisory services may be provided by a separate entity from the underwriter and broker/dealer. Or, management consulting services may be offered through a separate entity in a separate location from the parent in order to reassure customers that confidential information would not be used in lending decisions or to aid other firms in which the parent might have an ownership position. Equally, corporate separateness may provide greater flexibility for operating units that would otherwise be constrained by conflict-of-interest concerns or burdensome reporting requirements.

Kroszner and Rajan (1997) found evidence of this behavior in the way in which US banks organized their investment banking operations before the 1933 Glass–Steagall Act forced a separation between commercial and investment banking. During this period, some banks organized their investment banking operations as an internal department within the bank, while others formed separately incorporated affiliates with separate boards of directors. They found that the market attached a higher risk premium to issues underwritten by internal departments. Krozner and Rajan (1997, p. 475) conclude that this is consistent with "investors discounting for the greater likelihood of conflicts of interest when lending and underwriting are within the same structure" and that a separate affiliate structure is "an effective commitment mechanism" to reassure customers that the underwriter will not abuse its information advantage.

4.3.5 Costs of Financial Distress: Protecting the Group from a Risky Subsidiary

When costs of financial distress are substantial, firms may prefer to segregate risky activities in separately incorporated subsidiaries even though information is shared equally between corporate insiders and capital markets. A holding company structure, in which subsidiaries are separately funded, can limit the damage to the rest of the group from financial distress in one of its affiliates. Corporate separateness provides the option of partial liquidation when losses in one of the subsidiaries would otherwise jeopardize the solvency of the rest of the

---

[19] For a detailed study on conflicts of interest in the financial industry, see Walter (2004).

group. Bianco and Nicodano (2002) show that both shareholders of the financial group and the rest of society are better off when external debt is raised through separately incorporated subsidiaries instead of through the holding company and then downstreamed to the subsidiaries.[20] In either case, gains from coinsurance could be realized: the holding company may choose to rescue a faltering subsidiary with profits from the rest of the group. But, if funding is primarily from the holding company, a group-threatening loss that hits a subsidiary will certainly inflict the costs of financial distress on the rest of the group. In contrast, if subsidiaries are separately funded in external capital markets, the loss could be stopped at the subsidiary directly affected, reducing the costs of financial distress to the rest of the group. Of course, the providers of debt will charge a higher risk premium when they lend to the subsidiary. But, as long as the premium does not include a substantial, adverse-selection premium, both shareholders and society should be better off. (Of course, this depends crucially on the authors' assumption of full information. If lenders are concerned that they are less-well-informed about risk, then the Kahn and Winton model discussed above is more relevant.)

It is sometimes asserted that a financial group could not afford to walk away from a faltering subsidiary because it would undermine confidence in the rest of the group (Baxter and Sommer, 2005, p. 187). While it is true that a loss of reputation may be more costly to financial firms than to other, less leveraged firms, limited liability does have option value. In some instances, banks have walked away from insolvent subsidiaries without notable detrimental impact on the rest of their business (Herring and Schuermann, 2005; Dermine, 2006).

Moreover, banks sometimes appear to isolate riskier activities in separate subsidiaries. Dermine (2006) and Cerutti, Dell'Ariccia, and Martínez-Pería (2005), for example, have observed that banks tend to prefer to organize as subsidiaries (rather than branches) in riskier countries. Herring and Santomero (1990) reported that some banks chose to join clearing and settlement schemes that had open-ended loss-sharing agreements with separately capitalized subsidiaries in order to limit potential losses. The panic that swept through Asian securities markets after the collapse of Barings stemmed, in part, from the fear that a number of institutions would abandon their subsidiaries if losses should exceed their capital investments in memberships in some of the exchanges (Herring, 2003). But, in other cases—for example in dealing with troubled special investment vehicles (SIVs) or special purpose vehicles (SPVs)-financial institutions have provided additional funds to protect their reputations even though they were under no legal obligation to do so.

In some jurisdictions, moreover, the limited liability option is constrained by regulation. The Federal Reserve Board has long held that the failure of a parent bank holding company to act as a source of strength to a troubled banking subsidiary would be considered "an unsafe and unsound banking practice" (Ashcraft, 2004). The source-of-strength doctrine

---

[20] The choice on where to raise external funding is one of the key features impacting the level of centralization or decentralization of the banking business model (CGFS, 2010b); two other relevant factors are the centralization/decentralization of risk management and the choice to expand through branches or subsidiaries (Schoenmaker, 2013). On internal funding for US global banks see Cetorelli and Goldberg (2012); on the choice between branches and subsidiaries see Fiechter et al. (2011). Bertay, Demirgüç-Kunt, and Huizinga (2012) found that the cost of funding for a foreign subsidiary is between 1.5% and 2.4% higher than the cost of funds for a domestic bank. Note too that the Bianco-Nicodano result suggests that the single-point-of-entry resolution strategy proposed by the regulators may impose substantial costs.

is intended to enhance the position of the bank within a holding company. It implies that during periods of financial stress, the regulatory authorities should be permitted to use the resources of the holding company and its subsidiaries to support the bank. In essence, the source-of-strength doctrine would give the regulatory authorities an option on the assets of the rest of the holding company to prevent the default of the bank. Nonetheless, the Fed's attempt to enforce this doctrine in the 1989–1991 Mcorp case was thwarted by the courts, and the Federal Deposit Insurance Corporation settled two cases where the parent of a failed bank sued the receivership to recover funds and assets that were downstreamed by the holding company to a faltering bank subsidiary. But, subsequently, Congress enacted two laws that enhanced the ability of the regulatory authorities to force bank holding companies to act as a source-of-strength in some circumstances. First, the Financial Institutions Reform, Recovery and Enforcement Act (FIRREA) of 1989 contained a cross-guarantee provision that permitted the FDIC to charge off any expected losses from a failing banking subsidiary to the capital of non-failing affiliate banks. Second, under the prompt corrective action section of the Federal Deposit Insurance Corporation Improvement Act (FDICIA) of 1991, the Federal Reserve Board was given authority to force a parent bank holding company to guarantee the performance of a troubled affiliate as part of a capital restoration plan. Finally, the 2010 Dodd–Frank Act transformed the Fed source-of-strength doctrine into law (Sec. 616(d)).

4.3.6 Costs of Financial Distress: Protecting a Subsidiary from the Rest of the Group

The growth of securitization has led to a proliferation of special purpose vehicles (SPVs),[21] which are designed to be financially insulated from the rest of the group. An SPV is a legal entity set up by a corporate sponsor for a specific, limited purpose. It buys pools of assets, usually originated by the sponsor, and issues debt to be repaid by cash flows from that pool of assets. It is tightly bound by a set of contractual obligations that ensure the activities of the entity are essentially predetermined at the inception of the vehicle. SPVs tend to be thinly capitalized, lack independent management or employees, and have all administrative functions performed by a trustee who receives and distributes cash according to detailed contracts. Most SPVs involved in securitization are organized as trusts, although they may also be organized as limited-liability companies, limited partnerships, or corporations. For some kinds of transactions substantial tax benefits can be achieved if an SPV is domiciled offshore—usually in Bermuda, the Cayman Islands, or the British Virgin Islands (Gorton and Souleles, 2006).

G-SIBs have been at the heart of the growth of the structured credit markets and have dominant shares in arranging residential mortgage-backed and other asset-backed securitizations that rely heavily on SPVs. It is evident from Table 4.2 that trusts may represent a very substantial number of subsidiaries for each of the 13 G-SIBs, those LCFIs that survived the crisis. Some of these trusts are SPVs, but most securitization vehicles are unlikely to be

---

[21] The term "special purpose entity" (SPE) is used more or less interchangeably.

Table 4.2 Breakdown by industry of subsidiaries of G–SIBs, 2013 (2007 in parenthesis)

	Banks	Insurance companies	Mutual & pension funds/ nominees/trusts/ trustees	Other financial subsidiaries[1]	Non-financial subsidiaries[2]	Total subsidiaries
Bank of America	72 (32)	17 (24)	584 (396)	322 (282)	915 (673)	1,910 (1,407)
Barclays	54 (49)	16 (21)	465 (309)	380 (239)	824 (385)	1,739 (1,003)
BNP Paribas	103 (88)	68 (74)	323 (102)	760 (433)	1,338 (473)	2,592 (1,170)
Citigroup	111 (101)	41 (35)	456 (706)	650 (584)	1,039 (1,009)	2,297 (2,435)
Credit Suisse	30 (31)	4 (4)	89 (91)	52 (63)	67 (101)	242 (290)
Deutsche Bank	68 (54)	8 (9)	541 (458)	618 (526)	889 (907)	2,124 (1,954)
Goldman Sachs	15 (7)	10 (4)	74 (48)	121 (151)	200 (161)	420 (371)
HSBC	89 (85)	37 (37)	309 (246)	298 (381)	832 (485)	1,565 (1,234)
JPMorgan Chase	54 (38)	13 (17)	305 (229)	205 (145)	518 (375)	1,095 (804)
Morgan Stanley	19 (19)	12 (22)	245 (225)	236 (170)	799 (616)	1,311 (1,052)
Royal Bank of Scotland	33 (31)	5 (29)	162 (168)	206 (450)	393 (483)	799 (1,161)
Société Générale	95 (81)	20 (13)	97 (93)	405 (270)	296 (387)	913 (844)
UBS	28 (29)	4 (2)	108 (121)	152 (66)	166 (199)	458 (417)
Total by industry	771 (720)	255 (310)	3,758 (3,490)	4,405 (4,263)	8,276 (6,729)	17,465 (15,512)
% by industry	4% (5%)	1% (2%)	22% (22%)	25% (27%)	47% (43%)	100% (100%)

Note: May 2013 and December 2007.

[1] "Other financial subsidiaries" include hedge funds, private equity, and venture capital subsidiaries.

[2] "Non-financial subsidiaries" include all companies that are neither banks nor insurance companies nor financial companies. They can be involved in manufacturing activities but also in trading activities (wholesalers, retailers, brokers, etc.). We have allocated foundations and research institutes to this category as well.

Source: Bankscope. Majority-owned subsidiaries.

included in our count of majority-owned subsidiaries because sponsors generally seek to avoid the appearance of voting control.[22]

SPVs are constructed to be bankruptcy remote. The objective is to reassure investors in the SPV that their rights to the promised cash flows will not be compromised by financial distress or insolvency in the sponsor or its affiliates. Similarly, the SPV itself is structured so that it cannot be taken through bankruptcy. Typically, any shortfall of cash that would otherwise cause an event of default will trigger, instead, an early amortization of the pool of assets. The benefit of this structure is that it should avoid the deadweight costs of financial distress and so the debt issued by the SPV should not be subject to a bankruptcy premium. By separating the control rights over assets from the financing of these assets, the SPV reduces the costs of financial distress and thus the cost of debt financing (Gorton and Souleles, 2006).

Although the desire to avoid the deadweight costs of financial distress may be the primary motive for securitizing assets, Tufano (2006) notes that other factors may also be important. For example, SPVs may be formed to achieve more favorable accounting treatment for the sponsor, to increase tax efficiency, to avoid regulatory capital requirements, to tap new pools of capital through changing the risk characteristics of a pool of assets, or to reduce the deadweight costs of information asymmetry by separating the funding of a more transparent pool of assets from the rest of the sponsor's balance sheet.

Protection of the bankruptcy-remote status of SPVs requires that the sponsor refrain from making any commitment to support the SPV. The concern is that a legal commitment might undo the bankruptcy-remote structure. If a sponsor should enter a bankruptcy proceeding, the judge might recharacterize the sale of assets to the SPV as a secured financing, which would bring the assets back onto the sponsor's balance sheet. Attempts to minimize this possibility account for a considerable amount of the complexity of securitization vehicles. For example, sponsors often employ a two-tiered SPV structure to provide an extra layer of insulation between the claims of the investors and the sponsor (Gorton and Souleles, 2006, p. 558).

If SPVs are, in fact, bankruptcy-remote, would they complicate the unwinding of a G-SIB? Perhaps not, but Gorton and Souleles (2006) present evidence that sponsors have supported their SPVs and, based on the pricing of debt issued by SPVs and the credit rating of the sponsoring institution, conclude that investors rely on this implicit support. Gorton and Souleles (2006) argue that this implicit commitment is essential to deal with moral hazard and adverse selection problems implicit in the asymmetric information between the originator of the assets and investors in the SPV. Nonetheless, the efforts by several LCFIs to support their SIVs and asset-backed commercial paper (ABCP) conduits during the turmoil in financial markets in the latter half of 2007 appear to have surprised shareholders and some regulators. In any event, this disconnect between explicit and implicit contracts complicates any analysis of how the existence of SPVs might affect the resolution of a G-SIB experiencing extreme financial distress. Moreover, many of the innovative securitization structures have not been tested in a bankruptcy proceeding. Although these bankruptcy-remote structures may well turn out to be "bulletproof," they are likely to complicate the resolution of a faltering G-SIB, nonetheless.

---

[22] For example, in its 2013 resolution plan Deutsche Bank (2013, p. 20) reports to have 1,541 special purpose entities.

4.3.7 The Legacy of Mergers and Acquisitions

Mergers and acquisitions may have a significant impact on the degree of complexity of corporate structure. Relative to a firm of equal size that has grown organically, an acquisitive financial conglomerate is likely to have many more subsidiaries, if only because it may be costly to close or consolidate them. G-SIBs have engaged in a large number of mergers, some of them exceptionally large. For example, since 1990, Bank of America, Deutsche Bank, JPMorgan Chase, and UBS have implemented mergers in which the target institution was larger than 10% of the acquiring firm's total assets (Thomson Securities Data Company).

The acquiring firm may choose to retain a considerable amount of corporate separateness in the target firm for two reasons. First, it may perceive value in the brand and hope to retain the reputational capital of the target firm. Second, the willingness to retain the existing corporate structure may facilitate acceptance of the merger. As Dermine (2006) notes, by committing to keep in place a local structure and staff, local shareholders and the board of directors of the target may be reassured about the future of the target firm. Also, as we discuss below, host country regulatory authorities sometimes require that the acquiring bank maintain the target bank as a separate, locally chartered corporation. Dermine (2006) observes, however, that this decision to maintain a separate entity is often tactical rather than strategic. Over time, G-SIBs generally decide to build a global brand identity, which may be inconsistent with the retention of separate subsidiaries bearing legacy names. Based on his interviews with ING and Nordea, Dermine (2006) found that even though both firms initially left many legacy organizations intact, they were also committed to building a global brand over time.

It may simply take a significant amount of time to rationalize the structure of the larger group. For example, litigation involving the legal entity may oblige the acquirer to maintain it as a separate entity until the litigation is resolved. Finally, since simplification of the structure may be costly and time-consuming, it may sometimes be easier to create a new legal entity than to identify and make use of an existing one. As a result, some of the proliferation of subsidiaries may simply be attributable to lackadaisical housekeeping of corporate structures. To the extent that growth in complexity may have been the result of inadequate attention to the growing complexity of corporate structures, the living will process should be effective in encouraging banking groups to simplify and rationalize their corporate structures.

JPMorgan Chase provides a good example of how mergers may increase corporate complexity. The current organization is the result of a series of mergers of very large banks that began in 1991 with the merger of Chemical Bank Corporation and Manufacturers Hanover Corporation. This merger resulted in a near doubling of the size of the surviving institution, Chemical Bank, and, in 1996, was followed by the merger of Chemical Bank with the Chase Manhattan Corporation. The resulting institution merged with JPMorgan & Co., forming JPMorgan Chase & Co. (JPMC) in 2000. This series of mergers culminated in July 2004 with the merger of JPMC and Bank One Corporation (BOC) before the crisis, and during the crisis included mergers with Bear Stearns and Washington Mutual. According to Federal Reserve/National Information Center data, at year end 2003 JPMC had 1,569 subsidiaries; after acquiring BOC it had 3,406 subsidiaries at year end 2004, an increase of 117%. At year end 2007 JPMC had 3,683 subsidiaries. After the acquisitions of Bear Stearns and Washington Mutual in 2008, the figure rose to 5,384, a 46% increase. Subsequently, JPMC has undergone a process of simplification of its structure. By June 2013 it had succeeded in reducing its number of subsidiaries to 4,059.[23] A similar pattern can be observed for Bank of America, with a doubling of the number of subsidiaries after the 2008 acquisitions, followed by a significant reduction (about −25% from year end 2009 to June 2013); and for Wells Fargo, which had 1,112 subsidiaries at year end 2007 and 2,698 at year end 2008 (+143%), after the acquisition of Wachovia.

The efforts to reduce corporate complexity are consistent with evidence presented by Klein and Saidenberg (2005) that bank holding companies with many bank subsidiaries are valued at a discount relative to similar bank holding companies with fewer bank subsidiaries. Although this conglomerate discount has sometimes been attributed to inefficient internal capital markets, they find that affiliated banks benefit from access to internal capital markets by lending more and holding less capital than comparable unaffiliated banks. Since activity and geographic diversification is broadly similar for their sample of affiliated and unaffiliated banks, they infer that the valuation discount is attributable mainly to greater complexity of organizational structure rather than diversification. Laeven and Levine (2007) adopt a different approach, but also find a diversification discount in financial conglomerates. They identify agency problems and insufficient economies of scope as probable causes. This finding may help explain why several large banks have attempted to simplify their corporate structures. Rosengren (2003, p. 111) presented evidence that from 1993 to 2002 eight large US bank holding companies reduced their number of subsidiaries relative to the number of subsidiaries in their predecessor organizations. These efforts notwithstanding, continuing merger activity undoubtedly adds to corporate complexity.

4.4 Tax Frictions

Taxes can have a major impact on the choice of corporate structure for all firms, especially international financial firms, because they tend to have more flexibility to shift profits from one entity to another (Demirgüç-Kunt and Huizinga, 2001, p. 430). The choice of corporate structure, including the location and organizational form of SPEs, may be influenced by income taxes (and the details of permissible deductions and credits), capital gains taxes, taxes on interest and dividends, value-added taxes, withholding taxes, transactions taxes, and stamp duties.[24]

Tax considerations are especially important for internationally active financial groups. Because home countries often tax groups on their consolidated worldwide income and, at the same time, most host countries tax locally generated income as well, cross-border transactions are usually subject to double taxation. Without some sort of relief, multiple taxes could stifle cross-border transactions completely.

---

[23] Note that the data in Tables 4.1 and 4.2 reflect majority-owned subsidiaries based on Bankscope data and are not directly comparable with the FED/NIC database, which employs a different methodology.

[24] Banks are often subject to a number of implicit taxes as well, which may include the obligation to hold required reserves at the central bank at less than the market rate of interest or deposit insurance premiums that exceed the fair value of insurance.

When foreign source income is not exempt from taxation in the home country, firms are often permitted to credit foreign taxes paid against domestic tax owed. Generally, the foreign tax credit is limited by the amount of taxes that the firm would have paid if the income had been earned at home. Thus, firms have a strong incentive to reduce the average tax rate on foreign source income by shifting profits from relatively high-tax countries to tax havens (permissible foreign tax credits may be constrained in other ways as well; see Demirgüç-Kunt and Huizinga (2001) for restrictions imposed on profit shifting by the US).

A crude indication of the extent to which tax issues may have contributed to the corporate complexity of G-SIBs may be seen in the number of entities located in tax havens. Our list of tax havens is based on the 42 countries/ territories/ jurisdictions classified by the Financial Stability Forum as offshore financial centers (Financial Stability Forum, 2000; International Monetary Fund, 2000). The list includes countries/ territories/ jurisdictions that provide low or zero taxation, moderate or light financial regulation, and/or banking secrecy and anonymity. Of course, the impact of tax issues on organizational complexity is much more pervasive and complex than can be represented by a count of the number of subsidiaries in these centers. Nonetheless, even this number is substantial for some of the G-SIBs (see Table 4.1). Nine of our G-SIBs each have more than 100 subsidiaries located in these booking centers. Moreover, six of the G-SIBs have located 20% or more of their subsidiaries in tax havens.

4.5 REGULATORY CONSTRAINTS

All of the preceding rationales for corporate separateness—asymmetric information problems, insulation against risk, the legacy of mergers and acquisitions, and taxes—apply to large corporations in general, not just financial groups. But financial groups are subject to an additional source of constraints that complicates their corporate structures—regulation. This may help explain, at least in part, why they have a substantially greater number of subsidiaries than non-financial groups of comparable size. On average, the number of majority-owned subsidiaries of the 28 G-SIBs identified by the Financial Stability Board as of November 2012 was 2.6 times the number of majority-owned subsidiaries of the biggest 28 non-financial firms by market capitalization (as of year end 2012).[25]

Banks are among the most regulated institutions in every country, although countries differ with regard to the constraints imposed on banks' expansion into other lines of business. Broadly, three different regulatory models can be discerned: (1) complete integration; (2) parent bank with non-bank operating subsidiaries; and (3) holding company parent with bank and non-bank affiliates.[26] Universal banking countries tend to follow the first model, with only minimal corporate separateness imposed for regulatory reasons. For example, Germany allows the combination of bank and securities businesses in a single legal entity, while the third model is dominant in the US, where the corporate separateness imposed on bank holding companies and financial services holding companies is reinforced by restrictions on the flows of credit between different functional units and the bank, set out in Sections 23A and 23B of the updated Federal Reserve Act and the 1999 Gramm–Leach–Bliley Act.

---

[25] Number of subsidiaries of G-SIBs as of May 2013 (source: Bankscope); number of subsidiaries of the non-financial firms as of August 2013 (source: Osiris).

[26] See Herring and Santomero (1990) for a more detailed discussion of these models and their variations.

In a survey of 143 countries Čihák et al. (2012, p. 31) find that of 93% of countries that permit banks to engage in some securities activities, 43% impose some form of corporate separateness on these activities. Of the 83% of countries that permit banks to engage in the insurance business, 78% impose some form of corporate separateness. Finally, of the 60% of countries that permit banks to engage in the real estate business, 44% require some form of corporate separateness.

Different functional regulators may require that the activities that they regulate be conducted in separate legal entities. This not only facilitates oversight, but makes it easier to ring-fence those activities should it become necessary to intervene.[27] Thus, even without consideration of the complexities introduced by international expansion, financial conglomerates may be required to adopt a certain amount of corporate separateness for regulatory purposes.

G-SIBs have established subsidiaries in numerous countries (see column 10 in Table 4.1) and international expansion may require substantial additional corporate complexity for two reasons. First, host countries that apply some variation of model three noted above (holding company parent with bank and non-bank affiliates) to domestic financial conglomerates generally impose the same restrictions on foreign firms to maintain a level playing field. The fact that the US, the largest market in the world for financial services, applies model three to domestic and foreign firms can account for a significant amount of the complexity of the corporate structure of G-SIBs headquartered outside the US.

Second, even if the host country has not adopted a variation of model three for domestic firms, it may require that foreign-owned firms incorporate locally to ensure that the domestic authorities can intervene to protect domestic residents. New Zealand, where more than 85% of the banking system is controlled by foreign-owned banks, provides perhaps the most extreme example of the second rationale (Woolford and Orr, 2005).

Čihák et al. (2012, p. 25) find that in their sample of 143 countries only 4% of countries prohibit entry by foreign subsidiaries, but 14% prohibit entry by foreign branches. Moreover, even if foreign branch entry is not prohibited, host countries often impose stricter regulatory requirements on foreign branches that make the formation of a separate subsidiary relatively attractive.

Functional and national regulators frequently employ corporate separateness as a means of regulating, supervising, and monitoring the part of a financial conglomerate that falls in their bailiwick. While this may enhance local regulatory oversight, an unintended consequence may be that international financial conglomerates may have significantly more complex corporate structures than domestic firms of comparable size.

More broadly, G-SIBs often respond to new regulations with still more corporate complexity. Kane (1977, 1981, 1984) has characterized this dynamic as a regulatory dialectic, in which regulators impose a rule (or implicit tax) and the regulated firms react within their constrained environment to minimize the burden of the implicit tax. The regulators in turn react to perception of regulatory avoidance with still more regulations. This kind of dynamic has undoubtedly increased the corporate complexity of G-SIBs.[28] In the event of financial distress, however, this complexity could impede an effective regulatory response.

---

[27] In some jurisdictions it is possible to ring-fence entities that are not separately incorporated; for example, the US regulatory authorities can ring-fence a foreign branch.

[28] See Tröger (2013) for a discussion of how regulation may create incentives to change corporate structures in order to maximize efficiency or adjust to the new regulatory environment: he observes that

4.6 Implications of Corporate Complexity for Safety and Soundness of the Financial System

Despite their corporate complexity, G-SIBs tend to be managed in an integrated fashion along lines of business with only minimal regard for legal entities, national borders, or functional regulatory authorities. Moreover, there are often substantial interconnections among the separate entities within the financial group. Baxter and Sommer (2005) note that, in addition to their shared (although possibly varying) ownership structure, the entities are likely to be linked by cross-affiliate credit relationships, cross-affiliate business relationships, and reputational relationships.

What would happen should one of these G-SIBs experience extreme financial distress? Quite apart from the difficulty of disentangling operating subsidiaries that provide critical services to other affiliates and mapping an integrated firm's activities into the entities that would need to be taken through a bankruptcy process, the corporate complexity of such institutions would present significant challenges. The fundamental problem stems from conflicting approaches to bankruptcy across regulators, across countries, and, sometimes, even within countries. There are likely to be disputes over which law and which set of bankruptcy procedures should apply. Some authorities may attempt to ring-fence the parts of the G-SIB within their reach to satisfy their regulatory objectives without necessarily taking into account some broader objective such as the preservation of going concern value or financial stability. At a minimum, authorities will face formidable challenges in coordination and information sharing across and among jurisdictions. Losses that spill across national borders will intensify conflicts between home and host authorities and make it difficult to achieve a cooperative resolution of an insolvent financial group. Experience has shown that, in times of stress, information-sharing agreements are likely to fray (Herring, 2007).

Despite more than 30 years of harmonization initiatives by the BCBS, approaches to bank resolution differ substantially across countries. For example, countries differ with regard to the point at which a weak bank requires resolution and to what entity initiates the resolution process. Clearly cross-border differences in regard to how and when the resolution process is initiated can cause delays that may be costly in a crisis.

The choice of jurisdiction may also have important implications for the outcome of the insolvency proceedings. Most countries have adopted a universal approach to insolvency in

some large European banks have recently undergone a process of transformation of subsidiaries into branches through a cross-border merger of the foreign subsidiaries into the parent banks. Banks claim that the main driver for such changes in organizational structures is efficiency and simplification of their corporate structures, but the transformation also provides an effective means of avoiding host country regulation and supervision. In the United States, the stricter requirements on foreign bank holding companies imposed by the Dodd-Frank Act, for example in terms of higher capital on a standalone basis, and the proposed rule to require intermediate holding companies for foreign banking groups were followed in a few cases by a choice by foreign banks to reorganize their legal structure in the US and end their bank holding company status by transferring the ownership of deposits to the parent bank and leaving only non-depository business with the US entity.

which one jurisdiction conducts the main insolvency proceedings and makes the distribution of assets, while other jurisdictions collect assets to be distributed in the main proceedings. But the US follows a more territorial approach with regard to US branches of foreign banks and will conduct its own insolvency proceedings based on local assets and liabilities. Assets are transferred to the home country only after (and if) all local claims are satisfied. The choice of jurisdiction will also determine a creditor's right to set off claims on the insolvent bank against amounts that it owes the bank. The Bank of Credit and Commerce International (BCCI) case revealed striking differences across members of the BCBS (BCBS, 1992). Similarly, the ability to exercise close-out netting provisions under the International Swap Dealers Association (ISDA) Master Contracts may vary from jurisdiction to jurisdiction, although ISDA has achieved a remarkable degree of international harmonization.

The outcome of insolvency proceedings will also depend on the powers and obligations of the resolution authority, which may differ from country to country. For example, does the resolution authority have the power to impose "haircuts" on the claims of creditors without a lengthy judicial proceeding? Does the resolution authority have the ability (and access to the necessary resources) to provide a capital injection? With regard to banks, is the resolution authority constrained to choose the least costly resolution method, as in the US? Or is the resolution authority obliged to give preference to domestic depositors as the law requires in Australia and the US? More fundamentally, what is the objective of the supervisory intervention and the resolution process? The priority that supervisors will inevitably place on domestic objectives in the event of insolvency is the essential source of conflict between home and host authorities.

Three asymmetries between the home and host country may create additional problems even if procedures could be harmonized. First is asymmetry of resources: supervisory authorities may differ greatly in terms of human capital and financial resources, implying that the home supervisory authority may not be able to rely on the host supervisory authority (or vice versa) simply because it may lack the capacity to conduct effective oversight. Second, asymmetries of financial infrastructure may give rise to discrepancies in the quality of supervision across countries. Weaknesses in accounting standards and the quality of external audits may impede the efforts of supervisors just as informed, institutional creditors and an aggressive and responsible financial press may aid them. The legal infrastructure matters as well. Inefficient or corrupt judicial procedures may undermine even the highest quality supervisory efforts.

Perhaps the most important conflict, however, arises from asymmetries of exposures: what are the consequences if the entity should fail? Perspectives may differ with regard to whether a specific entity jeopardizes financial stability. This will depend on whether the entity is systemically important in either or both countries and whether the foreign entity is economically significant within the parent group.

4.6.1 The Collapse of Lehman Brothers and the Impetus for Reform

The collapse of Lehman Brothers (LB) on 15 September 2008 demonstrated that these potential conflicts are not just theoretical. After trying to broker a merger of LB with other, stronger institutions, the US authorities declined to bail it out and sent the holding company, Lehman Brothers Holdings Inc. (LBHI), to the bankruptcy courts for protection under Chapter 11 of the US bankruptcy code. This became the largest (and undoubtedly the most unprepared) bankruptcy in US history. Although LB was only the fourth largest US investment bank it was of sufficient systemic importance that its collapse led to substantial spillovers on global and national capital markets.

In its bankruptcy petition Lehman reported assets totaling $634 billion; it had more than 25,000 employees and over 7,000 subsidiaries in more than 40 countries (Lehman Brothers, 2009). Interestingly, during the bankruptcy proceedings courts determined that fewer than 1,000 subsidiaries had any active relationship to ongoing business. Lehman operated in such an integrated fashion that employees were largely ignorant about which legal entity employed them. A trader on the New York equities desk might book trades with a Lehman entity anywhere in the world (Miller and Horwitz, 2012). This corporate complexity greatly impeded the orderly resolution of the firm and led to significant spillovers to other institutions and markets.

The fundamental problem was that LB was managed as an integrated entity with minimal regard for the legal entities that would need to be taken through the bankruptcy process. LBHI issued the vast majority of unsecured debt and invested the funds in most of its regulated and unregulated subsidiaries. This approach is typical of global corporations and is designed to facilitate control over global operations, while reducing funding, capital, and tax costs. LBHI, in effect, served as banker for its affiliates, running a zero-balance cash-management system. LBHI lent cash to its operating subsidiaries at the beginning of each day and then swept the cash back to LBHI at the end of each day. The bankruptcy petition was filed before most of the subsidiaries had been funded on September 15 and so most of the cash was tied up in court proceedings in the US and the subsidiaries had no choice but to declare bankruptcy or be put in administration.

Lehman also centralized its information technology so that data for different products and different subsidiaries were co-mingled. This was an efficient way of running the business as a going concern, but presents an enormous challenge in global bankruptcy proceedings. LB stored data in 26,666 servers, 20,000 of which contained accumulated emails, files, voicemail messages, instant messages, and recorded calls that were necessary for ongoing operations and for allocating assets and liabilities in bankruptcy. The largest data centers were in New York, London, Tokyo, Hong Kong, and Mumbai. The UK Administrator closed down one of Lehman's critical information and operational systems, which disrupted the rest of the information network and impeded retrieval of essential information to identify assets and liabilities. Moreover, LB used approximately 2,700 proprietary, third-party, and off-the-shelf programs, each of which interacted with or created transactions data.

The bankruptcy administrators have the responsibility to preserve, extract, store, and analyze data relevant to the entities they are charged with resolving. This challenge was exacerbated by the success of the administrators of LBHI in selling two important entities that were rapidly declining in value because of loss of human capital: its investment banking operations and its asset management business, which owned much of the critical data.

Most of the US investment banking operations—the assets, not the legal entities—were sold to Barclays. This necessitated bringing a Securities Investor Protection Corporation

(SIPC) proceeding, which put all LBI accounts under the control of the SIPC Trustee and permitted the broker-dealer to be liquidated. Nomura bought most of the investment banking business in Asia and continental Europe, and LB's asset management business was sold in a management buyout. But this meant that the data were owned by Barclays, Nomura, and the now independent asset management division, and so bankruptcy administrators were dependent on the new owners for access to data in order to determine the assets and liabilities of each legal entity. The administrator of the four London subsidiaries complained that nine weeks after the bankruptcy, he had yet to receive a confirmation of the assets owned by these subsidiaries.

The US administrators expressed the optimistic view that they would be able to complete the resolution within 18 to 24 months, but the presiding judge reminded the administrator that the biggest impediments to a timely completion of the administration are the timetables of the other insolvency fiduciaries around the world. The administrators in London warned that it may take years for creditors to get their money back, noting that they were continuing to work on Enron, which had failed seven years earlier and was about one-tenth the size and complexity of Lehman (Hughes, 2008). Today there are more than 100 insolvency proceedings involving various remnants of Lehman under way in at least 16 different jurisdictions.

Although members of the G7 had expressed the view that the US authorities should have bailed out Lehman, they began to realize that bailouts create expectations of still greater bailouts and may create huge taxpayer liabilities that cannot be justified on political or economic grounds. Haldane (2009) estimated that at the height of the crisis over $14 trillion (about one-quarter of world GDP) had been committed by the United States, the United Kingdom, and the Eurozone to support their banking systems.

By the time of the first meeting of the G20, a consensus had formed that a policy of TBTF had become too expensive to sustain. The rallying cry was that taxpayers should never again be put at risk of such loss. And leaders began to realize that they lacked effective tools to deal with a faltering financial giant. Without an effective resolution policy they were left with two bad choices: a bailout or the risk of widespread financial disorder. This perception proved a turning point with regard to policy toward large, complex financial institutions. In the next section we will review some of the policy reforms initiated to ameliorate the TBTF problem.

4.7 Policy Reforms to Deal With G-Sibs: An Overview

The most notable change since the original edition of this chapter is that the issue of size and complexity has risen from obscurity to the top of the policy agenda. A virtual cascade of proposals and regulations has flowed from international organizations and from the regulatory authorities in the US, the EU, and many other countries. The sheer quantity and range of such proposals have been so vast that this overview must be very selective, focusing only on those initiatives directed explicitly at the too-complex/ too-big-to-fail problem at the international level and in the United States.[29]

4.7.1 Global Initiatives

At the international level the Basel Committee on Banking Supervision responded quickly to the mounting evidence that Basel capital rules had not worked. The definition of capital in the numerator was much too broad, including many instruments that could not serve as going-concern capital. Risks in the denominator were underweighted and the required minimums were much too low. The Committee began work immediately on a new Basel III framework to address these problems. Some adjustments were made to increase risk weights and especially to strengthen them for complex instruments in the trading book. Since G-SIBs account for a disproportionate amount of trading activity, this increased the regulatory measure of risk for them. Similarly, the measures to push out derivatives activity from banks to exchanges by increasing the risk weights on such exposures that remain off banks' balance sheets will have particular impact on the G-SIBs, which account for most of the activity in over-the-counter derivatives trading.

The most important change, however, was in the numerator. The BCBS determined that banks should have more and higher quality capital. The focus was on Tier 1 equity capital, which tended to be what the market monitored once it became clear that regulatory measures were unreliable. This higher quality capital then became the basis for additional layers of capital requirements. The minimum common equity Tier 1 capital was increased to 4.5% of risk-weighted assets (RWA), an additional conservation buffer of 2.5% was added, and a discretionary, countercyclical buffer varying from 0–2.5% could be required by a national authority that was concerned about excessively rapid credit expansion. These capital requirements applied to all internationally active banks. But, in addition, a surcharge was aimed directly at G-SIBs: this additional Tier 1 equity capital charge can vary from 1% to 3.5%. Each November, when G-SIBs are identified, they are allocated into five different buckets according to the degree of systemic risk they pose. So far, G-SIBs have been assigned to the 1%, 1.5%, 2.0%, and 2.5% buckets. The 3.5% bucket has been left empty, but is held out as a potential sanction to be used against institutions that become more systemically important.

This is a complete reversal of the philosophy underlying Basel II. In Basel II the risk-weighting scheme was designed to reduce risk-weighted assets for large institutions in order to give them an incentive to adopt the most advanced approaches to risk measurement and management (SRC, 2013a). These weights were calibrated to give a lower risk weight than if the standardized approach were used. Of course, this approach completely neglected the fact that very large institutions are likely to pose a greater systemic

---

[29] We will touch on some policy proposals in the European Union, focused on insulating retail banking from riskier businesses within a banking group, but space constraints prevent us from discussing the broader EU banking union project. It should be noted, however, that the European Union is attempting to resolve many of the cross-border problems we have highlighted within the context of the Eurozone. For further discussion of the EU banking union see, for example, Goddard, Molyneux, and Wilson (2014) and Herring (2013).

risk than smaller institutions and should be required to hold higher, not lower capital buffers. Thus the Basel III reforms impose a penalty on banks that become more systemically important.

In addition, the BCBS has proposed a 3% Tier 1 leverage capital ratio. This will be a constraint for several of the largest banks that had operated on leverage ratios as high as 50:1. The leverage ratio will also provide a safeguard against the manipulation of internal models to lower risk weights (Carmassi and Micossi, 2012; Admati and Hellwig, 2013; Bair, 2013; Hoenig, 2013; SRC, 2013b, 2013c). Some very large banks will be compelled to raise significantly more equity or downsize their balance sheets. In addition, the denominator of the leverage ratio is being redefined to take into account off-balance-sheet exposures as well as on-balance-sheet exposures. This, too, will raise the hurdle for the G-SIBs, which conduct much more of their business off-balance sheet than most other banks.

While the BCBS focused on capital requirements, the FSB concentrated on resolution policies. Perhaps its most important accomplishment has been the agreement on "Key Attributes of Effective Resolution Policy" and the development of a methodology for assessing the degree to which member countries have adopted these attributes. An effective resolution regime should (FSB, 2011a):

- ensure continuity of systemically important functions;
- protect insured depositors and ensure rapid return of segregated client assets;
- allocate losses to shareholders, unsecured and uninsured creditors in a way that respects payment priorities in bankruptcy;
- not rely on public support for solvency and not create an expectation that it will be available;
- avoid unnecessary destruction of value;
- provide for speed, transparency, and as much predictability as possible based on legal and procedural clarity and advanced planning for orderly resolution;
- provide legal mandate for cooperation, information exchange, and coordination with foreign resolution authorities;
- ensure that non-viable firms can exit the market in an orderly fashion;
- achieve and maintain credibility to enhance market discipline and provide incentives for market solutions.

During the crisis many countries found that they had no coherent resolution regime and so these key attributes set very ambitious goals, and have been quite influential as countries have begun to establish or reform their resolution regimes. To encourage progress in meeting these goals the FSB monitors each country's progress (FSB, 2013d) and makes an annual report to the G20 (FSB, 2013e). The Financial Stability Board, chaired by Mark Carney, made the optimistic assessment that: "Good progress has been made in putting this international policy framework in place and there are signs that firms and markets are beginning to adjust to authorities' determination to end 'too-big-to-fail'" (FSB, 2013f). But it goes on to observe than many jurisdictions have not yet undertaken the necessary reforms to meet the standards set by the key attributes.

4.7.2 The US Response

The main response of the United States to the financial crisis was passage of the sprawling and complex Dodd–Frank Wall Street Reform and Consumer Protection Act (DFA) in July 2010. The DFA, 2,319 pages of legislation, required that agencies make 500 rules and prepare 81 studies and 93 reports. Even now scarcely half of these provisions of the law have been implemented. We will focus on aspects of the DFA that are aimed particularly at G-SIBs.

Although the DFA abolished one regulatory agency, it created a new Financial Stability Oversight Council (FSOC), chaired by the Secretary of the Treasury, with the responsibility to identify threats to financial stability and gaps in regulation. FSOC also designates the non-bank financial companies that are deemed systemically important and thus should be subject to heightened supervision by the Fed. The DFA defined the threshold for bank holding companies to be designated as SIFIs, setting the hurdle at $50 billion, which most observers consider to be much too low.

FSOC is also charged with limiting the size and complexity of SIFIs. It can recommend heightened regulatory standards for institutions that grow in size and complexity and it must approve (by a two-thirds majority) any decision by the Fed to compel asset sales by SIFIs that have failed to submit satisfactory resolution plans.

The DFA attempted to reduce the scope for discretion that the authorities exercised during the crisis by establishing a new two-tier resolution regime.[30] Congress wanted to discourage the presumption that any SIFI was too-big-to-fail, by requiring that every SIFI demonstrate that it could be taken through the bankruptcy process like any other firm. Each SIFI is required to file an annual "living will" describing how it could be taken through bankruptcy without creating intolerable spillovers. If a particular SIFI's living will is not persuasive, the Fed and FDIC are required to return it with suggestions for improvement that may include selling businesses, consolidating subsidiaries, or other measures to make the SIFI easier to resolve in bankruptcy. If the SIFI is unresponsive these suggestions may become requirements.

Although bankruptcy is the preferred mode of resolution, Congress provided for the possibility of an administrative alternative misleadingly titled the Orderly Liquidation Authority (OLA). The intent of this administrative process is not to liquidate the group, but rather to preserve going concern value by executing a rapid good bank/bad bank split in which the assets with going concern value, along with the liabilities ranking highest in repayment priority, are transferred to a new bridge institution. The bridge institution would continue the systemically important operations of the group until all or parts of the business can be sold to third parties or wound down in an orderly fashion. The bad bank would be liquidated over time with the intent of maximizing the value of the assets for the creditors left behind in the bad bank. In many respects this approach is parallel to that which has been and will continue to be employed by the FDIC to resolve insured depository institutions. Indeed, the OLA represents an expansion of the FDIC's powers to manage the process for potentially any financial institution. Its powers under the OLA, however, differ in some important respects from those it has exercised over insured banks:

---

[30] For a discussion of the new US approach to bank resolution see Tarullo (2013). For a discussion on the current state of resolution planning in the US see Norton (2013).

the OLA is intended to be used only in extreme cases involving turbulent financial conditions. Congress intends that no financial institution should know ex ante that it will be resolved under the OLA rather than bankruptcy (and, it does not relieve SIFIs from the responsibility of conducting their businesses so that they can be subjected to the normal bankruptcy processes). Congress has attempted to impose some high procedural hurdles that must be surmounted before the OLA can be used. Before the FDIC can be appointed as receiver, the US Secretary of the Treasury (in consultation with the US President) must make three determinations supported by two-thirds of the Federal Reserve Board and two-thirds of the FDIC Board. First, the financial company is in default or in danger of default. Second, resolution under bankruptcy would have serious adverse effects on financial stability in the United States. Third, no viable private sector alternative to default can be found. If the board of the company in financial distress consents, the FDIC can be appointed as receiver. If the board does not consent it can challenge the Secretary of the Treasury in a secret proceeding before the US District Court in Washington DC, but only on the narrow grounds of whether the institution is a financial institution within the meaning of the DFA and whether it is in default or in danger of default. The court must reach a decision within 24 hours.

Once it is appointed as receiver the FDIC has considerable scope for cherry-picking assets and liabilities that will be transferred to the bridge institution, but its actions are limited by the requirement that creditors that are left behind will be at least as well off as they would have been under a Chapter 7 liquidation proceeding. To limit moral hazard in the exercise of OLA powers the FDIC is required to remove the management and board, which may be harsher than the treatment that managers and some board members might receive under bankruptcy.

In order to fund the bridge institution the FDIC may borrow from the Treasury an amount no greater than it expects to receive from the ultimate disposition of the bridge institution. In the event the loan cannot be repaid from this source, the shortfall will be covered by a special assessment on firms with more than $50 billion in assets. This is intended to provide assurances that the taxpayers will not be put at risk through exercise of OLA authority.

Two other features of the DFA have particular relevance for G-SIBs. First, the Collins Amendment establishes a floor for both risk-based and leverage capital requirements equal to the ratios in effect when the DFA was passed. Since the US had not yet adopted Basel II, this means that risk-weighted assets calculated under the advanced approaches (expected to be used by the largest institutions) can be no lower than they would be under the standardized approach (expected to be used by most other institutions). This means that the Basel III capital requirements in the US can be more stringent, but must be no less stringent than the capital requirements in effect during July 2010. In addition, the Collins Amendment requires that regulators raise capital requirements for firms with significant activity in derivatives, securitization products, financial guarantees, securities borrowing and lending, and repos. Higher capital requirements must also be imposed on firms with concentrations of assets for which reported values depend on internal models. These are all characteristics that tend to distinguish the G-SIBs and other larger SIFIs from smaller banks and so the Collins Amendment effectively mandates US regulators to impose higher capital requirements on the larger SIFIs. In the final quarter of 2013 the Fed announced the way in which it will implement Basel III and has introduced a new leverage ratio that is significantly higher for large banks and for large bank holding companies (Switzerland and Great Britain have also increased capital requirements by substantially more than the Basel minimums).

Second, the Volcker Rule, which has not yet been implemented, was focused on limiting the scope and scale of large SIFIs. The Volcker Amendment was not part of the original DFA, but was inserted by the US Administration in response to exit polls, which showed that voters were so angry with what they perceived as lenient treatment of Wall Street that they elected a Republican to the Senate seat that had been held for decades by a Kennedy. The principal rationale for the Volcker Rule was to protect insured deposits from activities that were thought to be especially risky. The Volcker Rule prohibits proprietary trading but permits trading to serve the interests of customers. This distinction has proved difficult to transform into an implementing regulation and has delayed imposition of the Volcker Rule for more than three years. The Volcker Rule also limits investments in and sponsorship of hedge funds and private equity funds: SIFIs can invest no more than 3% of their Tier 1 capital in such funds and their investment can account for no more than 3% of the financing in any given fund. Finally, the Volcker Rule constrains the ability of SIFIs to grow through mergers and acquisitions: no SIFI may undertake a merger that would result in a financial institution with liabilities greater than 10% of the total liabilities of all US financial institutions at the end of the previous year.

The basic intent of the Volcker Rule is to limit the benefits of public guarantees of deposits to core banking services that are believed to be systemic and to shield them from riskier activities. Implicitly, the Volcker Rule takes the view that some activities are so risky and so complex to monitor that they should be prohibited. Regulators in the UK and the European Union have also sought to shield a core set of activities from activities that are thought to be riskier, but they have chosen to rely on subsidiarization (or corporate separateness) buttressed by constraints on intra-group exposures. The Vickers Report has sought to ring-fence retail banking by pushing other activities out of the deposit-taking institution. But these activities can continue to be conducted by affiliates so long as they do not take retail deposits in the UK. The EU's Liikanen Report (HLEG, 2012) would prohibit depository institutions from engaging in market making, proprietary trading, and investment in hedge funds and private equity, but other subsidiaries in the same banking group would be free to conduct these lines of business.

The French and German governments have adopted a somewhat weaker version of the Liikanen model that allows depository institutions to engage in market making. All of these approaches attempt to protect the depository institutions from shocks to other activities, but the details of each approach are quite different.[31] This is, in fact, characteristic of virtually every aspect of bank regulation and especially resolution policy. That is why the FDIC has faced a special challenge in implementing OLA in a way that would be effective for cross-border banks.

This is an important challenge because all of the largest US SIFIs have substantial operations outside the United States. If the FDIC cannot specify how OLA can work across borders, it will lack credibility. The FDIC has been actively engaged in supervisory colleges and crisis management groups organized by the BCBS and it has signed several

---

[31] For a detailed overview of structural bank regulation initiatives see Gambacorta and van Rixtel (2013); they also provide an in-depth analysis of the closely related issue of economies of scale and scope in banking.

memoranda of understanding with their counterparts (when they can be identified) in other countries. But it is unclear whether any of these measures will be effective under the stress of an actual crisis. One solution might be to harmonize resolution regimes across the world. The key attributes approach set up by the FSB is, in fact, a step in that direction, but when the question of allocating losses arises few people have confidence that this approach would hold up. Countries are understandably reluctant to allocate losses ex ante—no country is willing to make an open-ended fiscal commitment. And cross-border losses will be even more difficult to allocate ex post since it will always be possible to argue that the losses would not have occurred if home country supervision had been more effective. There is probably no better example of this problem than the reluctance of the EU to even consider the possibility of a common deposit insurance fund. Yet, so long as the safety of a deposit depends on the strength of the deposit insurance system and the creditworthiness of the country where the deposit was placed, the lethal link between bank risk and country risk cannot be broken. One reaction to this lack of a robust cross-border system for resolving G-SIBs is to prepare to ring-fence the parts of the banking group that are within one country's borders. The US has proposed that foreign banks with substantial operations in the United States be required to establish a US holding company that would be subject to prudential rules in the US, including capital adequacy requirements, and could, in principle, be resolved in the US if the home country's resolution procedures do not seem to treat US interests fairly.

But the FDIC, in cooperation with the Bank of England (FDIC and Bank of England, 2012), has proposed an alternative that might finesse the issues of corporate complexity and differences in national resolution regimes, by requiring the top-level entity in the group (in the US, the bank holding company) to hold sufficient capital to recapitalize its subsidiaries in the event of a near default. In essence, the holding company would be taken through bankruptcy court and for the rest of the group would be placed in a bridge institution and continue operation under the supervision of the FDIC. All of the operating entities would continue to function. Of course, this approach depends on at least three important assumptions: (1) that the top-level holding company is sufficiently well capitalized to recapitalize the rest of the group; (2) that counterparties of the subsidiaries would not deem the change in control to be an event of default that would enable them to net and close-out their existing contracts; and (3) that host country governments would be confident that the subsidiaries operating in their country would continue in operation without imposing loss on local creditors or counterparties. This, however, places the FDIC in a very tricky position. To make the single-point-of-entry (SPE) approach work, the creditors, counterparties, and foreign regulators of the subsidiaries must believe that the bridge institution can and will continue to operate the subsidiaries. But the FDIC cannot make such a guarantee, particularly if resources at the holding company level are not sufficient. If it should issue such a guarantee, the opponents of OLA would justifiably claim that OLA was yet another way to subsidize large SIFIs. In essence, the DFA would have failed to remove the special access of large SIFIs to government resources (even if such resources are to be repaid by levies on the remaining large banks in the end). If the FDIC does not make such a guarantee, however, each creditor, counterparty, and regulator of a foreign subsidiary will question whether the subsidiary with which they are dealing will be supported. Given the lack of transparency of such groups, the suspicion that a subsidiary might fail could precipitate behavior that will ensure that it does.

4.8 Concluding Comment

We can no longer claim that the authorities have ignored the issue of complexity. The problem is now widely recognized and numerous initiatives have been taken at both the international and national levels to reduce corporate complexity and constrain the size of G-SIBs. Higher capital requirements, heightened supervision, restrictions on activities, and improved resolution regimes accompanied by living wills should help reduce the problem. All of these new policies take time to implement, but financial institutions usually try to achieve compliance with new regulations even before the date they are effective because markets will reward financial institutions that are prepared for the new regimes. Nonetheless, our analysis of what little public data there is regarding complexity suggests that progress has been quite uneven. Some institutions appear to have simplified their structures and downsized, while others have become still larger and more complex. This raises several questions about whether the new policies will succeed.

One issue the authorities must face is whether markets believe they will implement the new policies rigorously. Here they face an enormous credibility gap. Despite decades of rhetoric asserting that no institution was too-big-to-fail, the only instance in which the doctrine was applied, the bankruptcy of Lehman Brothers, was widely criticized as hugely disruptive to world financial markets. Moreover, when it became clear that several banks were too big to save without placing impossible financial burdens on their home countries, these countries chose to bailout their banks even at the cost of serious damage to their own credit ratings. In addition, when faced with an actual crisis, the authorities proved reluctant to use the powers they already had. In the US, even subordinated debtors at troubled institutions were protected (except in the case of Lehman Brothers). Whether the authorities have the will to use the new powers they have been given remains an open question. Perhaps this doubt can only be resolved by a crisis of just the right size in which the authorities can demonstrate that they have the will and ability to carry out their new powers without disrupting markets. So far, credit rating agencies and markets appear to have significant doubts.

Will the crisis management groups, memoranda of understanding, and resolution strategies such as the SPE withstand the strain of crisis? Here, again, experience during the crisis leads one to be skeptical. Perhaps the most obvious example is the collapse of Fortis, a large bank that was owned by interests in Belgium, the Netherlands, and Luxembourg—a trio of countries known as the Benelux group that had maintained a currency union long before the euro was introduced. When faced with the challenge of resolving Fortis in a way that might conserve its going concern value, however, cooperation collapsed and each country grabbed the assets that it could control. If an SPE regime is adopted and if the home country has the resources and will to implement it, this problem might be overcome. But so far, it is a clever, but untested idea.

What is most troubling in the progress to date is the complete lack of public disclosure. This means that markets lack the information to discipline banks that have excessively complex structures or, indeed, to monitor whether regulators are implementing their new powers. The US has led the way in disclosure by requiring a public section of living wills, but it is of little value because it contains no new data. Other countries, however, have not even taken this limited step. Worse still, markets lack a clear understanding of how each G-SIB would be resolved. If resolution regimes are to succeed they should enlist market discipline ex ante. Creditors and counterparties should know how resolution plans will be implemented in order to price claims appropriately. This could strengthen regulatory efforts markedly. Equally importantly, the resolution should not surprise the market when it is implemented. It is unwise to surprise creditors ex post by imposing unexpected losses on them. Although regulators are often enamored with the doctrine of "constructive ambiguity," one of the clear lessons of the 2007–2008 crisis is that when regulators surprise the market by taking unexpected actions that cause loss (or by failing to act when expected to prevent loss), financial instability is intensified. Investors will tend to flee to safety and secondary markets will evaporate until investors once again believe they understand the rules of the game. Of the key objectives for effective resolution regimes, the one that appears to have received the least attention is to "Achieve and maintain credibility to enhance market discipline and provide incentives for market solutions." Although this appears last on the list of key objectives, it is most certainly not last in importance.

Finally, the authorities should take this opportunity to examine their own regulations and tax laws. It is clear that these provide strong incentives for overly complex transactions and corporate structures. The authorities should continually question whether their objectives can be accomplished with taxes and regulations that cause fewer distortions and less counter-productive behavior.

References

Admati, A. and Hellwig, M. (2013). *The Bankers' New Clothes—What's Wrong with Banking and What to Do About It*. Princeton: Princeton University Press.

Aron, D. (1991). Using the Capital Market as a Monitor: Corporate Spinoffs in an Agency Framework, *RAND Journal of Economics* 22, 505–518.

Ashcraft, A. (2004). Are Bank Holding Companies a Source of Strength to Their Banking Subsidiaries?, Federal Reserve Bank of New York Staff Report No. 189, June.

Avraham, D., Selvaggi, P., and Vickery J. (2012). A Structural View of US Bank Holding Companies, *Federal Reserve Bank of New York Economic Policy Review* 65–81.

Bair, S. (2013). *Bull by the Horns—Fighting to Save Main Street from Wall Street and Wall Street from Itself*. New York: Free Press.

Baxter, T. and Sommer, J. (2005). Breaking Up is Hard to Do: An Essay on Cross-Border Challenges in Resolving Financial Groups. In: D. Evanoff and G. Kaufman (Eds.), *Systemic Financial Crises, Resolving Large Bank Insolvencies*, 175–191. Singapore: World Scientific.

BCBS (Basel Committee on Banking Supervision) (1992). The Insolvency Liquidation of a Multinational Bank, BCBS Compendium of Documents, International Supervisory Issues III, 1–21.

BCBS (Basel Committee on Banking Supervision) (2011). Global Systemically Important Banks: Assessment Methodology and the Additional Loss Absorbency Requirement—Rules Text. Bank for International Settlements, Basel, November.

BCBS (Basel Committee on Banking Supervision) (2013). Global Systemically Important Banks: Updated Assessment Methodology and the Higher Loss Absorbency Requirement. Bank for International Settlements, Basel, July.

Berger, A. N., Herring, R. J., and Szegö, G. P. (1995). The Role of Capital in Financial Institutions, *Journal of Banking & Finance* 19: 393–430.

Bertay, A. C., Demirgüç-Kunt, A., and Huizinga, H. (2012). Is the Financial Safety Net a Barrier to Cross-Border Banking?, The World Bank Development Research Group, Finance and Private Sector Development Team Policy Research Working Paper No. 5947, January.

Bianco, M. and Nicodano, G. (2002). Business Groups and Debt. Universitá di Torino Working Paper, January 29.

Carmassi, J. and Herring, R. J. (2013). Living Wills and Cross-Border Resolution of Systemically Important Banks, *Journal of Financial Economic Policy* 5, 361–387

Carmassi, J. and Micossi, S. (2012). *Time to Set Banking Regulation Right.* CEPS Paperback, Brussels, March.

Cerutti, E., Dell'Ariccia, G., and Martinez Peria, M. S. (2005). How Banks Go Abroad: Branches or Subsidiaries?, World Bank Policy Research Working Paper No. 3753, October.

Cetorelli, N. and Goldberg, L. S. (2012). Liquidity Management of US Global Banks: Internal Capital Markets in the Great Recession, *Journal of International Economics* 88, 299–311.

CGFS (Committee on the Global Financial System) (2010a). Long-term Issues in International Banking, Bank for International Settlements, Basel CGFS Papers No. 41, July.

CGFS (Committee on the Global Financial System) (2010b). Funding Patterns and Liquidity Management of Internationally Active Banks, Bank for International Settlements, Basel, CGFS Papers No. 39, May.

Čihák, M., Demirgüç-Kunt, A., Martínez Pería, M. S., and Mohseni-Cheraghlou, A. (2012). *Bank Regulation and Supervision Around the World—A Crisis Update,* World Bank Policy Research Working Paper No. 6286, December.

Claessens, S., Herring, R. J., and Schoenmaker, D. (2010). A Safer World Financial System: Improving the Resolution of Systemic Institutions, International Center for Monetary and Banking Studies, Geneva Reports on the World Economy No. 12, July.

Claessens, S. and Van Horen, N. (2012). Foreign Banks: Trends, Impact and Financial Stability, International Monetary Fund, Washington DC, IMF Working Paper No. 12/10, January.

Demirgüç-Kunt, A. and Huizinga, H. (2001). The Taxation of Domestic and Foreign Banking, *Journal of Public Economics* 79, 429–453.

Dermine, J. (2006). European Banking Integration: Don't Put the Cart before the Horse, *Financial Markets, Institutions & Instruments* 15, 57–106.

Deutsche Bank (2013). Deutsche Bank Resolution Plan Section 1. Public Section, October 1.

Elliott, D. J. and Litan, R. E. (2011). Identifying and Regulating Systemically Important Financial Institutions: The Risks of Under and Over Identification and Regulation. Brookings Institutions Policy Brief, Washington DC, January 16.

FDIC (Federal Deposit Insurance Corporation) and Bank of England (2012). Resolving Globally Active, Systemically Important, Financial Institutions. Joint Paper, December 10, <http://ww.fdic.gov/about/srac/2012/gsifi.pdf.>.

Fiechter, J., Ötker-Robe, I., Ilyina, A., Hsu, M., Santos, A., and Surti, J. (2011). Subsidiaries or Branches: Does One Size Fit All?, International Monetary Fund, Washington DC, IMF Staff Discussion Note No. 11/04, March 7.

Financial Stability Forum (2000). Press Release, May 26.

Frame, W. S. and White, L. J. (2014). Technological Change, Financial Innovation, and Diffusion in Banking. In: A. N. Berger, P. Molyneux, and J. O. S. Wilson, *Oxford Handbook of Banking.* 2nd edition. Oxford: Oxford University Press.

FSB (Financial Stability Board) (2011a). Key Attributes of Effective Resolution Regimes for Financial Institutions, October.

FSB (Financial Stability Board) (2011b). Policy Measures to Address Systemically Important Financial Institutions, November 4.

FSB (Financial Stability Board) (2012a). Resolution of Systemically Important Financial Institutions—Progress Report, November.

FSB (Financial Stability Board) (2012b). Update of Group of Global Systemically Important Banks (G-SIBs), November.

FSB (Financial Stability Board) (2013a). Recovery and Resolution Planning for Systemically Important Financial Institutions: Guidance on Developing Effective Resolution Strategies, July 16.

FSB (Financial Stability Board) (2013b). Recovery and Resolution Planning for Systemically Important Financial Institutions: Guidance on Identification of Critical Functions and Critical Shared Services, July 16.

FSB (Financial Stability Board) (2013c). Recovery and Resolution Planning for Systemically Important Financial Institutions: Guidance on Recovery Triggers and Stress Scenarios, July 16.

FSB (Financial Stability Board) (2013d). Thematic Review on Resolution Regimes, April 11.

FSB (Financial Stability Board) (2013e). Implementing the FSB Key Attributes of Effective Resolution Regimes—How Far Have We Come? Report to the G20 Finance Ministers and Central Bank Governors, April 15.

FSB (Financial Stability Board) (2013f). FSB Reports to the G20 on Progress and Next Steps Toward Ending Too-Big-To-Fail. Press Release, September 2.

Fulghieri, P. and Hodrick, L. (2005). Synergies and Internal Agency Conflicts: The Double-Edge Sword of Mergers. Kenan-Flagler Business School Working Paper.

Gambacorta L. and van Rixtel, A. (2013). Structural Bank Regulation Initiatives: Approaches and Implications, Bank for International Settlements, Basel, BIS Working Papers No. 412, April.

Goddard, J., Molyneux, P., and J. O. S Wilson (2014). Banking in the European Union: Deregulation, Crisis and Renewal. In: A. N. Berger, P. Molyneux, and J. O. S. Wilson (Eds.). *Oxford Handbook of Banking*. 2nd edition. Oxford: Oxford University Press.

Gorton, G. and Souleles, N. (2006). Special Purpose Vehicles and Securitization. In: M. Carey and R. Stulz (Eds.), *The Risks of Financial Institutions*, 549–597. Chicago: National Bureau of Economic Research.

Habib, M., Johnsen, B., and Naik, N. (1997). Spinoffs and Information, *Journal of Financial Intermediation* 6, 153–176.

Haldane, A. (2009). Banking on the State. Paper Based on Presentation to the Federal Reserve Bank of Chicago, September 25.

Haldane, A. (2012). On Being the Right Size. The Beesley Lectures Delivered to the Institute of Directors, October 25.

Herring, R. J. (1993). BCCI: Lessons for International Bank Supervision, *Contemporary Policy Issues* 11, 1–11.

Herring, R. J. (2003). International Financial Conglomerates: Implications for National Insolvency Regimes. In: G. Kaufman (Ed.), *Market Discipline and Banking: Theory and Evidence*, 99–129. New York: Elsevier.

Herring, R. J. (2007). Conflicts between Home and Host Country Prudential Supervisors. In: D. Evanoff, G. Kaufman, and J. LaBrosse (Eds.), *International Financial Instability, Global Banking and National Regulation*, 201–219. New Jersey: World Scientific.

Herring, R. J. (2013). The Danger of Building a Banking Union on a One-Legged Stool. In: F. Allen, E. Carletti, and J. Gray (Eds.), *Political, Fiscal and Banking Union in the Eurozone?*, 9–28. Florence: European University Institute and Philadelphia: Wharton Financial Institutions Center, University of Pennsylvania.

Herring, R. J. and Carmassi, J. (2010). The Corporate Structure of International Financial Conglomerates: Complexity and Its Implications for Safety & Soundness. In: A. N. Berger, P. Molyneux, and J. O. S. Wilson (Eds.), *Oxford Handbook of Banking*, 195–229. Oxford: Oxford University Press.

Herring, R. J. and Santomero, A. (1990). The Corporate Structure of Financial Conglomerates, *Journal of Financial Services Research* 4, 471–497.

Herring, R. J. and Schuermann, T. (2005). The Regulation of Position Risk in Banks, Securities Firms and Insurance Companies. In: H. Scott (Ed.), *Capital Adequacy Beyond Basel, Banking, Securities and Insurance*, 15–86. Oxford: Oxford University Press.

HLEG (High-Level Expert Group on Reforming the Structure of the EU Banking Sector) (2012). Final Report, Group Chaired by Erkki Liikanen, Brussels, October 2.

Hoenig, T. (2013). Basel III Capital: A Well-Intended Illusion. Remarks to the International Association of Deposit Insurers 2013 Research Conference, Basel, April 9.

Holod, D. and Peek, J. (2006). Capital Constraints, Asymmetric Information and Internal Capital Markets in Banking: New Evidence. Working Paper available on SSRN Website, December.

Huertas, T. F. (2009). The Rationale and Limits of Bank Supervision, Unpublished Manuscript.

Hughes, J. (2008). Lehman Creditors to Face Years of Waiting, *Financial Times November* 14.

International Monetary Fund (2000). Offshore Financial Centers. IMF Background Paper, Washington DC, June 23.

Jensen, M. (1986). Agency Costs of Free Cash Flow, Corporate Finance, and Takeovers, *The American Economic Review* 76, 323–329.

Kahn, C. and Winton, A. (2004). Moral Hazard and Optimal Subsidiary Structure for Financial Institutions, *Journal of Finance* 59(6), 2531–2575.

Kane, E. (1977). Good Intentions and Unintended Evil: The Case against Selective Credit Allocation, *Journal of Money Credit and Banking* 9, 55–69.

Kane, E. (1981). Accelerating Inflation, Technological Innovation, and the Decreasing Effectiveness of Banking Regulation, *Journal of Finance* 36, 355–367.

Kane, E. (1984). Technological and Regulatory Forces in the Developing Fusion of Financial Services Competition, *Journal of Finance* 39, 759–772.

Klein, P. and Saidenberg, M. (2005). Organizational Structure and the Diversification Discount: Evidence from Commercial Banking, University of Missouri CORI Working Paper No. 2005–2006, April.

Kroszner, R. and Rajan, R. (1997). Organization Structure and Credibility: Evidence from Commercial Banks Securities Activities before the Glass-Steagall Act, *Journal of Monetary Economics* 39, 475–516.

Laeven, L. and Levine, R. (2007). Is There a Diversification Discount in Financial Conglomerates?, *Journal of Financial Economics* 85, 331–367.

Lehman Brothers (2009). Press Release on Cross-border Insolvency Protocol, May 26.

Merton, R. and Perold, A. (1993). Management of Risk Capital in Financial Firms. In: S. Hayes (Ed.), *Financial Services: Perspectives and Challenges*, 215–245. Boston MA: Harvard Business School Press.

Miller, H. and Horwitz, M. (2012). Lehman—An Unnecessary Tragedy—Lessons that Should Have Been Learned. Cross-Border Resolution Policy: Issues and Opportunities.

A Presentation at Joint Penn/Wharton Financial Institutions Center & Stanford/Hoover Resolution Project Workshop, July 25.

Modigliani, F. and Miller, M. (1958). The Cost of Capital, Corporation Finance and the Theory of Investment, *American Economic Review* 48, 261–297.

Morgan, D. P. (2002). Rating Banks: Risk and Uncertainty in an Opaque Industry, *American Economic Review* 92: 874–888.

Norton, J. O. (2013). Discussion on the Current State of Resolution Planning. Remarks to the American Bankers Association, New Orleans, Louisiana, October 21.

Rajan, R., Servaes, H., and Zingales, L. (2000). The Cost of Diversity: The Diversification Discount and Inefficient Investment, *Journal of Finance* 55: 35–80.

Rosengren, E. (2003). Comment. In: V. Gaspar, P. Hartmann, and O. Sleijpen, (Eds.), The Transformation of the European Financial System. Second ECB Central Banking Conference, October, 109–115.

Schoenmaker, D. (2013). *Governance of International Banking—The Financial Trilemma*. New York: Oxford University Press.

Smith, C. and Stulz, R. (1985). The Determinants of Firms' Hedging Policies, *The Journal of Financial and Quantitative Analysis* 20, 391–405.

SRC (Systemic Risk Council) (2013a). Letter to Bank Regulators about Delayed and Weakened Global Capital and Liquidity Standards, Washington, DC, January 23.

SRC (Systemic Risk Council) (2013b). Systemic Risk Council Comment Letter to Bank Regulators on Proposed Enhanced Supplementary Leverage Ratio, Washington, DC, October 15.

SRC (Systemic Risk Council) (2013c). Systemic Risk Council Comments to Discussion Paper Issued by Basel Committee on Banking Supervision, Washington, DC, October 15.

Tarullo, D. (2013). Toward Building a More Effective Resolution Regime: Progress and Challenges. Speech at the Federal Reserve Board and Federal Reserve Bank of Richmond Conference, Planning for the Orderly Resolution of a Global Systemically Important Bank, Washington, DC, October 18.

Tröger, T. H. (2013). Organizational Choices of Banks and the Effective Supervision of Transnational Financial Institutions, *Texas International Law Journal* 48(2), 177–221.

Tufano, P. (2006). Comment. In: M. Carey and R. Stulz (Eds.), *The Risks of Financial Institutions*, 597–602. Chicago: National Bureau of Economic Research.

Walter, I. (2003). Strategies in Financial Services, the Shareholders, and the System: Is Bigger and Broader Bettter?, *Brookings/Wharton Papers on Financial Services* 8, 1–36.

Walter, I. (2004). Conflicts of Interest and Market Discipline among Financial Service Firms, *European Management Journal* 22, 361–376.

Woolford, I. and Orr, A. (2005). The Limits to Hospitality, *The Financial Regulator* 10, 41–46.

CHAPTER 5

....

UNIVERSAL BANKING*

....

ALAN D. MORRISON

5.1. INTRODUCTION

....

UNIVERSAL banks are institutions that combine the lending and payment services of commercial banks with a wider range of financial services. In particular, universal banks underwrite securities, and hence can offer their client firms access to a broader range of sources of funds than can specialist commercial or investment banks. Universal banking was commonplace in nineteenth-century Germany, but not in the United Kingdom or the United States. Indeed, universal banks were outlawed in the United States for the last two-thirds of the twentieth century. This institutional difference has been a preoccupation of economists since Schumpeter (1939) and Gerschenkron (1962), who argued that early universal banks in Germany substituted financial capital for limited human capital.

This chapter outlines Gerschenkron's ideas, and relates them to more recent developments in universal banking. In particular, I argue that one of the reasons for the recent widespread adoption of the universal banking model is a general change in relationship between human and financial capital in modern economies. Nevertheless, I argue that the institutional context in which universal banks operate remains important. Hence, for example, universal banks require effective regulation if their effectiveness is not to be undermined by conflicts between their component businesses. The need for such regulation was thrown into sharp relief by the financial crisis of 2008–2009; I outline the current state of the regulatory debate, and I highlight the challenges inherent in designing and implementing effective rules for the structure of universal banking.

* Many of the ideas concerning human capital in this chapter arose during joint work with Bill Wilhelm, to whom I am extremely grateful for numerous conversations and insights. I am also grateful to Alexander Gümbel and Dimitri Tsomocos for comments on an earlier draft.

5.2. UNIVERSAL BANKING, INDUSTRIAL DEVELOPMENT, AND HUMAN CAPITAL FORMATION

Numerous authors have pointed to the large-scale and well-capitalized universal banks that played an important role in the pre-World War I financing of German industry. These banks held the equity as well as the debt securities of their clients; Schumpeter (1939) argues that this resulted in long-term relationship formation, which facilitated efficient resource direction. In contrast, the finance required for British industrialization was garnered partly from commercial banks, and also from stock market flotations, which were brought to market by small-scale merchant houses which lacked the financial capital of the commercial banks.

In a famous essay, Gerschenkron (1962) explains these differences as consequences of the ways in which the respective economies developed. He argues with reference to "economic backwardness"; this is a term that he never defines precisely, but he uses it to describe economies that were relatively late adopters of modern methods of production and distribution. He argues that development in these economies was hampered by a number of "institutional obstacles." First, entrepreneurs had not accumulated capital in the earlier stages of development. Second, the workforce in "economically backward" economies had little experience of new technologies and ways of doing things. In the language of modern labor economics, they lacked human capital and, in particular, they lacked tacit human capital, acquired through on-the-job experience but not easily taught at arm's length, for example in a classroom.[1]

Gerschenkron's observation about human capital is central to his argument, although it has been little discussed by modern authors. Lack of labor skill renders development difficult; in some cases, as for example with the serfdom of peasants in pre-1861 Russia, he argues that it renders it impossible.[2] In general, Gerschenkron argues, industrialization in backward economies can proceed only when technology reaches a sufficiently advanced stage to substitute for human capital: it is easier to teach a worker to operate very advanced production machinery than it is to teach him the tacit production skills he needs to obtain any benefit from a less sophisticated machine.

Gerschenkron argues that nineteenth-century Germany, and also France and Russia, were "economically backward"; he contrasts them with England, which industrialized earlier, and, hence, was not. According to Gerschenkron, industrialization in economically backward nations relied upon technologies that rendered hard-to-transmit tacit skills sufficiently unimportant. But these technologies operated at a very large scale. They could only function effectively if an adequate infrastructure developed to support them: factories required railways to ensure adequate levels of throughput, railways required coal, and so on.[3]

---

[1] Becker (1964) discusses human capital; its importance to development has been stressed by many authors. Tacit skill is discussed by Polanyi (1966).

[2] One might expect serfdom to provide the owners of peasants with incentives to invest in human capital. Gerschenkron argues that serfdom was symptomatic of a social sclerosis that undermined any tendency toward innovation.

[3] More recently, Chandler (1990) stresses the importance to the development of industrial capitalism of a large-scale infrastructure that can service expensive capital.

Industrialization therefore had to proceed on a "broad front," and this required capital on a scale that, by virtue of their economic backwardness, local entrepreneurs had not accumulated. Hence appropriate institutions were required to pool capital, and to direct it toward the technologies that would underpin economic development. These institutions were the universal banks.

In sum, Gerschenkron argues that universal banks arose naturally in countries that had to play economic catch-up, because a lack of human capital generated a pressure toward bigness which could only be satisfied if dispersed sources of capital were combined. And, because capital came from dispersed sources, it had to be closely watched by the banks that directed it. Gerschenkron (p. 225) claims that the German banks established "the closest possible relations with industrial enterprises," and that they "accompanied an industrial enterprise from the cradle to the grave, from establishment to liquidation throughout all the vicissitudes of its existence."

Gerschenkron's analysis extends to what modern writers call industrial organization, but which he calls the "industrial structure" of the economy. He argues that concentration of power and relations in the universal banks served to reinforce the basic tendencies inherent in backward countries, so that attention was devoted to the heavy industry where large-scale financial capital was most useful. Moreover, Gerschenkron argues that the late nineteenth-century cartelization movement in German industry was a natural result of the amalgamation of German banks which "refused to tolerate fratricidal struggles amongst their children." In contrast, while English banks also consolidated at this time, the process was not mirrored to the same extent in industry.

Gerschenkron does not discuss the US banking sector. America industrialized later than Britain; although it lacked some of the institutional features that Gerschenkron argues were a brake on development elsewhere, one might expect America's banking system to have developed along German lines. Indeed, while the US financial system owed rather more to the British system of financing than did the German one and, moreover, the extent of universal banking in the US was restricted by regulation, US banking had some features that, at least at the level of casual empiricism, were consistent with Gerschenkron's stories. At the end of the first decade of the twentieth century, Redlich (1968, pp. 381–382) argues that not more than six banking firms were responsible for managing the organization of the American economy.[4] Lamoreaux (1985) documents the merger wave that the US experienced between 1895 and 1904: it saw 1,800 firms disappear into merged entities, and many of the firms formed at this time continued to dominate their industries for the following century: examples are US Steel, DuPont, International Harvester, Pittsburgh Plate Glass, American Can, and American Smelting and Refinery. As discussed by Morrison and Wilhelm (2007, pp. 182–184), these mergers were largely orchestrated by bankers, and in particular by J. P. Morgan & Co. In line with Gerschenkron's observations, Morgan was concerned throughout his career to avoid what he regarded as destructive competition between competitors, and this concern informed his deal-making at this time.

As far as I am aware, Gerschenkron's assertion that the rate of human capital formation affected the way in which the banking sector developed in Germany (and, arguably, in the

---

[4] They were J. P. Morgan & Co., First National and the National City Bank of New York, Kuhn, Loeb & Co. and, to a lesser extent, Kidder, Peabody & Co., and Lee, Higginson & Co.

United States) has not been subjected to a formal empirical analysis. His assertion that universal banks formed closer and longer-term relationships than their counterparts elsewhere has however been discussed.

Calomiris (1993, 1995) examines the effect of laws that prevented US banks from consolidating and branching during the second Industrial Revolution (1870–1914). He argues that these laws increased the informational and transactions costs of issuing securities, and, hence, he argues that there was a lower propensity to issue equities in the US than in Germany where, he argues, universal banks were better able to extract valuable information from their borrowers. Moreover, he presents evidence that the costs of financing German industrialization were lower than in the US, precisely because there were universal banks in Germany. He argues that institutional changes that increased bank concentration in the US lowered the costs of finance there.

Calomiris' conclusions are challenged in a series of papers by Caroline Fohlin. If long-term relationships with banks eased financing conditions, then one should see less contemporary evidence of credit rationing in firms with such a relationship. Fohlin (1998b) tests whether a relationship with one of the nine "Great Banks" of nineteenth-century Germany eased access to credit by examining the cash flow sensitivity of investment for firms with and without such a relationship. Her approach follows Fazzari, Hubbard, and Petersen (1988) and Hoshi, Kashyap, and Scharfstein (1990): firms that have easy access to capital should be less reliant upon retained earnings to finance investment, and hence, after controlling for the quality of their investment opportunities, their investment levels should be independent of the cash that their operations generate. Fohlin faces an endogeneity problem, in that association with a universal bank may be related to the quality of investment opportunities. But, even after controlling for this effect, she finds, in an apparent contradiction of the relationship hypothesis, that a bank relationship actually increases the sensitivity of investment to holdings of liquid assets. In another paper (Fohlin, 1998a), she shows that universal bank affiliation in Italy did nothing to ameliorate a liquidity sensitivity of investment, and finds little support from performance data for the notion that universal banks provided screening services to investors.

In other papers, Fohlin presents evidence that first indicates that German banks held more liquid assets than British banks, and that, while they held a limited number of securities in their portfolios, this was often merely because they could not place new issues in their entirety (Fohlin, 2001), and second that bank affiliation in Germany was about securities issuance and stock market listings, rather than the monitoring of debt contracts and the provision of consultancy services (Fohlin, 1997).

Edwards and Ogilvie (1996) also examine the role of universal banks in German industrialization. In contrast to Gerschenkron's claims, they find that universal banking accounted for a relatively small proportion of the total assets of financial institutions in Germany before 1914. At this time, joint stock companies never accounted for more than 20% of the industrial capital stock; for at least 80%, then, the special skills of universal banks were not relevant. In most cases, internally generated funds were the most important source of finance for joint stock companies, and much of the rest came from non-universal financial intermediaries, such as savings and mortgage banks, and credit cooperatives.

The evidence to support a close monitoring interpretation of Gerschenkron's universal banking story therefore seems rather shaky. Interestingly, however, Ramirez (1995) finds evidence that supports it in the American context. He finds, in contrast to Fohlin's (1998b)

German analysis, that a relationship with J. P. Morgan significantly reduced the cash flow sensitivity of investment for American firms. Whether this reflects active monitoring or skilled screening is harder to establish, but it does suggest that a universal banking relationship could ease access to the credit markets. Indeed, it was concerns that the wrong types of firms might be helped into the capital markets by their investment banks that led the American authorities to separate commercial from investment banking. Their reasoning, and the evidence concerning it, is examined in Section 5.3.

5.3. Universal Banking and Conflicts of Interest

Commercial banks had a significant presence in the United States securities markets of 1900. Although the Comptroller of the Currency ruled in 1902 that national banks were not permitted to engage in the securities business, the First National Bank of Chicago managed in 1903 to circumvent this ruling by creating a securities affiliate. Securities affiliates were state banks with their own capital, owned by the shareholders of the national bank in proportion with their shares in the national bank. As state banks were not the concern of the Comptroller, affiliates were able to operate in the securities markets, and consequently the national banks functioned as de facto investment banks.[5]

However, while commercial banks were able to operate via securities affiliates in the securities markets, their activities were viewed with some skepticism by populist regulators and legislators. A series of investigations into the governance of investment houses brought the state into conflict with the securities industry in the first quarter of the twentieth century:[6] the Armstrong Committee of 1905 expressed concerns regarding excessively close relations between large investment banks and insurance companies, and the Pujo Committee of 1912 tried but failed to prove the existence of a "money trust" that suppressed competition in finance. In the wake of the 1929 stock market crash, the investment banks were again in the line of fire, this time from the Pecora Commission, established in 1932 by Herbert Hoover in an attempt to substantiate his belief that the stock market was being undermined by pools of short sellers.

Ferdinand Pecora was far from neutral: Morgan remarked at the time that "Pecora has the manner and the manners of a prosecuting attorney who is trying to convict a horse thief."[7] Nevertheless, he found some evidence of governance failures, most notably at National City Bank.[8] His findings fed a public mood that demanded changes to the regulatory framework of the investment banking industry, and which found its voice in New Deal

---

[5] Carosso (1970, p. 276) discusses at some length the operation of securities affiliates.

[6] Morrison and Wilhelm (2007, pp. 196–215) discuss the hearings, and their consequences, in some detail.

[7] See Leuchtenburg (1963, p. 59).

[8] Charles E. Mitchell, the president and board chairman of National City Bank, was paid a salary of $25,000, but awarded himself bonuses of $1 million in 1927 and 1928. Seligman (1982) discusses the hearings, and their legislative consequences, in detail.

legislation that both established a regulatory framework for the securities industry, by creating the Securities and Exchange Commission, and that also profoundly altered the industrial organization of the industry.

The Banking Act of June 1933, popularly known as the Glass–Steagall Act, abolished securities affiliates by requiring a total separation of investment from commercial banking. The
Act had a massive impact, since at the end of the 1920s over half of all new securities issues
were sponsored by security affiliates. In the wake of the Act, all issues had to be brought to
market by specialist investment houses. J. P. Morgan & Co. remained in deposit banking and
hence had to leave the securities industry.[9]

While some academic articles debate the point,[10] the Glass–Steagall Act appears to have
been motivated by concerns that commercial banks were using their securities affiliates
to place low-quality securities on the market in order to avoid taking losses on their own
loan portfolios. For example, the Pecora Commission uncovered evidence that when the
National City Bank's securities affiliate, the National City Company, pushed Peruvian debt,
it did so despite knowing that it was a poor investment. There is, however, evidence that
commercial banks lost heavily on unsold stock when underwriting issues by their debtors
(see Kroszner and Rajan, 1994).

The claim that securities affiliates pushed low-quality issues that benefited their parent
firms at the expense of their investors went unchallenged in the academic literature for
many years. But it is rather incredible: if securities affiliates were pushing low-quality issues
then, if they were dealing with rational investors, the low quality should have been reflected
in share prices. Hence, if the securities affiliates were pushing poor securities, either they
were dealing with naïve investors who failed to learn from experience, or they were making
no profits from their actions. Neither story is particularly convincing. Moreover, the fact
that investment banks faced conflicts of interest is not necessarily evidence of institutional
failure: Morrison and Wilhelm (2007, chs 2 and 3) argue that investment banks are economically useful precisely because, by placing their reputations at risk, they are able to manage
conflicts of interest.

Conflicts of interest in pre-1933 investment banking were examined carefully in the 1990s,
as pressure mounted for a repeal of the Glass–Steagall Act. Kroszner and Rajan (1994) test
the "naïve investor" theory by examining the performance of affiliate-underwritten securities. They find that there were fewer defaults among affiliate-underwritten securities, which
mitigates against the hypothesis that these securities were of systematically lower quality.

Kroszner and Rajan also point to evidence about the pattern of securities issuance that
suggests strongly that investors were perfectly aware of the conflicts that their investment
banks faced. Precisely because they faced a potential conflict of interest, it was harder
for securities affiliates credibly to signal the quality of their issues to the ratings agencies.
Kroszner and Rajan support this assertion by showing that ratings were a less accurate predictor of default for affiliate-underwritten bonds than for those underwritten by specialist
investment banks. I argue above that conflicts of interest have fewer adverse consequences

---

[9] A year later, partners from Morgan and from Drexel founded the new firm of Morgan Stanley & Co.
as an investment bank. See Carosso (1970) for a discussion of the industry changes that the Act caused.

[10] For example, Macey (1984) argues that the Act was intended to protect investment bankers at the
expense of commercial bankers; Langevoort (1987) argues that Carter Glass believed that his bill would
encourage banks to channel money toward small companies, rather than into the securities markets.

within a bank that has significant reputational capital at stake. Hence, one would expect the informational problems to be particularly problematic for small affiliates with a lower reputational stake. A sophisticated investor should therefore be unwilling to buy complex and opaque securities that are underwritten by a small affiliate. Consistent with this argument, Kroszner and Rajan find first that affiliates in general underwrote larger issues where information asymmetry was less likely to be a problem, and second, that smaller affiliates underwrote more senior issues by less-risky firms than did larger affiliates.

Kroszner and Rajan's results suggest strongly that investors were too smart to be taken in by an affiliate pushing poor quality stock. Affiliates with less to lose could not underwrite informationally sensitive issues, and hence could not make as much from their securities business as competitors with more reputational capital. It is even possible that combining commercial with investment banking improved incentives, as commercial banks strove to build reputations which would allow them to enter the lucrative securities markets.

Ang and Richardson (1994) present evidence that is consistent with Kroszner and Rajan's. They find that bank affiliate issues had lower default rates, lower ex ante yields, and higher ex post prices than those issued by pure investment houses; moreover, they find that the relative ability of ex ante yields to predict ex post performance was no different for affiliate issues than for investment bank issues. Even issues underwritten by the National City Company and the Chase Securities Corporation, both of which were targets of the Pecora hearings, while of lesser quality than other bank affiliate issues, were no worse than those underwritten by the investment banks. Puri (1994) also presents evidence that pre-1933 bank underwritten issues defaulted less than non-bank underwritten issues.

In contrast to other papers written on this subject, Puri (1996) bases conclusions regarding the quality of affiliate issues on ex ante pricing, rather than on ex post default performance. She finds that pre-1933 investors paid higher prices for securities underwritten by banks than for those underwritten by securities houses. Puri argues that these results are indicative of a certification role for banks, which arose because banks had superior information about the firms to which they lent, and because they faced reputational risk.

In short, recent research suggests strongly that pre-1933 commercial banks in the United States did not use their securities affiliates to float securities that would repay their lowest quality loans. The Glass–Steagall Act rendered it impossible to perform precisely this type of research on contemporary US firms. However, Gompers and Lerner (1999) are able to come close, by examining the underpricing of initial public offerings (IPOs) brought to market between December 1972 and December 1992 by investment banks that held equity in the issuing firm via a venture capital subsidiary. Once again, they find no support for the "naïve investor" hypothesis; investors appear rationally to account for the quality of securities. IPOs underwritten by affiliated investment banks in their sample perform at least as well as those in which underwriters have no position. Investors demand a greater discount for investing in affiliated issues and, consistent with the evidence in Kroszner and Rajan (1994), investment bank-affiliated venture capital firms seem to invest in less information-sensitive issues.

Another opportunity to perform research on modern data was provided by a partial relaxation of the Glass–Steagall Act in 1987, under which some banks were allowed to set up subsidiaries ("Section 20 subsidiaries") to underwrite corporate securities. The subsidiaries were subject to firewalls that limited information flows, and they were limited in size: initially to 5% of the gross revenues of the parent bank, and ultimately to 25%. Gande et al.

(1997) examine the operations of Section 20 subsidiaries. Their findings are in line with all of the research cited above, in that they find no evidence of malfeasance. They control in their work for the use to which the proceeds of the issue are put. When the securities are issued for purposes other than debt repayment, spreads for sub-investment grade issues are 42 basis points lower than for investment houses; when the stated purpose is refinancing, the spreads are statistically indistinguishable. Moreover, and in contrast to some of the earlier papers cited, Gande et al. 1997 find that Section 20 subsidiaries tend to underwrite smaller issuers than investment houses. The evidence of this work is therefore that, if anything, the informational advantage of lending banks serves to attract investors, rather than to repel them: Puri (1999) presents a model along these lines, in which the information that commercial banks acquire through lending allows them to obtain better prices for securities. Gande, Puri, and Saunders (1999) find moreover that the entry of Section 20 subsidiaries lowered fees for security underwriting, particularly among lower-rated and smaller issues, where Section 20 subsidiaries were particularly active. Evidence largely consistent with the results of these papers is presented by Roten and Mullineaux (2002), who find that Section 20 subsidiaries charged lower fees than investment bank underwriters, who were able to capitalize upon their stronger reputational capital, but that there was no significant overall difference in yield spreads between the two types of underwriters.

More recent work by Focarelli, Marques-Ibanez, and Pozzolo (2011) examines outcomes, rather than initial yields, for securities underwritten immediately before Glass–Steagall was revoked, and draws differing conclusions. Focarelli, Marques-Ibanez, and Pozzolo find that securities underwritten by the Section 20 subsidiaries of commercial banks had higher default rates than those underwritten by investment houses. They conclude that, on the basis of their evidence, it is impossible to reject either the hypothesis that the repeal of Glass–Steagall led to weaker credit screening by universal banks attempting to gain market share, or that those banks had less ability to evaluate security riskiness.

Focarelli, Marques-Ibanez, and Pozzolo's results run against the bulk of research on US underwriting, which suggests first, that the market accounts for conflicts of interest when US banks underwrite securities; and second, that such conflicts are seldom a significant concern. There is little comparable evidence in other countries. However, a paper by Ber, Yafeh, and Yosha (2001) generates results for the modern Israeli market that are somewhat at variance with those for the United States of the 1930s. The Israeli banking industry is highly concentrated, and it is universal, with banks managing investment funds as well as controlling subsidiaries that specialize in underwriting. While most pre-Glass–Steagall data is for bond issues, Ber, Yafeh, and Yosha focus on straight equity issues. They find that the post-issue accounting performance of firms underwritten by their lender is significantly better than average. However, they find that the same firms exhibit negative stock excess returns in the first day and year after issuance, which suggests that these issues are systematically overpriced. If buyers are not naïve, we must look elsewhere for an explanation for this persistent mispricing. The authors suggest that it arises because the buyers are investment funds controlled by issuers. Hence, they argue that, at least in the Israeli market, the combination of bank lending, underwriting, and investment fund management in a single institution is potentially harmful.

The findings of Ber, Yafeh, and Yosha are worrisome. They suggest that, while managed funds are controlled by entirely rational agents, they are able to find and to exploit naïve retail investors; hence, financial infrastructure needs to be designed in order to ensure that fund managers' incentives are properly aligned with their investors. Arguably, then, the efficiency consequences of allowing universal banking in one economy could be different to those in another which has different institutional and legal features. While research into the pre-Glass–Steagall US economy helped to justify the repeal of the Banking Act, it should be applied to other economies with caution.

5.4. SCALE AND SCOPE IN TWENTY-FIRST-CENTURY BANKING

Gerschenkron's (1962) account of German industrialization emphasizes the importance of institutional context in explaining the emergence of universal banking in Germany. Specifically, as discussed above, Gerschenkron stresses the relative importance of human and financial capital in nineteenth-century Germany. Universal banking became an increasingly dominant model for financial services firms around the world in the last decade of the twentieth century. I argue in this section that an important driver of this phenomenon was a technological change that, *pace* Gerschenkron, increased the importance of financial relative to human capital in many financial firms.

The investment banking industry became increasingly reliant upon financial capital in the second half of the twentieth century. Morrison and Wilhelm (2008) report data for the US: on a CPI-adjusted basis (1983 dollars), the combined capitalization of the top ten investment banking firms rose at an increasing rate from $821 million in 1955 to $2,314 million in 1970, $6,349 million in 1980, $31,262 million in 1990 and $194,171 million in 2000. Over the same period the industry became increasingly concentrated, with the capitalization of the 11th to 25th largest investment banks as a proportion of that of the top ten dropping from 80% to 10%. Moreover, it appears that the importance of financial capital significantly increased relative to human capital over this period: while the average number of employees in the largest five banks quadrupled between 1979 and 2000, the mean capitalization per employee in these banks increased by a factor of more than 15. I will argue in this section that the imperative for universal banking at the end of the twentieth century was created by the same economic forces that increased both concentration and capitalization in the investment banking industry.

Starting from its origins in the nineteenth-century Atlantic trade, investment banks provided services over which it was very hard to contract: while clients may be able to distinguish a well-priced IPO from a poorly priced one, good advice from bad, or a well-executed security transaction from a botched deal, making this distinction stick in court is very hard. It is precisely for this reason that investment banks depended upon their reputations: because clients would pay a significant premium to a trustworthy bank, investment bankers would work hard to retain their reputations, so that a strong reputation could underpin agreements that were not enforceable under black-letter law. The need for a reputation created a substantial barrier to entry into the business, and, arguably, explained the very long-lived supernormal profits that the early investment bankers made.[11]

---

[11] De Long (1991) argues that the impossibility of matching J. P. Morgan's reputation gave the firm a strong competitive position in the nineteenth century. Morrison and Wilhelm (2007, chs 4–8) trace the evolution of the modern investment bank.

When investment bankers relied upon reputation to underpin tacit agreements with their counterparties, their business was inevitably based upon close relationships. Many of the skills that investment bankers needed were tacit: that is, they were best learned on-the-job, through a close mentoring relationship with a senior banker. Morrison and Wilhelm (2004) argue that partnership firms provide the strongest possible incentives to maintain these relationships, and hence the early investment banks were constituted as partnerships. While partnership status assisted in human capital formation, it limited the size and capitalization of investment banks (Morrison and Wilhelm, 2008).[12]

Starting in the early 1960s, a number of factors undermined the traditional structure of the investment banking firm. First, the advent of transistor-based mainframe computers in the early 1960s rendered cost-effective the overnight batch processing of the large-scale repetitive tasks associated with settlement. This type of processing was particularly valuable to "retail" firms such as Merrill Lynch, which performed high volumes of small-value transactions. Mainframe computing was extremely costly, but retail firms that failed to adopt it found it impossible to cope with a massive increase in trading volumes at the end of the decade: they ultimately failed, or were absorbed by larger institutions (see Morrison and Wilhelm, 2007, pp. 235–238). The retail firms acquired the capital needed to acquire mainframe computers by floating in the early 1970s (see Morrison and Wilhelm, 2008).

Further advances in information technology were more applicable to investment banks that specialized in wholesale business and, ultimately, to universal banks. The cost of computing started to plummet in the late 1970s as microcomputers found their way into banks and allowed traders and relationship managers to interrogate databases and to perform complex pricing calculations in real time. For example, the ability rapidly to create spreadsheet-based financial models revolutionized the operation of the LBO market, and made it far easier to price new offerings. At the same time, advances in financial economic theory were transforming the financial market place. The Black–Scholes–Merton framework for financial options valuation became a practical tool rather than an academic exercise when it could be implemented with a desktop computer; risk management practices could be hard-coded into computers, rather than based upon judgment and recruitment practices; trading and hedging strategies could be driven by computer algorithms rather than by humans.[13]

Unlike mainframe computers, microcomputers were cheap and they substituted for a great deal of human expertise. One might expect them to lower the minimum scale at which investment banks could operate. Indeed, Rajan (1996) makes this point, arguing that there is no a priori reason to assume that better information technology should increase the optimal scale of a bank. But better information technology not only automated tasks that previously were the province of the human expert; it also changed the nature of investment banking skill. Activities that could be expressed in the formal language of financial economics could be taught in a classroom. Trading results that could be captured with computers and analyzed using portfolio theory could be contracted upon. As a result, businesses that previously were the preserve of a few specialists operating in businesses with reserves of human capital and reputation started to be open to any firm that could hire a smart financial engineer. Precisely because information technology and the codification of skills combined

---

[12] The reason for this is twofold: first, partnership capital is provided by the partners, who have limited resources; and second, the number of partners is limited by a free-rider problem amongst partners.

[13] Morrison and Wilhelm (2007, pp. 238–249) discuss the phenomena outlined in this paragraph.

to render market entry easy for any firm, large or small, financial markets became extremely competitive. In the end, it was because the financial markets had become so contestable by small firms that they could no longer sustain small-scale trade: bid-ask spreads narrowed to such an extent that participation in the markets became cost-effective only for firms that could operate at a large scale. The consequence was the massive increase in investment bank capitalization and concentration that I highlighted in the opening paragraph of this section.[14]

In short, distributed microcomputers and advances in financial economics lowered the value of tacit skill relative to technical, codifiable skill in many investment banking activities. It also facilitated entry, and hence lowered the minimum scale at which these activities were economically viable. Morrison and Wilhelm (2008) argue that these effects combined to cause the demise of the traditional investment banking partnership. They also opened the door to commercial bank entry into investment banking. Commercial banks had greater reserves of capital than the investment banks. Where they were legally allowed to underwrite, they could bundle their services with lending business in a way that investment banks could not. Particularly when underwriting bond issues, whose prices are most susceptible to codification, commercial banks therefore had advantages that were denied to investment banks. Similarly, commercial banks were playing to their strengths when they invested in derivatives trading partnerships in the late 1980s: derivatives trading was a technical, computer-oriented activity that required capital on a huge scale.[15]

Gerschenkron argued in the 1960s that "economically backward" economies relied for development upon codified knowledge that was embedded in large-scale and capital-intensive production technologies; it was for this reason that he believed that universal banking was common in economies that historically had developed from a backward state. The arguments of this section suggest that something similar is afoot in the modern banking sector, where production techniques have been revolutionized by new computer-based technologies that formalize many formerly tacit skills. As in Gerschenkron's work, the new technologies require very high levels of capital investment, which arise in this case because they generate competitive pressures that significantly raise the minimum operating scale in banking. The commercial pressures for universal banking seem unsurprising in the light of this argument; the steady erosion of the Glass–Steagall Act, which started in 1986 with the Fed's approval of an application by Banker's Trust to underwrite commercial paper, was perhaps inevitable.

The immense scale and scope of the modern universal bank does not come without challenges, however. It may be very hard for an institution to run large-scale codified businesses side-by-side with those that rely upon more traditional tacit skills. When universal banks build systems and procedures around "hard" codifiable information that can be fed into a computer, their decision making becomes increasingly remote from the loan officers who forge relationships with their customers. As a result it becomes hard for them to accommodate lending

---

[14] This argument is given in greater detail, and with more supporting statistics, in Morrison and Wilhelm (2008).

[15] The most prominent derivatives trading partnerships were O'Connor, CRT, and Cooper Neff, which were acquired by Swiss Bank, Nations Bank and BNP respectively: see Morrison and Wilhelm (2007, p. 279).

based upon "soft" relationship-based information that cannot easily be computerized. Stein (2002) argues that, as a result, loan officers in banks that rely upon formal systems to make decisions may be less inclined to gather information at all. Berger et al. (2005) find evidence consistent with Stein's hypothesis, stating that "large banks are less willing to lend to informationally 'difficult' credits, such as firms with no financial records." Of course, whether or not information is hard is to some extent a decision variable: Petersen (2004) argues that ratings agencies emerged in the nineteenth century as ways of hardening previously soft information about borrowers. But there are presumably limits to this process, and it may prove difficult in general to reconcile small-scale relationship lending with the needs of the universal bank.

5.5. Universal Banks and Economic Efficiency: The Repeal of the Glass–Steagall Act

The technological developments of the preceding section generated competitive pressure for the adoption of universal banking around the world. The second Banking Co-ordination Directive of 1989 made universal banking the norm in the European Union by introducing a single banking license valid throughout the EU, and limiting product mix restrictions to those imposed by home regulators.[16] After the passage of the Co-ordination Directive, European banks responded to the changing technological environment through a steady process of financial conglomeration.[17] The technological imperative for conglomeration was recognized in the United States when the Federal Reserve Board approved the 1998 merger of Citicorp and Travellers. This approval was rapidly followed by the passage in November 1999 of the Gramm–Leach–Bliley Act, which dismantled the barriers to universal banking that had been erected in the United States by the Glass–Steagall Act.

The Gramm–Leach–Bliley Act could be passed, and universal banking could be introduced to the United States, only when two concerns had been assuaged. First, legislators had to be convinced that universal banking would improve resource allocation. In particular, the conflicts of interest that motivated the passage of the Glass–Steagall Act had to be addressed. Second, regulators and legislators had to be convinced that universal banking would not create new systemic risks that threatened the stability and efficiency of the financial sector. I discuss these points in turn below.

5.5.1. Conflicts of Interest and Efficiency

As discussed above, a growing body of research in the 1990s suggested that the deleterious consequences of the conflicts of interest facing universal banks may have been more

[16] See Berger, De Young, and Udell (2001) for a discussion of this directive, and of the consolidation of financial services in the European Union.
[17] See Lown et al. (2000) for a survey.

perceived than real. Indeed, a more recent body of evidence suggests that universal banks enhance efficiency. For example, Barth, Brumbaugh, and Wilcox (2000) point to technological advances that open new economies of scope in large banks. Berger et al. (2000) discuss economies of scale: universal institutions can share offices, computers, information systems, investment departments, account service centers, or other operations; they can economize on the fixed costs of raising capital, and they can re-use information about a client in several business lines.[18] On the other hand, like any other organization, universal banks may experience diseconomies of scale (see Winton, 1999, for a model incorporating this effect): the extent to which universal banks can realize economies of scale and scope is of course an empirical question.

Gorton and Schmid (2000) use data from 1975 to 1985 to examine the consequences of universal banking for the real economy in Germany. They account for control rights, voting restrictions, and the effects of co-determination.[19] They find that banks affect firm performance beyond the effect they would have as non-banks, and that the concentration of control rights in banks improves firm performance. A number of authors have suggested that introducing universal banking into other countries would bring benefits that mirrored the German experience. Indeed, in an analysis of 60 countries, Barth, Caprio, and Levine (1999) find that restricting securities activities reduces bank efficiency and raises the likelihood of a banking crisis. Their data contains no evidence that restricting financial firms assists financial development, or that it increases industrial competition.

Specifically European evidence on scope economies is mixed. Allen and Rai (1996) and Vander Vennet (1999) find only limited evidence of scope economies in European universal banks; Cyberto-Ottone and Murgia (2000) find evidence that scope-expanding mergers in European banking markets increase shareholder wealth; and Rime and Stiroh (2003) find no evidence to suggest that any efficiency benefits are being derived from the trend toward universal banking in Switzerland. Nevertheless, the main thrust of an expanding literature on share price effects appears supportive of the hypothesis that universal banking makes investors richer. Using 1998–2002 data on 836 banks from 43 different countries, Laeven and Levine (2007) find evidence of a diversification discount in financial conglomerates. But van Lelyveld and Knot (2009) note that Laeven and Levine are concerned with diversification within traditional banking businesses; Lelyveld and Knot find no consistent evidence of a diversification discount in universal banks that perform banking and insurance. Similarly, Schmid and Walter (2009) find a diversification discount in businesses that perform lending and securities trading, but identify a significant diversification premium between commercial banking and insurance, and between commercial banking and investment banking. Elsas, Hackethal, and Holzhäuser (2010) also find evidence of a conglomerate premium in banking. They examine the source of the premium, and find that it derives from higher margins in non-interest business.

Of course, the revenue effects that Elsas, Hackethal, and Holzhäuser identify need not be evidence of efficiencies. They could equally derive from an abuse of market power, which allows investment banks to extract more surplus from their clients. In line with this hypothesis, Fang, Ivanisha, and Lerner (2013) find that bank-affiliated private equity groups do

[18] For related discussions, see Milbourn, Boot, and Thakor (1999) and Dierick (2004).
[19] Co-determination gives German workers a right of representation on the Board of all but the very smallest companies. Gorton and Schmid find that it worsens firm performance.

not make superior equity investments, but derive superior returns from expansion to take advantage of cross-selling opportunities during credit booms. More generally, policymakers have expressed concern that universal banking may result in more "tying": that is, in selling one product, such as a commercial loan, conditional upon the sale of another, such as a security underwriting. For example, in 2002 US congressman John Dingell wrote an open letter to Alan Greenspan, then chairman of the Federal Reserve system, suggesting that financial institutions were using loans as "loss leaders" to attract more profitable investment banking business. This strategy is illegal under Sections 23A and 23B of the Federal Reserve Act, but it is hard to prove, and the Association for Financial Professionals (2004, p. 2) states that "Financial professionals continue to report that commercial banks frequently make access to credit contingent upon the purchase of other financial services, despite assertions by regulatory bodies to the contrary."

Even if tying occurs, it is not obvious that it is damaging. Lóránth and Morrison (2012) argue that tying may serve to alleviate credit rationing, because the returns from cross-selling ensure banks of an adequate share of the social surplus that their lending generates. Supportive evidence is presented by Ferreira and Matos (2012), who note that banks are more likely to act as lead arrangers in loans when they exert some control, either through board representation or by holding shares. Such links improve the profitability of the relationship, as witnessed in Ferreira and Matos' work by higher lending spreads throughout the 2003–2006 credit boom and, hence, in a greater willingness to lend when credit conditions are tight, which manifests itself in Ferreira and Matos' data through reduced credit spreads through the 2007–2008 financial crisis. Moreover, Neuhann and Saidi (2012) report a total factor productivity improvement of 9% for firms funded by universal banks; this effect is particularly pronounced when there is a close relationship with cross-selling.

The evidence of this subsection indicates strong evidence that universal banking is efficiency enhancing, at least at the level of the individual borrower. Financial markets appear rationally to discount conflicts of interest within universal banks. Hence, as Kanatas and Qi (1998) argue, borrowers will choose to deal with universal banks only if the costs of conflict are outweighed by the scope economies that the universal banks can realize. Only if universal banking generates an unpriced social cost is there a case for restricting it. Kanatas and Qi suggest that this cost might arise because conflicts of interest give rise to a soft budget constraint: they argue that, because borrowers from a universal bank anticipate that they will be bailed out via a stock issue in the event of poor performance, they choose lower quality investments. However, the empirical evidence reviewed in the previous section suggests that, in fact, ex post conflicts are relatively small. In advanced economies, one can arguably deal with other potential problems, such as anti-competitive behavior and abuse of the deposit insurance safety net, through careful regulation.

5.5.2. Systemic Effects

I argue in Subsection 5.5.1 that recent evidence indicates that, considered at the level of the individual firm, universal banking can enhance the efficiency of the financial sector. But it is nevertheless possible that an economy-wide shift toward universal banking comes at a cost, in the shape of heightened systemic fragility. In this subsection I discuss the systemic risks associated with universal banks.

One concern is that, because universal banks are large and operate across a range of markets and products, they may suppress competing institutions and markets. Rajan (1996) argues that good regulation can probably counteract this effect, but, in developing countries with less-advanced regulatory systems, he argues that the concentration of financial power in a few universal banks could act as a brake on economic activity. As discussed above, Gerschenkron made a similar point, identifying a tendency in late nineteenth- and early twentieth-century banks to suppress competition in the real sector of the economy. Unlike Rajan, of course, Gerschenkron argued that universal banks aided development, and hence that the danger of anti-competitive behavior was worth accepting. In any case, Benston (1994) argues that modern universal banks serve such a broad constituency that they are unlikely to favor one interest group over another, and hence that they are less likely to be a source of damaging rent-seeking than more specialized institutions.

Boot and Thakor (1997) identify another competitive effect. They argue that borrowers choose between bank and market finance by weighing up the relative benefits of bank monitoring, which attenuates moral hazard and more informative price signals, which facilitate efficient resource allocation. Financial innovations that increase price informativeness result in a shift from bank to market finance. These innovations raise welfare, but their effect within a universal bank is to transfer revenues from one part of the business to another. Hence, Boot and Thakor argue that the incentive to innovate in a universal bank is lower than in an investment bank, which can hope to attract new customers by innovating.

Another systemic concern relates not to competitive effects, but to stability. Legislators and regulators were concerned before the passage of the Gramm–Leach–Bliley Act that large universal banks would prove too central to the operation of the economy to be allowed to fail, so that a moral hazard problem would arise between bank shareholders, who stand to gain from taking too much underpriced risk, and regulators, who use taxpayer funds to pick up the costs of excessive risk-taking.

The danger that some banks might be treated as too-big-to-fail was reflected in market prices after the Comptroller of the Currency acknowledged in testimony to Congress that 11 of the largest US national banks could expect to receive the sort of $1 billion bailout extended in 1984 to the insolvent Continental Illinois Bank: Avery, Belton, and Goldberg (1988) show that subsequently, bank bond spreads were barely related to ratings, and Boyd and Gertler (1993) find that large banks took on bigger risks than smaller commercial banks.

Legislators responded to the too-big-to-fail (TBTF) problem by attempting to improve regulation. The Federal Deposit Insurance Corporation Insurance Act (FDICIA) of 1991 was landmark legislation partly intended to address the TBTF problem. It requires regulators to take prompt corrective action against distressed banks, and places checks and balances upon the decision to declare a bank too-big-to-fail. Stern and Feldman (2004) argue that FDICIA did little to resolve the too-big-to-fail problem, claiming that regulators still have the incentive and the ability to bail out insolvent banks.

Even prior to the financial crisis, some evidence indicated that the FDICIA did not entirely resolve the TBTF problem: Morgan and Stiroh (2005) find that the spread-rating relationship for banks identified in the mid-1980s as too-big-to-fail was little changed by FDICIA, although they find more sensitivity than did Avery, Belton, and Goldberg, and Brewer and Jagtiani (2007) show that banks are prepared to pay a premium for acquisitions that will push them over perceived too-big-to-fail boundaries. Nevertheless, there was some cause to be optimistic. Mishkin (2006) argues in an essay reviewing Stern and Feldman's book that the weight of evidence does not support their assertion: Ennis and Malek (2005) find no evidence in the wake of FDICIA of the excessive risk-taking documented in large banks by Boyd and Gertler (1993), and Flannery and Sorescu (1996) find stronger market discipline in the subordinated debt market for banks in the post-FDICIA period. Hence, even if large universal banks are systematically so important that the regulator cannot credibly commit to deny them access to the government safety net, many academics were prepared prior to the financial crisis to make a case that the concomitant incentive problems could be addressed by well-designed regulatory institutions. Mishkin (1999) adopts this position, arguing that universal banking should be accompanied by greater regulatory vigilance, coupled with some constructive ambiguity regarding bailout policy.

The TBTF problem is related to the discussion on increasing scale in banking for two reasons. First, regulators have increasingly to deal with the distortionary impact of a de facto TBTF policy as banks expand in respond to technological factors; I have already presented pre-crisis evidence that regulation has been only partially successful in this respect. Second, to the extent that a TBTF problem renders bank investors less sensitive to risk, bankers face a strong incentive to expand beyond their efficient scale in pursuit of TBTF status.

The evidence on this latter point is hard to interpret. Early work on bank size suggested that the efficient scale for a bank was no more than $25 billion (Berger and Mester, 1997). But this research occurred before the internet transformed the financial services industry: DeYoung (2005) suggests that this transformation may significantly have increased bank efficient scale. Recent work identifies economies of scale in very large banks: these are partly attributable to new technology, and are in part effects uncovered by new econometric techniques. For example, Hughes and Mester (2013) find that, after accounting for the endogenous risk-taking incentives in diversified financial conglomerates,[20] very large banks generate economies of scale that are not driven by their TBTF status. Wheelock and Wilson (2011) show that credit unions operate on increasing returns to scale, and argue that this effect has strengthened as the unions have adopted new information technology, and they show in later work (Wheelock and Wilson, 2012) that, as recently as 2006, most US banks faced increasing returns to scale.

Hence, recent evidence indicates that even very large banks may achieve economies of scale. Furthermore, they may even fail to internalize some of the social benefits of scale: DeYoung and Jiang (2013) present evidence suggesting that, while product-specific economies of scale are exhausted fairly quickly in lending and deposit-taking, very large banks that combine these activities nevertheless experience significant economies of scale in the socially important production of macro economy-wide liquidity. But this evidence merely points to some of the benefits of large-scale banking. It does not demonstrate that banks are not TBTF, nor does it disprove the hypothesis that the TBTF problem generates serious resource misallocation. That banks have become very much larger in recent years[21] could be evidence of both scale efficiencies and a TBTF problem: indeed, Hughes and Mester's (2013) work appears to suggest that the two effects roughly cancel each other out.

---

[20] These incentives are modeled in a paper by Freixas, Lóránth, and Morrison (2007), which I discuss below.

[21] This expansion is documented in the US by DeYoung (2010), and in Europe by Goddard, Molyneux and Wilson (2010).

The TBTF problem results in underpriced risk and so results in a socially excessive share-holder risk appetite. A similar effect, specific to universal banks, arises when the securities arm of a universal bank is able to access the deposit insurance safety net provided to the commercial banking arm. Precisely as with the TBTF effect, the consequence of such an extension of deposit insurance cover is underpriced debt and, hence, excessive risk-taking. Furthermore, as Boyd, Chang, and Smith (1998) note, banks that hold equity stakes in their borrowers have strong incentives to take advantage of the deposit insurance safety net. On the other hand, because a universal bank is more diversified, it may be better able to with-stand financial shocks and, hence, may be less likely to call upon the deposit insurance fund.

A number of academic studies prior to the 2008–2009 financial crisis argued that the above tradeoff resolved itself in favor of financial stability. For example, Benston (1994) argues that there is no evidence that universal banks are more risky than focused banks. Cornett, Ors, and Tehranian (2002) support Benston's assertion, finding that bank riskiness around the introduction of a Section 20 subsidiary does not change. Mälkönen (2004) and Allen and Jagtiani (2000) both perform simulations using portfolios of commercial bank loans and insurance company investments, and show that combining the two generates inter-divisional diversification. This work is however subject to a Lucas-style critique: Freixas, Lóránth, and Morrison (2007) show that the non-bank divisions of financial conglomerates could take more risk in order to profit from the deposit insurance put option than they would have done as standalone firms. Whether or not the diversification effect outweighs the enhanced risk-shifting incentive is context specific. With the appropriate capital adequacy policy, Freixas, Lóránth, and Morrison demonstrate that optimal regulation forces the deposit-taking and non-deposit-taking arms of the bank to maintain separate balance sheets: although this reduces diversification opportunities, it enhances market discipline sufficiently to compen-sate. I discuss practical moves toward this type of regulation in the next section.

The experience of the 2008–2009 financial crisis suggests that, at least in extreme market conditions, diversification effects do not outweigh risk-taking incentives. Wilmarth (2009) notes that 17 large universal banks accounted for more than half of the $1.1 trillion of losses reported by the world's banks and insurance companies.[22] He argues that the source of these problems were an originate-to-distribute strategy in the large banks, which fueled a credit boom whose effects were further exacerbated by the speculative activities of the same institutions.

Of course, one cannot consider universal banks outside of their institutional con-text. Deutsche Bank was one of Wilmarth's large universal banks, and emerged relatively unscathed from the financial crisis. Indeed, the only German universal bank to experience severe problems was Commerzbank, which has now almost repaid the government support it received. Dietrich and Vollmer (2012) present some evidence that Germany's economic crisis was not caused by universal banks, which, they argue, served in Germany to reduce financial fragility and to dampen the macroeconomic consequences of the crisis. Hence, to the extent that universal bank effects contributed to the crisis, they may have done so as part of a broader institutional and legal story.

Universal banks are highly complex. One way in which this complexity could manifest itself is by opening new channels for financial contagion, through which instability could be

---

[22] Wilmarth's classifies the following firms as universal banks: Bank of America, Chase, Citigroup, Wachovia, Bear Stearns, Goldman Sachs, Lehman Brothers, Merrill Lynch, Morgan Stanley, Credit Suisse, Deutsche Bank, Barclays, RBS, HSBC, BNP Paribas, Société Générale, and AIG.

transmitted between banks and other financial institutions, for example in the insurance market. This contagion channel was laid bare by the 2008 failure of American International Group (AIG), a firm that, prior to the crisis, comprised approximately 70 US insurance companies and 175 non-US companies and insurers doing business in 130 countries.[23] AIG derived 4.5% of its revenues through financial services, including consumer finance, aircraft leasing, and the activities of its subsidiary AIG Financial Products (AIGFP). AIGFP was a major seller of default protection in the credit default swap market, and so exposed AIG to risks that were traditionally confined to the banking market. Those risks caused it to fail, and the firm received more than $182 billion of assistance from the US federal government (Harrington, 2009, p. 795).

The crisis experience highlighted the danger of financial contagion within universal banks. But evidence on this type of contagion prior to the financial crisis was rather mixed. In work that to some extent anticipated Kroszner and Rajan, White (1986) finds no evidence of greater instability in universal institutions at the start of the 1930s: while 26.3% of national banks failed between 1930 and 1933, only 6.5% of the 63 banks that had security affiliates in 1929 and 7.6% of the 145 banks with large-scale bond operations failed. Logit regressions on White's data confirm that the presence of a security affiliate reduced the probability of a bank failure. Colvin (2007) argues that the Netherlands experienced in the 1920s its only traditional banking crisis since 1600; he presents evidence that the relatively large difficulties that the Rotterdamsche Bankvereeniging experienced relative to its rival Amsterdamsche Bank were attributable to its universal status. Franke and Hudson (1984) find no evidence that universal banks were behind any of the major twentieth-century financial crises to affect West Germany. Canals (1997) cites Cuervo (1988) on the effect of the European recessions of the late 1970s and early 1990s upon Spanish banks. In both cases, the banks that experienced the biggest losses were universal banks with major stakes in the industrial sector.

In short, then, the evidence prior to 2008 indicated that universal banks had advantages in managing individual client relationships, and that the systemic risks associated with universal banking could be contained through appropriate regulation. The crisis suggested that, in fact, universal banks could be a significant source of financial fragility. They were frequently perceived as TBTF, they were widely believed to extend the deposit insurance net beyond the retail deposit business for which it was intended, and they appeared to serve as a source of financial contagion.[24] The consequence was intense political pressure for regulatory reform, whose effects are still playing out at the time of writing.

5.6. STRUCTURAL REGULATION OF UNIVERSAL BANKS

Very early in the financial crisis commentators started discussing the challenges of universal bank regulation, and suggesting in particular that financial stability would be best served

---

[23] For a detailed discussion of AIG and of its failure during the crisis, see Harrington (2009).

[24] For example, Wilmarth (2008) discusses early signs of deposit insurance creep, and Martin Wolf (2011), a member of the UK's Independent Commission on Banking, identifies "rogue universal banks" as "the biggest danger of all."

by a separation of deposit-taking from other financial businesses.[25] In an early regulatory response to the financial crisis, Adair Turner of the Financial Services Authority acknowledged the "theoretical clarity" of this idea, but noted that this would be a hard policy to pursue without international coordination and that, further, there are good economic reasons to allow commercial banks to participate in securities markets (Turner Review, 2009, p. 95). Other policymakers pushed the notion of separation of retail from non-retail banking harder: most notably, Paul Volcker, former Chairman of the US Federal Reserve, chaired a G-30 working group which suggested that deposit-taking banks should be prohibited from proprietary trading (Group of Thirty, 2009), a proposal frequently identified as the "Volcker Rule."

Regulators around the world appear increasingly to believe that retail and risky (or "casino") banking should be separated. The Volcker Rule entered the US statute books as Section 619 of the Dodd–Frank Wall Street Reform and Consumer Protection Act (2010). It prohibits deposit-funded, licensed commercial banks in the United States, or bank holding companies with US affiliates from proprietary trading, or investing in or sponsoring hedge funds and private equity funds.[26] In the United Kingdom, the Vickers Report (2011) of the Independent Commission on Banking requires banking groups headquartered in the UK to "ring-fence" retail and small business deposits and overdrafts from investment banking operations, such as derivatives trading, debt and equity underwriting, and securities trading. And the European Community's Liikanen Report (2012) recommends the mandatory separation of proprietary trading, along with tighter capital requirements on trading and real estate assets and some changes to the corporate governance of banks.[27]

But the implementation of these recommendations is proving far from trivial. The Volcker Rule cannot be enacted until the relevant administrative agencies write a detailed rule. The scale of this task appears massive. Regulators are struggling to agree definitions of apparently simple terms like "market making", and, according to press comment, the process is further complicated by political fighting between the agencies concerned. The first draft of the rule was published in October 2011; it was 280 pages long, and sought comment on more than 380 questions. It sparked disagreement over the definitions of "hedge funds" and "private equity funds." At the time of writing US regulators say that they may be able to write a rule to implement the Volcker Rule be the end of 2013; the finished rule could be as much as 900 pages long. Implementation is likely to occur in July 2014. It is hard to see

---

[25] For example, both Will Hutton and Jon Moulton argued in evidence to the UK's House of Commons Treasury Select Committee on January 13, 2009 that the repeal of Glass–Steagall fanned the flames of the credit boom and, ultimately, that it was a contributing factor to the credit crunch. Geoffrey Wood made a similar point in evidence to the House of Lords Economic Affairs Committee on January 20, 2009, stating that complexity allows for rapid bank failure, which in turn creates systemic problems. John Kay (2009) argued in a widely cited report that the adoption of narrow banking would allow the state to commit not to rescue non-deposit-taking institutions, and so restore market discipline to their activities. Pennacchi (2012) surveys theory and evidence relating to narrow banks, and concludes that a properly designed system of mandatory narrow banking would reduce moral hazard, without losing any of the traditional benefits associated with traditional full-service banking.

[26] There are a number of exemptions, relating to certain US government, or government-sponsored securities, to market making, hedging, and agency trading.

[27] For a survey of the Volcker Rule and the Vickers and Liikanen Reports, see Gambacorta and van Rixtel (2013).

how it could be trouble-free: there will most likely be further debate, in and out of court.[28] The Liikanen Report is intended to serve as the basis of future EU directives. A consultation process is under way to determine the extent of the separation of business (see for example European Commission, 2013); precisely how the definitional questions that have plagued the US implementation process will be resolved has yet to be determined. The UK government has adopted the recommendations of the Vickers Report and, at the time of writing, they are being enacted as the Financial Services (Banking Reform) Bill 2014. UK banks will have until 2019 to implement the Vickers ring-fence; precisely how this requirement will be affected by any EU directives has yet to be spelled out.

In summary, the 2008–2009 financial crisis presented apparently strong evidence that large universal banks could generate severe too-big-to-fail problems, that they could introduce new deposit insurance-related moral hazard problems, and that they might open new channels for contagion. Legislators have responded by attempting to separate traditional retail and commercial banking from market-based trading and securities market activities. The changes do not constitute a fresh Glass–Steagall Act, as commercial banks are prohibited from speculative trading rather than from underwriting.[29]

It is too early to say whether the regulatory changes will be effective. The crisis certainly highlighted problems in large and complex universal banks. But many failed institutions were specialist retail finance firms operating in the mortgage market, and in some cases it proved necessary to extend support to firms operating in non-retail finance. We have early indications from the US of the enormous regulatory challenge of writing rules intended to restrict bank activities and, in the longer run, there is a danger that those rules will become the focus of regulatory arbitrage. There is clearly scope for further research in this area.

5.7. CONCLUSION

Historically, universal banking was common in some economies, but not in others. Gerschenkron (1962) argued that this variation could be explained with reference to the way in which development occurred: economies that had to play "catch-up" did so by adopting technologies on a broad front that could compensate for the lack of a deep human capital pool, and the institution that collected and directed capital into these technologies was the universal bank.

Notwithstanding the success of universal banking, it was regarded with suspicion in the United States for much of the twentieth century, where it was outlawed by the 1933 Banking Act. Toward the end of the century an increasing body of evidence suggested that this suspicion was largely misplaced. Moreover, commercial pressures were for large, complex financial intermediaries that offered services that encompassed security market

[28] For a summary of the rule making process for the Volcker Rule, see for example Patterson and Solomon (2013).
[29] Although Senators John McCain and Elizabeth Warren have tabled legislation in the US that attempts to reintroduce a version of the Glass–Steagall Act. See "Split the Banks," *Financial Times* Comment section, July 12, 2013.

business as well as traditional commercial banking. I have argued that these pressures contained an echo of the forces studied by Gerschenkron: simultaneous advances in information technology and financial economies codified traditional knowledge and created massive pressure for scale. These pressures resulted ultimately in the 1999 repeal of the Banking Act.

Today's universal banks exist against an institutional backdrop that is significantly different to the one that was obtained when the Banking Act was passed. In particular, most developed economies provide retail depositors with insurance against bank default, and it is today appreciated that large banks are unlikely to be allowed to fail completely. These facts were thrown into sharp relief by the financial crisis of 2008–2009, and they have inspired a raft of regulatory measures that seem likely to alter the universal banking model by preventing retail banks from assuming significant speculative position risk, either through straightforward prohibition or by ring-fencing part of the bank's operations. The long-term effects of these regulations are hard to predict. They run up against serious codification problems, and may ultimately be the focus of regulatory arbitrage. The future universal bank may be simpler, but its supervision is likely to remain very complex.

References

Allen, L. and Jagtiani, J. (2000). The Risk Effects of Combining Banking, Securities, and Insurance Activities, *Journal of Economics and Business* 52, 485–497.

Allen, L. and Rai, A. (1996). Operational Efficiency in Banking: An International Comparison, *Journal of Banking and Finance* 20, 655–672.

Ang, J. S. and Richardson, T. (1994). The Underwriting Experience of Commercial Bank Affiliates Prior to the Glass-Steagall Act: A Re-Examination of Evidence of Passage of the Act, *Journal of Banking and Finance* 18, 351–395.

Association for Financial Professionals (2004). Credit Access Survey: Linking Corporate Credit to the Awarding of Other Financial Services.

Avery, R., Belton, T., and Goldberg, M. (1988). Market Discipline in Regulating Bank Risk: New Evidence from the Capital Markets, *Journal of Money, Credit, and Banking* 3, 597–619.

Barth, J. R., Brumbaugh Jr., R. D., and Wilcox, J. A. (2000). The Repeal of Glass-Steagall and the Advent of Broad Banking, *Journal of Economic Perspectives* 14, 191–204.

Barth, J. R., Caprio Jr., G., and Levine, R. (1999). *Banking Systems Around the Globe: Do Regulation and Ownership Affect Performance and Stability?*, World Bank, Washington, DC Policy Research Working Paper No. 2325.

Becker, G. S. (1964). *Human Capital: A Theoretical and Empirical Analysis, with Special Reference to Education*. Chicago: University of Chicago Press.

Benston, G. J. (1994). Universal Banking, *Journal of Economic Perspectives* 8, 121–143.

Ber, H., Yafeh, Y., and Yosha, O. (2001). Conflict of Interest in Universal Banking: Bank Lending, Stock Underwriting, and Fund Management, *Journal of Monetary Economics* 47, 189–218.

Berger, A. N. and Mester, L. J. (1997). Inside the Black Box: What Explains Differences in the Efficiencies of Financial Institutions?, *Journal of Banking and Finance* 21, 895–947.

Berger, A. N., De Young, R., Genay, H., and Udell, G. F. (2000). Globalization of Financial Institutions: Evidence from Cross-Border Banking Performance, *Brookings-Wharton Papers on Financial Services* 3, 23–125.

Berger, A. N., De Young, R., and Udell, G. F. (2001). Efficiency Barriers to the Consolidation of the European Financial Services Industry, *European Financial Management* 7, 117–130.

Berger, A. N., Miller, N. H., Petersen, M. A., Rajan, R. G., and Stein, J. C. (2005). Does Function Follow Organizational Form? Evidence from the Lending Practices of Large and Small Banks, *Journal of Financial Economics* 76, 237–269.

Boot, A. W. A. and Thakor, A. V. (1997). Banking Scope and Financial Innovation, *Review of Financial Studies* 10, 1099–1131.

Boyd, J. H., Chang, C., and Smith, B. D. (1998). Moral Hazard Under Commercial and Universal Banking, *Journal of Money, Credit and Banking* 30, 426–468.

Boyd, J. H. and Gertler, M. (1993). U.S Commercial Banking: Trends, Cycles, and Policy. In: O. J. Blanchard and S. Fisher (Eds.), *NBER Macroeconomics Annual 1993*. Cambridge, MA: MIT Press.

Brewer, III, E. and Jagtiani, J. (2007). *How Much Would Banks be Willing to Pay to Become "Too-Big-to-Fail" and to Capture Other Benefits?*, Federal Reserve Bank of Kansas City Research Working Paper No. 07–05.

Calomiris, C. W. (1993). Corporate Finance Benefits from Universal Banking: Germany and the United States, 1870–1914, NBER, Cambridge, MA Working Paper No. 4408.

Calomiris, C. W. (1995). Universal Banking and the Financing of Industrial Development, World Bank, Washington, DC Policy Research Working Paper No. 1533.

Canals, J. (1997). *Universal Banking: International Comparisons and Theoretical Perspectives.* New York, NY: Oxford University Press.

Carosso, V. P. (1970). *Investment Banking in America: A History.* Cambridge, MA: Harvard University Press.

Chandler, A. D. (1990). *Scale and Scope; The Dynamics of Industrial Capitalism.* Cambridge, MA: Harvard University Press.

Colvin, C. L. (2007). Universal Banking Failure? An Analysis of the Contrasting Responses of the Amsterdamsche Bank and the Rotterdamsche Bank to the Dutch Financial Crisis of the 1920s, London School of Economics Economic History Working Paper No. 98.

Cornett, M. M., Ors, E., and Tehranian, H. (2002). Bank Performance around the Introduction of a Section 20 Subsidiary, *Journal of Finance* 57, 501–521.

Cuervo, Á. (1988). *La Crisis Bancaria en Espana, 1977-1985.* Barcelona: Ariel.

Cyberto-Ottone, A. and Murgia, M. (2000). Mergers and Shareholder Wealth in European Banking, *Journal of Banking and Finance* 24, 831–859.

De Long, J. B. (1991). Did J. P. Morgan's Men Add Value? An Economist's Perspective on Financial Capitalism. In: P. Temin (Ed.), *Inside the Business Enterprise: Historical Perspectives on the Use of Information.* Chicago, IL: University of Chicago Press.

DeYoung, R. (2005). The Performance of Internet-Based Business Models: Evidence from the Banking Industry, *Journal of Business* 78, 893–947.

DeYoung, R. (2010). Banking in the United States. In: A. N. Berger, P. Molyneux, and J.O. S. Wilson (Eds.), *Oxford Handbook of Banking*, 777–806. Oxford: Oxford University Press.

DeYoung, R. and Jiang, C. (2013). Economies of Scale and the Economic Role of Banks. University of Kansas: Mimeo.

Dierick, F. (2004). The Supervision of Mixed Financial Services Groups in Europe, Frankfurt European Central Bank Occasional Paper No. 20.

Dietrich, D. and Vollmer, U. (2012). Are Universal Banks Bad for Financial Stability? Germany during the World Financial Crisis, *Quarterly Review of Economics and Finance* 52, 123–134.

Edwards, J. and Ogilvie, S. (1996). Universal Banks and German Industrialization: A Reappraisal, *Economic History Review* 49, 427–446.

Elsas, R., Hackethal, A., and Holzhäuser, M. (2010). The Anatomy of Bank Diversification, *Journal of Banking and Finance* 34, 1274–1287.

Ennis, H. M. and Malek, H. S. (2005). Bank Risk of Failure and the Too-Big-To-Fail Policy, *Federal Reserve Bank of Richmond Economic Quarterly* 21–44.

European Commission (2013). Report on Stakeholders' Meeting—Reforming the Structure of the EU Banking Sector, Brussels, May 17.

Fang, L., Ivanisha, V., and Lerner, J. (2013). Combining Banking with Private Equity Investing, *Review of Financial Studies* 26, 2139–2173.

Fazzari, S. M., Hubbard, R. G., and Petersen, B. C. (1988). Financing Constraints and Corporate Investment, *Brookings Papers on Economic Activity* 1988, 141–195.

Ferreira, M. A. and Matos, P. (2012). Universal Banks and Corporate Control: Evidence from the Global Syndicated Loan Market, *Review of Financial Studies* 25, 2703–2744.

Focarelli, D., Marques-Ibanez, D., and Franco Pozzolo, A. (2011). *Are Universal Banks Better Underwriters? Evidence from the Last Days of the Glass-Steagall Act*, European Central Bank Working Paper No. 1287.

Flannery, M. J. and Sorescu, S. M. (1996). Evidence of Bank Market Discipline in Subordinated Debenture Yields, *Journal of Finance* 51, 1347–1377.

Fohlin, C. (1997). Universal Banking Networks in Pre-War Germany: New Evidence from Company Financial Data, *Research in Economics* 51, 201–225.

Fohlin, C. (1998a). Fiduciari and Firm Liquidity Constraints: The Italian Experience with German-Style Universal Banking, *Explorations in Economic History* 35, 83–107.

Fohlin, C. (1998b). Relationship Banking, Liquidity, and Investment in the German Industrialization, *Journal of Finance* 53, 1737–1758.

Fohlin, C. (2001). The Balancing Act of German Universal Banks and English Deposit Banks, 1880-1913, *Business History* 43, 1–24.

Franke, H.-H. and Hudson, M. (1984). *Banking and Finance in West Germany*. New York, NY: St. Martin's Press.

Freixas, X., Lóránth, G., and Morrison, A. D. (2007). Regulating Financial Conglomerates, *Journal of Financial Intermediation* 16, 479–514.

Gambacorta, L. and van Rixtel, A. (2013). Structural Bank Regulation Initiatives: Approaches and Implications, Bank for International Settlements Working Paper No. 412.

Gande, A., Puri, M., and Saunders, A. (1999). Bank Entry, Competition, and the Market for Corporate Securities Underwriting—A Survey of the Evidence, *Journal of Financial Economics* 54, 165–195.

Gande, A., Puri, M., Saunders, A., and Walter, I. (1997). Bank Underwriting of Debt Securities: Modern Evidence, *Review of Financial Studies* 10, 1175–1202.

Gerschenkron, A. (1962). *Economic Backwardness in Historical Perspective*. Cambridge, MA: Harvard University Press.

Goddard, J., Molyneux, P., and Wilson, J. O. S. (2010). Banking in the European Union. In: A. N. Berger, P. Molyneux, and J. O. S. Wilson (Eds.), *Oxford Handbook of Banking*, 807–843. Oxford: Oxford University Press.

Gompers, P. and Lerner, J. (1999). Conflict of Interest in the Issuance of Public Securities: Evidence from Venture Capital, *Journal of Law and Economics* 42, 1–28.

Gorton, G. and Schmid, F. A. (2000). Universal Banking and the Performance of German Firms, *Journal of Financial Economics* 58, 29–80.

Group of Thirty (2009). Financial Reform: A Framework for Financial Stability.

Harrington, S. E. (2009). The Financial Crisis, Systemic Risk, and the Future of Insurance Regulation, *Journal of Risk and Insurance* 76, 785–819.

Hoshi, T., Kashyap, A., and Scharfstein, D. (1990). Corporate Structure, Liquidity and Investment: Evidence from Japanese Industrial Groups, *Quarterly Journal of Economics* 106, 33–60.

Hughes, J. P. and Mester, L. J. (2013). *Who Said Large Banks Don't Experience Scale Economies? Evidence from a Risk-Return-Driven Cost Function*, Federal Reserve Bank of Philadelphia Working Paper No. 13–13.

Kanatas, G. and Qi, J. (1998). Underwriting by Commercial Banks: Incentive Conflicts, Scope Economies, and Project Quality, *Journal of Money, Credit and Banking* 30, 119–133.

Kay, J. (2009). *Narrow Banking: The Reform of Bank Regulation*, Center for the Study of Financial Innovation Report No. 88.

Kroszner, R. S. and Rajan, R. G. (1994). Is the Glass-Steagall Act Justified? A Study of the US Experience with Universal Banking before 1933, *American Economic Review* 84, 810–832.

Laeven, L. and Levine, R. (2007). Is There a Diversification Discount in Financial Conglomerates?, *Journal of Financial Economics* 85, 331–367.

Lamoreaux, N. R. (1985). *The Great Merger Movement in American Business, 1895–1904*. Cambridge, UK: Cambridge University Press.

Langevoort, D. C. (1987). Statutory Obsolescence and the Judicial Process: The Revisionist Role of the Courts in Federal Banking Regulation, *Michigan Law Review* 85, 672–733.

Leuchtenburg, W. E. (1963). *Franklin D. Roosevelt and the New Deal, 1932-1940*. New York, NY: Harper and Row.

Liikanen Report (2012). High Level Expert Group on Reforming the Structure of the EU Banking Sector Final Report.

Lóránth, G. and Morrison, A. D. (2012). Tying in Universal Banks, *Review of Finance* 16, 481–516.

Lown, C. S., Osler, C. L., Strahan, P. E., and Sufi, A. (2000). The Changing Landscape of the Financial Services Industry: What Lies Ahead?, *Federal Reserve Bank of New York Economic Policy Review* 6, 39–55.

Macey, J. R. (1984). Special Interest Groups Legislation and the Judicial Function: The Dilemma of Glass-Steagall, *Emory Law Journal* 33, 1–40.

Mälkönen, V. (2004). *Capital Adequacy Regulations and Financial Conglomerates*, Bank of Finland, Helsinki, Discussion Paper No. 10.2004.

Milbourn, T. T., Boot, A. W. A., and Thakor, A. V. (1999). Megamergers and Expanded Scope: Theories of Bank Size and Activity Diversity, *Journal of Banking and Finance* 23, 195–214.

Mishkin, F. S. (1999). Financial Consolidation: Dangers and Opportunities, *Journal of Banking and Finance* 23, 675–691.

Mishkin, F. S. (2006). How Big a Problem is Too Big to Fail? A Review of Gary Stern and Ron Feldman's Too Big to Fail: The Hazards of Bank Bailouts, *Journal of Economic Literature* 91, 988–1004.

Morgan, D. and Stiroh, K. J. (2005). *Too Big to Fail After All These Years*. Federal Reserve Bank of New York Staff Report No. 220.

Morrison, A. D. and Wilhelm Jr., W. J. (2004). Partnership Firms, Reputation and Human Capital, *American Economic Review* 94, 1682–1692.

Morrison, A. D. and Wilhelm Jr., W. J. (2007). *Investment Banking: Institutions, Politics and Law*. Oxford, UK: Oxford University Press.

Morrison, A. D. and Wilhelm Jr., W. J. (2008). The Demise of Investment Banking Partnerships: Theory and Evidence, *Journal of Finance* 63, 311–350.

Neuhann, D. and Saidi, F. (2012). The Rise of the Universal Bank: Financial Architecture and Firm Volatility in the United States. University of Pennsylvania and New York University: Mimeo.

Patterson, S. and Solomon, D. (2013). Volcker Rule to Curb Bank Trading Proves Hard to Write, *Wall Street Journal*, September 10.

Pennacchi, G. (2012). Narrow Banking, *Annual Review of Financial Economics* 4, 1–36.

Petersen, M. A. (2004). Information: Hard and Soft. Kellogg School of Management, Northwestern University Working Paper.

Polanyi, M. (1966). *The Tacit Dimension*. Garden City, NY: Doubleday.

Puri, M. (1994). The Long-term Default Performance of Bank Underwritten Security Issues, *Journal of Banking and Finance* 18, 397–418.

Puri, M. (1996). Commercial Banks in Investment Banking. Conflict of Interest or Certification Role?, *Journal of Financial Economics* 40, 373–401.

Puri, M. (1999). Commercial Banks as Underwriters: Implications for the Going Public Process, *Journal of Financial Economics* 54, 133–163.

Rajan, R. G. (1996). The Entry of Commercial Banks into the Securities Business: A Selective Survey of Theories and Evidence. In A. Saunders and I. Walter (Eds.), *Universal Banking: Financial System Design Reconsidered*, 282–302. Chicago: Richard D. Irwin.

Ramirez, C. D. (1995). Did J. P. Morgan's Men Add Liquidity? Corporate Investment, Cash Flow, and Financial Structure at the Turn of the Twentieth Century, *Journal of Finance* 50, 661–678.

Redlich, F. (1968). *The Molding of American Banking: Men and Ideas*. New York, NY: Johnson Reprint Corporation.

Rime, B. and Stiroh, K. J. (2003). The Performance of Universal Banks: Evidence from Switzerland, *Journal of Banking and Finance* 27, 2121–2150.

Roten, I. C. and Mullineaux, D. J. (2002). Debt Underwriting by Commercial Bank-Affiliated Firms and Investment Banks: More Evidence, *Journal of Banking and Finance* 26, 689–718.

Schmid, M. M. and Walter, I. (2009). Do Financial Conglomerates Create or Destroy Economic Value?, *Journal of Financial Intermediation* 18, 193–216.

Schumpeter, J. A. (1939). *Business Cycles: A Theoretical, Historical and Statistical Analysis of the Capitalist Process*. New York: McGraw-Hill.

Seligman, J. (1982). *The Transformation of Wall Street: A History of the Securities and Exchange Commission and Modern Corporate Finance*. Boston, Mass: Houghton Mifflin Company.

Stein, J. C. (2002). Information Production and Capital Allocation: Decentralized versus Hierarchical Firm, *Journal of Finance* 57, 1891–1921.

Stern, G. H. and Feldman, R. J. (2004). *Too Big to Fail: The Hazards of Bank Bailouts*. Washington, DC: Brookings Institution Press.

The Turner Review (2009). *A Regulatory Response to the Global Banking Crisis*. London: Financial Services Authority.

van Lelyveld, I. and Knot, K. (2009). Do Financial Conglomerates Create or Destroy Value? Evidence for the EU, *Journal of Banking and Finance* 33, 2312–2321.

Vander Vennet, R. (1999). The Effect of Mergers and Acquisitions on the Efficiency and Profitability of EC Credit Institutions, *Journal of Banking and Finance* 20, 1531–1558.

Vickers Report (2011). Independent Commission on Banking: Final Report Recommendations.

Wheelock, D. C. and Wilson, P. W. (2011). Are Credit Unions Too Small?, *Review of Economics and Statistics* 93, 1343–1359.

Wheelock, D. C. and Wilson, P. W. (2012). Do Large Banks Have Lower Costs? New Estimates of Returns to Scale for US Banks, *Journal of Money, Credit and Banking* 44, 171–199.

White, E. N. (1986). Before the Glass-Steagall Act: An Analysis of the Investment Banking Activities of National Banks, *Explorations in Economic History* 23, 33–55.

Wilmarth Jr., A. E. (2009). The Dark Side of Universal Banking: Financial Conglomerates and the Origins of the Subprime Financial Crisis, *Connecticut Law Review* 41, 9631–105.

Winton, A. (1999). Don't Put All Your Eggs in One Basket? Diversification and Specialization in Lending. Carlson School of Management, University of Minnesota Working Paper.

Wolf, M. (2011). Of Course it's Right to Ringfence Rogue Universals, *Financial Times* September 15.

CHAPTER 6

....

CORPORATE GOVERNANCE IN BANKING

....

JENS HAGENDORFF

6.1 INTRODUCTION

....

CORPORATE governance deals with the ways in which outside investors and other stakeholders, such as government and employees, exercise control over senior management and other corporate insiders in order to protect their interests. The seminal work by Jensen and Meckling (1976) describes the frictions between corporate insiders and shareholders as well as between equity holders and external firm creditors over the desired level of firm risk. In a nutshell, since shareholders hold residual claims over a firm's assets, they have incentives to increase firm risk. While shareholders benefit from pursuing risk-increasing policies (they benefit from any upside potential in the value of their equity), external firm creditors stand to bear losses without the prospect of wealth gains from higher risk.

Banks differ from non-banking institutions in many important ways. The nature of their core activities is information-based and highly opaque, their capital structure is geared toward debt much more than any other major industry, and governments are an important stakeholder in banks both as regulators and as a fiscal backstop, for instance, through the lender of last resort function. This suggests that the corporate governance of banks should be different from that of non-financial firms to reflect the differences between banks and non-banking firms.

Perhaps surprisingly, it is not the case that bank governance is greatly different from the corporate governance arrangements of other firms. While certain aspects of bank governance are unique for banks (for instance, there are restrictions on bank ownership or bank capital structure when regulators limit leverage in some countries), most key aspects such as the organization of the board of directors or the way in which senior executives are paid is more or less in line with that of non-financial firms. Hence, many governance devices in the banking sector mimic those of non-financial firms quite closely without taking the unique features of banks sufficiently into account. As this chapter will argue, this can be problematic if, for instance, overly shareholder-focused governance is applied to a highly leveraged industry such as banking.

Before the financial crisis started in 2007, research into the nature and effects of corporate governance in banks was disparate and scattered across different journals and subdisciplines of finance, management, and economics (see Haan and Vlahu, 2013 for an overview of these different streams of research). With some exceptions, work on the corporate governance of banks rarely made it into the most prestigious academic journals, perhaps reflecting what until recently was a widespread view that the corporate governance of banks is a niche subject and that banks are not sufficiently different from other firms to warrant a separate investigation of their corporate governance arrangements. The result is that a coherent body of empirical findings, which advances our understanding of this subject area and serves as a basis for sound policy advice, has been missing to date.

However, in terms of governance rules and regulations, banking is increasingly becoming an industry with separate corporate governance standards from other countries. This demonstrates that, from a policymaking view, a new consensus has emerged that the corporate governance of banking firms deserves special and separate attention because of its importance for bank creditors, the taxpayer, and the real economy.

Some examples of recent governance rules and codes targeted at the banking industry include the following. In the UK, a review conducted by Sir David Walker regarding the corporate governance in UK banks and other financial institutions has made recommendations on board arrangements and the qualifications of board members as well as on the compensation arrangements of UK banks and financial firms. Similarly, the Netherlands has had a Banking Code in place since 2010 that contains guidelines on the make-up of bank boards, including the qualification and training of board members and their remuneration. Additionally, US compensation guidelines for CEOs and other senior executives at large banks come close to dictating compensation structures in banking (Board of Governors et al., 2010, p. 33). The flurry of new bank governance rules has meant that in a number of countries, banks now have separate corporate governance codes from other industries.

However, as this chapter will argue, there are reasons to rethink the corporate governance of banks more profoundly. This chapter will survey the key literature on the governance of banking institutions and argues that the differences between banks and non-financial firms necessitate governance arrangements that reflect these differences. Crucially, governance arrangements that do not sufficiently take the unique features of banks into account risk exacerbating existing agency conflicts that may have contributed to excessive risk-taking by banks before the recent crisis.

As an illustration of this, banks are highly leveraged firms. Equity funding in banking makes up the smallest proportion of the balance sheet of any major industry. However, equity holders control the key governance mechanisms of banks such as the board of directors (shareholders enjoy the power to appoint and remove directors) and set remuneration of senior management just like in any other industry where equity makes up a much more substantial proportion of funding and where equity holders jointly have greater loss exposure (more "skin in the game"). As a result, with risk-based profits going to equity holders, equity holders have strong incentives to put in place monetary risk-taking incentives that lead to higher payoffs for them at the expense of debtholders (and by extension, the deposit insurer or taxpayer that acts as a fiscal backstop in the event of bank failure).

The divergent interests between equity and debtholders as regards risk is just one example where owing to the highly geared capital structure of banks, shareholder-oriented corporate governance leads to risky strategies that may hurt the interests of other stakeholders in banks. Consistent with this, Beltratti and Stulz (2012) show that banks that underperformed during the crisis had "better" (i.e., more shareholder-focused) corporate governance arrangements in place before the crisis. Therefore, as this chapter will argue, banks warrant separate governance arrangements that take their unique features into account above and beyond what is currently being proposed.

This chapter proceeds as follows. Section 6.2 discusses the manner in which banks differ from non-financial firms and why this matters for the corporate governance of banks. The sections after that discuss the literature on how the compensation of senior executives, the independence, and the composition of the board of directors, the shareholder structure, and risk management practices affect the performance and risk of banks.

6.2 WHY BANKS ARE DIFFERENT AND THE IMPLICATIONS FOR BANK GOVERNANCE

Banking theory explains that the nature of financial intermediation makes bank assets informationally opaque and difficult to assess and monitor for outsiders and banks vulnerable to runs (e.g., Diamond and Dybvig, 1983; Diamond and Rajan, 2001). While there are many factors that make banks different from non-financial firms, not all of these factors have corporate governance implications. However, two aspects that make banks special and that have implications for the corporate governance of banks are the capital structure of banks (banks are highly leveraged) and the tightly regulated nature of many of their activities. Why both of these aspects make banks different in terms of their governance is the focus of this section.

One of the reasons why bank governance warrants separate analysis is that banks, by the standards of other industries, issue little equity. While equity investors are a lot less important than creditors in terms of the funding they provide to banks, equity investors still control key governance devices such as the board of directors, director appointments (and dismissals), and executive pay. Hence, it is shareholders who can put in place monitoring mechanisms and incentives designed to bring about shareholder-focused outcomes. This matters because shareholders have different risk preferences (they are risk neutral) from creditors (who are risk averse) and because the negative externalities caused by bank failures mean that bank risk-taking is clearly a policy-relevant issue.

It is important to emphasize just how unusual banks are in terms of their levels of financial leverage. Figure 6.1 illustrates that the average listed US firm in 2007 (before the crisis) was funded by around 30% equity (relative to total assets). However, for banks it is not unusual to have a balance sheet where liabilities account for in excess of 90% of total assets. Some large European banks entered the recent crisis with equity accounting for less than 3% of total assets. As Figure 6.1 shows, no other major industry has leverage ratios as high as the banking industry.

The high leverage of banks has two important corporate governance implications. The first implication is that high leverage can lead to excessive risk-taking if bank shareholders become too dominant in the governance of the bank. Going back to at least Jensen and Meckling (1976),

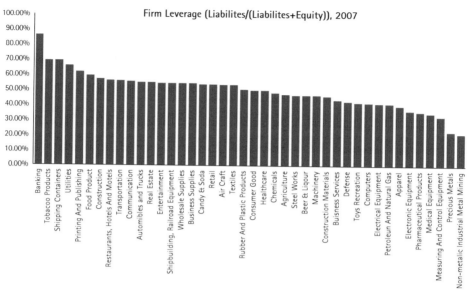

FIGURE 6.1 Firm leverage [liabilities/ (liabilities+equity)], 2007.

it is well known that there are conflicts between equity holders and external firm creditors over the desired level of firm risk. Since shareholders hold residual claims over a firm's assets, they have incentives to increase firm risk. While shareholders benefit from pursuing risk-increasing policies (they benefit from any upside potential in the value of their equity), external firm creditors stand to bear losses without the prospect of wealth gains from higher risk.

The second implication from high leverage is that, in the banking industry, risk-taking incentives linked to equity are further intensified by the presence of guarantees advanced by regulators and governments. Therefore, it is a widely held view that the financial safety net (and by extension regulators) are at least in part responsible for the high leverage of banks. The view is that regulators subsidize bank leverage and thus induce banks to issue larger amounts of liabilities than they otherwise would. For instance, since the prospect of large externalities caused by bank failures raises the expectation of bank bailouts, banks may increase their implicit claim on the financial safety net through higher risk-taking. Both explicit deposit insurance and implicit bailout guarantees shield bank creditors from market discipline and induce banks to "lever up" at low costs.

Consistent with public bank guarantees inducing leverage, Berger, Herring, and Szegö (1995) show drastic increases in the leverage of US banks since the mid-nineteenth century. The leverage increases coincide with various changes in regulation that made the financial safety net more generous. Examples are the Federal Reserve Act of 1914, which let banks obtain liquidity via discounting assets at the Federal Reserve, and the creation of deposit insurance in 1933, which guaranteed depositors' repayments in the event of a bank failing.

Naturally, high bank leverage is not only the result of safety-net subsidies but also in part the result of the role of banks as providers of liquidity, which is intrinsic to the process of financial intermediation (see Diamond and Dybvig, 1983; Diamond and Rajan, 2001 and others). Essentially, if financially constrained businesses and households demand liquid claims (in the form of deposits and other short-term liquid instruments) and do so at a premium, banks will produce substantial amounts of liabilities. DeAngelo and Stulz (2013) show that demand for bank liabilities (i.e., deposits) causes banks to be highly leveraged even in the absence of frictions such as deposit insurance and implicit bailout guarantees.

Nonetheless, the financial safety net in part subsidizes bank leverage and bank risk-taking more generally because regulators act as a fiscal backstop when bailing out failing banks. This turns regulators into stakeholders in the corporate governance of banks in a way that is different from other industries. The presence of regulators as stakeholders is the second aspect that sets the corporate governance of banks apart from that of non-banking organizations.

To sum up, among the various aspects that make banks stand out from non-financial firms, this section has identified the capital structure of banks and relatively tight regulation of bank activities as key characteristics with important implications for the corporate governance of banks. Section 6.3 examines the pay arrangements in banking and their effect on bank risk.

6.3 COMPENSATION IN BANKING

Executive compensation policy may serve as a mechanism to reduce conflicts between managers and shareholders over the deployment of corporate resources and the riskiness of the firm (Jensen and Meckling, 1976). Public and academic interest in CEO compensation in the banking industry has increased exponentially in the aftermath of the financial crisis of 2007–2008. While this is partly motivated by public outrage over the levels of CEO remuneration in an industry that has become increasingly reliant on public funds, the view that the structure of executive pay has given rise to socially harmful risk-taking by banks is gaining ground. Thus, the use of incentive pay in banking is widely believed to have motivated excessive risk-taking and to have acted as a contributory factor to the recent financial crisis (e.g., Bebchuk and Spamann, 2009; Federal Reserve Bank, 2010).

This section critically reviews existing empirical work on the relationship between CEO pay and bank risk-taking and argues that previous work has been too narrow in its focus on equity-linked CEO compensation (mainly share and option grants) while neglecting common forms of CEO compensation that are not equity-linked and that could make a valuable contribution to promoting more socially optimal risk-taking by banks. Research that examines non-equity components of CEO compensation, particularly pensions and other forms of deferred compensation, is still in its infancy. However, many of the findings proffered by this stream of research are consistent with the view that, where equity-based pay encourages risk-taking, non-equity-linked pay makes CEOs more risk averse (see Edmans and Liu, 2011). This section argues that it is regrettable that not more is empirically known about the risk effects generated by non-equity (and essentially more debt-like) forms of compensation and calls for debt-like components of CEO compensation to be examined in greater detail.

6.3.1 Cash and Bonus Compensation

Most of the extant literature largely overlooks the role of CEO cash bonuses as a risk-taking incentive. The lack of empirical work on CEO bonus plans on bank risk is unfortunate for two reasons. First, CEO cash bonuses are an important component of executive pay. CEO bonus payments make up around a third of total CEO compensation (Murphy, 2000). Second, the effect of bonus payments on managerial risk preferences is likely to differ from that exerted by option grants.

Figure 6.2 illustrates the shape of a typical bonus function. CEO cash bonuses generally become payable once an earnings-based target over a one-year period has been met. After exceeding this threshold, the CEO payoffs from bonus plans increase in line with performance until capped at a maximum payout. Therefore, for earnings performances exceeding the threshold at which bonus payments become payable, CEO bonus plans do not provide convex payoffs (Smith and Stulz, 1985) and should not promote excessive risk-taking (see Noe, Rebello, and Wall, 1996; Duru, Mansi, and Reeb, 2005). This is in sharp contrast to CEO holdings of stock options. Since the payoffs from option holdings are convex functions of the volatility of stock returns, options incentivize CEOs to increase the volatility of share prices by engaging in riskier activities (Guay, 1999; Rajgopal and Shevlin, 2002; Coles, Daniel, and Naveen, 2006; Hagendorff and Vallascas, 2011).

Theoretical work posits that CEO cash bonuses can play an important role in mitigating managerial incentives to engage in risk-shifting. In a theoretical model, Smith and Stulz (1985) show that as long as cash bonuses increase linearly with corporate performance, the payoffs linked to a bonus plan are non-convex and therefore not inherently risk-rewarding.

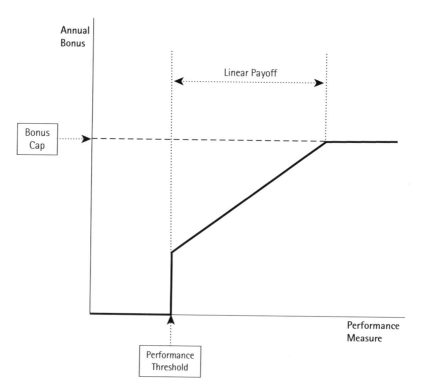

FIGURE 6.2 A typical cash bonus function.

However, when performance is below the earnings-based threshold at which bonuses become payable, bonus plans resemble a call option on the performance measure. In this case, bonus plan payoffs will be convex and offset the concavity of the CEO's risk-averse utility function. By contrast, when performance is above the threshold at which bonuses become payable (and below the bonus cap), the slope of a bonus plan is linear with respect to performance and will not incentivize risk-averse CEOs to increase bank risk in order to secure higher bonus payments.

Other work suggests that, rather than having no effect on risk-taking, bonuses may lower the risk preferences of the CEO. One such argument suggests that, because bonus payments can only be received in a state of solvency, they incentivize CEOs to avoid bankruptcy (John and John, 1993). Consistent with this, Duru, Mansi, and Reeb (2005) find that earnings-based cash bonuses make managers seek stable cash flows to meet contractual debt obligations. The authors show that the costs of debt financing decrease for firms that pay higher CEO cash bonuses and contend that this reflects the lower agency costs of debt and reduced risk-shifting incentives in these firms.

In spite of the arguments above, claims that cash bonuses encourage banks to engage in "excessive" risk-taking continue to be made (for instance, in the Financial Stability Board, 2009). However, the case for bonuses increasing risk tends to rest on two assumptions, both of which have recently been challenged by empirical evidence. The first assumption is that cash bonus contracts do not sufficiently expose managers to downside risk and therefore reward managers for taking on more risk to achieve the performance goals underlying bonus contracts. In contrast to this, empirical studies have shown that bonus contracts tend to punish underperformance more than they reward strong performance (Indjejikian et al., 2011).

The second assumption is that, by making bonus payments contingent on annual performance targets, shareholders design bonuses to affect short-term behavior and managers pursue higher risk-taking strategies to achieve these short-term goals. While some evidence exists that managers may ration productive effort in order to maximize bonus payments (Bouwens and Kroos, 2011), this does not rule out that bonuses can be designed as long-term compensation tools. In fact, Indjejikian et al. (2011) show that bonus plans provide managers with long-term incentives to exert effort. These studies document that companies consider a tradeoff between bonuses and career incentives over time horizons of multiple years when devising managerial compensation packages.

The narrow empirical evidence available for the banking industry reaches conflicting conclusions on the role of CEO bonus payments and bank risk. Harjoto and Mullineaux (2003) report a positive association between bonus payments and return volatility (risk). Balachandran, Kogut, and Harnal (2010) proffer some evidence that the sum of bonus and other cash incentives reduces the probability of bank default.

Fahlenbrach and Stulz (2011) do not find that CEO cash bonus payments affect the performance of US banks during the recent crisis. Looking at risk, Vallascas and Hagendorff (2013) show that increases in CEO cash bonuses lower the default risk of banks. They explain this finding by arguing that, because bonus payments are contingent on bank solvency, they lower the risk preferences of CEOs. They then demonstrate that the risk-reducing effect of cash bonuses disappears as banks move closer to the point of default. At the most risky banks, the results show that bonus payments promote rather than mitigate bank risk-taking. This finding is consistent with the view that financially distressed banks seek to maximize the value of the financial safety net.

Evidently, cash bonuses are not the only form of incentive compensation that may affect CEO risk-taking. Stock and stock options may cause CEOs to overcome their risk aversion and incentivize them to engage in risk-increasing projects. Section 6.3.2 examines the role of equity-based compensation and its effect on bank risk-taking.

6.3.2 Equity-Based Compensation

Over recent decades, the use of equity-linked compensation has increased rapidly, both inside and outside the banking industry. Equity-linked CEO compensation takes the form of grants of the firm's shares as well as call options on the firm's equity. Option grants in particular make CEO wealth sensitive to risk-taking.

Pay-based incentives that make compensation more sensitive to risk (*vega*) and pay-based incentives that make compensation more sensitive to performance (*delta*) are captured by a method described in Guay (1999). The measure captures the partial derivative of the value of the CEO's portfolio of options (estimated using the dividend-adjusted Black–Scholes value) or stock holdings, respectively:

$$\text{vega} = \frac{\partial \text{value}}{\partial \sigma} \times .01 = e^{-dT} N'(Z) S \sqrt{T} \times .01 \tag{6.1}$$

$$\text{delta} = \frac{\partial \text{value}}{\partial S} \frac{S}{100} = e^{-dT} N(Z) \frac{S}{100} \tag{6.2}$$

where $Z = \left[\ln(S/X) + \left(r_f - d + 0.5\sigma^2 \right) T \right] / \sigma\sqrt{T}$. $N'(\cdot)$ and $N(\cdot)$ are the normal probability density function and the cumulative normal distribution respectively. S is the closing stock price at the fiscal year end, X is the exercise price of the option, σ is the annualized standard deviation of daily stock returns, r is the risk-free rate for a maturity value equal to that of the option contract, d is the dividend yield, and T is the time to maturity of the option grant.

DeYoung, Peng, and Yan (2013) show that the use of equity-linked compensation in US banking has increased so rapidly over the last decade that CEO payoffs linked to increases in firm risk (vega) are higher in the banking industry than in non-financial firms. DeYoung, Peng, and Yan (2013) calculate that the average bank CEO saw his or her wealth increase by around $300,000 in 2004 as a result of a 0.01% increase in stock return volatility.

Previous evidence on vega and the investment decisions made by managers is equivocal. For instance, the non-financial literature finds that higher CEO vegas lead to riskier investment choices and bind corporate resources to riskier activities (Guay, 1999; Rajgopal and Shevlin, 2002; Coles, Daniel, and Naveen, 2006). For the banking industry, Mehran and Rosenberg (2007) and DeYoung, Peng, and Yan (2013) show that high-vega banks engage in riskier types of activities. By contrast, Fahlenbrach and Stulz (2011) do not find that CEO vegas explain the performance of bank stocks (i.e., previous managerial risk-taking) during the recent financial crisis. Hagendorff and Vallascas (2011) find that CEOs are responsive to the vega embedded in their compensation when engaging in acquisitions. Thus, higher pay risk sensitivity causes CEOs to engage in risk-increasing deals.

As regards the levels of pay-performance sensitivity (delta), delta may exacerbate managerial risk aversion (Amihud and Lev, 1981; Smith and Stulz, 1985). DeYoung, Peng, and Yan (2013) find some evidence that delta reduces the riskiness of bank activities, while Mehran and Rosenberg (2007) do not detect any robust influence of delta on bank risk-taking. As regards the effect of CEO delta on the riskiness of merger decisions, Datta, Iskander-Datta, and Raman (2001) find that higher deltas lead to acquisitions that are associated with higher increases in stock return volatility after a merger. For the banking industry, Bliss and Rosen (2001) and Minnick, Unal, and Yang (2011) show that high-delta banks are less likely to engage in acquisitions, which is consistent with high-delta CEOs foregoing risky investment projects such as mergers and acquisitions.

Berger at al. (2013) examine the role of managerial stock holdings (the primary component of delta above) and bank failures during the crisis. The results show that stock holdings of lower-level management (such as vice-presidents) increase default risk while the shareholdings of CEOs and other senior executives do not affect the probability of failure. Even though the authors focus on stock holdings rather than compensation, the findings raise the possibility that pay and other governance variables ought to be examined not only at the level of the board of directors but also at hierarchical levels below the board.

6.3.3 Debt-Based Compensation

Debt as a form of executive remuneration is widespread. It tends to take the shape of deferred compensation, most notably in the form of defined benefit pensions (see Sundaram and Yermack, 2007; Wei and Yermack, 2011). These company promises of fixed sums at some future point in time are unfunded and unsecured CEO claims. In the USA and many other countries, the deferred compensation claims of executives take no priority over the claims of other unsecured creditors in the event of bankruptcy, effectively turning the holders of inside debt into unsecured firm creditors.

The value of deferred compensation claims by CEOs—also known as "inside debt" (Jensen and Meckling, 1976)—can make up a substantial share of a CEO's overall remuneration. Wei and Yermack (2011) report that out of the S&P 1,500 firms, more than two-thirds of CEOs hold some form of inside debt and that for those who hold inside debt, the holdings were worth an average of $5.7 million in 2006.

A small number of empirical studies report evidence consistent with inside debt curbing CEO risk-taking behavior. Sundaram and Yermack (2007) find that large inside debt positions by a CEO reduce the probability of default on a firm's debt. More recently, Wei and Yermack (2011) examine the bond and share price reaction to the disclosure of inside debt holdings in 2007 as mandated by the Security and Exchange Commission (SEC). The authors find that large CEO pensions (as well as other forms of deferred payments to CEOs) are associated with gains for bond holders and losses for shareholders.

Few studies have been conducted to examine the effects of inside debt on bank behavior. Tung and Wang (2012) show that bank CEOs with higher inside debt holdings engaged in less risk-taking before the financial crisis (as indicated by better stock market performance during the financial crisis). Bennett, Guntay, and Unal (2012) show that larger CEO inside debt holdings before the crisis are associated with lower bank default risk during the crisis.

There is a clear need for further research to look at the risk-taking effects of inside debt holdings over longer examination periods. The recently enhanced disclosure requirements by the SEC as regards deferred compensation claims by CEOs will provide a wealth of new opportunities for researchers to examine the effects of paying CEOs with debt. However, even before the enhanced disclosure requirements became active in 2007, the proxy statements filed with the SEC contain sufficient information to estimate the expected present value of a CEO's pension using actuarial computations (see Sundaram and Yermack, 2007).

6.4 THE BOARD OF DIRECTORS AND SHAREHOLDER-ORIENTED GOVERNANCE

In all economic sectors, the board of directors of publicly traded companies is among the most important internal control mechanisms for promoting and protecting shareholder interests due to the board's role in providing expertise and monitoring managerial discretion. More specifically, boards have the authority to ratify or obstruct managerial initiatives, to assess the performance of top management, and to determine managerial compensation packages and career paths at a particular firm.

For a board to be effective in mitigating self-serving managerial behavior, its independence from management needs to be ensured. A common assumption is that boards that are more independent (in the sense that a larger proportion of directors has no family, social, or business connections to management) are more likely to bring about shareholder-oriented outcomes such as higher risk or better performance.

Adams and Mehran (2003) report that US bank boards between 1986 and 1999 were both larger and more independent than those of S&P 500 manufacturing firms: the average board size was 12 for manufacturing firms and 18 for banks. Given shareholders are risk neutral and managers are risk averse with respect to firm-specific and idiosyncratic risk (managers' human capital is invested in their own firm and cannot be diversified), banks that are more shareholder-controlled should be riskier. Powerful bank boards should therefore be associated with increased risk-taking activities, while powerful bank CEOs who face a less shareholder-oriented board should be associated with less risk-taking.

Consistent with shareholder-aligned boards increasing risk, Pathan (2009) shows that as the boards of bank holding companies reflect shareholder interests to a larger degree (e.g., when they are smaller and more independent), bank risk-taking increases. Similarly, Laeven and Levine (2009) show that bank risk-taking increases with the comparative power of shareholders within the corporate governance structure of a bank.

Examining the recent crisis period, the evidence is not consistent with the view that the crisis has roots in the "weak" corporate governance, if weakness is defined in terms of how aligned boards are with shareholders. Thus, Erkens, Hung, and Matos (2012) find that firms with more independent boards realized lower stock returns during the crisis period. Similarly, for an international sample of banks, Beltratti and Stulz (2012) show that banks that underperformed during the crisis had altogether more shareholder-oriented boards.

Beltratti and Stulz offer an intriguing explanation for their results. The authors argue that better governed banks outperformed before the crisis by engaging in a number of activities that at the time were value-enhancing but later on turned out to be a source of underperformance. Since Beltratti and Stulz (2012) control for various indicators of shareholder-oriented corporate governance, the authors argue that the risk of investments could not have been anticipated at the time the investments were made (since it does not seem plausible that shareholder-oriented boards were intent on diminishing shareholder value during the crisis). Hence, they suggest that shareholder-focused banks suffered from "bad luck" (rather than ill-intent).

Beltratti and Stulz's (2012) study is important because it demonstrates the pitfalls of overly shareholder-oriented corporate governance. Such a governance system can bring about outcomes that at the time appear to be in the interests of shareholders but that may turn out to be not optimal for other stakeholders including governments. Therefore, shareholder-focused governance should not be viewed as a major component in the regulatory response to the recent crisis. If anything, it may even have played a role in the buildup to leading to the crisis.

Finally, Berger et al's (2013) findings encourage future corporate governance research to shift toward middle and higher management levels situated below the board of directors. The authors find managerial ownership can be linked to bank failures during the crisis if ownership is measured for managers (e.g., vice-presidents or treasurers) but not when ownership is measured for top executives (e.g., CEO or chief financial officer).

6.5 BOARD DIVERSITY: DOES IT MATTER WHO RUNS BANKS?

It is a widely accepted view that the composition of the board of directors could play a vital role in determining corporate performance (see, e.g., Hermalin and Weisbach, 2003). In the past decade, boards inside and outside the banking sector have made an increasing number of appointments from a wider range of demographic, educational, and social backgrounds. Following the recent crisis, the view has taken hold that the responsibility of bank boards to monitor managerial risk-taking should be improved and that board diversity can play an important part in improving board decision making.

This view has some traction with policymakers and the general public. For instance, following the aftermath of the recent crisis, the quote that Lehman Brothers would not have collapsed if it had been "Lehman Sisters" has been attributed to European commissioner Viviane Reding and former UK minister Harriet Harman among others. This section seeks to make the case for and against board diversity based on theoretical grounds as well as the rather limited evidence to date that has examined the effects of more diverse bank boards in the banking industry.

6.5.1 The Case for Board Diversity?

The case for diversity in the boardroom essentially centers around two main types of arguments: ethical and economic. Ethical arguments regard board diversity as a desirable end in itself and emphasize that it is inequitable to exclude certain groups from corporate elites on the basis of gender, race, or other non-performance-related characteristics (Singh, Vinnicombe, and Johnson, 2001). In the same vein, promoting board diversity is one means to empower constituencies of society that have historically been excluded from positions of power. Therefore, the concept of board diversity is linked to the notion of equality of representation and, ultimately, to the ideal of "fair" outcomes in society (Brammer, Millington, and Pavelin, 2007). It follows from this that diverse boards create legitimacy and improve a firm's bargaining power vis-à-vis its various stakeholders.

As regards the economic case for board diversity, a central argument is that diversity enhances the functional abilities of a board, particularly its ability to engage in complex problem-solving, strategic decision making, and management monitoring (Forbes and Milliken, 1999). Boards may be viewed as a knowledge-based asset that creates value for shareholders by linking an organization to its external environment (Pfeffer and Salancik, 1978). For example, board diversity expands the networks of existing board members and helps place firms in a network of other firms. This network may lead firms to benefit from improved access to their various external constituents (see Hillman, Cannella, and Paetzold, 2000). Specifically, board networks may provide access to capital, a nation's business elite, and—in the case of a regulated industry such as banking—industry regulators (Macey and O'Hara, 2003).

As well as placing a firm within a network of external contacts, board diversity may improve the internal workings of the board. Owing to their idiosyncratic experiences and values, diverse board members bring privileged economic resources to organizations that help them comprehend a firm's dynamic industry context (Hambrick and Mason, 1984). For example, the presence of knowledge and specific skills that cater to a board's specialized needs may further an organization's understanding of its marketplace and thus improve corporate performance when a board matches its diversity with that of customers or suppliers. However, calls by policymakers to appoint directors with more sector-specific knowledge run contrary to recent attempts by banks to increase the diversity of their boards.

However, there may also be costs associated with board diversity. The presence of different viewpoints on less homogeneous boards may cause coordination problems (Forbes and Milliken, 1999). Further, diversity may corrode group cohesion and lead to a board whose members are less cooperative and experience increased emotional conflict. Consistent with this, Adams and Ferreira (2009) show that female board directors engage in more monitoring but are unable to improve performance. The authors argue that too much monitoring causes conflict and lowers overall performance.

6.5.2 Empirical Evidence on Board Diversity in Banking

There is little empirical evidence on the effects of diversity in banking. However, the work that has been done to date is interesting because it shows that gender, education, and director characteristics do indeed affect performance and risk-taking in the banking industry. Since the banking sector is relatively opaque, complex, and skill-intensive, education and other director characteristics that may correlate with abilities could be particularly important in the banking sector.

Beck, Behr, and Guettler (2013) analyze gender differences in the performance of loan officers. Consistent with the view that female loan officers make more cautious decisions, the authors show that default rates for loans originated by female loan officers tend to be lower than for those originated by male loan officers.

Berger, Imbierowicz, and Rauch (2013) link changes in board composition to measures of bank portfolio risk. Specifically, the authors relate board-level measures of age, gender, and education (the latter measured by the fraction of directors on the board holding a PhD) to the proportion of risk-weighted assets on a bank's balance sheet. The authors show that younger executive teams and teams with more females take more portfolio risks. The authors show this is due to female directors being on average less experienced than male appointments and less experienced directors taking on additional risks.

As regards board diversity, Hagendorff and Keasey (2012) measure the value of board diversity in the US banking industry. They employ a sample of bank mergers and find positive announcement returns to mergers approved by boards whose members are diverse in terms of their occupational background. By contrast, Erkens, Hung, and Matos (2012) do not find a significant relationship between financial experience of board members and firms' stock returns during the crisis.

Nguyen, Hagendorff, and Eshraghi (2013) examine the announcement effects of new bank director appointments and find that age, education, and prior experience of executive directors create shareholder wealth in the US banking sector. In contrast, gender, experience outside the banking sector, and a PhD degree do not have measurable market returns. In addition, the appointment of directors who hold non-executive directorships with an unaffiliated firm at the time of the appointment attracts negative returns, consistent with the view that these directors are too busy to be effective monitors.

In summary, while the ethical arguments for board diversity appear strong, the economic case for board diversity has yet to stand on more solid empirical grounds. Therefore, more work needs to be done to establish stronger causal links between who the members of the board are and corporate outcomes such as bank risk and returns.

6.6 Bank Ownership: Does it Matter who Owns Banks?

This section analyzes the effects of bank ownership on bank risk. It distinguishes between concentration of ownership stakes and government versus other types of ownership in banking. In essence, this section asks the question: Does it matter which institutions own banks?

6.6.1 Ownership Concentration

Saunders, Strock, and Travlos (1990) and Laeven and Levine (2009) show that banks with larger management control engage in less risk-taking than banks controlled by shareholders. Gropp and Köhler (2010) add to this by showing that bank managers prefer less risk compared to shareholders irrespective of whether shareholders are dispersed or concentrated. Further, Gropp and Köhler show that shareholder-controlled banks had higher profits in the years before the crisis, incurred larger losses, and were more likely to require government assistance during the crisis compared with manager-controlled banks. Again, this shows that shareholder-aligned governance leads to outcomes that may be privately optimal (they bring about higher expected shareholder returns) but not necessarily socially optimal.

Erkens, Hung, and Matos (2012) analyze the impact of institutional ownership on stock performance and find that banks with greater institutional ownership engaged in more risk-taking before the crisis and, consequently, suffered lower stock returns during the crisis. Beltratti and Stulz (2012) report qualitatively similar findings. Aebi, Sabato, and Schmid (2012) find that institutional investors and other large investors are associated with lower bank performance. Their analysis indicates that large shareholders are less able to provide effective monitoring with respect to the risks taken by banks before the crisis.

It is important to bear in mind that, in many countries, ownership concentration in the banking industry is substantially lower than in non-financial firms (Adams and Mehran, 2003). This is mainly because regulators put implicit and explicit restrictions in place on which type of firms can hold significant shareholdings in banks thus restricting the pool of potential investors and making their equity investment significantly less liquid. In the USA, only financial firms can own banks and most countries require regulatory approval for substantial shareholdings (that is, shareholdings in excess of 20%) in banks.

6.6.2 Governments as Shareholders

To some extent, institutional owners and governments are similar in that both have significant resources and influence over the firms they invest in. Nonetheless, these investor groups have different objectives, most notably that profit-making is seldom the key objective when governments invest in firms. Therefore, government ownership of banks is a special case that warrants separate discussion of its implications for the risk and governance of banks.

Studies on the performance and risk effects when governments are the only or the dominant shareholder in a bank have been quite equivocal in reporting that state control causes banks to underperform (Barth, Caprio, and Levine, 2004; Beck, Demirgüç-Kunt, and Maksimovic, 2004; Berger, Hasan, and Klapper, 2004). Among other reasons, state-owned banks are likely to be relatively inefficient as a result of pressures to provide finance for state-sponsored projects (see Altunbas, Evans, and Molyneux, 2001).

The finding that government-owned banks underperform has been confirmed in different geographical settings. For instance, Iannotta, Nocera, and Sironi (2007) confirm that government-owned banks are less profitable than private-sector banks in a sample of European banks from 15 countries. Similarly, Lin and Zhang (2009) show that large state-owned banks in China have lower asset quality compared with joint stock and city-level commercial banks. Government ownership can also affect bank risk-taking. Cornett et al. (2010) analyze the effect of government ownership and government involvement in a country's banking system. They show that state-owned banks operate less profitably, hold less core capital, and have greater credit risk than privately-owned banks. Interestingly, any performance differences become more significant with greater government involvement in the banking system.

However, this literature has received renewed impetus following the recent crisis, which brought about very strong, and in some countries, unprecedented levels of state ownership of the banking sector. The question of if and how government ownership affects banks has therefore re-entered the spotlight.

In the US, the Troubled Asset Relief Program (TARP) has led to taxpayer-funded equity injections into hundreds of banking firms since 2008. A frequently raised concern is that TARP, by extending the financial safety net, has encouraged additional bank risk-taking. Consistent with this view, recent evidence suggests that TARP banks have indeed approved riskier loans (Black and Hazelwood, 2013) and shifted investment portfolios toward riskier securities (Duchin and Sosyura, 2011). Additionally, a number of countries had to take troubled lenders into public ownership (e.g., Royal Bank of Scotland and Lloyds in the UK or Germany's Commerzbank). The emerging literature is only just beginning to understand the risk-taking incentives linked to the government ownership of these institutions (see Gropp, Gruendl, and Guettler, 2014). Next to any isolated effect of government ownership of individual banks, government ownership may also have wider implications for the industry by causing competitive distortions.

Further, it is important and interesting to study the implications for bank behavior once governments have embarked on the process of re-privatizing banks previously taken into public ownership. Gropp, Gruendl, and Guettler (2014) and Fischer et al. (2012) study a related topic by analyzing the effects of the removal of state guarantees for German Landesbanken. In particular, Fischer et al.'s (2012) results show that between the time the removal was announced (in 2001) and the time it became effective (in 2005), Landesbanken engaged in higher risk-taking by lending to riskier borrowers. These results raise interesting implications for the eventual removal of government ownership and related guarantees once government ownership is withdrawn.

Regarding the interaction between corporate governance and government ownership, Borisova et al. (2012) show government ownership affects corporate governance based on a sample of 373 European companies (including banks) between 2003 and 2008. They find that government ownership lowers governance quality but this effect varies with the legal framework of a country. Government intervention is negatively related to governance quality in civil law countries, but positively related to governance quality in common law countries.

In summary, government ownership of the banking industry is a special type of ownership that has recently risen to more prominence given the widespread equity injections into banks by governments around the globe. Increasing government ownership of the banking sector is an important topic because it is a well-established empirical fact that government-controlled banks underperform private banks. Also, the impending re-privatization of banks recently taken into public ownership is likely to have risk-taking implications for banks, which warrants further empirical investigation.

6.7 Risk Management Inside and Outside the Board of Directors

In a report on governance failings, the OECD (2009) argues that weak corporate governance in banks leads to inadequate risk management, especially insufficient risk monitoring through the board, and that this has contributed greatly to bank instability during the crisis. A small number of studies have started to examine how risk management practices, especially the workings of the risk management committee and its members, affect corporate outcomes. Given the high leverage of banking firms and the concerns over excessive risk-taking incentives for shareholders, strong risk management practices inside and outside the board of directors should be an important governance device.

Keys et al. (2009) show that lenders with relatively powerful risk managers created mortgage portfolios with lower ex post default rates. The study measures the importance of risk managers using the risk manager's share of the total compensation relative to the five highest-paid executives. Similarly, Aebi, Sabato, and Schmid (2012) demonstrate that banks in which the chief risk officer directly reports to the board of directors and not to the CEO (or other corporate entities) exhibit significantly higher (i.e. less negative) stock returns and return on investment during the crisis.

Ellul and Yerramilli (2013) study the relationship between risk management practices outside the board and tail risk for the largest 100 US banks between 1995 and 2010. They develop a Risk Management Index (RMI) based on five variables related to the strength of a bank's risk management. Their findings show that banks with a high RMI value in 2006 were less risky and performed better while they also had better operating and stock return performance during the financial crisis years. Therefore, a strong and independent risk management function can curtail risk exposures at banks.

In summary, while risk management has not been explored in any great level of detail, certainly not at the level of scrutiny afforded to the working of the board of directors, the evidence so far suggests that risk management has an important role to play in mitigating bank shareholder incentives to increase risk. Further, what makes the risk management literature particularly interesting is that it moves away from simply looking at the board of directors and instead offers insights on how important other corporate governance devices further down the corporate hierarchy are in terms of mitigating risk-taking.

6.8 Policy Implications and Conclusions

This chapter surveys the literature on the corporate governance of banking firms with a particular focus on the compensation arrangements of bank executives, the composition of the board of directors, and the ownership of banks. One of the main conclusions of this chapter is that the unique features of banks should lead to more unique governance arrangements for the banking industry than can be presently observed. For instance, given the high leverage of banks, pay incentives should align managers more with creditors than shareholders in the banking industry compared with other industries. However, US-based evidence suggests that, compared with CEOs in non-financial firms, CEOs in the banking industry have been more aligned with equity holders than debtholders (see DeYoung, Peng, and Yan, 2013).

Equally, and as a direct result of the high leverage and the resulting importance of bank creditors in the financing of banks, creditors should be given a more prominent role in the corporate governance of banks. At present, equity holders control the key governance mechanisms of banks such as the board of directors (shareholders have the exclusive power to appoint and remove directors) and set the remuneration of senior management just like in any other industry. One possibility would be to allow for creditor representation on bank boards. The simple intuition behind such an initiative would be that, if the capital structure of banks is different from non-financial firms, the governance structure within a bank should reflect this.

While creditor representation on bank boards is at odds with the principle of proportional shareholder representation on boards ("one share one vote"), it is important to bear in mind that a number of companies have long represented stakeholders other than shareholders on the board. For instance, Germany's *Mitbestimmungsgesetz* (Codetermination Act) mandates that half of the board seats at large German corporations are reserved for employee representatives. One possibility would be to allow for a sliding scale of creditor representation starting beyond a threshold level of leverage and increasing with higher leverage up to a certain point. This would ensure that creditor representation would increase in line with bank leverage and give creditors the opportunity to exert more influence over governance aspects such as executive director appointments, risk management, and remuneration policy.

Overall, the evidence surveyed does not back the conclusion that the recent crisis has been brought about by a lack of shareholder-oriented corporate governance and that, following this line of argument, future banking crises can be prevented by improving the influence that shareholders have on the corporate governance of banks. If anything, the literature surveyed in this chapter shows that shareholder-oriented governance leads to risky outcomes and has therefore contributed to unsustainable bank policies that played a major role in the buildup of the crisis.

This chapter also highlights two particularly important lines for future research into the corporate governance of banks. First, future research should do more to understand the effectiveness of individual directors and their personal characteristics. Empirical work has only recently begun to examine issues around individual director characteristics and board heterogeneity. Some findings are consistent with the view that it matters who runs banks, but not all these findings are in line with current policy discussions around board composition. For instance, empirical support for the view that female board participation or more banking sector experience lower risk (as is often asserted) is weak at best.

Second, research into the corporate governance of banks has so far been overly focused on the board of directors. While no doubt a key governance device, there are other institutions outside the board that are important for reducing agency conflict over bank risk. For instance, studying the risk management culture and risk management practices inside banks (see Ellul and Yerramilli, 2013) or studying middle- and high-ranking management instead of the board level of executives (see Berger, Imbierowicz, and Rauch, 2013) can provide useful avenues for further research.

The corporate governance of banks is clearly an important topic both for investors and for policymakers. However, much of what is known about the governance of banks has relied on replicating research based on the non-financial sector without adequately taking the unique features of banks into account. However, these unique features of banks call for a more profound rethink of the corporate governance of banks, one that centers around debtholders rather than equity holders, to bring forward the literature on this topic and to base the impending regulatory changes to the banking sector on a solid empirical footing.

References

Adams, R. and Mehran, H. (2003). Is Corporate Governance Different for Bank Holding Companies?, *Economic Policy Review* 9, 123–142.

Adams, R. B. and Ferreira, D. (2009). Women in the Boardroom and Their Impact on Governance and Performance, *Journal of Financial Economics* 94, 291–309.

Aebi, V., Sabato, G., and Schmid, M. (2012). Risk Management, Corporate Governance, and Bank Performance in the Financial Crisis, *Journal of Banking and Finance* 36, 3213–3226.

Altunbas, Y., Evans, L., and Molyneux, P. (2001). Bank Ownership and Efficiency, *Journal of Money, Credit and Banking* 33, 926–954.

Amihud, Y. and Lev, B. (1981). Risk Reduction as a Managerial Motive for Conglomerate Mergers, *Bell Journal of Economics* 12, 605–617.

Balachandran, S., Kogut, B., and Harnal, H. (2010). The Probability of Default, Excessive Risk, and Executive Compensation: A Study of Financial Services Firms from 1995 to 2008. Columbia University Unpublished Working Paper.

Barth, J., Caprio, G., and Levine, R. (2004). Bank Supervision and Regulation. What Works Best?, *Journal of Financial Intermediation* 13, 205–248.

Bebchuk, L. A. and Spamann, H. (2009). Regulating Bankers' Pay. *Georgetown Law Journal* 98, 247–287.

Beck, T., Behr, P., and Guettler, A. (2013). Gender and Banking: Are Women Better Loan Officers?, *Review of Finance* 17, 1279–1321.

Beck, T., Demirgüç-Kunt, A., and Maksimovic, V. (2004). Bank Competition and Access to Finance: International Evidence, *Journal of Money, Credit and Banking* 36, 627–648.

Beltratti, A. and Stulz, R. M. (2012). The Credit Crisis Around the Globe: Why Did Some Banks Perform Better during the Credit Crisis?, *Journal of Financial Economics* 105(1), 1–17.

Bennett, R., Guntay, L., and Unal, H. (2012). Inside Debt, Bank Default Risk and Performance during the Crisis. University of Maryland Unpublished Working Paper.

Berger, A. N., Hasan, I., and Klapper, L. F. (2004). Further Evidence on the Link between Finance and Growth: An International Analysis of Community Banking and Economic Performance, *Journal of Financial Services Research* 25, 169–202.

Berger, A. N., Herring, R. J., and Szegö, G. P. (1995). The Role of Capital in Financial Institutions, *Journal of Banking & Finance* 19, 393–430.

Berger, A., Imbierowicz, B., and Rauch, C. (2013). *The Roles of Corporate Governance in Bank Failures during the Recent Financial Crisis*. European Banking Center.

Black, L. K. and Hazelwood, L. N. (2013). The Effect of TARP on Bank Risk-Taking, *Journal of Financial Stability* 9, 790–803.

Bliss, R. and Rosen, R. (2001). CEO Compensation and Bank Mergers, *Journal of Financial Economics* 61, 107–138.

Board of Governors of the Federal Reserve System, Federal Deposit Insurance Corporation, Office of the Comptroller of the Currency, Treasury, and Office of Thrift Supervision. (2010). Guidance on Sound Incentive Compensation Policies. June 25,<http://www.fdic.gov/news/news/press/2010/pr10138a.pdf.>.

Borisova, G., Brockman, P., Salas, J. M., and Zagorchev, A. (2012). Government Ownership and Corporate Governance: Evidence from the EU, *Journal of Banking and Finance* 36, 2918–2934.

Bouwens, J. and Kroos, P. (2011). Target Ratcheting and Effort Reduction, *Journal of Accounting and Economics* 51, 171–185.

Brammer, S., Millington, A., and Pavelin, S. (2007). Gender and Ethnic Diversity among UK Corporate Boards, *Corporate Governance: An International Review* 15(2), 393–403.

Carbo-Valverde, S., Kane, E. J., and Rodriguez-Fernandez, F. (2012). Regulatory Arbitrage in Cross-Border Banking Mergers within the EU, *Journal of Money, Credit and Banking* 44, 1609–1629.

Coles, J. L., Daniel, N. D., and Naveen, L. (2006). Managerial Incentives and Risk-Taking, *Journal of Financial Economics* 79, 431–468.

Cornett, M. M., Guo, L., Khaksari, S., and Tehranian, H. (2010). The Impact of State Ownership on Performance Differences in Privately-Owned versus State-Owned Banks: An International Comparison, *Journal of Financial Intermediation* 19(1), 74–94.

Datta, S., Iskandar-Datta, M., and Raman, K. (2001). Executive Compensation and Corporate Acquisition Decisions, *Journal of Finance* 56, 2299–2336.

DeAngelo, H. and Stulz, R. (2013). Why High Leverage is Optimal for Banks. Fisher College of Business Working Paper.

DeYoung, R., Peng, E., and Yan, M. (2013). Executive Compensation and Business Policy Choices at US Commercial Banks, *Journal of Financial and Quantitative Analysis* 48, 165–196.

Diamond, D. and Dybvig, P. (1983). Bank Runs, Deposit Insurance, and Liquidity, *Journal of Political Economy* 99, 689–721.

Diamond, D. and Rajan, R. (2001). Liquidity Risk, Liquidity Creation, and Financial Fragility: A Theory of Banking, *Journal of Political Economy* 109, 287–327.

Duchin, R. and Sosyura, D. (2011). Safer Ratios, Riskier Portfolios: Banks' Response to Government Aid. Ross School of Business Paper.

Duru, A., Mansi, S. A., and Reeb, D. M. (2005). Earnings-Based Bonus Plans and the Agency Costs of Debt, *Journal of Accounting and Public Policy* 24, 431–447.

Edmans, A. and Liu, Q. (2011). Inside Debt, *Review of Finance* 11, 75–102.

Ellul, A. and Yerramilli, V. (2013). Stronger Risk Controls, Lower Risk: Evidence from US Banking Holding Companies, *Journal of Finance* 68, 1757–1803.

Erkens, D. H., Hung, M., and Matos, P. (2012). Corporate Governance in the 2007–2008 Financial Crisis: Evidence from Financial Institutions Worldwide, *Journal of Corporate Finance* 18(2), 389–411.

Fahlenbrach, R. and Stulz, R. (2011). Bank CEO Incentives and the Credit Crisis, *Journal of Financial Economics* 99, 11–26.

Federal Reserve Bank (2010). *Guidance on Sound Incentive Compensation Policies*. Washington, DC: Board of Governors of the Federal Reserve System.

Financial Stability Board. (2009). Principles for Sound Compensation Practices, Basel, Switzerland, <http://www.financialstabilityboard.org/publications/r_0904b.pdf.>.

Fischer, M., Hainz, C., Rocholl, J., and Steffen, S. (2012). Government Guarantees and Bank Risk Taking Incentives. University of Frankfurt Unpublished Working Paper.

Forbes, D. P. and Milliken, F. J. (1999). Cognition and Corporate Governance: Understanding Boards of Directors as Strategic Decision-Making Groups, *The Academy of Management Review* 24(3), 489–505.

Guay, W. R. (1999). The Sensitivity of CEO Wealth to Equity Risk: An Analysis of the Magnitude and Determinants, *Journal of Financial Economics* 53, 43–71.

Gropp, R., Gruendl, C., and Guettler, A. (2014). The Impact of Public Guarantees on Bank Risk-Taking: Evidence from a Natural Experiment, *Review of Finance* (Forthcoming).

Gropp, R. and Köhler, M. (2010). Bank Owners or Bank Managers: Who is Keen on Risk? Evidence from the Financial Crisis, Centre for European Economic Research Discussion Paper No. 10–013, 1–36.

Haan, J. De and Vlahu, R. (2013). Corporate Governance of Banks: A Survey, De Nederlandsche Bank Working Paper No. 336/2013.

Hagendorff, J. and Keasey, K. (2012). The Value of Board Diversity in Banking: Evidence from the Market for Corporate Control, *The European Journal of Finance* 18, 41–58.

Hagendorff, J. and Vallascas, F. (2011). CEO Pay Incentives and Risk-Taking: Evidence from Bank Acquisitions, *Journal of Corporate Finance* 17, 1078–1095.

Hambrick, D. C. and Mason, P. A. (1984). Upper Echelons: The Organization as a Reflection of its Top Managers, *Academy of Management Review* 9, 193–206.

Harjoto, M. A. and Mullineaux, D. J. (2003). CEO Compensation and the Transformation of Banking, *Journal of Financial Research* 26, 341–354.

Hermalin, B. and Weisbach, M. (2003). Boards of Directors as an Endogenously Determined Institution: A Survey of the Economic Literature, *Economic Policy Review* 9, 7–26.

Hillman, A. J., Cannella, A. A., and Paetzold, R. L. (2000). The Resource Dependence Role of Corporate Directors: Strategic Adaptation of Board Composition in Response to Environmental Change, *Journal of Management Studies* 37(2), 235–256.

Iannotta, G., Nocera, G., and Sironi, A. (2007). Ownership Structure, Risk and Performance in the European Banking Industry, *Journal of Banking & Finance* 31, 2127–2149.

Indjejikian, R., Matějka, M., Merchant, K., and Van Der Stede, W. (2011). Earnings Targets and Annual Bonus Incentives. Arizona State University Unpublished Working Paper.

Jensen, M. C. and Meckling, W. H. (1976). Theory of the Firm: Managerial Behavior, Agency Costs and Ownership Structure, *Journal of Financial Economics* 3, 305–360.

John, T. A. and John, K. (1993). Top-Management Compensation and Capital Structure, *Journal of Finance* 48, 949–974.

Keys, B. J., Mukherjee, T., Seru, A., and Vig, V. (2009). Financial Regulation and Securitization: Evidence from Subprime Loans, *Journal of Monetary Economics* 56, 700–720.

Laeven, L. and Levine, R. (2009). Bank Governance, Regulation, and Risk-Taking, *Journal of Financial Economics* 93, 259–275.

Lin, X. C. and Zhang, Y. (2009). Bank Ownership Reform and Bank Performance in China. *Journal of Banking and Finance* 33, 20–29.

Macey, J. R. and O'Hara, M. (2003). *The Corporate Governance of Banks*, Federal Reserve Bank of New York Economic Policy Review No. 9(1), 91–107.

Mehran, H. and Rosenberg, J. V. (2007). *The Effect of Employee Stock Options on Bank Investment Choice, Borrowing, and Capital*, Federal Reserve Bank of New York Staff Report No. 305.

Minnick, K., Unal, H., and Yang, L. (2011). Pay for Performance? CEO Compensation and Acquirer Returns in BHCs, *Review of Financial Studies* 24, 439–472.

Murphy, K. J. (2000). Performance Standards in Incentive Contracts, *Journal of Accounting and Economics* 30, 245–278.

Nguyen, D. D., Hagendorff, J., and Eshraghi, A. (2013). The Value of Executive Director Heterogeneity in Banking: Evidence from Appointment Announcements. University of Edinburgh Unpublished Working Paper.

Noe, T. H., Rebello, M. J., and Wall, L. D. (1996). Managerial Rents and Regulatory Intervention in Troubled Banks, *Journal of Banking & Finance* 20, 331–350.

OECD. (2009). The Corporate Governance Lessons from the Financial Crisis, *Financial Markets Trends* 2009/1.

Pathan, S. (2009). Strong Boards, CEO Power and Bank Risk-Taking, *Journal of Banking & Finance* 33, 1340–1350.

Pfeffer, J. and Salancik, G. R. (1978). *The External Control of Organizations: A Resource Dependence Perspective*. New York: Harper & Row.

Rajgopal, S. and Shevlin, T. (2002). Empirical Evidence on the Relation between Stock Option Compensation and Risk-Taking, *Journal of Accounting and Economics* 33, 145–171.

Saunders, A., Strock, E., and Travlos, N. (1990). Ownership Structure, Deregulation and Bank Risk Taking, *Journal of Finance* 45, 643–654.

Singh, V., Vinnicombe, S., and Johnson, P. (2001). Women Directors on Top UK Boards, *Corporate Governance: An International Review* 9(3), 206–216.

Smith, C. W. and Stulz, R. M. (1985). The Determinants of Firms' Hedging Policies, *The Journal of Financial and Quantitative Analysis* 20, 391–405.

Sundaram, R. K. and Yermack, D. L. (2007). Pay Me Later: Inside Debt and Its Role in Managerial Compensation, *Journal of Finance* 62, 1551–1588.

Tung, F. and Wang, X. (2012). Bank CEOs, Inside Debt Compensation, and the Global Financial Crisis. Working Paper.

Vallascas, F. and Hagendorff, J. (2013). CEO Bonus Compensation and Bank Default Risk: Evidence from the US and Europe, *Financial Markets, Institutions & Instruments* 22, 47–89.

Wei, C. and Yermack, D. (2011). Investor Reactions to CEOs' Inside Debt Incentives, *Review of Financial Studies* 24, 3813–3840.

CHAPTER 7

....

RISK MANAGEMENT IN BANKING

....

LINDA ALLEN AND ANTHONY SAUNDERS

7.1 INTRODUCTION

....

IF you open the vaults of any bank, you might think you would know what you'd find there. You would be wrong. What is really there, hidden behind the stacks of currency, is the bank's inventory of risk. The bank exists to take on the risks of its customer base. By offering its clients risk management products, the bank absorbs an inventory of risk that is added to with each transaction. The bank prices those products by estimating its costs of managing the risks inherent in each transaction. Financial institutions are specialists in risk management. Indeed, their primary expertise stems from their ability to both measure and manage risk exposure on their own behalf and on behalf of their clients—either through the evolution of financial market products to shift risks or through the absorption of their clients' risk into their risk inventory on their own balance sheets. Because financial institutions are risk intermediaries, they maintain an inventory of risk that must be measured carefully so as to ensure that the risk exposure does not threaten the intermediary's solvency. Thus, accurate measurement of risk is an essential first step for proper risk management, and financial intermediaries, because of the nature of their business, tend to be leading developers of new risk measurement and risk pricing techniques.

When financial institutions misprice risk, however, as was the case of subprime mortgage securities in the run-up to the 2007–2008 banking crisis, the size of the risk inventory may overwhelm the financial system's capacity to absorb risk, thereby resulting in global market failures such as the credit crisis of 2007. For example, banks provided equity and backup lines of credit to the structured investment vehicles (SIVs) that they formed during the build-up of the subprime mortgage securitization bubble. The SIV is a structured operating company that invests in assets that are designed to generate higher returns than the SIV's cost of funds. Rather than selling the asset-backed securities directly to investors in order to raise cash (as special purpose vehicles, SPVs, do in standard securitizations), the SIV sells bonds or commercial paper to investors in order to raise cash. The SIV then holds the loans purchased from originating banks on its own balance sheet until maturity. These loan assets held by the SIV back the debt instruments issued by the SIV to investors. Thus, in essence the SIV itself becomes an asset-backed security, and the SIV's commercial paper liabilities are considered asset-backed commercial paper. Investors buy the SIV's liabilities (most often, asset-backed commercial paper, ABCP), providing the proceeds for the purchase of loans from originating banks. The SIV's debt is backed by the loan portfolio held by the SIV. However, the SIV does not simply pass through the payments on the loans in its portfolio as in a traditional collateralized mortgage obligation (CMO). Indeed, investors have no direct rights to the cash flows on the underlying loans in the portfolio. They are entitled to the payments specified on the SIV's debt instruments. The SIV's ABCP obligations carry interest obligations that are independent of the cash flows in the underlying loan portfolio. Thus, in the traditional form of securitization, the SPV pays out only what it receives from the underlying loans in the pool of assets backing the asset-backed securities. In the newer form of securitization, the SIV is responsible for payments on its ABCP obligations whether or not the underlying pool of assets generates sufficient cash flow to cover those costs. Of course, if the cash flow from the asset pool exceeds the cost of ABCP liabilities, then the SIV keeps the spread and makes a profit. However, if the assets in the underlying pool do not generate sufficient cash flows, the SIV is still obligated to make interest and principal payments on its debt instruments.

The SIV's operating methodology should seem very familiar to bankers. SIVs are banks minus the regulations! The SIV acts like a traditional bank—holding loan assets until maturity and issuing debt instruments (such as ABCP) to fund its asset portfolio. The major difference between a SIV and a traditional bank is that the SIV cannot issue deposits to fund its asset base (i.e., it's not technically a "bank"). However, to the extent that many of these SIVs used commercial paper and interbank loans (such as repurchase agreements) to finance their asset portfolios, then they were subject to even more liquidity risk than are traditional banks.[1] This is because in the modern world of banking, sophisticated lenders (so-called suppliers of "purchased funds") are prone to "run" at the first sign of trouble, whereas depositors are slower to react. That is, interbank lenders and commercial paper buyers will withdraw funds (or refuse to renew financing) quicker than traditional "core" depositors, who may rely on their bank deposits for day-to-day business dealings or may be protected by government deposit insurance. Thus, the well-publicized problems of UK's Northern Rock Bank in August 2007 were precipitated by the withdrawal of funds by interbank lenders and other purchased fund suppliers. Core depositors represented only approximately 25% of Northern Rock's funded assets. The liquidity risk problem is exacerbated when the SIV relies on short-term sources of funding, such as commercial paper, which must be renewed within nine months, and repurchase agreements, which must be fully backed by collateral at all points in time. Thus, if the value of the portfolio declines due to credit conditions worsening for example, then the SIVs are forced to sell long-term, illiquid assets at fire sale prices in order to meet its short-term debt obligations.

Many SIVs prior to the 2007–2008 crisis were sponsored and originated by banks anxious to remove the risky subprime mortgages (and other obligations) from their balance

---

[1] A repurchase agreement allows a bank to borrow against collateral (securities) transferred to a counterparty. This transaction is typically reversed within a short time period—from a week to three months. Moreover, the collateral is marked-to-market on a daily basis.

sheets. The banks and bank regulators believed that these off-balance-sheet SIVs posed little risk to the bank itself. However, most of these SIVs had ABCP programs that were backed with bank lines of credit. When the ABCP market seized up during the summer of 2007, the SIVs took down their lines of credit and, all of a sudden, the risks that were believed to be off the balance sheet came back to haunt the banks. The banks were exposed to the risks associated with the poorly underwritten subprime mortgage securities because they were forced to lend to SIVs that had no assets other than these risky securities. Bank shareholders and stakeholders suffered, top executives lost their jobs, global credit markets dried up, and the SIV experiment ended—all because risk was improperly measured and priced in the mortgage securities market.

Banks are exposed to several major sources of risk. The first, market risk, includes interest rate risk. Thus, if, for example, interest rates increase unexpectedly, the bank's cost of funds may increase and the value of its longer-term, illiquid assets may fall, to the detriment of both the bank's profitability (net interest margin) and the market value of the bank's equity.

A second source of risk is credit risk. Since the most substantial asset classification on the bank's balance sheet consists of loans (whether to businesses, residential households or even sovereign governments), banks face the risk of default or deterioration in the borrower's credit quality.[2] As many of the subprime mortgages in the pools originated in 2005 and 2006 began to show delinquencies as early as one year or less after origination, there were concerns in the market about the credit risk exposure of the securities, despite their AAA and AA credit ratings.

A third source of risk, described above in the context of the 2007 credit crisis, is liquidity risk. Banks transform short-term, liquid liabilities (such as demand deposits) into longer-term, illiquid assets (such as loans). If there is a sudden demand for liquidity, the bank will be unable to meet all withdrawal demands because of the costs of selling an illiquid portfolio at fire sale prices.

Another source of risk is operational risk. Banks undertake clearing and custodial transactions on behalf of their customers. Fraud, mismanagement, computer failure, and human error can result in losses to customers, which the bank may have to reimburse in order to protect its reputation. Strategic business errors cause catastrophic losses that may threaten the bank's viability. Loss of reputation may spell the end of the firm's independence for a financial institution—as in the case of the venerable Barings Bank. In the context of the credit crisis of 2007, HSBC absorbed $45 billion in assets from its SIVs in order to protect its reputation in the market. Moreover, firms such as Citi, Merrill Lynch, UBS, and Bear Stearns had their reputations tarnished by their participation in the subprime mortgage debacle.

This brief thumbnail survey of risk exposures highlights the importance of measuring the amount of risk in the bank's risk inventory on a continual basis. Thus, before we can even talk about risk management, we first have to discuss risk measurement. Section 7.2 of this chapter will describe a commonly used model of risk measurement for banks—Value at Risk (VaR). Only after the bank's risk exposure is measured can we discuss how to manage that risk. It is a common perception that is was models such as VaR that led to, if not caused, the global financial crisis that began in 2007–2008. Flaws in risk measurement models presumably misled banks and other financial institutions, thereby reassuring them by obscuring the actual risk

---

[2] For example, in July 1998, Russia defaulted on its debt, followed by Argentina in 2001.

levels in the system. Undoubtedly, there are flaws in the models. However, there is evidence that banks were aware of their extreme risk exposures in 2006. For example, Goldman Sachs actively hedged its mortgage risk exposure months before the crisis broke during the summer of 2007. Most financial institutions, on the other hand, ignored the red alert future risk signals sent by their internal models in favor of the lucrative prospects immediately in front of them. Rather than the models failing the financial community, it could be said that it was the financial community that failed the models by failing to respond to signals sent by the models. Indeed, in this chapter, we will show how financial professionals blithely ignored warning signals and took actions that actually exacerbated risk exposure.

What if, upon measuring the amount of risk in the bank's risk inventory, we find that the exposure is too high from the perspective of top management's risk tolerance? Can banks simply refuse to take on more risk? The answer is no. The business of banking requires that banks stand ready to absorb the risks of their customers, but at a price. If customers are willing to pay that price, it is bad business practice to refuse it. Customers will be forced to go elsewhere and it may be impossible to win them back. Instead, the bank should continue to take on their customers' risk exposures—whether by making loans with credit risk, or absorbing currency risk by offering import/export firms cross-currency letters of credit, or by executing trust agreements, thereby exposing the bank to operational risk. However, once that risk is placed into inventory, the bank's risk management team can then decide whether to hold that risk or resell it in the global marketplace. This "risk reselling" is accomplished using financial derivatives. Banks can manage their risk inventory using financial futures, forward contracts, options and swaps. This is a much more efficient way for the bank to manage risk than disappointing longstanding customers. Thus, risk management takes place almost exclusively using derivatives transactions, rather than balance sheet adjustments. After reviewing risk management opportunities available to banks in the derivatives markets in Section 7.3, Section 7.4 discusses the risk management failures of the 2007–2008 global financial crisis, which is what happens when financial intermediaries ignore the signals sent by their risk measurement models. Finally, the chapter concludes in Section 7.5 with a discussion of the economic importance of banking sector risk.

7.2 RISK MEASUREMENT

Risk measurement has preoccupied financial market participants since the dawn of financial history. However, many past attempts have proven to be impractically complex. For example, upon its introduction, Harry Markowitz's Nobel prize-winning theory of portfolio risk measurement was not adopted in practice because of its onerous data requirements.[3]

---

[3] Modern portfolio theory is based on Markowitz's insight that diversification can reduce, but not generally eliminate, risk, thereby necessitating a risk-reward guide to portfolio selection. To estimate the efficient investment frontier in a mean-variance world requires data on expected returns, standard deviations of returns and correlations between returns for every possible pair of financial securities. On the occasion of the 50th anniversary of the publication of the seminal Markowitz's (1952) paper, Rubinstein (2002) offers an interesting discussion of the development of modern portfolio theory by Markowitz and others.

Indeed, it was Bill Sharpe who, along with others,[4] made portfolio theory the standard of financial risk measurement in real-world applications through the adoption of the simplifying assumption that all risk could be decomposed into two parts: systematic, market risk and the residual, company-specific or idiosyncratic risk. The resulting Capital Asset Pricing Model (CAPM) theorized that, since only undiversifiable market risk is relevant for securities pricing, only the market risk measurement β is necessary, thereby considerably reducing the required data inputs. This model yielded a readily measurable estimate of risk that β could be practically applied in a real-time market environment. The only problem was that β proved to have only a tenuous connection to actual security returns, thereby casting doubts on β's designation as the true risk measure.[5]

With β questioned, and with asset pricing in general being in some disarray with respect to whether the notion of "priced risk" is really relevant, market practitioners searched for a replacement risk measure that was both accurate and relatively inexpensive to estimate. Despite the consideration of many other measures and models, VaR has been widely adopted. Part of the reason leading to the widespread adoption of VaR was the decision of JP Morgan to create a transparent VaR measurement model, called RiskMetrics. RiskMetrics was supported by a publicly available database containing the critical inputs required to estimate the model.[6] Another reason behind the widespread adoption of VaR was the introduction in 1998 by the Bank for International Settlements (BIS) of international bank capital requirements that allowed relatively sophisticated banks to calculate their capital requirements based on their own internal modes such as VaR.[7]

In the past, many of the risk measurement models were private, internal models, developed in-house by financial institutions. Internal models were used for risk management in its truest sense. Indeed, the VaR tool is complementary to many other internal risk measures—such as RAROC developed by Bankers Trust in the 1970s.[8] However, market forces during the late 1990s created conditions that led to the evolution of VaR as a dominant risk measurement tool for financial firms.

The US financial environment during the 1990s was characterized by the de jure separation of commercial banking and investment banking that dating back to the Glass–Steagall

---

   [4] For example, Sharpe's (1963) paper was followed by Mossin (1968).
   [5] Dissatisfaction with the β measure began as early as Douglas (1969), with mounting doubts leading to Roll's (1977) paper. The practitioner world closely followed the academic debate with articles such as Wallace (1980). Beta's death knell was sounded by Fama and French's (1992) paper, which found that, after controlling for firm size and the market to book ratio, the firm's β had no statistically significant power to explain returns on the firm's equity.
   [6] In their introduction Mina and Xiao (2001) stress that RiskMetrics is not strictly a VaR model, although it can be used to estimate a VaR model. RiskMetrics' critical role in the dissemination of VaR among financial market practitioners stems in large part from the availability of real-time data on financial market fluctuations provided freely in the public domain. Recognizing that value added, RiskMetrics has currently formed a separate data service, DataMetrics which covers almost 100,000 data series.
   [7] The market risk amendment to the Basel capital requirements was adopted in November 1996 in Europe and in January 1998 in the US.
   [8] RAROC (risk-adjusted return on capital) models are risk-sensitive measures of economic performance that can be used to allocate risk capital within the firm. See chapter 11 of Saunders and Allen (2010).

Act of 1933.[9] However, these restrictions were undermined in practice by Section 20 affiliates (that permitted commercial bank holding companies to engage in investment banking activities up to certain limits), mergers between investment and commercial banks, and commercial bank sales of some "insurance" products, especially annuities. Thus, commercial banks competed with investment banks and insurance companies to offer financial services to clients in an environment characterized by globalization, enhanced risk exposure, and rapidly evolving securities and market procedures. Concerned about the impact of the increasing risk environment on the safety and soundness of the banking system, bank regulators instituted (in 1992) risk-adjusted bank capital requirements that levied a capital charge for both on—and off-balance-sheet credit risk exposures.

Risk-adjusted capital requirements initially applied only to commercial banks, although insurance companies and securities firms had to comply with their own reserve and haircut regulations as well as with market forces that demanded capital cushions against insolvency based on economic model-based measures of exposure—so called economic capital.[10] Among other shortcomings of the BIS capital requirements were their neglect of diversification benefits in measuring a bank's risk exposure. Thus, regulatory capital requirements tended to be higher than economically necessary, thereby undermining commercial banks' competitive position vis à vis largely unregulated investment banks. To compete with other financial institutions, commercial banks had the incentive to track economic capital requirements more closely, notwithstanding their need to meet regulatory capital requirements. The more competitive the commercial bank was in providing investment banking activities, for example, the greater its incentive to increase its potential profitability by increasing leverage and reducing its capital reserves.

JP Morgan (now JP Morgan Chase) was one of a handful of globally diversified commercial banks that were in a special position relative to the commercial banking sector on the one hand and the investment banking sector on the other. In one sense, these banks were caught in between. On the one hand, from an economic perspective, they could be thought of more as investment banks than as commercial banks, with large market risks due to trading activities, as well as advisory and other corporate finance activities. On the other hand, this group of globally diversified commercial banks was holding a commercial banking license, and, hence, was subject to commercial bank capital adequacy requirements. This special position gave these banks, JP Morgan being a particular example, a strong incentive to come out with an initiative to remedy the capital adequacy problems that they faced. Specifically, the capital requirements for market risk in place were not representative of true economic risk, due to their limited account of the diversification effect. At the same time competing financial institutions, in particular, investment banks such as Merrill Lynch, Goldman Sachs, and Salomon Brothers, were not subject to bank capital adequacy requirements. As such, the capital they held for market risk was determined more by economic and investor considerations than by regulatory requirements. This allowed these institutions to bolster significantly more impressive ratios such

---

[9] The Gramm–Leach–Bliley Act of 1999 permitted the creation of financial service holding companies that could include commercial banking, investment banking and insurance subsidiaries under a single corporate umbrella, thereby effectively repealing the Glass–Steagall Act.

[10] Insurance regulators in the US adopted their own risk-based capital requirements for life and property-casualty insurers in the mid-to the late 1990s.

as return on equity (ROE) and return on assets (ROA) compared with banks with a banking charter.

In response to the above pressures, JP Morgan took the initiative to develop an open architecture (rather than in-house) methodology, called RiskMetrics. RiskMetrics quickly became the industry benchmark in risk measurement. The publication of RiskMetrics was a pivotal step in moving regulators toward adopting economic capital-based models in measuring a bank's capital adequacy. Indeed, bank regulators worldwide allowed (sophisticated) commercial banks to measure their market risk exposures using internal models that were often VaR-based. The market risk amendments to the Basel accord made in-house risk-measurement models a mainstay in the financial sector. Financial institutions worldwide moved forward with this new approach and never looked back.

The basic question that is the basis for VaR as we know it today is "how much can we lose on our trading portfolio by tomorrow's close?" Note that this is a risk-measurement, not a risk-management question. Furthermore, it is not concerned with obtaining a portfolio position to maximize the profitability of the bank's traded portfolio subject to a risk constraint, or any other optimization question. Instead, this is a pure question of risk measurement. VaR takes a statistical or probabilistic approach to answering Mr Weatherstone's question of how much could be lost on a "bad day." That is, we define a "bad day" in a statistical sense, such that there is only an x% probability that daily losses will exceed this amount given a distribution of all possible daily returns over some recent past period. That is, we define a "bad day" so that there is only an x percent probability of an even worse day. Moreover, VaR models can be used to estimate the expected average loss on such bad days (expected shortfall).

Implementing VaR models requires estimation of a probability distribution of returns (or losses) so that we can measure the cutoff point that designates the loss that will be exceeded with an x% probability on any given day. The simplest forms of RiskMetrics—for example, the Rule 415 model—assume that financial securities are normally distributed. This makes estimation of VaR quite easy because all we have to do is estimate the mean and standard deviation of securities prices using historical data. Unfortunately, it is often the case that the simplicity of the VaR measures—used to analyze the risk of the equity portfolio, for example—is in large part obtained with assumptions that are not supported by empirical evidence. The most important (and most problematic) of these assumptions is that daily equity returns are normally distributed. In general, there is a tradeoff between the accuracy of assumptions and ease of calculation, such that greater accuracy is often accompanied by greater complexity.[11]

This problem of complexity is exacerbated when there is a paucity of data available to be used to estimate the model's fundamental assumptions. Market risk exposure arises from unexpected security price fluctuations, estimated using long histories of daily price fluctuations. Unfortunately, measuring a loan's credit risk exposure is far more difficult. Since loans are not always traded, and even when traded they trade infrequently, there is often no history of daily price fluctuations available to build a (loan) loss distribution. Moreover, credit events such as default or rating downgrades are rare, often non-reoccurring events. Thus, we often have insufficient statistical power to estimate a daily VaR for credit risk exposure; that

[11] For specific methodologies used to estimate VaR models, see Allen, Boudoukh, and Saunders (2004).

is, data limitations create special challenges in adapting VaR techniques to estimate credit risk exposure. However, we can use VaR techniques to estimate losses due to credit events if the time interval we consider is longer. Indeed, the convention in the new generation of credit risk models is to assume that the credit risk time horizon is one year, thereby estimating losses during the next year if it is a "bad" year, defined according to a specified VaR level; for example, a 99.5 percentile VaR (i.e., x% equals 0.5%) estimates the minimum losses in the worst five years out of 1,000. A VaR model, such as CreditMetrics, measures the probability that the credit rating of any given debt security will change over the course of the one year credit horizon. The tabulation of potential changes in credit ratings—known as the credit migration matrix—considers the entire range of credit events, including upgrades and downgrades as well as actual default. Historical migrations of publicly traded debt instruments, such as corporate bonds, are used to tabulate the annual probability of any given change in credit risk. These loss probabilities are then applied to specific debt instruments, such as untraded loans, to calculate the loan portfolio's VaR.

Because of the problems applying the VaR model to credit risk assessment, banks often use other credit risk measurement models. There has been widespread adoption of credit scoring models in all arenas of bank lending—such as mortgage lending, commercial lending, credit card and revolving debt. Credit scoring models (e.g., FICO scores) apply discriminant analysis to a class of borrowers by identifying certain key factors that determine the probability of default (as opposed to repayment), and combine or weight them into a quantitative score. In some cases, the score can be literally interpreted as a probability of default; in others, the score can be used as a classification system: it places a potential borrower into either a good or a bad group, based on a score and a cutoff point.

VaR models are probably best suited to measuring operational risk exposure. VaR measures losses from unexpected, extreme shocks that are in the tail of the probability distribution (i.e., at the end of outcomes that are extremely unlikely to occur). Thus, the probability of a VaR-size event (x%) is very small (i.e., 5%, or 1%, or 0.5%). However, when these improbable events occur, they are catastrophic for the firm and typically result in insolvency. Indeed, Allen and Bali (2007) find that operational risk events are likely to be the cause of large unexpected catastrophic losses. They use a comprehensive approach to measuring operational risk that includes reputational risk and strategic business risk and shows that approximately 18% of financial institutions' returns represent compensation for operational risk. In contrast, Basel II mandates a narrow definition of operational risk for regulatory purposes that focuses on day-to-day loss events emanating from computer failures and human error, for example, while excluding catastrophic operational risk events resulting from reputational losses and strategic business errors. Although this definitional decision may be warranted on pragmatic grounds (e.g., the absence of reliable industry databases on extreme tail operational loss events), the eventual goal is to develop a more comprehensive measure of operational risk that is more consistent with the designation of regulatory capital as a cushion against unexpected loss. Frame and White (Chapter 11 of this *Handbook*) describe operational issues arising from technological innovation and diffusion in financial firms. VaR enables banks to measure operational risk (for economic capital, if not for regulatory capital purposes) because of the methodology's focus measuring the impact of extremely unlikely, but catastrophic risk events. Thus, the VaR methodology can be used to measure market risk, credit risk and operational risk.

7.3 Risk Management

Suppose that the VaR model implemented by the bank provides a measure of risk exposure that is enormous—even in excess of the bank's capital position. What can be done? The first thing is not to panic. The second is to fire up the derivatives traders. The bank can manage its risk position by trading in derivatives markets. If the initial risk inventory is too high, the bank can undertake hedging transactions to reduce its risk exposure without turning away profitable and longstanding customers. On the other hand, if the initial risk inventory is too low, and therefore not sufficiently profitable, the bank can undertake speculative transactions to increase its risk exposure. Derivatives markets are the thermostat used by the bank to control its risk temperature.

Warren Buffett has termed derivatives "financial weapons of mass destruction."[12] He has decried the "daisy chain of risk" that is facilitated by derivatives requiring little payment up front but which can represent large and uncertain obligations in the future. This point of view has led some to call for a ban on certain derivatives, although Warren Buffett admits (in the Berskshire Hathaway Annual Report of 2002) that "the derivatives genie is out of the bottle, and these instruments will almost certainly multiply in variety and number until some event makes their toxicity clear." However, the fundamental question is whether derivatives are the cause of this "toxic" behavior, or merely the vehicle for excessive risk-taking. If it is the latter, there will always be financial players who exploit the system for personal gain, whether or not they have derivatives to accomplish their nefarious goals.

In either extreme, pure hedging or pure speculating, the derivatives transaction is tied to, indeed motivated by, another transaction, or series of transactions that constitute the underlying cash position. The Commodity Futures Trading Commission (CFTC) estimates that up to 85% of all futures trades are explicitly linked to other transactions. If the cash flows on the derivatives transaction are opposite to those of the underlying cash position, we consider the derivatives trade to be a hedge. If, on the other hand, the cash flows move in the same direction, we consider the derivatives trade to be speculative. The cash flows on derivatives are determined by fluctuations in interest rates, exchange rates, equity prices, default probabilities, and so on. That is, derivatives can be used to manage all types of risk exposure.

Suppose, for example, the bank has an underlying cash position that is exposed to interest rate increases. This is a very common position for a bank, as a result of the process of "borrowing short to lend long." Thus, the bank's assets have a longer maturity (duration) than the bank's liabilities, leading to a positive duration gap. Under these circumstances, the underlying cash position (the bank's portfolio) will decline in value and profitability will fall if interest rates go up. To hedge that risk, the bank can undertake a derivatives position that generates positive (offsetting) cash flows when interest rates go up—that is, a short position. Short positions can be implemented by selling interest rate futures or forwards, buying put options on interest rate sensitive instruments and/or buying fixed-for-floating swaps. We examine each of these markets briefly.

---

[12] Warren Buffett's quotes have been taken from the 2002 Berkshire Hathaway Annual Report.

7.3.1 Financial Futures and Forwards

The concept of a forward contract originated in sixteenth-century Japan when landown-ers raised money by selling rice in advance of delivery to rice merchants. A more formal, exchange-based contract, the precursor to the modern futures contract, originated in the US Midwest during the early nineteenth century. In 1848, some 82 merchants met above a flour store on Chicago's South Water Street and formed the Chicago Board of Trade (CBOT). Today, merged with the Chicago Mercantile Exchange (CME), the CBOT trades millions of futures contracts, as well as options and swaps.

Financial futures or forwards are obligations to make (sell) or take (buy) delivery of some underlying financial asset at a predetermined price (i.e., futures or forward price) on a spec-ified delivery date. The counterparty that buys the contract agrees to buy the underlying financial asset and holds a long position. The counterparty that sells the contract is obligated to sell the underlying financial asset and holds a short position. The long position gains if the price upon delivery date is higher than the predetermined price, whereas the short posi-tion gains if the price declines below the predetermined price. Typically, there is no actual delivery of the underlying financial asset in financial futures/forward contracts (in contrast to commodity futures/forwards). Instead of physical delivery, the contracts are usually cash settled, with the losing party paying the winning party for the difference between the spot price upon delivery minus the predetermined futures/forward price.

For example, if the bank has a positive duration gap and wants to hedge its exposure to rising interest rates, it may take a short position in an interest rate futures contract, such as the US Treasury bills futures contract or the three-month Eurodollar futures contract.[13] If interest rates go up, the price of the contract falls and the short (selling) counterparty gains. For each basis point increase in interest rates, the Treasury bill and Eurodollar futures contracts gain $25 per $1 million face value. This cash inflow would offset some (or all) of the losses on the underlying cash position emanating from the bank's positive duration gap.[14]

Banks can hedge interest rate risk, currency risk, equity price risk, commodity risk, credit risk, and operational risk using futures and forward contracts. The methodology is the same as illustrated above; that is, short futures/forwards positions hedge underlying cash expo-sures to price declines and long futures/forwards positions hedge underlying cash expo-sures to price increases. The only difference is the identity of the reference security. Thus, when hedging currency risk, the reference security's value must fluctuate with shifts in for-eign exchange rates. When hedging credit risk, the derivative's underlying security fluctu-ates with shifts in default risk.

---

[13] The Eurodollar CD is not related to the currency named the euro. Eurodollar CDs refer to US dollar-denominated deposits held by banks outside the US or in international banking facilities within the US. LIBOR (the London Interbank Offered Rate) is the offer rate on interbank loans of Eurodollar deposits. See Allen (1997, ch. 12).

[14] If all the losses are hedged, we consider that a "perfect" or "naïve" hedge. In practice, we do not observe such hedges because (1) they are difficult to get exactly right and (2) they are undesirable since, while a "perfect" futures/forward hedge eliminates all possibility of loss, it also eliminates all possibility of gain.

7.3.2 Financial Options

Financial futures and forwards are useful tools to protect an underlying cash position from losses due to risk exposure. However, because of their symmetric cash flow payout, they also protect an underlying cash position from gains. That is, when the positive duration gap bank puts on a short futures position, and interest rates decline rather than increase, the bank's portfolio will make money, but the hedge will lose money. Thus, there is a demand for a hedging instrument that protects against losses, but not against gains—that is, an insurance policy against losses. This insurance policy is an options contract.

An options contract is a derivative that gives the holder the right, not the obligation, to buy (call option) or sell (put option) an underlying reference financial asset at a predetermined price (the exercise or strike price) for a time period up to the specified expiration date.[15] The buyer (holder) of the option retains the right to exercise the option if it is worthwhile. That is, if the holder has a call option, they will benefit when prices increase above the exercise price. If prices do not exceed the exercise price at expiration date, the option expires worthless. Thus, if the bank wants to use an option to hedge its exposure to rising interest rates, it would purchase a put option on an interest rate sensitive instrument (such as a Eurodollar futures contract),[16] which would generate positive cash flows if interest rates increase (and prices fall), thereby offsetting the bank's loss due to its underlying cash position with a positive duration gap. If, however, interest rates decline, the positive duration gap bank generates positive cash flows and the option hedge expires worthless, thereby allowing the bank to keep its gains.

The exception to this is that the options buyer must pay an upfront cost—the premium— which is nonrefundable to the buyer if the option expires worthless.[17] Options premiums are quite substantial. For this reason, we have seen the development of compound options positions, such as straddles, collars, and butterflies that were originated in order to reduce the upfront premium cost of options trades. As market participants experimented with these "lower cost options hedges," however, they found that they were viable products in their own right. Therefore, today, collars are sold as stand-alone risk management products to the customers of financial institutions. Alternatively, they can be packaged with other financial products, as in adjustable-rate mortgages that contain collars.

---

[15] An American option can be exercised at any time up until expiration date, whereas a European option cannot be exercised prior to expiration date. Unless are interim cash flows (such as dividend payments), it would not desirable to exercise an American option prior to expiration since the option is worth more alive than dead because of its time value. Therefore, in practical terms, there is no difference between American and European options on financial securities with no interim cash flows (e.g., zero coupon bonds).

[16] In general, financial options on futures contracts tend to be more liquid than financial options on cash instruments. Thus, for example, we see more activity in the market for US Treasury bill futures options than in the market for US Treasury bill options.

[17] In contrast, futures contracts require an upfront margin (paid to the exchange's clearing corporation, which acts as third-party guarantor) which is a good faith deposit and is refunded to the contract holders (both buyer and seller) upon fulfillment of their obligations under the futures contract. Because forward markets are limited to financial intermediaries with reputations to uphold, there is no margin or third-party guarantor in the forwards market.

7.3.3 Swaps

The process of financial innovation leading to the introduction of cross-currency swaps is described in Box 7.1. It did not take long for financial market professionals to see the extensions—to fixed-for-floating rate swaps (to hedge interest rate risk) and credit default swaps (to hedge credit risk exposure). A swap is essentially a portfolio of forward contracts with predetermined payment dates, called reset dates, and predetermined prices. In a fixed-for-floating rate swap, for example, the buyer of the swap exchanges floating rate payments (say, tied to LIBOR) for fixed rate payments. If interest rates increase, the swap buyer gains because instead of paying the higher LIBOR payments the swap buyer pays the lower, predetermined fixed rate. Thus, the positive duration gap bank can purchase fixed-for-floating rate swaps in order to hedge its exposure against increasing interest rates.

Upon reset dates (which can occur monthly, quarterly, semi-annually, annually) for the life of the swap (which can last for up to five or ten years), the swap intermediary calculates the payments required, nets them out and supervises the transfer of the net cash flow (the difference between the fixed and floating rate as of the reset date) between the counterparties. Thus, if interest rates have increased, the swap seller pays the swap buyer an amount equal to the difference between the fixed rate minus the floating rate times the notional value of the swap, and vice versa if interest rates have declined. The swap intermediary also acts as the guarantor to insure that each swap counterparty meets its obligations. In exchange for setting up the transaction, monitoring its cash flows and guaranteeing the counterparty credit risk, the swap intermediary receives a fee that is paid on each reset date.

The dominant credit derivative to date has been the credit default swap (CDS). CDSs are essentially insurance policies on the face value (notional value) of corporate debt (bonds or loans) such that the CDS buyer pays a premium in exchange for protection against loss from

---

Box 7.1 Introduction of Cross–Currency Swaps

It was August 1981. The US dollar was entering a period of strength against European currencies. In 1979, IBM had issued debt denominated in Swiss francs and Deutschemarks, in the course of its regular financing program. With the increase in the dollar, the dollar cost of IBM's liabilities declined significantly. IBM could realize a significant cash inflow if only the liabilities could be repurchased and converted into US dollars. But the retirement of debt at a discount would expose IBM to considerable tax liability. Moreover, in the European bearer bond market, it would have been difficult for IBM to find the bonds for repurchase. It seemed that the opportunity would pass IBM by.

Enter the World Bank. The World Bank typically borrows in all major currencies to finance its activities. Because of the upheaval in the European currencies, the World Bank was concerned that future borrowing would soak up the credit available in those markets. How could the World Bank borrow Swiss francs and Deutschemarks without competing with other borrowers?

Enter Salomon Brothers, who saw the opportunity to match the needs of IBM and the World Bank. IBM wanted to replace DM and Swiss franc borrowings with US dollar borrowings. The World Bank wanted those DM and Swiss franc borrowings and was willing to borrow US dollars in order to avoid disrupting the European debt markets. The synergies were obvious, at least once someone point them out, and a new financial instrument was born—the cross-currency swap.

credit events (e.g., default) on the underlying (reference) debt instrument.[18] That is, in the event of default, the CDS seller must pay the CDS buyer either some cash amount or transfer physical securities, depending upon the method of settlement. CDSs are customizable, over-the-counter (OTC) contracts, although standardization enhances the tradability (liquidity) of the contract.[19] Thus, five-year CDS contracts are most prevalent, although one-, three-, seven-, and ten-year contracts are also traded.[20]

In contrast to actual insurance policies, there is no requirement that the CDS buyer actually own the underlying reference securities, and therefore the notional value of CDS contracts in recent years has exceeded the total value of the outstanding debt instruments. For example, Helwege et al. (2009) report that the number of General Motors outstanding debt was $20 billion less than the $65 billion CDS notional value. As of the end of 2006, the Bank of England estimated total global corporate debt instruments (bonds plus loans) outstanding at $17.1 trillion. In contrast, the BIS reported that single name CDS outstanding during the first half of 2007 had a total notional value exceeding $20 trillion.[21] This has implications both for settlement of the CDS contract and systemic risk exposure.

The credit derivatives market has grown from an ad hoc attempt by banks to transfer their risk exposure to an innovative dealer system that has evolved into a standardized global market.[22] As of December 2012, Figure 7.1 shows that OTC derivatives notional value totaled $633 trillion, almost up to pre-crisis levels of over $680 trillion as of mid-2008. Out of this, CDS represented notional value of $25 trillion as of year end 2012, substantially reduced

[18] The credit event can be specified as default, failure to pay, restructuring, etc. However, the use of restructuring as a credit event is ambiguous when the reference security is a loan, since loan restructuring is a fairly common occurrence that may be triggered by something other than the borrower's financial distress. Thus, restructuring is known as a "soft" credit event. Repudiation or moratorium is used as a credit event for credit derivatives based on government obligations.

[19] There have been several proposals to move credit derivatives trading to organized exchanges. It is unclear whether the benefits of exchange trading (enhanced transparency and liquidity) will be offset by the costs of basis risk and lack of customization as the standardized contracts diverge from the underlying risks to be hedged.

[20] The increased presence of hedge funds (since the late 1990s' investment in credit instruments in the US and London) led to an agreement that enhanced the liquidity of the CDS market in 2006. Liquidating a CDS position typically required either offsetting transactions or an agreement by both counterparties to terminate (tear up) the transaction. However, hedge funds preferred to transfer their shares via assignment—a process known as novation. However, there were problems in coordinating novation agreements and getting confirmation. In September 2006, the ISDA Novation Protocol was announced to standardize novation procedures requiring parties to obtain prior consent, which could be communicated electronically. The results were to dramatically reduce confirmation backlogs.

[21] Single-name CDSs specify a single reference security. In contrast, multi-name CDSs reference more than one name, as in a portfolio or basket CDS or CDS index, such as the Dow Jones CDX. Baskets are credit derivatives based on a small portfolio of loans or bonds, such that all assets included in the underlying pool are individually listed. In contrast, the contents of larger portfolios are described by their characteristics. A basket CDS, also known as a first-to-default swap, is structured like a regular CDS, but the reference security consists of several securities. The first reference entity to default triggers a default payment of the par value minus the recovery value and then all payments end. As of the first half of 2007, there was an additional $20 trillion notional value in multi-name CDS.

[22] See Smithson (2003) and Mengle (2007) for a discussion of the stages of development of the market for credit derivatives. The standardized contracts, terms and dispute resolution provided by the International Swap and Derivatives Association (ISDA) played a role in that evolution.

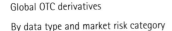

Global OTC derivatives

By data type and market risk category   Graph 1

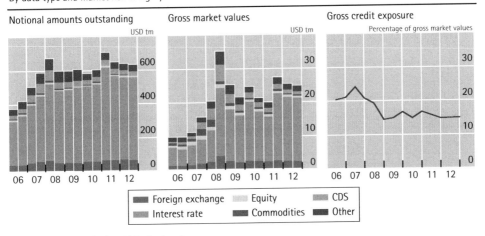

FIGURE 7.1 Global OTC derivatives.

Source: Bank for International Settlements, "Statistical Release: OTC Derivatives Statistics at End December 2012," May 2013.

from pre-crisis levels exceeding $40 trillion. The gross market replacement value (middle panel of Figure 7.1) amounted to $24.7 trillion as of December 2012.

In September 2003, the Dow Jones CDX (DJ CDX) North American Investment Grade Index was introduced. In November 2004, Markit initiated a credit index data service, which included the DJ CDX (which also includes indexes covering emerging market credit derivatives) and the International Index Company's (IIC) iTraxx (which covers the EU, Japan and non-Japan Asia). Both sets of indexes are made up of 125 of the most liquid, investment grade credits in the form of CDS. For example, the DJ CDX consists of a basket of 125 CDS contracts on US firms with liquid, investment grade corporate debt. The identity of the components in the index changes every six months—every March and September for the DJ CDX. Companies may be dropped from the index if they are downgraded or become illiquid. For example, Ford and General Motors were dropped from the DJ CDX in September 2005 when their debt fell below investment grade. The index is equally weighted, and so each CDS component makes up 0.8% of the index value. Using indexed CDS to hedge credit risk may be less expensive because of the liquidity of these instruments, although it does expose the hedger to basis risk.[23] Synthetic CDOs are comprised of tranches of indexed CDS. Thus, CDS are used as building blocks in financial securities design as well as risk management.[24]

Similar to options, but different from non-credit-related swaps, the risks on a credit swap are not symmetrical. That is, the protection buyer receives a payment upon the occurrence of a

[23] Basis risk results when the fluctuations in the value of the reference security underlying the derivative do not move in lock step with the hedge position. For example, there is basis risk if indexed CDS is used to hedge a portfolio of loans to firms that are not identical to the 125 firms in the index.

[24] The most popular CDS indexes consist of 125 corporate entities. Multi-name, or basket CDSs contain more than one reference security, most commonly between three and ten. The most common form of multi-name CDS is the first-to-default CDS, which compensates the protection buyer for losses

credit event trigger, but the swap "expires worthless" if no trigger occurs.[25] In that event, the protection seller keeps the periodic premiums paid for the swap, similar to the convex cash flows that characterize options. Thus, the protection buyer transfers the credit risk to the protection seller in exchange for a premium. The size of the premium, known as the swap spread, is the internal rate of return that equates the periodic premium payments to the expected payments in the event of a credit event trigger. The spread is quoted per annum, but paid quarterly throughout the year.[26]

Although the credit protection buyer hedges exposure to default risk, there is still counterparty credit risk in the event that the seller fails to perform their obligations under the terms of the contract (as was the concern in September 2008 with regard to AIG, an active CDS seller).[27] A pure credit default swap is similar to buying credit insurance and/or a multiperiod credit option. The growth in trading of these credit derivatives has facilitated a net overall transfer of credit risk from banks to non-banks, principally insurance companies. Banks, securities firms and corporations are net buyers of credit protection, whereas insurance companies, hedge funds, mutual funds, and pension funds are net sellers. Insurance companies view credit derivatives as an insurance product, in which their relatively high credit ratings can be used to insure the buyers of credit protection (e.g., banks) against risk exposure to their loan customers. Credit derivatives such as CDS allow a bank to alter the risk-return tradeoff of a loan portfolio without having to sell or remove loans from the balance sheet. Apart from avoiding an adverse customer relationship effect, the use of credit derivatives (rather than loan sales or other portfolio methods for reducing the bank's credit risk exposure) may allow a bank to avoid adverse timing of tax payments, as well as liquidity problems related to buying back a similar loan at a later date if risk-return considerations so dictate. Thus, for customer relationship, tax, transaction cost, and liquidity reasons, a bank may prefer the credit derivative solution to loan portfolio optimization rather than the more direct (loan trading) portfolio management solution.

7.4 THE 2007–2008 GLOBAL FINANCIAL CRISIS

The economy relies on financial institutions to act as specialists in risk measurement and risk management. The importance of this is demonstrated by the aftermath of the banks' failure to perform this critical function: the 2007–2008 global financial crisis, resulting in the worldwide breakdown in credit markets, as well as an astonishing level of equity market

---

on the first default among the basket of reference entities, after which the swap automatically terminates. Tranched synthetic CDOs comprised of indexed CDS also prioritize credit protection, but are more flexible than first-to-default swaps.

[25] In contrast, an interest rate swap (fixed for floating rate swap) will entail symmetric payments such that the swap buyer (the fixed rate leg of the swap) earns positive cash flows when interest rates increase and the swap seller (the floating rate leg) earns positive cash flows when interest rates decrease.

[26] OTC CDS have standardized spread payment dates on March 20, June 20, September 20, and December 20. The spread is constant for the life of the swap, with the exception of a constant maturity CDS in which the spread is reset periodically to the market rate for newly issued CDS.

[27] Swap spreads incorporate counterparty credit risk. For example, Hull and White (2001) find a range of around 50 basis points when they simulate the impact of counterparty credit risk exposure.

volatility. When banks fail to perform their critical risk measurement and risk management functions, the result is a crisis of confidence that paralyzes the entire economy. Even overnight credit markets seize up. Banks are unwilling to lend to other banks because of uncertainty about their own and their competitors' precarious financial condition. This hoarding of liquidity prevents banks from providing the fundamental credit required to keep businesses moving. Commercial paper and other debt markets cease to function, thereby leaving even creditworthy firms without a source of either working capital or investment capital. These firms are then unable to do business and the financial contagion is transmitted to the real economy in terms of loss of jobs and declines in economic activity.

In analyzing the global financial crisis that began in 2007, we delineate three separate phases and three different types of risk: (1) the initial credit risk crisis, (2) the following liquidity risk crisis, and (3) the realization of an operational risk crisis.

The first phase began in the beginning of the year 2007 with the realization of rising delinquencies on subprime residential mortgage-backed securities (RMBS). As of February 2007, the percentage of subprime mortgage-backed securities delinquent by 90 days or more was 10.09%, up from 9.08% in October 2006, which was substantially higher than the 5.37% rate in May 2005 (Shenn, 2007). The second largest subprime lender, New Century Financial, was hit by large number of mortgage defaults, and filed for bankruptcy on April 2, 2007, after it was unable to meet its lenders' calls for more collateral on its credit lines. Bear Stearns High-Grade Structured Credit Master Fund (the investment vehicle for four Bear Stearns hedge funds heavily invested in subprime CMOs, CLOs, and CDOs) and Dillon Read Capital Management (DRCM), a subsidiary of UBS, both experienced substantial losses during the spring of 2007 and were ultimately closed down several months later.

The roots of these credit problems can be found in the overheated market conditions that characterized the housing bubble. While it is difficult to date the genesis of the 2007 credit crisis, the preconditions for such a crisis were building from 2001 and, in particular, the terrorist attacks on 9/11. In fact, the immediate response by regulators to the terrorist attacks was to create stability in the financial markets. For example, the Federal Reserve lowered the short-term money market rate that banks and other financial institutions pay in the federal funds market, the market for overnight borrowings among major banks, and even made lender of last resort funds available to non-bank financial institutions such as investment banks. This had the immediate effect of lowering short-term borrowing rates for other market instruments, such as short-term borrowings of dollars abroad (LIBOR). In fact, very soon nominal short-term rates fell to close to 1%, that is, to historically low levels. Perhaps not surprisingly, given low interest rates and the increased liquidity provided by central banks such as the Federal Reserve, there ensued a rapid expansion in borrowing or debt levels in the economy, both among consumer borrowers and commercial borrowers. Thus, consumer demand for mortgages and credit card debt ballooned. Moreover, commercial demand for loans increased, and it became increasingly less expensive for private equity firms to undertake takeovers financed via commercial loans (often in the form of syndicated bank loans).

However, what is important is that it was not just the *quantity* of consumer and commercial debt that increased, but also the *quality* of debt simultaneously declined. Specifically, as the demand for mortgage debt grew, especially among those who had previously been excluded from participating in the market because of their poor credit quality, banks and other financial institutions began lowering their credit quality cutoff points. Moreover, to boost their earnings in the relatively new area of the market now popularly known as the "subprime market," banks and other mortgage-supplying institutions often offered relatively low "teaser" rates or adjustable rate mortgages (ARMs) at exceptionally low initial interest rates, but with substantial step-up rates after the initial rate expired and if market rates rose in the future, in addition to low-documentation or no-documentation loans, now known as "liar loans" because they did not verify borrowers' claims. Under the traditional banking structure, banks might have been reluctant to court low credit quality borrowers so aggressively for fear that the loans would default prior to maturity. However, asset securitization and loan syndication allowed banks to retain little or no part of the loans they originated. Thus, banks were able to pass along the risk without performing their fundamental risk measurement and management functions. This approach to bank risk management has been called the "originate-to-distribute" model.

The crisis started with the downturn in US housing prices during the second half of the year 2006. Most importantly, the geographic impact of the subprime mortgage crisis spread across the US, thereby undermining the geographic diversification assumptions used in constructing the subprime asset-backed mortgage pools. At around the same time as housing prices began to fall, the Federal Reserve started to raise interest rates in the money market as it began to fear inflation. Since many subprime mortgages that originated in the 2001–2005 period had floating rates (i.e., were ARMs) with high step-up rates, the cost of meeting mortgage commitments rose to unsustainable levels for many low-income households. The result was a dramatic increase in delinquencies and defaults. This was the credit risk phase of the crisis.

Phase Two began in the late summer of 2007 as the crisis spread to the banking community and to the money markets. The British bank Northern Rock and the German Bank IKB experienced runs and were bailed out by their respective regulatory agencies. The major US subprime mortgage lender, Countrywide, announced in August that it was drawing down on backup lines of credit because of its growing losses. Ultimately, a liquidity run on Countrywide was stemmed only after a $2 billion equity investment by Bank of America on August 23, 2007. However, a number of Asset-Backed Commercial Paper issuers also began having difficulty refinancing their short-term commercial paper issues because of investors' concerns about the quality of the underlying collateral of subprime mortgages and other assets, despite the AA or AAA ratings these issues may have received from the rating agencies.

Liquidity hoarding forced overnight interbank rates to very high levels and for some banks became unavailable. Investors began to lose confidence in the quality of credit ratings and the rating agencies, until an AAA security did not mean what it appeared to suggest.[28] Thus, all debt issues—from the interbank market to the corporate bond market, including the so-called investment grade market—were negatively affected by a "flight to quality." A flight to quality implies a move away from privately issued debt to default-risk free securities issued by the government, such as US Treasury securities. This resulted in falling prices (rising interest rates or "credit spreads") on privately issued debt securities and rising prices and lower rates on government issued securities. Thus, credit markets throughout the world suffered from high spreads and drastically curtailed liquidity.

---

[28] In 2006, Moody's earned 44% of its revenues from rating structured finance deals—see Tomlinson and Evans (2007). Thus, the rating agencies may have had been disinclined to scrutinize the quality of the loans in the ABS, thereby contributing to the large number of defaults on highly rated securities.

It is at this stage in the crisis that the vulture funds and workout specialists typically hunt for bargains to purchase securities by selling at depressed prices. During November–December 2007, there was evidence that this process had begun, thereby firming up some debt prices and lowering credit spreads. Sovereign wealth funds made investments in prominent investment and commercial banks. It appeared that the market was finding a bottom. That was when the third, and perhaps most devastating, phase hit. The year 2008 opened to news that a low level employee of Societe Generale, Jerome Kerviel, managed to run up almost €5 billion of losses without being detected by the bank's state-of-the-art internal risk measurement systems. One sophisticated bank after another announced enormous write-downs, only to find that additional huge write-downs were required weeks after the "final" damage was announced. For example, after reassuring markets in February 2008 that it had only minimal losses, Credit Suisse was forced to announce a $2.85 billion write-down that had somehow been overlooked because the traders didn't properly value the securities in the portfolio.

The credibility of the banks and financial community was undermined by a string of rogue traders with eye-popping losses, the poor state of the due diligence conducted by underwriters of asset-backed securities, credit default swap holders who did not know the identity of their counterparties to extract payment, liens against property in mortgage pools that were not perfected, and the Keystone Cops quality to the write-downs (ironically called "death by a thousand cuts" by a Merrill Lynch analyst). It was becoming apparent to the market that the banks themselves did not know the value of the dodgy securities on their own books. The securitizations were done so hastily, without the proper due diligence or legal protections that working out the loans would be difficult and time consuming. Operational corners were cut when the deals were originally done, thereby imposing operational risk on the entire market. Thus, the vulture funds and workout specialists pulled back. When the originators themselves do not know the contents (never mind the valuation) of a security, no one can step in with a bid to put a floor under the market—so it just keeps falling. This is what happens in an operational risk crisis. The result was that the credit markets tightened up even further than they had during the first two phases of the crisis.

Indeed, this third operational risk phase has proved to be the most devastating phase of the crisis. Years after the initial credit shock, banks' balance sheets remain filled with troubled and non-performing loans that cannot be sold or packaged into securitizations.[29] To date, six years after the start of the global financial crisis, banks are still holding billions of dollars of non-performing loans in which the borrowers have made no payments of either interest or principal for extended periods of time. However, rather than resolving these loans via foreclosure or property sale (e.g., short sale), the banks are holding the loans "in limbo" for extended periods of time. Allen, Peristiani, and Tang (2012) examine the phenomenon of "limbo loans," defined as loans that have been delinquent for extended periods of time, but have not progressed to any form of resolution.[30] The recovery of macroeconomic conditions to pre-crisis levels is impeded by the existence of these limbo loans on bank balance sheets,

---

[29] "Over the past two years less than $25 billion of delinquent mortgages have been sold to investors who specialize in the area.... This is only about 0.25% of U.S. home loans outstanding" Hagerty (2010).

[30] We do not take a stand on the issue of whether loan resolution takes the form of property repossession and sale, modification or foreclosure. Instead, we examine loans that are stuck in limbo and remain delinquent without resolution of any kind.

since they increase bank risk exposure, drain bank capital resources and restrict aggregate lending activity.[31]

There appears to be little incentive for banks to delay resolution of non-performing loans, as even a partial recovery of loan value should be preferred to the zero recovery value of a limbo loan. Allen, Peristiani, and Tang (2012) find that 21.79% of the subprime mortgage loans originated in Florida during 2004–2008, totaling $24.8 billion in original mortgage value, can be classified as limbo loans. Most of these loans (representing 19.07% of the total number of mortgages in our sample) were in foreclosure limbo for close to 26 months (as of the end of 2010).[32] Operational risk is found to be at the root of the limbo loan phenomenon.

Back-office operations in the mortgage origination business consist of verifying liens and titles and obtaining the proper legal documentation for the loans in ABS issues. In the frenzy of the recent housing boom, lenders got careless about keeping track of the paperwork. For example, in a sample of recent Chapter 13 bankruptcy filings, Porter (2008) finds that a majority of residential property loans are missing at least one piece of the required paperwork; more than 40% of residential property loans were missing the promissory note while 20% of residential property loans were missing evidence of security interest in the property (either a mortgage or a deed of trust). As loans got packaged into mortgage-backed securities (MBS), repackaged, and then sold perhaps several times, the paperwork required to establish the existence of the debt (the promissory note) or the lender's right to foreclose if the terms of the note are not met (the mortgage or deed of trust) may not have been passed to the holder of the security or the trustee for all of the loans in each pool of mortgages.[33]

Operational risk is behind the limbo loan phenomenon when banks delay the resolution of foreclosures because of the missing paperwork backing the loans. Lenders fear that either they will be challenged in foreclosure proceedings or that title will be clouded subsequent to the foreclosure proceeding. Moreover, if fraud or lack of due diligence is shown for government-insured mortgages, the bank may be liable for treble damages, thereby making pursuit of delinquency claims risky. These concerns increase the transaction costs associated with resolving non-performing loans and may explain the incidence of limbo loans.

When the foreclosing bank lacks critical documents, such as the original note, some jurisdictions require the filing of a lost note affidavit to attest that the bank owns the mortgage and should be permitted to proceed with the foreclosure.[34] During October 2010, it was revealed that these affidavits themselves were often inaccurate, having been signed by "robo-signers" who were responsible for the signing of hundreds of affidavits each day, and therefore could not be expected to investigate and verify each affidavit's claims. The

---

[31] Allen, Bali, and Tang (2012) show that excessive risk-taking in the financial sector forecasts macroeconomic downturns one year into the future.

[32] Allen, Peristiani, and Tang (2012) consider a loan to be delinquent if CoreLogic specifies its status as 90 days delinquent and there are no cash flows in the following months. Thus, an additional three months should be added to our descriptive statistics in order to determine the length of time from the date at which the loan first became delinquent.

[33] Hunt, Stanton, and Wallace (2011) describe the legal requirements that require two contracts (the promissory note and the deed of trust) to establish property rights under a "mortgage."

[34] In most states, residential property lenders are required to have at a minimum the promissory note and evidence of a lien to foreclose. In some states (for example, Florida) the lender is required to have the original promissory note, rather than simply a copy. Further, some states (such as Florida) are judicial states that require all foreclosures to be granted by a judge.

robo-signer scandal, however, understates the severity of potential operational problems in mortgage originators and underwriters. Many jurisdictions do not require the foreclosing bank to produce the original note. Moreover, banks may rationally decide not to initiate foreclosure proceedings for limbo loans with missing documentation for fear that their operational problems will be revealed, or may choose not to re-file foreclosure proceedings once a case has been dismissed. Thus, the extent of operational risk in the bank system is probably more pervasive than the incidence of lost note affidavits would suggest.

Another aspect of the operational risk emanates from the origination of the MBS. In 1995, a group of financial institutions (including Fannie Mae, Freddie Mac, Bank of America, and JP Morgan Chase) banded together to create the Mortgage Electronic Registration System, or MERS. The objective was to streamline the mortgage recording process by bypassing county offices that were slow to process legal documents regarding ownership of mortgages. Rather than record the mortgage with the county clerk, it was instead registered in the name of MERS, which became the owner of record. MERS could transfer the mortgage at will as many times as desired to accommodate the speed of securitization that characterized the boom years. Transfers were to be recorded in the MERS database. Thus, MERS was a form of book entry for mortgages. However, MERS did not actually build the computer infrastructure required to carefully record and monitor the transfers of all of the mortgages in its system. Indeed, although MERS has a full-time staff of fewer than 50, it claims to hold 60 million loans.[35] Moreover, Hunt, Stanton, and Wallace (2011) show that the MERS structure violates legal requirements and may undermine the bankruptcy remoteness legal foundation crucial to the viability of mortgage securitization.[36] Allen, Peristiani, and Tang (2012) find that a loan is significantly more likely to remain in limbo if it has been assigned to MERS, and the presence of MERS in county-level foreclosures increases the length of time a loan spends in limbo by around ten months. By failing to address operational risk issues in a timely fashion, the banking system has created a costly and stubborn problem that shows no signs of resolution in the near future.

7.5   WHY DO WE CARE ABOUT RISK IN THE BANKING SECTOR?

Until this point, we have focused on the risks inherent within individual financial firms that impact the bank's shareholders and other stakeholders. We have not considered the risk that financial institutions impose on the economic system at large—that is, we have neglected

---

[35]   Powell and Morgenson (2011).

[36]   Bankruptcy remoteness protects the special purpose vehicle (SPV), or any other party, from claims by securitization investors in the event of ABS default, so that only the underlying assets themselves are available to make payments to the ABS investors. Moreover, bankruptcy remoteness insures that ABS investors can obtain clear title to the assets underlying the securitization without undergoing bankruptcy proceedings even if the SPV or the originator becomes insolvent. Hunt, Stanton, and Wallace (2011) show that by violating legal registration requirements, the presence of MERS may violate the "true sale" requirements necessary to secure bankruptcy remoteness.

systemic risk. Viewing the economic wreckage in the aftermath of the financial debacle that began in 2007, it is almost self-evident that systemic risk is important. For this reason, bank regulators have focused in recent years on ways to measure systemic risk. Focus has been on correlations among pairs of financial firms to determine the most interconnected banks, since these interconnected, "systemically important" banks can set off a chain reaction of financial contagion when they become distressed.[37] These "micro-level" systemic risk measurements measure the contribution of each bank to overall systemic risk.

However, Allen, Bali, and Tang (2012) show that proposed micro-level systemic risk measures have no macroeconomic forecasting power. Thus, they develop a new macro-index of systemic risk that predicts future real economic downturns six to eight months in advance. The index measures the aggregate level of systemic risk in the entire financial sector (rather than an individual bank's systemic risk exposure), and is calculated using a cross-sectional analysis of equity returns of financial firms in the US, Europe, and Asia.

A macro-measure of systemic risk complements micro-level systemic risk measures focusing on direct interbank connections, because systemic risk can emerge through general economic factors that cause financial markets to freeze up and/or banks to substantially reduce the supply of credit. Kashyap, Berner, and Goodhart (2011) and Korinek (2011) describe financial amplification effects resulting from fire sales of financial assets by individual banks that trigger the catastrophic declines in asset prices and reduced liquidity that accompany a systemic crisis. These effects transcend pairwise interconnections between banks (particularly if many bank portfolios are overly invested in assets exposed to rollover risk: see Acharya, Gale, and Yorulmazer, 2011). Indeed, Bekaert et al. (2011, p. 5) show that international contagion during the 2007–2009 crisis did not spread through direct trade and financial linkages, but rather through a "wake-up call" that "provides new information that may prompt investors to reassess the vulnerability of other market segments or countries, which spreads the crisis across markets and borders."

More generally, financial institutions are "special" since when they are in distress, banks tend to cut back on all of their activities, including lending to their customers (see Ivashina and Scharfstein, 2010 for evidence of this in 2008), who in turn reduce their investment activity and hiring, which impacts employment and expenditure on a macroeconomic level. If there are only a limited number of troubled banks at any one point in time, competitor banks may overcome the information destruction inherent in these disruptions in bank–customer relationships, and meet the demands of customers formerly served by a distressed bank. However, as more banks enter into crisis, these spillover effects become substantial and competitor banks are unable to prevent macroeconomic contagion (e.g., Jermann and Quadrini, 2009 link reductions in credit availability to macroeconomic downturns). This chain reaction of systemic effects extends beyond the web of individual interbank relationships and impacts the entire macroeconomic system.

Systemic risk could conceivably bubble up from widespread catastrophic risk among smaller, less directly interrelated banks with common risk factors. Indeed, Kashyap and

---

[37] Micro-level systemic risk proposals include Marginal Expected Shortfall (*MES*, see Acharya et al. (2010)), *CoVaR* (Adrian and Brunnermeier, 2009), conditional tail risk (*CTR*, Kelly, 2011), co-risk (Chan-Lau, 2009), a contingent claims approach (Gray and Jobst, 2009), Shapely values (Tarashev, Borio, and Tsatsaronis, 2009) and the IMF risk budgeting and standardized approaches (Espinosa-Vega, Kahn, and Sole, 2010).

Stein (2000) find that aggregate declines in loan supply are driven by smaller banks (in the bottom 95th percentile of the size distribution) that are liquidity constrained. Thus, focus on the largest financial firms omits an important potential source of systemic risk. Banks, large and small, tend to take on excessive risk since they do not consider the external costs of their risk taking on non-financial firms and on society at large. That is, financial contagion is spread through risk and illiquidity in the financial sector (Longstaff, 2010), as liquidity constrained banks transmit financial shocks to the real economy (Duchin, Ozbas, and Sensoy. 2010), thereby creating systemic risk (e.g., through bank transmission of fluctuations in investor sentiment as in Shleifer and Vishny, 2010). Indeed, it is because of the risk of macroeconomic contagion that regulators and governments are so concerned about systemic risk. Thus, regulators require a systemic risk measure that determines the macroeconomic implications of aggregate risk taking in the financial system.

The crisis of 2007–08 demonstrates that we still have a lot to learn about risk measurement and risk management. However, no system will be effective if financial institutions ignore the warning signals flashed by their risk measurement models in their rush to join in the latest market frenzy—whether it is subprime mortgage-backed securities, high tech, international government securities, or whatever happens to be the next mania. Risk measurement and management requires a steady eye and a firm hand as well as effective quantitative and analytical tools. Indeed, macroeconomic conditions around the world will be improved if the banking sector controls its systemic risk.

References

Acharya, V., Gale, D., and Yorulmazer, T. (2011). Rollover Risk and Market Freezes, *Journal of Finance* 66, 1177–1209.

Acharya, V., Pedersen, L., Philippon, T., and Richardson, M. (2010). Measuring Systemic Risk. New York University Working Paper.

Adrian, T. and Brunnermeier, M. K. (2009). *CoVaR*, Federal Reserve Bank of New York Staff Reports No. 348, August.

Allen, L. (1997). *Capital Markets and Institutions: A Global View*. New York: John Wiley and Sons.

Allen, L. and Bali, T. (2007). Cyclicality in Catastrophic and Operational Risk Measures, *Journal of Banking and Finance* 31(4), 1191–1235.

Allen, L., Bali, T., and Tang, T. (2012). Does Systemic Risk in the Financial Sector Predict Future Economic Downturns?, *Review of Financial Studies* 25, 3000–3036.

Allen, L., Boudoukh, J., and Saunders, A. (2004). *Understanding Market, Credit and Operational Risk: The Value at Risk Approach*. Oxford: Blackwell Publishing.

Allen, L., Peristiani, S., and Tang, Y. (2012). Bank Delays in the Resolution of Delinquent Mortgages: The Problem of Limbo Loans. Working Paper, March.

Bekaert, G., Ehrmann, M., Fratzscher, M., and Mehl, A. (2011). Global Crises and Equity Market Contagion. Columbia University Working Paper.

Berkshire Hathaway Annual Report (2002).

BIS Monetary and Economic Department (2012). OTC Derivatives Statistics at end-December, <http://www.bis.org>.

Chan-Lau, J. (2009). Regulatory Capital Charges for Too-Connected-To-Fail Institutions: A Practical Proposal. IMF Working Paper, November.

Douglas, G. W. (1969). Risk in Equity Markets: An Empirical Appraisal of Market Efficiency, *Yale Economic Essays* 9, 3–45.

Duchin, R., Ozbas, O., and Sensoy, B. A. (2010). Costly External Finance, Corporate Investment and the Subprime Mortgage Credit Crisis, *Journal of Financial Economics* 97, 418–435.

Espinosa-Vega, M. A., Kahn, C. M., and Sole, J. (2010). Systemic Risk and the Redesign of Financial Regulation. IMF Global Financial Stability Report, April.

Fama, E. F. and French, K. R. (1992). The Cross-Section of Expected Stock Returns, *Journal of Finance* 47, 427–465.

Gray, D. and Jobst, A. A. (2009). New Directions in Financial Sector and Sovereign Risk Management, *Journal of Investment Management* 8, 22–38.

Hagerty, J. (2010). Vultures Save Troubled Homeowners, *Wall Street Journal* August 18, A6.

Helwege, J., Maurer, S., Sarkar, A., and Wang, Y. (2009). *Credit Default Swap Auctions*, Federal Reserve Bank of New York Staff Report No. 372, May.

Hull, J. and White, A. (2001). Valuing Credit Default Swaps II: Modeling Default Correlations, *Journal of Derivatives*, 8, 12–21.

Hunt, J. P., Stanton, R., and Wallace, N. (2011). *The End of Mortgage Securitization? Electronic Registration as a Threat to Bankruptcy Remoteness*, UC Davis Legal Studies Research Paper No. 269, August.

Ivashina, V. and Scharfstein, D. (2010). Bank Lending During the Financial Crisis of 2008, *Journal of Financial Economics* 97, 319–338.

Jermann, U. and Quadrini, V. (2009). *Macroeconomic Effects of Financial Shocks*, NBER Working Paper No. 15338.

Kashyap, A. K., Berner, R. B., and Goodhart, C. A. (2011). The Macroprudential Toolkit, *IMF Economic Review* 59, 145–161.

Kashyap, A. K. and Stein, J. C. (2000). What a Million Observations on Banks Say About the Transmission of Monetary Policy, *American Economic Review* 90, 407–428.

Kelly, B. (2011). Tail Risk and Asset Prices. University of Chicago Working Paper.

Korinek, A. (2011). Systemic Risk-Taking: Amplification Effects, Externalities, and Regulatory Responses, European Central Bank Working Paper No. 1345.

Longstaff, F. A. (2010). The Subprime Credit Crisis and Contagion in Financial Markets, *Journal of Financial Economics* 97, 436–450.

Markowitz, H. (1952). Portfolio Selection, *Journal of Finance* 7, 77–91.

Mengle, D. (2007). Credit Derivatives: An Overview, *Federal Reserve Bank of Atlanta Economic Review* Fourth Quarter, 1–24.

Mina, J. and Xiao, J. Y. (2001). *Return to RiskMetrics: The Evolution of a Standard.* New York: RiskMetrics.

Mossin, J. (1968). Optimal Multiperiod Portfolio Policies, *Journal of Business* 41, 215–229.

Porter, K. (2008). Misbehavior and Mistake in Bankruptcy Mortgage Claims, *Texas Law Review* 87, 121–182.

Powell, M. and Morgenson, G. (2011). MERS? It May Have Swallowed Your Loan, *New York Times, Sunday Business* March 6.

Roll, R. (1977). A Critique of the Capital Asset Theory Tests: Part I: On Past and Potential Testability of the Theory, *Journal of Financial Economics* 4, 129–176.

Rubinstein, M. (2002). Markowitz's "Portfolio Selection": A Fifty-Year Retrospective, *Journal of Finance* 57(3), 1041–1045.

Saunders, A. and Allen, L. (2010). *Credit Risk Measurement: New Approaches to Value at Risk and Other Paradigms.* 3rd edition. New York: John Wiley and Sons.

Sharpe, W. F. (1963). A Simplified Model for Portfolio Analysis, *Management Science* 9, 277–293.

Shenn J. (2007). Subprime Loan Defaults Pass 2001 Peak, *Bloomberg Markets* February 2, <http://www.bloomberg.com/apps/news?pid=newsarchive&sid=aFGf71vlQkWM>.

Shleifer, A. and Vishny, R. W. (2010). Unstable Banking, *Journal of Financial Economics* 97, 306–318.

Smithson, C. (2003). *Credit Portfolio Management*. Hoboken, NJ: John Wiley & Sons.

Tarashev, N., Borio, C., and Tsatsaronis, K. (2009). The Systemic Importance of Financial Institutions, *BIS Quarterly Review* September, 75–87.

Tomlinson, R. and Evans, D. (2007). CDO Boom Masks Subprime Losses, Abetted by S&P, Moody's, Fitch, *Bloomberg News* May 31, <http://www.bloomberg.com/news/2007-05-31/cdo-boom-masks-subprime-losses-abetted-by-s-p-moody-s-fitch.html>.

Wallace, A. (1980). Is Beta Dead?, *Institutional Investor* 14, 22–30.

CHAPTER 8

....

LIQUIDITY

How Banks Create it and How it Should

Be Regulated*

....

CHRISTA H. S. BOUWMAN

8.1 INTRODUCTION

....

THIS chapter provides a review and synthesis of key issues related to "liquidity creation" by banks, including prudential regulation. The questions addressed are: How do banks create liquidity and how does this improve welfare? What risks does liquidity creation generate for the bank? How does the bank cope with these risks in the traditional originate-to-hold (OTH) model and in the originate-to-distribute (OTD) model that is closely linked to the shadow banking system? Does managing these risks call for regulation in the form of capital requirements and regulatory reserve/liquidity requirements?

"Liquidity creation" refers to the fact that banks provide illiquid loans to borrowers while giving depositors the ability to withdraw funds *at par value* at a moment's notice (e.g., Bryant, 1980; Diamond and Dybvig, 1983). Banks also provide borrowers liquidity off the balance sheet through loan commitments and similar claims to liquid funds (e.g., Boot, Greenbaum, and Thakor, 1993; Holmstrom and Tirole, 1998; Kashyap, Rajan, and Stein, 2002; Thakor, 2005). There is now a large theoretical literature on bank liquidity creation and an emerging literature on its empirical measurement (e.g., Berger and Bouwman, 2009)

Bank liquidity creation is important for the macroeconomy (e.g, Bernanke, 1983; Dell'Ariccia, Detragiache, and Rajan, 2008), and becomes even more prominent during financial crises (e.g., Acharya, Shin, and Yorulmazer, 2009). However, the creation of liquidity exposes the bank to a variety of risks, including liquidity risk. This risk can be mitigated

* I thank Allen Berger, Charlie Calomiris, Martin Hellwig, Antoine Martin, Matthew Osborne, René Stulz, Scott Sumner, Elu von Thadden, and John Wilson for useful comments, and Harald Benink for helpful comments.

to some extent by holding liquid assets such as cash. Cash-asset reserves are not sufficient if depositors withdraw simply because they are afraid that the bank will shut down due to a run by others on its deposits. A regulatory safety net (including deposit insurance and the Federal Reserve discount window) can deal with such fears, but its existence reduces the bank's incentive to keep cash-asset reserves. Safety nets also give rise to moral hazard in that the bank has a perverse incentive to increase risk at the expense of the deposit insurer. This can increase the risk of future asset-value impairment, an event that would trigger liquidity risk by causing depositors to run the bank; the empirical suggest that liquidity problems are often triggered by concerns that the bank is insolvent due to poor asset quality (e.g., Gorton, 1988). To improve the bank's asset portfolio choices and risk management, regulatory monitoring and capital requirements can be used.

This highlights that both liquidity requirements and capital requirements are useful as part of the regulation of banks' liquidity creation. The predominant focus, however, of the macro- and micro-prudential regulation leading up to the subprime lending crisis has been on capital requirements rather than liquidity requirements. The same holds for the theories. As a result, while I am able to discuss the past, present, and future of both capital and liquidity regulation and implementation issues in the US and Europe, the discussions on how they should be regulated will focus largely on capital.

To properly understand the roles of both capital requirements and liquidity requirements in influencing bank liquidity creation in the present-day economy, I also examine the economics of traditional banking (which focuses on relationship lending and the OTH model) and its evolution to modern-day banking, characterized by a mix of the OTH and the OTD models, and a rapid growth of the shadow banking system. I describe this system and how it interacts with traditional banking in its liquidity creation role.

While one could argue that the absence of bank runs in US commercial banking indicates the effectiveness of the regulatory safety net and the redundancy of liquidity requirements, the rapid drying up of liquidity in the shadow banking system during the recent subprime lending crisis suggests that regulators need to look beyond the traditional boundaries of deposit-based banking when thinking about capital and liquidity requirements. Basel III requires banks to operate with more and higher-quality capital, and introduces two liquidity ratios. I discuss these new standards, how they are adopted in the US and Europe, and how they may affect liquidity creation. I also turn to the possible theoretical linkages between liquidity requirements and capital requirements, how one should think about these requirements for both traditional deposit-funded banks and for shadow banks, and identify open research questions.

8.2 BANKS AS LIQUIDITY CREATORS

8.2.1 Theories

Standard textbooks on financial intermediation (e.g., Greenbaum and Thakor, 2007; Freixas and Rochet, 2008) explain that banks are institutions that make loans funded by a combination of deposits from the public and equity supplied by the banks' shareholders.

More formally, banks engage in "liquidity creation," which is a form of "qualitative asset transformation."

To understand liquidity creation, picture a firm in need of long-term financing in a world without banks. In such a world, savers would directly finance the funding needs of the firm, and they would end up with an illiquid claim against the firm. In contrast, in a world with banks, it is the bank that provides the long-term loan to the firm, and the bank is able to offer savers demand deposits.[1] So it is the bank that holds the illiquid claim against the firm and savers end up with a liquid claim against the bank. Because of this difference in liquidity between what banks do with their money and the way they finance their activities, banks are said to create liquidity. Inherent in the liquidity creation in these models is maturity transformation; see Bhattacharya and Thakor (1993) and Hellwig (1994) for discussions on this topic. Formal models of banks as liquidity creators in this sense were developed by Bryant (1980) and Diamond and Dybvig (1983). In those models, depositors can suffer interim liquidity shocks, so being able to hold liquid (demand) deposit claims improves welfare.

In Diamond and Dybvig (1983), this liquidity creation exposes banks to withdrawal risk.[2] Fear that other depositors may rush in to withdraw their deposits prematurely even though they may not have liquidity needs can cause all depositors to withdraw, precipitating a bank run as one of two possible equilibria.[3] It is impossible for the bank to "provision" for such an event, short of practicing 100% reserve banking, that is, keeping all deposits as cash in vault. But such an institution would be merely a safe-deposit box, rather than a bank that creates liquidity. Diamond and Dybvig (1983) argue that federal deposit insurance can eliminate bank runs, thereby ridding banks of the prospect of the large-scale deposit withdrawals that characterize such runs.[4] But of course, the intent of deposit insurance is to help banks deal with panic runs, *not* substitute for the liquidity banks need to keep on hand to meet day-to-day routine deposit withdrawals. Thus, even with deposit insurance, banks need to worry about having enough liquidity on hand to meet the normal liquidity needs of depositors.

---

[1] There are alternative theories as to why banks fund with so much short-term debt. Some argue that short-term debt has a disciplining role in that the threat of non-renewal of funding makes bank managers behave (Calomiris and Kahn, 1991; Dewatripont and Tirole, 1994; Diamond and Rajan, 2001). Others argue it may be the outcome of a maturity rat race (Brunnermeier and Oehmke, 2013) or debt overhang problem (Admati et al., 2014).

[2] In practice, it also exposes banks to credit risk and interest rate risk (both are absent in Diamond and Dybvig, 1983) related to maturity transformation. Hellwig (1994) discusses the relation between both in a model of maturity transformation.

[3] In Diamond and Dybvig (1983), a bank run is a "sunspot" phenomenon, not attributable to any specific economic trigger. Chari and Jagannathan (1988) show that a bank run can arise as a unique equilibrium that is triggered by adverse fundamental information. Diamond and Dybvig (1983) take the sequential servicing constraint (SSC: first-come, first-served rule) as a given. Calomiris and Kahn (1991) provide an endogenous rationale. They show that demandable debt disciplines the manager because depositors can vote with their feet, and that the SSC gives depositors an incentive to monitor (avoids free-riding).

[4] Kane, Laeven, and Demirgüç-Kunt (2008) examine deposit insurance in 170 countries from 1960–2003. They document that explicit deposit insurance schemes were not available in most countries before 1960. The number of countries with such schemes had grown to 45 by the beginning of 1995 and to 87 by year end 2003. They argue that countries that do not have explicit schemes typically have some form of implicit deposit insurance.

Because the level of even routine withdrawals on any given day is stochastic, the liquidity reserves a bank keeps may either be too high or too low in light of the realized level of withdrawals. Moreover, absent panic runs and financial crises, the daily withdrawal levels across banks will not be perfectly correlated, suggesting gains from diversification. To take advantage of these diversification gains, an interbank market in trading cash reserves emerged in the early 1920s (Board of Governors of the Federal Reserve System, 1959). The fed funds rate is the rate at which banks borrow and lend on an overnight basis in this market in the US.[5] Banks with excess reserves are lenders and those with reserve deficiencies are borrowers.[6]

In addition to the fed funds market, banks can also avail themselves of short-term borrowing at the discount window to meet their short-term liquidity needs. The Federal Reserve's willingness to provide banks with discount window access is an important potential source of liquidity for banks.

Banks face costs in accessing the federal funds market and in borrowing at the discount window. One of these costs is that eligible collateral must be posted. Accessing the discount window may in addition be associated with a stigma—such borrowing may be perceived as a sign of weakness, which may make banks reluctant to obtain funds.[7] Banks thus have an incentive to keep some cash on hand to deal with the liquidity risk that is an unavoidable companion to the bank's basic economic function of being a liquidity creator.

While the financing of banks through liquid demand deposits leads to withdrawal risk for banks, it also provides an opportunity for banks to provide liquidity to borrowers off the balance sheet. This was formalized by Kashyap, Rajan, and Stein (2002) who argue that banks face a demand for liquidity from their depositors as well as from customers who purchase loan commitments that can be exercised in the future, thereby obligating the bank to lend when customers exercise these commitments. This means that a pool of liquid assets that the bank keeps on hand can serve two purposes—meeting the liquidity needs of borrowers as well as those of depositors. And there are diversification benefits associated with this costly holding of liquidity if the liquidity needs of borrowers and depositors are not perfectly correlated.[8]

[5] In the UK, the analogous rate is LIBOR, the London InterBank Offered Rate.

[6] Allen, Peristiani, and Saunders (1989) show that small banks tend to act as lenders while large banks tend to act as borrowers in this market. They argue this may be because small banks: prefer to use deposits to fund their activities; can attract deposits more cheaply due to local monopoly power; and face greater information asymmetries which makes fed funds more expensive for them than for large banks.

[7] In the words of the Chairman of the Federal Reserve, Bernanke (2008): "the efficacy of the discount window has been limited by the reluctance of depository institutions to use the window as a source of funding. The 'stigma' associated with the discount window, which if anything intensifies during periods of crisis, arises primarily from banks' concerns that market participants will draw adverse inferences about their financial condition if their borrowing from the Federal Reserve were to become known." Ennis and Weinberg (forthcoming) provide a theoretical model on the origin and implications of stigma. Furfine (2001) provides some empirical evidence on stigma by examining data on a special Y2K Federal Reserve liquidity facility. In an attempt to quantify the costs associated with stigma using data from the recent subprime lending crisis, Armantier et al. (2011) show that banks were on average willing to pay a 37-basis-point premium over a similar funding source (term auction facility) during the height of the crisis. Information on who obtains funds from the central bank is generally not available. However, data on access during the recent subprime lending crisis were recently made available. Berger, Black et al. (2013) examine which kinds of banks obtained such funds from the Federal Reserve. Drechsler et al. (2013) instead focus on banks that used funds from the European Central Bank.

[8] As evidence, they report that loan commitments and transaction deposits are positively correlated across banks. Gatev, Schuermann, and Strahan (2009) test whether this leads to a diversification benefit

The fact that banks make loan commitments is related to the seminal contributions of Diamond (1984) and Ramakrishnan and Thakor (1984) which provided the microfoundations of banks as specialists in screening credit information and monitoring borrowers.[9] Thus, banks as primary lenders make commitments to lend in the future. Such commitments create liquidity as they provide borrowers (partial) insurance against being rationed in the spot credit market (James, 1981; Blackwell and Santomero, 1982; Morgan, 1994; Thakor, 2005), so that a commitment can give a borrower access to future liquidity even when it is unavailable in the spot credit market.[10]

Boot, Greenbaum, and Thakor (1993) show that loan commitments improve ex ante welfare, even though they represent only "illusory promises" in that the bank may choose not to honor its commitment when the borrower attempts a takedown. They model the bank's choice as a tradeoff between reputational and financial capital—when the bank honors a loan commitment, it provides liquidity for the borrower but uses up its financial capital, and when it does *not* honor a commitment, it essentially "liquefies" its illiquid reputation capital and preserves its financial capital.

8.2.2 Empirical Evidence

Comprehensive empirical measures of liquidity creation were non-existent until recently. To measure the output of the banking sector, studies typically focused on total assets, total lending, or different types of lending. Taking a cue from the theories, Berger and Bouwman (2009) develop several measures of liquidity creation.[11] Using data on banks in the US, they show that large banks (assets over $1 billion) create over 80% of the banking sector's liquidity despite accounting for only a small percentage of all banks. They also document that banks create almost half of their liquidity off the balance sheet through loan commitments and similar claims to liquid funds. Most of the empirical studies in this area examine the relationship between capital and liquidity creation (see Section 8.5.1.2). More recently, Bai, Krishnamurthy, and Weymuller (2013) develop a liquidity mismatch index (LMI), which is conceptually similar even though it measures the exact opposite: the LMI is a liquidity measure whereas the Berger and Bouwman (2009) measures capture illiquidity (creating

and find it does: bank risk (stock return volatility) increases in unused commitments except for banks with high deposit levels. Building on this, Gatev, Schuermann, and Strahan (2006) argue that transaction deposits and loan commitments may be negatively correlated during crises since banks enjoy deposit inflows and greater demand for loan commitments during such times. Such inflows occur because banks are viewed as a safe haven given explicit government guarantees, access to the discount window and other emergency liquidity facilities, and additional support for banks that are To-Big-To-Fail (e.g., O'Hara and Shaw, 1990).

[9] See also Leland and Pyle (1977), Millon and Thakor (1985), Allen (1990), and Coval and Thakor (2005).

[10] Other explanations for the existence of loan commitments include: they provide a mechanism for optimal risk sharing (Campbell, 1978; Ho and Saunders, 1983), and they ameliorate informational frictions between the borrower and the bank (Berkovitch and Greenbaum, 1991; Boot, Thakor, and Udell, 1991).

[11] Quarterly data on liquidity created by virtually every bank in the US from 1984:Q1 until "now" are available for research purposes on my website (updated regularly).

liquidity for customers makes the bank illiquid). They calculate liquidity mismatch for the universe of bank holding companies (BHCs) in the US and show that the banking sector's liquidity condition is largely determined by the top 50 BHCs.

Empirical studies on the use of loan commitments have generally focused on corporate customers and document that over 80% of commercial and industrial lending is in the form of drawdowns under commitments. Melnik and Plaut (1986), Shockley and Thakor (1997), and Sufi (2009) provide detailed descriptions of loan commitment contracts and their specific features. Berger and Udell (1992) and Morgan (1994) document that credit lines reduce the risk of credit rationing during downturns. Consistent with this, Ivashina and Scharfstein (2010) show that after Lehman collapsed during the subprime lending crisis, there was a "run" by borrowers who drew down their loan commitments. There is also evidence, however, that banks renegotiated the terms for credit lines in their own favor during the crisis (Campello et al., 2011).

8.3 THE NEED FOR REGULATION

Given the demand for liquidity by both its (on- and off-balance-sheet) borrowers and depositors, the bank will trade off the costs and benefits of keeping liquidity on hand in deciding how much cash and other liquid assets to hold. However, just as deposit insurance lessens the bank's need to worry about events that might induce depositors to run the bank, the discount window can cause banks to keep too low a level of liquidity to meet routine withdrawal risk. Why keep cash lying around earning nothing if you know you can borrow at the discount window at a cost lower than the return you would earn by investing the cash?[12]

Of course, the central bank can eliminate this moral hazard by removing the deposit insurance and discount window safety nets. But this entails social costs because it could result in disruptive banking panics. Moreover, it might even disrupt the bank's relationship loans if core deposits are withdrawn in large amounts, and this can add to the welfare losses (Song and Thakor, 2007). Rather than throwing out the baby with the bathwater, the central bank can deal with the moral hazard created by these back-stop liquidity safety nets by imposing a minimum cash-asset reserve.

8.3.1 Cash Reserve Requirements

Feinman (1993) documents that cash reserve requirements have been imposed in the US as early as 1820, when commercial banks were state-chartered and did not have large amounts of deposits. However, they did issue bank notes which were often used as a medium of exchange. This initially only happened locally because it was challenging to gauge the solvency of banks located at greater distances. To facilitate their usage over greater distances, banks voluntarily agreed to accept each other's notes, provided that the issuing bank kept

[12] This assumes that the return earned exceeds the costs associated with posting eligible collateral and the possible stigma associated with borrowing from the discount window mentioned above.

enough liquid funds at the redeeming bank as backing. A few states subsequently mandated that banks hold reserves against their notes and deposits.

Reserve requirements were launched at the national level in 1863 with the passage of the National Bank Act. This Act enabled banks with a national charter to issue national bank notes and required them to hold a 25% reserve against such notes and deposits.[13] In 1864, this was reduced to 15% for banks located outside the largest cities. An Act of 1874 replaced reserve requirements on bank notes with a required redemption fund (banks were to deposit money equal to 5% of the notes with the Treasury) which counted toward fulfilling reserve requirements on deposits (Champ, 2007).[14] Reserve requirements did stay in place for deposits, which replaced bank notes as the preferred medium of exchange.

Various bank runs and panics in the late nineteenth and early twentieth centuries demonstrated that reserve requirements could not safeguard the convertibility of deposits for the entire banking system (e.g., Calomiris and Gorton, 1991), in essence because a dollar of reserves could not concurrently meet a customer's demand for cash and also satisfy reserve requirements. To maintain stability of the financial system, the Federal Reserve System was created in 1913: in it, Reserve Banks could act as lenders of last resort by accommodating banks' temporary liquidity needs. While this seemingly eliminated the need for reserve requirements, they continued to be imposed on transaction and time deposits, albeit at lower levels than during the national banking era. Starting in 1917, banks could only satisfy these requirements by keeping non-interest-bearing balances at the Federal Reserve.

By 1931, reserves were not viewed only as a source of liquidity for deposits anymore but also as a monetary policy tool used by the central bank to influence the expansion of bank lending (Federal Reserve, 1933). To reduce the burden on small banks, which tended to hold high cash balances, banks were able to count vault cash to meet reserve requirements from 1950 onward. In the late 1960s, new liabilities that were functionally equivalent to deposits also became subject to reserve requirements.

In the 1970s, rising interest rates increased the cost that banks incurred for satisfying reserve requirements, since the Federal Reserve paid no interest on reserves. This caused banks to leave the Federal Reserve System (Feinman, 1993). To stop this trend, Congress adopted the Depository Institutions Deregulation and Monetary Control Act (DIDMCA or MCA) of 1980 which mandated that all depository institutions—regardless of membership status—be subject to reserve requirements and be given access to the discount window. Regulation D of the Act specifies the reserve requirements. Initially, they were set at 3% on the first $25 million of transaction deposits and 12% on the rest, and 3% on non-transaction deposits. Over time, these percentages have declined, possibly to avoid disintermediation due to non-payment of interest on reserves. The Garn–St. Germain Act of 1982 introduced an exemption amount for transaction deposits, initially set at $2 million. The reserve requirement on non-transaction accounts was lowered to 0% in December 1990 and has been at that level ever since. In April 1992, the 12% rate was reduced to 10% and has stayed at that level. As of 2013, the exemption amount is $12.4 million, a 3% rate is imposed on transaction deposits between $12.4 million and $79.5 million, and amounts above that are subject to a 10% rate.

---

[13] They also had to deposit 111% of (the lesser of) the face or market value of these notes in US government bonds with the US Treasury. In 1900, this was reduced to 100%.

[14] Calomiris and Mason (2008) argue that this created economies of scope between note issuance and deposit taking because banks that issued notes had lower marginal costs of maintaining reserves associated with deposit taking.

Figure 8.1 Panel A shows the dollar amounts of required reserves and vault cash for the US banking sector from January 1960 through April 2013. While both required reserves and vault cash have increased over time, the banking system's cash balances exceeded the reserve requirements from the late 1990s until the beginning of 2009, suggesting that depository institutions were able to satisfy their entire reserve requirement with vault cash during that period. Panel B contrasts the dollar amounts of required reserves with the total amount of reserves held by the US banking sector. The picture is striking. Before the subprime lending crisis, total reserves of the banking sector showed a steady increase (from $18.8 billion

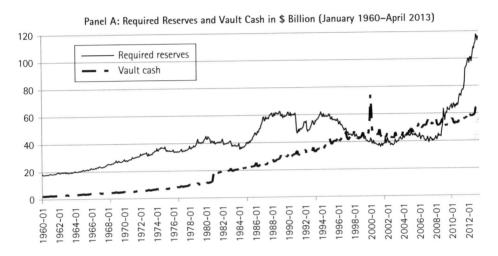

FIGURE 8.1 Total reserve, required reserves, and vault cash over time. This figure focuses on reserves of the US banking sector from January 1960–April 2013. Panel A shows both the US$ amounts of required reserves and vault cash, while Panel B contrasts the US$ amounts of required reserves with the total amount of reserves held.

Source: Aggregate Reserves of Depository Institutions and the Monetary Base, Not Seasonally Adjusted—H.3 Table 2.

in January 1960 to $49.9 billion in July 2007) and were on average a mere 2% higher than required reserves. During the initial phase of the crisis, total reserves increased somewhat, but they exploded after the collapse of Lehman Brothers in September 2008, reaching a level of $860 billion by January 2009 (almost 14 times the required level of $63.4 billion) and a record $1,885 billion by April 2013 (over 16 times the required level of $115.9 billion).

The dramatic increase in reserves during the crisis coincided with the Federal Reserve's decision to pay interest on reserve balances for the first time in its history.[15] This has led many (e.g., Edlin and Jaffee, 2009; McTague, 2009; Auerbach, 2010) to conclude that banks are simply "parking" funds at the Federal Reserve—they do not want to lend anymore since earning a sure return by sitting on funds kept at the Federal Reserve is more lucrative.[16] In stark contrast, others (e.g., Keister and McAndrews, 2009) suggest that this perspective is incorrect, arguing that the increase in reserves merely mirrors the unprecedented scale of the Federal Reserve's liquidity facilities and other credit programs. That is, it is simply driven by an accounting identity: the Federal Reserve's liabilities need to equal its assets.

8.3.2 Capital Requirements Prior to the Subprime Lending Crisis

As discussed above, safety nets can facilitate liquidity creation. But these safety nets give rise to moral hazard in that the bank has a perverse incentive to increase risk at the expense of the deposit insurer—see Merton's (1977) analysis showing that deposit insurance gives the bank a put option on its assets, and that the value of this option is decreasing in the bank's capital. The observation that safety nets induce banks to lower their capital ratios is supported by the sharp drop in capital ratios after the adoption of federal deposit insurance in the US in 1934 (see Figure 8.2).

To increase bank capital and reduce the bank's risk-taking appetite, regulatory monitoring and capital requirements can be used (e.g., Campbell, Chan, and Marino, 1992; Chan, Greenbaum, and Thakor, 1992; Merton and Bodie, 1992; Bhattacharya and Thakor, 1993; Thakor, 1996; Hellmann, Murdock, and Stiglitz, 2000).[17]

Formal capital requirements were introduced for the first time in the US only in 1981. Prior to the 1980s, supervisors merely applied informal and subjective measures, including

[15] The Financial Services Regulatory Relief Act (FSRRA) of 2006 authorized the Federal Reserve to pay interest on balances held by or on behalf of depository institutions starting October 1, 2011. Section 128 of the Emergency Economic Stabilization Act (EESA) of 2008 moved the effective date forward to October 1, 2008. The Federal Reserve indicated (press release: <http://www.federalreserve.gov/ newsevents/press/monetary/20081006a.htm>) that paying interest on reserves would give it "greater scope to use its lending programs to address conditions in credit markets while also maintaining the federal funds rate close to the target established by the Federal Open Market Committee." The Federal Reserve initially set the interest rate on required (excess) reserves at 10 (75) basis points below the average target fed funds rate over the reserve maintenance period. From December 18, 2008 onward it has paid a fixed rate of 25 basis points on both required and excess reserves.

[16] Some suggest that to curb this, excess reserves should be subject to a maximum (Dasgupta, 2009) or taxed (Sumner, 2009).

[17] Higher capital requirements may increase portfolio risk in certain circumstances (Koehn and Santomero, 1980; Kim and Santomero, 1988; Genotte and Pyle, 1991; Besanko and Kanatas, 1996). Mailath and Mester (1994) examine the regulator's incentive to close banks and how that affects its ability to influence the riskiness of banks' asset portfolios.

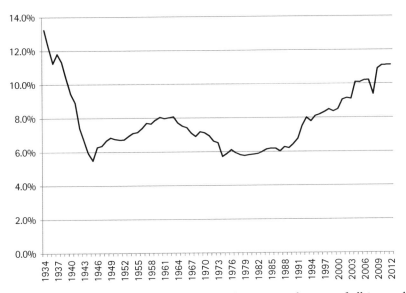

FIGURE 8.2 Capital ratios over time. This figure shows capital ratios of all insured commercial banks in the US from 1934 to 2012. The capital ratios are measured as aggregate book equity normalized by aggregate book assets of the banking sector.

Source: Table CB14 of FDIC's Historical Statistics on Banking.

managerial capability and loan portfolio quality, because they could not agree on a framework (FDIC, 2003). Starting in 1981, banks were subject to a leverage ratio of primary capital (mainly equity and loan loss reserves) to average total assets. The minimum requirements were not uniform across the three regulators (Federal Reserve, the Office of the Comptroller of the Currency, and the Federal Deposit Insurance Corporation) but ranged from 5% to 6%. There were differences at the international level as well. Over the next few years, regulators from the US and around the world worked together to devise a uniform capital framework necessary to ensure that banks had adequate capital and were operating in a level playing field.

The Basel Capital Accord (commonly referred to as Basel I), adopted in 1988, became partially effective for all US banks and thrifts at year end 1990, and was fully implemented at year end 1992. Basel I primarily focused on credit risk and forced banks to risk-weight their assets and off-balance-sheet items based on their perceived credit risk. While loans to private borrowers and stand-by letters of credit serving as financial guarantees for loans were risk-weighted at 100%, residential mortgages and long-term loan commitments were weighted at 50%, claims on or guarantees by qualifying banks were weighted at 20%, and very low-risk assets (including cash, government debt, and short-term loan commitments) were weighted at 0%. So banks had to hold more capital if they chose riskier assets. Banks were required to hold tier 1 capital of at least 4% of risk-weighted assets and total capital of at least 8% of risk-weighted assets.[18] Tier 1 capital is the purest form of capital, comprised of shareholders' equity and non-redeemable non-cumulative preferred stock. Total capital also

[18] They had to meet interim minimum standards of 3.625% (tier 1 capital) and 7.25% (total capital) by year end 1990.

includes capital/debt hybrids such as long-term subordinated debt (which counts as capital because it is at risk before deposits and other bonds). In 1991, US bank regulators (OCC, FRB, FDIC, and OTS) also passed the Federal Deposit Insurance Corporation Improvement Act (FDICIA), which introduced an additional leverage requirement and specified that to operate without regulatory restrictions, a bank must be adequately or well capitalized. To be adequately (well) capitalized, it must have a Tier 1 leverage ratio of at least 4% (5%), a Tier 1 risk-based ratio of at least 4% (6%), and a total risk-based capital ratio of at least 8% (10%).

Soon after the introduction of Basel I, shortcomings became apparent. For example, capital requirements were the same on loans to highly rated corporations and much riskier distressed firms. Furthermore, capital requirements were typically higher for on-balance-sheet loans than for off-balance-sheet exposures to the same borrowers even when the risks to the bank were similar. These shortcomings gave banks incentives to engage in regulatory capital arbitrage, that is, they tried to find ways to reduce their risk-weighted assets without truly lowering risk.

Basel II, initially published in June 2004, aimed to better align the minimum capital required with the underlying risks and focused on the denominator of the capital ratios. It introduced three pillars. Pillar 1 encompasses risk-based capital requirements for credit risk, market risk, and operational risk (risks arising from people, systems, or processes). Unlike Basel I, it does not prescribe one approach, but offers banks three approaches for credit risk (standardized approach, foundation internal ratings-based approach (F-IRB), and advanced IRB approach (A-IRB)[19] and for operational risk (basic indicator approach, standardized approach, and advanced measurement approaches (AMA). The A-IRB for credit risk and the AMA for operational risk together are called the "Advanced Approaches." Pillar 2 involves a supervisory review of banks' internal assessments of capital and risk, giving regulators discretion to impose higher capital requirements. Pillar 3 promotes market discipline by mandating banks to increase public disclosure of capital and risk.

The European Parliament approved Basel II for *all* banks in the EU in 2005 and formally adopted it in 2006 (European Parliament, 2011).[20] While most banks in Europe can choose any of the three approaches, many member states require the very largest banks to adopt at least the A-IRB. In contrast to the EU, the US never fully implemented Basel II. US banking regulators adopted a final regulation only in late 2007 (Federal Reserve, 2007). It required the very largest banks (11 or 12 "core banks" with consolidated total assets of at least $250 billion or with consolidated total on-balance-sheet foreign exposure of at least $10 billion) to apply the Advanced Approaches; other banks could obtain authorization to use those approaches ("opt-in banks") or had to stay on Basel I. The rule stipulated that banks would first be subject to a one-year parallel run of Basel I and Basel II, and would then start a three-year transition period. However, the subprime lending crisis happened, and the focus shifted to Basel III and the Dodd–Frank Act, which outlawed the use of credit

---

[19] The standardized approach groups exposures into several risk categories (as Basel I does), but the risk weights for loans to corporates, sovereigns, and banks depend on external credit ratings assigned to the borrower instead of being fixed. The F-IRB approach allows banks to use their own models to estimate probabilities of default (PD), while relying on the supervisor to provide estimates of loss given default (LGD), exposure at default (EAD), and maturity (M). The A-IRB approach allows banks with the most advanced risk management and modeling skills to provide all the estimates (PD, LGD, EAD, and M) needed to determine their capital requirement.

[20] Benink and Benston (2005) provide a more detailed discussion on changes in EU banking regulation.

ratings in regulations while Basel II heavily used such ratings (to be discussed in "Basel III" below). As of March 2013, all of the 27 Basel Committee member countries except for the US, Argentina, and Russia had fully implemented Basel II (BIS, 2013c).

8.4 From Originate-to-Hold (OTH) to a Mix of OTH and Originate-to-Distribute (OTD) and the Emergence of the Shadow Banking System

As discussed above, cash-asset reserve requirements steadily declined in the US until the subprime lending crisis for two main reasons. First, as a tool of prudential regulation, they simply became too costly since the Federal Reserve did not pay interest on reserves and market interest rates—the shadow price of holding reserves—spiked up dramatically in the 1970s. Second, as a tool of monetary policy, reserve requirements were hardly ever used because they represented a rather blunt instrument compared to other tools like the discount window and fed funds borrowing rates. Thus, reliance on reserve requirements has fallen over the years and we are now in a period in which banks are largely subject to capital requirements. Yet, as discussed below, there may be a role for both in moderating bank liquidity creation in an efficient way in the present-day economy. To properly understand these issues, we first need to step back and take a closer look at the economics of traditional banking and its evolution to modern-day banking.

8.4.1 Originate-To-Hold

The research on financial-intermediary existence implied that banks generate proprietary information about their borrowers.[21] This then suggested that banks could use their information to resolve informational frictions and increase the surplus generated by the bank–borrower relationship. This insight paved the way for the emergence of a literature on relationship banking which highlights the benefits of deep relationships between banks and their borrowers. The pioneering contributions in this area are Greenbaum, Kanatas, and Venezia (1989), Sharpe (1990), Rajan (1992), and Boot and Thakor (1994, 2000). Boot (2000, p. 10) defines relationship banking as "the provision of financial services by a financial intermediary that: (i) invests in obtaining customer-specific information, often proprietary in nature; and (ii) evaluates the profitability of these investments through multiple interactions with the same customer over time and/or across products." The first part highlights that banks obtain information while providing screening and/or monitoring services. The

---

[21] Using unique data on small-business borrowers, Mester, Nakamura, and Renault (2007) show that transaction accounts provide banks with ongoing information regarding borrowers' activities, thereby facilitating bank monitoring.

second part emphasizes the fact that information can be used in multiple interactions with the same customer, which allows the bank to reuse information.

To address whether relationships benefit borrowers, empirical studies have typically included measures of duration, scope, and/or the number of bank relationships in regressions to explain the cost and availability of credit. While the international evidence is at times mixed, most US studies tend to find clear benefits: stronger relationships result in lower cost, lower collateral requirements, and better access to credit (e.g., Petersen and Rajan, 1994; Berger and Udell, 1995; for a review, see Degryse, Kim, and Ongena, 2009, and the Chapter on Small Business Lending in this Handbook). Consistent with this, bank loan announcements are associated with significantly positive abnormal returns (e.g., James, 1987; Billett, Flannery, and Garfinkel, 1995) even in the presence of loan sales (Gande and Saunders, 2012).[22] Banks benefit as well—stronger lending relationships are associated with a higher probability of winning SEO underwriting business (Drucker and Puri, 2005) and future lending and investment banking business (Bharath et al., 2007).[23] Small banks tend to form stronger relationships with customers than large banks, likely because they are better at processing soft information (Berger et al., 2005).

Relationship banking involves the bank making the loan and holding it on its balance sheet. This is the so-called "originate-to-hold" model, in which banks fund relationship loans with core deposits. The loans are illiquid—banks keep them on their balance sheets until maturity. This reduces moral hazard on the side of the bank—the fact that the loans stay on the balance sheet gives the bank incentives to perform upfront screening and then monitor on an ongoing basis.

Relationships can lose a lot of value if they have to be liquidated prematurely due to a bank run; often, a bank's failure will result in the resolution authority arranging for the bank to be acquired by another institution, which results in a loss of the original relationship and its associated economic surplus, even if the loan is not liquidated.[24] To prevent such runs and protect the value of relationships, deposit insurance and lender of last resort facilities were introduced.

8.4.2 Originate-To-Distribute

During the 1990s and 2000s, loan sales and securitization skyrocketed, in essence moving banks more and more away from the OTH model toward a mix of OTH and the OTD model. While loan sales are easy to grasp, it is helpful to show how securitization works and how it contrasts with traditional banking (see Figure 8.3). As shown in Panel B, the bank originates loans as it does in the traditional OTH model, but then transfers the loans to a trust called a special purpose vehicle (SPV), which issues various tranches of debt claims called asset-backed securities (ABS) against this pool of loans. These ABS are sold to institutional investors and the

---

[22] In contrast to the short-run effect, Billett, Flannery, and Garfinkel (2006) find significant long-run underperformance after firms have obtained bank loans.

[23] In contrast to evidence provided by Drucker and Puri (2005), Calomiris and Pornrojnangkool (2009) show that banks may charge higher prices when combining lending and underwriting.

[24] Song and Thakor (2007) show theoretically how this influences the bank's choice of funding mix between core deposits and purchased money. Berlin and Mester (1999) provide empirical evidence that banks with greater reliance on core deposits give their borrowers better insurance against negative shocks to their creditworthiness. Consistent with this, Ivashina and Scharfstein (2010) and Cornett et al. (2011) show that banks that relied more on (stable) deposits, cut their lending less during the subprime lending crisis.

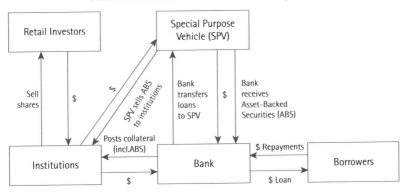

FIGURE 8.3 Traditional banking versus securitization in the shadow banking system. This figure compares the originate-to-hold (OTH) model of traditional banking (Panel A) with the originate-to-distribute (OTD) model of the shadow banking system (Panel B).

money received by the SPV is transferred in part to the bank.[25] Thus, like loan sales, securitization provides banks with extra funding that can be used to originate new loans.

Greenbaum and Thakor (1987) examine which assets banks will securitize, and show that with asymmetric information about borrowers' payoffs, they securitize higher-quality assets (see also Gorton and Pennacchi, 1995). Boot and Thakor (1993) show that banks may want to create tranches of claims against pooled assets, so as to diversify away idiosyncratic noise and then create information-sensitive claims that maximize issuer revenue. The push to split up securities in Gorton and Pennacchi (1990) is demand driven instead: uninformed investors can reduce their trading losses if they can trade relatively information-insensitive securities. While these papers focus on the bright side of securitization, recent papers point to a dark side:[26] securitization may negatively affect screening incentives since it allows lenders to pass onto others the loans they have originated (Aghion, Bolton, and Tirole, 2004; Stiglitz, 2007).[27] Evidence from the subprime lending crisis of 2007–2009 tends to support

[25] The bank may also purchase some of these ABS and use them as collateral to obtain repo funding from institutional investors like money-market mutual funds.

[26] Gorton and Haubrich (1990) argue that this is a natural way in which a market develops: initially, easy-to-value assets are sold; later on, increasingly complex and risky contracts are made. Loutskina (2011) points at another dark side—securitization makes banks more susceptible to funding shocks when the securitization market is disrupted.

[27] These problems may be more severe when the economy is doing well: Thakor (2005) and Dell'Ariccia and Marquez (2006) show that lending standards decline during economic booms. Hellwig (1994) focuses on the incentive effects of securitization and argues that it should be structured such that

this view (e.g., Mian and Sufi, 2009; Demyanyk and Van Hemert, 2011; Purnanandam, 2011; Dell'Ariccia, Igan, and Laeven, 2012; Keys, Seru, and Vig, 2012; Dai, Zhang, and Zhao, 2013), although skin in the game seems to improve banks' screening incentives (Demiroglu and James, 2012). In Gennaiolo, Shleifer, and Vishny (2013), securitization leads to bank interconnected and raises their exposure to tail risks.

Banks may benefit from loan sales. Pennacchi (1988) shows that selling banks have an advantage in originating loans and a disadvantage in providing funding; the reverse holds for buying banks. James (1988) finds that loan sales can reduce underinvestment problems of banks with risky debt. Firms may also benefit from loan sales. It may enable them to borrow more (Drucker and Puri, 2009), and it can lower their cost of capital due to increased liquidity in the secondary loan market (Gupta, Singh, and Zebedee, 2008) or risk-sharing benefits between the originating bank and loan buyers (Parlour and Winton, 2013). There is also a dark side. Firms whose loans are sold by banks underperform their peers (Berndt and Gupta, 2009), maybe because banks sell loans of lower-quality borrowers and/or loan sales reduce bank monitoring since the bank–borrower relationship is broken.

8.4.3 OTD and the Shadow Banking System

The OTD model fueled the development of the so-called "shadow banking system."[28] While a consensus definition does not exist, Bernanke (2010) defines shadow banks as "financial entities other than regulated depository institutions (commercial banks, thrifts, and credit unions) that serve as intermediaries to channel savings into investment." Adrian and Ashcraft (2012, p. 4) add that such channeling takes place "through a range of securitization and secured funding techniques," highlighting the importance of securitization in shadow banking.[29] The shadow banking system includes institutions such as investment banks, brokerage houses, and finance companies; securitization structures such as ABS and asset-backed commercial paper (ABCP); and key investors in securitized structures, such as money market mutual funds (MMMFs), which heavily rely on short-term funding like tri-party repurchase agreements (repos) and commercial paper (CP). Appendix 8.1 briefly describes key shadow banking actors and discusses their roles during the subprime lending crisis. See Gorton and Metrick (2010), Adrian and Ashcraft (2012), Claessens et al. (2012), and Martin, Skeie, and von Thadden (2014a) for more elaborate discussions.[30]

---

the bank retains asset-specific return risks to ensure proper screening and monitoring of clients, i.e., the securitizing bank needs the right kind of "skin in the game."

   [28] The term "shadow banking" is attributed to money manager Paul McCulley (2007).

   [29] The Financial Stability Board (FSB, 2012c) describes the shadow banking system more broadly as "credit intermediation involving entities and activities (fully or partially) outside the regular banking system" or non-bank credit intermediation.

   [30] Calomiris, Himmelberg, and Wachtel (1995) discuss how growth of the CP market was driven by growth of finance companies, and how it fuelled disintermediation by providing high-quality firms a low-cost alternative to short-term debt.

As in the case of the OTH model, banks create liquidity in the OTD model as well, since they continue to originate the loans that are subsequently sold or securitized. There are two key differences, however, from a liquidity creation perspective. The first is that with the OTH model the risk associated with liquidity creation is borne by the bank, whereas with the OTD model this risk is borne largely by the investors who purchase the loans or securities created by securitization.[31] The second difference is that funding for loans in the OTH model tends to come from (core) deposits, while funding for securitized structures in the OTD model typically comes eventually from repos and CP, even though the pre-securitization origination of the loan may have involved deposit funding. Unlike core deposits, there is no deposit insurance backing repos and CP funding, so runs are possible. Various papers document that such runs indeed occurred during the subprime lending crisis—see Gorton and Metrick (2012) for evidence on a "run on repos,"[32] and Covitz, Liang, and Suarez (2013) for evidence on "runs on ABCP."[33] These differences aside, loan sales and securitization do not alter the fact that bank-intermediated liquidity creation occurs in the economy—it merely reflects a change in the *process* by which this liquidity creation is occurring.

Bord and Santos (2012) assess the impact of the OTD model on corporate lending. They document that while lead banks retained 21% of the term loans they originated in 1988, that share had dropped to a mere 3.4% by 2010. Banks' increasing use of the OTD model helped to fuel the syndicated loan market from $339 billion in 1988 to an all-time high of $2.2 trillion in 2007. The secondary loan market transformed from a market in which banks hardly participated to an active market with volumes that rose from $8 billion in 1991 to $176 billion in 2005.

Another indication of how much the OTD market has grown is to examine funding of the shadow banking system and bank deposit funding over time. Figure 8.4 below shows that while they were roughly equal in 1988 ($2.7 trillion versus $2.4 trillion), shadow bank funding grew much more rapidly until the subprime lending crisis, peaking at $23.0 trillion in 2007 (versus bank deposit funding of $7.3 trillion in that year). While shadow bank funding dropped somewhat during the crisis, bank deposit funding increased, likely because of a flight to quality.

---

[31] Banks typically continue to bear some risk—they often provide guarantees and keep (part of) the lowest-rated tranche.

[32] They focus on the bilateral (i.e., interdealer) repo market and interpret an increase in margin requirements ("haircuts") as a run. Copeland, Martin, and Walker (2012) find that no such run seemed to have taken place in the tri-party repo market, which may have accounted for 50–60% of all outstanding repo in the US Krishnamurthy, Nagel, and Orlov (2013) find similar results and argue that Gorton and Metrick's (2012) "run on repo" is not the equivalent of a traditional bank run by depositors—to establish that, one should not analyze inter-dealer data but rather examine whether investors run on dealers. Martin, Skeie, and Von Thadden (2014a) show that increasing margin requirements can be stabilizing: while it results in some loss of funding, it is better than losing all funding, as seemed to have happened with Lehman.

[33] Martin, Skeie, and Von Thadden (2014b) show under what conditions short-term funding markets such as the repo market are immune to expectation-driven runs and discuss the scope of regulation to stabilize such markets.

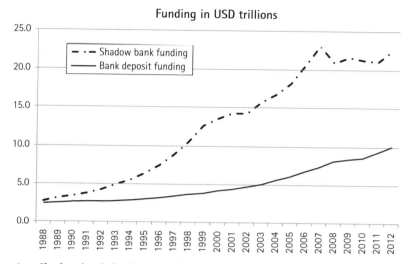

FIGURE 8.4 Shadow bank funding and bank deposit funding over time. This figure shows shadow bank funding and traditional bank deposit funding in US$ trillions in the US from 1988 to 2012. Shadow bank funding is defined as in Adrian and Ashcraft (2012) and is created using data from the Federal Reserve Flow of Funds Table L.107. It is the sum of money market mutual funds (line 31), repos (line 32), commercial paper (line 34), agency- and GSE-backed securities (line 35), and security broker-dealer payables plus credit (lines 41 and 42). Bank deposit funding is total deposits of insured banks as provided in Table CB14 of the FDIC's Historical Statistics on Banking.

8.5 REGULATION TO PRESERVE UNINTERRUPTED LIQUIDITY CREATION GOING FORWARD

Liquidity creation occupies an important seat at the table in both the OTH and OTD models. But for liquidity creation to not be ruptured, it is critical that banks operate with sufficiently high equity capital and liquidity. That became apparent during the subprime lending crisis, which brought issues regarding both to the forefront of the discussions, and has prompted a call for revised capital regulation and new liquidity regulation. I now discuss some of the key regulatory issues and the progress made in the implementation of new regulations in the US and Europe.

8.5.1 Capital Requirements for Traditional OTH Banking and for OTD Shadow Banking

8.5.1.1 Basel III

The subprime lending crisis of 2007–2009 revealed important weaknesses in Basel I and II. Both Accords seemed to provide inadequate incentives for banks to hold sufficient capital.

Moreover, these accords failed to appropriately incorporate the risks posed by securitization, lacked liquidity standards, and failed to incorporate systemic risks associated with the buildup of leverage in the financial system. Inadequate levels of capital may have led to imprudent asset choices by banks, which then raised solvency concerns that contributed to the drying up of liquidity for banks during the recent crisis.

In response to these perceived shortcomings, various academics have written proposals which essentially argue that there are externalities due to the safety net provided to banks and thus social efficiency can be improved by requiring banks to operate with more capital, especially during financial crises (e.g., Kashyap, Rajan, and Stein, 2008; Admati et al., 2012; Calomiris and Herring, 2011; Hart and Zingales, 2011; Acharya, Mehran, and Thakor, 2013).

Consistent with the academic perspective, Basel III—released in December 2010—proposes higher capital requirements and raises the quality of capital to address the seeming deficiencies of the prior Basel Accords (BIS, 2010, 2013b). Figure 8.5 compares Basel II and III capital requirements.

First, it increases the minimum Tier 1 risk-based capital ratio from 4% to 6%, and requires that the common equity component of Tier 1 capital goes up from 2% to 4.5% to ensure that a bank holds sufficient truly loss-absorbing capital (both requirements fully phased in by January 1, 2015). It leaves the minimum total risk-based capital ratio unchanged at 8%. Second, to reduce procyclicality and better withstand future periods of stress, it introduces a capital conservation buffer (additional common equity Tier 1 of 2.5% of risk-weighted assets, fully phased in by January 1, 2019). Third, to reduce systemic risk that has built up as a result of excessive credit growth, a country's regulator may impose a countercyclical capital buffer (additional common equity Tier 1 of 0%–2.5% of risk-weighted assets). Fourth, to constrain leverage in the banking sector and to introduce extra safeguards against model risk and measurement error, it supplements the risk-based capital requirements with a minimum leverage ratio (based on Tier 1 capital to on—and off-balance-sheet assets) of 3% by 2018.[34] Fifth, it subjects globally systemically important banks (G-SIBs) to additional loss absorbency requirements (extra common equity Tier 1 of 1%–2.5% of risk-weighted assets depending on assessed systemic importance, fully phased in by January 1, 2019).[35]

All 27 member jurisdictions of the Basel Committee were supposed to translate the Basel III standards into their own national laws and regulations by January 1, 2013. As of April 2013, only 14 had done so (BIS, 2013c). The other 13 had published their draft regulations.

The EU intends to apply Basel III to all financial institutions. The US proposes to apply it to all US insured depository institutions, BHCs with at least $500 million in assets, and savings and loan holding companies. It plans to retain the distinction between the Advanced Approaches Banks and other banks for certain purposes (e.g., the countercyclical capital buffer would only apply to the Advanced Approaches Banks). Maybe surprisingly in light of the major role played by liquidity during the subprime lending crisis and as further

---

[34] As discussed above, US banks had already been subject to a minimum leverage ratio since the early 1980s. However, the US ratio is defined differently since it is based on tier 1 capital relative to on-balance sheet assets.

[35] G-SIBs are banks whose distress or disorderly failure would significantly disrupt the wider financial system and economic activity (BIS, 2011). G-SIBs are identified every year in November (starting in 2011) based on five equally-important characteristics: bank size, complexity, interconnectedness, lack of substitutability, and cross-jurisdictional activity. As of November 2012, there are 28 G-SIBs (see FSB, 2012b) of which 4 are subject to 2.5% extra capital (Citigroup, Deutsche Bank, HSBC, and JP Morgan

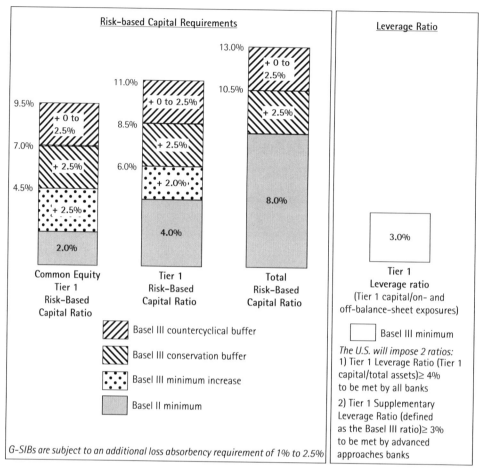

FIGURE 8.5 Comparison of Basel II and Basel III capital requirements. This figure shows the Basel II and Basel III risk-based capital requirements, and the Basel III tier 1 minimum leverage ratio. It also explains the US plans to impose two leverage ratios.

discussed below, the US proposals only see a role for Basel III's liquidity requirements for the very largest financial institutions.

Some argue that Basel III is not aggressive enough, that even higher capital requirements are needed and that they need to be imposed sooner (e.g., Admati et al., 2011; Haldane and Madouros 2012; Hoenig, 2012).[36] In deciding on the appropriate level (and form) of future

Chase), 2 need to hold 2% extra capital (Barclays and BNP Paribas), 8 are subjected to 1.5% extra capital (Bank of America, Bank of New York Mellon, Credit Suisse, Goldman Sachs, Mitsubishi UFJ FG, Morgan Stanley, Royal Bank of Scotland, and UBS), and the remaining 14 have to keep 1% extra capital (Bank of China, BBVA, Groupe BPCE, Group Crédit Agricole, ING Bank, Mizuho FG, Nordea, Santander, Société Générale, Standard Chartered, State Street, Sumitomo Mitsui FG, Unicredit Group, and Wells Fargo).

[36] The Systemic Risk Council, chaired by former FDIC Chairman Sheila Bair, proposes a minimum leverage ratio of 8% (2012). Admati and Hellwig (2013) propose it should be 20% to 30%.

capital requirements, two key issues need to be considered: the effect on bank output, and the need for capital regulation in the shadow banking system.

8.5.1.2 *Key Issue #1: Effect of Higher Capital Requirements on Bank Output*

The first issue is the effect of higher capital requirements on bank output (alternatively measured as lending or liquidity creation).[37] Bankers are vocal in this respect—they claim that increases in capital would negatively affect their performance and lead to less lending. The academic literature suggests a more complex picture.

The theories produce opposite predictions. Some argue that the relationship between capital and bank liquidity creation or lending should be negative (e.g., Diamond and Rajan, 2001) because demandable deposits help to resolve a hold-up problem that cannot be resolved by bank capital. Others argue that capital will facilitate liquidity creation and other forms of bank output because it helps to absorb the risks associated with those activities (e.g., Bhattacharya and Thakor, 1993; Allen and Santomero, 1998; Allen and Gale, 2004; Repullo, 2004; Von Thadden, 2004; Coval and Thakor, 2005).

The US evidence is mixed. In the early 1990s, US regulators imposed new leverage requirements, as well as the Basel I risk-based capital standards. Many studies conclude that the leverage requirements may have reduced lending (e.g., Berger and Udell 1994; Hancock, Laing, and Wilcox 1995; Peek and Rosengren 1995), while Thakor (1996) shows that the risk-based capital requirements may have had a similar effect, at least in the short run. However, the unusual combination of several major changes in capital regulation and a recession makes it challenging to separate the different effects and draw general conclusions.

European evidence suggests that the effect of higher capital requirements differs by bank type and the state of the business cycle. Using data from the UK, Aiyar, Calomiris, and Wieladek (2012) find that increases in minimum capital requirements are associated with a decline in lending by some (UK banks and branches of foreign banks) and an increase in lending by others (subsidiaries of foreign banks). Using unique data from changes in capital regulation in Spain, Jiménez et al. (2013) show that countercyclical capital buffers mitigate the effect of business cycles—while such buffers lead to less credit in good times, they result in more lending in bad times.

The studies discussed above focus on capital requirements, but many others focus on capital per se. Several studies find a significant reduction in lending following a decline in capital arising from loan losses in the 1920s to 1930s (e.g., Calomiris and Wilson, 2004) and late 1980s to early 1990s (e.g., Peek and Rosengren, 1995), consistent with a positive relationship between capital and lending during a period of distress. Using data on 165 large US BHCs from 1992 to 2009, Berrospide and Edge (2010) also find that higher capital (the actual level or measured relative to an estimated target) is associated with higher loan growth, although the effect seems to be small. Francis and Osborne (2012) use data on banks in the UK from 1989 to 2007 to show that banks with greater surplus capital have higher growth in lending and off-balance-sheet activities. They argue that higher capital requirements would reduce the amount of surplus capital and that a positive relationship between surplus capital and lending should be viewed as evidence that higher capital requirements reduce lending.

---

[37] For an earlier discussion on this, see Berger, Herring, and Szego (1995).

While this argument may be valid in the short run in which capital is hard to adjust, it does not seem appropriate in the long run. Some recent contributions in this area define bank output as liquidity creation instead of lending. Berger and Bouwman (2009) examine the relationship between bank capital and the amount of liquidity they create using data on banks in the US from 1993 to 2003. For large banks, which create by far most of the liquidity, they find a positive relationship (driven largely by the effect on off-balance-sheet activities), whereas for small banks, the relationship is negative. European evidence on this topic is starting to emerge (e.g., Distinguin, Roulet, and Tarazi, 2013; Horvath, Seidler, and Weill, forthcoming) and tends to suggest that capital and on-balance sheet liquidity creation are negatively related in Europe.

While the papers discussed above examine the effect of higher capital requirements and higher capital on bank output, it is useful to briefly address two related issues in closing. First, higher capital requirements may affect loan rates. Specifically, if higher capital requirements cause banks to operate with more capital, then two effects may be generated. First, the replacement of tax-advantaged debt with equity may increase the bank's weighted average cost of capital, putting upward pressure on loan rates. But second, higher capital will reduce the bank's debt funding cost (due to the cushioning effect of capital and also its incentive effects), and this reduction may be large enough to increase the bank's return on equity, so that higher capital in the bank may exert downward pressure on loan rates.[38] The overall effect of bank capital on loan rates may thus turn out to be small. Simulations by Hanson, Kashyap, and Stein (2011) support this notion— depending on the chosen scenario, a 10% point increase in the capital ratio would cause loan rates to increase by a mere 25 to 45 basis points. Second, it is important to remember that a key reason to impose higher capital requirements is to obtain a safer and less fragile banking sector.[39] Consistent with this objective, Mehran and Thakor (2011) show theoretically and find empirically that bank capital and bank value are positively related in the cross-section. Beltratti and Stulz (2012) provide evidence that banks which had higher tier 1 capital ratios before the recent subprime lending crisis showed better stock performance during the crisis. Berger and Bouwman (2013) show that capital helps small banks to survive at all times (during crises and normal times), and helps large banks primarily during banking crises. Baker and Wurgler (2013) document that in the past 40 years, banks with higher capital had lower betas risks but higher stock returns, leading them to conclude that higher capital requirements will increase the cost of capital in banking, although they will also make banks systematically safer.

In sum, it appears that the effects of higher *capital requirements* on bank output are mixed, but in the US this is in part because the introduction of higher capital requirements in the early 1990s coincided with changes in the type of capital requirements and a recession which

---

[38] Cross-country studies on the relationship between capital (not: capital requirements) and loan rates tend to find evidence consistent with this (e.g., Demirgüç-Kunt and Huizinga, 1999; Saunders and Schumacher, 2000). Osborne, Fuertes, and Milne (2012) document that, for UK banks, the positive relationship between capital and loan rates exists only in non-crisis periods, and becomes negative during a crisis.

[39] Several recent papers examine how capital injections by the government affect bank lending in the US (e.g., Black and Hazelwood, 2013; Duchin and Sosyura, forthcoming; Li, forthcoming) or liquidity creation in Germany (Berger, Bouwman, and Kick et al. 2013).

makes it harder to interpret the results. In contrast, it seems that higher *capital* generally benefits banks and their borrowers, reduces bank-specific and systemic risks (e.g., Acharya and Thakor, 2012; Farhi and Tirole, 2012), and reduces the need for taxpayer-funded bailouts (e.g., Farhi and Tirole, 2012).

8.5.1.3 Key Issue #2: Capital Requirements and the Shadow Banking System

A second issue is that imposing higher capital requirements might lead to widespread migration of financial intermediation towards the less regulated shadow banking system (Hanson, Kashyap, and Stein, 2011; FSB, 2012c). This is a concern since the subprime lending crisis showed that the absence of an explicit government safety net in this market can cause runs and that liquidity can dry up for institutions in the shadow banking system, which can then threaten overall liquidity creation in the economy. Many of these institutions are considered "systemically important," so the government has an (ex post) incentive to rescue them, as we saw with non-deposit-insured institutions like Bear Stearns and American International Group (AIG) in the subprime lending crisis.

One way to address this issue is to impose capital requirements on shadow banks. Basel III includes steps in this direction (FSB, 2012c): it increases capital requirements for short-term liquidity facilities provided to securitization vehicles, and for exposures to unregulated financial institutions regardless of size. The Basel Committee decided against increasing capital requirements related to banks' short-term liquidity facilities to money market funds (MMFs), fearing this could have unintended consequences and might be unnecessary in light of the introduction of the liquidity coverage ratio. The Dodd–Frank Act imposes capital requirements on shadow banks that are considered SIFIs. The Financial Stability Oversight Council proposed in early June 2013 to designate AIG, Prudential Financial, and GE Capital as such.

More steps are likely needed to prevent migration toward the shadow banking system. Gorton and Metrick (2010) discuss several additional proposals, including the conversion of MMFs that offer bank-like services (transaction accounts and the ability to withdraw funds on demand at par) into "narrow savings banks" with appropriate supervision, government insurance, and access to lender of last resort facilities.

8.5.2 Liquidity Requirements—International and US Developments

Although reserve requirements have taken a back seat in US regulation, there is now growing momentum for having explicit liquidity requirements for financial institutions, both in the US and in other countries. Some of these developments are briefly reviewed here.

The Basel Committee is introducing liquidity regulation as part of Basel III. This is a departure from Basel I and II, which focused on strengthening capital regulation. The original December 2010 liquidity framework (BIS, 2010) specifies two minimum liquidity requirements with complementary objectives. The first is the liquidity coverage ratio (LCR) which promotes short-term resilience—to survive a specified stress scenario which lasts one month, banks have to operate with enough high-quality liquid assets. The second is the net stable funding ratio (NSFR) which promotes long-run resilience—to be able to survive an extended closure of wholesale funding markets, banks have to operate with a minimum acceptable amount of "stable funding" based on the liquidity characteristics of the bank's assets and activities over a one-year period. The Basel Committee initially focused on operationalizing the LCR and an amended proposal was endorsed by its oversight body in January 2013 (BIS, 2013a). It is currently working on operationalizing the NSFR. The discussion below reflects this two-step approach: it discusses the LCR in depth but only briefly describes the NSFR.

The LCR requires that a bank's stock of unencumbered high-quality liquid assets (HQLA) generally equals or exceeds its projected net cash outflows (NCOF) over a 30-day horizon under a stress scenario prescribed by the supervisors:

$$LCR = \frac{HQLA}{NCOF} \geq 100\%.$$

The numerator includes so-called Level 1 assets (cash, central bank reserves, and certain marketable securities backed by sovereigns and central banks), Level 2A assets (certain government securities, covered bonds and corporate debt securities), and Level 2B assets (lower-rated plain-vanilla senior corporate bonds and certain residential mortgage-backed securities). Level 2 (2B) assets may not account for more than 40% (15%) of the bank's total stock of HQLA. The denominator is defined as total expected cash outflows minus total expected cash inflows in the specified stress scenario for the next 30 days. Total expected cash outflows are calculated by multiplying the outstanding balances of different types of liabilities and off-balance-sheet commitments by the rates at which they are expected to run off or be drawn down in the prescribed stress scenario. For example, unsecured interbank loans are assumed to run off fully if they come due during the stress scenario, while deposits are assumed to run off by 5% or 10%, depending on the type of deposit. To ensure a minimum level of HQLA holdings at all times, total cash inflows are subject to a cap of 75% of total expected cash outflows. While banks are expected to keep their LCR above 100% at all times, the latest proposal suggests that banks' LCR may drop below the minimum requirement during times of stress (BIS, 2013b). The LCR will be introduced internationally on January 1, 2015, with a minimum requirement starting at 60%, increasing gradually in 10% annual increments to 100% on January 1, 2019.

The Federal Reserve intends to implement some form of the LCR, but the scope, timing and nature of such implementation is unclear. In its proposals to implement parts of the Dodd–Frank Act's systemic risk regulation framework, the Federal Reserve indicates that it intends to apply the LCR to: (a) all or a subset of the US systemically important financial institutions or SIFIs (US BHCs with consolidated assets of at least $50 billion and US non-bank financial companies that the Financial Stability Oversight Council designates as systemically important) (Federal Reserve, 2012a); and (b) the US operations of all or a subset of large foreign banking organizations (with combined US assets of at least $50 billion) (Federal Reserve, 2012b).

If implemented, it is unclear how the LCR will interact with the liquidity risk management standards proposed in the Dodd–Frank enhanced prudential standards for large US and foreign institutions. There are some fundamental differences. First, while the LCR makes one-size-fits-all liquidity run-off assumptions which all banks have to use to determine the size of the liquidity buffer, the Federal Reserve's proposed internal stress testing would require each institution to conduct internal liquidity stress tests which are tailored to its capital structure, riskiness, complexity, size, and activities, and to use the results of these tests to calculate the size of its liquidity buffer. Second, the LCR requires banks to apply prescribed haircuts to specific asset classes when establishing its stock of HQLA, whereas the Federal Reserve's proposals merely ask an institution to discount the fair market value of assets included in its liquidity buffer to reflect any market volatility and credit risk. Third, the LCR relies on external ratings and requires a bank to calculate the amount of collateral it would have to post after a three-notch downgrade of the bank's rating, whereas Section 939A of the Dodd–Frank Act demands that regulations do not rely on external ratings and replace them with alternative standards of creditworthiness.

The NSFR requires that a bank's available stable funding (ASF) exceeds the required amount of stable funding (RSF) based on the liquidity characteristics of the bank's assets and activities over a one-year bank-specific stress scenario:

$$NSFR = \frac{ASF}{RSF} > 100\%.$$

Stable funding includes equity, preferred stock with a maturity of at least one year, liabilities with effective maturities of at least one year, and demand deposits/term deposits/ wholesale funding with maturities of less than one year that are expected to stay with the bank in case of idiosyncratic stress. The numerator is determined by assigning weights to the amounts of stable funding the bank has. For example, tier 1 and tier 2 capital receive weights of 100% (fully stable), stable deposits are weighted at 80%, while less stable deposits obtain a weight of 50%. The denominator is calculated as the sum of the bank's assets and off-balance-sheet activities multiplied by an RSF factor assigned to each asset and off-balance-sheet activity type. Activities that are more liquid receive the lowest RSF factors (and require less stable funding) because they can act as a source of extended liquidity in case of stress. For example, cash receives a weight of 0%, conditionally revocable and irrevocable credit and liquidity facilities to any client are weighted at 5% of the undrawn portion, loans to non-financial corporates/sovereigns/central banks with a remaining maturity of less than one year are weighted at 50%, residential mortgages that qualify for a risk weight of up to 35% under Basel II's standardized approach obtain a weight of 65%, while loans to retail customers and small business customers with a remaining maturity of less than one year are weighted at 85% (see BIS (2010) for more detail).

8.5.3 Understanding Better How Liquidity Requirements Interact with Capital Requirements

Liquidity requirements and capital requirements are designed to address two different problems and they affect different sides of the bank's balance sheet—liquidity requirements deal with withdrawal risk on the liability side by stipulating that a fraction of the bank's assets be held as cash or deposits with the central bank, whereas capital requirements deal with asset-substitution risk by stipulating that a fraction of the bank's liabilities be in the form of equity. Nonetheless, liquidity requirements and capital requirements may interact. Little academic research has been done in this important area.

Two recent papers address this issue theoretically. Acharya, Mehran, and Thakor (2013) examine optimal capital regulation for banks that face two moral hazard problems: shirking by managers (i.e., underprovision of monitoring) and risk shifting by shareholders. They show that a simple minimum capital requirement can rule out the second problem, but not the first problem, since it makes debt so safe that it eliminates market discipline related to loan monitoring. To deal with both moral hazards, they propose that regulators impose two kinds of capital requirements: a regular minimum capital requirement and a "special capital account." The regular capital can be used to invest in any type of assets. In contrast, the special capital has to be invested in relatively safe and liquid assets (which can be monitored and do not cause a downward price spiral in case of liquidation) such as Treasuries, and can thus be viewed as a liquidity requirement. The key innovation in the paper's proposal is that the special capital belongs to the bank's shareholders as long as the bank is solvent, but when the bank is insolvent, this capital goes to the regulator, not the bank's creditors. This means that this special capital is "invisible" to the bank's creditors and does not dilute their incentive to discipline the bank.

Calomiris, Heider, and Hoerova (2013) incorporate two unique aspects of cash relative to capital: the value of cash is observable at all times, and cash is riskless, making it impervious to risk shifting. These two features mean that cash does not only mitigate liquidity risks associated with exogenous withdrawal shocks, but also mitigates endogenous asset risk. Specifically, the market recognizes that banks with higher cash holdings make more prudent risk-management decisions and thus will be more willing to provide funds, which implies that in bad states of the world, banks will avoid higher asset risk and increase their cash holdings to preserve market confidence. A key insight of the paper is that liquidity requirements should not be viewed as a mere insurance policy to deal with liquidity risk that may occur in a financial crisis, but also as a prudential regulatory tool that—like capital requirements—can limit default risk and encourage good risk management. That is, liquidity requirements and capital requirements act as (imperfect) substitutes.

The optimal design of both capital and liquidity requirements can only be addressed with a good understanding of the nature of government intervention in financial crises. It would be preferable to acknowledge up-front that such intervention is unavoidable and ask how capital and liquidity requirements should be designed ex ante, conditional on knowing that bailouts will occur ex post in circumstances that can be identified ex ante.

8.6 CONCLUSION

This chapter has covered the theory and empirical evidence related to bank liquidity creation to shed light on the underlying economics of this central aspect of the financial system. It has also covered regulatory issues and how these are affected by the evolution of banking from an OTH model to one that has a mix of OTH and OTD. These developments have profound implications for regulatory policy that is designed to ensure that liquidity creation continues without the costly breaches associated with financial crises.

As discussed, much work remains to be done. Foremost is the question of how capital requirements ought to be designed for both traditional OTH banking activities as well as for the newly emerged shadow banking system. A second question is the design of liquidity requirements. These two issues should not be addressed in isolation. It is critically important to develop a good understanding of how capital and liquidity requirements interact. Finally, Farhi and Tirole (2012) highlight the fact that inefficient bailouts of banks by regulators may occur because regulators cannot distinguish between insolvency and illiquidity even ex post, so research that informs regulators about how to distinguish between insolvency and illiquidity as a precursor to intervening in what looks like a crisis would be very useful.

Appendix 8.1: The Shadow Banking System

The types of activities and institutions that are part of the shadow banking system continue to evolve. Important players include the following (for a review, see Adrian and Ashcraft, 2012).

First, asset-backed securities (ABS): ABS are securities backed by claims on pools of assets such as loans and mortgages. The cash flows of the underlying assets are sliced and diced in different ways into several tranches, which are typically rated. The most senior tranche receives the highest rating (e.g., AAA) and the most junior tranche is the equity tranche, which may be retained by the issuer. Often, a special purpose vehicle (SPV) is created to handle the securitization. The SPV is bankruptcy-remote, which allows the structure to receive off-balance-sheet treatment. Collateralized debt obligations (CDOs) are a special form of ABS in which lower-rated tranches (e.g., the BBB tranches) of several securitizations can be pooled together and again split in various ways, creating yet again tranches which may have higher ratings including AAA and AA. Some blame the financial woes of the subprime lending crisis on the complexity of CDOs and a failure of the models used by rating agencies to value them. The first CDO was created by Drexel Burnham Lambert Inc. in 1987. CDO issuance was at its highest in 2007 and fully collapsed during the crisis.

Second, asset-backed commercial paper (ABCP) conduits: an ABCP conduit is a bankruptcy-remote entity that issues CP to finance the purchase of a pool of financial assets (such as trade receivables). To make the CP more appealing or to get a higher rating, a program sponsor typically arranges some form of credit enhancement (e.g., overcollateralization or excess cash) and/or a backup-borrowing facility. ABCP experienced a run in the summer of 2007, when American Home, sponsor of a conduit, declared bankruptcy, and three of its mortgage programs extended the maturity of their paper. Not being able to value ABCP holdings, BNP Paribas stopped redemptions at two money market mutual funds on August 7, 2007. A run by investors on more than 100 programs (1/3 of the market) followed (see Covitz, Liang, and Suarez, 2013).

Third, tri-party repurchase agreements (repos): repos are collateralized deposits. A depositor puts funds in a bank for a short period (typically overnight) and the bank promises to pay the overnight repo rate. Since the funds tend to be too big to qualify for deposit insurance, the depositor demands collateral, which it can sell if the bank fails. Repos are overcollateralized—the difference between the collateral value and the sale price is the repo haircut. In a tri-party repo, a clearing bank holds the collateral, ensuring that both the lender and the borrower are protected against the other party's default. A 1984 law exempted repos on "safe" collateral from the automatic stay in bankruptcy, meaning that lenders would get quick access to their collateral in case of dealer default, fueling growth of the market. In 2005, mortgage-backed repos were given similar treatment. Their prevalence led to runs on repo during the subprime lending crisis.

Fourth, money market funds (MMFs): MMFs are open-ended mutual funds which invest in short-term securities like treasuries, CP, and repos. From 1971 onward, MMFs have acted as an alternative to bank deposits from the investors' perspective. In that year, Regulation Q restricted the interest rates that banks could pay on deposits. The MMF sector reached an all-time high at \$3.5 trillion in 2008. The net asset value of MMFs is typically constant at \$1. If it drops below \$1, it is "breaking the buck." This can happen when its investment income does not cover its operating expenses, for example, because interest rates have dropped. The day after Lehman Brothers went bankrupt in September 2008, the Reserve Primary Fund broke the buck, triggering a run on MMFs. In reaction to this, other fund managers sold assets or reallocated to treasuries, thus exacerbating the funding problems for other instruments such as repos and CP.

REFERENCES

Acharya, V. V., Mehran, H., and Thakor, A. V. (2013). Caught between Scylla and Charybdis? Regulating Bank Leverage when there is Rent Seeking and Risk Shifting. Working Paper.

Acharya, V. V., Shin, H. S., and Yorulmazer, T. (2009). Endogenous Choice of Bank Liquidity: The Role of Fire Sales. Working Paper.

Acharya, V. V. and Thakor, A. V. (2012). The Dark Side of Liquidity Creation: Leverage and Systemic Risk. Working Paper.

Admati, A. R., DeMarzo, P. M., Hellwig, M. F., and Pfleiderer, P. (2011). Fallacies, Irrelevant Facts, and Myths in the Discussion of Capital Regulation: Why Bank Equity is Not Expensive. Working Paper.

Admati, A. R., DeMarzo, P. M., Hellwig, M. F., and Pfleiderer, P. (2014). The Leverage Ratchet Effect. Working Paper.

Admati, A. R. and Hellwig, M. F. (2013). *The Bankers' New Clothes: What's Wrong with Banking and What to Do about It*. Princeton, NJ: Princeton University Press.

Adrian, T. and Ashcraft, A. B. (2012). Shadow Banking: A Review of the Literature. In: S. N. Durlauf and L. E. Blume (Eds.), *The New Palgrave Dictionary of Economics*. New York, NY: Palgrave Macmillan

Aghion, P., Bolton, P., and Tirole, J. (2004). Exit Options in Corporate Finance: Liquidity versus Incentives, *Review of Finance* 8, 327–353.

Aiyar, S., Calomiris, C. W., and Wieladek, T. (2012). Does Macropru Leak? Evidence from a UK Policy Experiment, Bank of England Working Paper No. 445.

Allen, F. (1990). The Market for Information and the Origin of Financial Intermediation, *Journal of Financial Intermediation* 1, 3–30.

Allen, F. and Gale, D. (2004). Financial Intermediaries and Markets, *Econometrica* 72, 1023–1061.

Allen, F. and Santomero, A. M. (1998). The Theory of Financial Intermediation, *Journal of Banking and Finance* 21, 1461–1485.

Allen, L., Peristiani, S., and Saunders, A. (1989). Bank Size, Collateral, and Net Purchase Behavior in the Federal Funds Market: Empirical Evidence, *Journal of Business* 62, 501–515.

Armantier, O., Ghysels, E., Sarkar, A., and Shrader, J. (2011). Stigma in Financial Markets: Evidence from Liquidity Auctions and Discount Window Borrowing during the Crisis. Federal Reserve Bank of New York Working Paper.

Auerbach. R. (2010). Malpractice at the Bernanke Federal Reserve, *Huffington Post* September 13.

Bai, J., Krishnamurthy, A., and Weymuller, C.-H. (2013). Measuring Liquidity Mismatch in the Banking Sector. Working Paper.

Baker, M. and Wurgler, J. (2013). Would Stricter Capital Requirements Raise the Cost of Capital? Bank Capital Regulation and the Low Risk Anomaly. Working Paper.

Beltratti, A. and Stulz, R. M. (2012). The Credit Crisis Around the Globe: Why Did Some Banks Perform Better?, *Journal of Financial Economics* 105, 1–17.

Benink, H. and Benston, G. (2005). The Future of Banking Regulation in Developed Countries: Lessons from and for Europe, *Financial Markets, Institutions & Instruments* 14, 289–328.

Berger, A. N., Black, L. K., Bouwman, C. H. S., and Dlugosz, J. (2013). The Federal Reserve's Discount Window and TAF Programs: Pushing on a String? Working Paper.

Berger, A. N. and Bouwman, C. H. S. (2009). Bank Liquidity Creation, *Review of Financial Studies* 22, 3779–3837.

Berger, A. N. and Bouwman, C. H. S. (2013). How Does Capital Affect Bank Performance During Financial Crises?, *Journal of Financial Economics* 109, 146–176.

Berger, A. N., Bouwman, C. H. S., Kick, T., and Schaeck, K. (2013). Bank Risk Taking and Liquidity Creation Following Regulatory Interventions and Capital Support. Working Paper.

Berger, A. N., Herring, R. J., and Szego, G. P. (1995). The Role of Capital in Financial Institutions, *Journal of Banking and Finance* 19, 393–430.

Berger, A. N., Miller, N. H., Petersen, M. A., Rajan, R. G., and Stein, J. C. (2005). Does Function Follow Organizational Form? Evidence from the Lending Practices of Large and Small Banks, *Journal of Financial Economics* 76, 237–269.

Berger, A. N. and Udell, G. F. (1992). Some Evidence on the Empirical Significance of Rationing, *Journal of Political Economy* 100, 1047–1077.

Berger, A. N. and Udell, G. F. (1994). Did Risk-Based Capital Allocate Bank Credit and Cause a "Credit Crunch" in the United States?, *Journal of Money, Credit, and Banking* 26, 585–628.

Berger, A. N. and Udell, G. F. (1995). Relationship Lending and Lines of Credit in Small Firm Finance, *Journal of Business* 68, 351–381.

Berkovitch, E. and Greenbaum, S. I. (1991). The Loan Commitment as an Optimal Financing Contract, *Journal of Financial and Quantitative Analysis* 26, 83–95.

Berlin, M. and Mester, L. J. (1999). Deposits and Relationship Lending, *Review of Financial Studies* 12, 579–607.

Bernanke, B. S. (1983). Nonmonetary Effects of the Financial Crisis in Propagation of the Great Depression, *American Economic Review* 73, 257–276.

Bernanke, B. S. (2008). Liquidity Provision by the Federal Reserve. Remarks at the Federal Reserve Bank of Atlanta Financial Markets Conference, Sea Island, Georgia, May 18.

Bernanke, B. S. (2010). Causes of the Recent Financial and Economic Crisis. Statement before the Financial Crisis Inquiry Commission, Washington, DC, delivered on September 2.

Berndt, A. and Gupta, A. (2009). Moral Hazard and Adverse Selection in the Originate-to-Distribute Model of Bank Credit, *Journal of Monetary Economics* 56, 725–743.

Berrospide, J. M. and Edge, R. M. (2010). The Effects of Bank Capital on Lending: What Do We Know, and What Does It Mean?, *International Journal of Central Banking* 6, 5–54.

Besanko, D. and Kanatas, G. (1996). The Regulation of Bank Capital: Do Capital Standards Promote Bank Safety?, *Journal of Financial Intermediation* 5, 160–183.

Bharath, S., Dahiya, S., Saunders, A., and Srinivasan, A. (2007). So What Do I Get? The Bank's View of Lending Relationships, *Journal of Financial Economics* 85, 368–419.

Bhattacharya, S. and Thakor, A. V. (1993). Contemporary Banking Theory, *Journal of Financial Intermediation* 3, 2–50.

Billett, M. T., Flannery, M. J., and Garfinkel, J. A. (1995). The Effect of Lender Identity on a Borrowing Firm's Equity Return, *Journal of Finance* 50, 699–718.

Billett, M. T., Flannery, M. J., and Garfinkel, J. A. (2006). Are Bank Loans Special? Evidence on the Post-Announcement Performance of Bank Borrowers, *Journal of Financial and Quantitative Analysis* 4, 733–751.

BIS (Bank for International Settlements) (2010). Basel III: International Framework for Liquidity Risk Measurement, Standards and Monitoring, December.

BIS (Bank for International Settlements) (2011). Global Systemically Important Banks: Assessment Methodology and the Additional Loss Absorbency Requirement, July.

BIS (Bank for International Settlements) (2013a). Group of Governors and Heads of Supervision Endorses Revised Liquidity Standards for Banks, January.

BIS (Bank for International Settlements) (2013b). Basel III: The Liquidity Coverage Ratio and Liquidity Risk Monitoring Tools, January.

BIS (Bank for International Settlements) (2013c). Report to G20 Finance Ministers and Central Bank Governors on Monitoring Implementation of Basel III Regulatory Reform, April.

Black, L. K. and Hazelwood, L. N. (2013). The Effect of TARP on Bank Risk-Taking, *Journal of Financial Stability*, 9, 790–803.

Blackwell, N. R., and Santomero, A. M. (1982). Bank Credit Rationing and the Customer Relation, *Journal of Monetary Economics* 9, 121–129.

Board of Governors of the Federal Reserve System (1959). The Federal Funds Market: A Study by a Federal Reserve System Committee, Washington, DC.

Boot, A. W. A. (2000). Relationship Banking: What Do We Know?, *Journal of Financial Intermediation* 9, 7–25.

Boot, A. W. A., Greenbaum, S. I., and Thakor, A. V. (1993). Reputation and Discretion in Financial Contracting, *American Economic Review* 83, 1165–1183.

Boot, A. W. A. and Thakor, A. V. (1993). Security Design, *Journal of Finance* 48, 1349–1378.

Boot, A. W. A. and Thakor, A. V. (1994). Moral Hazard and Secured lending in an Infinitely Repeated Credit Market Game, *International Economic Review* 35, 899–920.

Boot, A. W. A. and Thakor, A. V. (2000). Can Relationship Banking Survive Competition?, *Journal of Finance* 55, 679–714.

Boot, A. W. A., Thakor, A. V., and Udell, G. F. (1991). Credible Commitments, Contract Enforcement Problems and Banks: Intermediation as Credibility Assurance, *Journal of Banking and Finance* 15, 605–632.

Bord, V. M. and Santos, J. A. C. (2012). The Rise of the Originate-to-Distribute Model and the Role of Banks in Financial Intermediation, *FRBNY Economic Policy Review* July, 21–34.

Brunnermeier, M. K. and Oehmke, M. (2013). The Maturity Rat Race, *Journal of Finance* 6, 483–521.

Bryant, J. (1980). A Model of Reserves, Bank Runs, and Deposit Insurance, *Journal of Banking and Finance* 4, 335–344.

Calomiris, C. W. and Gorton, G. B. (1991). The Origins of Banking Panics: Models, Facts, and Bank Regulation. In: R. G. Hubbard (Ed.), *Financial Markets and Financial Crises*, 109–174. NBER: University of Chicago Press.

Calomiris, C. W., Heider, F., and Hoerova, M. (2013). A Theory of Bank Liquidity Requirements. Working Paper.

Calomiris, C. W. and Herring, R. J. (2011). Why and How to Design a Contingent Convertible Debt Requirement. Working Paper.

Calomiris, C. W., Himmelberg, C. P., and Wachtel, P. (1995). Commercial Paper and Corporate Finance: A Microeconomic Perspective, *Carnegie—Rochester Conference Series on Public Policy* 45, 203–250.

Calomiris, C. W. and Kahn, C. M. (1991). The Role of Demandable Debt in Structuring Optimal Banking Arrangements, *American Economic Review* 81, 497–513.

Calomiris, C. W. and Mason, J. R. (2008). Resolving the Puzzle of the Underissuance of National Bank Notes, *Explorations in Economic History* 45, 327–355.

Calomiris, C. W. and Pornrojnangkool, T. (2009). Relationship Banking and the Pricing of Financial Services, *Journal of Financial Services Research* 35, 189–224.

Calomiris, C. W. and Wilson, B. (2004). Bank Capital and Portfolio Management: The 1930s "Capital Crunch" and the Scramble to Shed Risk, *Journal of Business* 77, 421–455.

Campbell, T. S. (1978). A Model of the Market for Lines of Credit, *Journal of Finance* 33, 231–244.

Campbell, T. S., Chan, Y.-S., and Marino, A. M. (1992). An Incentive-Based Theory of Bank Regulation, *Journal of Financial Intermediation* 2, 255–276.

Campello, M., Giambona, E., Graham, J. R., and Harvey, C. R. (2011). Liquidity Management and Corporate Investment During a Financial Crisis, *Review of Financial Studies* 24, 1944–1979.

Champ, B. (2007). The National Banking System: A Brief History. Working Paper.

Chan, Y.-S., Greenbaum, S. I., and Thakor, A. V. (1992). Is Fairly Priced Deposit Insurance Possible?, *Journal of Finance* 47, 227–245.

Chari, V. V. and Jagannathan, R. (1988). Banking Panics, Information, and Rational Expectations Equilibrium, *Journal of Finance* 43, 749–761.

Claessens, S., Pozsar, Z., Ratnovski, L., and Singh, M. (2012). Shadow Banking: Economics and Policy, IMF Staff Discussion Note No. SDN/12/12.

Copeland, A., Martin, A., and Walker, M. (2012). *Repo Runs: Evidence from the Tri-Party Repo Market*, Federal Reserve Bank of New York Staff Reports No. 506.

Cornett, M. M., McNutt, J. J., Strahan, P. E., and Tehranian, H. (2011). Liquidity Risk Management and Credit Supply in the Financial Crisis, *Journal of Financial Economics* 101, 297–312.

Coval, J. and Thakor, A.V (2005). Financial Intermediation as a Beliefs-Bridge between Optimists and Pessimists, *Journal of Financial Economics* 75, 535–570.

Covitz, D. M., Liang, N., and Suarez, G. A. (2013). The Evolution of a Financial Crisis: Collapse of the Asset-Backed Commercial Paper Market, *Journal of Finance* 68, 815–848.

Dai, Z., Zhang, H., and Zhao, F. (2013). Tug-of-War: Incentive Alignment in Securitization and Loan Performance. Working Paper.

Dasgupta, S. (2009). Comment on L. Zingales: Why Not Consider Maximum Reserve Ratios?, *The Economist's Voice* 6(4), Art. 6.

Degryse, H., Kim, M., and Ongena, S. (2009). *Microeconometrics of Banking: Methods, Applications, and Results*. Oxford: Oxford University Press.

Dell'Ariccia, G., Detragiache, E., and Rajan, R. G. (2008). The Real Effects of Banking Crises, *Journal of Financial Intermediation* 17, 89–112.

Dell'Ariccia, G., Igan, D., and Laeven, L. (2012). Credit Booms and Lending Standards: Evidence from the Subprime Mortgage Market, *Journal of Money, Credit, and Banking* 44, 367–384.

Dell'Ariccia, G. and Marquez, R. (2006). Lending Booms and Lending Standards, *Journal of Finance* 61, 2511–2546.

Demirgüç-Kunt, A. and Huizinga, H. (1999). Determinants of Commercial Bank Interest Margins and Profitability: Some International Evidence, *World Bank Economic Review* 13, 379–408.

Demiroglu, C. and James, C. M. (2012). How Important is Having Skin in the Game? Originator-Sponsor Affiliation and Losses on Mortgage-Backed Securities, *Review of Financial Studies* 25, 3217–3258.

Demyanyk, Y. and Van Hemert, O. (2011). Understanding the Subprime Mortgage Crisis, *Review of Financial Studies* 24, 1848–1880.

Dewatripont, M. and Tirole, J. (1994). A Theory of Debt and Equity: Diversity of Securities and Manager-Shareholder Congruence, *Quarterly Journal of Economics* 109, 1027–1054.

Diamond, D. W. (1984). Financial Intermediation and Delegated Monitoring, *Review of Economic Studies* 51, 393–414.

Diamond, D. W. and Dybvig, P. H. (1983). Bank Runs, Deposit Insurance, and Liquidity, *Journal of Political Economy* 91, 401–419.

Diamond, D. W. and Rajan, R. G. (2001). Liquidity Risk, Liquidity Creation, and Financial Fragility: A Theory of Banking, *Journal of Political Economy* 109, 287–327.

Distinguin, I., Roulet, C., and Tarazi, A. (2013). Bank Regulatory Capital and Liquidity: Evidence from US and European Publicly Traded Banks, *Journal of Banking and Finance* 37, 3295–3317.

Drechsler, I., Drechsel, T., Marques-Ibanez, D., and Schnabl, P. (2013). Who Borrows from the Lender of Last Resort? Evidence from the European Financial Crisis. Working Paper.

Drucker, S. and Puri, M. (2005). On the Benefits of Concurrent Lending and Underwriting, *Journal of Finance* 60, 2763–2799.

Drucker, S. and Puri, M. (2009). On Loan Sales, Loan Contracting, and Lending Relationships, *Review of Financial Studies* 22, 2835–2872.

Duchin, R. and Sosyura, D. (Forthcoming). Safer Ratios, Riskier Portfolios: Banks' Response to Government Aid. Working Paper.

Edlin, A. S. and Jaffee, D. M. (2009). Show Me the Money, *The Economists' Voice* 6, 1–5.

Ennis, H. M. and Weinberg, J. A. (Forthcoming). Over-the-Counter Loans, Adverse Selection, and Stigma in the Interbank Market, *Review of Economic Dynamics*.

European Parliament (2011). US Implementation of Basel II: Final Rules Issued, but No Supervisory Approvals to Date. Briefing Note Requested by the European Parliament's Committee on Economic and Monetary Affairs.

Farhi, E. and Tirole, J. (2012). Collective Moral Hazard, Maturity Mismatch, and Systemic Bailouts, *American Economic Review* 102, 60–93.

FDIC (Federal Deposit Insurance Corporation) (2003). Basel and the Evolution of Capital Regulation: Moving Forward, Looking Back. A Study by S. Burhouse, J. Feid, G. French, and K. Ligon.

Federal Reserve (1933). Member Bank Reserves—Report of the Committee on Bank Reserves of the Federal Reserve System. In: *19th Annual Report of the Board of Governors of the Federal Reserve System*, 260–285.

Federal Reserve (2007). Risk-Based Capital Standards: Advanced Capital Adequacy Framework—Basel II, *72 Federal Register 235* December 7.

Federal Reserve (2012a). Enhanced Prudential Standards and Early Remediation Requirements for Covered Companies, 77 *Federal Register 594* January 5.

Federal Reserve (2012b). Enhanced Prudential Standards and Early Remediation Requirements for Foreign Banking Organizations and Foreign Nonbank Financial Companies, 77 *Federal Register 76627* December 28.

Feinman, J. N. (1993). Reserve Requirements: History, Current Practice, and Potential Reform, *Federal Reserve Bulletin* June, 569–589.

Francis, W. A. and Osborne, M. (2012). Capital Requirements and Bank Behavior in the UK: Are There Lessons for International Capital Standards?, *Journal of Banking and Finance* 36, 803–816.

Freixas, X. and Rochet, J.-C. (2008). *Microeconomics of Banking*. 2nd edition. Boston, MA: MIT Press.

FSB (Financial Stability Board) (2011). Shadow Banking: Strengthening Oversight and Regulation. Recommendations of the Financial Stability Board.

FSB (Financial Stability Board) (2012a). Securities Lending and Repos: Market Overview and Financial Stability Issues. Interim Report of the FSB Workstream on Securities Lending and Repos, April 27.

FSB (Financial Stability Board) (2012b). Update of Group of Global Systemically Important Banks (G-SIBs), November 1.

FSB (Financial Stability Board) (2012c). Strengthening Oversight and Regulation of Shadow Banking: An Integrated Overview of Policy Recommendations, November 18.

Furfine, C. (2001). The Reluctance to Borrow from the Fed, *Economics Letters* 72, 209–213.

Gande, A. and Saunders, A. (2012). Are Banks Still Special when There is a Secondary Market for Loans?, *Journal of Finance* 67, 1649–1684.

Gatev, E., Schuermann, T., and Strahan, P. E. (2006). How do Banks Manage Liquidity Risk? Evidence from the Equity and Deposit Markets in the Fall of 1998. In: M. Carey and R. Stulz (Eds.), *Risks of Financial Institutions*, 105–127. Chicago, IL: University of Chicago Press.

Gatev, E., Schuermann, T., and Strahan, P. E. (2009). Managing Bank Liquidity Risk: How Deposit-Loan Synergies Vary with Market Conditions, *Review of Financial Studies* 22, 995–1020.

Gennaioli, N., Shleifer, A., and Vishny, R. W. (2013). A Model of Shadow Banking, *Journal of Finance* 68, 1331–1363.

Genotte, G. and Pyle, D. H. (1991). Capital Controls and Bank Risk, *Journal of Banking and Finance* 15, 805–824.

Gorton, G. B. (1988). Banking Panics and the Business Cycle, *Oxford Economic Papers* 40, 751–781.

Gorton, G. B. and Haubrich, J. G. (1990). The Loan Sales Market. In: George Kaufman (Ed.), *Research in Financial Services*, 85–135. Greenwich, US: Jai Press.

Gorton, G. B. and Metrick, A. (2010). Regulating the Shadow Banking System, *Brookings Papers on Economic Activity* 41, 261–312.

Gorton, G. B. and Metrick, A. (2012). Securitized Banking and the Run on Repo, *Journal of Financial Economics* 104, 425–451.

Gorton, G. B. and Pennacchi, G. G. (1990). Financial Intermediaries and Liquidity Creation, *Journal of Finance* 45, 49–71.

Gorton, G. B. and Pennacchi, G. G. (1995). Banks and Loan Sales: Marketing Non-Marketable Assets, *Journal of Monetary Economics* 3, 389–411.

Greenbaum, S. I., Kanatas, G., and Venezia, I. (1989). Equilibrium Loan Pricing under the Bank-Client Relationship, *Journal of Banking and Finance* 13, 221–235.

Greenbaum, S. I. and Thakor, A. V. (1987). Bank Funding Modes: Securitization versus Deposits, *Journal of Banking and Finance* 11, 379–401.

Greenbaum, S. I. and Thakor, A. V. (2007). *Contemporary Financial Intermediation.* 2nd edition. Amsterdam: North Holland, Elsevier/Academic Press.

Gupta, A., Singh, A. K., and Zebedee, A. A. (2008). Liquidity in the Pricing of Syndicated Loans, *Journal of Financial Markets* 11, 339–376.

Haldane, A. G. and Madouros, V. (2012). The Dog and the Frisbee. Speech at the Jackson Hole Economic Policy Symposium, August 31.

Hancock, D., Laing, A. J., and Wilcox, J. A. (1995). Bank Balance Sheet Shocks and Aggregate Shocks: Their Dynamic Effects on Bank Capital and Lending, *Journal of Banking and Finance* 19, 661–677.

Hanson, S. G., Kashyap, A. K., and Stein, J. C. (2011). A Macroprudential Approach to Financial Regulation, *Journal of Economic Perspectives* 25, 3–28.

Hart, O. and Zingales, L. (2011). A New Capital Regulation for Large Financial Institutions, *American Law and Economics Review* 13, 453–490.

Hellmann, T. F., Murdock, K. C., and Stiglitz, J. E. (2000). Liberalization, Moral Hazard in Banking, and Prudential Regulation: Are Capital Requirements Enough?, *American Economic Review* 90, 147–165.

Hellwig, M. (1994). Liquidity Provision, Banking, and the Allocation of Interest Rate Risk, *European Economic Review* 39, 1363–1389.

Ho, T. S. Y. and Saunders, A. (1983). Fixed Rate Loan Commitments, Take-Down Risk, and the Dynamics of Hedging with Futures, *Journal of Financial and Quantitative Analysis* 18, 499–516.

Hoenig, T. (2012). Get Basel III Right and Avoid Basel IV, *Financial Times* December 12.

Holmstrom, B. and Tirole, J. (1998). Public and Private Supply of Liquidity, *Journal of Political Economy* 106, 1–40.

Horvath, R., Seidler, J., and Weill, L. (Forthcoming). Bank Capital and Liquidity Creation: Granger-Causality Evidence, *Journal of Financial Services Research.*

Ivashina, V. and Scharfstein, D. (2010). Bank Lending during the Financial Crisis of 2008, *Journal of Financial Economics* 97, 319–338.

James, C. M. (1981). Self-Selection and the Pricing of Bank Services: An Analysis of the Market for Bank Loan Commitments and the Role of the Compensating Balance Requirements, *Journal of Financial and Quantitative Analysis* 16, 725–746.

James, C. M. (1987). Some Evidence on the Uniqueness of Bank Loans, *Journal of Financial Economics* 19, 217–236.

James, C. M. (1988). The Use of Loan Sales and Standby Letters of Credit by Commercial Banks, *Journal of Monetary Economics* 22, 395–422.

Jiménez, G., Ongena, S., Peydró, J.-L., and Saurina, J. (2013). Macroprudential Policy, Countercyclical Bank Capital Buffers and Credit Supply: Evidence from the Spanish Dynamic Provisioning Experiments. Working Paper.

Kane, E., Laeven, L., and Demirgüc-Kunt, A. (2008). Determinants of Deposit Insurance Adoption and Design, *Journal of Financial Intermediation* 17, 407–438.

Kashyap, A. K., Rajan, R. G., and Stein, J. C. (2002). Banks as Liquidity Providers: An Explanation for the Coexistence of Lending and Deposit-Taking, *Journal of Finance* 57, 33–73.

Kashyap, A. K., Rajan, R. G., and Stein, J. C. (2008). Rethinking Capital Regulation. In: *Federal Reserve Bank of Kansas City Symposium on Maintaining Stability in a Changing Financial System*, 431–471. Kansas City: Federal Reserve Bank of Kansas City.

Kashyap, A. K., Stein, J. C., and Hanson, S. (2010). An Analysis of the Impact of "Substantially Heightened" Capital Requirements on Large Financial Institutions. Working Paper.

Keister, T. and McAndrews, J. J. (2009). Why Are Banks Holding So Many Excess Reserves?, *Current Issues in Economics and Finance—Federal Reserve Bank of New York* 15, 1–10.

Keys, B. J, Seru, A., and Vig, V. (2012). Lender Screening and the Role of Securitization: Evidence from Prime and Subprime Mortgage Markets, *Review of Financial Studies* 25, 2071–2108.

Kim, D. and Santomero, A. M. (1988). Risk in Bank and Capital Regulation, *Journal of Finance* 43, 1219–1233.

Koehn, M. and Santomero, A. M. (1980). Regulation of Bank Capital and Portfolio Risk, *Journal of Finance* 35, 1235–1244.

Leland, H. E. and Pyle, D. H. (1977). Informational Asymmetries, Financial Structure and Financial Intermediation, *Journal of Finance* 32, 371–387.

Li, L. (Forthcoming). TARP Funds Distribution and Bank Loan Supply, *Journal of Banking and Finance*.

Loutskina, E. (2011). The Role of Securitization in Bank Liquidity and Funding Management, *Review of Financial Studies* 100, 663–684.

McCulley, P. (2007). Teton Reflections. PIMCO Global Central Bank Focus.

McTague, J. (Ed.). (2009). Where's the Stimulus, *Barrons* February 2.

Mailath, G. J. and Mester, L. J. (1994). A Positive Analysis of Bank Closure, *Journal of Financial Intermediation* 3, 282–299.

Martin, A., Skeie, D., and von Thadden, E.-L. (2014a). Repo Runs, *Review of Financial Studies* 27, 957–989.

Martin, A., Skeie, D., and von Thadden, E.-L. (2013). The Fragility of Short-Term Secured Funding Markets, *Journal of Economic Theory* 149, 15–42.

Mehran, H. and Thakor, A. V. (2011). Bank Capital and Value in the Cross-Section, *Review of Financial Studies* 24, 1019–1067.

Melnik, A. and Plaut, S. (1986). Loan Commitment Contracts, Terms of Lending, and Credit Allocation, *Journal of Finance* 41, 425–435.

Merton, R. C. (1977). On the Pricing of Contingent Claims and the Modigliani-Miller Theorem, *Journal of Financial Economics* 5, 241–249.

Merton, R. C. and Bodie, Z. (1992). On the Management of Financial Guarantees, *Financial Management* 21, 87–109.

Mester, L. J., Nakamura, L. I., and Renault, M. (2007). Transactions Accounts and Loan Monitoring, *Review of Financial Studies* 20, 529–556.

Mian, A. and Sufi, A. (2009). The Consequences of Mortgage Credit Expansion: Evidence from the US Mortgage Default Crisis, *Quarterly Journal of Economics* 124, 1449–1496.

Millon, M. H. and Thakor, A. V. (1985). Moral Hazard and Information Sharing: A Model of Financial Information Gathering Agencies, *Journal of Finance* 40, 1403–1422.

Morgan, D. P. (1994). Bank Credit Commitments, Credit Rationing, and Monetary Policy, *Journal of Money, Credit and Banking* 26, 87–101.

O'Hara, M. and Shaw, W. (1990). Deposit Insurance and Wealth Effects: The Benefit of being Too Big to Fail, *Journal of Finance* 45, 1587–1600.

Osborne, M., Fuertes, A.-M., and Milne, A. K. L. (2012). In Good Times and In Bad: Bank Capital Ratios and Lending Rates. Working Paper.

Parlour, C. A. and Winton, A. (2013). Laying Off Credit Risk: Loan Sales versus Credit Default Swaps, *Journal of Financial Economics* 107, 25–45.

Peek, J. and Rosengren, E. S. (1995). The Capital Crunch: Neither a Borrower nor a Lender Be, *Journal of Money, Credit and Banking* 27, 625–638.

Pennacchi, G. G. (1988). Loan Sales and the Cost of Bank Capital, *Journal of Finance* 43, 375–396.

Petersen, M. A. and Rajan, R. G. (1994). The Benefits of Lending Relationships: Evidence from Small Business Data, *Journal of Finance* 49, 3–37.

Purnanandam, A. (2011). Originate-to-Distribute Model and the Subprime Mortgage Crisis, *Review of Financial Studies* 24, 1881–1915.

Rajan, R. G. (1992). Insiders and Outsiders: The Choice between Informed and Arm's-Length Debt, *Journal of Finance* 47, 1367–1400.

Ramakrishnan, R. T. S. and Thakor, A. V. (1984). Information Reliability and a Theory of Financial Intermediation, *Review of Economic Studies* 51, 415–432.

Repullo, R. (2004). Capital Requirements, Market Power, and Risk-Taking in Banking, *Journal of Financial Intermediation* 13, 156–182.

Saunders, A. and Schumacher, L. (2000). The Determinants of Bank Interest Rate Margins: An International Study, *Journal of International Money and Finance* 19, 813–832.

Sharpe, S. A. (1990). Asymmetric Information, Bank Lending and Implicit Contracts: A Stylized Model of Customer Relationships, *Journal of Finance* 45, 1069–1087.

Shockley, R. and Thakor, A. V. (1997). Bank Loan Commitments: Data, Theory, and Tests, *Journal of Money, Credit and Banking* 29, 517–534.

Song, F. and Thakor, A. V. (2007). Relationship Banking, Fragility and the Asset-Liability Matching Problem, *Review of Financial Studies* 20, 2129–2177.

Stiglitz, J. E. (2007). Houses of Cards, *The Guardian* October 9.

Sufi, A. (2009). Bank Lines of Credit in Corporate Finance: An Empirical Analysis, *Review of Financial Studies* 22, 1057–1088.

Sumner, S. (2009). Comment on Brad Delong: Can We Generate Controlled Reflation in a Liquidity Trap?, *The Economists' Voice* 6(4), Art. 7.

Systemic Risk Council (2012). Comment Letter Regarding: Regulatory Capital Rules, October 4.

Thakor, A. V. (1996). Capital Requirements, Monetary Policy and Aggregate Bank Lending: Theory and Empirical Evidence, *Journal of Finance* 51, 279–324.

Thakor, A. V. (2005). Do Loan Commitments Cause Overlending?, *Journal of Money, Credit and Banking* 37, 1067–1100.

Von Thadden, E.-L. (2004). Bank Capital Adequacy Regulation under the New Basel Accord, *Journal of Financial Intermediation* 13, 90–95.

CHAPTER 9

....

DIVERSIFICATION IN BANKING*

....

KEVIN J. STIROH

9.1 INTRODUCTION

....

THE turbulence in financial markets since mid-2007 continues to reshape the industry and raises fundamental questions about how large, complex financial firms operate. Greater scale and scope and wide diversification, both geographically and across products, were expected by some to reduce risk and insulate larger firms from macroeconomic or financial market shocks. While the crisis has affected financial firms of all sizes, it is notable that many large, diversified firms have been among the most impaired as real estate-related problems spread across a wide range of products, markets, and geographies.

While it is too early to fully understand the implications of the financial crisis, it is useful to review what is known about the impact of diversification on the risk and return of US financial institutions. This view is informed by the performance of the largest financial firms during and after the financial crisis. This can help policymakers to both better understand the potential and limitations of diversification across alternative business models and to implement a more effective policy response when thinking about longer-term regulatory reform issues.

Section 9.2 examines potential explanations for why banks diversify in the first place. This is a natural first step because classical finance theory suggests that internal diversification is not efficient since investors can easily shed any firm-specific risk by holding a well-diversified portfolio. There are good reasons reflecting market frictions, however, that explain why managers may choose to diversify and why this may be valuable to a wide range of stakeholders including equity-holders, borrowers, regulators, and the managers themselves.

Section 9.3 reviews the empirical literature that investigates the impact of diversification on the risk and return of financial firms. Both the earlier literature that examined US banks

* I thank Matt Botsch and the editors for helpful comments on an earlier draft of this chapter.

in a relatively regulated environment and the more recent literature that examined their performance in the last few years provide no consensus view—some studies report evidence of significant diversification gains, while others do not.

To summarize broadly, studies that looked at counterfactual mergers between banks and non-bank firms tended to find evidence of potential diversification benefits. These studies, however, cannot account for the endogeniety of risk-taking and thus must be interpreted cautiously. In contrast, studies that focused on accounting measures tended to showed evidence of greater risk after product diversification, particularly when measured by the growth of non-interest income. Studies that examine equity market returns, however, showed mixed evidence about the impact of diversification on the total risk of financial firms. This divergence undoubtedly reflects differences in methodology, data, sample, and time period and is consistent with basic finance theory, but raises interesting issues about the impact of adopting a more diversified set of financial activities

Section 9.4 concludes with potential interpretations of the results and a discussion of implications for financial market participants. I raise some questions for bank supervisors interested in maintaining financial stability and a healthy banking sector in the future, and for researchers interested in better understanding the impact of diversification on financial institutions.

9.2 UNDERSTANDING DIVERSIFICATION

The fundamental motivation for this chapter is the observation that large banks, particularly in the US, have become substantially more diversified in terms of product mix and geography over the last two decades. To provide some perspective, Table 9.1 reports summary statistics for the five largest bank holding companies (BHCs) in 1986, 1996, 2006, and 2012 in the US (identified by total BHC assets in Y-9C reports in December of each year). In 1986, the five largest BHCs held about 21% of aggregate bank assets with about two-thirds of those assets in the form of traditional loans. Approximately 40% of their net operating revenue (defined as net interest income plus non-interest income) in 1986 came from non-interest sources such as fees and commissions, trading, and fiduciary income. Even the largest firms in the banking industry were relatively concentrated geographically, operating in only five states on average.

Over the following few decades, the industry changed dramatically as regulatory constraints loosened and market pressures evolved. The largest BHC grew relative to the industry due to a steady stream of consolidation and a wave of mega-mergers in the last decade. By 2006, the five largest BHCs accounted for half of aggregate banking assets. Along with greater size came changes in strategy and focus—loans became a smaller share of the balance sheet and non-interest income grew to dominate the income statement. DeYoung and Rice (2004a) show a similar trend for the industry as whole, with the relative importance of non-interest income more than doubling between 1970 and 2003. These large banks operated in a much wider geographic footprint with branches in more than 20 states on average. Indeed, an explicit motivation for many of the large bank mergers in recent years has been the desire to create a nationwide franchise (Clark et al. 2007; Hirtle and Stiroh, 2007).

Table 9.1 Evolution of large bank holding companies

	Total assets ($B)	Share	Loan/assets	Non-interest income/ net operating revenue	States	Branches	Concentration Product	Concentration Geography
1986								
Citicorp	196	7.6	67.0	39.6	13	537	4,623	6,176
BankAmerica Corp	104	4.0	70.9	39.9	2	1,145	4,489	8,140
Chase Manhattan Corp	95	3.7	70.0	34.2	6	394	4,864	8,555
J.P. Morgan and Co.	76	3.0	45.6	42.2	3	7	3,930	8,881
Manufacturers Hanover Corp	74	2.9	75.3	39.3	3	231	4,616	9,189
Sum	546	21.2						
1996								
Chase Manhattan Corp	336	7.9	49.5	46.8	7	755	3,840	6,364
Citicorp	281	6.6	63.8	47.3	11	395	3,970	5,073
BankAmerica Corp	251	5.9	67.6	40.3	12	1,983	4,327	4,495
J.P. Morgan and Co.	222	5.2	12.7	72.5	3	4	2,671	9,282
Nationsbank Corp	186	4.4	66.7	37.0	11	1,854	4,440	1,596
Sum	1,276	29.9						
2006								
Citigroup	1,884	15.4	38.1	56.2	14	886	4,113	4,309
Bank of America Corp	1,464	11.9	49.4	54.4	31	5,598	3,658	1,045
J.P. Morgan Chase and Co.	1,352	11.0	35.7	64.7	19	2,545	2,891	2,764
Wachovia Corp	707	5.8	62.0	46.2	17	3,058	4,046	1,456
Wells Fargo & Co.	482	3.9	73.6	44.5	23	3,068	4,162	1,719
Sum	5,889	48.0						

(Continued)

Table 9.1 (Continued)

	Total assets		Loan/assets	Non-interest income/net operating revenue	States	Branches	Concentration	
	($B)	Share					Product	Geography
2012								
J.P. Morgan Chase and Co.	2,359	13.1	32.2	52.7	24	5,449	3,269	2,411
Bank of America Corp	2,212	12.2	43.8	43.4	35	5,499	4,193	1,003
Citigroup	1,865	10.3	36.1	32.0	16	1,035	5,409	3,788
Wells Fargo & Co.	1,423	7.9	59.2	51.2	40	6,047	4,292	856
The Goldman Sachs Group	939	5.2	7.4	85.2	1	1	3,902	10,000
Sum	8,798	48.7						
1986 Mean	109	4.2	65.8	39.0	5	463	4,504	8,188
1996 Mean	255	6.0	52.0	48.8	9	998	3,850	5,362
2006 Mean	1,178	9.6	51.8	53.2	21	3,031	3,774	2,259
2012 Mean	1,760	9.7	35.7	52.9	23	3,606	4,213	3,612

Notes: Data for individual bank holding companies are from Y-9C reports in December of each year. Share of total assets is total assets for the individual bank holding company as a percentage of aggregate banking assets reported by the FDIC in the Historical Statistics on Banking for 1986, and as a percentage of aggregate bank holding company assets from the Y-9C for 1996, 2006, and 2012. Net operating revenue N is defined as net interest income plus non-interest income. Each concentration measure is the sum of the squared shares (multiplied by 100) of all items in a category. Product concentration is calculated as the HHI using revenue shares from net interest income, fiduciary income, services, trading, and fee and other income. Geographic concentration is calculated as the HHI using the distribution of a BHC's deposits across states (excluding Puerto Rico, Guam, and the Virgin Islands, but including DC) as reported in the FDIC's Summary of Deposits for June 30th of each year.

Looking past the financial crisis, this perspective shows a new wave of fundamental change. Most notably, the industrial organization changed dramatically with some large firms incorporating others (Wachovia into Wells Fargo, Merrill Lynch into Bank of America, Bear Stearns into JPMorgan Chase, etc.), while investment firms such as Goldman Sachs and Morgan Stanley (not shown) became bank holding companies (BHCs). By 2012, the five largest BHCs held nearly nearly $9 trillion in assets, which was almost half the industry total.

To quantify how diversification for the largest BHCs changed across both product mix and geography, I calculated bank-level measures of concentration via Herfindahl–Hirschman indices (HHI) that are based on variation in revenue sources and in interstate activities over time.[1] Both measures show increases as these BHCs became increasingly diversified by offering a wider range of financial products that generated a more varied income streams and by operating in a wider geographic area.

What might explain the trend toward provision of broader financial services and geographic expansion? Most obviously, earlier regulations may have prevented banks from entering profitable business lines or forced them to enter in inefficient ways, so consolidation and increased diversification could be the normal response of profit-maximizing firms to the relaxation of external constraints. Berger, Demsetz, and Strahan (1999) review the consolidation wave in the 1990s in the US. More fundamentally, these gains could reflect production synergies between lending and other financial activities that create a comparative advantage for the integrated financial services firm. Alternatively, diversification across products may improve the risk-return frontier by expanding the investment opportunity set.

9.2.1 Why Do Firms Diversify?

Portfolio theory shows that diversification—the expansion of investments into activities that are not perfectly correlated—can reduce the risk of the portfolio. In the context of a firm's strategic decisions, managers can diversify by offering new products or entering new markets. This should reduce risk that is specific to each activity and leave only risk that is common to all activities. That is, internal diversification can eliminate a firm's idiosyncratic risk and leave only its systematic risk.

To be clear about terminology, consider the simple case of a bank's return $(R_{i,t})$ that depends linearly on a single risk factor, the market $(R_{M,t})$, and an idiosyncratic component $(\varepsilon_{i,t})$ through the familiar capital asset pricing model (see Fama and French, (2004) and Roll (1988) for reviews). In this case:

$$R_{i,t} = \alpha_i + \beta_M R_{M,t} + \varepsilon_{i,t} \qquad (9.1)$$

The independence of the residuals implies that the variance of returns can be decomposed as:

---

[1] An HHI index is calculated as the sum of the squared shares (measured in percentages). I used revenue shares from net interest income, fiduciary income, services, trading, and fee and other income for the measure of product concentration. I used the distribution of a BHC's deposits across states for the measure of geographic concentration, i.e., the share of a particular BHC's deposits that come from each state in which it operates.

$$\sigma_i^2 = \hat{\beta}_M^2 \, \sigma_M^2 + \sigma_{\varepsilon,i}^2 \tag{9.2}$$

where σ^2 reflects the variance of the subscripted variable. Following convention, the variance of total returns, σ_i^2, is called "total" risk and the variance of the residuals, $\sigma_{\varepsilon,i}^2$, is called "idiosyncratic" or "firm-specific" risk. The part explained by the market factor, $\hat{\beta}_M^2 \, \sigma_M^2$, is called "systematic" risk.

Portfolio theory suggests that internal diversification will reduce the idiosyncratic component of volatility, but not systematic risk, so firm diversification can, in principle, reduce idiosyncratic and therefore total risk. But, should firm pursue this strategy? Is it efficient to expend valuable resources in the pursuit of lower overall volatility and risk?

A natural starting point is the perfect capital market world of Modigliani and Miller. An implication is that firms should not expend valuable resources diversifying, hedging, or on other risk-management activities because investors can always buy or sell positions themselves to adjust their exposure. As pointed out by Sharpe (1964), an investor need not be concerned with a firm's idiosyncratic risk because it can be eliminated by holding a well-diversified portfolio. An implication is that investors should not price idiosyncratic risk and should only be concerned with the non-diversifiable, systematic component.

Despite these well-grounded arguments, questions remain. Cummins, Phillips, and Smith (1998, p. 33) ask why "managers of widely held corporations, acting in the interest of their stockholders, should manage risk that their shareholders could presumably manage themselves." Winton (1999, p. 46) phrases the question differently: "Should lenders diversify, as suggested by the intermediation literature, or specialize, as suggested by the corporate finance literature (abstract)?" Said still differently, is it useful to reduce idiosyncratic risk through internal diversification?

A large body of research has concluded that there are sound reasons why risk management may be optimal. This is true for investors due to capital market frictions that make the textbook case inappropriate for many firms, particularly financial intermediaries. It is also true for other market participants such as managers, supervisors, or bank counterparties, all of whom have an interest in the total risk of the financial firm. For these participants, both systematic and idiosyncratic risks impose real costs; to the extent that diversification reduces a firm's idiosyncratic risk, then diversification is desirable.

In a discussion focused on financial institutions, Froot, Scharfstein, and Stein (1993) and Froot and Stein (1998) highlight several of these channels. One factor is that the costs of external funds may be non-linear, so the value of the firm will depend on the total volatility of returns. If the marginal cost of adjustment rises with the amount of external financing raised, then optimization requires that an adverse shock to cash flow induces both an increase in external finance and a decrease in real investment. Thus, lower variability in cash flow can impact real investment positively, raise the value of the firm, and be desirable for shareholders.

A second friction is that some risks are not marketable; for example, an investor may not be able lay off the risk associated with all idiosyncratic shocks such as the introduction of new products. Froot and Stein (1998) argue that risk associated with this type of illiquid asset is particularly relevant for financial firms; for example, a loan to a small company that is information-intensive and difficult to trade in the secondary market. While recent financial innovations such as a more liquid loan-sale market or securitization may have reduced this as a concern, it remains relevant for many firms not actually involved in these markets.

Acharya, Hasan, and Saunders (2006) provide additional motivation for financial firms. One, banks are highly regulated entities and these regulations often provide conflicting incentives to diversify or focus activities—such as capital restrictions tied to the risk of the loan portfolio or branching restrictions. Two, inherent agency problems within a bank, which stem from imperfect information and conflicts between bank owners and bank managers, are likely to be influenced by the risk of insolvency, what they call "downside riskiness," and a bank's diversification strategy can affect this.

More broadly applicable to all firms, Smith and Stulz (1985) point to the convex nature of the tax code and conclude that firm value will be higher if earnings are more stable. This suggests that shareholders will prefer lower overall volatility, which can be achieved by internal diversification. Smith and Stulz (1985) also show that if there are costs of financial distress such as bankruptcy costs, loss of value during asset sales, and search costs for new management, then shareholders will care about total risk. This may be particularly relevant for financial firms where assets are relatively "opaque" and hard to value from the outside.

Firm managers may have additional incentives to manage risk and reduce the overall volatility of returns that go beyond value-maximizing motives. Stulz (1984) and Cummins, Phillips, and Smith (1998) suggest that firms manage risks because their managers are risk-adverse and cannot completely diversify when a substantial fraction of their wealth is tied up in a firm's equity. Hughes and Mester (2002) provide evidence that bank managers behave as if they are risk-adverse. As a result, managers may prefer to diversify and reduce total volatility even if this is not in the best interest of shareholders. Berger, Demsetz, and Strahan (1999), Milbourn, Boot, and Thakor (1999), Bliss and Rosen (2001), Houston, James, and Marcus (2001), and Aggarwal and Samwick (2003) also discuss manager's incentives related to empire-building, corporate control problems, or managerial hubris and self-interest, all of which could also lead to inefficient diversification.

Diversification and risk-reduction may also be desirable from the perspective of other participants. Borrowers, for example, will care about the viability of their lenders if the intermediation process is built on private information and long-term relationships. Slovin, Sushka, and Polonchek (1993) show that borrower stock prices fell after the de facto failure of Continental Illinois and interpret this as evidence of the costs of severing intangible banking relationships that are valuable to borrowers. In this view, borrowers are bank stakeholders who care about the total risk of the institution. Similarly, Houston, James, and Marcus (1997) show that diversification of internal capital markets benefits borrowers through the efficient allocation of scarce capital resources. If banks have large variation in revenue, for example, positive net present value project may not be funded in periods of low realized cash flows. Bank-dependent borrowers, therefore, care about the volatility of revenues and total risk. This may be particularly true for small firms that are dependent on small banks for financing

Finally, total risk is the most relevant metric for supervisors who are concerned with the probability of default and the associated bankruptcy costs. The idea that a more geographically diversified banking system increases financial and economic stability goes back at least to Sprague (1903). From the regulator's perspective, concern is for the costs associated with failure including transaction and liquidation costs related to bankruptcy, systemic risk concerns, and direct costs to the insurance fund from the tax distortions implicit in its funding or increased supervisory resources needed to offset moral hazard. As a result, supervisory interest is not in a diversified portfolio of firms, but in the total risk of each individual institution that is supervised. This is especially true when looking at the "systemic risk" of the financial system as a whole.

This can be seen directly in Merton-type portfolio models of credit risk, developed by Merton (1974) and implemented in KMV risk models, which are driven by assumptions about total asset return volatility. Moreover, Haubrich (1998) emphasizes that the deposit insurance fund is likely to be more concerned with the expected value of future insurance payments rather than just the probability of a given bank failure, so if diversification benefits are gained along with size, a more diversified (and larger) bank may still be more risky from the deposit insurance fund's perspective. Thus, there are good reasons for supervisors and regulators to be concerned with the total risk of an institution.

A second factor reflects banks' supervisory ratings such as the CAMEL rating, which depend on supervisors' assessment of a bank's ability to absorb future losses, the sensitivity of earnings to economic changes, and management's ability to measure, monitor, and control risk (Berger, Hasan, and Zhou, 2010). Because the degree of supervisory oversight and regulatory burden depend on these ratings, managers will care about total risk due to this supervisory effect.

Taken together, these arguments suggest that there are good reasons why shareholders, managers, borrowers, and supervisors are all concerned with the total risk of individual US banks. As a consequence, this suggests that internal diversification may be efficient and desirable as it can reduce idiosyncratic risk and total risk.

9.2.2 Two Decades of Deregulation and the Expansion of Bank Activities

The summary statistics in Table 9.1 show a trend toward more diversified banking activities in the US over the last two decades, both in terms of revenue sources and geographic exposure. Given the previous arguments for why financial firms may desire to be diversified, the next step is to consider how regulatory constraints may have hindered earlier attempts to diversify and how the massive deregulation of US financial markets over the last two decades facilitated it. This discussion is largely based on the more detailed treatment in Spong (1994, 2000), Berger, Demsetz, and Strahan (1999), and Strahan and Sufi (2000).

In the aftermath of the stock market crash of 1929 and in fear of conflicts of interest between commercial and investment banking, regulators moved to sever the link. The Banking Act of 1933 (the Glass–Steagall Act) limited financial integration by preventing any firm that accepts demand, time, or saving deposits from also engaging in most investment banking activities such as issuing, underwriting, selling, or distributing stocks, bonds, or other financial securities. This essentially prohibited the universal banking model common in other countries, particularly Europe.

The McFadden Act of 1927 granted national banks the same ability as state banks to branch within their own state, which limited interstate branching because most states had branching restrictions. Moreover, this was interpreted as preventing national bank branches on an interstate level (Spong, 1994). Several decades later, in response to attempts by some banks to circumvent existing constraints, the Bank Holding Company Act of 1956 imposed geographic restrictions; for example, the Douglass Amendment prohibited interstate acquisition unless state law specifically authorized it. Most states did not authorize it, however, so interstate banking through the holding company structure was halted. The Bank

Table 9.2 Major events in bank deregulation

Date	Event
April 30, 1987	Federal Reserve authorizes underwriting activity for Bankers Trust, JP Morgan, and Citicorp with a 5% revenue limit in "ineligible" activities.
January 18, 1989	Federal Reserve expands Section 20 underwriting permissibility to corporate debt and equity securities, subject to revenue limit.
September 13, 1989	Federal Reserve raises limit on revenue from Section 20 ineligible activities from 5 to 10%.
July 16, 1993	Court Ruling in Independent Insurance Agents of America v. Ludwig upholds OCC decision to allow national banks to sell insurance from small towns.
July 26, 1994	Interstate Banking and Branching Efficienct Act (Riegle-Neal Act) passed by Joint Congressional Committee.
January 18, 1995	Court ruling in Nationsbank v. VALIC allows banks to sell fixed and variable annuities.
March 26, 1996	Court ruling in Barnett Bank v. Nelson upholds Ludwig and overturns states' remaining restrictions on national bank insurance sales.
October 30, 1996	Federal Reserve announces the elimination of many firewalls between bank and nonbank remaining restrictions on national bank insurance sales.
December 20, 1996	December 20, 1996 Federal Reserve raises limit on revenue from Section 20 ineligible activities from 10 to 25%.
August 22, 1997	Federal Reserve eliminates many of the remaining firewalls between bank and nonbank subsidiaries within BHCs.
April 6, 1998 October 22, 1999	Citicorp and Travelers Group announce intentions to merge. Administration and congressional leaders announce compromise legislation on the Financial Services Modernization Act (Gramm-Leach-Bliley Act).

Notes: Information from Table 1 in Strahan and Sufi (2000).

Holding Company Act also prevented bank holding companies from owning or controlling non-bank activities except under very specific circumstances.

As a result of this long history of regulation, US banks in the 1970s were highly restricted in terms of both the products that they could offer and where they could operate geographically, although the 1970 amendment of the Bank Holding Company Act did allow bank subsidiaries to engage in bank-related services that offered public benefits. In the 1980s, however, the regulatory environment began to loosen and banks were able to expand both in terms of the financial products they offered and their geographic footprint; Table 9.2 provides a chronology of this deregulation. The Federal Reserve in 1987, for example, allowed BHCs to underwrite certain securities on a limited basis through their Section 20 subsidiaries.[2] Revenue from these activities, however, could not exceed 5% of total revenue for the

---

[2] Section 20 was the portion of the Glass–Steagall Act that split commercial and investment banking and "Section 20 subsidiaries" was the name given to a bank holding company subsidiary that engaged in a limited amount of securities activities. See Kwan (1998) and Cornett, Ors, and Tehranian (2002) for detailed descriptions.

subsidiary. Banks also gradually obtained the power to provide investment advisory services along with securities brokerage activities.

Over the next few years, additional statutory and regulatory change further expanded the scope of activities such as broader underwriting abilities, increased revenue from non-traditional banking activities, and expansion into insurance sales in certain cases. By 1996, the Federal Reserve allowed Section 20 subsidiaries of BHCs to earn up to 25% of the subsidiaries' revenue from underwriting. This progression culminated in the Financial Services Modernization Act of 1999 (also known as the Gramm–Leach–Bliley Act [GLBA]), which effectively dismantled the Glass–Steagall restrictions and allowed the combination of banking, insurance, and securities activities within the same "financial holding company" structure. See Furlong (2000) for an overview of GLBA.

In terms of geographic restrictions, a similar path of gradual expansion unfolded. Several states passed laws allowing interstate entry in the 1970s. Maine, for example, passed a bill in 1975 allowing interstate entry, conditional on other states granting reciprocity (Spong, 1994). Over the next decade, several state "compacts" formed, which allowed interstate banking and some states also amended interstate branching prohibitions. Moreover, the Garn-St. Germain Depository Institutions Act of 1982 authorized interstate acquisitions of certain failed banks and the Competitive Equality Banking Act of 1987 broadened this to include a wider set of troubled institutions. This steady relaxation of restrictions culminated in the Riegle–Neal Interstate Banking and Branching Efficiency Act of 1994, which allowed interstate mergers and branching after 1997 subject to concentration restrictions, CRA requirements, and all capital adequacy standards.

The cumulative impact was that two decades of deregulation allowed the creation of financial holding companies that offer a wider range of financial products and operate in broad geographic markets. This fundamental change paved the way for the type of widely diversified mega-banks that now dominate US banking markets.

In response to the financial crisis, the Dodd–Frank Wall Street Reform and Consumer Protection Act (the Dodd–Frank Act) imposed new constraints on bank size and activities. For example, Section 622 establishes a concentration limit that prohibits a firm from merging or acquiring another company if the combined liabilities exceed 10% of the industry total (US Treasury, 2011). A section example is Section 165, which requires enhanced prudential standards such as higher capital and liquidity standards for the most systemically important banking companies. A third example is Section 619, commonly known as the Volcker Rule, which limits banks' ability to engages in proprietary trading, private fund sponsorship, and certain relationships with hedge funds and private equity funds.

These sections, like other parts of the Dodd–Frank Act, are meant to reduce risks to financial stability and limit potential problems such as moral hazard that may be associated with very large financial firms. One possible outcome is pressure on the largest firms to reduce their size and limit their product diversity.

9.2.3 A Framework for Interpreting Broader Activities

This section concludes with a brief discussion of how one can interpret the expansion of bank activities—either across products or geography—in an expected risk and return framework. Morgan and Samolyk (2005) use this approach and describe the opportunities to expand geographically as shifts of the risk/return frontier, as does Haubrich (1998).

This familiar framework is useful because it allows a clear illustration of an important point—expansion of a banks' opportunity set and greater diversification need not lower observed risk.

As shown in Figure 9.1, a given set of regulatory, market, and technological constraints allows banks to earn higher expected returns only by taking on additional risk. This opportunity set is shown by line A. As is standard, the marginal expected return for increased risk declines with the level of risk. The bank owners' preferences are given by the utility curve 1, where owners trade off risk for expected return, but increasing amounts of expected return are required as compensation as risk rises. The optimal point is given by the tangent at X_1.

Expansion in a bank's ability to produce a broader set of products or enter new markets expands the opportunity set. Assuming that these activities are less than perfectly correlated with the existing set, this ability to diversify allows lower risk without surrendering expected return and effectively shifts the opportunity set up and in to B. Importantly, this expansion need not lead to lower risk-taking and the actual outcome will depend on the preferences of bank owners and managers. For example, bank owners that are more risk averse (with the relatively steep indifference curve 2) may choose to increase returns and reduce risk by shifting from X_1 to X_2. Owners who are less risk averse (with the relatively flat indifference curve 2') may choose a combination of higher risk and higher return and shift to X_3.[3] This observation—risk-taking is endogenous and diversification need not lead to lower observed levels of risk—is a fundamental implication of standard portfolio theory.

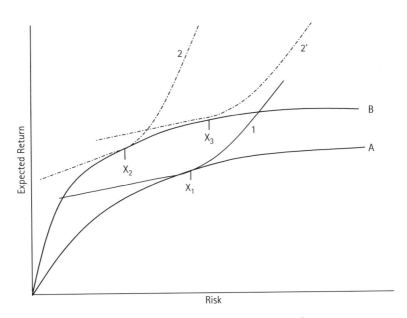

FIGURE 9.1 Risk and return when the opportunity set expands.

[3] Of course, indifference curves 2 and 2' are incompatible with each other. The proper comparison is between either 2 or 2' with 1. Both are shown here for illustrative purposes only.

As an example from US bank holding companies, Demsetz and Strahan (1997) showed that larger BHCs were indeed more diversified than smaller ones, e.g., bank size was negatively correlated with idiosyncratic risk and positively correlated with the explanatory power of a market model regression like the one in Equation (9.1). These large banks, however, also held less capital and made riskier loans such as commercial and industrial loans, so size was uncorrelated with total risk. In essence, managers seemed to use up the diversification gains to take on more risk and earn higher returns. Demsetz and Strahan concluded that "large BHCs have not used their superior diversification to reduce risk" (Demsetz and Strahan, 1997, p. 306).

As a second example from an earlier era, Carlson (2004) argues that branch banks in the 1930s tended to use their diversification advantage to reduce reserves and thereby increase risk, rather than reduce the risk within their loan portfolios. Again, the key point, emphasized by Hughes et al. (1996), is that risk-taking is endogenous, chosen by bank managers, so the increased ability to diversify need not be correlated with observed declines in measured risk.

9.3 DIVERSIFICATION AND RISK

The question of whether or not diversified financial institutions outperform their more concentrated peers is an area of active research and researchers have examined the link between diversification and performance from a variety of perspectives. Given the previous discussion about the endogeneity of risk-taking, it is perhaps not surprising that it has been difficult to find a clear and stable link between measures of diversification and measures of risk. In an early survey, for example, Saunders and Walter (1994) reviewed 18 studies that examined whether non-bank activities reduced BHC risk and found no consensus: 9 answered yes, 6 answered no, and 3 were mixed.

Both the earlier and the more recent studies approach the diversification/risk question with a variety of methods: creation of counterfactual mergers of banks with non-banks, analysis of accounting results, and analysis of equity market reactions to variation in diversification. This section reviews the literature over the last two decades on the link between diversification and risk from each of these perspectives, while Santomero and Chung (1992), Saunders and Walter (1994), Reichert and Wall (2000), and DeYoung and Roland (2001) review the earlier literature.

Note, however, that I do not cover research that examines the impact of diversification on other variables such as the cost of debt (Deng, Elyasiani, and Mao, 2007), loan pricing or interest margins (LePetit et al. 2005, 2006) and Valverde and Ferndandez (2007), bond returns (Penas and Unal, 2004), merger returns (DeLong, 2001), market reaction to regulatory reform (Strahan and Sufi, 2000; Yu, 2003), market values (Klein and Saidenberg, 2005; Laeven and Levine, 2007), or franchise values (Baele, De Jonghe, and Vennet, 2007). Nor do I directly discuss the broader literature on the "diversification discount," summarized for example by Campa and Kedia (2002), Laeven and Levine (2007), Elsas, Hackethal, and Holzhauser (2010), or the increased market power and potential anti-trust challenges from more consolidated and larger institutions.

9.3.1 Counterfactual Mergers

Due to the highly regulated nature of US financial services in the 1980s and early 1990s, many early studies of diversification performed counterfactual mergers across industries by combining income statement and balance sheet information in a pro forma manner. The idea was that by simulating mergers and combining revenue streams one could gauge the impact on volatility from various combinations of banks, securities firms, and insurance firms. If revenue volatility from the combined entity were lower than for the stand-alone entities, then this suggests diversification benefits exist.

Boyd and Graham (1988) and Boyd, Graham, and Hewitt (1993) simulated mergers between BHCs and non-bank financial firms using data from the 1970s and 1980s. Their primary conclusion was that the biggest gains from diversification in the form of lower risk would likely come from combinations between BHCs and life insurance firms. In contrast, bank mergers with securities firms or real estate firms would likely increase risk, they found. Saunders and Walter (1994) also found reduced risk, measured as less volatile market returns, for diversified firms through simulated mergers. Rose (1996) compared financial and non-financial firms from 1966 to 1985 and reported that the observed cash-flow correlation between banking and financial-service lines was positive and small, which suggested some diversification benefits.

Lown, Morgan, and Rohatgi (2000) performed similar counterfactual combinations of BHCs with other financial firms and also concluded that life insurance company mergers provided the greatest potential for risk reduction. Allen and Jagtiani (2000) found evidence of significant diversification benefits in the form of lower total risk from the potential merger of a bank, a securities firm, and an insurance firm. Systematic risk, however, would likely rise as securities firms in particular bring greater market risk, which limits the combined firm's ability to diversify. This two-sided impact from the expansion of bank powers—reduced risk from diversification and increased risk from greater exposure to more volatile activities—is a common finding and is echoed in subsequent research.

Emmons, Gilbert, and Yeager (2004) performed a counterfactual merger exercise focusing on potential diversification benefits for community banks. These banks are typically quite small and geographically focused, so they are heavily exposed to potentially diversifiable risk because of the small number of borrowers and geographic concentration. They concluded, however, that idiosyncratic risk associated with the small number of customers is quantitatively much larger than the local market risk associated with the geographic concentration. Thus, for these community banks, the evidence pointed toward scale effects rather than diversification effects as a means to reduce failure risk.

Santomero and Chung (1992) took a different approach to the simulation strategy by employing option pricing theory to estimate the implied volatilities of asset returns from possible mergers between bank and non-bank firms. Their results indicated that consolidation between bank and non-bank businesses would lead to a lower probability of failure. In particular, they concluded that bank mergers with securities firms would not materially increase risk, while potential mergers with property/casualty insurance would increase risk but also increase expected returns. Perhaps most interesting, they estimated that a universal bank that provided all financial activities would be the most stable of all.

Estrella (2001) extended this approach to a later time period with a somewhat different empirical method. Using option pricing techniques, he found evidence of bilateral diversification gains from mergers involving banks and insurance firms. Using arbitrage pricing theory to provide more intuition, the data showed that financial sector returns are driven by only a few factors and there is not much difference in the most important factors across industries. Estrella concluded that there was strong evidence for potential diversification gains between banks and insurance firms.

Slijkerman, Schoenmaker, and de Vries (2005) also used market data to examine the potential for diversification benefits in Europe, but their focus was on extreme events. In particular, they used extreme value theory to consider whether downside risk (the probability of a crash) is the same for European banks as for European insurance firms, and whether diversification can reduce this risk Using market data from 1992 to 2003, they concluded that diversification benefits for financial conglomerates (banks/insurance firms) exceeded those for large, stand-alone banks due to the relatively low dependence of returns across financial sectors.

Taken together, these counterfactual merger studies generally found evidence of diversification benefits, particularly between banks and insurance firms. An important caveat, however, is that their counterfactual nature necessarily ignores the endogeneity of risk-taking and changes in behavior that managers may make in response to diversification gains. Moreover, they ignore both potential benefits such as scale and scope economies and the potential costs of mergers such as increased agency costs or culture conflicts that could impact both returns and volatility. These concerns are reasonably compelling and suggest considerable caution when interpreting the results, so I now turn to the empirical evidence on the actual performance of diversified financial firms.

9.33.2. Accounting Studies

The second strand of research examined actual return and volatility data for banking firms involved in a broad set of financial activities using accounting data, primarily from published regulatory reports such as the Call Reports for US banks or the Y-9C data for US bank holding companies (BHCs). These data are popular because they are readily available for a large number of institutions and are reported on a relatively consistent basis over time.

9.3.2.1 Product Market Diversification

Several studies examined variation in performance across different types of BHC subsidiaries. Kwast (1989) studied the impact of the steady expansion of bank securities activities described in Section II by comparing returns on securities and non-securities activities from 1976 to 1985. He concluded that there were only limited diversification benefits. Kwan (1998) performed a similar exercise and found that Section 20 subsidiaries of BHCs were riskier but not more profitable, on average, than other subsidiaries. Return correlations, however, were low so some diversification benefits likely existed.

DeYoung and Roland (2001) compared bank profitability and volatility with revenue shares for large commercial banks from 1988 to 1995 and concluded that increased reliance on fee-based activities (revenue from all sources except loans, investment, deposit, and trading activities) did not reduce the volatility of earnings. Similarly, Stiroh (2004b) concluded that a greater reliance on non-interest income, particularly trading revenue, was associated with higher volatility and lower risk-adjusted profits in a cross-section of banks for the period 1979 to 2000.

Stiroh and Rumble (2006) performed a similar analysis with BHC data and concluded that diversification benefits existed when looking across BHCs, but these gains were more than offset by increased exposure to more volatile activities so risk-adjusted performance suffered. To be more precise, consider the return volatility on a portfolio of bank activities. If the bank can engage in two activities, A and B, then the expected return of the portfolio, $E(R_P)$, and variance, σ_P^2, are:

$$E(R_P) = wE(R_A) + (1-w)E(R_B)$$
$$\sigma_P^2 = w^2\sigma_A^2 + (1-w)^2\sigma_B^2 + 2w(1-w)Cov(R_A, R_B)$$
(9.3)

where w is the weight, $E(R)$ and σ^2 are the expected return and variances of the subscripted variables and $Cov(R_A, R_B)$ is the covariance between returns on A and B.

Consider the impact of regulatory or technological change that induces an increase in the relative importance of activity A. If activity A offers higher and more volatile returns, then a shift toward A has several effects: higher expected portfolio returns because $E(R_A) > E(R_B)$, a direct increase in portfolio variance if the weighted variance of A exceeds the weighted variance of B, and an indirect diversification benefit if there is less than perfect correlation. The results in Rosen et al. (1989) and Stiroh and Rumble (2006) both indicated that the increased share of volatile non-interest activities outweighed the diversification benefits.

Stiroh (2004a) found consistent results for community banks in the US, although he also reported evidence of diversification gains both within the loan portfolio and within non-interest income streams. Goddard, McKillop, and Wilson (2008) showed similar results for US credit unions where greater exposure to non-interest income was linked with more volatile accounting returns, while diversification tended to lower volatility. On net, the direct impact of more exposure to non-interest income essentially offset the diversification gains.

For Europe, LePetit et al. (2008) and LePetit et al. (2005) examined European banks from 1996 to 2002 and found that increased non-interest income exposure was positively linked with measures of risk (both accounting and equity-market-based measures). This link was strongest for small banks and was driven by activities that generated commissions and fees. Similarly, Hayden, Porath, and Westernhagen (2006) examined German banks for the same period and concluded that benefits of diversification are difficult to find. Using a more detailed measure of diversification for German banks, Kamp et al. (2007) concluded that specialized lending banks tended to have slightly higher returns and better asset quality, but also more volatile provisions and asset quality.

Mercieca, Schaeck, and Wolfe (2007) examined a set of small European credit institutions from 1997 and 2003 and found no evidence of direct diversification benefits. This result is similar to the analysis of US community banks by Stiroh (2004a) as a greater reliance on non-interest income was associated with weaker risk-adjusted performance in both studies.

Berger, Hasan, and Zhou (2010) examine Chinese bank in the pre-crisis period and introduce a new concept "economies of diversification" to measure the impact across four dimensions: loans, deposits, assets, and geography. They find that all four dimensions are associated with lower profits and higher costs.

DeYoung and Rice (2004b) compared a variety of banking strategies such as traditional banks, non-traditional banks, corporate banking, community banks, and diversified banks and found a clear risk/return tradeoff using both accounting and equity market return data for 1993 to 2003. This suggests that many strategies are viable—for example, high risk and high return in corporate banking vs. low risk and low return in community banking, and the choice will reflect managers' preferences. This view is supported by evidence in Hirtle and Stiroh (2007), who found that retail banking activities offered a combination of relatively low returns and low volatility, and suggests that is important to recognize that these banks will operate at different points along the risk/return frontier.

Looking at the financial crisis, DeYoung and Torna (2013) examine whether income from non-traditional activities contributed to the occurrence of bank failures during the crisis. Their results indicate that overall bank risk-taking likely drove outcomes, rather than exposure to specific revenue streams. For example, the probability of a distressed bank failure declined with fee-based activities such as brokerage and insurance sales, but increased with less traditional activities such as venture capital, investment banking, and securitization. Moreover, banks that engaged in risky non-traditional activities also had more risky traditional businesses.

Loutskina and Strahan (2011) examine behavioral differences between concentrated and diversified lenders and conclude that lenders who concentrate in a few markets devoted more effort in information collection. One implication is that the decline in borrower screening as lenders diversified in the 1990s and 2000s may have contributed to the excesses that led to the financial crisis.

Landskroner, Ruthenberg, and Zaken (2005) examined the link between diversification and performance for universal banks in Israel from 1992 to 2001. This has an advantage relative to US studies due to the longer time period when these institutions actually engaged in a broad range of financial services such as mortgage banking, international banking, investment banking, insurance, and commerce, but the sample size is much smaller. They found strong evidence of diversification benefits and concluded that the banks appear to be operating near the efficient frontier.

Jorion (2005) focused on the diversification benefits of trading activities for large banks from 1995 to 2003 by examining trading revenues and Value at Risk (VaR) based market risk charges. He found substantial diversification across business lines associated with trading.

Demirigüç-Kunt and Huizinga (2010) focus on short-term funding strategies for international banks prior to the financial crisis and found that a shift toward non-interest income-generating activities generally increases the return on assets, but offers diversification benefits only at very low levels. They conclude that strategies focused on generating non-interest income or attracting non-deposit funding are highly risky.

Acharya, Hasan, and Saunders (2006) looked for diversification within the loan portfolio by examining the expansion of loans into new sectors for a set of Italian banks from 1993 to 1999. They concluded that loan diversification tended to reduce returns (both accounting and equity market return data), while also producing riskier loans for high-risk banks and offering no or only modest improvements for low risk-banks. They concluded that "diversification is not guaranteed to produce superior performance and/or greater safety for banks" (p. 1355). Their explanation is that bank monitoring loses its effectiveness with diversification as a bank expands into areas with more competition or where it lack expertise. This can also be viewed as another example of the endogeneity of risk-taking as managers use up their diversification gains by taking on more risk elsewhere, in this case by monitoring less effectively.

A general conclusion from these studies is that the growing reliance on non-interest income has not been associated with reduced volatility in earnings. Summarizing the literature, DeYoung and Rice (2004a) concluded that "increased reliance on fee-based activities tends to increase rather than decrease the volatility of banks' earnings streams (p. 34)." DeYoung and Roland (2001) offer three potential explanations. First, lending is typically relationship-based, so there are high switching costs for both borrowers and lenders. This tends to make the lending relationship sticky, and therefore more stable. Second, non-interest income is often associated with increased operating leverage, that is, high fixed costs relative to variable costs. As result, a given amount of revenue volatility is transformed into even more earnings volatility. Third, the activities that generate non-interest income do not typically have a substantial regulatory capital charge. This allows banks to operate with greater financial leverage, which can generate volatility. The increase in leverage is another example of the endogeneity of risk-taking discussed earlier.

A second general conclusion is that expansion to new activities has two effects on volatility—a direct effect through the changing weights and an indirect effect through diversification. Both affect overall volatility and the evidence suggests that the recent expansion toward non-interest income has offsetting effects at best.

9.3.2.2 Geographic Diversification

Laderman, Schmidt, and Zimmerman (1991) were among the first to examine the impact of geographic diversification in the 1980s when US states began to materially allow wider expansion. They found that the relaxation of statewide branching restrictions led rural banks to hold more non-agricultural loans and urban banks to hold more agricultural loans. While this is not a direct test of the benefits of geographic diversification, it does show that banks responded to the changing constraints and moved to diversify their portfolios.

Rose (1996) examined US banks between 1980 and 1992 and concluded that geographic expansion generally led to higher risk, but that some diversification gains emerged when firms expanded into at least four distinct regions. Hughes et al. (1996) examined US banks in 1994 and searched for a link between geographic diversification and measures of insolvency risk measured as a Z-score and inefficiency. They found mixed results—more branches tended to lower insolvency risk for inefficient banks, but raise it for efficient banks, while operations across more states increased risk for efficient banks.

Pilloff and Rhoades (2000) concluded that geographically diversified banks do not have a net competitive advantage, while Morgan and Samolyk (2005) reported that a broader geographic scope would increase risk-adjusted returns. In particular, Morgan and Samolyk found a U-shaped relationship between geographic diversification and risk-adjusted returns, which implies that further broadening of the geographic footprint may be optimal.

Carlson and Mitchener (2006) studied the impact of geographic expansion in the US during the 1920s and 1930s. They emphasized that increased geographic scope through, for example, deregulation generally has two effects—increased ability to diversify and increased competitive pressures from potential entry. They concluded that the competitive effects were quantitatively more important in terms of reducing bank failures than the diversification effect. They found no evidence that diversification reduced bank failures for national banks.

Deng and Elyasiani (2008) look at the impact of geographic diversification for BHCs and find that geographic diversification—measured by the number of locations, level of activity across locations, and distance among a BHC's branches—is associated with higher value and lower risk. An interesting result is that geographic diversification to more remote areas increases value, but has smaller risk reductions.

9.3.3 Market Studies

A third strand of research focused on equity market measures of risk and return. Relative to the studies that focused on accounting data, there are clear reasons to prefer this perspective. To the extent bank managers have choices in how economic activities are reported in an accounting sense, market data provide a clearer view on the risk impact. If accounting data are manipulated to generate a smoother revenue stream or if different revenue streams are subject to different accounting treatments—for instance, the trading portfolio is marked-to-market on a daily basis which may induce volatility in non-interest income—then accounting returns may be misleading indicators of true risk. Second, market data provide a more forward-looking perspective on the expected returns of new activities, while accounting data are necessarily backward-looking and reflect actual performance in the past.

9.3.3.1 *Product Market Diversification*

Brewer (1989) examined the diversifying benefits of banks from 1978 to 1986 by comparing the equity market return volatility to a measure of non-bank activity implied by the holding company's balance sheet. He found mixed results, although the risk-reducing benefits of non-bank activities seemed largest for high-risk banks. Rosen et al. (1989) focused particularly on the real estate activities of banks from 1980 to 1985 and concluded that greater real estate investment would likely increase risk.

Templeton and Severiens (1992) examined financial market data for BHCs from 1979 to 1986 and measured diversification benefits as the share of market value not attributed to bank assets. They concluded that this measure was correlated with a lower variance of shareholder returns (total risk), but not with systematic risk, suggesting that diversification reduced only the idiosyncratic component.

Similar to the previously discussed studies of the impact of Section 20 subsidiaries on bank performance, several papers have examined the link between equity market measures of risk and return and the presence of Section 20 subsidiaries. Cornett, Ors, and Tehranian (2002) found evidence of gains from Section 20 subsidiaries as the industry-adjusted operating cash flow return on assets rises, while both total and systematic risk did not change significantly. They concluded that the improved cash-flow associated with establishing a Section 20 subsidiary reflects increased revenue and decreased costs, rather than increased risk-taking.

Geyfman (2005a) also examined the impact of having Section 20 subsidiaries for very large BHCs in the late 1980s and 1990s. She found that the presence of Section 20 subsidiaries was associated with lower idiosyncratic risk (evidence of diversification benefits), but higher systematic risk. Total risk tended to fall with Section 20 subsidiaries, however. Geyfman (2005b) utilized a portfolio approach and found that Section 20 subsidiaries provided strong diversification benefits. She concluded that US BHCs should reduce their commercial banking exposure and increase their securities underwriting exposure.

Other papers have examined the link between activity diversification again as measured by revenue streams and equity market returns. Stiroh (2006a) used a simple portfolio framework and found that activities that generate non-interest income do not raise average equity market returns, but are correlated with higher total risk, idiosyncratic risk, and systematic risk. These findings indicate that the higher weight on relatively volatile non-interest activities outweighs the diversification benefits, so overall volatility rises with a great non-interest exposure. Idiosyncratic risk, however, did fall with BHC assets, suggesting diversification benefits along other dimensions associated with size.

Stiroh (2006b) extended this analysis to control for variation within both the loan portfolio and the revenue stream. He found a negative link between total risk and diversification of both the loan portfolio and the sources of revenue, but that a greater reliance on non-interest income was linked to more volatile returns. Baele, De Jonghe, and Vennet (2007) performed a similar exercise for European banks with supporting results; shifts of revenue into non-interest income were correlated with higher market betas and idiosyncratic risk fell with size.

Looking across countries, Elsas, Hackethal, and Holzhauser (2010) report that diversification leads to higher market values, a so-called "conglomerate premium," which differs from much of the prior work. The authors attribute this to differences in how diversification is measured and the failure in prior studies to incorporate an indirect value effect through higher bank profitability.

9.3.3.2 *Geographic Diversification*

Buch, Driscoll, and Ostergaard (2005) examined the investment choices of banks located in France, Germany, the UK, and the US from 1995 to 1999. Using returns to different country investments that are approximated by broad bond indices, they found that banks tended to overinvest domestically and there were considerable, unexploited gains from international diversification. As an explanation, they point to cultural, legal systems, and capital control frictions.

Finally, there is evidence from the merger literature. DeLong (2001) used equity return data to gauge the reaction of investors to different types of bank mergers—those that diversify versus that specialize the bank. She found that diversifying mergers, by activity and/or by geography, do not create market value at the time of the merger announcement. In contrast to DeLong (2001), Laeven and Levine (2007), and the broader literature on the diversification discount, Elsas, Hackethal, and Holzhauser (2010) concluded that revenue diversification through both organic growth and through mergers and acquisitions leads to higher market values in a study of international banks from 1996 to 2003, which they attributed to revenue and cost economies of scope.

Mishra et al. (2005) examined the impact of diversification for a small set of US bank mergers. They found no evidence that systematic risk changed after a merger, but significant evidence that idiosyncratic and total risk declined. They interpret this as evidence of diversification gains or a "risk synergy benefit" from the combined entity.

9.4 CONCLUSIONS

US banks have clearly become more diversified over the last two decades as regulatory barriers fell, financial innovation progressed, and opportunities to expand into new products lines and new geographic areas opened. This diversification, however, has not provided an obvious advantage to large firms during the ongoing financial crisis as real estate-related problems spread over a range of products, markets, and geographies.

The empirical evidence suggests that observers should not be too surprised as there is no consensus on the impact of diversification on bank risk in the US and around the world. In some sense, this is predictable. Risk-taking is endogenous and optimizing managers may choose to exploit any diversification gains by increasing returns or adding risk in another dimension. Moreover, banks are shifting into precisely those activities that are relatively volatile, which can offset and obscure any diversification benefits.

Many papers, however, have found that risk-adjusted returns actually declined with the expansion of activities. This is harder to explain and requires some speculation. One possible explanation is that US bank managers may have simply gotten the diversification idea wrong. Managers and analysts, for example, have extolled the virtues of "cross-selling" to lower costs, increase income, and add diversification. But, if banks are simply selling more products to the same core customers, then this might not be true diversification if business lines have simply become exposed to the same underlying shocks.

An alternative explanation may be the non-profit maximizing motives discussed by Berger, Demsetz, and Strahan (1999), Milbourn, Boot, and Thakor (1999), Bliss and Rosen (2001), and Aggarwal and Samwick (2003). These motives include managers' zeal for empire building, overdiversification to protect firm-specific human capital, corporate control problems, or managerial hubris and self-interest, all of which could lead to inefficient diversification.

Excess risk-taking could also reflect a standard principal-agent explanation if traders, brokers, and underwriters (agents) like volatility more than shareholders (principals) do. Laeven and Levine (2007), for example, argued that the discount that the market applies to diversified financial firms is consistent with the idea of severe agency problems within financial institutions. These market failures would be exacerbated by any implicit government guarantee that reduces the incentives for debt holders to monitor and discipline managers. Many observers have raised this concern in the "originate-to-distribute" (OTD) and securitization model of mortgage finance that came to prominence in the 2000s and there is some evidence that bank behavior related to diversification may have contributed to the financial crisis—for example, less screening of borrowers (Loutskina and Strahan, 2011).

Finally, the disappointing results could be a short-run phenomenon due to adjustment costs associated with the recent expansion or simply bad luck reflecting recent market conditions. Gramm–Leach–Bliley and the ability to offer full-scale financial services was passed less than a decade ago and the US economy experienced a series of financial market shocks over this period such as the Asian crisis and LTCM in 1998, the bursting of the NASDAQ bubble in 2000, the events of September 11, 2001, corporate accounting scandals in 2002, and the recent financial crisis. If true, risk-adjusted performance could improve as the necessary business practices, expertise, technology, and scale are developed, and banks more successfully manage their expanded operations in a more stable environment. The performance of many larger, diversified financial firms during the current crisis, however, makes this explanation increasingly untenable.

These potential explanations are speculative, and it is critical to better understand the risk and stability of the largest financial firms. There is ample evidence that disruptions in the provision of credit can have real economic consequences (e.g., Ashcraft, 2005), so supervisors and regulators should have strong incentives to understand the motivations for and impact of increasing diversification by financial services firms.

Continuing change in financial markets, however, makes this a considerable challenge. The shift toward an OTD model of credit and the increased reliance on complex securitization practices, for example, altered traditional lending practices and made them more integrated with capital markets. The long-run impact of the more recent failure of several large institutions and the fundamental restructuring of others remains unclear. Moreover, the broad range of regulatory and legislative changes that were implemented after the financial crisis makes this increasingly difficult to test. This suggests that historical studies may not prove particularly insightful when assessing the potential for future diversification benefits among the largest financial institutions, but opens an exciting opportunity for continued research in this area.

As a final point, it is important to note the recent focus on the link between diversification of financial institutions and the financial stability. This literature, reviewed by Wilson et al. (2010), has grown recently and clearly reflects the need to better understand the underlying causes of the recent financial crisis. Battiston et al. (2012a, 2012b) and Ibragimov, Jaffee, and Walden (2011), for example, look at the interlinkages among financial institutions and point out a range of potential externalities that could impact financial stability. De Jonghe (2010) explores the relationship between diversification, specialization and systemic risk exposure. Wagner (2010) and van Oordt (2013) look at the interplay between diversification, securitization, and systemic risk. The recent experience clearly shows the critical importance of these connections and this represents a significant opportunity for researchers interested in bank behavior and diversification.

REFERENCES

Acharya, V. V., Hasan, I., and Saunders, A. (2006). Should Banks be Diversified: Evidence from Individual Bank Loan Portfolios, *Journal of Business* 79, 1355–1412.

Aggarwal, R. K. and Samwick, A. A. (2003). Why do Managers Diversify their Firms? Agency Reconsidered, *Journal of Finance* 58, 71–118.

Allen, L. and Jagtiani J. (2000). The Risk Effects of Combining Bank, Securities, and Insurance Activities, *Journal of Economics and Business* 52, 485–497.

Ashcraft, A. B. (2005). Are Bank Failures Really Special? New Evidence from the FDIC-Induced Failure of Healthy Banks, *American Economic Review* 95, 1712–1930.

Baele, L., De Jonghe O., and Vennet R. V. (2007). Does the Stock Market Value Bank Diversification?, *Journal of Banking and Finance* 31, 1999–2023.

Battiston, S., Delli Gatti, D., Gallegati M., Greenwald, B., and Stiglitz J. E. (2012a). Liasons Dangereuses: Increasing Connectivity, Risk Sharing, and Systemic Risk, *Journal of Economic Dynamics and Control* 36(8), 1121–1141.

Battiston, S., Delli Gatti, D., Gallegati M., Greenwald, B., and Stiglitz J. E. (2012b). Default Cascades: When Does Risk Diversification Increase Stability? *Journal of Financial Stability* 8(3), 138–149.

Berger, A. N., Demsetz, R. S., and Strahan, P. E. (1999). The Consolidation of the Financial Services Industry: Causes, Consequences, and Implications for the Future, *Journal of Banking and Finance* 23, 135–194.

Berger, A. N., Hasan, I., and Zhou, M. (2010). The Effects of Focus versus Diversification on Bank Performance: Evidence from Chinese Banks, *Journal of Banking and Finance* 34(7), 1417–1435.

Bliss, R. T. and Rosen, R. J. (2001). CEO Compensation and Bank Mergers, *Journal of Financial Economics* 61, 107–138.

Boyd, J. H. and Graham, S. L. (1988). The Profitability and Risk Effects of Allowing Bank Holding Companies to Merge with Other Financial Firms: A Simulation Study, *Quarterly Review Federal Reserve Bank of Minneapolis* 12, 3–20.

Boyd, J. H., Graham, S. L, and Hewitt, R. S. (1993). Bank Holding Company Mergers with Nonbank Financial Firms: Effects on the Risk of Failure, *Journal of Banking and Finance* 17, 43–63.

Brewer III, E. (1989). Relationships between Bank Holding Company Risk and Nonbank Activity, *Journal of Economics and Business* 41, 337–353.

Buch, C., Driscoll, J. C., and Ostergaard, C. (2005). Cross-Border Diversification in Bank Asset Portfolios, ECB Working Paper Series No. 429.

Campa, J. M. and Kedia, S. (2002). Explaining the Diversification Discount, *Journal of Finance* LVII, 1731–1762.

Carlson, M. (2004). Are Branch Banks Better Survivors: Evidence from the Depression Era, *Economic Inquiry* 42, 111–126.

Carlson, M. and Mitchener, K. J. (2006). Branch Banking, Bank Competition, and Financial Stability, *Journal of Money, Credit, and Banking* 38, 1293–1328.

Clark, T., Dick, A., Hirtle, B. J., Stiroh, K. J., and Williams, R. (2007). The Role of Retail Banking in the US Banking Industry: Risk, Return, and Industry Structure, *Federal Reserve Bank of New York Economic Policy Review* 13, 39–56.

Cornett, M. M., Ors, E., and Tehranian, H. (2002). Bank Performance around the Introduction of a Section 20 Subsidiary, *The Journal of Finance* LVII, 501–521.

Cummins, J. D., Phillips, R. D., and Smith, S. D. (1998). The Rise of Risk Management, *Federal Reserve Bank of Atlanta Economic Review* First Quarter, 30–40.

De Jonghe, O. (2010). Back to the Basics in Banking? A Micro-Analysis of Banking System Stability, *Journal of Financial Intermediation* 19, 387–417.

DeLong, G. L. (2001). Stockholder Gains from Focusing versus Diversifying Bank Mergers, *Journal of Financial Economics* 59, 221–252.

Demsetz, R. S. and Strahan, P. E. (1997). Diversification, Size, and Risk at Bank Holding Companies, *Journal of Money, Credit and Banking* 29, 300–313.

Demirgüç-Kunt, A. and Huizinga, H. (2010). Bank Activity and Funding Strategies: The Impact on Risk and Returns, *Journal of Financial Economics* 98(3), 626–650.

Deng, S. and Elyasiani, E. (2008). Geographic Diversification, Bank Holding Company Value, and Risk, *Journal of Money, Credit and Banking* 40(6), 1217–1238.

Deng, S., Elyasiani, E., and Mao, C. X. (2007). Diversification and the Cost of Debt of Bank Holding Companies, *Journal of Banking and Finance* 31, 2453–2473.

DeYoung, R. and Rice, T. (2004a). How do Banks Make Money? The Fallacies of Fee Income, *Federal Reserve Bank of Chicago Economic Perspectives* Q4, 34–51.

DeYoung, R. and Rice, T. (2004b). How do Banks Make Money? A Variety of Business Strategies, *Federal Reserve Bank of Chicago Economic Perspectives* Q4, 52–67.

DeYoung, R. and Roland, K. P. (2001). Product Mix and Earnings Volatility at Commercial Banks: Evidence from a Degree of Total Leverage Model, *Journal of Financial Intermediation* 10, 54–84.

DeYoung, R. and Torna, G. (2013). Nontraditional Banking Activities and Bank Failures during the Financial Crisis, *Journal of Financial Intermediation* 22, 397–421.

Elsas, R., Hackethal, A. and Holzhauser, M. (2010). The Anatomy of Bank Diversification, *Journal of Banking and Finance* 34(6), 1274–1287.

Emmons, W. R., Gilbert, R. A., and Yeager, T. J. (2004). Reducing the Risk at Small Community Banks: Is it Size or Geographic Diversification that Matters?, *Journal of Financial Services Research* 25, 259–281.

Estrella, A. (2001). Mixing and Matching: Prospective Financial Sector Mergers and Market Valuation, *Journal of Banking and Finance* 25, 2367–2392.

Fama, E. F. and French, K. R. (2004). The Capital Asset Pricing Model: Theory and Evidence, *Journal of Economic Perspectives* 18(3), 25–46.

Financial Stability Oversight Council (2011). Study and Recommendations Regarding Concentration Limits on Large Financial Companies, January.

Froot, K. A., Scharfstein, D. S., and Stein, J. C. (1993). Risk Management: Coordinating Corporate Investment and Financing Policies, *Journal of Finance* XLVIII, 1629–1658.

Froot, K. A. and Stein, J. C. (1998). Risk Management, Capital Budgeting, and Capital Structure Policy for Financial Institutions: An Integrated Approach, *Journal of Financial Economics* 47, 55–82.

Furlong, F. (2000). The Gramm-Leach-Bliley Act and Financial Integration, *FRBSF Economic Letter* 2000–10.

Geyfman, V. (2005a). Banks in the Securities Business: Market-Based Risk Implications of Section 20 Subsidiaries, Federal Reserve Bank of Philadelphia Working Paper No. 05-17.

Geyfman, V. (2005b). Risk-Adjusted Performance Measures at Bank Holding Companies with Section 20 Subsidiaries, Federal Reserve Bank of Philadelphia Working Paper No. 05-26.

Goddard, J., McKillop, D., and Wilson, J. O. S. (2008). The Diversification and Performance of U.S. Credit Unions, *Journal of Banking and Finance* 32(9), 1836–1849.

Haubrich, J. G. (1998). Bank Diversification: Laws and Fallacies of Large Numbers, *Federal Reserve Bank of Cleveland Economic Review*, Q2, 2–9.

Hayden, E., Porath, D., and Westernhagen, N. V. (2006). Does Diversification Improve the Performance of German Banks: Evidence from Individual Bank Loan Portfolios. Deutsche Bundesbank Working Paper, June.

Hirtle, B. J. and Stiroh, K.J. (2007). The Return to Retail and the Performance of US Banks, *Journal of Banking and Finance* 31, 1101–1133.

Houston, J. C., James, C., and Marcus, D. (1997). Capital Market Frictions and the Role of Internal Capital Markets in Banking, *Journal of Financial Economics* 46, 135–164.

Hughes, J. P., Lang, W., Mester, L. J., and Moon C.-G. (1996). Efficient Banking Under Interstate Branching, *Journal of Money, Credit, and Banking* 28, 1045–1071.

Hughes, J. P. and Mester, L. J. (2002). Bank Capitalization and Cost: Evidence of Scale Economies in Risk Management and Signaling, *Review of Economics and Statistics* 80, 314–325.

Ibragimov, R., Jaffee, D., and Walden, J. (2011). Diversification Disasters, *Journal of Financial Economics* 99(2), 333–348.

Jorion, P. (2005). Bank Trading Risk and Systemic Risk, NBER Working Paper No. 11037, January.

Kamp, A., Pfingsten, A., Memmel, C., and Behr, A. (2007). *Diversification and the Banks' Risk-Return Characteristics—Evidence from Loan Portfolios of German Banks*, SSRN No. 906448.

Klein, P. G. and Saidenberg, M. R. (2005). Organizational Structure and the Diversification Discount: Evidence from Commercial Banking, CORI Working Paper No. 2005-06, SSRN No. 721566.

Kwan, S. (1998). Risk and Return of Banks' Section 20 Securities Affiliates, *FRBSF Economic Letter* 98–32.

Kwast, M. (1989). The Impact of Underwriting and Dealing on Bank Returns and Risk, *Journal of Banking and Finance* 13, 101–125.

Laderman, E. S., Schmidt, R. H., and Zimmerman, G. C. (1991). Location, Branching, and Bank Portfolio Diversification: The Case of Agricultural Lending, *Federal Reserve Bank of San Francisco Economic Review*, Winter 4–38.

Laeven, L. and Levine, R. (2007). Is There a Diversification Discount in Financial Conglomerates?, *Journal of Financial Economics* 85, 331–367.

Landskroner, Y., Ruthenberg, D., and Zaken, D. (2005). Diversification and Performance in Banking: The Israeli Case, *Journal of Financial Services Research* 27, 27–49.

LePetit, L., Nys, E., Rous, P., and Tarazi, A. (2005). *Product Diversification in the European Banking Industry: Risk and Loan Pricing Implications*, SSRN No. 873490, December.

LePetit, L., Nys, E., Rous, P., and Tarazi, A. (2006). The Provision of Services, Interest Margins, and Loan Pricing in European Banking, December, 1–25.

LePetit, L., Nys, E., Rous, P., and Tarazi, A. (2008). Bank Income Structure and Risk: An Empirical Analysis of European Banks, *Journal of Banking and Finance* 32(8), 1452–1467.

Loutskina E. and Strahan P. E. (2011). Informed and Uninformed Investment in Housing: The Downside of Diversification, *Review of Financial Studies* 24(5), 1447–1480.

Lown, C., Morgan, D., and Rohatgi, S. (2000). Listening to Loan Officers: Commercial Credit Standards, Lending, and Output, *Federal Reserve Bank of New York Economic Policy Review* 1–16.

Mercieca, S., Schaeck, K., and Wolfe, S. (2007). Small European Banks: Benefits from Diversification, *Journal of Banking and Finance* 31, 1975–1998.

Merton, R. C. (1974). On the Pricing of Corporate Debt: The Risk Structure of Interest Rates, *Journal of Finance* 29, 449–470.

Milbourn, T. T., Boot, A.W. A., and Thakor, A. V. (1999). Megamergers and Expanded Scope: Theories of Bank Size and Activity Diversity, *Journal of Banking and Finance* 23, 95–214.

Mishra, S., Prakash, A. J., Karels, G. V., and Peterson, M. (2005). Bank Mergers and Components of Risk: An Evaluation, *Journal of Economics and Finance* 29, 84–96.

Morgan, D. P. and Samolyk, K. (2005). Bigger and Wider: The (Neglected) Benefits of Geographic Diversification in Banking. Federal Reserve Bank of New York Working Paper, June.

Penas, M. F. and Unal, H. (2004). Gains in Bank Mergers: Evidence from the Bond Market, *Journal of Financial Economics* 74, 149–179.

Pilloff, S. J. and Rhoades, S. A. (2000). Do Large, Diversified Banking Organizations Have Competitive Advantages?, *Review of Industrial Organization* 16, 2873–3302.

Reichert, A. K. and Wall, L. D. (2000). The Potential for Portfolio Diversification in Financial Services, *Federal Reserve Bank of Atlanta Economic Review* Third Quarter, 35–51.

Rose, P. S. (1996). The Diversification and Cost Effects of Interstate Banking, *The Financial Review* 31, 431–452.

Rosen, R. J., Lloyd-Davies, P. R., Kwast, M. L. and Humphrey, D. B. (1989). A Portfolio Analysis of Bank Investment in Real Estate, *Journal of Banking and Finance* 13, 355–366.

Santomero, A.W. and Chung, E. (1992). Evidence in Support of Broader Banking Powers, *Financial Markets, Institutions, and Instruments* 1, 1–69.

Saunders, A. and Walter, I. (1994). *Universal Banking in the United States: What Could We Gain? What Could We Lose?*. New York, NY: Oxford University Press.

Sharpe, W. F. (1964). Capital Asset Prices: A Theory of Market Equilibrium Under Conditions of Risk, *The Journal of Finance* 19, 425–442.

Slijkerman, J. F., Schoenmaker, D., and de Vries, C. G. (2005). Risk Diversification by European Financial Conglomerates, Tinbergen Institute Discussion Paper No. 110/2, December 7.

Slovin, M. B., Sushka, M. E., and Polonchek, J. A. (1993). The Value of Bank Durability: Borrowers as Bank Stakeholders, *Journal of Finance* XLVIII, 247–266.

Smith, C. W. and Stulz, R. M. (1985). The Determinants of Firms' Hedging Policies, *Journal of Financial and Quantitative Analysis* 20, 391–405.

Sprague, O. M. W. (1903). Branch Banking in the United States, *Quarterly Journal of Economics* 27, 242–260.

Spong, K. (1994, 2000). *Banking Regulation: Its Purpose, Implementation, and Effects, Monograph.* 4th and 5th editions. Kansas, Missouri: Federal Reserve Bank of Kansas City.

Stiroh, K. J. (2004a). Do Community Banks Benefit from Diversification?, *Journal of Financial Services Research* 25, 135–160.

Stiroh, K. J. (2004b). Diversification in Banking: Is Noninterest Income the Answer?, *Journal of Money, Credit, and Banking* 36, 853–882.

Stiroh, K. J. (2006a). A Portfolio View of Banking with Interest and Noninterest Activities, *Journal of Money, Credit, and Banking* 38, 1351–1361.

Stiroh, K. J. (2006b). New Evidence on the Determinants of Bank Risk, *Journal of Financial Services Research* 30, 237–263.

Stiroh, K. J. and Rumble, A. (2006). The Darkside of Diversification: The Case of US Financial Holding Companies, *Journal of Banking and Finance* 30, 2131–2161.

Strahan, P. E. and Sufi A. (2000). The Gains from Financial Sector Modernization, Federal Reserve Bank of New York Mimeo, May.

Stulz, R. (1984). Optimal Hedging Policies, *Journal of Financial and Quantitative Analysis* 19, 127–140.

Templeton, W. K. and Severiens, J. T. (1992). The Effect of Nonbank Diversification on Bank Holding Companies, *Quarterly Journal of Business and Economics* 31(4), 3–16.

Valverde, S. C. and Fernandez, F. R. (2007). The Determinants of Bank Margins in European Banking, *Journal of Banking and Finance* 31, 2043–2063.

Van Oordt, M. R. C. (2013). Securitization and the Dark Side of Diversification, *Journal of Financial Intermediation* (Forthcoming).

Wagner, W. (2010). Diversification at Financial Institutions and Systemic Crises, *Journal of Financial Intermediation* 2, 173–193.

Wilson, J. O. S., Casu, B., Garardone, C., and Molyneux, P. (2010). Emerging Themes in Banking: Recent Literature and Directions for Future Research, *The British Accounting Review* 42(3), 153–169.

Winton, A. (1999). *Don't Put All Your Eggs in One Basket? Diversification and Specialization in Banking,* SSRN No. 173615, 1–43.

Yu, L. (2003). On the Wealth and Risk Effects of the Glass-Steagall Overhaul: Evidence from the Stock Market, AFA Meetings.

PART II

BANK PERFORMANCE AND OPERATIONS

CHAPTER 10

MEASURING THE PERFORMANCE OF BANKS

Theory, Practice, Evidence, and
*Some Policy Implications**

JOSEPH P. HUGHES AND
LORETTA J. MESTER

10.1 INTRODUCTION

WHAT do commercial banks do? What are the key components of banking technology? What determines whether banks operate efficiently? Banks' ability to ameliorate informational asymmetries between borrowers and lenders and to manage risks are the essence of bank production. The literature on financial intermediation suggests that commercial banks, by screening and monitoring borrowers, can help to solve potential moral hazard and adverse selection problems caused by the imperfect information between borrowers and lenders. Banks are unique in issuing demandable debt that participates in the economy's payments system. This debt confers an informational advantage to banks over other lenders in making loans to informationally opaque borrowers. In particular, the information obtained from checking account transactions and other sources allows banks to assess and manage risk, write contracts, monitor contractual performance, and, when required, resolve non-performance problems. Bhattacharya and Thakor (1993) review the modern theory of financial intermediation, which takes an informational approach to banking.

* The authors thank the editors Allen Berger, Phillip Molyneux, and John Wilson for helpful comments. The views expressed here are those of the authors and do not necessarily reflect those of the Federal Reserve Bank of Cleveland or of the Federal Reserve System.

That banks' liabilities are demandable debt also gives banks an incentive advantage over other intermediaries. The relatively high level of debt in a bank's capital structure disciplines managers' risk-taking and their diligence in producing financial services by exposing the bank to an increased risk of insolvency. The demandable feature of the debt, to the extent that it is not fully insured, further heightens performance pressure and safety concerns by increasing liquidity risk. These incentives tend to make banks good monitors of their borrowers. Thus, banks' unique funding by demandable debt that participates in the economy's payments system gives banks both an incentive advantage and an informational advantage in lending to firms too informationally opaque to borrow in public debt and equity markets. The uniqueness of bank production, in contrast to the production of other types of lenders, is derived from the special characteristics of banks' capital structure: the funding of informationally opaque assets with demand deposits.[1] Calomiris and Kahn (1991) and Flannery (1994) discuss the optimal capital structure of commercial banks.

But banks' ability to perform efficiently—to adopt appropriate investment strategies, to obtain accurate information concerning their customers' financial prospects, and to write and enforce effective contracts—depends in part on the property rights and legal, regulatory, and contracting environments in which they operate. Such an environment includes accounting practices, chartering rules, government regulations, and the market conditions (e.g., market power) under which banks operate. Differences in these features across political jurisdictions can lead to differences in the efficiency of banks across jurisdictions.[2]

Banks' unique funding by demand deposits motivates key components of the legal and regulatory environments that influence managerial incentives for risk-taking and efficiency. The participation of banks in the payments system leads to their regulation and, in particular, to restrictions on entry into the industry. The need to obtain a charter to open a bank confers a degree of market power on banks operating in smaller markets and, in general, permits banks to exploit valuable investment opportunities related to financial intermediation and payments. Government regulation and supervision promote banks' safety and soundness with the aim of protecting the payments system from bank runs that contract bank lending and threaten macroeconomic stability. Protecting the payments system frequently involves deposit insurance. To the extent that the insurance is credible, it reduces depositors' incentive to run banks when they fear banks' solvency. Consequently, it reduces banks' liquidity risk and, to the extent it is underpriced, gives banks the incentive to take additional risk for higher expected return.

---

[1] Berlin and Mester (1999) find empirical evidence of an explicit link between banks' liability structure and their distinctive lending behavior. As discussed in Mester (2007), relationship lending is associated with lower loan rates, less stringent collateral requirements, a lower likelihood of credit rationing, contractual flexibility, and reduced costs of financial distress for borrowing firms. Banks' access to core deposits, which are rate inelastic, enable banks to insulate borrowers with whom they have durable relationships from exogenous credit shocks. Mester, Nakamura, and Renault (2007) also find empirical evidence of a synergy between the liability and asset sides of a commercial bank's balance sheet, showing that information on the cash flows into and out of a borrower's transactions account can help an intermediary monitor the changing value of collateral that a small-business borrower has posted.

[2] Demirgüç-Kunt, Kane, and Laeven (2007) use a sample of 180 countries to study the external and internal political features that influence the adoption and design of deposit insurance, which, in turn, affects the efficiency of the domestic banking system.

10.2 BANKING TECHNOLOGY
AND PERFORMANCE

10.2.1 Banks' Risk Menu and Conflicting Incentives for Risk-Taking

Mispriced deposit insurance and policies that are too-big-to-fail (TBTF) can create a cost-of-funds subsidy that gives banks an incentive to take additional risk.[3] But banks also have an incentive to avoid risk to protect their valuable charter from episodes of financial distress. Distress involves liquidity crises resulting from runs by uninsured depositors, regulatory intervention in banks' investment decisions, and even the loss of the charter when distress results in insolvency. As discussed in Hughes and Mester (2013b), Marcus (1984) finds that banks with high-valued investment opportunities maximize their expected market value by pursuing lower-risk investment strategies that protect their charters and thereby preserve their ability to exploit these opportunities. On the other hand, banks with low-valued investment opportunities maximize their expected value by adopting higher-risk investment strategies that exploit the cost-of-funds subsidy of mispriced deposit insurance (Keeley, 1990). Mid-range risk strategies do not maximize value. These dichotomous investment strategies as well as other sources of risk-taking and risk-avoidance fundamentally shape production decisions and must be taken into account when modeling bank production.

The risk environment banks face can be characterized by a frontier of expected return and return risk, which shows a bank's menu of efficient investment choices.[4] In Figure 10.1 from Hughes and Mester (2013b), a smaller bank's menu of investment choices is given by the lower frontier. Consider a smaller bank that operates at point A.[5] To illustrate scale-related diversification, suppose a larger bank is created by scaling up the assets of this smaller bank. In principle, the larger bank can obtain better diversification of its assets, which reduces credit risk, and better diversification of its deposits, which reduces liquidity risk. Thus, the larger bank can efficiently produce the expected return of the smaller bank (point A) with less return risk (point A'). In fact, the larger bank will likely take advantage of its better diversification and produce a different (and perhaps more complicated) mix of financial services. Nonetheless, the risk-expected-return frontier of the larger bank lies above that of

[3] FDIC (2013) summarizes some of the estimates of the subsidy found in the literature.

[4] For expository purposes, in this discussion we are assuming that only the first two moments of the distribution of returns matter for bank production. More generally, however, higher moments, such as skewness and kurtosis, can be expected to influence, for example, calculations of Value at Risk (VaR) and the choice of investment strategies that minimize the probability of financial distress or that exploit the federal safety net. Thus, risk resulting from higher moments likely plays an important role in bank production.

[5] To simplify the discussion, we assume that the smaller bank operates efficiently; therefore point A lies on the frontier rather than beneath it. See Hughes and Mester (2013b) for an analysis of how inefficiency is related to scale economies in banking.

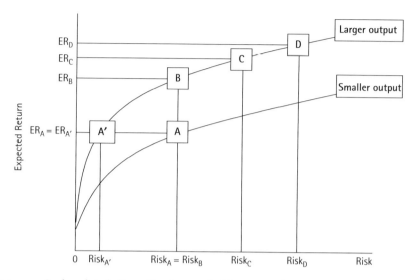

FIGURE 10.1 Scale-related diversification and risk-return frontiers.

Source: Hughes and Mester (2013b)

the smaller bank because the larger bank has a better menu of investment choices resulting from improved diversification.

Textbooks point to better diversification, which reduces the costs of risk management, as a key source of scale economies. The link between better diversification and scale economies is apparent when comparing a larger bank operating at point A′ with one operating at point B. A larger bank operating at point A′ has the same expected return but lower risk than the smaller bank operating at point A, while a larger bank at point B operates with the same return risk as the smaller bank but obtains a higher expected return. At point B, the better diversification of deposits allows the larger bank to economize on liquid assets without increasing liquidity risk, while the better diversification of loans allows it to economize on equity capital without increasing insolvency risk. Thus, its expected return for the same risk as the smaller bank is higher.

Better diversification, however, does not necessarily mean that the larger bank operates with less risk; rather, it means the larger bank experiences a better risk-expected-return frontier. Heightened competition and lower-valued growth opportunities in the larger bank's markets, or lower marginal costs of risk management might induce the larger bank to choose to produce its output with more risk in order to obtain a higher expected return—say the strategy at point C or point D.

A bank's risk-taking is also influenced by external and internal mechanisms that discipline bank managers. Internal discipline can be induced or reduced by organizational form, ownership and capital structure, governing boards, and managerial compensation. External discipline might be induced or reduced by government regulation and the safety net, capital market discipline (takeovers, cost of funds, stakeholders' ability to sell stock), managerial labor market competition, outside blockholders of equity and debt, and product market competition.[6] This operating environment can also create agency conflicts that

---

[6] LaPorta, Lopez-de-Silanes, and Shleifer (2002) examine banking systems in 92 countries and find that government ownership is correlated with poorer countries and countries with less developed

influence managers' incentives to pursue value-maximizing risk strategies. Managers whose wealth consists largely of their undiversified human capital tend to avoid riskier investment strategies that maximize the value of banks with poorer investment opportunities. However, the presence of a diversified outside owner of a large block of stock might encourage the board of directors to put in place a compensation plan that overcomes managers' risk aversion and encourages value-maximizing risk-taking (Laeven and Levine, 2009).

Thus, in order to measure the efficiency of bank production it is important to account for bank risk-taking and its efficiency.

10.2.2 The Empirical Measurement of Banking Technology and Performance

There are two broad approaches to measuring technology and explaining performance: non-structural and structural. Using a variety of financial measures that capture various aspects of performance, the non-structural approach compares performance among banks and considers the relationship of performance to investment strategies and other factors such as characteristics of regulation and governance. For example, the non-structural approach might investigate technology by asking how performance measures are correlated with such investment strategies as growing by asset acquisitions and diversifying or focusing the bank's product mix. It looks for evidence of agency problems in correlations of performance measures and variables characterizing the quality of banks' governance. While informal and formal theories may motivate some of these investigations, no general theory of performance provides a unifying framework for these studies.

The structural approach is choice-theoretic and, as such, relies on a theoretical model of the banking firm and a concept of optimization. The older literature applies the traditional microeconomic theory of production to banking firms in much the same way as it is applied to non-financial firms and industries. The newer literature views the bank as a financial intermediary that produces informationally intensive financial services and takes on and diversifies risks—unique, essential aspects of financial intermediation that are not generally taken into account in traditional applications of production theory.[7] For example,

---

financial systems, poorer protection of investors' rights, more government intervention, and poorer performance of institutions. They also find that government ownership is associated with higher cost ratios and wider interest rate margins. Aghion, Alesina, and Trebbi (2007) provide evidence that democracy has a positive impact on productivity growth in more advanced sectors of the economy, possibly by fostering entry and competition.

[7] This framework often guides the choice of outputs and inputs in the bank's production structure. For example, as discussed in Mester (2008), the traditional application of efficiency analysis to banking does not allow bank production decisions to affect bank risk, which rules out the possibility that scale—and scope-related improvements in diversification could lower the cost of borrowed funds and induce banks to alter their risk exposure. Also, much of the traditional literature does not account for the bank's role in producing information about its borrowers in its underwriting decisions when specifying the bank's outputs and inputs. An exception is Mester (1992), who directly accounted for banks' monitoring and screening role by measuring bank output treating loans purchased and loans originated as separate outputs entailing different types of screening, and treating loans held on balance sheet and loans sold as separate outputs entailing different types of monitoring.

the traditional theory defines a cost function by a unique cost minimizing combination of inputs for any given level of outputs. Thus, the cost function gives the minimum cost of any given output vector without regard to the return risk implied by the cost-minimizing input vector. Ignoring the implied return risk may be appropriate for non-financial firms, but for financial institutions, return risk plays an essential role in maximizing the discounted flow of expected profits. First, return risk influences the rate at which future expected profits are discounted. Second, return risk affects the expected cost of financial distress. The bank with high-valued investment opportunities may find the level of risk associated with the cost-minimizing vector too high. If so, it may choose to reduce the credit risk of the given output vector by adding more labor and physical capital to improve credit evaluation and loan monitoring. In doing so it trades higher cost (lower profit) for lower profit risk to reduce the expected costs of financial distress and the discount rate on its expected cash flow, thus maximizing its market value. This tradeoff suggests that measuring bank performance by a cost metric or a profit metric that fails to account for endogenous risk-taking is likely to be seriously biased.

Notice in this example that risk influences the decision of how to produce a given output vector and, thus, must influence the cost of producing it. In Figure 10.1, when the risk-expected-return frontier for the larger bank is narrowly interpreted as showing different investment strategies for producing the same output vector—the scaled-up outputs of the smaller bank—it is clear that larger banks with higher-valued investment opportunities are likely to choose a lower risk-expected-return strategy, say point B or A′, than banks with lower-valued opportunities, say point C or D. Since the cost of producing the scaled-up output vector is likely to differ along the frontier, the value-maximizing input vector and, hence, cost of the output, will be driven in part by risk considerations. And, these risk considerations imply that *revenue influences cost when risk matters.* How, then, can managers' preferences for these production plans and their implied risk be represented?

Letting the output vector be represented by q, the input vector by x, and equity capital by k, the technology for producing a given output vector is represented by transformation function $T(x, k; q) \le 0$. Points C and D in Figure 10.1 arise from different input vectors (x, k) that produce the given output q. Let z represent the production plan and price environment. Managers' beliefs about how production plans interact with a given state of the world, s, to yield profit, π, imply a realization of profit, $\pi = g(z, s)$, that is conditioned on the state of the world. And managers' beliefs about the probability distribution of states of the world imply a subjective distribution of profit that is conditional on the production plan: $f(\pi; z)$. Under well-known restrictive conditions, this distribution can be represented by its first two moments, $E(\pi; z)$ and $S(\pi; z)$.[8]

The traditional literature on bank production and efficiency assumes banks choose their production plan to minimize expected cost and maximize expected profit: managers rank production plans by their *expected* profit and cost, the first moment of their subjective probability distribution of profit, $f(\pi; z)$, attached to each production plan. The newer research assumes bank managers maximize the utility of their production plans. Rather than define the utility function over the first two moments, the newer literature defines it over profit and

---

[8] See Hughes et al. (2000) for further discussion of this model.

the production plan, $U(\pi; z)$, which is equivalent to defining it over the conditional probability distributions $f(\pi; z)$. Utility maximization is a more general objective that subsumes profit maximization and cost minimization (e.g., Hughes, 1999; Hughes et al., 1999; Hughes et al., 2000; and Hughes, Mester, and Moon, 2001). However, when higher moments of the profit distribution influence managers' preferences, managers may trade profit to achieve other objectives involving risk, say, value maximization. The model treats the choice of risk as endogenous.

Note, however, that the other objectives might reflect agency problems: Managers might take on too little risk in order to protect their jobs, or they might consume private benefits that reduce shareholder wealth. Thus, the utility-maximizing framework can explain inefficient as well as efficient production. When the output vector is held constant, the utility-maximizing cost of output can be derived from the utility-maximizing input demands. This cost function accounts for the choice of whether to produce the particular output vector using a method that has lower risk and lower expected return or a method with higher risk and higher expected return (e.g., point B versus point C in Figure 10.1). This choice depends on differences in the value of investment opportunities. In this case, managers' ranking of production plans captures the profit and profit-risk environment they face.

How one gauges performance in structural models, then, depends on whether one views bank managers as ranking production plans by their first moments (i.e., minimum expected cost or maximum expected profit), or, more generally, by higher moments as well as the first moment, i.e., considerations involving risk. In the latter case, one would want to gauge the tradeoffs between risk and expected return being made by banks where there is less of an agency problem between owners and managers—that is, banks with strong corporate controls (see Hughes, Mester, and Moon, 2001). In both the structural and non-structural approaches, the performance metric and the specification of the performance equation reflect implicitly or explicitly an underlying theory of managerial behavior.

As a general specification of the structural and non-structural approaches, let y_i represent the measure of the ith bank's performance. Let z_i be a vector of variables that capture key components of the ith bank's technology (e.g., output levels and input prices) and τ_i be a vector of variables affecting the technology (e.g., the ratio of nonperforming to total loans). Jensen and Meckling (1979) add a vector, θ_i, of characteristics of the property-rights system, contracting, and regulatory environment in which the ith firm operates (e.g., whether the country has a deposit insurance scheme and the degree of investor protection that exists) and a vector, ϕ_i, of characteristics of the organizational form and the governance and control environment of the ith firm (e.g., whether the bank is organized as a mutual or stock-owned firm, the degree of product market concentration, and the number of outside directors on its board). When the sample of banks used in the estimation includes financial institutions located in environments with different property rights and contracting environments or with different governance and control structures, estimating this model permits one to investigate how these differences are correlated with differences in bank performance.

Allowing for random error, the performance equation to be estimated takes the form,

$$y_i = f(z_i, \tau_i, \phi_i, \theta_i \mid \beta) + \varepsilon_i \tag{10.1}$$

The specification of the vectors z_i and τ_i differs between the structural and non-structural approaches.

10.2.3 The Structural Approach to Bank Efficiency Measurement: Cost Minimization, Profit Maximization, and Managerial Utility Maximization

The traditional *structural approach* usually relies on the economics of cost minimization or profit maximization, where the performance equation (1) denotes a cost function or a profit function. Occasionally, the structural performance equation denotes a production function. While estimating a production function might tell us if the firm is *technically efficient*, that is, if managers organize production such that the firm maximizes the amount of output produced with a given amount of inputs (so that the firm is operating on its production frontier), we are more interested in *economic efficiency*, that is, whether the firm is responding to relative prices in choosing its inputs and outputs to minimize cost and/or to maximize profit, which subsumes technical efficiency. Risk plays no explicit role in these performance functions, although some papers include one or more dimensions of risk in the estimation as control variables (see Berger and Mester, 1997 and 2003, and Mester, 2008, for further discussion). Including risk components as controls does not fully capture the tradeoff between risk and expected return that banks face. While including risk, e.g., the variance of profit, in the cost function would control for the second moment of return, higher moments would not be taken into account, and these higher moments may be an important element in the bank's production decision. So the standard cost function conditioned on risk is unlikely to capture important considerations in banking production and value maximization. In addition, as discussed below, the assumptions of cost minimization and profit maximization underlying the standard structural approach have been tested and rejected by some papers in the literature. See, for example, Evanoff (1998), Evanoff, Israilevich, and Merris (1990), Hughes et al. (1996, 2000), Hughes, Mester, and Moon (2001), and Hughes and Mester (2013b).

In the newer literature, the optimization problem is managerial utility maximization, where the manager ranks production plans not just by their first moment—expected profit—but also by higher moments, such as skewness and kurtosis risk, as well as variance risk, that characterize profit risk. The utility-maximizing cost function is derived from the profit function, conditioned on the output vector. As such, the cost function includes arguments that characterize revenue. In Figure 10.1 the larger bank can produce its scaled-up output vector with a menu of production plans that differ by their expected profit and profit risk. The utility-maximizing cost function captures the plan that maximizes managerial utility and thus, reflects a risk-expected return tradeoff.

To specify the utility-maximizing performance equation (1), Hughes et al. (1996, 1999, 2000) adapt the Almost Ideal Demand System to derive a *utility-maximizing* profit equation and its associated input demand equations. This profit function does not necessarily maximize profit, since it follows from managers' assessment of risk and risk's effect on asset value; it might also reflect managers' concerns about their job security. Profit maximization (cost minimization) can be tested by noting that the standard translog profit (cost) function and share equations are nested within the model and can be recovered by imposing the parameter restrictions implied by profit maximization (cost minimization) on the coefficients of this adapted system. Hughes et al. (1996, 1999, 2000) and Hughes and Mester (2013b) test these restrictions in their applications and reject the hypothesis of profit maximization (and cost minimization).

Both newer and traditional performance functions can differ by the definition of cost they use: accounting (cash-flow) cost excludes the cost of equity capital, while economic cost includes it. The challenge of specifying economic cost is in estimating the cost of equity capital. McAllister and McManus (1993) arbitrarily pick the required return and assume it is uniform across banks. Clark (1996) and Fiordelisi (2007) use the Capital Asset Pricing Model to estimate it. Fiordelisi (2007) describes the resulting profit function as "economic value added." Alternatively, the quantity of equity capital can be substituted for its price. In these cases of restricted cost and profit functions, the expense of equity capital is excluded from the empirical measure of cost and profit.

The traditional structural performance equation can be fitted to the data as an average relationship, which assumes that all banks are equally efficient at minimizing cost or maximizing profit, subject to random error, ε_i, which is assumed to be normally distributed. Alternatively, it can be estimated as a *frontier* to capture best observed practice and to gauge X-inefficiency, the difference between the best-observed practice performance and achieved performance. The literature has used four basic methods for estimating the frontier: stochastic frontier, the distribution-free approach, the thick frontier, and data envelopment analysis (DEA). Berger and Mester (1997) review the estimation methods and present evidence on scale economies, cost X-inefficiency, and profit X-inefficiency using the stochastic frontier and distribution-free methods.[9]

In the stochastic frontier method, the error term, ε_i, consists of two components; one is a two-sided random error that represents noise (v_i), and the other is a one-sided error representing inefficiency (μ_i). The stochastic frontier approach disentangles the inefficiency and random error components by making explicit assumptions about their distributions. The inefficiency component measures each bank's extra cost or shortfall of profit relative to the frontier—the best-practice performance observed in the sample.[10] Let y_i denote either the cost or profit of firm i. The stochastic frontier gives the highest or lowest potential value of y_i given z_i, τ_i, ϕ_i, and θ_i,

$$y_i = F(z_i, \tau_i, \phi_i, \theta_i \mid \beta) + \varepsilon_i, \tag{10.2}$$

where $\varepsilon_i \equiv \mu_i + v_i$ is a composite error term comprising v_i, which is normally distributed with zero mean, and μ_i, which is usually assumed to be half-normally distributed and negative when the frontier is fitted as an upper envelope in the case of a profit function and positive when the frontier is fitted as a lower envelope as in the case of a cost function. β are parameters of the deterministic kernel, $F(z_i, \tau_i, \phi_i, \theta_i \mid \beta)$, of the stochastic frontier. The ith bank's

---

[9] Note that the literature often uses the term "best-practice performance" and sometimes calls it "potential performance." However, this is somewhat of an abuse of terms since measured best-practice performance does not necessarily represent the best possible practice, but merely the best practice observed among banks in the sample (see Berger and Mester, 1997, and Mester, 2008).

[10] Leibenstein (1966) called such inefficiency, which can result from poor managerial incentives or the failure of the labor market to allocate managers efficiently and to weed out incompetent managers, *X-inefficiency*. Jensen and Meckling (1976) called such inefficiency *agency costs* and provided a theoretical model of managerial utility maximization to explain how, when incentives between managers and outside stakeholders are misaligned, managers may trade off the market value of their firm to enjoy more of their own private benefits, such as consuming perquisites, shirking, discriminating prejudicially, and taking too much or too little risk to enhance their control.

inefficiency is usually estimated by the mean of the conditional distribution of μ_i given ε_i, i.e., $E(\mu_i|\varepsilon_i)$. The difference between best observed practice and achieved performance gauges managerial inefficiency in terms of either excessive cost—*cost inefficiency*—or lost profit—*profit inefficiency*. Expressing the shortfall and excess as ratios of their frontier (best observed practice) values yields profit and cost inefficiency ratios. While the fitted stochastic frontier identifies best-observed-practice performance of the banks in the sample, it cannot explain the behavior of inefficient banks. A number of papers have surveyed investigations of bank performance using these concepts: for example, Berger and Humphrey (1997), Berger and Mester (1997), and Berger (2007).

As discussed in Hughes et al. (2000) and Mester (2008), since inefficiency is derived from the regression residual, selection of the characteristics of the banks and the environmental variables to include in the frontier estimation is particularly important. These variables define the peer group that determines best-practice performance against which a particular bank's performance is judged. If something extraneous to the production process is included in the specification, this might lead to too narrow a peer group and an overstatement of a bank's level of efficiency. Moreover, the variables included determine which type of inefficiency gets penalized. If bank location, e.g., urban versus rural, is included in the frontier, then an urban bank's performance would be judged against other urban banks but not against rural banks, and a rural bank's performance would be judged against other rural banks. If it turned out that rural banks are more efficient than urban banks, all else equal, the inefficient choice of location would not be penalized. An alternative to including the variable in the frontier regression is to measure efficiency based on a frontier in which it is omitted and then see how it correlates with efficiency. Several papers have looked at the correlations of efficiency measures and exogenous factors, including Mester (1993), Mester (1996), Mester (1997), and Berger and Mester (1997). Mester (1997) shows that estimates of bank cost efficiency can be biased if bank heterogeneity is ignored. See also Bos et al. (2005) on the issue of whether certain differences in the economic environment belong in the definition of the frontier.

Since the utility-maximizing profit function explains inefficient as well as efficient production, it cannot be fitted as a frontier. To gauge inefficiency, Hughes et al. (1996) and Hughes, Mester, and Moon (2001) estimate a best-observed-practice risk-return frontier and measure inefficiency relative to it. The estimated utility-maximizing profit function yields a measure of expected profit for each bank in the sample, and, when divided by equity capital, the expected profit is transformed into expected return on equity, $E(\pi_i/k_i)$. Each bank's expected (or, predicted) return is a function of its production plan and other explanatory variables. When the estimation of the profit function allows for heteroscedasticity, the standard error of the predicted return (profit), σ_i, which is a measure of econometric prediction risk, is also a function of the production plan and other explanatory variables and varies across banks in the sample.[11] The estimation of a stochastic frontier similar to (2) gives the highest expected return at any particular risk exposure:

$$E(\pi_i / k_i) = \alpha_0 + \alpha_1\,\sigma_i + \alpha_2\,\sigma_i^{\,2} - \mu_i + v_i, \qquad (10.3)$$

---

[11] Note that the estimated profit (or return) function resembles a multi-factor model where the factors are the explanatory variables in the profit function. The regression coefficients can be interpreted as marginal returns to the explanatory variables, and the standard error of the predicted return, a function of the variance-covariance matrix of the estimated marginal returns, resembles the variance

where v_i is a two-sided error term representing noise, and μ_i is a one-sided error term representing inefficiency. A bank's *return inefficiency* is the difference between its potential return and its noise-adjusted expected return, gauged among its peers with the same level of return risk. (Note, however, that if a bank's managers are taking too much or too little risk relative to the value-maximizing amount, this inappropriate level of risk is not taken into account by this measure of inefficiency.)

Koetter (2006) uses the model of managerial utility maximization and the associated measure of risk-return efficiency developed in Hughes et al. (1996, 1999, 2000) to investigate the efficiency of universal banks in Germany between 1993 and 2004. Comparing the measure of return efficiency with cost and profit efficiency estimated by standard formulations, he finds evidence that *efficient* banks using a low-risk investment strategy score poorly in terms of standard profit efficiency measures, since they also expect lower profit.

Hughes, Mester, and Moon (2001) take this a step further by recognizing that the utility-maximizing choices of bank managers need not be value maximizing to the extent that there are agency problems within the firm and managers are able to pursue their own, non-value-maximizing objectives. To identify the value-maximizing banks among the set of all banks, they select the quarter of banks in the sample that have the highest predicted return efficiency. These banks are the mostly likely group to be maximizing value or, at least, producing with the smallest agency costs. One can use this set of efficient banks to gauge characteristics of the value-maximizing production technology. For example, mean scale economies across this set of banks would indicate whether there were scale economies as banks expand output along a path that maximizes value. In contrast, mean scale economies across *all* banks would indicate whether there were scale economies as banks expand output along a path that maximizes managers' utility, but this can differ from the value-maximizing expansion path to the extent that managers are able to pursue their own objectives and these objectives differ from those of outside owners.

While the model of managerial utility maximization yields a structural utility-maximizing profit function that includes as special cases the standard maximum profit function and a value-maximizing profit function, it is, nevertheless, based on accounting measures of performance. An alternative model developed by Hughes and Moon (2003) gauges performance using the market value of assets. They develop a *utility-maximizing q-ratio function* derived from a model where managers allocate the potential (frontier) market value of their firm's assets between their consumption of agency goods (market-value inefficiency) and the production of market value, which, given their ownership stake, determines their wealth. The utility function is defined over wealth and the value of agency goods and is conditioned on capital structure, outside blockholder ownership, stock options held by insiders, and other managerial incentive variables. The authors derive a utility-maximizing demand function for market value and for agency goods (inefficiency). Hence, their *q*-ratio equation

of a portfolio return. Hughes (1999) and Hughes, Mester, and Moon (2001) report that the regression of *ln*(market value of equity) on $ln(E(\pi_i/k_i))$ and $ln(\sigma_i)$ for 190 publicly traded bank holding companies has an R-squared of 0.96, which implies that the production-based measures of expected return and risk explain a large part of a bank's market value. For a regression of the market value of equity on $E(\pi_i/k_i)$ and σ_i, Hughes and Mester (2013b) report R-squareds of 0.99, 0.94, and 0.97 for samples of data from 2003, 2007, and 2010, respectively. These values of R-squared are significantly higher than those obtained by regressing the market value on the accounting net income before and after taxes.

is *structural* and, consequently, enjoys the properties of a well-behaved consumer demand function. The authors use these properties to analyze the relationship between value (or inefficiency) and the proportion of the firm owned by insiders, which is their opportunity cost of consuming agency goods.

10.2.4 The Non-Structural Approach to Bank Efficiency Measurement

The *non-structural approach* to bank performance measurement usually focuses on achieved performance and measures y_i, in equation (10.1) by a variety of financial ratios, e.g., return-on-asset, return-on-equity, or the ratio of fixed costs to total costs. However, some applications have used measures of performance that are based on the market value of the firm (which inherently incorporates market-priced risk), for example, Tobin's q-ratio (which is the ratio of the market value of assets to the book value of assets); the Sharpe ratio (which measures the ratio of the firm's expected excess return over the risk-free return to the volatility of this excess return (as measured by the standard deviation of the excess return)); or an event study's cumulative abnormal return, CAR (the cumulative error terms of a model predicting banks' market return around a particular event). Other applications have measured performance by an inefficiency ratio obtained by estimating either a non-structural or structural performance equation as a frontier. The non-structural approach then explores the relationship of performance to various bank and environmental characteristics, including the bank's investment strategy, location, governance structure, and corporate control environment. For example, the non-structural approach might investigate technology by asking how performance ratios are correlated with asset acquisitions, the bank's product mix, whether the bank is organized as a mutual or stock-owned firm, and the ratio of outside to inside directors on its board. While informal and formal theories may motivate some of these investigations, no general theory of performance provides a unifying framework for these studies.

Using the frontier methods in a non-structural approach, Hughes et al. (1997) proposed a proxy for Jensen and Meckling's agency cost: a frontier of the market value of assets fitted as a potentially nonlinear function of the book-value investment in assets and the book value of assets squared. This frontier gives the highest potential value *observed* in the sample for any given investment in assets. For any bank, the difference between its highest potential value and its noise-adjusted achieved value represents its lost market value—a proxy for agency cost (X-inefficiency). Several studies have used either this systematic lost market value or the resulting noise-adjusted q-ratio to measure performance: Hughes et al. (1999), Hughes, Mester, and Moon (2001), Hughes et al. (2003), Hughes and Moon (2003), DeJonghe and Vander Vennet (2005), Baele, De Jonghe, and Vander Vennet (2006), and Hughes and Mester (2013b).

Habib and Ljungqvist (2005) specified an alternative market-value frontier as a function of a variety of managerial decision variables, including size, financial leverage, capital expenditures, and advertising expenditures. Thus, the peer grouping on which the frontier is estimated is considerably narrower than the wide grouping based on investment in assets, and inefficient choices of these conditioning values are not accounted for in the measurement of agency costs.

10.2.5 Specifying Outputs and Inputs in Structural Models of Production

In estimating the standard cost or profit function or the managerial utility maximization model, one must specify the outputs and inputs of bank production. The intermediation approach (Sealey and Lindley, 1977) focuses on the bank's production of intermediation services and the total cost of production, including both interest and operating expenses. Outputs are typically measured by the dollar volume of the bank's assets in various categories. As mentioned above, an exception is Mester (1992), who, to account for the bank's screening and monitoring activities, measured outputs as loans previously purchased (which require only monitoring), loans currently originated for the bank's own portfolio, loans currently purchased, and loans currently sold. Inputs are typically specified as labor, physical capital, deposits and other borrowed funds, and, in some studies, equity capital. While the intermediation approach treats deposits as inputs, there has been some discussion in the literature about whether deposits should be treated as an output since banks provide transactions services for depositors. Hughes and Mester (1993) formulated an empirical test for determining whether deposits act as an input or output. Consider variable cost, VC, which is the cost of nondeposit inputs and is a function of the prices of nondeposit inputs, w, output levels, y, other variables affecting the technology, τ, and the level of deposits, x. If deposits are an input, then $\partial VC/\partial x < 0$: Increasing the use of some input should decrease the expenditures on other inputs. If deposits are an output, then $\partial VC/\partial x > 0$ Output can be increased only if expenditures on inputs are increased. Hughes and Mester's empirical results indicate insured and uninsured deposits are inputs at banks in all size categories.

10.2.6 Specifying Capital Structure in Performance Equations

Typically, cost and profit functions are measured without considering the bank's capital structure, which results in a seriously mis-specified model that omits an important funding input, equity capital. However, the newer literature recognizes the importance of bank managers' choice of risk and capital structure on bank performance. Some of the first structural models to include equity capital as an input are Hancock (1985, 1986), Hughes and Mester (1993), McAllister and McManus (1993), Clark (1996), and Berger and Mester (1997).

As discussed in Hughes and Mester (1993), Berger and Mester (1997), Hughes (1999), and Mester (2008), a bank's insolvency risk depends not only on the riskiness of its portfolio, but also on the amount of financial capital it has to absorb losses. Insolvency risk affects bank costs and profits through (1) the risk premium the bank has to pay for uninsured debt, (2) the intensity of risk management activities the bank undertakes, and (3) the discount rate applied to future profits. A bank's capital level also directly affects costs by providing an alternative to deposits as a funding source for loans.

Most studies use the cash-flow (accounting) concept of cost, which includes the interest paid on debt (deposits) but not the required return on equity, as opposed to economic cost, which includes the cost of equity. Failure to include equity capital among the inputs can bias efficiency measurement. If a bank were to substitute debt for some of its financial equity capital, its accounting (cash-flow) costs could rise, making the less capitalized bank appear to be more costly than a well-capitalized bank. To solve this problem, one can include the level of equity capital as a quasi-fixed input in the cost function. The resulting cost function captures the relationship of cash-flow cost to the level of equity capital, and the (negative) derivative of cost with respect to equity capital—the amount by which cash-flow cost is reduced if equity capital is increased—gives the shadow price of equity. The shadow price of equity will equal the market price when the amount of equity minimizes cost or maximizes profit. Even when the level of equity does not conform to these objectives, the shadow price nevertheless provides a measure of its opportunity cost. Hughes, Mester, and Moon (2001) find that the mean shadow price of equity for small banks is significantly smaller than that of larger banks. This suggests that smaller banks over-utilize equity relative to its cost-minimizing value, perhaps to protect charter value. On the other hand, larger banks appear to under-utilize equity relative to its cost-minimizing value, perhaps to exploit a deposit subsidy and the subsidy due to the TBTF doctrine. In both cases, these capital strategies, while not minimizing cost, may be maximizing value.

10.2.7 Specifying Output Quality in the Performance Equation

In measuring efficiency, one should control for differences in output quality to avoid labeling unmeasured differences in product quality as differences in efficiency. Controls for loan quality, such as non-performing loans to total loans by loan category or loan losses, are sometimes included in the cost or profit frontier as controls (see Mester, 2008, for further discussion). As discussed in Berger and Mester (1997), whether it is appropriate to include nonperforming loans or loan losses in the cost or profit function depends on the extent to which these variables are exogenous. They would be exogenous if caused by economic shocks (bad luck), but could be endogenous to the extent that management is inefficient or has made a conscious decision to cut short-run expenses by cutting back on loan origination and monitoring resources. Berger and Mester (1997) attempt to solve this problem by using, as a control variable, the ratio of nonperforming loans to total loans in the bank's state. This state average would be nearly entirely exogenous to any one bank, but can control for negative shocks that affect bank output quality.

The variable, nonperforming loans, can also play a role as a quasi-fixed "input" whose quantity rather than price is included in the performance equation. As such, its "cost" is excluded from the performance metric, either cost or profit. Its price is the expected loan-loss rate. Hence, when the cost of nonperforming loans, i.e., loan losses, is excluded from the performance measure, a case can be made for including the level of nonperforming loans, and when the performance measure is net of loan losses, the logic suggests that the loss rate be included in the specification of the performance equation.

10.3 APPLICATIONS OF THE STRUCTURAL APPROACH

10.3.1 Performance in Relation to Organizational Form, Governance, Regulation, and Market Discipline

An increasing number of papers using structural models are exploring the importance of governance and ownership structure to the performance of banks. The structural model is first used to obtain a frontier-based measure of inefficiency. Then inefficiency is regressed on a set of explanatory variables.

Using confidential regulatory data on small, closely held commercial banks, DeYoung, Spong, and Sullivan (2001) use a stochastic frontier to measure banks' profit efficiency. They find banks that hire a manager from outside the group of controlling shareholders perform better than those with owner-managers; however, this result depends on motivating the hired managers with sufficient holdings of stock. They calculate an optimal level of managerial ownership that minimizes profit inefficiency. Higher levels of insider holdings lead to entrenchment and lower profitability.

Berger and Hannan (1998) consider the relationship of bank cost efficiency, estimated by the distribution-free technique and a stochastic frontier, to product market discipline, gauged by a Herfindahl index of market power. They find that the reduced discipline of concentrated markets is associated with a loss of cost efficiency far more significant than any welfare loss due to monopoly pricing.

DeYoung, Hughes, and Moon (2001) use the model of managerial utility maximization developed by Hughes et al. (1996, 2000) to estimate expected return and return risk. Using these values, they estimate a stochastic risk-return frontier as in equation (3) to obtain each bank's return inefficiency. They consider how banks' supervisory CAMEL ratings are related to their size, their risk-return choice, and their return inefficiency. They find that the risk-return choices of efficient banks are not related to their supervisory rating, while higher-risk choices of inefficient banks are penalized with poorer ratings. Moreover, the risk-return choices of large inefficient banks are held to a stricter standard than smaller banks and large efficient banks.

Two studies by Mester (1991, 1993) investigate differences in scale and scope measures for stock-owned and mutual savings and loans by estimating average cost functions. She finds evidence of agency problems at mutual S&Ls, as evidenced by diseconomies of scope, prior to the industry's deregulation, and evidence that these agency costs were lessened after the deregulation in the mid-1980s.

Using data for the period 1989–1996, Altunbas, Evans, and Molyneux (2001) estimate separate and common frontiers for three organizational forms in German banking: private commercial, public (government-owned) savings, and mutual cooperative banks. They argue that the same technology of intermediation is available to all so that the choice of technology is a management decision whose efficiency should be compared among all types of forms. The private sector appears to be less profit and cost efficient than the other two sectors. These results are especially clear in the case of the common frontier, but they are also obtained from the estimation of separate frontiers.

10.3.2 Uncovering Evidence of Scale Economies by Accounting for Risk and Capital Structure

Former Federal Reserve Chairman Alan Greenspan (2010) summarized the literature on scale economies in banking: "For years the Federal Reserve had been concerned about the ever-growing size of our largest financial institutions. Federal Reserve research had been unable to find economies of scale in banking beyond a modest size." (p. 231) But in fact, many investigators, including some at the Fed, have found evidence of scale economies even at the largest financial institutions. This research includes, for example, Hughes et al. (1996), Berger and Mester (1997), Hughes and Mester (1998), Hughes, Mester, and Moon (2001), Berger and Mester (2003), Bossone and Lee (2004), Feng and Serletis (2010), Wheelock and Wilson (2012), and Hughes and Mester (2013b).

The Greenspan observation raises the fundamental question: Are scale economies in banking illusive or elusive? The investment strategies of many of the largest financial institutions constituted ground zero in the recent banking crisis, and their rescue under the TBTF doctrine has prompted some prominent policymakers to call for breaking up the largest banks. For example, Fisher and Rosenblum (2012) assert, "Hordes of Dodd-Frank regulators are not the solution; smaller, less complex banks are. We can select the road to enhanced financial efficiency by breaking up TBTF banks—now." Hoenig and Morris (2012) call for limiting the government safety net to the core activities of commercial banks including lending, deposit taking, providing liquidity and credit intermediation services, and disallowing banks from doing certain non-core banking activities, including engaging in broker-dealer activities, making markets in derivatives or securities, trading derivatives and securities for their own account or their customers, or sponsoring hedge funds or private equity funds. Tarullo (2011), however, questions whether breaking up banks would lead to efficiency and suggests there is a tradeoff between concerns for systemic risk and efficiency: "An additional concern would arise if some countries made the tradeoff by limiting the size or configuration of their financial firms for systemic risk reasons at the cost of realizing genuine economies of scope or scale, while other countries did not. In this case, firms from the first group of countries might well be at a competitive disadvantage in the provision of certain cross-border activities." And Powell (2013) indicates that if the current regulatory reform agenda succeeds in substantially reducing the likelihood of bank failure and minimizing the externalities caused by a large bank failure, then in his view this would be preferable to breaking up the banks, since such a break-up would "likely involve arbitrary judgments, efficiency losses, and a difficult transition."

While textbooks assert that scale economies characterize banking (e.g., Kohn, 2004 and Saunders and Cornett, 2010), these economies elude many empirical studies because the studies generally fail to account for the effects of endogenous risk-taking on banks' cost as bank size increases. Textbooks cite diversification as one component of the technology that generates scale economies. As discussed above, in Figure 10.1, the larger bank enjoys a better risk-expected-return tradeoff and chooses its risk exposure on that improved frontier to maximize managerial utility, which is likely associated with *expected* shareholder value in the absence of severe agency problems. The increase in cost due to the larger output will depend on the investment strategy the larger bank chooses. For example, as a bank scales up its output and moves from point A to point A′, diversification has resulted in lower risk and cost is likely to have increased less than proportionately than the increase in output. If risk-taking is costly, then the investment strategy at point C may result in, say, a proportional increase in cost compared to operating at point A, while the investment strategy at point D may imply a more than proportional increase in cost. Hughes (1999) contends that studies of how cost varies with output that ignore the effects of endogenous risk-taking on cost are likely to identify the technology as constant returns to scale when larger banks tend to produce at point C and as scale diseconomies when larger banks tend to produce at point D. To the extent that larger banks are generally more risky than smaller banks (Demsetz and Strahan, 1997), the naïve econometric investigation of banking cost that ignores endogenous risk-taking is likely to find that larger banks experience constant returns to scale or even scale diseconomies. Hughes, Mester, and Moon (2001) call the effect on cost from moving from point A to point A′, the *diversification effect*—diversification leads to a decline in risk for the same level of expected profit. They call the effect on cost of moving from point A′, which resulted from better scale-related diversification, to point C or D, the *risk-taking effect*.

Accounting for endogenous risk-taking—isolating the diversification effect—in estimating scale economies requires controlling for revenue as well as cost. While the traditional cost function does not incorporate any revenue terms, the utility-maximizing cost function incorporates revenue because it is derived from the utility maximizing profit function, conditioned on the output vector and as noted earlier, it reflects bank managers' choice of risk as well as expected return. In Figure 10.1, suppose that the smaller bank chooses to produce its output vector with the investment strategy at point A and the large bank chooses to produce its output vector with the strategy at point D. Scale economies estimated in the neighborhood of point A refer to the increase in cost for a small proportional increase in outputs given the investment strategy at point A. If expanded output allows for better diversification that lowers costs for given expected return, then the estimated scale economies would compare cost at point A to cost at point A′. In this way, it would isolate the diversification effect and avoid the bias of measuring scale economies at point D relative to point A.[12]

Hughes and Mester (2013b) estimate several traditional cost functions and the risk-return-driven cost function for US bank holding companies in the years 2003, 2007, and 2010. In all three years, estimates derived from the traditional minimum cost functions, which do not take into account the banks' risk-expected return choice, indicate modest scale economies or in some cases constant returns to scale. In contrast, the utility-maximizing cost function, which takes into account the banks' risk-expected return choice, yields evidence of large scale economies that increase with the scale of the bank. For example, in 2007, for the smallest banks (with less than $0.8 billion in assets), estimated scale economies is 1.12, which means that a 10% increase in output levels is associated with an 8.8% increase in cost. For

---

[12] Demsetz and Strahan (1997) demonstrate that a larger scale of operations leads to better diversification of banking risk—in particular, bank-specific risk estimated from a multifactor asset pricing model. To isolate this diversification effect, they regress bank-specific risk on asset size and find a small, negative association. When they control for the many ways banks take risk, the relationship between risk and asset size becomes much more negative and statistically significant. They note that isolating the scale-related diversification effect requires controlling for differences in business strategies that influence risk exposure. Finding the effect of scale-related diversification on scale economies requires a similar approach to controling for endogenous risk-taking.

the largest banks (with greater than $100 billion in assets), estimated scale economies is 1.34, which means that a 10% increase in output levels is associated with a 7.5% increase in cost.

This evidence of large scale economies at the largest financial institutions suggests that breaking them up into smaller institutions with the goal of reducing the systemic risk they pose would reduce their competitiveness in global financial markets. Using their 2007 estimates, Hughes and Mester (2013a) consider breaking each of the 17 institutions that exceed $100 billion in consolidated assets in half to create 34 banks with total assets equal to those of the 17 larger institutions. Holding product mix constant, that is, assuming the smaller institutions produce the same product mix as the larger ones, their costs are 23% higher. In a similar exercise, Wheelock and Wilson (2012), who also find large scale economies at banks of all sizes, scale back the four largest US institutions in 2009 to a size of $1 trillion and increase their numbers so that the total assets of the smaller institutions equal those of the larger institutions. They find that the cost of the smaller institutions is approximately 19% higher. These two exercises suggest that breaking up the largest institutions into smaller institutions will limit their global competitiveness and provide incentives to produce their financial services offshore where such limits are not operative.

A related issue in this literature questions whether the estimated scale economies at the largest financial institutions result from cost-of-funds subsidies due to the TBTF doctrine. Davies and Tracey (2014) answer affirmatively; however, Hughes and Mester (2013b) point to flaws in the methods used by Davies and Tracey. Hughes and Mester (2013b) present several pieces of evidence indicating that the large scale economies they find are not driven by a TBTF cost-of-funds subsidy. First, they find large scale economies at small banks in their sample as well as large banks. Second, when they re-estimate their model excluding banks with assets greater than $100 billion, and then calculate scale economies out of sample for the largest banks, their results are unchanged. Finally, they calculate scale economies for the largest bank if they faced the cost-of-funds of smaller banks. Again, their results are unchanged. Hughes and Mester (2013b) conclude that the underlying technology, not TBTF subsidies, account for the scale economies of the largest financial institutions.

10.4 APPLICATIONS OF THE NON-STRUCTURAL APPROACH

10.4.1 Measuring the Value of Investment Opportunities ("Charter Value")

The value of a bank's investment opportunities is often measured by Tobin's q-ratio; however, in the presence of agency cost the q-ratio captures only the ability of the incumbent managers to exploit these opportunities. Ideally, the value of investment opportunities should be gauged independently of the ability and actions of the current management. Hughes et al. (1997) and Hughes et al. (2003) propose a measure based on fitting a stochastic frontier to the market value of assets as a function of the book value of assets and variables characterizing the market conditions faced by banks. These conditions include a Herfindahl index of market power and the macroeconomic growth rate. The fitted frontier gives the highest potential value of a bank's assets in the markets in which it operates. Thus, this potential value is conditional on the location of the bank and represents the value the bank would fetch in a competitive auction. Hughes et al. (1997) define this value as the bank's "charter value"—its value in a competitive auction.

10.4.2 Measuring the Performance of Business and Capital Strategies

Several papers have used the non-structural performance equation to examine the relationship between bank value and bank capital structure. Hughes et al. (1997) regress performance measured by Tobin's q-ratio and market-value inefficiency on a number of variables characterizing bank production. Calomiris and Nissim (2007) regress the ratio of the market value of equity to its book value on a similar list of variables. De Jonghe and Vander Vennet (2005) apply the market-value frontier of Hughes et al. (1997) to derive a noise-adjusted measure of Tobin's q, which they use to evaluate how leverage and market power are related to value. All three studies find evidence that banks follow dichotomous strategies for enhancing value as predicted by Marcus (1984): a lower risk, lower leverage strategy and a higher risk, higher leverage strategy.

10.4.3 Relationship of Ownership Structure to Bank Value

In an influential study, Morck, Shleifer, and Vishny (1988) hypothesized that managerial ownership creates two contrasting incentives: A higher ownership stake, first, better aligns the interests of managers and outside owners and, second, enhances managers' control over the firm and makes it harder for managers to be ousted when they are not efficient. Measuring performance by Tobin's q-ratio, these authors provide evidence that the so-called alignment-of-interests effect dominates the entrenchment effect at lower levels of managerial ownership, while the entrenchment effect dominates over a range of higher levels.

Studies that attempt to measure the *net* effect of the alignment and entrenchment effects on firm valuation cannot identify these effects individually—only their sum in the form of the sign of a regression coefficient or a derivative of a regression equation. Adams and Santos (2006) cleverly isolate the entrenchment effect by considering how the proportion of a bank's common stock that is controlled but not owned by the bank's own trust department is statistically related to the bank's economic performance. The voting rights exercised by management through the trust department enhance management's control over the bank but do not align their interests with outside shareholders', since the beneficiaries of the trusts, not the managers, receive the dividends and the capital gains and losses.

Caprio, Laeven, and Levine (2003) study the effect of ownership, shareholder protection laws, and supervisory and regulatory policies on the valuations of banks around the world. The authors construct a database of 244 banks across 44 countries. They measure performance by Tobin's q-ratio and by the ratio of the market value of equity to the book value of equity. They find evidence that (1) banks in countries with better protection of minority shareholders are more highly valued, (2) bank regulations and supervision have no signifi-cant effect on bank value, (3) the degree of cash-flow rights of the largest owner has a sig-nificant positive effect on bank value, and (4) an increase in ownership concentration has a larger positive effect on valuation when the legal protection of minority shareholders is weak.

Laeven and Levine (2009) consider a sample of large banks in 48 countries in 2001 and investigate how the cash flow rights of the largest shareholder and various regulatory provi-sions affect the probability of insolvency. They find that the cash-flow rights of the largest shareholder are positively related to the risk of insolvency. They also find that when there is a shareholder with large cash-flow right, deposit insurance and activity restrictions are asso-ciated with increased insolvency risk, but they are uncorrelated with insolvency risk when the bank is widely held.

Hughes et al. (2003) examine US bank holding companies and find evidence of mana-gerial entrenchment among banks with higher levels of insider ownership, more valuable growth opportunities, poorer financial performance, and smaller asset size. When manag-ers are not entrenched, asset acquisitions and sales are associated with reduced market value inefficiency. When managers are entrenched, sales are associated with smaller reductions in inefficiency, while acquisitions are associated with greater inefficiency.

10.4 CONCLUSIONS

Great strides have been made in the theory of bank technology in terms of explaining banks' comparative advantage in producing informationally intensive assets and financial services and in taking, diversifying, and offsetting a variety of risks. Great strides have also been made in explaining sub-par managerial performance in terms of agency theory and in applying these theories to analyze the particular environment of banking. In recent years, the empirical modeling of bank technology and the measurement of bank performance have begun to incorporate these theoretical developments and yield interesting insights that reflect the unique nature and role of banking in modern economies.

This new literature recognizes that the choice of risk influences banks' production deci-sions, (including their mix of assets, asset quality, off-balance-sheet hedging activities, capi-tal structure, debt maturity, and resources allocated to risk management), and so, in turn, affects banks' cost and profitability. Measures of bank performance should take account of this endogeneity. The estimation of structural models that incorporate managerial prefer-ences for expected return and risk have uncovered significant scale economies in banking, a finding that differs from the earlier literature but accords with the consolidation of the banking industry that has been occurring worldwide.

Performance studies based on structural models of managerial utility maximization, as well as those based on non-structural models of bank production, have incorporated vari-ables designed to capture incentive conflicts between managers and outside stakeholders. These studies have shown that factors associated with enhanced market discipline are also associated with improved bank performance and that improved bank performance is not necessarily associated with improved financial stability. The incentive of larger banks to take extra risk to exploit the federal safety net and increase their expected market value may undermine financial stability.

REFERENCES

Adams, R. B. and Santos, J. A. C. (2006). Identifying the Effect of Managerial Control on Firm Performance, *Journal of Accounting and Economics* 41, 55–85.

Aghion, P., Alesina, A., and Trebbi, F. (2007). Democracy, Technology, and Growth. Department of Economics, Harvard University Working Paper.

Altunbas, Y., Evans, L., and Molyneux, P. (2001). Bank Ownership and Efficiency, *Journal of Money, Credit, and Banking* 33, 926–954.

Baele, L., DeJonghe, O., and Vander Vennet, R. (2006). Does the Stock Market Value Bank Diversification?, Department of Financial Economics, Ghent University Working Paper No. 2006/402.

Berger, A. N. (2007). International Comparisons of Banking Efficiency, *Financial Markets, Institutions and Instruments* 16, 119–144.

Berger, A. N. and Hannan, T. H. (1998). The Efficiency Cost of Market Power in the Banking Industry: A Test of the "Quiet Life" and Related Hypotheses, *Review of Economics and Statistics* 80, 454–465.

Berger, A. N. and Humphrey, D. B. (1997). Efficiency of Financial Institutions: International Survey and Directions for Future Research, *European Journal of Operational Research* 98, 175–212.

Berger, A. N. and Mester, L. J. (1997). Inside the Black Box: What Explains Differences in the Efficiencies of Financial Institutions, *Journal of Banking and Finance* 21, 895–947.

Berger, A. N. and Mester, L. J. (2003). Explaining the Dramatic Changes in Performance of US Banks: Technical Change, Deregulation, and Dynamic Changes in Competition, *Journal of Financial Intermediation* 12, 57–95.

Berlin, M. and Mester, L. J. (1999). Deposits and Relationship Lending, *Review of Financial Studies* 12, 579–607.

Bhattacharya, S. and Thakor, A. (1993). Contemporary Banking Theory, *Journal of Financial Intermediation* 3, 2–50.

Bos, J. W. B., Heid F., Koetter, M., Kolari, J. W. and Kool, C. J. M. (2005). Inefficient or Just Different? Effects of Heterogeneity on Bank Efficiency Scores, Deutsche Bundesbank Discussion Paper No. 2.

Bossone, B. and Lee, J.-K. (2004). In Finance, Size Matters: The 'Systemic Scale Economies' Hypothesis, IMF Staff Papers No. 51.1.

Calomiris, C. W. and Kahn, C. M. (1991). The Role of Demandable Debt in Structuring Optimal Banking Arrangements, *American Economic Review* 70, 312–326.

Calomiris, C. W. and Nissim, D. (2007). Activity-Based Valuation of Bank Holding Companies, National Bureau of Economic Research Working Paper No. 12918.

Caprio, G., Laeven, L., and Levine, R. (2003). Governance and Bank Valuation, National Bureau of Economic Research Working Paper No. 10158.

Clark, J. (1996). Economic Cost, Scale Efficiency and Competitive Viability in Banking, *Journal of Money, Credit, and Banking* 28, 342–364.

Davies, R. and Tracey, B. (2014). Too Big to Be Efficient? The Impact of Too-Big-To-Fail Factors on Scale Economies for Banks, *Journal of Money, Credit, and Banking* 46, 219–253.

DeJonghe, O. and Vander Vennet, R. (2005). Competition versus Agency Costs: An Analysis of Charter Values in European Banking. Ghent University Working Paper.

Demirgüç-Kunt, A., Kane, E. J. and Laeven, L. (2007). Determinants of Deposit-Insurance Adoption and Design, NBER Working Paper No. 12862.

Demsetz, R. S. and Strahan, P. E. (1997). Diversification, Size, and Risk at Bank Holding Companies, *Journal of Money, Credit, and Banking* 29, 300–313.

DeYoung, R. E., Hughes, J. P. and Moon, C.-G. (2001). Efficient Risk-Taking and Regulatory Covenant Enforcement in a Deregulated Banking Industry, *Journal of Economics and Business* 53, 255–282.

DeYoung, R. E., Spong, K., and Sullivan, R. J. (2001). Who's Minding the Store? Motivating and Monitoring Hired Managers at Small, Closely Held Commercial Banks, *Journal of Banking and Finance* 25, 1209–1243.

Evanoff, D. D. (1998). Assessing the Impact of Regulation on Bank Cost Efficiency, Federal Reserve Bank of Chicago, *Economic Perspectives* 22, 21–32.

Evanoff, D. D., Israilevich, P. R., and Merris, R. C. (1990). Relative Price Efficiency, Technical Change, and Scale Economies for Large Commercial Banks, *Journal of Regulatory Economics* 2, 281–298.

FDIC. (2013). TBTF Subsidy for Large Banks—Literature Review, Prepared for Thomas Hoenig, Vice Chair, Federal Deposit Insurance Corporation.

Feng, G. and Serletis, A. (2010). Efficiency, Technical Change, and Returns to Scale in Large US Banks: Panel Data Evidence from an Output Distance Function Satisfying Theoretical Regularity, *Journal of Banking and Finance* 34, 127–138.

Fiordelisi, F. (2007). Shareholder Value Efficiency in European Banking, *Journal of Banking and Finance* 31, 2151–2171.

Fisher, R. and Rosenblum, H. (2012). How Huge Banks Threaten the Economy. *Wall Street Journal* April 4.

Flannery, M. J. (1994). Debt Maturity and the Deadweight Cost of Leverage: Optimally Financing Banking Firms, *American Economic Review* 84, 320–331.

Greenspan, A. (2010). The Crisis, *Brookings Papers on Economic Activity*, Spring, 201–246.

Habib, M. A. and Ljungqvist, A. (2005). Firm Value and Managerial Incentives: A Stochastic Frontier Approach, *Journal of Business* 78, 2053–2093.

Hancock, D. (1985). The Financial Firm: production with Monetary and Nonmonetary Goods, *Journal of Political Economy* 93, 859–880.

Hancock, D. (1986). A Model of the Financial Firm with Imperfect Asset and Deposit Liabilities, *Journal of Banking and Finance* 10, 37–54.

Hoenig, T. M. and Morris, C. S. (2012). Restructuring the Banking System to Improve Safety and Soundness, Federal Deposit Insurance Corporation, <https://www.fdic.gov/about/learn/board/Restructuring-the-Banking-System-05-24-11.pdf>.

Hughes, J. P. (1999). Incorporating Risk into the Analysis of Production, Presidential Address to the Atlantic Economic Society, *Atlantic Economic Journal* 27, 1–23.

Hughes, J. P. and Mester, L. J. (1993). A Quality and Risk-Adjusted Cost Function for Banks: Evidence on the "Too-Big-To-Fail" Doctrine, *Journal of Productivity Analysis* 4, 293–315.

Hughes, J. P. and Mester, L. J. (1998). Bank Capitalization and Cost: Evidence of Scale Economies in Risk Management and Signaling, *Review of Economics and Statistics* 80, 314–325.

Hughes, J. P. and Mester, L. J. (2013a). A Primer on Market Discipline and Governance of Financial Institutions for Those in a State of Shocked Disbelief. In: F. Pasiouras (Ed.), *Efficiency and Productivity Growth: Modelling in the Financial Services Industry*, 19–47. Chicester: Wiley.

Hughes, J. P. and Mester, L. J. (2013b). Who Said Large Banks Don't Experience Scale Economies? Evidence from a Risk-Return-Driven Cost Function, *Journal of Financial Intermediation* 22, 559–585.

Hughes, J. P., Mester, L. J., and Moon C.-G. (2001). Are Scale Economies in Banking Elusive or Illusive? Evidence Obtained by Incorporating Capital Structure and Risk-Taking into Models of Bank Production, *Journal of Banking and Finance* 25, 2169–2208.

Hughes, J. P. and Moon C.-G. (2003). Estimating Managers' Utility-Maximizing Demand for Agency Goods, Department of Economics, Rutgers University Working Paper No. 2003-24.

Hughes, J. P., Lang, W., Mester, L. J. and Moon C.-G. (1996). Efficient Banking Under Interstate Branching, *Journal of Money, Credit, and Banking* 28, 1045–1071.

Hughes, J. P., Lang, W., Mester, L. J., and Moon C.-G. (1999). The Dollars and Sense of Bank Consolidation, *Journal of Banking and Finance* 23, 291–324.

Hughes, J. P., Lang, W., Mester, L. J., and Moon C.-G. (2000). Recovering Risky Technologies Using the almost Ideal Demand System: An Application To US Banking, *Journal of Financial Services Research* 18, 5–27.

Hughes, J. P., Lang, W., Mester, L. J., Moon C.-G., and Pagano, M. (2003). Do Bankers Sacrifice Value to Build Empires? Managerial Incentives, Industry Consolidation, and Financial Performance, *Journal of Banking and Finance* 27, 417–447.

Hughes, J. P., Lang, W., Moon C.-G., and Pagano, M. (1997). Measuring the Efficiency of Capital Allocation in Commercial Banking, Federal Reserve Bank of Philadelphia Working Paper No. 98-2 (revised as Rutgers University Economics Department Working Paper No. 2004-1).

Jensen, M. C. and Meckling, W. H. (1976). Theory of the Firm: Managerial Behavior, Agency Costs and Ownership Structure, *Journal of Financial Economics* 5, 305–360.

Jensen, M. C. and Meckling, W. H. (1979). Rights and Production Functions: An Application to Labor-Managed Firms and Codetermination, *Journal of Business* 52, 469–506.

Keeley, M. C. (1990). Deposit Insurance, Risk, and Market Power in Banking, *American Economic Review* 80, 1183–1200.

Koetter, M. (2006). The Stability of Efficiency Rankings when Risk-Preferences and Objectives Are Different, Banking and Financial Studies, Deutsche Bundesbank Discussion Paper No. 08/2006 Series 2.

Kohn, M. (2004). *Financial Institutions and Markets*. Oxford: Oxford University Press.

La Porta, R., Lopez-de-Silanes, F., and Shleifer, A. (2002). Government Ownership of Banks, *Journal of Finance* 57, 265–301.

Laeven, L. and Levine, R. (2009). Bank Governance, Regulation, and Risk Taking, *Journal of Financial Economics* 93, 259–275.

Leibenstein, H. (1966). Allocative Efficiency vs. "X-Efficiency," *American Economic Review* 56, 392–415.

McAllister, P. H. and McManus, D. (1993). Resolving the Scale Efficiency Puzzle in Banking, *Journal of Banking and Finance* 17, 389–406.

Marcus, A. J. (1984). Deregulation and Bank Financial Policy, *Journal of Banking and Finance* 8, 557–565.

Mester, L. J. (1991). Agency Costs Among Savings and Loans, *Journal of Financial Intermediation* 1, 257–278.

Mester, L. J. (1992). Traditional and Nontraditional Banking: An Information-Theoretic Approach, *Journal of Banking and Finance* 16, 545–566.

Mester, L. J. (1993). Efficiency in the Savings and Loan Industry, *Journal of Banking and Finance* 17, 267–286.

Mester, L. J. (1996). A Study of Bank Efficiency Taking Into Account Risk-Preferences, *Journal of Banking and Finance* 20, 1025–1045.

Mester, L. J. (1997). Measuring Efficiency at US Banks: Accounting for Heterogeneity is Important, *European Journal of Operational Research* 98, 230–242.

Mester, L. J. (2007). Some Thoughts on the Evolution of the Banking System and the Process of Financial Intermediation, *Federal Reserve Bank of Atlant, Economic Review*, First and Second Quarter, 67–75.

Mester, L. J. (2008). Optimal Industrial Structure in Banking. In: A. Boot and A. Thakor (Eds.), *Handbook of Financial Intermediation and Banking*, 133–162. Amsterdam: North-Holland/ Elsevier.

Mester, L. J., Nakamura, L. I., and Renault, M. (2007). Transactions Accounts and Loan Monitoring, *Review of Financial Studies* 20, 529–556.

Morck, R., Shleifer, A., and Vishny, R. W. (1988). Management Ownership and Market Valuation: An Empirical Analysis, *Journal of Financial Economics* 20, 293–315.

Powell, J. H. (2013). Ending "Too Big To Fail." Remarks at the Institute of International Bankers 2013 Washington Conference, Washington, DC.

Saunders, A. and Cornett, M. (2010). *Financial Institutions Management: A Risk Management Approach*. New York: McGraw-Hill Higher Education.

Sealey, C. W. and Lindley, J. T. (1977). Inputs, Outputs, and a Theory of Production and Cost at Depository Financial Institutions, *Journal of Finance* 32, 1251–1266.

Tarullo, D. K. (2011). Industrial Organization and Systemic Risk: An Agenda for Further Research. Remarks at the Conference on the Regulation of Systemic Risk, Federal Reserve Board, Washington, DC.

Wheelock, D. and Wilson, P. (2012). Do Large Banks have Lower Costs? New Estimates of Returns to Scale for US Banks, *Journal of Money, Credit, and Banking* 44, 171–199.

CHAPTER 11

....

TECHNOLOGICAL CHANGE, FINANCIAL INNOVATION, AND DIFFUSION IN BANKING

....

W. SCOTT FRAME AND LAWRENCE J. WHITE

11.1 INTRODUCTION

....

THE commercial banking business has changed dramatically over the past 30 years, due in large part to technological change.[1] Advances in telecommunications, information technology, and financial theory and practice have jointly transformed many of the relationship-focused intermediaries of yesteryear into data-intensive risk management operations of today. Consistent with this, we now find many commercial banks embedded as part of global financial institutions that engage in a wide variety of financial activities.

To be more specific, technological changes relating to telecommunications and data processing have spurred financial innovations that have altered bank products and services and bank production processes. For example, the ability to use applied statistics cost-effectively (via software and computing power) has markedly altered the process of financial intermediation. Retail loan applications are now routinely evaluated using credit scoring tools, rather than using human judgment. Such an approach makes underwriting much more transparent to third parties and hence facilitates secondary markets for retail loans, such as credit card debt and mortgages, via securitization. Statistically based risk measurement tools are also used to measure and manage other types of credit risks—as well as market

---

[1] Restrictions on commercial banks' ability to diversify geographically and across product space were also significantly relaxed during this time, especially in the United States. This trend has significantly reinforced technological change in terms of driving the observed evolution of commercial banking over the past 30 years. See Berger, Kashyap, and Scalise (1995) for discussion of the role of technological and regulatory changes in transforming the US banking industry.

risks—on an ongoing basis across entire portfolios.[2] After the global financial crisis, these tools have been leveraged to comply with new regulatory stress-testing requirements for systemically important financial institutions.

This chapter describes how technological change has spurred financial innovations that have driven the aforementioned changes in commercial banking over the past 30 years. In this respect, our survey is similar to that of Berger (2003). However, our analysis distinguishes itself by reviewing the literature on a larger number of new banking technologies and synthesizing these studies in the context of the broader economics literature on innovation. In this way, the chapter is more like our own previous survey of empirical studies of financial innovation (Frame and White, 2004). We note that this survey is largely US-centric, owing to our own experiences, the fact that many financial innovations originate in the US, and the fact that most studies of such innovations rely on US data. Before proceeding, it will be helpful to understand better what is meant by financial innovation.

11.2 BACKGROUND: THE ROLE OF FINANCE AND FINANCIAL INNOVATION

As noted by Merton (1992, p. 12), the primary function of a financial system is to facilitate the allocation and deployment of economic resources, both spatially and across time, in an uncertain environment. This function encompasses a payments system with a medium of exchange; the transfer of resources from savers to borrowers; the gathering of savings for pure time transformation (i.e., consumption smoothing); and the reduction of risk through insurance and diversification.

The operation of a financial system involves the real resource costs (labor, materials, and capital) employed by financial intermediaries (e.g., commercial banks) and by financial facilitators (e.g., mortgage brokers). Many of these resources are expended in the data collection and analyses in which financial market participants engage so as to deal with problems of asymmetric information. There are also uncertainties about future states of the world that generate risks, which for risk-averse individuals represent costs. In this environment, new financial products and services that can better satisfy financial system participants' demands should generally be welcomed by those participants.

Hence, we define a financial innovation as something new that reduces costs, reduces risks, or provides an improved product/service/instrument that better satisfies financial system participants' demands. Financial innovations can be grouped as new products or services; new production processes; or new organizational forms. Of course, if a new intermediate product or service is created and used by banks, it may then become part of a new financial production process.

---

[2] Related to this, there has been important innovation in the development of indexes—such as house price indexes, securities price indexes, and volatility indexes—that have aided in the measurement and management of risks, including the innovative development of financial instruments that are based on these indexes. The importance of such indexes is a theme that underlies many of the essays in Haliassos (2013).

The centrality of finance in an economy and its importance for economic growth (e.g., Levine 1997) naturally raises the importance of financial innovation—and its diffusion. Since finance is a facilitator of virtually all production activity and much consumption activity, improvements in the financial sector will have direct positive ramifications throughout an economy. Further, since better finance can encourage more saving and investment and can also encourage better (more productive) investment decisions, these indirect positive effects from financial innovation add further to its value for an economy. This positive view of financial innovation has been discussed in a number of articles, most notably: Van Horne (1980), Miller (1986, 1992), Merton (1992, 1995), Tufano (2003), Frame and White (2004), and Allen (2012).

The recent global financial crisis has led some observers to cast doubt on the usefulness of most financial innovation—seeing such activity as being largely associated with financial instability and financial malpractice.[3] For example, Paul Volcker (2009) famously remarked "the most important financial innovation that I have seen [in] the past 20 years is the automatic teller machine" after earlier highlighting two financial innovations—"credit-default swaps and collateralized debt obligations—which took us right to the brink of disaster." Similarly, Paul Krugman (2007) characterized "financial innovation" as "two words that should, from now on, strike fear into investors' hearts" since the recent innovations "were sold on false pretenses...[and instead] spread confusion, luring investors into taking on more risk than they realized."

While such a reevaluation is natural in light of the financial crisis, it is important to recognize that not every financial innovation will be welfare enhancing or successful. Innovation involves trial-and-error, and failures can be costly—especially for widely diffused innovations (e.g., Lerner and Tufano, 2011). So, when one suggests that financial innovation is beneficial, this should be viewed as "on net."[4] Consistent with these conjectures, Beck et al. (2012) conduct a cross-country analysis and find that financial innovation is associated with higher (but more volatile) economic growth and with greater bank fragility.

Given the importance of financial innovation, identifying the environmental conditions that are conducive to such changes is worthwhile. The general innovation literature in economics has sought to uncover the environmental conditions that affect the stream of innovations—focusing on hypotheses concerning roughly five structural conditions: (1) the market power of enterprises; (2) the size of enterprises; (3) technological opportunity; (4) appropriability; and (5) product market demand conditions (see Cohen and Levin, 1989; and Cohen, 1995 for comprehensive surveys of this literature).

Campbell (1988) offers four such conditions specifically in the context of financial innovation. The first relates to underlying technologies and the ability of technological improvements to increase efficiency. Here we point to how the information technology revolution has facilitated the use of applied statistics for risk measurement and management in banking. A second condition is an unstable macroeconomic environment, since the concomitant fluctuating asset prices are likely to spur risk-transfer innovations. Third, regulation

---

[3] Thakor (2012) and Gennaioli, Shleifer, and Vishny (2012) are recent examples of theoretical research that attempts to tie financial innovation and financial instability. Both provide models where banks innovate by making new loans or creating new securities; but then altered information or beliefs results in runs or panics. Henderson and Pearson (2011) provide recent empirical analysis of a welfare-reducing financial innovation.

[4] A similar perspective can be found in Smith (2013) and Ackerman (2013).

can inhibit some innovations and encourage others (as a mechanism to avoid regulation) as consistent with Kane's (1981, 2012) "regulatory dialectic." For example, regulatory capital arbitrage—or the ability to hold a particular risk in a different form and receive regulatory capital relief for doing so—has been a key driver of US mortgage securitization activity for two decades. Finally, taxes can spur financial innovations to the extent that they create incentives to repackage (or re-label) specific income streams so as to reduce tax liability. Over the past 30 years, each of the environmental conditions (1)–(5) that were noted above was markedly altered—resulting in substantial changes to the commercial banking industry.

Furthermore, as noted previously by Molyneux and Shamroukh (1999) and Frame and White (2004), there has been a surprising dearth of empirical studies that test hypotheses with respect to financial innovation in general. This is especially true for hypotheses that focus on the structural conditions that encourage innovation. For example, Frame and White (2004) identified only two papers that tested hypotheses concerning structural conditions that encourage financial innovation (Ben-Horim and Silber, 1977; and Lerner, 2002), although Lerner (2006) has made a more recent contribution.

Instead, the comparatively few empirical studies that have been done tend to focus on the characteristics of users/adopters of innovations—sometimes on a cross-sectional basis and other times in the context of the diffusion of the innovation. In surveying the literature in preparation for this chapter, we find that more empirical studies have appeared, but the field is still relatively sparse, and the studies still focus largely on the characteristics of users/adopters. This finding represents a supplementary contribution of this chapter.

11.3 FINANCIAL INNOVATION AND BANKING: 1980–2010

In this section, we survey the literatures pertaining to several specific financial innovations that have appeared over the past 30 years or so that were specifically driven by technological change. We have organized our discussion along the lines of the three major categories that we described in Section 11.2: new products and services; new production processes; and new organizational forms.

11.3.1 Products

Mortgage loans were one suite of products that experienced a great deal of change in the United States during the 25 years leading up to the financial crisis. In 1980, long-term fully amortizing fixed-rate mortgages were the norm; and this product was offered primarily by thrift institutions. Moreover, these loans required substantial down payments and a good credit history; and the accumulated equity was relatively illiquid.

These characteristics have markedly evolved.[5] The first big change occurred in the early 1980s with the widespread introduction of various types of adjustable rate mortgages

---

[5] Gerardi, Rosen, and Willen (2012) provide an overview of the changes in the mortgage market since the 1970s and argue that these changes—especially mortgage securitization (which will be discussed later

(ARMs), which had previously been banned by federal regulators. The Tax Reform Act of 1986, which ended federal income tax deductions for non-mortgage consumer debt, spurred substantial growth in home equity lending. One mortgage innovation that is more directly tied to technological change is subprime lending, which was originally predicated on the use of statistics for better risk measurement and risk-based pricing to compensate for these higher risks. However, the subprime mortgage crisis has uncovered significant short-comings in the underlying statistical models.

11.3.1.1 *Subprime Mortgages*

Subprime mortgage lending, broadly defined, relates to borrowers with poor credit histories (e.g., a FICO score below 620) and/or high leverage as measured by either debt/income (personal leverage) or loan-to-value (property leverage). Some analysts also may view certain mortgage characteristics (such as adjustable rates with near-term resets or prepayment penalties) as being subprime. Mortgages guaranteed by the Federal Housing Administration (FHA) are generally not considered subprime, although the borrower profiles are similar.

The subprime mortgage market grew rapidly in the US during the first decade of the twenty-first century—averaging about 20% of residential mortgage originations between 2004 and 2006. At the end of 2006, subprime mortgages outstanding stood at $1.2 trillion. Subprime mortgage lending then markedly receded in 2007 and virtually disappeared thereafter, as falling house prices led to a wave of subprime mortgage defaults (and associated foreclosures). By the end of 2012, subprime mortgages outstanding totaled only $475 billion. Foote, Gerardi, Goette, and Willen (2008) and Mayer, Pence, and Sherlund (2009) provide excellent overviews of the subprime mortgage crisis.

Subprime mortgage lending acts to expand the pool of potential homeowners and helped to lead the US to a record homeownership rate in 2004 of 69.2%—even in the face of declining housing affordability in many areas of the country. On the other hand, subprime mortgages typically come with more onerous terms, such as higher interest rates and prepayment penalties. This led to some concern that subprime lending can be "predatory" in nature, especially since lower-income and/or minority households are much more likely to have subprime mortgages. In the years leading up to the crisis, many state and local governments enacted predatory lending laws that restricted certain lending practices. Post-crisis, the Dodd–Frank Act created a new Consumer Financial Protection Bureau and required the regulator to establish the definition of a "qualified mortgage" (QM), which requires the lender to verify a borrower's ability to pay and to have limited up-front fees and points and forbids the lender from including contract features such as interest-only payments, negative amortization, balloon payments, and most prepayment penalties. Non-QMs face much higher legal risks if the borrower can demonstrate that the mortgage was originated without regard to the borrower's ability to repay.

Some research has sought to explain the existence and efficiency of the subprime mortgage market. Crews-Cutts and Van Order (2005) explain various stylized facts pertaining to subprime loan pricing and performance in the context of financial contracting theory. Chinloy and Macdonald (2005) discuss how the subprime market helps to

in this chapter)—helped reduce imperfections in mortgage lending. To support this claim, the authors demonstrate that the links between future household incomes and current home purchases became substantially tighter between 1970 and 2001.

complete the credit supply schedule and therefore enhance social welfare, while Nichols, Pennington-Cross, and Yezer (2005) explain why prime and subprime mortgage markets are distinct and not continuous. More recent research has focused on the importance of rising home prices in facilitating subprime mortgage financing (e.g., Goetzmann, Peng, and Yen, 2012; Bhardwaj and Sengupta, 2012; and Brueckner, Calem, and Nakamura 2012).

Other papers have documented the characteristics of subprime borrowers and mortgages. Lax et al. (2004) find that, relative to prime borrowers, subprime borrowers are more likely to have poor credit, lower incomes, less education, and belong to minority groups. Chomsisengphet and Pennington-Cross (2006) provide several stylized facts about subprime mortgage loans over time, including borrower credit quality, interest rates, down payment requirements, and the presence of prepayment penalties. Other papers look at the geographic distribution of subprime borrowers (Calem, Gillen, and Wachter, 2004; Mayer and Pence, 2008) and the incidence of subprime mortgage features (Farris and Richardson, 2004; Rose, 2013). Finally, there are a number of papers that study how local predatory lending laws affect subprime mortgage credit supply: Elliehausen and Staten, (2004); Harvey and Nigro, (2003, 2004); Quercia, Stegman, and Davis, (2004); and Ho and Pennington-Cross, (2006).

Another strand of research studied subprime loan termination by jointly estimating empirical models of prepayment and default (e.g., Alexander et al. 2002; Pennington-Cross, 2003; Danis and Pennington-Cross, 2005; Ho and Pennington-Cross, 2006b, 2010; and Pennington-Cross and Chomsisengphet, 2007). Related papers have sought to explain the length of time between delinquency and default (Danis and Pennington-Cross, 2008); time in foreclosure (Capozza and Thomson, 2006; Pennington-Cross, 2006; Pennington-Cross, 2010); and loss given default (Capozza and Thomson, 2005).

Since the onset of the subprime mortgage crisis, research has attempted to identify various sources of the problem. Mayer, Pence, and Sherlund (2009) and Gerardi et al. (2008) among others point to a significant increase in borrower leverage during the mid-2000s, as measured by combined loan-to-value (CLTV) ratios, which was soon followed by falling house prices.[6] CLTV is important because economic theory predicts that borrowers with positive home equity will not default. That is, distressed borrowers with positive equity could borrow against this equity or simply sell the home and pocket any net proceeds. Hence, negative equity (owing more than the home is worth) is a *necessary condition* for mortgage default (see, for example, Foote, Gerardi, and Willen, 2008). As US house prices declined in many parts of the US during 2007 and 2008, an increasing number of homeowners found themselves with negative equity in their homes. Many borrowers facing negative income shocks—especially financially fragile subprime mortgage borrowers—subsequently defaulted on their loans.

But how did such financially fragile borrowers obtain mortgage financing in the first place? Some research attention has been paid to the evolution of subprime mortgage underwriting standards. In particular, the focus has been on declining underwriting standards as measured by observable characteristics (e.g. Gerardi et al. 2008; Mayer, Pence, and

---

[6] Unfortunately, only the loan-to-value ratio of the first lien mortgage at origination is typically observed in commercially available mortgage data. Second mortgages, such as home equity loans and home equity lines of credit, were unreported and became increasingly popular in the US during the housing boom.

Sherlund, 2009) or by increased forecast errors from empirical default models (Demyanyk and Van Hemert, 2011; An et al. 2012). The declining underwriting standards likely emanated from the sizeable rise in US house prices between 2001 and 2006, which likely masked much of the weakness.

11.3.2 Services

Recent service innovations primarily relate to enhanced account access and new methods of payment—each of which better meets consumer demands for convenience and ease.[7] Automated teller machines (ATMs), which were introduced in the early 1970s and diffused rapidly through the 1980s, significantly enhanced retail bank account access and value by providing customers with around-the-clock access to funds. ATM cards were then largely replaced through the 1980s and 1990s by debit cards, which bundle ATM access with the ability to make payment from a bank account at the point-of-sale. Over the past two decades, remote access has migrated from the telephone to the personal computer and most recently to the mobile smart phone. Online banking, which allows customers to monitor accounts and originate payments using "electronic bill payment," is now widely used. Stored-value, or prepaid, cards have also become ubiquitous.[8]

11.3.2.1 Debit Cards

Debit cards are essentially "pay-now" instruments linked to a checking account whereby transactions can happen either instantaneously using online (PIN-based) methods or in the near future with offline (signature-based) methods. Consumers typically have the choice of using online or offline methods, and their selection often hinges on the respective benefits: Online debit allows the cardholder also to withdraw cash at the point-of-sale, and offline provides float. According to ATM & Debit News, there were approximately 40.8 billion debit transactions in the US during 2012 that totaled almost $1.6 trillion.

Much of the research that pertains to debit cards relates to identifying the most likely users of this payment instrument. Such demand-side explorations have been conducted individually as well as jointly across multiple payment options. Stavins (2001), for example, uses data from the 1998 Survey of Consumer Finances (SCF) and finds that debit usage is positively related to educational attainment, homeownership status, marital status, business ownership, and being a white collar worker; and is negatively related to age and net worth. Klee (2006) extends this analysis to consider the 1995, 1998, and 2001 SCFs and reports a secular increase in adoption driven by similar demographic factors.[9] Additional US evidence is

---

[7] The discussion in this section complements the overview that is found in Chapter 17 ("Payments and Payment Systems") by David Humphrey in this volume.

[8] Other small-dollar payment options have emerged in recent years, such as smart cards and PayPal. However, we do not discuss these further due to their limited penetration and a dearth of research relating to "electronic cash."

[9] See also Anguelov, Hilgert, and Hogarth (2004) for the relevant statistics that pertain to these surveys. Also, using data across four SCFs, Zinman (2009) reports that, other things being equal, the choice of using debit cards is positively related to being a "revolver" of credit card balances (as opposed to paying off such balances each month).

provided by: Mantel and McHugh (2001), who use survey data from Vantis International; by Hayashi and Klee (2003), who use data from a 2001 survey conducted by Dove Consulting; as well as by Borzekowski and Kiser (2008) and Borzekowski, Kiser, and Ahmed (2008), who use 2004 data from the Michigan Surveys of Consumers.

Some additional analysis by Hayashi and Klee (2003) studied the circumstances under which consumers are likely to use debit cards and found that these are more often used at grocery stores and gas stations than at restaurants. Related to this, the authors also find that debit card usage is positively related to the incidence of self-service transactions.

11.3.2.2 Online Banking

As households and firms rapidly adopted Internet access during the late 1990s, commercial banks established an online presence. According to DeYoung (2005), the first bank websites were launched in 1995; and by 2002 nearly one-half of all US banks and thrifts operated transactional websites. As of 2012, bank call report data suggests that 90.0% of commercial banks offer transactional websites (and these banks control 95.3% of commercial bank deposits).

The primary line of research that relates to online banking has been aimed at understanding the determinants of bank adoption and how the technology has affected bank performance. In terms of online adoption, Furst, Lang, and Nolle (2002) find that US national banks (by the end of the third quarter of 1999) were more likely to offer transactional websites if they were: larger, younger, affiliated with a holding company, located in an urban area, and had higher fixed expenses and non-interest income. Sullivan (2000) and Courchane, Nickerson, and Sullivan (2002), who use smaller samples, present evidence that is consistent with these findings.

Similar analysis is provided by Hernández-Murillo, Llobet, and Fuentes (2010), who look at Internet banking adoption at US banks during the mid-2000s. These authors confirm many of the previous findings, but also that transactional website adoption is positively related to county-level demographics (median household income, education, Internet access) and market concentration and negatively related to additional bank characteristics (branching intensity, ratio of capital-to-total assets, and nonperforming loans). Further, Dow (2007) analyzes data for US credit unions and finds that online banking adoption is related to institution size and having a lower proportion of nonperforming loans. On the flip side, Goddard, McKillop, and Wilson (2008, 2009) find that credit unions that do not provide transactional websites are more likely to fail and/or be acquired.

With respect to online bank performance, DeYoung, Lang, and Nolle (2007) report that Internet adoption improved US community bank profitability—primarily through deposit-related charges. In a related study, Hernando and Nieto (2007) find that, over time, online banking was associated with lower costs and higher profitability for a sample of Spanish banks. Both papers conclude that the Internet channel is a complement to—rather than a substitute for—physical bank branches. Additional evidence is offered by Ciciretti, Hasan, and Zazzara (2009), who also find that Italian banks that offered Internet-related services had higher profitability (and stock returns) relative to their peers. However, a contemporaneous study of US credit unions found no relationship between online banking adoption and profitability, but did find significantly higher operating expenses (Dandapani, Karels, and Lawrence, 2008).

Other studies look at the demand-side for online banking services. Mantel (2000) studies the demographic characteristics of users of electronic/online bill payment. Among other things, the author finds that electronic bill payers tend to be: older, female, higher income, and homeowners. Bauer and Hein (2006), who analyze data from the Survey of Consumer Finances, find that younger customers and those with previous experience with remote banking technologies are more likely to use online banking.

11.3.2.3 *Prepaid Cards*

As the name implies, prepaid cards are instruments whereby cardholders "pay early" and set aside funds in advance for future purchases of goods and services. (By contrast, debit cards are "pay-now", and credit cards are "pay later".) The monetary value of the prepaid card resides either on the card or at a remote database.

Prepaid cards can be generally delineated as either "closed" systems (e.g., a retailer-specific gift card, such as a card for Macy's or Best Buy) or "open" systems (e.g., a payment-network branded card, such as Visa or MasterCard). Closed-system prepaid cards have also been effective as a cash substitute on university campuses, as well as for mass transit systems and retailers. Open-card systems, while less effective in some of these contexts to date, may ultimately have greater promise owing to their wider functionality, which more resembles traditional debit and credit cards. For example, these prepaid cards can be used to withdraw money from an ATM and to make purchases or pay bills in person, over the phone, or online. Cheney and Rhine (2006) discuss two types of open-system prepaid programs—payroll cards and general spending reloadable cards—each of which provides functions that are similar to deposit accounts. Payroll cards, which were first introduced in 2001, are particularly attractive for unbanked workers and their employers because of lower transactions costs (McGrath, 2005). Such cards have also been used to deliver welfare benefits and disaster relief. Reloadable cards, which are typically offered through grocery stores and convenience stores, have most often been promoted to immigrants for remittances, to travelers, or to parents for teen purchases. Wilshusen et al. (2012) use transactions-level data to summarize consumers' use of prepaid cards.

Some descriptive research on prepaid cards is focused on certain public policy issues that are related to this payments medium. Furletti and Smith (2005) note the lack of state and federal consumer protections, but mention that card associations and bank-issuers have voluntarily extended some safeguards in practice, such as "zero liability" and "charge-back" provisions. Keitel (2008) looks more broadly at consumer protections for prepaid gift cards by studying state statutes and Federal Trade Commission rulings. Sienkiewicz (2007) discusses the potential for prepaid cards to be used in money laundering schemes. The author notes instances with offshore card issuance and the ability to access cash at ATMs as being the most vulnerable to illicit activity.

11.3.3 Production Processes

The past 30 years have witnessed important changes in banks' production processes. The use of electronic transmission of bank-to-bank retail payments, which had modest beginnings in the 1970s, has exploded owing to greater retail acceptance, online banking, and check conversion. In terms of intermediation, there has been a steady movement toward a reliance on statistical models. For example, credit scoring has been increasingly used to substitute for manual underwriting—and has been extended even into relationship-oriented products, such as small business loans. Similar credit risk measurement models are also used when creating structured financial products through "securitization". Statistical modeling has also become central in the overall risk management processes at banks through portfolio stress-testing and Value at Risk (VaR) models—each of which is geared primarily to evaluating portfolio value in the face of significant changes in macro-financial environments.

11.3.3.1 Automated Clearinghouse (ACH)

An automated clearinghouse (ACH) is an electronic funds transfer network that connects banks and is primarily used for recurring, small-dollar payments. While several ACH networks emerged in the 1970s, volumes grew only modestly through the 1980s, with the networks' being used almost exclusively for direct payroll deposits. Over the past 20 years, however, consolidation has occurred, and volumes have soared. According to the National Automated Clearing House Association, the number of ACH payments has increased from just under 2 billion in 1991 to 21 billion in 2012. (Over the same timeframe, the dollar value of ACH items transmitted rose from $6.9 trillion to $36.9 trillion.) These payments, in turn, are now made through only two ACH networks: the New York Clearinghouse's Electronic Payments Network, and the Federal Reserve System's FedACH.

The modest literature on ACH networks has been aimed at understanding supply and demand conditions in support of FedACH pricing policies. Bauer and Hancock (1995) found that over the 1979–94 period the cost of processing an ACH item fell dramatically owing to scale economies, technological change, and lower input prices. Using a much smaller sample, Bauer and Ferrier (1996) also found support for the existence of ACH scale economies as well as significant allocative inefficiencies. Stavins and Bauer (1999), on the other hand, estimated ACH demand elasticities by exploiting FedACH price changes over time—finding ACH demand to be highly inelastic.

The two most recent papers studied network externalities for ACH. Gowrisankaran and Stavins (2004) find support for significant network externalities, which they ascribe to technological advancement, peer-group effects, economies of scale, and market power. Ackerberg and Gowrisankaran (2006) identify large fixed costs of bank adoption as the barrier to greater use of ACH transactions and thus to society's capturing the accompanying potential cost savings.

11.3.3.2 Small Business Credit Scoring

Banks use a number of different lending technologies to lend to informationally opaque small businesses (for a summary of these technologies, see Berger and Udell, 2006). One new technology that was introduced in the 1990s and continues to evolve is small business credit scoring (SBCS). This technology involves analyzing consumer data about the owner of the firm and combining it with relatively limited data about the firm itself using statistical methods to predict future credit performance. Credit scores had long been pervasive in consumer credit markets (e.g., mortgages, credit cards, and automobile credits)—and resulted in widely available, low-cost, commoditized credits that are often packaged and sold into secondary markets.

The empirical literature that has studied SBCS has focused on the determinants of bank adoption and diffusion of this technology, as well as on how SBCS has affected credit availability. Two studies have statistically examined the determinants of the probability and timing of large US banks' adoption of SBCS. Frame, Srinivasan, and Woosley (2001) and Akhavein, Frame, and White (2005) both find an important role for size and organizational structure in the adoption decision: Larger banking organizations with fewer bank charters and more bank branches were more likely to adopt and also to adopt sooner. This suggests that large banks with a more "centralized" structure were more likely to adopt SBCS. While the use of the SBCS technology still appears to be mostly limited to large banking organizations, one recent study suggests that small banks now often make use of the consumer credit score of the principal owner of the firm (Berger, Cowan, and Frame, 2007).

Several studies have focused on the relationship between SBCS adoption and credit availability. Three studies documented increases in the quantity of lending (Frame, Srinivasan, and Woosley, 2001; Frame, Padhi, and Woosley, 2004; Berger, Frame, and Miller, 2005). One found evidence that is consistent with more lending to relatively opaque, risky borrowers (Berger, Frame, and Miller, 2005); another with increased lending within low-income as well as high-income areas (Frame, Padhi, and Woosley, 2004); and another with lending over greater distances (DeYoung et al. 2011). In instances in which SBCS is used in conjunction with other lending technologies to reduce information asymmetries, it is also shown to result in increased loan maturity (Berger, Espinosa-Vega, et al. 2005) and reduced collateral requirements (Berger and Espinosa-Vega, et al. 2011).

11.3.3.3 Asset Securitization

Asset securitization refers to the process by which nontraded assets are transformed into tradable "asset-backed securities" (ABS) by repackaging cashflows.[10] Today, in the US, securitization is widely used by large originators of retail credit—specifically mortgages, credit cards, and automobile loans. As of year end 2012, federally sponsored mortgage pools and privately arranged ABS issues (including private-label mortgage-backed securities) totaled almost $8.0 trillion of the $56.9 trillion in US credit market debt outstanding.

A large number of books and articles have been devoted to the process of securitization and the analytics required to structure and value the resulting assets. As a result, we provide only a cursory review of the issues. Generally speaking, asset securitization involves several steps. The first is the sale of a pool of financial assets to a legally separate ("bankruptcy remote") trust against which liabilities (the ABS) are issued.[11] In this way, the original holder of the assets

---

[10] The Government National Mortgage Association ("Ginnie Mae") was the first "modern" issuer of ABS—residential mortgage-backed securities (RMBS)—in 1970. The Federal Home Loan Mortgage Corporation ("Freddie Mac") was a "fast second," with its RMBS appearing in 1971. As Goetzmann and Newman (2010) have documented, commercial mortgages were securitized at least as early as the 1920s, and some of these commercial mortgages appear to have included multi-family (i.e., apartment) residential structures; see also Snowden (2010a). And a form of securitization appears to have been attempted for farm mortgages in the late nineteenth century (Snowden, 2010b).

[11] This discussion implicitly assumes a "liquidating pool" of assets with fixed (but prepayable) terms to maturity. Some assets, like credit cards, are placed into "revolving pools," which allow for the ex post addition of assets, since these loans have no fixed payment amount or term.

receives a cash payment, thereby liquefying its position. However, since the seller presumably has better information about the assets than does the buyer of the ABS (who thus faces the potential for "adverse selection"), the buyer requires some form of "credit enhancement" in the form of third-party guarantees, overcollateralization, or the creation of subordinate claims through "tranching."[12] While the first two forms of credit enhancement are straightforward, the last one requires some explanation.

Tranching involves the creation of two or more security types that are defined by their priority of claims.[13] The original seller often retains the most junior ("equity") security—the one with the lowest payment priority (and thus the first absorption of losses)—as a way of assuaging skeptical investors about the quality of the assets in the pool.[14] However, sophisticated investors—such as hedge funds—sometimes also purchase and hold such positions.[15]

In addition to providing liquidity, securitization may be socially beneficial insofar as it allows for lower-cost financing of loans: Efficiencies from greater specialization can arise when (through securitization) origination, funding, and servicing are separated (as compared with the "traditional" vertically integrated structure of these functions within a depository institution); also, the separation of funding allows a wider array of investors to access mortgage payment streams more directly, rather than being confined to indirect access through deposits or other investments in depository institutions. In addition, securitization may also hold private benefits for depository institutions that seek to manage their required capital positions.[16] Thomas (2001) presents empirical evidence that the stockholders of certain ABS issuers benefit from securitization—that is, first-time issuers, large issuers, frequent issuers, lower-quality issuers, and bank-issuers.[17]

Some analysts have pointed to incentive conflicts inherent in securitization as a key reason for the magnification of the recent financial crisis. Ashcraft and Schuermann (2008) identify seven key informational frictions that arise in the subprime securitization model; discuss how market participants work to minimize such frictions; and speculate as to how this process broke down. One particular conflict was that of mortgage originators' no

---

[12] Investors may also believe that deal sponsors are additionally providing some level of implicit recourse as a method to maintain their reputation in the market. Higgins and Mason (2004) and Gorton and Souleles (2005) provide empirical evidence consistent with this conjecture—higher-rated sponsors execute ABS deals at tighter spreads.

[13] The case of two securities (senior and junior) is generally sufficient to make the stylized points about securitization, but in practice much more granular structures are observed.

[14] This is consistent with important theoretical work in financial economics by Leland and Pyle (1977) and Myers and Majluf (1984) that is related to capital structure more generally. See DeMarzo and Duffie (1999) and DeMarzo (2005) for similar discussions that are specific to asset-backed securities.

[15] Boot and Thakor (1993) and Plantin (2004) provide theoretical explanations for the sale of tranched securities to investors of differing financial sophistication.

[16] For example, as Frame and White (2005) and others have demonstrated, the ability of banks bound by risk-based capital requirements to swap residential mortgages (on which there is a risk-based capital requirement of 4%) for the mortgage-backed securities (MBS) that are issued and guaranteed by Fannie Mae or Freddie Mac (on which there is a risk-based capital requirement of only 1.6%) and that contain exactly the same mortgages provides the banks with a regulatory capital arbitrage (RCA). See Jones (2000) for a more general discussion of the RCA phenomenon.

[17] Prior empirical work by Lockwood, Rutherford, and Herrera (1996) and Thomas (1999) had used subsamples of the data and had found conflicting evidence: The former paper focused on 1985 to 1992 and the latter paper on 1991 to 1996.

longer routinely holding equity tranches of their securitizations and hence having little "skin-in-the-game." The Dodd–Frank Wall Street Reform and Consumer Protection Act of 2010 now requires that loan originators hold 5% of their securitization deals (in one form or another). The law includes a carve-out exception for "qualified residential mortgages", which are meant to be extremely safe (i.e., low-risk) mortgages but which (ironically) regulators have subsequently proposed to define as encompassing almost the entire mortgage market.

11.3.3.4 Risk Management

Advances in information technology (both hardware and software) and financial theory spurred a revolution in bank risk management over the past two decades. Two popular approaches to measuring and managing financial risks are stress-testing and VaR. In either case, the idea is to identify the level of capital required for the bank to remain solvent in the face of unlikely adverse environments.

Stress-testing involves the construction of adverse scenarios for credit and/or interest rate conditions and then the valuation of assets and liabilities—and thus solvency—under these stressed circumstances.[18] These tests can be conducted assuming either one or multiple periods. Fender and Gibson (2001) provide a pre-crisis survey of stress-testing in financial institutions.

Stress tests have become increasingly important following the recent financial crisis and the formal adoption of these methods by bank supervisory authorities around the world. In the US, stress tests are carried out as part of the Federal Reserve's annual "Comprehensive Capital Assessment Review" for its largest banking organizations. These stress tests involve the creation of hypothetical near-term macroeconomic scenarios, which are then used by banking organizations as inputs into their risk measurement models to produce estimates of credit losses, income, expenses, and capital under stress. The resulting capital estimates, in turn, act as the basis for each institution's capital plan, which is required to be submitted annually to the Federal Reserve. Concurrently, the Federal Reserve applies the same macroeconomic projections to its own risk measurement models to produce independent supervisory estimates of required capital for each banking organization. These supervisory estimates, along with a qualitative assessment of the quality of the banking organization's own capital planning process, are used as the basis for evaluating the capital plan submissions.

As stress-testing has recently become a critical risk-management tool for both financial institutions and their regulators, research should be aimed at better understanding stress-test limitations and offering improvements for current practice. Pre-crisis analysis by Berkowitz (1999–2000) and Kupiec (2000) both discuss certain shortcomings of stress-testing for risk management, including whether the results of such tests will generally achieve equity capital allocations that are sufficient to stave-off default under duress. More recently, research has considered the use of empirical likelihood to generate macroeconomic scenarios (Glasserman, Kang, and Kang, 2012) and the need to expand the set

---

[18] Related stress-testing procedures are also used by some central banks as a method of evaluating financial system resiliency in the face of shocks. See, for example, Čihák (2007), Goodhart (2006), Elsinger, Lehar, and Summer (2006), and Majnoni et al. (2001).

of scenarios to other banking-sector shocks (Pritsker, 2012). Acharya, Engle, and Pierret (2013) compare capital requirements suggested by stress tests using market data to outcomes reported by US and European regulators and note deficiencies related to regulatory risk weights. Frame, Gerardi, and Willen (2013) analyze how the risk-based capital stress test for Fannie Mae and Freddie Mac failed to warn regulators of massive impending losses. Research is also being aimed at understanding the implications of the breadth and depth of supervisory disclosures—both in terms of the supervisory models and parameters ex ante (e.g., Frame, Gerardi, and Willen, 2013) and stress test results ex post (e.g., Goldstein and Sapra, 2012; Leitner and Goldstein, 2013).

VaR relies on a probabilistic approach that evaluates the return distributions of assets. In this case, a bank would define a probability level of the return distribution (e.g., 99.9%) as an outer limit of exposure and then calculate the economic losses that are associated with that point on the distribution. Because of the focus on return distributions, VaR has been applied most widely to trading portfolios, which are populated by readily marketable securities. Nevertheless, the principles involved have also been applied to credit portfolios more generally. A large number of books and articles have been devoted to VaR—primarily centered on the appropriate characterization of return distributions for various assets and the use of VaR principles in the Basel II Capital Accord.

11.3.4 Organizational Forms

New bank organizational forms have emerged in the United States over the past few decades. Securities affiliates (so-called "Section 20" subsidiaries or the creation of "financial holding companies") for very large banks and Subchapter S status for very small banks, were the byproduct of regulatory/legal evolution.[19] Indeed, only one new organizational form, the Internet-only (or Internet-primary) bank, arose from technological change. These institutions, which quickly emerged and disappeared, may represent an interesting laboratory for the study of "failed" financial innovations. We believe that understanding such experimental failures may hold important insights for understanding the keys to successful financial innovations.

The dramatic increase in individuals' use of the Internet in the 1990s created the possibility of a new organizational form in banking: the Internet-only (Internet-primary) bank. According to Delgado, Hernando, and Nieto (2007), as of mid-year 2002, there were some 35 Internet-only banks operating in Europe and another 20 in the US. However, in Europe, virtually all of these banks were affiliated with existing institutions, while in the US they tended to be de novo operations. This may explain why most/all of the US Internet-only

---

[19] Another important, but short-lived, organizational innovation driven by regulation was the structured investment vehicle (SIV). This was an entity sponsored by a large financial institution that typically held relatively long-term assets and issued relatively short-term liabilities and held little or no capital (but with some understanding that the sponsor would provide liquidity or capital infusions, if necessary. Many SIVs became distressed during the financial crisis and were repatriated onto sponsor balance sheets. Contemporaneous changes to accounting standards forced remaining entities to be consolidated. See Acharya, Schnabl, and Suarez (2013) for an analysis of SIV performance during the crisis.

banks have disappeared (through acquisition, liquidation, or closure) or established a physical presence to supplement their Internet base. This suggests that the dominant technology is one of "clicks and mortar."

DeYoung (2001, 2005) finds that, as compared with conventional de novo banks, the Internet de novo banks are less profitable due to low business volumes (fewer deposits and lower non-interest income) and high labor expenditures. However, the author also reports that the financial performance gaps narrow quickly over time due to scale effects. Relatedly, Cyree, Delcoure, and Dickens (2009) find that Internet-primary banks are larger and have lower net interest margins and loan losses. While the authors also find these institutions to be less profitable, they do find them to be more profit efficient (as measured by the distance from a best-practice frontier that involves outputs and inputs). Delgado, Hernando, and Nieto (2007) similarly find that European Internet banks demonstrate technology-based scale economies.

11.4 CONCLUSIONS

This chapter has reviewed the literature on technological change and financial innovation in banking since 1980. This quarter century has been a period of substantial change in terms of bank services and production technologies, but much less so with respect to organizational form. As this survey indicates, although much has been learned about the characteristics of users and adopters of financial innovations and the attendant welfare implications, *we still know little about how and why financial innovations are initially developed.* This remains an important area for further research.

REFERENCES

Acharya, V., Engle, R., and Pierret, D. (2013). Testing Macroprudential Stress Tests: The Risk of Regulatory Risk Weights, <http://papers.ssrn.com/sol3/papers.cfm?abstract_id=2254221.>.

Acharya, V., Schnabl P., and Suarez, G. (2013). Securitization Without Risk Transfer, *Journal of Financial Economics* 107(3), 515–536.

Ackerberg, D. A. and Gowrisankaran, G. (2006). Quantifying Equilibrium Network Externalities in the ACH Banking Industry, *RAND Journal of Economics* 37(3), 738–761.

Ackerman, J. (2013). Financial Innovation: Balancing Private and Public Interests. In: M. Haliassos (Ed.), *Financial Innovation: Too Much or Too Little?*, 213–230. Cambridge, MA: MIT Press.

Akhavein, J., Frame, W. S., and White, L. J. (2005). The Diffusion of Financial Innovation: An Examination of the Adoption of Small Business Credit Scoring by Large Banking Organizations, *Journal of Business* 78(2), 577–596.

Alexander, W. P., Grimshaw, S. D., McQueen, G. R., and Slade, B. A. (2002). Some Loans Are More Equal Than Others: Third-Party Originations and Defaults in the Subprime Mortgage Industry, *Real Estate Economics* 30(4), 667–697.

Allen, F. (2012). Trends in Financial Innovation and Their Welfare Impact: An Overview, *European Financial Management* 18(4), 493–514.

An, X., Deng, Y., Rosenblatt, E., and Yao, V. (2012). Model Stability and the Subprime Mortgage Crisis, *Journal of Real Estate Finance and Economics* 45(3), 545–568.

Anguelov, C. E., Hilgert, M. A., and Hogarth, J. M. (2004). US Consumers and Electronic Banking, 1995-2003, *Federal Reserve Bulletin* 90(1), 1–18.

Ashcraft, A. B. and Schuermann, T. (2008). *Understanding the Securitization of Subprime Mortgage Credit*, Federal Reserve Bank of New York Staff Study No. 318.

Bauer, K. and Hein, S. (2006). The Effect of Heterogeneous Risk on the Early Adoption of Internet Banking Technologies, *Journal of Banking & Finance* 20(6), 1713–1725.

Bauer, P. W. and Ferrier, G. D. (1996). Scale Economies, Cost Efficiencies, and Technological Change in Federal Reserve Payment Processing, *Journal of Money, Credit, and Banking* 28(4), 1004–1039.

Bauer, P. W. and Hancock, D. (1995). Scale Economies and Technological Change in Federal Reserve ACH Payment Processing, *Federal Reserve Bank of Cleveland Economic Review* Third Quarter, 14–29.

Beck, T., Chen, T., Lin, C., and Song, F. M. (2012). Financial Innovation: The Bright and the Dark Sides. SSRN Working Paper, <http://papers.ssrn.com/sol3/papers.cfm?abstract_id=1991216.>.

Ben-Horim, M. and Silber, W. L. (1977). Financial Innovation: A Linear Programming Approach, *Journal of Banking & Finance* 1(3), 277–296.

Berger, A. N. (2003). The Economic Effects of Technological Progress: Evidence from the Banking Industry, *Journal of Money, Credit, and Banking* 35(2), 141–176.

Berger, A. N., Cowan, A., and Frame, W. S. (2007). The Surprising Use of Credit Scoring in Small Business Lending by "Community Banks" and the Attendant Effects on Credit Availability, Risk, and Profitability, *Journal of Financial Services Research* 39(1), 1–17.

Berger, A. N., Espinosa-Vega, M., Frame, W. S., and Miller, N. (2005). Debt Maturity, Risk, and Asymmetric Information, *Journal of Finance* 60(6), 2895–2923.

Berger, A. N., Espinosa-Vega, M., Frame, W. S., and Miller, N. (2011). Why Do Borrowers Pledge Collateral? New Empirical Evidence on the Role of Asymmetric Information, *Journal of Financial Intermediation* 20, 55–70.

Berger, A. N., Frame, W. S., and Miller, N. (2005). Credit Scoring and the Availability, Price, and Risk of Small Business Credit, *Journal of Money, Credit, and Banking* 37(2), 191–222.

Berger, A. N., Kashyap, A. K., and Scalise, J. M. (1995). The Transformation of the US Banking Industry: What a Long, Strange Trip It's Been, *Brookings Papers on Economic Activity* 2, 55–218.

Berger, A. N. and Udell, G. F. (2006). A More Complete Conceptual Framework for SME Finance, *Journal of Banking & Finance* 30(11), 2945–2966.

Berkowitz, J. (1999–2000). A Coherent Framework for Stress Testing, *Journal of Risk* 2(2), 5–15.

Bhardwaj, G. and Sengupta, R. (2012). Subprime Mortgage Design, *Journal of Banking & Finance* 36(5), 1503–1519.

Boot, A. W. A. and Thakor, A. V. (1993). Security Design, *Journal of Finance* 48(4), 1349–1378.

Borzekowski, R. and Kiser, E. (2008). The Choice at the Checkout: Quantifying Demand Across Payment Instruments, *International Journal of Industrial Organization* 26(4), 889–902.

Borzekowski, R., Kiser, E., and Ahmed, S. (2008). Consumers' Use of Debit Cards: Patterns, Preferences, and Price Response, *Journal of Money, Credit, and Banking* 40(1), 149–172.

Brueckner, J. K., Calem, P. S., and Nakamura, L. I. (2012). Subprime Mortgages and the Housing Bubble, *Journal of Urban Economics* 71(2), 230–243.

Calem, P. S., Gillen, K., and Wachter, S. (2004). The Neighborhood Distribution of Subprime Mortgage Lending, *Journal of Real Estate Finance and Economics* 29(4), 393–410.

Campbell, T. S. (1988). *Money and Capital Markets*. Glenview, IL: Scott, Foresman.

Capozza, D. R. and Thomson, T. A. (2005). Optimal Stopping and Losses on Subprime Mortgages, *Journal of Real Estate Finance and Economics* 30(2), 115–131.

Capozza, D. R. and Thomson, T. A. (2006). Subprime Transitions: Lingering or Malignant in Default? *Journal of Real Estate Finance and Economics* 33(3), 241–258.

Cheney, J. S. and Rhine, S. L. W. (2006). Prepaid Cards: An Important Innovation in Financial Services, Federal Reserve Bank of Philadelphia Payment Card Discussion Paper No. 06-07.

Chinloy, P. and Macdonald, N. (2005). Subprime Lenders and Mortgage Market Completion, *Journal of Real Estate Finance and Economics* 30(2), 153–165.

Chomsisengphet, S. and Pennington-Cross, A. (2006). The Evolution of the Subprime Mortgage Market, *Federal Reserve Bank of St. Louis Review* 88(1), 31–56.

Ciciretti, R., Hasan, I., and Zazzara, C. (2009). Do Internet Activities Add Value? Evidence from Traditional Banks, *Journal of Financial Services Research* 35(1), 81–98.

Čihák, M. (2007). Introduction to Applied Stress Testing, IMF Working Paper No. 07/59.

Cohen, W. M. (1995). Empirical Studies of Innovative Activity. In: P. Stoneman (Ed.), *Handbook of the Economics of Innovation and Technological Change*, 182–264. Cambridge: Blackwell.

Cohen, W. M. and Levin, R. C. (1989). Empirical Studies of Innovation and Market Structure. In: R. Schmalensee and R. Willig (Eds.), *Handbook of Industrial Organization*, Vol. 2, 1059–1107. Amsterdam: North-Holland.

Courchane, M., Nickerson D., and Sullivan R., (2002). Investment in Internet Banking as a Real Option: Theory and Tests, *Journal of Multinational Financial Management* 12(4), 347–363.

Crews-Cutts, A. and Van Order, R. (2005). On the Economics of Subprime Lending, *Journal of Real Estate Finance and Economics* 30(2), 167–196.

Cyree, K. B., Delcoure, N., and Dickens, R. (2009). An Examination of the Performance and Prospects for the Future of Internet-Primary Banks. *Journal of Economics & Finance* 33(2), 128–147.

Dandapani, K., Karels, G. V., and Lawrence E. R. (2008). Internet Banking Services and Credit Union Performance, *Managerial Finance* 34(6), 437–446.

Danis, M. A. and Pennington-Cross, A. (2005). A Dynamic Look at Subprime Loan Performance, *Journal of Fixed Income* 15(1), 28–39.

Danis, M. A. and Pennington-Cross, A. (2008). The Delinquency of Subprime Mortgages, *Journal of Economics and Business* 60(1–2), 67–90.

Delgado, J., Hernando, I., and Nieto, M. J. (2007). Do European Primarily Internet Banks Show Scale and Experience Efficiencies?, *European Financial Management* 13(4), 643–671.

DeMarzo, P. (2005). The Pooling and Tranching of Securities: A Model of Informed Intermediation, *Review of Financial Studies* 18(1), 1–35.

DeMarzo, P. and Duffie, D. (1999). A Liquidity-Based Model of Security Design, *Econometrica* 67(1), 65–99.

Demyanyk, Y. and Van Hemert, O. (2011). Understanding the Subprime Mortgage Crisis, *Review of Financial Studies* 24(6), 1848–1880.

DeYoung, R. (2001). The Financial Performance of Pure Play Internet Banks, *Federal Reserve Bank of Chicago Economic Perspectives* 25, 60–75.

DeYoung, R. (2005). The Performance of Internet-Based Business Models: Evidence from the Banking Industry, *Journal of Business* 78(3), 893–947.

DeYoung, R., Frame, W. S., Glennon, D., and Nigro, P. (2011). The Information Revolution and Small Business Lending: The Missing Evidence, *Journal of Financial Services Research* 39(1), 19–33.

DeYoung, R., Lang, W. W., and Nolle, D. L. (2007). How the Internet Affects Output and Performance at Community Banks, *Journal of Banking & Finance* 31(4), 1033–1060.

Dow, J. P. (2007). The Adoption of Web Banking at Credit Unions, *The Quarterly Review of Economics and Finance* 47(3), 435–448.

Elliehausen, G. and Staten, M. E. (2004). Regulation of Subprime Mortgage Products: An Analysis of North Carolina's Predatory Lending Law, *Journal of Real Estate Finance and Economics* 29(4), 411–433.

Elsinger, H., Lehar, A., and Summer, M. (2006). Using Market Information for Banking System Risk Assessment, *International Journal of Central Banking* 2(1), 137–165.

Farris, J. and Richardson, C. A. (2004). The Geography of Subprime Mortgage Prepayment Penalty Patterns, *Housing Policy Debate* 15(3), 687–714.

Fender, I. and Gibson, M. S. (2001). Stress Testing in Practice: A Survey of 43 Major Financial Institutions, *BIS Quarterly Review* June, 58–62.

Foote, C. L., Gerardi, K., Goette, L., and Willen P. S. (2008). Just the Facts: An Initial Analysis of Subprime's Role in the Housing Crisis, *Journal of Housing Economics* 17(4), 1–24.

Foote, C. L., Gerardi, K., and Willen, P. S. (2008). Negative Equity and Foreclosure: Theory and Evidence, *Journal of Urban Economics* 64(2), 234–245.

Frame, W. S., Gerardi, K., and Willen, P. S. (2013). Supervisory Stress Tests, Model Risk, and Model Disclosure: Lessons from OFHEO. Federal Reserve Bank of Atlanta Working Paper.

Frame, W. S., Padhi, M., and Woolsey, L. (2004). The Effect of Credit Scoring on Small Business Lending in Low-and Moderate-Income Areas, *Financial Review* 39(1), 35–54.

Frame, W. S., Srinivasan, A., and Woosley, L. (2001). The Effect of Credit Scoring on Small Business Lending, *Journal of Money, Credit, and Banking* 33(3), 813–825.

Frame, W. S. and White, L. J. (2004). Empirical Studies of Financial Innovation: Lots of Talk, Little Action? *Journal of Economic Literature* 42(1), 116–144.

Frame, W. S. and White, L. J. (2005). Fussing and Fuming Over Fannie and Freddie: How Much Smoke, How Much Fire? *Journal of Economic Perspectives* 19(2), 159–184.

Furletti, M. and Smith, S. (2005). The Laws, Regulations, and Industry Practices That Protect Consumers Who Use Electronic Payment Systems: ACH E-Checks and Prepaid Cards, Federal Reserve Bank of Philadelphia Payment Card Discussion Paper No. 05-04.

Furst, K., Lang, W., and Nolle, D. (2002). Internet Banking, *Journal of Financial Services Research* 22(1/2), 95–117.

Gennaioli, N., Shleifer, A., and Vishny, R. W. (2012). Neglected Risks, Financial Innovation, and Financial Fragility, *Journal of Financial Economics* 104(3), 452–468.

Gerardi, K., Lehnert, A., Sherlund, S. M., and Willen, P. S. (2008). Making Sense of the Subprime Mortgage Crisis, *Brookings Papers on Economic Activity* 39, 69–159.

Gerardi, K., Rosen, H. S., and Willen, P. S. (2012). The Impact of Deregulation and Financial Innovation on Consumers: The Case of the Mortgage Market, *Journal of Finance* 65(1), 333–360.

Glasserman, P., Kang, C., and Kang, W. (2012). Stress Scenario Selection by Empirical Likelihood, <http://papers.ssrn.com/sol3/papers.cfm?abstract_id=2101465.>.

Goddard, J., McKillop, D., and Wilson, J. O. S. (2008). Consolidation in the US Credit Union Sector: Determinants of Failure and Acquisition. SSRN Working Paper, <http://papers.ssrn.com/sol3/papers.cfm?abstract_id=1200262.>.

Goddard, J., McKillop, D., Wilson, J. O. S. (2009). Which Credit Unions Are Acquired? *Journal of Financial Services Research* 36(2–3), 231–252.

Goetzmann, W. N. and Newman, F. (2010). Securitization in the 1920s, NBER Working Paper No. 15650, <http://cid.bcrp.gob.pe/biblio/Papers/NBER/2010/enero/w15650.pdf.>

Goetzmann, W. N., Peng, L., and Yen, J. (2012). The Subprime Crisis and House Price Appreciation, *Journal of Real Estate Finance and Economics* 44(1–2), 36–66.

Goldstein, I. and Sapra, H. (2012). Should Banks' Stress Test Results Be Disclosed? An Analysis of the Costs and Benefits. Chicago Booth Working Paper.

Goodhart, C. A. E. (2006). A Framework for Assessing Financial Stability? *Journal of Banking and Finance* 30(12), 3415–3422.

Gorton, G. and Souleles, N. (2005). Special Purpose Vehicles and Securitization, National Bureau of Economic Research Working Paper No. 11190.

Gowrisankaran, G. and Stavins, J. (2004). Network Externalities and Technology Adoption: Lessons from Electronic Payments, *RAND Journal of Economics* 35(2), 260–276.

Haliassos, M. (2013). *Financial Innovation: Too Much or Too Little?* Cambridge, MA: MIT Press.

Harvey, K. D. and Nigro, P. J. (2003). How do Predatory Lending Laws Influence Mortgage Lending in Urban Areas? A Tale of Two Cities, *Journal of Real Estate Research* 25(4), 479–508.

Harvey, K. D. and Nigro, P. J. (2004). Do Predatory Lending Laws Influence Mortgage Lending? An Analysis of the North Carolina Predatory Lending Law, *Journal of Real Estate Finance and Economics* 29(4), 435–456.

Hayashi, F. and Klee, E. (2003). Technology Adoption and Consumer Payments: Evidence from Survey Data, *Review of Network Economics* 2(2), 175–190.

Henderson, B. J. and Pearson, N. D. (2011). The Dark Side of Financial Innovation: A Case Study of the Pricing of a Retail Financial Product, *Journal of Financial Economics* 100(2), 227–247.

Hernández-Murillo, R., Llobet, G., and Fuentes, R. (2010). Strategic Online Banking Adoption, *Journal of Banking & Finance* 34(7), 650–1663.

Hernando, I. and Nieto, M. J. (2007). Is the Internet Delivery Channel Changing Banks' Performance? The Case of Spanish Banks, *Journal of Banking & Finance* 31(4), 1083–1099.

Higgins, E. J. and Mason, J. R. (2004). What is the Value of Recourse to Asset-Backed Securities? A Clinical Study of Credit Card Banks, *Journal of Banking & Finance* 28(4), 875–899.

Ho, G. and Pennington-Cross, A. (2006a). The Impact of Local Predatory Lending Laws on the Flow of Subprime Credit, *Journal of Urban Economics* 60(2), 210–228.

Ho, G. and Pennington-Cross, A. (2006b). Loan Servicer Heterogeneity and the Termination of Subprime Mortgages, Federal Reserve Bank of St. Louis Working Paper No. 2006-24.

Ho, G. and Pennington-Cross, A. (2010). The Termination of Subprime Hybrid Fixed-Rate Mortgages, *Real Estate Economics* 38(3), 399–426.

Jones, D. (2000). Emerging Problems with the Basel Capital Accord: Regulatory Capital Arbitrage and Related Issues, *Journal of Banking & Finance* 24(1), 35–58.

Kane, E. J. (1981). Accelerating Inflation, Technological Innovation, and the Decreasing Effectiveness of Banking Regulation, *Journal of Finance* 36(2), 355–367.

Kane, E. J. (2012). The Inevitability of Shadowy Banking. SSRN Working Paper, <http://papers.ssrn.com/sol3/papers.cfm?abstract_id=2026229.>

Keitel, P. L. (2008). The Laws, Regulations, Guidelines, and Industry Practices That Protect Consumers That Use Gift Cards. SSRN Working Paper, <http://papers.ssrn.com/sol3/papers.cfm?abstract_id=1266789.>.

Klee, E. (2006). Families' Use of Payment Instruments During a Decade of Change in the US Payment System, Federal Reserve Board, Finance and Economics Discussion Series No. 2006-01.

Krugman, P. R. (2007). Innovating Our Way to Financial Crisis, *New York Times* December 3, <http://www.nytimes.com/2007/12/03/opinion/03krugman.html?_r=0.>.

Kupiec, P. H. (2000). Stress Tests and Risk Capital, *Journal of Risk* 2(4), 27–39.

Lax, H, Manti, M., Raca, P., and Zorn, P. (2004). Subprime Lending: An Investigation of Economic Efficiency, *Housing Policy Debate* 15(3), 533–571.

Leitner Y. and Goldstein, I. (2013). Stress Tests and Information Disclosure, Federal Reserve Bank of Philadelphia Working Paper Nos. 13–26.

Leland, H. E. and Pyle, D. H. (1977). Informational Asymmetries, Financial Structure, and Financial Intermediation, *Journal of Finance* 32(2), 371–387.

Lerner, J. (2002). Where Does State Street Lead? A First Look at Finance Patents, 1971–2000, *Journal of Finance* 57(2), 901–930.

Lerner, J (2006). The New New Financial Thing: The Origins of Financial Innovations, *Journal of Financial Economics* 79(2), 223–255.

Lerner, J. and Tufano, P. (2011). The Consequences of Financial Innovation: A Counterfactual Research Agenda, *Annual Review of Financial Economics* 3(1), 41–85.

Levine, R. (1997). Financial Development and Economic Growth: Views and Agenda, *Journal of Economic Literature* 35(2), 688–726.

Lockwood L. J., Rutherford, R. C., and Herrera, M. J. (1996). Wealth Effects of Asset Securitization, *Journal of Banking & Finance* 20(1), 151–164.

Majnoni, G., Martinez-Peria, M. S., Blaschke, W., and Jones, M. T. (2001). Stress Testing of Financial Systems: An Overview of Issues, Methodologies, and FSAP Experiences, IMF Working Paper No. 01/88.

Mantel, B. (2000). Why Do Consumers Pay Bills Electronically? An Empirical Analysis, *Federal Reserve Bank of Chicago Economic Perspectives* Fourth Quarter, 32–47.

Mantel, B. and McHugh, T. (2001). Competition and Innovation in the Consumer E-Payments Market? Considering Demand, Supply, and Public Policy Issues, Federal Reserve Bank of Chicago, Emerging Payments Occasional Working Paper No. EPS-2001-4.

Mayer, C. and Pence, K. (2008). Subprime Mortgages: What, Where, and to Whom?, Federal Reserve Board Working Paper No. 2008–29.

Mayer, C., Pence, K., and Sherlund, S. (2009). The Rise in Mortgage Defaults, *Journal of Economic Perspectives* 23(1), 27–50.

McGrath, J. C. (2005). The Cost Effectiveness of Stored Value Cards for Unbanked Consumers, Federal Reserve Bank of Philadelphia Payment Card Discussion Paper No. 05-06.

Merton, R. C. (1992). Financial Innovation and Economic Performance, *Journal of Applied Corporate Finance* 4(4), 12–22.

Merton, R. C. (1995). Financial Innovation and the Management and Regulation of Financial Institutions, *Journal of Banking & Finance* 19(3–4), 461–481.

Miller, M. H. (1986). Financial Innovation: The Last Twenty Years and the Next, *Journal of Financial and Quantitative Analysis* 21(4), 459–471.

Miller, M. H. (1992). Financial Innovation: Achievements and Prospects, *Journal of Applied Corporate Finance* 4(4), 4–12.

Molyneux, P. and Shamroukh, N. (1999). *Financial Innovation*. New York: John Wiley & Sons.

Myers, S. C. and Majluf, N. S. (1984). Corporate Financing and Investment Decisions When Firms Have Information That Investors Do Not Have, *Journal of Financial Economics* 13(2), 187–221.

Nichols, J., Pennington-Cross, A., and Yezer, A. (2005). Borrower Self-Selection, Underwriting Costs, and Subprime Mortgage Credit Supply, *Journal of Real Estate Finance and Economics* 30(2), 197–219.

Pennington-Cross, A. (2003). Credit History and the Performance of Prime and Subprime Mortgages, *Journal of Real Estate Finance and Economics* 27(3), 279–301.

Pennington-Cross, A. (2006). The Value of Foreclosed Property, *Journal of Real Estate Research* 28(2), 193–214.

Pennington-Cross, A. (2010). The Duration of Foreclosures in the Subprime Mortgage Market: A Competing Risks Model with Mixing, *The Journal of Real Estate Finance and Economics* 40, 109–129.

Pennington-Cross, A. and Chomsisengphet, S. (2007). Subprime Refinancing: Equity Extraction and Mortgage Termination, *Real Estate Economics* 35(2), 233–263.

Plantin, G. (2004). Tranching, <http://ssrn.com/abstract=650839.>.

Pritsker, M. (2012). Enhanced Stress Testing and Financial Stability, <http://papers.ssrn.com/sol3/papers.cfm?abstract_id=2082994.>.

Quercia, R. G., Stegman, M. A., and Davis, W. R. (2004). Assessing the Impact of North Carolina's Predatory Lending Law, *Housing Policy Debate* 15(3), 573–601.

Rose, M. J. (2013). Geographic Variation in Subprime Loan Features, Foreclosures, and Prepayments, *Review of Economics and Statistics* 95(2), 563–590.

Sienkiewicz, S. (2007). Prepaid Cards: Vulnerable to Money Laundering?, Federal Reserve Bank of Philadelphia Payment Card Discussion Paper No. 07-02.

Smith, S. J. (2013). Crisis and Intervention in the Housing Economy: A Tale of Three Markets. In: M. Haliassos (Ed.), *Financial Innovation: Too Much or Too Little?*, 71–10. Cambridge, MA: MIT Press.

Snowden, K. A. (2010a). The Anatomy of a Residential Mortgage Crisis: A Look Back to the 1930s. In: L. E. Mitchell and A. E. Wilmarth Jr. (Eds.), *The Panic of 2008: Causes, Consequences, and Implications for Reform*, 51–74. Northampton, MA: Edward Elgar Publishing.

Snowden, K. A. (2010b). Covered Farm Mortgage Bonds in the Late Nineteenth Century US, *Journal of Economic History* 70(4), 783–812.

Stavins, J. (2001). Effect of Consumer Characteristics on the Use of Payment Instruments, *Federal Reserve Bank of Boston New England Economic Review* 3, 19–31.

Stavins, J. and Bauer, P. W. (1999). The Effect of Pricing on Demand and Revenue in Federal Reserve ACH Payment Processing, *Journal of Financial Services Research* 16(1), 27–45.

Sullivan, R. J. (2000). How Has the Adoption of Internet Banking Affected Performance and Risk in Banks?, Federal Reserve Bank of Kansas City, *Financial Industry Perspectives* December, 1–16.

Thakor, A. (2012). Incentives to Innovate and Financial Crises, *Journal of Financial Economics* 103(1), 130–148.

Thomas, H. (1999). A Preliminary Look at the Gains From Asset Securitization, *Journal of International Financial Markets, Institutions, and Money* 9(3), 321–333.

Thomas, H. (2001). The Effect of Asset Securitization on Seller Claimants, *Journal of Financial Intermediation* 10(3/4), 306–330.

Tufano, P. (2003). Financial Innovation. In: G. M. Constantinides, M. Harris, and R. Stulz (Eds.), *Handbook of the Economics of Finance: Volume 1A Corporate Finance*, 307–335. Amsterdam: North Holland.

Van Horne, J. C. (1980). Of Financial Innovations and Excesses, *Journal of Finance* 40(3), 621–636.

Volcker, P. A. (2009). Paul Volcker: Think More Boldly, *Wall Street Journal* December 14, 2009, <http://online.wsj.com/article/SB10001424052748704825504574586330960597134.html.>.

Wilshusen, S. M., Hunt, R. M., van Opstal, J., and Schneider, R. (2012). Consumers' Use of Prepaid Cards: A Transaction-Based Analysis, Federal Reserve Bank of Philadelphia Payment Card Discussion Paper No. 12-02.

Zinman, J. (2009). Debit or Credit?, *Journal of Banking & Finance* 33(2), 358–366.

CHAPTER 12

....

SMALL BUSINESS LENDING BY BANKS

Lending Technologies and the Effects of Banking Industry Consolidation and Technological Change*

....

ALLEN N. BERGER

12.1 INTRODUCTION

....

SMALL businesses are engines of growth in the modern economy and bank lending provides much of the fuel for this growth. Banks provide 57% of debt financing to US small businesses, according to the last Survey of Small Business Finance (SSBF) in 2003, and banks also provide critical funding to recent startups according to the Kaufman Firm Survey (Robb and Robinson, 2014). Small business lending differs from lending to large corporations because small businesses are generally much more informationally opaque, lacking certified audited financial statements, and market prices for traded equity or debt. As a result of this opacity, small firms often face significant difficulties in accessing funding for positive net present value projects.

These difficulties are recognized by the US Small Business Administration (SBA), whose 7(a) Loan Program is designed to help eligible small businesses receive credit financing when they cannot obtain "credit elsewhere." The Program provides financing for general business purposes through guaranties of loans made by about 4,500 participating lenders. In fiscal year 2012, 44,377 such loans were approved for $15.2 billion, bringing the total

---

  * The author thanks Lamont Black, Ken Brevoort, Nate Miller, Phil Molyneux, Raluca Roman, Herman Saheruddin, Greg Udell, John Wilson, and John Wolken for helpful comments and suggestions.

outstanding unpaid principal balances to $59.4 billion.[1] In some cases, the guaranteed loans are securitized.

The difficulties in obtaining credit by small businesses appear to have worsened during the financial crisis of 2007–09. To illustrate, consider the Thomson Reuters/ PayNet Small Business Lending Index, which measures the volume of new US small business loans monthly since January 2005 and is normalized at a value of 100 that month. The index peaked at a value of 131.7 in January 2007 and fell to a minimum of 66.0 in May 2009, and did not rise back to 100 until August 2011, and stood at 111.0 as of February 2014.[2] Consistent with this, DeYoung, Gron, Torna, and Winton (2014) find significant decreases in small business lending by community banks during the crisis. It is not known, however, how much of the decline in credit during the crisis was due to supply versus demand reductions. Consistent with a decrease in supply were reports of small business owners' difficulty in obtaining access to credit over the crisis period.[3] Perhaps in response to some of these problems, the Small Business Jobs Act of 2010 was passed and signed into law in September 2010. It expanded the SBA 7(a) program to make bigger loans (from $2 million to $5 million) and created the Small Business Lending Fund (SBLF), which is designed to provide capital to qualified community banks and community development loan funds to encourage small business lending. The Treasury invested over $4.0 billion in 332 institutions through the SBLF program. As of March 31, 2013, SBLF participants had increased their small business lending by $9.0 billion over a $36.3 billion baseline, although as above, it is unclear how much of this increase was due to an increase in supply by the program versus other sources of supply and demand expansions.

Banks address the informational opacity problem using a number of different lending technologies, which are described later. The basic research model for analyzing bank small business lending has evolved considerably since the early 1990s. Early theoretical studies (e.g., Sharpe, 1990; Rajan, 1992) and subsequent empirical analyses (e.g., Petersen and Rajan, 1994; Berger and Udell, 1995) helped to bring about a broad recognition of the special methods that banks use to lend to small businesses. These studies focused on the differences between relationship lending and transactions lending technologies.

Under the technology of relationship lending, a loan officer collects proprietary information through contact over time with the small business, its owner, and other members of its local community. The bank uses these data to make decisions on underwriting and contract terms with the firm. Thus, a bank with an existing relationship with the firm may be able to provide credit that other banks cannot because of the relationship bank's informational advantage from past contact. Under transactions lending technologies, by contrast, loans are underwritten primarily on the basis of information collected at the time of the loan application.

The research model for small business lending has become much more sophisticated over time. Perhaps the most important change is that the model has been broadened to include many more lending technologies that may be used to lend to opaque small businesses, each based on a different combination of "hard" (quantitative) and "soft" (qualitative)

[1] These statistics are from <http://www.fas.org/sgp/crs/misc/R41146.pdf> (table 1, p. 17).

[2] This is available at <http://www.paynetonline.com/SmallBusinessInsights/. ThomsonReutersPayNetSmallBusinessLendingInde.aspx.>.

[3] For example, see the testimony of Governor Elizabeth A. Duke before the Committee on Financial Services and Committee on Small Business, US House of Representatives, Washington, DC, February 26, 2010 (<http://www.federalreserve.gov/newsevents/testimony/duke20100226a.htm.>).

information (discussed further below). For example, small business credit scoring can be used to provide credit to very opaque firms by relying on hard data derived largely from consumer information about the owners of these firms. Notably, however, this technology also allows for judgmental overrides based on soft information known to the loan officer, although the application of this soft information sometimes results in higher loan defaults (Berge, Puri, and Rochell, 2014). Similarly, even when lending decisions are largely based on collateral values, banks often keep monitoring the firm after the loan is issued (Cerqueiro, Ongena, and Roszbach, forthcoming). The lending technologies may be thought of as the basic building blocks of the modern research model of small business lending. Virtually all of the analyses of credit availability, contract terms, and type of bank that provides the funding revolve around the lending technologies employed in the underwriting process.

The research on small business lending raises a number of issues of research and policy importance. One such issue is the effect of the consolidation of the banking industry on small business credit availability, particularly for opaque firms that might rely on relationship lending. As discussed below, the early research suggested potentially serious declines in small business lending as a result of consolidation, but the current research on this topic yields more ambiguous predictions.

Another key issue is the effect of technological progress on small business lending. Technological progress may increase overall small business credit availability through the innovation of new lending technologies, such as small business credit scoring, and through improvements in existing lending technologies. Enhancements in information technology more broadly defined may also improve the ability of banks to process and transmit hard information over distances between the bank and the small business, and between the loan officer and the management of the bank. This may allow for more and better use of hard-information lending technologies to serve opaque small businesses, particularly those located distantly from the bank.

We acknowledge that there are many other important issues regarding small business lending, including the effects of financial crises, credit crunches, the business cycle, monetary policy, the interest rate cycle, minority access to credit, and the regulatory and legal rules and conditions regarding bank lending. However, space constraints restrict the number of topics that can be adequately covered here.

The remainder of the chapter is organized as follows. Section 12.2 discusses the lending technologies that form the building blocks of the modern research model. We also discuss the information on which these technologies are based and the types of borrowers these technologies are designed to serve.

Section 12.3 discusses the issue of bank consolidation and small business lending. We include summaries of research on the comparative advantages of different types of banks in small business lending—small versus large banks, single market versus multi-market institutions, local versus non-local lenders, and domestically owned versus multinational organizations. Consolidation tends to shift banking resources from the former set of banks (small, single market, local, and domestically owned) to the latter set of organizations (large, multi-market, non-local, and multinational, respectively). In addition, we cover research on the effects of changes in competitiveness associated with mergers and acquisitions (M&As) on small business credit availability. The discussion in this section is also designed to help illustrate some of the main elements of the current research model of small business lending.

Section 12.4 discusses the "hardening" of small business lending information over time because of technological progress, banking industry consolidation, and other causes. We cover research that shows that distances between small businesses and their lending institutions has generally increased over time and the method of contact between the firm and its institution has become more impersonal over time, consistent with a greater use of hard information in lending. Section 12.5 concludes.

12.2 Lending Technologies

12.2.1 Classification of the Technologies

A lending technology is a unique combination of the primary information source used in the underwriting process, a set of screening and underwriting policies and procedures, a loan contract structure, and monitoring strategies and mechanisms. A technology is typically identified by the primary source of information employed in the credit underwriting process, but we do not rule out that some important information may be generated using other technologies in secondary roles. Thus, a commercial mortgage would generally be classified as generated using the commercial real estate lending technology, even if the bank also obtained a credit score and used information from an existing relationship as secondary information in underwriting the credit. This taxonomy of lending technologies is largely based on Berger and Udell (2006) and Berger and Black (2011).

We also distinguish between hard- and soft-information technologies. Hard-information technologies are based principally on quantitative data that may be relatively easily processed and transmitted within a banking organization. Examples of hard information include valuations of collateral, financial ratios from certified audited financial statements, and credit scores generated by outside parties. Soft-information technologies, in contrast, are based mainly on qualitative information that may not be easily processed and transmitted beyond the loan officer or other bank employee that collects it. Examples of soft information include evidence on the character and reliability of the owner of the firm gathered through personal contact by the loan officer, and the personal experience and training of the loan officer that helps in judging the firm's creditworthiness.

There are at least ten lending technologies used by banks to lend to small businesses. Included are five fixed-asset technologies—leasing, commercial real estate lending, residential real estate lending, motor vehicle lending, and equipment lending—as well as asset-based lending, financial statement lending, small business credit scoring, relationship lending, and judgment lending, all of which are described below. All of these technologies employ some combination of both hard and soft information. At a minimum, underwriting any loan requires some numbers about the firm, the owner, and/or the collateral (hard information), and some judgment of the loan officer based on experience and training (soft information). A key implication of this fact is that even if large banks have a comparative advantage in processing and transmitting hard information due to economies of scale, large institutions will not necessarily have an advantage in all of the hard-information technologies. The reason is that their comparative advantage in using the hard-information component of a technology may be offset by their comparative disadvantage in using the soft-information component. Similarly, an advantage for small banks in processing soft information—due to having fewer layers of management over which to transmit the soft information—may not always translate into an advantage for small institutions in every soft-information technology because of a disadvantage in the hard-information component. The comparative advantages may also depend on the type of firm being served. It may be expected that the hard-information component would generally be greater for larger firms and the soft-information component would tend to be greater for smaller firms. It is an empirical question as to whether large or small banks have a comparative advantage in using a given technology to lend to a given class size of firms.

Turning to the specific technologies, fixed-asset lending is a set of technologies that are based primarily on the values of fixed assets that are leased or pledged as collateral. Fixed assets are long-lived assets that are not sold in the normal course of business (i.e., are "immovable"), and are uniquely identified by a serial number or a deed. These include commercial and residential real estate, motor vehicles, and equipment. Leasing is considered to be a fixed-asset lending technology, because the leased assets are generally fixed. Other fixed-asset technologies include commercial real estate lending, residential real estate lending, motor vehicle lending, and equipment lending, which are based primarily on the valuations of the corresponding fixed assets pledged as collateral. Fixed-asset lending technologies may be applied to both transparent and opaque small businesses, as long as the firms have easily valued fixed assets to pledge.

Asset-based lending is another hard-information technology based principally on the value of collateral, in this case accounts receivable and/or inventory. The amount of credit extended is linked to the estimated liquidation value of the assets, so that the credit exposure is always below the estimated liquidation value. This technology also may be applied to both transparent and opaque small businesses, as it is based primarily on the value of the collateral, rather than on the ability of the firm to generate cash flow to repay the loan.

Financial statement lending is a hard-information technology based primarily on the strength of a borrower's financial statements and the quality of those statements. The latter condition generally implies that the statements must be audited by an outside accounting firm. In addition to having informative financial statements, the borrower must have a sufficiently strong financial condition, as reflected in the financial ratios calculated from these statements to justify credit. Unlike the fixed-asset and asset-based lending technologies, financial statement lending is based primarily on an assessment of the firm's ability to repay, rather than the value of the collateral that may be taken in the event of non-payment. Unlike all the other lending technologies, financial statement lending is limited to relatively transparent firms.

Small business credit scoring is a technology based primarily on hard information about the firm's owner as well as the firm. Owner information from consumer credit bureaus is combined with data on the firm collected by the bank and often from commercial credit bureaus to produce a score, or summary statistic for the loan. The US models are usually designed for credits up to $250,000, but many institutions use them only for credits up to $100,000. In most cases, the scores are purchased from an outside party, rather than generated by the bank. In some cases, banks—particularly small community banks—use consumer credit scores on the owner of the business, rather than scores that include business information (Berger, Cowan, and Frame, 2011). As already discussed, small business credit scoring may be applied to very opaque small firms.

Relationship lending relies primarily on soft information gathered through contact over time with the firm, its owner, and its local community. Information may be acquired from the provision of loans, deposits, and other services to the firm and to the owner over time.

Much of the soft information may be acquired through personal contact by the loan officer with the firm, its owner, local suppliers, customers, and so forth. Relationship lending may be used for relatively opaque small businesses without significant hard information being available.

Another soft-information technology employed by banks to lend to small businesses is judgment lending, which is based primarily on the loan officer's training and personal experience. When firms do not have sufficient hard information on which to base their credit, and they have not established a strong relationship to generate soft information, their loans may require a high degree of judgment on the part of the loan officer. The officer makes a judgment based on whatever limited information is available about the firm, plus the officer's training and personal experience with regard to the type of business, location, local demand for the product, and so forth. The training and experience of the loan officer are primarily soft information, as they generally cannot be reduced to credible hard numbers that may be easily communicated. Similar to relationship lending, judgment lending may be applied to opaque small businesses without significant available hard information.[4]

12.2.2 Empirical Studies of the Technologies

Most empirical studies of small business lending identify only one or two lending technologies or simply analyze small business lending without identifying the technologies employed. Two of the lending technologies, relationship lending and small business credit scoring, are extensively studied. A number of studies examine the effects of relationship strength, generally measured by the duration, breadth, or exclusivity of the relationship, or whether the institution is the firm's "main" bank. The technology of relationship lending is generally not explicitly identified, but stronger relationships are assumed to be more often associated with this technology. For example, even if a loan is underwritten primarily based on the value of fixed-asset collateral, it is considered to be a relationship loan if the firm has a long relationship with the bank.

Most of these studies find benefits to borrowers from stronger relationships. The research often finds that stronger relationships are associated with better credit availability, as measured by a higher loan application acceptance rate, less dependence on expensive trade credit, or more loans without collateral requirements (e.g., Petersen and Rajan, 1994; Berger and Udell, 1995; Petersen and Rajan, 1995; Cole, 1998; Elsas and Krahnen, 1998; Harhoff and Korting, 1998; Machauer and Weber, 2000; and Berger, Frame, and Ioannidou, 2011), although the effects on loan interest rates are mixed. Some studies find that stronger relationships may result in lower loan interest rates (e.g., Berger and Udell, 1995; Hernández-Cánovas and Martínez-Solano, 2006; Bharath et al., 2011), others find that stronger relationships may induce higher loan interest rates (e.g., Angelini, Di Salvo, and Ferri, 1998; Degryse and Van Cayseele, 2000; Calomiris and Pornrojnangkool, 2009), while still other studies find insignificant or mixed effects of relationships on loan interest rates (e.g., Petersen and Rajan, 1994; Elsas and Krahnen, 1998; Harhoff and Korting, 1998; Machauer and Weber, 2000; Schenone, 2010; Berger, Frame, and Ioannidou, 2011). Other

[4] Judgment lending was first introduced by Berger and Black (2011).

research finds benefits from strong relationships during banking crises (e.g., Horiuchi and Shimizu, 1998; Watanabe, 2010; Park, Shin, and Udell, 2007; and Jiangli, Unal, and Yom, 2008). Some recent studies also discover favorable effects of strong relationships on firm performance in terms of recovery from distress and bankruptcy, and fostering innovation (Dahiya et al., 2003; Herrera and Minetti, 2007; Rosenfeld, 2011). Finally, a recent meta-analysis of relationship lending finds that the benefits of this technology vary across countries in some systematic ways, including that the benefits are generally higher in the US, where competition is more intense (Kysucky and Norden, 2012).[5]

Strong relationships—particularly when they are exclusive—may also involve costs. The private information generated by an exclusive banking relationship may give the bank market power over the firm, yielding a hold-up problem and extraction of rents from the firm (e.g., Sharpe, 1990; Rajan, 1992). Firms may mitigate the rent extraction by engaging in multiple relationships (e.g., von Thadden, 1992; Boot, 2000; Elsas, Heinemann, and Tyrell, 2004), by adding a relationship at the margin (Farinha and Santos, 2002), and/or by paying a higher interest rate at a different bank (Degryse and Van Cayseele, 2000). Exclusive relationships also bring about the potential for premature withdrawal of services if the bank becomes financially distressed or fails. The empirical literature on this topic is mixed, with studies in some cases finding positive, negative, and/or no consistent effect of bank fragility on the probability of multiple banking (e.g., Detragiache, Garella, and Guiso, 2000; Ongena and Smith, 2000; Berger, Klapper, and Udell, 2001; Berger et al. 2008; and Berger, Goulding, and Rice, 2014).[6]

As noted, the small business credit-scoring technology has also been extensively studied. Banks that use this technology are identified based on survey data regarding whether, when, and how US banks employ this lending technology (Frame, Srinivasan, and Woosley, 2001; Cowan and Cowan, 2006). Banks appear to differ significantly in how they use credit scoring. Large banks often use small business credit scores that include firm information (Frame, Srinivasan, and Woosley, 2001), while small banks often use the consumer credit scores of the owner of the business alone (Berger, Cowan, and Frame 2011). Some institutions essentially follow "rules" and use the scores automatically to accept or reject loan applications and set loan terms (subject to judgmental overrides). Other banks use more "discretion" and combine the scores with information generated using other technologies. The use of "rules" likely reduces underwriting costs significantly, and the use of "discretion" may add costs, but also provide more information. Some studies find an increase in lending associated with the technology, but this increase appears to be primarily by "rules" banks, and is probably driven by lower costs (e.g., Frame, Srinivasan, and Woosley, 2001; Frame, Padhi, and Woosley, 2004; Berger, Frame, and Miller, 2005; Berger, Cowan, and Frame, 2011). Several studies also find results consistent with the hypothesis that use of small business credit scoring with "discretion" significantly reduces informational opacity—specifically, "discretion" banks may be associated with reduced borrower risk (Berger, Frame, and Miller, 2005), longer maturities (Berger, Espinosa-Vega et al., 2005), and reduced use of collateral (Berger, Espinosa-Vega et al., 2011). Finally, some studies also find that small business credit scoring tends to be used for more distant or "out-of-market" borrowers, consistent

---

[5] Some studies also find that banks benefit from strong relationships in terms of future lending and underwriting business (Drucker and Puri, 2005; and Bharath et al., 2011).

[6] Other motives for multiple banking relationships are discussed in Berger et al. (2008).

with the use of hard information that requires relatively little personal contact (e.g., Frame, Padhi, and Woosley, 2004; DeYoung, Glennon, and Nigro, 2008; and DeYoung, Frame et al., 2011). Another study finds that the observed increases in out-of-market small business lending are concentrated in loans of $100,000 or less—the limit on small business credit scoring amounts imposed by many banks—consistent with the use of small business credit scoring as a key technology for providing small business credit at a distance (Brevoort, 2006).

Some recent studies identify the use of multiple technologies. One study identifies all five of the fixed-asset lending technologies—leasing, commercial real estate lending, residential real estate lending, motor vehicle lending, and equipment lending—from the loan contract data in the 1998 Survey of Small Business Finance (SSBF) (Berger and Black, 2011). The authors find that more than 40% of the loans in the survey can be identified as made using the fixed-asset lending technologies. The identification procedure uses only information on whether the contract type was a lease and the type of fixed asset pledged as collateral. Similar to the relationship-lending literature, the authors also examine the effects of relationship strength using lines of credit that are not secured by fixed assets. This method may be more accurate in identifying the effect of relationship strength than the conventional relationship-lending literature, because of the removal from the sample of the loans made using the fixed-asset lending technologies. They find that small banks have a comparative advantage in relationship lending, but this appears to be strongest for lending to the largest firms. A study of Japanese firms identifies six lending technologies—financial statement lending, equipment lending, real-estate-based lending, relationship lending, leasing, and factoring—using information from the borrowing firms, and finds that in many cases, multiple lending technologies are employed for lending to the same firm (Uchida, Udell, and Yamori, 2006). Finally, one study of minority access to small business credit in the US finds that such access differs according to the technology used (line-of-credit versus non-line of credit loans, presumably mostly representing relationship lending versus transactions lending technologies),[7] as well as the degree of local market loan competition (Mitchell and Pearce, 2011).

12.3 EFFECTS OF BANK CONSOLIDATION ON SMALL BUSINESS CREDIT AVAILABILITY

12.3.1 Early Research on Consolidation and Small Business Lending

Some of the early research on small business lending suggested a generally unfavorable effect of the consolidation of the banking industry on small business credit availability, particularly for opaque firms that might rely on relationship lending. Studies testing the effect of bank size on the supply of small business credit find that large banks allocate much lower proportions of their assets to small business loans than do small banks (e.g., Berger, Kashyap,

---

[7] Berger and Udell (1995) argue that lines of credit are ideally suited for relationship lending and support this by showing that small firms are more likely to have all of their lines consolidated at a single lender than other types of loans.

and Scalise, 1995; Keeton, 1995; Strahan and Weston, 1998). A second key finding is that the ratio of small business loans to assets declines after large banks are involved in M&As (e.g., Berger, Saunders et al., 1998; Strahan and Weston, 1998). A third key finding is that large banks appear to reject small business loans much more frequently than small banks. According to the Biz2Credit survey of 1,000 small businesses with credit scores above 680, the loan approval rate was only 16.9% for banks with over $10 billion in assets, while smaller banks approved 49.8% of applications in June 2013.[8] As a result of findings such as these, large banks were thought to be disadvantaged in relationship lending, with a potential consequence of significantly reduced credit availability to informationally opaque small businesses as a result of consolidation.[9]

This early research may be misleading for at least two main reasons. First, although the research finds that consolidating institutions often substantially reduce their ratios of small business loans to total assets, this does not necessarily imply that small business lending by these banks declines significantly. The ratios may decrease primarily because of an increase in other assets in the denominators of the ratios, such as large business loans. Consistent with this possibility, some evidence suggests that small businesses' ability to borrow is unrelated to the presence of large banks in their markets (Jayarante and Wolken, 1999). Other findings suggest that the likelihood of borrowing from a large bank is roughly proportional to the local deposit market share of large banks, consistent with small businesses simply borrowing from the most convenient bank, independent of bank size (Berger, Rosen, and Udell, 2007). Other research confirms the importance of convenience, and suggests that opaque small businesses are not more likely to have a small bank as their main bank, and that the strength of the relationship also does not depend in an important way on bank size (Berger, Goulding, and Rice, 2014). Another study finds that the effect of the market presence of banks of different sizes depends on economic conditions—a higher local market share for small banks is associated with more bank credit to recent startups during normal times, but this did not hold during the recent financial crisis that began in 2008 (Berger, Cerqueiro, and Penas, 2014).

Second, even if M&As do significantly reduce the supplies of small business credit of the consolidating banks, there may be offsetting "external effects" or general equilibrium effects in the local market. Empirical evidence suggests that other incumbent banks in the same local market substantially increase their supplies of small business credit after M&As (e.g., Berger, Saunders et al., 1998; Avery and Samolyk, 2004). In addition, de novo or newly chartered banks—which tend to specialize in small business lending—often enter the market after M&A activity, potentially offsetting any cutbacks in small business lending by consolidating banks (e.g., Berger, Bonime et al., 2004). A recent study by Jagtiani, Kotliar, and Maingi (2014) finds that small business lending has not declined over time due to consolidation.[10]

---

[8] These data are from the Biz2Credit website, <http://www.biz2credit.com/small-business-lending-index/june-2013.html.>.

[9] Also consistent with the early research, a recent study finds that a higher local market share for small banks increases the number of establishments in industries most dependent on external finance when local deposits increase (Gilje, 2012).

[10] Notably, these findings—as are most of the results reported here—are based on US data and may not apply to other nations, particularly developing nations, where opacity problems are worse and hard information is more often lacking. An international comparison finds greater market shares for large banks are associated with lower small business employment and less overall bank lending (Berger, Hasan, and Klapper, 2004).

12.3.2 Current Research on Consolidation and Small Business Lending

Under the current research model of small business lending, the effects of banking industry consolidation on credit availability to opaque small businesses is even more ambiguous for two additional reasons. First, even if the consolidated banks have a comparative disadvantage in relationship lending, they may have advantages in hard-information technologies that may also be used to lend to opaque small businesses. Second, consolidation may affect the competitiveness of markets for small business borrowers, which may have either favorable or unfavorable effects on small business credit availability.

In the remainder of this section, we first discuss the comparative advantages of different types of banks in the technologies used in small business lending. We look at the advantages of small versus large banks, single-market versus multi-market institutions, local versus non-local lenders, and domestically owned versus multinational organizations. Consolidation often shifts banking resources from the former set of banks (small, single market, local, domestically owned) to the latter set of organizations (large, multi-market, non-local, multinational, respectively). We then review the findings on the effects of competitiveness on small business credit availability.

Large institutions are likely to have a comparative advantage in hard-information technologies, and small institutions are likely to have the advantage in soft-information technologies. Large banks may be able to exploit economies of scale in the processing and transmission of hard information within the bank, but be relatively poor at processing and transmitting soft information through the communication channels of large organizations (e.g., Stein, 2002). An additional problem for large banks with soft-information technologies may be the number of layers of management required for loan approval. This is because the loan officer is the prime repository of the soft information that cannot be easily communicated, giving a comparative advantage to small institutions with fewer layers of management (e.g., Berger and Udell, 2002) or less hierarchical distance between the loan officer and the manager who approves the loans (e.g., Liberti and Mian, 2009). Finally, large banks may suffer Williamson-type (Williamson, 1988) organizational diseconomies associated with providing hard-information loans to more transparent large businesses, together with soft-information loans to less transparent small businesses.

Recent empirical research is consistent with the hypothesis that large and small banks have comparative advantages in using hard and soft information, respectively (e.g., Cole, Goldberg, and White, 2004; Scott, 2004; Berger, Miller et al., 2005). However, these advantages do not necessarily extend to all of the individual hard- and soft-information technologies, and do not necessarily apply to all types of firms. As discussed above, all technologies incorporate some hard and some soft information; the advantage of a large bank in the hard information may be overwhelmed by the advantage of a small bank in the soft information, and vice versa. To illustrate, one empirical study finds that large banks have a greater comparative advantage in leasing relative to other fixed-asset technologies, but this advantage is dissipated for the smallest firms in the sample (Berger and Black, 2011).

The arguments regarding single-market versus multi-market banks are similar to those regarding the size of banks. Single-market banks are likely to have a comparative advantage over multi-market banks in using soft information, because of the physical proximity of their headquarters to small business customers (Degryse and Ongena, 2005). Single-market institutions may be better able than multi-market competitors to play the role of "community bank" that knows better the local borrowers, their customers and suppliers, and local business conditions (DeYoung, Hunter, and Udell, 2004). In addition, single-market banks may also have an advantage in processing soft information because of the physical proximity of the loan officer to the management of the bank that must approve the credits. It may be easier to transmit soft information to someone in the same location who may also have knowledge of the local conditions. Some recent empirical evidence is consistent with these arguments. One study of the lending of a US bank finds that borrower proximity facilitates the production of proprietary information by the bank, which gives the bank significant advantages over competitors (Agarwal and Hauswald, 2010). A study of an Argentine bank finds that soft information was most difficult to use when the loan officer and manager that approves the loans are located in different offices of the bank (Liberti and Mian, 2009). Similarly, it may be more difficult to transmit soft information between different regions of a country with significant cultural differences. Consistent with this, one study of Italian banking finds more credit rationing of small businesses when their banks are headquartered in another province (Alessandrini, Presbitero, and Zazzaro, 2009). As discussed in Section 12.4 below, lending distances are increasing over time, consistent with a "hardening" of information and potentially reduced importance of the distinction between single-market and multi-market banks over time.

The arguments about single-market versus multi-market banks also apply to local versus non-local banks. Local banks should have comparative advantages in collecting and processing soft information over non-local institutions. One research paper that examines the effects of both single-market versus multi-market and local versus non-local banks suggests that, contrary to expectations, opaque small businesses are not more likely to have a single-market or local bank as their main bank, and that the strength of the relationship also does not depend in an important way on whether the bank is single market or local (Berger, Goulding, and Rice, 2014).

The same arguments regarding size and geography generally apply to foreign bank ownership, as foreign-owned banks are generally quite large, have headquarters that are geographically distant, and often have different cultures and languages from the host nation. Thus, it is expected that foreign-owned banks have comparative advantages in hard-information technologies and disadvantages in soft-information technologies relative to domestically owned banks. There is little evidence on the use of technologies, but the empirical research generally suggests that foreign banks make relatively few small business loans in developed nations, but may increase small business credit availability in developing nations due to access to superior hard-information technologies. See Berger and Udell (2006) for a summary of this research.

Finally, consolidation may affect the competitiveness of markets for small business borrowers, with M&As within markets likely reducing competition and M&As across markets more likely increasing competition. Reduced competition would restrict the supply of small business credit through any technology under the standard structure-conduct-performance hypothesis, but it may increase the supply through relationship lending. This is because limits on competition help banks enforce implicit contracts in which relationship borrowers receive subsidized rates in the short term, and pay higher rates in later periods (e.g., Sharpe, 1990; Petersen and Rajan, 1995). The empirical evidence on this point is mixed, with some studies finding favorable effects of concentration and other restrictions on competitiveness on measures of credit availability, activity, and general economic performance (e.g., Petersen and Rajan, 1995; Cetorelli and Gambera, 2001; Bonaccorsi di Patti and Dell'Ariccia, 2004; and Cetorelli, 2004), others finding unfavorable effects (e.g., Black and Strahan, 2002; Berger, Hasan, and Klapper, 2004; Karceski, Ongena, and Smith, 2005; Cetorelli and Strahan, 2006; de la Torre, Martinez Peria, and Schmukler 2009; Canales and Nanda, 2012; Noth, Koetter, and Inklaar, 2012), and some finding different effects based on alternative measures of competition (e.g., Carbo-Valverde, Rodriguez-Fernandez, and Udell, 2009; Scott and Dunkelberg, 2010) or alternative types of small business loans (e.g., Berger, Cerqueiro, and Penas, 2014).[11]

12.4 THE "HARDENING" OF SMALL BUSINESS LENDING INFORMATION OVER TIME

A potentially important development in small business lending is the "hardening" of the information used in making these loans. As discussed below, there is evidence that, on average, the distance between small business borrowers and their banks has increased and the percentage of borrowers who have personal contact with their banks has decreased. These findings are consistent with a greater use of hard information in lending or a "hardening" of the information used, given that soft information is difficult to learn and transmit over long distances and through impersonal methods of contact. For example, a loan officer often needs to have face-to-face contact with the small business owner and members of the local community in order to gather soft information to use in the relationship lending technology.

One reason for the hardening of information is technological progress. Many studies have documented significant technological progress in the banking industry, as banks take advantage of improvements in information processing, telecommunications, and financial technologies (e.g., Berger, 2003). The improvements in information processing and telecommunication technologies likely have improved banks' abilities to process and transmit hard quantitative information about loan customers over longer distances. New financial technologies that use this information, such as small business credit scoring, may have further facilitated the ability of banks to expand their range of lending. Some research has specifically linked the use of the relatively new small business credit-scoring technology to additional out-of-market lending and longer-distance lending (e.g., Frame, Padhi, and Woosley, 2004; DeYoung et al. 2007; DeYoung, Frame et al. 2008; DeYoung, Frame et al. 2011) and reduced default rates on longer-distance small business loans (e.g., DeYoung et al. 2008). It seems unlikely that technological change has had as much effect in improving soft-information technologies, which are by their nature more labor intensive, and the qualitative data are less subject to improvements in processing and transmission.

[11] Consolidation may also affect the lending technologies used by local rivals. One study of Belgian banking finds that when local banks are larger, their rival bank tends to lend over a smaller geographic area, consistent with a focus on soft-information technologies (Degryse, Laeven, and Ongena, 2009).

A second reason for the hardening of information is the consolidation of the banking industry. As discussed above, large financial institutions may have comparative advantages in using hard-information lending technologies. Thus, consolidation may have increased lending distances because the hard-information lending technologies in which large banks specialize tend to be associated with longer distances and more impersonal contact methods. Recent research is consistent with the notion that large banks are associated with longer-distance small business loans (e.g. Berger, Miller et al. 2005; Brevoort, 2006).

Similarly, the hardening of information may be related to a shift in lending among the different types of financial institutions. Recent research suggests that increasing proportions of small business loans are made by non-depository institutions (finance and factoring, brokerage and pension, leasing, insurance, and mortgage companies) rather than depositories (commercial banks, thrifts, and credit unions) and that non-depositories tend to lend at longer distances and use more impersonal means of contact with small businesses (Brevoort and Wolken, 2009).

The hardening of information and increase in lending distance over time may also be related to a shift in the mix of lending technologies. There is evidence that soft information is associated with relatively short distances between borrowers and lenders, as loan officers need a close geographic proximity to observe soft information such as owner character and reliability (e.g., Degryse and Ongena, 2005). Lending distances may be expected to increase to the extent that financial institutions shift from "softer" lending technologies that are associated with relatively short distances to "harder" technologies associated with longer distances.

There may also be important complementarities among technological progress, consolidation, and the shift to harder lending technologies. It is likely that large banks gained more from technological progress than small banks for a number of reasons, including that technological progress probably improved the hard-information lending technologies in which these banks specialize more than the soft-information technologies in which small banks specialize. Other empirical research on bank performance is consistent with this hypothesis, finding that, over time, large banks: (1) improved their productivity more than small banks (e.g., Berger and Mester, 2003); (2) reduced their agency costs of managing affiliates at greater distances (e.g., Berger and DeYoung, 2006); and (3) competed more effectively against small banks (e.g., Berger, Dick, et al. 2007).[12] It may also be argued that the shift to harder-lending technologies is related to both technological progress and consolidation. Technological progress may have resulted in new hard-information technologies, such as small business credit scoring, and lowered the relative cost of other hard-information technologies relative to soft-information technologies. Bank consolidation may also facilitate shifting into harder technologies, as large banks tend to have comparative advantages in these technologies.

In the remainder of this section, we briefly review some of the research on the changes in small business lending distance over time and give some updates from the 1993, 1998, and 2003 Surveys of Small Business Finances (SSBFs).[13]

---

[12] However, there may be limits to consolidation. It may be argued that consolidation may not proceed beyond the point where there are sufficient small banks to provide relationship lending (DeYoung, Hunter, and Udell, 2004).

[13] The SSBF was discontinued by the Federal Reserve after 2003.

Petersen and Rajan (2002) use the 1993 SSBF to construct a synthetic panel based on the year in which the lender–borrower relationship started and find that the average distance between small firms and their lenders increased by 3.4% per year from the 1970s to the early 1990s. They also find that the most frequent method of contact between the small business and its lender was less often personal and more often by phone or mail. Wolken and Rohde (2002) compare lending distances between the 1993 and 1998 SSBFs and find that the average firm–lender distance increased from 115 miles in 1993 to 244 miles in 1998, an annual growth rate of 15%. However, the median distance only increased from 9 miles in 1993 to 10 miles in 1998, suggesting that the increase in mean distance was largely from increases in out-of-market distances that affected a minority of small businesses.

Brevoort and Hannan (2006) focus on in-market distances using Community Reinvestment Act data from 1997 to 2001, and find little change in distance over the sample period. Hannan (2003) uses Community Reinvestment Act data from 1996 to 2001 and finds a significant increase in out-of-market lending. He also finds that more loans in metropolitan markets are extended by out-of-market lenders over time. Brevoort (2006) uses Community Reinvestment Act data from 1998 to 2003 and finds a large increase in out-of-market commercial lending. However, Brevoort also finds that the effects are limited to large banks and loans of $100,000 or less, consistent with the effects of small business credit scoring by large banks to lend to small borrowers.

Using data on SBA's 7(a) loan program discussed above and the 1998 Atlanta Federal Reserve Survey on the use of the small business credit-scoring technology, DeYoung et al. (2007), DeYoung, Frame, et al. (2008), and DeYoung et al. (2011) find that average distances between small business borrowers and their lenders grew between 1984 and 2001 and that these observed increases were larger at banks that had adopted credit scoring by the time of the 1998 survey. These results are consistent both with the earlier observed increases in mean distances and with the likelihood that the adoption of the small business credit-scoring technology has played an important role in the increase.

Next, we turn to the most recent information on changes in lending distance and personal contact with small businesses from Brevoort and Wolken (2009), who provide detailed comparisons of the data from the 1993, 1998, and 2003 SSBFs. They find that mean lending distance more than doubled in five years, from 110.6 miles in 1993 to 242.9 miles in 1998, and then surprisingly fell to 180.6 miles in 2003. The exact reason for the drop between 1998 and 2003 is not known, but apparently it is concentrated at the top end of the distribution, since the median lending distance rose modestly from 8 miles to 11 miles, and the loans of over 30 miles increased slightly from 34% to 34.6% of the total. The proportion of financial institutions conducting business in person with small business borrowers dropped from 49% in 1993 to 48% in 1998 to 44% in 2003, consistent with a continuing hardening of information over time. As noted above, the data also show important differences in lending distances and personal versus impersonal contact between depositories (commercial banks, thrifts, and credit unions) and non-depository institutions (finance and factoring, brokerage and pension, leasing, insurance, and mortgage companies). For example, in 2003, the mean distance to depository lenders was 74.6 miles versus 357.4 miles for non-depositories, and the percentage conducting business in person was 71% for depositories and only 15% for non-depositories, consistent with a much greater use of soft information by depositories and a much greater use of hard information by non-depositories. This is again consistent with expectations that loan officers at commercial banks and other depositories tend to specialize in relationship lending and judgment lending, while other types of financial institutions rely more on hard-information techniques. Finally, the data in Brevoort and Wolken (2009) suggest some interesting differences in the use of hard and soft information in different lending products that are consistent with expectations. For example, in 2003, the mean distance for lines of credit was 77.1 miles, while the mean distance for leases was 438 miles. This is consistent with findings that lines of credit are associated with relationship lending (e.g., Berger and Udell, 1995) and with arguments that leasing is one of the "hardest" lending technologies (e.g., Berger and Black, 2011).

Finally, some recent papers have documented a shift away from relationship lending over time. Using the different waves of the SSBF, Durguner (2012) shows that the importance of small business lending relationships in determining loan contract terms has diminished over time. Consistent with this, van Ewijk and Arnold (Forthcoming) find that US banks have shifted from relationship-oriented models towards transactions-oriented models over time.

12.5 CONCLUSIONS

This chapter covers some of the issues regarding bank lending to small businesses. We briefly discuss the lending technologies used by banks to lend to small businesses. These technologies form the building blocks of the modern research model of small business lending. We also look at the effects of banking industry consolidation and technological progress on the use of the lending technologies and their effects on small business credit. We find, for example, that the effects of consolidation on small business credit availability is ambiguous for several reasons, including the possibility that the consolidated banks may have comparative advantages in hard-information lending technologies that may be used to lend to opaque small businesses. We also find that consolidation, technological progress, their interactions, and other factors appear to have resulted in a "hardening" of small business lending information over time. This is reflected in greater distances between financial institutions and their loan customers and greater use of impersonal methods of contact between the parties.

REFERENCES

Agarwal, S. and Hauswald, R. (2010). Distance and Private Information in Lending, *Review of Financial Studies* 23, 2757–2788.

Alessandrini, P., Presbitero A. F., and Zazzaro, A. (2009). Banks, Distances and Financing Constraints for Firms, *Review of Finance* 13, 261–307.

Angelini, P., Di Salvo, R., and Ferri, G. (1998). Availability and Cost of Credit for Small Businesses: Customer Relationships and Credit Cooperatives, *Journal of Banking and Finance* 22, 925–954.

Avery, R. B. and Samolyk, K. A. (2004). Bank Consolidation and the Provision of Banking Services: Small Commercial Loans, *Journal of Financial Services Research* 25, 291–325.

Berg, T., Puri, M., and Rocholl, J. (2014). *Loan Officer Incentives, Internal Ratings and Default Rates*, Bonn University Working Paper.

Berger, A. N. (2003). The Economic Effects of Technological Progress: Evidence from the Banking Industry, *Journal of Money, Credit, and Banking* 35, 141–176.

Berger, A. N. and Black, L. K. (2011). Bank Size, Lending Technologies, and Small Business Finance, *Journal of Banking and Finance* 35, 724–735.

Berger, A. N., Bonime, S. D., Goldberg, L. G., and White, L. J. (2004). The Dynamics of Market Entry: The Effects of Mergers and Acquisitions on Entry in the Banking Industry, *Journal of Business* 77, 797–834.

Berger, A. N., Cerqueiro, G., and Penas, M. F. (2014). Market Size Structure and Small Business Lending: Are Crisis Times Different from Normal Times? University of South Carolina Working Paper.

Berger, A. N., Cowan, A. M., and Frame, W. S. (2011). The Surprising Use of Credit Scoring in Small Business Lending by Community Banks and the Attendant Effects on Credit Availability, Risk, and Profitability, *Journal of Financial Services Research* 39, 1–17.

Berger, A. N. and DeYoung R. (2006). Technological Progress and the Geographic Expansion of the Banking Industry, *Journal of Money, Credit, and Banking* 38, 1483–1513.

Berger, A. N., Dick, A. A., Goldberg, L. G., and White, L. J. (2007). Competition from Large, Multimarket Firms and the Performance of Small, Single-Market Firms: Evidence from the Banking Industry, *Journal of Money, Credit, and Banking* 39, 331–368.

Berger, A. N., Espinosa-Vega, M. A., Frame, W. S., and Miller, N. H. (2005). Debt, Maturity, Risk, and Asymmetric Information, *Journal of Finance* 60, 2895–2923.

Berger, A. N., Espinosa-Vega, M. A., Frame, W. S., and Miller, N. H. (2011). Why Do Borrowers Pledge Collateral? New Empirical Evidence on the Role of Asymmetric Information, *Journal of Financial Intermediation* 20, 55–70.

Berger, A. N., Frame, W. S., and Ioannidou, V. (2011). Tests of Ex Ante versus Ex Post Theories of Collateral using Private and Public Information, *Journal of Financial Economics* 100, 85–97.

Berger, A. N., Frame, W. S., and Miller, N. H. (2005). Credit Scoring and the Availability, Price, and Risk of Small Business Credit, *Journal of Money, Credit, and Banking* 37, 191–222.

Berger, A., Goulding, W., and Rice, T. (2014). Do Small Businesses Still Prefer Community Banks? *Journal of Banking & Finance* 44, 264–278.

Berger, A. N., Hasan, I., and Klapper, L. F. (2004). Further Evidence on the Link between Finance and Growth: An International Analysis of Community Banking and Economic Performance, *Journal of Financial Services Research* 25, 169–202.

Berger, A. N., Kashyap, A. K., and Scalise, J. M. (1995). The Transformation of the US Banking Industry: What a Long, Strange Trip Its Been, *Brookings Papers on Economic Activity* 2, 55–218.

Berger, A. N., Klapper L. F., Martinez Peria, M. S., and Zaidi, R. (2008). Bank Ownership Type and Banking Relationships, *Journal of Financial Intermediation* 17, 37–62.

Berger, A. N., Klapper L. F., and Udell, G. F. (2001). The Ability of Banks to Lend to Informationally Opaque Small Businesses, *Journal of Banking & Finance* 25, 2127–2167.

Berger, A. N. and Mester, L. J. (2003). What Explains the Dramatic Changes in Cost and Profit Performance of the US Banking Industry?, *Journal of Financial Intermediation* 12, 57–95.

Berger, A. N., Miller, N. H., Petersen, M. A., Rajan, R. G., and Stein, J. C. (2005). Does Function Follow Organizational Form? Evidence from the Lending Practices of Large and Small Banks, *Journal of Financial Economics* 76, 237–269.

Berger, A. N., Rosen, R. J., and Udell, G. F. (2007). Does Market Size Structure Affect Competition? The Case of Small Business Lending, *Journal of Banking & Finance* 31, 11–33.

Berger, A. N., Saunders, A., Scalise, J. M., and Udell, G. F. (1998). The Effects of Bank Mergers and Acquisitions on Small Business Lending, *Journal of Financial Economics* 50, 187–229.

Berger, A. N. and Udell, G. F. (1995). Relationship Lending and Lines of Credit in Small Firm Finance, *Journal of Business* 68, 351–381.

Berger, A. N. and Udell, G. F. (2002). Small Business Credit Availability and Relationship Lending: The Importance of Bank Organizational Structure, *Economic Journal* 112, 32–53.

Berger, A. N. and Udell, G. F. (2006). A More Complete Conceptual Framework for SME Finance, *Journal of Banking & Finance* 30, 2945–2966.

Bharath, S., Dahiya, S., Saunders, A., and Srinivasan, A. (2011). Lending Relationships and Loan Contract Terms, *Review of Financial Studies* 24, 1141–1203.

Black S. E. and Strahan, P. E. (2002). Entrepreneurship and Bank Credit Availability, *Journal of Finance* 57, 2807–2833.

Boot, A. W. A. (2000). Relationship Banking: What Do We Know?, *Journal of Financial Intermediation* 9, 7–25.

Bonaccorsi di Patti, E. and Dell'Ariccia, G. (2004). Bank Competition and Firm Creation, *Journal of Money, Credit, and Banking* 36, 225–251.

Brevoort, K. P. (2006). An Empirical Examination of the Growth of Out-of-Market Lending: The Changing Competitive Landscape and the Role of Asymmetric Information. Federal Reserve Board Working Paper.

Brevoort, K. P. and Hannan, T. H. (2006). Commercial Lending and Distance: Evidence from Community Reinvestment Act Data, *Journal of Money, Credit, and Banking* 38, 1991–2012.

Brevoort, K. P. and Wolken, J. D. (2009). Does Distance Matter in Banking?. In: A. Zazzaro, M. Fratianni, and P. Alessandrini (Eds.), *The Changing Geography of Banking and Finance*, 27–56. Vienna: Springer Publishing.

Calomiris, C. W. and Pornrojnangkool, T. (2009). Relationship Banking and the Pricing of Financial Services, *Journal of Financial Services Research* 35, 189–224.

Carbo-Valverde, S., Rodriguez-Fernandez, F., and Udell, G. F. (2009). Bank Market Power and SME Financing Constraints, *Review of Finance* 13, 309–340.

Canales, R. and Nanda, R. (2012). A Darker Side to Decentralized Banks: Market Power and Credit Rationing in SME Lending, *Journal of Financial Economics* 105, 353–366.

Cerqueiro, G., Ongena, S. and Roszbach, K. (forthcoming). Collateralization, Bank Loan Rates and Monitoring, *Journal of Finance*.

Cetorelli, N. (2004). Bank Concentration and Competition in Europe, *Journal of Money, Credit, and Banking* 36, 543–558.

Cetorelli, N. and Gambera, M. (2001). Banking Market Structure, Financial Dependence and Growth: International Evidence from industry Data, *Journal of Finance* 56, 617–648.

Cetorelli, N. and Strahan, P. E. (2006). Finance as a Barrier to Entry: Bank Competition and Industry Structure in Local US Markets, *Journal of Finance* 61, 437–461.

Cole, R. A, (1998), The Importance of Relationships to the Availability of Credit, *Journal of Banking & Finance* 22, 959–977.

Cole, R. A., Goldberg, L. G., and White, L. J. (2004). Cookie-Cutter versus Character: The Micro Structure of Small Business Lending by Large and Small Banks, *Journal of Financial and Quantitative Analysis* 39, 227–251.

Cowan, C. D. and Cowan, A. M. (2006). *A Survey-Based Assessment of Financial Institution Use of Credit Scoring for Small Business Lending*, Small Business Administration Office of Advocacy Report No. 283.

Dahiya, S., Bharath, S., Saunders, A., and Srinivasan, A. (2007). So What Do I Get? The Banks View of Lending, *Journal of Financial Economics* 85, 368–419.

Dahiya, S., John, K., Puri, M., and Ramirez, G. (2003). Debtor-in-Possession Financing and Bankruptcy Resolution: Empirical Evidence, *Journal of Financial Economics* 69, 259–280.

de la Torre, A., Martinez Peria, M. S., and Schmukler, S. L. (2009). Drivers and Obstacles to Banking SMEs: The Role of Competition and the Institutional Framework, CESifo Working Paper Series No. 2651.

Degryse, H., Laeven, L., and Ongena, S. (2009). The Impact of Organizational Structure and Lending Technology on Banking Competition, *Review of Finance* 13, 225–259.

Degryse, H. and Ongena, S. (2005). Distance, Lending Relationships, and Competition, *Journal of Finance* 60, 231–266.

Degryse, H. and van Cayseele, P. (2000). Relationship Lending within a Bank-Based System: Evidence from European Small Business Data, *Journal of Financial Intermediation* 9, 90–109.

Detragiache, E., Garella, P., and Guiso, L. (2000). Multiple versus Single Banking Relationships: Theory and Evidence, *Journal of Finance* 55, 1133–1161.

DeYoung, R., Frame, W. S., Glennon, D., McMillen, D. P., and Nigro, P. (2008). Commercial Lending Distance and Historically Underserved Areas, *Journal of Economics & Business* 60, 149–164.

DeYoung, R., Frame, W. S., Glennon, D., and Nigro, P. (2007). What's Driving Small Borrower-Lender Distance? Federal Reserve Bank of Atlanta Working Paper.

DeYoung, R., Frame, W. S., Glennon, D., and Nigro, P. (2011). The Information Revolution and Small Business Lending: The Missing Evidence, *Journal of Financial Services Research* 39, 19–33.

DeYoung, R., Glennon, D., and Nigro, P. (2008). Borrower-Lender Distance, Credit Scoring, and the Performance of Small Business Loans, *Journal of Financial Intermediation* 17, 113–143.

DeYoung, R., Gron, A., Torna, G., and Winton, A. (2014). Risk Overhang and Loan Portfolio Decisions: Small Business Loan Supply Before and During the Financial Crisis, University of Kansas Working Paper.

DeYoung, R., Hunter, W. C., Udell, G. F. (2004). The Past, Present, and Probable Future for Community Banks, *Journal of Financial Services Research* 25, 85–133.

Drucker, S. and Puri, M. (2005). On the Benefits of Concurrent Lending and Underwriting, *Journal of Finance* 60, 2763–2799.

Durguner, S. (2012). Effects of Changes in Borrower-Lender Relationships on Small Business Loan Contract Terms and Credit Availability. University of Illinois at Urbana-Champaign Working Paper.

Elsas, R., Heinemann, F., and Tyrell, M. (2004). Multiple but Asymmetric Bank Financing: The Case of Relationship Lending, CESifo Series Working Paper No. 1251.

Elsas, R. and Krahnen, J. P. (1998). Is Relationship Lending Special? Evidence from Credit-File Data in Germany, *Journal of Banking & Finance* 22, 1283–1316.

Farinha, L. A. and Santos, J. A. C. (2002). Switching from Single to Multiple Bank Lending Relationships: Determinants and Implications, *Journal of Financial Intermediation* 11, 124–151.

Frame, W. S., Padhi, M., and Woolsey, L. (2004). The Effect of Credit Scoring on Small Business Lending in Low—and Moderate-Income Areas, *Financial Review* 39, 35–54.

Frame, W. S., Srinivasan, A., and Woosley, L. (2001). The Effect of Credit Scoring on Small Business Lending, *Journal of Money, Credit, and Banking* 33, 813–825.

Gilje, E. (2012). Does Local Access To Finance Matter?: Evidence from US Oil and Natural Gas Shale Boom. Boston College Working Paper.

Hannan, T. H. (2003). Changes in Non-Local Lending to Small Business, *Journal of Financial Services Research* 24, 31–46.

Harhoff, D. and Korting, T. (1998). Lending Relationships in Germany: Empirical Evidence from Survey Data, *Journal of Banking & Finance* 22, 1317–1353.

Hernández-Cánovas, G. and Martínez-Solano, P. (2006). Banking Relationships: Effects on Debt Terms for Small Spanish Firms, *Journal of Small Business Management* 44, 315–333.

Herrera, A. M. and Minetti, R. (2007). Informed Finance and Technological Change: Evidence from Credit Relationships, *Journal of Financial Economics* 83, 223–269.

Horiuchi, A. and Shimizu, K. (1998). The Deterioration of Bank Balance Sheets in Japan: Risk-Taking and Recapitalization, *Pacific-Basin Finance Journal* 6, 1–26.

Jagtiani, J., Kotliar, I., and Maingi R. Q. (2014). The Evolution of U.S. Community Banks and Its Impact on Small Business Lending, Federal Reserve Bank of Philadelphia Working Paper No. 14–16.

Jayaratne, J. and Wolken. J. (1999). How Important are Small Banks to Small Business Lending? New Evidence from a Survey of Small Firms, *Journal of Banking & Finance* 23, 427–458.

Jiangli, W., Unal, H., and Yom, C. (2008). Relationship Lending, Accounting Disclosure and Credit Availability during the Asian Financial Crisis, *Journal of Money, Credit, and Banking* 40, 25–55.

Karceski, J., Ongena, S., and Smith, D. (2005). The Impact of Bank Consolidation on Commercial Borrower Welfare, *Journal of Finance* 60, 2043–2082.

Keeton, W. R. (1995). Multi-Office Bank Lending to Small Businesses: Some New Evidence. *Federal Reserve Bank of Kansas City Economic Review* 80, 45–57.

Kysucky, V. and Norden, L. (2012). The Benefits of Relationship Lending in a Cross-Country Context: A Meta-Analysis. Erasmus University Working Paper.

Liberti, J. M. and Mian, A. R. (2009). Estimating the Effect of Hierarchies on Information Use, *Review of Financial Studies* 22, 4057–4090.

Machauer, A. and Weber, M. (2000). Number of Bank Relationships: An Indicator of Competition, Borrower Quality or Just Size?, Johan Wolfgang Goethe-Universitat Center for Financial Studies Working Paper No. 2000/06.

Mitchell, K. and Pearce, D. K. (2011). Lending Technologies, Lending Specialization, and Minority Access to Small-Business Loans, *Small Business Economics* 37, 277–304.

Noth, F., Koetter, M., and Inklaar, R. (2012). Who's Afraid of Big Bad Banks? Bank Competition, SME, and Industry Growth. Goethe University Frankfurt Working Paper.

Ongena, S. and Smith, D. (2000). What Determines the Number of Bank Relationships? Cross-Country Evidence, *Journal of Financial Intermediation* 9, 26–56.

Park, S. Y., Shin, B. S., and Udell, G. F. (2007). Lending Relationships, Credit Availability and Banking Crises. Indiana University Working Paper.

Petersen, M. A. and Rajan, R. G. (1994). The Benefits of Lending Relationships: Evidence from Small Business Data, *Journal of Finance* 49, 3–37.

Petersen, M. A. and Rajan, R. G. (1995). The Effect of Credit Market Competition on Lending Relationships. *Quarterly Journal of Economics* 110, 407–443.

Petersen, M. A. and Rajan, R. G. (2002). The Information Revolution and Small Business Lending: Does Distance Still Matter? *Journal of Finance* 57, 2533–2570.

Rajan, R. G. (1992). Insiders and Outsiders: The Choice between Informed and Arms Length Debt, *Journal of Finance* 47, 1367–1400.

Robb, A. and Robinson, D. (2014). The Capital Structure Decisions of New Firms, *Review of Financial Studies* 27, 153–179.

Rosenfeld, C. M. (2011). The Effect of Banking Relationships on the Future of Financially Distressed Firms. College of William and Mary Working Paper.

Schenone, C. (2010). Lending Relationships and Information Rents: Do Banks Exploit Their Information Advantages?, *Review of Financial Studies* 23, 1149–1199.

Scott, J. A. (2004). Small Business and Value of Community Financial Institutions, *Journal of Financial Services Research* 25, 207–230.

Scott, J. A. and Dunkelberg, W. C. (2010). Competition for Small Firm Banking Business: Bank Actions versus Market Structure, *Journal of Banking and Finance* 34, 2788–2800.

Sharpe, S. A. (1990). Asymmetric Information, Bank Lending, and Implicit Contracts: A Stylized Model of Customer Relationships, *Journal of Finance* 45, 1069–1087.

Stein, J. C. (2002). Information Production and Capital Allocation: Decentralized vs. Hierarchical Firms, *Journal of Finance* 57, 1891–1921.

Strahan, P. E. and Weston, J. (1998). Small Business Lending and the Changing Structure of the Banking Industry, *Journal of Banking & Finance* 22, 821–845.

Uchida, H., Udell, G. F., and Yamori, N. (2006). SME Financing and the Choice of Lending Technology. Research Institute of Economy, Trade, and Industry (REITI) Working Paper.

Van Ewijk, S. and Arnold, I. (Forthcoming). How Bank Business Models Drive Interest Margins: Evidence from US Bank-Level Data. *European Journal of Finance*.

von Thadden, E. (1992). The Commitment of Finance, Duplicated Monitoring, and the Investment Horizon, Center for Economic Policy Research Working Paper No. 27.

Watanabe, W. (2010). Does a Large Loss of Bank Capital Cause Evergreening? Evidence from Japan, *Journal of the Japanese and International Economies* 24, 116–136.

Williamson, O. (1988). Corporate Finance and Corporate Governance, *Journal of Finance* 43, 567–591.

Wolken, J. and Rohde, D. (2002). Changes in the Location of Small Businesses Financial Services Suppliers between 1993 and 1998. Federal Reserve Board Memo.

CHAPTER 13

···

CONSUMER LENDING

···

THOMAS A. DURKIN AND
GREGORY ELLIEHAUSEN

13.1 INTRODUCTION

···

BEYOND deposit services and monetary transfers, the most prevalent financial service in developed countries is consumer lending. Terminology sometimes differs according to the user, but most often the term "consumer lending" refers to the advance of cash to a consumer by a financial institution or permission by a retail seller of goods and services to delay payment for a purchase. The term does not normally include credit for purchase of a residence or collateralized by real estate or by specific financial assets such as stocks and bonds or extended for business financing. Most consumer lending involves repayment in periodic payments sometimes called "installments," at set intervals such as monthly. Besides loans of cash, credit for purchase of substantial goods and services such as automobiles, home improvements, appliances, recreational goods such as boats, movable housing, and educations all fall within this definition, as does credit on credit cards. Credit of this kind has been growing worldwide in recent decades; in the US alone $3.1 trillion of credit arising from consumer lending was outstanding at the end of 2013. This amount is in addition to $9.4 trillion of credit outstanding on real estate collateral there, and is not counted in "consumer lending" as the term is used here.

Within this definition of consumer lending there are many ways to classify the loans, including by purpose of credit use (automobile lending, student education loans, etc.), by institutional source of the funds (e.g., bank, credit union, or store), according to method of credit generation and repayment (closed-end single advances versus multiple-advance revolving credit arrangements such as credit cards), and by mechanics of extension (directly from the financial institution or indirectly from a seller of goods that relies on a financial institution for funding). In earlier decades, another classification method was according to agreed timing of repayment; at that time, a further common differentiation was between non-installment credit and installment credit. Non-installment credit referred to single-payment loans, charge accounts at retail stores and dealers without an extended payments feature, and service credit granted by physicians, hospitals, lawyers, and other professionals where payment was expected in one lump sum. Today, credit cards substitute for many kinds of non-installment credit and most consumer lending is installment credit.

Consumer lending is sometimes controversial among people who believe its use is merely an attempt by consumers to live beyond their means, but most informed observers agree that consumer lending provides a number of important economic benefits. First, consumer credit use makes it easier and more timely for many families to purchase household investment goods and services such as automobiles and education. In this context, the term "household investments" using credit does not refer to financial investment in such assets as stocks or bonds. Rather, it means making expenditures for high-value goods or services that provide their benefits over a period of time and whose cash purchase does not usually fit comfortably into monthly budgets. By facilitating such investment spending, consumer lending enables consumers to change the timing of their saving and consumption flows to a preferred pattern. Specifically, rather than postponing the purchase of household investment goods and services, and the consumption benefits they provide, until funds are available from savings (a difficult task for many families, especially in the earlier stages of their earning years), consumers have been able to use credit to purchase the investment goods and services first and pay for them while using them. In effect, they can save for them by making payments while actually using the goods and services.

Second, consumer lending has contributed to the growth of durable goods industries where new technologies, mass production, and economies of scale historically have produced employment growth and new wealth. It is simply hard to imagine development of the suburbs or the automobile and appliance industries in the twentieth century, or for that matter the higher education system as it now exists in many places, without the simultaneous rise of consumer credit to facilitate sale of the output.

Third, consumer lending provides an important outlet for employing financial resources available from net surplus components of the economy, notably from consumers themselves, through the financial intermediation process. Ultimately, the source of funds for consumers who borrow is other (or even the same) consumers who have a financial surplus they can hold as deposits, as life insurance and pension reserves, or as portfolios of securities, including bonds, stocks, and mutual fund shares.

Evidence from the Federal Reserve Board's periodic Surveys of Consumer Finances shows that the bulk of consumer lending arises in the course of undertaking household investments that provide a return over time, especially purchase of automobiles, education, home repair, and modernization and other purchases of durable goods including mobile home housing (see Durkin et al., 2014, ch. 1). Much credit-card credit appears to be a substitution of traditional installment credit for this newer form of revolving credit for these purposes.

However, long-term growth of consumer lending has for decades been a matter of concern to some observers. Much of this concern appears to overlook the growth of household income and assets that also has occurred since the end of World War II (see Durkin et al., 2014, ch. 2). Although consumer credit use in the US has grown sharply in the post-World War II era, it has not grown very much relative to income or assets since the early 1960s. Historical patterns in these ratios have been intensely cyclical, however, which likely at least partially explains why there are expressions of concern when they rise, despite lack of firm evidence that rising debt ratios have led to economic calamity. Debt growth has occurred in all income and age groups, but the bulk of consumer credit outstanding currently is owed by the younger and higher-income population segments, much as in the past.

13.2 Demand for Consumer Lending

The intertemporal investment–consumption economic model developed by Irving Fisher (1930), and extended by Hirschleifer (1958) and Juster and Shay (1964), provides the neoclassical analytical framework for consumers' borrowing decisions. The investment–consumption framework explored by these economists, including their extensions to encompass uncertainty and credit rationing, relates consumer investment opportunities, time preference, the possibility of lending and borrowing, and the market interest rate to solve the problem of maximizing and allocating consumption over time. It also shows formally when borrowing is a rational economic decision for consumers, as well as for investors in commercial and industrial enterprises (the latter being the main focus of much of the theoretical economics derived from the Fisher approach). Since this theory also shows that there are many common circumstances when credit use by consumers is rational, it leads immediately to the inference that there will be widespread rational economic demand for consumer lending. (Durkin et al., 2014, especially chs 3, 4, and 5, discusses many of these issues at greater length.)

The investment–consumption theory based on the work of Fisher provides the formal basis in economics for consumer lending demand, but the fundamentals are also intuitive: an individual will borrow to purchase investment-type goods and services if doing so has a favorable impact on consumption possibilities after repaying the loan with any necessary interest. This is merely an informal rendering of the Fisher–Hirschleifer–Juster-Shay theoretical conclusion: borrowing to undertake the investment is rational for consumers, as for business enterprises, if there is a positive net present value from the investment under consideration. Under the condition of a positive net present value from borrowing and investing, the individual is better off by undertaking the transaction. If, in contrast, borrowing to purchase the investment goods or services does not produce a positive net return, then the rational choice is not to undertake the investment. Limited amounts of empirical work on uses of consumer loans show that returns can be quite high (see, e.g., discussion in Poapst and Waters, 1964; Dunkelberg and Stephenson, 1974; Elliehausen and Lawrence, 2001).

During the post-World War II period, and certainly since at least the 1960s, when Juster and Shay were formally analyzing the rationality conditions behind consumers' credit-use behavior, the view that consumer credit use is a normal development in a modern economy seems also to have gained traction with the public at large. Consumer lending is not without its problems and its critics, however, including analysts advancing hypotheses of fundamental consumer irrationality in credit use, especially focusing in recent years upon the modern phenomenon of credit cards.

Behavioral economists and psychologists actually have studied consumers' credit decisions for decades, especially using consumer survey methodologies pioneered by George Katona and his colleagues John B. Lansing, James N. Morgan, Eva Mueller, and others at the University of Michigan's Survey Research Center, founded by Katona in 1946. For consumer credit, passage of the US "Truth in Lending" Act in 1968, designed to require transaction-specific information disclosures to borrowers, further stimulated research using psychology-based models to study the role of information in the credit decision process (see Day and Brandt, 1973, 1974; Day, 1976). Added to this, the work by Tversky and Kahneman (1974) and Kahneman and Tversky (1979) on decision making under uncertainty has further reawakened the interest of economists in psychological influences on consumer behavior, including credit-use behavior. Survey research on the processes of spending supports the theoretical economic analyses that treat consumer credit as a part of consumers' investment and consumption decisions. Although some consumer lending arises from the financial consequences of hardship or distress—such as medical expenses, paying recurring bills, or the burden of already existing debts—surveys show that most arises in the consumer investment process involving acquisition of consumer durable goods and services such as automobiles, home repairs, and education, which provide for both a return and a repayment process over time. Consistent with the theories of the economists, surveys have found that credit use is greatest in early family life cycle stages when the rate of return on additional durable goods and services that might be financed using consumer credit is probably quite high.

Another major focus of the survey research has been to investigate the extent to which consumers' durable goods purchasing decisions are deliberative and rational. The research indicated that few purchases include all of the elements of rational decision making—namely planning for purchases, extensive search for information, formulation of evaluation criteria, and careful consideration of alternatives before making decisions. In fact, consumers often simplify, take shortcuts, or use heuristics. Consumers may focus on one or a few product characteristics or rely on the experience of friends, for example, or their own experience.

Nevertheless, most consumers use one or more elements of deliberative behavior in decisions about consumer durables and credit. The research also identified several circumstances that lead to more or less deliberation in durable goods purchases, including purchase of an item that is considered expensive or particularly important, purchase of a new or unfamiliar product, dissatisfaction with a previous purchase, and situations involving a strong new stimulus that causes uncertainty about previous attitudes or experience. In these situations, consumers are more likely to gather additional information, formulate or revise evaluative criteria, and deliberate on alternatives, although they may still take shortcuts, simplify, or use heuristics. Few consumers collect all available information or carefully consider all possible choices. But even in the context of the optimizing models of traditional economics, consumers may not want to collect all available information. Consumers will collect additional information only as long as the perceived cost of search is less than its expected benefits (see Stigler, 1961; Durkin and Elliehausen, 2011, ch. 3). Lowering the cost of search is a main argument in favor of disclosure rules such as "Truth in Lending."

Behavioral research indicates that consumers do make cognitive errors (Ausubel 1999, for example) and exhibit time-inconsistent behavior (Frederick, Loewenstein, and O'Donohue, 2002). However, the extent to which these phenomena impair actual credit decisions in markets is not at all clear. Evidence based on actual behavior in markets suggests that consumers' credit use is sensitive to interest rates (Gross and Souleles, 2002); many consumers accurately assess their future credit use (Agarwal et al. 2006; Mann, 2013); and when mistakes occur, they are usually small, and large mistakes are corrected (Agarwal et al. 2006; Agarwal et al. 2008). At the time of writing neither existing behavioral evidence nor conventional economic evidence supports a general conclusion that consumers' credit behavior is not rational or that markets do not work reasonably well. (Durkin et al. 2014, ch. 4, discusses further implications of behaviorally influenced research for consumer credit use.)

13.3 SUPPLY OF CONSUMER LENDING

Production of consumer lending involves the transfer of funds from savers who have them to borrowers who have need of them, along with the subsequent collection of loan repayments from the borrowers. For consumer lending, the transfers from savers to borrowers and back are usually effected not directly from one to the other, but rather by financial firms through a production process called financial intermediation. As this term suggests, financial intermediaries are institutions that stand between the ultimate suppliers of funds (savers) and the ultimate users (investors). In common parlance, financial intermediaries are usually referred to simply as financial institutions; many kinds are broadly familiar including banks, credit unions, insurance companies, pension funds, mutual funds, and finance companies.

Many financial intermediaries are active in specialized areas of financial markets, and they do not all operate in the same way. Among those undertaking consumer lending, banks and credit unions obtain funds directly from consumers and businesses by providing deposit accounts, and they lend the funds obtained back to consumers and businesses, sometimes the same ones. In contrast, other intermediaries involved in consumer lending obtain most or a good portion of their funds from other intermediaries. Finance companies, for example, obtain most of their funds in capital markets from other institutions such as insurance companies and pension funds. Ultimate funds sources always are savers, however, typically consumers, but also businesses and governments, both domestic and foreign.

Financial intermediaries perform several functions that facilitate the transfer of funds from savers to borrowers, none of which individuals probably want, or are able, to provide for themselves. These functions include: (1) information processing; (2) risk intermediation; (3) monitoring; (4) temporal intermediation; and (5) size intermediation (see Benston and Smith, 1976). In performing these functions, financial intermediaries produce distinct financial products for one or both groups of market participants: borrowers, savers, or both. As indicated, banks and credit unions produce products for both savers (deposits) and investors (loans). Finance companies primarily produce products for borrowers, although the securities they issue to obtain their lending funds provide an outlet for other intermediaries. Mutual funds are examples of financial intermediaries that produce primarily a savings product, raising funds from many savers to purchase a diversified portfolio of securities. Through economies of scale and specialization, financial intermediaries are able to perform these functions in financial markets at a lower cost than individuals could do so on their own (see Gurley and Shaw, 1960; Benston and Smith, 1976). That financial intermediaries use funds obtained either directly from savers or indirectly in financial markets— and then use them as inputs to produce their own distinct products for borrowers—is what distinguishes financial intermediaries from brokers. Brokers match sellers of a product with buyers—buyers and sellers of a house, for example. Financial intermediaries do not match borrowers and savers but rather obtain funds from one source for use by another, typically in much different form.

Whether or not a lending transaction involves an intermediary, it consists of an advance of funds to a borrower by a lender—in exchange, the lender receives from the borrower a promise to repay in the future the amount advanced plus a finance charge. On average, the amount of the finance charge must cover at least the lender's operating and non-operating expenses, including cost of funds.

Operating expenses in a lending transaction include costs of originating the loan, processing payments, and collection and bad debt expenses. All types of credit availability share the same basic activities, although the extent of specific activities depends on a variety of factors such as whether or not the credit is open end or closed end, the amount of credit and the term to maturity, whether or not collateral is taken, and the credit quality of the customers. For consumer lending, operating costs can be more substantial in relation to the size of the loan than on larger loans more typical of lending to business and governments, and research evidence suggests there are substantial economies of scale in operating costs associated with larger loan amounts.

Non-operating expenses of consumer lending include taxes, interest expense for share of the advance financed from borrowed funds, and a return on the owners' equity share of the advance. Although economic theory, as well as experience, suggests that intermediation lowers the overall cost of the transfer of resources from ultimate savers to borrowers, it is obviously still true that the prices charged for loans cannot go below some minimum that must fully cover operating and non-operating costs of the transfer process, if the intermediary is to remain in business.

The importance of operating costs associated with loan origination, together with the high costs of losses on consumer lending, has kept the goal of reducing expenses constantly in the sight of the managers of lending intermediaries. It is, of course, possible to reduce both operating costs and losses to zero, or close to zero, by not making any loans or making very few loans only to individuals who pose virtually no default risk. Not surprisingly, managers have not found this approach very useful, however, because it naturally also relegates profits to zero, or very close to zero. More useful over the years have been attempts to lessen operating costs and losses while keeping lending volume the same or increasing it. Managers have instituted a variety of approaches with this in mind, among them office automation, improved employee quality and training rather than more employees, and, especially, sophisticated statistical approaches to evaluating the risk of customers, an approach generally referred to as "credit scoring."

13.4 Default Risk and the Supply of Credit

Because all credit transactions share the common feature of involving an intertemporal transaction in which the lender provides funds, there must be an expectation that future cash flows will be sufficient to replenish the funds and provide satisfactory capital return. For consumer lending, as with all lending, this means proper management of the possibility of default risk. Models of credit supply were originally developed to study the rationality of credit rationing, which was believed to be an important channel through which monetary policy transmitted to the economy. Credit rationing occurs when the price of credit is less than the equilibrium price. In such situations, the amount of credit demanded is more than the amount offered. Normally, an excess of demand over supply leads to a price increase. A model of credit supply was needed to explain why lenders would limit credit rather than raise the price of credit when monetary policy was tightened.

13.4.1 The Default Risk Model of Credit Supply

The basic theoretical model of the supply of credit to an individual borrower (also known as the loan offer curve) starts with the quite reasonable assumption that the borrower's final wealth, and thus his or her ability to repay, is limited and not known with certainty. Under these conditions, increasing the amount of credit extended increases the likelihood of default. Indeed, beyond a certain amount of credit, default may be virtually certain, so that no offer to pay a higher interest rate would induce a lender to extend additional credit. As a consequence, the supply curve for an individual borrower becomes completely inelastic or even backward bending at some rate of interest.

Several variants of this model have been developed. Perhaps the best-known variant is the model of Jaffee and Modigliani (1969). Other variants are by Hodgman (1960), Miller (1962), and Freimer and Gordon (1965). The default risk model was developed originally for commercial loans, but the critical feature of the model—the assumption that the borrower's ability to repay the loan is finite—clearly applies also to consumer loans.

Jaffee and Modigliani considered a lender's loan amount and interest rate decision when the borrower's wealth—and hence ability to repay—is a random variable. They demonstrated that an optimal loan is one that equates the probability of default to the discounted difference between the loan interest rate and the opportunity rate. This result gives the loan-supply curve for an individual borrower its specific shape.

Normally, supply curves have a positive slope as higher prices elicit larger quantities supplied. In contrast, the loan-supply curve has several distinct features. For very small loan amounts, where repayment is virtually a certainty, the loan-supply curve is horizontal. That is, larger loan amounts do not entail higher interest rates. At some loan amount, default risk becomes a consideration, however. Greater loan amounts entail greater default risk and hence higher interest rates. Thus, the supply curve has a positive slope. But, the maximum loan amount is limited because, as mentioned, the borrower's wealth is finite. Based on the level of this finite wealth, a promise to pay a larger amount of interest is not credible. The borrower cannot possibly pay a larger amount even under the best of circumstances. Indeed, beyond the maximum loan amount, higher interest rates entail smaller loan amounts. Consequently, the loan offer bends backward.

The existence of a maximum loan amount is not credit rationing, though. Credit rationing requires consideration of demand and the determinants of the interest rate. Jaffee and

Modigliani argued that credit rationing occurs because legal restrictions and considerations of good will and social mores prevent charging different rates to different customers. Instead, they suggested, lenders group customers in a small number of risk classes based on a few objective and verifiable criteria and charge a single rate to all customers in the class. Within these classes, borrowers whose individual rate is less than the common class rate will not be rationed, and borrowers whose individual rate more than the class rate will be rationed.

13.4.2 Asymmetric Information and Adverse Selection

The basic default risk model of Jaffee and Modigliani does not consider the possibilities that lenders' information about borrowers may be imperfect or that the terms of a loan may affect borrowers' choices regarding risk or performance. Numerous models of credit markets with asymmetric information and adverse selection now exist. The models of Jaffee and Russell (1976) and Stiglitz and Weiss (1981) are among the best known and most influential.

Focusing on the latter, Stiglitz and Weiss demonstrate that adverse selection and moral hazard may cause credit rationing even in the absence of usury ceilings or community norms as suggested by Jaffee and Modigliani. Stiglitz and Weiss assume that the credit market is characterized by asymmetric information. Lenders observe only expected income but not the risk associated with income. In contrast, borrowers know both the expected value and risk.

Borrowers subsequently either realize income and repay the loan, or default if income plus any assets pledged as collateral is less than interest and principal. The borrower keeps any surplus income above the amount of loan repayment but cannot lose more than the amount of assets pledged as collateral. This limit to the borrower's downside risk gives rise to the possibility of adverse selection and moral hazard.

Higher interest rates reduce the amount of income available after loan repayment, but lower-risk individuals are less likely to default and, therefore, would be less likely than higher-risk individuals to benefit from the limitation in downside risk or to receive large surpluses. Thus, rises in the interest rate would cause fewer lower-risk individuals to apply for loans. The resulting worsening of the risk distribution of applicants caused by rising interest rates is called adverse selection.

The lender cannot receive any more than the repayment amount of interest and principal if there is no default, and may lose up to the repayment amount less than the value of any assets pledged as collateral. Thus, greater risk due to adverse selection would increase the likelihood for the lender of receiving less than the contracted amount of principal and interest and, other things equal, would reduce the lender's profit per loan. Consequently, raising the lending interest rate might increase the lender's profit per loan for a while, but eventually a higher interest rate causes lower-risk borrowers to drop out of the market, worsening credit risk through adverse selection and thereby reducing profit overall. In other words, the lender's profit would not always rise with increases in the interest rate but may fall at some point because at a higher interest rate lower-risk borrowers do not apply for credit.

Credit rationing may then occur because lenders' supply of funds depends on lenders' profit, but borrowers' demand depends on the loan interest rate. Lenders will not increase interest rates to equilibrate supply and demand if doing so reduces their profits, which as described above may occur when higher interest rates cause lower-risk borrowers to leave the market.

Stiglitz and Weiss considered several extensions to their model. Among the extensions are the effects of the interest rate on borrowers' subsequent choices, differences among borrowers in attitudes toward risk, and collateral or equity requirements. For example, the interest rate may influence the subsequent behavior of a borrower. Specifically, a higher interest rate may induce a borrower to choose a riskier income prospect, a change in behavior called moral hazard. The reason is due fundamentally to the same difference in borrower and lender incentives that cause adverse selection. That is, the riskier income prospect becomes more attractive to the borrower as the interest rate rises but less profitable for the lender. The presence of moral hazard then provides another incentive for the lender to ration credit rather than raise the interest.

13.4.3 Credit Scoring and Current Significance of Models of Default Risk, Asymmetric Information, and Adverse Selection

The default risk model of loan supply for individual borrowers establishes the importance of default risk in determination of the interest rate, but the empirical significance of credit rationing is likely less today than it was when the model was developed. Interest rate ceilings have relaxed by many lenders and effectively have disappeared for some types of lenders. Special rate ceilings have been enacted by some lenders explicitly to allow small, short-term loans (payday loans, for example, in some American states and in other countries). Furthermore, information asymmetries between borrowers and lenders have been reduced as advances in technology made collection, storage, and analysis of comprehensive credit information possible and economical. Automated credit bureaus contain virtually complete credit use and payment performance information for nearly all credit users in some places, and the development of statistical credit bureau risk scores provide highly accurate predictions of future payment performance and can be available to any lender. Availability of comprehensive credit reports and credit bureau scores also facilitates risk-based pricing, which reduces the significance of rationing within broad risk classes, as posited by Jaffee and Modigliani. Because of their usefulness for these purposes, public and private automated credit-reporting agencies have developed in many countries (see Japelli and Pagano, 2002 Tables 1 and 2).

Through most of the twentieth century, lenders trying to assess a borrower's creditworthiness were guided by their own judgment and experience following industry folklore known as the five "Cs" of lending: character (of borrowers), their capacity, capital, and collateral, and conditions (largely economic conditions). Until fairly recently, consumer lending decisions were generally made individually by loan officers who exercised their individual judgment with each application. Loan officers gathered information from and about the applicant in each of the five critical areas and applied lessons from their personal lending experience to decide whether an application should be approved.

As already indicated, more recently a number of factors have combined to push the consumer credit industry away from this "judgmental" model of underwriting. Competitive pressures on lending institutions to process efficiently the rising tide of loan applications undermined the slow and typically labor-intensive judgmental credit evaluation process. The result was a search for methods of automation, including statistical methodologies of credit evaluation that have come to be known as credit scoring, to take over the evaluation process from the older labor-intensive methods. Statistical methods consisting of advanced forms of multiple regression and correlation analysis have become the norm in credit evaluation, along with extensive automated information sources, to feed necessary information to the statistical evaluation models. Besides lowering the costs of the credit evaluation process, the automated statistical approaches also have the advantage of consistent application across loan applicants in a way that simplifies management of an intermediation/ lending enterprise. On this basis, they are unlike judgmental lending approaches that in the past were at least somewhat idiosyncratic to each individual loan officer. Statistical approaches do not invalidate the need for application of judgment to development of overall systems, however. Overreliance on data about past relationships in mortgage lending and excess faith in relatively new forms of financial engineering contributed to credit market difficulties in 2007–09.

Advances in information availability and in the technology to manage and analyze large amounts of information have improved lenders' ability to assess risk, and today many consumers are able to finance household investment and manage liquidity needs through primary lenders at the lower rates they offer. Nonetheless, there exists various "subprime" versions of credit cards, automobile financing, mortgage loans, and other credit. As the term "subprime" suggests, such products are mostly used by those who exhibit greater amounts of credit risk than mainstream consumers and likely are more credit constrained at low rates. There also are new short-term subprime cash-lending products to go with the small loan industry that has existed for decades and the pawn lenders that have been prevalent for centuries. The payday lending industry allows consumers to obtain an advance on their next paycheck, and 'automobile title' lenders offer small loans secured by consumers' automobiles. These newer lenders have been controversial, since the single-payment nature of their repayment sometimes can make timely repayment difficult for some borrowers. Consumer finance companies still make small installment loans, and small installment loans are different from these other products because their multi-payment nature suggests they can be better adapted to the budgets of rationed borrowers, especially when somewhat larger amounts of credit are needed over a longer period of time (see discussion of these institutions in Durkin et al., 2014, ch. 8).

13.5 REGULATION OF CONSUMER LENDING

Lending to individuals is as old as recorded human history and the interest of governments in regulating it is at least as old. For centuries this meant either absolute prohibition of consumer lending at interest or legal ceilings on the legal rate of interest, known respectively as usury laws and usury ceilings. In modern times, as interest and the economics of commercial activities have come to be better understood, usury restrictions have come to be less influential in many countries, although still important for consumer lending in some jurisdictions, including France, Italy, Portugal, and Switzerland (see Masciandaro, 2001).

Of more significance in recent decades is the growing governmental interest in ensuring transparency of consumer lending transactions and in regulating specific lending practices of financial institutions. An example of transparency regulation is the massive Truth in Lending Act of 1968 in the US, which covers most lending transactions involving consumers, including real estate transactions not generally within the definition of "consumer lending" employed here. The Truth in Lending Act and similar statutes elsewhere have a number of distinct advantages over other forms of government regulation. Improving transparency refers not only to the generic educational or credit-related educational materials in the lending area but rather to the governmental requirement of specific disclosures on details of lending transactions.

It seems that the importance of improved transparency and specific lending disclosures to government policy for protecting consumers in important transactions stems ultimately from at least three potential advantages over other methods of regulation (see Durkin and Elliehausen (2011) for more extended discussion). First, information protections often are compatible with existing market forces already at work to protect consumers. Financial services providers with good reputations and favorable pricing have an incentive to make these facts known, and required disclosures can provide for common standards and terminology, such as the finance charge and annual percentage rate (APR) under Truth in Lending in the US. Mandatory standards can then enhance the power of existing market incentives to provide information, advancing consumers' learning process, lowering its cost, and making it more efficient. Under the circumstances, required disclosures in a standard format help highlight the performance of the best institutions and expose the inadequacies of the poorer ones.

Second, if what consumers really lack is information in particular areas, then it seems logical that consumer protection should focus on providing what is missing rather than engaging in some other protection method. If consumers need information about pricing or terms of consumer credit contracts, for example, then it seems more reasonable to require disclosure of the information than to regulate prices or contract terms. Providing information rather than directly intervening does not require that the government knows, or presumes to know, the product-feature preferences of all consumers. With disclosures, consumers can decide for themselves what their own preferences are for the tradeoff between price and product features, and success of the disclosure approach does not depend on consumers' preferences being the same.

Third, required disclosures may be relatively lower in cost—both in terms of market disruption and out-of-pocket government expenditures—than other approaches to consumer protection, although some observers may argue this point. Lower expected costs of this sort from disclosure schemes undoubtedly have been instrumental in encouraging their adoption in some countries as political compromises between those demanding greater consumer protection and those arguing that more substantive market interference is too wrenching and costly or too harmful to the benefits that arise from a market-based system.

In contrast to transparency initiatives, an example of restrictions on lending practices to protect consumers is the Equal Credit Opportunity Act in the US, which prohibits taking into account in any credit-granting evaluation system (judgmental or statistical) certain individual characteristics such as sex, marital status, race, or national origin. Although implementation of this law in the 1970s required lenders to engage in costly review of all their evaluation practices and record-keeping procedures, few lenders today either disagree with the principles of equal credit opportunity or find compliance especially difficult. Although there are occasional claims that correlations between measures of lending experience, such as lending turndowns or loan pricing, with personal characteristics such as race or national origin are indicative of illegal discrimination, most observers of lending markets believe there are different reasons, including differential income and assets that support lending (see Avery, Brevoort, and Canner, 2006).

There also are many additional governmental restrictions on lending practices in the US and elsewhere, including the US federal Fair Credit Reporting Act (1970, with major revision in 2003) that regulates activities of credit-reporting agencies, the Fair Debt Collection Practices Act (1978) that governs third-party debt collection agencies, the Federal Trade Commission's rule on Credit Practices (1984), and the consumer lending codes of the 50 individual states. The federal requirements are quite extensive in their coverage, as are many of the state laws.

The 2008 financial crisis and ensuing recession stimulated further federal regulation of consumer credit. The Credit Card Accountability, Responsibility, and Disclosure Act (2009) mandated additional disclosures and imposed substantive restrictions on credit card accounts. Notable among the substantive restrictions are limits on interest rate increases and on the amount of fees that may be charged that were historically left to state regulation. The Dodd–Frank Wall Street Reform and Consumer Protection Act (2010) created a new regulatory agency, the Consumer Financial Protection Bureau, to enforce existing consumer financial regulations and implement new consumer protections deemed to be necessary to ensure fair, transparent, and competitive markets. The Dodd–Frank Act also contains many new requirements and restrictions on mortgage credit to consumers.

The 2008 financial crisis appeared to exacerbate somewhat the normal recessionary conditions restraining demand and restricting supply of consumer lending that occur in more typical cyclical downturns. Net change (normally growth) in consumer lending typically approaches zero briefly during recessionary periods due to these demand and supply influences taken together. Net change in consumer credit in the US in 2009 was slightly negative but not a great deal different than in typical cyclical episodes (see Durkin et al., 2014, ch. 2). The upturn since that time has followed the normal cyclical pattern.

13.6 CONCLUSION

Consumers have taken on debt obligations since antiquity, and lenders and the consumer lending marketplace have evolved over the centuries into today's very modern and sophisticated financial providers. The essential elements of consumer lending and borrowing are well established in economics, and it is possible to study many features of the lending process and its governmental regulation with the tools of modern economic analysis. Because so many people today use the products of consumer lending, however, and because of ongoing political interest in the nature of markets and institutions in this area, widespread public discussion of both the benefits and costs of consumer lending seems likely to continue, despite their familiarity. For this reason, continued attention to this area from economic analysts should continue to prove beneficial.

REFERENCES

Agarwal, S., Chomsisengphet, S., Liu, C., and Souleles, N. S. (2006). Do Consumers Choose the Right Credit Contracts?, Federal Reserve Bank of Chicago Working Paper No. 2006–11.

Agarwal, S., Driscoll, J. C., Gabaix, X., and Laibson, D. (2008). Learning in the Credit Card Market, National Bureau of Economic Research Working Paper No. 13822, <http://www.nber.org/papers/w13822.>.

Ausubel, L. (1999). Adverse Selection in the Credit Card Market. University of Maryland Working Paper.

Avery, R. B., Brevoort, K. P., and Canner, G. B. (2006). Higher-Priced Home Lending and the 2005 HMDA Data, *Federal Reserve Bulletin* 92, A123–A166.

Benston, G. J. and Smith Jr., C. W. (1976). A Transactions Cost Approach to the Theory of Financial Intermediation, *Journal of Finance* 31, 215–231.

Day, G. S. (1976). Assessing the Effects of Information Disclosure Requirements, *Journal of Marketing* 40, 42–52.

Day, G. S. and Brandt, W. K. (1973). A Study of Consumer Credit Decisions: Implications for Present and Prospective Legislation. In: *National Commission on Consumer Finance, Technical Studies of the National Commission on Consumer Finance*, Vol. I, 2. Washington, DC: US Government Printing Office, 1–123.

Day, G. S. and Brandt, W. K. (1974). Consumer Research and the Evaluation of Information Disclosure Requirements: The Case of Truth in Lending, *Journal of Consumer Research* 1, 21–32.

Dunkelberg, W. C. and Stephenson, J. (1974). Durable Goods Ownership and the Rate of Return. In: *National Commission on Consumer Finance, Technical Studies of the National Commission on Consumer Finance*, Vol. 6. Washington, DC: US Government Printing Office, 31–65.

Durkin, T. A. and Elliehausen, G. (2011). *Truth in Lending: Theory, History, and a Way Forward*. Oxford and New York: Oxford University Press.

Durkin, T. A., Elliehausen, G., Staten, M. E., and Zywicki, T. J. (2014). *Consumer Credit and the American Economy*. New York: Oxford University Press.

Elliehausen, G. and Lawrence, E. C. (2001). *Payday Advance Credit in America: An Analysis of Customer Demand*. Georgetown University, McDonough School of Business, Washington, DC, Credit Research Center Monograph No. 35.

Fisher, I. (1930). *The Theory of Interest*. New York: Macmillan.

Frederick, S., Loewenstein, G., and O'Donohue, T. (2002). Time Discounting and Time Preference: A Critical Review, *Journal of Economic Literature* 40, 351–401.

Freimer, M. and Gordon, M. J. (1965). Why Bankers Ration Credit, *Quarterly Journal of Economics* 79, 397–416.

Gross, D. B. and Souleles, N. B. (2002). Do Liquidity Constraints and Interest Rates Matter for Consumer Behavior, *Quarterly Journal of Economics* 117, 149–185.

Gurley, J. G. and Shaw, E. S. (1960). *Money in a Theory of Finance*. Washington, DC: The Brookings Institution.

Hirschleifer, J. (1958). On the Theory of Optimal Investment Decision, *Journal of Political Economy* 66, 329–352.

Hodgman, D. R. (1960). Credit Risk and Credit Rationing, *Quarterly Journal of Economics* 74, 258–278.

Jaffee, D. M. and Modigliani, F. (1969). A Theory and Test of Credit Rationing, *American Economic Review* 59, 850–872.

Jaffee, D. M. and Russell, T. (1976). Imperfect Information, Uncertainty, and Credit Rationing, *Quarterly Journal of Economics* 90, 651–666.

Japelli, T. and Pagano, M. (2002). Information Sharing, Lending, and Defaults: Cross-Country Evidence, *Journal of Banking and Finance* 26(10), 2017–2045.

Juster, F. T. and Shay, R. P. (1964). Consumer Sensitivity to Finance Rates: An Empirical and Analytical Investigation, New York, National Bureau of Economic Research Occasional Paper No. 88.

Kahneman, D. and Tversky, A. (1979). Prospect Theory: An Analysis of Decision under Risk, *Econometrica* 47, 263–292.

Mann, R. (2013). Assessing the Optimism of Payday Loan Borrowers, Columbia University School of Law, Center for Law and Economic Studies Working Paper No. 443.

Masciandaro, D. (2001). In Offense of Usury Laws: Microfoundations of Illegal Credit Contracts, *European Journal of Law & Economics* 12, 193–215.

Miller, M. H. (1962). Credit Risk and Credit Rationing: Further Comment, *Quarterly Journal of Economics* 76, 480–488.

Poapst, J. V. and Waters, W. R. (1964). Rates of Return on Consumer Durables, *Journal of Finance* 19, 673–677.

Stigler, G. J. (1961). The Economics of Information, *Journal of Political Economy* 69, 213–225.

Stiglitz, J. E. and Weiss, A. (1981). Credit Rationing in Markets with Imperfect Information, *American Economic Review* 71, 393–410.

Tversky, A. and Kahneman, D. (1974). Judgment under Uncertainty: Heuristics and Biases, *Science* 185, 1124–1131.

CHAPTER 14

....

RESIDENTIAL MORTGAGES

....

GREGORY DONADIO AND
ANDREAS LEHNERT[*]

14.1 INTRODUCTION

....

A *mortgage* is a legal arrangement in which a lender (the *mortgagee*) has some kind of legal claim on an underlying piece of real property held by a borrower (the *mortgagor*). Interested parties other than the mortgagee may have claims to the property; such claims (as well as the mortgagor's) are often referred to as *liens*. A separate legal document, sometimes known as the *note*, sets out the terms and conditions under which the borrower will satisfy the lender and discharge the debt. In practice, most research tends to conflate the mortgage, lien, and note into a single entity known simply as a mortgage. Except where required for technical reasons, we will follow this convention.

The precise legal arrangements vary across jurisdictions, depending both on the underlying legal tradition of the jurisdiction (e.g., common vs. civil law) and on specific statutes enacted by the jurisdiction. For example, even jurisdictions with similar legal traditions, such as individual states in the US, differ markedly in their statutory treatment of *foreclosure*, the legal process by which lenders seize property from borrowers in default of the terms of their notes.

Mortgage banking traditionally consists of three related businesses: origination, funding, and servicing. Origination is the extension of new credit to borrowers; funding refers to the mix of debt, equity, and market-based instruments used to finance portfolios of mortgages; and servicing is the day-to-day business of managing payments from borrowers. These three businesses can be separated; indeed, many banks prefer to use their retail presence

[*] Board of Governors of the Federal Reserve System. The views expressed here are solely those of the authors and do not reflect the views of the Federal Reserve Board or its staff. We thank Helen Keil-Losch for bibliographic assistance.

to concentrate on originating mortgages, then selling them to investors on the secondary market for loans rather than funding them internally. Mortgage servicing, because it features large fixed costs, can exhibit significant scale economies. Thus, many of the functions of mortgage banking can be done outside of traditional depository institutions.

The US mortgage market was the initial locus of the turmoil that hit financial markets beginning in August 2007. The US housing market appears to be recovering: originations increased in 2012 relative to 2011, when they hit their lowest level since 1995. However, the level of activity remains well below pre-crisis levels (Avery et al., 2012; Bhutta and Canner, 2013). Research since the crisis has addressed several topics, including the causes of the credit boom, the connection between credit and house prices, the optimal strategy for modifying mortgages, and the scope for regulation to minimize the financial stability consequences of future housing market disruptions.

This chapter aims to provide the reader with an introduction to residential mortgages and their relationship to banking. It will describe the common features of residential mortgages (Section 14.2); factors influencing household behavior (Section 14.3); the market for mortgages as a financial asset (Section 14.4); bank capital regulation and its treatment of residential mortgages (Section 14.5). Finally, Section 14.6 addresses the financial stability implications of mortgage market developments, including the so-called "macroprudential" approach to regulating housing finance.

14.2 RESIDENTIAL MORTGAGE FEATURES

Mortgages are a specialized asset class, with their own jargon and specific concerns. We describe how to compute payments on mortgages, the terminology and key concepts in the decision to extend credit to a borrower, the issues surrounding the seizure of collateral, and, finally, the little-studied back-office work of processing payments and contacting borrowers.

14.2.1 Mortgage Payments

In principle, mortgages describe a series of payments to be made by the borrower; with the successful completion of these payments the borrower usually holds clear title to the property (hence the term "mortgage," or "dead pledge"). The process of decreasing the principal balance owed on a mortgage is known as *amortization*. In addition, mortgages carry an interest rate that can vary over time, usually in line with a published index. Mortgages can differ in how interest rates are determined and in their amortization schedules.

A mortgage will carry a *note rate*, r_t, the interest rate on the loan, usually expressed as an annual percentage. The actual rate applied to the loan for a month's borrowing is, by convention, the annual rate divided by 12. The mortgage will have a remaining maturity, T_t. Given a payment at the end of the month, x_t, and an unpaid principal balance at the end of the previous period, P_{t-1}, the unpaid principal balance at the end of period t is $(1+r_t)P_{t-1} - x_t$.

If the payment is designed to amortize the loan over the remaining maturity of T_t periods, it must be the case that $P_{T_t} = 0$. Substituting, the payment x_t must satisfy:

$$x_t = r_t P_{t-1} \frac{(1+r_t)^{T_t}}{(1+r_t)^{T_t} - 1}. \tag{14.1}$$

This formula assumes that the note rate r_t remains constant over time. As the note rate fluctuates, the payment will fluctuate, both to pay for the higher cost of borrowing a month's worth of the principal, but also to amortize the loan over the remaining maturity. Alternatively, the maturity could adjust to offset changes in interest rates to keep the payment constant, as in *variable maturity mortgages*.

Mortgages may offer varying amounts of interest rate protection. A *fixed rate* mortgage (FRM) carries a constant note rate. An *adjustable rate* mortgage (known as an ARM) carries a note rate that is usually computed as a fixed margin over a published index; ARMs vary in the frequency of adjustment. For example, the note rate on an ARM could adjust every six months and be computed as a 2% margin over the average value of the six-month Libor prevailing in the month prior to adjustment. *Hybrid* mortgages carry a fixed rate for an extended period before converting to an ARM. The term *variable rate* mortgage is sometimes used to encompass traditional ARMs and hybrids.

Mortgages may have provisions that allow the principal balance to remain constant (*interest-only payments* where $x_t = r_t P_t$) or even grow (*negative amortization payments* where $x_t < r_t P_t$). Some mortgages allow borrowers to choose the amount of amortization from month to month. All of these loans have a cap on the principal balance. When amortization schedules are recomputed, loans are said to *recast*. Often, mortgage payments then rise to the so-called fully amortizing rate, sufficient to pay off the total principal balance over the remaining life of the loan.

Variable-rate mortgages may have caps on how much the scheduled payment can rise at a time; however, these caps may be coupled with a provision that the difference between the fully indexed payment $r_t P_t$ and the capped payment $\bar{r}_t P_t$ be added to the principal.

As an alternative to non-amortizing loans, some loans amortize on a longer schedule than their contractual maturity. For example, a loan's principal payments may be computed as if the principal were to be repaid over 40 years, while the loan in fact is only set to last 30 years. The final payment of such a mortgage, consisting of all unpaid principal, is called a *balloon payment*.

The maturity of the loan, T_t, can vary over time. However, the traditional or typical maturity varies across countries as well. In the US, the standard maturity is 30 years, in many other countries it is shorter, while in some countries, notably Japan, it can be longer.

Mortgages can also have balloon payments due in a relative short amount of time, such as five years after origination. Typically, borrowers do not actually make the balloon payment; instead, they take out a new loan to pay the balloon payment. Since the mortgage crisis, balloon payments—typically defined as terminal payments more than twice as large as earlier payments—have become quite rare in the US. These arrangements were seen by some as unfair and deceptive because some borrowers appeared to focus only on the payments required in the first few months of the mortgage's life. Such borrowers would thus be surprised when faced with the prospect of paying off the balance or refinancing the loan. In addition, even fully informed and rational borrowers found it difficult to refinance ahead of their balloon payments in the tight credit conditions that prevailed following the financial crisis.

14.2.2 The Credit-Extension Decision

Lenders are said to *underwrite* a loan when they decide whether or not to extend credit (or *originate* a loan) to a potential borrower, and, if so, on what terms. There are four main variables that commonly enter the underwriting decision, as well as a host of other considerations.

First, because mortgages are collateralized debt, the lender must value the property. Ideally, properties would be sold at auction, and the lender would value the property using the second-highest bid. In the event the borrower defaults, the lender could seize the property and sell it to that second-highest bidder. Yet, in most countries (with some notable exceptions), houses are not usually sold at auction. Further, borrowers may want to get a loan to refinance an existing mortgage rather than to purchase a home. To value the property, then, lenders must rely on an independent valuation, known as an *appraisal*. Evidence suggests that, as one might expect, appraisers are under pressure to report a value high enough to enable the deal to go through (see LaCour-Little and Malpezzi, 2003). Indeed, Ben-David (2008) suggests that, in some instances, appraisers systemically over-report home values as part of a broader scheme to defraud lenders.

Appraisals can enter house price indexes as if they were true arm's-length transactions. Several major house price indexes now routinely strip out appraisals from their base data when constructing their indexes. However, Leventis (2006) points out that appraisals, even though flawed, may give some information on price movements, and hence excluding them needlessly increases the standard error of the estimate. He describes a procedure for removing this "appraisal bias"—the tendency of appraisals to overvalue properties—from house price indexes. Leventis argues, based on findings in the literature, that appraisals are more likely to be inflated for refinancings where the borrower liquidates equity, that is, cash-out refinancings, relative to refinancings where the borrower merely wants to take advantage of lower interest rates (so-called "rate/term" refinancing). Leventis estimates a model in which reported house prices are inflated by a constant proportion each period, depending on the type of refinancing. He finds that his improved price index has a lower variance and the same mean as a "purchase only" index.

Second, lenders must decide how much of an equity cushion to require. This is usually measured as the *loan to price* or *loan to value* (LTV) ratio, defined as the mortgage principal divided by the property's value. Given a low enough LTV and foreclosure laws that permit the timely seizure of collateral, mortgage lending could in principle be risk-free. For example, with an LTV at origination of 75%, even if house prices declined 20% and the borrower defaulted, the lender would still be unlikely to take a loss on the loan.

However, potential homebuyers often find onerous the large down payments required to achieve low LTVs (see Haurin, Herbert, and Rosenthal (2007), among others). In principle, lenders should be, and have been, willing to accept the increased risk associated with higher LTVs in exchange for higher note rates (Edelberg, 2006). For institutional reasons, in the US, borrowers seeking an LTV above 80% often resort to either *mortgage insurance*, in which a third party guarantees repayment of principal to the lender in exchange for monthly insurance premiums paid by the borrower, or to *piggyback mortgages* or *junior liens*, in which the borrower makes a down payment of less than 20%, but splits the mortgage into a loan with an LTV of 80% and a second loan for the remaining amount. (This is sometimes also known, rather confusingly, as "borrowing the downpayment.") Operationally, investors and other market participants can find it difficult to determine whether a given mortgage has an associated junior lien, making it difficult for them to determine the total debt on a property. These junior liens were a major source of leverage in the credit boom and contributed to difficulties in resolving mortgage defaults (Cordell et al., 2010).

Third, lenders consider the borrower's ability to make the scheduled mortgage payments. Usually, lenders compute various payment-to-income ratios (also known as debt-to-income or DTI ratios) and compare them to thresholds determined by underwriting guidelines. A commonly used ratio, known as the *back end ratio*, compares monthly payments associated with all debts on a household's balance sheet (including property taxes and insurance, credit card, auto loans, and so on) to the household's post-tax income. However, measuring and verifying a borrower's income is not straightforward. Before the 2008 crisis some lenders considered expected future income such as unrealized bonuses while some borrowers preferred not to document certain income sources. In many cases, lenders relied in part on the borrower's own estimation of their ability to make mortgage payments. This difficulty in verifying income led to the rise of lending with incomplete verification of income and assets, known as *low doc* or *no doc* loans. These loans—which came to be known as "liar loans" during the crisis—have since vanished.

Fourth, lenders often consider a borrower's history of making all debt payments on time, including payments on credit cards, auto, and student loans. In the US a popular summary measure of borrower credit quality developed by Fair, Isaac Company, known as the FICO score, has become a quick rule of thumb for determining whether a borrower is prime quality or below prime, in other words, "subprime." (However, note that most underwriting engines use more than just the FICO score to determine a borrower's credit risk.) Barakova et al. (2003), using data on US households, find that wealth and income apparently decreased in importance as barriers to homeownership during the 1990s, while credit scores increased in importance. This result underscores lenders' increased willingness to accept the risks associated with high LTV loans and reliance on credit histories.

Since the financial crisis, underwriting standards have tightened dramatically, both because of new regulations and because of lenders' increased caution following the outsized credit losses of the financial crisis. These tightened underwriting standards are illustrated in Figure 14.1; borrowers with impaired credit histories have been effectively unable to get new loans.

14.2.3 Seizure of Collateral

Mortgage lending is unlike other consumer lending because it is secured; however, if lenders cannot easily seize the underlying collateral, this advantage wanes. However, policymakers may also want to design legal systems that delay collateral seizure in order to provide homeowners with some crude insurance and bargaining power to protect them against shocks to income and house prices.

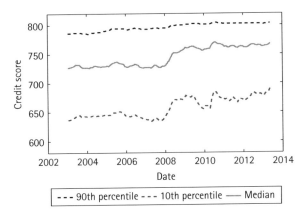

FIGURE 14.1 Credit scores for prime mortgage borrowers.

Note: Figure shows the FICO scores on prime purchase mortgage originations.
Federal Reserve staff calculations based on data provided by McDash Analytics, LLC,
a wholly owned subsidiary of Lender Processing Services, Inc.

Mortage borrowers are typically not considered as seriously delinquent, and hence at risk for having their home seized, until they have missed three consecutive mortgage payments. What happens at this point varies by state within the US, and, even more, across countries. Laws and regulations can be designed to hinder or ease the transfer of ownership from the borrower to the lender, a process known as *foreclosure*. In the US, a lender typically starts the foreclosure process with a *notice of default*. Using cross-state variation in the length of time between the foreclosure start and the final transfer of property, Pence (2006) shows that more defaulter-friendly foreclosure laws lead lenders to demand higher down payments, and thus restrict credit access, because more defaulter-friendly laws delay repossession of the property and impose additional costs on the lender. Pence also cites a 1938 study that found higher foreclosure costs in states with defaulter-friendly foreclosure laws by the Home Owner's Loan Corporation (the original New Deal entity that became Fannie Mae). Clauretie and Herzog (1990) use data from mortgage insurers to estimate losses from more defaulter-friendly foreclosure laws. They find that lenders lose more money on loans that default in states with laws that hinder the foreclosure process. Certain jurisdictions permit loans to be made *with recourse*; that is, lenders have a legal right to pursue judgments against borrowers for any deficiency between the foreclosure proceeds and the outstanding loan balance at the time of default. Such arrangements are thought to decrease the strategic default motive (discussed in greater detail in Section 14.3.2).

Pence (2006) cites estimates of the financial losses to mortgage holders following a foreclosure ranging between 30% and 60% of the unpaid principal balance on the loan. Not only do lenders have to incur legal costs and expenses associated with maintaining a property, they have to face a sometimes-substantial delay before they can repossess the property and resell it. An extensive literature documents these foreclosure costs (see, among others, Clauretie, 1989; Capone, 1996; Ciochetti, 1997).

The large increase in foreclosures following the collapse in house prices in 2009—foreclosures jumped from a pre-crisis average of 1.2 million per year to a peak of over 8 million in 2009—strained the capacity of servicers and the legal system as well as prompted a variety of formal and informal government interventions. Cordell et al. (2013) estimate that the

time-related costs of foreclosure have increased about eight percentage points since the financial crisis; from a pre-crisis level of 11% to a post-2012 level of 19% of the loan's unpaid balance.
The authors also show that these costs are even higher in defaulter-friendly states and present
evidence that foreclosure delays can have other negative effects on neighborhoods.

The dramatic rise in the number of foreclosures following the collapse of house prices in
the US focused attention on the spillover effects of foreclosures. If a foreclosure drives down
the prices of neighboring properties, default could become contagious (see Campbell and
Giglio, 2011).

14.2.4 Mortgage Servicing

Mortgage servicing is the business of computing scheduled payments on mortgages, collecting these payments from borrowers and transmitting the proceeds to the mortgage
owners or holders. In addition, servicers monitor borrowers' credit records for events that
can threaten the value of the collateral, such as failure to pay property insurance, personal
bankruptcy filing, or liens filed by other creditors, such as *mechanics liens* or liens filed by
homeowners' associations. Finally, servicers are usually responsible for handling delinquent
borrowers, whether by foreclosing on the property or some other course of action.

Mortgage servicers are usually paid by allowing them to retain a portion of the borrower's
monthly payment; for example, a servicer's fee might be quoted as "25 basis points," indicating that, on a mortgage with a note rate of 6.75%, the servicer transmits 6.50% to the mortgage holder and retains 0.25% for itself. However, servicers are typically required to advance
scheduled principal and interest payments to the mortgage holders even if the borrower has
stopped paying. The servicer can recoup the value of these advances as well as out-of-pocket
expenses incurred during a foreclosure proceeding (see Cordell et al., 2010 for more information on the incentives faced by mortgage servicers).

Mortgage servicers charge more to handle loans that require them to contact borrowers more often. For example, borrowers with weaker credit histories can routinely miss
one payment per year. While such borrowers are in technical violation of the terms of their
mortgage, mortgage servicers typically respond by reminding the borrower of his missed
obligation, and most of these borrowers subsequently make good on the missed payment.
However, this kind of repeated contact is expensive, and explains part of the larger fee
charged to service such loans.

When a borrower misses several payments in a row, servicers must decide whether to
pursue a foreclosure to allow the borrower an opportunity to make good the missed payments. Stegman et al. (2007) argue that such forbearance, and even more aggressive policies
known as *modifications*, which involve permanent changes to the terms of a mortgage to
decrease monthly payments, increase the net present value of a mortgage. Rather than seizing a property whose value has likely fallen, Stegman et al. point out that by changing the
terms of the mortgage to better suit a borrower's circumstances (which had perhaps changed
since origination), the servicer is more likely to realize continued timely payments, albeit
smaller than before, and avoid the expense of seizing the property. Eggert (2007) points out
that while loan modifications may indeed make broad economic sense, the incentives of
servicers are far from clear in this case and that the ultimate owners of the mortgage may
disagree on how best to proceed.

Since the 2008 financial crisis, mortgage modification has become a part of US policy. In response to the dramatic increase in foreclosures, the government started the Home Affordable Modification Program (HAMP) as part of the Financial Stability Act of 2009. The goal of the program is to help borrowers modify their mortgage payments to affordable levels, defined as a household debt-to-income ratio of 31%. Since its implementation, HAMP has modified loans for over 1.2 million households (US Dept. of the Treasury, 2013). According to the Mortgage Bankers Association National Delinquency Survey, during the same period over 7.7 million foreclosures were started.

14.3 Household Decision Making

In this section we analyze household decision making regarding mortgages. First, we consider the various choices a borrower faces before taking on a mortgage: how much to borrow, how much interest rate risk to accept, what kind of amortization structure to use, and whether to accept a prepayment penalty. Second, we consider the various choices a borrower faces if they are in difficulty after taking on a mortgage: whether to refinance the loan or whether to default on the loan.

14.3.1 Choice of Mortgage Contract Features

Households face a menu of options when taking out mortgages, with the items on this menu differing radically across countries. Research has focused on choices made by consumers in the US because of the relatively large number of options available and because of the presence of several useful data sources with which to study decisions. Despite setbacks, the trend across countries appears to be towards ever-greater choice, suggesting that the US experience can be a useful lesson elsewhere. A comprehensive list of cross-country differences in mortgage systems, as well as differing household choices among options, is available from the Bank for International Settlements (2006) and the International Monetary Fund (2011).

Since the 2008 crisis, the willingness of lenders to accept mortgage credit risk has diminished sharply, limiting the availability of credit relative to pre-crisis norms. As shown in Figure 14.1, tightened credit terms have limited mortgages to borrowers with higher credit scores.

Mortgage debt typically moves in line with house prices; the correlation coefficient between the annual percentage change in house prices and mortgage debt is 0.81. However, this cannot be taken as evidence of a causal relationship between borrowing and house prices—unobserved common factors, such as expected future house price growth, likely influence both households' willingness to pay for a house *and* their willingness to borrow to finance the purchase. Thus, causation is likely to run in both directions.

Household borrowing may be constrained by caps on LTVs, as discussed in the previous section. In principle, borrowers should face an interest rate trade-off between increased leverage and higher mortgage rates. Edelberg (2006) shows that such risk-based pricing increased in the 1990s in the US; Bucks, Kennickell, and Moore (2006) document that household leverage increased since the late 1990s. Stein (1995) and Lamont and Stein (1999) argue that leverage constraints are binding for the marginal homebuyer, and that when buyers can use greater leverage, equilibrium house prices move more in response to a shock to fundamentals, such as unemployment. Thus, the mortgage market acts as an amplification mechanism.

In addition, some national tax codes, including that in the US, permit the deduction of mortgage interest, which may encourage households to use more debt than is optimal. (Technically, a mortgage interest deduction should not distort households' debt choice if it is coupled with a tax on the imputed income derived from the service flow of housing financed by the debt.) Amromin, Huang, and Sialm (2007) find that US households forgo a potentially lucrative tax arbitrage between tax-exempt debt (mortgages) and tax-preferred savings (401(k) plans). They ascribe this in part to debt-aversion, as described by Graham (2000). This suggests that, at the margin at least, the tax code may not exert as great an effect on household mortgage choice as one might expect.

The next choice faced by households concerns the level of interest rate risk they are willing to accept. National mortgage systems differ markedly in the amount of interest rate protection available. Mortgages with contract rates that are fixed for five or more years are widely available in Canada, Germany, France, Belgium, Switzerland, the Netherlands, and the US, although these mortgages may carry prepayment penalties—clauses in the contracts charge borrowers for paying off loans early—and other features. The UK has attempted to encourage fixed-rate borrowing, although with mixed success (see Miles, 2004).

To illustrate this choice, consider a hypothetical homebuyer who wishes to borrow $100,000 in January 2006 using either a hypothetical one-year Treasury ARM or a standard fixed-rate mortgage: here, the hypothetical ARM resets to the one-year Treasury rate plus, by assumption, 2% every year (see Stanton and Wallace, 1999, for more details of common features of ARMs). The homebuyer will remain in the home for seven years. The note rate on the ARM adjusts essentially in line with US monetary policy over the period. The rate on the FRM is constant except when the borrower refinances during the extremely low rate environment of early 2012. (Here, refinancing is assumed to cost 1% of the loan balance and borrowers refinance when current rates fall 1.5% below their current contract rate; we discuss refinancing in greater detail below.) Assuming the borrower has a constant 3% discount rate, the present discounted value (PDV) of his interest and refinancing expenses would have totaled about $41,000 had he taken the fixed rate loan, and $35,000 had he taken the adjustable rate loan.

Figure 14.2 shows the PDV of interest payments for the same hypothetical fixed and adjustable rate loans originated each month from January 1972 to May 2007. As shown, the relative advantage of one mortgage type over the other is dwarfed by the low-frequency trend in US interest rates. This is particularly clear since 2008 as US Treasury rates neared zero. Further, this is an ex post exercise and does not reflect the ex ante conditions faced by the household when making the decision between fixed rate and adjustable rate mortgages. Finally, no consideration is made here for the very important issue of household risk aversion. That said, homebuyers in the 1970s would, generally speaking, have been much better off using fixed rate mortgages, while homebuyers in the 1990s would have been slightly better off using adjustable rate mortgages. However, this difference is relatively small, sensitive to assumptions, and does not reflect all the considerations faced by households). Earlier studies (see Shilling, Dhillon, and Sirmans 1987; Brueckner and Follain, 1988; Brueckner, 1993) focused on the relative risks of the two mortgage types, while Campbell and Cocco (2003) find that the real cost of nominal fixed rate mortgages is extremely sensitive to

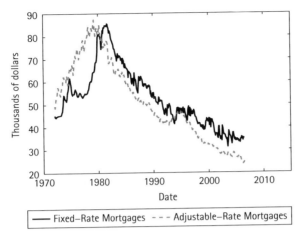

FIGURE 14.2 Present discounted value of interest and refinancing expenses for hypothetical fixed rate and adjustable rate mortgages.

Note: Figure shows the present discounted value of interest payments for a hypothetical homebuyer financing
$100,000 using either a fixed rate (solid line) or adjustable rate (dashed line) mortgage. See text for details on the
hypothetical mortgages.

realized inflation. They argue that inflation-indexed fixed rate mortgages offer the benefits of stable payments without requiring an inflation premium. In their follow-up work
Campbell and Cocco (2012) show that borrowers who take adjustable rate mortgages are
more prone to default when interest rates rise, from the combination in increased required
mortgage payments and tighter borrowing constraints.

The next choice faced by households concerns the mortgages' amortization schedule.
Amortization can be seen as a form of portfolio shuffling; households are building their
home equity at the expense of other forms of saving. In this view, households pay down
their mortgage, taking into account the risk/return profiles of other investment opportunities (see Fu, LaCour-Little, and Vandell, 1997). Alternatively, mortgages with deferred amortization schedules are marketed as *affordability products*, emphasizing their lower payments
relative to fully amortizing mortgages. LaCour-Little and Yang (2010) find that borrowers
with greater expected income growth, or those purchasing homes in areas with rapidly
appreciating prices, are more likely to select loans with deferred amortization, suggesting
that borrowers do indeed value the decreased payment burden associated with deferred
amortization. LaCour-Little and Yang (2010) also show that, over the course of many years,
the lack of amortization on a mortgage leaves the borrower with less equity on the property
and hence more likely to default. Piskorski and Tchistyi (2010) argue that, within the context
of a mechanism design problem, the optimal mortgage contract can be characterized as a
loan with amortization under the control of the borrower, including negative amortization
options, which are used to offset shocks to household income. During the 2008 financial crisis, non-traditional repayment mortgages, such as interest-only or other alternate amortization products, faced much higher delinquency and default rates than standard mortgages
(Mayer, Pence, and Sherlund, 2009). Subsequent financial reforms, including the Dodd–
Frank Act in the United States, have included provisions to restrict mortgages with negative
amortization and other non-traditional means of repayment.

The final choice that a household makes is whether to enter into a mortgage that carries some form of a prepayment penalty or other feature that makes refinancing less desirable. As we discuss in Section 14.4, lenders funding mortgages with non-callable liabilities (such as deposits or standard loans) must carefully manage prepayment risk when holding leveraged portfolios of fixed rate mortgage assets. In the absence of a well-developed market for fixed income derivatives, such lenders will require extra compensation to hold fixed rate mortgages without prepayment penalties. In countries such as the US with relatively liquid fixed income markets, prepayment penalties can spare the lender the cost of hedging. In practice, however, prepayment penalties are usually not even offered to prime borrowers, and there is considerable debate as to whether prepayment penalties offer any net benefits to borrowers. Elliehausen, Staten, and Steinbuks (2008) find that loans with prepayment penalties carry lower rates and fees than equivalent loans without them. However, if enough borrowers actually refinance, and hence must pay the fee, this benefit could be offset. Borrowers have the option of paying *points*; that is, buying down the contract rate on their loan by paying an upfront fee. Brueckner (1994) argues that points are an effective signal of a borrower's unwillingness to refinance.

Given the various dimensions discussed in this section along which a mortgage contract can differ, it is reasonable to wonder whether the typical borrower understands the terms of their mortgage. Bucks and Pence (2008) find that most borrowers understand the broad terms of their mortgages. However, some borrowers with adjustable rate mortgages underestimated the size of the caps on potential changes in their note rates.

14.3.2 Household Decisions to Refinance or Default

Borrowers who already have a mortgage can decide to *refinance* or *remortgage*; that is, take out a new mortgage under different terms than the existing loan and use the proceeds to pay off the existing loan. Borrowers may also decide, or be forced by a negative shock, to *default*; that is, to violate the agreed-upon terms of the note by failing to make adequate or timely payments of principal or interest.

Standard models treat the refinance and default decisions as options embedded in the mortgage. In this view, refinancing corresponds to an option to call the mortgage at par (assuming no prepayment penalties), while default corresponds to an option to put the mortgage back to the lender at the value of the house (assuming non-recourse lending). From period to period, mortgages terminate in a default, terminate in a refinancing, or continue to the next period. Thus, the standard empirical model is a modified version of the duration model known as a *competing hazards* model. Deng, Quigley, and van Order (2000) added unobserved borrower heterogeneity; their model, and its subsequent adumbrations, is the workhorse model used in mortgage-level analysis. Gerardi, Shapiro, and Willen (2008) constructed a dataset of homeownership experiences, rather than mortgages; in their research paper, a homeowner goes through multiple mortgages, and the competing hazards are voluntary sale and loss of the home involuntarily through foreclosure.

Borrowers refinance for other reasons besides the desire to lower their note rate (i.e., at times when new mortgages carry substantially lower rates than existing mortgages): they may wish to increase their mortgage principal. Such *cash out* refinancings often are the cheapest form of financing available to borrowers, even if the new mortgage carries a rate higher than the mortgage it is replacing. Hurst and Stafford (2004) document that households with few liquid assets are more likely to undertake a cash-out refinancing following an employment shock. Such refinancings allow households to tap their accumulated home equity and thus smooth consumption.

Because most refinancing occurs when rates are relatively low and most refinancers at such times are simply seeking to lower their contract interest rates, the two series—until the 2008 financial crisis—exhibit an inverse correlation. At that time the fraction of cash-out refinancing dropped to low levels in part because cash-out refinancings carried additional credit risk and lenders were sharply tightening underwriting standards.

The Federal Reserve Board has conducted a series of surveys of borrowers undertaking a cash-out refinancing. Canner, Dynan, and Passmore (2002) find that the most popular reported uses of funds raised were, first, to repay other debts (presumably carrying higher interest rates), second, to finance a home improvement project, third, to purchase consumer items, and fourth to invest the proceeds. Weighted by dollars raised, home improvement projects became the most popular use of funds. It is interesting to note that French mortgage law typically does not allow borrowers to increase their mortgage balance after the purchase of a property (Bank for International Settlements, 2006).

Mortgage defaults appear to be primarily driven by house prices or, more precisely, the borrower's equity in the home. Indeed, if a borrower has a significant amount of equity in the home, default is unlikely because the borrower would prefer to sell the home and realize the equity rather than have it repossessed by the lender. However, there is some debate over whether borrower behavior is best characterized as the exercise of the put option in the mortgage, with borrowers walking away from the property once its price dropped below a critical threshold, or whether defaults are ultimately driven by cash flow considerations.

The former view is sometimes characterized as *ruthless default* while the latter view is known as the *double trigger* or *borrower solvency* theory of default. In the double trigger view, negative equity is a necessary but not sufficient condition for default; the underlying pace of adverse life events such as job loss, uninsured medical expenses, divorce, and so on, show through to default rates only when borrowers do not have an equity cushion to rely on. The two views can be reconciled if one assumes that there are substantial transaction costs from default, pushing the optimal default trigger price extremely low. Indeed, Foote, Gerardi, and Willen (2008) document that a large number of homeowners in Massachusetts endured several years of negative equity in the early 1990s without defaulting.

Quigley and van Order (1995) conduct one of the first empirical tests of the pure "ruthless default" model and find that observed defaults imply fairly high transaction costs. Ambrose, Capone, and Deng (2001) estimate the trigger values of a put option and find that, again, a frictionless model of option exercise does a poor job of explaining the data, suggesting that borrowers weigh more than the narrow financial benefit of defaulting. However, the authors also find evidence that forward-looking borrowers consider the state of the housing market and thus emphasize the importance of expectations in the borrower decision. Campbell and Cocco (2012) focus on adjustable rate and fixed rate mortgage defaults, also showing that borrowers do not default as soon as they face negative home equity. Rather intuitively, they find that adjustable rate mortgage defaults increase when interest rates increase and when there are shocks to labor income. Fixed rate mortgages, by comparison, have a higher probability of default when inflation and interest rates are low.

14.4 RESIDENTIAL MORTGAGES AS A FINANCIAL ASSET

In the same way that a mortgage is a household liability as discussed in Sections 14.2 and 14.3, it is an asset held by the lender. Like any other asset, mortgages can be sold individually or used to back larger securities. Indeed, lenders, investors, and other financial market participants value mortgages using the standard tools for valuing any asset that generates a series of scheduled and largely fixed payments. A description of the fixed income valuation toolkit is beyond the scope of this chapter. Nonetheless, we discuss approaches to valuing the options embedded in residential mortgages and the inherent challenges of valuing individual mortgages. Because whole loans are relatively illiquid and hard-to-value financial instruments, investors prefer to buy securities backed by thousands of individual mortgages, often with extra protections to make valuation easier. Again, there is an enormous practical and scientific literature on mortgage-backed securities, which is outside the scope of this chapter. We instead describe some of the important organizing principles and institutional features of mortgage securitization.

14.4.1 Valuing a Mortgage

The primary concern in valuing the cash stream generated by a mortgage is determining the probability that the mortgage will either default or prepay conditional on realizations of the appropriate aggregate variables thought to determine state prices (see Duffie, 1992). If cash flow in future states is valued based on just the prevailing risk-free rate, the key issue is how the mortgage cash flow varies with changes in interest rates. This in turn requires modeling the behavior of the underlying borrower in reaction to aggregate variables. (State prices might also depend on house prices or other aggregate variables that can affect borrower behavior.)

The most common borrower choice is to refinance an existing mortgage when rates drop. Without refinancing, and ignoring default risk for a moment, fixed rate mortgages would tend to rise (fall) in value as spot rates fell (rose). If borrowers refinance when rates fall, however, the cash flow from the mortgage may terminate in precisely those cases when the mortgage is most valuable.

Aggregate refinancing volume is mainly driven by the *refinancing incentive*, defined in the US as the difference between the currently prevailing rate on new 30-year fixed-rate prime mortgages and the average rate on all outstanding mortgages. When the refinancing incentive is large, most existing borrowers could lower their note rates by refinancing; when it is low only a few existing borrowers could lower their note rates. As an empirical matter, there is a strong positive relationship between refinancing volume and the refinancing incentive. In the aftermath of the financial crisis of 2007–09, the refinancing incentive grew quite large because prevailing interest rates on new mortgages fell to historic lows; while the volume of refinancing at the time was quite large, it was perhaps not as large as might have been expected given the tighter prevailing underwriting standards.

To describe the importance of the relationship between refinancing activity and interest rates, we first define some key terms. The change in an asset's value with respect to shifts in the risk-free rate, that is, the first derivative of the asset's value with respect to the spot rate, is known as an asset's *duration*. The change in duration, in other words, the second derivative of an asset's value with respect to the spot rate, is known as an asset's *convexity*. A mortgage's duration is lower (in absolute value) with respect to declines in interest rates than with respect to increases in interest rates. Thus, fixed rate mortgages exhibit *negative convexity*. Negative convexity is illustrated in Figure 14.3. The dashed lines give the value of two mortgages (actually, of two mortgage-backed securities) with respect to parallel shifts in the yield curve.

This negative convexity underlies the difficulty faced by financial institutions when funding portfolios of fixed rate mortgages. If the portfolio is funded with non-callable debt (the solid line in the figure represents the value of a hypothetical zero-coupon bond with seven-year maturity), *any* changes in interest rates will decrease the net value of portfolio because the liability's value falls less (rises more) than the asset's value when rates rise (fall). If the portfolio is funded with demand deposits the situation is more complex. In principle, the value of the liability is constant with respect to interest rate changes. Thus, the holder could benefit from falls in interest rates, but will suffer larger drops in net value if interest rates increase. Intuitively, the portfolio manager is paying the prevailing rate while receiving payments from the mortgage borrower that are insensitive to interest rates. If rates rise, the portfolio manager may have to pay more than he receives from the mortgage borrower, a situation known as *negative carry*. Thus, holders of fixed rate mortgages must carefully manage their exposure to convexity. Perli and Sack (2003) argue that portfolio managers' desire to hedge US convexity risk is large enough to amplify shocks to interest rates.

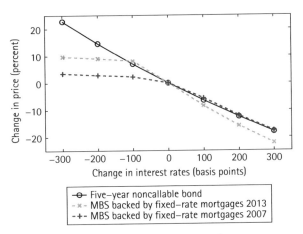

FIGURE 14.3 Price response of MBS and corporate bond to interest rates.

Note: Figure compares the percentage changes in the values of a Fannie Mae MBS backed by fixed rate mortgages from 2007 and 2013. The 2007 asset is a five-year Fannie Mae noncallable bond paying a coupon of 3.875% issued on June 6, 2008 and the 2013 asset is a five-year Fannie Mae noncallable bond paying a coupon of 3% issued on June 15, 2013. The bonds are compared to a hypothetical seven-year, non-coupon bond to indicate parallel shifts in the Treasury yield curve. Results based on Bloomberg's duration model; values retried on June 12, 2008 and June 23, 2013.

Note that the difficulty in funding fixed rate mortgages increases the more sharply kinked the value of the asset: that is, the greater the negative convexity. In turn, this implies that the more sensitive borrowers are to the incentive to refinance, the more expensive it is to hold unhedged portfolios of fixed rate mortgages. This is why prepayment penalties or other means of lessening a borrower's incentive to refinance when rates drop can be valuable to investors.

To illustrate the changes in the valuation of MBS in the US mortgage market since the financial crisis, Figure 14.3 displays two lines that represent the change in the values of two mortgage-backed securities issued in 2007 and 2013 (at approximately the same age) with respect to changes in interest rates. In each case, the value of the MBS is normalized to par if rates are unchanged. If rates *increase*, the MBS issued in 2007 declines less in value than the MBS issued in 2013. Mortgages carrying below-market interest rates terminated more rapidly in 2007 than in 2013: in 2007, housing sales were greater and borrowers were more mobile, often choosing to sell homes and move even if their new mortgage would carry a higher interest rate than the mortgage on their old property. However, if rates *decrease*, the MBS issued in 2007 increases less in value than the MBS issued in 2013. While fixed income securities rise in value when rates decrease, borrowers' ability to refinance mitigates the rise. The relatively tight underwriting standards prevailing in 2013 made refinancing more difficult for borrowers, keeping them locked in mortgages with relatively higher rates. By contrast, the relatively loose underwriting standards prevailing in 2007 allowed borrowers to quickly take advantage of any fall in rates.

14.4.2 Mortgage-Backed Securities

Mortgage-backed securities (MBSs) are simply financial assets backed by some claim on the cash flow from a group of mortgages. These come in a wide variety of flavors, depending on the differences in prevailing national mortgage institutions and financial regulations. We focus here on the institutions and markets in the United States. As with mortgage valuation, an enormous and highly specialized literature has sprung up around mortgage-backed securities, including both theoretical contributions and those designed for industry participants (see Fabozzi and Modigliani, 1992). For a broader discussion of securitization, see Chapter 15. Here we focus on the relationship of mortgage-backed securities to banks.

Broadly speaking, there are two main types of mortgage-backed securities in the United States. First are MBS issued by Fannie Mae, Freddie Mac, and Ginnie Mae, which are known as *agency securities*. Fannie Mae and Freddie Mac were private corporations with Congressional charters; they are known as the housing-related government-sponsored enterprises, or GSEs. Since August 2008, Fannie and Freddie have been in government conservatorship, effectively controlled by and their liabilities largely backed by the US government. Thus, agency MBS are to some degree more like covered bonds than stand-alone asset-backed securities. The second main type of MBS are *private-label securities*, which, by contrast, are backed primarily by the pool of underlying mortgages. (Sometimes higher-rate tranches of these MBS will carry third-party guarantees from bond insurance companies.)

For historical reasons, the great majority of prime loans with balances below the *conforming loan limit* (in 2013, this limit was back to $417,000 after having been temporarily raised during the recent financial crisis) are securitized by Fannie Mae and Freddie Mac. (Loans with balances in excess of the conforming loan limit are known as *jumbos*.) Thus subprime, near-prime, non-traditional and prime jumbos are securitized by issuers in the private-label market. Agency security issuance far outpaced private-label issuance, except for a brief period around 2005 at the peak of the US credit boom.

Private-label MBS were typically divided into *tranches* that varied in the seniority of their claims. The most senior tranches had first claim to any payment made by a borrower, while the most junior tranche had last claim. Alternatively, the most junior tranche took the first loss from any defaults. Tranches were rated by the major rating agencies (Moody's, S&P, and Fitch) and marketed based on their rating. In 2007, securities backed by mortgages were rapidly downgraded as the rating agencies grappled with higher-than-expected defaults. The large amount of loan defaults effectively closed the private-label MBS market, with issuance falling to near zero.

An increasing fraction of mortgages were held in securities over time (either in private-label MBS, on GSE portfolios, or securitized by the GSEs), at the expense of whole loans held on bank portfolios. Since the crisis, GSEs (including the Federal Housing Association, FHA)—which have historically originated a large portion of the loans in the home mortgage market—now hold more than half of the US residential mortgage debt (Avery et al., 2012).

This secular shift in mortgage funding away from bank portfolios and toward non-bank sources owes to several factors. First, as we discuss in Section 14.5, mortgage-backed securities can carry lower capital charges than the equivalent portfolio of whole loans. Thus, the financial system taken as a whole (banks and GSEs) lowers its regulatory capital charge when a bank swaps a portfolio of mortgages for an MBS guaranteed by a GSE backed by those same mortgages.

Second, as we discussed earlier, holding fixed rate mortgages on portfolio can be difficult for banks because of the mortgages' negative convexity. Of course, mortgage-backed securities have the same problem. However, MBS are easier and cheaper to sell than whole loans, thus allowing banks to liquidate their holdings if required. Further, pools of MBS can be structured into new securities with more desirable interest rate risk characteristics.

Third, securitization allowed a fundamental change in the industrial organization of mortgage lending. Previously, the three components of mortgage banking (origination, funding, and servicing) had been linked. Securitization allowed lenders to turn over the funding to financial markets.

Securitization could, in principle, lower the cost of funds to the ultimate mortgage borrower. Financial market participants differ in the premium they require to hold certain kinds of risk; by splitting out these risks into separate securities, securitization in theory allows mortgages to be funded at a lower cost than if a single institution had to hold all of the risks bundled with a mortgage. For example, a specialist hedge fund might feel that it can accurately predict defaults better than most market participants. Thus, it would be willing to pay a higher price than other participants for assets carrying credit risk. This hedge fund would be interested in buying the riskiest tranches of MBS.

Finally, most market participants require a liquidity premium, that is, extra compensation to hold an asset that they might not be able to sell quickly. To the extent that securitization permits mortgages to be traded in a more liquid environment, it can lower the cost of funds to the ultimate borrowers.

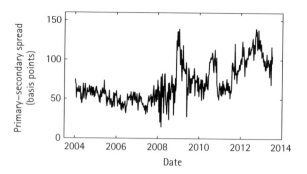

FIGURE 14.4 Primary–secondary mortgage market spread.

Note: Figure shows the spread between primary and secondary mortgage rates for 30-year, fixed rate conventional home loans. Source. FHLMC, FRBNY, and Barclays.

Since the 2008 financial crisis the spread between rates paid on the underlying loans and the yield on the MBS backed by those loans has widened. Fuster et al. (2013) point out that this spread rose from about 30 basis points from the late 1990s to over 100 basis points during the financial crisis and again in 2012, as shown in Figure 14.4. When the Federal Open Market Committee made the announcement of additional MBS purchases in 2012, the spread briefly approached 150 basis points. The authors go into considerable detail to discuss the reasons for this increase, concluding that the widening gap in the spread is due to a rise in unmeasured costs and originator profits.

14.5 BANK CAPITAL REGULATION OF MORTGAGES

Financial institutions hold capital to ensure solvency in the face of undiversified, or undiversifiable, risk. Regulators require banks to hold capital for the same reason, but also because, in part, they fear that their status as regulated institutions lessens market discipline. A complete discussion of bank capital regulation is beyond the scope of this chapter. Here, we focus on the key attributes that affect the economic capital required to back a portfolio of residential mortgages.

Bank capital regulation as described in the New Basel Capital Accord (or Basel II) adopts the terminology of portfolio credit risk management. Here, expected losses equal the probability of default (PD) times the loss given default (LGD) and the exposure at default (EAD), with a correction for the maturity of the obligation. For mortgages with a fixed maturity and a principal that cannot grow over time, the EAD is essentially fixed because the borrower cannot increase the principal value of their mortgage (this is not true for mortgages with a negative amortization option). Thus, we will focus on the PD and LGD associated with individual mortgages.

The first key attribute of residential mortgages is that credit risk (both PD and LGD) depends heavily on house prices. While geographic diversification can provide some protection for a portfolio, the current US experience, as well as other national house price cycles, suggests that during severe swings, local house price growth can be explained by a national factor (see Del Negro and Otrok, 2007).

Second, credit risk varies significantly by mortgage characteristics. Calem and LaCour-Little describe a model for computing the economic capital required to back 30-year fixed rate mortgages in the US. Hancock et al. (2006) adapt the Calem and LaCour-Little model to compute the "prudent economic capital" required to back mortgages with a variety of borrower credit scores and loan-to-value ratios. Portfolios of mortgages backed by "prudent economic capital" are typically rated BBB+ to A–. Hancock et al. (2006) find that the lowest-risk loans require very little capital backing—on the order of 20 to 65 basis points. However, higher-risk loans (those with loan-to-value ratios above 90 or severely impaired borrower credit histories) require much more capital, between 1.90% and 7.25%, depending on the risk characteristics.

Third, regulatory capital under the older bank capital regime (Basel I) was typically much greater than the prudent economic capital required to hold most residential mortgages. This gave banks a strong incentive to convert whole mortgage loans into securities; the housing-related GSEs known as Fannie Mae and Freddie Mac, for example, had to hold only 45 basis points of capital against credit risk during the regulatory regime that existed prior to the GSE accounting scandals of the mid-2000s. The fraction of mortgage debt outstanding held as whole loans on banks' balance sheets declined significantly, falling from 67.9% in 1980 to 34.6% in 1995, while that securitized or held by the GSEs grew over the same period. Starting in mid-2000s, private-label mortgage-backed securities issuers began to account for a significant fraction of mortgage debt outstanding—a shift that was consistent with the lower capital required on securitized assets.

The most recent change to capital rules came with Basel III. With regard to residential mortgages, the US implementation initially proposed risk weights that varied with the LTV of the loan and other risk characteristics and were, in general, higher than the existing risk weights. However, ultimately, this proposal was not adopted out of concerns that the higher risk weights would restrict lending to creditworthy borrowers and thus inhibit the recovery of the housing market. Thus, the previous risk weights remain in place.

Related, as one might expect under capital regulation that was broadly insensitive to credit risk, banks also had an incentive to hold riskier mortgages. Alternatively, if they were securitizing a large fraction of their loans, they had an incentive to hold the riskier loans in order to maintain their reputation with secondary market investors for not selling risky loans. Ambrose, LaCour-Little, and Sanders (2005) examined the performance of the loans that a major lender securitized as opposed to those that it chose to hold on portfolio and found that, as expected, it chose to keep the riskier loans.

Finally, estimating the correct capital required to back mortgage portfolios requires data on the performance of a wide variety of mortgages under many different circumstances. Banks may not have access to a long-enough time series of performance, or performance data on new types of mortgages that they are considering making. Further regulatory capital has to be estimated using so-called *stress LGDs*; that is, losses experienced during severe economic downturns. Yet suitable events are relatively rare, and it may be hard to generalize from a narrow set of mortgages that underwent the stress event to a broader set of mortgages that exist at a later time or in a different geographic area.

14.6 FINANCIAL STABILITY AND RESIDENTIAL MORTGAGES

Residential mortgages were at the heart of the global financial crisis of 2007–09, and have played a role in the more recent banking and sovereign debt crises in Europe. Moreover, the recent upsurge of interest in so-called "macroprudential" regulation—that is, financial regulation designed to bolster broad systemic financial stability rather than the safety and soundness of individual institutions—has many implications for the regulation of mortgage credit going forward. Indeed, several governments have adopted policies to restrain mortgage credit growth for reasons explicitly related to financial stability, rather than broader macro performance. These policy actions implicate a related set of questions that are currently the subject of active research: (1) How does credit backed by real property pose a threat to financial stability? (2) Can increases in mortgage credit supply have negative consequences, including sparking or contributing to a property price bubble? (3) Can policies related to mortgage credit directly address the threat to financial stability or should they instead aim to build resilience in the financial system?

14.6.1 How Can Mortgages Pose a Threat to Financial Stability?

As an empirical matter, Reinhart and Rogoff (2009) identify five banking crises prior to the 2007–09 episode to have seriously affected advanced economies since World War II. Each of these so-called "Big Five" crises appears to have been linked to an episode of credit-fueled asset price growth. Property prices and associated mortgage debt played at least a supporting role in all five, although stock prices and exchange rate movements also played important roles. Nonetheless, it appears that property financing is almost always involved to a certain degree in financial crises.

Real property makes an attractive asset with which to collateralize debt: even taking into account the recent decline in house prices, the volatility of property values is substantially below that of stock prices, the other major asset category on household balance sheets. (Using quarterly data from the US from the period 1976–2012, the standard deviation of the log difference in nominal house prices is 1.94, of stock prices it is 6.40.) Creditor's rights to real property are usually fairly clear, in part because mortgages are largely exempt from bankruptcy proceedings (such as the Chapter 11 proceedings in the United States) that might interfere with claims on assets such as business equipment; Perotti (2010) emphasized the importance of such exemptions in enhancing the liquidity of instruments backed by such assets. Finally, because originating, servicing and funding mortgages is often tied to the purchase of a primary residence, it is a well-understood and common transaction, particularly in countries with high homeownership rates.

Thus, because mortgages are a common form of debt—indeed, often second only to sovereign credit in terms of total credit outstanding in a country—they affect financial stability in the same way that any large source of debt does. In addition, the securitization of mortgages makes them attractive collateral to back other financial instruments, and investors may unwittingly find themselves holding mortgage-related assets. Finally, mortgage-related securities can play a role in maturity transformation in the shadow banking system; that is, intermediation outside the standard banking industry.

Borio and Lowe (2002) argued that sustained rapid credit growth, particularly when associated with asset price gains, pose a threat to financial stability and ought to be a focus of policymakers. This so-called "BIS view" stood in contrast to the standard central bank view that policy should only react to the indirect macroeconomic effects of a bubble: for example, through standard wealth effects. At most, credit was seen as a passive amplifier of shocks. Of course, policymakers understood that housing might have an unusual effect on the real economy as well as affecting the monetary transmission mechanism; Mishkin (2007) explores the implications for policy when considering these effects in a standard macro modeling framework. Figure 14.5 shows total US household assets around the two most recent asset price bubbles—the Internet bubble of the late 1990s and the house price bubble. As shown, wealth grew roughly the same amount during the build-up phase of each bubble, but the subsequent drop was much greater—and more persistent—following the house price crash. Thus, it would appear that the house price bubble was qualitatively different than the stock price bubble.

A more recent literature has more formally linked credit booms to subsequent financial crises, usually identified as banking crises. Schularick and Taylor (2012) use historical evidence from several developed economies over more than 130 years to show that lending booms often precede financial crises. A number of other research papers have developed similar arguments using different definitions, data, and methodologies (see Dell'Ariccia et al. 2012, and the references therein). These papers, for the most part, do not single out mortgage credit booms as particularly culpable, in part because data that distinguish between loans backed by real property and other loans are difficult to assemble in comparable fashion across countries and over long periods of time. Ferrero (2012) notes that, in the recent financial crisis, countries that experienced house price

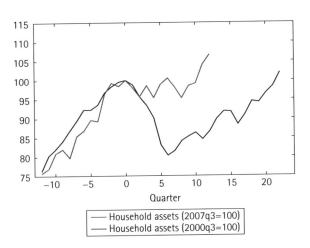

FIGURE 14.5 US household assets.

Note. Figure shows the total assets of households and non-profit organizations indexed at the peaks of the Internet (2000) and housing (2007) bubbles. Source. Federal Reserve Board Flow of Funds.

booms also experienced substantial current account deficits and deeper subsequent recessions.

A somewhat different view emphasizes the role of mortgage-related securities in funding markets outside of the traditional banking system. A hallmark of the US mortgage credit boom was the funding of novel residential mortgages in the secondary markets. Keys et al. (2010) argue that securitization per se encouraged lenders to screen borrowers less closely and to focus on making riskier loans. However, Foote, Gerardi, and Willen (2012) argue that financial innovations such as securitization cannot explain the US mortgage credit boom and bust.

Whether or not securitization per se contributes to credit booms, mortgage-backed securities were commonly used as collateral in funding markets. Gorton (2010) emphasized that, in the years before the 2008 financial crisis, large corporations, wealthy individuals, and sovereign wealth funds sought assets with deposit-like characteristics—liquidity, safety, and some transaction services. Poszar et al. (2010) describe how this so-called "shadow banking system" transformed residential mortgages into deposit-like liabilities. The intermediation, maturity transformation, and risk transformation conducted in the shadow banking system proved fragile for a variety of reasons. As documented by Adrian and Shin (2009), contractions in liabilities of the shadow banking system have tended to precede declines in real economic growth. Thus, the deleveraging in the shadow banking system during the crisis contributed to the contraction in credit supply and activity. Ramcharan, Van den Heuvel, and Virane (2013) provide direct evidence of this effect in consumer credit markets.

14.6.2 Consequences of an Increase in Mortgage Credit Supply

Credit supply, measured as the willingness of lenders to extend credit on improved terms or to classes of borrowers previously excluded from credit markets, can increase as the result of technological advances (Edelberg, 2006), increased credit market competition (see e.g., Dick and Lehnert, 2010), or government policies (see e.g., Elliehausen and Durkin, 1989). Given the major expansion of mortgage credit supply that preceded the financial crisis, it is worth investigating the financial stability consequences of such expansions.

An obvious channel for mortgage credit supply to affect financial stability is through house prices. One might conjecture that exogenous forces that more easily permit households to take out mortgages, and thus purchase their primary residence rather than rent it, might spark or fuel a rise in house prices, which could ultimately escalate into a speculative bubble. Because lenders are more willing to originate loans, particularly to high-risk borrowers, when they expect house prices to rise, identifying the treatment effect of credit supply on house prices is extremely challenging. Indeed, Gerardi et al. (2008) document that market participants shared the view that nominal house prices would not fall. Adelino, Schoar, and Severino (2012) use the maximum size of loans eligible for guarantee by Fannie Mae and Freddie Mac, which was set by a formula based on lagged house prices, as an instrument for credit supply; they find a sizable effect of credit supply on house prices.

14.6.3 Macroprudential Policies and Mortgages

Given that mortgages are common culprits in financial crises, one would expect that regulatory policies aimed at promoting financial stability should take special note of them. The general class of regulatory policies designed to promote financial stability have come to be known as macroprudential policies. There is some debate about whether macroprudential policies should aim simply to build resilience in the financial system during good times or whether they should attempt to constrain the asset prices or credit growth of concern. In a related way, policies are often divided into structural—those that address weaknesses in the financial system that are always present—and cyclical—those that address vulnerabilities that build over time. Finally, the toolkit of macroprudential policies remains somewhat unclear. While a complete discussion of these issues is beyond the scope of this chapter, we focus on the developments related to mortgage credit.

A raft of new approaches to regulating and structuring mortgage markets has emerged from the 2008 financial crisis. Some of these can be thought of as structural macroprudential policies; that is, policies aimed at enhancing the inherent stability of the mortgage market. The most obvious failing of the previous system was the inadequate preparation for house price risk among market participants. As Frame, Gerardi, and Willen (2013) document, at the US government-sponsored enterprises this was due in part to a capital regime based on a stress test that featured a mild and gradual decline in house prices. In the 2009 US bank stress tests, by contrast, house prices were assumed to fall sharply and immediately (see Board of Governors of the Federal Reserve System, 2009). The subsequent US bank stress tests have also featured scenarios in which national house prices fall sharply and, consequently, loss rates on residential and commercial mortgages that are extremely high by historical standards.

Authorities in the US and Europe identified the putative misaligned incentives between issuers of mortgage-backed securities and their purchasers as a contributing factor to the 2008 financial crisis. Under this theory, issuers of MBS had diminished incentives to monitor the underlying riskiness of borrowers because all of the loans they originated were sold to investors in the form of securities. Indeed, many of the firms at the center of the mortgage credit boom in the United States, such as New Century Financial Corporation, were thinly capitalized and had little capacity to hold mortgages, yet were among the largest originators of mortgages. As a response to this, European and US regulators instituted so-called "risk retention" rules prohibiting issuers of securities from selling all the assets derived from a pool of residential mortgages.

Of the somewhat nebulous set of dynamic macroprudential tools, capital regulation deserves particular notice because it is the most explicitly used macroprudential tool in developed economies. The Basel III capital standards include a so-called countercyclical buffer (see Basel Committee on Banking Supervision, 2011). Under the proposed framework, countries are supposed to impose additional capital requirements on banks when their national credit-to-GDP ratios remain above-trend for a certain amount of time. A number of authors, including Edge and Meisenzahl (2011) and Repullo and Saurina (2011) have demonstrated that real-time credit-to-GDP measures are unreliable predictors of financial crises and, indeed, would have led to counterproductive policies such as relaxing credit standards in 2007, at the leading edge of the financial crisis. Nonetheless, the general idea of requiring financial intermediaries to accumulate capital during boom times and to draw down capital during busts is attractive. During good times capital is relatively cheap, and higher capital requirements might mitigate credit growth. During busts, allowing financial intermediaries to dip into these cyclical buffers might mitigate their tendency to shrink loan supply during bad times.

The effectiveness of countercyclical capital requirements in counteracting mortgage-related threats to financial stability remains somewhat unclear. In theory, the ability of capital requirements to lean against a mortgage credit boom depends on the effect of capital on loan pricing and availability, and the elasticity of mortgage demand with respect to such terms. During credit booms investors willingly take on risk, so it is unclear how much loan costs would increase with higher capital requirements in such an environment. Further, a general increase in capital requirements may have less effect on a particular class of loans, such as mortgages, that are in the midst of a boom. Finally, in economies with large market-based systems of mortgage funding, increased capital requirements on banks may simply drive more activity to the non-bank sector.

Dynamic loan-loss provisioning, which can be thought of as a form of capital regulation, was in use in Spain prior to the 2008 crisis. To the extent that loss provisions on mortgages held by banks were too low because of the Spanish house price bubble, such provisioning should in principle have made banks more resilient to the unwind of the bubble and to have made mortgages less cheap and available than they otherwise would have been. While the Spanish experience is still unfolding, the consensus is that, without dynamic provisioning, mortgage credit would have grown more and the subsequent capital shortfalls at banks would have been greater (see Saurina, 2009).

Sectoral capital requirements (SCRs) allow policymakers to target particular bank assets for higher capital requirements. In effect, SCRs can be thought of as asset-specific risk weights. Thus, in the midst of a mortgage boom, policymakers could raise the capital required to back just these loans without affecting the provision of other forms of credit: for example, loans to small and medium-sized enterprises. The Bank of England's macroprudential policymaking body, the Financial Policy Committee, has been granted some control over SCRs (see Bank of England, 2013).

14.7 CONCLUSION

Mortgage lending is one of the oldest forms of intermediation; it is often the largest credit transaction undertaken by a household, and is an important part of the financial services sector. Mortgage banking comprises three functions: origination, funding, and servicing. Advances in technology and financial market developments have allowed institutions to split these three parts. Mortgages can now be originated by small-scale operators using web-based underwriting applications, sold to financial institutions who in turn package the loans and sell them to investors, and serviced by specialty operations that take advantage of economies of scale. Many of the tensions inherent in the new mortgage business model were highlighted by the recent turmoil in the US subprime market.

Residential mortgages are collateralized obligations of the household sector. They tend to carry longer maturities and lower interest rates than unsecured borrowing. However, the advantages of mortgages over other forms of borrowing depend on the ability of lenders to seize the underlying collateral. When originating loans, lenders must consider the value of the underlying asset, the amount of equity used by the borrower, the borrower's income and assets, and the borrower's history of making timely payments on other debt obligations.

Households face two types of decisions regarding mortgages: decisions made before origination regarding the characteristics of the household's preferred loan, and decisions made after origination regarding whether to refinance or default. Before origination, households face a menu of choices that varies across countries. Broadly speaking, households must decide on how much to borrow, how much interest rate risk to accept, and what kind of amortization schedule to use.

Once in a mortgage, households may be able to refinance the mortgage, or they may decide, or be forced by circumstances, to default on the mortgage. Economists generally view these choices as options embedded in the mortgage. However, pure option-theoretic models have difficulty matching borrowers' actual decisions, especially the decision to default, suggesting that transaction costs play a big role in household decision making.

Of course, any options embedded in a mortgage and available to the household were placed there by the lender, who must price these options and determine appropriate compensation. A large and diverse literature has grown up around the problem of accurately modeling the household's refinancing decision. The more sensitive the borrower is to changes in the spot interest rate, the more care must be taken by the ultimate holder of a leveraged portfolio of mortgages in matching the duration of the mortgage assets and the liabilities used to fund them. Sudden changes in interest rates can decrease the net value of the portfolio.

Bank capital regulators face the problem of matching the regulatory capital on mortgages to their economic capital. Indications are that capital charges under the older Basel I scheme are higher than warranted by the credit risk on most mortgages. This provides an incentive for regulated banks to move some mortgages off balance sheet.

Finally, because the 2008 financial crisis stemmed in part from developments in mortgage markets, a great deal of attention has focused on the financial stability consequences of mortgage credit growth and institutional features. Historical evidence suggests that rapid credit growth often precedes financial crises, suggesting a role for policy in constraining credit growth. Moreover, mortgages make attractive assets for use in the shadow banking system, which has proved fragile in the past.

REFERENCES

Adelino, M., Schoar, A., and Severino, F. (2012). Credit Supply and House Prices: Evidence from Mortgage Market Segmentation, NBER Working Paper No. 17832.

Adrian, T. and Shin, H. S. (2009). Money, Liquidity, and Monetary Policy, *American Economic Review* 99(2), 600–605.

Ambrose, B. W., Capone Jr., C. A. and Deng, Y. (2001). Optimal Put Exercise: An Empirical Examination of Conditions for Mortgage Foreclosure, *Journal of Real Estate Finance and Economics* 23(2), 213–234.

Ambrose, B. W., LaCour-Little, M., and Sanders, A. B. (2005). Does Regulatory Capital Arbitrage, Reputation, or Asymmetric Information Drive Securitization?, *Journal of Financial Services Research* 28(1), 113–133.

Amromin, G., Huang, J., and Sialm, C. (2007). The Tradeoff between Mortgage Prepayments and Tax-Deferred Retirement Savings, *Journal of Public Economics* 91(10), 2014–2040.

Avery, R., Bhutta, N., Brevoort, K., and Canner, G. (2012). The Mortgage Market in 2011: Highlights from the Data Reported under the Home Mortgage Disclosure Act, *Federal Reserve Bulletin* 98(6), 1–46.

Bank for International Settlements (2006). Housing Finance in the Global Financial Market, Committee for the Global Financial System Papers No. 26.

Bank of England (2013). The Financial Policy Committee's Powers to Supplement Capital Requirements. A Draft Policy Statement.

Basel Committee on Banking Supervision (2011). Basel III: A Global Regulatory Framework for More Resilient Banks and Banking Systems, Bank for International Settlements Consultative Paper No. 189.

Barakova, I., Bostic, R., Calem, P., and Wachter, S. (2003). Does Credit Quality Matter for Homeownership?, *Journal of Housing Economics* 12(4), 318–336.

Ben-David, I. (2008). Manipulation of Collateral Values by Borrowers and Intermediaries. Graduate School of Business, University of Chicago, Chicago, IL Manuscript.

Bhutta, N. and Canner, G. (2013). Mortgage Market Conditions and Borrower Outcomes: Evidence from the 2012 HMDA Data and Matched HMDA-Credit Record Data *Federal Reserve Bulletin* 99, 1–58.

Board of Governors of the Federal Reserve System (2009). The Supervisory Capital Assessment Program, Design and Implementation.

Borio, C. and Lowe, P. (2002). Asset Prices, Financial and Monetary Stability: Exploring the Nexus, BIS Working Paper No. 114.

Brueckner, J. (1993). Why Do We Have ARMs?, *American Real Estate and Urban Economic Associations Journal* 21(3), 333–345.

Brueckner, J. (1994). Borrower Mobility, Adverse Selection and Mortgage Points, *Journal of Financial Intermediation* 3(4), 416–441.

Brueckner, J. and Follain, J. R. (1988). The Rise and Fall of the ARM: An Econometric Analysis of Mortgage Choice, *Review of Economics and Statistics* 70(1), 93–102.

Bucks, B., Kennickell, A., and Moore, K. (2006). Recent Changes in US Family Finances: Evidence from the 2001 and 2004 Survey of Consumer Finances, *Federal Reserve Bulletin* 92, A1–A38.

Bucks, B. and Pence, K. (2008). Do Homeowners Know Their House Values and Mortgage Terms?, *Journal of Urban Economics* 62(2), 57–70.

Campbell, J. Y. and Cocco, J. (2003). Household Risk Management and Optimal Mortgage Choice, *Quarterly Journal of Economics* 118(4), 1449–1494.

Campbell, J. Y. and Cocco, J. (2012). A Model of Mortgage Default, NBER Working Paper No. 17516.

Campbell, J. Y. and Giglio, S. (2011). Forced Sales and House Prices, *American Economic Review* 101(5), 2108–2131.

Canner, G., Dynan, K., and Passmore, W. (2002). Mortgage Refinancing in 2001 and Early 2002, *Federal Reserve Bulletin* 88(12), 469–490.

Capone Jr., C. A. (1996). *Providing Alternatives to Mortgage Foreclosure: A Report to Congress.* Washington, DC: US Department of Housing and Urban Development.

Ciochetti, B. A. (1997). Loss Characteristics of Commercial Mortgage Foreclosure, *Real Estate Finance* 14(1), 53–69.

Clauretie, T. M. (1989). State Foreclosure Laws, Risk Shifting, and the PMI Industry, *Journal of Risk and Insurance* 56(3), 544–554.

Clauretie, T. M. and Herzog, T. (1990). The Effect of State Foreclosure Laws on Loan Losses: Evidence from the Mortgage Insurance Industry, *Journal of Money, Credit and Banking* 22(2), 221–233.

Cordell, L., Dynan, K., Lehnert, A., Liang, N., and Mauskopf, E. (2010). The Incentives of Mortgage Servicers: Myths and Realities. In: R. W. Kolb, (Ed.), *Lessons from the Financial Crisis*, 231–237. Hoboken, NJ: John Wiley & Sons.

Cordell, L., Geng, L., Goodman, L., and Yang, L. (2013). The Cost of Delay, Federal Reserve Bank of Philadelphia Working Paper No. 13–15.

Del Negro, M. and Otrok, C. (2007). 99 Luftballons: Monetary Policy and the House Price Boom across US States, *Journal of Monetary Economics* 54(7), 1962–1985.

Dell'Ariccia, G., Igan, D., Laeven, L., and Tong, H. (2012). Policies for Macrofinancial Stability: How to Deal with Credit Booms and Busts, IMF Staff Discussion Note No. 12/06.

Deng, Y., Quigley, J. M., and van Order, R. (2000). Mortgage Terminations, Heterogeneity and the Exercise of Mortgage Options, *Econometrica* 68(2), 275–307.

Dick, A. and Lehnert, A. (2010). Personal Bankruptcy and Credit Market Competition, *Journal of Finance* 65(2), 655–686.

Duffie, D. (1992). *Dynamic Asset Pricing Theory*. Princeton, NJ: Princeton University Press.

Edelberg, W. (2006). Risk-Based Pricing of Interest Rates for Consumer Loans, *Journal of Monetary Economics* 53(8), 2283–2298.

Edge, R. and Meisenzahl, R. (2011). The Unreliability of Credit-to-GDP Ratio Gaps in Real Time: Implications for Countercyclical Capital Buffers, *International Journal of Central Banking* 261–298.

Eggert, K. (2007). Comment: What Prevents Loan Modifications?, *Housing Policy Debate* 18(2), 279–297.

Elliehausen, G. and Durkin, T. (1989). Theory and Evidence of the Impact of Equal Credit Opportunity: An Agnostic Review of the Literature, *Journal of Financial Services Research* 2(2), 89–114.

Elliehausen, G., Staten, M. E., and Steinbuks, J. (2008). The Effect of Prepayment Penalties on the Pricing of Subprime Mortgages, *Journal of Economics and Business* 60(1–2), 33–46.

Fabozzi, F. J. and Modigliani, F. (1992). *Mortgage and Mortgage-Backed Securities Markets*. Boston, MA: Harvard Business School Press.

Ferrero, A. (2012). House Price Booms, Current Account Deficits, and Low Interest Rates, Federal Reserve Bank of New York Staff Report No. 541.

Foote, C., Gerardi, K., and Willen, P. (2008). Negative Equity and Foreclosures: Theory and Evidence, *Journal of Urban Economics* 64(2), 234–245.

Foote, C., Gerardi, K., and Willen, P. (2012). Why Did So Many People Make So Many Ex-Post Bad Decisions? The Causes of the Foreclosure Crisis, Federal Reserve Bank of Atlanta Working Paper No. 2012–7.

Frame, W. S., Gerardi, K., and Willen, P. (2013). Supervisory Stress Tests, Model Risk, and Model Disclosure: Lessons from OFHEO. Federal Reserve Bank of Atlanta Manuscript.

Fu, Q., LaCour-Little, M., and Vandell, K. (1997). Retiring Early: An Empirical Analysis of the Mortgage Curtailment Decision, University of Wisconsin Center for Urban Land Economic Research Working Paper No. 97–09.

Fuster, A., Goodman, L., Lucca, D., Madar, L., Molloy, L., and Willen, P. (2013). The Rising Gap between Primary and Secondary Mortgage Rates, *Economic Policy Review* 19, 17–39.

Gerardi, K., Lehnert, A., Sherlund, S., and Willen, P. (2008). Making Sense of the Subprime Crisis, *Brookings Papers on Economic Activity*, Fall, 69–145.

Gerardi, K., Shapiro, A. H., and Willen, P. (2008). Subprime Outcomes: Risky Mortgages, Homeownership Experiences, and Foreclosures, Federal Reserve Bank of Boston Working Paper No. 07–15.

Gorton, G. (2010). *Slapped by the Invisible Hand*. New York: Oxford University Press.

Graham, J. R. (2000). How Big are the Tax Benefits of Debt?, *The Journal of Finance* 55(5), 1901–1942.

Hancock, D., Lehnert, A., Passmore, W., and Sherlund, S. M. (2006). The Competitive Effects of Risk-Based Capital Regulation: An Example from US Mortgage Markets, Federal Reserve Board, Finance and Economics Discussion Series No. 2006–46.

Haurin, D. R., Herbert, C. E., and Rosenthal, S. S. (2007). Homeownership Gaps among Low-Income and Minority Households, *Cityscape* 9(2), 5–52.

Hurst, E. and Stafford, F. (2004). Home Is Where the Equity Is: Mortgage Refinancing and Household Consumption, *Journal of Money, Credit, and Banking* 36(6), 985–1014.

International Monetary Fund (2011). Global Financial Stability Report. World Economic Surveys, Washington DC.

Keys, B. J., Mukherjee, T., Seru, A., and Vig, V. (2010). Did Securitization Lead to Lax Screening? Evidence from Subprime Loans, *Quarterly Journal of Economics* 125(1), 307–362.

LaCour-Little, M. and Malpezzi, S. (2003). Appraisal Quality and Residential Mortgage Default: Evidence from Alaska, *Journal of Real-Estate Finance and Economics* 27(2), 211–233.

LaCour-Little, M. and Yang, J. (2010). Pay Me Now or Pay Me Later: Alternative Mortgage Products and the Mortgage Crisis, *Real Estate Economics* 38(4), 687–732.

Lamont, O. and Stein, J. (1999). Leverage and House-Price Dynamics in US Cities, *RAND Journal of Economics* 30(3), 498–514.

Leventis, A. (2006). Removing Appraisal Bias from a Repeat-Transactions House Price Index: A Basic Approach, OFHEO Working Paper No. 06–1.

Mayer, C., Pence, K., and Sherlund, S. M. (2009). The Rise in Mortgage Defaults, *Journal of Economic Perspectives* 23(1), 27–50.

Miles, D. (2004). *The UK Mortgage Market: Taking a Longer-Term View*. Norwich, UK: HM Stationery Office.

Mishkin, F. (2007). Housing and the Monetary Transmission Mechanism, Federal Reserve Board Finance and Economics Discussion Series No. 2007–40.

Pence, K. (2006). Foreclosing on Opportunity: State Laws and Mortgage Credit, *Review of Economics and Statistics* 88(1), 177–182.

Perli, R. and Sack, B. (2003). Does Mortgage Hedging Amplify Movements in Long-Term Interest Rates?, *The Journal of Fixed Income* 13(3), 7–17.

Perotti, E. (2010). *Systemic Liquidity Risk and Bankruptcy Exemptions*, Centre for Economic Policy Research Policy Insight No. 52.

Piskorski, T. and Tchistyi, A. (2010). Optimal Mortgage Design, *Review of Financial Studies* 23(8), 3098–3140.

Quigley, J. and van Order, R. (1995). Explicit Tests of Contingent Claims Models of Mortgage Default, *Journal of Real Estate Finance and Economics* 11(2), 99–117.

Ramcharan, R., Van den Heuvel, S., and Virane, S. (2013). From Wall Street to Main Street: The Impact of the Financial Crisis on Consumer Credit Supply, Federal Reserve Board Finance and Economics Discussion Series No. 2013–10.

Reinhart, C. and Rogoff, K. (2009). *This Time is Different: Eight Centuries of Financial Folly*. Princeton, NJ: Princeton University Press.

Repullo, R. and Saurina, J. (2011). The Countercyclical Capital Buffer of Basel III: A Critical Assessment, CEMFI Working Paper No. 1102.

Saurina, J. (2009). *Loan Loss Provisions in Spain: A Working Macroprudential Tool*, Banco de España Estabilidad Financiera No. 17.

Schularick, M. and Taylor, A. (2012). Credit Booms Gone Bust: Monetary Policy, Leverage Cycles, and Financial Crises, 1870–2008, NBER Working Paper No. 15512.

Shilling, J. D., Dhillon, U. S., and Sirmans, C. F. (1987). Choosing between Fixed and Adjustable Rate Mortgages, *Journal of Money, Credit, and Banking* 19(2), 260–267.

Stanton, R. and Wallace, N. (1999). Anatomy of an ARM: The Interest Rate Risk of Adjustable Rate Mortgages, *Journal of Real Estate Finance and Economics* 19(1), 49–67.

Stegman, M. A., Quercia, R. G., Ratcliffe, J., Ding, L., and Davis, W. R. (2007). Preventive Servicing is Good for Business and Affordable Homeownership Policy, *Housing Policy Debate* 18(2), 243–278.

Stein, J. (1995). Prices and Trading Volume in the Housing Market: A Model with Downpayment Effects, *Quarterly Journal of Economics* 110(2), 379–406.

US Department of the Treasury (2013). May 2013 Making Home Affordable Program Performance Report.

CHAPTER 15

....

SECURITIZATION

....

BARBARA CASU AND ANNA SARKISYAN

15.1 INTRODUCTION

....

SECURITIZATION is a structured process that involves a bank transforming its (usually) illiquid assets, traditionally held until maturity, into marketable securities by pooling these assets and transferring them into a special purpose vehicle (SPV), a bankruptcy-remote entity that in turn finances the purchase through the issuance of securities backed by the pool (generally referred to as asset-backed securities or ABSs).[1] Between the early 1990s and the mid-2000s there was a tremendous increase in the size of securitization markets, driven by factors on the sides of both supply and demand. On the supply side, banks had been operating in increasingly competitive markets and as such had to take on more risks and to seek out higher margin activities. Securitization facilitated this quest for higher margin business, by allowing banks to convert illiquid loans into marketable securities and therefore release capital for other investment opportunities. The dynamics of the US housing market facilitated this expansion (Baily, Elmendorf, and Litan, 2008). On the demand side, the growth of securitization was fueled by the increase in the amount of money under management of institutional investors, which were looking to invest in safe assets (that is, high quality AAA-rated debt instruments) (Acharya and Schnabl, 2010). Because of their intrinsic characteristics, ABSs were particularly suited to the investment needs of institutional cash pools seeking out deposit-like safe investments (Pozsar, 2011; Claessens et al. 2012).[2] Gorton

---

[1] In narrow terms, asset-backed securities (ABSs) are securities backed by loans other than mortgages; securities backed by the latter are referred to as mortgage-backed securities or MBSs.

[2] The term institutional cash pool refers to large, centrally managed, short-term cash balances of global non-financial corporations and institutional investors such as asset managers, securities lenders, and pension funds (see Pozsar, 2011).

and Metrick (2013) argue that the rise in demand for ABSs was also linked to the growth in demand for collateral, both in the derivatives and in the repo markets.[3]

After this prolonged period of rapid expansion, securitization markets froze in late 2008, following the collapse of Lehman Brothers, as institutional investors and market participants lost confidence in ABSs. The impact of the 2007–09 financial crisis on securitization markets has since been well documented (Brunnermeier, 2009; Gorton, 2010; BIS, 2011).

Despite the controversial role of securitization during the financial crisis, its economic importance is undeniable. This structured finance technique has fundamentally changed the role of banks as financial intermediaries, by modifying the functioning of banking markets from the traditional "originate-to-hold" model (whereby banks originated loans and then held them on their balance sheet till maturity) to the "originate-to-distribute" model, where loans are bundled and sold to outside investors. In this respect, securitization significantly changed banks' intermediation function by blurring the boundaries between loans and bonds and by fragmenting banks' traditional role as intermediaries into several specific functions, increasingly outsourced to specialized non-bank financial entities. In addition, securitization increased the reliance of banks on capital markets as a source of finance. Starting from the late 1990s, banks began expanding their funding sources away from retail deposits to include bond financing, commercial paper financing, and repo financing. On the asset side of their balance sheet, banks started to distribute increasing portions of the loans they had originated, not only at the time of the loan origination, but also in the years after origination (Bord and Santos, 2012). This trend not only led to the growth of financial intermediation outside the banking system (or shadow banking), but also had important implications for the roles banks still perform in financial markets.[4] Some have argued that the originate-to-distribute model undermines financial stability and emphasized the misalignment of incentives between banks and investors in the securitization process. This stems from the fact that the structure of securitization can create adverse selection (low quality loans are securitized) and moral hazard problems (as loans can be sold, lenders lack incentives to screen and monitor borrowers). A number of recent research papers provide evidence to suggest that securitization led to a weakening of lending standards (Mian and Sufi, 2009; Keys et al., 2010; Elul, 2011; Dell'Ariccia, Igan, and Laeven, 2012).

Despite the weaknesses in the securitization process, which became apparent during the financial crisis, policymakers and market practitioners also recognize its potential benefits and are currently attempting to revive the market by increasing transparency and by introducing changes in terms of simplicity and standardization. Regulatory efforts notwithstanding, the future of securitization is uncertain. Will the market restart? Will this structured finance technique still have an important role to play in future developments of financial markets? Will the proposed regulatory reforms achieve their aim to minimize the risks, realign the incentives, and maximize the benefits of securitization?

---

[3] Both the use of derivatives and repo transactions require the use of collateral. Gorton and Metrick (2013) argue that due to the growth in both markets, there was an insufficient amount of US Treasuries available for use as collateral and asset-backed securities had design features that made them a substitute "safe asset."

[4] Adrian, Ashcraft, and Cetorelli provide a thorough account of the shadow banking market in Chapter 16, "Shadow Bank Monitoring," in this *Handbook*.

Against this background, this chapter aims to address some of the key issues in securitiza-tion markets. We start with a brief analysis of the history of securitization and chart its rise and fall in Section 15.2. In Section 15.3 we provide some technical definitions of the secu-ritization process as well as a discussion of the issues that each stage of the securitization process raises. A discussion of the private and social costs and benefits of securitization is provided in Section 15.4. Finally, Section 15.5 discusses the future of securitization both from a policy and market perspective, and offers concluding remarks.

15.2 THE EVOLUTION OF SECURITIZATION

The origins of securitization are traditionally traced back to the US financial markets in the 1970s, with the structured financing of mortgage loans by a US government agency, the Government National Mortgage Association (GNMA, also called Ginnie Mae), followed by the Federal Home Loan Mortgage Corporation (FHLMC, or Freddie Mac), and the Federal National Mortgage Association (FNMA, or Fannie Mae) in the early 1980s (Baily, Elmendorf, Litan, 2008). Government agencies and government-sponsored enterprises (GSEs) remained the main issuers in the market for mortgage-backed securities until the mid-1980s, when other financial and non-financial institutions entered the market. This was made possible by the Tax Reform Act of 1986, which enabled the creation of real estate mort-gage investment conduits (REMICs). The reform spurred the growth of the US securitiza-tion market, by allowing the transfer of assets into a bankruptcy-remote accounting vehicle. Following the 1986 Act, the issuance of non-agency (also known as private label) securitiza-tion increased steadily and reached a peak in 2005. Following the outbreak of the 2007–09 financial crisis, non-agency origination decreased dramatically (from around $739 billion in 2007 to $37 billion in 2008, as illustrated in Table 15.1).

The tremendous growth experienced by the US securitization market from the mid-1990s up until the financial crisis is charted in Figure 15.1. The market for MBSs increased from around $2.4 trillion outstanding in 1995 to $7.1 trillion at year end 2006. The outstanding volume of ABSs reached around $1.9 trillion at year end 2006, up from $258 billion in 1995. In 2002, securitization issuance (excluding agency securitization) exceeded the issuance of corporate bonds and continued to be larger until the onset of the financial crisis in 2007 (Gorton and Metrick, 2013).

The market expanded in both the size and the range of securitized assets, securitizing firms, and investors in securitized products. The first transaction for ABSs in 1985 was backed by automobile loans, the most straightforward type of collateral. This was followed by the first issuance of securities backed by credit card debt in 1986. The latter became the cornerstone of the ABS market, due to the revolving nature of credit card debt (OCC, 1997). Since then, the process and the structure of securitization have evolved significantly, including the development of private credit enhancements (such as over-collateralization, third-party, and structural support), fostering the growth of the asset-backed securitization market.

Table 15.1 shows the historical US securitization issuance (1985 to 2013). Looking at MBSs, agency issuance has remained the main source of MBS origination throughout the years (with comparable amounts pre- and post-crisis). On the other hand, private label

Table 15.1 US securitization issuance, USD billions

Year	MBS			ABS								TOTAL
	Agency	Non-Agency	Total MBS	Auto	Credit Card	Equipment	Home Equity	Manufactured Housing	Other	Student Loans	Total ABS	
1985	110.56	—	110.56	1.04	—	0.19	—	—	—	—	1.23	111.79
1986	267.98	—	267.98	9.76	—	0.17	—	—	0.07	—	10.00	277.98
1987	249.90	—	249.90	6.20	2.30	—	—	0.18	0.23	—	8.91	258.81
1988	187.97	—	187.97	5.84	6.92	0.10	—	0.79	0.62	—	14.27	202.24
1989	294.70	—	294.70	6.14	10.99	—	2.70	1.95	0.29	—	22.07	316.77
1990	358.26	—	358.26	13.38	22.58	—	5.53	1.07	0.64	—	43.21	401.47
1991	451.37	—	451.37	17.47	21.82	0.48	10.29	1.38	0.46	—	51.91	503.28
1992	750.82	—	750.82	24.77	17.40	2.28	6.65	2.59	1.51	—	55.20	806.02
1993	956.13	—	956.13	24.67	19.61	3.67	8.26	2.49	3.14	0.34	62.18	1018.31
1994	514.03	—	514.03	19.52	31.52	4.32	11.01	4.66	8.10	2.40	81.54	595.57
1995	288.40	—	288.40	29.97	47.39	3.46	15.76	6.14	7.24	2.86	112.81	401.21
1996	444.10	52.62	496.70	35.74	48.74	12.39	37.52	8.12	16.20	8.05	166.76	663.45
1997	544.50	68.69	613.19	42.12	40.57	8.32	69.03	9.58	19.87	12.56	202.07	815.26
1998	954.90	194.48	1149.40	40.90	43.07	10.14	87.07	11.89	43.80	10.23	247.10	1396.51
1999	887.10	139.43	1026.58	46.58	40.68	12.53	75.71	15.01	34.50	11.09	236.10	1262.67
2000	583.30	101.68	684.99	71.03	57.14	11.46	75.52	11.28	36.06	18.56	281.05	966.05
2001	1480.40	212.93	1693.28	83.95	68.62	8.50	112.21	7.15	30.90	14.88	326.21	2019.49
2002	2044.30	293.50	2337.82	94.66	70.34	6.42	150.77	4.62	19.35	27.74	373.90	2711.72
2003	2757.20	415.37	3172.59	82.53	66.73	9.45	229.07	0.40	30.37	42.99	461.54	3634.13
2004	1393.00	523.57	1916.60	79.38	53.74	8.46	425.03	0.37	36.50	48.04	651.53	2568.13
2005	1347.70	882.74	2230.46	106.10	67.83	10.44	460.49	0.44	44.97	63.24	753.52	2983.97

(Continued)

Table 15.1 (Continued)

Year	MBS			ABS								TOTAL
	Agency	Non-Agency	Total MBS	Auto	Credit Card	Equipment	Home Equity	Manufactured Housing	Other	Student Loans	Total ABS	
2006	1239.10	871.22	2110.31	90.44	66.90	8.78	483.91	0.20	36.52	67.13	753.88	2864.19
2007	1465.60	738.72	2204.27	78.60	99.53	5.77	216.89	0.41	44.39	61.37	506.96	2711.23
2008	1366.80	36.79	1403.59	36.16	59.06	3.07	3.82	0.31	8.87	28.20	139.49	1543.09
2009	2022.90	18.12	2041.07	62.75	46.09	7.66	2.07	0.00	10.25	22.10	150.91	2191.98
2010	1941.10	34.60	1975.75	59.32	7.37	7.83	4.57	–	14.92	15.45	109.46	2085.21
2011	1623.10	37.07	1660.17	68.22	16.15	9.53	4.10	–	14.27	13.96	126.24	1786.41
2012	2016.20	39.87	2056.12	90.10	39.70	19.35	4.08	0.00	20.09	26.09	199.41	2255.54
2013*	1415.20	55.30	1470.54	61.17	19.79	9.60	7.76	–	15.66	12.38	126.36	1596.90

Notes: *Up to and including August 2013. The table reports US securitization issuance (in $ billions), including mortgage-related securities (MBS), asset-backed securities (ABS), and a total of the two categories. Agency includes agency (FHLMC, FNMA, GNMA, NCUA, and FDIC) MBSs and CMOs. Non-agency includes private label CMBSs and RMBSs, and re-REMICs. Auto includes prime, near-prime, subprime auto loans and leases; auto dealer floorplans; RV; motorcycle; fleet lease. Credit card includes credit cards, resecuritizations of credit card securities. Equipment includes equipment, resecuritizations of equipment securities. Home equity includes home equity loans; home improvement loans; HELOC; servicing advances; home equity NIMs and other home equity resecuritizations; Res BtC loans; and certain performing and non-performing seasoned loans; does not include NIMs of Alt-A or other non-agency RMBSs. Manufactured housing includes lease agreements; manufactured housing floorplans. Student loans includes all student loans, public and private. Other includes anything that does not fit into any of the above categories, including those with mixed asset categories (e.g., tax liens, trade receivables, boat loans, aircraft, etc.).

Source: Federal Agencies (FHLMC, FNMA, GNMA, NCUA, and FDIC), Bloomberg, Dealogic, Thomson Reuters; data compiled by SIFMA.

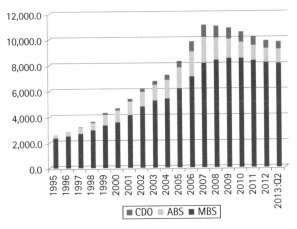

FIGURE 15.1 US securitization outstanding 1995–2013: Q2, USD billions.

Notes: The graph plots outstanding US securitization (in $ billions) between 1995 and 2013, quarter
2. The total outstanding volume includes mortgage-backed securities (MBS),
asset-backed securities (ABS), and collateralized debt obligations (CDO).

Source: US Department of Treasury, Federal Reserve System, Federal agencies, Dealogic,
Thomson Reuters, Bloomberg, Loan Performance, SIFMA; data compiled by SIFMA.

issuance has not recovered since the crisis. ABS issuance peaked in 2005–06; following the crisis-induced plunge in new issuance in 2007 and 2008, there are recently signs of (mild) recovery. In addition, Table 15.1 illustrates the breakdown of ABS issuance in terms of the main types of assets being securitized; the largest category is auto loans, followed by credit cards, and student loans.

Although in the initial phase securitization was relevant mainly in the US, from the late 1990s onward this technique started to grow significantly in other countries as well. The development of the European securitization market was driven primarily by the increased demand from institutional investors, technological and financial innovation, and the introduction of the euro, rather than by government agencies as in the US (Altunbas, Gambacorta, Marques-Ibanez, 2009). The European securitization market has remained relatively heterogeneous across countries, with the UK, Italy, the Netherlands, and Spain dominating the market (see Figure 15.2 and Figure 15.3).

While ABSs and MBSs are the "original" fixed income securities,[5] from the early 2000s a so-called "second wave" securitization started to acquire market share in the US and Europe, both in terms of new issuance and total amount outstanding. The creation of securities known as collateralized debt obligations (CDOs) formed a new phase in the securitization process. CDOs are securitization vehicles that depart from the traditional securitization model toward the creation of instruments backed by fewer but larger and more heterogeneous assets, including high yield bonds, leveraged loans, and tranches of other securitizations. The CDO market experienced an unprecedented growth from its inception in the mid-1990s and reached a high of nearly $2 trillion by 2006 (Longstaff and Rajan, 2008); however, the growth came to a halt by 2008 and the market has been shrinking from 2008–09 onward (see Figure 15.1 and Figure 15.2).

---

[5] MBSs include residential mortgage-backed securities (RMBSs).

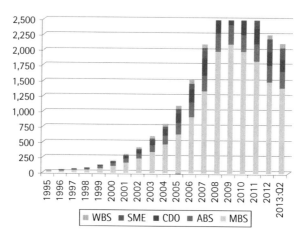

FIGURE 15.2 European securitization outstanding 1995–2013: Q2, USD billions.

Notes: The graph plots outstanding European securitization (in $ billions) between 1995 and 2013, quarter 2. The total outstanding volume includes mortgage-backed securities (MBS), asset-backed securities (ABS), collateralized debt obligations (CDO), small and medium enterprises (SME), and whole business securitization (WBS).

Source: AFME/SIFMA Members, Bloomberg, Thomson Reuters, prospectus filings, Fitch Ratings, Moody's, S&P, AFME, SIFMA; data compiled by SIFMA; data compiled by SIFMA.

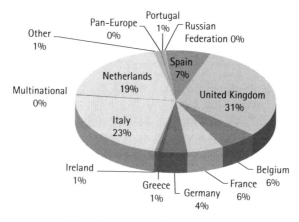

FIGURE 15.3 European securitization issuance by country, year 2012.

Notes: The graph plots European securitization issuance by country of collateral, as of year 2012. "Other" includes countries too small to be displayed: Austria, Sweden, Denmark, Finland, the Channel Islands, Hungary, Iceland, Poland, Switzerland, Turkey, Ukraine, and the US. Pan-Europe consists of collateral predominantly sourced from multiple European countries. Multinational contains collateral from multiple and/or unknown countries; most CDOs are bucketed in this group.

Source: AFME & SIFMA Members, Bloomberg, Thomson Reuters, prospectus filings, Fitch Ratings, Moody's, S&P, AFME & SIFMA; data compiled by SIFMA.

While there is a substantial literature on credit derivatives, relatively little attention has been paid to CDOs. Longstaff and Rajan (2008) present the first extensive empirical analysis of the CDO market and its pricing characteristics, while Deng, Gabriel, and Sanders (2011) evaluate the effects of the emergence of the CDO market on the pricing of MBSs and discuss how the abrupt halt of the global CDO markets in 2008 affected MBS spreads and contributed to a slowdown in the global securitization markets. Benmelech, Dlugosz, and Ivashina (2012) instead focus on collateralized loan obligations (CLOs), which are CDOs backed by corporate loans, and find no consistent evidence of underperformance of loans securitized using this vehicle.

Other significant securitized products that enjoyed a boom in the pre-crisis period are asset-backed commercial paper (ABCP) conduits and structured investment vehicles (SIVs). ABCP conduits initially appeared in the US in the 1980s, and were primarily sponsored by major commercial banks as means of providing trade receivable financing to their corporate customers. Marques-Ibanez and Scheicher (2010) note that typically an ABCP uses short-term debt (with maturities starting from one day to several months) to finance a pool of credit assets such as trade receivables, corporate loans, mortgage loans, CDO tranches, or other credit assets obtained from the market. The underlying assets in ABCP have relatively long maturities compared with the funding liabilities and, as such, ABCP structures have large maturity mismatches. The conduit finances the assets by selling ABCP to outside investors. The outside investors are primarily money market funds and other "safe asset" investors. In general, the originator will provide liquidity support (enhancement and other guarantees) to allay investors' fears about the liquidity mismatch. Many US banks used this type of structure to hold large pools of medium-term loans in SPVs financed by the issue of short-term commercial paper.

In January 2007, ABCP was the largest short-term debt instrument with more than $1.2 trillion outstanding (compared with about $940 billion outstanding for Treasury bills). However, between July and December 2007, the ABCP market experienced the equivalent of a bank run, when the ABCP outstanding dropped from $1.3 trillion to $833 billion, as documented by Covitz, Liang, and Suarez (2013) and Acharya, Schnabl, and Suarez (2013). Kacperczyk and Schnabl (2010) provide a detailed analysis of the crisis of the ABCP market.[6]

After the extended period of growth and development, global securitization markets collapsed during the financial crisis, as market participants lost confidence in structured products. As a result, from mid-2007 onward the issuance of securitized products has been confined to the agency sector in the US and to refinancing operations with the European Central Bank in the EU (Fender and Mitchell, 2009). As of the second quarter of 2013, the outstanding volumes of US mortgage- and asset-backed securitization and CDOs are around $8.1 trillion, $1.1 trillion, and 591 billion, respectively; the corresponding volumes for the European market are around $1.4 trillion, $275 billion, and $202 billion, respectively (see Figure 15.1 and Figure 15.2).

---

[6] Prior to 2007, ABCP was popular with investors as it offered higher returns than Treasury bills and was considered a safe asset, due to its short maturity and high credit rating. This view changed following the bankruptcy of two Bear Stearn's hedge funds in July 2007, followed by BNP Paribas' decision to halt withdrawals from three of its investment funds. These events caused a fall of nearly 40% of the total value of ABCP outstanding. The event that caused the run on the ABCP market was the announcement that the Reserve Primary Fund had suffered large losses on its holding of Lehman Brothers' commercial paper. This news triggered the equivalent of a bank run, which was contained only by the announcement concerning the provision of deposit insurance to investments in money-market funds by the US government (Kacperczyk and Schnabl, 2010).

15.3 MECHANICS OF SECURITIZATION

Securitization is a structured process whereby homogenous financial assets are pooled, underwritten, and sold to outside investors in the form of securities. A typical securitization transaction involves an originator pooling assets with fixed or nearly fixed cash flows and subsequently transferring the pool to a special purpose vehicle (SPV), a bankruptcy-remote entity that in turn finances the purchase through the issuance of securities backed by the pool. A simplified securitization transaction is illustrated in Figure 15.4. It typically consists of five main stages.

15.3.1 Asset Selection

The first stage of a securitization transaction is choice of the assets to be sold to the SPV, with the view to create an asset pool whose expected performance is consistent with the required quality of the final ABSs. This stage is also known as the design stage of the process. One

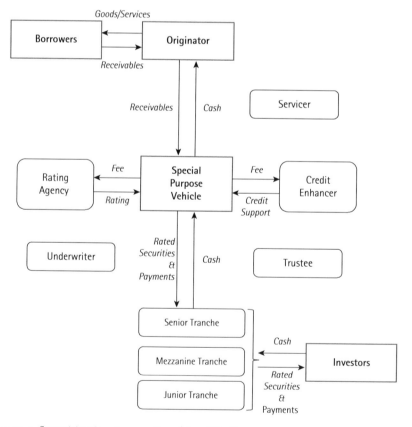

FIGURE 15.4 Securitization transaction (simplified).

peculiarity of the securitization design is that it always involves assets that are homogenous in nature (i.e., mortgages, auto loans, credit card receivables, etc.), even when the bank originates several different asset classes. Although standard finance theory assumes that asset diversification is important to reduce risk, different asset classes are always kept apart in securitization. Once assets are selected to be part of a pool, they are then scrutinized by rating agencies and underwriters, with the aim to evaluate the expected performance of the pool. One or more credit enhancement facilities are usually required in order to receive a high enough credit rating to make the resulting ABSs readily marketable.

This first stage of the securitization process can raise issues of adverse selection as a result of asymmetric information between originators and investors. Originators may have an incentive to exploit their informational advantage and select lower quality assets for securitization, while retaining higher quality assets on the balance sheet. Overall, recent research seems to find evidence to support the view that securitization is a "market for lemons." Downing, Jaffee, and Wallace (2009) provide consistent evidence that RMBSs sold by GSEs (Fannie Mae and Freddie Mac) to SPVs over the period 1991–2002 were of lower quality ("lemons") compared to retained assets and were subsequently priced at a "lemons discount." This result is also confirmed by the findings of An, Deng, and Gabriel (2011). Agarwal, Chang, and Yavas (2012) suggest that in the prime mortgage market prior to the crisis (2004–06) originators were securitizing lower default risk and higher prepayment risk loans while retaining higher default risk and lower prepayment risk loans on the balance sheet. This strategy changed with the onset of the crisis in 2007, when originators were no longer willing to retain high default risk loans on their books. Interestingly, there seems to be no evidence for adverse selection in the subprime mortgage market where loans securitized/retained exhibit no significant differences in default and prepayment risks. Analysing data on loans used as CLO collateral, Benmelech, Dlugosz, and Ivashina (2012) also find evidence contrary to the adverse selection hypothesis and conclude that adverse selection is not an inevitable consequence of securitization. Gorton and Metrick (2013) argue that while originators may well have an informational advantage, they might also have little discretion over the choice of loans to enter a pool, as eligibility criteria are set out in pooling and servicing agreements (the main contractual documents of securitization) and loans are scrutinized by servicers and rating agencies, who evaluate the expected performance of the assets before entering these into the pool to be sold to the SPV.

Another issue that arises in the first stage of the securitization process relates to the role of credit rating agencies (CRAs). This has spurred a large literature as credit ratings were assigned to structured products with significant errors. Ashcraft and Schuermann (2008) provide a detailed overview of how the rating agencies assign credit ratings on tranches of a securitization issuance. White (2010) discusses how the securitization of subprime mortgages only happened because of the high ratings assigned to the more senior tranches, thereby ensuring a market for the resulting securities. An analysis of credit ratings on subprime and Alt-A MBS deals issued between 2001 and 2007 is provided by Ashcraft, Goldsmith-Pinkham, and Vickery (2010). Their results seem to reject the simple story that credit rating standards deteriorated uniformly over the pre-crisis period. However, they do find evidence of a significant decline in risk-adjusted subordination levels between the start of 2005 and mid-2007, when incentive problems were likely to be most severe. The credit rating of CLOs is analyzed by Benmelech and Dlugosz (2009), to uncover the reasons why these have not experienced the downgrades suffered by MBSs, ABSs, and CDOs. Results seem to point to the quality of the collateral and evidence possible issues in the CLO market.

An overall analysis of the role of credit rating agencies in the subprime crisis is provided by Pagano and Volpin (2010), who focus on rating inflation and coarse information disclosure, and discuss how regulation can be designed to mitigate these problems in the future. They propose a model where rating agencies are paid by investors rather than by originators. Herring and Kane (2012) argue that the solution is to create accountability in the rating process. Both these suggestions have been incorporated in the design of the new EU Directive on credit rating agencies (Directive 2013/14/EU).

15.3.2 Creation of an SPV and Transfer of Assets

The second stage in the securitization process involves the creation of a special purpose vehicle, a separate legal entity that is normally set up as a trust and is tax neutral and bankruptcy remote from the originator, and the transfer of the pool of assets to the SPV. The SPV is created for the sole purpose of holding on its balance sheet the assets transferred by the originator and subsequently issuing ABSs. Typically, the SPV is thinly capitalized; it has no independent management or employees; the administrative functions are performed by a trustee; and the assets are serviced via a servicing arrangement (Gorton and Souleles, 2006). Ayotte and Gaon (2011) focus on the "bankruptcy remoteness" of SPVs and demonstrate that it provides creditor protection that is not available with secured debt, and this protection is valued by lenders when pricing these contracts. Originally, a new SPV was set up for each securitization issuance, but it is no longer the case and originators utilize a "master" SPV to transfer assets originated at different times.

Having created an SPV, the pool of assets is transferred from the originator's balance sheet onto the balance sheet of the SPV. The transfer of assets must be in the form of a "true sale," where the transferor (i.e., the originator) surrenders control over the financial assets and can, therefore, remove the assets from its balance sheet. This true sale condition serves as a protection of the SPV's and eventually investors' rights on the cash flows generated by the underlying pool of assets in the case of the originator's bankruptcy.

Originators tend to violate the true sale condition by providing implicit recourse, or non-contractual performance guarantees, to investors with the purpose to maintain reputation in the securitization market for repeated sales. However, implicit recourse also provides scope for regulatory capital arbitrage and is, consequently, of concern for regulators (OCC, 2002). In addition, as a result of implicit recourse, risks may remain with the securitizing banks (Calomiris and Mason, 2004; Higgins and Mason, 2004; Vermilyea, Webb, and Kish, 2008).

15.3.3 Structuring the Transaction

The third stage in the securitization process is the structuring of the transaction, to modify the risk and return to investors. This structuring process constitutes the main difference between securitization and conventional loan sales and it is commonly done by tranching and the provision of credit enhancements and guarantees.[7] Tranching is a technique used by issuers to create securities with a subordinated structure, that is, to create bond classes with different degrees of priority and therefore redistribute the risk of the underlying assets among the different tranches and subsequently among different investors. In addition to tranching, in order to reduce credit risk for investors, thereby increasing the credit rating (and therefore the pricing and marketability) of the ABSs, the SPV can obtain credit enhancements. Credit enhancements are contractual provisions, which aim to reduce the likelihood that losses from the underlying assets are borne by investors.

Credit enhancements may take different forms and can be provided internally, externally, or a combination of both. Internal credit enhancements, also known as contractual retained interests, can be generated by the cash flows from the underlying assets (excess spread), by the structure of the transaction (subordinated securities), or can be provided by the originating bank (liquidity provisions, over-collateralization, standby letters of credit). External credit enhancements include the credit support provided by other institutions and may take the form of a third-party letter of credit, cash collateral account, and surety bonds (OCC, 1997).

A typical securitization structure may contain one or more contractual credit enhancements, with varying subordination (first-loss) arrangements. The nature and the amount of credit enhancements required to obtain the credit ratings sought for ABSs are determined by the rating agency and depend on characteristics and quality of underlying assets, but (importantly) not of the originator.

Figure 15.5 illustrates the waterfall structure of claims (in order from junior to senior). The priority of claims is an important feature of a structured transaction. However, apart from the subordination of tranches of different credit ratings, there is little consensus among industry practitioners and regulators over a clear waterfall structure as it is specific to each individual securitization transaction.

Credit enhancements are present in all securitization transactions. They are also used to maintain the assigned rating levels and therefore can vary during the lifetime of a structured transaction. Recent figures indicate an upward trend in the use of credit enhancements: total enhancements provided by US bank holding companies, including both those provided to own and to third-party securitizations, increased from $25 billion in 2001, Quarter 2, to $70 billion in 2009, Quarter 1 (Mandel, Morgan, and Wei, 2012). The growth in the provision of credit enhancements raises the question of the role of retained interests in the securitization process and ultimately their resultant effect on bank risk.

The interest retention theme is relatively new in the securitization literature. Theoretical studies on interest retention in securitization mainly focus on the impact it has on the screening and monitoring effort by the originating institution. In particular, early studies by Pennacchi (1988) and Gorton and Pennacchi (1995) suggest that retention of interest in securitized assets helps to mitigate the moral hazard problem. Based on the assumption that retaining an interest in the securitized assets (also known as retaining "skin in the game") induces banks to improve the screening and monitoring of borrowers, recent regulatory initiatives call for mandatory risk retention. Examples of the proposed rules

---

[7] Loan sales (or secondary loan participations) occur when a bank originates a loan and then sells the cash stream from the loan without explicit contractual recourse, guarantee, insurance, or other credit enhancement, to a third party (Gorton and Pennacchi, 1995).

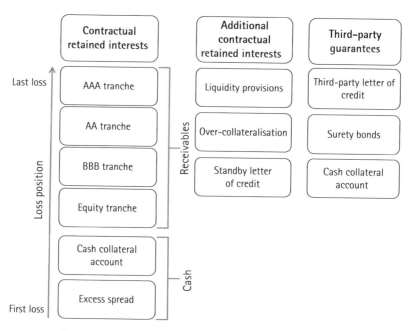

FIGURE 15.5 Credit enhancements.

Source: Asset Securitization, The Comptroller's Handbook (OCC 1997); adapted and updated.

requiring securitizers to retain a portion of the credit risk in the assets that they securitize include Section 941 of the 2010 Dodd–Frank Act in the US, and Article 122a of the Capital Requirements Directive (CRD II) in the EU. Notwithstanding their potential to minimize asymmetric information problems and foster a better alignment of incentives between banks and investors, retained interests also expose banks to the risk of the securitized assets. In addition, given the lower capital requirements associated with retained interests, the structuring of transactions created a significant concentration of risks, thereby increasing banks' insolvency risk (Shin, 2009; Acharya, Schnabl, and Suarez, 2013). In many cases, the simple act of securitizing loans decreased a bank's capital requirements substantially. The fact that the risk inherent to securitized assets was not passed on to investors but remained on banks' balance sheets, in the form of credit enhancements and other forms of retained interests, is considered one of the key reasons for the severity of the 2007–09 financial crisis (Shin, 2009). Using US bank holding company data for the pre-crisis period, Sarkisyan and Casu (2013) analyze the relationship between the total economic interests retained by banks in off-balance-sheet securitizations and insolvency risk. They find that the provision of credit enhancements and guarantees significantly increases bank insolvency risk, albeit this varies for different levels of securitization outstanding. In addition, they find that the type of facility provided is relevant, as those facilities with the most subordinated (first-loss) position have the greater impact on banks' default risk. These results suggest that, when designing the optimal risk retention framework for securitization, regulators should consider bank risk at the institutional level, with a view to balancing the incentive structure embedded in the risk retention regulation with the use of securitization as a risk management tool.

15.3.4 Issuance of Asset-Backed Securities

In the fourth stage, ABSs are issued by the SPV. In the most common case, the securities are issued in tranches of different risk, duration, and other characteristics, with the senior tranche of investment grade being supported by mezzanine tranches, which in turn are supported by an unrated subordinated equity tranche. The equity tranche is the most risky tranche of the securitization transaction; in early securitizations it was commonly retained by the originator on its balance sheet. Over time, an active market for equity tranches developed, resulting from both the increased investors' confidence in securitized products and the growth of a liquid market for credit derivatives that made it possible to hedge the risk exposure of equity tranches. This in turn might have contributed to weakening the incentives that the retention of the equity tranche should have generated for originators (Fender and Mitchell, 2009).

As discussed in Section 15.3.3, tranching is essentially a way of transferring credit risk; the intuition behind the practice of tranching is that it allows originators to concentrate the default risk in one part of the securitization structure, therefore resulting in a large share of liabilities becoming almost risk free. This in turn should decrease the overall lemons discount demanded by investors (Boot and Thakor, 1993; Gorton and Pennacchi, 1995). DeMarzo (2005)'s model demonstrates that when the number of assets is large and their returns are imperfectly correlated, the originators can maximize their revenue from the sale by pooling and tranching. More recently, Van Oordt (2014) models the securitization of loan portfolios as a diversification strategy. The model shows that tranching offers non-linear diversification strategies, which can reduce the risk of failure of individual institutions beyond the minimum level attainable by linear diversification, without increasing systemic risk.

15.3.5 Allocation of Cash Flows

Finally, in the fifth stage of the securitization process, the cash flows received from the underlying pool are disbursed among the investors in ABSs. The cash flows are distributed following a waterfall structure, where payments are first allocated to the holders of senior tranches, then to the holders of subordinated tranches, and last to the junior tranche holders.

The modeling of the cash flows is a crucial stage in the valuation and pricing of fixed income securities, including MBSS and ABSS. Due to the complexity of the cash flow structure in most securitization issues, it is often difficult for investors to evaluate the performance of ABSs and how this is impacted by the performance of the underlying assets. This has resulted in the overreliance on credit ratings, as discussed in Section 15.3.1 above.

15.4 BENEFITS AND RISKS OF SECURITIZATION

Securitization can offer substantial benefits to all the major parties in the transaction, which explains the growth of the market. However, it also introduces some frictions that might impede the potential benefits. Below we provide some discussion of the benefits and risks inherent in securitization from the perspectives of originators, borrowers, investors, and the general economy.

15.4.1 Originators

Securitization provides financial institutions with a way to: (1) lower the cost of funding, as ABSs are typically assigned a higher credit rating than that of the originator; (2) diversify funding sources, by establishing themselves in the market; (3) improve credit risk management, by shifting the credit risk of the originated assets to external credit enhancers and investors; (4) diversify portfolios, by reducing firm-specific exposure, as well as asset-class, sectoral, and geographic concentration; (5) manage interest rate risk, by selling assets to reduce the interest rate mismatch of balance sheet assets and liabilities; (6) reduce regulatory capital requirements, by transferring assets off the balance sheet; (7) earn origination and servicing fee income, by originating assets to securitize and subsequently servicing the ABSs; (8) enhance performance indicators as a result of the above.

The realization of the benefits offered by securitization requires prudent underwriting and credit risk management—when performed poorly, these may undermine the potential performance benefits of using the securitization market (FDIC, 2007). For example, while securitization may allow banks to raise funds at a lower cost, non-performing asset pools may impair banks' access to the market and require higher credit enhancements, thereby considerably increasing the cost of this funding source. This might lead to significant funding constraints when banks become overly reliant on securitization and overgrow traditional funding sources; especially so when securitization markets become disrupted, as witnessed during the 2007–09 financial crisis (FDIC, 2007; Loutskina, 2011). In addition, while securitization may allow banks to reduce their credit risk exposure by transferring the unexpected portion of the default risk to credit enhancers and outside investors, management's incentives to ensure the performance of the securitized pool—and thereby establish and maintain their reputation in the market—may result in "cherry-picking" of assets when designing the securitization transaction and in providing implicit and/or explicit recourse to the structure (Higgins and Mason, 2004; Gorton and Souleles, 2006; Vermilyea, Webb, and Kish, 2008).[8] As a consequence, in the short term, the potential benefits to banks in terms of reduced cost of funding and reduced credit risk might be outweighed by the implicit and explicit costs of structuring the transaction. In the longer term, there is evidence in the literature that securitization may also trigger lax origination and monitoring processes (Mian and Sufi, 2009; Keys et al. 2010; Elul, 2011; Dell'Ariccia, Igan, and Laeven, 2012). This could eventually offset the potential credit risk reduction achieved through securitization. Finally, the additional capital released through securitization can be used by banks for expansion purposes or to retire existing debt, which in turn might increase profitability. However, poor underwriting and credit risk management practices might offset the potential positive effect

---

[8] The reputation of a bank in a securitization market is of great importance and depends mainly on the quality of the underlying assets and the efficiency at which the bank can service those assets. Poorly performing assets or servicing failures on existing securitizations may increase the costs and decrease the profitability of future transactions.

on profitability. Additionally, the effect on profitability of securitization may be distorted by managers' discretion afforded under fair value accounting rules (Dechow, Myers, and Shakespeare, 2010).

To sum up, while the performance benefits from the originator's perspective can be substantial, in practice the net impact of securitization remains ambiguous. In a recent research paper, Casu et al. (2013) use a propensity score-matching technique to estimate the effects of securitization on a number of bank performance indicators, including cost of funding, credit risk, and profitability. To evaluate the effects of securitization, the authors estimate the counterfactual performance of securitizing banks (that is, the performance securitizing banks would have had, had they not securitized) using a sample of matched non-securitizing banks. The analysis shows that securitizing banks would have had comparable performance had they not securitized, that is, it does not provide evidence to suggest that securitization had an impact upon bank performance. Casu et al. (2013) conclude that in the run-up to the 2007–09 crisis the risks associated with increasingly complex securitizations might have outweighed the benefits to originators.

15.4.2 Borrowers

Borrowers may benefit from securitization as a result of: (1) increased credit supply, as lenders are able to raise additional capital for new loans via the market; (2) reduced borrowing costs, as lenders can pass the lower funding costs to the borrowers in the form of lower interest rates on loans; and (3) enhanced availability of credit on terms more favourable than lenders would have been able to offer, had they kept the loans on their balance sheets.[9]

With regards to the first point, overall the literature provides evidence to support the view that securitization increases credit supply. Using data on CLOs issued between 1995 and 2004, Goderis et al. (2007) find that banks that adopt advanced credit risk transfer techniques experience a permanent increase in their target loan level of around 50%.[10] Altunbas, Gambacorta, and Marques-Ibanez (2009) also find that securitization increases bank lending by providing banks with a source of capital relief and additional funding; however, this capacity is found to change over time and to depend on the business cycles and the banks' risk positions. Loutskina (2011) finds that securitization reduces banks' holdings of liquid assets on balance sheet and subsequently increases the supply of lending per dollar of capital. The author also finds that, by increasing the liquidity of loans, securitization reduces the sensitivity of lending growth to cost of funding shocks, thereby increasing credit availability across sectors; for example, banks' ability to securitize liquid mortgage loans tends to increase their willingness to supply illiquid business loans. Loutskina and Strahan (2009) show that securitization reduces the impact of banks' financial condition on credit supply. Specifically, the authors find that the banks' cost of deposits and on-balance sheet holdings

---

[9] As an example of the latter, the existence of securitization markets may allow lenders to extend fixed rate debt preferred by many borrowers over variable rate debt without exposing themselves to interest rate risk (OCC, 1997).

[10] The authors note that equity capital would have to increase by around 60% to have a similar impact on the target loan level.

of liquid assets impact the supply of illiquid loans (the so-called jumbo mortgages, defined as mortgage loans above a given size threshold), while having no effect on the supply of relatively liquid loans (non-jumbo mortgages).

Regarding the cost of borrowing, a study by Sabry and Okongwu (2009) finds that securitization lowered the cost of consumer credit, including mortgages, credit card receivables, and auto loans. Specifically, the evidence shows that, in the period between 1999 and 2006, a 10% increase in the securitization rate was associated with a decrease in yield spreads of 24–38 basis points for subprime mortgages, 4–12 basis points for jumbo mortgages, 22–64 basis points for auto loans, and 8–54 basis points for credit card loans; however, there seems to be no consistent long-term relationship between securitization and yield spreads for conforming mortgage loans. This evidence is consistent even during the crisis period, between 2007 and June 2008, and suggests a negative association between securitization rates and yield spreads for all the products, except for conventional conforming mortgages and credit card receivables. Overall, the authors conclude that the benefits of securitization to originators in the form of lower funding costs are passed on to borrowers in the form of lower cost of consumer credit. Nadauld and Weisbach (2012) investigate whether securitization has an impact on the cost of debt for borrowers in the primary corporate debt market. Their results indicate that over the period 1995–2008 the yield on a loan that is subsequently securitized is around 15 basis points lower than that on an otherwise identical loan that is held on the balance sheet. This provides evidence to support the view that securitization also leads to a reduction in the cost of corporate debt.

While securitization offers benefits to borrowers, the 2007–09 financial crisis, and ensuing unprecedented levels of mortgage foreclosures, reignited the discussion of a potential adverse impact of securitization on loan renegotiation. This motivated a growing research examining whether securitization impedes servicers' willingness to renegotiate delinquent loans, thereby causing more foreclosures. Among the reasons why securitized loans might have a different renegotiation treatment compared to loans held on the balance sheet (the so-called portfolio loans) is the fact that servicers do not internalize losses on securitized loans and therefore are not incentivized to renegotiate a delinquent securitized loan. Other reasons include potential legal restrictions on renegotiations imposed by the pooling and servicing agreements, dispersion in property rights and subsequent coordination difficulties in altering mortgage contracts, and institutional constraints faced by lenders (Adelino, Gerardi, and Willen, 2009; Piskorski, Seru, and Vig, 2010).

The empirical evidence on the issue of securitization and loan renegotiation is mixed. Adelino, Gerardi, and Willen (2009) find no evidence to suggest that securitization affects servicers' loan renegotiation. The authors find that in general the servicers renegotiate a small fraction of residential mortgage loans, regardless of whether a loan is securitized or held in their portfolios. However, most of the recent literature finds evidence to suggest that securitization introduces frictions in the market that impede effective loan renegotiation. In particular, Piskorski, Seru, and Vig (2010) consider a wider definition of loan renegotiation and find that seriously delinquent securitized mortgage loans have higher foreclosure rates than comparable portfolio loans. Agarwal et al. (2011) find that distressed securitized residential mortgage loans are significantly less likely to be renegotiated (up to 36% in relative terms) than portfolio loans. Furthermore, the renegotiation of securitized loans appears to be less efficient with higher post-modification default rates. A recent study by Zhang (2013) examines both redefault and self-cure rates of residential mortgage loans depending on their securitization status, and suggests that previously delinquent securitized loans are more likely to redefault and less likely to self-cure than comparable portfolio loans. However, this difference in the rates persists in the intermediary time frame only and diminishes afterwards. In general, the study finds that previously cured loans have similar redefault and self-cure rates over time, regardless of their securitization status.

15.4.3 Investors

Investors may benefit from ABSs as they: (1) offer higher yields compared to other financial instruments of a similar credit quality,[11] and generally better credit risk protection by means of credit enhancements; (2) provide a measure of flexibility as the payment streams can be structured to meet an investor's particular requirements; and (3) release investors from the need to gain a detailed understanding of the underlying assets as a result of structural credit enhancements and diversified asset pools (OCC, 1997). These features of ABSs meet the requirements of pension funds, insurance companies, and other institutional investors for safe fixed income securities with specific payment streams and attractive yields and, therefore, boost institutional investors' demand.

While ABSs are attractive to investors for the reasons discussed above, it is important to reiterate the moral hazard problem arising from asymmetric information between the originators and investors. To recall, as loans can be securitized, originators are likely to lack incentives to effectively screen and monitor borrowers and thereby minimize the defaults on securitized loans. Supporting this argument, a number of empirical papers have found evidence of lax screening by originators (Mian and Sufi, 2009; Keys et al. 2010). A number of theoretical papers have attempted to derive the optimal security design under moral hazard. Among the recent papers, Hartman-Glaser, Piskorski, and Tchistyi (2012) consider the optimal design of MBSs in the presence of initial moral hazard in a dynamic setting, where a mortgage originator can choose the level of the costly screening effort for assets to be securitized. Their optimal contract calls for the investors to receive the entire pool of mortgages and to make a single payment to the originator of the loans after a waiting period conditional on no defaults on the loans. Interestingly, it also calls for pooling mortgages rather than selling them individually, as it would allow investors to learn about the screening effort of the originator more quickly. Building on the work by Hartman-Glaser, Piskorski, and Tchistyi (2012), Malamud, Rui, and Whinston (2013) also consider the optimal dynamic contract in the presence of initial moral hazard, where the originator chooses the optimal effort level when screening the assets to be securitized. Their optimal contract calls for multiple waiting periods, where the originator is partially paid conditional on no defaults in every subsequent waiting period. The authors show that when there is optimal contracting between the originator and outside investors, securitization can improve originators' screening incentives, even when originators are completely unregulated and have all the bargaining power in designing the optimal contract.

---

[11] Higher yields are offered as a compensation for a possible prepayment risk and restricted secondary market for these securities.

15.4.4 Economy

Finally, securitization may affect the general economy through a number of channels, including its impact on originators, borrowers, and investors discussed earlier, as well as that on government policy and financial stability.

Securitization may benefit the general economy by increasing credit availability and reducing the cost of credit in areas prioritized by social policy; for example, increasing the supply of funds for homeownership, developing access to finance for small businesses, or reducing regional disparities within a country. Securitization increases banks' flexibility to tap additional sources of funding, which in turn broadens the pool of cash that can be tapped to support economic growth. On the other hand, there is evidence that in a number of countries securitization reinforced the feedback effect between increases in housing prices and the expansion of credit, therefore contributing to a housing bubble (Carbo-Valverde, Marques-Ibanez, and Rodríguez-Fernández, 2011). Furthermore, securitization may have a mitigating impact upon the effect of monetary policy on real economic activity through the lending channel. A stream of research has analyzed this issue and found evidence that securitization reduces the efficacy of monetary policy; specifically, results suggest that securitization appears to shelter banks' loan supply from cost of funding shocks induced by monetary policy (Altunbas, Gambacorta, and Marques-Ibanez, 2009; Loutskina and Strahan, 2009; Loutskina, 2011).

With regards to financial stability, prior to the 2007–09 financial crisis, a predominantly positive view of securitization emphasized its role in enhancing the resilience of the financial system to shocks by distributing credit risk across diverse parties (Adrian and Shin, 2008; Duffie, 2008; Shin, 2009). However, the financial crisis has shown that this spreading of risks led to an increase in correlations across sectors of the financial system, thereby increasing systemic risk. Post-crisis, a number of studies have investigated the impact of securitization on financial stability. Some have argued that securitization increased the risk appetite of banks, which led to increased leverage, increased expected returns, and decreased liquidity premia; and therefore ultimately resulted in bank failures and financial instability. Brunnermeier and Sannikov (2012) argue that the increase in endogenous risk taking triggered by the securitization process may make the financial system less stable. While a sound understanding of the ultimate impact of securitization on financial stability is of crucial importance, there is little empirical research on the topic.

Despite the fact that the securitization markets have been severely affected by the financial crisis, and the macroeconomic volatility in the Eurozone, the overall view of policymakers and industry participants is that securitization remains a key funding tool for banks and that it can positively contribute to the recovery of the global economy (AFME, 2012). This is particularly important in Europe, as the economy is highly dependent on banks for funding. IMF (2012) estimates that if securitization provides funding that increases the ability of banks to raise debt, and if the cash raised is then used to support new lending, even a small increase in securitization would have a positive impact on gross domestic product (GDP). However, the mechanisms behind this relationship are not fully understood and require further research. Specifically, the aim is to ensure high-quality securitizations that can lead to increased volumes of lending and lower credit prices to borrowers, without triggering the excessive risk taking witnessed in the run-up to the 2007–09 financial crisis.

15.5 CONCLUDING REMARKS: REGULATORY REFORMS AND THE FUTURE OF SECURITIZATION

Despite the frictions inherent in the securitization process and the ensuing potential adverse effects, policymakers as well as market practitioners also acknowledge its potential benefits and are currently attempting to revive the market.

The economic rationale for securitization is still a valid one: it alleviates credit constraints and facilitates risk transfer. While many of the incentive problems inherent in the securitization process remain to be resolved, if the market remains depressed, banks might not be able to replace maturing securitized products and might therefore face a contraction of their funding sources, which in turn may exacerbate already tight credit conditions and impede economic growth. In addition, as securitization offered banks a credit risk transfer mechanism, the absence of this channel can worsen, deleveraging pressures on already constrained bank balance sheets.

Ongoing regulatory reforms are aimed at minimizing some of the perceived frictions, but much still remains to be done. In order to address the key structural weaknesses of the securitization process the following have been identified as necessary conditions: (1) align incentives; (2) reduce complexity; (3) increase transparency; and (4) improve the use of credit ratings.

A key issue that regulators are currently trying to address relates to the alignment of incentives associated with securitization. This resulted in the introduction of "risk retention rules" that require banks to maintain an interest in their own securitizations, based on the assumption that retaining "skin in the game" induces banks to improve screening and monitoring of borrowers. Examples of the proposed rules requiring securitizers to retain a portion of the credit risk in the assets that they securitize include Section 941 of the 2010 Dodd–Frank Act in the US and Article 122a of the Capital Requirements Directive (CRD II) in the EU.

With the aim of reducing complexity and increasing transparency, a number of changes have been proposed in terms of accounting standards. While a detailed description of proposed changes in accounting standards is outside the scope of this chapter, we refer the reader to recent proposals by the Financial Stability Board and by the International Organization of Securities Commissions (FSB, 2012; IOSCO, 2012).

The issue of improving credit rating has also been tackled by regulators. As of June 2013, new EU legislation on credit rating agencies has come into force (Directive 2013/14/EU) and CRAs will now have to follow stricter rules, which will make them more accountable for their actions. The new rules also aim to reduce overreliance on credit ratings, while at the same time improving the quality of the rating process. Credit rating agencies will have to be more transparent when rating sovereign states. The 2010 Dodd–Frank Act also contains provisions for "Improvements to the Regulation of Credit Rating Agencies."

Whether these regulatory initiatives will suffice to restart the securitization market is still uncertain. A return of trust in the market will take time. Banks and investors are still dealing with the so called "legacy of toxic assets." It is also predicted that the market will not return to the dizzy pre-crisis heights, but products and process will be simplified, to improve both liquidity and valuation. There is a concern that the interaction of domestic and international regulatory initiatives will overburden market participants and therefore stifle recovery. Securitization has many potential advantages, as it can provide banks with cost-effective, market-based funding. It can more closely align the needs of banks and investors and therefore result in credit growth and economic expansion. The key to reaping these benefits is to ensure all parties have the relevant information and price risks appropriately.

References

Acharya, V. V. and Schnabl, P. (2010). Do Global Banks Spread Global Imbalances? Asset-Backed Commercial Paper During the Financial Crisis of 2007–09, *IMF Economic Review* 58, 37–73.

Acharya, V. V., Schnabl, P., and Suarez, G. (2013). Securitization without Risk Transfer, *Journal of Financial Economics* 107, 515–536.

Adelino, M., Gerardi, K., and Willen, P. S. (2009). Why Don't Lenders Renegotiate More Home Mortgages? Redefaults, Self-Cures, and Securitization, Federal Reserve Bank of Atlanta Working Paper No. 2009–17.

Published as Adelino, M., Gerardi, K., and Willen, P.S. (2009). Why Don't Lenders Renegotiate More Home Mortgages? Redefaults, Self-Cures, and Securitizatio', *Journal of Monetary Economics* 60, 835–853.

Adrian, T. and Shin, H. S. (2008). Liquidity and Financial Contagion, *Banque de France Financial Stability Review* 11, 1–7.

AFME (Association for Financial Markets in Europe) (2012). The Economic Benefits of High Quality Securitisation to the EU Economy, November.

Agarwal, S., Amromin, G., Ben-David, I., Chomsisengphet, S., and Evanoff, D. (2011). The Role of Securitization in Mortgage Renegotiation, *Journal of Financial Economics* 102, 559–578.

Agarwal, S., Chang, Y., and Yavas, A. (2012). Adverse Selection in Mortgage Securitization, *Journal of Financial Economics* 105, 640–660.

Altunbas, Y., Gambacorta, L., and Marques-Ibanez, D. (2009). Securitisation and the Bank Lending Channel, *European Economic Review* 53, 996–1009.

An, X., Deng, Y., and Gabriel, S. A. (2011). Asymmetric Information, Adverse Selection, and the Pricing of CMBS, *Journal of Financial Economics* 100, 304–325.

Ashcraft, A. B., Goldsmith-Pinkham, P., and Vickery, J. (2010). MBS Ratings and the Mortgage Credit Boom, Federal Reserve Bank of New York Staff Report No. 449.

Ashcraft, A. B. and Schuermann, T. (2008). Understanding the Securitization of Subprime Mortgage Credit, Federal Reserve Bank of New York Staff Report No. 318.

Published as Ashcraft, A. B., and Schuermann, T. (2008). 'Understanding the Securitization of Subprime Mortgage Credit, *Foundations and Trends(R) in Finance* 2, 191–309.

Ayotte, K. and Gaon, S. (2011). Asset-Backed Securities: Costs and Benefits of "Bankruptcy Remoteness," *Review of Financial Studies* 24, 1299–1335.

Baily, M. N., Elmendorf, D. W., and Litan, R. E. (2008). The Great Credit Squeeze: How It Happened, How to Prevent Another. Brookings Institution Discussion Paper.

Benmelech, E. and Dlugosz, J. (2009). The Alchemy of CDO Credit Ratings, *Journal of Monetary Economics* 56, 617–634.

Benmelech, E., Dlugosz, J., and Ivashina, V. (2012). Securitization without Adverse Selection: The Case of CLOs, *Journal of Financial Economics* 106, 91–113.

BIS (Bank for International Settlement) (2011). Report on Asset Securitisation Incentives, July.

Boot, A. W. A. and Thakor, A. V. (1993). Security Design, *Journal of Finance* 48, 1349–1378.

Bord, V. M. and Santos, J. A. C. (2012). The Rise of the Originate-to-Distribute Model and the Role of Banks in Financial Intermediation, *FRBNY Economic Policy Review* 8, 21–34.

Brunnermeier, M. K. (2009). Deciphering the Liquidity and Credit Crunch 2007–2008, *Journal of Economic Perspectives* 23, 77–100.

Brunnermeier, M. K. and Sannikov, Y. (2012). A Macroeconomic Model with a Financial Sector, National Bank of Belgium Working Paper No. 236.

Published as Brunnermeier, M. K., and Sannikov, Y. (2012). 'A Macroeconomic Model with a Financial Sector', *American Economic Review* 104, 379–421.

Calomiris, C. W. and Mason, J. R. (2004). Credit Card Securitization and Regulatory Arbitrage, *Journal of Financial Services Research* 26, 5–27.

Carbo-Valverde, S., Marques-Ibanez, D., and Rodríguez-Fernández, F. (2011). Securitization, Bank Lending and Credit Quality: The Case of Spain, European Central Bank Working Paper No. 1329.

Casu, B., Clare, A., Sarkisyan, A., and Thomas, S. (2013). Securitization and Bank Performance, *Journal of Money, Credit and Banking* 45, 1617–1658.

Claessens, S., Pozsar, Z., Ratnovski, L., and Singh, M. (2012). Shadow Banking: Economics and Policy, International Monetary Fund Staff Discussion Note No. 12/12.

Covitz, D., Liang, N., and Suarez, G. A. (2013). The Evolution of a Financial Crisis: Collapse of the Asset-Backed Commercial Paper Market, *Journal of Finance* 68, 815–848.

Dechow, P. M., Myers, L. A., and Shakespeare, C. (2010). Fair Value Accounting and Gains from Asset Securitizations: A Convenient Earnings Management Tool with Compensation Side-Benefits, *Journal of Accounting and Economics* 49, 2–25.

Dell'Ariccia, G., Igan, D., and Laeven, L. (2012). Credit Booms and Lending Standards: Evidence from the Subprime Mortgage Market, *Journal of Money, Credit and Banking* 44, 367–384.

DeMarzo, P. M. (2005). The Pooling and Tranching of Securities: A Model of Informed Intermediation, *Review of Financial Studies* 18, 1–35.

Deng, Y., Gabriel, S., and Sanders, A. B. (2011). CDO Market Implosion and the Pricing of Subprime Mortgage-Backed Securities, *Journal of Housing Economics* 20, 68–80.

Downing, C., Jaffee, D. M., and Wallace, N. (2009). Is the Market for Mortgage-Backed Securities a Market for Lemons?, *Review of Financial Studies* 22, 2257–2294.

Duffie, D. (2008). Innovations in Credit Risk Transfer: Implications for Financial Stability, No. 255.

Elul, R. (2011). Securitization and Mortgage Default, Federal Reserve Bank of Philadelphia Working Paper No. 09–21.

FDIC (Federal Deposit Insurance Corporation) (2007). Credit Card Securitization Manual, March.

Fender, I. and Mitchell, J. (2009). Incentive and Tranche Retention in Securitisation: A Screening Model, Bank for International Settlements Working Paper No. 289.

FSB (Financial Stability Board) (2012). Strenghtening Oversight and Regulation of Shadow Banking. An Integrated Overview of Policy Recommendations. Consultative Document, November.

Goderis, B., Marsh, I. W., Castello, J. V., and Wagner, W. (2007). Bank Behavior with Access to Credit Risk Transfer Markets, Bank of Finland Discussion Paper No. 4/2007.

Gorton, G. B. (2010). *Slapped by the Invisible Hand: The Panic of 2007*. New York: Oxford University Press.

Gorton, G. and Metrick, A. (2013). Securitization. In: G. Constantinides, M. Harris, and R. Stulz (Eds.), *Handbook of the Economics of Finance*. 2nd edition. Amsterdam: Elsevier, 1–70.

Gorton, G. B. and Pennacchi, G. G. (1995). Banks and Loan Sales: Marketing Nonmarketable Assets, *Journal of Monetary Economics* 35, 389–411.

Gorton, G. B. and Souleles, N. S. (2006). Special Purpose Vehicles and Securitization. In: R. M. Stulz and M. Carey (Eds.), *The Risks of Financial Institutions*. Chicago: University of Chicago Press, 549–602.

Hartman-Glaser, B., Piskorski, T., and Tchistyi, A. (2012). Optimal Securitization with Moral Hazard, *Journal of Financial Economics* 104, 186–202.

Herring, R. and Kane, E. J. (2012). How to Reform the Credit-Rating Process to Support a Sustainable Revival of Private-Label Securitization, *Quarterly Journal of Finance* 02, 1299–1301.

Higgins, E. J. and Mason, J. R. (2004). What Is the Value of Recourse to Asset-Backed Securities? A Clinical Study of Credit Card Banks, *Journal of Banking and Finance* 28, 875–899.

IMF (International Monetary Fund) (2012). Growth Resuming, Dangers Remain. World Economic Outlook, April.

IOSCO (International Organization of Securities Commissions) (2012). Global Developments in Securitisation Regulation, November.

Kacperczyk, M. and Schnabl, P. (2010). When Safe Proved Risky: Commercial Paper During the Financial Crisis of 2007–2009, *Journal of Economic Perspectives* 24, 29–50.

Keys, B. J., Mukherjee, T., Seru, A., and Vig, V. (2010). Did Securitization Lead to Lax Screening? Evidence from Subprime Loans, *Quarterly Journal of Economics* 125, 307–362.

Longstaff, F. A. and Rajan, A. (2008). An Empirical Analysis of the Pricing of Collateralized Debt Obligations, *Journal of Finance* 63, 529–563.

Loutskina, E. (2011). The Role of Securitization in Bank Liquidity and Funding Management, *Journal of Financial Economics* 100, 663–684.

Loutskina, E. and Strahan, P. E. (2009). Securitization and the Declining Impact of Bank Finance on Loan Supply: Evidence from Mortgage Originations, *Journal of Finance* 64, 861–889.

Malamud, S., Rui, H., and Whinston, A. (2013). Optimal Incentives and Securitization of Defaultable Assets, *Journal of Financial Economics* 107, 111–135.

Mandel, B. H., Morgan, D., and Wei, C. (2012). The Role of Bank Credit Enhancements in Securitization, *Federal Reserve Bank of New York Economic Policy Review* 18, 35–46.

Marques-Ibanez, D. and Scheicher, M. (2010). Securitisation: Causes and Consequences. In: A. N. Berger, P. Molyneux, and J. O. S. Wilson (Eds.), *Handbook of Banking*, 599–633, 1st edition. Oxford: Oxford University Press.

Mian, A. R. and Sufi, A. (2009). The Consequences of Mortgage Credit Expansion: Evidence from the US Mortgage Default Crisis, *Quarterly Journal of Economics* 124, 1449–1496.

Nadauld, T. and Weisbach, M. S. (2011). Did Securitization Affect the Cost of Corporate Debt?, Fisher College of Business Working Paper No. 2010–03–16.

Published as Nadauld, T. D., and Weisbach, M. S. (2012). Did Securitization Affect the Cost of Corporate Debt?, *Journal of Financial Economics* 105, 332–352.

OCC (Office of the Comptroller of the Currency) (1997). Asset Securitization. Comptroller's Handbook, November.

OCC (Office of the Comptroller of the Currency) (2002). Interagency Guidance on Implicit Recourse in Asset Securitizations, No. 2002–20.

Pagano, M. and Volpin, P. (2010). Credit Ratings Failures and Policy Options, *Economic Policy* 25, 401–431.

Pennacchi, G. G. (1988). Loan Sales and the Cost of Bank Capital, *Journal of Finance* 43, 375–396.

Piskorski, T., Seru, A., and Vig, V. (2010). Securitization and Distressed Loan Renegotiation: Evidence from the Subprime Mortgage Crisis, *Journal of Financial Economics* 97, 369–397.

Pozsar, Z. (2011). Institutional Cash Pools and the Triffin Dilemma of the US Banking System, International Monetary Fund Working Paper No. 11/190.

Sabry, F. and Okongwu, C. (2009). Study of the Impact of Securitization on Consumers, Investors, Financial Institutions and the Capital Markets. NERA Economic Consulting, June.

Sarkisyan, A. and Casu, B. (2013). Retained Interests in Securitisations and Implications for Bank Solvency, European Central Bank Working Paper No. 1538.

Shin, H. S. (2009). Securitization and Financial Stability, *Economic Journal* 119, 309–332.

Van Oordt, M. R. C. (2014). Securitization and the Dark Side of Diversification, *Journal of Financial Intermediation* 23, 214–231.

Vermilyea, T. A., Webb, E. R., and Kish, A. A. (2008). Implicit Recourse and Credit Card Securitizations: What Do Fraud Losses Reveal?, *Journal of Banking and Finance* 32, 1198–1208.

White, L. J. (2010). Markets: The Credit Rating Agencies, *Journal of Economic Perspectives* 24, 211–226.

Zhang, Y. (2013). Does Loan Renegotiation Differ by Securitization Status? A Transition Probability Study, *Journal of Financial Intermediation* 22, 513–527.

CHAPTER 16

SHADOW BANK MONITORING

TOBIAS ADRIAN, ADAM B. ASHCRAFT, AND NICOLA CETORELLI

16.1 WHAT IS SHADOW BANKING?

TRADITIONAL financial intermediaries are centralized entities brokering the flow of funds between households and borrowers. Households could certainly bypass intermediaries and directly invest in equity or debt of borrowers. However, direct finance requires dealing with well-known informational and liquidity frictions. In particular, it is usually costly to screen, select, monitor, and diversify across investment projects. Moreover, direct investments may be constrained by the need by households for liquidity: that is, the need to access funds before the investments comes to fruition, resulting in wasteful liquidation costs. Financial intermediaries exist to minimize on all of these costs. In the traditional model, intermediaries are centralized agents performing under one roof multiple roles of screening, selection, monitoring, and diversification of risk, while simultaneously providing liquidity services to the providers of funds. The simultaneous provision of these services to multiple agents through maturity, liquidity, and credit transformation provides for a better allocation of risk between households and firms.

While financial intermediation facilitates more efficient risk sharing between borrowers and the suppliers of funds, it does create new risks, the most relevant one being the well-known exposure to "runs" and premature liquidation of projects when the suppliers of funds pull out en masse. Hence, financial intermediation activity is intrinsically fragile, and most importantly it carries a significant social externality, represented by the risk of systemic disruptions in the case of contagion of run events.

The official sector has attempted to minimize this systemic risk through the use of its own balance sheet, by providing credit guarantees on the liabilities of these intermediaries as well as by providing contingent liquidity to these institutions from the lender of last resort. However, the risk-insensitive provision of credit guarantees and liquidity backstops creates well-known incentives for excessive risk-taking, leverage, and maturity transformation, motivating the need for enhanced supervision and prudential regulation. This traditional form of financial intermediation, with credit being intermediated through banks and insurance companies, but with the public sector standing close by to prevent destabilizing runs, dominated other forms of financial intermediation from the Great Depression well into the 1990s.

Over time, financial innovation has transformed intermediation from a process involving a single financial institution to a process now broken down among several institutions, each with their own role in manufacturing the intermediation of credit. With specialization has come significant reductions in the cost of intermediation, but the motive to reduce costs has also pushed financial activity into the shadows in order to reduce or eliminate the cost associated with prudential supervision and regulation, investor disclosure, and taxes. Over the course of three decades, the shadow banking system quickly grew to become equal in size to that of the traditional system, improving on the terms of liquidity traditionally offered to households and borrowers. However, it was only a matter of time before intermediation designed to evade public sector oversight would end badly, as occurred during the post-2007–08 credit cycle. Consequently, while financial innovation is naturally associated with the more efficient provision of financial services, it is this dark side of non-traditional intermediation that has come to define shadow banking.

The term "shadow banking" was coined by McCulley (2007) and was picked up by policymakers (see, for example, Tucker, 2010). The first articles on shadow banking are by Pozsar (2008) and Adrian and Shin (2009). In this chapter, we provide a structured overview of the literature to date. In Section 16.2, we provide a definition of shadow banking, and review attempts to measure its size. In Section 16.3, we explore reasons why shadow banking exists, and in Section 16.4, discuss why regulators and academics should care about shadow banking. In Section 16.5, we provide an approach for monitoring risks in the shadow banking system, with a detailed discussion for each of agency mortgage-backed securities (MBS), real estate investment trusts (REITS), reinsurance, leveraged lending, tri-party repo, money market mutual funds, and off-balance-sheet activity of Chinese banks. Concluding remarks are made in Section 16.6.

16.2 How Does One Define and Measure Shadow Banking?

The official definition of shadow banking was recently formulated by the Financial Stability Board (FSB) as "the system of credit intermediation that involves entities and activities outside the regular banking system." In the words of the FSB: "This implies focusing on credit intermediation that takes place in an environment where prudential regulatory standards and supervisory oversight are either not applied or are applied to a materially lesser or different degree than is the case for regular banks engaged in similar activities" (FSB, 2011). This regulatory approach fully recognizes the complexity of the credit intermediation chain, as well as the fact that banks themselves may be an integral component in the shadow system. For that reason, the FSB approach also emphasizes examining the connections between bank and non-bank activities. At the same time, and in the interest of effective monitoring and regulation, while the FSB approach "casts a wide net"—incorporating potentially any entity, market, or activity at work along the credit intermediation chain—it also called for a narrower focus, calling attention on activities involving four key risk factors: maturity transformation, liquidity transformation, imperfect credit risk transfer, and leverage.

An alternative definition of shadow credit intermediation is outlined by Pozsar et al. (2010). This definition is focused on the nature of financial intermediary liabilities. In particular, liabilities that are explicitly guaranteed by the official sector are not part of shadow credit intermediation, as they benefit from the strongest form of official sector support.[1] Second, if an uninsured liability is consolidated onto the balance sheet of an institution with access to the lender of last resort, that uninsured liability is not part of shadow credit intermediation.[2] The focus on accounting consolidation as part of the definition is important, as liabilities not consolidated are presumed to be structured to avoid regulatory taxes that would apply if showing directly on the intermediary's balance sheet. Uninsured liabilities are part of the shadow banking system since they do not benefit from access to official sector liquidity, thus making them vulnerable to concerns about credit as well as runs by investors.

While these two definitions appear quite different, they are in fact complementary. Each is focused on activities that evade regulatory taxes. The FSB approach focuses on intermediation activities outside of banks, while Pozsar et al. (2010) focuses on the funding of credit without official sector credit and liquidity support.

How large is the shadow banking system? And how do we measure it? The FSB, as part of its mandate to investigate shadow banking and propose enhanced monitoring and regulation, has been conducting yearly global data mappings of the shadow banking system, in order to conduct surveillance of potential emergence of new shadow banking risks. The mapping exercise is difficult for a number of reasons. First, by its own nature, data on entities and activities that may be in the shadow of the regulator may just be missing. Second, and this is perhaps less obvious, cross-country aggregations are rendered arduous by the simple reason that the definition of certain entities or activities may have very different legal and/or regulatory meaning within each local confine.

Despite these difficulties, the FSB has conducted annual monitoring exercises since 2011. In the 2012 exercise it presented data coverage for 25 countries plus the Eurozone as a whole. In aggregate, coverage represented 90% of global financial system assets. According to the FSB exercise, the global shadow banking system, defined in the data as the aggregate total assets of "Other Financial Intermediaries," grew exponentially in the years prior to the crisis, rising from $26 trillion in 2002 to $62 trillion in 2007. The system shrunk during the crisis,

---

[1] This class of liabilities includes insured deposits and guaranteed amounts of insurance contracts, mortgage-backed securities issued by Ginnie Mae which, as well as coin and currency in circulation. This definition clearly excludes liabilities that benefit from implicit official sector support, such as the liabilities of the government-sponsored enterprises or Federal Home Loan banks. It also excludes liabilities that do not benefit from explicit or implicit support, such as corporate bonds or private-sector bond insurance.

[2] This class of liabilities includes uninsured deposits and trading liabilities of depository institutions. While these activities are associated with fragility, they are subject to capital and liquidity regulation, and the holders of those liabilities benefit from the institution's access to contingent official liquidity, reducing the scope for runs. This second standard clearly excludes securitization or asset management activities sponsored by institutions with access to the lender of last resort, which is not consolidated onto their balance sheet. It also excludes liabilities issued by non-bank finance companies, which do not benefit from access to the lender of last resort.

Share of assets of non-bank financial intermediaries
20 jurisdictions and euro area   Exhibit 2-4

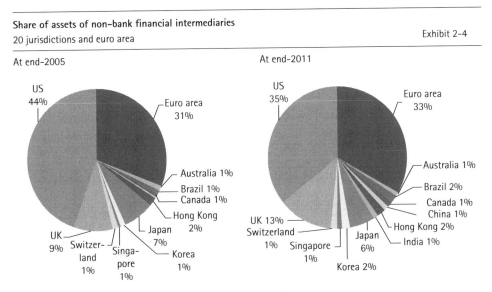

FIGURE 16.1 Share of assets of non-bank financial intermediaries.

but it is reported at $67 trillion in 2011. Moreover, the data indicates that the shadow bank-
ing system represents about 25% of total financial intermediation, down from its peak at
27% in 2007. Across countries, the largest share is for the US, with assets of $23 trillion in
2011, followed by the Eurozone ($22 trillion) and the UK ($9 trillion). Interestingly, the US
share declined from 44% in 2005 to 35% in 2011, while the Eurozone and the UK exhibited
an equivalent increase in their share (Figure 16.1). The global mapping also indicates significant heterogeneity across countries in terms of growth of non-bank financial intermediaries
(FIs) across countries, and also in terms of specific type of subsectors within the population of non-bank FIs. As shown in Figure 16.2, the largest growth rates have been observed
among certain emerging market economies. China is one such example, with substantial
growth in money market mutual funds and finance companies. This is a clear indication
that shadow banking is global and that its growth is associated with both overall economic
growth (a natural response to the growing need for intermediated funds) but also that it may
be fostered by weaker regulatory environments.[3]

16.3 WHY DOES SHADOW BANKING EXIST?

As a whole, the academic literature suggests that shadow credit intermediation is largely
motivated by the confluence of specialization by financial intermediaries, financial innovation in the composition of money supply, and regulatory cost avoidance. We briefly review

---

[3] A different approach is taken by Fiaschi, Kondor, and Marsili (2013), estimating the size of the
shadow banking system using differences in the size of the financial sector and that predicted by a
power law.

Average annual growth of OFI sector pre- and post-crisis

By jurisdiction, in percent   Exhibit 3–3

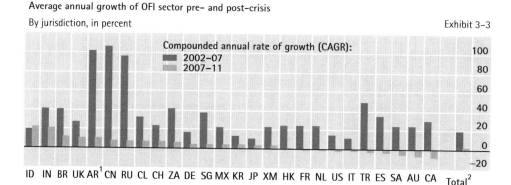

AR = Argentina; AU = Australia; BR = Brazil; CA = Canada; CH = Switzerland; CI = Chile; CN = China; DE = Germany; ES = Spain; FR = France;
HK = Hong Kong; ID = Indonesia; IN = India; IT = Italy; JP = Japan; KR = Korea; MX = Mexico; NL = Netherland; RU = Russia; SA = Saudi Arabia;
SG = Singapore; TR = Turkey; UK = United Kingdom; US = United States; XM = Euro area; ZA = South Africa.

[1] The unusually high growth rate over the period 2002–2007 for Argentina (101% per year) reflects the strong recovery after the very deep financial crisis that affected the Argentine economy in 2001–2002, and is therefore not comparable with other countries. Besides this, the aforementioned variation is affected by the inclusion of intermediaries with incomplete information for the entire reference period. Considering only those intermediaries, among OFIs, with complete information for the entire 2002–2007 period, the average annual change goes down from 101% to 67% [2] 20 jurisdictions plus euro area.

FIGURE 16.2 Average annual growth of OFI sector pre- and post-crisis.

each of these explanations here, but refer to Adrian and Ashcraft (2012a, 2012b) for an extended discussion.

16.3.1 Specialization

Through the shadow intermediation process, the shadow banking system transforms risky, long-term loans (subprime mortgages, for example) into seemingly credit-risk-free, short-term, money-like instruments. Unlike the traditional banking system, where the entire process takes place within the walls of a single institution, the shadow banking system decomposes the credit intermediation into a chain of wholesale-funded, securitization-based lending. Shadow credit intermediation is performed through chains of non-bank financial intermediaries in a multistep process that can be interpreted as a "vertical slicing" of the traditional bank's credit intermediation process into seven steps. Pozsar et al. (2010) explain the seven steps of shadow bank credit intermediation, illustrated in Figure 16.3:

1. Loan origination (auto loans and leases, non-conforming mortgages, etc.) is performed by non-bank finance companies.
2. Loan warehousing is conducted by single—and multi-seller conduits and is funded through asset-backed commercial paper (ABCP).
3. The pooling and structuring of loans into term asset-backed securities (ABSs) is conducted by broker-dealers' ABS syndicate desks.
4. ABS warehousing is facilitated through trading books and is funded through repos, total return swaps, or hybrid and repo conduits.
5. The pooling and structuring of ABS into collateralized debt obligations (CDOs) is also conducted by broker-dealers' ABSs.

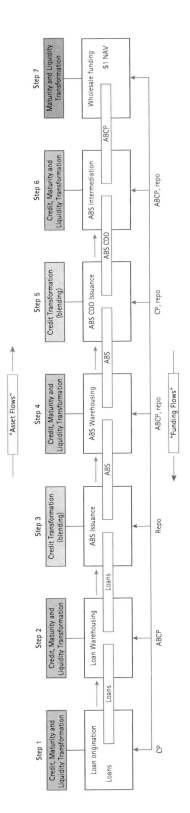

FIGURE 16.3 The credit intermediation chain.

6. ABS intermediation is performed by limited-purpose finance companies (LPFCs), structured investment vehicles (SIVs), securities arbitrage conduits, and credit hedge funds, which are funded in a variety of ways including, for example, repo, ABCP, medium term notes (MTNs), bonds, and capital notes.
7. The funding of all the above activities and entities is conducted in wholesale funding markets by funding providers such as regulated and unregulated money market intermediaries (for example, 2(a)-7 money market mutual funds (MMMFs) and enhanced cash funds, respectively) and direct money market investors (such as securities lenders). In addition to these cash investors, which fund shadow banks through short-term repo, commercial paper (CP), and ABCP instruments, fixed-income mutual funds, pension funds, and insurance companies also fund shadow banks by investing in their longer-term MTNs and bonds.

Why does the shadow banking system involve so many more institutions than the traditional banking system?

Part of the answer likely involves economies of scale. When it comes to the structuring and underwriting securities, it seems clear that this could be done at a lower cost by a specialized entity such as a broker-dealer than by a non-bank originator, given the common components to structuring across issues, as well as the need to create relationships with investors to distribute, as well as a cheap funding source through tri-party repo to support market making. When it comes to warehouse funding, Kashyap, Rajan, and Stein (2002) demonstrated that due to the imperfect correlation between deposit withdrawals and the demand for credit, banks have a cost advantage over non-banks in the provision of contingent liquidity necessary to make lines of credit work effectively.

Another part of the answer must be that transformation of risky loans on the balance sheet of a non-bank finance company with an investment grade bond rating into securities with AAA credit ratings requires bankruptcy remoteness. While the non-bank lender could issue commercial paper directly to fund loans on its balance sheet, there will be a significant cost advantage to selling loans to a special purpose vehicle that is independent of the credit risk profile of the sponsor through securitization. As bankruptcy remoteness is an essential component of securitization, shadow credit intermediation naturally involves a larger number of entities than traditional credit intermediation through depository institutions.

A final part of the answer is likely related to the unique opaqueness of traditional credit intermediaries, which combine lots of different types of financial activities into a single financial intermediary. The relative opaqueness of banks to other types of firms has been well-documented in the academic literature. See Flannery, Kwan, and Nimalendran (2004) for analysis and literature review. It seems reasonable to suspect that the relative opaqueness of banks is facilitated in part through explicit and implicit support of bank liabilities by the official sector, permitting banks to engage in a wider range of activities that would not be possible if funded entirely by the market without such support. As an example, money market mutual funds, which also offer demandable debt, typically have a significantly smaller range and higher quality assets than the typical commercial bank. Along this line of thinking, the specialization that exists outside of the traditional banking system might be a more natural order.

16.3.2 Innovation in Composition of Money

Gorton and Metrick (2010) portray shadow credit intermediation as financial innovation in the composition of aggregate money supply. Money plays a crucial role in the economy, acting not only as a store of value, but also as a unit of account and means of exchange. The rapid loss of confidence in the value of money has been a root cause of financial panics across countries and over time. See Reinhart and Rogoff (2009, 2011) for a review of financial panics across the globe over eight centuries. In particular, the shift from commodity money to fiat money was an important innovation, but for decades it was associated with panics driven by speculation over its convertibility into commodities, which only ended in the US with the full backing of the taxpayer through the National Banking Acts in 1863 and 1864. As continued innovation prompted the replacement of fiat money by deposits, the threat of large-scale banking panics returned, and was only mitigated through the backing of deposits through federal deposit insurance through the Federal Deposit Insurance Corporation (FDIC) and the Federal Reserve as lender of last resort.

Despite the effectiveness of these policy interventions in creating financial stability for decades following the Great Depression, significant innovations in the composition of the aggregate money supply have made the financial system more vulnerable to a loss of confidence by the holders of money. This is illustrated in Figure 16.4, which illustrates the composition of liabilities of financial business from the flow of funds into four major categories: (1) traditional maturity transformation, including bank deposits and interbank liabilities; (2) traditional credit transformation, including term debt issued by banks and bank holding companies as well as reserves of pensions and life insurance companies, in addition to depository loans not elsewhere classified; (3) shadow maturity transformation, including MMMFs, repo, open market paper, and security broker-dealer credit and payables; and (4) shadow credit transformation, including government-sponsored entities (GSEs), term debt issued by non-banks, mutual fund shares, REIT mortgage debt, and loans categorized as "other."

Figure 16.4 suggests several striking patterns. First, the amount of maturity transformation in the financial system has been declining significantly since backing by the official sector. While almost 75% of intermediated credit was funded by short-term bank liabilities in the mid-1940s, including both banks and non-banks, that number has fallen as low as 15% in recent years before rebounding to 21% in 2011. The decline in maturity transformation, which largely occurred in banks, is offset by the increased role of term debt markets in funding credit. In particular, the amount of shadow credit transformation increased from zero in 1945 to as much as 36% of total financial sector liabilities in 2007 before declining to 31% in 2011. The increase in market funding for credit is driven not only by the GSEs and securitization, but also by the increased importance of mutual funds and REITs. Shadow credit transformation increased from only 5% of total credit transformation in 1945 to a peak amount of 60% in 2008 before declining to 55% in 2011.

Second, while maturity transformation by banks has declined significantly in line with the overall financial sector, maturity transformation by non-banks has increased significantly. The consequence is that the fraction of the aggregate money supply issued by shadow intermediaries has increased significantly, peaking at 45% in the early 2000s before declining sharply to 28% in 2011, a level not seen since 1993. The increased amount of maturity transformation is explained in part by the development of money market mutual funds in the 1970s in response to limits on the ability of depository institutions to pay interest on

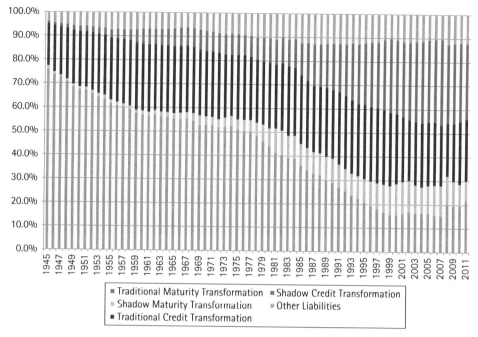

FIGURE 16.4 Composition of liabilities of financial business.

Source: Federal Reserve Flow of Funds, Tables L107 and L212. Traditional maturity transformation includes net interbank liabilities (line 28) plus checkable (line 29) and savings (line 30) deposits of depository institutions. Traditional credit transformation includes reserves of life insurance companies (line 43) and pensions (line 44) plus corporate debt issued by banks and holding companies plus loans from depository institutions NEC (line 37). The latter is calculated by subtracting from total corporate debt (line 36) the amount issued by holding companies (line 10) and banks (line 5) from L212. Shadow maturity transformation includes from L107 MMMFs (line 31), repo (line 32), commercial paper (line 34), and security broker-dealer credit (line 41) and payables (line 42). Shadow credit transformation includes GSEs (line 35), REITs (line 39), mutual fund shares (line 40), and other loans (line 38).

checking accounts, as well as in response to a need for limits on deposit insurance, which left large depositors exposed to bank risk. While Figure 16.4 illustrates that the amount of credit funded through shadow intermediation even at the peak was never larger than 10%, the growing importance of shadow money in the aggregate supply of money was an important factor in amplifying the shocks to the financial system more broadly.

The role of shadow liabilities in the overall money supply is beginning to be explored in the academic literature. Sunderam (2012) analyses the extent to which shadow banking liabilities constitute substitutes for high-powered money. He shows in a simple model that shadow banking liabilities should constitute substitutes for money in the private sector's asset allocation. Empirically, Sunderam shows that shadow banking liabilities respond to money demand, extrapolating that heightened money demand can explain about half of the growth of ABCP in the mid-2000s. He also confirms that regulatory changes to ABCP played a significant role in the growth of the shadow banking system.

Moreira and Savov (2013) study the impact of shadow money creation on macroeconomic fluctuations. Intermediaries create liquidity in the shadow banking system by levering up the collateral value of their assets. However, the liquidity creation comes at the cost of financial fragility as fluctuations in uncertainty cause a flight to quality from shadow liabilities to safe assets. The collapse of shadow banking liquidity has real effects via the pricing of credit and generates prolonged slumps after adverse shocks.

16.3.3 Regulatory Arbitrage

One clear motivation for intermediation outside of the traditional banking system is for private actors to evade regulation and taxes. The academic literature documents that motivation explains part of the growth and collapse of shadow banking over the past decade. In particular, Acharya, Schnabl, and Suarez (2010) document that the rapid expansion of ABCP since 2004 resulted in part from changes in regulatory capital rules. In particular, Financial Accounting Standards Board (FASB) issued a directive in January 2003 (FIN 46) and updated the directive in December 2003 (FIN 46A) suggesting that sponsoring banks should consolidate assets in ABCP conduits onto their balanced sheets. However, US banking regulators clarified that assets consolidated onto balance sheets from conduits would not need to be included in the measurement of risk-based capital and instead used a 10% credit conversion factor for the amount covered by a liquidity guarantee. The authors documented that the majority of guarantees were structured as liquidity-enhancing guarantees aimed at minimizing regulatory capital, instead of credit guarantees, and that the majority of conduits were supported by commercial banks subject to the most stringent capital requirements. Moreover, the authors documented that conduits were sponsored by banks with low economic capital as measured by the ratio of the book value of equity to assets. Finally, the authors find that investors in conduits with liquidity guarantees were repaid in full, while investors in conduits with weaker guarantees suffered small losses, suggesting there the absence of risk transfer despite the capital relief.

The motivation for capital arbitrage is consistent with the mispricing of explicit credit and liquidity put options associated with deposit insurance and access to official liquidity, as well as the presence of a perception that large banks are "too-big-to-fail," which permits them to engage in excessive leverage maturity transformation. As discussed by Adrian and Ashcraft (2012a), the presence of minimum capital and liquidity standards mitigates these incentives, and the ability of banks to evade binding standards permits them to maximize the value of these put options.

16.4 What is the Role of Banks in Shadow Banking?

The standard narrative of shadow banking is that traditional banks lose their centrality in the process of intermediation, and they get replaced by specialized providers of intermediation services along the chain. It seems possible that incumbent intermediaries (the banks) could in fact adapt to the changing "technology" of intermediation. As described earlier, asset securitization allows the development of new markets and activities, a longer intermediation chain and the emergence of—or strengthened role of already existing—specialized intermediaries. In light of this evolution, we should at least allow for the possibility that banks adapt to the change to maintain a central role in the intermediation system. A way to do that is by engaging in a process of organizational restructuring: if modern intermediation requires an enhanced role for, say, specialty lenders, underwriters, asset managers, money market funds, insurance companies, etc., then an existing banking organization may adapt by incorporating such entity types under common ownership and control. This conjecture thus suggests that as the concept of intermediation is redefined, banks adapt by expanding the traditional boundaries of the intermediation firm. Consequently, the locus of intermediation activity is not confined within the balance sheet of a commercial bank, but it is to be found within the broader footprint of more complex bank holding company organizations.

Understanding the extent to which banks adapt to the changing environment is crucial as it allows a better understanding of the actual transformations that have occurred in the industry. Moreover, it highlights from a different perspective the connections between the regulated world and what developed in the shadow. Finally, it really informs the debate on the concept of what really should be defined as shadow banking.

Defining shadow banking from an organizational perspective requires drawing an alternative map of the credit intermediation chain. Instead of describing the steps of the intermediation chain as in Figure 16.3 above, it highlights the roles that are needed along the intermediation chain to allow the match between supply and demand. The map is shown in Figure 16.5 and illustrates that there is a loan originator at the beginning of the chain. However, also needed is an issuer of securities, an underwriter that is in charge of the placement of the securities, a servicer that takes care of the revenue stream associated with the securities, a trustee, which is essentially a delegated monitor for the ultimate investors of the securities, and an entity providing the role of enhancer, providing liquidity and/or credit guarantees to boost the quality of these issuances.

This alternative mapping is complementary to that focused on the steps of the chain, but it allows a quantification of what—from an organizational perspective—lies in the shadow. In the US the Federal Reserve Bank is the regulator of bank holding companies, implying that the extent to which one can actually assess the role of bank holding companies in modern financial intermediation allows potentially important quantifications about the degree of shadiness of shadow banking. Cetorelli and Peristiani (2012) provided for the first time such quantification. Using data from the universe of non-agency asset-backed securitization

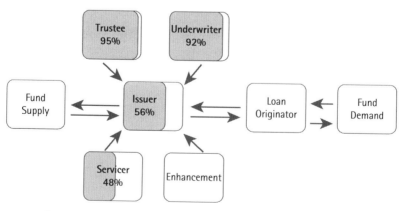

FIGURE 16.5 Alternative map of the credit intermediation chain.

activity from 1978 to 2008, the authors were able to identify for each tranche in each secu-rity the role of issuer, underwriter, servicer, and trustee. Subsequently, they matched the identity of the entities providing these services to bank holding company identifiers. Still, as Figure 16.5 illustrates, in percentage of dollar amount securitized, the extent to which bank holding companies played one or multiple roles with their subsidiaries along the credit intermediation chain. The main result is that there was very little securitization activity that was done without some roles played by regulated bank entities.[4]

Regulated bank entities also maintained an important role in "feeding" the shadow bank-ing systems, in their role at loan origination. Bord and Santos (2012) show this in their study of the role of banks in the originate-to-distribute model of credit intermediation. The authors document that more than 75% of syndicated credit lines are bought by syndicate participant banks and that they stay with those banks after three years. The share of term loans owned by syndicate banks has fallen from around 75% in the mid-1990s to around 30% in the mid-2010s. For term loans, shadow banking organizations have thus emerged as more and more important investors over the past 20 years. Buyers of term loans that are particularly important are investment managers and collateralized loan obligations (CLOs). Bord and Santos conclude that the share of term loans sold to the shadow banking system amounted to less than 10% in 1993 and rose to over 30% by 2007. While loan originations were conducted almost exclusively by commercial banks, the ultimate owners of term loans were thus split among banks and shadow banks.

Avraham, Selvaggi, and Vickery (2012) provide evidence that bank holding companies are transforming with the advent of shadow credit intermediation. Figure 16.6 compares the organizational structure, by simple count of subsidiaries, of the top US bank holding companies (BHCs) in 1990, arguably a time when the traditional model of intermediation was the most relevant, to that in 2012. BHCs, at least the largest, are shown to have increased many times over the number of entities for which they retain control. For example, each of the five largest BHCs in the US had over 1,500 subsidiaries in 2012, with the largest one

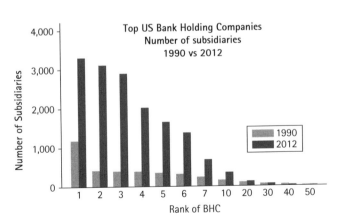

FIGURE 16.6 Top US bank holding companies number of subsidiaries 1990 vs. 2012.

[4] This view is reinforced through work by Mandel, Morgan, and Wei (2012), suggesting that traditional banks were also intimately involved in shadow credit intermediation activity through the provision of credit enhancements to securitization trusts.

Table 16.1 Consolidation dynamics in the US financial industry, 1983–2012

Target Buyer	Asset Manager	Bank	Broker-Dealer	Finance Tech	Insure Broker	Insure Uwriter	Invest Co	Real Estate	Savings/ Thrift	Special Lender	Total	On Diagonal	Off Diagonal
Asset Manager	459	2	38	110	27	24	6	17	1	51	735	459	276
Bank	518	6067	291	164	759	38	3	1	1304	664	9809	6067	3742
Broker-Dealer	127	6	613	78	59	9	4	9	6	42	953	613	340
Finance Tech	13	2	23	1123	60	8	0	0	0	13	1242	1123	119
Insure Broker	31	4	12	35	1760	20	0	0	1	6	1869	1760	109
Insure Uwriter	138	14	55	126	533	1451	0	4	18	54	2393	1451	942
Invest Co	19	2	4	4	4	2	11	4	1	42	93	11	82
Real Estate	3	1	3	0	0	1	0	111	1	12	132	111	21
Savings/Thrift	45	359	28	8	114	21	0	2	704	140	1421	704	717
Special Lender	10	19	26	20	11	5	3	2	21	771	888	771	117
Total	1363	6476	1093	1668	3327	1579	27	150	2057	1795	19535	19535	19535
On Diagonal	459	6067	613	1123	1760	1451	11	111	704	771	13070		
Off Diagonal	904	409	480	545	1567	128	16	39	1353	1024	6465		

owning more than 3,000. The majority of these subsidiaries are funds, trusts, and financial vehicles that are typically engaging in shadow banking activities.[5]

A more in-depth study of organizational adaptation by BHCs, by Cetorelli, McAndrews, and Traina (2014), focuses on the full dynamics of mergers and acquisitions observed in the entire US financial industry from the early 1990s. Table 16.1, reproduced from their research, summarizes such dynamics, capturing by year the extent of cross-type consolidation initiated by financial firms over time, that is the extent to which, say, banks have been buying non-bank targets such as asset managers, insurance underwriters, insurance brokers, etc., and the extent to which these other entity types have engaged in similar organizational changes. As Table 16.1 indicates, banks represented the bulk of such expansion.

Besides the subsidiaries associated with BHC involvement in securitization activities, the largest non-bank BHC subsidiaries consist of finance companies, broker-dealers, and wealth management units including mutual, hedge, and money market mutual funds. While the two decades in the run-up to the financial crisis saw the emergence of a shadow banking system that was partially independent from BHCs, the financial crisis led, perhaps paradoxically, to a migration of independent shadow banking activity into BHCs. Cetorelli (2012) mentions that, as of 2011, BHCs controlled about 38% of the assets of the largest insurance companies, 41% of total money market mutual fund assets, and 93% of the assets of the largest brokers and dealers. Moreover, very little securities lending and related cash collateral reinvestments take place without the services provided by the main custodian banks.

The takeaway from these contributions is that at closer inspection, regulated bank entities have kept a considerable footprint in modern financial intermediation. This is not to say that the risks associated with intermediation activities have not migrated in the shadow. Taking an organizational perspective, however, does underscore the necessity to give weight to forms of adaptation of regulated intermediaries and it does suggest a key to complement a forward-looking oversight approach (Cetorelli, 2012): regulated bank entities have proven to be resilient and adaptable in the face of innovation. Following their evolution may offer insights on the ways intermediation activities, and the related risks, evolve as well. The trend toward consolidation of shadow banking in BHCs since the crisis is, however, counteracted by a powerful force: the enhanced prudential standards of BHCs. Tighter capital and liquidity requirements will arguably lead to an increased incentive for some forms of credit intermediation to migrate out of BHCs and into the shadow banking system.

16.5 WHY SHOULD WE CARE ABOUT SHADOW BANKING?

While intermediation of credit in the shadows is different than intermediation through traditional banks, it is worth highlighting how shadow credit intermediation can lead to inefficient outcomes.

[5] Copeland (2012) shows that these shadow banking activities of bank holding companies have been increasing over time and represent a quantitatively important share of the holding companies' total earnings.

16.5.1 Regulatory Arbitrage

Regulation typically forces private actors to do something that they would otherwise not do: pay taxes to the official sector, disclose additional information to investors, or hold more capital against financial exposures. Financial activity that has been restructured to avoid taxes, disclosure, and/or capital requirements, is referred to as arbitrage activity. While arbitrage generally refers to the simultaneous buying and selling of instruments for a riskless profit, regulatory arbitrage is generally a change in structure of activity that does not change the risk profile of that activity, but increases the net cash flows to the sponsor by reducing the costs of regulation.

There is a small literature investigating the impact of taxes and tax avoidance activity on the recent financial boom and bust. Alworth and Arachi (2012) provide a broad discussion of the role of the tax advantages of homeownership, the use of debt in mergers and acquisitions by private equity, the use of hybrid debt instruments as capital by financial institutions, and the use of tax havens to structure securitization vehicles. Mooij, Keen, and Orihara (2013) document an empirical link between corporate tax rates and the probability of crises. Finally, Davis and Stone (2004) document that the severity of crises is larger when pre-crisis leverage is higher, suggesting that tax policy could have effects both on incidence and severity of financial stress.

While high corporate taxes can have adverse effects on financial stability, it appears that low corporate taxes can also have adverse effects. In an attempt to attract foreign capital and create jobs, several jurisdictions have enacted relatively low corporate income tax rates. Corporations in high tax countries have worked to restructure their activity in order to take advantage of these low tax rates, to the frustration of the official sector in those regimes. Beyond shifting the burden of taxes, it is likely that differences in corporate tax rates can lead to global financial instability related to rapid and short-term capital flows to those countries. For example, many of the developed countries with the lowest tax rates, including Ireland, Iceland, and Cyprus, have recently experienced significant boom and bust cycles related to inflows of hot money. The relationship between capital mobility and banking crises is not a new phenomenon, and has been discussed extensively by Reinhart and Rogoff (2009, 2011).

16.5.2 Neglected Risks

Because shadow banking institutions are tailored to take advantage of mispriced tail risk, they accumulate assets that are particularly sensitive to tail events. At a deep level, the question becomes: how can the mispricing of tail risk exist in a world with fully rational actors? Shouldn't financial market participants be able to calculate tail risk probabilities, implicit guarantees, and various tail risk enhancements? And shouldn't these calculations lead to the proper assessment of tail risk? The literature has provided two distinct, complementary answers. The first relies on the behavioral explanation of "neglected risk." The second relies on information opacity in a rational world. We will discuss each of these explanations in turn.

Evidence from psychology and behavioral finance argues that market participants are fundamentally biased against the rational assessment of tail risk. Gennaioli, Shleifer, and Vishny (2012a) develop a theory of individual decision making based on the behavioral evidence, positing that actors neglect risk. In a later paper, Gennaioli, Shleifer, and Vishny (2013) apply this theory to the economics of the shadow banking system. They model a world where investors systematically ignore the worst state of the world, generating over-investment and overpricing during the boom and excessive collapse of real activity and the financial sector during the bust.

Their theory is possibly the most parsimonious narrative of the boom and bust of the shadow banking system. In fact, much empirical evidence is consistent with such a theory. Credit rating agencies modeled only small or no declines in aggregate housing prices, and investors in securitized products often did not understand the amount of risk exposure that was embedded in the products. Meanwhile, the prices of tail risk far into the future, far out of the money options relating to mortgage credit, were surprisingly cheap. An early paper warning of the financial system's exposure to such tail risk was presented by Rajan (2005), who pointed to precisely this phenomenon by asking whether financial innovation had made the world riskier.

Neglected risks are one way to interpret the widely perceived risk-free nature of highly rated structured credit products, such as the AAA tranches of ABS. Coval, Jurek, and Stafford (2009) point out that these AAA tranches behave like catastrophe bonds that load on a systemic risk state. In such a systemic risk state, assets become much more correlated than in normal times. The underestimation of correlation enabled financial institutions to hold insufficient amounts of liquidity and capital against the puts that underpinned the stability of the shadow banking system, which made these puts unduly cheap to sell. As investors tend to overestimate the value of private credit and liquidity enhancement purchased through these puts, the result is an excess supply of cheap credit. Neglected risk can manifest itself through overreliance on credit ratings by investors. For example, Ashcraft et al. (2011) document that subprime MBS prices are more sensitive to ratings than ex post performance, suggesting that funding is excessively sensitive to credit ratings relative to informational content.

Dang, Gorton, and Holmström (2009) present an alternative theory where, in a world with fully rational market participants, assets are highly exposed to tail risk. Theirs is a theory of information opacity that can serve as a rationalization of credit problems for the shadow banking system. According to this theory, debt contracts are optimal because they generate opacity. Opacity, in turn, minimizes adverse selection and provides the least possible incentives to collect information. This insight justifies the growth of relatively opaque securitized products in the run-up to the 2007–08 crisis. Mortgages and loans were packaged into MBS and ABS and funded by CDOs, SIVs, and MMMFs that had relatively little information about the underlying credit quality. However, Dang, Gorton, and Holmström show that systemic risk is exacerbated once a bad shock hits informationally opaque, debt-funded economies. The intuition is that a bad shock leads to an increase in private information collection, which exacerbates the incorporation of adverse information in market prices. As a result, adverse selection starts to accumulate as systemic crises deepen.

The above theory complements the explanation by Gennaioli, Shleifer, and Vishny (GSV) discussed earlier. While Dang, Gorton, and Holmström (DGH) (2009) emphasize adverse selection as an amplification mechanism, GSV emphasize awareness of risk. In GSV, the riskiness of the worst state of the world is simply neglected, and this neglect is based on behavioral arguments. In contrast, on DGH's model, the opacity of financial contracts in good times is an equilibrium outcome that maximizes the liquidity of financial contracts. The commonality between the two theories is that the severity of financial crisis is neglected, either rationally or behaviorally. As a result, the tail risk embedded in debt securities is underpriced from an ex post point of view. In both DGH and GSV, the assets that are accumulated during the boom experience large asset price declines during times of crisis. Such theories of neglected risk thus provide a rationalization for the accumulation of risk exposure to the housing market that was the major aggregate risk of the shadow banking system. In the theories of DGH and GSV, securities such as ABS and CDOs that obscure the underlying credit risks arise naturally. Such securities, in turn, generate large losses in times of crisis.

16.5.3 Funding Fragilities

The financial frictions that lead to excessive risk-taking and exacerbated credit losses during downturns also interact with the fragility of funding. Per definition, funding sources for shadow banking activities are uninsured and thus runnable. In many ways, the fragility of shadow banks due to the runability of liabilities resembles the banking system of the nineteenth century, prior to the creation of the Federal Reserve and the FDIC. During that time, bank runs were common, and they often had severe consequences for the real economy.

The shadow banking system's vulnerability to runs bears resemblance to bank runs as modeled by Diamond and Dybvig (1983). Shadow banks are subject to runs because assets have longer maturities than liabilities and tend to be less liquid as well. While the fundamental reason for commercial bank runs is the sequential servicing constraint, for shadow banks the effective constraint is the presence of fire sale externalities. In a run, shadow banking entities have to sell assets at a discount, which depresses market pricing. This provides incentives to withdraw funding—before other shadow banking depositors arrive.

However, the analogy between bank runs and shadow bank runs goes only so far. The reason is that shadow banking entities do not offer demand deposits, but instead obtain funding in wholesale money markets such as commercial paper or repo. Martin, Skeie, and von Thadden (2012) provide a model for a run in repo markets that takes the empirical facts of the Bear Stearns and Lehman crises as a starting point. On their model, repo borrowers face constraints due to the scarcity of collateral and the liquidity of collateral. Under sufficiently adverse conditions, self-fulfilling runs can occur. The model focuses in particular on the differences between the tri-party repo market and the bilateral repo market (see Adrian et al. (2013) for an overview of both markets). Arguably, runs occurred in both markets, but they were of very different natures. While the run in the bilateral market was characterized by a sharp increase in haircuts (as documented by Gorton and Metrick, 2012), the run in the tri-party repo market materialized as a simple withdrawal of funding with a rather limited impact on the level of haircuts (see Copeland, Martin, and Walker, 2011). Runs in the ABCP market were equally characterized by a withdrawal of funding (see Covitz, Liang, and Suarez, 2012).

Gallin (2013) provides a comprehensive map of the amount of short-term funding from the shadow banking system to the real economy, based on the flow of funds statistics. Gallin's framework shows that much of the decline in credit supply in the crisis was due to the decline of short-term shadow bank funding. Gallin's work can be used to quantify the amount of fragility in shadow bank funding over time.

16.5.4 Leverage Cycles

The fragility of shadow banking institutions can also be interpreted as the result of the leverage cycles of market-based financial institutions. Such leverage cycles refer to equilibrium outcomes, where asset values and balance sheet capacity of intermediaries are determined endogenously. The friction in models of leverage cycles is due to the funding constraints of intermediaries, which reflect the incentive problems discussed earlier. Theories of intermediary leverage cycles have been proposed by Fostel and Geanakoplos (2008), Brunnermeier and Pedersen (2009), Brunnermeier and Sannikov (2012), Garleanu and Pedersen (2011), and Adrian and Boyarchenko (2012). Such theories of leverage cycles have the commonality that intermediaries are subject to collateral constraints, as is the case for repo and ABCP funding. The tightness of the collateral constraints depends on the underlying risk of assets, the liquidity of assets, and the collateral values. As economic conditions deteriorate, the leverage cycle acts as an amplification mechanism to underlying shocks.

Adrian and Boyarchenko (2012) show that their theory of intermediary leverage cycles has strong empirical support. Intermediary balance sheets exhibit strongly procyclical leverage, meaning that leverage expands in booms. This procyclical behavior of leverage is a hallmark of shadow banking, as documented by Adrian and Shin (2009). Shadow bank leverage tends to be high when balance sheets are large and credit intermediation is expanding. Furthermore, equity is countercyclical, both in the theory and in the data, as intermediaries tend to hold as little equity as possible during booms, but are forced to raise equity during downturns when the market risk increases. Adrian and Boyarchenko (2012) also document the close link between intermediary balance sheets and asset prices. Over time, expanding leverage tends to coincide with compressed risk premia and inflated asset prices. In busts, risk premia widen, generating asset price busts. In addition, market volatility is countercyclical. As a result, the funding of intermediaries tends to collapse during times of crisis. Similarly, Meeks, Nelson, and Alessandri (2012) show that a macroeconomic model with shadow credit intermediation via asset-backed securities exacerbates fluctuations due to the increased amplitude in the leverage cycle of the shadow banking entities.

16.5.5 Agency Problems

The splitting up of intermediation activity across multiple institutions, as is done in the shadow banking system, has the potential to aggravate underlying agency problems. In particular, it is typically costly to convey between financial institutions the complete and accurate private information about the credit quality of a borrower, and the transfer of credit risk without a complete transfer of this information creates agency problems leading to inefficient outcomes. Ashcraft and Schuermann (2008) describe seven important informational frictions that existed in the securitization of subprime mortgage credit prior to the financial crisis, although these frictions can be generalized to all securitization transactions. They include asymmetric information problems between the lender and originator (predatory lending and borrowing), between the lender and investors, between the servicer and investors, between the servicer and borrower, between the beneficiary of invested funds and asset managers, and between the beneficiary of invested funds and credit rating agencies. In addition, asymmetric information between investors and issuers results in risk-insensitive cost of funding. For example, Keys et al. (2010) document that mortgage borrowers with FICO scores just above a threshold of 620 perform significantly worse than borrowers with FICO scores just below 620. As it is more difficult to securitize loans below that threshold, the authors argue that this result is consistent with issuers exploiting asymmetric information, disrupting the otherwise monotone relationship between borrower credit scores and performance.

Although securitization has a relatively short history, it is a troubled one. The first known securitization transactions in the United States occurred in the 1920s, when commercial real estate (CRE) bond houses sold loans to finance CRE to retail investors through a vehicle known as CRE bonds. Wiggers and Ashcraft (2012) document the performance of these bonds, which defaulted in large numbers following the onset of the Great Depression. Although the sharp deterioration in economic conditions played an important part in explaining their poor performance, so did aggressive underwriting and sales of the bonds in small denominations to unsophisticated retail investors.

Overreliance on credit ratings can create problems when the rating agencies face their own agency problems. For example, Mathis, McAndrews, and Rochet (2009) analyze a dynamic model of ratings where reputation is endogenous and the market environment may vary over time. The authors' model predicts that a rating agency is likely to issue less accurate ratings in boom times than it would during recessionary periods. Moreover, the authors demonstrate that competition among rating agencies yields similar qualitative results. Xia and Strobl (2012) document that the conflict of interest caused by the issuer-pays rating model leads to inflated corporate credit ratings. Finally, Cohen (2011) documents significant relationships between variables that should not affect a credit rating agency's (CRA) view of the credit risk of conduit/fusion commercial mortgage-backed security (CMBS) transactions issued during 2001–2007, but that would affect issuers' and CRAs' incentives in an environment where rating shopping was present.

16.6 How Can Risks in the Shadow Banking System be Monitored?

In this section we provide examples of monitoring particular shadow banking activities and entities. These examples are for illustrative purposes. Shadow banking activities are ever evolving, and what appears important at some point might lose importance over time. For example, many of the activities listed in Pozsar et al. (2010) are no longer in existence: ABCP conduits are being unwound due to changes in regulations and accounting standards, structured investment vehicles have disappeared due to changes in capital requirements, and the credit default swap wraps for subprime mortgages that played an important role as tail risk repository are either extinct (in the case of large insurance companies) or have shrunk dramatically (in the case of monoline insurers).

However, many shadow banking activities continue to exist, and new activities have emerged, or have gained in importance. Agency mortgage REITS, leveraged finance intermediation, and captive insurance companies have, arguably, gained in importance since the financial crisis. The repo market and money market mutual funds continue to represent major building blocks of the shadow banking system. Shadow bank intermediation is thus constantly evolving, partly in reaction to regulatory changes.

In order to provide for a more dynamic framework to identify shadow banking, the FSB has formulated a functional approach to shadow bank monitoring, which means that activities—which might be conducted by a variety of different institutions—are being constantly monitored according to their location in the intermediation chain. The functional approach is particularly important as there are significant differences in legal and regulatory frameworks across countries. The FSB (2012) identifies five broad economic functions that are meant to capture the broad spectrum of intermediation activities:

1. management of client cash pools with features that make them susceptible to runs such as credit investment funds, credit mutual funds, and mortgage REITs;
2. loan provisions that depend on short-term funding such as finance companies;
3. intermediation of market activities that depend on short-term funding or on secured funding of client assets;
4. facilitation of credit creation such as insurance guarantors; and
5. securitization-based credit intermediation and funding of financial entities such as securitization vehicles.

In the remainder of this section, we provide examples of particular entities and activities, and outline the way in which they can be monitored for the build-up of risk.

16.6.1 Agency Mortgage REITS

Real estate investment trusts (REITs) are investment vehicles that primarily invest in real estate related assets. Agency mortgage REITs (agency REITs) are specialized REITs that invest in mortgage-backed securities (MBSs) issued by US government-sponsored agencies, particularly the government-sponsored enterprises. While REITs can generally be either public or private, agency REITs are publicly traded. While US REITs are regulated by the Securities Exchange Commission (SEC), agency REITs structure their operations in a way to be excluded from specific regulations in the Investment Company Act. As a result, agency REITs have virtually no prudential regulation, though, as publicly listed entities, they are subject to the SEC's investor protection rules and have to file reports such as 10Qs.

While there are several hundred publicly listed REITs in the US, the agency REIT market consists of only a handful of companies, the majority of which have been created since the financial crisis (though the oldest agency REIT was created in the mid-1980s). The sector holds over $350 billion of agency MBSs, which corresponds roughly to 7% of the total agency MBS market. The size of agency MBS has been growing rapidly in recent years.

The business model of agency REITs relies on liquidity and leverage, but not credit transformation. Mortgage REITs obtain leverage in the bilateral repo market, from the security broker-dealer sector. The repo contracts limit the amount of leverage that REITs can obtain. Since the financial crisis, haircuts for agency MBSs have increased dramatically, so that leverage of the largest mortgage REITs is currently less than 10% according to their 10K filings. The current leverage of agency REITs is in contrast to pre-crisis levels, when lower haircuts allowed for considerably higher leverage, often above 15%.

The rapid growth of agency REITs since the financial crisis can be primarily attributed to the interest rate environment. As expansionary monetary policy has resulted in low yields across the maturity spectrum, levered investments have attracted outsized funds under management. In addition to agency REITs, high-yield mutual funds and exchange traded funds (ETFs) as well as collateralized loan obligations have grown rapidly in size in recent years. The relatively high degree of leverage of agency REITs allows them to generate dividend yields that are among the highest among traded stocks. The largest agency REITs have achieved dividend yields around 20% in recent years, despite longer-term interest rates that are only around 2%. An additional reason for the success of the REIT industry in general is the special tax treatment. Earnings are not taxed at the corporate level, but only when equity holders receive earnings in the form of dividends. In order to maintain REIT status, agency REITs return in excess of 90% of their earnings to equity holders.

Agency REITs are exposed to two main sources of risk: duration risk and liquidity risk. Duration risk arises as their assets are longer term MBSs, while liabilities are repos. Hence when the slope of the yield curve steepens, agency REITs experience mark to market losses on their mortgage holdings, which translates into a falling equity value. Historically, the return on assets of agency REITs correlates tightly with the slope of the yield curve. In addition to slope risk, agency REITs hold convexity risk. Convexity risk arises also in a rising yield environment. As agency mortgage pools consist of mortgages that can be prepaid, rising interest rates makes prepayment less likely, extending the duration of mortgages. The duration extension in a rising yield environment generates "negative convexity," meaning that the price of MBS is more and more sensitive to increasing rates, the higher the rates are. Negative convexity has been linked to past bond market selloffs, particularly in 1994 and 2003.

Liquidity risk arises for agency REITs because their repo funding is short term, typically with either an overnight or a month-long maturity. If money market investors suddenly withdraw funding to dealers, those can no longer pass funding onto agency REITs, exposing the REITs to liquidity risk. In addition, dealers might increase haircuts when liquidity and rate risk of agency MBS is judged higher, exposing REITs to the possibility of forced deleveraging. In fact, during the financial crisis, repo funding of agency MBSs became severely distorted, leading the Federal Reserve to start a special financing program called "Term Securities Lending Facility."

From a systemic point of view, the main concern is that a significantly larger agency REIT sector might contribute to the magnitude of selloffs in a rising rate environment. Rising interest rates might force REITs to fire sale agency MBSs, increasing slope and duration risk. In addition, agency MBS liquidity might become impaired. The adverse rate and liquidity effects might in turn spill over to other institutions, such as MBS mutual funds, money market funds, insurance companies, and pension funds. The evidence from the bond market selloff in the spring of 2013 did not show significant forced deleveraging by agency REITs. However, if the sector grew significantly, endogenous adverse feedback loops in the agency MBS market might be exacerbated by the presence of leveraged investment vehicles that do not have access to lender of last resort facilities.

16.6.2 Reinsurance

Reinsurance is the sale of risk from an insurance company to a reinsurance company. There are several motivations for reinsurance. First, reinsurance helps an insurer avoid concentrations in its own portfolio, permitting it to underwrite larger insurance policies by relaxing regulatory and economic capital constraints. Second, solicitation of third-party evaluation and pricing of risk can supplement the insurer's own evaluation and pricing, reducing uncertainty about the risk. Third, when markets are segmented, the insurer can earn arbitrage profits. Segmentation can be driven by reinsurers who have more expertise or better diversification, permitting them to have better pricing. However, reinsurers can have a cost advantage for other reasons, including lower taxes and/or regulatory costs, as well as a greater risk appetite.[6]

One particular form of reinsurance is captive reinsurance, where an insurance company purchases reinsurance from an affiliate, reducing the cost of regulation of the insurer. In particular, captives are subject to different accounting rules, which facilitate lower reserves; do not face regulatory capital requirements; do not face restrictions on assets that permit greater risk and less liquidity; face weaker transparency requirements, which limit market and regulatory discipline; and unlike insurance companies are able to back reinsurance with low-cost letters of credit or parental guarantees instead of more expensive capital. In a typical captive insurance arrangement, risk is simply transferred from the insurance company to the parent, which reduces the insurance company's regulatory capital requirements. The arrangement permits the consolidated organization to evade binding regulatory capital requirements, and instead face market capital requirements by investors and credit rating agencies on the parent. Note that insurance company regulators do have the authority to reject transactions with a captive, but typically approve as they are focused on regulation of the insurance company, not the broader holding company, and these transactions reduce risk in the regulated entity. Insurance companies argue that captive insurance is used to reduce the cost of excessively conservative regulation, which require them to hold reserves above the actuarial risk of their insurance policies. Moreover, captive reinsurance helps to protect the insurance company from the capital market volatility of variable-rate annuities. As the insurer provides a guaranty on the principal value of these investments, they are required to increase reserves when the market value of those investments declines in value, which reduces earnings and capital of the insurance company. The use of a captive insurance reduces volatility in regulatory capital ratios of the regulated entity.[7]

Life insurers' reinsurance to captives has grown significantly in recent years, from $130 billion in 2006 to an estimated $394 billion in 2012, and this growth is starting to attract attention of regulators. The New York State Department of Financial Services recently issued a report (June 2013) highlighting findings from reinsurance captives.[8] The regulators have referred to the activity as "shadow insurance," noting broader financial stability concerns, and calling for a moratorium on new activity. In the report, the regulators note significant volume of activity, significant reductions in regulatory capital ratios,

---

[6] Wikipedia entry for "Reinsurance."

[7] Julia Gouny and Robert McMenamin: "Life Insurers use Captive Reinsurance for Regulatory Arbitrage," Marketsource, July 3, 2013.

[8] <http://www.dfs.ny.gov/reportpub/shadow_insurance_report_2013.pdf.>.

inconsistent and incomplete disclosure to the market and regulators, and evidence of a regulatory race to the bottom. NYS is working on disclosure requirements for captives of New York-based insurers and their affiliates, is pressing the National Association of Insurance Commissioners to develop enhanced disclosure requirements for all jurisdictions, has called for the Federal Insurance Office to conduct similar investigations in order to help understand the aggregate picture across states, and finally has called for an immediate national moratorium on approvals of shadow insurance transactions until investigations are complete.

16.6.3 Leveraged Finance

Loans to firms with non-investment-grade credit ratings are generally referred to as leveraged lending, and include two broad loan purposes. The first is regular corporate lending, including the funding of capital expenditures and working capital. The second is event-driven financing, for example to fund a leveraged buyout of a publicly traded company by a private equity firm. Leveraged loans are typically structured as five- to seven-year floating-rate balloon loans with limited amortization, which makes their performance highly dependent on refinancing conditions and the state of equity markets. Defaults on leveraged lending are highly sensitive to the macroeconomic conditions, varying at an annual rate from as low as 1% to as high as 12%. However, recoveries on loans, which average 70%, are generally much higher than on bonds, which average 50%, given the seniority and collateral of the lender.

While leveraged lending collapsed in 2008 from a peak of $680 billion in 2007, it has rebounded very quickly, and is now at record levels of volume, projected to be larger than $1 trillion in 2013. However, as at the time of writing (March 2014), the total amount of leveraged loans outstanding has remained flat since 2007, suggesting that the flow is largely related to refinancing of loans, in part due to lower interest rates, but also due to maturities. The level of overall leveraged buyout (LBO) activity in the economy has remained muted, and there has been very little leveraged lending to support new LBOs. Credit metrics of LBOs have not deteriorated, with average debt-to-EBITA (earnings before interest, tax, and amortization expenses) and EBITA-to-debt service within historical norms.

One area of concern, however, is the significant increase in the fraction of covenant lite loans, which have increased dramatically from 0% in 2010 to 60% in 2013. This deterioration in loan underwriting has come hand-in-hand with an increased presence of retail investors in the leveraged loan market, through both CLOs and prime funds, as relatively sophisticated investors, like banks and hedge funds, are exiting the asset class. The funding of long-term opaque and risky loans through mutual funds and exchange-traded funds, which engage in liquidity and maturity transformation, help to define this activity clearly as shadow credit intermediation.

Banking agencies have recently issued new regulatory guidance on leveraged lending through SR 13-03.[9] This provides specific guidance to examiners when criticizing leveraged lending, including standards for underwriting of specific loans, as well as overall risk

---

[9] <http://www.federalreserve.gov/bankinforeg/srletters/sr1303.htm.>.

management. The underwriting guidelines will raise scrutiny in the face of excessive leverage, limited amortization, and overreliance on refinancing. Importantly, these underwriting standards apply both to loans intended for distribution as well as for the bank's own portfolio. Guidance related to risk management requires institutions to have a clearly articulated risk appetite, limits for pipeline and commitments, as well as for the aggregate book and individual borrower concentration. Banks must stress-test both the pipeline and retained portfolio, and hold adequate capital against all positions.

16.6.4 Tri-Party Repo

A repurchase agreement (repo) is the sale of securities together with an agreement that the seller will buy back the securities at a later date. Most repo contracts are short term—between 1 and 90 days—although there are repos with much longer maturities. Repos are over-collateralized, and the difference between the value of the collateral and the sale price is called the repo haircut. In addition, the repurchase price is greater than the sale price, the difference constituting the repo rate, which is, in economic terms, an interest rate on a collateralized loan. In a repo transaction, the party buying the collateral acts as a lender.

The distinguishing feature of a tri-party repo is that a clearing bank acts as an intermediary between the two parties to the repo. The clearing bank is responsible for the administration of the transaction, including collateral allocation, marking to market, and substitution of collateral. The tri-party structure ensures that both the borrower and the lender are protected against the default of the other, as the collateral resides with a third party. The US tri-party repo market represents a major source of funding for security broker-dealers. The market peaked at slightly above $2.8 trillion in 2008 and is currently slightly below $1.7 trillion.

Investors in tri-party repo are primarily money market mutual funds and other cash-rich investors such as corporate treasury functions, while the borrowers are large securities dealers with inventories of securities to finance. Clearing banks unwind these trades each afternoon and return the cash to the investors. But because the dealers retain a portfolio of securities that need financing on a 24-hour basis, they must extend credit to the other dealers against these securities for several hours between that afternoon unwind and the settlement of new repos in the early evening. That way, those dealers can repay their investors and avoid defaulting on the obligations.

Since the enactment of the Bankruptcy Amendments and Federal Judgeship Act of 1984, repos on Treasury, federal agency securities, bank certificates of deposits, and bankers' acceptances have been exempted from the automatic stay in bankruptcy. The bankruptcy exemption ensures the liquidity of the repo market by assuring lenders that they would get speedy access to their collateral in the event of a dealer default. In 2005, the safe harbor provision was expanded to repos written on broader collateral classes, including certain mortgage-backed securities. This broadening of acceptable collateral for the exemption from the automatic stay for repos allowed the repo market to fund credit collateral—and thus directly fund the shadow banking system.

It should be noted that the tri-party repo market is only a subset of other repo and short-term, collateralized borrowing markets. While broker-dealers conduct their funding primarily in the tri-party repo market, their lending occurs mainly in DVP (delivery vs. payment) repo or GCF (general collateral finance) repo. In contrast to a tri-party repo,

DVP repos are bilateral transactions that are not settled on the books of the clearing banks. Instead, settlement typically occurs when the borrower delivers the securities to the lender. Adrian et al. (2013) discuss various forms of repo and securities lending.

Copeland, Martin, and Walker (2011) document the collateral composition in the tri-party market, as well as the repo market conventions, using data from July 2008 to early 2010. They show that, during this period, several hundred billion dollars of collateral in the tri-party repo market consisted of collateral such as equities, private-label ABSs, and corporate credit securities without any eligibility for public sources of liquidity or credit backstops. Krishnamurthy, Nagel, and Orlov (2011) complement this finding by looking directly at the collateral of MMMFs. While they find that the majority of the $3.5 trillion MMMFs' collateral is of high quality, they do document several hundred billion dollars of private-label ABS securities funded by MMMFs. However, the overall amount of private-label ABS funded in the repo market by MMMFs is less than 3% of total outstanding.

16.6.5 Money Market Funds

Money market mutual funds are open-ended mutual funds that invest in short-term securities such as Treasury bills, commercial paper (including ABCP), and repo. MMMFs were first created in 1971 in response to Regulation Q, which restricted the interest that commercial banks can pay on deposits. Since then, money market funds have represented an alternative to bank deposits from investors' point of view, with yields that are typically more attractive than bank deposits. The money market sector peaked at around $3.5 trillion in 2008. MMMFs are regulated by the SEC under the Investment Company Act of 1940.

Money market funds seek a stable net asset value (NAV), which is generally $1.00, meaning that they aim never to lose money. If a fund's NAV drops below $1.00, it is said to "break the buck." In September 2008, the day following the Lehman Brothers bankruptcy, the Reserve Primary Fund broke the buck and triggered a run on MMMFs. Other fund managers reacted by selling assets and investing at only the shortest of maturities or by reallocating to Treasury bills, thereby exacerbating the funding difficulties for other instruments such as commercial paper and repo.

Wermers (2011) investigates in more detail the role of investment flows into and out of money market mutual funds, focusing particularly on the period of the financial crisis. Wermers shows that institutional investors were more likely to run than retail investors, and institutional investors tended to spread such run behavior across various MMMF families. Institutional MMMF investors can thus be viewed as a transmission channel for contagious runs. Kacperczyk and Schnabl (2011) analyze the impact of the organizational structure of MMMFs on their risk-taking behavior. In particular, they ask how the risk-taking differs between stand-alone funds and the funds that are owned by larger holding companies, such as bank holding companies. Kacperczyk and Schnabl find significant differences in the risk-taking of stand-alone MMMFs relative to the funds that have implicit guarantees from financial conglomerates. During the financial crisis of 2008, when systemic risk increased and conglomerates became relatively more exposed to systemic risk, stand-alone mutual funds increased their risk-taking behavior relatively more. Conversely, in the run-up to the crisis, when measured systemic risk was low, MMMFs that were part of conglomerates took on relatively more risk.

16.6.6 Chinese Shadow Banking

While shadow credit intermediation in the United States and Europe has been contracting since the onset of the recent global financial crisis in 2007, one area where shadow banking has been growing significantly is in China. In response to rapid growth in bank credit and concerns about inflation, in 2010 the Chinese government put in place significant restrictions on the traditional banking system through higher interest rates, tougher reserve requirements, and more conservative credit quotas. Combined with reductions on the maximum permitted loan to value (LTV) on second home purchases, the intervention had a significant impact in slowing the growth rate of credit on bank balance sheets. However, it did not take long for the banking system to find ways to continue to originate credit off balance sheet. In particular, while bank credit growth has slowed from a peak of 35% in 2010 to 15% in recent years, the slowdown in total financing, including off-balance-sheet credit, has been less, falling to only 20%.

The difference is largely off-balance-sheet lending by banks, which is broken into three large components. First, there are trust loans. Here, bank loans are sold into trust companies, which in turn sell wealth management products to retail depositors. Banks earn fees on the origination of loans and management of these products, but since they are off balance sheet, they do not have to hold capital against them. While some of these products have principal guaranteed balances, most do not, and instead benefit from perception of implicit support by the banks, and in turn by the official sector. Consequently this activity appears to fall squarely within the definition of shadow banking outlined above. Second, there are undiscounted banker's acceptances. These instruments are obligations of a bank customer to pay a third party on a future date that is guaranteed by the bank, like a post-dated check. The third party can redeem this acceptance with the bank for a discount to its face value, at which point the bank needs to advance funds not yet advanced to it by the original customer, effectively extending credit to that customer. To protect itself from the risk of customer default, the bank requires cash collateral from the customer in the form of deposits. In the end, undiscounted acceptances are contingent liabilities of the bank, while discounted liabilities are extensions of credit. However, only the latter are subject to capital requirements and count toward loan quota, making this activity shadow credit intermediation. Finally, there are entrusted loans. These are loans originated by non-banks, but sold to trust companies, and serviced by banks. Banks that are restricted by loan quotas can also use entrusted loans to continue origination but fund off balance sheet. Consequently, banks have increased their ownership stakes in trust companies to facilitate this distribution channel.

The rise of shadow credit intermediation in China thus seems less the result of financial innovation and more driven by the response of the regulated sector to heightened restrictions to traditional intermediation activity, in an environment no less where official monitoring is still in the early stages of development. Chinese shadow banking also seems to have a more local nature than what was observed in the years prior to the financial crisis. This is not to imply that disruptions to Chinese intermediation infrastructure would not generate global ripple effects, but it does suggest different implications regarding global monitoring and regulation. For instance, containment of potential global propagation of shocks in this instance might be better addressed through enhanced monitoring of activities of the largest Chinese financial intermediaries. This would be achieved by applying the current methodologies for the identification of global, systemically important financial institutions. Such methodologies have been developed for the identification of global systemically important banks (G-SIBs) and for insurance companies (G-SIIs) and it is work in progress at the time of publication of this Handbook for other type of institutions.[10]

16.7 CONCLUSION

In this chapter, we have provided a definition of shadow credit intermediation, and provided an overview of a recent attempt by the FSB to measure it. We have drawn on existing literature to explain motivations for this activity, which include specialization, innovation in the composition of money, and regulatory arbitrage. We review literature on the role of banks in shadow banking, then explore reasons why academics and regulators should care. These include regulatory arbitrage, neglected risks, funding fragilities, leverage cycles, and agency problems. Finally, we provide an overview of recent developments in shadow credit markets: agency mortgage REITS, reinsurance, tri-party repo, money market mutual funds, and shadow banking in China.

REFERENCES

Acharya, V., Schnabl, P., and Suarez, G. (2010). Securitization Without Risk Transfer, NBER Working Paper No. 15730.

Adrian, T. and Ashcraft, A. B. (2012a). Shadow Bank Regulation, *Annual Review of Financial Economics* 4, 99–140.

Adrian, T. and Ashcraft, A. B. (2012b). Shadow Banking: A Review of the Literature, *Palgrave Dictionary of Economics*. Basingstoke: Palgrave Macmillan.

Adrian, T., Begalle, B., Copeland, A., and Martin, A. (2013). Repo and Securities Lending. In: J. G. Haubrich and A. W. Lo (Eds.), *Quantifying Systemic Risk Measurement: NBER Research Conference Report Series*, 1–62. Chicago: University of Chicago Press.

Adrian, T. and Boyarchenko, N. (2012). Intermediary Leverage Cycles and Financial Stability, Federal Reserve Bank of New York Staff Reports No. 567, 1–62.

Adrian, T. and Shin, H. S. (2009). The Shadow Banking System: Implications for Financial Regulation, *Banque de France Financial Stability Review* 13, 1–10.

Alworth, J. S. and Arachi, G. (2012). *Taxation and the Financial Crisis*. Oxford: Oxford University Press.

Ashcraft, A., Goldsmith-Pinkham, P., Hull, P., and Vickery, J. (2011). Credit Ratings and Security Prices in the Subprime MBS Market, *American Economic Review* 101(3), 115–119.

Ashcraft, A. B, and Schuermann, T. (2008). Understanding the Securitization of Subprime Mortgage Credit, *Foundations and Trends in Finance* 2(3), 191–309.

Avraham, D., Selvaggi, P., and Vickery, J. (2012). A Structural View of Bank Holding Companies, *Federal Reserve Bank of New York Economic Policy Review* 18(2), 65–82.

---

[10] See http://www.bis.org/publ/bcbs207.pdf for G-SIBs and www.iaisweb.org/view/element_href.cfm?src=.1/15384.pdf for G-SIIs.

Bord, V. and Santos, J. C. (2012). The Rise of the Originate-to-Distribute Model and the Role of Banks in Financial Intermediation, *Federal Reserve Bank of New York Economic Policy Review* 18(2), 21–34.

Brunnermeier, M. K. and Pedersen, L. H. (2009). Market Liquidity and Funding Liquidity, *Review of Financial Studies* 22(6), 2201–2238.

Cetorelli, N. (2012). A Principle for Forward-Looking Monitoring of Financial Intermediation: Follow the Banks!, Federal Reserve Bank of New York. Liberty Street Economics Blog, July 23.

Cetorelli, N., McAndrews, J., and Traina, J. (2014). Evolution in Bank Complexity, *Federal Reserve Bank of New York Economic Policy Review* 20(2), 1–40.

Cetorelli, N. and Peristiani, S. (2012). The Role of Banks in Asset Securitization, Federal Reserve Bank of New York, *Economic Policy Review* 18(2), 47–64.

Cohen, A. (2011). Rating Shopping in the CMBS Market. Presented at Regulation of Systemic Risk, Washington, DC, September 15–16.

Copeland, A. (2012). Evolution and Heterogeneity among Larger Bank Holding Companies: 1994 to 2010, *Federal Reserve Bank of New York Economic Policy Review* 18(2), 83–93.

Copeland, A., Martin, A., and Walker, M. (2011). Repo Runs: Evidence from the Tri-Party Repo Market, Federal Reserve Bank of New York Staff Report No. 506.

Coval, J., Jurek, J., and Stafford, E. (2009). The Economics of Structured Finance, *Journal of Economic Perspectives* 23(1), 3–25.

Covitz, D., Liang, N., and Suarez, G. (2013). The Evolution of a Financial Crisis: Panic in the Asset-backed Commercial Paper Market, *Journal of Finance* 68, 815–843.

Dang, T. V., Gorton, G., and Holmström, B. (2009). Opacity and the Optimality of Debt for Liquidity Provision. Yale/MIT Working Paper.

Davis, E. P. and Stone, M. (2004). Corporate Financial Structure and Financial Stability. International Monetary Fund, Washington, DC, IMF Working Paper No. 4/124, 1–49.

Diamond, D. and Dybvig, P. (1983). Bank Runs, Deposit Insurance, and Liquidity, *Journal of Political Economy* 91, 401–419.

Fiaschi, D., Kondor, I., and Marsili, M. (2013). The Interrupted Power Law and the Size of Shadow Banking. PLOS ONE. PONE-D-13-45366R1.

Financial Accounting Standards Board (2012). *Briefing Document*, FASB Statement Nos. 166 and 167.

Financial Stability Board (FSB) (2011). Shadow Banking: Strengthening Oversight and Regulation, October 27, <https://www.financialstabilityboard.org/publications/r_111027a.pdf.>.

Financial Stability Board (FSB) (2012). Progress Report to the G20 on Strengthening the Oversight and Regulation of Shadow Banking, April 16, <http://www.financialstability board.org/publications/r_120420c.pdf.>.

Flannery, M. J., Kwan, S. H., and Nimalendran, M. (2004). Market Evidence on the Opaqueness of Banking Firms' Assets, *Journal of Financial Economics* 71, 419–460.

Fostel, A. and Geanakoplos, J. (2008). Leverage Cycles and the Anxious Economy, *American Economic Review* 98(4), 1211–1244.

Gallin, J. (2013). Shadow Banking and the Funding of the Nonfinancial Sector, Federal Reserve Board Finance and Economics Discussion Series No. 2013–50.

Garleanu, N. and Pedersen, L. H. (2011). Margin-Based Asset Pricing and Deviations from the Law of One Price, *Review of Financial Studies* 24(6), 1980–2022.

Gennaioli, N., Shleifer, A., and Vishny, R. (2012a). Neglected Risks, Financial Innovation, and Financial Fragility, *Journal of Financial Economics* 104, 452–468.

Gennaioli, N., Shleifer, A., and Vishny, R. (2013). A Model of Shadow Banking, *Journal of Finance*, 68, 1331–1364.

Gorton, G. and Metrick, A. (2010). Regulating the Shadow Banking System, *Brookings Paper on Economic Activity*, 41, 261–312.

Gorton, G. and Metrick, A. (2012). Securitized Banking and the Run on Repo, *Journal of Financial Economics* 104, 425–451.

Kacperczyk, M. and Schnabl, P. (2011). Does Organizational Form Affect Risk Taking? Evidence from Money Market Mutual Funds. New York University Working Paper.

Kashyap, A. K., Rajan, R., and Stein, J. C. (2002). Banks as Liquidity Providers: An Explanation for the Coexistence of Lending and Deposit-Taking, *Journal of Finance* 57, 33–73.

Keys, B., Mukherjee, T., Seru, A., and Vig, V. (2010). Did Securitization Lead to Lax Screening? Evidence from Subprime Loans, *Quarterly Journal of Economics* 125(1), 307–362.

Krishnamurthy, A., Nagel, S., and Orlov, D. (2011). Sizing Up Repo. NBER/CEPR/Stanford/Northwest Working Paper.

Mandel, B., Morgan, D., and Wei, C. (2012). The Role of Bank Credit Enhancements in Securitization, *Federal Reserve Bank of New York Economic Policy Review* 18(2), 35–46.

Martin, A., Skeie, D., and von Thadden, E. (2012). Repo Runs, Federal Reserve Bank of New York Staff Report No. 444, 1–42.

Mathis, J., McAndrews, J., and Rochet, J. C. (2009). Rating the Raters: Are Reputation Concerns Powerful Enough to Discipline Rating Agencies?, *Journal of Monetary Economics* 57(5), 657–674.

McCulley, P. (2007). Teton Reflections, *PIMCO Global Central Bank Focus* September, 1–11

Meeks, R., Nelson, B., and Alessandri, P. (2012). Shadow Banks and Macroeconomic Instability, Bank of England Working Paper No. 487, March.

Mooij, R., Keen, M., and Orihara, M. (2013). Taxation, Bank Leverage, and Financial Crises, International Monetary Fund, Washington DC, IMF Working Papers No. 13/48.

Pozsar, Z. (2008). The Rise and Fall of the Shadow Banking System, *Regional Financial Review* 44, 13–15.

Pozsar, Z., Adrian, T., Ashcraft, A. B., and Boesky, H. (2010). Shadow Banking, Federal Reserve Bank of New York Staff Report No. 458, July, 1–38.

Rajan, R. (2005). Has Financial Development Made the World Riskier? Proceedings of the Federal Reserve Bank of Kansas City Economics Symposium. Federal Reserve Bank of Kansas City Report, August, 313–369.

Reinhart, C. M. and Rogoff, K. S. (2009). *This Time Is Different: Eight Centuries of Financial Folly*, Princeton, NJ: Princeton University Press.

Reinhart, C. M. and Rogoff, K. S. (2011). From Financial Crash to Debt Crisis, *American Economic Review* 101, 1676–1706.

Reinhart, C. M. and Rogoff, K. S. (2013). Banking Crises: An Equal Opportunity Menace, *Journal of Banking & Finance* 37, 4557–4573.

Sunderam, A. (2012). Money Creation and the Shadow Banking System. Harvard Business School Working Paper.

Tucker, P. (2010). Shadow Banking, Financing Markets and Financial Stability. Remarks by Mr Paul Tucker, Deputy Governor for Financial Stability at the Bank of England, at a Bernie Gerald Cantor (BGC) Partners Seminar, London, January 21.

Wermers, R. (2011). Runs on Money Market Mutual Funds. University of Maryland Working Paper.

Wiggers, T. and Ashcraft, A. B. (2012). Defaults and Losses on Commercial Real Estate Bonds during the Great Depression Era, Federal Reserve Bank of New York Staff Report No. 544, 1–44.

Xia, H. and Strobl, G. (2012). The Issuer-Pays Rating Model and Ratings Inflation: Evidence from Corporate Credit Ratings.

CHAPTER 17

....

PAYMENTS AND PAYMENT SYSTEMS*

....

DAVID HUMPHREY

17.1 INTRODUCTION

....

THE many different payment instruments are best distinguished by their average transaction value, since this largely determines the type of transaction they are used for. Smaller value "retail" transactions include cash, checks, and debit and credit cards (some tied to a mobile phone) and are used at the point of sale. Another type of retail payment concerns medium-value consumer and business bill payments using checks and electronic automated clearing house (ACH) transfers in the US or giro networks in Europe. This includes direct debits for consumer bill payments (with cards used on the Internet) along with credit transfers for business employee disbursements. Large-value or "wholesale" payments primarily use wire transfers (in the US and Europe). These represent large-value transactions among businesses, between business and government, and importantly lie behind almost all large-value financial transactions in the foreign exchange, government security, corporate bond, equity, and derivative markets. As retail and wholesale transactions and the main policy issues they present are different, they are treated separately in most of the sections below, with retail payments covered first followed by wholesale transactions.

17.1.1 Production Structure

A country's payment system is comprised of the payment instruments listed above and the banking institutions directly involved in offering transaction services. In addition, there

---

* James McAndrews contributed to an earlier version of this chapter.

are bank and non-bank firms processing the payments, the transportation firms (for cash), and telecommunications facilities (for electronic payments) needed to move the payment information between individual and business deposit accounts at banks, and between individual bank reserve accounts at central banks for final settlement of retail and wholesale transactions. Cash does not require final settlement—the transfer of good and final funds between accounts—since coin and currency already represents final payment. Central banks are used for final settlement, rather than private banks, due to their low cost and the presumption that they cannot fail (as governments could print money or tax to support them if needed).

In the US and Europe, banks—or organizations owned by banks—have an effective monopoly in offering retail and wholesale payment services, as deposit accounts contain the funds needed for almost all types of transactions. This is enforced by the legal definition of what a bank is and does, since typically only banks are allowed access to central bank payment settlement accounts. In some countries (e.g., Canada, Australia) non-bank financial firms can have limited access to central bank settlement services and in many countries non-bank institutions may offer limited payment services (e.g., money order firms, money transmitters of intercountry remittances) outside of usual banking channels.

A different arrangement exists for large-value payments. In the US (and similarly in Europe) large-value payment volumes are less than 0.6% of all non-cash retail transactions but over 15 times the value of retail payments. Due to the importance of these transactions underpinning financial markets, central banks are typically the primary supplier of wire transfers (Fedwire in the US, Target in Europe, and BOJ-NET in Japan). However, in some specialized financial markets bank-owned organizations initiate and process large-value transactions among their members for themselves and their customers (CHIPS in the US, Euro1 and CLS Bank for Europe, CHAPS in the UK). In this process they use a portion of central bank reserve account funds for initial funding (in the US) or post collateral for intraday exposures (in the UK and Europe) with later final settlement at the central bank. This is an improvement over practices some 30 years ago when there was almost no cover for intraday credit exposures on these networks.

International payments are made via SWIFT, a message transfer network. Here funds are "moved" using accounting entries to interbank correspondent accounts at banks in sending and receiving countries. As there is no world central bank, there is no final settlement in the usual sense: banks in different countries carry as an asset (liability) the various "due from" ("due to") amounts of other banks in their interbank correspondent accounts in order to pay foreign exchange for customer imports, receive foreign exchange from customer exports, or facilitate foreign investment.

17.2 Retail Payments

17.2.1 Payment Theory

Using simplified models for mathematical tractability, payment theory largely focuses on how different payment arrangements evolved among transactors as a substitute for barter and how they tradeoff with one another today. These analyses offer insights on the reasons for the development of different types of retail payment instruments—cash vs. different types of debit or credit instruments (checks, cards)—and on their efficiency in facilitating transactions via attributes of transferability and finality (Kahn and Roberds, 2007). Recent theoretical work on wholesale payments has explored the risk, liquidity benefits, and costs of different settlement arrangements on large-value deferred net settlement vs. real-time gross settlement systems as well as exposure limits and collateralization. In contrast, most empirical analysis of payments relies on well-accepted microeconomic theory dealing with payment pricing principles, demand estimation, analysis of payment cost, scale economies, and assessing competition among payment suppliers.

The most novel development in payment theory concerns recasting traditional demand theory into a two-sided market framework (Rochet and Tirole, 2003). It is applied to credit and debit card pricing arrangements (the interchange fee) as well as to other markets and forms the basis for recent theoretical work in the retail payments area (a survey is provided by Chakravorti, 2003; numerous models are outlined and critized in Katz, 2001). Most theoretical developments in this field are related to antitrust and competition issues that have dominated policy debates, regulatory actions, and legal cases. Papers on these topics can be found in the *Review of Network Economics* (2005, 2006).

17.2.2 Differences in Payment Structure

Current payment instruments evolved from earlier forms (sea shells, pepper corns, precious metals) because they are easier to transfer and store, have an agreed-upon stable nominal value, and are more easily divisible, as well as safer to use. The current transition from paper (checks, paper giros) to electronic non-cash payments (cards, electronic giros) is mostly due to technical change allowing greater convenience and lower costs in making payments. Often, an electronic transaction costs only one-third to one-half as much as the all-in social or private cost of a paper-based one for the same purpose. Even though payment transactions are not usually priced, in Europe checks (except for the UK and France) and paper giro transactions have been effectively eliminated and replaced with electronic giro payments and cards. In contrast, checks markedly reduced cash use in the US and only relatively recently has check use been falling with the expansion of cards and ACH. This is occurring even as checks are now being collected electronically, a development that took place much earlier in Germany.

Use of cash is approximated by the ratio of cash in circulation to gross domestic product (GDP) or the value of cash to population (other methods are more involved). The cost of delivering cash acquisition services to depositors has fallen significantly as banks have progressively augmented branch networks with networks of automated teller machines (ATMs) for cash acquisition. Indeed, in some countries the number of expensive stand-alone bank offices has fallen absolutely. Cash use in 2011 is approximated in Table 17.1 and suggests that European countries in the Eurozone use two to three times as much cash as does the US, while Japan uses twice as much as Europe (US data has been corrected for the approximately 60% of cash held overseas rather than used domestically). The six countries/areas shown in Table 17.1 have been ranked according to their approximate cash use, which except for the Eurozone is generally the reverse of the ranking of their total use of non-cash instruments at the point of sale, for bill payments, and other disbursements (in the last column).

Table 17.1 Payment instrument use, 2011

	Cash/GDP	Cash/Population	Annual Transactions Per Person			
	Percent	Value Held	Check	Card	Giro/ACH	Total Non-Cash
US*	2.4	$1,381	68	211	63	342
UK	3.8	$1,391	21	133	104	258
Canada	3.9	$1,897	25	210	50	285
Euro Area**	9.7	$3,571	52	435	610	1,097
Japan	18.9	$8,947	1	64	11	76

* US cash data reduced by 60% (the percent estimated to be held overseas).

** Some smaller Eurozone countries are missing from the BIS statistical tables.

Estimates of the share of cash in point of sale payments are 20% for the US but can be more than three times higher in Europe (Humphrey, Snellman, and Vesala, 2001). This is consistent with a general aversion to consumer debt in Europe (hence their relatively low use of credit cards—not shown) and a history of relying on giro credit transfers for bill payments (where funds have to be in an account in order to make a transfer). One area where cash is the clear instrument of choice is in tax evasion and other illegal transactions. Here large denomination notes are heavily used and in some countries the share of these notes in the value of cash in circulation is in rough agreement with statistical and survey-based estimates of the value of illegal activity. Estimates of such activities differ greatly but averages 13% of GDP for 11 European countries (with some values larger than 25%), 11% for Japan, and 9% for the US (Schneider, 2005, Table B.1). More recently, the European Union commissioner for taxation has estimated that around €1 trillion is lost annually to tax evasion and avoidance within the EU.

Differences in non-cash payment instrument use across countries are best seen when expressed as numbers of annual transactions per person. In Table 17.1, 68 checks are written per person per year in the US (about evenly divided between consumers and businesses), 52 per person in the Eurozone (almost all from France), but only 1 in Japan. While Japan has 64 card transactions per person per year and cards are used more than twice as much in the UK and the US (133 and 211, respectively), they are most heavily used in the Eurozone with 435 card transactions per person. The Eurozone is also a heavy user of Giro/ACH transactions at 610 payments per person per year, 10 times the level of the US, while Japan hardly uses them at all. The main trend in recent payment instrument use has been the reduction in checks in all countries and the continued expansion of debit card and Giro/ACH transactions.

These differences in the intensity of payment instrument use across countries are associated with historical institutional "accidents" rather than any clear plan to shape payment use. One major institutional difference was the development of a postal giro system in Europe before 1900 but never in the US. Another was the low cost of obtaining a US banking charter over 100 years ago compared to a very high charter cost in Canada and a history of royal or state monopolies in most European countries. These two institutional differences resulted in many thousands of small banks in the US compared to a far more concentrated banking structure in Europe and Canada. In turn, Europe was able to offer nationwide paper-based giro payments using postal banks (and now also commercial banks) while the US had no alternative but to rely on checks for transactions among thousands of small banks since no national payment supplier existed. And when technology made electronic payments possible, Europe—with a national giro network already in place—was able to shift more rapidly to electronics for bill payments and business disbursements than was the US. Similarly, the heavy use of cash in Japan compared to either Europe or the US was facilitated by the fact that Japan was and still is considered to be a safer country.

Another institutional development concerned the early US practice of discounting the face value of a check to cover the cost of collection (non-par checking). This resulted in payment delays that were at times inordinately long and disrupted commerce. One reason the Federal Reserve was established was to transport and process checks at face (par) value and at no charge to eliminate circuitous routing of checks that hindered commerce. Non-par checking was eliminated but today the Federal Reserve, alone among central banks, processes about one-half of all check and ACH payments (now for a fee). Europe, not having an overabundance of checks (debit transfers) to begin with, due to a reliance on cash and giro (credit transfer) payments, instead covered payment costs by debiting accounts prior to the value date in order to earn float revenues. This helps to explain why Europe's central banks are not involved in processing retail transactions in competition with banks but do provide final settlement for interbank giro and other transactions.

17.2.3 Payment Costs

The cost of a nation's payment system has been estimated to be 0.5% to 0.9% of GDP annually (Hayashi and Keeton, 2012) while the social cost of making a $50 or €50 payment is around 1% to 5% of the transaction value, depending on the instrument used. Banks know their payment production costs, but fees per transaction are rarely assessed. Consequently consumers, without prices to influence them, choose different payment instruments for different applications (e.g., local point of sale transactions vs. more distant bill payments) based on non-price influences such as convenience, availability, and perceived safety. The availability of terminals is a clear precondition for use of cards, while consumer cash flow considerations and reward programs influence the use of credit cards. On the merchant side, some limit cash use due to counterfeiting concerns with high-value notes, while others exclude card use for low-value payments in order to cover better bank card interchange fees.

On the supply side, cost considerations have induced banks to shift consumer cash acquisition away from branch offices to cheaper ATMs and away from checks and cash to less expensive debit cards or more profitable credit cards. Averaging two European cost accounting studies (for the Netherlands and Belgium) suggests that the bank plus merchant average cost of a cash transaction at the point of sale is around €0.42 while a debit card is €0.52 with incremental costs of €0.12 and €0.20, respectively (c.f. Brits and Winder, 2005). In contrast, average credit card costs are €3.11 with an incremental cost of €0.68.

As the ratio of marginal to average cost reflects scale economies, these figures also suggest that cash and cards realize strong cost economies. Cash cost economies are 0.29 and those for debit cards are 0.38 while credit card economies are better still at 0.22. These estimates suggest that a doubling of debit card transaction volume would raise debit card costs by only 38%, so average cost falls. Similar payment scale economy estimates for Europe have been obtained in statistical estimation using bank-based as well as payment processor-based data

(Bolt and Humphrey, 2007). Thus consolidation of payment processors across countries in Europe offers the opportunity for substantial reductions in payment costs, a result that will facilitate the emergence of a more competitive cross-country product market as envisioned by the Single Euro Payments Area policy promoted by the European Commission (EC) and the European Central Bank (ECB).

Payment scale economies have long been identified (and realized) for US checks, ACH, and wire transfers (using Federal Reserve data) and debit cards (private source). With scale economies, card, and giro/ACH unit costs should continue to fall as volume expands. Although US checks are still initiated as paper items, almost all are now processed and collected electronically. Check-processing costs fell by 70% and faster collection saved business payees at least one day in payment float. This lowered bank-processing and business payee working capital costs by upwards of $3 billion annually (Humphrey and Hunt, 2013).

17.2.4 Direct vs. Indirect Pricing of Payment Services

Most pricing of consumer payments in the US and Europe is indirect and relies on fixed monthly account fees, minimum balance requirements, no or low interest paid on deposits, and/or payment float. Payment services, such as deposits, are not viewed as a profit center but as a means to provide lower-cost funding for bank loans compared to purchased funds or other bank debt. The lack of price data or detailed information on deposit account non-price characteristics has limited the application of microeconomic theory to assess payment or other banking service demand and substitution relationships. However, some of these relationships have been inferred from US consumer payment survey data (Borzekowski, Kiser, and Ahmed, 2008) while in Europe the focus has been on Norway, which has directly priced their payment services for over a decade (Norges Bank, various years). Per transaction pricing in Norway apparently speeded up the shift to electronic card payments from cash and checks by about 20% compared to the Netherlands, which did not price (Bolt and Humphrey, 2008). Payment demand elasticities here are typically inelastic and non-price characteristics of electronic payments seem to be more important than pricing in explaining volume growth. In this regard, terminal availability is a good summary indicator for the non-price attributes of card use, since mere availability is quickly followed by use. For ATMs, convenience trumps pricing, which is why in the US for instance, non-banks offer ATM services to any bank depositor for a fee, and customers of one bank use another bank's ATMs even though a surcharge applies (Hannan, Prager, and McAndrews, 2003).

17.2.5 Payment Instrument Developments

An improved way to make a payment at the point of sale is with e-money, such as a card with a chip, which is well advanced in Europe due to significant fraud losses with cards with only a magnetic strip. Widespread implementation in the US is not expected until 2015 due to the higher cost of issuing a card with a chip and changing terminals. Another development involves the use of the Internet in Europe to initiate giro bill payments (credit transfers). However, online banking has lagged in the US since, unlike Europe, many business payees are not set up to accept ACH transactions from individual consumers, and potential users are wary of current security safeguards.

More recently, there has been much interest in how payments can be initiated by tapping or waving a mobile phone at a retail point of sale terminal. As mobile payments are basically just card-based payments using a mobile phone rather than swiping a card, any substitution here is more form than substance and may add little value for most users (Katz, 2012). Efforts to incorporate many different card numbers, passwords, and other financial information into either a mobile phone or on a single card (e.g., Google wallet) may offer some convenience value to a subset of users but the key for widespread adoption will be improved security over what users currently have.

17.2.6 Effect on Monetary Policy

The substitution of electronic payments for cash is slow enough to not have an important effect on monetary policy. The oft predicted "cashless society" is still a long way off, especially in Europe, which uses more than twice as much cash per person than the US (and even further off for Japan, which uses twice as much as Europe). So far, population growth and inflation have typically offset the reduction in the share of cash in total payments, so its absolute value is still expanding or is relatively stable. Once the value of cash falls absolutely, however, tax revenues will have to be used for its redemption and seigniorage revenues will be correspondingly reduced. Singapore has raised the possibility that a government could redeem currency and replace it with a government-issued card and account of equal value, effectively retaining seigniorage revenues as well as saving tax revenues otherwise needed for currency redemption.

17.2.7 Fraud

Payment fraud is a significant expense borne by consumers, merchants, and banks. Neglecting wire transfers, credit card fraud is the largest source and US consumers are reported to have lost $128 million in 2011 (Federal Trade Commission, 2012). As many as 10% of US citizens have been victims of credit card fraud, with 7% experiencing debit card or ATM fraud. Card fraud includes card theft, theft of card numbers from card processors or merchants in a data breech, card counterfeiting, and fraudulent use of cards (identify theft). Fraud losses tradeoff with user convenience and illustrate the difficulty in restricting improper use, especially when card information is compromised through data breeches at merchants and payment processors. Solutions exist but are expensive: pin numbers that are not observed or saved by merchants; chips that encrypt card information; and randomly varied transaction verification numbers for each payment.

Europe has reduced card fraud by replacing magnetic stripe cards—which only require a signature—with cards embedded with a chip that use a PIN instead of a signature and improve security. Adoption of cards with a chip is extensive in Europe and merchants find that "chip and pin" cards mean quicker transactions and shorter lines. European banks issued chip and PIN cards not only because they are more secure, but also because it allowed banks to shift the liability for fraudulent charges associated with lost or stolen cards to consumers (when a PIN is used) and to merchants (when it is not). This is not possible in the US: Regulation E limits consumer liability to $50 for lost and stolen cards when promptly reported to the issuing bank. While US banks, consumers, and merchants would all benefit from having cards with a chip instead of a magnetic stripe, banks would incur large costs as cards with a chip are many times more expensive to issue and millions of existing card terminals would need to be replaced or modified. Consequently, this replacement has only been offered to US depositors who extensively travel overseas and is not expected to be generally available to all current card holders until 2015.

17.2.8 Availability of Payment Data

There are little more than 20 years of annual data on the volume and value of non-cash payment instrument use by country (Bank for International Settlements, various years; European Central Bank, various years). This is all at the national level. Only Norway has collected payment use, cost, and pricing data at the individual bank level. No country has time-series information on the number and value of cash transactions, and the value of cash outstanding is only an approximate indicator of its domestic use in the US. European cash data are better in this regard, as are their check data. Card information is usually good but the split between debit and credit is often missing for Europe. The US does not have accurate time-series check volume or value data except after 2000, and then only at three-year increments. Instead, there is considerable survey information on the demographic characteristics of people who use different payment instruments (cf. recurring University of Michigan surveys). This has been used to infer payment preferences (Hayashi and Klee, 2003; Schuh and Stavins, 2010) and sometimes intimate convenience and price responsiveness.

More recently, cost accounting analysis has been applied to determine the unit cost of payment instruments at the bank and merchant level (costs only: Brits and Winder, 2005; costs and benefits: Garcia-Swartz, Hahn, and Layne-Farrar, 2004, and Shampine, 2007; cost concepts: Hayashi and Keeton, 2012; literature survey: Koivuniemi and Kemppainen, 2007). Consumer benefits from using the various payment instruments, however, remain difficult to value accurately. Consequently, comparing calculated net benefits with observed relative usage may be an indicator of how inaccurate these calculations are and/or reflect the fact that most payment instruments are only indirectly priced (via lost float, fixed monthly bank account fees, mostly free ATM cash withdrawals, hidden interchange fees, etc.) so relative use is not strongly based on actual relative resource cost.

17.2.9 Payment Card Pricing

Central banks are responsible for the safety and soundness of payment systems and profess a concern for their cost efficiency as well. Australia has a specific legislative mandate regarding payment efficiency, Europe is getting involved, but the US has been much less active. All countries, however, have regulations, legislation, and case law that spell out the various rights and liabilities of consumer, merchant, and bank participants of a payment transaction.

One current policy example is the Single Euro Payments Area initiative noted above, which seeks to lower the cost of within and cross-border payments in Europe. Another cost-related issue concerns debit and credit card interchange fees. The theory of two-sided markets outlines the logic behind interchange fees between a merchant-acquiring bank and a card-issuing bank. As expenses are incurred by both acquiring and issuing banks, the interchange fee collected by the issuing bank when its customer uses its card is shared with the acquiring bank. If the issuing bank is also the acquiring bank, the "interchange fee" becomes an internal (and less obvious) transfer rather than an external one.

The interchange controversy exists because (1) merchant costs of accepting credit cards tend to be much higher than for other payment instruments and (2) interchange fees have often not fallen as volume has expanded even though scale economies, the stated reason for past mergers resulting in just a few large card processors, are seemingly being realized. Merchant costs are higher still for cards that offer a reward when consumers use them and, since these costs are factored into what the merchant sells, users of cash, checks, and even debit cards effectively cross-subsidize credit card users' reward programs. The Reserve Bank of Australia mandated a reduction in interchange fees (Reserve Bank of Australia, 2005) while competition authorities in Europe are putting pressure on banks to reduce and/or justify better the interchange fees they charge. As well, legal action by merchants is underway in the US to achieve the same end, with some success since acceptance of a credit card no longer requires that the issuer's debit card—and interchange fee—also be accepted. Work in this area has focused on trying to determine the effect on relative payment instrument use as a result of these regulatory changes as well as the effects of card loyalty programs and merchants surcharging card use (Simon, Smith, and West, 2010).

Merchant-promoted legislation in the US (Durbin amendment) mandated close to a 50% reduction in debit card interchange fees but (for now) left credit card fees unaffected. In Europe, regulators are mulling over a possible cap on card interchange fees based on a "tourist test" in which a merchant would be more willing to accept the card of a non-returning customer (a tourist) if the interchange fee did not exceed the cost of accepting a non-card payment such as cash (Rochet and Wright, 2010). However, the merchant cost of accepting cash rises with the value of the transaction. A different card issue currently being addressed in some countries is the so-called no surcharge rule in contracts between card issuers and merchants. This rule restricts merchants from charging a customer a separate fee— on top of the price of a sale—for using a card for payment rather than some other instrument. Australia has allowed merchants to surcharge for paying with a card but most do not surcharge, perhaps because some or many customers would decide to shop elsewhere. Although a recent US legal settlement between merchants and Visa and MasterCard would allow merchants to impose a credit card surcharge, ten states currently have laws that ban card surcharging (and more states are considering similar bans).

Competition in providing payment services has received little attention. While the issue has been raised in Europe and many apparent influences on competition differ across countries, much of the data collected remains confidential (European Commission, 2007). Fortunately, recent improvements in banking data reported to regulators in the US (which is public) has suggested that banks most competitive in providing payment services are relatively small billion-dollar banks, as are the banks that are least competitive. The conventional wisdom that the largest banks are the least competitive is apparently not supported (Bolt and Humphrey, 2012). This conclusion is controversial, as the standard summary measure of competition used by antitrust regulators (a Herfindahl-Herschman Index) is unrelated to more theoretically supported measures of competition (Lerner Index, H-Statistic).

Other card policy issues deal with money laundering using prepaid payment cards (although industry initiatives have largely contained this problem) and use of government-issued cards to replace cash and checks for welfare and food stamp programs (Electronic Benefit Transfer in the US). Overall, the use of stored value cards for general purposes (rather than narrow gift or special promotion applications) has been stalled at a relatively low level of acceptance in both the US and Europe (Van Hove, 2006). More recently, since payment card interchange fees were not limited by the Durbin Amendment that cut bank debit card merchant interchange fees by half, their use has been promoted by banks and has expanded.

17.2.10 Financial Inclusion

Some 10% of US adults and between 15 and 23% of UK adults do not have a bank check-ing/ transaction account, while markedly higher percentages of adults do not have a savings account (Carbo, Gardener, and Molyneux, 2005; Federal Deposit Insurance Corporation, 2012). These are the so-called "unbanked" that typically have lower incomes. The concern is that they incur higher costs in obtaining cash for transactions and money orders (or similar instruments) for bill payments from non-bank firms as compared to banks, just as they pay higher rates when borrowing from a non-bank firm rather than a bank (usually due to hav-ing a lower credit rating, indicating greater default risk).

Although it has been demonstrated that the unbanked would incur lower transaction costs from a bank, these cost comparisons typically assume that account holders keep track of their balances and do not overdraw their accounts, which triggers overdraft fees. Over the period 2008–10, overdraft fees generated $35 billion annually in bank fee income. These fees were paid primarily by lower-income depositors who also have lower account balances and often unsteady incomes, making it more difficult not to overdraw a transaction account (Federal Deposit Insurance Corporation, 2008).

While the cost of transaction services from a non-banking firm may be higher, their offices are typically open on weekends, have longer operating hours, and are more con-veniently located for lower-income individuals. In addition, many of the unbanked have an unfavorable opinion of banks and/or wish to keep their financial situation more pri-vate. Government efforts to promote financial inclusion tend to focus on cost compari-sons but the most effective programs to bring the unbanked into the financial system have been pursued by credit unions that combine community outreach programs with financial education.

17.3 WHOLESALE PAYMENTS

Wholesale payments are quite different from retail payments in two important respects. First, the values transferred are very large. Second, in the shift to electronic processing of these large payments, and the establishment of private net settlement networks for these payments, it was cheaper and indeed easier to arrange if settlement was made at the end of the day rather than at the time a payment was sent. Doing otherwise would have meant that the sender would have to actually have the funds on hand to make the payment being sent (by liquidating other assets or by interbank borrowing). Similarly, receivers of funds would much rather use the funds when they were received during the day rather than wait for end-of-day settlement and be forced to borrow intraday to make payments needed for that day. Thus an unexpected failure of a sending bank prior to settlement, under past rules, regulation, and bankruptcy law, could disrupt the smooth operation of the payment system.

The value of wholesale payments is so overwhelmingly large that any major interruption in their daily payment flows could severely impact economic activity and even financial market stability. The total value transferred over the four major large-value payment networks—Fedwire, Target, CHIPS, and Euro1—was $1,939 trillion in 2011 while the total value of GDP in the US and Europe was only $29 trillion (Bank for International Settlements, 2013). Payments over large-value payment system (LVPS) networks are extensive and include daily interbank funding; loan sales and syndications; large-value business and government payments; securities transactions by large commercial and financial firms; and daily settlement of foreign-exchange, equity, derivative, and other financial asset trades. These transactions typically occur as payments among commercial banks move funds from payor to payee deposit accounts. Although savings institutions and credit unions also initiate large-value payments, they often are routed through large commercial banks in major financial centers. The values that flow through LVPS networks are much better protected from fraud and operational failure than are retail payment networks using dedicated telecommunication arrangements, message encryption and, in some cases, passwords that are changed daily.

Large-value payment transactions and settlements can occur in real time using central bank reserve or deposit accounts. Here each payment is separately settled in "good and final funds," which denotes a RTGS (real-time gross settlement) system, such as Fedwire in the US and Target in Europe. Other large-value transactions are made over DNS (deferred net settlement) systems where intraday transactions are netted—rather than each transaction settled in real time—and usually settled at the end of the business day also using central bank reserve or deposit accounts. This includes CHIPS in the US and Euro1 in Europe, which are owned and operated by groups of large banks or a combined bank-central bank network such as CHAPS in the UK. Intraday liquidity flows in the US are outlined in Payments Risk Committee (2012). This is where the risk lies.

17.3.1 Systemic Risk

By far the most important issue concerning large-value networks is the risk that payments initiated during the day may not be finalized or settled due to bank or operational failure. Reducing these risks has been a focus of government policy for almost all central banks and national banking systems as well as academic research for the past 30 years. Most of the procedures adopted for reducing LVPS risk have been initiated by individual central banks with dissemination and policy coordination through the Bank for International Settlements. The risk-reducing policies adopted have raised bank costs and limited bank flexibility in making uncovered payments—a flexibility that had occurred in the transition from a partially manual transaction and monitoring system to a fully electronic one.

The major risk-reducing procedures include intraday net debit caps tied to individual bank capital positions, the collateralization of intraday credit exposures, rules requiring a certain percentage of each day's payments be sent before a stipulated time period, charging higher prices for sending payments at later times in the day, and the use of specialized payment queues in which algorithms are used to match or net pending payment transactions before they are sent. Currently, the emphasis is on better management of posted collateral by transferring excess liquidity on one network to other networks where it can be used to cover desired payments. So far, an intraday interbank funds market has failed to gain traction, probably because the cost to buy daily cover is viewed to be too large (although the procedures involved would be similar to transferring collateral).

In order to understand why different risk-reduction procedures were adopted on different LVPS networks, it is necessary to see how LVPS risk arose in the first place. In the US, the shift to making wire transfers fully electronic during the late 1970s and early 1980s did not initially include real-time monitoring of reserve account positions. This was deemed to be too expensive, especially since, when wire transfers required more manual intervention and balances were effectively monitored both during and at the end of the day, daylight overdrafts were relatively rare. However, the unique combination of an unconcentrated US banking system, the institutional practice favoring overnight (rather than one week, or "good till canceled") interbank borrowing, the practice of purchasing and accumulating securities during the day until the entire order could be delivered and paid for (as partial deliveries were not then allowed), along with a reduction in reserve balances (through lower reserve requirements and, later, deposit sweep accounts) all contributed to a daylight overdraft problem by increasing the demand for settlement balances while decreasing the supply. To illustrate, if rollovers, continuing contracts, term settlement, and on-the-books settlement, which accounted for 52% of all federal funds settlement in the late 1980s, had replaced the funding requirements portion of overnight interbank funding settled on Fedwire, then daylight overdrafts (and systemic risk) would have been at a manageable level (Humphrey, 1989). For the US, systemic risk is largely an institutional funding issue rather than a necessary outcome of a large-value payment network.

Other countries have more concentrated banking systems where internal transfers among customer accounts replace what would otherwise be external funding/payment transactions between accounts at different banks in a less concentrated environment. As well, there are simply more large-value payment transactions in countries where money centers are located but balances to fund these payments did not expand in tandem. In sum, once the full dimension of the daylight overdraft problem was recognized, it was not possible to "put the genie back in the bottle," for the reasons just noted. Instead, central banks took steps to limit their credit risk on the RTGS networks they operated using the procedures noted above.

Although the same intraday exposures occurred on commercial bank-operated LVPS networks such as CHIPS, they arose from a more deliberate decision to save costs. In the beginning, some banks wanted to fund CHIPS in the morning with enough initial funding so that all transactions could be settled as they were made, as occurs on a RTGS network. Others wanted to save the funding cost and instead allow intraday exposures to occur but settle these net exposures at the end of the day using reserve accounts at the central bank. This latter view was a DNS approach that, logically, was just an extension of the daily check-clearing and settlement arrangement already in place and operated by the same group of large New York banks that form CHIPS.

As it now stands, bilateral pending payments on CHIPS are often able to be netted so that only the bilateral net amount need be sent. If one bank is set to pay another $1.6 million while the second bank around a similar time is set to pay the first bank $1.2 million, the two payments are netted and only $0.4 million is sent. CHIPS members also transfer some of their central bank reserve balances to CHIPS' network accounts in the morning to fund payments during the day. Through these two mechanisms, the vast majority of CHIPS payments are now settled intraday. Those that cannot be so settled are settled at the end of the day.

The main problem with a DNS system is that the rules stipulated that if any bank could not settle their net position at the end of the day, its payments to all other banks and its payments from all other banks would be "unwound" from the settlement. This would alter the net settlement positions of all the other banks on the network that received payments from or sent payments to the failed bank. While such a settlement failure has never occurred, simulations of such a possible failure indicated that many other banks would also fail to settle, since in many cases the change in their net exposure would exceed their total capital position. A simulation in the 1980s using actual payment data suggested that the unexpected failure to settle on CHIPS could lead to the unwinding of as much as one-third of that day's payments (Humphrey, 1986).

Other simulations using data from other countries were far less extreme because their banking systems were more concentrated (generating more internal transfers among customer accounts within banks) so their bank-to-bank external daylight credit exposures were lower. More recent simulations (in the 2000s) show that a much lower level of unwinding would occur given today's payment activities, likely because of increased levels of bank capital, more stringent net debit limits, and bank mergers, which make previously external payments among two banks into internal account transfers of the merged institution.

Systemic risks exist in financial markets outside of large-value net settlement payment networks. Unfortunately, information on the web of cross-bank and non-bank financial institution exposures is currently either too limited or non-existent (as in the case of credit default swaps during the credit crisis of 2008) to permit authorities to monitor continuously or simulate in near-real-time the systemic effects of financial institution failure on the financial system. Analyses of risks on LVPS networks have identified several sources of risk in addition to systemic risk. These include liquidity risk, legal risk, time-gap risk, and operational risk.

17.3.2 Wire Transfers

Most LVPSs use wire transfers as the payment instrument. A wire transfer is a credit transfer in which the originating bank directs funds to be sent to a recipient bank. Wholesale, or interbank, wire transfer systems (to be distinguished from retail systems that are often used for cross-country remittances in Europe) limit access by requiring participant banks to use dedicated hardware to initiate payments that are transferred over dedicated communication links using encryption. In addition, back-up payment processing centers have been established that can, with no or only a small delay, take over processing in the event of an operational failure. Fedwire is the wire transfer system in the US, owned and managed by the Federal Reserve System, and Target is the wire transfer system used in many countries in Europe, and which is owned and managed by the European Central Bank.

Fedwire and Target are RTGS networks, and payments are final and cannot be reversed when made. If a payment is made in error, the receiving party is requested to wire the return funds. In contrast, payments over a DNS system are final typically only when all the net debits are paid to net creditors at the end of the day using funds from central bank reserve or deposit accounts. Although bankruptcy law has been changed to not require that funds sent by a failed bank be reversed on the day of failure, contractual agreements that banks have with a net settlement network can require a settlement unwind anyway if posted collateral is insufficient. A comparative analysis of the settlement risk on gross and net systems is provided by Kahn, McAndrews, and Roberds (2003) while a comprehensive analysis of the risk, liquidity, and public policy issues associated with large-value payment networks is covered in Manning, Nier, and Schanz (2009).

17.3.3 Liquidity and Other Risks

In 1985 only three central banks had adopted RTGS systems while by 2006 fully 93 of the world's 174 central banks had adopted them. RTGS systems require real-time monitoring of account balances and efficient and timely communication infrastructures to support their operations relative to the netting systems they often displaced. Subsequent advances in computing power and communication links, as well as consolidation of operating centers over time, have allowed central banks to lower their costs and the fees they charge (Bech, Preisig, and Soramaki, 2008).

As funds are transferred immediately in RTGS systems, and because the values transferred in the systems are so large, banks must make provisions to have funds available in their central bank reserve or deposit accounts in order for the payments to occur. To accommodate this need for covering funds, most central banks provide "daylight credit" to banks during system operating hours. Daylight credit is different from an overnight loan by the central bank through a discount window facility. Most often central banks provide daylight credit at a zero interest rate against collateral provided by commercial banks in order to assure the funding of payments during the day. The US is an anomaly as it provides limited amounts of daylight credit at a very small fee, but (generally) without the requirement that the credit be collateralized. In either case, the provision of daylight credit by central banks is performed at a subsidized rate compared to what one bank would charge another for intraday funding. In the past when some banks offered to fund intraday exposures for a fee, there were no takers. While the current provision of daylight credit allows banks to conserve on working capital for their large-value payment services, it also benefits the businesses that make large-value payments and entities that transact in bond, equity, and other financial markets.

The major legal risks on LVPS networks have been addressed through: (1) a change in bankruptcy law (noted above) so payments made earlier in the day by a sending bank that fails are not reversed, and (2) by strengthening the legal underpinnings of netting (by novation) contracts through changes in statutory laws. Time-gap risk, which occurs in the foreign exchange market, has been addressed through the development of the Continuous Linked Settlement (CLS) bank (discussed below). Real-time monitoring of payment accounts, improved bank supervision, and enhanced regulation of bank capital have improved risk exposures on both RTGS and DNS networks. Importantly, pools of collateral that can be used to cover the largest single net debit of one participant on a DNS network have markedly reduced the likelihood that an unexpected failure of a participant will lead to the failure to settle of other participants on the same network on the same day. Expected participant failures can be handled by restricting the participant's net debit position to either a small value or to zero (although quite rare, this has been done in the past).

17.3.4 Liquidity Savings Mechanisms

Cost is still the main issue for LVPS networks and has concerned the expense of implementing the various risk-reduction procedures noted earlier. As these procedures have been largely implemented, the cost issue is now focused on the ability to process more payments with a lower expenditure or tie-up of funding or collateral. Although central banks offer daylight credit to meet payment needs, most limit the amount provided to the level of posted collateral. However, some central banks have expanded their definition of acceptable collateral, which has allowed a wider range of collateral to be posted. Even so, the restrictions on acceptable collateral have fostered the development of liquidity-savings mechanisms.

One procedure allows banks to submit a payment for either immediate settlement or to place it in a queue of pending payment orders. The payment order remains pending until the bank receives offsetting funds (after which the payment is sent) or until the bank's queued payment order is met by an offsetting payment order in the queue of another bank (or a combination of banks). In this latter case, both payments settle simultaneously as funds are provided to settle one another's payment. These systems have been implemented in the German Bundesbank's RTGS^PLUS system, as well as on the LVPS networks in Italy, Japan, and in the European Central Bank's Target 2 system (Bank for International Settlement, 2005). The adoption of these systems has reduced the liquidity/ collateral costs associated with RTGS systems.

Similar arrangements have been applied to DNS networks, with the result that many payments are effectively netted and made final prior to the end of the day. A few DNS networks have instead chosen to settle the net positions of all their participants at least once before the end of the day. This not only reduces risk, but also saves posted collateral since net debits on the network are correspondingly reduced. A newer liquidity savings arrangement involves the ability of banks to move collateral from a network where it is not being fully utilized to another network to support expanded payments on that network.

17.3.5 Continuous Linked Settlement (CLS) Bank

The CLS bank began operation in 2002 and was created to provide a means for banks to settle both legs of a foreign exchange trade simultaneously in a payment vs. payment (PVP) environment. This addresses the time-gap risk that existed earlier when foreign exchange transactions between countries used different DNS networks in different time zones and thus settled at different times, since the end of the business day also differed. The development of foreign exchange (FX) settlement risk and procedures adopted to deal with it from 1980–2000 is outlined in Galati (2002).

Time-gap risk was graphically illustrated with the failure of Bankhaus Herstatt at the end of the business day in Germany in 1974 before CHIPS payments the same day were to be settled. The Herstatt failure is important because it illustrated how fragile the international payment system was at that time. Some details of this failure are contained in a Basel Committee on Banking Supervision working paper (2004).

At that time, bankruptcy law voided all out (sent) payments of a failed bank on the day it failed but retained all the in (received) payments. SWIFT instructions received by Herstatt to credit its "due to" account with deutsche marks for a US bank were reversed following then existing bankruptcy law. But SWIFT instructions to the US bank—as the counterparty to the mark–dollar trade—to correspondingly credit its "due from" Herstatt account with dollars, and then release these dollars to a US customer, remained. As any dollar payment would no longer be backed by a corresponding Herstatt asset, the dollar payment was not initially made and CHIPS settlement was delayed until the early morning hours of the next day. The delay concerned who was going to stand in line as creditor to the failed bank—the US bank customer who was to be the final recipient of the $150 million traded for deutsche marks that day with Herstatt or the receiving correspondent bank in New York? In the end, the dollar payment was made and the losses from the Herstatt failure were minimal. Even so, the value of payments through CHIPS fell by some 60% in the following days because of fears of foreign exchange counterparty default.

The CLS bank uses multilateral net settlement to settle its member banks' foreign exchange trades (spot, forward, swap). CLS, its member banks, and central bank RTGS networks communicate using SWIFT. CLS is open simultaneously, in all the countries whose currency it trades, for approximately five hours during the day with final settlement through CLS accounts it holds with central banks of the traded currencies. Member banks each have a multicurrency account with CLS and make payments into these accounts to cover the trades they wish to make. The trades are transacted by simultaneously debiting the account of the bank in the currency being sold, and crediting the account of another bank in the currency being purchased. Trades take place if, and only if, both sides of the trade successfully complete all the requirements of the payment.

Over its ten years of operation, CLS bank has grown rapidly with daily average settlement values exceeding $5.2 trillion and trade volume exceeding 1.1 million. It settles trades in the world's 17 most traded currencies, has more than 60 direct bank members, and over 700 indirect participants. CLS bank represents a significant innovation in the practice of large-value payment systems by linking the systems in multiple countries and eliminating the time-gap risk noted above.

17.3.6 Related Systems

Securities settlement systems are complementary networks to LVPSs and are designed specifically to settle securities trades. The Depository Trust and Clearing Corporation provide settlement services for the trades of most stock and bond trades in the US along with commercial paper. These systems represent another source of demand for wholesale payments on RTGS or DNS networks. Security settlement systems employ a wide variety of approaches for settlement, often using a technique that assures the delivery of the security if, and only if, the payment for the security occurs, a technique known as delivery vs. payment (DVP). This also eliminates time-gap risk, this time between security delivery and payment for securities.

17.3.7 Current LVPS Issues

The major current policy issue on LVPS networks is the efficient use of bank-posted collateral across different networks for banks that participate in more than one LVPS network. As banks conduct business and participate in LVPSs in different countries, they can find themselves with idle collateral available in one country even though they have a binding collateral constraint in a different country in which they operate. This has led some central banks to expand their acceptance of foreign collateral against which they offer daylight credit. However, many technical and legal difficulties prevent banks from completely overcoming restrictions on use of collateral posted in one country for obtaining daylight credit in another country (Bank for International Settlements, 2006).

A second current issue concerns security settlement systems, which are often affiliated with a particular securities trading system such as a stock exchange. For securities that are traded over the counter (e.g., through a bilateral or dealer trading system), trades are often settled on a bilateral basis. This lack of centralization and standardization in settlement can lead to less efficient mechanisms for securities settlement. With the growth in derivatives trading, many parties recognized that settlement of these trades was subject to large back-office backlogs and delays. These backlogs have been reduced, but verifying and reconciling these trades still lags the rapid growth in trading volume, creating risks for participants (Bank for International Settlements, 2007).

Finally, there is the ongoing effort to harmonize financial market infrastructures in terms of risk-limiting procedures as well as bank regulation and supervision across countries (Bank for International Settlements, 2012a). This concerns systemically important payment networks, securities settlement systems and depositories, as well as specialized financial instrument clearing houses. The goal is to bring each of the various links in a payment system up to the current practice of the strongest links. Some efforts to measure/ forecast systemic risk, in its different manifestations, are contained in a special issue of the *Journal of Financial Services Research* (2012).

17.4. PAYMENT ACTIVITIES OF NON-BANKS

Non-bank firms also provide certain specialized payment services. On the retail level, there are money orders, traveler's checks, telegraph transfers or other remittances, as well as merchant charge cards and bill aggregation services. In addition, large credit card firms such as Visa and MasterCard now operate as non-bank firms. While not offering the full range of banking services, these firms provide valuable services to customers in narrow market segments.

There are also "money transmitters" in the US and elsewhere who accept currency from customers and, using the services of a correspondent bank, allow the customer's designated recipient of a payment to withdraw cash from a bank or branch of the firm in a different city. Money transmitter payment services are priced to be profitable and earn revenue through transaction fees. This stands in contrast to banks who typically charge low fees per transfer for retail customers, but encourage the customer to maintain large balances on account, on which the bank aims to earn a net interest margin.

Firms that offer charge cards or bill aggregation allow consumers to purchase goods from merchants and to pay for the goods only at the end of a billing cycle, such as a one-month period. The charge card firm makes the payment to the merchant earlier, and earns fees by collecting both from the merchant and the consumer. The consumer is expected to pay the charges in full at the end of the billing cycle; this is in contrast to credit cards, which offer the consumer the opportunity to incur a revolving balance loan. In addition, consumer prices in charge card arrangements are often made up of fixed fees, rather than variable interest charges.

Visa and MasterCard are both for-profit public firms but both began their institutional life as associations of banks. Their roles in the credit and debit card industries are far-reaching. They sponsor the systems of branding and acceptance of cards by banks (and bank customers, the cardholders) and merchants. Together with telecommunications and computer-processing firms, they route transaction information from a merchant ultimately to the cardholder's bank. Their activities have been pivotal in the worldwide acceptance of credit and debit cards.

17.5 THE FUTURE

In retail payments, debit and credit cards will continue to replace cash (in Europe) and checks (in the US). The expanded use of cards will not only intensify efforts to reduce fraud, but will also increase the friction between merchants and card suppliers regarding the level of card interchange fees. This will likely intensify disputes related to the competitive effects of retail card pricing and efforts to price payment services to consumers on a per transaction basis (already done for higher volume business users) in order to induce consumers to adopt instruments with the lowest bank/ merchant costs. And since card transactions are not anonymous, the continuing replacement of cash will raise privacy issues, especially in countries with high sales taxes where cash is still heavily used (facilitating tax evasion).

Similar rapid growth and privacy concerns will likely be seen in specialized electronic retail payment systems used for transportation services such as toll roads. The future of stored value cards, a potentially lower cost replacement for small-value cash transactions, is uncertain and has not expanded beyond their currently narrow applications (subway rides, public phone calls, gift cards, and merchants close to college campuses). Finally, the expansion of Internet bill payments and transactions using mobile phones for most potential users will depend on improvements in transaction security.

Future developments in wholesale payments will be on ways that excess collateral or liquidity on one LVPS network can be used on other networks within and across countries as well as reducing backoffice delays and counterparty risk in handling derivative trades. Achieving greater integration of backoffice systems and uses of LVPSs will continue to be a goal of LVPS design. And given the recent financial crisis, there will be efforts to improve the ability of LVPS networks and their participants to deal with and respond to unexpected and serious financial market disruption (e.g., Bank for International Settlements, 2012b).

The 2007–2008 financial crisis had no real effect on small-value retail payment systems and only affected large-value network volume due to bank reliance on short-term funding sources, which initially "dried up" as a result of the uncertainty concerning which banks in the US and Europe could be in trouble. While the crisis affected the payments routed through LTPSs, the systems themselves worked fine. New bank regulations following the crisis have focused on increasing bank capital and liquidity (reducing, somewhat, the reliance on short-term funding) as well as reducing risky bank activities (such as using insured deposits for risky trading activities and moving some over-the-counter derivative trading to centralized exchanges).

References

Bank for International Settlements (2005). New Developments in Large-Value Payment Systems, Basle, No. 67, May.

Bank for International Settlements (2006). Cross Border Collateral Arrangements, Basle, No. 71, January.

Bank for International Settlements (2007). New Developments in Clearing and Settlement of OTC Derivatives, Basle, No. 77, March.

Bank for International Settlements (2012a). Principles for Financial Market Infrastructures. Basle, CPSS-IOSCO, April.

Bank for International Settlements (2012b). Recovery and Resolution of Financial Market Infrastructures—Consultative Report, Basle, July.

Bank for International Settlements (2013). Statistics on Payment, Clearing and Settlement Systems in CPSS Countries—Figures for 2011, January.

Bank for International Settlements (Various Years). Statistics on Payment Systems in the Group of Ten Countries, Basle.

Basel Committee on Banking Supervision (2004). Bank Failures in Mature Economies, Bank for International Settlements Working Paper No. 13.

Bech, M., Preisig, C., and Soramaki, K. (2008). Global Trends in Large-Value Payments, *Federal Reserve Bank of New York Economic Policy Review* 14, 59–81.

Bolt, W. and Humphrey, D. (2007). Payment Network Scale Economies, SEPA, and Cash Replacement, *Review of Network Economics* 6, 453–473.

Bolt, W. and Humphrey, D. (2008). Transaction Pricing and the Adoption of Electronic Payments: A Cross-Country Analysis, *International Journal of Central Banking* 4, 89–123.

Bolt, W. and Humphrey, D. (2012). Competition in Bank-Provided Payment Services. De Nederlandsche Bank Working Paper.

Borzekowski, R., Kiser, E., and Ahmed, S. (2008). Consumers' Use of Debit Cards: Patterns, Preferences, and Price Response, *Journal of Money, Credit and Banking* 40, 149–172.

Brits, H. and Winder, C. (2005). *Payments Are No Free Lunch*. Occasional Studies, Vol 3/Nr 2, De Nederlandsche Bank.

Carbo, S., Gardener, E., and Molyneux, P. (2005). *Financial Exclusion*. Basingstoke: Palgrave Macmillan.

Chakravorti, S. (2003). Theory of Credit Card Networks: A Survey of the Literature, *Review of Network Economics* 2, 50–68.

European Central Bank (Various Years). Payment and Securities Settlement Systems in the European Union, Frankfurt.

European Commission (2007). Report of the Retail Banking Industry, Brussels Commission Staff Working Document SEC No. 106.

Federal Deposit Insurance Corporation (2008). FDIC Study of Bank Overdraft Programs, November.

Federal Deposit Insurance Corporation (2012). 2011 FDIC National Survey of Unbanked and Underbanked Households, September.

Federal Trade Commission (2012). Consumer Sentinel Network Data Book, Washington, DC, February.

Galati, G. (2002). Settlement Risk in Foreign Exchange Markets and CLS Bank, *BIS Quarterly Review* 6, 55–65.

Garcia-Swartz, D., Hahn, R., and Layne-Farrar, A. (2004). The Move Toward a Cashless Society: A Closer Look at Payment Instrument Economics, *Review of Network Economics* 5, 175–198.

Hannan, T., Prager, R., and McAndrews, J. (2003). To Surcharge or Not to Surcharge: An Empirical Investigation of ATM Pricing, *Review of Economics and Statistics* 85, 990–1002.

Hayashi, F. and Keeton, W. (2012). Measuring the Costs of Retail Payment Methods, *Federal Reserve Bank of Kansas City Economic Review*, 2nd Quarter, 37–77.

Hayashi, F. and Klee, B. (2003). Technology Adoption and Consumer Payments: Evidence from Survey Data, *Review of Network Economics* 2, 175–190.

Humphrey, D. (1986). Payments Finality and Risk of Settlement Failure. In: A. Saunders and L. White (Eds.), *Technology and the Regulation of Financial Markets*, 97–120. New York: Lexington Books/Solomon Brothers Center Series on Financial Institutions and Markets.

Humphrey, D. (1989). Market Responses to Pricing Fedwire Daylight Overdrafts, *Federal Reserve Bank of Richmond Economic Review* 75, 23–34.

Humphrey, D. and Hunt, R. (2013). Cost Savings from Check 21 Electronic Payment Legislation, *Journal of Money, Credit and Banking* 45, 1415–1429.

Humphrey, D., Snellman, J., and Vesala, J. (2001). Substitution of Noncash Payment Instruments for Cash in Europe, *Journal of Financial Services Research* 19, 131–145.

Journal of Financial Services Research (2012). Issue Containing Papers Attempting to Measure and Forecast Aspects of Systemic Risk, 42, 1–2.

Kahn, C., McAndrews, J., and Roberds, W. (2003). Settlement Risk Under Gross and Net Settlement, *Journal of Money, Credit, and Banking* 35, 591–608.

Kahn, C. and Roberds, W. (2007). Transferability, Finality, and Debt Settlement, *Journal of Monetary Economics* 54, 955–978.

Katz, M. (2001). Network Effects, Interchange Fees, and No-Surcharge Rules in the Australian Credit and Charge Card Industry. Reform of Credit Card Schemes in Australia II, Reserve Bank of Australia, August.

Katz, M. (2012). Increasing Connectedness and Consumer Payments: An Overview. Conference on Consumer Payment Innovation in the Connected Age, Federal Reserve Bank of Kansas City, March.

Koivuniemi, E. and Kemppainen, K. (2007). On Costs of Payment Methods: A Survey of Recent Studies. Bank of Finland Working Paper.

Manning, M., Nier, E., and Schanz, J. (Eds.). (2009). *The Economics of Large-Value Payments and Settlement*. Oxford: Oxford University Press.

Norges Bank (Various Years). Annual Report on Payment Systems, Norway.

Payments Risk Committee (2012). Intraday Liquidity Flows. Federal Reserve Bank of New York, March 30.

Reserve Bank of Australia (2005). Common Benchmark for the Setting of Credit Card Interchange Fees, November, <http://www.rba.gov.au/.

Review of Network Economics (2005, 2006). 4(4) and 5(1).

Rochet, J-C. and Tirole, J. (2003). Platform Competition in Two-Sided Markets, *Journal of the European Economic Association* 1, 990–1029.

Rochet, J-C and Wright, J. (2010). Credit Card Interchange Fees, *Journal of Banking and Finance* 34, 1788–1797.

Schneider, F. (2005). Shadow Economies Around the World: What Do We Really Know?, *European Journal of Political Economy* 21, 598–642.

Schuh, S. and Stavins, J. (2010). Why Are (Some) Consumers (Finally) Writing Fewer Checks? The Role of Payment Characteristics, *Journal of Banking and Finance* 34, 1745–1758.

Shampine, A. (2007). Another Look at Payment Instrument Economics, *Review of Network Economics* 6, 495–508.

Simon, J., Smith, K., and West, T. (2010). Price Incentives and Consumer Payment Behaviour, *Journal of Banking and Finance* 34, 1745–1758.

Van Hove, L. (2006). Why Electronic Purses Should be Promoted, *Banking and Information Technology* 2, 20–31.

PART III

REGULATORY AND POLICY PERSPECTIVES

CHAPTER 18

....

CENTRAL BANKING*

....

MICHEL AGLIETTA AND BENOIT MOJON

18.1 INTRODUCTION

....

CENTRAL banks perform several tasks. They provide settlement services to high-value payments, oversee banks for the sake of financial stability, act as lenders of last resort, and implement monetary policy. These tasks and their mode of operation have been repeatedly redefined in order to resolve specific monetary and financial crises: all major stages in the shaping of central bank functions have been responses to monetary or financial crises. It is necessary to analyze these crises and their competing interpretations in order to understand the functions that central banks need to embody and implement for a monetary economy to prosper.

The genesis of central banks as bankers' banks took place in nineteenth-century England. Two opposing theoretical conceptions of money—the currency principle and the banking principle—implied radically different roles for central banks. For the former, strict convertibility of money into a "special commodity," of which the supply is independent of the government, is an insurance against the secular manipulation of the unit of account to raise an inflation tax. The role of the central bank is to enforce convertibility of its bills into gold, as the Bank of England was assigned to do in 1846. However, a repetition of liquidity crises in 1847, 1857, and 1866 demonstrated the need of flexibility in the supply of money.

Such flexibility is more consistent with the banking principle, whereby money is a debt that financial intermediaries endogenously issue as the counterpart to their credit operations. Yet if the means of payments are debts issued by competing banks, payments between banks call for high-powered money to settle inter-bank transactions. This is precisely the

* This text reflects the authors' opinions alone, not those of the Banque de France. We would like to thank Doug Evanoff, Philippe Moutot, and the editors for their comments and suggestions. All remaining errors are ours. Benoit Mojon worked on this text mainly while working at the Chicago Fed.

role of the money issued by the central bank, money that the sovereign designates as legal tender for all debts.

However, the trust of economic agents in central bank money cannot be imposed by law. It is essentially to preserve this trust that central banks have developed their functions. They supervise the banks to ensure the integrity of the payment system and prevent liquidity crises. In the event of liquidity crises, they stand ready to lend as a last resort. They conduct monetary policies to stabilize the unit of account and thereby provide a nominal anchor to the economy.

Section 18.2 explores the evolution of central bank attributes as a bankers' bank, relating them to the centralization of payments. Section 18.3 outlines how central banks have been committed to different monetary regimes from the gold standard to the present inflation targeting. It also points out the monetary doctrines underlying the different practices to deliver the nominal anchor that preserves trust in money. Finally, Section 18.4 explores some potential issues that may necessitate the continuing development of central banks in the twenty-first century.

18.2 The Centralization of Payments and the Emergence of Central Banks as Bankers' Banks

The idea of a central bank, that is, a bankers' bank, was slow to emerge in monetary thinking. It was an offshoot of devastating financial crises that became international in scope in the mid-nineteenth century. The expansion of industrial capitalism had intertwined credit networks, making contagion more virulent. In the crises of 1847, 1857, and 1866, the Bank Act of 1844, which had split the Bank of England into two departments—the issue and the banking departments—had to be de facto suspended, although no provision had been enacted to do so de jure. In contrast, the Banque de France had acknowledged responsibility to the financial system earlier. However, in 1868, when Crédit Mobilier was still recovering from the 1866 crisis, the Banque de France refused to discount its paper. The French central bank was involved in the rivalry between the Rothschilds and the Péreire Brothers, owners of Crédit Mobilier. By taking the side of the Rothschilds to preserve the privilege of the *Haute Banque* (merchant banks) against the emergence of modern commercial banking, the Banque de France failed to pursue the stability of the financial system as a whole in the circumstances, since this would have implied rescuing Crédit Mobilier.

The financial centers of the main European countries initially resented that the banks created to manage the public debt and to regulate currency should have superior status relative to other banks. Because bank money is a debt, it is the counterpart of credit. Because debts have to be settled in other forms of debts, there is a hierarchy of debts and, indeed, of the institutions that issue them. The central bank is the bank that issues the debt in which all other debts are settled. The hierarchy of the banking system whereby the central bank issues the high-powered money that can be used for the settlement of inter-bank debts appeared as a necessary condition for the integrity of the system of payments. The latter can allow means of payments issued as liabilities by competing commercial banks to coexist if three general rules are respected.

The first and foremost rule is the institution of the unit of account. In a decentralized market economy, market participants discover relative prices through nominal prices denominated in the unit of account. As long as it can be trusted over time, the monetary standard reduces transaction costs efficiently in avoiding offer prices to be announced in incompatible numéraires.

The second rule is that issued debts can be made eligible to means of payments, that is, debts can circulate amongst third parties to redeem other debts and buy commodities. In a developed market economy, producers necessarily incur debts because they must buy resources, not least the human resource (i.e., pay wages), before they can sell their products. The quality of being accepted by third parties is the liquidity of debts, which in turn depends on the financial strength and the reputation of the issuer. The selection and verification of the liquidity of debts make the financial system hierarchical. Banks are financial agents specialized in the issuance of the most liquid debts.

The third rule is the one that makes the verification of debt liquidity a social process: the settlement. It is the process by which payments are made final, that is, by which any kind of debt used as a means of payment in any private transaction proves that it can be transferred against a unanimously accepted form of money. Depending on the definition of the unit of account, the ultimate liquidity in a payment system can be a commodity minted by the sovereign (or a foreign currency), or it can be the liability of a financial institution empowered by society as a whole or by its highest political authority—the sovereign. This institution is a central bank. It has become the paramount monetary institution.

How do the rules make a monetary system? If the ultimate liquidity is the liability of the central bank, the unit of account is purely abstract.[1] It is the name given to the numerical unit of liability issued by the central bank. Such are the US dollar, the euro, the pound sterling, the yen, and the yuan, to cite the most important world currencies today. In that case all forms of money are issued as liabilities of a financial agent. The banking system is hierarchical. The central bank is the bankers' bank because its liability is the means of settlement of all commercial bank debts.

18.2.1 The Law of Reflux, Multilateral Clearing Systems, and the Emergence of Central Banks

Under free banking, that is, when there were no central banks, commercial banks could issue notes and open deposit accounts against their assets over and above their reserves of species. Notes and deposits were convertible on demand in gold coins. Convertibility (into gold or silver) was the rule that validated bank money. The law of reflux was the settlement mechanism whereby convertibility limited the issuance of competing bank monies. It saved the use of species, while, at the same time, it vetted the quality of bank issued notes. A free banking payment system without a central bank was conceivable as long as settlement in gold coins could be made viable. The law of reflux effectively centralized the relationships

---

[1] It was not so when the ultimate liquidity was minted into a commodity, let us say gold. Debts used as means of payments had to be redeemed in gold coins.

between inter-bank correspondents within multilateral clearing systems. The question arises of the modus operandi of the law of reflux, both historically and theoretically.

Historically, such a system was successful in Scotland in the late eighteenth century, because banks were few and highly capitalized. It also operated for a long time in the United States in the nineteenth century. Nevertheless, in the latter, free banking was evolving under acute tensions. Solving settlement crises induced the development of institutions called clearing houses. They were incomplete surrogates of central banks, as far as settlement issues were concerned.

Banks were competing to increase their market share in the discounting of trade bills, as a counterpart to which they issued bank notes. The law of reflux implied that a bank that issued too many notes would face a liquidity shortage when the redemption of excess notes at par would be exercised. Theoretically three mechanisms can be at work. First, the excess notes are immediately canceled when customers demand redemption in species and the bank loses an equal amount of reserves. Second, the note owners prefer to buy other banks' notes. Therefore those banks increase their claims on the issuing bank in the inter-bank market, that is, the exchange market for bank notes, which leads to a net settlement demand in species after clearing. The destruction of the excess notes arises via correspondent banks. Third, the notes remain active balances for future expenditures. In the latter case, a multiplier effect of payments arises and diffuses the excess issue on more banks, as long as more individuals buy the bank notes they prefer. However, the pressure to redeem the notes will eventually be exerted via the former mechanisms, by either public demand for species or bank clearing.

The law of reflux was the process emphasized by the Banking School to advocate regulation of the quality of money counterparts rather than the quantity of money. Since the law of reflux automatically restrained the banks from their loss of ultimate liquidity, the appropriate oversight was to check that banks discounted good assets. Only solvency might be problematic, while the interplay of the banks would assume the regulation of liquidity. In their own interest, banks would maintain a ratio of liquidity that balanced the marginal cost of relative illiquidity and the marginal gain of asset building. Reconstituting the optimal ratio of reserves to notes triggered an adjustment toward balance sheet equilibrium. The payment system was theoretically viable. Macroeconomically, the optimal amount of bank money was determined by the desired demand for species and the general level of prices in terms of gold, which was actually largely independent from the banking system.

Such a system had functioned without a central bank. However, central banks progressively emerged as banks for banks in order to remedy two essential limits of self-organized, non-hierarchical payment systems.

First, the law of reflux with 100% redemption in specie on a bilateral basis is a straitjacket that becomes incompatible with the needs of trade in a growing market economy. The monetary system was under various form of stress when the law of reflux failed to discipline a bank.

In the case where bank notes dominate, the failing banks suffer a discount in the value of the notes they issued. The consequence is a fragmented payment system levying crippling information costs on the economy. People always wondered in which bank money they should have their income paid, with self-fulfilling prophecies often destroying many banks in time of stress. The payment system was plagued by recurring runs on weak banks with contagion creating bank panics.

The case where checkable deposit accounts dominate is different because the means of payments (the checks) are dissociated from the liquidity registered on the account. This form of money became prevalent in the second half of the nineteenth century, when banking business went beyond discounting trade bills to meet the financing needs of industrial capitalism. Banks became intermediaries. On the asset side, they made illiquid credit requiring investment in specific information whose quality depositors were not able to assess. On the liability side, they offered non-marketable deposits combined with the provision of payment services. This asymmetric information structure, coupled with network effects in the payment system, implied that valuing deposits at par in unit of accounts and securing their convertibility at par into the base currency (e.g., into gold coins) made the most efficient contract.

However, in contrast with the mechanisms whereby bank notes dominated payment systems, pricing bank money in a crisis became impossible. The law of reflux could not work without an innovation in the technology of payments that allows a drastic saving of species. This innovation was the multilateral clearing system. It *ipso facto* differentiated the community of banks because some banks become clearing houses.

A clearing house is a centralized organization that introduces collective rationality into payment systems. Clearing houses appeared in the leading business centers of the United States in the midst of the free banking era (1838–1863). Free banking developed after the Second Bank of the US lost its federal charter in 1836. [2] It ended in 1863 while the civil war was raging, when the huge increase of liquidity needs induced the creation of the Comptroller of the Currency to regulate the quality of money. Clearing and settlement of the banks that were members of the system were made on the books of clearing houses. Clearing houses issued settlement certificates on behalf of their members who deposited reserves with them. Multilateral clearing and net settlement saved a huge amount of specie and reduced the cost of check collection.

Moreover, clearing houses managed to insulate the execution of payments at the time of liquidity stringency by suspending convertibility into species. As Goodfriend (1988) pointed out, they acted as de facto surrogates of central banks. The higher status of settlement money gave the clearing houses hierarchical authority over their members. The responsibility of preserving the integrity of payments among the club of retail banks led the clearing houses to guarantee the irrevocability of payments in return for the banks' compliance with restrictive obligations. The system of the Suffolk Bank in Boston, Massachusetts, was the first to reach such a degree of centralization while it was evolving between 1825 and 1861.

The second limit that required the emergence of central banks appeared in the incapacity the of the large banks that acted as clearing houses to separate their profit maximization objectives from the interest of the community of banks participating in the clearing houses. In addition, in the case of the United States, the clearing houses did not protect non-member banks that were located outside large financial centers from liquidity crises.

The National Bank Act of 1863 aimed at homogenizing the quality of money by instituting a Comptroller of the Currency and granting national charter to banks that respected

---

[2] The Second Bank was granted a charter in 1818 after the expiration of the First Bank of the United States. It was closed by President Andrew Jackson, who accused the bank of political corruption and fraud. Jacksonian democracy, which leaned toward libertarian policies, favored free banking.

stipulated obligations. Despite the extension of regional clearing houses, the US payment system remained vulnerable to bank panics until the paroxysm of the 1907 crisis. The financial debacle persuaded Congress to undertake a radical reform to provide the country with a single institution capable of securing the payment system under a dual mandate: supplying elastically unique settlement money and assuming the responsibility of a lender of last resort. In countries where a government-sponsored bank already existed for a long time or had been enacted in the wake of political unification (such as in Germany and Italy), they took over the role of clearing houses more smoothly. In England and France, the former bank of the sovereign already played a special role in the banking system and this role evolved, in spite of the financial community's resistance, to the one of bankers' bank.

18.2.2 Central Banks and the Regulation of Payment Systems in Tranquil Times

Since its emergence as the bankers' bank, the central bank is the institution at the heart of payment systems. It safeguards settlement, prevents systemic failures against operational risks ($50 billion of liquidity was injected a single day in November 1985 to offset the destruction of liquidity owing to a computer breakdown at the Bank of New York), and imposes safety rules on banks that are members of high-value payment systems.

Commercial banks may pertain to different clearing systems linked to retail payments or payments of securities and other financial transactions (including the national currency leg of foreign exchange transactions). But the balances resulting from those payment services contribute to build inter-bank positions. They must register on the books of the central bank for multilateral clearing and settlement in central bank money. To honor their settlement obligations, banks with net negative positions must secure central bank money by all means available before settlement time, depending on the technique of settlement (net end-of-day, or gross in real time). They can draw on their reserve account at the central bank, borrow overnight money from surplus banks, or use repo facilities with the central bank against eligible collateral. All those devices connect the central bank to the channels of liquidity provision to the whole banking system. From this unique position, the central bank can draw superior information on the situations of banks regarding liquidity ease or stringency. They can detect anomalies in the inter-bank market, as they did on August 9, 2007 when they observed a spike in overnight interest rates.

In the last 30 years or so, payment flows generated by financial transactions have swelled ominously. High-value payments concentrate risks that have a strong likelihood of becoming systemic. As a result, central banks have reformed inter-bank payment systems to deal with credit and liquidity risks in order to guarantee final settlement, that is, the irrevocability of the payment for the beneficiaries whatever the situation of the payers. The central bank, which is the only player that can do so, guarantees unconditionally the payments it settles.

The path towards centralization of payments goes on unabated with the creation of a wider range of private means of payments, such as the increasing role of credit cards. Contrary to popular opinion, innovation in payment systems does not undermine central bank leadership in the control of money. It reinforces central bank power because more complex payments, ever larger volumes and shorter lead times increase systemic risk. Such risk in payment systems threatens trust in money at its most fundamental level. Therefore the integrity of payment systems is much more than a merely technical issue. It must be seen as part of the broader objective of financial stability and the sustainability of the financial system.

18.2.3 The Central Bank in Stressful Times: The Lender of Last Resort

Lending in last resort has been pinpointed as the gist of the art of central banking. This is not a new concept—it has long been recognized as such. As early as 1802, Thornton had highlighted the responsibility of the Bank of England in supplying liquidity to sound banks in time of panic. But there was no follow-up to his advice. Recurring panics arose with ever more devastating outcomes. The Banking Act of 1844 worsened financial crises in making it harder for the Bank of England to issue notes while losing gold reserves. De facto, the Bank Act was overruled with the suspension of convertibility in 1847, 1857, and 1866, without any complementary legislation. It permitted the Bank of England's banking department to expand its loans over the limit fixed by the gold stock in the issue department. But the easing in money markets was too little too late. This unsatisfactory state of affairs prompted Bagehot (1873) to elaborate his doctrine that is defined below.

Indeed lending in last resort is an extraordinary operation that violates market rules. It is a unilateral and discretionary decision to provide potentially unlimited amounts of the ultimate means of payment/settlement to the money markets. It escapes market contracts and is therefore an act of sovereignty that keeps afloat debtors who otherwise would have failed to settle their debts. This operation allows other perfectly sound liabilities to perpetuate, whereas they would have been destroyed by the spillover of the failed debts. Therefore the economic impact of lender of last resort interventions is ambivalent. On the one hand, it forestalls systemic risk, because the social cost of letting insolvency spread is higher than the private cost of the original failure. On the other hand, it can induce moral hazard if it strengthens reckless behavior against which it provides collective insurance. The purpose of Bagehot's principles and prescriptions was to stop contagion while keeping moral hazard at bay.

According to Bagehot, the lender of last resort is concerned about the overall stability of the financial system, not by the fate of any particular financial firm. It must lend without limit to solvent but illiquid firms, who cannot borrow in the market because the mistrust of potential lenders dries up liquidity. Insolvent institutions must be sold to new owners for what they are worth. However, these objectives require operational principles to distinguish intrinsic insolvency from threats of failure due to liquidity stringency.

Bagehot (1873) proposed as a distinctive criterion the quality of the collateral presented by borrowers. The central bank should accept the collateral and evaluate the solvency of banks at pre-crisis value. Furthermore, to better safeguard against moral hazard, Bagehot insisted that the central bank should lend at punitive rates. This disposition would be both a risk premium for the central bank and a deterrent for borrowers. Finally, central bank interventions in last resort should be made unpredictable. This is the constructive ambiguity that central bankers are fond of. It is an attribute of the radical discretion that is the essence of sovereignty.

Nowadays banks have to comply with capital regulation and accept the ongoing supervision of activity by either the central bank or an independent supervisory authority. These requirements are counterparts of the "insurance" that the central bank would provide, as a lender of last resort, to insulate banks that have not taken excessive risks from crises that threaten the integrity of payments.

Failure to lend in last resort can have the most dramatic consequences. A prominent example is the Great Depression. The Wall Street crash of October 1929 had led to a scramble for liquidity. By the year end the deflation in equity prices had been communicated to primary commodities and durable goods industries. The Federal Reserve lowered the discount rate from 6% in August 1929 to 2.5% in June 1930. But the money stock continued to shrink unabated. According to Friedman and Schwartz (1963), it should have undertaken blanket open-market operations to avoid the seizure of the credit markets. After mid-1930, the financial crisis changed in nature and in magnitude. Three waves of extended bank failures, one every year, wrecked the banking system completely, leading to the Bank Holiday in March 1933. A drastic change in regulation severed commercial banks from financial markets.

With the comeback of financial crises in deregulated financial systems, the lender of last resort has returned to fashion since the Penn Central failure in the US in 1970 and the secondary banking crisis in the UK in 1972. Since that time there have been innumerable banking and financial market crises worldwide that have solicited the interventions of central banks in last resort. There has been a diversification of such central bank interventions, ranging from securing the payment systems to, in recent history, spectacular interventions by the Federal Reserve System to restore confidence or attempt to limit the chances of financial crises before they occur.

Innovation in last resort lending has been spectacularly pursued since August 2007 after a global credit crisis in securitized markets struck, following and propagating a surge of insolvency in the US subprime mortgage market, the bankruptcy of Lehman Brothers in September 2008 and the euro sovereign debt crisis since mid-2010. The most striking common feature of interventions of last resort since 2007 has been the increase of central banks balance sheets, which have increased by a factor of three in the US, the euro area, Japan, and the UK. For instance, the Fed balance sheet has increased from $891 billion in December 2007 to $2,311 billion in December 2008 and the ECB balance sheet also increased from €1,286 billion to €2,089 billion over the same period.

During the first stage of the crisis, this increase in the supply of central bank money has supported banks as well as some emblematic non-depository institutions either directly in the form of loans by the central bank to banks, or via open-market operations, including, in some cases the support of depressed assets. It is only later, as we will see shortly, that it increased for supporting asset prices through quantitative easing.

The Fed set up a number of new facilities to address the new developments of the financial strain. Some involved marginal adjustments. The Term Auction Facility introduced in December 2007 consisted just of avoiding the stigma that plagued the discount window. Others were more radical, such as the decision to support individual institutions such as AIG, only two days after having decided to let Lehman fail, in September 2008, or extending a $300 billion non-recourse loan to Citigroup in November 2008, or authorizing non-depository institutions such as Goldman Sachs, Morgan Stanley and American Express to become banks overnight so that they could access the Fed provision of liquidity. Specific markets were also targeted. Money Market mutual funds, also in September 2008, were offered an implicit guarantee to counter a run after one counterparty fund of Lehman broke the buck. And the commercial paper market saw a massive purchase by the Fed in October 2008 with a capital guarantee of the Treasury.

Last but not least, as rolling over short-term financing in dollars had become close to impossible, the Fed extended swap agreements with no less than 14 central banks, including the European Central Bank, the Bank of Japan, and the Bank of England, so that they could facilitate the unfolding of dollar funding of the structured finance set up by their domestic counterparties.

In the US, strict lending in last resort came to an end in 2009. The volume of transactions on the inter-bank market then resumed between private banks. In contrast, the ECB allocation of liquidity at will to banks, at fixed price, which started in October 2008, is still ongoing. In May 2013, the governing council committed to expand this fixed-rate full allotment mode of liquidity supply until at least June 2014 and many expect it to be further extended still.

The ECB also undertook two other new forms of lending in last resort. First, it has extended the maturity of its liquidity loans to banks. It offered three 12-month Very Long Term Refinancing Operations (VLTRO) in June, September, and December 2009, and two 36-month VLTROs in December 2011 and February 2012. Second, the ECB intervened on distressed sovereign debt markets in 2010 for Greece, Ireland, and Portugal, and in 2011 for Italy and Spain. Also related to distressed sovereign debt, it issued a conditional insurance to support the public debt of maturity between one and three years, should a country wish to have her support.

The Lehman financial crisis led major central banks to take a number of unprecedented steps to tame the financial turmoil. Central banks worldwide have extended their lending facilities and widened the range of collateral they accept. They modified their lending facility to fixed-rate tenders with full allotment. They substituted the decentralized money markets that ceased to function by providing liquidity to banks on a bilateral basis. In these processes, they took onto their balance sheet larger and larger amounts of risky assets.

This unprecedented asset structure implies a credit risk that may make the central bank technically insolvent, and therefore at the mercy of the fiscal authority.

Central banks have also repeatedly coordinated their crisis management actions (lowering interest rates together on October 8, 2008, extending the maturity of their liquidity provision, setting up currency swaps to extend the provision of dollars outside the US, etc.). This coordination of "lender of last resort" operations is however not new. Financial markets are typically integrated internationally and more typically so in times of financial stress. In the current crisis, the banks' distress has occurred or spread across major financial markets at each and every stage of the crisis. This echoes, for instance, the 1907 crisis resolution when the Banque de France lent gold to the Bank of England to allow her to provide enough emergency liquidity to the US banking system. While not new, this emphasizes once more that the contagious nature of financial crises eventually requires the coordination of central banks in crisis management.

Last but not least, they slashed interest rates in order to facilitate the deleveraging process now engaged by financial intermediaries, households, and firms. It is meant to avoid credit crunches in the downward stages of financial cycles. It was spectacular both after the turning point of the real estate bubble in 1991–1993 and the stock market bubble in 2001–2003. In both cases, US short-term interest rates were driven much lower and for much longer than the easing in monetary policy that would have been warranted by the arbitrage between the medium-run objectives of anchoring inflation expectations and of keeping economic activity close to potential. The stance of monetary policy was motivated by concern about the macroeconomic impact of financial distress. Risk management was then the primary objective of US monetary policy. Turning to the 2007–2009 crisis, it is too early to assess the effectiveness of the changes in monetary policy stance on economic activity.

Our inquiry into central bank policy as a bankers' bank leads to monetary policy. It highlights the consistency in all aspects of central bank behavior due to its pivotal position in the monetary system. The roundabout dynamic between credit expansion and asset price appreciation in global financial systems entails a macroeconomic risk that is both endogenous and procyclical. The central bank is the sole institution able to handle it.

18.3 Nominal Anchor and Monetary Policy

The most well-known function of central banks is to conduct monetary policy. The objectives of monetary policy can include price stability, sustainable growth of output, full employment, and financial stability. The monetary policy legal mandates of central banks may specify that price stability is the primary objective (1992 Maastricht Treaty for the European Central Bank), or that sustainable growth is a side benefit of price stability, but they do not always do so (as in the case of the 1913 United States Federal Reserve Bank Act).

The monetary policy function of central banks relates directly to the unit of account attribute of monies. Economic agents engage in current and intertemporal exchanges at nominal prices, that is, at prices expressed in terms of the unit of account. Monetary policy therefore consists of issuing money in a quantity that would stabilize the value of the unit of account, hence avoiding both inflation and deflation of the general price level. The central banks aim to provide a nominal anchor for economic agents to set prices in their current and planned transactions.

Monetary policy has also evolved with major innovations in the technology of payments and of financial instruments more generally. This evolution started centuries before the emergence of central banks as the institutions in charge of monetary policies. The main distinctions in monetary systems, as far as the determination of the unit of account is concerned, lie between metallic standards and fiat money.

However a vast majority of central banks enforce convertibility into the currency that is central to a region or to the world. It is therefore essential to make a distinction between the central banks that dominate the international monetary system and the vast majority of central banks on the periphery. For central banks at the periphery, the value of the currency remains largely defined in terms of an external object over which the central bank has little control. Nonetheless they peg against standards that are not fixed benchmarks. The pound sterling, the US dollar, the euro, or the basket of currencies chosen to peg the domestic currency against may change value similarly, although for entirely different reasons, as precious metals have at the time of the gold standard and earlier. Hence, the value of the domestic currency hinges on the country's ability to maintain enough reserves in the center's currencies to sustain the credibility of the peg.

18.3.1 Control of the Unit of Account in Earlier Times/Under Metallic Standards

For centuries Europe's monies worked under dualist systems. Units of account were separated from coins in use. Defined in old coins that are no longer circulated, they became abstract units. Dualist systems were established in which the sovereign could change the value of the unit of account in terms of the galaxy of coins without having to alter the latter.[3] Whenever the king devalued the unit of account, he increased the purchasing power of the coins in use, because prices were slow to adjust. He did so to increase the money supply, but also to alleviate the burden of the public debt that was denominated in the unit of account. Monetary conditions were highly dependent on the availability of metal.[4]

In the seventeenth century, the Nation States' eagerness to build large-scale factories required the immobilization of savings in long-run investments. However, when the unit of account was depreciated, hoarders of species gained at the expense of creditors holding nominal claims. In England, the silversmiths speculated on the recurrent devaluations of the pound sterling and on the debasement of species. They aggravated the monetary chaos by exporting the best coins. The Orange Revolution of 1688 promoted a drastic change spurred on by the need to finance the War of the Spanish Succession. In 1694 the merchants created the Bank of England and lent its entire capital of £1.2 million to the king. In return the bank was granted the right to discount bills and issue notes that later became legal tender.

However, in 1694–1695, an inflationary spike was a bad omen for the acceptance of the Bank of England's notes. A hot debate raged about the means to restore the trust in money. On one side, Chancellor Lowndes advocated another devaluation of Sterling. On the other side, Locke pleaded for a complete revamp of coinage, which would entail getting rid of debased species entirely. This deflationary solution was finally accepted by the king. It resulted in a terrible recession in 1697–1698 and triggered a huge loss for the Crown. Nonetheless the chosen ratio of gold to silver was 15:9 against 15 in Continental Europe. It attracted species from abroad and put the newly founded United Kingdom on a de facto gold standard. The dualist system was replaced by the convertibility rule that was only suspended during the wars against France, starting in 1797 and lasting beyond the Vienna Treaty of 1815, to the complete monetary recovery in 1821.

The gold standard became an international monetary order much later. Meanwhile gold and silver coexisted as long as Central Europe was on silver and France was the bimetallic center of the system. It was not until 1871 that the new German Empire adopted the gold

---

[3] In France the "*livre tournois*" dates back to Charlemagne, around ad 800. In Great Britain the pound sterling originates in a Norman silver penny brought in with the conquest of 1066.

[4] For instance, the dualist system worked to mitigate the destructive forces of deflation in the terrible era that encompassed 150 years from the Black Death of 1348 to the end of the fifteenth century. However, in the sixteenth century, the inflow of silver from the Potosi in Peru launched a long inflation exacerbated by the manipulation of the units of accounts that the sovereigns indulged in their rivalries for the supremacy in Europe.

standard. Not long after, France decided to abandon silver coinage and the United States to redeem the greenbacks issued in the Civil War in gold. In 1880 the world was on the gold standard.

The international monetary stability that prevailed until World War I is another example of the importance of hierarchy in payment systems, though this time at the international level, with a central role for the Bank of England. The gold standard was in essence a key currency system legitimated by gold convertibility. Sterling bills of exchange were the universal means of payment in international trade, while long-run capital exports from the City were negatively correlated with investment cycles in the UK. Since the rule of convertibility was considered everywhere as an intangible common good over national policy objectives, short-run capital flows were stabilizing. Banks all over the world held deposits in London because they discounted sterling bills and received sterling payments. Therefore sterling was *primus inter pares*. In handling its rate to keep the ratio of gold reserves to notes close to the required level, the Bank of England *ipso facto* regulated international liquidity because all other countries kept their exchange rates against sterling within gold points.

The working of convertibility was so entrenched in the minds of people that trust in the nominal value of contracts was never shattered. In times of stress, such as the Baring crisis of 1890 and the crisis of 1907, ad hoc cooperation between the Banque de France and the Bank of England, in the form of gold loans by the former to the latter, helped to build up international rescues that retrieved confidence.

The City of London centralized the market for international bills of exchange. The bank rate had a paramount influence on other countries via the discount houses in London. It is why the financial conditions in London summed up the degree of tightness in world liquidity. Liquid balances of foreign banks in London were highly sensitive to bank rates. The latter triggered stabilizing capital flows and synchronized the business cycle.

18.3.2 Monetary Policy Implementation in Purely Fiat Monetary Systems

The implementation of monetary policy since World War II is fundamentally different in the sense that money has effectively lost its physical, metallic reference. The high-powered money issued by the central bank has become purely fiat with the suspension of convertibility of dollars into gold in 1971. However, even before 1971, the convertibility into gold has had only a very marginal role in the conduct of monetary policies. The gold standard had been replaced by a gold exchange standard in the 1930s. Under the exchange standard, only monetary authorities could exchange gold for currencies among themselves. The system was put under pressure in the 1960s as financial markets became progressively convinced that the US treasury could not sustain an artificially low peg of dollars into gold. Bickering arose on both sides of the Atlantic while European central banks had begun accumulating excess dollar reserves. In 1965, president de Gaulle of France accused the US of buying French assets cheaply and ordered the Banque de France to sell dollar reserves against Fort Knox gold at the official rate of $35 an ounce.

The growing abstraction of money takes the form of new means of payments and savings instruments that become nearly as liquid as the more traditional deposits that are used for payments. These evolutions led to the definition and measurement of several monetary aggregates (e.g., M1, M2, and M3). This multiplication of operational definitions of money reflects the increasing difficulty of identifying the relevant set of financial instruments that best reflect the liquidity available in the economy.

18.3.2.1 *Monetary Policy Doctrines*

Monetary policy, concerned with the money supply and the value of the unit of account, has always been the object of intense debates among economists and commentators of public policies. Throughout history, the main axis of division in this debate opposes those who consider that money is essentially exogenous and to those who consider it essentially endogenous. For the former, discretion in the supply of money should be avoided because it tends to be used by the political power to raise an inflation tax that spoils the people and destabilizes the economy. For the latter, rules imposed on the money supply, such as strict convertibility into species in metallic standards or quantity of money in fiat monetary systems, lack the flexibility to accommodate changes in the money demand needed for the economy's growth. Interestingly, the doctrine underlying the current consensus that dominates the conceptualization of monetary policy, of which a prominent example is inflation targeting, claims that it strikes a balance between rules and discretion (Bernanke and Mishkin, 1997; Woodford, 2003; Goodfriend, 2007).

The quantity theory of money is a milestone of the debate on monetary policy. First expressed by Cantillon (1755) and Hume (1752), the quantity theory implies that increases in the supply of money are eventually reflected in higher prices with no effects on output. An important consequence of the quantity theory is that monetary policy should strictly focus on price stabilization because in any case, manipulating the money supply can only affect prices. In line with the quantity theory, the Currency School of nineteenth-century England considered that only strict convertibility of bank notes into gold would prevent over-issuance of notes and inflation. A century later, while the straitjacket of strict convertibility into gold was no longer an essential feature of the monetary system, Milton Friedman and other monetarists argued that the supply of money should follow strict rules, for example, increase the money supply at a pre-announced, k-percent rate. Authorities should not use monetary policy to fine tune the business cycle, because, although money was not neutral in the short run, the transmission from changes in the money stock to output and prices "took long and variable lags." As a result, fine-tuning policies paradoxically risked introducing volatility, in complete opposition to their objective.

These views have been opposed by economists who believe that the money stock is evolving endogenously in response to changes in the liquidity needs of the economy. An important consequence of the endogenous character of money implies that strict rules on the money supply can abruptly curtail transactions and growth if conditions that determine the demand of money are changing. Monetary policy authorities should therefore have discretion in supplying liquidity.

To start with, the Banking School advocates considered that the bank notes in circulation were secured by their counterparts on the asset side of a bank's balance sheet. The law of reflux would warrant that, as credit (at the time Merchant's bills) was reimbursed to banks with bank notes, over-issuance was prevented. In addition, the major flaw of strict convertibility lay in the mismatch between the amount of money needed for economic growth and the stock of metal available for minting money. With neither flexible nominal prices nor rapidly adjusting velocity of money, the nineteenth century saw a repetition of monetary crises where the shortage of metal limited the expansion of output. These crises pointed to the need to free up money supply from the restraints of strict convertibility.

Wicksell (1907, 1935) is the first to introduce the notion that the supply of money should depend on the rhythm at which production capacity grows. The money interest rate, set by the monetary authority, ought to be equal to the real interest rate, which itself reflects the expected return on newly produced capital goods. This approach of monetary policy can avoid both overexpansion of money, credit, and, henceforth, inflation, and a contraction of credit and deflation. The central bank should accommodate the private sector demand for liquidity at the chosen level of money interest rate. It is easy to understand that, in this conceptual framework, non-contingent rules of money supply turn out to be destabilizing because the real rate can change over time with economic circumstances.

However, it took another two major monetary crises, in the 1930s and in the 1970s before the Wicksellian approach became the dominant monetary policy doctrine. The notion that monetary policy (as well as fiscal policy) should be articulated in order to stabilize the business cycle became popular largely because of the trauma of the 1930s Great Depression and its interpretation by Keynes.[5] From World War II to the mid-1970s the common wisdom had been that monetary policy (and fiscal policy) may have to stimulate demand and let inflation increase, so that real wages would permit full employment. In the event of a slowdown of the business cycle, monetary and fiscal policies should stabilize output by exploiting the tradeoff between inflation and unemployment (what became known as the Philips curve).

However, the experience of the 1970s Great Inflation discarded the fine-tuning policies of Keynesian inspiration. Besides, in spite of their success in stabilizing inflation in Germany and Switzerland, monetarist approaches (e.g., targeting a fixed rate of growth for money aggregates) appeared difficult to generalize because of the instability of money demand.

On the conceptual front, the increasing importance of expectation formation in the analysis of macroeconomic policies led the Rational Expectation School to argue that monetary policy may actually be neutral even in the short run. Kydland and Prescott (1977) demonstrated that, as long as agents believe that the central bank would try to exploit an inflation–unemployment tradeoff, the economy would converge to higher inflation because the expectation of eventual stimulating monetary policy would induce higher wages and prices, in order for agents to preserve their purchasing power. Issues with the credibility of the central bank's anti-inflation commitment led economists and policymakers to consider that independence of central banks from governments could be desirable. However, this independence, which freed central banks from the influence of elected governments, also called for the development of monetary policy frameworks that would enhance their accountability.

These considerations led to a new consensus of monetary policymaking, whose ingredients include a credible commitment to low inflation, adequate flexibility of the money supply in the pursuit of this objective, and an effort toward transparency in the communication

---

[5] Keynes' interpretation of the Great Depression was exactly opposite to the one of the monetarist. He stressed in particular that, beyond a certain threshold, increasing the money supply would have no effect on the level of interest rates (the liquidity trap). His policy recommendation was instead to manage demand through active fiscal policy.

of monetary policy decisions. This consensus is exemplified by, but not exclusive to, inflation targeting.

An inflation-targeting central bank announces a target level for inflation and engineers the monetary policy that would drive inflation near this level. The inflation target is either a point or a range that sets a low and positive level of inflation for a given consumer price index, and the horizons vary, across countries, from a couple of years to the business cycle or indefinitely. This pre-announcement helps anchor inflation expectations and provides a benchmark against which the central bank can be held accountable.

Inflation targeting has been portrayed as a compromise between rules and discretion. Bernanke and Mishkin (1997) actually used the term "constrained discretion" to describe the monetary policy strategy of inflation targeting. They argue that commitment of the central bank to keep inflation near a pre-announced inflation target provides a nominal anchor for economic agents. The latter can therefore engage in nominal contracts even at relatively long horizons, for example, a mortgage interest rate, with a fair assessment of the real purchasing power of future flows of income and payments. The inflation target is also a benchmark to evaluate the monetary policy performance of the central bank. It is a discipline device that should prevent, and so far that has prevented, the inflation bias allegedly inherent to unconstrained discretion in the conduct of monetary policy.

However, an inflation target does not provide prescriptions for the money supply. The latter has to be decided by the central bank with the aim of keeping inflation close to its target. A good framework to analyze such monetary policy decisions is to consider a benchmark interest rate rule, whereby the central bank increases the real interest rate proportionally to deviations of inflation from the inflation target in order to weigh up effective aggregate demand and bring inflation back to the target. Likewise, one can conceive that the central bank should increase the interest rate when it observes tensions on prices, as measured, for instance by an output gap, that is, the demand–supply gap. Taylor (1993) has actually showed that a contingent interest rate rule such that the real interest rate increases equally with respect to inflation and to the output gap provided a good model of effective monetary policy in the US. This framework is also fully consistent to a Wicksellian approach to monetary policy, where the central bank sets its monetary instrument, the interest rate, in reference to a neutral interest rate (Woodford, 2003).

Such lean "against the wind" state contingent policy rules provide benchmarks to evaluate the stance of monetary policy by comparing the interest rate to a contingent hypothetical rate that is fully consistent with the aim to bring inflation back to its official target level. Moreover, interest rules that depend on the output gap, and conceivably other indicators of tensions on prices, can indicate whether the current stance of monetary policy tends to counteract these tensions or, on the contrary, accommodate them (Woodford, 2003).

However, inflation targeting is better described by a framework for the conduct of policy than by a strict rule. For one, inflation targets are often defined as ranges and it is generally understood that point targets are indicative of the region where inflation should be, approximately. Inflation can be expected to be close to the target, on average on the business cycle and as close as possible to the target, but it can deviate temporarily because of specific supply shocks, for instance to energy or food prices. In addition, inflation targeting does not provide a strict operational rule (Goodfriend, 2007). The central bank can adjust the stance of monetary policy and the rate of growth in the money stock to accommodate either changes in the velocity of money or unexpected shocks that could harm the other objectives of monetary policy, such as stabilizing output and employment at their maximal non-inflationary levels. Finally, the central bank ought to acknowledge the uncertainty of the environment in which it operates. This uncertainty may entail temporary deviations of the monetary policy stance from the one required under a baseline scenario to prevent the risks of less likely outcome, typically a crisis on financial markets, the occurrence of which would imply prolonged economic unrest. This risk management approach to monetary policy, which has been formulated by Alan Greenspan (2004), has been particularly useful to describe the reaction of monetary policies to changes in the economic outlook that are outside the scope of standard macroeconomic models. In particular, the financial crises that we discussed in the previous section led central banks to alter the path of interest rates to restore confidence on financial markets. The risk management doctrine was effectively implemented only toward the loosening of monetary policy stance in times of financial stress and never to defend a tightening path in times of financial exuberance.

The new monetary policy consensus looked successful insofar as muting inflation did not entail higher variability of output and employment for some time.[6] The reason lay in the very success of the flexible target inflation doctrine, which delivered both stable prices and stable growth—the so called Great Moderation. The neo-Keynesian model that underpinned this achievement hardly gave attention to financial developments. The Great Moderation of inflation and output fluctuations between the mid-1980s and the mid-2000s reinforced the perception that the focus of monetary policy on securing price stability was a necessary and sufficient condition of macroeconomic stability. Financial asset bubbles might happen, but it was enough to countervail the subsequent disturbances in reducing the interest rate more than the indication of the Taylor rule to stem the disturbances induced by the bust that followed the bubble. The apparent success of Greenspan's risk management doctrine superimposed to the Wicksellian view of endogenous money embodied in the neo-Keynesian model entailed a complacent view that a new economy had emerged, whereby the business cycle had been tamed and financial disturbances were taken care of by the financial markets themselves.

This contention proved to be massively wrong. The huge global crisis bursting out in August 2007 and still lingering in 2014 has blatantly shown the failure of the risk management approach worked out by Alan Greenspan. In recommending a hands-off approach in the upward phase of asset price rise and setting a floor under plummeting prices after bubbles had burst, he created a huge moral hazard. Contrary to the hypothesis that finance was self-regulating whenever shocks occurred, deregulated financial markets proved to be intrinsically unstable, as Minsky (1986) stated, following Keynes's view on coordination failures induced by uncertainty that can spill over into systemic crises.

The impact on central banks of the apex of the financial crisis in September–October 2008 was dramatic. So large and widespread were the losses in credit markets that inter-bank transactions froze entirely, threatening to paralyze the flow of international trade. The extent of capital depreciation was so severe that the return on capital, and therefore the natural interest rate, turned negative. It follows that the conduct of monetary policy according to the Wicksellian framework entailed, in view of the relatively low levels if inflation targets,

[6] For instance, the Bank of England announced an inflation target of 2.5% in 1992. UK inflation was brought from 5% in 1991 to 2% in 1993 and close to its 2.5% target since then.

a negative nominal interest rate. But the latter ends up being difficult to deliver when investors can turn to cash. The central banks lowered their leading rate to zero, the lowest possible level. This is the zero lower bound. Because at that rate, the opportunity cost of holding money falls to zero, money and short-term assets become perfect substitutes, so that the demand for money becomes extremely unstable. Facing this unusual constraint, central banks had to devise non-conventional means of keeping monetary policy active. They tried, and largely succeeded, to influence long-term interest rates via their components: the expectation of future short-term rates with the so-called forward guidance and the term premium with targeted asset purchases. In the last section of this chapter we will spell out the intricate problems related to non-conventional policies, both for the exiting of such policies and for the future, as far as financial stability is entitled to become an objective of monetary policy in its own right.

18.3.2.2 *Instruments of Monetary Policy*

Central banks mainly use three instruments to influence the pace of money creation in the economy. Reserve requirements are the first type of instrument. By law, central banks stipulate that banks keep a fraction of their balance sheets (typically a specified money aggregate) in reserve at their account at the central bank. The reserve requirement ratio can be used to affect the cost of issuing deposits.[7] Given that the central banks often choose to pay no or a low interest rate on the reserve, the cost of issuing any liability subject to reserve is directly affected by the level of reserve and their opportunity cost.

The second type of monetary policy instruments are standing facilities (also called discount windows) for banks to obtain liquidity in a bilateral transaction with the central bank. The interest rate of these transactions is typically called the discount rate. This rate can be superior to the money market interest rate so that these standing facilities are essentially insurance in case of unforeseen liquidity shortages. However, the discount window has been, and still can be, the foremost channel of central bank liquidity to the banking sector in countries where decentralized money markets are not mature.

The last major instrument of monetary policy is open market operations. These operations take different forms. The European Central Bank organizes regular auctions where it provides reserve at a target interest rate. The Federal Reserve directly purchases and sells public sector securities against central bank money in order to achieve a certain overnight interest rate.

These three instruments are used to varying degrees to control money supply. However, open market operations are not usually described in terms of the interest rate they are meant to achieve, rather than in terms of the resulting level of monetary aggregates. One reason for this development is that the unpredictable rhythm of financial innovation alters the link between money growth and inflation. Another is that the control of monetary aggregates may require volatile short-term interest rates, as experienced in the US between 1979 and

---

[7] A prominent example of such implementation of monetary policy is the ongoing increase of required reserve ratio in mainland China. The People's Bank of China increased its reserve requirement ratio nearly every month in 2007 in order to contain the expansion of credit and deposit, while, at the same time limiting increases in interest rates.

1982. And, targeting larger monetary aggregates, while less conducive to financial instability, largely reflect the evolution of deposits, on which the central bank has a much looser grip.

Effectively, the level of the target interest rate has progressively become the dominant operational instrument of monetary policy. While the amount of liquidity exchanged by central banks is relatively small in comparison with the overall amounts of debt securities, the monopoly of the central bank over the supply of monetary base guarantees that the overnight interest rate rarely deviates from the target interest rate of the central bank for more than a day. Hence, at the frequency that is relevant for production, consumption and financial planning, that is, over months or years, the central bank does control the level of short-term interest rates. Moreover, because this control of the cost of liquidity is ongoing, the central bank both controls the short end of the yield curve and influences the full maturity spectrum through the market expectations of future short-term rates.

Central banks therefore need to pick a level for this interest rate and explain the reason for this choice to market participants and the economic agents at large. The conceptual framework used to decide on the level of short-term interest rate and the supply of central bank money is precisely the object of the monetary doctrines discussed above.

The 15 years before the financial crisis saw a large convergence in the conduct of monetary policy. Explicit inflation targeting was first introduced in New Zealand, Canada, the UK, and Sweden in the early 1990s. More than 20 countries have adopted it since (see Crowe and Meade, 2007, for a list). The European Central Bank which conducts monetary policy for 17 European countries, has a quantified inflation objective that has a level close to the inflation targets of inflation-targeting countries. Even the US Federal Reserve Bank, which stands out because it has a dual mandate of price stability and full employment, adopted a formal inflation target, also at 2% for the year on year increase of consumer prices, in January 2012.

Central banks announce and explain changes in the level of the short-term interest rates with reference to inflationary and deflationary pressures that follow from the degree of tensions demand puts on the productive capacity of the economy. Changes in the price of liquidity are hence typically associated with the risks of both inflation and economic activity, though the path of inflation is always sustainable at the low level of the explicit or implicit inflation target. This approach to monetary policy succeeds in providing a nominal anchor although money has become a purely abstract concept that, potentially, can grow or shrink without limit. In normal times central banks tie the price of liquidity, the nominal interest rate, through a state contingent rule, to the degree of tensions on the economy's productive capacity. An explicit nominal anchor is pursued, and, to a very large extent, achieved, through tailoring the money supply to the economy's changing need for liquidity.

For reasons explained above, this framework did not preclude the accumulation of financial imbalances that led to the financial crisis. Because the aftermath of the crisis, which started in August 2007, has been lingering for years, the framework has endured substantial changes due to the leading interest rate hitting or approaching the zero lower bound in 2009. In Section 18.2.3 we analyzed the early responses as extended lender of last resort operations. However the private sector embarked in long and painful deleveraging and credit demand remained weak. Central banks had to innovate within the framework of monetary policy with so-called non-conventional policies. These policies have consisted in further expanding the supply of central bank liquidity even when their effects on the short-term interest rate was exhausted after it reached the zero lower bound.

Since the usual transmission channel of monetary policy going through the structure of interest rates via the change of the policy short rate was weakened by the variation in the term premium due to the higher price of risk, central banks, which wanted to flatten the whole yield curve, had to complement their usual channel via expected future short rates with quantitative means aiming at lowering risk premiums.

First, the central bank expended liquidity to buy or rent assets and stir their price, typically longer-maturity assets of which the interest rate is still above zero, but also assets with specific forms of credit risk, that can be purchased directly or indirectly as collateral in repo transactions with the central bank. Changes in collateral policies are effectively changing the "price of central bank liquidity." Central banks focused on different types of assets, depending on the transmission channels they wanted to activate and the credit mechanisms most affected by the crisis. The Fed bought mainly Treasury bonds and mortgage-backed securities. The ECB embarked on heavy operations to provide long-term liquidity to commercial banks.

Second, central banks can commit to the future price of liquidity. A typical form of such policy is the so-called forward guidance, whereby the central bank commits to the future path of interest rates, keeping them at zero for an extended period of time, that can be specified explicitly or contingent on an explicit objective. For instance, in December 2012 the Fed committed to purchase $85 billion of mortgage-backed securities (MBS) per month until expected inflation and unemployment remained below 2.5% and above 6.5% respectively.

18.4 Looking Forward: The Challenges of a Renewed Doctrine of Monetary Policy[8]

As we have shown in this text, structural changes, technological developments, and the occurrence of new crises constantly raise new challenges for central banks. We therefore now turn to what we consider to be major threats for central banks at this current juncture.

---

[8] This conclusion focuses on the current financial crisis, the innovations in monetary policy implied by the zero lower bound of interest rate over many years, and by the unknown market responses to the so-called exit from these peculiar circumstances. There are, however, other important challenges. First, means of payments have been evolving for a long time from coins, to notes, checks, plastic cards, and electronic transfers. E-money poses several new forms of risk because it uses open networks to communicate instructions and transfer value, in contrast to the closed nature of the inter-bank market. Open networks can remain efficient only if they maintain a critical mass of users while they may collapse suddenly if would-be users anticipate that this threshold will not be reached. In that event, losing customers triggers a self-fulfilling flight from the network. Chaos could then spread through interconnection between networks. The control by the central bank of the degree of liquidity in the economy would be severely hampered if issuers of e-monies were freed from the reserves and supervision requirements that apply to banks. Second, while there is a broad agreement that monetary policies have contributed to general stabilization of inflation since 1995, this remarkable performance may also result from globalization. The worldwide organization of production may indeed diminish the traditional bottlenecks that translated tensions on local factors of production into local inflation pressure. As a consequence, central banks may need to reconsider the geographic base of supply and demand in analyzing inflation tensions and envisage international coordination of monetary policies.

Because it has turned systemic, the financial crisis has stirred prolonged adverse consequences for the financial system and for the economy in many countries. Recurrent episodes of liquidity stringency have induced central banks to devise new ways of lending in
last resort. However, more pervasive distortions have occurred between finance, the public
sector, and the non-financial private sector. The narrow view of monetary policy, that is,
gearing the interest rates in the exclusive pursuit of price stability, which was the dominant
view in the three decades to 2010, is unlikely to prevail.

The first structural change has been the massive transfer of debts to the public sector. It
has occurred in all developed countries, along with the stimulating plans engineered in 2009
to save the world from depression. It took a dramatic course when the financial crisis spilled
over the Eurozone in 2010. The specific design of this monetary union, with entrenched
financial polarization between debtor and creditor countries and no institutional mechanism for fiscal transfers, made the banking system the main intermediary between debtor
and creditor countries. When creditor country banks became unwilling or unable to carry
the liabilities of debtor countries, a vicious circle spread between sovereign debt that can
turn from illiquid to insolvent and banks' balance sheets.

Since the beginning of the crisis, the Eurosystem has taken charge of banking system
liquidity to eschew the fragmentation of the European financial system that could have led
to the breakup of the euro. In September 2012, the liquidity policy of the central bank also
took a new form: the insurance to that she would buy public debt of short maturity provided
commitments of sound fiscal policies by governments. The path of public debt in the euro
area may crucially depend on the success of this policy of the central bank, especially in
times of financial stress.

In other countries (US, UK, and Japan to cite the largest) the linkage between the state
and the central bank has been more direct. Central banks have bought large quantities of
sovereign bonds to immunize the public debt from market liquidity stress that could have
sent bond rates to levels where public debt becomes unsustainable. Because high public
debt/GDP ratios are here to stay for a long time in many countries, let alone future contingent liabilities of pension systems, the subsequent interdependence between the state and
the central bank could lead governments and parliaments to question the independence of
central banks.

Indeed, independence has proved effective in circumstances where the primary assignment of central banks has been the pursuit of price stability to secure the value of the nominal anchor. Preserving the sustainability of public debt may however become an overriding
priority for governments. When public debt approaches 100% of GDP, as it has, on average, in the OECD, a 2% increase in public debt implies, if one wants to stabilize the debt, a
2% increase in fiscal revenues. Such fiscal implications of interest rate policies, while always
there, have increased considerably in proportion to the increase of public debts.

Central banks and political authorities are facing two intertwined problems: how to deal
with the legacy of high public debts in the long run and how to achieve the twin objectives of
price and financial stability, considering that the one is not contained in the other?

The post-World War II era has however seen at least several episodes of public debt
reduction (during the two decades after the war, under the Clinton administration in the
US, and under the first Prodi government in the 1990s in Italy, to name a few). Such adjustments would ideally combine long-term interest rates inferior to the nominal growth rate
of GDP. This combination need not bring inflation, especially because fiscal surpluses are

disinflationary. However, in the event of a conflict between the price stability objective and a reborn objective to maintain low levels of long-term interest rates, governments and parliaments are likely to reconsider the benefits of central bank independence. An alternative for central banks would be to adopt the long-term interest rate as a secondary or a complementary objective.

In addition to much higher levels of public debt, the second legacy of the Lehman financial crisis is the social demand for financial stability and more stringent ruling of financial markets. Financial stability is now widely understood as an objective in its own right. However, unlike the price stability objective of monetary policy, it is not an objective that can be defined by a single quantitative measure.

At the very least, taking care of financial stability should reduce systemic risk both ex post and ex ante. Ex post management of crises, especially in the form of lender of last resort interventions are a classic attribute of central banks. However, such interventions remain inductive of moral hazard by financial market participants in the upward phase of financial cycles—hence the crucial role for ex ante policies. Authorities ought to prevent the buildup of financial vulnerabilities that accumulate in the financial system in the upward euphoric stage of the financial cycle (Adrian, Covitz, and Liang, 2013). This is what macro prudential policy is all about. It is meant to keep the generic price of risk sufficiently high in the upward phase of the financial cycle to avoid its destructive rise in downward phases.

Financial vulnerabilities are partly structural and partly dynamic. The first must be eradicated by proper regulation (high enough capital and liquidity ratios for banks, tighter regulation for systematically important financial intermediaries, a ban on toxic synthetic financial products, derivatives transactions cleared and settled on organized markets, and the like). The second are responsible for momentous dynamics fostered by ever higher leverage, maturity mismatches, and denser webs of counterparty risks that lead to vicious procyclical circles between aggregate credit growth in the private non-financial sector and asset prices.

Because financial dynamics are sensitive to the level of interest rates, the conduct of monetary policy cannot pursue price stability in isolation, ignoring its effects on the financial developments. Financial stability will most likely become an explicit or implicit secondary objective of monetary policy. And central banks will rediscover the multiplicity of monetary policy tools (counter-cyclical capital buffers, required reserve ratios, special bond issuance to mop up excess bank reserves, etc.) that can be mobilized to lean against financial winds should they prefer to gear short-term interest rates predominantly to price stability.

All in all, the Lehman crisis and its longlasting replica will most likely reassign central banks their original role on top of being the conservators of the value of money including through guaranteeing the proper financing of the state and guarding financial stability.

REFERENCES

Adrian, T., Covitz, D., and Liang, N. (2013). Financial Stability Monitoring, Fed NY Staff Reports No. 601, February.

Bagehot, W. (1873). *Lombard Street: A Description of the Money Market*. London: H. S. King.

Bernanke, B. and Mishkin, F. (1997). Inflation Targeting: A New Framework for Monetary Policy?, *Journal of Economic Perspectives* 11, 97–117.

Cantillon, R. ([1755] 1964). *Essai sur la nature du commerce en général*, ed. H. Higgs and A. M. Kelley. Basel: Bank for International Settlements.

Crowe, C. and Meade, E. (2007). The Evolution of Central Bank Governance around the World, *Journal of Economic Perspectives* 21, 69–90.

Friedman, M. and Schwartz, A. J. (1963), *A Monetary History of the United States*. Princeton, NJ: Princeton University Press.

Goodfriend, M. (1988). Money, Credit Banking and Payment Systems Policy. In: D. Humphrey (Ed.), *The US Payments System: Efficiency, Risk and the Role of the Federal Reserve*. Dordrecht: Kluwer Academic.

Goodfriend, M. (2007). How the World Achieved Consensus on Monetary Policy, *Journal of Economic Perspectives* 21, 47–68.

Greenspan, A. (2004). Risk and Uncertainty in Monetary Policy, *American Economic Review* 94, 33–40.

Hume, D. (1752). Banks and Paper Money. In: F. H. Capie (Ed.), *History of Banking*. Vol. 1. London: Pickering & Chatto.

Kydland, F. and Prescott, E. (1977). Rules Rather than Discretion: The Inconsistency of Optimal Plans, *Journal of Political Economy* 85(3), 473–491.

Minsky, H. P. (1986). *Stabilizing an Unstable Economy*. New Haven, CT: Yale University Press.

Taylor, J. (1993). Discretion versus Policy Rules in Practice, *Carnegie-Rochester Conference Series on Public Policy* 39, 195–214.

Thornton, H. (1802). *An Inquiry into the Nature and Effects of Paper Credit of Great Britain*, ed. F. A. Hayek. Fairfield: Augustus M. Keley.

Wicksell, K. (1907). The Influence of the Rate of Interest on Prices, *The Economic Journal* 17, 213–220.

Wicksell, K. (1935). *Lectures on Political Economy*. London: Routledge.

Woodford, M. (2003). *Interest and Prices, Foundation of a Theory of Monetary Policy*. Princeton, NJ: Princeton University Press.

CHAPTER 19

··

THE ROLE OF BANKS IN
THE TRANSMISSION OF
MONETARY POLICY*

··

JOE PEEK AND ERIC S. ROSENGREN

19.1 INTRODUCTION

WHILE macroeconomists have traditionally focused on the role of inside money in the transmission of monetary policy, over the past two decades an increased emphasis has been placed on the other side of bank balance sheets. Although the traditional interest rate channel for the transmission of monetary policy remains intact, the importance of the credit channel in augmenting the impact of monetary policy on the economy has gained credibility. Nevertheless, while the broad credit channel version has gained widespread acceptance, the narrower bank lending channel remains somewhat controversial. The main points of contention are whether a shift in monetary policy affects bank loan supply, and, if it does, the extent to which a change in bank loan supply can affect economic activity. Here we describe the mechanisms by which the banking system transmits changes in monetary policy and provide an overview of the evidence on the efficacy of the view that bank lending plays an important role in determining the magnitude of the effect of monetary policy on the economy.

Several factors may explain the renewed interest in the role played by bank lending in the transmission mechanism of monetary policy. First, financial innovation has resulted in a shift in the focus of monetary policy from a focus on money aggregates to a focus on interest rates, as the Federal Reserve relied on the federal funds rate as its policy instrument until

* The views expressed are the authors' and do not necessarily reflect those of the Federal Reserve Bank of Boston, Federal Reserve System, or the Federal Open Market Committee (FOMC).

hitting the zero lower bound in the recent financial crisis. Second, in the early 1990s, the US experienced significant banking problems that resulted in banks limiting their lending as a result of capital constraints.[1] Similar concerns with a bank "capital crunch" help to explain some of the reaction of monetary policymakers to their own banking problems in countries as diverse as Japan, Sweden, and Argentina.[2] Third, episodes of liquidity problems in the United States, such as those associated with the failure of Penn Central, the 1987 stock crash, the Long-Term Capital Management crisis, the events of 9/11, and the Lehman failure, have highlighted the important role of bank lending during liquidity and financial crises.[3] Fourth, the concerns about the bank capital crunch of the early 1990s have once again been raised as numerous banks and non-bank lending institutions became capital constrained as a result of the credit problems that became apparent in August 2007.

The subsequent financial crisis caused countries around the world to intervene in an effort to stabilize the banking system and credit markets more generally. In addition to the standard interest rate reductions, these interventions included significant capital injections, such as the Troubled Asset Relief Program (TARP) capital injections in the United States, and extensions of broad liability guarantees to ensure that banks would have the ability to roll over debt. Finally, as traditional interest rate policies became limited by the zero lower bound, countries increasingly looked to alternative monetary policy tools, with major central banks undertaking quantitative easing policies and engaging in forward guidance on interest rates. In the United States, the extensive use of lending facilities was adopted in an effort to stimulate lending by financial institutions with the intent, in some cases, to impact financial markets more broadly, for example the commercial paper and asset-backed commercial paper (ABCP) markets. While our recent experience has highlighted the observation that problems that generated major banking reforms in the past, for example concerns about asset-liability management and liquidity runs, were not unique to banks, the financial crisis has also focused attention on the importance of banks for the shadow banking market and in the securitization of assets, two areas badly disrupted by the crisis. However, another important lesson is that understanding the role of banks in lending and in financial markets more generally is critically important for explaining both the onset of the financial crisis and the severity of the ensuing economic crisis.

This chapter provides an overview of recent research about the role played by bank lending in the transmission of monetary policy. Section 19.2 begins with a description of the mechanisms, under both the money view and the credit view, by which monetary policy is transmitted to the economy through the banking sector. Section 19.3 examines the empirical evidence on how bank lending responds to changes in monetary policy. This literature has focused both on changes in firms' borrowing and on changes in the amounts and composition of bank assets following a change in the stance of monetary policy. In particular, we discuss the evidence concerning which banks and which firms are likely to play key roles in transmitting monetary policy to the macroeconomy through the bank lending channel. This section also includes a discussion of how the effects emanating from the bank lending

---

[1]   See Chapter 29 in this volume for a discussion of earlier episodes and the role of banking distress in exacerbating adverse macroeconomic shocks.

[2]   See Chapter 28 in this volume for a thorough discussion of banking crises.

[3]   See Strahan (2009) and Chapter 8 in this volume for a discussion of the important role of banks in providing "funding" liquidity.

channel can be derailed by bank capital constraints that limit the extent to which banks are able to expand their balance sheets in response to an easing of monetary policy. Section 19.4 briefly reviews some of the literature on the role of banks in other countries, many of which are far more dependent on bank lending than in the United States. The fifth section, 19.5, discusses how the role of bank lending may have been altered by recent financial innovations and provides observations on the implications of the events associated with the recent financial crisis for the effectiveness of the bank lending channel. Section 19.6 provides some conclusions.

19.2 HOW IS MONETARY POLICY TRANSMITTED THROUGH THE BANKING SYSTEM?

19.2.1 Traditional Interest Rate, or Money, View

The traditional interest rate, or money, view of the transmission of monetary policy focuses on the liability side of bank balance sheets. The important role played by banks in this transmission mechanism arises from the reserve requirement constraint faced by banks. Because banks rarely hold significant excess reserves, the reserve requirement constraint is typically considered to be binding at all times.[4] Thus, shifts in monetary policy that change the quantity of outside money result in changes in the quantity of inside money in the form of the reservable deposits that can be created by the banking system.

The transmission mechanism functions as follows. When the monetary authority undertakes open-market operations in order to tighten monetary policy (by selling securities), the banking industry experiences a decline in reserves. The fractional reserve system then forces banks (as a whole) to reduce reservable deposits in order to continue to meet the reserve requirement. This shock, which is exogenous to the banking sector, thus constrains bank behavior. To induce households to hold smaller amounts of reservable deposits (transactions accounts), interest rates on other deposits and non-deposit alternatives must rise. That is, since the supply of transactions deposits has declined relative to the supply of alternative assets, interest rates on these alternative assets would have to rise to clear the market for transactions deposits. As the increase in the short-term interest rate is transmitted to longer-term interest rates, aggregate demand declines. However, an important characteristic of the recent financial crisis has been the substantial expansion of excess reserves in the US banking system. Consequently, with the reserve requirement failing to serve as a binding constraint on most institutions, an increasing focus has been placed on the important role of alternative transmission mechanisms.

---

[4] While that accurately describes non-crisis times, two recent notable exceptions are the episodes of quantitative easing policies undertaken by the Bank of Japan in response to the crises experienced by Japan in the 1990s and, in response to the most recent financial crisis, also by the Federal Reserve, the Bank of England, and the European Central Bank.

19.2.2 The Broad Credit Channel

The broad credit channel, also referred to as the balance sheet effect or financial accelerator, does not require that a distinction be drawn among the alternative sources of credit. Instead, it is predicated on credit market imperfections associated with asymmetric information and moral hazard problems. Research on the credit channel was motivated, in large part, by the puzzle that monetary policy shocks that had had relatively small effects on long-term real interest rates appeared to have had substantial effects on aggregate demand. This literature attributes the magnification, or propagation, of monetary policy shocks to frictions in the credit markets (see, for example, Gertler and Gilchrist, 1993; Bernanke and Gertler, 1995; Cecchetti, 1995; Hubbard, 1995; Bernanke, Gertler, and Gilchrist, 1996; and Oliner and Rudebusch, 1996a). Because of the information asymmetries between borrowers and lenders, external finance is an imperfect substitute for a firm's internal funds.

The broad credit channel posits that an increase in interest rates associated with a tightening of monetary policy causes a deterioration in firm health, in terms of both net income and net worth. A firm's net income is impaired both because its interest costs rise and because its revenues deteriorate as the tighter monetary policy slows the economy. A firm's net worth is adversely impacted as the lower cash flows emanating from the firm's assets are discounted using the higher interest rates associated with the tightening of monetary policy. The deterioration in the firm's net income and the reduction in the collateral value of the firm's assets, in turn, cause an increase in the external finance premium that must be paid by the firm for all sources of external finance. This increase in the cost of external funds for borrowers over and above the risk-free interest rate then results in a reduction in aggregate demand in addition to that due to the increase in the risk-free interest rate associated with the interest rate channel of the transmission of monetary policy.

19.2.3 The Bank Lending Channel

With the bank lending, or credit, view, in contrast to the money view, the focus of the transmission mechanism operating through bank balance sheets shifts from bank liabilities to bank assets. When monetary policy tightens, the reduction in available bank reserves forces banks to create fewer reservable deposits. Banks must then either replace the lost reservable deposits with non-reservable liabilities, or shrink their assets, such as loans and securities, in order to keep total assets in line with the reduced volume of liabilities. Typically, one would expect to observe some combination of these responses, although Romer and Romer (1990) question the extent to which banks, in an age of managed liabilities, are unable to easily replace reservable deposits. However, to the extent that banks are unable or unwilling to fully insulate their loan portfolio, the interest rate effect on aggregate demand is supplemented with an additional effect stemming from a reduction in the availability of bank loans that further slows aggregate demand.

In a simple world with three assets—money, government bonds, and bank loans—three conditions must be satisfied for the bank lending channel to be operational in the transmission of monetary policy (see, for example, Bernanke and Blinder, 1988; and Kashyap and Stein, 1994). First, as with the interest rate view, prices must not adjust fully and instantaneously to a change in the money supply. That is, money is not neutral, at least in the short run. Second, open-market operations must affect the supply of bank loans. Third, loans and bonds must not be perfect substitutes as a source of credit for at least some borrowers. Of course, the set of assets can be expanded to include private sector bonds and non-bank intermediated loans, in which case the narrower bank lending channel is distinguished from the broad credit channel by requiring that private sector bonds and non-bank intermediated loans not be perfect substitutes for bank loans as a source of credit for at least some borrowers. Because only the second and third conditions distinguish the bank lending view from the money view, and because substantial evidence exists that wages and prices are not perfectly flexible, it will be assumed for the purposes of this discussion that the first condition holds.

With respect to the second condition, when open-market operations reduce the quantity of bank reserves, the banking system has no choice but to reduce reservable deposits, given the reserve requirement. However, banks do have choices, and individual banks do differ with respect to how, and to what extent, they respond to this decline in reserves. Banks must raise non-reservable liabilities to replace the lost reservable deposits, reduce assets such as securities and loans, or make some combination of these two types of portfolio adjustments. To the extent that banks do not regard non-reservable sources of funds as perfect substitutes for reservable deposits, they will not fully replace the lost reservable deposits, and thus must shrink their assets in order to keep their total assets in line with their reduced volume of liabilities.

Asymmetric information and credit market frictions play an important role in determining how an individual bank responds on the liability side of its balance sheet. Banks primarily use uninsured non-reservable liabilities, such as large time deposits, as the marginal source of funds during periods of monetary policy tightening. However, the ease of raising large time deposits varies by bank. For example, one would expect that more transparent (for example, publicly traded), larger, and healthier banking organizations would have relatively better access to external (uninsured) funds, and thus would tend to replace a higher proportion of their lost reservable deposits, resulting in a relatively smaller shrinkage in their assets.

Given that some shrinkage in bank assets will occur, a bank must then decide on the distribution of that shrinkage across the various assets held in its portfolio. Because securities are relatively liquid and considered to be secondary reserves, one would certainly expect banks to shrink their holdings of securities. However, to the extent that banks do not consider securities and loans to be perfect substitutes in their asset portfolio, one would expect that at least part of the adjustment in assets would come from a shrinkage in the volume of their loan portfolio, although initially the loan portfolio might temporarily grow as a result of distress borrowing, as loan customers access credit from previously established loan commitments and lines of credit (Morgan, 1998).

Asymmetric information and credit market frictions also play an important role in determining the extent to which firms consider bonds, or, more generally, publicly issued credit market instruments, and non-bank intermediated loans to be perfect substitutes for bank loans. That is, to distinguish the broad credit channel from the bank lending channel, one must address the degree to which borrowers consider non-bank sources of credit as perfect substitutes for bank loans. To the extent that non-bank sources of credit are perfect substitutes for bank loans from the viewpoint of borrowers, borrowers will merely substitute these alternative sources of credit for bank loans when a tightening of monetary policy reduces the availability of bank loans. In this case, one would observe no impact on aggregate demand arising from the reduction in bank credit beyond that due to the increase in the external finance premium associated with the broad credit channel.

Although non-bank financial intermediaries provide loans, open-market instruments are available for short-term credit, and trade credit is available to some firms, these alternative sources of credit are not perfect substitutes for bank credit for a variety of institutional reasons. With respect to the substitutability of intermediated loans and publicly issued credit market instruments, not all firms have access to public credit markets. In particular, smaller firms are unable to issue such debt because the issue size would be too small to outweigh the fixed costs of issuance at a reasonable interest rate. Similarly, firms that are sufficiently opaque or have a sufficiently low credit standing to require close monitoring by a financial intermediary would not have direct access to the credit markets. Nevertheless, even though large, highly rated firms can directly access public credit markets by issuing commercial paper, issuing unsecured commercial paper may still involve participation by banks, insofar as the issuing firms obtain third-party guarantees from banks to enhance the credit rating of the commercial paper in order to lower the interest cost to the firm.

Similarly, alternative sources of intermediated loans are not perfect substitutes for bank loans for at least some borrowers. While for firms bank loans share the attributes of many of the alternative forms of intermediated loans, there are important differences. For example, insurance companies are very active in the commercial real estate market and are important providers of term financing that allows them to better match the maturities of their assets and liabilities. Similarly, finance companies provide asset-backed financing—for example, for loans collateralized by inventories and accounts receivable. Yet, for a small, opaque firm with few tangible assets, bank loans may be the only source of an unsecured line of credit or of a loan secured by an asset that might not be easily commoditized. As a result, the clientele effect in bank lending results in many firms being bank-dependent, with few alternatives to banks should their bank credit be curtailed.

19.3 Empirical Evidence on the Role of Bank Lending for the Transmission of Monetary Policy

Empirical researchers investigating the bank lending view face several challenges. First, they need to determine whether a change in monetary policy affects bank lending. Then, if bank lending is affected, the issue becomes the extent to which shifts in bank loan supply do, in fact, affect aggregate demand. The difficulties in establishing the first point are twofold. First, to what extent are banks able to insulate their loan portfolios from monetary policy shocks by adjusting other components of their balance sheet? The second difficulty concerns identifying a bank-loan supply shock, insofar as a decline in bank loans following a tightening of monetary policy may simply reflect a decline in loan demand rather than a decline in the supply of loans.

19.3.1 The Effect of Monetary Policy on Bank Loan Supply

While the theoretical conditions required for bank loan supply to be affected by changes in monetary policy are clear, it is not straightforward empirically to disentangle shifts in loan supply from shifts in loan demand. At an aggregate level, Bernanke and Blinder (1992), among others, show that bank lending does contract when monetary policy becomes tighter. However, such an observed correlation may reflect a reduction in loan demand as the economy weakens in response to the tighter monetary policy, rather than reflecting a reduction in bank loan supply. Furthermore, even if one observed an initial increase in bank loans or a notable delay in the decline in bank loans following a tightening of monetary policy, such evidence would not necessarily conflict with an inward shift in bank loan supply in response to a tightening of monetary policy. For example, the initial response of firms to a tightening of monetary policy may be an increase in loan demand resulting from the need to finance the buildup of inventories, as aggregate demand initially declines faster than production. Even though banks may decrease loan supply immediately to borrowers without loan commitments, the total amount of bank loans may temporarily increase, as banks are forced to honor existing loan commitments (Morgan, 1998). Thus, the endogeneity issues associated with using aggregate data for total loans make it impossible to obtain a clear answer.

Kashyap, Stein, and Wilcox (1993) provide an alternative approach for identifying an effect of monetary policy on bank loan supply, although the analysis is still based on aggregated data. They investigate the change in the mix of bank loans and commercial paper in the composition of firms' external finance, with the argument being that if the decline in loans is due to a general decline in credit demand associated with a slowing of the real economy, then demand for other types of credit should decline similarly. Finding that a tightening of monetary policy is associated with an increase in commercial paper issuance and a decline in bank loans, they conclude that a tightening of monetary policy does reduce bank loan supply rather than the decline in bank loans simply reflecting a reduction in credit demand as the economy slows. In the same vein, Ludvigson (1998) investigates the composition of automobile finance between bank and non-bank providers of credit. She finds that, in fact, a tightening of monetary policy reduces the relative supply of bank loans, consistent with the bank lending channel. In contrast, Oliner and Rudebusch (1996b) revisit the Kashyap, Stein, and Wilcox (1993) approach using a different measure of the mix of external finance and disaggregating the data into two separate components, one for small firms and one for large firms. They argue that their evidence is consistent with the broad credit channel rather than with the more narrowly defined bank lending channel. However, this only highlights the weaknesses associated with attempting to isolate bank loan supply shocks from shifts in credit demand using aggregate data. In fact, in their reply, Kashyap, Stein, and Wilcox (1996) close by suggesting that a more definitive answer will have to rely on an analysis using micro data at the individual bank and firm levels.

By advancing the analysis to focus on panel data, the literature has been able to obtain more definitive results about the impact of changes in monetary policy on bank loan supply. The key has turned out to be relating cross-sectional differences in bank, or banking organization, characteristics to differences in the extent to which banks were able to insulate their loan portfolios from a tightening of monetary policy. Two aspects of bank characteristics appear to have been the primary focus. First, the ability of banks to raise non-reservable liabilities to replace the lost reservable deposits is a key factor in determining the extent to which a bank must adjust its loan portfolio when monetary policy is tightened. Because these funds are, for the most part, uninsured liabilities, bank characteristics related to banks' access to external funds—for example, size, health, and direct access to capital markets—play an important role in determining the ability of banks to insulate their loan portfolios from the effects of changes in monetary policy. Second, because banks face a capital require-ment constraint in addition to the reserve requirement constraint on their activities, they may differ in their response to a change in the stance of monetary policy, depending on which constraint is more binding. If the capital ratio requirement is the binding constraint, easing the reserve requirement constraint through open-market operations should have little, if any, effect on bank lending. That is, because the binding constraint has not been eased, expansionary monetary policy, at least if operating through the bank lending chan-nel, would be like "pushing on a string."

Kashyap and Stein (1995) note that with a tightening of monetary policy and the associ-ated loss in reservable deposits, it is costly for banks to raise uninsured deposits. However, banks differ in the degree to which they have access to external funds. Kashyap and Stein hypothesize that bank size is a reasonable proxy for the degree of access to uninsured lia-bilities, with smaller banks having more limited access, and thus having their loan portfolio impacted more by a tightening of monetary policy. Indeed, they find empirical support for the proposition that small banks are more responsive (shrink their loan portfolios by more) than large banks to a monetary policy tightening.

Subsequently, Kashyap and Stein (2000) extend their analysis of the relative ease with which banks can raise uninsured deposits following a tightening of monetary policy, noting that the bank loan response will also differ depending on the liquidity position of the bank. A bank that finds it relatively costly to raise uninsured deposits but that has large securi-ties holdings has the option of adjusting to the shrinkage of reservable deposits by selling some of its securities, while a less liquid bank may be forced to shrink its loan portfolio by a greater degree. In a large cross-section of banks, they find evidence that the loan portfolios of smaller, more illiquid banks are the most responsive to monetary policy shocks.

Campello (2002) distinguishes among these smaller banks based on whether the bank is affiliated with a large multibank holding company, finding that the lending of small banks that are affiliated with large multibank holding companies reacts less to a tightening of mon-etary policy than does the lending of similar small (standalone) banks that are not affili-ated with multibank holding companies. Although this evidence indicates that small banks affiliated with multibank holding companies are better able to insulate their lending from a tightening of monetary policy, the extent to which this is due to the channeling of internal holding company funds to bank subsidiaries rather than due to the fact that large multi-bank holding companies have easier access to external funds is not clear. Campello tries to address this issue by using capital-to-asset ratios to distinguish among bank holding com-panies. Similarly, Kishan and Opiela (2000) use the capital-to-asset ratio as the proxy for a bank's ability to raise uninsured deposits, finding that the loan portfolios of well-capitalized banks are less sensitive to monetary policy shocks than are those of poorly capitalized banks of the same size. However, for reasons discussed below, capital-constrained banks may behave differently for reasons other than their ability to raise uninsured deposits.

Holod and Peek (2007) utilize the distinction between publicly traded and non-publicly traded banks to classify banks by the ease with which they can access external funds. They find that after controlling for size, capitalization, and other factors, the loan portfolios of publicly traded banks shrink less than those of non-publicly traded banks when monetary policy tightens due to the banks' ability to raise external funds, including by issuing large time deposits. Furthermore, as one would expect, when a distinction is made between tightening and easing monetary policy, the estimated effect can be attributed to the effects of monetary policy tightening (tightening a binding constraint) rather than to monetary policy easing (possibly pushing on a string).

While substantial evidence supports the existence of an operational lending channel that amplifies the transmission of monetary policy, recent studies have suggested that the lending channel may have been weakened in recent years by developments in financial markets that allow banks to be less dependent on reservable deposits to fund their lending. For example, Loutskina and Strahan (2009) argue that growth in loan securitization, in particular the expansion of the secondary mortgage market, has weakened the transmission of monetary policy through the lending channel by increasing bank balance sheet liquidity. Similarly, Cetorelli and Goldberg (2012) argue that the domestic amplification of monetary policy through the lending channel has been mitigated by the increasing globalization of banking. Banking organizations with international operations are able, at least partially, to insulate themselves from domestic liquidity shocks, such as from a tightening of monetary policy, through the cross-border operation of their internal capital markets. That is, multinational banks can react to a tightening of monetary policy by using internal flows of funds to offset the impact on their domestic banks. On the other hand, this mechanism also suggests that the total effect of the lending channel has been understated by focusing only on domestic lending, insofar as changes in monetary policy are propagated internationally through the internal capital markets of global banks.

The second important characteristic of banks that can affect the extent to which the bank lending channel is operative is whether banks face a binding capital constraint. As a result of the "headwinds in monetary policy" noted by Chairman Greenspan during the recovery from the 1990 recession, a variety of authors have examined the impact that significant bank health problems can have on the transmission of monetary policy. For example, Peek and Rosengren (1995a) examine the impact that being capital constrained had on a bank's ability to lend during the period of significant banking problems in the early 1990s in New England. Using a simple static model, they show that banks facing a binding capital constraint are limited in altering the size of their balance sheet, restricting the ability of capital-constrained banks to respond to monetary policy shocks. They document that experiencing an adverse capital shock that makes the capital constraint binding will cause banks to shrink both assets and liabilities. Peek and Rosengren (1995a) also show that the behavior of capital-constrained banks in New England differed from that of unconstrained banks, with the loan portfolios of unconstrained banks responding more to monetary policy shocks than those of the capital-constrained banks.

In a subsequent study, Peek and Rosengren (1995b) focus on the direct impact of the enforcement of capital regulations by bank supervisors on the ability of capital-constrained banks to lend, and thus to be able to increase loans in response to an easing of monetary policy. They examine the impact on bank lending of formal regulatory actions (cease and desist orders and written agreements) imposed on banks that experienced asset quality problems. They find that the enforcement actions by bank regulators included explicit capital targets that needed to be achieved over a short time frame. The result was an immediate and significant reduction in bank loan portfolios associated with the imposition of the enforcement action that persisted for some time thereafter while the bank continued to operate under the enforcement action.

Alternatively, banks can become capital constrained as a consequence of changes in capital regulations. A number of authors have examined whether such changes can cause banks to be particularly responsive to their capital constraint, and, by implication, less responsive to changes in monetary policy. For example, Hall (1993) finds that the introduction of the Basel I Accord had a significant impact on bank portfolios. Hancock and Wilcox (1994) also find that the implementation of the Basel I Accord affected banks' willingness to lend. However, Berger and Udell (1994) do not find evidence that the Basel I Accord created a bank capital crunch. More recently, a concern raised with the proposed Basel II Accord has been that the new capital regulations would magnify potential capital constraints during recessions (for example, Kashyap and Stein, 2004), making banks less responsive to an easing of monetary policy. Thus, a very real concern with the effectiveness of the bank lending channel, and thus the overall effectiveness of monetary policy, is whether banks are capital constrained at the time of an easing of monetary policy.

19.3.2 Real Effects of Shifts in Bank Loan Supply

Given that the empirical evidence generally supports the proposition that banks, particularly those that may find it relatively expensive to raise uninsured liabilities, respond to a monetary policy tightening by reducing loans, we turn to the next link in the bank lending channel mechanism. For the reduction in bank loans to have an impact on economic activity, firms must not be able to easily substitute other sources of external finance when bank loan supply is cut back. Gertler and Gilchrist (1994) find, at a somewhat aggregated level, that the investment of an aggregate of small firms is more responsive to changes in monetary policy than is the investment of an aggregate of large firms, a set of firms that presumably is less bank dependent. Similarly, Ludvigson (1998), comparing bank and non-bank sources of automobile loans, finds that the composition of automobile credit impacts automobile sales, even after controlling for the standard factors that probably impact automobile demand.

Additional evidence at an aggregate level is provided by Driscoll (2004), who uses a panel of state-level data to investigate the extent to which shocks to bank loan supply affect output. Using state-specific shocks to money demand as an instrumental variable to address the endogeneity problem, he does not find a meaningful effect of loan supply shocks on economic activity at the state level. Ashcraft (2006), similarly basing his analysis on state-level data, attempts to exploit differences between standalone banks and banks affiliated with multibank holding companies in their degree of access to external funds in order to identify loan supply shocks related to changes in monetary policy. While he does find a difference between the two types of banks in their lending response to changes in monetary policy, he does not find a significant effect of these bank loan supply shocks on state income growth. In contrast, Ashcraft (2005), using the cross-guarantees of two failed Texas bank holding companies as his identification mechanism to address the endogeneity problems, finds that the failures of healthy banks forced by the cross-guarantee provisions were associated with reduced local economic activity. This suggests that bank lending is special, insofar as it appears that other lenders (even other banks) did not fill the gap created by the sharp reduction in lending by the failed banks, and is consistent with an operative lending channel.

Another approach that provides direct evidence that a reduction in bank loan supply adversely affects macroeconomic activity is provided by Peek and Rosengren (2000). Using the banking problems in Japan as the source of an exogenous loan supply shock in the United States, they are able to avoid the common endogeneity problem faced by studies that rely on domestic shocks to bank loan supply. Furthermore, by focusing on commercial real estate loans that tend to have local or regional markets, they are able to exploit cross-sectional differences across geographic regions to show that the decline in loans had real effects. That is, the pull-back by Japanese banks in local US markets was not fully offset by other lenders stepping in to fill the void.

Taking still a different tack, Peek, Rosengren, and Tootell (2003) obtain evidence of a macroeconomic effect of shifts in bank loan supply. They find that adverse shocks to bank health weaken economic activity in the major GDP components that one would expect to be most affected by bank loan supply shocks—for example, the change in business inventory investment—while not impacting other major components of GDP whose fluctuations would be correlated with demand shocks.

While such aggregate evidence is more than simply suggestive of an operative bank lending channel, to obtain even more convincing evidence about the efficacy of the bank lending channel, one must turn to disaggregated data, preferably at the firm level. One way to test whether bank lending is special is to determine whether a monetary policy tightening disproportionately impacts borrowers that are more reliant on bank lending as a source of external finance. A variety of authors have examined individual firm-level data to determine whether being subject to financial constraints cause non-financial firms to react more to monetary policy shocks, for example by reducing investment more in response to a monetary policy tightening (for example, Fazzari, Hubbard, and Petersen, 1988). The proxies for liquidity constraints have included dividend payouts (Fazzari, Hubbard, and Petersen, 1988), size (Gertler and Gilchrist, 1994), and bond ratings (Kashyap, Lamont, and Stein, 1994). The evidence tends to support the proposition that external funds are more costly to raise than internal funds, so that firms that depend more on external finance are likely to be impacted more adversely by a reduction in bank loan supply.

This, of course, presumes that bank loans are special to firms, so that such loans cannot be replaced easily with non-bank loans or by issuing credit market instruments. A large literature speaks precisely to this point. For example, James (1987) notes that the stock price of a firm rises in response to an announcement of a new loan agreement. Slovin, Sushka, and Poloncheck (1993) observe that the failure of Continental Illinois Bank adversely impacted borrowers that had a close banking relationship with that bank. However, this outcome did not hold if the Continental Illinois loan was part of a loan participation unless Continental Illinois was the lead underwriter of the loan. In terms of the strength of the banking relationship, Petersen and Rajan (1995) note that a firm's banking relationship often involves both a deposit and a lending relationship. They find that the strength of lending relationships, as indicated by a firm holding deposits at the bank, is indicative of how extensively the firm relies on bank lending. Finally, Fields et al. (2006) argue that the value of lending relationships has diminished substantially over time, due in part to the further development of financial markets and the increased availability of information about borrowers. However, their sample includes only publicly traded firms, precisely those firms that are the least likely to be bank-dependent. Consistent with the view of Fields et al. (2006), Gande and Saunders (2012) argue that the development of the secondary loan market has reduced to some extent the "specialness" of banks due to the weakening of banks' incentives to monitor borrowers.

Thus, the evidence from studies based on individual non-financial firms supports the proposition that many firms are, in fact, bank-dependent, and that their economic activity is adversely affected by reductions in bank loan supply. While other financial intermediaries provide external finance to firms, this credit tends to be directed to specific types of loans. Finance companies tend to focus on asset-backed lending, such as receivables, while insurance companies tend to make longer-duration loans that match more closely the duration of their liabilities. Thus, banks remain the primary source of funding for smaller firms that lack ready access to external finance from other sources.

19.4 Non-US Evidence on Bank Lending and the Transmission of Monetary Policy

The role of banks in the transmission of monetary policy is potentially more relevant in many other countries because of their relatively greater reliance on bank finance compared with the market-based system of finance in the United States. A good example is Japan, where banks continue to have a significant role in financing large as well as small companies, although because of deregulation of the Japanese bond markets the largest companies are increasingly able to tap directly into financial markets (for example, Hoshi and Kashyap, 2001). The Japanese economy also is particularly interesting because of a variety of characteristics that make bank–firm ties especially close; such characteristics include widespread cross-shareholding, bank representatives placed on firms' board of directors, and bank-centered keiretsu groups (see, for example, Kaplan and Minton, 1994; Kang and Shivdasani, 1995; and Morck and Nakamura, 1999).

Even before the Japanese banking problems that began in the early 1990s were able to have their full impact, Hoshi, Scharfstein, and Singleton (1993), using the mix-effect technique with aggregate data, found that when monetary policy tightened, the share of bank loans compared to insurance company loans declined. Furthermore, for Japanese firms not affiliated with bank-centered keiretsu groups, and thus less closely connected to banks, firm liquidity was a more important determinant of these firms' investment when monetary policy tightened and bank credit became less available.

After the stock market and real estate bubbles burst and bank health began to deteriorate, Japanese banks faced with potential capital constraints sought ways to continue to lend to domestic borrowers while still shrinking their balance sheets. Peek and Rosengren (1997, 2000) find that global Japanese banks initially shrank their assets abroad in order to insulate their domestic lending. As the Japanese banking problems continued, domestic borrowers and the lending channel were affected. For example, Ito and Sasaki (2002) find evidence of a credit crunch in Japan as binding capital constraints became an important factor in the ability of Japanese banks to continue to lend. Similarly, Kang and Stulz (2000) find that the banking problems in Japan had the greatest adverse impact, both in terms of stock prices and in terms of their investment expenditures, on the firms that were the most bank-dependent. In addition, several studies argue that problems were compounded by Japanese banks applying international bank capital standards that resulted in the need for Japanese banks to increase their capital ratios (see, for example, Hall, 1993; and Montgomery, 2005).

Given the relative importance of bank lending as a source of credit in Japan, it is likely that the severe banking problems weakened the bank lending channel and contributed to the prolonged malaise in the Japanese economy throughout the 1990s and early 2000s, even though monetary policy reduced interest rates to near zero. This was magnified by distortions that had a broader adverse impact on the economy. These distortions had their source in a combination of the prevailing lending relationships and the perverse incentives faced by banks that led to a misallocation of much of the credit that banks provided (Peek and Rosengren, 2005). In fact, Caballero, Hoshi, and Kashyap (2008) link the misallocation of credit to broader economic problems in Japan, finding that investment by firms was seriously distorted by the desire of banks to support "zombie" (insolvent) firms.

Similarly, the evidence suggests that the deterioration in bank health created similar problems when other Asian countries experienced financial difficulties in the late 1990s. For example, Ferri and Kang (1999) find that South Korean problems caused a significant credit crunch when bank capital became constrained. Given that the chaebols (business groups) in Korea have some similarities to the keiretsus in Japan, one might expect that some of the same results found in Japan also would hold in emerging market economies such as South Korea. Still, the banking consolidation in emerging market economies in Asia and Latin America has tended to weaken the bank lending channel of monetary policy transmission (Olivero, Li, and Jeon, 2011). Moreover, the rise in foreign bank penetration in emerging markets has been another factor weakening the lending channel, given that foreign banks respond less strongly than domestic banks in host countries to host-country monetary policy shocks due to the foreign banks' access to funding from their parent organizations, which can insulate them from an adverse liquidity shock in the host country (Wu, Luca, and Jeon, 2011).

Europe is somewhere between Japan and the United States in terms of bank dependence. While European countries do not have the formalized banking relationships of the Japanese keiretsus to the same degree, Europe has generally been considered to have bank-centered finance. Thus, European firms have not had the same direct access to financial markets as many US firms. However, the conversion to the euro and the consequent integration and deepening of European financial markets has moved the Eurozone to a more market-based model of corporate finance, improving the access of European firms to credit.

Even though bank lending is more important in Europe than in the United States, the evidence on the European bank lending channel is mixed. While Angeloni et al. (2003) find that most of the European evidence is consistent with a classic interest rate channel for the transmission of monetary policy, they do find some country-specific evidence supporting a bank lending channel, with bank loan supply reacting to changes in monetary policy in a number of countries. Ehrmann et al. (2001) also investigate the importance of the bank lending channel in Europe, applying a number of the empirical tests conducted on US data to European data. Consistent with the results in the United States, they find that monetary policy does alter bank loan supply, particularly for those banks that are liquidity constrained. However, they do not find that the size of the bank influences the bank's reaction to a monetary policy shock. Similarly, Gambacorta (2005), using Italian data, finds that a tightening of monetary policy reduces bank lending, with the effect mitigated for banks that are well capitalized, are relatively liquid, or can benefit from the operation of internal capital markets by being affiliated with a bank holding company. Again, bank size is not important.

More recently, a number of studies have specifically addressed the identification challenges that make it particularly difficult to obtain definitive evidence. Becchetti, Garcia,
and Trovato (2011), using Italian data, and Jimenez et al. (2012), using Spanish data, base
their analyses on individual loan application records. Becchetti, Garcia, and Trovato (2011)
investigate the relationship between the European Central Bank refinancing rate and credit
rationing by banks, using the difference between the amounts requested by borrowers and
the loan amounts granted by the banks. They find that the refinancing rate is positively
related to credit rationing, although they conclude that the effect arises from a borrower's
balance sheet effect rather than from a bank balance sheet effect. In contrast, Jimenez et al.
(2012) use the extensive margin for loan application decisions, finding an inverse relationship between short-term interest rates and loan approval that is stronger the weaker is bank
health, and concluding that the bank balance sheet effect is operative.

Maddaloni and Peydro (2011) take an alternative approach to addressing the identification challenges by relying on surveys of lending standards (for both the Eurozone and
the United States). They find that low short-term interest rates soften bank lending standards for loans to both firms and households, reinforcing the lending channel that operates
through banks. Moreover, this effect is amplified by securitization. In contrast, Altunbas,
Gambacorta, and Marques-Ibanez (2009) argue that the dramatic increase in securitization activity in Europe has weakened the efficacy of the bank lending channel. By increasing
banks' access to liquidity and ability to continue lending without expanding their balance
sheets, securitization contributes to the ability of banks to insulate their loan supply from
the effects of a tightening of monetary policy.

19.5 SOME OBSERVATIONS ON RECENT EVENTS

The severity of the Great Recession and the extremely slow recovery, both in the United
States and abroad, in the face of a dramatic and sustained easing of monetary policy have
highlighted the importance for the efficacy of monetary policy of the developments we
have been discussing. In particular, recent events have re-emphasized the important role
of financial intermediaries in the transmission of monetary policy. Particularly striking
has been the realization that most standard macroeconomic models had included little or
no role for financial institutions, resulting in very poor performance in forecasting events
around the financial crisis. Consequently, research in this area has been stimulated by a general agreement that reliance on macroeconomic models with no significant financial sector was a significant flaw in our understanding of macroeconomic dynamics. Adrian and
Shin (2011) provide a survey of some of this early research, and Brunnermeier and Sannikov
(2014) provide a good example of the difficulties posed by introducing a financial sector
into standard macroeconomic models. Moreover, in addition to recognition of the failure of
most large macroeconomic models to capture the dynamics of the financial crisis, there has
been a significant re-evaluation of the critical role that financial intermediaries can play in
the transmission of monetary policy and in amplifying the impact of financial shocks more
generally.

As a consequence, the important role of securitized lending is receiving much more attention. Prior to the financial crisis, it had frequently been assumed that collateralized credit

would be stable in a crisis because lenders would remain comfortable lending on a fully collateralized basis. The thinking was that relying less on the credit quality of the borrower, securitized lending would be relatively unaffected by a shock that impacted the perceived credit-worthiness of the borrower. However, the so-called originate-to-distribute model, whereby financial intermediaries make loans that are securitized while retaining a small proportion of the loan, turned out to be a particularly unstable source of financing during the crisis. While securitization can expand the supply of bank loans, it can also increase the cyclicality of the supply of credit and expose highly levered banks to a disruption of the securitization market (for example, Ivashina and Scharfstein, 2010b; Loutskina, 2011; and Gorton and Metrick, 2012). In particular, a drying up of the securitization pipeline can put pressure on bank liquidity, impair new bank lending, and potentially cause fire sales of securities. For example, Shleifer and Vishny (2010) show that if fire sales of securities cause security prices to fall below their fundamental values, banks may choose to hold on to their securities because of the very low valuations and may, in fact, expand their holdings at the expense of lending for new projects. Moreover, as haircuts are increased for repurchase agreements, highly levered financial intermediaries that rely on wholesale funding come under severe stress (for example, Adrian and Shin, 2009; and Gorton and Metrick, 2012). The consequent deleveraging actions by financial intermediaries further increase the downward pressure on securities valuations. In fact, the inability of most of the large investment banks to fund themselves during the crisis and the spectacular collapse of Bear Stearns and Lehman Brothers provided graphic examples that previous assumptions about the ability to roll over collateralized loans were deeply flawed.

The funding pressure on financial intermediaries was compounded by their increased reliance on wholesale funding. Although the role of financial runs had received very little attention prior to the crisis because it had been assumed that bank runs would likely be contained by deposit insurance, this area of research is being re-examined in light of the different nature of financial runs experienced during the crisis that severely limited credit extension after the failure of Lehman Brothers. A number of studies have highlighted the fact that these less traditional bank runs can have a significant impact on the supply of credit and that the effect of these supply constraints depends on the exact nature of the bank's business model. For example, Ivashina and Scharfstein (2010a) show that concerns with credit availability caused borrowers to draw down available lines of credit at the same time as banks themselves were having trouble rolling over their own short-term debt. As might be expected in such a situation, banks less dependent on wholesale funding cut their lending less than banks more dependent on wholesale funding. In fact, Gambacorta and Marques-Ibanez (2011) show that a funding model based on short-term market funding can, and did, alter banks' response to changes in monetary policy in both the United States and Europe. Adrian and Shin (2009) similarly note that capital market financing and bank lending behavior performed quite differently during the crisis. Banks that were funded by deposits expanded their credit as customers drew down their lines of credit, while market-based credit and securitization declined significantly as a result of the financial crisis. Going forward, this implies that the strength of the bank lending channel will depend in part on how bank funding models evolve in the wake of the financial crisis, as well as on how new bank regulatory regimes, such as the increasing regulatory attention being placed on the over reliance on wholesale funding by banks, evolve.

While earlier financial problems resulted in the academic literature focusing on the role of capital constraints in potentially impeding bank lending, that literature did not focus on the role of bank liquidity management. One of the key elements of the financial crisis in the fall of 2008 was how quickly banks and firms hoarded liquidity, compounding some of the collateral damage from the failure of large financial institutions. Studies have increasingly highlighted the fact that credit supply can be impeded by banks that are liquidity constrained. For example, Cornett et al. (2011) and Gambacorta and Marques-Ibanez (2011) show that banks were more likely to lend during the crisis if they were well capitalized and had significant core deposits. Banks that held more illiquid assets were less able to continue lending, particularly if their lines of credit were being drawn down by borrowers. Moreover, liquidity problems were an issue not only for banks. One of the motivations for the lending facilities established by the Federal Reserve was to ease liquidity constraints by providing liquidity to non-depository institutions through the Federal Reserve's discount window. One example of this was the run on money market funds after the Reserve Fund announced that it would no longer be able to pay a fixed net asset value to investors. Duygan-Bump et al. (2013) describe the role that discount window lending played in reducing the liquidity problems generated by runs on the money market fund industry. Because money market funds were an important source of short-term financing, including to banks, this facility helped relieve liquidity problems beyond just the money market fund industry.

In addition to the evolution of bank business models to rely more on both securitization and wholesale funding to enhance their liquidity, other dramatic changes in the financial environment associated with the financial crisis also are likely to weaken the efficacy of monetary policy operating through the lending channel. In particular, hitting the zero lower bound for short-term interest rates forced the Federal Reserve to rely on unconventional monetary policy actions to stimulate economic activity. The large-scale asset purchases undertaken by the Federal Reserve and other central banks have provided substantial excess reserves to the banking system. As a consequence, the reserve requirement is no longer a binding constraint on bank behavior. Thus, open-market purchases of securities are unlikely to have an effect on bank lending through the usual mechanism associated with the lending channel whereby banks would be forced to reduce reservable deposits. Instead, bank lending behavior will likely be governed by capital requirements and the effect of interest rates on the banks' cost of funds and the profitability of lending. In fact, recent studies have emphasized a risk-taking channel for monetary policy that places more emphasis on the willingness of banks to expand their balance sheets (for example Adrian and Shin, 2011; and Borio and Zhu, 2012). Adrian and Shin (2011) provide an overview of how changes in risk appetite, which is partly a function of monetary policy, generate a critical link between monetary policy changes, the actions of financial intermediaries, and the impact on the real economy. This connection between bank risk-taking and monetary policy will be an important topic for future research highlighting the role of banks in the conduct of monetary policy, as well as for broader financial stability issues.

19.6 CONCLUSION

Theoretical and empirical studies produced over the past two decades have emphasized the important role for banks in the transmission of monetary policy. Much of this work has highlighted a role for changes in bank assets in response to a monetary policy shock, above and beyond the familiar interest rate channel operating on the liability side of bank balance sheets. The empirical evidence provides substantial support for the view that liquidity-constrained banks and bank-dependent borrowers can be adversely impacted by a tightening of monetary policy. The evidence also indicates that a bank lending channel can be important in an international context, especially in countries where banks and firms have less direct access to financial markets.

In addition, a significant body of research highlights that during bank capital crunches the bank lending channel can be short-circuited. Again, the international evidence indicates that capital-constrained banks make it difficult for monetary policy to have as large an impact as it would have if banks were not capital constrained. Moreover, more recent evidence related to the financial crisis shows that liquidity crunches can similarly short-circuit the bank lending response to accommodative monetary policy, requiring larger modifications in monetary policy instruments to obtain the same desired change in aggregate demand.

As a result of our experiences during the recent financial crisis, we now have a better appreciation of the importance of financial intermediaries, both in their role in the transmission of monetary policy and in their impact on financial stability more generally. Given the extensive need for government support of banks and credit provision more generally, the financial crisis should provide a particularly fruitful laboratory for future research that can improve our understanding of the role of banks in the transmission of monetary policy. While alternative hypotheses are only beginning to be explored and it is too soon to fully evaluate the consequences of the changed financial and regulatory environments associated with the crisis, it is virtually certain that banks will continue to play an important, although changing, role in the transmission of monetary policy as financial markets continue to evolve.

REFERENCES

Adrian, T. and Shin, H. S. (2009). Money, Liquidity, and Monetary Policy, *American Economic Review Papers and Proceedings* 99(2), 600–605.

Adrian, T. and Shin, H. S. (2011). Financial Intermediaries and Monetary Economics. In: B. M. Friedman and M. Woodford (Eds.), *Handbook of Monetary Economics*, 601–650. Amsterdam: Elsevier.

Altunbas, Y., Gambacorta, L., and Marques-Ibanez, D. (2009). Securitization and the Bank Lending Channel, *European Economic Review* 53(8), 996–1009.

Angeloni, I., Kashyap, A. K., Mojon, B., and Terlizzese, D. (2003). Monetary Transmission in the Euro Area: Where Do We Stand?. In: I. Angeloni, A. K. Kashyap, and B. Mojon (Eds.), *Monetary Policy in the Euro-Area*, 383–412. Cambridge: Cambridge University Press.

Ashcraft, A. (2005). Are Banks Really Special? New Evidence from the FDIC-Induced Failure of Healthy Banks, *American Economic Review* 95, 1712–1730.

Ashcraft, A. (2006). New Evidence on the Lending Channel, *Journal of Money, Credit and Banking* 38(3), 751–775.

Becchetti, L., Garcia, M. M., and Trovato, G. (2011). Credit Rationing and Credit View: Empirical Evidence from an Ethical Bank in Italy, *Journal of Money, Credit and Banking* 43(6), 1217–1245.

Berger, A. N. and Udell, G. F. (1994). Did Risk-Based Capital Allocate Bank Credit and Cause a "Credit Crunch" in the United States?, *Journal of Money, Credit and Banking* 26(3), 585–628.

Bernanke, B. S. and Blinder, A. S. (1988). Credit, Money, and Aggregate Demand, *American Economic Review Papers and Proceedings* 78(2), 435–439.

Bernanke, B. S. and Blinder, A. S. (1992). The Federal Funds Rate and the Channels of Monetary Transmission, *American Economic Review* 82(4), 901–921.

Bernanke, B. S. and Gertler, M. (1995). Inside the Black Box: The Credit Channel of Monetary Policy Transmission, *Journal of Economic Perspectives* 9(4), 27–48.

Bernanke, B. S., Gertler, M., and Gilchrist, S. (1996). The Financial Accelerator and the Flight to Quality, *The Review of Economics and Statistics* 78(1), 1–15.

Borio, C. and Zhu, H. (2012). Capital Regulation, Risk-Taking and Monetary Policy: A Missing Link in the Transmission Mechanism?, *Journal of Financial Stability* 8(4), 236–251.

Brunnermeier, M. K. and Sannikov, Y. (2014). A Macroeconomic Model with a Financial Sector, *American Economic Review* 104(2), 379–421.

Caballero, R. J., Hoshi, T., and Kashyap, A. K. (2008). Zombie Lending and Depressed Restructuring in Japan, *American Economic Review* 98(5), 1943–1977.

Campello, M. (2002). Internal Capital Markets in Financial Conglomerates: Evidence from Small Bank Responses to Monetary Policy, *Journal of Finance* 57(6), 2773–2805.

Cecchetti, S. G. (1995). Distinguishing Theories of the Monetary Transmission Mechanism, *Federal Reserve Bank of St. Louis Review* May/June, 83–97.

Cetorelli, N. and Goldberg, L. S. (2012). Banking Globalization and Monetary Transmission, *Journal of Finance* 67(5), 1811–1843.

Cornett, M. M., Ncnutt, J. J., Strahan, P. E., and Tehranian, H. (2011). Liquidity Risk Management and Credit Supply in the Financial Crisis, *Journal of Financial Economics* 101(2), 297–312.

Driscoll, J. O. (2004). Does Bank Lending Affect Output? Evidence from the US States, *Journal of Monetary Economics* 51(3), 451–471.

Duygan-Bump, B., Parkinson, P., Rosengren, E., Suarez, G., and Willen, P. (2013). How Effective Were the Federal Reserve Emergency Liquidity Facilities? Evidence from the Asset-Backed Commercial Paper Money Market Mutual Fund Liquidity Facility, *Journal of Finance* 68(2), 715–737.

Ehrmann, M., Gambacorta, L., Martìnez-Pagès, J., Sevestre, P., and Worms, A. (2001). Financial Systems and the Role of Banks in Monetary Policy Transmission in the Euro Area, European Central Bank Working Paper No. 105.

Fazzari, S. M., Hubbard, R. G., and Petersen, B. C. (1988). Financing Constraints and Corporate Investment, *Brookings Papers on Economic Activity* 1, 141–195.

Ferri, G. and Kang, T. S. (1999). The Credit Channel at Work: Lessons from the Republic of Korea's Financial Crisis, World Bank Policy Research Working Paper No. 2190.

Fields, L. P., Fraser, D. R., Berry, T. L., and Byers, S. (2006). Do Bank Loans Relationships Still Matter?, *Journal of Money, Credit and Banking* 38(5), 1195–1209.

Gambacorta, L. (2005). Inside the Bank Lending Channel, *European Economic Review* 49(7), 1737–1759.

Gambacorta, L. and Marques-Ibanez, D. (2011). The Bank Lending Channel: Lessons from the Crisis, BIS Working Paper No. 345, May.

Gande, A. and Saunders, A. (2012). Are Banks Still Special When There Is a Secondary Market for Loans?, *Journal of Finance* 67(5), 1649–1684.

Gertler, M. and Gilchrist, S. (1993). The Role of Credit Market Imperfections in the Monetary Transmission Mechanism: Arguments and Evidence, *The Scandinavian Journal of Economics* 95(1), 43–64.

Gertler, M. and Gilchrist, S. (1994). Monetary Policy, Business Cycles, and the Behavior of Small Manufacturing Firms, *The Quarterly Journal of Economics* 109(2), 309–340.

Gorton, G. and Metrick, A. (2012). Securitized Banking and the Run on Repo, *Journal of Financial Economics* 104(3), 425–451.

Hall, B. J. (1993). How Has the Basel Accord Affected Bank Portfolios?, *Journal of the Japanese and International Economies* 7(4), 408–440.

Hancock, D. and Wilcox, J. A. (1994). Bank Capital and the Credit Crunch: The Roles of Risk-Weighted and Unweighted Capital Regulation, *Journal of the American Real Estate and Urban Economics Association* 22(1), 59–94.

Holod, D. and Peek, J. (2007). Asymmetric Information and Liquidity Constraints: A New Test, *Journal of Banking & Finance* 31(8), 2425–2451.

Hoshi, T. and Kashyap, A. N. (2001). *Corporate Financing and Governance in Japan.* Cambridge, MA: MIT Press.

Hoshi, T., Scharfstein, D., and Singleton, K. J. (1993). Japanese Corporate Investment and Bank of Japan Guidance of Commercial Bank Lending. In: K. J. Singleton (Ed.), *Japanese Monetary Policy*, 63–94. Chicago: University of Chicago Press.

Hubbard, R. G. (1995). Is There a "Credit Channel" for Monetary Policy?, *Federal Reserve Bank of St. Louis Review* May/June, 63–77.

Ito, T. and Sasaki, Y. N. (2002). Impacts of the Basel Capital Standard on Japanese Banks' Behavior, *Journal of the Japanese and International Economies* 16(3), 372–397.

Ivashina, V. and Scharfstein, D. (2010a). Bank Lending during the Financial Crisis of 2008, *Journal of Financial Economics* 97(3), 319–338.

Ivashina, V. and Scharfstein, D. (2010b). Loan Syndication and Credit Cycles, *American Economic Review Papers and Proceedings* 100(2), 57–61.

James, C. (1987). Some Evidence on the Uniqueness of Bank Loans, *Journal of Financial Economics* 19(2), 217–235.

Jimenez, G., Ongena, S., Peydro, J. L., and Saurina, J. (2012). Credit Supply and Monetary Policy: Identifying the Bank Balance-Sheet Channel with Loan Applications, *American Economic Review* 102(5), 2301–2326.

Kang, J. K. and Shivdasani, A. (1995). Firm Performance, Corporate Governance, and Top Executive Turnover in Japan, *Journal of Financial Economics* 38(1), 29–58.

Kang, J. K. and Stulz, R. M. (2000). Do Banking Shocks Affect Borrowing Firm Performance? An Analysis of the Japanese Experience, *Journal of Business* 73, 1–23.

Kashyap, A. K., Lamont, O. A., and Stein, J. C. (1994). Credit Conditions and the Cyclical Behavior of Inventories, *The Quarterly Journal of Economics* 109(3), 565–592.

Kaplan, S. N. and Minton, B. A. (1994). Appointments of Outsiders to Japanese Boards: Determinants and Implications for Managers, *Journal of Financial Economics* 36(2), 225–258.

Kashyap, A. K. and Stein, J. C. (1994). Monetary Policy and Bank Lending. In: N. G. Mankiw (Ed.), *Monetary Policy*, 221–256. Chicago: University of Chicago Press.

Kashyap, A. K. and Stein, J. C. (1995). The Impact of Monetary Policy on Bank Balance Sheets, *Carnegie-Rochester Conference Series on Public Policy* 42, 151–195.

Kashyap, A. K. and Stein, J. C. (2000). What Do a Million Observations on Banks Say about the Transmission of Monetary Policy?, *American Economic Review* 90(3), 407–428.

Kashyap, A. K. and Stein, J. C. (2004). Cyclical Implications of the Basel II Capital Standard, *Federal Reserve Bank of Chicago Economic Perspectives* First Quarter, 18–31.

Kashyap, A. K., Stein, J. C., and Wilcox, D. W. (1993). Monetary Policy and Credit Conditions: Evidence from the Composition of External Finance, *American Economic Review* 83(1), 78–98.

Kashyap, A. K., Stein, J. C., and Wilcox, D. W. (1996). Monetary Policy and Credit Conditions: Evidence from the Composition of External Finance: Reply, *American Economic Review* 86(1), 310–314.

Kishan, R. P. and Opiela, T. P. (2000). Bank Size, Bank Capital, and the Bank Lending Channel, *Journal of Money, Credit and Banking* 32(1), 121–141.

Loutskina, E. (2011). The Role of Securitization in Bank Liquidity and Funding Management, *Journal of Financial Economics* 100(3), 663–684.

Loutskina, E. and Strahan, P. (2009). Securitization and the Declining Impact of Bank Finance on Loan Supply: Evidence from Mortgage Originations, *Journal of Finance* 64(2), 861–922.

Ludvigson, S. (1998). The Channel of Monetary Transmission to Demand: Evidence from the Market for Automobile Credit, *Journal of Money, Credit and Banking* 30(3), 365–383.

Maddaloni, A. and Peydro, J. L. (2011). Bank Risk-Taking, Securitization, Supervision, and Low Interest Rates: Evidence from the Euro-Area and the US Lending Standards, *Review of Financial Studies* 24(6), 2121–2165.

Montgomery, H. (2005). The Effect of the Basel Accord on Bank Portfolios in Japan, *Journal of the Japanese and International Economies* 19(1), 24–36.

Morck, R. and Nakamura, M. (1999). Banks and Corporate Control in Japan, *Journal of Finance* 54(1), 319–339.

Morgan, D. P. (1998). The Credit Effect of Monetary Policy: Evidence Using Loan Commitments, *Journal of Money, Credit and Banking* 30(1), 102–118.

Oliner, S. D. and Rudebusch, G. D. (1996a). Is There a Broad Credit Channel for Monetary Policy?, *Federal Reserve Bank of San Francisco Economic Review* 1, 3–13.

Oliner, S. D. and Rudebusch, G. D. (1996b). Monetary Policy and Credit Conditions: Evidence from the Composition of External Finance: Comment, *American Economic Review* 86(1), 300–309.

Olivero, M. P., Li, Y., and Jeon, B. N. (2011). Consolidation in Banking and the Lending Channel of Monetary Transmission: Evidence from Asia and Latin America, *Journal of International Money and Finance* 30(6), 1034–1054.

Peek, J. and Rosengren, E. S. (1995a). The Capital Crunch: Neither a Borrower nor a Leader Be, *Journal of Money, Credit and Banking* 27(3), 625–638.

Peek, J. and Rosengren, E. S. (1995b). Bank Regulation and the Credit Crunch, *Journal of Banking & Finance* 19(3–4), 679–692.

Peek, J. and Rosengren, E. S. (1997). The International Transmission of Financial Shocks: The Case of Japan, *American Economic Review* 87(4), 495–505.

Peek, J. and Rosengren, E. S. (2000). Collateral Damage: Effects of the Japanese Bank Crisis on Real Activity in the United States, *American Economic Review* 90(1), 30–45.

Peek, J. and Rosengren, E. S. (2005). Unnatural Selection: Perverse Incentives and the Misallocation of Credit in Japan, *American Economic Review* 95(4), 1144–1166.

Peek, J., Rosengren, E. S., and Tootell G. M. B. (2003). Identifying the Macroeconomic Effect of Loan Supply Shocks, *Journal of Money, Credit and Banking* 35(6), 931–946.

Petersen, M. A. and Rajan, R. G. (1995). The Effect of Credit Market Competition on Lending Relationships, *The Quarterly Journal of Economics* 110(2), 407–443.

Romer, C. D. and Romer, D. H. (1990). New Evidence on the Monetary Transmission Mechanism, *Brookings Papers on Economic Activity* 1, 149–213.

Shleifer, A. and Vishny, R. W. (2010). Asset Fire Sales and Credit Easing, *American Economic Review Papers and Proceedings* 100(2), 46–50.

Slovin, M. B., Sushka, M. E., and Poloncheck, J. A. (1993). The Value of Bank Durability: Borrowers as Bank Stakeholders, *Journal of Finance* 48(1), 247–266.

Strahan, P. E. (2009). Liquidity Production in Twenty-first-Century Banking. In: A. Berger, P. Molyneux, and J. O. S. Wilson (Eds.), *Oxford Handbook of Banking*, 112–145. Oxford: Oxford University Press.

Wu, J., Luca, A. C., and Jeon, B. N. (2011). Foreign Bank Penetration and the Lending Channel in Emerging Economies: Evidence from Bank-Level Panel Data, *Journal of International Money and Finance* 30(1), 1128–1156.

CHAPTER 20

....

LENDER OF LAST RESORT AND BANK CLOSURE POLICY

A Post-Crisis Perspective*

....

XAVIER FREIXAS AND BRUNO M. PARIGI

20.1 INTRODUCTION

THE financial crisis that began in 2007 redefines the functions of the lender of last resort (LOLR) of the twenty-first century, first by placing it at the intersection of monetary policy, fiscal policy, supervision, and regulation of the banking industry; second, by giving regulatory authorities the additional responsibility of monitoring the interbank market; and, third, by extending its role to cover the possible bailout of non-bank institutions.

Since the creation of the first central banks (CB) in the nineteenth century, the existence of a LOLR has been a key issue for the structure of the banking industry. The banking system has to provide mechanisms to manage banks' liquidity risk because one of the major functions of banks is to offer access to the payment system and facilitate property rights transfer, and because it is efficient to combine these functions with opaque long-term investments on the asset side (delegated monitoring) and with demand deposits on the liability side (as justified by Diamond and Dybvig, 1983; Diamond, 1984; Calomiris and Kahn, 1991; Diamond and Rajan, 2001). Although in any developed economy the principal mechanism to cope with both excesses and shortages of liquidity will be the interbank market, the well functioning of the banking system might still require an additional mechanism to avoid that both aggregate and bank specific liquidity risk mismanagement result in a bank defaulting

* We would like to thank Falko Fecht, several conference audiences, and the editors for their comments. We gratefully acknowledge funding from the Italian Ministry of University and Research, and jointly from the Italian and Spanish Ministries of University and Research through a grant Azioni Integrate/Accion Integradas 2006–08.

on its contractual obligations. The terminology "of last resort" itself emphasizes that this institution is not intended to replace existing regular market mechanisms, but should make up for its possible failures. This justifies the existence of a discount window in the US and the marginal lending facility in Eurozone.

The basic objectives of lender of the LOLR were first formulated by Thornton (1802) and Bagehot (1873), who argued that the facility was necessary in order to support the whole financial system and to provide stable monetary growth (Humphrey, 1989). Since then, the role of the LOLR has become a more controversial issue. The debate is inherent to the fact that, by providing insolvent banks with liquidity, we both allow them to escape market discipline and promote forbearance. There is a consensus among academics and central bankers that a mechanism should exist to allow solvent banks to obtain liquidity if the interbank market fails to operate correctly. Further, there is general agreement that insolvent banks should not access standard liquidity facilities and that, if necessary, their insolvency should be dealt with on a case-by-case basis. Problems arise because liquidity shocks affecting banks might be undistinguishable from solvency shocks. So, the debate about the role of the LOLR is connected with the efficient bank closure policy and, more generally, with the costs of bank failures and of the safety net, which is more the domain of fiscal policy.

This connection between the LOLR and bank bailout policy is not yet fully accepted. This may be due to the fact that access to liquidity and the role of the LOLR have evolved through history. Those accepting Bagehot's view of the LOLR may argue that it relates to a world where solvent banks were to be protected against sudden deposit withdrawals without the recourse to a well developed repo market and without the CB privilege of issuing fiat money. With the emergence of a well-functioning repo market, today's conception of the role of the LOLR is completely different. The LOLR may step in exceptionally to prevent a collapse of the payment system that could be triggered by the lack of liquidity, but this should normally be dealt with by means of the appropriate monetary policy. So, *if* the money markets are well-functioning, the LOLR should manage aggregate liquidity only and leave the issue of solvency to the market that will eliminate the lame ducks.

The critical step in this argument is the assumption of perfect money markets. Once we consider imperfect money markets we are forced to consider cases where it is impossible to establish whether a bank is solvent or insolvent. So we have to acknowledge that in solvency cases the LOLR is sometimes acting to channel liquidity and therefore is improving the efficiency of the monetary policy framework, while in the second case it is part of the safety net and directly related to the overall regulatory framework. Therefore the design of an optimal LOLR mechanism has to take into account the monetary framework, the banking regulation context, and fiscal policy.

The panic of 2008, which originated with the 2007 subprime crisis in the US, vividly illustrates the new role of LOLR. Years of accommodating monetary policy, regulatory arbitrage to save capital and waves of financial innovations—which by definition tend to escape traditional prudential regulation—had created the conditions for slack credit standards without the rating agencies calling for adequate risk premia. The opacity of bank assets and the off-balance-sheet finance vehicles created to hold mortgages resulted at some point in a dramatic and sudden reappraisal of risk premia and the refusal to roll over the short-term debt issued to finance these assets. As with a thin market typical of the Akerlof lemons problem (Freixas and Jorge, 2008) financial intermediaries became reluctant to lend to each other if not for very short maturities. The fear that the interbank market might not work well and might fail to recycle the emergency liquidity provided by the CBs around the world in various and coordinated ways induced financial institutions to hoard some of the extra liquidity instead of recycling it by lending it to liquidity-deprived financial institutions, a rational equilibrium strategy. Thus, channeling emergency liquidity assistance through the interbank market did not work precisely because the interbank market did not function properly. To limit the systemic feedbacks of the sudden deleveraging of financial institutions in 2008, the Fed took the unprecedented steps of increasing the list of collateral eligible for CB discount lending, of extending emergency liquidity assistance to investment banks, government sponsored entities, money market mutual funds, a large insurance company, of entering swap agreements with other central banks to provide dollar liquidity to banks outside the US, and of acquiring bank capital. Preventing a complete meltdown of the financial system required that the CB guarantees (and accepts potential losses) that most, if not all claims, on financial institutions will be fulfilled, which is more the resort of the bank regulatory authority and fiscal policy than of the CB alone. As a consequence, the Fed balance sheet grew from about $900 billion in September 2008 to more than $2 trillion in December 2008 and to more than $3 trillion at the end of spring 2013, largely financed by the creation of high powered money and by loans from the US Treasury. Discount windowing lending grew from a few hundred million dollars under normal circumstances to more than $500 billion at the height of the crisis. In the four months from September to December 2008 the Fed put more than $600 billion of reserves into the private sector (against September's 2007 total outstanding level of reserves of about $50 billion) in what Lucas (2008) has described as the boldest exercise of the LOLR function in the history of the Fed.

Consequently, we argue that the 2008 panic has shown that it would be erroneous to adopt a narrow definition of the LOLR and to state that its role should be limited to funding illiquid but solvent depository institutions, while capital injections should be the Treasury responsibility. This would lead to a very simplistic analysis of the LOLR functions, as the complex decisions would be either ignored or handed over to the Treasury. In our view, such a narrow view of the LOLR would create an artificial separation between lending by the LOLR at no risk and the closure or bailout decision by the Treasury that could lead to incorrect policy assessments.

On the contrary, the view of the LOLR that we take here has to be a broad one, encompassing the closure or bailout decision defining the LOLR as *an agency that has the faculty to extend credit to a financial institution unable to secure funds through the regular circuit.* This definition omits any mention of the fact that the institution is illiquid or insolvent. Obviously, this does not preclude that a separation between LOLR and Treasury decisions might prove efficient. This broad definition has the additional benefit of encompassing the management of overall banking crises, which would be difficult to consider from the narrow perspective of pure liquidity provision.

Once we agree that the LOLR policy has to be part of the overall banking safety net, the interdependence of its different components becomes clear. First, the existence and the extent of the coverage of a deposit insurance system, as well documented in Santos (2006), limits the social cost of a bank's bankruptcy, and therefore, reduces the instances where a LOLR intervention will be required. Second, capital regulation reduces the probability of a bank in default being effectively insolvent, and so has a similar role in limiting the costly intervention of the LOLR. Third, the procedures to bail out or liquidate a bank, determined by the legal and enforcement framework, will determine the cost–benefit analysis of a LOLR intervention.

Obviously, the LOLR policy and its efficiency will depend upon the overall financial environment. When a liquid market for Certificates of Deposit (CDs), Treasury bill and securitized loans, or even simply for the loans themselves exists, banks will only exceptionally encounter difficulties in coping with their liquidity shocks. Adopting a perspective of an all-embracing safety net does not mean that the safety net has to be the responsibility of a unique agent. Often several regulatory agencies interact, because different functions related to the well functioning of the safety net are allocated to different agents. It is quite reasonable to separate monetary policy from banking regulation, and the separation of the deposit insurance company from the CB makes the cost of deposit insurance more transparent. Furthermore, the national jurisdiction of regulation makes cross-border banking a joint responsibility for the home and host regulatory agencies.[1] This implies that regulation will be the outcome of a game among different agents that may cooperate or may face conflicts.

Finally, as part of the financial environment, the regulatory structure will be crucial. In particular, LOLR functions are usually attributed to the CB, while another institution, often the Deposit Insurance Company, is in charge of closure. So how the two decisions are coordinated is clearly an issue to be considered.

The rest of this chapter is structured as follows: in Section 20.2 we examine the justification of LOLR lending in a simplified framework where only liquidity shocks arise. Section 20.3 considers contagion in the interbank market. Section 20.4 is devoted to the case where liquidity shocks cannot be disentangled from solvency ones. Section 20. 5 discusses the issues raised by the implementation of the LOLR policy within the safety net. Section 20.6 concludes.

20.2 PURE LIQUIDITY SHOCKS

As already mentioned, one of the major features of banks, and a justification of their existence, is that they combine assets with a long maturity with short-lived liabilities, as the investment and production schedules may not coincide with the consumption needs of the individuals. As a consequence, an institution providing liquidity to the banking system has a key role in the well-functioning of the whole credit, deposit, and payment system. We will study here what types of liquidity shocks might affect banks and how emergency liquidity assistance (ELA) may help them cope with those shocks. However, setting a framework that explains why banks might face liquidity risk does not mean that a LOLR should exist. First, it could be argued that monetary policy, jointly with peer monitoring could solve the problem. Second, even if a specific institution is required, a private LOLR without any privileged access to CB liquidity could provide liquidity to the banks that need it.

---

[1] In the fall of 2008 the Belgian–Dutch banking and insurance conglomerate Fortis was rescued by a joint financial effort of the monetary and fiscal authorities of the Benelux countries, and the good offices of the President of the European Central Bank. This rescue was subsequently complicated by the Belgian courts rejecting the legal structure of the deal on the ground that shareholders rights had not been respected.

We will first examine the different models of pure liquidity shocks, then turn to the analysis of a pure liquidity shock event, the disruption of the market as a result of the events of September 11, 2001, and close this section by using historical evidence to discuss the pros and cons of a private LOLR.

20.2.1 Maturities Transformation Risk for a Single Institution

The main motivation for LOLR in a modern economy is the need to prevent the threat of systemic risk whereby the crisis of one financial institution affects others.

The classical models of Bryant (1980) and Diamond and Dybvig (1983) show that consumers who face independent risks about the timing of their consumption needs can pool resources to form a bank that offers demand deposits, invests the proceeds in illiquid assets, and keeps an amount of liquidity equal to the expected value of the liquidity needs of its depositors and offers a valuable insurance function. However, the transformation of maturities exposes the bank to the threat of bank runs if a large number of depositors decide to withdraw their money for reasons other than liquidity.

In this approach there are two possible equilibria. In the efficient one depositors withdraw only to satisfy their interim consumption needs, thus allowing the illiquid investment to mature. But since the value of bank assets does not cover the contractual obligations of the bank with its depositors at the interim stage there is also an inefficient equilibrium, where it is optimal for all depositors to withdraw early (a run), even for those that have no immediate consumption needs. This may cause the "fire sale" of long-term or illiquid assets, which, if generalized, may further depress asset values and cause a vicious circle. Deposit insurance and prudential regulation for many decades have essentially confined bank runs to textbook phenomena. This has changed dramatically with the crisis that began in 2007. Even in sophisticated banking systems, runs have reappeared in the retail markets—witness the run on the deposits of the mortgage lender Northern Rock in 2007,[2] and in 2008 the runs on among others, IndyMack, a Californian bank, and of Washington Mutual, the largest US thrift. More so, runs appeared in the 2007–09 crisis on the repo market where large investors refused to roll over the short-term credit that financed asset-backed securities, and in the money market mutual funds (MMMF) from which institutional investors withdrew en masse after the Lehman failure.

The traditional way to address equilibrium selection is to imagine that depositors behave in one way or another according to an exogenous event (a "sunspot" in the jargon of this literature). Since in one equilibrium banks increase welfare and in the other they decrease welfare, the impossibility to establish which equilibrium will prevail makes it impossible to determine whether it is ex ante desirable that banks arise as providers of intertemporal consumption insurance. In other words it is not clear why consumers would find it optimal to deposit their money in a bank in the first place.[3] As a consequence, absent regulatory

---

[2] This was the first bank run in Britain since 1866. Northern Rock was later nationalized by the UK Government.

[3] In an attempt to obviate this problem Cooper and Ross (1998) study a modified Diamond and Dybvig model that permits comparison between the welfare properties of a run-proof economy and of an economy that allows runs.

safeguards, policy recommendations are based on the assumption that a particular equilibrium will prevail, an issue that more recent modeling approaches using global games are not faced with. Despite this shortcoming, the Bryant–Diamond–Dybvig approach has been the modern draught-horse for the study of financial instability and systemic risk.

In the modern economy, liquidity transformation takes on a different form from that envisioned in the classical Bryant–Diamond–Dybvig setup. Two major changes that have occurred are relevant here. First, banks have dramatically lowered the proportion of their liquid assets in their investment portfolio. Second, since long-term funding is more expensive than short-term funding, banks have funded an increasing proportion of long-term illiquid assets with short-term borrowing on the wholesale market. As a result, banks have replaced a relatively stable source of short-term funding (such as demand deposits) with short-term interest-sensitive wholesale funding and rolling over debt. Brunnermeier (2008) observes that in 2006 and 2007 the short-term overnight repos were around 25% of the assets of brokers–dealers, thus implying that the whole balance sheet must be refinanced every four days. These related changes have put a tremendous pressure on any financial institution in cases of funding problems.

One of the major features of the subprime crisis of 2007–08, the fact that with the widespread adoption of the so called "originate-and-distribute" model of banking, maturity transformation takes place in part off balance sheet, and therefore escapes banking regulation and the traditional regulatory mechanisms to prevent runs, is to be considered also from this perspective: a liquidity crisis in a conduit or special purpose vehicle (SPV), that is funded through a rollover of short-term debt is akin (from the point of view of liquidity) to a holding bank company with an unregulated subsidiary where bank runs can occur.

20.2.2 Systemic Risk

Financially fragile intermediaries are exposed to the threat of systemic risk. Systemic risk can arise from the existence of a network of financial contracts from several types of operations: the payment system, the interbank market, and the market for derivatives. The tremendous growth experienced by these operations increases the degree of interconnections among operators and among countries and thus increases the potential for contagion.

A number of papers have modeled contagion among banks and the ways to prevent it. The discussion here will focus on the two we consider most relevant. Allen and Gale (2000) show that financial contagion can emerge in a banking system of a multi-region economy. The interbank deposit market offers insurance against regional liquidity shocks but also provides a channel through which the shocks to the agents' preferences in one region can spread over other regions. Allen and Gale (2000) consider a version of the Diamond–Dybvig model with several regions in which the number of early consumers (those demanding liquidity at an interim stage) and late consumers fluctuate. An interbank market in deposits allows insurance as regions with liquidity surpluses provide it to regions with shortages. This constitutes an efficient mechanism, provided there is enough aggregate liquidity. But if there is shortage of aggregate liquidity, due to a larger proportion of early consumers than expected at the contracting stage, the interbank deposit market can turn into the channel through which a crisis spreads. When facing a liquidity crisis, before liquidating long-term investments, banks liquidate their deposits in other banks, a strategy that in the aggregate just cancels out. In cases of shortage of aggregate liquidity, the only way to increase the consumption good early is eventually to liquidate long-term investments. A financial crisis in one region can thus spread via contagion. Note that the nature of the crisis, and of the solution, is different with respect to the market for retail deposits as for example in the Diamond–Dybvig model. In the retail market runs occur because banks liquidate when they have insufficient liquidity to meet the fixed payment of the deposit contracts. Hence by making the contracts contingent or discretionary, the incentive to run can be eliminated. In the interbank markets by contrast, the reciprocal nature of the deposit agreements makes these solutions impossible. Moreover, the likelihood that contagion happens depends on the architecture of the interbank deposits. If each region is connected with all the others the initial impact of the crisis can be attenuated and contagion avoided. On the other hand, if each region is connected with few others the impact of the initial crisis may be felt strongly on the neighboring regions.

In Freixas, Parigi, Rochet (2000) a system of interbank credit lines arises because depositors face uncertainty about where they need to consume. Financial connections reduce the cost of holding liquidity but make the banking system prone to experience speculative gridlocks even if all banks are solvent. The mechanism of the gridlock is the following: if the depositors in one location, wishing to consume in another location, believe that there will be not enough resources for their consumption at the location of destination, their best response is to withdraw their deposits at their home location. This triggers the early liquidation of the investment in the home location, which, by backward induction, makes it optimal for the depositors in other locations to do the same. The CB can play a role of crisis manager: when all banks are solvent the CB's role is simply to act as a coordinating device by guaranteeing the credit lines of all banks. Since the guarantees are not used in equilibrium this action entails no cost. When, instead, one bank is insolvent because of poor returns on its investment, the CB's role is to close the bank in orderly manner.

Both Allen and Gale (2000) and Freixas, Parigi, Rochet (2000) emphasize the key role the interbank market plays in propagating a crisis through the intertwining of their balance sheets, the default of one bank generating an immediate loss to all its unsecured creditors. Both emphasize that the structure of payments, with more or less diversification or more or less relationship lending, will be a key characteristic of the resilience of the banking system. Yet from a policy point of view the two models have a crucial difference. In Allen and Gale any CB emergency liquidity injection allows solving the crisis no matter where the liquidity is injected, as it is profitable for one liquidity long institution to lend to a liquidity short one. In Freixas, Parigi, Rochet, since the crisis does not originate in an unpredicted liquidity shortage but in a rational alternative equilibrium strategy for depositors, injecting additional cash in the aggregate will not help. Even in the case where every bank has access to sufficient liquidity, the inefficient gridlock equilibrium exists where banks resources are used in an inefficient way. Solving the crisis in the Freixas, Parigi, Rochet model falls more to the bank regulatory authority than to the CB, as it requires guaranteeing that all claims on banks will be fulfilled. So, despite apparent similarities, the LOLR plays the role of liquidity provider in the Allen–Gale model, while it plays the role of crisis manager in the Freixas, Parigi, Rochet model.

The 2008 crisis offers a clear example of the distinction between systemic risk in Allen and Gale (2000) and Freixas, Parigi, Rochet (2000). The resulting equilibrium closely resembles the gridlock described by Freixas, Parigi, Rochet (2000) where the fear that a debtor bank will not honor its obligations induces the depositors of the creditor bank to withdraw deposits, thus triggering the liquidation of assets in a chain reaction style. This is the modern form of a "bank run" where financial intermediaries refuse to renew credit lines to other intermediaries, thus threatening the very survival of the system.

20.2.3 The LOLR and Liquidity Shocks: The 9/11 Case Study

An important criticism of the classical view of the LOLR in today's financial market has been raised by Goodfriend and King (1988). They argue that the existence of a fully collateralized repo market allows CBs to provide an adequate amount of liquidity, which is then allocated by the interbank market. Since individual interventions would no longer be necessary, the discount window is made obsolete. Well-informed participants in the interbank market are capable of distinguishing between illiquid and insolvent banks. These arguments have been so influential that the Bagehot view of the LOLR is often considered obsolete in well-developed financial markets. Yet Goodfriend and King's argument contradicts the asymmetric information assumption that is regarded as the main justification for financial intermediation.

The liquidity effects of the events of September 11, 2001 offer a clear example of a system-wide liquidity shock and illustrate well the systemic threats posed by the interdependencies in payment flows even in the absence of solvency shocks, thus allowing the Goodfriend and King view of the LOLR to be tested in a financially developed economy. McAndrews and Potter (2002) make the point that on September 11 banks experienced severe difficulties in making payments because of the widespread damage to the payments infrastructure. The nettable nature of payment flows allows banks to operate in the Fedwire system—a real-time gross payment system—with an amount of reserves which is about 1% of their total daily payments, with the rest coming from the inflows of payments from other banks. This high velocity of circulation exposes the system to great risk if the normal coordination and synchronization of payments collapses, as happened on September 11. The events of that day resulted in an uneven distribution of liquidity in the banking system. McAndrews and Potter (2002) observe that the incident that triggered the liquidity shortfall was well known to all market participants and was generally perceived as a pure liquidity shock, unrelated to the fundamental solvency of any major financial institution. However, the fear of a systemic threat due to the breakdown of the coordination mechanism that banks use in their normal handling of payment flows induced the Fed to act. McAndrews and Potter (2002) and Coleman (2002) document that, on September 11 and in the following days, the Fed took a number of steps to make sure that market participants would know that the Fed was ready to provide the liquidity that the market demanded. The Fed did not simply inject liquidity; it also invited the banks to benefit from the discount window by lifting the stigma that is usually attached to this type of borrowing. Nevertheless, it could be argued that, had all the operations been channeled through the open market, the effect would have been the same. If so, it would be impossible to see if the liquidity crisis was of the Allen and Gale type or of the Freixas, Parigi, Rochet type.

Of course, the effect of the damage to the infrastructure does not invalidate the Goodfriend and King thesis. Yet McAndrews and Potter (2002) point out another important lesson from these events that help discriminating between the two models. Banks that are reluctant to pay one another are also reluctant to lend one another. Thus, in these circumstances, injecting liquidity through open market operations (OMO) may be ineffective at redistributing balances because the additional funds may not be circulated where needed, contrary to discount window interventions. Only once coordination among banks has been re-established OMO may be preferred as they leave to the market the task to allocate liquidity.

20.2.4 Private LOLR

The financial history of the US before the creation of the Federal Reserve System in 1913 offers good examples of private arrangements to solve bank crises, namely the commercial bank clearinghouses (CBCs) (See Gorton, 1985, and Gorton and Mullineaux, 1987 for a detailed analysis of CBCs). Originally developed to facilitate check clearance, the CBCs became organizations that performed a variety of tasks. During bank panics the CBC ceased to behave as an authority-regulating competing banks and instead effectively combined the member banks into a single organization, with the group accepting corporate liability for the debts of each individual member. Among the most significant actions of the CBC during a bank panic were the suspension of the publication of individual banks' balance sheets and the publication instead of aggregate balance sheet information for the clearinghouse as a whole, the suspension of convertibility of deposits into currency, and the issuance of loan certificates. Loan certificates were clearinghouse liabilities that member banks could use in the clearing process and circulate as currency. These loan certificates, issued up to a fraction of the market value of the assets of the member bank seeking them, were in effect the clearinghouse's fiat money.

In the US, cooperation among banks produced stable interbank relationships, which in the case of the Suffolk system—an important example of a self-regulating bank clearing system operating throughout New England from the 1820s through the 1850s—were even more resilient than was anticipated by their proponents (Calomiris, Kahn, Kroszner, 1996). Many observers pointed out that the Federal Reserve System was a development of the existing CBCs (Timberlake, 1978, 1993; White, 1983; Gorton, 1985; and Calomiris, Kahn, Kroszner, 1996). However, one criticism of the functioning of the CBCs was that their membership criteria were too stringent and designed to reflect only the interest of the member banks, not the public interest. For example the New York Clearing House Association demanded a very high level of reserves to qualify for membership so that many banks preferred to opt out of the clearing system (Sprague 1910). In the panic of 1907, a solvent Trust Company, the Knickerbocker Trust—which did not belong to any CBC—was forced to suspend as a result of liquidity problems. As argued by Friedman and Schwartz (1963, p.159), "Had the Knickerbocker been a member of the Clearing House, it probably would have been helped, and further crisis developments might thereby have been prevented." The consequence was one of the severest contractions in US economic history, which gave the impetus for the founding of the Federal Reserve System.

So the evidence seems to indicate that, as expected, CBCs are more concerned about their own narrow interests than about the risk of contagion that may result from the bankruptcy of a bank outside their network. This is why a LOLR should have a mandate to preserve financial stability and should therefore encompass all banks, not only the ones affiliated with its network. Dang, Gorton, and Holmstrom (2012) use the example of the loan certificates issued by US CBCs to draw an important lesson about the current financial crisis. By issuing loan certificates the CBCs were offering new securities that were insensitive to private information. This made the private information about individual banks debt irrelevant and the loan certificates liquid. More generally, the role of the LOLR is to exchange information-sensitive debt for information-insensitive debt free from adverse selection issues and hence liquid. This process closely resembles the mutualization of large chunks of the private financial institutions' debts in the current crisis and it envisions a role for the LOLR that can only be conducted together with the fiscal authorities.

20.3 SYSTEMIC CRISES AND CONTAGION

The mismatch between asset and liabilities maturity makes it imperative that a mechanism for the interbank transfer of liquidity is in place. Banks are related to one another through a network of assets and liabilities, and a joint reputation. As a consequence, when assessing the cost-benefit of a LOLR operation, prevention of contagion and systemic risk will be the first factors to be considered. Central banks have been clear in asserting that they will bail out banks that are systemic, thus comforting the market prevailing view that banks are not equally treated, as some banks are systemically important.

The financial crisis of 2008 onward has changed our views of how a systemic banking problem can emerge. Before the crisis, the conventional wisdom was that the main mechanism was the "domino effect," whereby the default of one bank generated both a change in depositors' and investors' confidence in the banking system as well as losses and illiquidity for the banks that were the defaulting bank's creditors. The current crisis has shown that the decrease in the prices of the assets the banks were holding (ABS, CDOs but also mortgages) was the main driving force. As a consequence, the injection of public liquidity to substitute the sudden lack of inside liquidity based on securities that were to become "toxic" was even more important than previously thought.

We will therefore start by reviewing the literature on the "domino effect," then consider the recent literature on "fire sale prices" and its impact on financial institutions fragility, before analyzing some proposals to measure contagion. Indeed, since the prevention of systemic risk is one of the main rationales behind the LOLR it is important to assess and quantify it. Unfortunately, lack of data availability has limited the analysis so far.

20.3.1 The "Domino Effect" Approach

As the domino effect perspective on contagion is based on one bank bankruptcy triggering other banks' bankruptcies, the analysis takes as given the failure of a bank and tracks its effects through the whole banking system. From a theoretical perspective, this approach is perfectly justified. Nevertheless, the majority of studies show that the effect is quite limited.

Humphrey (1986) was the first to investigate the extent of contagion by using data from the Clearinghouse Interbank Payments System (CHIPS) at a time when the payment system led to important interbank credit and debit positions. The analysis was extended by Furfine (2003), which studied the US federal funds market and found that contagion was quite limited (in the worst case scenario the failure of the largest bank with a 40% loss given default, would have affected between two and six banks or 0.8% of total bank assets). Interestingly, Furfine pointed out that liquidity presents a greater threat: if a large federal funds debtor becomes unable to borrow, illiquidity could spread to banks representing almost 9% of the US banking system by assets.

Studies conducted for smaller economies and, or with a bigger size of cross-border transactions show a more pronounced risk of systemic repercussions (See Blavarg and Nimander, 2002, for Sweden, Wells, 2004, and Upper and Worms, 2004, for Germany). With hindsight, and with the particular view that the crisis has offered, it is easy to understand that all the computations were based on data corresponding to a low level of financial fragility. So more recent contributions also analyze the impact of financial architecture, and the availability of detailed confidential bank balance sheet data about Belgium allowed Degryse and Nguyen (2007) to go beyond the existing literature. By conducting a regression analysis they identify the major determinants of contagion. They find that a move from a "complete" structure—one where each bank lends to each other—towards a "multiple money centers" bank structure and the increase in concentration in the lending market decreases domestic contagion. They also find that an increase in the proportion of cross border assets decreases the risk and the impact of domestic contagion. These results contrast with those of Mistrulli (2005) for the Italian interbank market. Mistrulli finds that the importance of cross-border exposures has decreased and that the transition from a "complete" toward a "multiple money centers" structure has increased contagion risk.

Afonso and Shin (2008), using lattice-theoretic simulation methods, show that precisely as the synchronization and coordination of payments of real-time systems creates a virtuous circle of high-payment volumes, the decline in bank's willingness to pay and the decision to postpone payments to the end of the day to conserve liquidity can cause an increase in the demand of intraday liquidity and disruption of payments. In addition they show that when a bank is identified as vulnerable to failure, other banks may choose to stop payments to that bank with systemic repercussions. This chain of events has probably played a role in the disruption of interbank wholesale funding and in the near meltdown of the major US investment banks in the middle of September of 2008 leading to the collapse of Lehman Brothers: nobody wanted to do business with a company that could fail, in spite of Lehman satisfying Basel II capital requirements.

On the basis of the previous estimates, one might have been tempted to conclude right before the crisis of 2007–2009 that contagion was a myth. The exposures of banks one to another are limited and should not be a major concern for the regulator. But taking the estimates at their face value without considering the whole contributions that the theoretical models allow us to make would be an oversimplified view of contagion. From this point of view, four important criticisms should be formulated. They concern the indirect contagion through the behavior of depositors, the business cycle, the price of bank assets during a crisis, and the impact of liquidity.

First, the empirical evidence is based on the network of banks assets and liabilities which may well affect the behavior of demand depositors. Their rational updating of the chances of another bank of similar characteristics may lead them to withdraw their deposits in a flight to quality. Many banking crises illustrate this phenomenon, as during the Great

Depression in the US, or in the ethnic bank crisis in the aftermath of the Bank of Credit and Commerce International in the UK. The default of the Madhavpura Mercantile Cooperative Bank in India in 2001 was used as a case study by Iyer and Peydro (2011) to examine the contagion taking place through demand deposits. Similarly, Iyer and Puri (2012) examine the minute-by-minute depositors' withdrawals for a bank in India that experienced a run when a neighboring bank failed. Yet the overall analysis of the joint impact of a bank failure through the network of reciprocal liabilities and through depositor's reaction remains to be done.

The second remark is that the measure of contagion is different in good times and in bad times. The impact of an individual bank when the banking system is healthy is the object of the above analysis. Yet from the policy analysis point of view, it is not clear that this is the best measure of contagion. An individual bank is more likely to go bankrupt when all banks are in trouble. This, of course, makes the analysis complex, because in such a case, contagion-induced and macroeconomic-induced systemic risk are simply undistinguishable. So the new challenge in the measurement of contagion is to compute the impact of a bank bankruptcy conditionally on the banking sector health, a topic that we discuss in detail later in this section.

A third remark is the impact of a number of bank failures or large reduction of the size of their balance sheet on the value of assets. The main impact, first identified by Irving Fisher (1933), concerns the price of assets that are used as collateral. In a debt-deflation situation, the value of assets decreases, which lowers the amount of collateralized loans and therefore the amount of available credit, which, in turn, reduces output. This output declines will again impact into the price of assets, thus leading to a further reduction in asset prices until outside investors buy the assets (see also Kyotaki and Moore, 1997 and, more recently, Gorton and Huang, 2004, and Acharya and Yorulmazer, 2008).

Fourth, a number of studies show how the impact of a relatively small shock, like defaults on subprime mortgages in 2007, may be amplified in a full-blown financial crisis in a way that cannot be captured by domino models of financial contagion.

20.3.2 The Illiquidity View of Contagion

The simplest way to think about fire sales and illiquidity as triggering a systemic banking crisis is to assume the aggregate amount of liquidity in the market is fixed. This "cash in the market" extreme simplifying assumption, initially proposed by Allen and Gale (1994), has the benefit of providing the bare bones of the argument. When banks are confronted with a liquidity shock they will be forced to sell their assets independently of the market prices. With a given amount of cash in the market any increase in the sales is matched by a decrease in price. Consequently, if the number of defaulting banks is sufficiently large, this inevitably leads to some or all banks going bankrupt. Acharya and Yorulmazer (2007) consider a more sophisticated version of this approach and show the necessity of a LOLR intervention.

A more elaborated alternative to domino models of financial contagion is offered by Brunnermeier (2009) and Brunnermeier and Pedersen (2009) who argue that liquidity spirals may cause aggregate liquidity to dry up as a result of minor shocks. If leveraged informed investors suffer even minor losses on their assets, in order to maintain the same leverage they have to sell assets hence contributing to depress asset prices even further if *market liquidity* for the asset is low. In addition to this loss spiral, Brunnermeier and Pedersen (2009) identify a margin spiral arising from the fact that, typically, financial assets are purchased on credit (*funding liquidity*) using the purchased assets as collateral (margin) for the loan, often a short-term one. The margin spiral reinforces the loss spiral as investors suffering losses have to sell assets to meet higher margin demands, that is, to lower the leverage ratio. Adrian and Shin (2008) confirm this spiral empirically for the five major US investment banks in the period 1997–2007. They identify a strong positive relationship for investment banks between the value-weighted change in leverage and the change in assets hence showing that leverage is highly procyclical. This helps explain, according to Adrian and Shin (2008), how modest losses on US subprime mortgages triggered the most severe financial crisis since the Great Depression.

Finally, and more tentatively, the cross-banks link could also be underestimated if we restrict the analysis to solvency. In fact, a bank lending overnight to a peer financial institution that happens to be in default may not be fully satisfied with the knowledge that it will recover 95% of its claims in five years' time, after the liquidation of the failing institution is complete. This may trigger the lending bank to liquidate some of its assets later at "fire sale," possibly increasing the impact on the price of assets. Recently the possibility of contagion from the asset side of interlinked balance sheets has received explicit attention in the literature. Schnabel and Shin (2004) and Cifuentes, Shin, and Ferrucci (2005) show that changes in asset prices may interact with solvency requirements or with internal risk control and amplify the initial shock in a vicious circle in which the reduction of the value of a bank's balance sheet may force the sale of assets or the disposal of a trading position, thereby further depressing asset prices, as illustrated above. This point appears particularly relevant in the current crisis. While contagion was expected to occur through the interlinkages between the different banks assets and liabilities, it occurs through the financial institutions lack of liquidity. The lack of liquidity led banks to sell some of their assets, which, in turn led to a decrease in the value of those assets; banks were, therefore, confronted with losses and an increase in their risk, thus leading to reduced solvency. Thus, it seems that during the current crisis assets liquidity has been the channeling vehicle for solvency shocks to be transmitted from one bank to another.

The awareness of this risk is linked to a number of steps taken by the regulators to soften liquidity requirements in the face of crisis. Thus, for instance, the Financial Services Authority (FSA) responded to the decline in stock prices in the summer 2002 by diluting the solvency test for insurance companies and in 1998 the Fed orchestrated the rescue of the hedge fund LTCM to prevent the negative impact of asset values that would have resulted from the unwinding of its positions.

20.3.3 Assessing Systemic Risk with Risk Management Techniques

The classical analysis of the exposure of the LOLR to systemic risk was traditionally quantified using standard risk management techniques that take into account the correlations between banks assets portfolios. While most studies take the probability of default as given and trace the impact of a bank default on the rest of the system, a new methodology by Lehar (2005) and Bodie, Gray and Merton (2007) uses the classic framework of Merton (1977) of contingent claims analysis, taking into account the option component of equity, derivates, and guarantees. Using a maximum likelihood estimation procedure the value of the banks' assets is then obtained and the exposure of the regulator computed. Lehar (2005) uses a sample of 149 international banks from 1988 to 2002 to identify the banks with the highest contributions to systemic risk and the countries which threaten the stability of the global financial system. Correlations of North American banks asset portfolios have increased but the systemic risk of the North American banking system has decreased over time as banks have increased their capitalization. On the other hand, the capitalization of the Japanese banks has declined dramatically, causing that system to become very unstable. Not surprisingly, the estimated regulator's liabilities increased sharply at the time of the Asian crisis in 1997–98.

With the crisis these types of methodologies have come under close scrutiny. Indeed, one of the main criticisms to regulatory supervision was that it was limited to the analysis of credit risk for each single individual institution, and that macroprudential policy was needed to understand the full implications of many institutions being in distress.

Regarding the extent of contagion, it is clear that the form it takes will depend on macroeconomic conditions. The term "macroeconomic fragility" has been coined to express the vulnerability of financial institutions at some point in time, when a systemic crisis is possible. The extent of macroeconomic fragility depends upon a number of macroeconomic factors that are present in the current crisis, such as asset bubbles linked to exuberant expectations, expected stable interest rates, and expected high growth. It also depends on the level of procyclicality of the financial system. On this point it should be mentioned that the combination of the accounting standards that impose marking assets to market and Basle II has made the supply of credit more procyclical. In addition, banks have not taken into account the risks they were generating, nor have the regulatory authorities (possibly with the exception of the Bank of Spain) increased the required capital or loan loss provisions level, a prerogative they have under the pillar two of Basle II, to take into account the increased level of risk.

20.3.4 Measuring Links among Financial Institutions

A more recent strand of literature has proposed various measures of links among financial institutions to reflect the spillovers and amplification effects that materialize in a crisis.

Three alternative measures of financial fragility have been put forward. First, Adrian and Brunnermeier's (2011) CoVaR measures the Value at Risk (VaR) of financial institutions conditional on other institutions experiencing a financial distress. Second, Acharya et al. (2011) measure the expected loss to each financial institution conditional on the entire set of institutions' poor performance. Finally, Huang, Zhou, and Zhu's (2008) distressed insurance premium measures the insurance premium required to cover distressed losses in the banking system. Since these measures are conditional on the state of the economy they are very different before, during, and after a systemic shock occurs, which may make them of little help as an early warning signal of the buildup of systemic risk.

Instead, by using unconditional measures of connectedness Billio, Getmansky, and Pelizzon (2012) are able to detect new linkages between parts of the financial system and capture their dynamic. These authors use principal components analysis to estimate the importance of common factors driving the market returns of four groups of financial institutions: hedge funds, publicly traded banks, brokers/dealers, insurance companies. They use pair wise Granger-causality tests to identify the network of statistically significant Granger-casual relations among the 25 largest entities among the four groups of institutions. The Granger-causality network measures of Billio, Getmansky, and Pelizzon (2012) offer a time dimension of connectivity which is missing in contemporaneous relations. To illustrate some of their results, the total number of connections between financial institutions was 583 in the beginning of the sample (1994–1996) and more than doubled to 1244 at the end (2006–2008). In the 2006–2008 period hedge funds had significant bilateral relationships with insurers and brokers/dealers, and they were heavily affected by banks but did not greatly affect banks. This allows the authors to conclude that banks may be of more concern than hedge funds from the perspective of connectedness, but hedge funds, which experience losses first when financial crises hit, may offer early warning signals.

In sum, the generation of studies on systemic risk spurred by the recent crisis, portrays systemic risk in a different way from the first generation of studies. Clearly, systemic risk is considered a real threat to the stability of the whole economy, its magnitude is significant, and the need of regulatory action is warranted.

20.4 DISTINGUISHING BETWEEN INSOLVENT AND ILLIQUID BANKS

The difficulty of distinguishing between an illiquid and an insolvent bank has been acknowledged at least since Bagehot's *Lombard Street*, when he argued (1873, II.64) "Every banker knows that if he has to prove that he is worthy of credit, however good may be his arguments, in fact his credit is gone." Modeling such a framework has been done only recently. Two different approaches are possible, one based on unobservable liquidity and solvency shocks and the other based on the coordination of interbank market lenders' strategic responses to fundamental, public and private, solvency signals.

20.4.1 Unidentifiable Shocks

The difficulty of sorting out liquidity and solvency shocks stems also from the unique position that banks have in creating aggregate liquidity. Diamond and Rajan (2005)—building on their previous work (Diamond and Rajan, 2001) argue that banks perform two complementary functions: they have loan collection skills, without which borrowers could not credibly commit to repay their loans, and they issue demand deposits to commit not to extract rents from investors. If a sufficiently large proportion of banks' portfolio needs refinancing (a solvency problem) the bank will be unable to borrow against its future value. But in that case there will be a shortage of liquidity in the economy for funding current consumption (a liquidity problem). A solvency problem or a liquidity problem alone can lead to a run on a bank if depositors anticipate losses. A run, in turn, destroys a bank's ability to extract money from borrowers and thus the ability to channel funds from surplus to deficit agents. Thus, after a run, aggregate liquidity is destroyed (an effect not present in bank runs of the type of Diamond and Dybvig, 1983) and liquidity is also trapped in the wrong place, very similarly to what happened during the panic of 2008—hence the difficulty of distinguishing between illiquid and insolvent banks. The appropriate policy response depends on the cause of the problem. When the source of the problem is a liquidity shortage Diamond and Rajan (2005) advocate lending freely to prevent a drop in the money stock. When solvency is the problem their advice is to recapitalize banks. Recapitalization, however, can be harmful if the problem is the lack of liquidity since capital infusion will simply push interest rates up, thus potentially causing more bank failures. Liquidity infusion instead has the least harmful downside and thus fits the test of doing no harm.

The approach followed by Freixas, Parigi, and Rochet (2004) is also based on the impossibility of distinguishing illiquidity from insolvency. These authors consider that banks are confronted with shocks that may come from uncertain withdrawals by impatient consumers (liquidity shocks) or from losses on the long-term investments that they have financed (solvency shocks) and that the two types of shocks cannot be disentangled. In acting as a LOLR the CB faces the possibility that an insolvent bank may pose as an illiquid one and borrow either from the interbank market or from the CB itself. Then the bank may "gamble for resurrection," that is, it may invest the loan in the continuation of a project with a negative expected net present value. This assumption is in line with the criticism of the LOLR during the Savings and Loans (S&L) crisis in the US during the 1980s and justifies why CBs are reluctant to be more liberal in their use of ELA. This setting allows the authors to focus both on the incentive issues of ELA and under which macroeconomic conditions the CB should provide ELA, at the cost of abstracting from modeling contagion. In periods of crisis, when banks' assets are very risky, borrowing in the interbank market may impose a high penalty because of the high spread demanded on loans. Freixas, Parigi, and Rochet (2004) show that ELA should be made at a penalty rate so as to discourage insolvent banks from borrowing, as if they were illiquid, but it should happen at a rate lower than the interbank market. The reason the CB can lend at better rate than the market is that the CB can lend collateralized and thus override the priority of existing claims. By penalizing insolvent banks that demand ELA, the CB provides banks with the appropriate incentives to exert effort to limit the probability that a bank becomes insolvent in the first place.[4] The implications of this approach can be clearly seen in the assessment of the 2007–2009 crisis. The classical view of the interbank market, according to which the interbank market works perfectly, was that the spreads on interbank loans were understating risk, and that the observed turmoil was a correction in pricing on all assets and contracts that depended on the price of risk: real estate, mortgages and unsecured loans to banks. By contrast, the Freixas, Parigi, Rochet (2004) approach views the crisis as a joint one of liquidity and solvency, so that, absent CB intervention, the interbank market may exacerbate the adverse selection problems. Taking the argument to the extreme, as modeled, for instance, in Freixas and Holthausen (2005) or Freixas and Jorge (2008), this may lead to thin-market equilibrium as in the classical market for lemons. The policy implications are vital, since if the differential diagnostic is a correction back to the long-term price of risk, the optimal policy may be for the CB not to

---

[4] However, when the Fed made an emergency senior loan to the largest US insurance company AIG in the middle of September 2008 it caused a 40% loss for AIG's junior creditors. This may well be one the reasons why unsecured interbank markets fail as the CB's interventions have diluted the value of pre-existing loans dramatically.

intervene except in so far as to reduce the cost of banks failure. If, instead, adverse selection in the interbank market leads to a standstill, then the LOLR liquidity provision to individual institutions is capital.[5]

20.4.2 Adverse Selection Driven Liquidity Dry-Ups

A common feature of Freixas, Parigi, Rochet (2000), Rochet and Vives (2004) and Freixas and Jorge (2008) is the existence of hoarding, that is, liquidity that is not intended to be used in the market. A reason for hoarding may be the potential of adverse selection in the secondary market for assets. Malherbe (2014) constructs a model in the tradition of the Diamond and Dybvig (1983) where after investing agents are privately informed about the quality of their long-term project. They then may want to sell part of their project either because they want to consume early or because they want to exploit their private information. But because of adverse selection the price at which they can sell in the secondary market is determined by the average seller's motive for trading. This may depress the price and make it very costly to transform long-term assets into current consumption goods and provides a rationale for hoarding at the initial stage.

Crucially, the proportion of people selling in the secondary market because they have received negative information about their project's return increases when sellers exhibit hoarding behavior. In fact the more sellers hoard liquidity, the less probable it is that a given seller trades because he must consume at the interim stage, and the more likely it is that he trades because he knows that his asset is a lemon. The investment decisions of the agent at the initial stage present strategic complementarities leading to multiple equilibria. When agents expect the secondary market to be illiquid, they rationally choose to hoard more. This reduces market participation, worsens the average quality of the asset for sale in the secondary market, and makes the market illiquid, validating the initial belief held by the agents.[6] Hence liquidity dry-ups can then be self-fulfilling, which may help explain why some markets where the potential for adverse selection problems is serious like, for example, those for asset-backed-securities that were liquid before the 2007–2009 financial crisis dried up in the midst of the crisis and did not recover as cash became available again.

Malherbe (2014) argues that since the bad equilibrium happens because of coordination failure, a public insurance scheme that levies taxes to compensate for the losses agents incurred for not storing enough eliminates the incentive to hoard and the only remaining equilibrium is that with high liquidity.

---

[5] Using the global games methodology Rochet and Vives (2004) provide a theoretical foundation of Bagehot's doctrine in a modern context. For a detailed description see the first edition of this survey in Freixas and Parigi (2010).

[6] Holmström and Tirole (2011, p. 193) point out the counterintuitive feature of Malherbe's model that an agent benefits from being perceived week and thus forced to sell assets for genuine reasons, contrary to the stigma usually associated to these conditions.

20.5 LOLR POLICY

20.5.1 A New Background

The current crisis has witnessed an unprecedented level of activity related to the LOLR role. Its systemic dimension implies that the distinction between the LOLR interventions supporting financial stability often use the instruments of monetary policy. We have observed high levels of CBs' activism consisting in the injection of liquidity through specific procedures at record low interest rates. This raises a number of important questions regarding the objectives, the effectiveness, and the medium long-term negative effects of such a policy.

Furthermore, this is the first time since the Great Depression that LOLR operations have been conducted both in EU and US to address a systemic crisis. In contrast to the Great Depression, current LOLR operations occurred in economies with much more developed and sophisticated financial markets and instruments and a high level of shadow banking activity.

Two phenomena have characterized the behavior of CBs during the crisis: the injection of liquidity by substituting banks inside liquidity that was based on repos by central bank liquidity and the drastic decrease of interest rates as illustrated below. Regarding liquidity injection, the Federal Reserve and the Bank of England balance sheet increase was spectacular, while those of the ECB followed close behind (see Figure 20.1). The reason was the interbank market freeze both in its repo segment, once the ABS and CDOs were deemed as "toxic assets," and in the unsecured segment once the suspicion of banks' insolvency and the credible possibility of their bankruptcy was perceived by the market.

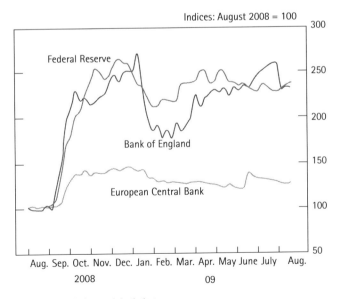

FIGURE 20.1 Central banks' total liabilities.

Source: Bank of England Quarterly Bulletin 2009 Q3 p.154. Reprinted with permission of the Bank of England

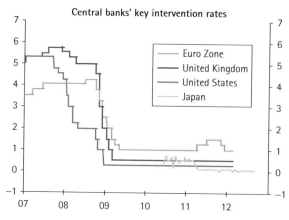

FIGURE 20.2 Central banks' key intervention rates.

Source: European Issue no. 240 - 14/05/2012, Robert Schuman Foundation, http://www.robert-schuman.eu/en/european-issues/0240-the-euro-crisis.

Furthermore, several CBs started to issue their own bills (Bank of England, Riksbank, and Swiss National Banks) and the Federal Reserve started to remunerate banks' reserves. Such an increase in monetary injection, as well as the cooperation between several CBs, contrasts with the policies followed during the Great Depression when, according to Friedman and Schwartz (1963), the money supply decreased by one-third between 1929 and 1933.

Regarding interest rates, the magnitude of the interest rate cuts as well as the frequency of interventions was unprecedented (see Figure 20.2). Of course, it may be argued that interest rate cuts reflect standard monetary policy, as the financial crisis was heralding a deep recession. Nevertheless, the departure from the classical Taylor rule response was clear: fighting financial fragility through the decrease of interest rates was the main objective, and the commitment to maintain low interest rates for a long period of times goes beyond the classical implementation of monetary policy. In addition, we observed how the Bank of England and the ECB narrowed the corridor between the rates of lending and deposit facilities, while in the US the Fed reduced the spread between the discount window rate and the Fed funds rate, thus signaling that extraordinary monetary policy measures were needed to cope with extraordinary times.

These massive interventions have generated a new view of the role of LOLR policy, interacting with monetary policy and with macro prudential policy; it is definitely impossible to imagine the LOLR operations without dealing with its interactions also with financial stability.

The final dramatic lesson from the current crisis is the link between banking fragility and sovereign risk. Indeed, a crucial implication of LOLR interventions, once we exclude the mythic case of perfect solvent institutions, is that the LOLR has to take risks in its liquidity injection operation, because of credit risk, collateral risk, and market risk. This raises the question of the extent of LOLR operations. An excessively generous policy may imply losses that are either too large, as happened in Ireland, or pile up in the worst possible moment, when fiscal revenue is low, leading to the implementation of an austerity program in a downturn. This leads to additional difficulties because the solvency of the country itself and its rating are at stake. The price increase in sovereign bonds will affect especially domestic banks that, for home biases, behavioral or cost reasons have invested a huge proportion of their portfolio in their countries sovereign bonds.

In the extreme case a country is confronted with the simple fact that implementing the required LOLR policy increases its sovereign risk because it constitutes a serious drain on public finances. This was the case in Iceland and in Cyprus, and in the first case it even led to defaulting on the deposit insurance scheme, thus generating losses to other European countries as well. This "diabolic loop," as Brunnermeier et al. (2011) called it, requires a fine-tuning of LOLR policy. As a consequence, in the context of the European sovereign debt crises, an even broader role and definition of the LOLR is emerging to address this vicious circle (see, for example, De Grauwe, 2011). In late 2011 the ECB has initiated a program of long-term refinancing operations (LTRO) providing liquidity to European banks, which was largely used to buy periphery sovereign debt. In the summer of 2012 the ECB announced a program of purchases of sovereign bonds of member states (Outright Monetary Transactions) with the aim of safeguarding appropriate monetary transmission.

The implications of a twin crisis where both banks and the country are in distress are dramatic not only because it increases the cost for the country to roll over its debt, but also because it affects lending by the domestic institutions involved. Bofondi, Carpinelli, and Sette (2013) show that after the Italian sovereign crisis lending by Italian banks grew by about 3% points less relative to foreign banks and the interest rate they charged was between 15 and 20 basis points higher. Van Horen and Popov (2013) establish that this was the case for all PIIGS countries (Portugal, Italy, Ireland, Greece, and Spain). The affected banks also drastically reduced their lending abroad, thus contributing to the credit crunch in the host countries, as shown by Correa, Sapriza, and Zlate (2012) in a study of the European banks' US branches behavior during the European sovereign crisis.

Nevertheless, a number of key issues are yet to be analyzed and some questions remain unanswered about this new perception of the role of the LOLR. First, why should the LOLR intervene and what are its objectives in doing so? Second, through what channels can a liquidity injection be implemented in order to address a systemic crisis? Third, how efficient has been the LOLR interventions so far and, fourth, what are the limitations and the negative effects of the new LOLR policy?

20.5.2 Why A New Role for Monetary Policy?

The explanation of the new role for monetary policy as a LOLR instrument comes quite naturally from the points we discussed in Section 20.5.1. The sudden change in defaults on subprime and Alt-A mortgages later extended to prime mortgages had two effects: first, it led the securities held by investment banks and some commercial banks (for example, ABS, CDOs) from being AAA information insensitive to becoming sensitive to private information and second it led to huge losses for banks either because they were holding the securities or because they had provided guarantees in special purpose vehicles that were holding the toxic assets. The same effect led to the collapse of both the repo market and the unsecured interbank market.

As a consequence, for banks to survive the liquidity shocks arising from the ordinary running of the payment system and the extraordinary shocks due to the systemic crisis, the injection of liquidity was critical. This could be interpreted as the need to replace the vanished inside liquidity provided by securities that were deemed safe, liquid and information insensitive in 2006, by outside liquidity provided by the CB. As a consequence the CB had to accept as collateral securities that could not be used in the repo market (as otherwise the banks themselves could have been using the securities to cope with their liquidity shocks). As mentioned in Section 2.4, such an exchange of information-sensitive debt for information-insensitive debt free from adverse selection and backed by fiscal revenues is quite related to the way central clearing houses coped with crises in the nineteenth century.

It is interesting to relate this to Goodfriend and King's proposal that the LOLR should intervene exclusively through OMO, as it elicits the implicit hypothesis that the collateral used in the implementation of monetary policy keeps the same characteristics of low credit risk and high liquidity throughout the crisis. When this feature is not fulfilled it is necessary to "think outside the box" and reinvent a role for the LOLR.

20.5.3 Implementing the LOLR Liquidity Injection

The question of how to implement monetary policy is largely irrelevant in normal times. In contrast, when confronted with a crisis, some channels may close down and, consequently, new channels may have to be designed. First, implementing LOLR requires coordination between different institutions that was not thought to be an important part of the regulatory design. Second, it implies dealing with the stigma effects of some mechanisms, like the discount window in the US that was in fact equivalent to a "name and shame" mechanism and, in the corresponding equilibrium, a clear sign that the bank asking for liquidity was already insolvent. Third, the way the liquidity injection was implemented in the US and in the Eurozone during the early phases of the financial crisis which began in 2008 has shown that it is possible to address the same issue in different ways even if it is impossible to assess categorically that one is better than the other.

Regarding institutional coordination, one of the major achievements of theoretical and empirical research in the last two decades has been to establish that the independence of CBs in setting monetary policy is a precondition for economic stability. Yet the issue of the independence of monetary policy and LOLR policy is more involved. To begin with, LOLR policy is part of the safety net; so a preliminary question would be to consider the pros and cons of having monetary policy and prudential regulation responsibilities delegated to two distinct institutions. The theoretical argument in favor of separation is the existence of possible conflicts of interest: like LOLR, the CB may feel compelled to bail out banks if this is necessary to prevent a systemic crisis. The conflict of interest is all the more serious in that monetary policy is countercyclical while prudential policy is procyclical, as bank bankruptcies occur in slowdowns (Goodhart and Schoenmaker, 1993). The cross-country empirical analysis of Goodhart and Schoenmaker (1993 and 1995) establishes that central banks that have supervisory responsibilities experience higher inflation rates. On the other hand, the empirical analysis of Peek, Rosengren, and Tootell (1999) shows that information obtained from bank supervision helps the CB to conduct monetary policy more effectively. More recently, Ioannidou (2005) examining the behavior of the three primary US federal regulators—the Federal Deposit Insurance Company (FDIC), the Office of the Comptroller of the Currency (OCC) and the Federal Reserve Board—shows that indicators of monetary policy do affect actions of the Federal Reserve Board, while it does not affect those of the FDIC or the OCC. Now, when we consider LOLR operations, the impact on monetary policy could, theoretically, be sterilized. So when the bailout operation concerns an individual bank crisis, monetary policy should not be affected. Of course, when facing a generalized crisis, as in the case of the 2007–2009 crisis, the CB has to consider the impact of the banking crisis on growth and inflation patterns and therefore is expected to intervene.

In summary, the empirical evidence indicates that whether the responsibilities of monetary policy and prudential regulation are joint or separate affects the way they are implemented. However, this does not tell us which of the two models, is more efficient and whether the choice of a model depends upon the context, normal times or during a systemic risk. The lesson of the crisis seems to be that the separation of functions vanishes so as to promote more efficient coordination.

The role of LOLR in liquidity creation is even more complex when not all assets can be used to purchase other assets. Gorton and Huang (2004) show that when there are such "liquidity-in-advance" constraints it is privately efficient for agents to hoard liquidity but it is not socially efficient given the opportunity cost of foregone investment opportunities. When the amount of the assets to be sold is so large that it would have been inefficient for private agents to have hoarded liquidity, the government can improve welfare by creating liquidity to bail out banks by taxing solvent projects. The drawback is that if the government tax capacity is too small, the government cannot bail out all banks, and forbearance arises. This is indeed the case for small countries (witness the crisis in Iceland in October 2008) and poses a serious risk for midsize countries with large banks, like Switzerland, where the assets of the banking system are several times larger than the country's GDP. The link with monetary policy and the conflict of interest it implies is clear. Banking crises will materialize in a downturn, under tight monetary policy. This puts pressure on the prices of assets, thus setting the stage for a debt-deflation. If, simultaneously, the LOLR has to bail out banks in distress, there is a clear case for coordination of policies and weighting of the cost of a higher inflation versus the cost of banking crises.

The second issue that has to be addressed is what channels should be used to inject liquidity. Before considering this point, it is interesting to recall that there may be a "stigma" associated with some sources of liquidity. In the US the discount window has long been thought to be the natural instrument for the LOLR to respond to financial strain. Yet it has become progressively obvious that a financial intermediary accessing the discount window would send a negative signal both to other banks from which the bank would normally borrow and to the Fed. In particular, before 2003, as the discount window rate was below the interbank rate it became clear that banks were reluctant to arbitrage the two markets, possibly because of the associated stigma. It was nevertheless expected that, in the midst of a systemic crisis, financial institutions would acknowledge that they were all facing the same liquidity shortages and the "stigma" would disappear. This was not the case. Attempts to stop the disclosure of Federal loans were useless once appeals courts ruled that the Fed must disclose recipients of certain loans extended through the discount window and other lending programs enacted in response to the financial crisis. Armantier et al. (2011), using the comparison between the TAF anonymous auction and the discount window, confirmed the existence of a stigma of at least 37 basis points on average.

Consequently, the channeling of funds to institutions may be restricted to mechanisms that are either anonymous or that all participants may attend in the current liquidity and solvency conditions. But the question of how to inject liquidity has still to be addressed. This may possibly be the most important issue, but it has not yet been the object of much research. The contrast between the EU and the US policies on this question illustrates that there seems to be no unique answer.

In the EU liquidity was injected through a unique entry door. The type of securities that were accepted as collateral was generously extended but still the liquidity injection went directly to banks and banks were then in charge of passing through the liquidity to the agents that require it. Contrasting this classical approach, the US created a number of liquidity facilities to channel liquidity directly to some critical players of the financial market, thus bypassing the traditional banking system. It is possible to identify three types of liquidity injection facilities.

The first corresponds to the classical role of the LOLR and emergency liquidity assistance. It consists of the term auction facility (TAF), term securities lending facility (TSLF), the primary dealer credit facility (PDCF), and swap lines. The second set of policy tools is intended to provide liquidity directly to borrowers and investors in key credit markets. It consists of the Term asset-backed securities loan facility (TALF), commercial paper funding facility (CPFF), asset-backed commercial paper money market mutual fund liquidity facility (AMLF) and the money market investment fund facility (MMIFF). The third liquidity channel aims to support the functioning of credit markets and involves the purchase of longer-term securities for the Fed's portfolio. To sum up, following Acharya and Richardson (2009) we can map these unconventional actions taken by the Fed to expand liquidity in three dimensions: expansion of the time duration of the CB loans, expansion of the eligible collateral accepted by the CB in exchange of liquidity, and expansion of the counterparties eligible for emergency liquidity assistance by the CB. These are described in Table 20.1.

After these interventions, by March 2009 the Fed held $1.75 trillion of bank debt, MBS, and Treasury notes, versus the $700–$800 billion in Treasury securities it held before the crisis, reaching $2.1 trillion by June 2010 and capping what later came to be known as quantitative easing, QE1. In November 2010 the Fed announced another round of quantitative easing, QE2, buying $600 billion of Treasury Securities by the end of the second quarter of 2011. In September 2012 the Fed launched a third round of quantitative easing, QE3, consisting in a $40 billion a month, open-ended, bond purchasing program of agency mortgage-backed securities, increased to $85 billion a month in December 2012. As a result of these rounds of interventions LOLR, fiscal, and monetary policies grew more and more intertwined. In a number of countries the observation that medium and small-size firms were deprived of credit led to the creation of new lending facilities, following the US model. Thus the Bank of Japan (BoJ) introduced in June 2010 a program to inject liquidity into those banks investing in growth areas.

A third approach different from both the US and the Eurozone approaches was developed in July 2012 by the Bank of England (BoE) and the HM Treasury with the Funding for Lending Scheme (FLS). Under FLS banks are able to borrow UK Treasury bills from the BoE for a period of up to four years against eligible collateral (including loans to households and businesses and other assets) for a fee. This exchange of securities allows the bank to improve the collateral they use in the repo market, although at some risk for the Central Bank.

The empirical analysis should help us understand whether the LOLR is effective in limiting the effects of the crisis. Berger et al. (2013) have recently produced some evidence on

Table 20.1 LOLR actions by the FED since 2007

Intervention	Objective	Period
Extension of Discount window (DW) duration	Extension of max term for depository institutions borrowing from DW to 30 days in Aug 2007, and 90 days in March 2008	From August 2007 to March 2008
Term Auction Facility (TAF)	Offer long-term liquidity to depository institutions given ineffectiveness of previous DW extension because of stigma	From December 12, 2007 to March 8, 2010
Primary Dealers Credit Facility (PDCF)	DW extended also to primary (i.e. systemically important) dealers after the collapse of Bear Stern	From March 16, 2008 to February 1, 2010
Term Securities Lending Facility (TSLF)	To provide medium-term liquidity to primary dealers Fed loaned liquid Treasury securities to Primary dealers for 1 month in exchange of less liquid collateral and a fee	From March 27, 2008 to February 1, 2010
Asset-Backed Commercial Paper Money Market Mutual Fund Liquidity facility (AMLF)	Introduced after failure of Lehman Brothers to extend loans to banking organizations to purchase asset-backed commercial paper from money markets mutual funds and help them meet investors' demand for redemptions	From September 19, 2008 to February 1, 2010
Money Market Investor Funding Facility (MMIFF)	Provides senior secured funding to special purpose vehicles to facilitate buying assets from money markets mutual funds and help them meet investors' demand for redemptions. No loans made under this facility	From October 21, 2008 to October 30, 2009
Commercial Paper Funding facility (CPFF)	To provide liquidity back stop to US issuers of commercial paper. It funds purchases of highly rated-unsecured and asset-backed commercial papers	From October 27, 2008 to February 1, 2010
Term Asset-Backed Securities Loan Facility (TALF)	To help market participants meet credit needs of households and small businesses, by supporting issuance of ABS collateralized by students loans, auto loans, credit cards loans, and loans guaranteed by the Small Business Administration in cooperation with Treasury.	From March, 2009 to June 30, 2010

the impact of the TAF auctions that shows a positive effect of the liquidity injection mechanism. First, liquidity helps small banks to improve their position by decreasing their imbalances. The authors show that "small banks receiving funds tended to have less capital and higher portfolio risk" (p. 1), which is consistent with the new role of the LOLR that grants risky loans the market cannot provide. In addition, they show that the TAF program fulfilled its objective since both small and large banks receiving funds increased their lending relative to banks that did not receive such funding. Examining the evidence in Europe, Ciccarelli, Maddaloni, and Peydró (2013) conclude that monetary policy during the crisis had a stronger impact on aggregate output, especially in countries facing increased sovereign financial distress. Their findings suggest that this amplification mechanism operates mainly through the credit channel, both the bank lending and the balance-sheet channel and that it took some time to be effective, as its impact starts to be felt in 2011.

Finally, the current crisis has also brought an important development in the cooperation between CBs. Since in 2007 banks in many countries were beginning to face severe shortage of dollar liquidity, the Fed extended large dollar swap lines to the ECB, the BoJ, the BoE, and the Swiss National Bank, to allow these CBs to provide dollar liquidity to their domestic banking systems. In fall 2008 the swap lines were extended to all advanced economies and to four major emerging markets, Brazil, Korea, Mexico, and Singapore. In turn, the ECB extended euro swap lines to Hungary, Poland, Denmark, and Iceland.

According to Obsfeld, Shambaugh, and Taylor (2009) this is the most notable example of CB cooperation in history. Obsfeld, Shambaugh, and Taylor (2009) document that the overall the size of swaps was around $1 trillion. For the banking systems of the advanced economies (except Japan) the intervention was sizeable as the dollar swap lines made up more than 50% of foreign reserves, while for the emerging economies swap lines accounted for less than 50% of their foreign reserves, and in some cases they were merely symbolic as the country already had significant reserves (e.g., Singapore, Brazil). Obsfeld, Shambaugh, and Taylor (2009) argue that resorting to swap lines to provide dollar liquidity to foreign banking systems avoids the drawbacks of the two alternatives. In one alternative the domestic CB provides domestic liquidity to its banking system and lets the banks sell the local currency in the open market against dollars, with the consequence, however, of exerting downward pressure on the exchange rate of the local currency. In another alternative, the CB uses its own dollar reserves to provide liquidity, with the risk of exhausting its own dollar reserves.

20.5.4 The Effects of Liquidity Injection

The emergence of new patterns of liquidity injection as a response to a systemic crisis raises many different questions, but two seem particularly relevant. First, is it possible to provide a theoretical underpinning of this type of policy that justifies its efficiency? Second, is there any empirical evidence on the impact of the policy?

Two recent theoretical contributions have challenged the traditional view of the separation of monetary policy and financial crises management by noting that during liquidity crises interbank markets cannot efficiently redistribute liquidity between banks with surplus and shortage of liquidity.

Allen, Carletti, and Gale (2009) consider an interbank market where banks can buy and sell long-term assets in the interim period to satisfy their liquidity shocks. However, to guarantee that banks have the incentive to hold both liquidity and long term assets, the interbank market bids up the price of the long-term asset in the interim period when aggregate liquidity demand is low. This induces asset price (and interest rate) volatility which hurts risk-averse consumers. The introduction of a CB that via OMO fixes the price of the long-term asset (or equivalently fixes the short-term interest rate) and removes the inefficiency associated with lack of hedging opportunities that aggregate liquidity uncertainty entails.

Freixas, Martin, and Skeie (2011) point out that during the current financial crisis banks faced tremendous disparity in liquidity needs: some banks were exposed to the risk to come up with billions of dollars on a same-day notice to honor the liquidity guarantees that they had offered to off balance sheets vehicles, while other banks were receiving large inflows of funds from investors fleeing other segments of the financial markets. To capture the variation in liquidity needs observed during the crisis their model consider two different states of the world regarding the uncertainty of the distribution of banks' liquidity needs: low uncertainty in normal times and high uncertainty during the crisis. The interest rate affects the ex ante decision to hold liquidity versus the long-term assets, and ex post it affects the terms at which banks can borrow in the interbank market. Only state-contingent interbank rates allow achieving the optimal allocation: in fact interest rates have to be low in crisis time to achieve the redistribution of liquidity, and higher than the return on the long-term asset under normal times to give banks the incentive to hold liquidity ex ante. Freixas, Martin, and Skeie (2011) argue then that interest rates set independently of prudential considerations cannot be optimal and thus criticize the notion that monetary policy should not be used to manage financial crisis.

On the other hand, these policies may be planting the seeds for the next crises if the policy is known in advance by market participants. One of the paradoxes of the policy interventions in the current financial crisis is that the banking sector, which is in large part responsible for the crisis, has been saved in various ways by the monetary and fiscal authorities (Gorton, 2012). That is, ex post it was deemed to be better for society as a whole to engage in the costly bailout of some of the financial institutions whose behavior triggered or exacerbated the crisis as opposed to engaging in the liquidation of large chunks of the financial industry. This type of time-inconsistency has been recognized at least since Bagehot. Two recent models offer new insights of how banks behave ex ante, thus anticipating future policy responses.

The lack of commitment by CBs to bail out failing banks increases the likelihood of banking crises. Acharya and Yorulmazer (2007) start from this intuition and show that regulators find it ex post optimal to bail out banks when the crisis assumes systemic proportions, i.e. when the number of failures is large. On the contrary if only few banks fail, their rescue can be arranged by having the surviving banks buy the failing ones. As the number of failing banks increases the number of banks that can be the potential acquirers shrinks and the chances that the failing banks have to be liquidated at a loss increases. Anticipating this too-many-to-fail guarantee induces banks to herd ex ante, for example lending to similar industries and/or bet on similar interest and mortgage rates risk. This problem focuses the attention on choices of banks as a group rather than on individual choices, and as such it suggests that also the category of small banks can be a source of systemic fragility.

Similarly, Fahri and Tirole (2012) argue that, since difficult economic conditions call for public policy to help financial institutions, strategic complementarities in banks' risk choices are generated. For example, the larger the number of banks exposed to the risk of a shock because of maturity mismatch, the more it is in the interest of an individual bank to do the same, as the fixed cost associated with the CB intervention declines when the number of banks involved increases, hence tilting the CB's incentives toward a lower interest rate policy.

More generally, in the debate about rules versus discretion in the conduct of the LOLR, Taylor (2012) criticizes the conduct of ELA by the Fed during the crisis. His point is that the on/off policies by the Fed led to confusion and contributed greatly to the panic of all 2008.

The issue of time inconsistency is closely linked to that of information sharing between different regulators and may prove useful in understanding the Northern Rock crisis in 2007. The Bank of England considers that the Northern Rock crisis was not systemic. Yet the market for liquidity dries. The FSA is in charge of solvency and issued a favorable report, confirming the "pure liquidity" assumption. The Bank of England could not institute a mechanism similar to the ECB or to the discount window that allows for a much larger class of admissible collateral, and was therefore forced to resort to a special LOLR operation that guaranteed all deposits. Without entering on the structure of deposit insurance in the UK or the fact that the actual terms and conditions of the credit facility are not public, the FSA had considered Northern Rock as following a safe banking strategy. The Bank of England had to rely on this information when choosing to extend a credit line. The Bank of England's difficulty in avoiding being perceived as encouraging moral hazard by not resisting to the lobbies of the uninsured debt holders is clear in this case. Despite previous official statement to the contrary, the images of depositors lined up to withdraw from Northern Rock branches in the end forced the UK authorities to guarantee all depositors. Since, at the same time, the credit line was guaranteed by HM Treasury, the incentives to find information contradicting the FSA are quite narrow. The Northern Rock case illustrates the notion that the commitment not to save lenders from their excesses is not realistic even in a sophisticated financial system once the CBs are confronted with the fragility of the banking system and the possibility of a systemic crisis.

20.6 CONCLUSIONS

To conclude, it is worthwhile comparing the classic view of the LOLR with the complexities of the above analysis and trying to summarize it by drawing the major lines of the recent advances in the contemporaneous approach of LOLR, as compared with the "wisdom of our ancestors." What is left today of the simple clear-cut guidelines suggested by Thornton and Bagehot that recommend to lend to solvent illiquid institutions against good collateral and at a penalty rate?

First, lending to the market through OMO is the standard way for a CB to prevent an aggregate liquidity shock. This is the contemporaneous version of "lending against good collateral," characteristic of developed financial markets. Yet recent models of interbank lending teach us that market imperfections can lead to other inefficiencies that require the LOLR support to extend beyond the pure CB responsibility of aggregate liquidity management and lend to individual banks, either unsecured or against collateral of lower quality, or guaranteeing their future liquidity.

The second classical recommendation was to lend at a penalty. This point is now clearly controversial. In the presence of ex ante moral hazard, as in Freixas, Parigi, Rochet (2004), a penalty provides managers with the right incentives to be diligent in their lending. Yet in Rochet and Vives (2004) the recommendation is the opposite, to lend at a rate inferior of the market rate. When, in addition, we consider decentralization between several regulatory agencies, a penalty on interest rates decreases the expected cost of the LOLR loan and imposes a better discipline in banks' liquidity management. This will therefore make the LOLR more prone to forbearance, which, as mentioned, could either increase or decrease the efficiency of LOLR. In the case of an unbiased regulator, this will be efficient, because in case of success, the LOLR will obtain a share of the bank's profits. So, on the penalty issue, there is no clear consensus yet and it is to be hoped that future work will help regulators to implement the efficient policy according to the economic and financial environment.

The recent turmoil in the financial markets offers several lessons regarding the role of the LOLR in a *systemic* crisis. First, we have witnessed how repeated and coordinated aggregate liquidity injections are not sufficient to solve the crisis: the illiquidity of financial institutions around the world is, in fact, directly linked not only to their solvency but also to asset prices. Second, it is important to notice that CBs around the world have been much more flexible in providing support to the banking industry than what was initially expected, or, in other words, that CBs cannot credibly commit to a well targeted bailout or liquidation policy. Indeed, the arguments in support of the bailout of banks only if their closure could have a systemic impact (too-big-to-fail), that were intended for an individual bank facing financial distress were soon discarded in favor of a more realistic approach. The case of Northern Rock, certainly not a systemic bank, illustrates this point. Its liquidation in such a fragile banking environment would have triggered a domino effect with contagion from one institution to another. From that perspective the lesson is that, when facing a systemic crisis, the LOLR has to take into account also the "too-many-to-fail," and consider how it will treat all banks that are in a similar position. A third point is that in a systemic crisis the perimeter of the safety net is extended to non-bank institutions. This may be the result of the waves of financial innovation. Yet because AIG had been issuing CDS, its bankruptcy would have affected the fragility of the banking industry by leading to losses and a lower capital.

In the end, the above discussion highlights the important notion that the LOLR of the twenty-first century lies at the intersection of monetary policy, supervision, and regulation of the banking industry, and the organization of the interbank market—a long way from the Bagehot doctrine.

References

Acharya, V. V., Pedersen, L. H., Philippon, T., and Richardson, M. (2011). Measuring Systemic Risk. New York University Working Paper.

Acharya, V. and Yorulmazer, T. (2007). Too Many to Fail. An Analysis of Time-Inconsistency in Bank Closure Policies, *Journal of Financial Intermediation* 16, 1–31.

Acharya, V. and Yorulmazer, T. (2008). Cash-in-the-Market Pricing and Optimal Resolution of Bank Failures, *Review of Financial Studies* 21, 2705–2742.

Adrian, T. and Brunnermeier, M. K. (2011). Co VaR, NBER Working Paper No. 17454.

Adrian, T. and Shin, H. S. (2008). Liquidity and Financial Contagion, Banque de France, *Financial Stability Review, Special Issue on Liquidity* 11, 1–7.

Afonso, G. M. and Shin, H. S. (2008). Systemic Risk and Liquidity in Payment Systems, *Federal Reserve Bank of New York Staff Report No. 352*, October.

Allen, F., Carletti, E., and Gale, D. (2009). Interbank Market Liquidity and Central Bank Intervention, *Journal of Monetary Economics* 56, 639–652.

Allen, F. and Gale, D. (1994). Limited Market Participation and Volatility of Asset Prices, *American Economic Review* 84, 933–955.

Allen, F. and Gale, D. (2000). Financial Contagion, *Journal of Political Economy* 108, 1–33.

Armantier, O., Ghysels, E., Sarkar, A., and Shrader, J. (2011). Stigma in Financial Markets: Evidence from Liquidity Auctions and Discount Window Borrowing during the Crisis, Federal Reserve Bank of New York Staff Report No. 483.

Bagehot, W. (1873). *Lombard Street: A Description of the Money Market*. London: H. S. King.

Berger, A., Black, L., Bowman, C., and Dlugosz, J. (2013). The Federal Reserve's Discount Window and TAF Programs: "Pushing on a String?". Case Western Reserve University: Mimeo.

Billio, M., Getmansky, M., Lo, A., and Pelizzon, L. (2012). Econometric Measures of Connectedness and Systemic Risk in the Finance and Insurance Sectors, *Journal of Financial Economics* 104, 535–559.

Blavarg, U. and Nimander, P. (2002). Inter-Bank Exposures and Systemic Risk, Sveriges Riksbank, *Economic Review* 2, 19–45.

Bodie, Z., Gray, D., and Merton, R. (2007). A New Framework for Measuring and Managing Macrofinancial Risk and Financial Stability, NBER Working Paper No. 13607.

Bofondi, A., Carpinelli, L., and Sette, E. (2013). Credit Supply during a Sovereign Crisis, Bank of Italy Working Paper No. 909.

Brunnermeier, M. K. (2008). Thoughts on a New Financial Architecture, http://www.prince ton.edu/~markus/research/papers/new_financial_architecture.pdf.>.

Brunnermeier, M. K. (2009). Deciphering the Liquidity and Credit Crunch 2007-08, *Journal of Economic Perspectives* 23, 77–100.

Brunnermeier, M. K., Garicano, L., Lane, P. R., Pagano, M., Reis, R., Santos, T., Van Nieuwerburgh, S., and Vayanos, D. (2011). European Safe Bonds (ESBies). The Euro-nomics Group, <http://euro-nomics.com/wp-content/uploads/.../ESBiesWEBsept262011.pdf.>.

Brunnermeier, M. K. and Pedersen, L. (2009). Market Liquidity and Funding Liquidity, *Review of Financial Studies* 22, 2201–2238.

Bryant, J. (1980). A Model of Reserves, Bank Runs and Deposit Insurance, *Journal of Banking and Finance* 4, 335–344.

Calomiris, C. W. and Kahn, C. M. (1991). The Role of Demandable Debt in Structuring Optimal Banking Arrangements, *American Economic Review* 81, 497–513.

Calomiris, C. W., Kahn, C. M., and Kroszner, R. S. (1996). The Efficiency of Self-Regulated Payments Systems: Learning from the Suffolk System, *Journal of Money Credit and Banking* 28(2), 766–797.

Ciccarelli, M., Maddaloni, A., and Peydró, J. L. (2013). Heterogeneous Transmission Mechanism Monetary Policy and Financial Fragility in the Euro Area, ECB Working Paper No. 1527.

Cifuentes, R., Shin, H. S., and Ferrucci, G. (2005). Liquidity Risk and Contagion, *Journal of the European Economic Association* 3, 556–566.

Coleman, S. P. (2002). The Evolution of the Federal Reserve's Intraday Credit Policies, *Federal Reserve Bulletin* 88, 67–84.

Cooper, R. and Ross, T. W. (1998). Bank Runs: Liquidity Costs and Investment Distortions, *Journal of Monetary Economics* 41, 27–38.

Correa, R., Sapriza, H., and Zlate, A. (2012). Liquidity Shocks, Dollar Funding Costs, and the Bank Lending Channel During the European Sovereign Crisis, Federal Reserve Board International Finance Discussion Paper No. 1059.

Dang, T. V., Gorton, G., and Holmström, B. (2012). Ignorance, Debt and Financial Crises. Yale: Mimeo.

De Grauwe, P. (2011). The European Central Bank: Lender of Last Resort in the Government Bond Markets?, CESifo Working Paper No. 3569.

Degryse, H. and Nguyen, G. (2007). Interbank Exposures: An Empirical Examination of Contagion Risk in the Belgian Banking System, *International Journal of Central Banking* 3, 123–171.

Diamond, D. (1984). Financial Intermediation and Delegated Monitoring, *Review of Economics Studies* 51, 393–414.

Diamond, D. and Dybvig, P. (1983). Bank Runs, Deposit Insurance, and Liquidity, *Journal of Political Economy* 91, 401–419.

Diamond, D. and Rajan, R. (2001). Liquidity Risk, Liquidity Creation and Financial Fragility: A Theory of Banking, *Journal of Political Economy* 109, 287–327.

Diamond, D. and Rajan, R. (2005). Liquidity Shortages and Banking Crises, *The Journal of Finance* 60, 615–647.

Fahri, E. and Tirole, J. (2012). Collective Moral Hazard, Maturity Mismatch, and Systemic Bailouts, *American Economic Review* 102, 60–93.

Fisher, I. (1933). Debt Deflation Theory of the Great Depression, *Econometrica* 4, 337–357.

Freixas, X. and Holthausen, C. (2005). Interbank Market Integration under Asymmetric Information, *Review of Financial Studies* 18, 459–490.

Freixas, X. and Jorge, J. (2008). The Role of Interbank Markets in Monetary Policy: A Model with Rationing, *Journal of Money, Credit and Banking* 40, 1151–1176.

Freixas, X., Martin, A., and Skeie, D. (2011). Bank Liquidity, Interbank Markets, and Monetary Policy, *Review of Financial Studies* 24, 2656–2692.

Freixas, X. and Parigi, B. M. (2010). Lender of Last Resort and Bank Closure Policy. In: A. Berger, P. Molyneux, and J. Wilson (Eds.), *Oxford Handbook of Banking*, 278–314. 1st edition. Oxford: Oxford University Press.

Freixas, X., Parigi, B. M., and Rochet, J.-C. (2000). Systemic Risk, Interbank Relations and Liquidity Provision by the Central Bank, *Journal of Money, Credit and Banking* 32(2), 611–638.

Freixas, X., Parigi, B. M., and Rochet, J.-C. (2004). The Lender of Last Resort: A 21st Century Approach, *Journal of the European Economic Association* 2, 1085–1115.

Friedman, M. and Schwartz, A. J. (1963). *A Monetary History of the United States, 1867-1960*. Princeton, NJ: Princeton University.

Furfine, C. H. (2003). Interbank Exposures: Quantifying the Risk of Contagion, *Journal of Money Credit and Banking* 35, 111–128.

Goodhart, C. A. E. and Schoenmaker, D. (1993). Institutional Separation between Supervisory and Monetary Agencies, LSE Financial Market Group Special Paper No. 52.

Goodhart, C. A. E. and Schoenmaker, D. (1995). Should the Functions of Monetary Policy and Bank Supervision be Separated?, *Oxford Economic Papers* 39, 75–89.

Goodfriend, M. and King, R. (1988). Financial Deregulation Monetary Policy and Central Banking. Financial Deregulation, Monetary Policy, and Central Banking, *Federal Reserve Bank of Richmond Economic Review*, May, 3–22.

Gorton, G. (1985). Clearinghouses and the Origin of Central Banking in the United States, *Journal of Economic History* 2, 277–283.

Gorton, G. (2012). *Misunderstanding Financial Crises. Why We Don't See Them Coming*. Oxford: Oxford University Press.

Gorton, G. and Huang, L. (2004). Liquidity, Efficiency and Bank Bailouts, *American Economic Review* 94, 455–483.

Gorton, G. and Mullineaux, D. (1987). The Joint Production of Confidence: Endogenous Regulation and Nineteenth Century Commercial-Bank Clearinghouses, *Journal of Money Credit and Banking* 4, 457–468.

Holmström, B. and Tirole, J. (2011). *Inside and Outside Liquidity*. Boston: MIT Press.

Huang, X., Zhou, H., and Zhu, H. (2008). Systemic Risk Contributions, Bank of International Settlements BIS Paper No. 60.

Humphrey, D. B. (1986). Payments Finality and Risk of Settlement Failure. In: A. Saunders and L. White (Eds.), *Technology and the Regulation of Financial Markets: Securities, Futures, and Banking*. Lexington, MA: Lexington Books.

Humphrey, T. (1989). The Lender of Last Resort: The Concept in History, *Federal Reserve Bank of Richmond Economic Review* 75, 8–16.

Ioannidou, V. P. (2005). Does Monetary Policy Affect the Central Bank's Role in Bank Supervision?, *Journal of Financial Intermediation* 14, 58–85.

Iyer, R. and Peydro, J. L. (2011). Interbank Contagion at Work: Evidence from a Natural Experiment, *Review of Financial Studies* 24, 1337–1377.

Iyer, R. and Puri, M. (2012). Understanding Bank Runs: The Importance of Depositor-Bank Relationship and Networks, *American Economic Review* 102, 1414–1445.

Kyotaki, N. and Moore, J. (1997). Credit Cycles, *Journal of Political Economy* 105, 211–248.

Lehar, A. (2005). Measuring Systemic Risk: A Risk Management Approach, *Journal of Banking and Finance* 29, 2577–2603.

Lucas, R. E. (2008). Bernanke is the Best Stimulus Right Now, *The Wall Street Journal* December 23.

Malherbe, F. (2014). Self-Fulfilling Liquidity Dry-Ups, *Journal of Finance* 69, 947–970.

McAndrews, J. and Potter, S. (2002). Liquidity Effects of the Events of September 11, 2001, *Federal Reserve Banks of New York Economic Policy Review* 8, 59–79.

Merton, R.C. (1977). An Analytic Derivation of the Cost of Deposit Insurance and Loan Guarantees: An Application of Modern Option Pricing Theory, *Journal of Banking and Finance* 1, 3–11.

Mistrulli, P. (2005). Interbank Lending Patterns and Financial Contagion. Bank of Italy: Mimeo.

Peek, J., Rosengren, E., and Tootell, G. (1999). Is Bank Supervision Central to Central Banking, *Quarterly Journal of Economics* 114, 629–653.

Rochet, J-C. and Vives, X. (2004). Coordination Failures and the Lender of Last Resort: Was Bagehot Right After All?, *Journal of the European Economics Association* 2, 1116–1147.

Santos, J. A. C. (2006). Insuring Banks against Liquidity Shocks: The Role of Deposit Insurance and Lending of Last Resort, *Journal of Economic Surveys* 20, 459–482.

Schnabel, I. and Shin, H. S. (2004). Liquidity and Contagion: The Crisis of 1763, *Journal of the European Economic Association* 2, 929–968.

Sprague, O. M. W. (1910). *History of Crises under the National Banking System*. Philadelphia: Government Printing Office.

Taylor, J. B. (2012). *First Principles. Five Keys to Restoring America's Prosperity*. New York: W.W. Norton & Company Inc.

Timberlake, R. H. (1978). *The Origins of Central Banking in the United States*. Cambridge, MA: Harvard University Press.

Timberlake, R. H. (1993). *Monetary Policy in the United States*. Chicago: University of Chicago Press.

Thornton, H. (1802). *An Enquiry into the Nature and Effects of the Paper Credit of Great Britain*. London: Hatchard.

Upper, C. and Worms, A. (2004). Estimating Bilateral Exposures in the German Interbank Market: Is There a Danger of Contagion?, *European Economic Review* 48, 827–849.

Van Horen, N. and Popov, A. (2013). The Impact of Sovereign Debt Exposure on Bank Lending: Evidence from the European Debt Crisis, De Nederlandsche Bank Working Paper No. 382.

Wells, S. (2004). Financial Interlinkages in the United Kingdom's Interbank Market and the Risk of Contagion, Bank of England Working Paper No. 230.

White, E. N. (1983). *The Regulation and Reform of the American Banking System, 1900-1929*. Princeton, NJ: Princeton University Press.

CHAPTER 21

....

REGULATION AND SUPERVISION
*An Ethical Perspective**

....

EDWARD J. KANE

PERHAPS the most intriguing feature of the so-called global financial crisis (GFC) of 2007–08 is that it is actually characterized as "global." While every country experienced adverse financial shocks, crisis events were geographically concentrated. Crisis severity proved far greater in the US and Western Europe than elsewhere.

This chapter develops a conceptual framework that seeks to tie national differences in crisis severity to a combination of differences in *regulatory cultures* and differences in taxpayers' capacity to observe and support costs generated by their country's safety net. The key insight is that safety nets and regulatory cultures generate and distribute politically determined regulatory burdens and subsidies across the citizenry in ways that rob Peter to pay Paul. Financial institutions whose net worth depends on subsidies hidden in a system of implicit and explicit guarantees are bound eventually to be tested from time to time by creditor runs. At such times, the political desirability of the loss-causing subsidy program is apt to be reconsidered.

Lists of countries that have experienced a banking crisis in recent years have been compiled by Caprio and Klingebiel (1996), Honohan and Klingebiel (2003), and Laeven and Valencia (2013). A high proportion of the crises that these authors identify were triggered by losses due to poor investments engendered by government efforts to channel bank credit disproportionally to politically influential sectors and firms. During the GFC in particular, the financial sectors of countries (such as the US) that used sizeable government credit-allocation schemes to subsidize homeownership seemed to suffer the most damage.

In their eagerness for votes and campaign contributions, it is not unusual for politicians to promote the goal of homeownership for all citizens. In some countries (such as Canada and Australia), politicians are accountable for the costs of pursuing this goal, because housing subsidies proceed principally through transparent on-budget grants to first-time

* This chapter extends and refocuses analysis first presented in Kane (1998). For helpful comments, the author wishes to thank Gerard Caprio, Robert Dickler, and John Wilson.

homeowners. But in most other countries (and especially in the US), housing subsidies are delivered more stealthily. Credit-allocation schemes encourage financial institutions and their regulators to support the activities of builders and realtors in off-budget ways that channel flows of credit to home buyers on favorable terms.

A major attraction of credit-allocation schemes is that they reduce political accountability by postponing the recognition of program costs for many years. This can lead to housing bubbles and crises, especially when the borrowers include an army of customers that careful loan officers could have identified either as serial flippers of houses or as households that some high-pressure realtor had saddled with more "house" than they could afford to service in the long run.

Until the credit-allocation bubbles began to burst, US and European investment banks were praised for fashioning assembly lines on whose conveyor belts they placed tradable (i.e., "securitized") instruments that represented trusteed claims to cash flows from pools of inadequately underwritten mortgage loans. To keep the belts moving at a high speed, securitizers pressured credit-rating organizations into over-rating large portions of the mortgage-backed securities (MBSs) being produced. Tranches of allegedly investment grade products were held by banks to exploit their favorable risk weighting, and by off-balance-sheet structured investment vehicles (SIV) which issued asset-backed commercial paper supported by credit lines that served as funding guarantees from banking organizations.

These destructive patterns of real-estate investment and finance were sustained—explicitly and implicitly—by shifting the downside risk of widespread defaults onto government safety nets. Although ostensibly meant to protect the savings of ordinary households from the ravages of possible banking crises, modern safety nets have devolved into schemes for rescuing important zombie firms. These rescues benefit financial-institution managers and uninsured creditors at the expense of other taxpayers. Politicians and regulators effected this transition by adopting de facto crisis-management policies that coerce domestic (and often even foreign) taxpayers into guaranteeing the debt of a country's major financial firms against the consequences of insolvency.

Policymakers' propensity to absorb the losses of distressed financial firms converts taxpayers into equity investors of last resort in so-called systematically important financial firms. In good times, the costs of contingent governmental rescues seem small, and it is easy for regulators and industry leaders to downplay their relevance. But when asset prices crash, it costs plenty for governments to rescue zombie firms. For this reason, the value of taxpayer guarantees surges in crisis. In countries where the government's tax-collection capacity is not strong enough to absorb the losses (e.g., in Iceland, Greece, Ireland, Portugal, Italy, Spain, and Cyprus), the resources of international organizations and foreign governments are apt to be brought into the picture.

The body of this chapter develops two key ideas. First, credit-allocation schemes are part of a regulatory culture that misallocates real resources and redistributes income across time and space in anti-egalitarian ways. To understand this, it is helpful to portray regulation, supervision, and government guarantees as costly economic services that trade within and across countries in politically constrained markets. Operative political constraints are a source of endless negotiation between differently informed and differently empowered politicians, financial regulators, financiers, and ordinary citizens. The second idea is that the force of individual political constraints fluctuates dialectically, depending on whether or not contradictions in egalitarian norms underlying the regulatory cultures of different countries are brought into play by a budgetary or economic crisis.

Different cultures work out their incentive conflicts in different ways and over different time frames. A unified way to look at regulatory evolution is to conceive of the process of regulatory wealth redistribution as a non-stationary and dialectical game (Kane, 1977, 1981, and 1988). Individual plays consist of infrequently changing patterns of regulation and supervision on the one hand, and correspondingly frequent adaptive changes in the forms of burden avoidance on the other. As financial markets globalize, cross-country regulatory competition intensifies. Firms that suffer prolonged or sudden losses that make doubts about the value of their implicit governmental guarantees or risk management increase greatly come under exit pressure. As this pressure grows, taxpayers in the chartering country (and often in financial-center countries as well) find themselves progressively more exposed. From this perspective, a cross-country crisis is an adverse outcome that political and economic markets for regulatory services have to work through.

This perspective features the possibility of a regulation-induced financial crisis and leads to the view that offshore regulatory competition can either reinforce or attenuate inefficient or anti-egalitarian elements in the regulatory schemes of individual countries. Cross-country regulatory competition does this mainly by inducing increases and decreases in the share of financial business a country's institutions can capture. With technological change intensifying the influence of offshore regulators, local mis-steps promise to come to a boil sooner, but may still have severe and long-lasting effects on the local citizenry.

This chapter illustrates the adaptive process by analyzing how regulatory competition simultaneously encouraged incentive-conflicted US and EU financial supervisors to outsource much of their due discipline to credit-rating firms and thereby encouraged mortgage securitizers and institutional asset managers to lobby rating firms for inflated ratings and use the counterfeit ratings to securitize their weakest loans (US Senate Subcommittee on Investigations, 2011). This perverse set of managerial incentives pushed credit risks deliberately into corners of the universe where supervisors and credit-ratings firms could not easily see them and could deny plausibly that assessment lay in their domain of responsibility.

21.1 THE ROLE OF INCENTIVE CONFLICTS AND REGULATORY SUBSIDIES IN FINANCIAL FRAGILITY

Financial environments and patterns of financial regulation vary greatly from country to country. Financial-institution supervision combines a capacity to observe fluctuations in balance-sheet values ("vision") with a capacity to influence managerial actions ("control") and an *incentive system* that governs the pursuit and exercise of these capacities. Even when portfolios and attendant risks are concentrated within a single country, it is difficult to establish a combination of adequate oversight of institutional balance sheets, adequate authority to intervene in timely fashion, and bureaucratic incentives to detect and resolve insolvent institutions in ways that adequately protect taxpayer interests. As a result, individual countries solve this contracting problem in different ways. Although some cross-country commonalities in interests exist, systems for setting and enforcing financial rules are infested with incentive conflict. Even within a country, conflicts exist between and among:

1. Regulators and the firms they regulate;
2. Particular regulators and other societal watchdogs;
3. Regulators and the politicians to whom they must report;
4. Taxpayers and the politicians and regulators they put in office.

How a country approaches and resolves these conflicts is in part hard-wired into its political and institutional structure. One issue is whether the central bank or another agency supervises banks. The first alternative is more common in Asia than elsewhere. But most EU countries supervise banks separately from other financial institutions. A few European countries (Austria, Denmark, Germany, Sweden, the Netherlands, and the United Kingdom [albeit temporarily]) established agencies that supervise bank and nonbank financial institutions in an integrated way; others have to some degree integrated the oversight of at least their bank and securities sectors (Schüler, 2003). More recently, the Eurozone has been taking steps to build a supervisory union.

Every country relies on its ethical norms, government regulators, and other professional watchdogs to bridge gaps in the bonding, deterrent rights (deterrency), and transparency inherent in its private contracting environment. Over time, the interaction of private and government watchdogs generates a *regulatory culture*. A culture may be defined as customs, ideas, and attitudes that members of a group share and transmit from generation to generation by systems of subtle and unsubtle rewards and punishments. A regulatory culture constrains the ways in which an uncooperative or even unscrupulous individual managers can be monitored and disciplined. It comprises a matrix of attitudes and beliefs about how regulators should act. These slowly changing attitudes and beliefs often express a distrust of government power that traces back to abuses observed in a possibly distant past when the country was occupied, colonized, or run by a one-party government. The culture's taboos and traditions define standards for the fair use of government power. Behind these standards are higher-order social norms that underlie a nation's political and legal environments.

The character of a country's regulatory culture is spanned by six specific components:

- legal authority and reporting obligations;
- formulation and promulgation of specific rules;
- technology of monitoring for violations & compliance;
- allowable penalties for material violations;
- duties of consultation: To guarantee fairness, regulated parties enjoy a right to procedural due process that specifies burdens of proof that regulators must meet before they can change rules or penalize violators;
- regulatee rights to judicial review: To bond the fairness guarantee, aggrieved parties have access to inside and outside appeals procedures.

In large part, the details of each component are shaped by:

1. recognition and response lags generated by the interaction of weakness in the transparency of the nation's accounting system with bureaucratic incentives and statutory and bureaucratic checks and balances;

2. regulatory competition brought about by the entry of foreign or differently regulated institutions;
3. regulatory personnel's exposure to influence activity from a discipline-resistant firm's political clout, consultation rights, and appeal privileges;
4. social norms that protect fraudsters and bumblers against prompt regulatory discipline.

Lobbying activity seeks to reshape the particular norms that officials enforce and to constrain the tradeoffs they make. Within limits set by a country's regulatory culture, how particular policy strategies officials adopt actually work is determined by regulatees' ability to delay or stymie decisive intervention and to find and exploit circumventive loopholes. Some of these loopholes involve the ability to relocate loss exposures that are more closely supervised either by the home country (or by a particular host) to venues that monitor or discipline this kind of risk-taking less effectively.

The regulatory cultures of almost every country in the world today are manifestations in one form or another of three core tactical assumptions:

1. Desirability of *Politically-Directed Subsidies to Selected Bank Borrowers*: The policy framework either explicitly requires—or implicitly rewards—banks for making credit available to selected classes of borrowers at a subsidized interest rate;
2. Feasibility of *Subsidies to Bank Risk-Taking*: The policy framework commits government officials to providing on subsidized terms explicit or implicit conjectural guarantees of repayment to depositors and other bank creditors;
3. Plausible deniability of *Defective Monitoring and Control of the Subsidies*: The contracting and accounting frameworks used by banks and government officials fail to make anyone directly accountable for reporting or controlling the size of either subsidy in a conscientious or timely fashion.

Taken together, the first two tactical assumptions tempt banks to use the safety net to extract (i.e., to *steal*) wealth surreptitiously from taxpayers and constrain loan officers to pass some of the benefits to politically favored borrowers (such as builders and would-be homeowners in the US). Favored borrowers tend to be blocks of voters regularly courted by candidates for political office and financial supporters or cronies of influential government officials.

The third piece of the underlying framework of shared beliefs minimizes regulators' exposure to blame when things go wrong. It makes it impossible for outsiders to hold supervisors culpable for violating their ethical duties. It prevents outsiders from readily monitoring the true costs and risks generated by the first two assumptions and interferes with efforts to subject the intersectoral flow of net regulatory benefits to informed debate. This gap exists because corporate and government accounting systems do not report the value of net regulatory benefits or burdens as a separate item on the accounting statements of banks that receive them. In modern accounting systems, the capitalized value of regulatory subsidies is treated instead as an *intangible* source of value that, if booked at all, is not differentiated from other elements of a bank's so-called franchise value. Of course, some of the subsidy is offset by *tangible* losses that politically influenced loans eventually force onto financial-institution balance sheets and income statements.

In principle, a tangible reserve for expected losses ought to be set up as part of the process of making a poorly underwritten or deliberately underpriced loan. Not reserving for losses imbedded in a loan's preferential terms may be conceived as planting a time bomb in the asset and net-worth values shown on conventional bank balance sheets. Over time, the cumulative damage from politically favored loans becomes harder and harder to hide. Between the end of one crisis and the beginning of the next, the amount of government-favored loans grows larger and larger in bank portfolios. Eventually, a short-fall of contractual cash flows makes it harder to gain the financing needed to carry pools of mispriced and poorly structured loans. This is how poorly documented mortgage-backed securitizations began to suffer in the US and Europe during the summer of 2007. Although officials resist the idea, creating an enforceable obligation for regulators to estimate in trans-parent and reproducible ways the ebb and flow of the dual subsidies would empower exter-nal watchdog organizations in the private sector to force authorities to explain whether and how these subsidies benefit taxpayers.

Sooner or later, savvy large-denomination creditors come to appreciate the unre-ported hole that overvalued loans imbed in the opportunity-cost value of their bank's *enterprise-contributed net worth* (NW_E). By NW_E, we mean the value that an informed buyer would pay for the bank if safety-net guarantees did not exist. If a bank's NW_E declines through zero, it becomes a "zombie" institution. A zombie is an insolvent institution that stays active only because the black magic of government guarantees leaves its creditors with no reason to force it into a corporate grave. A zombie's ability to renew its deposit funding and other debt depends entirely on the continuing credibility of the explicit and implicit government and central bank solvency and liquidity guarantees that safety-net managers attach to its obligations.

Accounting loopholes allow a zombie institution to show positive accounting net worth long after its NW_E has turned negative. For example, although we now know that in June 2007 the British mortgage lender Northern Rock PLC was well on its way to becoming a zombie, management was able to post an accounting net worth equal to roughly 2% of its assets.

Systemwide fragility F increases with the number of zombies or near-zombies (Z) and with the aggregate size of the losses thought to be imbedded in their economic balance sheets and the interconnectedness of non-zombies with core, systemically relevant banks that are zombies:

$$F = F[Z, \sum_{j=1}^{Z} NW_E(j), I_{CZ}]$$

(21.1)

Funding problems begin *not* when a bank becomes a zombie, but when suppliers of large-denomination funds begin to doubt whether officials can or will continue to support its existence. Funding problems for a region's or country's banking system are intensified when doubts arise about the adequacy of arrangements for making taxpayers absorb the cost of guaranteeing the area's potential zombie institutions. The triggering condition is that the upper bound on the uncertain value of implicit and explicit government guarantees G rises so high that taxpayer resistance threatens to make it hard for authorities to raise the funds needed to pay the bill promptly or in full. Massive withdrawals by sophisticated credi-tors are sometimes described as "silent runs," because servicing the demands that a troubled bank receives from large creditors generates far less publicity than the queue of panicked small depositors that impatiently mills about in a conventional run.

However, silent runs greatly weaken bank balance sheets. The deposit and interbank out-flows (including repos and commercial paper) that a troubled institution experience must be financed by selling liquid assets and issuing costly debt. A distressed firm's first line of defense against a silent run is to arrange loans from government institutions or from rela-tively well-informed banks with which it has correspondent relationships. Private rescuers usually insist on receiving appropriately high interest rates and demand collateralization and an upside potential for their claims. In deciding to help a correspondent bank in another country to survive a silent run, foreign banks are apt first to lobby the IMF, the host govern-ment, and even their own government for assurances that they will not be stuck with the bill for whatever losses the rescue effort might incur.

Until officials increase the transparency and credibility of their credit support, silent runs on weak institutions tend to escalate. Distressed institutions' sales of good assets and increasing funding costs reduce future income and make the fragility of their condition apparent to more and more outside observers. When an institution collateralizes its good assets at or below their market value, its undisclosed losses on poorly performing loans become a larger proportion of the assets that remain unpledged. The more funding a trou-bled bank obtains at high credit spreads, the more severely its future accounting and eco-nomic profits are squeezed and the more likely it is to engage in go-for-broke lending and funding activities ("gambling for resurrection") that severely pressure the profit margins of healthy competitors.

A silent run puts pressure on regulators because it progressively undermines the willing-ness of taxpayers and stronger banks to tolerate the regulatory status quo. As a silent run unfolds, reduced profit margins spread zombieness and disturbing information is revealed about the size and distribution of taxpayers' potential involvement. At the same time, net regulatory benefits for weak and strong banks diverge more and more widely. Weak banks receive safety-net subsidies from central bank loans and government guarantees that stronger banks and general taxpayers eventually have to pay for.

The longer a silent run proceeds, the more deeply supervisory efforts to retard the exit or to delay the formal recapitalization of inefficient and insolvent deposit institutions push the net regulatory benefits of other economic sectors into negative territory. The economic and political forces exerted when a large bank suffers open and silent runs are nicely illus-trated by the British government's response to the Northern Rock debacle. In September 2007, an open depositor run on this bank was stopped by the government's promise to pro-vide emergency funding to the £114 billion institution and to "guarantee all existing deposit arrangements." However, a silent run persisted. By yearend, emergency loans from the Bank of England reached about £25 billion and Treasury guarantees had been extended to cover most of the bank's non-deposit obligations as well. Well-publicized efforts to persuade stockholders and outside acquirers to inject private capital into the bank showed little pro-gress. Finally, in February 2008, the bank was "temporarily" nationalized.

21.2 ETHICS OF SUPERVISION

An institution's incentive to circumvent or violate a given rule increases with the weight of the burdens that full compliance threatens to impose on its efforts to create value and manage risk. Dutiful enforcement revises bank incentives by rewarding compliance, punishing evasion, and searching out and closing loopholes that regulatees might use to skirt the rules.

Loopholes are gaps in supervisory enforcement that generate an informal set of looser rules. These shadow rules are designed to discourage appeals to higher authority and are at least partially conjectural. For example, although the formal speed limit on a given highway might be posted at (say) 55 miles per hour, drivers confidently expect the limit that police actually enforce to be higher than the posted one and to adapt predictably to exceptional circumstances (such as personal emergencies) as these unfold.

Common law and common-sense ethical theory maintain that, across any contract in which one party delegates authority to one or more others, agents and principals owe one another duties of loyalty, competence, and care. On this hypothesis, financial supervisors owe four key duties to the community that employs them:

1. *A duty of vision*: they should continually adapt their surveillance systems to observe and counter regulatee efforts to disguise or mischaracterize their rule-breaking;
2. *A duty of prompt corrective action*: they should stand ready to discipline rule-breakers whenever a violation is observed;
3. *A duty of efficient operation*: they should produce their services at minimum cost;
4. *A duty of conscientious or loyal representation*: they should be prepared to put the interests of the community they serve ahead of their own.

In principle, supervisors committed to the fourth duty would bond themselves to disclose enough information about their decision making to enable the community to hold them accountable for neglecting or abusing these responsibilities. But in credit-allocation schemes, institutional arrangements do not hold supervisors strongly accountable for inefficiencies and adverse distributional effects generated by their performance. To the contrary and in country after country, politicians check only whether credit is flowing on favorable terms to privileged economic sectors. To obtain a *quid pro quo*, a lender's or securitizer's stakeholders expect its position in favored loans to be supervised with a lighter hand, especially in times of financial turmoil (Kane, 1989).

21.3 IMPERFECTION IN THE MARKET FOR REGULATORY SERVICES

Traditionally, supervisory duties have been exercised locally and—in a narrow and formal sense—schemes for regulating and supervising financial firms are still shaped and administered on a nation-by-nation basis. For compelling historical, cultural, economic, and political reasons, these duties and schemes vary across countries—often greatly (Barth, Caprio, and Levine, 2006, 2012, 2013).

Differences in rules and enforcement create opportunities for regulatory arbitrage. Savvy managers are aware that different suppliers of regulatory services offer different frameworks of advantages and constraints. Just as managers might investigate alternative suppliers for any service that they wish to outsource, financiers sort through alternative regulatory schemes to ascertain the particular jurisdiction that offers them the best mix of costs and benefits for the various pieces of their product lines. In the absence of switching costs, each firm would design an array of substitute asset, liability, and hedging instruments and negotiate with alternative suppliers so that each deal they write could be booked in the most favorable jurisdiction.

Today, national regulatory schemes and resulting regulatee burdens are increasingly influenced by competition from cross-border guarantees available from foreign regulatory systems. In world markets, movements of financial capital and changing asset values overlay onto the domestic policy scene a series of unfamiliar political, economic, and reputational pressures that individual-country regulatory decision-makers must take into account. Arguably, these pressures have persuaded authorities in financial center countries to supplement the resources of foreign safety nets and to acquiesce in loophole-ridden agreements (Basel I, II, and III) for coordinating cross-country supervision (see Goodhart, 2011).

To sort out cross-country and cross-product differences in the quality and offering prices of different suppliers of regulatory and safety-net services, it is helpful to think of a *market* in which supplier competition is constrained by each supplier's resources and incentive-conflicted regulatory culture. The observable details that constitute a particular *regulatory scheme* consist of a particular set of goals and policy instruments.

Although a large literature treats financial regulation as if it were simply a *tax* on bank income, industry executives understand that regulation is better conceived as a back-office financial *service* that, for participants in financial markets, generates benefits as well as costs. Its benefits lie in three realms: improving customer confidence, improving customer convenience, and supporting or resisting an institution's efforts to accumulate and exercise market power. Because regulation and supervision require resources to produce, authorities can both produce them more or less efficiently and finance their production more or less fairly. Whether or not the costs of producing regulatory services are minimized, political activity allocates their production costs across society and determines their level and visibility.

Regulation is supplied competitively and accepted voluntarily to the extent that entry and exit opportunities exist for regulated firms willing to incur the transaction costs of switching all or part of their regulatory business to another supplier. Hence, although a regulator's clientele is fixed in the very short run, the jurisdictions in which a regulatee operates are voluntary over longer periods. Jurisdictional overlaps in the global market for financial regulatory services have expanded as entry and exit costs for foreign financial institutions have declined around the world.

The price an entity pays for regulatory services corresponds to the difference between the benefits that firm or household receives from regulation and the costs that regulation imposes on it. Depending on whether the difference is positive or negative, we can describe this price as an entity's "net regulatory benefit (or burden) from financial regulation," or NRB.

Rules and enforcement systems are continually tested and reshaped by changes in the net regulatory benefits that other jurisdictions offer. Nevertheless, jurisdictional competition for most financial products is inherently imperfect. An incumbent regulator may be said to have market power in any line in which it can lower the NRB it offers clients without completely surrendering its clientele to another regulator. Alternatively, we might say that the *leaders* of a regulatory agency have market power whenever the various labor, capital, and political markets from which they draw economic resources cannot hold them (and the elected politicians who appoint and sustain them) accountable for policy decisions that simultaneously lower net regulatory burdens for their clientele of lenders and borrowers and increase them for other important economic sectors.

The vigor of regulatory competition is enhanced by technological change and diminished by information asymmetries, leadership turnover, and various sources of principal-agent conflict that are inherent in governmental decision making. Regulators routinely adopt reporting systems that make it difficult for citizens to gather information either about subsidiary goals that policymakers might be pursuing or about sectoral, bureaucratic, or personal benefits that regulatory activity might generate. As ongoing debates over the details of the 2010 Dodd–Frank Act and Basel III show, when evidence of discriminatory or inefficient performance surfaces, it is difficult to isolate its root causes and even harder to correct the incentive defects responsible for it.

The value of regulatory competition lies in supplying indirect economic checks on the even-handedness and efficiency of net regulatory burdens. On the demand side, competition encourages parties that feel overburdened by their government's system of regulation to reconfigure their business to slide it into the jurisdiction of a more advantageous supplier of regulatory services. It does not matter whether the new supplier is a domestic agency or a foreign one. What does matter is that the regulatees gain relief, the new regulator gains budgetary resources, and the old regulator loses them. The lower the transition costs of moving to a less burdensome regulatory supplier, the more complete the demand-side check becomes.

On the supply side, entry and exit costs confer competitive advantages on incumbent regulators. In competing with private regulatory enterprises such as securities and futures exchanges, government entities are advantaged by the financial strength imparted to them by the extent to which they can assign catastrophic losses to taxpayers and by their ready access to the coercive power of the state. To a non-traditional supplier, the costs of actively gearing up to oversee a new category of financial deal-making can be substantial. The existence of these costs means that the number of potential new entrants that can economically supply regulatory services to financial firms in a given country is relatively limited in the short run.

Successful entry requires more than a capacity for exercising disciplinary power. To displace a seasoned regulator, would-be entrants need specific skills, a source of moral authority, and substantial financial and reputational capital. Entrants must be able to promise credibly that they can fairly and efficiently produce regulatory services and that they are willing and able to sustain this promise for a long while. They must be able to manipulate a system of rewards and punishments whose force seems strong enough to improve the behavior of potential regulatees.

In brief, the inherited market structure for regulatory services and opportunities for entry are distorted by market power that the law freely gives to government enterprises and by reputational advantages enjoyed by incumbent private regulators. On the one hand, representative democracy confers renewable monopoly power on elected politicians and the regulatory leaders they appoint. Because policymaking authority may be canceled by voters or limited ex post by the courts, this authority becomes all the stronger, the more confidently incumbent politicians may count on holding power and the more that top bureaucrats may count on holding onto their offices and avoiding vigorous prosecution or public censure for questionable acts.

1. Rent-Seeking Generates Aggressive Loss Exposures at Highly Leveraged Institutions
   - Pursuit of Safety-Net Subsidies Tied to Government-Promoted Forms of Lending
   - Pursuit of Subsidies Tied to Other Kinds of Leveraged Risk-Taking
2. Adverse Events and Industry Problems Upset Financial Markets
   - Banks and Regulators Keep Losses from Registering on Bank Books by Accounting Trickery and Coverup
   - Large-Denomination Creditors Test the Strength of the Safety Net
   - Fragility of System Rises as Good Assets are Collateralized and Endgame Incentives Induce Go-For-Broke Gambling
   - Threat of Shortages in Safety-Net Funding Rises Over Time
3. Supplementation of Traditional Safety-Net Support Mechanisms
   - Loans from Central-Bank Discount Window Can't Carry the Load
   - Inventive Accounting Loopholes and Forms of Public Credit Expand
4. Recapitalization of Troubled Banks and Safety-Net Institutions
   - A. Stopgap Partial Recapitalizations: Half-Measures Move the Financial Sector Back into Stage Two of the Cycle
   - B. Transformation of Bank Losses into Explicit Taxpayer Obligations or Explicit Nationalization of Zombie Banks
5. Final Clean-Up of the Mess
   - Reprivatization of Zombie Institutions
   - Blame Heaped on Designated Scapegoats
   - Credible Safety-Net Reforms are Adopted

Figure 21.1 Five stages of a regulation-induced banking crisis.

Even in the private sector, market power is conferred in lasting fashion on a successful regulatory enterprise. It is interesting that in recent years a number of traditionally private regulators that are hard to dislodge (including several major stock and commodities exchanges) experienced cross-country takeovers of their franchise. It may be unfortunate that, for key regulatory bureaus, central banks, and ministries of finance, takeover discipline cannot be so direct.

21.4 EXCULPATORY NORMS IN THE CULTURE OF CRISIS MANAGEMENT

Capital requirements are based on the idea that an overleveraged financial system is an accident waiting to happen. A regulation-induced accident occurs when misfortune impacts a financial system whose regulators have incentivized their institutions to leave themselves vulnerable to this amount and type of bad luck.

Figure 21.1 breaks the evolution of a regulation-induced financial crisis into five stages or crisis generation and regulatory response. The 2007–2008 breakdown of arrangements for financing for structured securitizations in the US and Europe, and the lesser banking crises that rolled through Latin America, Japan, Korea, the Philippines, Malaysia, Indonesia,

Thailand, and Russia during 1997–98 passed through the first three and one-half stages of this model of crisis generation and response.

Crises often hang up in the stopgap partial recapitalization stage (stage 4A). Since the GFC began in 2007, German, British, and American authorities have shown again and again a reluctance to move beyond this stage. As long as the weakness of an institution's or government's financial situation can be covered up, outsiders cannot easily distinguish a wave of financial-institution insolvencies from a transitory shortage of aggregate liquidity. In either circumstance, a group of economically significant firms find it exceedingly difficult to roll over their liabilities privately on profitable terms. Standard first-response practice for central bankers and other regulators is to provide liquidity to distressed institutions as a way to buy time for supervisory staff to investigate the extent to which irreparable insolvency might underlie the distress. This time-buying strategy is supported ethically by three norms whose exculpatory force intensifies in times of political, market, or institutional turmoil: a mercy norm; a nationalistic norm; and a non-escalation norm.

The *mercy norm* holds that it is bad policy and unacceptably cruel behavior for regulators to abandon the employees, creditors, and stockholders of institutions they oversee before and unless they can convincingly establish that the distress is too deep to be remedied by subsidized loans. This norm gives regulators the discretion (if not the duty) to alleviate the initial pains of any client institution that experiences a silent run.

The *nationalistic norm* presupposes that regulators should help domestic institutions and market-makers to cope with foreign competition. In practice, this norm is reinforced by community resistance to foreign control of national credit decisions and by lobbying pressure from politically favored sectors who suspect that foreign firms will not serve their interests very well.

The *non-escalation norm* allows authorities to lend on subsidized terms to distressed institutions as long as they can popularize the view that doing anything else would invite a national or global financial disaster. In order to invoke this norm, officials must first spread fear. They must argue three things: (1) that, without a large injection of subsidized funds, markets will set prices for troubled assets that are unreasonably low; (2) that prices for private emergency credit to institutions that hold distressed assets are unreasonably high; and (3) that these further price movements would sweep strong and healthy institutions into the turmoil.

It is dangerous for government officials either to exaggerate the depth of a crisis or to understate the size of the increasingly transparent flow of subsidies that partial recapitalization entails. For high-ranking regulators to keep churning out safety-net subsidies, two further conditions must hold. First, they must be able to control the flow of information, so as to keep taxpayers and the press from convincingly assessing either the magnitude of the implicit capital transfer and the anti-egalitarian character of the subsidization scheme industry lobbyists hope to keep going. Second, the self-interest of top regulators must be continually nourished by praise and other forms of tribute from the financiers, borrowers, and investors whose losses are being shifted to other parties.

Authorities are reluctant to move to full recapitalization unless evidence of overwhelming losses keep bubbling up in the form of resurging crisis pressures. The longer the game goes on, the greater the risk that the reputations of incoming policymakers and the particular politicians that appoint them will be saddled unfairly with the sins of their predecessors.

Although it is unwise to draw inferences from small samples, the U.S. savings-and-loan mess and various Argentine crises cast some light on how costs are allocated during the final stages of the life cycle of a regulation-induced crisis.

21.4.1 A Formal Model

To think about this formally, we may analyze continuation and breakdown in the burden-shifting process as the two states of an evolutionary Markov process. Though small on any given day, the probability (p) of a breakdown during an incentive-conflicted regulator's term in office increases with the fragility of the system for making good on the safety net's implicit and explicit safety-net guarantees. It is convenient to represent the value of government credit support as G and the cumulative size of the taxpaying community's hidden responsibility for supporting the liabilities of troubled institutions as (T). T and G increase with system fragility (F). In turn, whenever F grows, p also rises. During the early stages of an incipient crisis, increments in the probability of breakdown depend on the informativeness (A) of the accounting principles that banks and safety-net officials use to report losses and loss exposures:

$$p = p[G, T, F; A]. \tag{21.2}$$

During these early stages, banks and their regulators are tempted to seek and provide incremental "accounting relief." However, once market participants begin to recognize partial recapitalizations and accounting coverups as half-measures, weaknesses in A compound the problem and improvements in A become a critical part of a genuine crisis-resolution process.

21.4.2 Costs of Modern Crises

Rolling and incompletely resolved crises sound at least three alarms. First, the frequency and geographic extent of financial crises convincingly demonstrate that, around the world, numerous institutions have found it reasonable to book potentially ruinous risks. Looking at the period 1977–1995, Caprio and Klingebiel (1996) cite 58 countries in which the net worth of the banking system was almost or entirely eliminated. Second, in country after country, domestic (and sometimes foreign) taxpayers have been billed to bail out banks, depositors, and deposit-insurance funds. Honohan and Klingebiel (2003) confirm that, in modern crises, taxpayers' bill for making good on implicit and explicit guarantees typically ran between 1% and 10% of gross domestic product (GDP). The size of these bailouts establishes that, at least in crisis countries, banks managed to put large bets on the table and were able to shift a substantial amount of the downside of these bets to taxpayers. In many cases, authorities were eventually blamed for the size of the bills taxpayers were asked to pay. Officials were seen to have shirked their duties to expose and stop loss-causing patterns of credit allocation and to have compounded the damage from credit losses by not addressing individual-bank insolvencies until their situation had deteriorated disastrously.

In times of financial turmoil, crisis-management norms and weaknesses in ethical controls on the job performance of government regulators responsible for protecting the safety and soundness of financial institutions encourage regulatory forbearance. The high cost of modern crises indicates how far the risk-taking preferences of officials responsible for managing taxpayer risk exposures diverge from those of large-denomination creditors in private financial markets. Although institutional mechanisms for financing safety-net loans and guarantees differ across countries, poor information flows and incentive conflict in government policymaking complicate the treatment of banking crises everywhere (Calomiris and Haber, 2014).

Special problems of accountability and incentive conflict arise in managing cross-country risk exposures. Financial regulators subject foreign banks and the foreign operations of domestic banks to patterns of regulation that differ in two important ways from those that apply to strictly domestic banking operations. First, most developed countries are willing to allow their domestic banks to book a wider range of risks in foreign subsidiaries than they are prepared to tolerate in home-country offices. This is because relationships with internationally active customers are a geographically footloose part of the banking business and because government officials don't expect to confront responsibility for foreign banking losses in domestic political arenas. This creates incentives for offshore banks to "overlend" into foreign markets. Second, though greatly weakened by technological change and outside political pressure, obstacles to the entry of foreign financial firms in most banking markets still exist.

21.5 Globalization and Securitization of Bank Funding Opportunities

Contemporary theories of industrial organization seek to explain that a product's market structure evolves through time to permit *efficient firms* and *efficient contracting instruments* to reshape or displace relatively less-efficient alternatives. The force of these theories is particularly easy to grasp when we focus on hypothetical markets that meet a set of ideal conditions that Baumol, Panzar, and Willig (1986) call "perfect contestability."

A market is perfectly contestable when entry and exit costs are each zero *and* incumbent firms exit quickly whenever they find themselves faced with negative profits. In perfectly contestable markets, low-cost firms readily displace high-cost firms and incumbent competitors are prevented from setting monopoly prices by the threat of hit-and-run entry by other equally-efficient firms.

Of course, financial markets are never perfectly contestable. New entrants must adapt and expand their information systems before they can safely expand their customer base. Incumbents cannot easily abandon the pipeline of loan commitments they have promised to customers and the regulatory foundations on which inherently non-transparent financial markets must be built are burdened with inescapable entry and exit costs.

During the last 40 years, particularly in wholesale banking markets, technological change has steadily lowered entry costs for foreign and non-traditional competitors. Most of these firms undertook banking activities in innovative ways, making creative use of substitute products, substitute organizational forms, and substitute offshore locations. In some countries, the viability of a new entrant's business plan was temporarily enhanced by longstanding restrictions on how banks could compete domestically.

Chief among the innovative methods of doing business was structured securitization. With help from investment banks, credit rating agencies, mortgage insurers, and hedge funds, banks sliced and securitized titles to the cash flows from their loans in ways that assigned the slicing (or "tranching"), reslicing, and servicing of flows of interest and principal to separately capitalized conduit vehicles. By placing important tranches of their loans through and with foreign and non-bank firms, banks greatly complicated the job of financial supervision by creating new links in their domestic funding chains and extending the geographic span of their funding arrangements.

Innovative funding technologies benefited borrowers by integrating bank loan pricing within and across countries. However, outsourcing the funding side of a bank's balance sheet lessened its staff members' due diligence by weakening the link between the income a lender could make from originating securitizable loans and the quality of its system for underwriting the loans it originated. Investors in a securitized pool of loans did not rely on either the lender's or their own due diligence. Instead, they expected credit rating agencies to assess the risks in the positions investors were offered and they expected investment banks and mortgage insurers to make sure that the returns offered would respond appropriately to differences in loan quality. Unfortunately, the naïveté with which these expectations were held undermined agents' incentives to meet them. Compensation for rating and pricing individual securities was collected as soon as the securities were floated, with little exposure to ex post blowback for personnel that might later be shown to have made a serious rating or pricing mistake. With supervisors closing their eyes to the erosion of this chain of agents' contractual incentives to execute faithfully their duties of loyalty, competence, and care, investors presumed that they were purchasing titles to well-rated and well-priced securities.

Securitization also brought firms that were supervised in different regulatory cultures and jurisdictions into sharper competition with one another. This mutual invasion of traditional markets by institutions headquartered in different regulatory cultures put pressure on particular regulatory enterprises (especially at enterprises whose leaders' remaining terms in office promised to be short) to relax vigilance as a way of defending their bureaucratic turf. In retrospect, it is clear that banking supervisors did this by regularizing and legitimating cutting-edge ways to hide or transfer risk without fully vetting the threats that these complex new contracting structures imposed on individual country safety nets.

Whenever a regulator acquiesced in innovative entry by a foreign or nontraditional firm, it had to relax restraints that might make it hard for its traditional clients to compete with the new entrants. Institutions pressed politicians to make this happen sooner rather than later.

Authorities' accommodative response to this competitive pressure has been labeled *financial deregulation*, but our ethical perspective makes it clear that the response is better described as *desupervision*. In most countries, regulatory competition and defects in accountability led banking supervisors to assess the risks of innovative instruments of risk transfer with less watchfulness than these instruments deserved. With respect to structured securitizations, banking supervisors and mortgage-insurance firms outsourced their duty of vision to accountants and credit rating agencies without adequately bonding the obligations they were asking them to perform. They did this despite these firms' obvious conflicts in goals and outsized delays in downgrading distressed securities in past downturns (Portes, 2008).

The contestability of financial markets is greatly reduced by the political clout that domestic banks and securities firms enjoy and by the ability of supervisory entities to bill government safety nets for the losses their heedlessness might engender. In crises, safety-net subsidies disadvantage less-subsidized competitors and unreasonably sustain the operations of decapitalized firms. The contestable-markets portrayal of market-structure evolution helps us to understand that in most countries deregulation focused on unblocking entry without addressing supervisory incentives to resist the exit of important domestic banks. Bank and supervisory exit resistance attenuates the benefits to society that entry relaxation would otherwise produce. Banking crises teach foreign and non-traditional competitors of the need to estimate the extent of supervisor-supported exit resistance. By standing ready to absorb the losses of unprofitable clients, a regulator (especially a central bank) can prevent low-cost entrants from earning the profits needed to justify hit-and-run entry.

21.6 DIALECTICS OF A REGULATION-INDUCED BANKING CRISIS

For any policymaker, a crisis may be described as a time of upheaval that generates strong pressure for decisive changes in policy strategy. Figure 21.2 portrays a regulation-induced banking crisis as an evolutionary process that is driven in Hegelian fashion by dialectical collisions of irreconcilable market and regulatory adjustments.

For any regulated institution, change—not rest—represents the path of profit-making equilibrium. The Hegelian model of regulation assumes that the conflict between regulated parties and their regulators can never be completely eliminated. The contradictory forces at work in each round of adjustments are labeled the "thesis" and the "antithesis." Every sequence of adjustment and response produces a temporary "synthesis" that serves in turn as the "thesis" for a new round of action and response.

In the US, policies designed to promote homeownership encouraged borrowers and lenders alike to operate with a "perilously high degree of leverage" (Shadow Financial Regulatory Committee, 2008). For borrowers, the value of the subsidies that they could derive both from tax deductions for mortgage interest and from federal programs supporting mortgage credit increased with the amount they borrowed. For lenders, federal programs supported the securitization of home mortgages by offering cheap guarantees and by making it possible for banks to avoid capital requirements on mortgages that they chose to securitize. Supervisors did not require banks or securities firms either to estimate or to hold capital against the implicit obligations that structured securitization vehicles passed through to a sponsor's net worth. The high degree of leverage on borrower positions meant that, if and when housing prices declined by more than a few percent, marginal borrowers would be unable to service their obligations. Once a sharp increase in delinquencies and foreclosures

THESIS: UNSUSTAINABLE POLICY MIX
- Expansionary Monetary Policy and Loss-Causing Credit-Allocation Scheme ("politically sabotaged loans") vs. Adverse Effects of Desupervising Risks on the Costs of Providing Safety-Net Support for Loss-Making Banks

ANTITHESIS: SKEPTICAL INVESTORS AND DEPOSITORS TEST GOVERNMENTS' ABILITY TO MANAGE THE EXPANDING COSTS OF NATIONAL SAFETY NETS
- In a Banking Crisis, Market Tests consist of Silent Runs (Symptomized by a Generalized Flight to Quality and Simplicity)
- The probability of a deepening crisis rises the longer authorities refuse to contain the damage and continue to help zombie institutions to stay in play

SYNTHESIS: REFORM OCCURS WHEN AUTHORITIES CAN NO LONGER QUELL MARKET DOUBTS ABOUT THEIR ABILITY TO SUSTAIN THE CONTRADICTORY POLICY MIX.
- Credit-allocation scheme unravels
- Costs of sustaining decapitalized institutions become manifest

Figure 21.2 Dialectics of a regulation-induced crisis.

by subprime borrowers occurred, savvy investors revalued and cut back their positions in securitized mortgage pools. When this revaluation wiped out the equity of mortgage securitization conduits, reputational concerns persuaded bank sponsors to move a good portion of conduit losses back onto their balance sheets. Besides being billed for conduit losses, banks that had been heavily involved in originating mortgages for sale to conduits were stuck with losses on pipelines of ongoing mortgage commitments that they could no longer profitably securitize. Inevitably, silent runs on these banks tested the ability of safety-net managers to manage a spreading crisis.

The appropriate policy response to crisis pressures depends on the nature of the policy contradictions that occasioned the crisis. A perennial issue is to assess the potential insolvency of troubled banks and to determine how rapidly their net worth is being undermined by falling prices on crisis-creating loans. Asset-price meltdowns are most likely to occur when incentives for overlending by domestic and offshore institutions confront a host-country policy regime that offers incentives for overborrowing at domestic households and firms. In such cases, pressure on asset prices is apt to generate a crisis-intensifying run from claims issued by the insolvent borrowers and lenders.

It is superficial to conceive of the silent runs that triggered the US securitization crisis as manifestations of an underprovision of aggregate "liquidity." In fact, the central bank has for many years accommodated overspending in the housing sector and also financed a long run of current-account deficits. A central bank can prolong a payments deficit by letting its currency decline and by drawing down the country's foreign-exchange reserves and foreign lines of credit. In any consumption-driven currency devaluation, the need to rebuild the central banks' currency reserves may or may not be urgent. If it is, authorities can shrink the current-account deficit in two complementary ways: (1) by allowing the exchange rate to decline even further and (2) by tightening their mix of fiscal and monetary policies.

But when a money-center country is experiencing a banking crisis, this prescription is unattractive. These policies would impose a sizeable opportunity loss on foreign and domestic holders of the country's financial assets. The currency-adjustment half of this strategy would put inflationary pressure on domestic prices. To pile on the tight-money half of the prescription would induce a decline in aggregate economic demand, whose effects would reduce the real value of a country's financial assets in general and the net worth of its banking system in particular. This would further undermine asset values by raising prospective rates of default and delinquency on troubled assets. In crisis circumstances, it is politically impossible for authorities to ignore the effects that these adjustments would have on safety-net loss exposures.

In a financial center country, authorities face a Three-Way Policy Dilemma about how to control a silent run:

1. *Choice One*: Try to finance the runs with minimal adjustment in the loss-causing parts of the policy mix. We may describe this strategy as gambling for resurrection. As in the US, authorities may temporarily nationalize one or more insolvent giants (such as Fannie Mae and Freddie Mac), resolve a few others, and deny that any other significant zombies exist. They may expand the central bank's balance sheet (see Figure 21.3) and possibly soften the potential decline in their exchange rate by drawing down reserves or borrowing from private and official foreign sources.
2. *Choice Two*: Rebalance the policy mix to make it more sustainable, but perhaps only with respect to a narrowly defined window of time (e.g., until after the next election). Authorities may resolve or strengthen some of the weakest institutions and may slow monetary growth. We have described this as a strategy of "partial recapitalization."

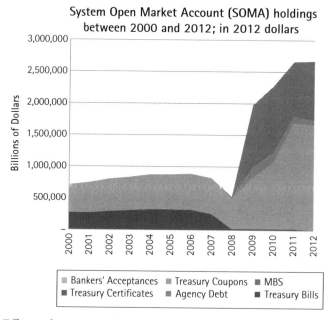

FIGURE 21.3 Effects of accepting choice one on the Federal Reserve's balance sheet.

3. *Choice Three* (unlikely to be chosen unless prior efforts to use one or both of the other strategies have failed dramatically): Face up to and eliminate the most obvious contradictions in the policy mix. The new policy regime would aim for a full cleanup of insolvent institutions and to establish a more incentive-compatible supervisory system going forward.

Leaving bank and corporate insolvencies partly unresolved fosters further malinvestment and enhances the likelihood that a deeper crisis will re-emerge down the line. The other side of the incentive conflict is that it is dangerous to acknowledge and resolve corporate and banking insolvencies in the midst of a national recession. In crisis circumstances, politicians are strongly tempted to reflate demand and to strengthen the credibility of safety-net guarantees, without doing much to resolve the incentive distortions that widespread insolvency creates.

21.7 THE ROLE OF REGULATORY COMPETITION IN BANKING CRISES

Contradictory policies misallocate capital in the household, financial, corporate, and government-planning sectors. The result is that asset values and industry net worth become overstated. Had asset values either been supported by a sustainable expansion in productive capacity or been written down promptly as unfavorable information surfaced, silent runs would not have become large enough to test the safety nets of financial-center countries.

The seeds of the 2007–2008 securitization crisis were sown over many decades. They did not flower into a crisis until doubts began to surface about authorities' willingness and ability to measure and absorb the losses and loss exposures confronting a suddenly decapitalized banking system. Measurement is important. As in the 1980s savings-and-loan mess, crisis costs were intensified by stubbornly delaying loss recognition at loss-making institutions.

What the press describes as a sudden "financial crisis" may be more accurately described as the surfacing of tensions caused by the longstanding efforts of loss-making institutions to force the rest of society to accept responsibility for their unpaid bills for making bad loans. In US mortgage markets, long-lived systems for subsidizing poorly underwritten loans to builders and overleveraged households imposed undisclosed losses on depository and securities firms and on taxpayer-financed safety nets.

Around the world, financial institutions and markets are supported by regulatory systems that show numerous country-specific features (Wilson, 1986; Dermine, 2003; Barth, Caprio, and Levine, 2006, 2012). Differences in patterns of financial regulation address differences that exist in the various economic, political, and bureaucratic deficiencies and inefficiencies that each country's regulatory system is overtly or covertly expected to correct (Garcia and Nieto, 2006; Herring and Schuermann, 2006).

However, the survival of differences in regulatory patterns is limited by the tendency of funding and loan-making opportunities to flow to markets and institutions that offer their customers the best deal. The extent to which net regulatory burdens on financial markets and institutions differ across countries is narrowed by the regulatory arbitrage that interjurisdictional deal flows entail. When and as technological change in information processing and telecommunications lowers the cost of transacting with foreign entities, adverse flows of capital and financial deal-making help to persuade a nation's authorities to lower the net burdens that their regulatory framework imposes on the savers and investors that book deals in its financial markets.

In recent years, rolling banking and currency crises have become frequent for three reasons. First, advances in information and communications technology have simultaneously globalized private financial markets and markets for government guarantees. Second, the globalization of markets for funding and guarantee services has made it less costly for domestic corporations and wealthy investors to mount silent runs on a country's zombie banks. Third, lenders, securitizers, credit-rating organizations, and supervisory authorities are not compensated in ways that make them accountable for the slow-developing but inevitable losses that their policies engender.

In 1997–1998, crises in Korea, Indonesia, Malaysia, the Philippines, and Thailand were hastened by the technologically driven absorption of these countries into an international market for loanable funds that allowed large depositors to protect themselves against the burdens of inefficient or discriminatory patterns of national regulation. Globalization put the costs and benefits of banking regulation in these countries into closer competition with the regulatory systems of offshore financial centers.

Exploitive regulation drives sophisticated depositors, unsubsidized borrowers, and other bank stakeholders to book at least some of their business elsewhere: either abroad or in informal or differently regulated domestic markets. Such regulatory arbitrage limits the extent to which politicians can promote a distribution of regulatory burdens that arbitrarily narrows opportunities for important sectors of a national economy to accumulate and manage their wealth.

Offshore banking competition shortened in two ways the crisis-gestation period featured in traditional crisis models (such as Krugman, 1979). First, even limited entry by outside banks expanded the stock of well-priced domestically available substitutes for deposits that local citizens had previously held in host-country banks. This lowered the cost to Asian depositors of participating in a silent run on domestic banks. Second, the relative safety of foreign-bank deposit substitutes demonstrated the greater reliability of the performance guarantees written for each offshore entrant by the regulatory systems of its homeland.

The normative goal of financial reform should be to induce nondiscriminatory and efficient patterns of regulation and supervision (Barth, Caprio, and Levine, 2012). Regulators should be made accountable not just for producing a stable financial economy, but for providing this stability fairly and at minimum long-run cost to society. In practice, this means establishing contractual incentives that would lead authorities to follow market-mimicking standards of supervisory performance. In the absence of explicit or implicit government guarantees, markets would insist that any institution that experiences a spate of opportunity-cost losses do one or more of three things: shrink, raise more equity capital, or pay higher interest rates for its debt. The public policy problem is to design employment contracts that would make it in regulators' and supervisors' self-interest to invoke "market-mimicking" disciplines when and as a country's important institutions weaken.

Officials understand that reworking financier incentives and strengthening bank supervision and corporate governance lie at the heart of genuine crisis resolution (Laeven and

Levine, 2009). But authorities remain reluctant to isolate and repair the behavioral norms and incentive structures that made a crisis country's and firm's supervision weak in the first place. They have proved willing to experiment with regulations for higher capital require-ments, expanded resolution authority, living wills (Goodhart, 2010), and contingent convert-ible debt (Calomiris and Herring, 2013), and are considering the possibility of regulatory size limits for too-big-to-unwind institutions. What authorities in the US and EU have not done is to delve into public-service and financial-institution contracting and information-disclosure regulatory reforms that would directly attack financiers' incentives to game the safety net and take steps to make their strategies of supervision not just tougher, but more efficient.

For any regime, the size of tolerable deviations from a fair and efficient distribution of net regulatory burdens increases with the opportunity costs its citizens face in engaging in capital flight. In turn, the benefits and costs of capital flight evolve with information tech-nology, the volatility of the real economy, and the fluidity of the political environment. The information revolution that is underway in finance today makes it short-sighted and inequi-table to adopt credit-allocation schemes that inexorably eat away at the capital of a country's financial institutions and that require taxpayers to subsidize weak megabanks and politi-cally driven patterns of real investment. Credit rating agencies and the Basel Committee on Banking Supervision would be well-advised to abandon sampling procedures that give little weight to adverse tail events and models that presume that asset risks are relatively sta-tionary over time. They should focus also on finding ways both to bond the scrupulousness with which staff members perform their supervisory duties and to enlist forward-looking stock and derivatives markets to help them track the changing odds of defaults in individual countries and industries (Kane, 2003).

References

Akerlof, G. and Romer, P. (1993). Looting: The Economic Underworld of Bankruptcy for Profit, *Brookings Papers on Economic Activity* 2.

Barth, J. R., Caprio, G., and Levine, R. (2006). *Rethinking Bank Regulation: Till Angels Govern.* New York, NY: Cambridge University Press.

Barth, J. R., Caprio, G., and Levine, R. (2012). Bank Regulation and Supervision in 180 Countries from 1999 to 2011, *Journal of Financial Economic Policy* 5(2), 111–219.

Barth, J. R., Caprio, G., and Levine, R. (2013). *Guardians of Finance: Making Regulators Work for Us.* Cambridge, MA: MIT Press.

Baumol, W., Panzar, J. C., and Willig, R. D. (1986). On the Theory of Contestable Markets. In: C. Frank Matthewson and Joseph E. Stiglitz (Eds.), *New Developments in the Theory of Industrial Structure,* 339–365. Cambridge, MA: MIT Press.

Calomiris, C. and Haber, S. (2014). *Fragile by Design: Banking Crises, Scarce Credit, and Political Bargains.* Princeton, NJ: Princeton University Press.

Calomiris, C. and Herring, R. (2013). How to Design a Contingent Convertible Debt Requirement that Solves Our Too-Big-To-Fail Problem, *Journal of Applied Corporate Finance* 25(2), 39–62.

Caprio, G. and Klingebiel, D. (1996). Bank Insolvency: Bad Luck, Bad Policy, or Bad Banking, In: *Annual Conference on Development Economics,* 79–104. Washington, DC: The World Bank.

Dermine, J. (2003). European Banking: Past, Present, and Future. In: V. Gaspar, P. Hartmann, and O. Sleijpen (Eds.), *The Transformation of the European Financial System*, 31–95. Frankfurt, Germany: European Central Bank.

Garcia, G. and Nieto, M. (2006). Banking Crisis Management in the European Union: Multiple Regulators and Resolution Authorities, *Journal of Banking Regulation* 6, 215–219.

Goodhart, C. (2010). How Should We Regulate Bank Capital and Financial Products? What Role for Living Wills? In: A. Turner and others (Eds.), *The Future of Finance: The LSE Report*. London: London School of Economics, http://harr123et.wordpress.com.>.

Goodhart, C. (2011). *The Basel Committee on Banking Supervision: A History of the Early Years, 1974-1997*. Cambridge, UK: Cambridge University Press.

Herring, R. and Schuermann, T. (2006). Capital Regulation for Position Risk in Banks, Securities Firms and Insurance Companies. In: H. Scott (Ed.), *Capital Adequacy: Law, Regulation, and Implementation*. Oxford, UK: Oxford University Press.

Honohan, P. and Klingebiel, D. (2003). The Fiscal Cost Implications of an Accommodating Approach to Banking Crises, *Journal of Banking and Finance* 27, 1539–1560.

Kane, E. J. (1977). Good Intentions and Unintended Evil: The Case against Selective Credit Allocation, *Journal of Money, Credit, and Banking* 9, 55–69.

Kane, E. J. (1981). Accelerating Inflation, Technological Innovation and the Decreasing Effectiveness of Banking Regulation, *Journal of Finance* 36, 355–367.

Kane, E. J. (1988). Interaction of Financial and Regulatory Innovation, *American Economic Review* 78, 328–334.

Kane, E. J. (1989). Changing Incentives Facing Financial-Services Regulators, *Journal of Financial Services Research* 2, 263–272.

Kane, E. J. (1998). Capital Movements, Asset Values, and Banking Policy in Globalized Markets. In: L. Seongtae (Ed.), *The Implications of Globalization of World Financial Markets*, 278–298. Seoul, Korea: Bank of Korea.

Kane, E. J. (2003). What Kind of Multinational Arrangements Might Best Enhance World Welfare?, *Pacific Basin Finance Journal* 11, 413–428.

Krugman, P. (1979). A Model of Balance-of-Payments Crises, *Journal of Money, Credit, and Banking* 11, 311–325.

Laeven, L. and Levine, R. (2009). Bank Governance, Ownership, and Risk Taking, *Journal of Financial Economics*, 93(2), 259–275.

Laeven, L. and Valencia, F. (2013). Systemic Banking Crises Database, *IMF Economic Review* 61, 225–270.

Portes, R. (2008). Ratings Agency Reform, January 12, http://www.voxeu.org>.

Schüler, M. (2003). How do Banking Supervisors Deal with Europe-wide Systemic Risk?, Centre for European Economic Research Discussion Paper No. 03-03.

Shadow Financial Regulatory Committee (2008). *Statement on Facilitating Mortgage Renegotiations: The Policy Issues*, Chicago, IL, Statement No. 255, February 11.

United States Senate Committee on Homeland Security and Governmental Affairs, Permanent Subcommittee on Investigations (2011). Wall Street and the Financial Crisis: Anatomy of a Financial Collapse. Majority and Minority Staff Report, April 23.

Wilson, J. A. G. (1986). *Banking Policy and Structure: A Comparative Analysis*. New York, NY: New York University Press.

....

CHAPTER 22

DEPOSIT INSURANCE ISSUES IN THE POST-2008 CRISIS WORLD*

....

ROBERT A. EISENBEIS AND
GEORGE G. KAUFMAN

22.1 INTRODUCTION

....

EVEN before the onset of the financial crisis of 2008, deposit insurance had become a central component of most country's financial safety net both in developed and developing countries. Demirgüç-Kunt, Karacaovali, and Laeven (2005) reported that at least 83 of 181 countries queried in 2004 prior to the crisis had explicit deposit-guarantee schemes in place just before the start of the crisis. The remainder effectively had implicit guarantees. Deposit insurance and the other parts of the safety net—such as the central bank discount window— were intended to enhance the safety of the financial system. Almost all countries with operating financial systems have some form of deposit insurance. However, the systems differ significantly, and some important characteristics of representative systems are provided in Tables 22.1 and 22.2.

History and recent experience demonstrate that the effectiveness of deposit insurance depends on how it is designed and implemented.[1] In other words, structure matters. Poorly implemented deposit-insurance or guarantee schemes combined with a lack of effective resolution policies contribute at least as much to increasing both the probability and costs of bank failures as to reducing them.

---

* We are particularly indebted to David Hoelscher, consultant and IMF (Retired), for a careful reading of the revised manuscript that has greatly improved the chapter.

[1] Kane, 1993; Kane and Yu, 1996; Kane, 2000;, Hovakimian, Kane and Laeven, 2003; Demirgüç-Kunt, Kane, and Laeven, 2008; Angkinand and Wihlborg, 2010; Hovakimian, Kane, and Leaven, 2012

Table 22.1 Selected characteristics of representative sample of deposit insurance schemes

Jurisdiction	Type of Financing	Deposit Coverage Level US$	Set-off	Provision of Coverage Local branches of Foreign	Foreign branches of domestic banks	Premiums Rate	Assessment Basis	Percentage of Deposits Fully Covered	Governing Structure Governing Body
Argentina	Ex ante	7,545	No	Yes	No	0.015–0.3%	Eligible deposits	94.9	Management Committee (Representative of the Central Bank acting as chairman, 4–7 members from financial institutions contributing to the Management Committee)
Australia	Ex post	1,0–6,300	No	No	Yes	n.a.	n.a.	>99	Members from prudential regulator
Brazil	Ex ante	42,000	No	No	No	0.0125% of average monthly balances	Covered deposits	n.a.	Board of Directors (5–9 representatives from member institutions)
Canada	Ex ante	100,000	No	No	No	2.8, 5.6, 11.1, and 22.2 basis points	Covered deposits	97	Board of Directors (11-member Board: heads of regulatory agencies, Governor of the Central Bank, Ministry of Finance and private non–ex-officio directors)
France	Ex ante	136,320	No	Yes	Yes	n.a.	Eligible deposits	n.a.	Supervisory Board/Executive Board (Elected private bankers for theSupervisory Board / Specific agreement of the Ministry of Finance for the Chairperson of the Executive Board)

Country	Funding						Liabilities of protected depositors		Governance
Germany 13/	Ex ante	136,920	Yes	Yes	Yes	0.016%		n.a.	Board of Directors (Members from banking associations. The DGS are legal persons under private law and are supervised by BaFin, which also checks the qualification and work of their directors)
Hong Kong	Ex ante	64,000	Yes	Yes	No	0.0175–0.049%	Covered deposits	n.a.	Board of Directors (8-member Board, including two ex-officio members from central bank and the government)
India	Ex ante	2,240	Yes	Yes	No	0.1%	Eligible deposits	92.9	Board (12-member Board; 2 from RBI, one from government, and 9 independents)
Indonesia	Ex ante	235,294	Yes	Yes	No	0.2%	Average monthly deposits	99.9	Board of Commissioners (6 members, appointed by the President including private and state bankers, one ex-officio of central bank and one ex-officio of ministry of finance)
Italy 14/	Ex post	136,920	Yes	Yes	Yes	n.a.	n.a.	n.a.	Board of Directors (24 members including the President of Italian Banking Association and officials of member banks. A representative from the Bank of Italy in its capacity as supervisor attends without vote.)
Japan	Ex ante	122,775	Yes	Yes	No	n.a.	Eligible deposits	98.9	Policy Board (Governor of the DICJ, representatives of Bankers Association, Regional Banks Association, Association of Regional Banks, National Association of Shinkin Banks, Community Bank, advisor of non-financial institution, news commentator,professor of University, and four DICJ executives)

(Continued)

Table 22.1 (Continued)

Jurisdiction	Type of Financing	Deposit Coverage Level US$	Set-off	Provision of Coverage Local branches of Foreign	Foreign branches of domestic banks	Premiums Rate	Assessment Basis	Percentage of Deposits Fully Covered	Governing Structure Governing Body
Korea	Ex ante	43,902	Yes	Yes	Yes	n.a.	Eligible deposits	n.a.	Deposit Insurance Committee (7 members: the President of the KDIC (Chairman), 3 ex officio members from the government and the central bank, and 3 others from the private sector)
Mexico	Ex ante	146,606	No	n.a.	n.a.	0.4%	A proxy of total bank liabilities	99.9	Governing Board (7 members: 3 officio members (Minister of Finance, Governor of the Central Bank, President of the Supervisory Commission) each of which can designate an alternate, and 4 independent members appointed by the President and ratified by 2/3 of the Senate (or by the same proportion of members of the Congressional Standing Committee when the Senate is in recess))
Netherlands	Ex post 5/	136,920	No	Yes	Yes	n.a.	n.a.	n.a.	Part of Central Bank/supervisor
Russia	Ex ante	23,064	Yes	n.a.	No	0.1% of average quarterly balances (~0.4% annually)	Eligible deposits	99.7	Board of Directors (13 members (7 from government, 5 from central bank, and CEO))

Singapore	Ex ante	38,835	No	Yes	No	0.02–0.07%	Covered deposits	n.a.	Board of Directors (5 members, with experience in public sector, banking, insurance, law and accounting)
Spain 18/	Ex ante	136,920	No	Yes	Yes	0.002 basis points	Eligible deposits	n.a.	Board of Directors (12 members (6 from industry and 6 from central bank))
Switzerland	Ex post	96,830	No	Yes	No	n.a.	n.a.	n.a.	Board of Directors (Bankers and securities dealers)
Turkey	Ex ante	32,341	No	Yes	No	11, 13, 15, or 19 points may be imposed based upon a firm's risk score and an additional 1 basis point for firms between TL55,545 million and TL 133,308 million and 2 basis points for firms greater than TL 133,308 million with the size breaks indexed to the price index	Insured deposits	88.7	Board of Directors (7 members (chairman, vice chairman and five appointees with experience in relevantdisciplines))
United Kingdom	Ex post	133,068	No	Yes	Yes	n.a.	n.a.	98	Board of Directors (13 appointed by FSA, nine nonexecutive and four executive directors (Chief Executive and the Directors of Corporate Affairs, Operations and Central Services))
United States	Ex ante	250,000	Yes 20/	No	Yes	2.5 – 45 basis points	Average consolidated total assets minus average tangible equity	99.7	Board of Directors (5 members (Chairman of the FDIC, Vice Chairman of the FDIC, Comptroller of the Currency, Director Consumer Financial Protection Bureau, and an independent director))

Source: Financial Stability Board (2012) and International Association of Deposit Insurers 2011 Survey

Table 22.2 Governance and powers of representative sample of deposit insurance schemes

Jurisdiction	Type of System	Type of Deposit Insurance Organization	System Mandates and Classification	Governing Body
Argentina	Government legislated and privately administered	Independent	Pay-box systems with extended, but still limited, roles and powers	Management Committee (Representative of the Central Bank acting as chairman, 4–7 members from financial institutions contributing to the Management Committee,
Australia	Government legislated and administered	Bank Supervisor	While Australia's deposit insurance scheme (the Financial Claims Scheme) is a pay-box, its administrator APRA has extensive powers in its capacity as the resolution authority.	Members from prudential regulator
Brazil	Government legislated and privately administered	Association of Banks	Pay-box systems with risk minimizing	Board of Directors (5–9 representatives from member institutions)
Canada	Government legislated and administered	Independent	Risk-minimizing	Board of Directors (11-member Board: heads of regulatory agencies, Governor of the Central Bank, Ministry of Finance and private non-ex-officio directors)
France	Government legislated and privately administered	Association of Banks under Governmental supervision	"Loss minimizing system" based on FSB Definition.	Supervisory Board/Executive Board (Elected private bankers for the Supervisory Board / Specific agreement of the Ministry of Finance for the Chairperson of Executive Board)
Germany	Government legislated and privately administered	Association of Banks	Pay-box systems with extended, but still limited, roles and powers	Board of Directors (Members from banking associations. The DGS are legal persons under private law and are supervised by BaFin, which also checks the qualification and work of their directors)

Hong Kong	NA	NA	NA	NA
India	Government legislated and privately administered Cretaed by an Act of the Parliament, DICGC is a wholly owned subsidiary of the Reserve Bank of India.	Within Central Bank Created by an Act of the Parliament, DICGC is a wholly owned subsidiary of the Reserve Bank of India.	Pay-box he DICGC Act, 1961 lays down the mandate for the Corporation to function as a "pay box" system. It has limited role in resolution of troubled banks by way of subvention in restructuring and merger of these banks with stronger bank, if considered	Board of Directors (8-member Board, including two ex-officio members from central bank and the government) Board (12-member Board; 2 from RBI, one from government, and 9 independents)

Source: Financial Stability Board (2012) and International Association of Deposit Insurers 2011 Survey

However, as the events of the recent near-global financial crisis have shown, even well-designed deposit insurance schemes are not sufficient, in themselves, to prevent a crisis from occurring or to limit contagion once a failure of a single systemically important institution occurs. Nevertheless, because all crises eventually come to an end, it is important to consider how deposit insurance and the financial safety net should be structured in non-crisis periods to achieve safe and efficient outcomes. The recent crisis also suggests that some large non-traditional bank financial institutions, like investment banks, insurance companies and finance companies can be perceived by policymakers as important as traditional banks as potential sources and propagators of systemic risk. That perception has led to extension of the safety net to these non-bank institutions.

Additionally, during a crisis, non-banking financial subsidiaries of bank holding companies can be important sources of financial distress and contagion. The recent crisis demonstrated that even though subsidiaries of financial institutions may be legally separate, and hence considered to bankruptcy remote, institutions may be motivated by reputational risks concerns that prompt the movement of assets within a bank holding company onto the books of on an insured bank subsidiary. This chapter briefly discusses the objectives of deposit insurance and how it should be structured in non-crisis periods for optimal results. It focuses primarily, but not totally, on the US. It also evaluates how well existing deposit insurance systems have functioned. In the process, the chapter notes critical conceptual weaknesses in the design of current systems.

The chapter proposes key features that well-functioning and efficient guarantee systems should have if they are to be an effective part of a country's broader financial safety net system in non-crisis periods. Finally, it raises some issues that can arise when banks are part of a more complex bank holding company structure and, in particular, when large, complex banking organizations operate in in a global environment. However, this chapter does not consider insurance or guarantees for financial firms that do not offer bank deposits, such as money market mutual funds, bank holding companies or insurance companies, whose failure may threaten financial stability. Nor does it consider the extension of government backstops for nonfinancial firms, such as General Motors of Chrysler, that received federal government support during the recent financial crisis in the US for reasons of maintaining employment and other objectives.

22.2 WHY DEPOSIT INSURANCE FOR BANKS AS A MATTER OF PUBLIC POLICY?

While the adoption of deposit insurance schemes in most countries is largely a late 1900s phenomenon, the concept is not new. The first government-sponsored deposit insurance scheme, at least in the US, was the New York State Safety Fund. It was initially created in 1829 to insure bank notes and deposits, (Chaddock, 1911; Calomiris, 1989; and Thies and Gerlowski, 1989). It experienced losses and went out of business in 1866. Five other states created funds before the start of the Civil War in 1865, but all failed and were closed before the turn of the century (Calormiris, 1989). State-sponsored systems were again created following the financial panic of 1907, but all had failed by 1930 (English, 1993). Some privately funded and managed, but widely perceived as state-sponsored, funds were resurrected in the US after World War II for smaller state-chartered banks and thrifts. But they also eventually failed. The last such fund for thrifts failed in the 1980s in Ohio and a fund for banks, credit unions, and loan and investment companies in Rhode Island failed in 1991s (Kane, 1987; Pulkkinen and Rosengren, 1993; and Todd, 1994).

The first central government-sponsored deposit insurance system was established in Czechoslovakia in 1924, followed in 1933 in the US with the establishment of the Federal Deposit Insurance Corporation (FDIC) (Camara and Montes-Negret, 2006).

The FDIC was created as one of a number of public initiatives instituted in the Banking (Glass–Steagal) Act of 1933 in response to the calamity of the Great Depression and the inability of the Federal Reserve to prevent the accompanying widespread bank failures. Between 1929 and 1933, the number of banks declined by nearly 10,000 from near 25,000 to near 15,000. By guaranteeing the par value of deposits up to the covered maximum, deposit insurance was intended to reduce the likelihood of bank runs that caused credit losses to depositors and could spill over to other banks, disrupt the payments system, and reduce the funding of economic activity. The insurance was designed to assure small (retail) depositors at banks that their funds would be protected from loss should their bank become insolvent. In this way, depositors would not have an incentive to run on their banks, thereby reducing the probability of banking panics that could adversely impact on economic activity (Demirgüç-Kunt and Detragiache, 1998). It was felt necessary to create a targeted safety net for banks but not for other firms because there is a perception that banks are "special."

22.2.1 Are banks "special"?

The rationale for a government-supported deposit-insurance scheme is rooted in the view that banks were and remain "special" when compared to most other business entities, because of greater positive externalities that flow to the economy from their activities, from interbank connections, and from greater and broader damage when they fail (Corrigan, 1982). That is, healthy banks are critical to a well-functioning and growing real economy for a long list of possible reasons that includes:

- banks provide a large share of financing for consumers, business firms, and governments;
- banks operate much of the nation's payments' system that transfers payments from buyers to sellers on a timely and certain basis; and
- as creators of deposits, banks function as the primary transmitter of monetary policy to the economy.

Because a healthy and efficient banking system is a prerequisite for a healthy and efficient macroeconomy, problems in the banking system that generate large losses and interfere with the smooth operation of their activities have important adverse effects, not only directly on the failed bank's customers but also indirectly on the health of the macroeconomy in the bank's market area and possibly beyond.

It follows that bank failures are widely perceived as more costly both to bank customers and to the economy at large than the failure of other firms of similar size and thereby require special prudential public policy attention. Moreover, unlike other firms, banks tend to be closely interconnected to each other through interbank deposits and loans. Thus, the failure of one bank is widely perceived to have the potential to spill over and infect other financially healthy banks (Benston, et al. 1986; Kaufman, 1988). These spillover effects were hypothesized to be rooted largely in the lack of information on the part of small depositors about the solvency of their bank when other neighboring banks were publicized as being in financial difficulty.

This idea of information interconnectedness was expanded to include the interbank deposits when Continental Illinois National Bank in Chicago was supported and ultimately failed in 1984 amidst concerns about its role in the interbank wholesale market for funds. In particular, Continental was a major correspondent bank that cleared and settled deposits for small rural Midwest banks. The Federal Reserve was concerned about the potential spillover effects that Continental's failure might have for small banks if it was unable to settle its positions with its correspondents and they would not be able to close their books. In the most recent financial crisis, interconnectedness was again a concern. But this time it was rooted in derivatives and other complex financial market instruments that had evolved. Specifically, as the crisis proceeded, uncertainty about liabilities for derivatives claims on troubled financial institutions and hypothecation of collateral in repo markets were the major rationales for the extraordinary measures that US policymakers took in injecting capital into large commercial banks in 2008 and 2009 through the Troubled Asset Relief Program (TARP), in supporting the mergers of banks and investment banks and in dealing the investment bank, Bear Stearns.

Banks and similar financial institutions are widely perceived to be more fragile and more susceptible to failure than most other firms because of four characteristics of their balance sheets:[2]

1. they have a high proportion of demandable (demand deposits) and other short-term debt relative to total debt;
2. the duration of their assets is typically longer than the duration of their liabilities (maturity intermediation);
3. they have a relatively small proportion of cash assets to total assets (fractional banking); and
4. they are highly leveraged with little capital relative to assets.

The first characteristic makes banks highly susceptible to runs by depositors and other short-term creditors. A large number of depositors can simultaneously attempt to withdraw funds with little if any advance notice. On the one hand, the threat of quick withdrawal of funds can serve as a useful ex ante source of market discipline on bank management (Calomiris and Kahn, 1991). On the other hand, problems may arise when large number of depositors believes that their bank may be insolvent or heading toward insolvency and may not be able to repay all of them in full and on time and try to withdraw their funds at the same time. Because those that are at the head of the line are more likely to get paid in full than those at the back of the line, physical or electronic lines may quickly form in front of the bank.

---

[2] Minsky (1976) argued that banks are inherently unstable. See also Diamond and Dybvig, 1983.

The second characteristic makes banks highly susceptible to losses both should interest rates rise and should depositors withdraw funds before the assets mature forcing hurried fire sales and large losses. The third characteristic implies that banks experiencing runs are unlikely to have sufficient cash to immediately pay all the claims of the running depositors. The banks may have to sell some of their earning assets. But, the less liquid are these assets and the faster the sales need to be made to meet the depositor demands, the larger would be any "fire sale" losses. The last factor implies that banks are not able to absorb very large "fire sale" losses before running through their entire capital buffer and becoming insolvent and unable to repay the remaining deposits on time and in full. At that point, the bank fails.

The appeal of deposit insurance is thus evident. When deposits are fully insured by a credible insurance agency then depositors will have fewer incentives to run. This reduces the need for banks to sell assets quickly and suffer "fire sale" losses that could drive a solvent bank into insolvency, generating losses to their deposit customers, potentially transmitting the problem to other banks, reducing credit availability, and interfering with the efficient operation of the payments' system (Rochet, 2004). Additionally, Morrison and White (2011) show that private sector risk monitoring is deficient and leads to moral hazard and adverse selection.[3] They argue that deposit insurance can mitigate these problems, generate social benefits that could not be achieved by the private sector alone.

22.2.2 The downside of deposit insurance

Deposit insurance clearly can improve financial stability, but extension of deposit insurance and other features of the federal safety nets also have a downside. They can induce moral hazard behavior by insured institutions and poor agency behavior by their regulators.[4] For example, Önder and Özyildirim (2008) show that in lesser developed economies, like Turkey, broad deposit insurance coverage can not only lead to moral hazard behavior but also by itself does not guarantee financial stability. Indeed, as the recent financial crisis has clearly demonstrated, government bailouts and rescues of major financial institutions have not only lead to still larger banking institutions and increased deposit concentration in US markets, but increased moral hazard and reduced market discipline Unless deposit insurance and federal guarantees more broadly are priced and administered correctly by the insurance and other responsible agencies, and also included credible and effective wind-down tools, they are likely to encourage increased risk-taking behavior by banks by enabling them to operate with less private capital and/or to adopt riskier portfolios than they would in the absence of insurance.

In particular, insurance can exacerbate endgame gambles, when banks approach or enter insolvency and insurance is poorly structured. Should these gambles pay off and the institution returns to financial health, managers and shareholders reap the benefits.[5] Should the institution fail, which is likely on average, the insurer suffers the losses. When the insurance is provided or ultimately supported by central governments, poor behavior in the form of

---

[3] Kane, Hovakimian, and Laeven, 2003; Kane, 2000.

[4] See Önder and Özyildirim, 2008; Angkinand and Wihlborg, 2010; Ioannidou and Penas, 2010.

[5] To this point, based on how Bear Stearns was rescued, it was clear that management of Lehmann Brothers expected that it would be rescued as well and hence pursued a risky endgame strategy.

forbearance by banking supervisors exacerbates the moral hazard problem and, by permitting insolvent banks to continue to operate, increases the losses that must ultimately be borne by taxpayers (Demirgüç-Kunt and Kane, 2001). Knowing that insured depositors are less likely to run and withdraw funding from their banks permits regulators not only to delay imposing sanctions on troubled institutions but also to postpone legally closing institutions and placing them in receivershipIn the absence of deposit insurance, depositors, like creditors of any firm, would monitor the financial performance of their banks and discipline them if they fail to maintain agreed-upon measures of financial health, either by charging a higher interest rate for their deposits or by withdrawing their deposits. The threat of either higher funding costs or loss of funding should induce managers to correct their problems well before a run begins.

Unfortunately, the record to date of federal safety net administration and deposit insurance in almost all countries, including the US, has on the whole been poorly structured and administered. As a result, moral hazard behavior by banks and poor agency behavior by regulators have caused deposit insurance to be excessively costly to the insurance agency and, often, to taxpayers.

22.2.3 The record of deposit insurance has been mixed

As noted earlier, in the US both before and after the introduction of the FDIC and federal government-sponsored deposit insurance in 1933, non-Federal, state-sponsored deposit insurance existed but was largely a failure. All state-sponsored funds either failed or were disbanded. None remain today. The main reason for this decline was that the funds available were insufficient to deal with a crisis when it occurred, the agencies' taxing powers were limited and their sponsoring state government were unwilling to increase taxes to honor the guarantees, and unlike the federal government, the states could not print money, For example, when the Ohio deposit insurance fund collapsed in 1988, the legislators in Ohio failed to support the fund fully, and many of the member institutions were eventually transferred to the FDIC at a cost to both the state and the FDIC. Federally sponsored deposit insurance widely appeared to have worked well for much of its early history. Indeed, federal deposit insurance was hailed by Milton Friedman and Anna Schwartz in their 1963 seminal book *The Monetary History of the United States*, 30 years after its introduction, as one of the most important and beneficial pieces of financial legislation in US history.

The ability of federal deposit insurance to prevent runs by insured depositors was evident immediately upon its introduction in 1933. However, it was not until many years later at the onset of the thrift crisis in the late 1970 and early 1980s that the potential limitations of deposit insurance that were described earlier became widely exposed. In particular, as interest rates rose in the late 1970s and thrift institutions' cost of short-term funds exceeded the fixed returns on their long-dated mortgage assets, they became insolvent in large numbers. And as they were not closed by the regulators in a timely manner they continued to generate losses. The thrift institution insurance fund at the time—the Federal Savings and Loan Insurance Corporation (FSLIC)—had insufficient assets to absorb the losses and it also became insolvent. The federal government had to step in and bail out the depositors at covered insolvent thrift institutions. Taxpayers contributed more than $150 billion, or nearly 3% of US GDP, at the time, to the rescue.

In response, among other legislation, Congress enacted the Federal Deposit Insurance Corporation Improvement Act (FDICIA) of 1991. That Act significantly reformed the nature of the US deposit insurance, required higher bank capital ratios, carefully defined the role and duties of the responsible supervisors in monitoring and resolving trouble institutions, including requiring the regulators to turn troubled institutions around through imposing sanctions on a timely basis—prompt corrective action (PCA)—and imposed greater accountability on the regulators for losses imposed upon the taxpayers. Unfortunately, as the most recent crisis and regulatory responses to it have demonstrated, significant flaws remained in the regulatory structure. This was particularly evident when it came to the achievement of low-cost failure resolution and in the effective expansion of the federal safety net to non-bank financial institutions and even to entire financial markets to minimize the probability of systemic risk, without at the same time strengthening other parts of the regulatory structure. Indeed, Jones and Oshinsky (2009) demonstrate that the risk that the FDIC would become insolvent has increased significantly due to the increased concentration of deposits, which occurred in part from crisis-induced and regulator promoted consolidations.

22.2.4 The Recent Evolution of US Deposit Guarantees Prior to the Financial Crisis of 2008

Starting in 1989, a series of US legislative acts reorganized the deeply insolvent FSLIC insurance fund for thrift institutions and merged it with the bank fund in the FDIC (Kaufman, 2002). The new fund is resourced by a combination of ex ante and ex post premiums paid by insured institutions. The funds were required to maintain, a minimum reserve ratio of 1.25% of insured deposits. If the reserve ratio declined below the fixed 1.25% target, the FDIC was required to increase premiums on insured institutions to recapitalize the fund to at least this ratio within a brief period of time. To increase flexibility, legislation in 2006 eliminated the 1.25% hard target percentage and established a target range between 1.15% and 1.50%. Should the reserve ratio fall below 1.15%, the FDIC is required to establish a recapitalization plan to bring it back to 1.15% within a longer five years. If the FDIC's reserve ratio exceeds 1.35% of estimated insured deposits, the FDIC generally must run down its reserves. It must pay dividends to banks that in aggregate equal to one-half of the amount by which the fund exceeds the 1.35%. If the reserve ratio increases further and exceeds 1.50%, the FDIC must pay dividends equal to the full amount by which the fund exceeds 1.50%.

Thus, the fund is effectively a mutual organization; losses to the FDIC from bank failures are shared among the surviving banks until the combined capital of the industry is exhausted. Only then would the Treasury and taxpayers be the remaining ultimate guarantors of insured deposits. In contrast, before FDICIA in 1991, premiums were difficult for the insurance agencies to increase, even when the FDIC incurred losses. The US Treasury and taxpayers served more as immediate guarantors of insured deposits.

FDICIA also required insurance premiums to be based on bank risk, rather than levied as a flat percentage of bank-asset size, as previously. From 1992 to 2005, the risk metric was a simple 9-cell formula based on the combination of a bank's CAMELS rating[6] from regulators

---

[6] Six components of a bank's condition that are assessed in CAMELS: (C)apital adequacy, (A)sset quality, (M)anagement, (E)arnings, (L)iquidity, and (S)ensitivity to market risk.

and its capital strength as defined in FDICIA's PCA provisions. Thereafter, the premium for-mula became more complex. It was based primarily on a model estimating the probability of supervisory downgrade developed by the FDIC using bank capital and other financial ratios and CAMELS ratings. For larger banks, the formula also used the banks' credit ratings from the rating agencies.

The FDIC was prohibited by the FDICIA from protecting de jure uninsured depositors, other creditors and equity owners. Insolvent institutions were required to be resolved at least cost to the FDIC. But an exception to this prohibition was made in case of a threat of systemic-risk that could destabilize the financial system. The systemic risk exemption (SRE) permits protecting uninsured creditors in cases where the lack of such protections would threaten financial and economic instability, and protecting them would prevent this. But, invoking this systemic-risk exemption was intended to be difficult for policymakers. It requires, among other actions, a two-thirds vote in favor by both the board of directors of the FDIC and the Board of Governors of the Federal Reserve, approval by the Secretary of the Treasury after consultation with the President of the United States. If the FDIC experi-enced losses from providing such protection, it would be required to levy a special assess-ment on all banks to reimburse it. No SREs were granted between 1991 and 2008, and only five have been granted thereafter through 2013.

22.3 WHAT ARE THE LESSONS FROM THE RECENT FINANCIAL CRISES?

The US experience with both state—and federally sponsored deposit insurance plans has several lessons for how insurance schemes both in the US and abroad should be structured, financed, and governed. This includes how the regulatory and supervisory process should operate and how the resolution of a failure should proceed. Particularly important is the legal structure and ability of the supervisors legally to close and resolve troubled institutions promptly and at minimum cost. This involves revoking the banks' charters, placing them in receivership, and disposing of their assets and liabilities before the losses to the uninsured depositors, other creditors, and the FDIC become large and without interrupting the provi-sion of important services.

22.3.1 Lessons for deposit-insurance fund structure and funding

The financial crisis which began in 2007 confirms that the existence of deposit insurance per se without the appropriate processes and procedures in place to limit excessive risk-taking and moral hazard behavior by the insured and bad behavior by the regulatory agents pre-sents costly problems. The experience provides little assurance that without reinforcing changes in the regulatory structure, either the frequency or costs of banking crises will be reduced significantly. Establishing a deposit insurance fund alone does not guarantee that it will be adequate to prevent or deal with a financial crisis or to weather even the failure of a single major institution. Rather, the fund may be viewed as a cash fund that provides regulators the time to deal with immediate problems and postpone the need for having to go to the industry or taxpayers for sufficient resources to make the guarantees credible to permanently deal with large problems and imbalances.

22.3.2 How deposit insurance funds have been funded

Countries have adopted different structures for providing resources to fund their deposit insurance schemes. Some are totally private, some are totally public, and others are a mix of the two (see Eisenbeis and Kaufman, 2008 for details of the deposit insurance structures in the European Union, Demirgüç-Kunt, Karacaovali, and Laeven, 2005 for a description of systems in other parts of the world and Financial Stability Board (2012) for a more current summary of key deposit insurance plans and resolution powers for selected countries. Some guarantee systems have actual monies collected from ex ante funding; others have no actual monies, and rely upon ex post premium levies on surviving participants, while still others rely on a combination of both ex ante and ex post. A few but growing number have risk-related premiums; while the remainder have some form of a flat-rate funding plan. Finally, some have an explicit draw on the central government, while other schemes, such as in the US, have temporary, debtors in possession type provisions but no lasting injection of public monies. Germany, for example, prohibits the injection of public monies.

As was pointed out in Section 22.2.3, the deposit insurance system in the US is effectively an industry-funded mutual institution. It is backed by the equity of the overall banking industry. The fund also has a small line of credit with the US Treasury to provide temporary working capital to finance resolutions.

Many of the deposit insurance funds in place in other countries have no explicit government support and are small. They tend to have meager funds relative to the risks that failure of large institutions might pose, especially since most of the countries do not have accompanying effective PCA and least cost resolution or structured early intervention and resolution (SEIR) provisions that are intended to reduce the magnitude of expected losses. They are effectively only cash boxes. This suggests that making good on their guarantees will require the potential commitment of taxpayer funds, despite strong denials beforehand. But as was pointed out earlier, experience with non-central government state-sponsored funds shows that legislatures are not always willing or able to live up to their perceived commitments, and the insured depositors and/or taxpayers at times suffer losses.

With large, cross-border banking organizations operating within the Europe that are often headquartered in relatively small countries, as in Iceland, Cyprus, the Netherlands, and Luxembourg, the ability or willingness of those countries to make good on their guarantees to depositors at their branches in other European countries, no less their own domestic branches, is problematic. Indeed, the crisis in Iceland and the more recent crisis in Cyprus illustrate the above point very clearly. Like many of financial institutions during the 2008–10 financial crises, the major Icelandic banks experienced very large losses and were subject to runs on large scale runs on deposits in their offices in the Netherlands and UK. The three largest private banks were huge relative to the size of the country's economy. Moreover, the country had been running a substantial government deficit and its debt was about 9.6 trillion Icelandic kronur as compared to the country's GDP of 1.3 trillion kronur. Eighty percent of that debt was held in its banking system and the assets of its three largest banks were more than 11 times Icelandic GDP. Thus, thus, the losses were likely greater in magnitude than the GDP of the countries. Neither the taxpayers nor the central bank had the capacity to cover the losses. The three largest banks failed and some half a million depositors in their foreign branches had their accounts frozen. These accounts were mainly in the UK and the Netherlands.

A diplomatic dispute ensued over the responsibility for deposit insurance in the Iceland banks' foreign branches in the UK and Netherlands. The end result was a controversial external rescue package in which funds were provided by the IMF and a loan from several Nordic countries, the Netherlands and the UK. Like Iceland, the banking system in Cyprus was huge relative to the size of the economy. It was about eight times the size of the country's GDP. Much of the funding for its institutions came from foreign depositors chasing high deposit rates. The banking system was deeply insolvent in part due to lax supervision of institutions. The banks had invested heavily in risky loans and securities, including Greek and Cyprus sovereign debt and experienced large losses. The country had been requested many times by EU authorities to get its banking system in order. Finally, in the midst of severe financial turmoil in the country, the European Central Bank (ECB) threatened to withdraw the emergency funding it had provided to the banks. In addition, the European finance ministers proposed that to fund the bank losses, Cyprus impose a tax of over 6% on insured deposits less than €100,000 and of over 12% on deposits over €100,000. The result not only contributed to increasing doubt about the solvency of the Cyprus banking system and the deposit insurance agency and thus called into question the quality of deposit guarantees other countries with weak financial systems. The Cyprus experience also demonstrates the fragility of national deposit insurance schemes that may be supported by the federal government but where the government does not issue its own currency. The experience was similar to that of some of the state sponsored schemes earlier in US history.

22.4 LESSONS FOR RESOLUTION POWERS AND BANKRUPTCY LAWS

The resolutions powers and processes that enable the administrators of insurance systems that have resolution authority to limit the costs of failure to shareholders rather than extending them to bank depositors, other bank customers, or taxpayers is widely underappreciated. This became readily evident from the experience in the UK with the depositor run on Northern Rock bank at the onset of the financial crisis in 2007. At the time, the UK had a federally mandated deposit insurance scheme that covered 100% of the first £2,000 (about $4,000) and 90% of the next £33,000 (about $67,500), compared with the US's 100% coverage of up to $100,000. Responsibility for supervising Northern Rock lay with the UK Financial Services Authority. Lender of last resort and responsibility for financial stability lay with the Bank of England. In addition, the Chancellor of the Exchequer had the authority to commit public funds, should it be necessary. But none of these entities had the legal authority to close Northern Rock and revoke its license should it become insolvent. Beyond nationalization, its fate was entrusted to the bankruptcy courts, as was the case for banks in virtually all countries outside the US. The judicial bankruptcy process, as currently structured, rather than an administrative process by bank regulators, generally produces a slower initiation and resolution procedure and likely larger losses (Bliss and Kaufman, 2007).

Nor need insured depositors receive their full funds promptly. In most European countries, the laws establishing deposit insurance provide that insured funds must be made available to depositors only within three months after failure. But often one or more extensions are permissible. A relatively low full guarantee combined with considerable uncertainty about when a troubled institution would be turned over to the courts and when uninsured and even insured depositors would receive their designated funds meant that it was rational for British depositors to run at the first hint of trouble to avoid possibly losing both a portion of their funds and ongoing access to the remaining portion. The specter on British television of lines at branches of Northern Rock, with the possibility of such lines of spilling over to other banks, forced the UK Treasury to step in and guarantee 100% of all deposits at Northern Rock and to suggest that other institutions would be granted similar guarantees should that be necessary. Northern Rock was eventually nationalized.

The Northern Rock incident shows that runs can occur even when there is a guarantee scheme in place, and even when there are strong assurances from the government that it will make good on the guarantee, if the scheme is designed poorly. It also has become clear that there is little benefit to co-insurance with depositors as a source of market discipline for retail depositors. Small (retail) depositors ran in Northern Rock's case long after funding had dried up for the institution in the interbank and commercial paper markets, when questions first arose about the quality of its assets. Retail depositors were the last to appreciate the depth of the problem and the run was a symptom, not the cause, of Northern Rock's difficulties.

In the 1800s, the US realized that the most adverse spillover effects from bank failures could be avoided by making banking failures isolated events. Importantly, insolvent banks needed to be legally closed more quickly than other firms to reduce runs—in those days by note holders trying to convert their notes into gold or silver specie—and additional credit losses. Furthermore, the closure decision should be made by regulators, not by the depositors or the courts to avoid delays. Thus, most states and the federal government enacted special bankruptcy codes. Legal closure powers were given to the chartering authority to revoke an institution's charter and to place it into receivership when there was evidence that the bank could not convert its notes in specie.

The FDIC is now appointed receiver for not only federally insured institutions but also, pursuant to the Dodd-Frank Act, directs the resolution process regardless of which regulatory agency in the US was responsible for supervising the institution. After its establishment, there has been no uncertainly as to where the responsibility lies for the resolution of a failed institution.

The FDIC provides all depositors—both insured and uninsured—at failed banks relatively quick access to some or all of their accounts. The deposits are not frozen until the institution or its assets were sold. The FDIC now pays insured depositors the full par value of their accounts, up to $250,000 on most accounts, the next business day after legal closure. This payment is regardless of when the proceeds of the sales of assets are received. These are the depositors least able to monitor their banks and most in need of accessing at least part of their balances to finance daily expenditures. Rapid payments serve to keep most retail depositors politically off the streets and simplify the resolution process. At the same time, the FDIC may pay uninsured depositors an advance against the estimated recovery value of the bank's assets before the proceeds are received for their sale. Thus, some uninsured depositors in the United States may also have immediate access to at least some of their funds and combined with credible attempts to minimize the credit losses reduce the incentive for uninsured depositors to run.

The bank resolution procedures in the Federal Deposit Insurance Act facilitates liquidation or reopening failed institutions as new, merged institutions with as small credit losses as possible and as quickly as possible—usually over the weekend—so as to make funds available to depositors and loan customers as promptly as possible (Bliss and Kaufman, 2007). To expedite this process for very large banks, the FDIC has authority to charter a temporary bridge bank to assume the activities of an insolvent bank, for which a private purchaser could not be found quickly.

22.5 MONITORING AND SUPERVISORY RESPONSIBILITIES

Timely and effective monitoring and attention to valuation of banks assets combined with appropriate remedial responses when problems are discovered are key to protecting the deposit insurance fund and ultimately the taxpayer against losses. One of the lessons of the US thrift crisis of the 1980s was that supervisory and regulatory responses to difficulties often involve forbearance and the use of accounting gimmicks to delay or avoid recognition of losses and even insolvencies. In an attempt to stop this practice, Congress enacted the FDICIA in 1991. The Act emphasized prompt corrective regulatory action to turn troubled banks around before insolvency and provided supervisors with stronger tools and incentives to do so. In particular, the Act attempted to refocus regulatory attention on remediation of troubled institutions as their capital declined, rather than only after they had become insolvent and imposed both mandatory and discretionary regulatory sanctions to limit forbearing. Banks are encouraged to hold more capital and regulators are incentivized to take actions promptly should capital fall below predefined levels. However, if a bank does not respond and lets its book equity capital decline below 2% of its assets, the regulators are legally obligated to close or otherwise resolve the bank within a maximum of nine months.

Evidence from the recent financial crisis suggests that some regulators apparently failed to learn this lesson. In a letter to the US Senate Finance Committee, the Inspector General of the US Treasury reported that the Office of Thrift Supervision (OTS) permitted the IndyMac Bank, a large thrift institution, to post-date a capital injection received May 2008 to March 2008 (Thorson, 2008). Had this been reported accurately, IndyMac, which failed in July 2008 with an estimated loss of $9 billion to the FDIC fund, would have had insufficient capital to qualify as "well-capitalized" by regulatory standards. Sanctions and closure would have been imposed earlier, and eventual losses may have been reduced. The Inspector General also noted similar backdating of capital injections in at least five other OTS-supervised institutions.

As noted above, under FDICIA in the US, in the event that supervisory efforts to engineer a turnaround of a troubled institution fail, the appropriate federal regulatory agency is legally authorized to close the institution before its book value capital is fully depleted and the FDIC is empowered to sell or liquidate the bank. If successful, losses would be confined to shareholders, who are paid to assume risk, while depositors and other creditors would remain whole. Thus, unlike deposit insurance that only shifts credit losses from insured depositors to the FDIC or taxpayers, PCA and the associated legal closure rule at positive capital attempts to eliminate credit losses to depositors and thus also to the FDIC. However, to be successful, the program requires timely and effective implementation by the regulators and more accurate measures of economic capital.

Since the institution of the FDICIA requirement that supervisors close troubled institutions once their capital falls below the critical value of 2% of total assets, the loss to the FDIC from bank failure depends largely on how successful the regulators are in promptly implementing the FDICIA requirements rather than on the risk exposure of the banks. With a well-functioning legal closure process at positive capital, there is little justification for imposing premiums based on the riskiness of the bank. Rather, the real risk is that the FDIC will not legally close the bank before its capital is depleted so that credit losses occur. For this reason it is not at all clear why insured institutions should be charged for this regulatory risk or that the risk is a function of bank portfolio composition. This view of risk contrasts with the original idea behind risk-based premiums, which was driven by the view that, when properly set, the premiums would serve as a deterrent to risk-taking by banks that would supplement the supervisory monitoring process (Flood, 1990; Flannery, 1991; Chan, Greenbaum, and Thakor, 1992; Allen and Saunders, 1993; Duan and Yu, 1994; Pennacchi, 2001).

However, this focus ignored the fact that there is an important distinction between portfolio risk, capital structure, and the probability of default on the one hand and the losses that the insurance fund might have to bear, should a default occur, on the other. The chief determinant of the losses to the insurance fund beyond fraud is regulatory risk. This risk is a function of examination frequency and policies and how quickly an institution is closed, once it becomes insolvent. That is, if the premiums are to be based on risk, they should be based primarily on the risk of delayed closure by the FDIC and not on the risk of individual banks, except to the extent that riskier banks may be more difficult for the FDIC to monitor, Flannery (1991). On average, the longer an insolvent institution is kept open and operating, the longer it will continue to realize losses and the larger the ultimate cost to the FDIC will be.

22.6 SUMMARY AND CONCLUSIONS: WHAT SHOULD AN EFFECTIVE DEPOSIT INSURANCE SYSTEM LOOK LIKE?

Deposit insurance schemes are an integral feature of the contemporary banking landscape and an important component of every nation's financial safety net. However, the guarantee systems in place frequently suffer from structural deficiencies that reduce their efficiency. In addition, as a consequence of the financial turmoil after 2007, many countries have temporarily provided 100% guarantees of all bank deposits and some other financial assets. But, once the crisis has abated, these countries will be faced with the need to reform their deposit-insurance systems to avoid the moral hazard problems that 100% guarantees create.

In considering possible reforms, it should be emphasized that an effective system consists not only of a credible guarantee, which in some countries is more dependent upon a government commitment than the existence of a deposit insurance fund or the ability to draw on the industry's equity. It also requires effective monitoring by supervisors, who are charged with the responsibility to protect the insurers and taxpayers against losses, and a legal system that empowers them to both intervene effectively before a troubled institution becomes insolvent and legally close them before their capital is fully depleted. Moreover, the structure should provide for quick resolution when failure occurs. Efficient resolution of insolvent and near-insolvent banks with minimum damage to the economy can be achieved when four conditions exist ((Eisenbeis and Kaufman, 2008).

First, an insolvent institution that cannot be recapitalized should be legally closed—charter revoked—when its equity-capital-to-asset ratio declines to a pre-specified and well-publicized positive minimum. If successful, no losses will accrue to depositors, only to stockholders. Second, once closed, recovery values should be estimated quickly and any losses from closure allocated to de jure uninsured in-the-money bank counterparties according to ex ante legal priorities. Third, institutions that are not liquidated should be reopened and the assets and deposits of those liquidated should be sold or valued as soon as possible, preferable the next business day, to enable depositors to have full access to their accounts on their due dates at their insured or present value of the estimated recovery amount and performing borrowers to access their pre-established credit lines. For large banks that cannot be sold quickly, these activities may be transferred to a newly chartered FDIC-operated temporary bridge bank. Finally, the institution should be re-privatized with adequate capital so that it does not quickly fall into insolvency again.

Under such a system both credit and liquidity losses, that generate the widespread fear of bank failures, are minimized. If there are no losses, deposit insurance becomes effectively redundant and necessary only when insolvent institutions are not closed promptly so that losses accrue, and the adverse moral hazard incentives inherent in deposit insurance become benign. Credit losses are minimized, if not eliminated altogether, rather than simply shifted to the insurer. Nevertheless, properly structured deposit insurance should be maintained in place for retail deposits in case regulators may not always be able to close the institutions before their capital turns negative. Redundancy has its uses. Moreover, the system only works to the extent that regulators are faithful agents for their healthy bank and taxpayer principals and enforce the rules in place in a timely manner.

Going forward, it is clear that before the beginning of the financial crisis world financial systems were becoming more integrated, more dependent upon capital markets, and less reliant upon banks for the bulk of financial intermediation. As a result, once the crisis is vanquished, deposit insurance limited to only bank liabilities is likely to assume a progressively smaller role as a key component of the overall federal financial safety net. Prudential financial regulatory agencies, to the extent they are charged with maintaining financial stability, will have to develop tools and techniques that extend beyond the current bank-deposit-insurance schemes. In addition, the rapid expansion of cross-border banking arrangements poses special burdens on regulators and deposit guarantee structures.

Differing legal and institutional structures and deposit guarantee systems in different countries complicate the resolution and settlement of claims when large cross-border institutions experience financial stress. Counterparties have proved reluctant to engage quickly in cost sharing for insolvent banks operating in more than one country. Such an expansion of prudential regulatory responsibilities will require greater thought to safety net and regulatory design than is developed for within border systems in this chapter.

References

Allen, L. and Saunders, A. (1993). Forbearance and Valuation of Deposit Insurance as Callable Put, *Journal of Banking & Finance* 17, 629–643.

Angkinand, A. and Wihlborg, C. (2010). Deposit Insurance Coverage, Ownership, and Banks' Risk-Taking in Emerging Markets, *Journal of International Money and Finance* 29(2), 252–274.

Benston, G. J., Eisenbeis, R. A., Horvitz, P. M., Kane, E. J., and Kaufman, G. G. (1986). *Perspectives on Safe and Sound Banking.* Cambridge, MA: MIT Press.

Bliss, R. R. and Kaufman, G. G. (2007). US Corporate and Bank Insolvency Regimes: Comparison and Evaluation, *Virginia Law and Business Review* 2, 143–177.

Camara, M. K. and Montes-Negret, F. (2006). Deposit Insurance and Banking Reform in Russia, World Bank Policy Research Working Paper No. 4056, November.

Calomiris, C. (1989). Deposit Insurance: Lessons from the Record, *Federal Reserve Bank of Chicago Economic Perspectives* 13, 10–30.

Calomiris, C. and Kahn, C. M. (1991). The Role of Demandable Debt in Structuring Optimal Banking Arrangements, *American Economic Review* 81, 497–515.

Chaddock, R. E. (1911). The Safety Fund Banking System in New York State, 1829-1866. In: *Publications of National Monetary Commission*, 227–388. Washington, DC: Government Printing Office.

Chan, Y. S., Greenbaum, S. I., and Thakor, A. V. (1992). Is Fairly Priced Deposit Insurance Possible?, *Journal of Finance* 47, 227–245.

Corrigan, G. (1982). Are Banks Special?. Federal Reserve Bank of Minneapolis Annual Report.

Demirgüç-Kunt, A. and Detragiache, E. (1998). The Determinants of Banking Crises in Developing and Developed Countries, IMP Staff Papers 45, 81–109.

Demirgüç-Kunt, A. and Kane, E. J. (2001). *Deposit Insurance around the Globe: Where Does It Work?*, World Bank Policy Research Working Paper No. 2679.

Demirgüç-Kunt, A., Kane, E. J., and Laeven, L. (2008). Determinants of Deposit-Insurance Adoption and Design, *Journal of Financial Intermediation* 17(3), 407–438.

Demirgüç-Kunt, A., Karacaovali, B., and Laeven, L. (2005). Deposit Insurance around the World: A Comprehensive Database, World Bank Policy Research Working Paper No. 3628, June.

Diamond, D. W. and Dybvig, P. H. (1983). Bank Runs, Deposit Insurance and Liquidity, *Journal of Political Economy* I, 401–419.

Duan, J. and Yu, M. T. (1994). Forbearance and Pricing Deposit Insurance in a Multiperiod Framework, *Journal of Risk and Insurance* 61, 575–591.

Eisenbeis, R. A. and Kaufman, G. G. (2008). Cross Border Banking: Challenges for Deposit Insurance and Financial Stability in the European Union. In: L. Jonung, C. Walkner, and M. Watson (Eds.), *Building the Financial Foundations of the Euro: Experiences and Challenges*, 355–403. New York and London: Taylor & Francis.

English, W. B. (1993). The Decline of Private Deposit Insurance in the United States, *Carneigie-Rochester Conference Series on Public Policy* 38, 57–128.

Financial Stability Board (2012). Thematic Review on Deposit Insurance Systems. Peer Review Report.

Flannery, M. J. (1991). Pricing Deposit Insurance When the Insurer Measures Bank Risk with Error, *Journal of Banking & Finance* 15, 975–998.

Flood, M. (1990). On the Use of Option Pricing Models to Analyze Deposit Insurance, *Federal Reserve Bank of St. Louis Review* 52, 217–232.

Friedman, M. and Schwartz, A. (1963). *A Monetary History of the United States, 1867-1960.* Princeton, NJ: Princeton University Press.

Hovakimian, A., Kane, E. J., and Laeven, L. (2003). How Country and Safety Net Characteristics Affect Bank Risk-Shifting, *Journal of Financial Services Research* 23, 177–204.

Hovakimian, A., Kane, E. J., and Laeven, L. (2012). Variation in Systemic Risk at US Banks during 1974-2012, NBER Working Paper No. 18043.

Ioannidou, V. P. and Penas, M. F. (2010). Deposit Insurance and Bank Risk-Taking: Evidence from Internal Loan Ratings, *Journal of Financial Intermediation* 19(1), 95–115.

Jones, K. D. and Oshinsky, R. C. (2009). The Effect of Industry Consolidation and Deposit Insurance Reform on the Resiliency of the US Bank Insurance Fund, *Journal of Financial Stability* 5(1), 57–88.

Kane, E. J. (1987). Who Should Learn What from the Failure and Delayed Bailout of the ODGF?. In: *1987 Proceedings of Conference on Bank Structure and Competition*, 306–326. Chicago: Federal Reserve Bank of Chicago.

Kane, E. J. (2000). The Dialectical Role of Information and Disinformation in Banking Crises, *Pacific Basin Finance Journal* 8, 285–308.

Kane, E. J. and Yu, M-T. (1996). How Much Did Capital Forbearance Add to the Cost of the S&L Insurance Mess?, *Quarterly Review of Economics and Finance* 36, 189–199.

Kaufman, G. G. (1988). Bank Runs: Causes, Benefits, and Costs, *Cato Journal* 7, 559–587.

Kaufman, G. G. (1992). Capital in Banking: Past, Present and Future, *Journal of Financial Services Research* 5, 385–402.

Kaufman, G. G. (2002). FDIC Reform: Don't Put Taxpayers Back at Risk, *Policy Analysis*, Cato Institute, April 16.

Kaufman, G. G. (2004). Basel II: The Roar that Moused. In: B. Gup (Ed.), *The New Basel Capital Accord*, 241–267. New York: Thomson.

Kaufman, G. G. (2006). Depositor Liquidity and Loss Sharing in Bank Failure Resolutions, *Contemporary Economic Policy* 22, 237–249.

Minsky, H. P. (1976). A Theory of Systematic Financial Fragility, In: E. J. Altman and A. W. Sametz (Eds.), *Financial Crises: Institutions and Markets in a Fragile Environment*, 138–152. New York: Wiley.

Morrison, A. D. and White, L. (2011). Deposit Insurance and Subsidized Recapitalizations, *Journal of Banking & Finance* 35(12), 3400–3416.

Önder, Z. and Özyildirim, S. (2008). Market Reaction to Risky Banks: Did Generous Deposit Guarantee Change It?, *World Development* 36(8), 1415–1435.

Pennacchi, G. G. (2001). Estimating Fair Deposit Insurance Premiums for a Sample of Banks under a New Long-Term Insurance Pricing Methodology. In: *The Financial Safety Net: Costs, Benefits, and Implications for Regulation*, Proceedings of the Conference on Bank Structure and Competition, 756–776. Chicago: Federal Reserve Bank of Chicago.

Pulkkinen, T. E. and Rosengren, E. S. (1993). Lessons from the Rhode Island Bank Crisis, *Federal Reserve Bank of Boston New England Economic Review* May/ June, 3–12.

Rochet, J. C. (2004). Bank Runs and Financial Crises: A Discussion. In: S. Bhattacha, A. W. A. Boot, and A. V. Thakor (Eds.), *Credit Intermediation and the Macro Economy*, 324–338. Oxford: Oxford University Press.

Thies, C. F. and Gerlowski, D. A. (1989). Deposit Insurance: A History of Failure, *CATO Journal* 8, 677–693.

Thorson, E. (2008). Letter to the Honorable Charles Grassley, Inspector General. Department of the Treasury, London, December 22.

Todd, W. F. (1994). Lessons from the Collapse of Three State-Chartered Private Deposit: Insurance Funds, *Federal Reserve Bank of Cleveland*, May, 1–6.

CHAPTER 23

....

RISK-BASED REGULATORY CAPITAL AND THE BASEL ACCORDS*

....

MICHAEL B. GORDY, ERIK A. HEITFIELD, AND JASON J. WU

23.1 MOTIVATION: BENEFITS OF COORDINATED, RISK-BASED BANK CAPITAL REGULATION

....

BANK solvency regulation is intended to reduce systemic risk and deadweight loss associated with bank failures and to address moral hazard problems arising from implicit or explicit government guarantees that interfere with effective market discipline. Bank supervisors in most countries impose minimum capital adequacy standards on banks as an important component of banking regulation. Banks that breach these standards may be subject to supervisory action and, in extreme cases, liquidation.

The most straightforward approach to regulating bank capital adequacy is to impose a floor on the ratio of banks' book equity to book assets, but this simple leverage ratio test has a number of critical drawbacks. By treating all bank assets the same regardless of risk, a simple leverage requirement effectively advantages those banks that invest in higher risk assets. These banks can anticipate earning higher expected returns on equity, but they are not required to hold extra capital to protect debtholders from the greater volatility of their investments. Thus, a capital rule that is not sensitive to risk can perversely encourage a bank to take on risk. Furthermore, a rule based solely on accounting leverage is relatively easy to circumvent, since sophisticated banks can efficiently gain exposure to risks that do not appear on their balance sheets by securitizing assets, providing credit guarantees, or trading

* The views expressed here are solely those of the authors and do not reflect the opinions of the Board of Governors of the Federal Reserve System or its staff. We thank Patrick de Fontnouvelle, David Jones, Mary Frances Monroe and John Wilson (the editor) for helpful discussion and suggestions.

in derivatives. For these reasons, regulators have sought to align regulatory capital requirements to measures of the risks associated with banks' business activities.[1]

In a globally integrated financial system, several benefits accrue to coordination in setting bank capital adequacy standards. First, coordination can help to solve a "prisoner's dilemma" faced by national banking authorities. All supervisors prefer a stable, well-capitalized banking system that is protected from adverse systematic shocks, but each country's banking authority also wants to see its own banks grow and compete aggressively in the international marketplace. Thus, each banking authority would prefer to see all other countries increase bank capital standards, but may have an incentive to advantage its own banks by keeping capital requirements relatively low. By working together to set common standards, national banking authorities can mitigate this coordination problem. Second, coordination can help reduce compliance costs and incentive problems that arise when internationally active banks must comply with different capital requirements in different jurisdictions. Third, a single international standard promotes transparency by facilitating comparison of banks under different jurisdictions. Finally, international coordination can help to facilitate the adoption of best practice standards by smaller or less experienced regulatory authorities who may have more limited access to technical expertise.

The rest of this chapter is organized as follows: Section 23.2 describes the 1988 Basel Accord. Sections 23.3, 23.4, and 23.5 provide an overview of Basel II, its theoretical foundations, and required model inputs, respectively. Section 23.6 describes the development and implementation of Basel III in the context of the global financial crisis. Some ongoing Basel Committee initiatives are discussed in Section 23.7.

23.2 THE 1988 BASEL ACCORD

National banking authorities began work to develop common bank capital adequacy rules in the late 1980s under the auspices of the Basel Committee on Banking Supervision (the Basel Committee). In 1988 the Basel Committee reached its first bank capital accord, now called Basel I. This accord, like all subsequent work by the Basel Committee, was not a treaty and carried no force of law. Then, as now, the Basel Committee relied solely on moral suasion to encourage countries to adopt its recommendations. Nonetheless, today, Basel Committee capital standards are used by virtually all countries with well-developed banking systems.

Basel I established standards for computing a measure of bank capital adequacy called a risk-based capital ratio (RBCR). Basel I's RBCR is similar to a standard equity-to-assets ratio, but it relies on more sophisticated definitions of capital and assets than are typically reported on firm balance sheets. The capital figure used in the numerator includes Tier 1 capital, which comprises mostly shareholders' equity and retained earnings, Tier 2 capital, which includes supplementary forms of capital such as undisclosed reserves and subordinated debt, and other forms of capital. The denominator—termed risk-weighted assets (RWA)—is calculated by taking a weighted sum of both on- and off-balance-sheet exposures. Following

---

[1] In the United States, both risk-based capital standards and a simple accounting leverage requirement are imposed on banks.

consultations with industry and its own analysis, the Basel Committee (1988, para. 44) determined that a minimum RBCR of 8% would be "consistent with the objective of securing over time soundly-based and consistent capital ratios for all international banks."

In a rudimentary way, the weights used in calculating RWA under Basel I were intended to reflect the underlying risks associated with different types of exposures. Low-risk OECD sovereign debt securities, for example, were given a zero-risk weight, so that banks were not required to hold capital against these assets. Residential mortgages, which at the time were typically highly collateralized, were given a 50% risk weight while corporate loans were weighted at 100%. By weighting different assets differently, Basel I attempted to link a bank's regulatory capital requirement to the riskiness of its asset portfolio. A bank invested primarily in assets that were believed to be relatively safe, such as sovereign debt or mortgages, had lower RWA and thus was required to hold less capital than a comparable bank invested primarily in higher-risk corporate debt.

Basel I's simple risk-weighting scheme was transparent and easy for banks and supervisors to implement, but it was somewhat arbitrary and was unable to capture important differences in risk across bank assets. For example, under Basel I, loans to highly rated "blue chip" corporations attracted the same capital requirements as junk bonds, and all home mortgages attracted the same level of capital regardless of the borrower's credit score or the amount of home equity backing the loan. The Basel I framework also could not be readily applied to loan securitization arrangements which allowed banks to move loans off their balance sheets while retaining much of the credit risk associated with those investments.

Within a decade of the introduction of Basel I, the limitations of its coarse risk-weighting approach became apparent. As best-practice risk-management systems continued to advance, bankers and their regulators observed significant and systematic differences between the regulatory capital charges imposed by Basel I, and the economic capital charges generated by banks' internal models. As anticipated by Merton (1995), and explored in detail by Jackson et al. (1999) and Jones (2000), such discrepancies give banks strong economic incentives to shift lending or to engage in regulatory capital arbitrages in order to bring regulatory and economic capital requirements closer together. Indeed, early collateralized debt obligation (CDO) structures were designed expressly for this purpose.

23.3 BASEL II

The limitations of Basel I led regulators to begin work on broad revisions to the accord in the late 1990s. After an extensive development and public consultation process, the Basel Committee published revised capital adequacy standards in 2004 and updated rules for the treatment of banks' trading and risk mitigation activities in 2005. Together, this revised framework, known as Basel II, sets forth detailed standards which need to be interpreted and implemented by national banking authorities (BCBS, 2006). European and Japanese banks began transitioning to Basel II rules in January and March of 2007, respectively. Transition in the United States began in 2008.

Basel II embodies a more comprehensive view of capital regulation than did Basel I. Whereas Basel I presents an unadorned rulebook for minimum capital standards, Basel II puts minimum capital standards in a broader context of supervisory and market discipline.

The "three pillars" of Basel II are intended to be mutually reinforcing. Pillar I establishes minimum risk-based capital requirements intended to cover the credit, trading and operational risks faced by well-diversified financial institutions. Pillar II establishes guidelines for supervising banks' internal risk management processes and encourages regulators to require that banks hold capital buffers above Pillar I minimums to cover those economic risks not explicitly addressed under Pillar I. Pillar III imposes new public disclosure requirements on banks with an eye toward increasing transparency and facilitating more effective market discipline of bank capital adequacy. Decamps, Rochet, and Roger (2004) analyze the complementary roles of the three pillars in a theoretical model of bank behavior under moral hazard. They show how market signals can allow supervisors to apply a lighter hand to inspection and closure. The stringency of Pillar I requirements and the intrusiveness of Pillar II supervision depend on the quality of Pillar III market disclosures. For the remainder of this chapter, as in the great majority of the literature on regulatory bank capital standards, we focus on Pillar I requirements.

Like Basel I, Basel II requires that a bank maintain a RBCR of at least 8%. While Basel II modestly updates the definitions of Tier 1 and Tier 2 capital for determining regulatory capital in the numerator of the RBCR, it dramatically changes the way RWA in the denominator or the RBCR are calculated. Basel II relies on a much more detailed and rigorous approach to determining RWA than Basel I. Pillar I capital requirements are specifically designed to cover credit risk embedded in a bank's traditional lending portfolio (the banking book), market and credit risk associated with its trading activities, and operational risk arising from a failure of the bank's internal financial controls. Under Basel II, RWA are defined as:

$$RWA = \frac{1}{0.08}\left(\sum_i k_i EAD_i + K_{TR} + K_{OR}\right),\qquad(23.1)$$

where k_i is the capital requirement per currency unit associated with the bank's i-th credit exposure, and EAD_i is an estimate of the value of that exposure at default. K_{TR} and K_{OR} are capital charges that cover a bank's trading risks and operational risks respectively. All capital charges are expressed as RWA by dividing through by 8%.

Basel II offers a menu of rulebooks of differing complexity and risk-sensitivity for each of the main categories of risk covered under Pillar I. In general, it is expected that large internationally active banks in all Basel II jurisdictions will migrate towards the most sophisticated approaches on the menu. Less sophisticated approaches may be preferred for smaller institutions with more traditional bank portfolios. The range of options for such institutions helps to accommodate cross-country differences in approaches to bank supervision.

For the more advanced menu options, capital charges are tied conceptually to Value at Risk (VaR), a measure of risk widely used by commercial and investment banks. VaR is defined as a specified percentile of a portfolio loss distribution over a given assessment horizon. For example, if L is a random variable representing portfolio losses over the chosen horizon, then q^{th} percentile VaR is:

$$VaR_q[L] = \inf\left\{k \mid P[L \geq k] \leq 1 - q\right\}.\qquad(23.2)$$

Capital requirements for the banking book are intended to cover the credit risk associated with debt instruments and related hedging instruments. Basel II proposes three separate options for calculating risk weights for positions in the banking book. The simplest
approach, called the Standardized Approach, derives credit-risk capital charges from broad
loan-type categories that are similar, though more refined, to those used in Basel I. The
most significant innovation in the Standardized Approach is that risk weights may be based
on *external* rating, where a public rating is available from a recognized rating agency. The
Foundation and Advanced Internal-Ratings-Based (IRB) Approaches go a step farther, and
rely on banks' own, or *internal*, measures of the credit quality of individual loans or pools
of retail loans to determine required capital. Under both IRB Approaches, a loan's capital
requirement depends on the bank's estimate of the likelihood that the loan will default. The
main difference between the Foundation and Advanced IRB Approaches is that in the latter
a loan's risk weight also depends on its remaining maturity (except in the case of retail loans)
and on the bank's estimate of the loss it expects to incur in the event that the loan defaults.
For Standardized and both IRB Approaches, rules are provided for recognition of risk mitigation in the form of financial collateral, third-party guarantees, and credit derivatives.

While banks' traditional lending business typically involves originating loans which are
then held to maturity and booked at historical cost, banks' trading activities can involve very
frequent buying and selling of marked-to-market assets. Recognizing the substantive differences between these two types of business, Basel II adopts a separate approach to assessing the capital required to cover banks' trading book exposures. K_{TR} has two components: a
general market risk charge covering changes in the market value of a bank's entire trading
portfolio arising from moves in market-wide risk drivers such as interest rates and equity
valuations, and a specific risk charge for each trading position covering changes in the value
of that position arising from idiosyncratic factors unrelated to broad market movements.
Subject to supervisory approval, a bank may either use a simple Standardized Approach
or a more advanced Internal-Models Approach to compute these charges. Under the
Standardized Approach, simple risk weights are applied to a bank's trading positions. Under
the Internal-Models Approach, a bank uses its own risk management systems to compute a
99th percentile VaR of its trading portfolio's exposure to market risk over a ten-day horizon.
The VaR measure for trading losses is multiplied by a factor of at least three to determine
the bank's general market risk capital charge. A scaling factor of larger than three may be
applied if the bank's VaR measure fails ex-post performance tests. Basel II provides formulas
for computing specific risk charges for trading book positions, but it also allows banks to use
internal models for this purpose. In addition to the market risk and specific risk charges, a
bank is also required to hold capital to cover the default risk of positions held in the trading
book to the extent that this risk is not captured in its ten-day VaR calculations. This incremental default risk charge was introduced to address new risks arising from the increasing
prevalence of credit risk-related products such as credit default swaps and less liquid structured credit products in banks' trading portfolios (BCBS, 2005a, para. 260–261).

Basel II also introduces a capital charge for operational risk (K_{OR}), defined as "the risk
of loss resulting from inadequate or failed internal processes, people and systems or from
external events" (2006, para. 644). Here too, Basel II offers a menu of options. The simplest,
called the Basic Indicator Approach, is based on the intuition that operational risk derives
from business activity, and so should increase in proportion with bank revenues. It sets a
capital charge of 15% of the average gross income over the past three years. The Standardized

Approach is a refined version of the Basic Indicator Approach in which bank activities are divided into eight broad business lines such as commercial banking, retail banking, asset management, and corporate finance. Capital charges that vary across these business lines (from 12% to 18%) are applied to average gross income by business line. Under the most advanced option, called the Advanced Measurement Approach (AMA), capital for operational risk is determined by the bank's own operational risk model. As a general principle, minimal structure is imposed on the AMA. The capital charge must correspond to 99.9 percentile VaR at a one-year horizon in the bank's internal operational risk model, but the bank is given broad discretion to tailor model design to its own unique organizational structure, business environment and internal controls. The flexibility of the AMA avoids stifling the development of what is still a nascent science. A potential cost to the approach, however, is that it may be difficult to discipline a bank that designs its AMA model opportunistically, as data constraints on statistical validation are severe and there is, as yet, no consensus among practitioners concerning what modeling assumptions are most appropriate. Supervisory oversight of the model is likely to be based instead on qualitative assessment and on-going dialogue. One popular approach to modeling operational risk is drawn from extreme-value theory (EVT), a branch of statistics widely used in actuarial sciences that examines the properties of extreme-event data. Fontnouvelle et al. (2006) estimate EVT models on two vendor-provided operational loss datasets. Seivold, Leifer, and Ulman (2006) and Embrechts and Hofert (2011) provide more detailed overviews of the regulatory treatment of operational risk under Basel II.

23.4 THEORETICAL FOUNDATIONS FOR THE INTERNAL-RATINGS-BASED APPROACHES

The primary motivation in developing Basel II was to achieve greater risk sensitivity in capital charges. This is desirable at the portfolio level, so that bank capital requirements are commensurate with bank portfolio risk. Banks with greater portfolio risk ought to face higher regulatory capital charges than banks with less risky portfolios, and, similarly, required capital for a bank should increase or decrease over time as the bank changes its risk profile. To reduce regulatory distortions in lending patterns and incentives for regulatory arbitrage, capital requirements should also be risk-sensitive at the *exposure* level. That is, the marginal capital charge for a particular credit exposure should be broadly consistent with banks' assessments of the risk contribution of that exposure. Banks allocate economic capital for credit risk as contributions to portfolio *unexpected loss*, defined as the difference between VaR and expected losses (the latter are assumed to be covered by interest income or reserves, and so excluded from required capital). Therefore Basel II capital charges would need to align risk weight formulae with those implied by bank credit VaR models.

The easiest way to align banks' internal risk management systems with regulatory capital requirements would be to allow banks to use their own internal models to calculate capital charges, much as they do for the trading book under the Market Risk Amendment of Basel I. A disadvantage of this internal models approach is that competitive pressures could induce banks to choose a model that delivers low capital charges over a more rigorous model that might demand higher capital. Given available data and supervisors' limited experience evaluating these models, it would be difficult for supervisors to impose much discipline on opportunistic behavior.

As an intermediate step between the broad category-based approach of Basel I and a full internal-models approach, the Basel Committee mandated that Basel II would offer an internal ratings based approach in which the risk weight for a banking book exposure would depend on the bank's assessment of the creditworthiness of the obligor and other risk characteristics of the instrument (e.g., collateral protection and maturity), but would not depend on the bank's assessment of how the exposure diversifies or concentrates risk in the context of its portfolio. That is, IRB risk weights would depend on the stand-alone characteristics of each exposure, but not the characteristics of the portfolio in which the exposure is held. This property is termed *portfolio invariance*.

A challenge in the design of Basel II was to reconcile portfolio invariance with the desire to align risk weights with contributions to VaR in widely used models of portfolio credit risk. In general, an exposure's marginal contribution to portfolio VaR depends on the composition of the portfolio as a whole. Thus, two banks with different asset portfolios may well assign different marginal capital requirements to the same risk exposure. However, Gordy (2003) shows that contributions to VaR are portfolio-invariant if one assumes that:

1. the portfolio is *asympototically fine-grained*, in the sense that no single obligor accounts for more than an infinitesimal share of portfolio exposure;
2. a single risk factor is the sole source of systematic risk in the portfolio; and
3. realizations of the systematic risk factor are monotonically related with the conditional expected losses associated with most risk exposures.

Under these assumptions, portfolio VaR is equal to the sum across exposures of the expected loss for that exposure conditional on a particular adverse draw of the systematic risk factor. Letting X denote the systematic factor and x_q denote the qth percentile of the distribution of X, and letting ℓ_i denote the loss on the ith exposure, we have

$$VaR_q[L] = \sum_i E[\ell_i \,|\, X = x_q].$$

(23.3)

This linear expression implies that contributions to VaR (both average and marginal) can be computed independently across exposures (i.e., that portfolio invariance is satisfied). Expected loss (EL) for the portfolio is similarly a linear aggregation of exposure EL, and so contributions to unexpected loss (UL) are portfolio invariant as well. This asymptotic-single-risk-factor (ASRF) framework serves as the theoretical foundation for IRB risk weights.

For simplicity, consider the treatment of a one-year bullet loan to a commercial enterprise. Let D be an indicator variable that is equal to one if an obligor defaults over a one-year horizon and zero otherwise, and let R be a random variable between zero and one that describes the proportion of an outstanding credit exposure to the obligor that will be recovered in the event of default. The default-related loss is $\ell = D \cdot (1 - R) \cdot EAD$. Under the ASRF framework, D and R may depend on a systematic risk factor X, but conditional on X, defaults and recoveries are assumed to be independent across obligors (EAD is here assumed to be non-random for simplicity). The marginal contribution of this position (per currency unit of exposure) to portfolio q-th-percentile UL is given by the difference between its conditional and its unconditional expected loss:

$$K = E\left[D\cdot(1-R)\mid X=x_q\right] - E\left[D\cdot(1-R)\right]. \tag{23.4}$$

The conditional expected loss term in equation (23.4) can be expressed as the product of a term measuring the probability of default under systematic stress conditions:

$$SPD = E\left[D\mid X=x_q\right]. \tag{23.5}$$

and a term measuring loss-given-default under the same stress conditions:

$$LGD = E\left[(1-R)\mid D=1, X=x_q\right]. \tag{23.6}$$

The decomposition is compatible with results from surveys by the Basel Committee (2000) and by Treacy and Carey (2000) which find that banks commonly evaluate credit exposures using two-dimensional rating systems that separately account for an obligor's likelihood of default and a loan's loss rate should default occur.

For exposures of one year maturity, the IRB capital formula may be derived as the solution to equation (23.4) in a one-factor version of the popular CreditMetrics model (Gupton, Finger, and Bhatia, 1997), which is a multi-firm generalization of the Merton (1974) structural model of default. The Basel Committee provides a more detailed derivation of the capital formula (BCBS, 2005c).

The actuarial perspective of equation (23.4) does not capture the full credit risk associated with exposures of maturity beyond the model's one-year horizon. Any credit migration short of default that is incurred within the year will imply a gain or loss on the exposure's market value. The longer the loan's remaining maturity, the greater the sensitivity of its market value to a rating change. In general, higher quality loans are less likely to experience default-related losses over a one year horizon but they are more likely to lose market value because of a ratings downgrade short of default. The IRB Approach includes a maturity adjustment function that rescales capital charges for corporate, bank, and sovereign credit exposures to reflect the effects of credit-related changes in market value on an exposure's marginal contribution to UL. The maturity adjustment is derived within a generalized mark-to-market version of this model that accounts for migration risk.

Equation (23.4) describes the ASRF capital charge for a whole loan, but the logic of the ASRF framework applies equally to any sort of credit exposure in a bank portfolio. Heitfield (2003) shows that the ASRF framework can also be used to derive capital requirements for loans that include a third-party credit guarantee or bonds whose default risk is hedged with a derivative instrument such as a credit default swap. Pykhtin and Dev (2002) and Gordy and Jones (2003) use the ASRF framework to derive capital requirements for structured finance products in which the credit performance of a security depends on the performance of an underlying pool of assets. These models are the basis of the IRB treatment of securitization exposures.

The three assumptions of the ASRF framework enumerated above are not inconsequential. Pillar II requires that banks and their supervisors consider ways in which these assumptions might be violated, and if necessary, hold additional capital beyond that implied by the Pillar I risk weight formulas. For the largest banks, characterization of the portfolio as asymptotically fine-grained (Assumption 1) may be a reasonable approximation. To the extent that the IRB Approach is applied to less well-diversified institutions, there will be a residual of undiversified idiosyncratic risk in the portfolio that is ignored by the IRB Approach, and so regulatory capital requirements may understate economic capital requirements. Analytic and semi-analytic approximations developed by Wilde (2001) and Martin and Wilde (2002) can be used to measure the effect of name concentration on capital requirements. Gordy (2004) reviews the mathematical foundations for granularity adjustment, and Gordy and Lütkebohmert (2013) develop simple algorithms for application of the granularity adjustment in the IRB context.

The "single factor" assumption (Assumption 2) is the more serious limitation of the ASRF framework. Heitfield, Burton, and Chomsisengphet (2006) and McNeil and Wendin (2006) find that credit losses associated with exposures to obligors in the same industry sectors are more highly correlated with one another than those associated with exposures to obligors in different sectors. So long as credit conditions across countries and industries do not move together in lockstep, diversification in the portfolio will depend not only on name concentration (i.e., granularity), but also on diversification across sectors. While this assumption limits the validity of *any* ratings-based method for assessing capital charges, Pykhtin (2004) shows how analytic methods can be used to adjust ASRF capital requirements for sector concentration effects and Garcia Cespedes et al. (2006) describe a practical approach to measuring the impact of sectoral diversification in a ratings-based capital framework.

23.5 Inputs To The IRB Risk-Weight Formula

Under the IRB Approach, the risk weight for a banking book exposure is a function of one regulatory parameter (the asset-value correlation) and four bank-supplied parameters: the probability of default (PD), downturn loss-given-default (LGD), expected exposure at default (EAD), and, in some cases, the expected maturity (M).

The asset-value correlation (AVC) parameterizes the relative importance of systematic risk in determining the obligor's likelihood of default, and is essentially the analog to beta in a CAPM setting. A value close to one implies that default by the obligor is determined primarily by the systematic risk factor X, while a value of close to zero implies that defaults are largely independent across obligors. For obligors with PD greater than the target bank solvency probability q, required capital increases with AVC. To understand why, consider two credit exposures that are equal in PD but differ in asset correlation. If a portfolio is well diversified, only adverse systematic shocks that do not average out across exposures can lead to higher than expected portfolio credit losses. Thus, the exposure with a lower asset correlation should contribute less to UL because a larger proportional of the uncertainty associated with the credit performance of that exposure can be diversified away.

The most direct approaches to estimating AVC rely on historical data on firm asset valuations or the credit performance of debt instruments. Early research simply used historical correlations in equity returns for public companies as proxies for asset correlation. A shortcoming of this approach is that equity values do not map directly to asset values, since, for example, different firms have different capital structures. Heitfield, Burton, and Chomsisengphet (2005), Düllmann, Scheicher, and Schmieder (2008), and others have estimated AVC using North American and European firm asset values imputed by Moodys/KMV from equity valuations and leverage information. This approach is simple and direct, but Zhu et al. (2007) show that estimated correlations may be sensitive to measurement errors in imputed asset values. Gordy (2000), Hamerle, Liebig, and Rösch (2003), and others estimate asset correlation parameters from data on the credit performance of bonds or other debt instruments by exploiting the fact that, all else equal, more volatile observed default rates imply higher underlying asset-correlation parameters. This approach does not rely on imputed firm asset values, but, as Frey and McNeil (2003) point out, results are sensitive to the functional form assumptions embedded in the single-factor Merton model. In general, studies that rely on imputed firm asset values tend to find higher asset correlations than those that employ historical default data.

A second strand of research infers average asset correlations for the simple single-factor Merton model from a more sophisticated multi-factor portfolio risk model. Under this approach, one fixes a benchmark portfolio, and then solves for a single-factor Merton asset-correlation parameter that equates VaR across the two models. Lopez (2004) uses this method to infer asset-correlation parameters from VaR estimates produced by the Moody's/KMV Portfolio Manager model. Instead of just one systematic factor, Portfolio Manager includes over a hundred factors that capture country- and industry-specific shocks. Lopez finds that for a portfolio of loans within a single country, the single-factor Merton model with asset correlations between 0.14 and 0.26 produce results similar to those generated by Portfolio Manager, and that portfolios of loans with higher default probabilities tend to have lower implied asset correlations.

Among the bank-supplied inputs, probability of default (PD) has received the most attention. A prerequisite for IRB adoption is that a bank has an internal rating system that assigns a credit rating to each corporate obligor commensurate with that obligor's "ability and willingness to contractually perform despite adverse economic conditions or the occurrences of unexpected events" (Basel Committee, 2006, para. 415). The PD associated with the obligor is a function of the credit rating grade assigned to that obligor. The rules require that the PD associated with a rating grade be "a long-run average of one-year default rates for borrowers in the grade" (Basel Committee, 2006, par 447). Although the IRB rules are fairly specific about how PDs should be computed, they give banks substantial latitude in determining how ratings are assigned.

In practice, approaches to slotting obligors into rating grades may differ widely across banks. For example, Treacy and Carey (2000) find that some banks rapidly update obligor ratings as business conditions change, while other use so-called through-the-cycle rating systems designed to produce ratings that remain stable even as aggregate business conditions change. Because an obligor's PD depends on the rating it is assigned, there is no guarantee that the PD associated with an obligor will be consistent across banks with different rating systems. Using samples of obligors rated by multiple banks in the US and Sweden respectively, Carey (2002) and Jacobson, Linde, and Roszbach (2003) find frequent cross-bank differences in the default probabilities associated with banks' ratings for the same obligors, and Rösch (2005) shows that differences in banks' rating philosophies can affect the level and volatility of portfolio-wide regulatory capital requirements.

LGD parameters are specified for banks on the Foundation IRB Approach. For example, senior, uncollateralized loans to corporations or government entities are assigned LGDs of 45%, while subordinated, uncollateralized loans are assigned LGDs of 75%. If a loan is secured, the LGD may be reduced by an amount tied to the value and quality of the collateral.

Banks on the Advanced IRB Approach are required to estimate LGD parameters using information from their credit rating systems. Recall that equation (23.6) implies that LGD must be estimated conditional on the systematic stress event ($X=x_q$). A large body of empirical evidence demonstrates that loss rates on defaulted corporate debt are indeed elevated during times of industry or economy-wide stress (e.g, Frye, 2000, 2003; Altman et al. 2005; Acharya, Bharath, and Srinivasan, 2007; Bruche and González-Aguado, 2010; Chen, 2010). In the mortgage market, Qi and Yang (2009) find that loss severities during distressed housing markets are significantly higher than under normal housing market conditions.

Pykhtin (2003) and Düllmann and Trapp (2005) propose parametric models that extend the one-period single-factor CreditMetrics model to incorporate correlation between the systematic risk factor and defaulted loan loss rates. However, since models of systematic recovery risk are not widely used in practice, banks are not required in Basel II to tie LGD estimates explicitly to an adverse draw of the systematic risk factor. Instead, Advanced IRB banks must report LGD estimates that "reflect economic downturn conditions where necessary to capture the relevant risks" (Basel Committee, 2006, para. 468). This qualitative requirement and clarifying guidance issued by the Basel Committee (2005b) give banks a great deal of flexibility in determining how to incorporate the effects of systematic risk in their LGD estimates.

EAD is the bank's expected legal claim on the borrower in the event of default. For bonds and term loans, EAD is the loan's face value plus expected accrued but unpaid interest. For undrawn commitments, EAD is more difficult to estimate. For revolving lines, banks are expected to specify EAD as the current drawn balance plus a "credit conversion factor" (CCF) applied to the remaining undrawn balance. The CCF is specified under the Foundation IRB Approach and depends on the type of credit facility. Advanced IRB banks are permitted to use their own estimates of CCFs. Banks must consider their ability and willingness to prevent drawdowns of unused commitments in the event of borrower distress. Treatment must reflect not only legal enforceability, but also the bank's systems and procedures for monitoring drawdowns. The CCFs used in practice are often based, at least in part, on the estimates of Asarnow and Marker (1995).

The maturity parameter, M, is calculated as a cashflow-weighted duration, and is subject to a floor of one year and a ceiling of five years. For banks on the Foundation IRB Approach, maturity is fixed at 2.5 years for corporate, bank, and sovereign exposures. Retail credit exposures, such as mortgages and credit cards, do not include an explicit maturity adjustment. For these exposures, average maturity effects are implicit in the calibration of the IRB risk-weight formulas.

23.6 THE FINANCIAL CRISIS AND BASEL III

The financial crisis of the late 2000s revealed a number of weaknesses in the way banks manage the risks arising system-wide financial and economic shocks. Banks were quite leveraged and the level and quality of the banks' capital bases were vulnerable to large credit and trading losses. Systemic institutions were highly interconnected, resulting in procyclical deleveraging and accelerated erosion of liquidity buffers as they all sought to shed the same types of risks at the same time (see, e.g., Shin, 2011). Many instruments in banks' trading books, particularly those exposed to credit risk, lacked price transparency and market liquidity, factors that banks did not take into account when making risk assessments. In June 2011, the Basel Committee introduced Basel III (BCBS, 2011b) to strengthen the risk-based capital framework by building on the three pillars of the Basel II framework. This section reviews three major areas of change in regulatory capital introduced by Basel III: enhancements to RWA calculations (the denominator in Pillar I RBCR), raising the quality, consistency and transparency of the capital base (the numerator), and the introduction of new macroprudential overlays on minimum capital requirements.

Basel III retains the IRB Approach of Basel II but imposes higher asset value correlation parameters, and hence higher risk weights, on certain types of exposures. Exposures to obligors that are regulated financial institutions with 100 billion dollars or more of assets, including but not limited to insurance companies, broker/dealers, banks, thrifts and futures commission merchants are subject to 25% higher AVCs (Basel Committee, 2011b: para. 102). This increase is intended to capture the heightened interconnectedness of large financial institutions during periods of stress. Realizing the important role of the shadow financial system during the crisis, the Basel Committee also increased asset correlations on exposures to obligors that are unregulated financial institutions such as asset managers, entities providing credit enhancements, and asset custodians. Standards to limit the reliance on external credit ratings in Standardized and IRB Approaches were also added (Basel Committee, 2011b: para. 118–121).

The value of traded products such as securities and derivatives deteriorated quickly during the financial crisis, amid substantial volatility and uncertainty in pricing. In response, Basel III substantively enhanced capital requirements associated with trading activities. Under Basel III, the ten-day VaR calculation is augmented by a Stressed VaR measure that is computed using data covering a "continuous 12-month period of significant financial stress relevant to the bank's portfolio" (Basel Committee, 2011a: page 21). This requirement carries the dual purposes of increasing the VaR-based capital, which was widely perceived to be inadequate leading up to the crisis, as well as dampening the volatility and procyclicality inherent in VaR calibrated only to the most recent data. In addition, new trading risk capital charges—the Incremental Risk Charge (IRC) and the Comprehensive Risk Measure (CRM)—were introduced in an effort to reduce the discrepancies in capital standards for credit products held in the trading and banking books. While the IRC focuses on capturing the issuer default and migration risks in non-securitized traded credit products, and is a natural extension of the incremental default risk framework in Basel II, the CRM aims to capture all price risks, including issuer default and migration risks, for certain securitization products designed to allow market participants to take positions on the correlation between the value of underlying reference assets.

Because derivatives involve future-dated cash flows, each party to a derivatives transaction bears the risk that its counterparty will not make good on its contractual obligations. Counterparty credit risk grew to unprecedented levels during the financial crisis. The Basel Committee introduced a host of new measures to strengthen the calculation of RWA for counterparty credit risk in Basel III. The most important change is the introduction a capital charge for credit valuation adjustments (CVA) on over-the-counter (OTC) derivatives. The CVA charge is designed to cover potential mark-to-market losses on derivatives positions as the credit quality of counterparties deteriorate. Requirements on the counterparty default risk have also been updated to account more effectively for wrong way risk through the use of stress periods to calibrate counterparty exposures, and to factor in longer margining periods during times of stress for collateralized trades.[2]

Basel III places new emphasis on the quality of capital, as well as its quantity. As evident during the financial crisis, some capital resources of banks did not prove very useful in buffering against losses. During the crisis, bank losses and write-downs were absorbed mostly by common equity and retained earnings. Consequently, Basel III requires banks to hold higher levels of Common Equity Tier 1 (CET1) capital, which consists primarily of common shares, retained earnings and accumulated other comprehensive income. The Minimum CET1 RBCR has been raised from 2% to 4.5%, and the Minimum Tier 1 RBCR from 4% to 6%, with transitional arrangements imposed through the full adoption date of January 2019. Basel III also eliminates Tier 3 capital from Total Capital, sets prudential adjustments and deductions to prevent banks from inflating the capital base with unqualified instruments, and resolves many of the ambiguities that surround the earlier definition of capital. Pillar III disclosure requirements have been strengthened to mitigate variation across jurisdictions in accounting definitions of capital (Basel Committee, 2011b: para. 91).

Leading up to the crisis, a number of banks continued to pay large dividends and generous bonuses, despite the deterioration in their financial conditions and the outlook on the financial sector (Basel Committee 2011b: para. 27). Banks were unwilling to hold back on these payments out of the concern that they would otherwise be perceived as financially vulnerable. To mitigate depletion of capital by distressed banks, Basel III explicitly restricts the amount of earnings that a bank is allowed to distribute as dividends, bonuses and share buy-backs, if the CET1 RBCR falls below the minimum requirement plus a 2.5% capital conservation buffer. In contrast to the stringent penalties on falling short of Minimum RBCR, failure to satisfy the buffer requirement triggers restrictions on distributions but not on the operation of the bank. As with the increases in the minimum RBCR requirements, the buffer requirement will be phased in over time.

Despite significant changes to both the RWA calculations and capital requirements, the RBCR remains largely a bank-specific "microprudential" tool. Both the literature and the regulatory community agree that microprudential tools alone are inadequate in achieving systemic financial stability. Hanson, Kashyap and Stein (2011) characterize microprudential regulation as partial equilibrium in its conception, contrasting the general equilibrium approach of "macroprudential" regulations which seek to safeguard the financial system as a whole. The new requirements of a leverage ratio and a countercyclical buffer in Basel III should be viewed as preliminary and limited attempts to supplement long-standing microprudential tools with macroprudential overlays.

As previously discussed, risk-based capital was largely motivated by the inability of a simple leverage ratio to capture accurately the riskiness of banks' asset holdings. While a leverage ratio cannot replace the RBCR for microprudential reasons, a leverage ratio serves

---

[2] Wrong way risk refers to the situation where the exposure to the counterparty is negatively correlated with its credit worthiness.

macroprudential purposes by limiting asset growth and setting limits on new lending (Shin, 2011). By design, it will constrain the buildup of leverage at banks and help avoid destabilizing deleveraging processes (Basel Committee, 2011b: para. 152). Furthermore, in contrast to the RBCR under the IRB Approach, a simple leverage ratio avoids model dependence, and can be calculated consistently across all banks. Basel III requires a 3% leverage ratio as a backstop measure to capital ratios. The numerator of this ratio will be the updated definition of Tier 1 capital, while the denominator will reflect simple measures of on- and off-balance-sheet exposures.

The potential procyclical effects of Basel II have received considerable attention. So long as bank rating systems are responsive to changes in borrower-default risk, capital requirements under the IRB Approach will tend to increase as the economy falls into recession and fall as the economy enters an expansion. To the extent that banks curtail or expand lending in response, Basel II could make it more difficult for policymakers to maintain systemic financial stability. Daníelsson et al. (2001) elaborate on this critique (among others) of Basel II. Kashyap and Stein (2004) and Gordy and Howells (2006) suggest modifications to Basel II rules that would mitigate procyclicality without sacrificing the risk-sensitivity of capital requirements or the quality of information in Pillar III market disclosures.

Pillar II of Basel II included generalized guidance instructing banks and their supervisors to ensure that banks accumulated sufficient capital above Pillar I minimums during cyclical expansions to allow for some drawdown of capital during more stressful conditions. Under Basel III, national authorities will monitor credit growth and other factors and may increase the required CET1 RCBR by up to 2.5% when credit growth is deemed excessive. This type of countercyclical buffer has received support from the literature. For instance, Angelini et al. (2011, p. 8) contend that the "[a] prudential rule that increases the capital requirement when the credit/output ratio rises seems capable of reducing output variance in a sizeable way." Internationally active banks will compute their countercyclical buffer as a weighted average of the buffers calculated for each geographic location where they hold exposures. The Basel Committee (2011b) offers some high level guidance on the operational aspects of the countercyclical buffer, but the implementation methods and timeline may vary across countries.

It will take some time before Basel III is fully implemented. While other countries have implemented Basel II Pillar I capital charges, advanced banks in the US continue to be in parallel run (Basel Committee, 2013). In many advanced economies, the implementation of Basel III is made more complex as the introduction of new capital rules needs to be coordinated with other financial regulatory reforms that have been adopted since the financial crisis (e.g., the Dodd–Frank Act in the US and the European Market Infrastructure Regulation in the EU).

23.7 LOOKING FORWARD

Basel capital rules continue to evolve. Proposals to address some of the weaknesses in Basel I and II revealed by the financial crisis are still under development and potential differences in the implementation of Basel III across jurisdictions are being closely monitored (Basel

Committee, 2012b). Additional work to refine the framework to address macroproduntial risks remains on the agenda of the Basel Committee.

The Basel Committee is conducting a number of ongoing reviews of risk-based capital. A Fundamental Review of the Trading Book (Basel Committee, 2012a) aims to more clearly define the boundary between trading book and banking book, and replace the separate and somewhat fragmented components of trading book capital requirements (i.e., Stressed VaR, IRC, and CRM) with a more coherent framework. The regulatory capital treatment of securitizations, including the role of external ratings, is also under review in light of the important role securitizations played in the financial crisis (Basel Committee, 2012d). Recognizing the dependence of financial stability on the safety and soundness of globally systemically important financial institutions (G-SIFIs), the Basel Committee is evaluating methods to identify institutions that would be required hold additional capital buffers (Basel Committee, 2012c).

Adequate capital is, of course, only one component of sound bank risk management. In addition to the capital rules aimed at protecting bank solvency, the Basel Committee has proposed new standards to safeguard bank liquidity. Broadly, these standards are intended to ensure that banks have the balance sheet liquidity and stable longer term funding to meet cash outflows during periods of stress. In collaboration with the International Organization of Securities Commissions, the Basel Committee is also developing standards governing minimum margin requirements for non-centrally cleared derivatives that would affect not only banks, but all financial firms and systemically important non-financial entities (BCBS and IOSCO, 2013). The goal is to ensure that OTC derivatives trade in a highly collateralized environment so that the losses due to the failure of a derivative counterparty would be limited.

References

Acharya, V. V., Bharath, S. T., and Srinivasan, A. (2007). Does Industry-Wide Distress Affect Defaulted Firms?—Evidence from Creditor Recoveries, *Journal of Financial Economics* 85(3), 787–821.

Altman, E. I., Brady, B., Resti, A., and Sironi, A. (2005). The Link between Default and Recovery Rates: Theory, Empirical Evidence, and Implications, *Journal of Business* 78(6), 2203–2228.

Angelini, P., Clerc, L., Curdia, V., Gambarcorta, L., Gerali, A., Locamo, A., Motto, R., Roeger, W., Van den Heuvel, S., and Vlcek, J. (2011). BASEL III: Long-Term Impact on Economic Performance and Fluctuations, BIS Working Papers No. 338.

Asarnow, E. and Marker, J. (1995). Historical Performance of the US Corporate Loan Market: 1988-1993, *Commercial Lending Review* 10(2), 13–32.

Basel Committee on Banking Supervision (BCBS) (1988). International Convergence of Capital Measurement and Capital Standards. Bank for International Settlements.

Basel Committee on Banking Supervision (BCBS) (2000). Range of Practices in Banks' Internal Rating Systems. Bank for International Settlements.

Basel Committee on Banking Supervision (BCBS) (2005a). The Application of Basel II to Trading Activities and the Treatment of Double Default Effects. Bank for International Settlements.

Basel Committee on Banking Supervision (BCBS) (2005b). Guidance on Paragraph 468 of the Framework Document. Bank for International Settlements.

Basel Committee on Banking Supervision (BCBS) (2005c). An Explanatory Note on the Basel II IRB Risk Weight Functions. Bank for International Settlements.

Basel Committee on Banking Supervision (BCBS) (2006). International Convergence of Capital Measurement and Capital Standards. A Revised Framework, Comprehensive Version, BCBS Publication No. 128, Bank for International Settlements.

Basel Committee on Banking Supervision (BCBS) (2011a). Revisions to Basel II Market Risk Framework. Bank for International Settlements.

Basel Committee on Banking Supervision (BCBS) (2011b). Basel III: A Global Regulatory Framework for More Resilient Banks and Banking Systems. Bank for International Settlements.

Basel Committee on Banking Supervision (BCBS) (2012a). Consultative Document: Fundamental Review of the Trading Book. Bank for International Settlements.

Basel Committee on Banking Supervision (BCBS) (2012b). Report to G20 Finance Ministers and Central Bank Governors on Basel III Implementation. Bank for International Settlements.

Basel Committee on Banking Supervision (BCBS) (2012c). Global Systemically Important Banks: Assessment Methodology and the Additional Loss Absorbency Requirement. Bank for International Settlements.

Basel Committee on Banking Supervision (BCBS) (2012d). Consultative Document: Revisions to the Basel Securitisation Framework. Bank for International Settlements.

Basel Committee on Banking Supervision (BCBS) (2013). Progress Report on Implementation of the Basel Regulatory Framework. Bank for International Settlements.

Basel Committee on Banking Supervision and Board of the International Organization of Securities Commissions (BCBS and IOSCO) (2013). Second Consultative Document: Margin Requirements for Non-Centrally Cleared Derivatives. Bank for International Settlements and the International Organization of Securities Commissions.

Bruche, M. and González-Aguado, C. (2010). Recovery Rates, Default Probabilities, and the Credit Cycle, *Journal of Banking and Finance* 34(4), 754–764.

Carey, M. (2002). Some Evidence on the Consistency of Banks' Internal Credit Ratings. In: M. Ong (Ed.), *Credit Ratings: Methodologies, Rationale, and Default Risk*, 449–470. London: Risk Waters.

Chen, H. (2010). Macroeconomic Conditions and the Puzzles of Credit Spreads and Capital Structure, *Journal of Finance* 65(6), 2171–2212.

Daníelsson, J., Embrechts, P., Goodhart, C., Keating, C., Muennich, F., Renault, O., and Shin, H. S. (2001). An Academic Response to Basel II, London School of Economics Financial Markets Group Special Paper No. 130.

Decamps, J-P., Rochet, J-C., and Roger, B. (2004). The Three Pillars of Basel II: Optimizing the Mix, *Journal of Financial Intermediation* 13(2), 132–155.

Düllmann, K., Scheicher, M., and Schmieder, C. (2008). Asset Correlations and Credit Portfolio Risk—An Empirical Analysis, *Journal of Credit Risk* 4(2), 37–62.

Düllmann, K. and Trapp, M. (2005). Systematic Risk in Recovery Rates of US Corporate Credit Exposures. In: E. I. Altman, A. Resti, and A. Sironi (Eds.), *Recovery Risk: The Next Challenge in Credit Risk Management*, 235–252. London: Riskbooks.

Embrechts, P. and Hofert, M. (2011). Practices and Issues in Operational Risk Modeling under Basel II, *Lithuanian Mathematical Journal* 51(2), 180–193.

Fontnouvelle, P. de, DeJesus-Rueff, V., Jordan, J. S., and Rosengren, E. S. (2006). Capital and Risk: New Evidence on Implications of Large Operational Losses, *Journal of Money, Credit, and Banking* 38(7), 1819–1846.

Frey, R. and McNeil, A. (2003). Dependent Defaults in Models of Portfolio Credit Risk, *Journal of Risk* 6(1), 59–92.

Frye, J. (2000). Collateral Damage, *Risk* 13(4), 91–94.

Frye, J. (2003). A False Sense of Security, *Risk* 16(8), 63–67.

Garcia Cespedes, J. C., de Juan Herrero, J. A., Kreinin, A., and Rosen, D. (2006). A Simple Multifactor "Factor Adjustment" for the Treatment of Credit Capital Diversification, *Journal of Credit Risk* 2(3), 57–86.

Gordy, M. B. (2000). A Comparative Anatomy of Credit Risk Models, *Journal of Banking and Finance*, 24(1–2), 119–149.

Gordy, M. B. (2003). A Risk-Factor Model Foundation for Ratings-Based Bank Capital Rules, *Journal of Financial Intermediation* 12(3), 199–232.

Gordy, M. B. (2004). Granularity Adjustment in Portfolio Credit Risk Measurement. In: G. Szego (Ed.), *Risk Measures for the 21st Century*, 109–122. New York: John Wiley & Sons.

Gordy, M. B. and Howells, B. (2006). Procyclicality in Basel II: Can We Treat the Disease Without Killing the Patient?, *Journal of Financial Intermediation* 15(3), 395–417.

Gordy, M. B. and Jones, D. (2003). Random Tranches, *Risk* 16(3), 78–83.

Gordy, M. B. and Lütkebohmert, E. (2013). Granularity Adjustment for Regulatory Capital Assessment, *International Journal of Central Banking* 9(3), 38–77.

Gupton, G., Finger, C. C., and Bhatia, M. (1997). *CreditMetrics—Technical Document*. New York: J. P. Morgan.

Hamerle A., Liebig, T., and Rösch, D. (2003). Benchmarking Asset Correlations, *Risk* 16(11), 77–81.

Hanson, S. G., Kashyap, A. K., and Stein, J. C. (2011). A Macroprudential Approach to Financial Regulation, *Journal of Economic Perspectives* 25(1), 3–28.

Heitfield, E. (2003). Using Credit Derivatives and Guarantees to Reduce Credit-Risk Capital Requirements under the New Basel Capital Accord. In: J. Gregory (Ed.), *Credit Derivatives: The Definitive Guide* 451–466. London: Risk Waters Group.

Heitfield, E., Burton, S., and Chomsisengphet, S. (2005). Risk Sensitive Regulatory Capital Rules for Hedged Credit Exposures. In: M. Pykhtin (Ed.), *Credit Risk Modeling: Pricing, Risk Management and Regulation*. London: Risk Waters Group.

Heitfield, E., Burton, S., and Chomsisengphet, S. (2006). Systematic and Idiosyncratic Risk in Syndicated Loan Portfolios, *Journal of Credit Risk* 2(3), 3–31.

Jackson, P., Furfine, C., Groeneveld, H., Hancock, D., Jones, D., Perraudin, W., Radecki, L., and Yoneyama, M. (1999). Capital Requirements and Bank Behaviour: The Impact of the Basle Accord, BIS Working Paper No. 1.

Jacobson, T., Linde, J., and Roszbach, K. (2003). Internal Ratings Systems, Implied Credit Risk and the Consistency of Banks' Risk Classification Policies, *Journal of Banking and Finance* 30(7), 1899–1926.

Jones, D. (2000). Emerging Problems with the Basel Capital Accord: Regulatory Capital Arbitrage and Related Issues, *Journal of Banking and Finance* 24(1–2), 35–58.

Kashyap, A. K. and Stein, J. C. (2004). Cyclical Implications of the Basel-II Capital Standards, *Federal Reserve Bank of Chicago Economic Perspectives* First Quarter, 18–31.

Lopez, J. (2004). The Empirical Relationship between Average Asset Correlation, Firm Probability of Default, and Asset Size, *Journal of Financial Intermediation* 13(2), 265–283.

McNeil, A. and Wendin, J. (2006). Dependent Credit Migrations, *Journal of Credit Risk* 2(3), 87–114.

Martin, R. and Wilde, T. (2002). Unsystematic Credit Risk, *Risk* 15(11), 123–128.

Merton, R. C. (1974). On the Pricing of Corporate Debt: The Risk Structure of Interest Rates, *Journal of Finance* 29(2), 449–470.

Merton, R. C. (1995). Financial Innovation and the Management and Regulation of Financial Institutions, *Journal of Banking and Finance* 19(3–4), 461–481.

Pykhtin, M. (2003). Unexpected Recovery Risk, *Risk* 16(8), 74–78.

Pykhtin, M. (2004). Multi-Factor Adjustment, *Risk* 17(3), 88–90.

Pykhtin, M. and Dev, A. (2002). Credit Risk in Asset Securitizations: An Analytical Model, *Risk* 15(5), S16–S20.

Qi, M. and Yang, X. (2009). Loss Given Default of High Loan-to-Value Residential Mortgages, *Journal of Banking and Finance* 33(5), 788–799.

Rösch, D. (2005). An Empirical Comparison of Default Risk Forecasts from Alternative Credit Rating Philosophies, *International Journal of Forecasting* 21(1), 37–51.

Seivold, A., Leifer, S., and Ulman, S. (2006). Operational Risk Management: An Evolving Discipline, *Supervisory Insights* 3, 4–11.

Shin, H. S. (2011). Macroprudential Policies Beyond Basel III, BIS Papers No. 60.

Treacy, W. and Carey, M. (2000). Credit Risk Ratings at Large US Banks, *Journal of Banking and Finance* 24(1–2), 167–201.

Wilde, T. (2001). Probing Granularity, *Risk* 14(8), 103–106.

Zhu, F., Dvorak, B., Levy, A., and Zhang, J. (2007). Using Asset Values and Asset Returns for Estimating Correlations. Moody's/KMV White Paper.

CHAPTER 24

....

MARKET DISCIPLINE IN FINANCIAL MARKETS
Theory, Evidence, and Obstacles *

....

ROBERT R. BLISS

24.1 INTRODUCTION

....

THE idea of using market discipline as an adjunct to supervision in the regulation of financial firms, and particularly banks, goes back to the mid-1970s. Since the financial crisis of 2008, market discipline has become a central issue in financial market reforms, both for specialists and in more general discussions in political forums and in the media. Some of the blame for the financial crisis of 2008 has been placed at the feet of market participants who failed to exert market discipline. Empirical investigations of market discipline in banking and the discussion of concrete regulatory proposals to enhance it have been important threads in the academic and regulatory banking literatures and in policy discussions. For all this, the concept of market discipline is not well defined or well understood. This may be because the term "market discipline" does not denote a theory but a collection of ideas as to how markets can be harnessed by regulators to assist them in supervising financial institutions and reducing the risk of financial failures.

"Market discipline" is not a term widely used in other areas of economics, although some of the ideas underlying it are. The term does crop up in trade theory, labor market theory, and in the discussion of alternative bankruptcy regimes, but not nearly to the extent that we see it in the banking literature. The reason for this may be that one of the driving forces behind the market discipline discussion in banking, and financial institutions more

* I would like to thank Mark Flannery, Sherry Jarrell, and the editors for their extremely helpful comments and suggestions. Any errors and omissions remain my own responsibility.

generally, is the concern that market discipline is not working as it should because of regulatory distortions such as deposit insurance and too-big-to-fail (TBTF). Since financial institutions are extremely important to modern capitalist economies, any failure of normal market mechanisms is a potentially serious problem.

The concept of market discipline, as it is used with respect to banks and financial institutions, focuses on the financial firm's security holders as the market agents involved in disciplining the firm. The risk of the activities in which the firm is engaged is the behavior to be disciplined. Thus, the term "market discipline" as used by regulators is rather narrow in its scope. Bliss and Flannery (2002) identify two steps in the market discipline process: *monitoring* and *influence*.[1] Monitoring is the process by which security holders and other market participants, such as derivatives counterparties and providers of short-term funding, observe the risk of the activities in which the firm is engaged. Their interest in doing so is to ensure that they are repaid. For traded securities, it is assumed that the market's risk assessments may be inferred from the prices of the securities which may be observed.

The second step, influence, can be divided into *direct influence* and *indirect influence*. Direct influence can occur when the actions of creditors and counterparties cause the firm to change its behavior when it has engaged in risk-taking of which the creditors disapprove. This is denoted *ex post market discipline*. This discipline occurs in response to an observed firm behavior. Alternatively, direct discipline can occur if the firm avoids taking certain risks because doing so would result in adverse responses from its creditors and counterparties. This is denoted *ex ante market discipline*. In the case of ex ante market discipline, there will be no signal of excessive risk-taking to observe, but that does not mean that direct market influence has not occurred. Indirect influence consists of supervisors using the signals in the market prices of securities issued by the firms they are supervising as additional sources of information beyond what their own examinations and required financial reports provide.[2] This allows supervisors to direct their resources appropriately and may provide early warning of problems. By definition, indirect influence is a form of ex post discipline as it cannot occur unless the market reacts to a firm's risk-taking to generate a signal for supervisors to observe and respond to. Indirect influence is not strictly speaking market influence. Nonetheless, indirect discipline is included in the scope of the market discipline debate

The first thread of the market discipline discussion, indirect market discipline, was originally proposed by Pettway (1976). The concern at the time was that banks had become too complex. The complexity and breadth of bank activities have greatly accelerated since then. The arguments for supplementing supervisory oversight with market discipline continue to emphasize the superior information that markets may provide.[3] It is believed that sophisticated market participants, who are thought to be the price setters for securities issued by banks, would be better able to assess the risk of these activities than supervisors who have little or no experience and training in these new markets.

---

[1] Most articles purporting to study market discipline actually study market monitoring. Claims some of these papers make of finding evidence of market discipline are therefore overstated.

[2] Supervisors are the members of financial regulatory authorities, such as the Federal Deposit Insurance Corporation (FDIC) or Federal Reserve, charged with ensuring that individual financial institutions comply with laws and regulations and operate in a safe and sound manner. They do this through on site examinations and off site monitoring.

[3] Pre- and post-2008 financial crisis examples of this argument include Kwast et al. (1999) and Evanoff, Jagtiani, and Nakata (2011).

The second thread of the market discipline discussion is that both monitoring and influence have been undermined by deposit insurance and market perceptions that some banks were TBTF. The belief that banks, which primarily funded themselves through deposits, are not sufficiently exposed to market discipline has been a major concern of regulators and financial economists. This concern also extended to large money center banks that rely to a greater extent on uninsured wholesale funding, and that might be perceived to be TBTF. To restore some degree of market discipline and to have securities whose prices would reflect bank risk correctly, it has been widely proposed that banks be required to issue unsecured subordinated notes and/or bonds (SND).[4] The argument is that bondholders, if they are credibly at risk of losses, are in a similar position to regulators, acting as agents for the deposit insurance fund. They share downside risk if the bank fails, but neither shares in the upside gains if the bank profits from excessive risk-taking.

A study of the mandatory SND idea by the Federal Reserve Board, Kwast et al. (1999), identified and discussed 11 specific proposals. These 11 are only a subset of the proposals that have been made in papers that advocate this idea. Proposals vary as to the amount, frequency, type of debt, maturity of required issues and who could or could not hold the issues.[5] The proposals also differed as to whether the purpose is to facilitate direct or indirect market influence. They agree that regular issuance is desirable both to increase liquidity and provide regular primary market price signals. A fixed issuance schedule also would prevent banks from gaming issue dates to minimize at-issue yields. A variant of the mandatory SND proposals would use the SND yields to trigger mandatory responses by either the banks or regulators.

The efforts of market discipline proponents have produced some successes, albeit not as far-reaching as many would wish. The Financial Services Modernization Act of 1999 (Pub.L. 106-102) also known as the Gramm–Leach–Bliley Act (GLB), requires that the 50 largest national banks have outstanding eligible debt rated A or better.[6] GLB also required the Federal Reserve and Treasury to conduct a study of mandatory subordinated debt proposals. The "Third Pillar" of the second Basel Accords issued by the Basel Committee on Banking Supervision (Basel II) in 2004 is entitled "Market Discipline." This addresses only transparency, intended to make market monitoring more effective. The regulatory and Treasury responses to the financial crisis of 2008 dealt a blow to attempts by regulators and legislators to eliminate market perceptions that some systemically important financial institutions are TBTF. The 2010 Wall Street Reform and Consumer Protection Act (H.R. 4173, a.k.a. Dodd–Frank) attempts to put the cat (TBTF) back in the bag by explicitly requiring the newly created Financial Stability Oversight Council to "promote market discipline" by imposing losses on creditors.[7]

---

[4] The D in SND stands for "debentures," another term for "bond."

[5] For example, Calomiris (1999) advocated that banks be required to have two % of their liabilities in uninsured two-year CDs to be held by foreign banks; 1/24th of the amount outstanding to be rolled over each month. Wall (1989) advocated that banks be required to issue puttable SNDs equal to 4–5% of their risk-weighted assets.

[6] 12 USC 24a(a)(3)(A)(i). Eligible debt is defined as "unsecured long-term debt," 12 USC 24a(g)(4).

[7] See Sec. 112 (a)(1)(B). Legislators see imposing losses on creditors of a failed financial institution as a moral issue: equity holders and creditors, not tax payers, should bear the first losses. Regulatory economists more often cite the moral hazard and market discipline arguments for this policy.

Most of the discussion of market discipline and related regulatory proposals took place before the financial crisis of 2008. As a result, these focused on banks as that was where regulatory attention was focused. The 2008 financial crisis made manifest the critical importance of non-bank financial institutions to the financial system. These non-bank financial institutions differ in important ways from banks. In particular, they have no insured deposits to protect them against runs. However, many non-bank financial institutions do rely heavily on short-term funding sources that are subject to runs. Absent bail outs, runs are, or at least have been, inevitably fatal to a firm relying substantially on short-term funding of illiquid assets, the usual case for financial institutions. Withdrawal of funding from a firm perceived to be too risky and its concomitant failure is the ultimate form of direct market discipline. We will denote this as *destructive market discipline*. From a regulatory perspective, this is the wrong kind of market discipline. Failure of firms that are inefficient or poorly managed is a normal mechanism in capital markets for improving the allocation of resources. Schumpter termed this "creative destruction." However, the failure of financial firms may involve serious externalities for the economy, particularly if the firms involved are systemically important. What financial regulators want is market discipline that either prevents excessive risk-taking (ex ante discipline) or influences managers to take corrective actions when markets signal their assessment that managers have taken on too much risk (ex post discipline), but before the adverse consequences become too serious. We will denote this as *corrective market discipline*.

Arguments as to why market discipline should occur have either been implicit or appeal has been made to intuitive arguments. This makes it difficult to critically examine the theoretical foundations on which the various types and components of market discipline are based. Section 24.2 of this chapter will attempt to clarify the intellectual foundations of market discipline and the different mechanisms by which it may operate. Section 24.3 will examine the empirical evidence that exists, or does not exist, for various components of market discipline. Section 24.4 will examine several problems in financial markets that impact the assumptions underlying the arguments for various applications of market discipline and the interpretation of the empirical evidence. The last section will draw conclusions.

24.2 Theory

In its most general sense, market discipline posits a feedback loop from market participants to firms that guides the choices that firms make. This is not a new idea. It goes back to the insight in Adam Smith's *The Wealth of Nations*, Smith (1776), that in a free and competitive market, buyers chose what and from whom to buy. This in turn forces producers to produce goods that buyers want at a price they are willing to pay. Firms that are inefficient or produce goods that are not wanted will fail. Capital and eventually labor will be redirected to more productive uses. Everyone is better off, except the owners of the firms that fail. Managers wishing to avoid failure have an incentive to change what they are doing, if they can. This theory is widely accepted in capitalist economies, with debate focusing on what happens when markets are not free or competitive, as is almost always the case to some degree.

There are two aspects of this standard theory of capital markets which differ from the feedback loop envisioned in the financial market discipline discussions. First, traditional capital market theory concerns buyers of goods (and services) produced by firms. The market discipline discussion in financial regulation focuses on buyers of securities, not buyers of products, and on the pricing of those securities. Creditors' choice whether to invest at all is usually ignored. Second, the important driving mechanism in the logic is firm failure. In the market discipline literature actual firm failure is rarely seen as part of the normal process of market discipline and from a regulatory perspective is undesirable.

Buyers of securities face an information problem that is substantially different from buyers of a firm's goods. They need to make assessments of the current and future prospects of the firm whose securities they are buying or already own, and in particular they need to ascertain the riskiness of the firm. This allows them to appropriately price the securities. But assessing the future prospects of a firm and the risk surrounding those prospects is a very different problem from assessing the quality, price, and alternatives of a particular product produced by a firm.

This brings us to the second theoretical foundation of market discipline—the efficient market hypothesis (EMH). Fama (1970) posited that the prices of securities in financial markets correctly reflect all available information. The basic argument underlying the EMH is that holders of financial securities have economic incentives to spend resources collecting information about the firm, that the collective efforts of large numbers of holders of a particular security will uncover all the relevant information, and that competition among investors (survival of the fittest) will find the correct valuations based on that information. The EMH too has been widely, though not universally, accepted.

Fama's EMH is qualified by the types of information encompassed by "all available." The weak form EMH includes only past prices, which should preclude abnormal profits based solely on past prices and trading rules. The semi-strong form EMH covers all publicly available information, and the strong form EMH covers all information, public or private, including insider information. Evidence for semi-strong form EMH is generally strong, with the exceptions of so-called anomalies.[8] Evidence supporting the strong form EMH is weaker indicating that stockholders are not always able to detect what is going on within the firm. The market discipline argument implicitly assumes the strong form EMH.

24.2.1 Indirect Market Influence

The indirect influence channel of market discipline relies on (1) the EMH, (2) the assumption that regulators will know how to respond appropriately to market signals, and (3) that they will do so. Flannery (2010) notes that, despite widespread discussions about using market signals in the supervisory process, actual use has been limited. This may reflect distrust of the accuracy of those signals or institutional conservatism.

Regulatory and political incentives can cause supervisors to not exert indirect discipline. Widespread forbearance by supervisors who failed to close distressed banks and savings and loans in a timely manner during the 1980s and occasional political interference in individual closure decisions is widely believed to have increased the costs of the S&L crisis.

---

[8] See Fama (1991) for a discussion.

This behavior also resulted in the legislation designed to force supervisors to take actions as banks and S&Ls conditions deteriorated.[9] These have not been entirely effective. For instance, Superior FSB was allowed to remain open until July 2001 despite massive losses while the OTS negotiated (unsuccessfully) with the politically influential Pritzker family, who were joint owners of the bank.

The tools available to supervisors to exert constructive discipline, while powerful, are not without problems. Orders to managers to recapitalize their banks depend on the feasibility of raising funds—which is not always easy for a distressed bank. Stopping dividends may result in a sharp drop in stock price that could trigger runs. Terminating access to brokered deposits may make the bank illiquid. The usual form of (terminal) discipline is to arrange a merger. During the financial crisis the market for distressed banks was overwhelmed. Potential buyers learnt that they could take advantage an FDIC that was forced to sell many failed institutions quickly by cherry picking assets and extracting loss guarantees for assets they accepted.

Where exercise of supervisory discipline is problematic, market signals (even if they are to be trusted) may do little to encourage such discipline. To provide incentives not to forbear without good reason, Bliss (2001) suggested using SND yield spreads to trigger required public explanations by supervisors as to why they were not taking action in individual situations if that was the case. On the other hand, Bond, Goldstein, and Prescott (2010) argue that if supervisors base corrective actions on markets signals, market participants' anticipation of these actions will make prices less informative.

24.2.2 Direct Market Influence

The direct influence channel of market discipline relies on a common assumption in finance: managers endeavor to maximize the value of stockholders' wealth. This starting point has several potential implications for how market discipline works. Theoretically, equity holders as owners of the firm should be in the strongest position to influence the firm. Unlike bondholders they have legal powers to vote for directors and to vote for or against mergers. But equity holder influence cut both ways, in theory, pushing the firm to either increase risk or to decrease it, depending on the situation.

Using a simple one-period option pricing model of the firm, Merton (1977) posited that stockholder/managers have incentives to increase the riskiness of a firm's assets to maximize the value of the option they hold. A more realistic multi-period model that considers lost future cash flows should the firm fail predicts that equity holders become increasingly risk averse as the firm approaches insolvency. Up to that point, their interests are aligned with those of the creditors, and thus the regulators. However, once the firm becomes insolvent, and before it is shut down, the equity holders and managers (seeking to protect their jobs) will wish to gamble for resurrection, increasing the potential losses to creditors.

---

[9] These were the prompt corrective action (PCA) provisions of the FDIC Improvement Act (FDICIA) of 1991. PCA consisted of a list of increasingly onerous restrictions on a distressed bank, some optional, some mandatory that were to be triggered by declining book capital.

Creditors are in a weak position to exert beneficial influence. They have no role in corporate governance and so cannot directly influence managers. The Trust Indenture Act of 1939 imposes a Trustee between the bondholders and the issuer and limits the actions that the Trustee may take to those related to the violation of terms of the bond indenture. Managers owe few duties to bondholders beyond those specified in the indenture (except abstaining from fraudulent misrepresentations). Bondholders can try to control firm risk through covenants, and markets can price the perceived risk of debt at time of issue, potentially impacting the net return on equity. Curiously, the second Basel Accord issued by the Basel Committee on Banking Supervision in 2004 (Basel II), while it encouraged the use of subordinate debt for Tier 2 capital purposes, limited the types of covenants that such debt may include. For instance, acceleration clauses are prohibited, which effectively prevents the trustee from being able to enforce other covenants.

The most potent mechanism of direct influence by bondholders, or creditors generally, is to withhold financing. However, even this source of direct influence may be weak when banks can shift between sources of funding, such as from CDs to insured deposits. But when banks or other financial institutions have to quickly find new sources of short-term borrowing (CDs and repos) to pay off prior borrowing coming due and creditors decline to rollover previously extended credit, the results are immediate and decisive as we saw during the 2007–08 financial crisis.

Notwithstanding intuitive arguments as to why managers should care what markets think about the risk they take, the finance literature is full of reasons why they may not. Smith (1776, p. 311) first identified the separation of ownership and control inherent in the corporate form as a source of problems:

> The directors of such [joint-stock] companies, however, being the managers rather of other people's money than their own, it cannot well be expected, that they should watch over it with the same anxious vigilance with which partners in a private copartnery frequently watch over their own . . . Negligence and profusion, therefore, must always prevail, more or less, in the management of the affairs of such a company.

This idea was developed into a formal theory of the principle-agent problem by Jensen and Meckling (1976) and Fama (1980). Besides separation of ownership and control, the other sources of the agency problem are information asymmetries and incomplete contracting. Managers' interests are not necessarily aligned with those of owners (stockholders); and as the equity-as-an-option model predicts, equity holders' interests are not necessarily aligned with those of creditors, who also suffer from information asymmetries. In a world with conflicting incentives and information problems, neither perfect monitoring nor direct influence will necessarily obtain.

Nonetheless, corporations are an extremely successful form of business organization and most corporations issue debt. So agency problems are not necessarily overwhelming. Agency costs are mitigated by various mechanisms. Delegated monitors include boards of directors (Fama, 1980), regulatory agency supervision, and rating agencies. Information asymmetries are reduced by legally required audited financial statements and regulatory filings. Fiduciary laws and laws against fraud and insider trading reduce the incentives of mangers to expropriate stockholders. The market for corporate control and threat of takeover helps to keep managers working in the stockholders' interests, as do performance incentives, such as stock options. Stockholder activism is a developing mechanism for influencing managers, though it is weak unless the stockholder has a large position. The managerial labor market may punish unsuccessful managers by reducing their future employment prospects.[10] All these mechanisms are useful devices, but necessarily imperfect.

24.3 Evidence

24.3.1 Indirect influence

For indirect influence to be effective, market monitoring must produce bond yields and or stock returns that reflect bank risk in a timely manner; that is, in sufficient time for regulators to take remedial actions. To justify imposing mandatory subordinated debt requirements on banks, the information provided by bond yields has to add to information already available from other sources, particularly accounting information. Finally, for indirect discipline the information embedded in prices has to be such as to allow supervisors to separate good banks from bad banks.

24.3.1.1 Do Market Signals Reflect Risk?

The majority of studies have examined whether debt yields reflect bank risk. The methodology employed in most of these studies has been to regress yield spreads against various measures of bank risk including accounting variables or, where available, supervisory ratings. These studies thus seek to demonstrate that a contemporaneous correlation exists between bond yields and other sources of information available to supervisors. They do not necessarily demonstrate that bond yields contain additional information over and above that available elsewhere, nor do they demonstrate the timeliness the information provided. A contrary finding that yield spreads are not correlated with firm risk, or are negatively correlated, would be inconsistent with market monitoring and hence market discipline. Very few studies have reached this conclusion.

Early studies found little evidence that bank risk was reflected in yield spreads.[11] This has been attributed to the effects of implicit guarantees arising out of the government's handling of bank failures (e.g., Continental Bank) in the 1980s. Subsequently, Flannery and Sorescu (1996), and numerous other studies find that bond yields do reflect bank risk, particular after FDICIA was passed in 1991. Sironi (2003) confirms this result for European banks as Pop (2006) does for North American, European and Japanese banks. On the other hand, Balasubramnian and Cyree (2011) found that bank sub-debt yields were sensitive to bank-specific risk factors prior to the LTCM intervention in 1998, but not afterwards. They attribute this in part to the increased issuance of Trust Preferred Securities, which are junior to subordinate debt in the event of failure and so provide an additional buffer to protect subordinate bondholders.

---

[10] Managers who leave troubled banks with multi-million golden parachutes may view such lost opportunities with equanimity.

[11] See, for instance, Avery, Belton, and Goldberg (1988); Gorton and Santomero (1990).

Evanoff, Jagtiani, and Nakata (2011) argue that the failure of some studies to find a significant relation between yield and risk is due to a lack of secondary market liquidity.[12] They divided their sample into observations around the time of issuance of the SND, when the bonds are most liquid and observed prices (and ratings) are timely, and later secondary market observations. They found that evidence of market monitoring was strongest at time of issuance. They attribute this to increased transparency and liquidity at time of issue. They conclude that a mandatory program of regular SND issuance would increase both factors and enhance market discipline.

Levels of both risk and yield spreads tend to be sticky. This means that it is difficult to infer whether yields are leading risk or vice versa. It also complicates statistical inference as successive observations of the same bank's risk and yields are not completely independent. A related line of inquiry is to look at changes rather than levels. Krishnan, Ritchken, and Thomson (2005) using bank subordinated bonds and Collin-Dufresne, Goldstein, and Martin (2001) using corporate bonds both conclude that changes in yields spreads are not correlated with changes in risk. On the other hand, Pop (2006) finds that rating changes are correlated with changes in SND yields.

The evidence that SND yields reflect contemporaneously measured risk is thus somewhat mixed. Studies of this type also fail to provide a strong rationale for mandatory SND issuance. The structure of these studies presumes that there are other available sources of information about firm risk against which to test the SND signals. They cannot show that SND signals add anything additional to the alternative risk measures used in the tests. SND yields can be observed more frequently than accounting information or examiner rating. However, contemporaneous correlations do not reveal whether this higher frequency data is helpful. To be useful for indirect discipline, SND signals must be timely. That is, they should anticipate adverse changes in firm conditions so that regulators have time to act on the information.

24.3.1.2 Do Market Signals Reflect Future Risks?

A second line of investigation therefore looks at whether debt yields and/or stock prices contain information about future changes in bank condition. Pettway (1980) found that stock returns anticipated supervisory bank examinations that resulted in bank closures by as much as 38 weeks. Jagtiani and Lemieux (2001) find the bank SND yields rise as much as 18 months prior to bank failures. Using CAMEL ratings, DeYoung et al. (2001) find that examiners have private information that is not captured in contemporaneous bond yields but is reflected in bond yields one or two quarters later. While CAMEL ratings are supposedly not public, the authors interpret their empirical results as reflecting a positive market reaction to supervisory recognition of developing problems. For this reason, DeYoung et al. (2001) conclude that supervisors have no informational advantage over bondholders. Krainer and Lopez (2004) find that equity returns anticipate future changes in supervisory ratings of bank holding

---

[12] Most bonds do not trade on frequently. Their observed secondary market "prices" are therefore inferred using a matched liquid bond and a fixed spread, called matrix pricing. The spread is updated only if the matrix-priced bond trades. As it is usually impossible to know when the matrix prices reflect new idiosyncratic information, most of the time observed prices changes are uninformative about changes in the credit risk of the matric-priced issue.

companies by up to four quarters, but that inclusion of equity returns in addition to supervisory variables does not improve the forecasts from using only supervisory variables.

24.3.1.3 Distress Prediction

Finding that SND yields and equity returns are correlated with future changes in risk is a second step towards establishing the usefulness of market monitoring for enhancing indirect discipline. The acid test, however, is the ability of market signals to discriminate between banks that will be "good" or "bad" in the future. This requires a logistic regression (logit) approach where the empirical exercise is to develop a model that predicts the future condition of a firm (e.g., "good" or "bad") and then comparing the results to the actual outcomes. This turns out to be a much more difficult task than simply establishing that market signals are correlated with future firm risk.

Evanoff and Wall (2001) use a logit model to predict supervisory ratings of banks (CAMEL) grouped into two classes, those with CAMEL ratings of 1 or 2 ("good") and those with ratings of 3 or 4 ("bad").[13] Their sample included 439 "good" banks and 13 "bad" banks. They test a number of specifications including those with and without SND yield spreads. They find that SND yields spread coefficients are statistically significant variables in their models. However, the rates of misclassification are high. Their best (lowest p-value) model correctly identifies 63% of the "good" banks and 76% of the "bad" banks. This means that their model falsely classified 169 "good" banks as "bad" (false negatives) and 3 of 13 "bad" banks as "good" (false positives).[14] Their model with the fewest number of misclassifications did not use SND yield spreads and had 16 false negatives and 2 false positives. A naïve model that predicts that all banks are "good" would have even fewer misclassifications, 13 false positives.

Gropp, Vesala, and Vulpes (2006) use SND yields and an equity-based distance-to-default (DD) measure developed by KMV Corporation, based on Merton (1974), as market signals to predict "serious weakening" of a bank's financial condition, which they define as a downgrade in the bank's Fitch/IBCA rating to C or below. Their sample covers 15 European countries and 87 banks, of which 25 were downgraded. Using monthly observations, their sample sizes were 5300 bank/months for the DD tests, and 3600 bank/months for the SND yield tests. As downgrades are not normally repeated, the number of "downgrade" observations is far less than the number of "no change" observations. Gropp, Vesala, and Vulpes (2006) use both logit regression and proportional hazard models to predict future downgrades. They find that both DD and SND yields are statistically significant regressors out to as many as 36 months. They find that their logit models using DD correctly predict 16 of 22 downgrades and 484 of 953 no changes, a prediction accuracy of 51%. The results for the SND yield spread logit model are 6 of 19, 235 of 331, and 70% respectively. Combining the DD measure and SND yield spreads and a third variable based on accounting information, they are able to increase the prediction accuracy to 85%. This still leaves a large number of false negatives.

Krainer and Lopez (2008) find that adjusted SND yields and equity returns contribute to their out-of-sample ordered logit models predicting "upgrade," "no change," and "downgrade," although the effect is weaker than in their in-sample tests. Examination of their

---

[13] There were no instances of banks with CAMEL rating of 5, the lowest rating, in their data.

[14] Here I am defining the null hypothesis as "no change" or "upgrade," that is "no need for concern," and the alternative as "downgrade."

578 REGULATORY AND POLICY PERSPECTIVES

prediction results, however, reveals that their model vastly over-predicts "no change." This results in the model misclassifying hundreds of actual "downgrades" as "no change" and a few as "upgrades."

In the above studies, the risk variables enter the logit specification in a linear manner. Evanoff and Wall (2002) consider that the relation may be non-linear by dividing their observations on the basis of the size of the SND yield spreads.[15] Starting with banks that have SND yield spreads that are 25 basis points above a Baa benchmark, they have a smaller (74) but more balanced dataset. They find that "almost one-half the banks that SND yield spreads suggested were high-risk, were also banks about which the supervisors had some concerns." This is better than their 2001 study, but still implies a 50% rate of false negatives. Evanoff and Wall further discuss the quality of SND signals as it may be related to issuer size and other factors that may make the signals noisy. They conclude that a mandatory SND requirement would be a useful source of indirect discipline, but do not favor SND signals as PCA triggers.

Notwithstanding the ambiguous implications of these papers for the usefulness of SND yields for indirect discipline, virtually all of the authors favor the use of SND yields as an input to regulatory discipline and many favor the mandatory issuance of SND by banks. One noteworthy exception to the support for mandatory SND issuance is Kwast et al. (1999). This Federal Reserve System study stopped short of recommending the adoption of a mandatory SND policy.

24.3.1.4 Sources of Prediction Problems

The above studies show that while market signals may be statistically significant as independent variables in prediction models, the prediction models do not do a very good job of correctly predicting future problem banks. This is actually not surprising. The available samples of "good" and "bad" banks are extremely unbalanced, so models are attempting to identify a few observations in the tail of a distribution of bank quality. As a simple simulation will show, the further out in the tail of the distribution the observations you are trying to identify lie, the greater the effect of any noise in the signal you are using to identify them. And market signals are very noisy signals indeed.

Models of the determinants of stock prices do not usually include idiosyncratic risk, which is what is of primary interest to supervisors and to discussions of market discipline. Nor do the majority of asset pricing models used to study stock returns contemplate bankruptcy, or the termination of the underlying stochastic process driving returns. As the primary focus of regulatory interest in market monitoring is failure prediction and/or avoidance the theoretical underpinnings of the equity markets literature are ill-suited to their purposes. This is not to say that stock prices cannot be empirically useful; just that we lack the models to explain any observed predictive power in a theoretical framework.

Tests of the EMH are necessarily joint tests of market efficiency and the assumed pricing model used to determine whether abnormal returns are possible. The focus of these tests is primarily on the means of the ex post risk adjusted returns.

---

[15] Bliss (2001) finds that there was little variation in yield-at-issue spreads for investment grade bonds, but that yields increased sharply for sub-investment grade issues, suggesting that the risk/yield relation is very non-linear.

Our interest is not so much in biasedness of stock price signals as in their accuracy. One strand of the empirical EMH literature is the investigation of whether stock prices are too volatile to be explained by the economic variables presumed to determine stock prices. Shiller (1989) reviews at length what was a vigorous debate in the 1980s. He concludes (in chapters 5 and 6) that the volatility of stock prices cannot reasonably be explained and therefore finds that this is evidence against the EMH. We are less concerned with accepting or rejecting the EMH than in noting that stock prices are more volatile than it appears from our models that they should be. There may be more to a stock price or return than just information about the firm's financial condition. Nonetheless, we note that default predictions models that are both widely used and commercially successful, such as Altman's z-scores and KMV distance to default, do rely on stock prices as inputs to their models.

Unlike the determinants of stock returns, we have a good deal of information about what bond yields contain. Advocates of using SND yields or spreads for indirect market discipline are making the assumption that yields or spreads primarily reflect default risk. Most discussions do not acknowledge that they could reflect anything else. Bliss (2001) lists studies finding that so called "credit spreads" reflect liquidity, slope and level of the Treasury term structure, perceived agency costs, and issuer opacity. Van Horne (1979) and Fama (1986) find that short and long credit spreads can be negatively correlated. This is inconsistent with credit spreads reflecting a single measure of risk. However, it is consistent with Duffee (1999), which finds that credit spreads cannot be explained by a single-factor model and hence incorporate more than a single "default risk" factor. Using yields-at-issue for financial company bonds of five or more years to maturity and measuring the spread over the contemporaneous BBB corporate bond benchmark, Bliss (2001) found that the variation within ratings group of investment grade bond spreads was 50–100 basis points above and below the mean, and that approximately 25% of bonds rated A+ through BBB+ had spreads above the BBB benchmark. Elton et al. (2001) decomposed corporate bond spreads over equivalent Treasury rates into default risk, tax effects, and systematic (market) risk. They found that default risk explained a small fraction of the observed variation, approximately 18% for ten-year A-rated bonds. Systematic risk explained the largest portion of the observed variation.

24.3.2 Direct Influence

24.3.2.1 *Ex Ante Influence*

Detecting ex ante influence is a difficult task. The logic of ex ante influence is that concern about negative market reactions dissuades managers from taking on too much risk. But negative market reaction is not the sole plausible reason for avoiding risk. Therefore, a low-risk profile does not necessarily imply effective ex ante influence. It may simply reflect a host of other reasons for conservative business conduct. Nonetheless, there are two places where ex ante influence (or its absence) may be directly observed: in covenants to restrict risk-taking and in the issuance of risky debt. The decision when and whether to issue SND may also cast light on ex ante discipline.

One should not infer from the evidence that debt yields are correlated with firm risk that bondholders are providing direct influence on firm risk-taking. The deterrent effect of risk sensitive bond yields depends on how much an increase in risk increases the cost of capital compared to how much the increase in risk increases the expected return on assets. If bond markets place a low premium on risk, as when credit spreads are cyclically low, or when risk sensitive debt is a small part of the capital structure (as is the case with most commercial banks), bond yields can be positively correlated with risk without necessarily impacting the choice of risk structure. The best evidence of this possibility is the large number of original issue high yield bonds that we see in the corporate bond world. Bliss (2001) notes that 16% of corporate bonds issued between 1993 and 1998 were rated below investment grade at time of issue.[16] This shows that bondholders are willing to invest in risky debt and firms are willing to pay the risk premium associated with such bonds. This does not mean that extremely risky firms could issue debt at an attractive yield, but it does show that the GLB A-rated floor for acceptable debt is routinely violated in the market.

Another piece of evidence for ex ante influence is the use of covenants. Goyal (2005) examined the types and frequency of restrictive covenants in bank SND issues from 1981–95. He found that restrictive covenants were negatively correlated with bank charter value in the period 1981–88. In other words, they were positively correlated with moral hazard incentives, consistent with bondholders exerting ex ante market influence. Over time, however, Goyal observes that the use of restrictive covenants has decreased. This is consistent with declining credit standards and anecdotal evidence of "covenant light" lending prior to the 2007 financial crisis.

Several papers have noted that currently the issuance and time of issue of bank SND is at the discretion of the firm and that this might affect the results of tests of risk sensitivity of SND yields to bank risk. Using a two-stage Heckman estimation procedure to first adjust for the decision to issue SND, Covitz, Hancock, and Kwast (2004) concluded that market discipline was operating through the primary debt market; that is, that firm risk partially explained issuance decisions. Their tests of the market monitoring hypothesis, conditioned on the issuance decision found monitoring to be strongest between 1988 and 1992, and weaker or insignificant before and after that period. They concluded that their own and other papers' weak results may be due to the prior effect of the issuance decision that biased the sample used to test for market monitoring. If only "good" firms issue SND and they time their issuance for optimal market conditions, the information content in the yield spreads, beyond the fact of the issuance itself, might be degraded.

24.3.2.2 Ex Post Influence

If looking for ex ante influence is akin to trying to explain why the dog did not bark, looking for ex post influence is search for a reaction to the dog's bark. This has proven to be surprisingly difficult to do. Bliss and Flannery (2002) looked at instances where an increase in SND yield spreads or negative stock returns followed an increase in one or more measures of bank risk (the dog barking). They then examined whether the increase in risk was subsequently reversed (the ex post discipline reaction). They found that risk changes following the adverse market signal were as apt to be further increases in risk as they were to be reversals of previous risk increases.

---

[16] Only two % of bank bonds were rated below investment grade at time of issue.

Calomiris and Powell (2001) studied the Argentine banking market in the period 1994:3 through 1999:1. This followed a period of financial crisis in the early 1990s, during which many banks were nationalized. The mid-1990s saw the introduction of a new central bank, financial reforms, including an SND issuance requirement for banks, and attempts to reduce perceptions of implicit government guarantees of deposit through the introduction of explicitly limited deposit insurance. Looking at mean reversion in individual bank deposit rates, they found evidence that ex post market discipline was effective in this case.

There have been a number of studies of depositor discipline, most of which look at changes in quantity as well as yields. As argued in Section 24.3.1.4 above, yields results are difficult to interpret. Quantity effects may be less ambiguous. Deposit insurance clearly undermines the potential effects of direct market discipline, where it is present. If banks can substitute insured deposits for other sources of funding, they can escape the full effect of the market discipline that might have been imposed by risk sensitive counterparties.

In a cross-country study, Demirgüç-Kunt and Huizinga (2004) found that deposit insurance undermined depositor discipline. Deposit growth was positively related to deposit rates paid by banks but only weakly related to risk measures. However, when the book capital ratio was interacted with a deposit insurance variable, they found a negative relation. This showed that weak banks could and did circumvent discipline when they could access insured funds.

Using a sample of central and eastern European banks, Distinguin, Kouassi, and Tarazi (2013) studied the effects of access to interbank deposit markets on bank risk-taking. They found that banks that had a higher proportion of interbank deposits had lower levels of risk. In an event study, Karas, Pyle, and Schoors (2013) looked at the effect of the introduction of deposit insurance for households, but not firms, in Russia in 2004 following a number of major bank failures. They found that deposit flows into and out of banks were less sensitive for insured depositors than for the uninsured depositors.

Berger and Turk-Ariss (2013) studied depositor discipline in the US, EU and Switzerland before and after the financial crisis. They found significant evidence of depositor discipline in the relation between deposit growth rates and bank capital ratios in large US banks. Large publically listed US banks however, showed lower levels of discipline. The effects were positive but weaker in smaller US banks. They interpret these results as consistent with TBTF perceptions for the largest (listed) US firms, more sophisticated creditors at the other large firms, and less use of uninsured funds at smaller firms. Non-US banks showed weak depositor discipline consistent with more widespread expectations of government intervention in distressed banks. In all cases, government interventions during times of financial crises weaken what depositor discipline there was before the crisis.

24.3.2.3 *Corporate Governance*

Stockholders' ability to realize their theoretical power to discipline managers directly by voting management out is undermined when stockholders are diffuse. Small individual holdings make information gathering is disproportionally costly. Even if adverse information is obtained, organizing a large number of like-minded stockholders is difficult. Laws and corporate bylaws governing access to the proxy process do not encourage the venture. Major stockholders, those who individually control a large fraction of the outstanding shares, are in a better position to influence management. In the case of banks, the situation is made even more difficult by the requirement that holders of a certain percentage of outstanding shares who act together must form a bank holding company and be subject to regulatory oversight. One of the few studies to examine corporate governance in banks was Prowse (1997). He concludes that:

> while market-based mechanisms of corporate control in BHCs appear to operate in the same[broad] fashion as manufacturing firms they may be weakened because hostile takeovers are precluded by regulation and bank boards of directors are not as aggressive in removing poorly performing managers. These weaknesses leave intervention by regulators as the primary force in disciplining management.

On the other hand, the managerial labor market does seem to function in banks as well as non-banks. Cannella, Fraser, and Lee (1995) and Farrell and Whidbee (2000) both find that subsequent to bank failures the market for bank managers is able to discriminate between managers who are likely to have been responsible for the failure and those who are not.

24.4 OBSTACLES

The conventional wisdom among regulators and bank economists is that the primary impediment to successful market discipline is the reduced incentives of market participants to engage in monitoring or effective influence due to deposit insurance and TBTF behavior on the part of regulators and politicians. The regulatory and administrative responses to the banking crisis, with the exception Lehman Brothers, supported this hypothesis. Dodd-Frank, therefore, set out to make bailouts illegal by prohibiting use of taxpayers' funds to prevent failures of large financial firms. It also sought to make failure more acceptable by creating a mechanism, the Orderly Liquidation Authority (OLA), which would be more predictable and less disruptive to markets than Chapter 11 bankruptcy.[17] Whether this legislative "this time we really mean it" assertion can weather an actual crisis with its attendant uncertainties, perceived catastrophic downside risks, and "better safe than sorry" reactions by authorities remains to be seen.

Placing blame for the failures that led to the financial crisis on creditors, stockholders and greedy managers who all took advantage of TBTF is somewhat simplistic. For one thing it ignores the enormous losses that were incurred by markets. Some creditors were indeed protected by government intervention, but many were not, including holders of mortgage-backed securities and CDOs. It was entirely predictable that the US. Government, while it might protect US counterparties of distressed banks, would not protect domestic hedge funds and foreign banks holding mortgage-backed securities originated in the US Kaufman (2013) has argued that the point of TBTF bail outs is to protect the creditors and counterparties of distressed firms, not the distressed firm itself. The systemic risk concerns that drove the bail outs during the financial crisis only concerned the

---

[17] Banks already had a smoothly functioning insolvency regime, on which OLA was modeled. This process handled the insolvency of the $180 billion Washington Mutual without disrupting markets, though five years after the fact the FDIC administrative process is continuing and unsecured debtors' claims remain unresolved.

systemically important counterparties, not incidental holders who did not present US systemic risks if they took losses. Stockholders were wiped out or their holding diluted down to trivial proportions. Why did those who lost so much ex post not monitor and influence as market discipline proponents says they should have done? It is difficult to understand why these losses were insufficient to generate market discipline, but greater losses for other counterparties in the future for would do so. It is also important not to forget that some sophisticated counterparties did exert market discipline, only that it was destructive market discipline. Clearly those who withdraw short term funding from floundering banks were not relying on being bailed out.

Moral hazard borne of presumptions that the government would rescue creditors and perhaps stockholders are not the only obstacles to market discipline. Indeed, since financial bubbles and crisis have long preceded deposit insurance and TBTF, the case can be made that the causes of the recent (regulatory and) market failures lie elsewhere—in cognitive failings of humans, or as Mackay (1841) memorably termed it "the madness of crowds."[18] These cognitive failings apply equally to market participants and regulators. Discussing crowds and whole markets is a departure from the firm-specific focus of the prior discussion of market discipline. But as we saw in Elton et al. (2001), systematic effects are a large component of bond prices. And individual securities are no less susceptible to the cognitive failures that lead to market bubbles than are the markets as a whole.

The literature of behavioral economics documents several regularly occurring behaviors that can help to explain the bubble that led to the financial crisis: the *availability heuristic* and *disaster myopia*. The availability heuristic says that people tend to focus on information and experiences that are available to them. Situations that are remote or that have not occurred within their experience are considered to be improbable or impossible. The classic example of this is the "black swan" of Taleb (2007)'s eponymous book. A black swan was considered to be an impossibility as all the swans in Europe were white. Black swans were eventually discovered in Australia. The equivalent belief leading up to the 2007 financial crisis was that a nationwide decline in housing prices was impossible. While local or regional housing price declines were common, a nationwide decline had not been observed, so housing price declines were attributed to uncorrelated local economic factors.[19] As housing prices continued to rise through the 1990s and early 2000s, the belief became wide spread that not only was a broad decline in housing prices impossible, but that housing prices would continue to rise. Various explanations were offered to explain why this had to be so.

Disaster myopia is an extension of the availability heuristic. It occurs when possible adverse events are uncertain in the Knightian sense of immeasurable probability and are extremely rare or have never occurred before. Normal behavioral biases in this situation are for people to assign a probability of zero to such an event. The possibility, therefore, does not enter into their calculations, and so is completely ignored. Guttentag and Herring (1986) discussed this effect in the context of the emerging market debt problems of the 1980s. They also note that the method of compensating managers can lead to a focus on short-term results and discourage investment in information to assess low probability risks. This carries

---

[18] Greenspan's 1996 term "irrational exuberance" is equally apt.
[19] People holding this belief did not recall or look back to the US in the 1930s or Japan in the 1990s.

over to other market participants. People want to believe and human brains are wired to provide this positive reinforcement.

Herring and Watcher (1999) studied disaster myopia in real estate markets across countries. Even though real estate is highly cyclical, developers lose sight of this and expect booms to continue. This leads to over building and another crash. Cornand and Gimet (2012), using an empirical model based on Guttentag and Herring (1986), tested for and found evidence of disaster myopia in the run-up to the 2007–08 US financial crisis. These behavioral biases cause market participants, including managers and regulators, to be less than objective calculators of risks, which in any case are often unknowable.

There is the further complication of rational irrationality. This describes the situation in the midst of a bubble, when even those who sense that prices are overvalued and risks underpriced, will rationally "ride the bubble" hoping to get out in time. As Charles Prince, Chairman of Citigroup until November 2007, famously said "As long as the music is playing, you've got to get up and dance." Trying to fight the bubble by betting against it can lead to losses if your timing is not perfect. Greenspan made his "irrational exuberance" remark in 1996, but it was not until the dot.com bubble burst in 2001 that he was proven to be correct.

Where housing prices seem to be growing at a perpetual prodigious rate, that is the world of recent experience circa 2005, the behavior of financial markets up to then did not seem unreasonable. Loose credit standards did not matter when collateral was appreciating. Mortgages were defaulting at low and manageable historical rates. Banks were profitable and apparently managing their risks well. In April of 2007 the IMF in its World Economic Outlook predicted that housing markets in developed countries were unlikely to cause problems, notwithstanding some high rates of price appreciation which it noted. That housing prices were shortly to fall 30 to 40% was completely beyond the imagination of all but a few Cassandras, who like the original Cassandra were ignored.

24.5 CONCLUSIONS

On the one hand, in retrospect, the accumulations of risks and imbalances were there in plain sight for everyone to see. Housing price inflation was evident and the subject of numerous articles and much discussion for several years before the bubble burst. On the other hand Greenspan rejected the idea that it was possible to detect a bubble in advance. Declining credit standards were well known to regulators if not to purchasers of mortgage-backed securities. Increasing leverage of financial institutions was evident in their financial statements, as was the reliance of short-term wholesale funding at the largest financial firms.

Providers of short-term finance did not price risks they did not perceive due to the above mentioned cognitive biases. Instead, they relied on the ability to recover their funds whenever they wished by declining to roll over their loans. In doing so they ignored the effects of the contagion that this would create, with all similar counterparties trying to recover their funds at the same time. One may argue that the purveyors of some mortgage-backed securities knew they were selling junk, but their firms were buying similar securities and lending to commercial and investment banks that held the securities they originated. The knowledge stayed on the trading desks and does not seem to have moved into "the market."

It is strange to expect that market participants outside the financial system could and should have known that ratings were flawed, and that mortgage credit quality was declining. Proponents of market discipline do not explain how information asymmetries are overcome or how the presumed knowledge of risks becomes incorporated into prices. These are simply assumed. Recent experience strongly suggests that sometimes this does not happen, even when the potential consequences of mispricing are severe. If the behavioral economists are correct and market participants are sometimes myopic, it is understandable that these key links in the chain of logic underpinning market discipline arguments may be missing.

Regulators have been quick to blame a failure of market discipline in substantial part for the 2007–08 financial crisis. They pin their hopes on restored market discipline to avoid a repeat of the mistakes that were made by market participants by seeking to ensure that these participants have proper incentives. This begs the question of how markets were supposed to see what regulators were unable to see with all their information, models, oversight authority and staff. And it ignores just how much regulators are themselves responsible for undermining the incentives that market participants would otherwise have to actively monitor firms. To be fair, regulators and the government face a problem of time inconsistency that is probably insurmountable. In the midst of a crisis they dare not risk a complete meltdown by letting systemically important firms fail, even if they believe that this will create morale hazard in the future.

In summary, the "failure of market discipline" explanation of the financial crisis is predicated on some very strong ideas as to what market discipline can reasonably be expected to do. I have argued here that these ideas rest on weak foundations, both theoretically and empirically. This is decidedly a minority view. If, however, behavioral biases rather than moral hazard were the proximate cause of the crisis, efforts to address future crises through haircuts to creditors and more efficient resolution methods will be disappointed. Worse yet, adequate efforts may not be undertaken to investigate, understand and mitigate the effects of behavioral biases on market participants and regulators.

References

Avery, R. B., Belton, T. M., and Goldberg, M. A. (1988). Market Discipline in Regulating Bank Risk: New Evidence from the Capital Markets, *Journal of Money, Credit & Banking* 20, 597–610.

Balasubramnian, B. and Cyree, K. B. (2011). Market Discipline of Banks: Why Are Yield Spreads on Bank-Issued Subordinated Notes and Debentures Not Sensitive to Bank Risks?, *Journal of Banking & Finance* 35, 21–35.

Berger, A. N. and Turk-Ariss, R. (2013). Do Depositors Discipline Banks and Did Government Actions during the Recent Crisis Reduce This Discipline?. An International Perspective. University of South Carolina Working Paper.

Bliss, R. R. (2001). Market Discipline and Subordinated Debt: A Review of Some Salient Issues, *Federal Reserve Bank of Chicago Economic Perspectives* 25, 24–45.

Bliss, R. R. and Flannery, M. J. (2002). Market Discipline in the Governance of US Bank Holding Companies: Monitoring Vs. Influencing, *European Finance Review* 6, 361–395.

Bond, P., Goldstein, I., and Prescott, E. S. (2010). Market-Based Corrective Actions, *Review of Financial Studies* 23(2), 781–820.

Calomiris, C. W. (1999). Building an Incentive-Compatible Safety Net, *Journal of Banking & Finance* 23, 1499–1519.

Calomiris, C. W. and Powell, A. (2001). Can Emerging Market Bank Regulators Establish Credible Discipline? The Case of Argentina, 1992–99, *Prudential Supervision: What Works and What Doesn't*. NBER Conference Report Series. Chicago and London: University of Chicago Press.

Cannella, A. A., Fraser, D. R., and Lee, D. S. (1995). Firm Failure and Managerial Labor Markets: Evidence from Texas Banking, *Journal of Financial Economics* 38(2), 185–210.

Collin-Dufresne, P., Goldstein, R. S., and Martin, J. S. (2001). The Determinants of Credit Spread Changes, *The Journal of Finance* 56, 2177–2207.

Cornand, C. and Gimet, C. (2012). The 2007–2008 Financial Crisis: Is There Evidence of Disaster Myopia?, *Emerging Markets Review* 13, 301–315.

Covitz, D. M., Hancock, D., and Kwast, M. L. (2004). A Reconsideration of the Risk Sensitivity of US Banking Organization Subordinated Debt Spreads: A Sample Selection Approach, *Federal Reserve Bank of New York Economic Policy Review* 10, 73–92.

Demirgüç-Kunt, A. and Huizinga, H. (2004). Market Discipline and Deposit Insurance, *Journal of Monetary Economics* 51, 375–399.

Deyoung, R., Flannery, M. J., Lang, W. W., and Sorescu, S. M. (2001). The Information Content of Bank Exam Ratings and Subordinated Debt Prices, *Journal of Money, Credit, and Banking* 33, 900–925.

Distinguin, I., Kouassi, T., and Tarazi, A. (2013). Interbank Deposits and Market Discipline: Evidence from Central and Eastern Europe, *Journal of Comparative Economics* 41, 544–560.

Duffee, G. R. (1999). Estimating the Price of Default Risk, *The Review of Financial Studies* 12, 197–226.

Elton, E. J., Gruber, M. J., Agrawal, D., and Mann, C. (2001). Explaining the Rate Spread on Corporate Bonds, *The Journal of Finance* 56, 247–277.

Evanoff, D. D., Jagtiani, J. A., and Nakata, T. (2011). Enhancing Market Discipline in Banking: The Role of Subordinated Debt in Financial Regulatory Reform, *Journal of Economics and Business* 63, 1–22.

Evanoff, D. D. and Wall, L. D. (2001). Sub-Debt Yield Spreads as Bank Risk Measures, *Journal of Financial Services Research* 20, 121–145.

Evanoff, D. D. and Wall, L. D. (2002). Measures of the Riskiness of Banking Organizations: Subordinated Debt Yields, Risk-Based Capital, and Examination Ratings, *Journal of Banking & Finance* 26, 989–1009.

Fama, E. F. (1970). Efficient Capital Markets: A Review of Theory and Empirical Work, *Journal of Finance* 25, 383–417.

Fama, E. F. (1980). Agency Problems and the Theory of the Firm, *Journal of Political Economy* 88, 288–307.

Fama, E. F. (1986). Term Premiums and Default Premiums in Money Markets, *Journal of Financial Economics* 17, 175–196.

Fama, E. F. (1991). Efficient Capital Markets: Ii, *The Journal of Finance* 46, 1575–1617.

Farrell, K. A. and Whidbee, D. A. (2000). The Consequences of Forced CEO Succession for Outside Directors, *Journal of Business* 73, 597–627.

Flannery, M. J. (2010). *Market Discipline in Bank Supervision*. In: A. Berger, P. Molyneux, and J. O. S. Wilson (Eds.), *Oxford Handbook of Banking*. Oxford: Oxford University Press.

Flannery, M. J. and Sorescu, S. M. (1996). Evidence of Bank Market Discipline in Subordinated Debenture Yields: 1983–1991, *The Journal of Finance* 51, 1347–1377.

Gorton, G. and Santomero, A. M. (1990). Market Discipline and Bank Subordinated Debt: Note, *Journal of Money, Credit and Banking* 22, 119–128.

Goyal, V. K. (2005). Market Discipline of Bank Risk: Evidence from Subordinated Debt Contracts, *Journal of Financial Intermediation* 14, 318–350.

Gropp, R., Vesala, J., and Vulpes, G. (2006). Equity and Bond Market Signals as Leading Indicators of Bank Fragility, *Journal of Money, Credit and Banking* 38, 399–428.

Guttentag, J. M. and Herring, R. J. (1986). Disaster Myopia in International Banking, Essays in International Finance No. 164.

Herring, R. J. and Watcher, S. (1999). *Real Estate Booms and Banking Busts: An International Perspective.* Pennsylvania: University of Pennsylvania.

Jagtiani, J. and Lemieux, C. (2001). Market Discipline Prior to Bank Failure, *Journal of Economics and Business* 53, 313–324.

Jensen, M. C. and Meckling, W. H. (1976). Theory of the Firm: Managerial Behavior, Agency Costs and Ownership Structure, *Journal of Financial Economics* 3, 305–360.

Karas, A., Pyle, W., and Schoors, K. (2013). Deposit Insurance, Banking Crises, and Market Discipline: Evidence from a Natural Experiment on Deposit Flows and Rates, *Journal of Money, Credit and Banking* 45, 179–200.

Kaufman, G. G. (2013). Too Big to Fail in Banking: What Does It Mean?. London School of Economics Special Paper Series.

Krainer, J. and Lopez, J. A. (2004). Incorporating Equity Market Information into Supervisory Monitoring Models, *Journal of Money, Credit, and Banking* 36, 1043–1067.

Krainer, J. and Lopez, J. A. (2008). Using Securities Market Information for Bank Supervisory Monitoring, *International Journal of Central Banking* 4, 125–164.

Krishnan, C. N. V., Ritchken, P. H., and Thomson, J. B. (2005). Monitoring and Controlling Bank Risk: Does Risky Debt Help?, *The Journal of Finance* 60, 343–378.

Kwast, M. L., Covitz, D. M., Hancock, D., Houpt, J. V., Adkins, D. P., Barger, N., Bouchard, B., Connolly, J. F., Brady, T. F., English, W. B., Evanoff, D. D., and Wall, L. D. (1999). Using Subordinated Debt as an Instrument of Market Discipline. Federal Reserve Board Board of Governors.

Mackay, C. (1841). *Extraordinary Popular Delusions and the Madness of Crowds.* London: Richard Bentley.

Merton, R. C. (1974). On the Pricing of Corporate Debt: The Risk Structure of Interest Rates, *The Journal of Finance* 29, 449–470.

Merton, R. C. (1977). An Analytic Derivation of the Cost of Deposit Insurance and Loan Guarantees an Application of Modern Option Pricing Theory, *Journal of Banking & Finance* 1, 3–11.

Pettway, R. H. (1976). Market Tests of Capital Adequacy of Large Commercial Banks, *Journal of Finance* 31, 865–875.

Pettway, R. H. (1980). Potential Insolvency, Market Efficiency, and Bank Regulation of Large Commercial Banks, *Journal of Financial and Quantitative Analysis* 15, 219–236.

Pop, A. (2006). Market Discipline in International Banking Regulation: Keeping the Playing Field Level, *Journal of Financial Stability* 2, 286–310.

Prowse, S. (1997). Corporate Control in Commercial Banks, *Journal of Financial Research* 20, 509–527.

Shiller, R. J. (1989). *Market Volatility.* Cambridge, MA: MIT Press.

Sironi, A. (2003). Testing for Market Discipline in the European Banking Industry: Evidence from Subordinated Debt Issues, *Journal of Money, Credit and Banking* 35, 443–472.

Smith, A. (1776). *An Inquiry into the Nature and Causes of the Wealth of Nations.* Dublin: Whitestone.

Taleb, N. N. (2007). *The Black Swan: The Impact of the Highly Improbable*. New York: Random House.

Van Horne, J. C. (1979). Behavior of Default-Risk Premiums for Corporate Bonds and Commercial Paper, *Journal of Business Research 7*, 301–313.

Wall, L. D. (1989). A Plan for Reducing Future Deposit Insurance Losses: Puttable Subordinated Debt, *Federal Reserve Bank of Atlanta Economic Review 74*, 2–17.

CHAPTER 25

···

COMPETITION IN BANKING*

···

HANS DEGRYSE, PAOLA MORALES ACEVEDO, AND STEVEN ONGENA

25.1 INTRODUCTION

···

THE degree of banking competition has implications for borrowers' access to finance, the allocation of funds in an economy and the resulting economic growth, and the degree of financial stability. Appropriately measuring the degree of banking competition over time within and across banking markets is important since if this is not done any policy measures may be misguided.

In this chapter we review the different *methodological approaches* taken to address competition in banking. We discuss the "traditional" and "new" empirical methods employed in industrial organization (IO), specifically applied to banking, and provide a detailed illustration in each section.[1]

We first discuss the traditional studies of structure-conduct-performance (SCP), the efficient-structure hypothesis, and economies of scale and scope. We then turn to the new empirical IO approaches taken by Panzar and Rosse (1987), Boone (2008), the conjectural variations and the structural demand models. We highlight the strengths and weaknesses of these different approaches and are naturally drawn to focus on the differences in data requirements and treatment of endogeneity in each method.

Table 25.1 shows how research on banking competition has evolved over time (Berger, Demirgüç-Kunt et al. 2004). The table highlights that in the early 1990s an important change took place in modeling competition, measuring concentration and conduct, and arriving at

* The authors thank Allen Berger, Philip Molyneux, and John Wilson (the editors) for their comments on an earlier draft. Degryse acknowledges financial support from the Fund for Scientific Research Flanders under FWO G.0719.13.

[1] For general overviews, see also Berger, Demirgüç-Kunt et al. (2004), Shaffer (2004), and Dick and Hannan (2010). We mention more specific reviews further in the text.

Table 25.1 Evolution of research on the impact of bank concentration and competition on bank performance

Element	Early 1990s	Current
Model	SCP Hypothesis	Various Models of Competition
Measures of Concentration	Herfindahl-Hirschman Index or Concentration Ratio for n Banks	Bank Size and Type (Foreign, State) Broader Measures of Competition
Measures of Conduct	Bank Prices Bank Profitability	Bank Efficiency, Service Quality, Risk Firms' Access to Credit Banking System Stability
Empirical Models	Static Cross Section Short Run	Dynamic Effects over Time of Bank Consolidation
Data	US Metropolitan Statistical Areas or Non-MSA Counties	Differently Defined US Markets Other Countries

The figures contrasts the models, the measures of concentration, the measures of conduct, the empirical models, and the data sources that were used in the early 1990s with those that are used today.

Source: Berger; Demirgüç-Kunt et al. (2004).

fruitful applications. The literature basically abandoned the traditional SCP paradigm, stating that banks in more concentrated markets behave less competitively and capture more profits.

The literature has pushed forward in two directions since. One strand of the literature embarked on modeling market structure as endogenous. A second development in the literature intended to capture the "special nature of banking competition" by also looking at non-price dimensions of banking products. We will review this part of the literature in Section 25.2. Section 25.3 summarizes the many empirical studies documenting the impact of competition on loan and deposit conditions and market presence. Section 25.4 deals with the current state of banking regulation and its relation to competition. Section 25.5 presents the relation between information-sharing and competition. Section 25.6 concludes.

25.2 MEASURING BANKING COMPETITION AND MARKET POWER

We start with a review of the different methodological approaches that have been employed to investigate banking competition.[2] This empirical research can be subdivided into the more *traditional IO* and the *new empirical IO* (NEIO) approaches. Within the traditional methods, we distinguish between the *structure-conduct-performance* (SCP) analyses, studies of *the efficient-structure hypothesis*, and studies of *scale and scope economies*. The NEIO

---

[2] Our discussion is partly based on Degryse and Ongena (2008).

methods aim to measure the degree of competition directly and not to employ market structure indicators. We differentiate between the approaches taken by *Panzar and Rosse (1987)*, the *Boone (2008)* indicator, the *conjectural variations* models and *structural demand* models. The usefulness of the different approaches hinges on data availability and the questions being addressed.

25.2.1 Traditional Industrial Organization

25.2.1.1 *Structure-Conduct-Performance*

The SCP model is originally developed by Bain (1956). SCP research was quite popular until the beginning of the 1990s. Table 25.1 summarizes the characteristics of SCP research. The SCP hypothesis argues that higher concentration in the banking market causes less competitive bank conduct and leads to higher bank profitability (but lower performance from a social point of view). To test the SCP hypothesis, researchers typically regress a measure of bank performance, for example, bank profitability, on a proxy for market concentration, that is, an *n*-bank concentration ratio or a Herfindahl–Hirschman Index (HHI).[3] A representative regression specification is:

$$\prod_{ijt} = \alpha_0 + \alpha_1 CR_{jt} + \sum_k \gamma_k X_{k,ijt} + \varepsilon_{ijt} \qquad (25.1)$$

where $\prod_{ijt}$ is a measure of bank *i*'s profitability, in banking market *j* at time *t*, CR_{jt} is the measure of concentration in market *j* at time *t*, and $X_{k,ijt}$ stands for a *k*-vector control variables that may affect bank profits (e.g., variables that control for the profitability implications of risk-taking). Banks operating in more concentrated markets are able (within the SCP paradigm) to set higher loan rates or lower deposit rates as a result of non-competitive behavior or collusion. Hence, the SCP hypothesis implies that $\alpha_1 > 0$, that is, that higher market concentration implies more market power and higher bank profits. The market structure itself, however, is assumed to be exogenous.

The specification taking the market structure as exogenous and the resulting use of the HHI, for instance, have been criticized by Berg and Kim (1998), who estimate a multi-output conjectural variation type of a model to show that concentration must not preclude substantially competitive conduct. In fact, their study of multi-output oligopolies shows that the (Norwegian) retail loan market is plagued by market power whereas the wholesale loan market lacks such power, contrary to the HHI, which produces opposite results.[4]

Numerous studies document a positive statistical relationship between measures of market concentration and bank profitability. As Gilbert (1984) and recently Berger, Demirgüç-Kunt et al. (2004) wrote excellent critical reviews of this early approach, there is no need to make another attempt in this setting. However, to illustrate SCP research in

---

   [3] See Alegria and Schaeck (2008) for a derivation of analytical relationships between the various concentration measures.
   [4] Their calculated HHI for the Norwegian retail and wholesale loan markets averaged between 866 and 2,155, respectively, for the period 1990–92. The US Department of Justice guidelines consider HHI < 1,000 as "unconcentrated" market and HHI > 1,800 as "highly concentrated" (Salop, 1987).

general, we briefly discuss Berger and Hannan (1989). While many studies focus on the *profitability*-concentration link, Berger and Hannan (1989) actually study the *deposit rate–concentration* link. Nevertheless their study is representative for the SCP approach given their measurement of concentration, reduced-form estimation, and interpretation. They use both a three-bank concentration ratio (CR3) and the HHI.[5] Their results overall show a negative impact of market concentration on deposit rates, independent of the concentration measure being used.

While the early SCP approach was successful in documenting the importance of market structure for various bank interest rates, Berger, Demirgüç-Kunt et al. (2004) surely presents the consensus view when they write that empirical banking literature "has now advanced well past this simple approach." We summarize the notable differences between the SCP and more recent studies both within an SCP framework and beyond in Table 25.1.

25.2.1.2 *Efficient-structure hypothesis*

The efficiency hypothesis provides an alternative explanation for the positive link between bank profitability and concentration or market share. The efficiency hypothesis (see Demsetz, 1973; Peltzmann, 1977) entails that more efficient banks will gain market share. Hence market concentration is driven (endogenously) by bank efficiency. Two types of efficiency can be distinguished (Berger, 1995). In an *X-efficiency* narrative, banks with superior management and/or production technologies enjoy higher profits and as a result grow larger market shares. Alternatively, some banks may produce at more *efficient scales* than others, again leading to higher per unit profits, larger market shares, and higher market concentration.

The positive relationship between structure and performance reported in the SCP literature is spurious in the two versions of the efficiency hypothesis, as both structure and performance are determined by efficiency. Initially, the empirical literature aimed to disentangle the SCP and efficiency hypotheses through the following regression specification:

$$\prod_{ijt} = \alpha_0 + \alpha_1 CR_{jt} + \alpha_2 MS_{ijt} + \sum_k \gamma_k X_{k,ijt} + \varepsilon_{ijt} \tag{25.2}$$

with MS_{ijt} the market share of bank i in market j for period t (the notation for the other variables remains the same). The coefficient α_2 will capture the effect of efficiency, due to production technologies or efficiency scales, on the bank's profits, but it may also reflect a bank's relative market power.

SCP implies that $\alpha_1 > 0$, whereas both efficiency hypotheses imply that $\alpha_2 > 0$. Most studies find a positive and statistically significant α_2, but an α_1 close to zero and insignificant. These findings support both efficiency hypotheses, that is, larger market shares go together with higher profitability.[6]

Berg and Kim (1994) argue that conduct has an important effect on both (in)efficiency and scale measurements and therefore the estimation of such should not be carried out

---

[5] As control variables they include time dummies, the one-year growth in market deposits, the proportion of bank branches in total number of branches of financial institutions (including S&L branches), a wage rate, per capita income, and a Metropolitan Statistical Area dummy variable.

[6] Hannan and Prager (2009), for example, combine market concentration with the market share of large (small) (not) primarily-out-of-market banks to account for the impact in the market of large banking organizations on the profitability of the small single-market banks.

independently of market structure and conduct. Berger (1995) goes one step further than the standard bank efficiency study and aims to further differentiate between the SCP and efficiency hypotheses by including direct measures of both X-efficiency and scale efficiency into the regression specification (as additional variables in the $X_{k.ijt}$ vector). He argues that after controlling for efficiency, MS_{ijt} only captures the relative market power of banks. Berger derives both efficiency measures from the estimation of a translog cost function. X-efficiency is separated from random noise by assuming that X-efficiency differences will persist over time while random noise will not. The X-efficiency measure for bank i then equals the ratio of the predicted costs for the most efficient bank in the sample to the predicted costs for bank i for any given vector of outputs and inputs.

Berger (1995) estimates a cost function using data from 4,800 US banks during the 1980s. Including both computed efficiency measures in the performance equation that also contains market share and concentration, Berger finds that in 40 out of 60 regressions, market share actually retains its positive sign. However, the economic significance of market share seems very small: a 1% increase in market share boosts return on assets by less than 0.1%. Nevertheless, Berger interprets these findings as evidence in favor of the relative market power hypothesis: market share does represent market power of larger banks, and their market power may be grounded in advertising, local networks, or business relationships. Results further show that X-efficiency also contributes positively in explaining profits, whereas the results on scale efficiency are mixed and never economically important.

Similarly, De Jonghe and Vander Vennet (2008) aim to discriminate between theories establishing a link between market structure and bank performance and alternative explanations based on efficiency considerations. They argue that the effects of competition and efficiency take time to materialize. Therefore, they analyze the competition–performance relationship using a longer-term concept of firm rents, the franchise value. They find that banks with better management or production technologies possess a long-run competitive advantage. They also find that bank market concentration does not affect all banks equally. Only the banks with a large market share in a concentrated market are able to generate non-competitive rents. For more on X-efficiency studies analyzing financial institutions, we refer the reader to surveys by Allen and Rai (1996), Molyneux, Altunbas, and Gardener (1996), Berger and Humphrey (1997), or work by Turati (2001). We turn to economies of scale and scope in the next subsection.

25.2.1.3   *Studies of Economies of Scale and Scope*

Studies of economies of scale and scope in banking address the question whether financial institutions produce the optimal output mix both in terms of size and composition. In an early paper, Kim (1986) develops cost function separability restrictions amenable for testing the existence of a consistent banking output aggregate. He concludes that such an aggregate fails to exist and thus the specification of a multi-output technology and its resulting economies of scope measure is necessary.

Allen and Rai (1996) estimate economies of scale and scope while controlling for X-efficiency. In particular, they estimate the following equation:

$$\ln(TC_{it}) = f(y_{it}, p_{it}) + \varepsilon_{it} \tag{25.3}$$

where TC_{it}, y_{it}, and p_{it} are total costs, outputs, and input prices of bank i at time t, respectively. They consider only one market (hence, j is dropped as a subscript). ε_{it} is a composite error term that can be decomposed into statistical noise and X-inefficiency. Allen and Rai pursue two identification strategies. First, they follow the so-called *stochastic cost frontier* approach (see also, e.g., Mester, 1993), whereby the error term is assumed to consist of random noise and a one-sided inefficiency measure. Second, they estimate a *distribution-free model*, whereby X-efficiency differences are assumed to persist over time while random noise is not (see also, e.g., Berger, 1993).

Allen and Rai (1996) estimate a translog cost function with total costs due to labor, capital, and borrowed funds, employing data from 24 countries for the period 1988–92. They obtain the price of labor by dividing staff expenses by the total number of employees; the price of fixed capital by dividing capital equipment and occupancy expenses by fixed assets; and interest costs by taking total interest expenses over total interest-bearing liabilities.

Allen and Rai (1996) find evidence of significant scale economies for *small banks* in all countries. Large banks in separated markets[7] on the other hand show significant diseconomies of scale amounting to 5% of optimal output levels. They do not find any evidence of significant economies of scope.[8] Many other papers present comparable results on economies of scale and scope (for detailed reviews, see Berger and Humphrey, 1997; Cavallo and Rossi, 2001).

25.2.2 New Empirical Industrial Organization

A fundamental criticism leveled against the SCP and the efficiency hypotheses relates to the embedded—assumed—one-way causality from market structure to performance. In other words, most SCP studies do *not* take into account the conduct of the banks in the market and the impact of performance of the banks on market structure. In fact, studies that have attempted to determine the degree of competition relying on various indexes of concentration such as the C3, the HHI, and the like, reach conflicting and troublesome results. Carbo et al. (2009) document that the coefficients of determination among these various indexes for both the within and between countries are very weak (most <40%). They use cross-country European data for the 1995–2001 period. The implication of these results is that the SCP nexus may not generate consistent results which make the assessment of the competitive state of the banking sector difficult to determine.

---

[7] *Separated* banking occurs in countries that prohibit the functional integration of commercial and investment banking.

[8] Vander Vennet (2002) revisits the issue employing a large European dataset. He distinguishes between universal banks, financial conglomerates (institutions that offer the entire range of financial services), and specialized banks. In contrast to previous studies, he nicely allows for heterogeneity in bank types within each country. In line with Allen and Rai (1996) he finds large unexploited *scale* economies for the small-specialized banks. But, in addition Vander Vennet (2002) also reports unexploited *scope* economies for the smallest specialized banks and for the largest financial conglomerates and universal banks.

New empirical industrial organization (NEIO) circumvents this problem and does not infer the degree of competition from "indirect proxies" such as market structure or market shares, or argue that market structure is the result of the degree of competition. Indeed, NEIO focuses directly on firms' conduct in response to changes in demand and supply conditions without even taking into account market structure – employing a variety of alternative methodologies with sometimes substantially different data requirements. We highlight a number of approaches.

25.2.2.1 *Panzar and Rosse (1987)*

Panzar and Rosse (1987) present a reduced form approach using industry or bank-level data to discriminate between three types of conduct, i.e., perfect competition, monopolistic competition, and monopoly. The Panzar and Rosse methodology investigates the extent to which changes in factor input prices are reflected in equilibrium industry or bank-specific revenues. The associated measure of competition, usually called the H-statistic, is obtained as the sum of elasticities of gross revenue of the banks with respect to their factor input prices. In most studies, three different input prices are considered: (1) the *deposit rate*, measured by the ratio of annual interest expenses to total assets; (2) *wages*, measured by the ratio of personnel expenses to total assets; and (3) *price of equipment or fixed capital*, measured by the ratio of capital expenditures and other expenses to total assets.

A monopoly situation yields an *H*-statistic that can be negative or zero. What will happen to a monopolist's revenues when all factor prices increase with 1%? For a monopolist such increase in factor prices leads to lower revenues (since the price elasticity of demand exceeds one). In other words, the sum of the elasticities should be negative. Perfect competition implies an *H*-statistic equal to 1. Indeed, an increase in input prices augments both marginal costs and total revenues to the same extent as the original increase in input prices. Monopolistic competition yields values of *H* in between 0 and 1. Banks will produce more but less than would be optimal in each individual case, leading to an *H*-statistic between 0 and 1.

Many studies bring the Panzar and Rosse (1987) methodology to banking. Bikker and Haaf (2002) offer a broad review of the results of many other studies (their table 4). By far the most comprehensive application to date of the Panzar and Rosse (1987) methodology is a paper by Claessens and Laeven (2004). They compute the Panzar and Rosse *H*-statistic for 50 countries for the period 1994–2001. Their results show that most banking markets are actually characterized by monopolistic competition with *H*-statistics ranging between 0.6 and 0.8. In addition, Claessens and Laeven aim to identify factors that determine banking competition across countries by regressing the estimated country *H*-statistics on a number of country characteristics. They find no evidence of a negative relationship between bank system concentration and H, but find that fewer entry and activity restrictions result in higher H-statistics and hence more competition.[9]

Recent studies have criticized the commonly used procedure on the estimation of the H-statistic. According to Goddard and Wilson (2009), the static revenue equation reported

---

[9] Consistently using the H-statistic as a measure of competition, Schaeck, Čihák, and Wolfe (2009) find that concentration and competition have independent effects on the likelihood and timing of systemic crisis, suggesting that these two measures describe different characteristics of banking systems.

widely in previous applications of the Panzar and Rosse test is misspecified. The reason for this is that the identification of the H-statistic, using a fixed effect panel model, relies upon the assumption that markets are in long-run equilibrium at each point in time. However, in practice, adjustment towards equilibrium is not instantaneous, and markets are out of equilibrium either frequently or always. A partial adjustment equation better describes adjustment towards equilibrium in response to factor input price shocks. Therefore, the revenue equation should contain a lagged dependent variable and dynamic panel estimation should be used instead of a static panel estimator.

Moreover, according to Bikker, Shaffer, and Spierdijk (2012), there is an inconsistency between the theoretical Panzar and Rosse model and its empirical application. The inconsistency appears when a price equation or a scaled revenue function is applied instead of a revenue equation. The authors show that the properties of the price and revenue equations are identical in the case of long-run equilibrium but different in the case of monopoly or oligopoly. Therefore, only an unscaled revenue equation yields a valid measure of the degree of competition.

25.2.2.2 *The Boone (2008) Competition Indicator*

Boone (2008) introduces a new way to measure competition. He develops the idea of the elasticity of profits toward marginal costs or "profit elasticity". In particular, they postulate the following specification:

$$\ln \pi_i = \alpha - \beta \ln(c_i) \qquad (25.4)$$

where β gives the profit elasticity, that is, the percentage drop in profits of bank i as a result of a percentage increase in bank i's marginal costs. The larger is β, the more intense the competition. Boone, van Ours, and van der Wiel (2007) review how several theoretical models show that both changes in entry conditions and strategic behavior influence in the correct way the profit elasticity.

van Leuvensteijn, Bikker, van Rixtel and Sørensen (2011) introduce two modifications to the specification. The first is that they employ a translog cost function to estimate the marginal cost c_i, while Boone, van Ours and van der Wiel (2007) employed average variable costs as a proxy. Second, van Leuvensteijn et al. (2011) use the bank's market shares as a left-hand-side variable instead of profits. They apply this methodology for several product categories for the time period 1994–04.

They find that competition in the bank loan market varies considerably across countries. In particular, the bank loan market in the Euro area is less competitive than the US market — where $\hat{\beta}$ equals 5.41 — but more competitive than in the United Kingdom ($\hat{\beta}$ = 1.05) and Japan ($\hat{\beta}$ = 0.72). Within the Euroarea, the German and Spanish market seems most competitive ($\hat{\beta}$ equals 3.38 and 4.15, respectively) and least competitive in France ($\hat{\beta}$ = 0.90).

Schaeck and Čihák (2010) estimate the Boone indicator for a European and US sample over the period 1995–2005. They find substantial heterogeneity in the degree of banking competition across Europe. Interestingly, they report that the Boone index captures over 80% of the variation in many other features of banking competition in Europe, suggesting that the Boone index truly is a comprehensive indicator of competition.

25.2.2.3 *Conjectural-Variations Method*

Another methodology to infer the degree of competition was introduced by Iwata (1974), Bresnahan (1982), and Lau (1982). This methodology is often referred to as the conjectural-variations method. It is based on the idea that a bank when choosing its output takes into account the "reaction" of rival banks. The equilibrium oligopoly price is then characterized by the following first-order condition:

$$P(Q,Y;\alpha) + \lambda QP'(Q,Y;\alpha) = C'(Q,Z;\beta) \tag{25.5}$$

where P is the market's equilibrium price, $P(Q,Y;\alpha)$ is the market inverse demand function, Q the market level quantity, and $C'(Q,Z;\beta)$ is the market marginal cost. α and β are vectors of unknown parameters associated with demand and costs, respectively. Y and Z are a vector of variables that affect demand and costs, respectively. λ is the conjectural elasticity of total bank industry output to variation of bank i output; that is, $\lambda = \dfrac{\partial Q}{\partial Q_i} \dfrac{Q_i}{Q}$. In other words, λ is the perceived response of industry output to a change in quantity by bank i (for more on this methodology, see Vives, 1999).

One can also compute the conjectural elasticity or conduct parameter as:

$$\lambda = \eta(P)\left[\frac{P-MC}{P}\right], \tag{25.6}$$

where $\eta(P)$ is the price elasticity of demand, and $MC[= C'(Q,Z;\beta)]$ the marginal cost. This implies that λ is the elasticity-adjusted Lerner index. An attractive feature of the conjectural variations model is the possibility to write different types of competition compactly. It nests the joint profit maximization (λ =1), perfect competition (λ =0), and the Cournot equilibrium or zero-conjectural variations model (λ =1/I with I the number of firms in the market; that is, the perceived variation of other participants in the industry to changes in bank i's output is zero).[10]

Shaffer (1993) applied this specific conjectural variations method to the Canadian banking sector, using annual data from 1965 to 1989.[11] Shaffer (1993) follows the so-called intermediation approach of banking. According to this view, banks use labor and deposits to originate loans. The quantity of output Q is the dollar value of assets and the price P is the interest rate earned on assets. Input prices are the annual wage rate and the deposit rate.[12] The exogenous variables are output and the three-month Treasury bill rate. The regression results show that λ is not significantly different from zero, implying that the estimates are consistent with perfect competition. Shaffer (1989) actually shows that US banking markets are even

[10] The conjectural variations approach has been subject to a number of important criticisms. Corts (1999) for example argues that the conduct parameter λ may not only hinge on the firm's static first-order condition, but also on the dynamics, i.e., the incentive compatibility constraints associated with collusion. In the dynamic case, the estimated λ may be biased when the incentive compatibility constraints are a function of demand shocks.

[11] For an earlier application of the conjectural variations method, see Spiller and Favaro (1984).

[12] In certain specifications, researchers also include the price of capital, since this price may vary over time.

more competitive than Cournot competition (λ is again close to zero and not statistically significant).

25.2.2.4 Structural Demand Models

Another strand of the NEIO uses characteristics-based demand systems. Dick (2008), for example, estimates a demand model for deposit services following a methodology prevalent in the discrete choice literature.[13] Consumers choose for a particular bank based on prices and bank characteristics. More formally, consider that consumers c and banks i populate markets j. The utility a consumer c derives from depositing at bank i stems both from individual and product characteristics. The consumer utility includes both the mean utility from buying at bank i in market j, δ_{ij}, and a mean zero random disturbance, ε_{cij}:

$$u_{cij} \equiv \delta_{ij} + \varepsilon_{cij} \equiv p_{ij}^d \alpha^s + X_{k,ij}\beta + \xi_i + \varepsilon_{cij} \tag{25.7}.$$

p_{ij}^d represents the deposit rate paid by bank i in market j; p_{ij}^s are the service charges on deposits by bank i in market j; $X_{k,ij}$ is a vector capturing k observed product characteristics for the (singular) product offered by bank i in market j; ξ_i are the unobserved bank product characteristics. The taste parameters to be estimated are α^d, α^s and β.

Making assumptions on the distribution of ε_{ci} then allows obtaining a closed form solution for the market share of bank i. A multinomial logit specification is obtained when assuming that ε_{ci} is identically and independently distributed (i.i.d) extreme value, yielding the bank i's market share s_i in market j:

$$s_i = \frac{\exp(\delta_i)}{\sum_{r=0}^{I_j} \exp(\delta_r)} \tag{25.8}.$$

Other assumptions may yield a nested logit model.[14]

Dick (2008) estimates this discrete choice model on US data for the period 1993–99. Her results indicate that consumers respond significantly to changes in deposit rates but to a lesser extent to changes in account fees. Bank characteristics such as geographic diversification, density of the local branch network, bank age, and size increase the attractiveness of a bank to consumers.

25.3 COMPETITION: CONDUCT AND STRATEGY

The previous section showed that the competition literature has made substantial progress by modeling market structure as endogenous. Furthermore, methodologies have

---

[13] See also Molnár (2007) and Molnár, Nagy, and Horvath (2007) for example.

[14] The idea in the nested logit model is that consumer tastes are correlated across bank products i. Making a priori groups G, a product i belonging to one of the groups then provides a utility to consumer c equal to $u_{cij} \equiv \delta_{ij} + \zeta_{cg} + [1-\delta]\varepsilon_{cij}$, where ζ_{cg} denotes the group specific component for individual c.

been developed to exploit the rich heterogeneity and different dimensions of the available datasets. However, it has been argued that the standard competitive paradigm is not appropriate for the banking industry (Vives, 1991; Vives, 2001; Allen et al. 2001; Carletti, 2008). Hence, to capture the "special nature of banking competition," we review the available empirical evidence and structure our discussion within a framework that finds its roots within the different theories explaining the existence of financial intermediation. We start discussing the impact of market structure on loan and deposit conditions and then turn to the question of whether market structure determines market presence.

25.3.1 Market Structure and Conduct

25.3.1.1 Loan Markets

Local Markets: There is ample empirical work starting from the SCP paradigm investigating the impact of bank market concentration on bank loan rates (for a review, see e.g., Gilbert and Zaretsky, 2003). Though mostly positive, the magnitude of the impact of the concentration index on loan rates varies widely. Recent studies, for example, indicate that a Δ HHI = 0.1 increases the loan rate by between 21 to 55 bp in the United States (Cyrnak and Hannan, 1999) and 59 bp in Italy (Sapienza, 2002), but only 3 bp in Norway (Kim, Kristiansen, and Vale, 2005) and –4 to 5 bp in Belgium (Degryse and Ongena, 2005). However, it remains difficult to compare results across specifications, banking markets, periods, and HHI measures that are alternatively based on loans, deposits, or branches, and vary widely (across studies) in geographical span (Morgan, 2002). Indeed, a serious related problem of interpretation is that local market concentration is often negatively correlated with market size.

In their seminal paper, Petersen and Rajan (1995) investigate the effects of competition between banks not only on the loan rate but also on the availability of bank credit to firms. Petersen and Rajan model how especially firms with uncertain future cash flows are negatively affected by competition between banks. Banks may be unwilling to invest in relationships by incurring initial loan losses that may never be recouped in the future (as firms can later on obtain a low loan rate in a competitive banking or financial market).

Petersen and Rajan provide evidence that young firms—having uncertain future cash flows—in more concentrated banking markets obtain substantially lower loan rates than firms in more competitive banking markets. The loan rates decreases by more than 150 bp for de novo firms, if the HHI increases by 0.1. They also document somewhat easier access to bank credit in more concentrated markets, but even for young firms the effects seem modest economically speaking and statistically not always significant.[15]

Similarly, Cetorelli (2004) using the sum of total assets of the three and of the five largest banks as a measure of concentration, find that firms that are more dependent on

---

[15] Carbó Valverde, Rodriguez Fernández, and Udell (2009) compare the "performance" of the HHI and Lerner index for the Petersen and Rajan (1995) credit availability hypothesis.

external finance (i.e. younger ones) enjoy a beneficial effect from a concentrated banking sector. Moreover, Bonaccorsi di Patti and Dell'Ariccia (2004) find that market power is more favorable to the emergence of new firms in industrial sectors where informational asymmetries are more important.

In contrast, Black and Strahan (2002) find that the deregulation of restrictions on branching and interstate banking stimulated rates of incorporation in the United States, suggesting that access to finance increases following deregulation. According to Kerr and Nanda (2009) this is particularly true for small startups. Similarly, Cetorelli and Strahan (2006) using data on US local markets for banking and non-financial sectors, find that policies that fostered competition, such as branching and interstate banking deregulation, increase the rate of new incorporations. In particular, the share of small firms increases substantially with better bank competition. Moreover, Jayaratne and Strahan (1996) find an increase in the rate of real, per capital growth following intrastate branch deregulation. They argue that improvement in bank lending quality is the main channel through which competition affect economic growth.

More recently, Rice and Strahan (2010) use differences in regulatory barriers to interstate branching as an instrument to test how credit competition affects credit supply to small firms. They find that in states where restrictions on out-of-state entry are tight, firms pay higher interest rates than similar firms operating where restrictions are loose. This suggests that branching expands competition and credit supply. They, however, do not find and effect on the loan amount. Similarly, using the Lerner index as a measure of market power in a sample of Spanish SMEs, Carbó Valverde, Rodriguez Fernández, and Udell (2009), find that market power is negatively related to credit availability.[16]

Multimarket: The presence of banks operating in several geographical areas or several industries—multimarket banks—may impact local loan rate conditions. The influence on the local loan rates depends on whether the multimarket banks apply uniform or discriminatory pricing across local markets and on the structure of each local banking market (including the importance of the multimarket banks present in that market).

Radecki (1998), for example, reports that most banks set uniform rates on auto loans and home equity loans *within* a US state. Loan rates, however, can differ *across* states. Berger, Rosen, and Udell (2007) address the issue of whether in the US large regional or nationwide banks compete in different ways than do small, local institutions. Their study is motivated by the observation that US banking consolidation over the period 1984–98 had only a minor impact on "local" HHI but a major effect on bank size because many "market-extension" mergers and acquisitions (M&As), that is, mergers between banks operating in different local markets, took place. Berger, Rosen, and Udell (2007) document that loan rates to SMEs (small and medium-size enterprises) are lower in markets with a large bank presence. They find that interest rate spreads charged in markets with a large bank presence are 35 bp lower than in other markets; on the other hand, the probability these SMEs obtain a loan may also be lower (Craig and Hardee, 2007).

---

[16] The effect of concentration on credit availability may further depend on how the bank–firm transactions are mediated, as in De Mello (2007) and Montoriol Garriga (2006).

A key paper by Sapienza (2002) investigates the impact of Italian bank M&As on interest rates to continuing borrowers. She actually compares the impact of "in-market" versus "out-of-market" bank mergers on loan rates. Interestingly enough, she finds that "in-market" mergers decrease loan rates but only if the acquired bank has a sufficiently low local market share. The decrease in loan rates is much less important for "out-of-market" mergers.

Panetta, Schivardi, and Shum (2009) study the link between firm risk, measured by bank credit ratings, and interest rates. They find that the risk-rate schedule becomes steeper after bank mergers (i.e., the merged bank prices risk sharper) and attribute this result to the informational benefits arising from bank mergers. Important in this context is their finding that the risk-rate schedules are even steeper for "out-of-market" than for "in-market" mergers, suggesting that "out-of-market" mergers even yield more informational benefits to the banks than "in-market" mergers. Finally, a paper by Berger, Hasan, and Klapper (2004) reports cross-country evidence on the importance of small, domestic, community banks for local economic activity in general. They find that higher shares of community banks in local bank markets are associated with more overall bank lending, faster GDP growth, and higher SME employment.

25.3.1.2 Deposit Markets

Local Market: There is also a long line of research, at least going back to Berger and Hannan (1989), investigating the impact of bank market concentration on bank deposit rates. Studies employ both the three-bank concentration ratio (CR3) and the HHI as concentration measures. Overall, most papers find a negative impact of an increase in concentration on time and savings deposit rates, but as with the loan rate studies, the effects vary across samples and specifications. We take a change in CR3 by 0.3 to be approximately comparable to a change in HHI by 0.1. The effect of the changes in either the CR3 or HHI on US time and savings deposits rates ranges then from –26 to –1 and from –27 to +5 bp, respectively. Rates on demand deposits seem less affected by market concentration with estimates varying from –18 to +10 bp. But there is evidence of more downward price rigidity and upward price flexibility in demand deposit rates than in time deposit rates especially in more concentrated markets (Neumark and Sharpe, 1992).

More recent studies typically find smaller negative effects for all deposit products, possibly reflecting the widening geographical scope of banking competition (Radecki, 1998) and the ensuing difficulties delineating the relevant local market (Heitfield, 1999; Biehl, 2002). Geographical markets in the United States for demand deposits may be currently "smaller than statewide" but not necessarily "local" (Heitfield and Prager, 2004), suggesting both local and statewide measures of concentration and multimarket contact variables should be included in the analysis. Heitfield and Prager (2004) find that the coefficients on "state" concentration measures became larger in absolute value over time than the coefficients on the "local" measures in particular for demand deposits. In 1999, for example, a 0.1 change in the local HHI affected the NOW deposit rate by only –1 bp while a similar change in the state HHI decreased the rate by 23 bp. Finally, Rosen (2007) finds that in addition to multimarket bank presence, market size structure also has an impact on deposit rates.

A paper by Corvoisier and Gropp (2002) studies European national banking markets, in geographical and economic span often comparable to US states. They find a substantial effect of −70 bp on demand deposit rates (corresponding an increase in HHI of 0.1), but a surprising increase of +50 and +140 bp for time and savings deposits rates. Corvoisier and Gropp argue that local markets are more relevant for demand deposits, whereas customers may shop around for time and savings deposits. Shopping around would imply an increase in contestability, breaking the expected link between HHI and this deposit rate. Demand deposit rates are often posted within a national market after being determined at the banks' headquarters where competition (or lack thereof) may be perceived to be nationwide. On the other hand, for the time and savings deposit markets the coefficient on HHI may actually pick up bank efficiency (even though various bank cost measures are included) or the effect of bank mergers caused by an unobservable increase in contestability. In any case, this study again underlines the methodological difficulties in interpreting the reduced form coefficients in interest rate-market concentration studies.

Multimarket: A number of papers explore the impact of multimarket banks on deposit pricing. Radecki (1998) provides evidence of uniform pricing across branches of banks operating throughout an entire US state or large regions of a state. He interprets this finding as evidence in favor of an increase of the geographic reach of deposit markets over time. Heitfield (1999) shows, however, that uniform pricing is practiced only by multimarket banks that operate statewide, and not between single-market banks that operate in different cities within the same state. Hence, "charging the same deposit rate" may result from a deliberate decision of uniform pricing and not mechanically from a geographical expansion of market boundaries. Heitfield and Prager (2004) further fine-tune the previous findings by exploring heterogeneity in the pricing of several deposit products. They report that the geographic scope of the markets for NOW accounts remains local, but that the scope of money market deposit accounts and savings accounts markets has broadened over time.

Hannan and Prager (2004) explore the competitive impact of multimarket banks on local deposit conditions, using US data for 1996 and 1999. They document that multimarket banks offer lower deposit rates than single-market banks operating in the same market. Moreover, a greater presence of multimarket banks relaxes competition as single-market banks offer lower deposit rates. On the other hand, Calem and Nakamura (1998) argue that multimarket banks mitigate localized market power in rural areas,[17] but that multimarket branching reduces competition in already competitive (urban) markets. Work by Barros (1999) reasons that the presence of banks across markets may lead to local interest rate dispersion, without implying different conduct of banks. Collusive behavior among banks could impact the degree of price dispersion. His empirical findings for Portugal provide strong support for Nash behavior, but given the small sample size, collusion cannot be rejected. Using a similar setup, collusive behavior among Spanish banks in the loan market in the early 1990s cannot be rejected (Jaumandreu and Lorences, 2002).

---

[17] Rosen (2007) finds that having more large banks in a market generally increases deposit rates at all banks but also increases their sensitivity to changes in the concentration ratio.

What about the impact of M&As? Focarelli and Panetta (2003) document that "in-market" mergers hurt depositors in the short run due to lower deposit rates—a drop of 17 bp. The short-run impact of "out-of-market" mergers, however, is negligible. In the long run, depositors gain from both "in-market" and "out-of-market" mergers as deposit rates increase with 14 and 12 bp, respectively, compared to the premerger level. Hence, in the long-run efficiency gains may dominate over the market power effect of bank mergers, leading to more favorable deposit rates for consumers. However, notice that Craig and Dinger (2009) do not find such an increase in rates.

25.3.1.3 *Interplay between Markets*

The links between the different banking markets have also been empirically investigated.[18] Park and Pennacchi (2009), for example, discuss the impact of the entry by large multimarket banks on competition in *both* loan and deposit markets. Park and Pennacchi (2009) posit that multimarket banks may enjoy a funding advantage in the wholesale market. As a result, they establish that a higher presence of the multimarket banks promotes competition in loan markets, but harms competition in deposit markets if these multimarket banks have funding advantages. Hence, their paper nicely shows that the impact of "size structure" could be asymmetric across markets.

25.4 BANKING REGULATION AND COMPETITION

Banking is an industry that in most countries is subject to a tight set of regulations (for reviews, see, e.g., Vives, 1991; Fischer and Pfeil, 2004). Some of the regulations tend to *soften competition*. Examples include restrictions on the entry of new banks or limitations of the free deployment of competitive tools by banks. Other regulations *restrict banking activities* in space and scope, putting limitations on the bank's potential to diversify and exploit scale/scope economies. Finally, there is *prudential* regulation that alters the competitive position of banks vis-à-vis other non-bank institutions (see, e.g., Dewatripont and Tirole, 1994). In the last two decades, several countries including the European Union countries and the United States have implemented a series of deregulatory changes with the objective to stimulate competition and to enhance financial integration.

25.4.1 Regulation and Market Structure

A number of papers investigate whether specific deregulatory initiatives have changed competition. Angelini and Cetorelli (2003), for example, consider the impact of the Second

---

[18] Kashyap, Rajan, and Stein (2002) for example link lending and deposit taking at the bank level, while Berg and Kim (1998) connect behavior in retail and corporate banking markets.

European Banking Directive on competition within the Italian banking industry, by analyzing data over the period 1983–97. Using a conjectural-variations model they compute a
Lerner index L for bank i:

$$L \equiv \frac{p_i - MC_i}{p_i} = \frac{-\dfrac{\theta_i}{\tilde{\varepsilon}}}{p_i}, \qquad (25.9)$$

with θ_i the conjectural elasticity of total industry output with respect to the output of bank

i, and $\tilde{\varepsilon} = \dfrac{\partial Q / \partial p}{Q}$ the market demand semi-elasticity to the price. The computed Lerner

index remained constant during the 1983–1992 period but steadily decreased thereafter, suggesting a substantial increase in the degree of competition after 1993.

Angelini and Cetorelli (2003) further explore whether the changes in the Lerner index
after 1993 can be attributed to the second banking directive. After controlling for changes
in market structure (HHI, number of banks operating in each regional market, number
of branches per capita) and some other exogenous variables, they find that a dummy variable equal to one for years in the period 1993–1997 explains a considerable fraction of the
drop in the Lerner index. The Lerner index drops from about 14 percentage points before
1992 to about 6% points after 1992. The deregulation dummy can explain about 5% points
of this drop.

Gual (1999) studies the impact of European banking deregulation over the period 1981–
1995 on the European banking market structure. He computes the elasticity of concentration to competition (which is directly measured by deregulation): evaluated at the sample
means, an increase in deregulation of 10% leads to an increase in the CR5 ratio of 0.86%.

Goddard et al. (2011) adopt a dynamic view of competition, in contrast with the essentially static SCP paradigm and NEIO approaches. They use the persistence of bank profit as
an indicator of the intensity of competition. They find that legal barriers to entry decrease
the intensity of competition, enabling banks to retain a significant portion of their abnormal
profits from year to year.

Finally, in a widely cited study Spiller and Favaro (1984) look at the effects of entry regulation on oligopolistic interaction in the Uruguayan banking sector. Before June 1978 entry
was totally barred. They find unexpectedly that following the relaxation of the legal entry
barriers the degree of oligopolistic interaction among the leading banks actually reduces,
pointing to less competition.

25.4.2 Regulation and Bank Conduct

How does banking regulation contribute to bank interest margins? Jayaratne and Strahan
(1998) find that permitting statewide branching and interstate banking in the United States
decreased operating costs and loan losses, reductions that were ultimately passed on to borrowers in lower loan rates. And using data from banks covering 72 countries a recent paper
by Demirgüç-Kunt, Laeven, and Levine (2004) examines the impact of banking regulation on bank net interest margins. The information on commercial banking regulation is
taken from Barth, Caprio, and Levine (2001). Regulatory variables include the fraction of

entry that is denied, a proxy for the degree to which banks face regulatory restrictions on their activities in, for example, securities markets and investment banking, and a measure of reserve requirements. They also employ an indicator of "banking freedom," taken from the Heritage Foundation, which provides an overall index of the openness of the banking industry and the extent to which banks are free to operate their business. The different regulatory variables are entered one at a time in a regression that also features bank-specific and macroeconomic controls.

The results in Demirgüç-Kunt, Laeven, and Levine (2004) indicate that restrictive banking regulation substantially hikes net interest margins. For example, a one standard deviation increase in entry or activity restrictions, reserve requirements, or banking freedom, result respectively in 50, 100, 51, and 70 bp extra for the incumbent banks. However, when including, in addition to the bank-specific and macroeconomic controls, also an index of property rights, the regulatory restrictions turn insignificant and do not provide any additional explanatory power. Demirgüç-Kunt, Laeven, and Levine (2004) interpret this result as indicating that banking regulation reflects something broader about the competitive environment. Their interpretation fits with findings in Kroszner and Strahan (1999) and Garrett, Wagner, and Wheelock (2005), who investigate the political and economic drivers of bank branching deregulation across US states, and with results in Jayaratne and Strahan (1996) showing that loan rates decrease with 30 bp on average following deregulation.

25.4.3 Regulation and Bank Strategy

How does the presence of *foreign banks* influence competition? Foreign-owned banks may not only compete in different ways than domestically owned institutions but could also be affected differently by domestic regulation. Levine (2004) distinguishes between entry restrictions for foreign versus domestic banks (he thus further refines the analysis by Demirgüç-Kunt, Laeven, and Levine, 2004). Levine substantiates that foreign bank entry restrictions determine interest rate margins,[19] while domestic bank entry restrictions do not. Foreign banks that are often more efficient than domestic banks could enter in many transition or developing countries, for example, because government officials did not try to encourage private, domestic institutions to combine into "National Champions" by delaying or denying foreign entry (Berger, 2007). In contrast to the contribution, then, of foreign ownership of domestic banks on the banking efficiency in these nations, the fraction of the domestic banking industry held by foreign banks does not determine bank interest margins.

Jeon, Olivero, and Wu (2011) analyze the impact of foreign bank penetration on the competitive structure of banking sectors in host emerging economies. They find that foreign bank penetration increases the level of banking competition. This effect becomes stronger when more efficient and less risky foreign banks enter the host banking markets, and when the market penetrated is less concentrated.

---

[19] Magri, Mori, and Rossi (2005) for example document that foreign banks successfully entered the Italian banking market following the lowering of the regulatory barriers under the Second Directive enacted in 1992.

State-owned banks may also compete in different ways than privately owned institutions. Government ownership of banks remains pervasive around the world, in particular in developing countries (La Porta, Lopez-de-Silanes, and Shleifer, 2002). Cross-country exercises indicate that more state ownership of the banking sector leads to less competition (Barth, Caprio, and Levine, 2004) and slower subsequent financial development (La Porta, Lopez-de-Silanes and Shleifer, 2002). However, firms that actually borrow from state-owned banks pay less than the firms that borrow from the privately owned banks (Sapienza, 2004). If this relatively lower interest rate is actually granted to the less productive firms, then state-owned banks may in fact contribute to the misallocation of credit eventually propagating stagnation and negatively affecting economic growth.[20]

In general bank supervisory policies could also affect the availability of credit. Beck, Demirgüç-Kunt, and Levine (2006b), for example, show that mandating official supervisory agencies to monitor, discipline and influence banks directly may actually increase the degree to which bank corruption is an obstacle to firms raising external finance. On the other hand, facilitating private monitoring by enforcing public disclosure of accurate information by banks tends to dissipate corruption as an obstacle.

25.4.4 Regulation and Financial Stability and Development

Do regulatory restrictions offer benefits/costs in other dimensions? The literature is divided in two different views of the link between competition and stability. On the one hand, according to the "competition-fragility" view, more competition decreases bank profit margins and therefore, in order to increase the returns, banks' might have incentives to take excessive risks. Thus, under this view regulatory restrictions are beneficial for the financial stability (e.g., Keeley, 1990; Besanko and Thakor, 1993; Marquez, 2002). On the other hand, according to the "competition-stability" view, more market power is associated with higher loan rates and lower repayment probability. Consequently, under this view regulatory restrictions are detrimental for financial stability (e.g., Boyd and De Nicolo, 2005).

A large empirical literature provides support for the "competition-fragility" view. Keeley (1990) finds that increased competition, following relaxation of state branching restrictions in the US, raised monopoly rents and resulted in an increase on bank failures. Consistently, Salas and Saurina (2003) find that greater market power is correlated with higher bank solvency ratios and lower credit risk losses, in the Spanish banking system. For Italy, Bofondi and Gobbi (2004) explore the link between entry in local credit markets and default rates of the loans extended by the entrants. They find that default rates increase as the number of participants in the market increases.

Dick and Lehnert (2010) analyze the variation from state-level banking deregulation in the US throughout the 1980s and early 1990s. They find that deregulation, by removing the barriers to out-of-state bank entry, increase credit market competition and therefore lead

---

[20] This issue is related to the so-called Zombie lending phenomenon (Caballero, Hoshi, and Kashyap, 2008).

banks to adopt better screening and monitoring technologies, facilitating the extension of credit to riskier and previously excluded borrowers. Levy Yeyati and Micco (2007) find that by increasing the degree of product differentiation, foreign penetration reduces competition and induce lower risk levels in eight Latin American countries.

Beck, De Jonghe, and Schepens (2013) examines the role of the regulatory framework in explaining the cross-country variation in the relationship between competition and stability in the banking system. As a measure of competition they use the Lerner index and as a measure of banks' stability they use the Z-score. They find, on average, a positive relationship between competition and bank's fragility. This relationship becomes stronger in countries where the deposit insurance is more generous and there are more restrictions on the permissible range of activities.

The "competition-stability" view is supported by more recent literature. Boyd, De Nicolo, and Jalal (2006) find cross-country empirical evidence of a negative relationship between bank risk, measure by the Z-score, and concentration, measure by the HHI. Thus, more concentrated banking systems are associated with a larger risk of bank failure. De Nicolò and Loukoianova (2007) find that this result is stronger when bank ownership is taking into account and it is strongest when state-owned banks have sizeable market shares.

Beck, Demirgüç-Kunt, and Levine (2006a) study the impact of bank concentration, bank regulation, and national institutions fostering, for example, competition or property rights on the likelihood of experiencing a banking crisis. They find that fewer regulatory restrictions—lower barriers to bank entry and fewer restrictions on bank activities—lead to less banking fragility, suggesting that regulatory restrictions are not beneficial in the stability dimension. Schaeck, Čihák, and Wolfe (2009), using the Panzar and Rosse H-statistic, find that competition reduces the likelihood of a crisis and increases time to crisis. This suggests that policies promoting competition among banks may have potential to improve also systemic stability.

Berger, Klapper, and Turk-Ariss (2009) regress measures of loan risk, bank stability, and bank equity capital on several measures of market power, using bank-level data for 23 countries. Consistent with the "competition-stability" view, their findings suggest that banks with higher degree of market power have riskier loan portfolios. However, they also find that due to additional holdings of equity capital, banks with more market power have less risk exposure. This result is consistent with the "competition-fragility" view.

Deregulation also generates interesting dynamic effects. When deregulation induces a more competitive outcome, then we can expect that "good banks" should survive and grow faster, whereas "weak banks" should shrink and eventually exit. Stiroh and Strahan (2003), for example, assess the competitive dynamics in terms of market share and industry exits after the deregulation in the US banking industry. Banks that are performing well are more likely to gain market share after deregulation. Moreover, they find an interesting heterogeneity in line with deregulatory forces: the strengthening in the performance-market share link is strongest in unit-banking states and in more concentrated markets. Branching deregulation had the largest impact for small banks whereas interstate deregulation had its greatest impact for large banks. They also find that the poorest performing banks were shrinking after deregulation, that the exit rate increased by 3.6% after a state removed its interstate banking restrictions, and that the relative profitability of banks exiting increased after deregulation. Finally, Buch (2003) explores the impact of deregulation on gross financial assets of banks. She finds that the EU single market program and the Basel Capital

Accord have a positive impact on intra-EU asset holdings and lending to OECD countries, respectively.

25.5 INFORMATION-SHARING AND COMPETITION

Theory suggests that information-sharing between banks is introduced to overcome asymmetric information problems. Lenders may be unable to observe the riskiness of the borrowers and this induces adverse selection problems. By sharing information, lenders are able to make more accruable prediction of repayment probabilities. Lenders may also be unable to control the actions taken by the borrowers after obtaining a loan and this induces moral hazard problems (see Berger, Klapper, et al. 2003 for a review on the objectives of public credit registers). Padilla and Pagano (1997) for example theoretically show that information-sharing serves as a commitment device by banks to engage in competition for borrowers. This reduces hold-up problems and allows incentivizing entrepreneurs, leading to lower default rates. Next to reducing moral hazard problems, information-sharing may also reduce adverse selection (Jappelli and Pagano, 1993), expand the credit market (i.e., when information is shared, the incentives of the borrower to perform are reinforced in Jappelli and Pagano, 2002), and shape the scope of bank entry and induce potential collusive behavior (Bouckaert and Degryse, 2006).

Using information on private credit bureaus and public credit registers around the world, Jappelli and Pagano (2002) find that information-sharing indicators are positively correlated with bank lending and negatively correlated with default rates. They also find that private and public information-sharing systems have no differential correlation with credit market performance. Similarly, using information on credit bureaus and public credit registries of 24 countries of Eastern Europe and the former Soviet Union, Brown, Jappelli, and Pagano (2009) find that information-sharing is associated with improved availability and with a lower cost of credit. The effect is stronger for opaque firms than for transparent ones and is present in countries with poor creditor protection. Moreover, Majnoni et al. (2004) analyze the public credit registers of Argentina, Brazil and Mexico. Their results show that public credit registers may improve credit access for borrowers for the same level of bank risk or reduce bank risk for the same level of credit access. They also find that small banks benefit more than larger institutions from sharing credit information. Love and Mylenko (2003) find that the existence of private credit registries is associated with lower financing constraints and higher share of bank borrowing in firm's financing structure. The effect is stronger for small and medium firms. They however do not find evidence that public credit registries have an effect on availability of financing.

Despite the aforementioned benefits of information-sharing, lenders' incentives to participate may be reduced by the fear of competition from potential entrants. Jappelli and Pagano (1993) develop a model in which banks have private information about the credit worthiness of local residents but no information about immigrants. If local banks agree to share information with all other lenders they learn how to distinguish between risky and safe borrowers among immigrants, but they lose their informational advantage concerning residents. They find that information-sharing makes competition tougher by depriving lenders of the monopoly power attached to exclusive customer information. Lender's incentive to share information is greater when competition is limited by cost or regulatory factors (barriers to entry).

Jappelli and Pagano (1993) further argue that the relationship between competition and information-sharing is evidenced on the differences observed between the regulatory framework of the United States and Britain. While in the United States branching regulations have traditionally limited competition among banks, in Britain banks are free to compete nationwide. Accordingly, in the United States credit bureaus have been used since 1920s and lenders share both "black" (or negative) and "white" (or positive) information. In contrast, in Britain a proposal from finance companies to share white information was refused in 1989. As a result, finance companies share only "black" information with banks.

Similarly and consistently with their findings, Chan, Greenbaum, and Thakor (1986) find that increased competition in banking has diminished bank's incentive to undertake costly screening of loans. Thus, more competition is associated with an increase on the interest rate spreads. Therefore, the surplus the bank can earn by identifying good borrowers is diminished.

Other empirical work shows that information-sharing per se and a greater coverage of any information-sharing mechanism that is in place promotes the competitiveness of banking systems. Countries such as Germany, Italy, and Spain, for example, have public credit registries that are operational since 1934, 1962, and 1962, respectively. This implies that a within-country difference-in-difference analysis (i.e., a before-and-after comparison) of the impact (of the introduction) of an information-sharing system on banking competition is not possible due to a lack of data (in addition one could also criticize such a study because it would have to employ historical data and therefore may lack external validity, i.e., insights for the current banking environment). Access to a micro-dataset that allows studying the characteristics of loans granted to the same firm right before and after the introduction or expansion of a public credit registry can make the identification of the impact of competition convincingly possible.

Recent work, however, has performed cross-country time series analysis of the impact of information-sharing on banking competition. Giannetti, Jentzsch, and Spagnolo (2010), for example, consider the EU-27 member states over the period 1990–2007. They perform a difference-in-difference analysis, but there is only a limited amount of variation in the information-sharing variable because there are (unfortunately) not many countries that have changed their systems of information reporting during the sample period. They find that after the introduction of a public register the C3 concentration ratio drops with about 12% due to new entry of banks. There is no impact on concentration when a private bureau is created. They also find that bank profitability as well as the net-interest margin declines. In sum, they find that public registries contribute to the intensification of competition (measured by various indicators) and these effects are more pronounced for highly concentrated markets.

Lin, Ma, and Song (2010) show in a cross-country study covering 60 countries that firms face fewer financing constraints in countries where an information-sharing mechanism is present and if so when the coverage of this mechanism is broader. Furthermore, they find that greater banking concentration induces more financing constraints but that its impact is mitigated when there is information-sharing and if so when coverage is broader. This shows that policymakers should be less concerned about the potential anti-competitive effects when the institutional environment contains other competitive forces such as information-sharing mechanisms.

Setting up and running public credit registries and/or private credit bureaus involves pecu-niary costs. Private bureaus are for-profit organizations and some of them are owned by banks. Their coverage is typically determined by their main shareholders as well as by the potential buyers of information. Public credit registers are typically owned by central banks and run on a non-profit basis. Reporting to public registries is mandated by law for specific items of data.

Who has access and the fees involved may differ substantially. The "devil truly is in the details here" as the fee structure (and/or the prevailing regulatory framework) may partly or completely undo the pro-competitive impact on the banking sector, for example when the fees that are charged are disadvantageous to (or in effect exclude) foreign banks, non-shareholders, smaller players or non-bank credit providers. Disadvantages may exist when there are high joining fees, high fixed access fees and/or discriminatory volume-based access fees. The European Commission (2007) led an inquiry into the joining and transac-tion fees and found that some (but not all) private bureaus charged high joining fees. The joining fees for public credit registries are typically zero. Transaction fees for access to most credit registries are generally below one euro per consultation, whether positive or negative data is requested. However, some private credit bureaus charge transaction fees significantly above these levels which may then hurt banking competition.

25.6 CONCLUSION

This chapter has reviewed the different methodological approaches that have been taken to measure competition in banking. While market structure indicators (e.g., HHI) are readily available and in line with the traditional SCP paradigm, these indicators may not be overly informative about the competitive conditions in banking markets. The empirical literature now aims to measure market conduct directly and employs "non-market structure" indica-tors such as the Panzar-Rosse H-statistic, the Lerner index, and the Boone indicator. We suggest that a thorough assessment of banking competition should be based on a wide set of different competition indicators.

Banking is "special" in many dimensions—asymmetric information, network effects, and switching costs. Our review has therefore also discussed many other specific approaches to infer banking competition. For example, we have reviewed how regulation and information-sharing between banks may impact on banking competition. The ongoing re-regulation of banks and the introduction and expansion of information-sharing mecha-nisms in many countries will certainly continue to put banking competition on the agenda of empirical banking researchers and policymakers.

REFERENCES

Alegria, C. and Schaeck, K. (2008). On Measuring Concentration in Banking Systems, *Finance Research Letters* 5, 59–67.

Allen, F., Gersbach, H., Krahnen, J. P., and Santomero, A. M. (2001). Competition among Banks: Introduction and Conference Overview, *European Finance Review* 5, 1–11.

Allen, L. and Rai, A. (1996). Operational Efficiency in Banking: An International Comparison, *Journal of Banking and Finance* 20, 655–672.

Angelini, P. and Cetorelli, N. (2003). Bank Competition and Regulatory Reform: The Case of the Italian Banking Industry, *Journal of Money, Credit, and Banking* 35, 663–684.

Bain, J. (1956). *Barriers to New Competition*. Cambridge MA: Harvard University Press.

Barros, P. P. (1999). Multimarket Competition in Banking, with an Example from the Portuguese Market, *International Journal of Industrial Organization* 17, 335–352.

Barth, J. R., Caprio, G., and Levine, R. (2001). *The Regulations and Supervision of Banks around the World: A New Database*. Washington DC: World Bank.

Barth, J. R., Caprio, G., and Levine, R. (2004). Bank Regulation and Supervision: What Works Best?, *Journal of Financial Intermediation* 13, 205–248.

Beck, T., De Jonghe, O., and Schepens, G. (2013). Bank Competition and Stability: Cross-Country Heterogeneity, *Journal of Financial Intermediation* 22, 218–244.

Beck, T., Demirgüç-Kunt, A., and Levine, R. (2006a). Bank Concentration, Competition, and Crises: First Results, *Journal of Banking and Finance* 30, 1581–1603.

Beck, T., Demirgüç-Kunt, A., and Levine, R. (2006b). Bank Supervision and Corruption in Lending, *Journal of Monetary Economics* 53, 2131–2163.

Berg, S. A. and Kim, M. (1994). Oligopolistic Interdependence and the Structure of Production in Banking: An Empirical Evaluation, *Journal of Money, Credit, and Banking* 26, 309–322.

Berg, S. A. and Kim, M. (1998). Banks as Multioutput Oligopolies: An Empirical Evaluation of the Retail and Corporate Banking Markets, *Journal of Money, Credit, and Banking* 30, 135–153.

Berger, A. N. (1993). Distribution Free Estimates of Efficiency in the US Banking Industry and Test of the Standard Distributional Assumptions, *Journal of Productivity Analysis* 4, 261–292.

Berger, A. N. (1995). The Profit-Structure Relationship in Banking. Tests of Market-Power and Efficient-Structure Hypotheses, *Journal of Money, Credit, and Banking* 27, 404–431.

Berger, A. N. (2007). Obstacles to a Global Banking System: "Old Europe" versus New Europe, *Journal of Banking and Finance* 31, 1955–1973.

Berger, A. N., Demirgüç-Kunt, A., Levine, R., and Haubrich, J. G. (2004). Bank Concentration and Competition: An Evolution in the Making, *Journal of Money, Credit, and Banking* 36, 433–451.

Berger, A. N. and Hannan, T. H. (1989). The Price-Concentration Relationship in Banking, *Review of Economics and Statistics* 71, 291–299.

Berger, A. N., Hasan, I., and Klapper, L. F. (2004). Further Evidence on the Link between Finance and Growth: An International Analysis of Community Banking and Economic Performance, *Journal of Financial Services Research* 25, 169–202.

Berger, A. N. and Humphrey, D. B. (1997). Efficiency of Financial Institutions: International Survey and Directions for Future Research, *European Journal of Operational Research* 98, 175–212.

Berger, A. N., Klapper, L. F., Miller, M. J., and Udell, G. F. (2003). Relationship Lending in the Argentine Small Business Credit Market. In: M. J. Miller (Ed.), *Credit Reporting Systems and the International Economy*, 255–270. Cambridge MA: MIT Press.

Berger, A. N., Klapper, L. F., and Turk-Ariss, R. (2009). Bank Competition and Financial Stability, *Journal of Financial Services Research* 35, 99–118.

Berger, A. N., Rosen, R. J., and Udell, G. F. (2007). Does Market Size Structure Affect Competition? The Case of Small Business Lending, *Journal of Banking and Finance* 31, 11–33.

Besanko, D. and Thakor, A. V. (1993). Relationship Banking, Deposit Insurance and Bank Portfolio Choice. In: C. Mayer and X. Vives (Eds.), *Capital Markets and Financial Intermediation*, 292–319. Cambridge UK: Cambridge University Press.

Biehl, A. R. (2002). The Extent of the Market for Retail Banking Deposits, *Antitrust Bulletin* 47, 91–106.

Bikker, J. A. and Haaf, K. (2002). Competition, Concentration and Their Relationship: An Empirical Analysis of the Banking Industry, *Journal of Banking and Finance* 26, 2191–2214.

Bikker, J. A., Shaffer, S., and Spierdijk, L. (2012). Assessing Competition with the Panzar-Rosse Model: The Role of Scale, Costs, and Equilibrium, *Review of Economics and Statistics* 94, 1025–1044.

Black, S. E. and Strahan, P. E. (2002). Entrepreneurship and Bank Credit Availability, *Journal of Finance* 57, 2807–2834.

Bofondi, M. and Gobbi, G. (2004). *Bad Loans and Entry into Local Credit Markets*. Rome: Bank of Italy.

Bonaccorsi di Patti, E. and Dell'Ariccia, G. (2004). Bank Competition and Firm Creation, *Journal of Money, Credit, and Banking* 36, 225–252.

Boone, J. (2008). A New Way to Measure Competition, *Economic Journal* 118, 1245–1261.

Boone, J., van Ours, J. C., and van der Wiel, H. (2007). *How (Not) to Measure Competition*. London: Centre for Economic Policy Research.

Bouckaert, J. and Degryse, H. (2006). Entry and Strategic Information Display in Credit Markets, *Economic Journal* 116, 702–720.

Boyd, J., De Nicolo, G., and Jalal, A. (2006). *Bank Risk-Taking and Competition Revisited: New Theory and New Evidence*. Washington, DC: International Monetary Fund.

Boyd, J. H. and De Nicolo, G. (2005). The Theory of Bank Risk Taking and Competition Revisited, *Journal of Finance* 60, 1329–1343.

Bresnahan, T. (1982). The Oligopoly Solution Is Identified, *Economics Letters* 10, 87–92.

Brown, M., Jappelli, T., and Pagano, M. (2009). Information Sharing and Credit: Firm-Level Evidence from Transition Countries, *Journal of Financial Intermediation* 18, 151–172.

Buch, C. M. (2003). What Determines Maturity? An Analysis of German Commercial Banks' Foreign Assets, *Applied Financial Economics* 13, 337–351.

Caballero, R. J., Hoshi, T., and Kashyap, A. K. (2008). Zombie Lending and Depressed Restructuring in Japan, *American Economic Review* 98, 1943–1977.

Calem, P. S. and Nakamura, L. I. (1998). Branch Banking and the Geography of Bank Pricing, *Review of Economics and Statistics* 80, 600–610.

Carbo, S., Humphrey, D., Maudos, J., and Molyneux, P. Y. (2009). Cross-Country Comparisons of Competition and Pricing Power in European Banking, *Journal of International Money and Finance* 28, 115–134.

Carbó Valverde, S., Rodriguez Fernández, F., and Udell, G. F. (2009). Bank Market Power and SME Financing Constraints, *Review of Finance* 13, 309–340.

Carletti, E. (2008). Competition and Regulation in Banking. In: A. V. Thakorand and A. W. A. Boot (Eds.), *Handbook of Financial Intermediation and Banking*, 449–482. London: North Holland.

Cavallo, L. and Rossi, S. (2001). Scale and Scope Economies in the European Banking Systems, *Journal of Multinational Financial Management* 11, 515–531.

Cetorelli, N. (2004). Bank Concentration and Competition in Europe, *Journal of Money, Credit, and Banking* 36, 543–558.

Cetorelli, N. and Strahan, P. E. (2006). Finance as a Barrier to Entry: Bank Competition and Industry Structure in Local US Markets, *Journal of Finance* 61, 867–892.

Chan, Y. S., Greenbaum, S. I., and Thakor, A. V. (1986). Information Reusability, Competition and Bank Asset Quality, *Journal of Banking and Finance* 10, 243–253.

Claessens, S. and Laeven, L. (2004). What Drives Bank Competition? Some International Evidence, *Journal of Money, Credit, and Banking* 36, 563–583.

Corts, K. S. (1999). Conduct Parameters and the Measurement of Market Power, *Journal of Econometrics* 88, 227–250.

Corvoisier, S. and Gropp, R. (2002). Bank Concentration and Retail Interest Rates, *Journal of Banking and Finance* 26, 2155–2189.

Craig, B. R. and Dinger, V. (2009). Bank Mergers and the Dynamics of Deposit Interest Rates, *Journal of Financial Services Research* 36, 111–133.

Craig, S. G. and Hardee, P. (2007). The Impact of Bank Consolidation on Small Business Credit Availability, *Journal of Banking and Finance* 31, 1237–1263.

Cyrnak, A. W. and Hannan, T. H. (1999). Is the Cluster Still Valid in Defining Banking Markets? Evidence from a New Data Source, *Antitrust Bulletin* 44, 313–331.

De Jonghe, O. and Vander Vennet, R. (2008). Competition versus Efficiency: What Drives Franchise Values in European Banking?, *Journal of Banking and Finance* 32, 1820–1835.

De Mello, J. M. P. (2007). *Can Lender Market Power Benefit Borrowers? Further Evidence from Small Firm Finance*. Stanford: Palo Alto.

De Nicolò, G. and Loukoianova, E. (2007). *Bank Ownership, Market Structure and Risk*. Washington, DC: International Monetary Fund.

Degryse, H. and Ongena, S. (2005). Distance, Lending Relationships, and Competition, *Journal of Finance* 60, 231–266.

Degryse, H. and Ongena, S. (2008). Competition and Regulation in the Banking Sector: A Review of the Empirical Evidence on the Sources of Bank Rents. In: A. V. Thakor and A. W. A. Boot (Eds.), *Handbook of Financial Intermediation and Banking*, 483–554. Amsterdam: Elsevier.

Demirgüç-Kunt, A., Laeven, L., and Levine, R. (2004). Regulations, Market Structure, Institutions, and the Cost of Financial Intermediation, *Journal of Money, Credit, and Banking* 36, 563–583.

Demsetz, H. (1973). Industry Structure, Market Rivalry, and Public Policy, *Journal of Law and Economics* 16, 1–9.

Dewatripont, M. and Tirole, J. (1994). *The Prudential Regulation of Banks*. Cambridge MA: MIT.

Dick, A. A. (2008). Demand Estimation and Consumer Welfare in the Banking Industry, *Journal of Banking and Finance* 32, 1661–1676.

Dick, A. A. and Hannan, T. H. (2010). Competition and Antitrust Policy in Banking. In: A. N. Berger, P. Molyneux, and J. O. S. Wilson (Eds.), *The Oxford Handbook of Banking*, 405–429. Oxford: Oxford University Press.

Dick, A. A. and Lehnert, A. (2010). Personal Bankruptcy and Credit Market Competition, *Journal of Finance* 65, 655–686.

European Commission (2007). *Sector Inquiry Retail Banking*. Brussels: European Commission.

Fischer, K. H. and Pfeil, C. (2004). Regulation and Competition in German Banking. In: J. P. Krahnen and R. H. Schmidt (Eds.), *The German Financial System*, 291–349. Frankfurt: Oxford University Press.

Focarelli, D. and Panetta, F. (2003). Are Mergers Beneficial to Consumers? Evidence from the Market for Bank Deposits, *American Economic Review* 93, 1152–1171.

Garrett, T. A., Wagner, G. A., and Wheelock, D. C. (2005). A Spatial Analysis of State Banking Regulation, *Papers in Regional Science* 84, 575–595.

Giannetti, C., Jentzsch, N., and Spagnolo, G. (2010). *Information-Sharing and Cross-Border Entry in European Banking*. Brussels: European Credit Research Institute.

Gilbert, R. (1984). Bank Market Structure and Competition: A Survey, *Journal of Money, Credit, and Banking* 16, 617–644.

Gilbert, R. A. and Zaretsky, A. M. (2003). Banking Antitrust: Are the Assumptions Still Valid?, *Review of the Federal Reserve Bank of St. Louis* November, 29–52.

Goddard, J., Liu, H., Molyneux, P., and Wilson, J. O. S. (2011). The Persistence of Bank Profit, *Journal of Banking and Finance* 35, 2881–2890.

Goddard, J. and Wilson, J. O. S. (2009). Competition in Banking: A Disequilibrium Approach, *Journal of Banking and Finance* 33, 2282–2292.

Gual, J. (1999). Deregulation, Integration and Market Structure in European Banking, *Journal of Japanese and International Economies* 12, 372–396.

Hannan, T. H. and Prager, R. A. (2004). The Competitive Implications of Multimarket Bank Branching, *Journal of Banking and Finance* 28, 1889–1914.

Hannan, T. H. and Prager, R. A. (2009). The Profitability of Small Single-Market Banks in an Era of Multi-Market Banking, *Journal of Banking and Finance* 33, 263–271.

Heitfield, E. A. (1999). What Do Interest Rate Data Say about the Geography of Retail Banking Markets, *Antitrust Bulletin* 44, 333–347.

Heitfield, E. A. and Prager, R. A. (2004). The Geographic Scope of Retail Deposit Markets, *Journal of Financial Services Research* 25, 37–55.

Iwata, G. (1974). Measurement of Conjectural Variations in Oligopoly, *Econometrica* 42, 947–966.

Jappelli, T. and Pagano, M. (1993). Information Sharing in Credit Markets, *Journal of Finance* 63, 1693–1718.

Jappelli, T. and Pagano, M. (2002). Information Sharing, Lending and Defaults: Cross-Country Evidence, *Journal of Banking and Finance* 26, 2017–2045.

Jaumandreu, J. and Lorences, J. (2002). Modelling Price Competition across Many Markets: An Application to the Spanish Loans Market, *European Economic Review* 46, 93–115.

Jayaratne, J. and Strahan, P. E. (1996). The Finance-Growth Nexus: Evidence from Bank Branch Deregulation, *Quarterly Journal of Economics* 111, 639–670.

Jayaratne, J. and Strahan, P. E. (1998). Entry Restrictions, Industry Evolution, and Dynamic Efficiency: Evidence from Commercial Banking, *Journal of Law and Economics* 41, 239–274.

Jeon, B. N., Olivero, M. P., and Wu, J. (2011). Do Foreign Banks Increase Competition? Evidence from Emerging Asian and Latin American Banking Markets, *Journal of Banking and Finance* 35, 856–875.

Kashyap, A., Rajan, R. G., and Stein, J. C. (2002). Banks as Liquidity Providers: An Explanation for the Co-existence of Lending and Deposit-Taking, *Journal of Finance* 57, 33–73.

Keeley, M. C. (1990). Deposit Insurance Risk and Market Power in Banking, *American Economic Review* 80, 1183–1200.

Kerr, W. R. and Nanda, R. (2009). Democratizing Entry: Banking Deregulations, Financing Constraints, and Entrepreneurship, *Journal of Financial Economics* 94, 124–149.

Kim, M. (1986). Banking Technology and the Existence of a Consistent Output Aggregate, *Journal of Monetary Economics* 18, 181–195.

Kim, M., Kristiansen, E. G., and Vale, B. (2005). Endogenous Product Differentiation in Credit Markets: What Do Borrowers Pay For?, *Journal of Banking and Finance* 29, 681–699.

Kroszner, R. S. and Strahan, P. E. (1999). What Drives Deregulation? Economics and Politics of the Relaxation of Bank Branching Restrictions, *Quarterly Journal of Economics* 124, 1437–1467.

La Porta, R., Lopez-de-Silanes, F., and Shleifer, A. (2002). Government Ownership of Banks, *Journal of Finance* 57, 265–301.

Lau, L. J. (1982). On Identifying the Degree of Competitiveness from Industry Price and Output Data, *Economic Letters* 10, 93–99.

Levine, R. (2004). Denying Foreign Bank Entry: Implications for Bank Interest Margins. In: L. A. Ahumada, J. R. Fuentes, N. Loayza, and K. Schmidt-Hebbel (Eds.), *Banking Market Structure and Monetary Policy*, 271–292. Santiago de Chile: Central Bank of Chile.

Levy Yeyati, E. and Micco, A. (2007). Concentration and Foreign Penetration in Latin American Banking Sectors: Impact on Competition and Risk, *Journal of Banking and Finance* 31, 1633–1647.

Lin, C., Ma, Y., and Song, F. M. (2010). *Bank Competition, Credit Information Sharing and Banking Efficiency*. Hong Kong: City University of Hong Kong.

Love, I. and Mylenko, N. (2003). *Credit Reporting and Financing Constraints*. Washington, DC: World Bank.

Magri, S., Mori, A., and Rossi, P. (2005). The Entry and the Activity Level of Foreign Banks in Italy: An Analysis of the Determinants, *Journal of Banking and Finance* 29, 1295–1310.

Majnoni, G., Miller, M. J., Mylenko, N., and Powell, A. (2004). *Improving Credit Information, Bank Regulation, and Supervision: On the Role and Design of Public Credit Registries*. Washington, DC: World Bank.

Marquez, R. (2002). Competition, Adverse Selection, and Information Dispersion in the Banking Industry, *Review of Financial Studies* 15, 901–926.

Mester, L. J. (1993). Efficiency in the Savings and Loan Industry, *Journal of Banking and Finance* 17, 267–286.

Molnár, J. (2007). *Market Power and Merger Simulation in Retail Banking*. Helsinki: Bank of Finland.

Molnár, J., Nagy, M., and Horvath, C. (2007). *A Structural Empirical Analysis of Retail Banking Competition: The Case of Hungary*. Budapest: Hungarian National Bank.

Molyneux, P. Y., Altunbas, Y., and Gardener, E. P. M. (1996). *Efficiency in European Banking*. London: John Wiley and Sons.

Montoriol Garriga, J. (2006). *Relationship Lending and Banking Competition: Are They Compatible?* Barcelona: Universitat Pompeu Fabra.

Morgan, D. (2002). *How Big are Bank Markets: Evidence Using Branch Sale Premia*. New York, NY: Federal Reserve Bank of New York.

Neumark, D. and Sharpe, S. A. (1992). Market Structure and the Nature of Price Rigidity: Evidence from the Market for Consumer Deposits, *Quarterly Journal of Economics* 107, 657–680.

Padilla, A. J. and Pagano, M. (1997). Endogenous Communication among Lenders and Entrepreneurial Incentives, *Review of Financial Studies* 10, 205–236.

Panetta, F., Schivardi, F., and Shum, M. (2009). Do Mergers Improve Information? Evidence from the Loan Market, *Journal of Money, Credit and Banking* 41, 673–709.

Panzar, J. C. and Rosse, J. N. (1987). Testing for Monopoly Equilibrium, *Journal of Industrial Economics* 35, 443–456.

Park, K. and Pennacchi, G. (2009). Harming Depositors and Helping Borrowers: The Disparate Impact of Bank Consolidation, *Review of Financial Studies* 22, 1–40.

Peltzmann, S. (1977). The Gains and Losses from Industrial Concentration, *Journal of Law and Economics* 20, 229–263.

Petersen, M. A. and Rajan, R. G. (1995). The Effect of Credit Market Competition on Lending Relationships, *Quarterly Journal of Economics* 110, 406–443.

Radecki, L. J. (1998). The Expanding Geographic Reach of Retail Banking Markets, *FRBNY Economic Policy Review* 4, 15–34.

Rice, T. and Strahan, P. E. (2010). Does Credit Competition Affect Small-Firm Finance?, *Journal of Finance* 65, 861–889.

Rosen, R. J. (2007). Banking Market Conditions and Deposit Interest Rates, *Journal of Banking and Finance* 31, 3862–3884.

Salas, V. and Saurina, J. (2003). Deregulation, Market Power and Risk Behavior in Spanish Banks, *European Economic Review* 47, 1061–1075.

Salop, S. C. (1987). Symposium on Mergers and Antitrust, *Journal of Economic Perspectives* 1, 3–12.

Sapienza, P. (2002). The Effects of Banking Mergers on Loan Contracts, *Journal of Finance* 57, 329–368.

Sapienza, P. (2004). The Effects of Government Ownership on Bank Lending, *Journal of Financial Economics* 72, 357–384.

Schaeck, K. and Čihák, M. (2010). *Competition, Efficiency, and Soundness in Banking: An Industrial Organization Perspective*. Tilburg: European Banking Center.

Schaeck, K., Čihák, M., and Wolfe, S. (2009). Are Competitive Banking Systems More Stable?, *Journal of Money, Credit and Banking* 41, 711–734.

Shaffer, S. (1989). Competition in the US Banking Industry, *Economics Letters* 29, 321–323.

Shaffer, S. (1993). A Test of Competition in Canadian Banking, *Journal of Money, Credit, and Banking* 25, 49–61.

Shaffer, S. (2004). Patterns of Competition in Banking, *Journal of Economics and Business* 56, 287–313.

Spiller, P. T. and Favaro, E. (1984). The Effects of Entry Regulation on Oligopolistic Interaction: The Uruguayan Banking Sector, *RAND Journal of Economics* 15, 244–254.

Stiroh, K. and Strahan, P. (2003). Competitive Dynamics of Deregulation: Evidence from US Banking, *Journal of Money, Credit, and Banking* 35, 801–828.

Turati, G. (2001). *Cost Efficiency and Profitability in European Commercial Banking*. Milan: Universita Cattolica del S. Cuore.

van Leuvensteijn, M., Bikker, J. A., van Rixtel, A. A. R. J. M., and Sørensen, C. K. (2011). A New Approach to Measuring Competition in the Loan Markets of the Euro Area, *Applied Economics* 43, 3155–3167.

Vander Vennet, R. (2002). Cost and Profit Efficiency of Financial Conglomerates and Universal Banks in Europe, *Journal of Money, Credit, and Banking* 34, 254–282.

Vives, X. (1991). Regulatory Reform in Europe, *European Economic Review* 35, 505–515.

Vives, X. (1999). *Oligopoly Pricing: Old Ideas and New Tools*. Cambridge MA: MIT Press.

Vives, X. (2001). Competition in the Changing World of Banking, *Oxford Review of Economic Policy* 17, 535–547.

CHAPTER 26

SYSTEMICALLY IMPORTANT BANKS
(SIBS) IN THE POST-CRISIS ERA

*The Global Response, and Responses
around the Globe for 135 Countries*[*]

JAMES R. BARTH, CHRISTOPHER BRUMMER,
TONG (CINDY) LI, AND DANIEL E. NOLLE

26.1 INTRODUCTION

POLITICAL leaders and regulatory authorities around the world responded to the global financial crisis which emerged in 2007–08 with a wide range of policies aimed at stabilizing and reforming national and international financial markets, institutions, and practices.[1] Six years and counting since its onset, policy responses to the crisis around the world continue to be debated, decided, and implemented, a reflection of its profound impact. A major policy focus for authorities—some would say "the" major focus—was initially, and continues

---

[*] The views expressed in this chapter are those of the authors alone, and should not be interpreted as reflecting those of the Office of the Comptroller of the Currency, the US Treasury Department, the Federal Reserve Bank of San Francisco, or the Board of Governors of the Federal Reserve System.

[1] Many researchers, analysts, market observers, and policymakers date "the" global financial crisis as covering the 2007–09 period or some significant subset of those three years. Others view the deepening seriousness of the sovereign debt-banking system stresses in the Eurozone as from 2010 as fundamentally a continuation of that same global financial system crisis; see, e.g., Lane (2012a), who designates the early period, ending in "Spring 2009," as the "market-panic phase of the global crisis," and explains that "subsequent crisis stages are still playing out, with Europe at the center of the current phase." For purposes of this chapter, it does not matter in which camp one places oneself, and indeed the authors believe that the information conveyed in this chapter is relevant to either point of view.

to be, risks to the financial system posed by systemically important financial institutions, or "SIFIs" as they quickly came to be called. These institutions, at both the global level ("G-SIFIs") and the domestic level ("D-SIFIs"), are institutions of such size, interconnectedness, and financial system importance that their failure, or even their severe distress, causes significant destabilization in the financial system and substantial adverse economic consequences. The distinction between D-SIFIs and G-SIFIs is that the former pose systemic risk to the national financial system but (probably) not beyond, while the latter pose systemic risk both within and across national borders.

At the national level, policymakers have been strengthening existing supervisory practices and regulations applying to SIFIs and, in country after country, new national laws and regulations aimed at SIFIs have been and are still being implemented. Some of these national efforts, such as the Dodd–Frank Act of 2010 in the United States, are sweeping in scope and widely known around the world. In addition, key policy responses to the global financial crisis have been deliberated upon and committed to at the international level. Among the most well known of these are the Basel III capital and liquidity standards for large, internationally active banks. Nevertheless, even many experienced financial market analysts and policymakers lack a clear and comprehensive picture of the nature of national and international policy responses to deal with SIFIs.

The purpose of this chapter is to address that lack of clarity and contribute to a better understanding of the nature and scope of SIFIs policies around the world. Our focus is on the regulation and supervision of systemically important banks (generically, "SIBs," including both D-SIBs and G-SIBs), a large and important subset of SIFIs. Indeed, as of the date of this chapter, SIBs have received by far the greatest attention by policymakers, both nationally and internationally. We look at this issue from two complementary perspectives: the "global" view focuses on the agenda of the dominant, if relatively little known, international entity engaged in reforming the financial system; and our country-specific review looks in detail at supervisory measures for SIBs in 135 countries around the world. For both perspectives, we present important new data and information.

Section 26.2 presents what we argue should be understood as "the" main international, or global, SIFIs policy agenda. Specifically, it describes the Group of Twenty (G20) and how, in response to the onset of the global financial crisis, it rapidly emerged as the premier forum for international cooperation on the development and implementation of policies aimed at reforming the world financial system, including in particular those aimed at SIFIs. The first part of the section explains what the G20 is and how, via its chief agent, the Financial Stability Board (FSB), the G20 exerts its lead policymaking role. The discussion in the second part of the section highlights the development of G20/FSB SIFIs initiatives, placing them within the context of the overall financial system reform agenda as it evolved from late 2008 to mid-year 2013, the five year "eve" of the full eruption of the global financial crisis in September 2008. That "story" is largely unknown and, as a consequence, there is a measure of ignorance and, perhaps, misunderstanding, even among serious financial system observers, analysts, and policymakers, about the hierarchical structure under which global banking and financial system policies are generated.

Section 26.3 starts by looking at the factors that are used to identify G-SIBs, and how those that are so-designated compare in asset size among the world's 100 biggest banks. The size of each of these banks is also gauged relative to the total assets of the banking system and the GDP of the country in which the given bank is headquartered. The section then turns to our second perspective: the post-crisis regulation and supervision of SIBs on a country-specific basis. Specifically, using new and comprehensive data collected by the World Bank, we look at the nature of policies applying to both D-SIBs and G-SIBs. Financial industry participants and policymakers are aware that numerous countries around the world have strengthened existing measures and/or introduced new measures to better regulate and supervise SIBs, but until very recently the lack of detailed data across a wide range of countries made it impossible to paint a comprehensive landscape. Using new World Bank banking system survey data, covering (among other things) the regulation and supervision of SIBs by 135 countries, this chapter addresses that deficiency.

The chapter's presentation of, on the one hand, "the global" agenda for identifying and controlling risks to the financial system posed by SIBs and, on the other hand, country-specific measures to accomplish the same objective raise the obvious question: "Do the global agenda and individual country measures dealing with SIBs mesh?" Section 26.4 considers this question. It begins with the observation that there is no single, all-encompassing "answer" to the question, and indeed even if there were, such a complex undertaking would provide sufficient material for another chapter, if not a (lengthy) separate book. With that in mind, our tack in this section is to provide a brief introduction to the nature of one important dimension of the issue, legal obstacles to cross-border regulation and supervision.

26.2 Systematically Important Financial Institutions: The G20 and Policy Development at the Global Level[2]

By the beginning of the fourth quarter of 2008, it had become apparent to most financial markets observers, analysts, and policymakers that the financial crisis triggered initially in the US subprime mortgage market had become global in scope. It was also widely recognized by then that a crucial corollary to that perspective was that national policy responses, however bold and innovative, would be inadequate to stabilize, much less repair, financial markets and networks reaching around the world. It was in this environment that the heads of government in the G20 countries met on November 14–15, 2008 at their first Leaders' Summit in Washington, DC. Note that although G20 finance ministers and central bank governors met annually since the group's founding in 1999, the November 2008 Summit was the first time G20 heads of state met as a group, precisely because of the gravity of the financial crisis.

That event represented a sea change in how, and by whom, internationally coordinated financial policy was made. In response to the previous global financial crisis in 1997–98, the Group of Seven (G7) rich industrial countries (Canada, France, Germany, Italy, Japan, the

---

[2] Our description of the G20, its policymaking structure, the FSB, and our brief history of the development of the G20/FSB financial system reform agenda all draw heavily on Nolle (2013).

UK, the US) held center stage, as had been the case for years. Little remarked at that time was the G7's decision to establish a new international economic forum with a wider and more economically varied membership, in particular in recognition of the rapidly increasing and important role in the world economy of several large emerging market and developing economies (EMDEs).[3] As the global financial crisis deepened and widened, that decision looked ever more prescient, especially because of the profound role reversals characterizing the crisis: the richest G20 members, with the biggest financial systems, were under duress while the traditionally less stable EMDE members had been little affected by the crisis. The next sub-section provides details on the composition of G20 membership, and describes the relationships between the G20 and other international policy fora, including in particular the more well-known Basel Committee on Banking Supervision (BCBS) and the International Monetary Fund (IMF). The final sub-section briefly describes the emergence and evolution of the G20's financial system reform policy agenda in response to the global financial crisis, highlighting the SIFIs-related portion of that agenda.

26.2.1 Who and What is the G20?

The term "G20" is used commonly to refer to the 19 member countries and the European Union that are represented in the group. More precisely however, as from its establishment by the G7 Finance Ministers and Central Bank Governors in September 1999, "the G20" specifically has meant the Finance Ministers and Central Bank Governors of the 19 member countries, plus an equivalent-level representative from the European Union—either the President of the European Council or the Head of the European Central Bank, serving on a rotating basis. The Finance Ministers and Central Bank Governors (henceforth in this chapter "Ministers & Governors") continue to function as the core group within the G20 but, as from the darkest days of the global financial crisis when the Ministers & Governors requested their direct and active participation in deciding upon the most important policy issues, the heads of state, or "Leaders," of the G20 countries are also called "the G20" in relevant situations. For clarity's sake, in this chapter our use of the simple term "G20" refers to the Ministers & Governors, and elsewhere we specify the "G20 Leaders" or "G20 [member] countries/ jurisdictions" as appropriate.

Table 26.1 lists the 19 member countries. That table also includes key measures of the economic and financial significance of individual member countries, as well as the combined significance of those countries. The largest economies in the world are included among G20 member countries (e.g., the US, China, Japan), but member countries also include smaller economies from every region of the world. Together, G20 member countries accounted for 86% of world GDP in 2012. Even more compelling is the G20 dominance over financial markets, where they accounted for 89% of world banking system assets, 81 percent of global stock market capitalization, and 94% of global bond markets. The far right-hand column in Table 26.1 presents an overall measure of global financial market activity by summing the bank, stock market, and bond market measures; using

[3] Foremost among the EMDEs asked to become original members of the G20 were China, Brazil, and India; see "What is the G20?" the G20 official website at <http://www.g20.org/docs/about/about_G20.html.>

that "financial market" construct, Table 26.1 shows that in 2012 the G20 member countries encompassed all but 10% of world finance.

The G20 defines itself as "the premier forum for international cooperation on the most important issues of the global economic and financial agenda," whose main objectives are to coordinate policies between its members "in order to achieve economic stability [and] sustainable growth;" "promot[e] financial regulations that reduce risks and prevent future financial crises;" and "moderniz[e] international financial architecture."[4] These objectives and, especially, the G20's unambigous assertion of its global leadership role seem somewhat at odds with common perceptions of lead roles traditionally played by other, better-known international policymaking groups, including in particular the BCBS and the IMF. It also constituted a change from the more limited role in financial regulatory measures played by the G7.[5]

Drawing on official G20 statements, including key passages in official communiqués and declarations issued by G20 Leaders at various Summits, Nolle (2013) addresses the issue of what he terms the "policymaking flow" underlying G20 initiatives. That study describes the perhaps surprisingly explicit hierarchical nature of the G20 policy deliberation and decision making process. Featured prominently in that process is the Financial Stability Board (FSB), which exercises tremendous influence on the substance of international financial system policy. When the G20 assumed global leadership at the depth of the Great Financial Crisis in late 2008, Ministers & Governors and Leaders were confronted with unparalleled demands to respond both rapidly and effectively and, under those circumstances moved quickly to establish a separate, strong, and permanent body to develop, initiate, and oversee their financial system stabilization and reform agenda. Specifically, at their London Summit in April 2009, G20 Leaders "establish[ed] a new Financial Stability Board (FSB) with a strengthened mandate, as a successor to the Financial Stability Forum (FSF)."[6] The FSB's mandate from G20 Leaders includes *not only coordination* of international work on financial system reform, but also to "*oversee* action needed" to actualize those reforms.[7]

The FSB exercises, on behalf of the G20, an implicit leadership role in cooperative work on selected issues with independent international organizations. These international organizations fall into two groups, the first of which is the "international

---

[4] "What is the G20?" at <http://www.g20.org/docs/about/about_G20.html.>

[5] For a full description of the international regulatory architecture, see Brummer (2012).

[6] *London Summit—Leaders' Statement*, 2 April 2009, point #15. The FSF was in essence an in-house think tank for G20 Ministers & Governors.

[7] See the FSB's *Mandate* at <http://www.financialstabilityboard.org/about/mandate.htm.> As explained in greater detail in Nolle (2013), FSB members include all G20 members, but membership is not limited to the G20. In addition, FSB members include major "international standard setting, regulatory, supervisory, and central bank bodies." Nevertheless, non-G20 FSB members play a small role on the FSB Plenary, and perhaps more importantly, on the Steering Committee, and G20 representatives lead most of the FSB committees and working groups. Also see Nolle (2013) for greater detail on the nature and operational structure of the Ministers & Governors. He notes that, although the G20 does not have a permanent secretariat and staff, it does have a well-defined internal operational structure. Specifically, the group designates a specific member as the group's president for a given year, and as such it is that member's responsibility to organize periodic meetings of the Ministers & Governors, and to organize, host, and chair the Leaders' Summit for that year. In addition, the designated member has the responsibility for official website design, maintenance, and content. In 2013, Russia held the G20 Presidency, with the Leaders' Summit to be held in St. Petersburg in September.

Table 26.1 G20 member countries in the global economic and financial systems (2012)

| | Real Economy | | | | Financial System | | | | | | | |
| | GDP | | Bank Assets | | Stock Market Capitalization | | Bond Market 1 | | Financial Market [Stocks + Bonds + Banks] | |
G20 Member	$US Trillion	% Total World	$US Trillion	% Total World	$US Trillion	% Total World	$US Trillion	% Total World	$US Trillion	% Total World
Argentina	0.47	0.7	0.16	0.1	0.03	0.1	0.05	0.0	0.24	0.1
Australia	1.54	2.1	3.34	2.6	1.37	2.5	4.04	2.9	8.74	2.7
Brazil	2.40	3.3	2.41	1.9	1.20	2.2	2.29	1.7	5.90	1.8
Canada	1.82	2.5	3.88	3.0	1.87	3.4	4.49	3.2	10.24	3.2
China	8.23	11.5	17.18	13.4	2.98	5.4	3.82	2.7	23.97	7.4
France	2.61	3.6	9.98	7.8	1.66	3.0	6.16	4.4	17.80	5.5
Germany	3.40	4.7	5.06	3.9	1.55	2.8	5.72	4.1	12.33	3.8
India	1.82	2.5	1.81	1.4	1.18	2.1	0.64	0.5	3.63	1.1
Indonesia	0.88	1.2	0.39	0.3	0.42	0.8	0.17	0.1	0.99	0.3
Italy	2.01	2.8	3.27	2.5	0.51	0.9	4.83	3.5	8.61	2.7
Japan	5.96	8.3	13.04	10.1	3.89	7.0	29.18	21.0	46.11	14.3
Mexico	1.18	1.6	0.47	0.4	0.56	1.0	0.68	0.5	1.71	0.5
Russia	2.02	2.8	1.13	0.9	0.83	1.5	0.79	0.6	2.74	0.9
Saudi Arabia	0.73	1.0	0.36	0.3	0.37	0.7	0.06	0.0	0.80	0.2

South Africa	0.38	0.5	0.38	0.3	0.49	0.9	0.25	0.2	1.12	0.3
South Korea	1.16	1.6	1.38	1.1	1.07	1.9	1.44	1.0	3.89	1.2
Turkey	0.79	1.1	0.75	0.6	0.31	0.6	0.60	0.4	1.66	0.5
UK	2.44	3.4	10.99	8.5	3.55	6.4	9.20	6.6	23.74	7.4
US	15.68	21.9	23.82	18.5	18.14	32.8	37.20	26.8	79.15	24.5
European Union Total	16.41	22.9	43.85	34.1	10.19	18.4	44.95	32.4	98.99	30.7
EU [excluding individual G20 Members] 2	5.95	8.3	14.55	11.3	2.92	5.3	19.04	13.7	36.51	11.3
G20 Total 3	61.47	85.7	114.35	88.9	44.90	81.2	130.64	94.2	289.90	89.8
Total World	71.71	100.0	128.63	100.0	55.32	100.0	138.75	100.0	322.70	100.0

1 Public + private debt securities.

2 Excludes data reported separately for France, Germany, Italy, and the UK; EU member countries which do not have separate individual representation in the G20 include Austria, Belgium, Denmark, Finland, Greece, Ireland, Luxembourg, the Netherlands, Portugal, Spain, and Sweden.

3 Sum of individual member countries + "EU—excluding individual G20 members" in order not to double count France, Germany, Italy, and the UK.

Source: IMF WEO; IMF IFS; Bankscope; Bloomberg, BIS.

standard setting bodies." International standard setting bodies are politically and legally independent groups of regulatory and supervisory authorities from member countries whose purpose is to "set out what are widely accepted as good principles, practices, and guidelines" under which firms and supervisory authorites in a given economic or financial sector should operate.[8] Perhaps the most prominent international standard setting entity is the BCBS; other major financial sector standard setters include the International Association of Insurance Supervisors (IAIS), the International Organization of Securities Commissions (IOSCO), and the International Accounting Standards Board (IASB). Each of these entities existed prior to the creation of the FSB, and each continues to pursue an independently determined agenda of work. Even so, an important operational corollary to the FSB's coordinating role with respect to the standard setting bodies is that it acts as a first-among-equals in aligning selected activities of the standard setters "to address any overlaps or gaps and clarify demarcations in light of changes in national and regional regulatory structures relating to prudential and systemic risk, market integrity, and investor and consumer protection, infrastructure, as well as accounting and auditing."[9]

The FSB's implicit leadership role on behalf of the G20 also extends to selected work with other major international organizations. Chief among these "other international organizations" is the IMF. Starting with the first Leaders' Summit in November 2008, the IMF has been named in every Summit communiqué for its important roles in the global financial system. Furthermore, as from the announcement of the creation of the FSB in the April 2009 London Summit communiqué, the FSB's collaboration with the IMF on several major intiatives has been featured; for example, the *London Summit—Leaders' Statement* (2 April 2009) states that "the FSB should collaborate with the IMF to provide early warning of macroeconomic and financial risks and the actions needed to address them." Nevertheless, there has also been a subtle, and perhaps somewhat implicit understanding that the G20 envisions the IMF deferring and reporting to the FSB in selected instances. This inference hinges in part on the fact that in addition to reforming the global financial system, another high-level post-crisis priority for the G20 has been, and continues to be, the reform of the "international financial architecture,"[10] characterized in particular by work to "modernize [the] IMF [to] better reflect the changes in the world economy" and to "enhance the IMF's legitimacy,

---

[8] See FSB, *What are Standards?* at <http://www.financialstabilityboard.org/cos/standards.htm.>; and FSB, *Who are the Standard-Setting Bodies?* at <http://www.financialstabilityboard.org/cos/wssb.htm.> Note that the FSB includes the IMF, the World Bank, and the OECD among the international standard setters. In this chapter we follow Nolle (2013) in categorizing those entities as "other international organizations" in recognition of the fact that their mission and work, while encompassing standard setting, is broader in scope.

[9] FSB, *Charter of the Financial Stability Board*, Article 2(2), June 2012.

[10] This phrase appears in the *G20 Leaders' Declaration* at the Los Cabos Summit, June 18-19, 2012. Other terminology covering this topic includes: "global architecture" (Pittsburgh Summit, September 24–25, 2009); "strengthening the IFIs" [international financial institutions] (Toronto Summit, June 26-27, 2010); "more stable and resilient International Monetary System" (Cannes Summit, November 3–4, 2011); and "the process to strengthen IMF resources to safeguard global financial stability and enhance the IMF's role in crisis prevention and resolution" (Ministers & Governors meeting in Mexico, November 4-5, 2012).

credibility, and effectiveness, making it an even stronger institution for promoting global financial stability and growth."[11] Such statements have typically been followed by specific G20 commitment to incease funding for the IMF.

26.2.2 G20/FSB SIFIs Initiatives

As from the first Leaders' Summit in Washington, DC in November 2008, G20 Leaders have pursued a broad and ambitious agenda, first to stabilize, and then to repair and reform the global financial system. One of their main targets has been the risks posed by the largest, most complex, and most interconnected financial firms, including in particular banking companies. In the five years since the full eruption of the global financial crisis, public documentation of G20/FSB financial system reform work has become extensive and complex; Nolle (2013) presents a tractable way to understand the nature and scope of that work, and we draw heavily on that study in the remainder of this section. Specifically, Nolle (2013) focuses on the major statements, declarations, and communiqués emerging from the seven Leaders' Summits, beginning with the first in November 2008.[12] Those Summit statements are in essence capstone summaries highlighting the nature and status of all relevant G20 and FSB workstreams, including those focusing on SIFIs. Together they provide a coherent picture of the emergence and evolution over time of both the overall financial system reform agenda and SIFIs-related initiatives.

When G20 Leaders met in Washington, DC in November 2008, all were urgently aware of the historic nature of the serious challenges to the world economy and financial markets, and indeed Leaders' began their main summit statement on that note. In that environment, Leaders' main focus at the Washington Summit was the stabilization of global financial markets, which many feared were near meltdown. In response, they hammered out an ambitious 47-point "action plan," which included a number of concrete, near-term, stabilization-aimed measures.[13] SIFIs received considerable attention in the 47-point plan, but no "SIFIs agenda" per se was constructed.

Less than half a year later, at the London Summit in April 2009, financial system stabilization continued to be the top priority for Leaders. Indeed, the London Summit communiqué begins by stating "We face the greatest challenge to the world economy in modern times; a crisis which has deepened since we last met." Nevertheless, the beginnings of a long-term financial system reform agenda began to take shape, including with respect to SIFIs. By the time Leaders met again in September 2009 in Pittsburgh—the one year anniversary, almost to the day, of the collapse of Lehman Brothers and the full eruption of the global financial crisis—the world financial system had turned the corner. As a consequence, beginning in Pittsburgh, Leaders were able to shift considerable attention to financial system reform

---

[11] *The G20 Seoul Summit Leaders' Declaration*, November 11-12, 2010, point #9, bullet #2.

[12] We note that this chapter was completed before the 8th Leaders' Summit in St. Petersburg, Russia in September 2013 took place. In his August 2013 draft (the most recent available for reference in this chapter), Nolle indicates that a subsequent, final version of that draft paper will cover the St. Petersburg Summit in a manner parallel to his treatment of the previous seven Leaders' Summits.

[13] See Nolle (2011) and (2012) for details on the 47-point action plan.

initiatives, officially declaring at that summit that the G20 had become "the premier forum" for international economic cooperation.[14]

The boldest financial system reform commitment Leaders made at the Pittsburgh Summit was aimed at SIFIs. Specifically, Leaders pledge to have developed, before the end of 2010, new international bank capital standards. In this manner, what became known as "Basel III" was launched. A commitment to develop a detailed plan for increasing the intensity of supervision of SIFIs was also announced at the Pittsburgh Summit, and Leaders began to refine their broad commitment to rationalize the process of the cross-border resolution of global banks.

In order to sustain momentum on their financial reform work, and given the still fragile nature of world financial markets, G20 Leaders decided to meet twice in 2010, as they had in 2009. In the event, the Toronto Summit in June 2010 served as a sort of "dress rehearsal" for the November 2010 Summit in Seoul, by which time substantial progress had been made across G20/FSB financial system reform initiatives, including in particular those focused on SIFIs. Front and center was the Leaders' sign-off on the just-completed Basel III program. The official protocol on the issuance of Basel III was that final public release of the main document came, by design, a few weeks after the standards were endorsed by G20 Leaders at the Seoul Summit. By that time, all of the details of the program were public and well-known; still, it is significant that, unlike in the case of the original Basel capital standards, or Basel II, the BCBS' was not the ultimate "stamp of approval" on the Basel III standards.

In addition to their ratification of Basel III, Leaders congratulated the FSB for its on-time completion of a comprehensive program of additional (non-Basel III) SIFIs initiatives, and endorsed the FSB's workplan for them. The FSB's "multi-pronged framework" covered five basic issues: (1) heightening prudential standards, with an emphasis on higher loss absorbency capacity; (2) making SIFI resolution a viable policy option for national authorities; (3) strengthening the supervision of SIFIs; (4) strengthening "core infrastructures" (including in particular payment and settlement systems); and (5) ensuring consistent implementation of national policies. Significantly, Leaders agreed with the FSB's strategy of focusing most intensely in the near-term on G-SIFIs, including the immediate task of developing methodology to identify which internationally active financial institutions should be designated as G-SIFIs.

Over the next year, as the Eurozone sovereign debt-cum-banking system distress situation became front-page financial news, the FSB made considerable progress on its SIFIs agenda, key parts of which relied heavily on the work of the BCBS.[15] By the November 3–4, 2011 Leaders' Summit in Cannes, that agenda had been reconfigured to emphasize four major workstreams focusing on G-SIFIs (detailed in Table 26.2). In Cannes, the workstream addressing international standards for resolution regimes was particularly highlighted, in view of the fact that the FSB had just completed (in October 2011) its *Key Attributes for Effective Resolution Regimes for Financial Institutions*. The FSB's development at the international level of those twelve requirements continues to be one of its most noteworthy successes and, as intended, has guided the dialogue at the national level in many countries, as

---

[14] *Leaders' Statement, the Pittsburgh Summit*, September 24-25, 2009, point # 19.
[15] For a description of the Eurozone crisis, see, e.g., Lane (2012b).

Table 26.2 The global response on SIFIs five years after the eruption of the global financial crisis: the G20/FSB SIFIs agenda—priorities and progress.[1]

Overall SIFIs project objective: Eliminate TBTF view and the moral hazard/excessive risk-taking behavior it elicits Establish and foster cooperation among countries, especially as it applies to the supervision and orderly cross-border resolution of G-SIFIs.[2]

SIFI Agenda Issue	Basic objective	Main achievements/progress
SIFIs identification and designation	Development of internationally consistent methodologies for determining financial firms of systemic importance at the relevant level (i.e. globally [G-SIFIs], or nationally/domestically [D-SIFIs]).	**G-SIBs**: In response to a major initiative of the G20 Leaders, BCBS published G-SIBs identification methodology, November 2011.[3] FSB designated first group of 29 G-SIBs in November 2011, and committed to updating those designations annually in November,[4] FSB published the first annual update of G-SIBs designations in November 2012.[5] **Globally systemically important *insurance* companies (G-SIIs)**: In a sequence intended to parallel the BCBS & FSB work on developing and applying identification methodology, annual updates, HLA requirements, and implementation schedule, the International Association of Insurance Supervisors (IAIS) committed to a program for globally systemically important *insurance* companies (G-SIIs). As of early July 2013, the IAIS' publication of the identification methodology was imminent, as was the use of that methodology by the FSB to name the initial list of G-SIIs; and as with G-SIBs, that list is to be updated annually in November, beginning in November 2014.[6] *Other Nonbank G-SIFIs*: The International Organization of Securities Commissions (IOSCO) committed to work in consultation with the FSB to produce a "proposed assessment methodology for identifying systemically important non-bank non-insurance financial institutions" by end-2013.[5]
Higher loss absorbency requirements for SIFIs	SIFIs "should have loss absorption capacity beyond the minimum agreed Basel III standards (and) should have a higher share of their balance sheets funded by capital and/or by other instruments which increase the resilience of the institution as a going concern."[2]	*Domestic systemically important banks (D-SIBs)*: In response to an FSB initiative, the BCBS began work at a mostly conceptual level on D-SIBs in late 2012. The BCBS published a high level "principles" discussion document on D-SIBs in October 2012.[7] For *Banks*—**Basel III** capital and liquidity standards, and implementation timeline, published in December 2010.[8] As of Q2 2013, 14 FSB member jurisdictions had issued final Basel III–based capital regulations, and 11 had final Basel III capital rules in force, with the remaining 3 committed to bringing the rules into force by end-2013; 4 FSB member countries (including the US) and the EU (covering FSB member countries France, Germany, Italy, Netherlands, Spain, and the UK) had published draft regulations.[9] *G-SIBs*: As from November 2012, banks designated as G-SIBs were grouped according to one of 5 "buckets," where each bucket indicates the higher loss absorbency (HLA) requirement applicable to G-SIBs in the given bucket. Specifically, the HLA is calculated as (additional) common equity loss absorbency as a percentage of risk-weighted assets, with the lowest bucket requiring 1.0% additional loss absorbency capital so calculated, and the remaining four buckets rising in 0.5 percentage point increments, as laid out in the November 2011 BCBS G-SIBs methodology document.[3] Note that, in effect, the November 2011 and 2012 G-SIBs designations were "trial runs" designed to make clear to the banking industry and regulators how the G-SIBs designations-cum-HLAs will work once fully in force in 2016, as applied to G-SIBs designated in November 2014.[5] *G-SIIs*: Work on specific HLA requirements and other standards for G-SIIs was slated for completion by the Leaders' Summit in 2014, with implementation beginning several years hence (in 2019, for example, for the application of the still-to-be-developed HLAs).[6]

(Continued)

Table 26.2 (Continued)

Overall SIFIs project objective: Eliminate TBTF view and the moral hazard/excessive risk-taking behavior it elicits. Establish and foster cooperation among countries, especially as it applies to the supervision and orderly cross-border resolution of G-SIFIs.[2]

SIFI Agenda

Issue	Basic objective	Main achievements/progress
SIFIs resolution framework	"SIFI resolution must be a viable option" ... "[an effective resolution] regime must be able to prevent the systemic damage caused by a disorderly collapse without exposing the taxpayer to the risk of loss."[2] In particular, G20 Leaders, and Ministers & Governors have committed "to ensure that all global systemically important financial institutions are resolvable."[10]	The FSB published in October 2011 its *Key Attributes of Effective Resolution Regimes* setting out the core elements necessary for an effective resolution regime.In April 2013, the FSB published its first comprehensive "thematic review" of resolution regimes in each of its 24 member countries. [10] The purpose of that and future reviews is "to support the timely and consistent implementation by FSB jurisdictions of agreed reforms."[11] The main findings were: (1) "some FSB jurisdictions have undertaken major reforms to their resolution regimes since the crisis;" (2) "several others are in the process of adopting reforms to further strengthen their regimes and align them to the *Key Attributes*;" but (3) especially with respect to "operational resolution plans and firm-specific cross-border cooperation agreements (COAGs) that set out a process for cooperation and information sharing for all G-SIFIs... progress has been relatively slow both because the issue is complex and because in many jurisdictions the powers necessary for implementing a preferred resolution strategy have not yet been provided."[12] The April 2013 thematic review identified 9 specific "areas in need of legislative or other action in FSB Members' jurisdictions" in order to fully implement the *Key Attributes*.[12] The thematic review specifically notes that the **banking industry** has so far been the FSB's priority focus, but the FSB laid out several broad nonbank initiatives on which future efforts will begin to focus.[12]
Increased supervisory intensity	"Every country must have a supervisory system that is up to the task of ensuring that the new regulation coming out of Basel III, are backed up by effective risk assessments and enforcement, especially as it relates to SIFIs."[2]	The FSB initially laid out principles for effective supervision of SIFIs in its 2010 report *Reducing the Moral Hazard Posed by Systemically Important Financial Institutions*. Since then, it has produced several major progress reports on Members' SIFIs' supervisory policies and practices, the most recent in November 2012.[13] The FSB has focused particularly on risk management, producing in February 2013 a thematic review on Members' supervisory practices in this respect.[14] **Banking Industry:** In its October 2010 report to the G20 on how Member countries had responded to the financial crisis, the BCBS committed to a thorough update of its *Core Principles for Effective Banking Supervision*; the BCBS published its revised **Core Principles** in September 2012. G-SIBs: G-SIBs designated by the FSB in either 2011 or 2012 are required, by January 2016, to meet higher supervisory standards, including in particular for "data aggregation capabilities and risk reporting."[5] **Nonbanks:** No deadline was set in the FSB's November 2012 G-SIBs designation report for nonbank G-SIFIs to begin to meet higher supervisory standards.[5] In April 2013, the FSB designated as one of its 5 "priority areas" "strengthening the oversight and regulation of shadow banking."[15] In general, FSB work on the supervision of nonbank SIFIs has progressed less than for SIBs.

[1] As of July 2013.

[2] FSB, *Reducing the moral hazard posed by systemically important financial institutions, FSB Recommendations and Time Lines* (October 20, 2010).

[3] BCBS, *Global systemically important banks: Assessment methodology and the additional loss absorbency requirement* (November 2011).

[4] FSB, *Policy Measures to Address Systemically Important Financial Institutions* (November 4, 2011). As explained in the text of this chapter, the first group of financial firms were all banking companies and for this reason, although originally called "G-SIFIs," subsequently came to be referred to as "G-SIBs."

[5] FSB, *Update of group of global systemically important banks (G-SIBs)* (November 1, 2012).

[6] FSB, *Meeting of the Financial Stability Board in Basel on 24 June*, Press release (June 25, 2013).

[7] BCBS, *A framework for dealing with domestic systemically important banks* (October 2012).

[8] BCBS, *Basel III: A global regulatory framework for more resilient banks and banking systems* (December 2010).

[9] FSB, *Progress of Financial Reforms*, Letter from the FSB Chairman to G20 Ministers and Central Bank Governors (April 15, 2013).

[10] FSB, *Thematic Review on Resolution Regimes*, Peer Review Report (April 11, 2013).

[11] FSB, FSB publishes peer review on resolution regimes, Press release (April 11, 2013).

[12] FSB, *Implementing the FSB Key Attributes of Effective Resolution Regimes—how far have we come?* (April 15, 2013).

[13] FSB, *Increasing the Intensity and Effectiveness of SIFI Supervision*, Progress Report to the G20 Ministers and Governors (November 1, 2012).

[14] FSB, *Thematic Review on Risk Governance* (12 February 2013).

[15] FSB, FSB reports to G20 on progress of financial regulatory reforms, Press release (April 19, 2013).

Source: Adapted from Nolle, Daniel E. (2013) "Who's in Charge of Fixing the World's Financial System? The Under Appreciated Lead Role of the G20 and the FSB," *Economics Working Paper—DRAFT*, Office of the Comptroller of the Currency. The draft of that paper available to this chapter's authors was written prior to the St. Petersburg Summit of September 5–6, 2013 (but note that in that draft Nolle indicates he intends to produce a revised version after the St. Petersburg Summit to take account of developments there).

policymakers grapple with the many challenges inherent in shaping and implementing programs and processes for the resolution of SIFIs.

Leaders also congratulated the FSB on hitting the target set after the Seoul Summit on the first-ever identification and designation of G-SIFIs. Those designations were based on methodology developed for that purpose by the BCBS (in close consultation with the FSB), details of which were released to the public at almost the same time as the FSB's G-SIFIs designations.[16] It is important to note that, although the 29 institutions designated by the FSB were explicitly listed as "G-SIFIs," all of them were banking companies.[17] Over the next year, as FSB-directed work began to focus to some extent on nonbank institutions, banking companies designated as globally significant came to be referred to by the more accurate term "G-SIBs."

The policy paper in which the FSB made its initial G-SIFIs designations also covered other concrete measures that have closely guided SIFIs work through the June 2012 Leaders' Summit in Los Cabos and, indeed, up to the present.[18] Drawing on that document, its sequel published one year later, and recent progress reports, the G20/FSB SIFIs program on the eve of the five-year anniversary of the full eruption of the global financial crisis in September 2008 is summarized in Table 26.2 under the four main workstreams first outlined in Cannes: (1) SIFIs identification and designation; (2) higher loss absorbency requirements for SIFIs, especially G-SIFIs; (3) effective resolution regimes aimed at eliminating both moral hazard behavior and taxpayer bailouts; and (4) enhanced supervision for SIFIs. It is clear that by far the most progress has been made with respect to banks, especially G-SIBs. The "Higher Loss Absorbency Requirements" row in Table 26.2 indicates that by Q3 2013 the majority of FSB member countries had either issued final Basel III regulations or had published draft regulations and so were on track for implementation in 2013. For G-SIBs, as discussed above, the BCBS established an internationally-agreed methodology for their identification, which the FSB used, and will continue to use, to make its annual G-SIBs designations. In consequence of being designated as G-SIBs, these institutions will be subject to higher capital requirements. In addition, the last row in Table 26.2 also shows that higher supervisory standards for banks had been agreed by the BCBS in 2012, and implementation of the standards laid out in the BCBS' *Core Principles for Effective Banking Supervision* was underway across G20 member countries.

The FSB has begun to turn attention to nonbank G-SIFIs, as well as to domestic systemically important banks (D-SIBs). Of note, as of early Q3 2013, the publication by the IAIS of identification methodology for globally significant insurance companies (G-SIIs) was imminent, as was the FSB designation of the initial group of G-SIIs. Nevertheless, as of Q3 2013, work had progressed less far for systemically important non-banks than for banks across all major SIFIs agenda components. With that in mind, we now turn from the global SIFIs agenda to a review of actual policies at the country-specific level, targeting the most important subset of SIFIs, SIBs.

---

[16] The BCBS' initial identification methodology was published as BCBS, *Global systemically important banks: Assessment methodology and additional loss absorbency requirements* (November 2011), but it was and remains the FSB's prerogative to publish the names of G-SIFIs (including G-SIBs).

[17] Specifically, see the terminology used in the one page *Annex* at the end of the FSB's *Policy Measures to Address Systemically Important Financial Institutions* report.

[18] In the context of this chapter, "the present" refers to the beginning of Q3 2013, the deadline for the production of this chapter.

26.3 REGULATION AND SUPERVISION OF SYSTEMICALLY IMPORTANT BANKS: CROSS-COUNTRY COMPARISONS

26.3.1 The SIBs Landscape around the World

As in Section 26.2, using methodology developed by the BCBS, the FSB took the lead in identifying those banks which are deemed to be globally systemically important banks (G-SIBs). Figure 26.1 describes the five factors that are used in making the determination. These factors include size, complexity, cross-jurisdictional activity, interconnectedness, and substitutability/financial institution infrastructure, with each of these factors equally weighted. The various subcomponents that underlie each of the five factors are also listed in the figure.[19]

Since size is only weighted at 20%, the list of G-SIBs will not necessarily simply include the biggest banks in the world. This point is made clear in Table 26.3, which lists the world's 100 biggest publicly trade banks, ranked by reported total assets as of 2012.[20] These banks are headquartered in only 26 countries and account for 83% of all publicly traded bank assets worldwide. At the same time, their aggregate assets are 112% of global GDP. Of the 100 banks, however, only 27 were identified by the FSB as G-SIBs in November 2012.[21] The total assets of these G-SIBs account for 55% of the total assets of the world's 100 biggest banks. Table 26.3 also shows that the biggest and tenth biggest bank as measured by total assets (Industrial and Commercial Bank of China and China Construction Bank, respectively) have not been designated as G-SIBs. More generally, the smallest G-SIB is State Street Corporation, with $223 billion in total assets, ranks 82nd on the list, while the biggest G-SIB, HSBC, with $2.7 trillion in total assets, ranks second. This illustrates the importance of factors other than asset size in the designation of G-SIBs.

One problem that arises in ranking the world's biggest banks by total assets is that not every country uses the same accounting standard. Table 26.3 shows that banks in most countries follow International Financial Reporting Standards (IFRS). However, banks in the United States follow Generally Accepted Accounting Principles (US GAAP). This is important because, dependent upon whether IFRS or US GAAP is followed, the two accounting systems may produce different measures of total assets. In particular, derivative assets are measured on a gross basis under IFRS, but on a net basis under US GAAP.[22]

---

[19] The determination of which banks are to be classified as G-SIBs requires a substantial amount of data and, ultimately, expert judgment. See BCBS (2013a) for the most recent classification methodology.

[20] Note that we focus on publicly traded banks due to their more readily available data.

[21] Group BPCE (Banque Populaire CdE) was also identified as a G-SIB, but is not on the list because it is not publicly traded.

[22] It is useful to elaborate on the importance of this distinction. The Europe-based International Accounting Standards Board (IASB), for example, allows less balance sheet offsetting than the US-based Financial Accounting Standards Board (FASB). The different offsetting requirements result in a significant difference between assets presented in accordance with IFRS and assets in accordance with US GAAP. This is particularly the case for entities that have large derivative activities (see ISDA, 2012).

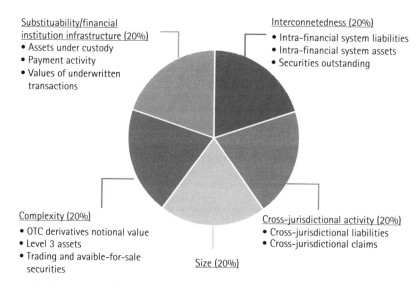

Substituability/financial
institution infrastructure (20%)
- Assets under custody
- Payment activity
- Values of underwritten
  transactions

Interconnetedness (20%)
- Intra-financial system liabilities
- Intra-financial system assets
- Securities outstanding

Complexity (20%)
- OTC derivatives notional value
- Level 3 assets
- Trading and avaible-for-sale
  securities

Cross-jurisdictional activity (20%)
- Cross-jurisdictional liabilities
- Cross-jurisdictional claims

Size (20%)

FIGURE 26.1 Factors used to identify globally systemically important banks.

Table 26.3 shows that if derivatives are measured on a gross basis for US banks, total assets for some of these banks increase substantially. For example, the assets of JP Morgan Chase increase to $3.9 trillion under IFRS from $2.4 trillion under US GAAP, and it then ranks as the biggest bank in the world. Figure 26.2 shows the impact of the different accounting treatments on total assets for the 8 US G-SIBs and 6 other US banks included among the world's 100 biggest banks. Clearly, whether derivatives are measured on a gross or net basis has important implications for the amount of capital banks must hold under the standards set by Basel III.[23]

There are different ways to assess the importance of the biggest banks in the world. Two of these ways are to compare the share of total bank assets accounted for by a big bank in a country and to compare the total assets of a big bank to the GDP of a country. The first way measures the degree to which bank assets are concentrated in one or a few institutions. The higher the concentration ratio, the greater the performance and stability of the banking sector depends upon one or a few big institutions. A bank or a few banks with a relatively high concentration ratio may therefore be deemed to be too-big-to-fail. Table 26.4 shows that the concentration ratios for individual banks range from a low of 1.1% for Suntrust Bank in United States to a high of 92% for ING in Netherlands. It is interesting that the ratios for the G-SIBs are not always the highest among all the banks. The second way to measure the importance of big banks is the size of a bank relative to GDP. The higher the ratio, the greater the strain placed upon a country if a big bank or a few big banks were to fail and require a bail out. Table 26.4 shows that the total asset-to-GDP ratios for individual banks range from a low of 1.1% for Suntrust bank in United States to a high of 217% for UBS in Switzerland. Again, the ratios for the G-SIBs are not always the highest among all banks.

---

[23] Table 26.3 indicates that some of the banks on our list choose to present their total assets under more than one accounting standards in their annual reports.

Table 26.3 The world's 100 biggest publicly traded banks ranked by reported total assets and total assets when derivatives are on a gross, not net (US GAAP), basis (IFRS). 2012 (G–SIBs, identified by the Financial Stability Board as of November 2012 are highlighted)

	Bank name	Country	Accounting standard	Total assets ($billions)	Total reported derivative assets on balance sheet ($billions)	Total derivative assets when based on gross rather than net basis ($ billions)	Total assets when derivatives based only on gross basis ($billions)
1	Industrial & Commercial Bank of China	China	IAS/IFRS	2,789	2.3	–	2,789
2	HSBC	United Kingdom	IAS/IFRS	2,693	357.5	–	2,693
3	Deutsche Bank	Germany	IAS/IFRS	2,655	1013.7	–	2,655
4	BNP Paribas	France	IAS/IFRS	2,517	560.6	–	2,517
5	Crédit Agricole S.A.	France	IAS/IFRS	2,431	626.3	–	2,431
6	Mitsubishi UFJ Financial Group	Japan	JP GAAP	2,410	n.a.	–	2,410
7	JP Morgan Chase	United States	US GAAP	2,359	75.0	1662.4	3,947
8	Barclays	United Kingdom	IAS/IFRS	2,352	740.3	–	2,352
9	China Construction Bank Corp.	China	IAS/IFRS	2,222	2.0	–	2,222
10	Bank of America Corp.	United States	US GAAP	2,210	53.5	1383.5	3,540
11	Agricultural Bank of China	China	IAS/IFRS	2,106	0.8	–	2,106
12	Royal Bank of Scotland Group	United Kingdom	IAS/IFRS	2,071	697.3	–	2,071
13	Bank of China	China	IAS/IFRS	2,016	6.4	–	2,016

(Continued)

Table 26.3 (Continued)

	Bank name	Country	Accounting standard	Total assets ($billions)	Total reported derivative assets on balance sheet ($billions)	Total derivative assets when based on gross rather than net basis ($ billions)	Total assets when derivatives based only on gross basis ($billions)
14	Citigroup	United States	US GAAP	1,865	54.6	1063.6	2,874
15	Mizuho Financial Group	Japan	JP GAAP	1,841	47.6	—	1,841
16	Sumitomo Mitsui Financial Group	Japan	JP GAAP	1,791	n.a.	—	1,791
17	Banco Santander S.A.	Spain	IAS/IFRS	1,675	159.0	—	1,675
18	Société Générale	France	IAS/IFRS	1,650	314.6	—	1,650
19	ING	Netherlands	IAS/IFRS	1,542	91.2	—	1,542
20	Lloyds Banking Group	United Kingdom	IAS/IFRS	1,459	89.2	—	1,459
21	Wells Fargo	United States	US GAAP	1,423	23.8	85.9	1,485
22	UBS	Switzerland	IAS/IFRS	1,374	456.1	—	1,374
23	UniCredit	Italy	IAS/IFRS	1,223	135.5	—	1,223
24	Credit Suisse Group	Switzerland	IAS/IFRS	1,008	40.5	910.1	1,878
25	Goldman Sachs	United States	US GAAP	939	71.2	839.1	1,707
26	Nordea Bank	Sweden	IAS/IFRS	894	155.8	—	894
27	Intesa Sanpaolo	Italy	IAS/IFRS	889	74.8	—	889
28	Banco Bilbao Vizcaya Argentaria S.A.	Spain	IAS/IFRS	842	71.0	—	842
29	Commerzbank	Germany	IAS/IFRS	839	148.6	—	839
30	Bank of Communications	China	IAS/IFRS	838	1.0	—	838
31	Metlife	United States	US GAAP	837	-0.161	9	846

32	Royal Bank of Canada	Canada	CA GAAP	825	91.3	—	825
33	Toronto-Dominion Bank	Canada	CA GAAP	811	60.9	—	811
34	National Australia Bank	Australia	IAS/IFRS	798	46.6	—	798
35	Morgan Stanley	United States	US GAAP	781	36.2	108.8	854
36	Commonwealth Bank of Australia	Australia	IAS/IFRS	732	39.7	—	732
37	Westpac Banking Corp.	Australia	IAS/IFRS	706	37.1	—	706
38	Natixis	France	IAS/IFRS	697	92.2	—	697
39	Australia and New Zealand Banking Group	Australia	IAS/IFRS	672	51.2	—	672
40	Bank of Nova Scotia	Canada	CA GAAP	668	30.3	—	668
41	Standard Chartered	United Kingdom	IAS/IFRS	637	49.5	—	637
42	Danske Bank	Denmark	IAS/IFRS	616	72.3	—	616
43	Banco do Brasil S.A.	Brazil	IAS/IFRS	563	0.7	—	563
44	China Merchants Bank	China	IAS/IFRS	547	0.3	—	547
45	Bank of Montreal	Canada	CA GAAP	526	48.1	—	526
46	Industrial Bank	China	CN GAAP	521	0.5	—	521
47	China Minsheng Banking Corp.	China	IAS/IFRS	515	0.2	—	515
48	Shanghai Pudong Development Bank	China	CN GAAP	505	0.1	—	505
49	Sberbank of Russia	Russia	IAS/IFRS	494	2.4	—	494
50	China CITIC Bank Corp.	China	IAS/IFRS	475	0.7	—	475
51	Dexia	Belgium	IAS/IFRS	471	44.9	—	471
52	Itau Unibanco Holdings	Brazil	IAS/IFRS	467	5.7	—	467
53	Caixa Bank	Spain	IAS/IFRS	460	27.4	—	460
54	Resona Holdings	Japan	JP GAAP	458	n.a.	—	458
55	DnB ASA	Norway	IAS/IFRS	407	17.3	—	407

(Continued)

Table 26.3 (Continued)

	Bank name	Country	Accounting standard	Total assets ($billions)	Total reported derivative assets on balance sheet ($billions)	Total derivative assets when based on gross rather than net basis ($ billions)	Total assets when derivatives based only on gross basis ($billions)
56	Nomura Holdings	Japan	JP GAAP	403	n.a.	–	403
57	Sumitomo Mitsui Trust Holdings	Japan	JP GAAP	395	n.a.	–	395
58	Canadian Imperial Bank of Commerce	Canada	CA GAAP	394	27.0	–	394
59	State Bank of India	India	IN GAAP	392	n.a.	–	392
60	Banco Bradesco S.A.	Brazil	IAS/IFRS	391	1.6	–	391
61	Skandinaviska Enskilda Banken	Sweden	IAS/IFRS	377	26.2	–	377
62	Bankia S.A.	Spain	IAS/IFRS	373	54.8	–	373
63	Svenska Handelsbanken	Sweden	IAS/IFRS	367	17.9	–	367
64	China Everbright Bank	China	CN GAAP	366	0.3	–	366
65	Bank of New York Mellon Corp.	United States	US GAAP	359	4.3	26.6	381
66	US Bancorp	United States	US GAAP	354	1.4	1.8	354
67	KBC	Belgium	IAS/IFRS	339	17.7	–	339
68	Shinkin Central Bank	Japan	JP GAAP	323	n.a.	–	323
69	Capital One Financial Corp.	United States	US GAAP	313	n.a.	–	313
70	PNC Financial Services Group	United States	US GAAP	305	8.6	–	305
71	Woori Finance Holdings	Korea, Rep.	IAS/IFRS	304	3.8	–	304
72	DBS Group Holdings	Singapore	IAS/IFRS	289	14.1	–	289
73	Banca Monte dei Paschi di Siena	Italy	IAS/IFRS	289	17.2	–	289

74	Swedbank	Sweden	IAS/IFRS	15.7	—	284	284
75	Erste Group Bank	Austria	IAS/IFRS	17.5	—	282	282
76	Shinhan Financial Group	Korea, Rep.	IAS/IFRS	2.0	—	281	281
77	Hana Financial Group	Korea, Rep.	IAS/IFRS	3.8	—	265	265
78	Ping An Bank	China	CN GAAP	0.0	—	258	258
79	VTB Bank	Russia	IAS/IFRS	3.1	—	243	243
80	Oversea-Chinese Banking Corp.	Singapore	IAS/IFRS	4.2	—	242	242
81	Huaxia Bank Co.	China	CN GAAP	0.0	—	239	239
82	State Street Corporation	United States	US GAAP	4.6	9.6	223	228
83	Banco de Sabadell SA	Spain	IAS/IFRS	8.8	—	213	213
84	Banco Popular Espanol S.A.	Spain	IAS/IFRS	3.6	—	208	208
85	United Overseas Bank	Singapore	IAS/IFRS	4.5	—	207	207
86	Daiwa Securities Group	Japan	JP GAAP	29.2	—	203	203
87	Bank of Ireland	Ireland	IAS/IFRS	7.7	—	196	196
88	Cathay Financial Holdings	Taiwan	TW GAAP	0.1	—	187	187
89	BB&T Corp.	United States	US GAAP	n.a.	—	184	184
90	Standard Bank Group	South Africa	IAS/IFRS	18.1	—	182	182
91	Raiffeisen Bank International	Austria	IAS/IFRS	10.8	—	180	180
92	Bank of Beijing	China	CN GAAP	0.0	—	180	180
93	Industrial Bank of Korea	Korea, Rep.	IAS/IFRS	2.6	—	179	179
94	National Bank of Canada	Canada	CA GAAP	6.7	—	178	178
95	UBI Banca	Italy	IAS/IFRS	3.9	—	175	175

(Continued)

Table 26.3 (Continued)

	Bank name	Country	Accounting standard	Total assets ($billions)	Total reported derivative assets on balance sheet ($billions)	Total derivative assets when based on gross rather than net basis ($ billions)	Total assets when derivatives based only on gross basis ($billions)
96	Banco Popolare	Italy	IAS/IFRS	174	8.8	–	174
97	SunTrust Bank	United States	US GAAP	173	1.9	2.6	174
98	Malayan Banking Berhad	Malaysia	MY GAAP	162	0.9	–	162
99	Allied Irish Banks plc	Ireland	IAS/IFRS	162	3.7	–	162
100	Macquarie Group	Australia	IAS/IFRS	157	15.3	–	157

Note: n.a.= not available and "–" means not applicable. IAS denotes International Accounting Standards.

1. Data from Q3 2012 is used for Japanese banks, whose fiscal year ends on March 31.

2. Group BPCE was identified as a G-SIB, but is not publicly traded.

3. Switzerland allows companies the choice of reporting derivatives on a net or gross basis.

4. BB&T, PNC Financial and Capital One report derivative assets on a gross basis, unlike other US banks.

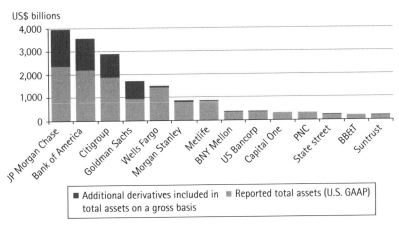

US$ billions

Additional derivatives included in   Reported total assets (U.S. GAAP)
total assets on a gross basis

FIGURE 26.2 Application of different accounting standards for derivatives has huge impact on measured assets-size of large US banks (2012).

26.3.2 The World Bank Survey Data

As noted at the outset, in response to the global financial crisis countries around the world have taken steps to reform the regulation and supervision of financial institutions. Until recently, detailed data to illuminate this fact did not exist. Fortunately, economists at the World Bank were quick to realize the importance of such data. As a consequence, the Bank augmented its periodic survey of banking regulations and supervisory practices around the world by asking regulatory authorities about their regulation and supervision of SIBs.[24] Specifically, the Bank's most recent (fourth) survey, completed in 2011, collected that new information from 135 countries.

Table 26.5 highlights new information on individual countries' treatment of SIBs. Of the 135 countries, 45% indicate that they now supervise systemic institutions in a different way than non-systemic ones. Furthermore, the countries employ different combinations of tools to oversee more closely and/or limit the activities of large/interconnected institutions. Some countries rely upon several tools, while others rely on relatively few tools. It is interesting that 11 countries do place restrictions/limits on the size of institutions. Countries that do not supervise systemic institutions in a different way than non-systemic ones almost always indicate that they do not have any tools to oversee more closely and/or limit the activities of large/interconnected institutions. Of course, it is not surprising that smaller countries do not supervise systemic institutions differently given the relatively small number of institutions in such countries.

Some countries have established a specialized department within the regulatory agency to deal with financial stability and systemic supervision. Table 26.6 shows that among the 135 countries surveyed, 61% have established such a department. In addition, some countries

[24] For a more comprehensive discussion of the surveys and how the information from them may be used to assess the impact of regulation and supervision on bank performance and bank stability, see Barth, Caprio, and Levine (2013) and the references therein.

Table 26.4 The world's 100 biggest banks: size relative to banking system assets and GDP, 2012

	Bank name	Country	Total assets ($billions)	Total assets (% of country bank assets)	Total assets (% of country GDP)	Cumulative assets (% world publicly traded bank assets)	Cumulative assets (% of world GDP)
1	Industrial & Commercial Bank of China	China	2,789	21.1	33.9	2.9	3.9
2	HSBC	United Kingdom	2,693	29.1	110.3	5.7	7.6
3	Deutsche Bank	Germany	2,655	71.8	78.1	8.5	11.3
4	BNP Paribas	France	2,517	31.9	96.5	11.1	14.9
5	Crédit Agricole S.A.	France	2,431	30.9	93.2	13.6	18.2
6	Mitsubishi UFJ Financial Group	Japan	2,410	32.4	40.4	16.1	21.6
7	JP Morgan Chase	United States	2,359	15.6	15.0	18.6	24.9
8	Barclays	United Kingdom	2,352	25.4	96.4	21.0	28.2
9	China Construction Bank Corp.	China	2,222	16.8	27.0	23.3	31.3
10	Bank of America Corp.	United States	2,210	14.6	14.1	25.6	34.4
11	Agricultural Bank of China	China	2,106	15.9	25.6	27.8	37.3
12	Royal Bank of Scotland Group	United Kingdom	2,071	22.3	84.9	30.0	40.2
13	Bank of China	China	2,016	15.2	24.5	32.1	43.0
14	Citigroup	United States	1,865	12.3	11.9	34.0	45.6
15	Mizuho Financial Group	Japan	1,841	24.8	30.9	35.9	48.2
16	Sumitomo Mitsui Financial Group	Japan	1,791	24.1	30.0	37.8	50.7
17	Banco Santander S.A.	Spain	1,675	43.2	123.9	39.5	53.0
18	Société Générale	France	1,650	20.9	63.3	41.2	55.3
19	ING	Netherlands	1,542	92.0	199.4	42.8	57.4
20	Lloyds Banking Group	United Kingdom	1,459	15.7	59.8	44.3	59.5
21	Wells Fargo	United States	1,423	9.4	9.1	45.8	61.5
22	UBS	Switzerland	1,374	50.3	217.2	47.3	63.4
23	UniCredit	Italy	1,223	35.4	60.7	48.5	65.1
24	Credit Suisse Group	Switzerland	1,008	36.9	159.5	49.6	66.5
25	Goldman Sachs	United States	939	6.2	6.0	50.5	67.8
26	Nordea Bank	Sweden	894	46.3	169.8	51.5	69.0

(Continued)

Table 26.4 (Continued)

	Bank name	Country	Total assets ($billions)	Total assets (% of country bank assets)	Total assets (% of country GDP)	Cumulative assets (% world publicly traded bank assets)	Cumulative assets (% of world GDP)
27	Intesa Sanpaolo	Italy	889	25.7	44.1	52.4	70.3
28	Banco Bilbao Vizcaya Argentaria S.A.	Spain	842	21.7	62.2	53.3	71.5
29	Commerzbank	Germany	839	22.7	24.7	54.1	72.6
30	Bank of Communications	China	838	6.3	10.2	55.0	73.8
31	Metlife	United States	837	5.5	5.3	55.9	75.0
32	Royal Bank of Canada	Canada	825	23.1	45.4	56.7	76.1
33	Toronto-Dominion Bank	Canada	811	22.7	44.6	57.6	77.2
34	National Australia Bank	Australia	798	24.5	51.8	58.4	78.4
35	Morgan Stanley	United States	781	5.2	5.0	59.2	79.5
36	Commonwealth Bank of Australia	Australia	732	22.4	47.5	60.0	80.5
37	Westpac Banking Corp.	Australia	706	21.6	45.8	60.7	81.5
38	Natixis	France	697	8.8	26.7	61.5	82.4
39	Australia and New Zealand Banking Group	Australia	672	20.6	43.6	62.2	83.4
40	Bank of Nova Scotia	Canada	668	18.7	36.7	62.8	84.3
41	Standard Chartered	United Kingdom	637	6.9	26.1	63.5	85.2
42	Danske Bank	Denmark	616	83.0	196.4	64.2	86.0
43	Banco do Brasil S.A.	Brazil	563	32.1	23.5	64.7	86.8
44	China Merchants Bank	China	547	4.1	6.6	65.3	87.6
45	Bank of Montreal	Canada	526	14.7	28.9	65.9	88.3
46	Industrial Bank	China	521	3.9	6.3	66.4	89.1
47	China Minsheng Banking Corp.	China	515	3.9	6.3	66.9	89.8
48	Shanghai Pudong Development Bank	China	505	3.8	6.1	67.5	90.5
49	Sberbank of Russia	Russia	494	44.9	24.4	68.0	91.2
50	China CITIC Bank Corp.	China	475	3.6	5.8	68.5	91.8
51	Dexia	Belgium	471	56.6	97.3	69.0	92.5

(Continued)

Table 26.4 (Continued)

	Bank name	Country	Total assets ($billions)	Total assets (% of country bank assets)	Total assets (% of country GDP)	Cumulative assets (% world publicly traded bank assets)	Cumulative assets (% of world GDP)
52	Itau Unibanco Holdings	Brazil	467	26.6	19.5	69.4	93.1
53	Caixa Bank	Spain	460	11.9	34.0	69.9	93.8
54	Resona Holdings	Japan	458	6.2	7.7	70.4	94.4
55	DnB ASA	Norway	407	66.2	81.3	70.8	95.0
56	Nomura Holdings	Japan	403	5.4	6.8	71.2	95.5
57	Sumitomo Mitsui Trust Holdings	Japan	395	5.3	6.6	71.6	96.1
58	Canadian Imperial Bank of Commerce	Canada	394	11.0	21.6	72.1	96.6
59	State Bank of India	India	392	29.8	21.5	72.5	97.2
60	Banco Bradesco S.A.	Brazil	391	22.3	16.3	72.9	97.7
61	Skandinaviska Enskilda Banken	Sweden	377	19.6	71.7	73.3	98.3
62	Bankia S.A.	Spain	373	9.6	27.6	73.6	98.8
63	Svenska Handelsbanken	Sweden	367	19.0	69.8	74.0	99.3
64	China Everbright Bank	China	366	2.8	4.4	74.4	99.8
65	Bank of New York Mellon Corp.	United States	359	2.4	2.3	74.8	100.3
66	US Bancorp	United States	354	2.3	2.3	75.1	100.8
67	KBC	Belgium	339	40.7	69.9	75.5	101.3
68	Shinkin Central Bank	Japan	323	4.3	5.4	75.8	101.7
69	Capital One Financial Corp.	United States	313	2.1	2.0	76.2	102.2
70	PNC Financial Services Group	United States	305	2.0	1.9	76.5	102.6
71	Woori Finance Holdings	Korea, Rep.	304	27.4	26.3	76.8	103.0
72	DBS Group Holdings	Singapore	289	38.7	104.5	77.1	103.4
73	Banca Monte dei Paschi di Siena	Italy	289	8.4	14.3	77.4	103.8
74	Swedbank	Sweden	284	14.7	54.0	77.7	104.2
75	Erste Group Bank	Austria	282	47.1	70.8	78.0	104.6
76	Shinhan Financial Group	Korea, Rep.	281	25.3	24.3	78.3	105.0
77	Hana Financial Group	Korea, Rep.	265	23.8	22.9	78.6	105.4

(Continued)

Table 26.4 (Continued)

	Bank name	Country	Total assets ($billions)	Total assets (% of country bank assets)	Total assets (% of country GDP)	Cumulative assets (% world publicly traded bank assets)	Cumulative assets (% of world GDP)
78	Ping An Bank	China	258	1.9	3.1	78.8	105.7
79	VTB Bank	Russia	243	22.1	12.0	79.1	106.1
80	Oversea-Chinese Banking Corp.	Singapore	242	32.4	87.6	79.3	106.4
81	Huaxia Bank Co.	China	239	1.8	2.9	79.6	106.7
82	State Street Corporation	United States	223	1.5	1.4	79.8	107.0
83	Banco de Sabadell SA	Spain	213	5.5	15.8	80.0	107.3
84	Banco Popular Espanol S.A.	Spain	208	5.4	15.4	80.2	107.6
85	United Overseas Bank	Singapore	207	27.7	74.9	80.5	107.9
86	Daiwa Securities Group	Japan	203	2.7	3.4	80.7	108.2
87	Bank of Ireland	Ireland	196	54.7	92.9	80.9	108.5
88	Cathay Financial Holdings	Taiwan	187	16.0	38.9	81.1	108.7
89	BB&T Corp.	United States	184	1.2	1.2	81.3	109.0
90	Standard Bank Group	South Africa	182	32.7	47.4	81.4	109.2
91	Raiffeisen Bank International	Austria	180	30.0	45.1	81.6	109.5
92	Bank of Beijing	China	180	1.4	2.2	81.8	109.7
93	Industrial Bank of Korea	Korea, Rep.	179	16.1	15.5	82.0	110.0
94	National Bank of Canada	Canada	178	5.0	9.8	82.2	110.2
95	UBI Banca	Italy	175	5.1	8.7	82.4	110.5
96	Banco Popolare	Italy	174	5.0	8.6	82.6	110.7
97	SunTrust Bank	United States	173	1.1	1.1	82.7	111.0
98	Malayan Banking Berhad	Malaysia	162	26.3	53.4	82.9	111.2
99	Allied Irish Banks plc	Ireland	162	45.3	76.8	83.1	111.4
100	Macquarie Group	Australia	157	4.8	10.2	83.2	111.6

Note: Total assets are based on individual countries' accounting policies. Total assets from previous quarter are used if the year end 2012 data are not available.

Sources: BankScope; International Monetary Fund; Milken Institute.

Table 26.5 Information on regulations for SIBs, by country

Country	Do you supervise systemic institutions in a different way than non-systemic ones?	If yes, do you have any tools to oversee more closely and/or limit the activities of large/interconnected institutions?								
		Additional capital requirements	Additional liquidity requirements	Asset/risk diversification requirements	Restrictions/ limits on activities	Restrictions/ limits on size of institution	Additional corporate taxes for large institutions	Closer or more frequent supervision	Restrictions on the group's legal structure	Other
Argentina	Yes	No	No	No	No	No	No	Yes	No	No
Australia	Yes	No	No	No	No	No	No	Yes	No	No
Brazil	Yes	No	No	No	No	No	No	Yes	No	Yes
Canada	No	--	--	--	--	--	--	--	--	--
China	Yes	Yes	Yes	Yes	--	--	--	Yes	--	--
France	Yes	No	No	No	No	No	Yes	Yes	No	No
Germany	--	--	--	--	--	--	--	--	--	--
India	Yes	No	No	No	No	No	No	No	No	No
Indonesia	Yes	No	No	No	No	No	No	Yes	No	No
Italy	Yes	Yes	No	Yes	Yes	No	No	Yes	No	--
Japan	n.a.	n.a.	n.a.	n.a.	n.a.	n.a.	n.a.	n.a.	n.a.	n.a.
Mexico	Yes	No	No	Yes	No	No	No	No	No	Yes
Russia	Yes	No	No	No	No	No	No	Yes	No	No
Saudi Arabia	n.a.	n.a.	n.a.	n.a.	n.a.	n.a.	n.a.	n.a.	n.a.	n.a.
South Africa	Yes	Yes	Yes	Yes	Yes	Yes	No	Yes	Yes	No
South Korea	No	--	--	--	--	--	--	--	--	--
Turkey	No	--	--	--	--	--	--	--	--	--

United Kingdom	Yes	Yes	Yes	Yes	Yes	No	No	Yes	No	---
United States	Yes	Yes	Yes	Yes	Yes	No	No	Yes	No	Yes
European Union Total	"Yes": 15 "No": 9 "---": 1 n.a.: 2	"Yes": 6 "No": 9 "---": 10 n.a.: 2	"Yes": 5 "No": 10 "---": 10 n.a.: 2	"Yes": 4 "No": 11 "---": 10 n.a.: 2	"Yes": 5 "No": 9 "---": 11 n.a.: 2	"Yes": 3 "No": 11 "---": 11 n.a.: 2	"Yes": 2 "No": 13 "---": 10 n.a.: 2	"Yes": 15 "No": 0 "---": 10 n.a.: 2	"Yes": 3 "No": 12 "---": 10 n.a.: 2	"Yes": 3 "No": 8 "---": 14 n.a.: 2
Rest of the world	"Yes": 36 "No": 55 "---": 6	"Yes": 15 "No": 21 "---": 61	"Yes": 10 "No": 26 "---": 61	"Yes": 12 "No": 24 "---": 61	"Yes": 18 "No": 20 "---": 59	"Yes": 7 "No": 28 "---": 62	"Yes": 0 "No": 35 "---": 62	"Yes": 35 "No": 5 "---": 57	"Yes": 10 "No": 26 "---": 61	"Yes": 4 "No": 25 "---": 68

Note: Japan, Saudi Arabia, Czech Republic and Sweden did not complete this particular survey. "---" denotes no answer for this question.

Sources: World Bank Survey IV; Barth, Caprio and Levine (2013).

Table 26.6 Information on factors considered for SIBs, by country

Country	Is there a specialized department in your agency dealing with financial stability and systemic supervision?	Which of the following factors do you consider in assessing systemic risk?											
		Bank capital ratios	Bank leverage ratios	Bank profitability ratios	Bank liquidity ratios	Growth in bank credit	Sectoral composition of bank loan portfolios	FX position of banks	Bank non-performing loan ratios	Bank provisioning ratios	Stock market prices	Housing prices	Other
Argentina	Yes	No	No	No	No	No	No	No	No	No	No	No	Yes
Australia	No	Yes	Yes	Yes	Yes	Yes	Yes	Yes	Yes	Yes	Yes	Yes	Yes
Brazil	Yes	Yes	Yes	Yes	Yes	Yes	Yes	Yes	Yes	Yes	Yes	No	Yes
Canada	Yes	Yes	Yes	Yes	Yes	Yes	Yes	Yes	Yes	Yes	Yes	Yes	Yes
China	--	--	--	--	--	--	--	--	--	--	--	--	--
France	Yes	No	No	No	No	No	No	No	No	No	No	No	Yes
Germany	--	--	--	--	--	--	--	--	--	--	--	--	--
India	Yes	Yes	Yes	Yes	Yes	Yes	Yes	Yes	Yes	Yes	Yes	Yes	No
Indonesia	Yes	Yes	No	No	No	No	No	No	No	No	No	No	No
Italy	No	Yes	Yes	Yes	Yes	Yes	Yes	No	Yes	Yes	Yes	Yes	No
Japan	n.a.	n.a.	n.a.	n.a.	n.a.	n.a.	n.a.	n.a.	n.a.	n.a.	n.a.	n.a.	n.a.
Mexico	Yes	Yes	Yes	No	Yes	No	Yes	Yes	Yes	Yes	Yes	No	Yes
Russia	Yes	Yes	No	Yes	Yes	No	No	Yes	Yes	Yes	Yes	Yes	No
Saudi Arabia	n.a.	n.a.	n.a.	n.a.	n.a.	n.a.	n.a.	n.a.	n.a.	n.a.	n.a.	n.a.	n.a.

	1	2	3	4	5	6	7	8	9	10	11	12	13
South Africa	Yes	Yes	Yes	Yes	Yes	Yes	No	Yes	Yes	No	No	No	Yes
South Korea	No	No	No	No	No	No	No	No	No	No	No	No	No
Turkey	Yes	Yes	Yes	Yes	Yes	Yes	Yes	Yes	Yes	Yes	No	No	No
United Kingdom	Yes	Yes	Yes	Yes	Yes	Yes	Yes	Yes	Yes	Yes	Yes	Yes	No
United States	No	Yes	Yes	Yes	Yes	Yes	Yes	Yes	Yes	Yes	Yes	Yes	Yes
European Union Total	"Yes": 17	"Yes": 16	"Yes": 19	"Yes": 22	"Yes": 20	"Yes": 20	"Yes": 19	"Yes": 15	"Yes": 20	"Yes": 20	"Yes": 13	"Yes": 16	"Yes": 5
	"No": 7	"No": 8	"No": 5	"No": 2	"No": 4	"No": 4	"No": 5	"No": 9	"No": 4	"No": 4	"No": 11	"No": 8	"No": 19
	"---": 1	"---": 1	"---": 1	"---": 1	"---": 1	"---": 1	"---": 1	"---": 1	"---": 1	"---": 1	"---": 1	"---": 1	"---": 1
	n.a.: 2	n.a.: 2	n.a.: 2	n.a.: 2	n.a.: 2	n.a.: 2	n.a.: 2	n.a.: 2	n.a.: 2	n.a.: 2	n.a.: 2	n.a.: 2	n.a.: 2
Rest of the world	"Yes": 56	"Yes": 53	"Yes": 59	"Yes": 73	"Yes": 68	"Yes": 66	"Yes": 68	"Yes": 56	"Yes": 63	"Yes": 57	"Yes": 27	"Yes": 28	"Yes": 23
	"No": 33	"No": 40	"No": 34	"No": 20	"No": 25	"No": 27	"No": 25	"No": 37	"No": 30	"No": 36	"No": 66	"No": 65	"No": 70
	"---": 8	"---": 4	"---": 4	"---": 4	"---": 4	"---": 4	"---": 4	"---": 4	"---": 4	"---": 4	"---": 4	"---": 4	"---": 4

Note: Japan, Saudi Arabia, Czech Republic and Sweden did not complete this particular survey. "---" denotes no answer for this question.

Sources: World Bank Survey IV; Barth, Caprio and Levine (2013).

have indicated the specific factors that they consider in assessing systemic risk, as shown in Table 26.6. Perhaps not surprisingly, nearly every country considers bank capital ratios important in assessing systemic risk.

26.3.3 Capital Requirements: Major Trends/Tendencies among Countries

It is a widespread view that one of the key factors that contributed to the global financial crisis was that many of the banks in countries around the world held too little capital relative to the riskiness of their on- and off-balance-sheet assets. To address this issue, the Basel III Capital Accord puts forth more stringent capital standards. Table 26.7 lists those new and higher capital standards, and shows the schedule for their full implementation by 2019. One feature that is important to emphasize is that there is a new leverage ratio, which is the ratio of equity to non-risk based assets. The other ratios are based upon equity to risk-based assets. Of course, not all countries have yet agreed to adopt such a leverage ratio. Most, however, have indicated they will adopt risk-based capital ratios. Another feature that is important to emphasize is that the new capital standards call for a capital surcharge for G-SIBs.

Table 26.7 Basel III new capital standards

	2013	2014	2015	2016	2017	2018	2019
Leverage ratio[1]	3% Parallel run Jan. 2013–Jan. 2017 Public disclosure starts Jan. 2015				Migration to pillar 1		
Minimum common equity capital ratio	3.5%	4.0%	4.5%				4.5%
Capital conservation buffer				0.625%	1.25%	1.875%	2.5%
Minimum common equity plus capital conservation buffer	3.5%	4.0%	4.5%	5.125%	5.75%	6.375%	7.0%
Phase-in of deduction from CET1	—	20%	40%	60%	80%	100%	100%
Minimum Tier 1 Capital	4.5%	5.5%					6.0%
Minimum Total Capital	8.0%	8.0%					8.0%
Minimum Total Capital plus conservation buffer	8.0%	8.0%	8.0%	8.625%	9.25%	9.875%	10.5%
Countercyclical buffer (discretionary)[2]	Up to 2.5%						
Surcharge of global SIBs	—	—	—	1.0–2.5% (in theory: 0–3.5%)			

Note: [1]. The Basel Committee will continue to test a minimum requirement of 3% for the leverage ratio during the parallel run period (from 1/1/2013 to 1/1/2017). Any final adjustments to the definition and calibration of the leverage ratio will be made by 2017, with a view to migrating to a Pillar 1 treatment on 1/1/2018 based on appropriate review and calibration.
[2]. Only applies to "Advanced Approaches Banking Organizations." The countercyclical capital buffer in the US would initially be set to zero, but it could increase if the agencies determine that there is excessive credit in the markets, possibly leading to subsequent widespread market failures.

Sources: Bank for International Settlements; Barth, Caprio, and Levine (2012); authors.

Table 26.8 provides information on the composition of the balance sheets of the world's 100 biggest banks as well as three different capital ratios. It is clear from this information that these banks have quite different business models and different capital ratios. This is the case for both G-SIBs and non-G-SIBs.

26.3.4 Resolution Regimes: Major Trends/Tendencies among Countries

In response to the global financial crisis, regulators in many countries have focused more intensely on their resolution regimes for banks that become insolvent. Table 26.9 provides information on whether banks are treated separately from nonfinancial firms in the event of any insolvency. It also provides information on whether banks are treated differently than bank holding companies. In addition, the powers and the authority possessing those powers whenever a bank becomes insolvent are identified. As shown, 11 of the 19 G20 countries have a separate bank insolvency framework that is distinct from that of non-financial firms, and 10 of the 19 G20 countries have a different insolvency framework for bank holding companies than banks. In terms of powers and the agency possessing these powers, the majority of the countries grant the most powers to resolve problem banks to bank supervisors. The courts, however, also seem to play an important role in many countries with respect to declaring insolvency. Furthermore, in most of the G20 countries shareholders can appeal to the court against a resolution decision of the banking supervisor.

Table 26.10 shows that most of the G20 countries do indeed provide for mechanisms to resolve problem banks prior to their closure and liquidation, including open bank assistance and government intervention in the form of conservatorship or nationalization. In terms of new approaches to resolving banks, most of the G20 countries have not introduced separate bank insolvency frameworks, but several of them have nevertheless implemented coordination arrangements among domestic authorities.

26.4 CROSS-BORDER LEGAL ISSUES

The challenges of greater coordination with regards to the supervision and regulation of G-SIBs are considerable. Unlike other traditional areas of international economic coordination, international financial regulation is not populated by treaties, but instead by non-binding protocols and accords. These "soft law" arrangements espouse best practices and codes of conduct that are geared towards outlining sound practices for governments and market participants, to memoranda of understanding in which financial authorities commit to sharing information with one another where they conduct cross-border investigations.

Among the most prominent of such agreements is the Basel III Accord. As we have already discussed above, the implementation process for Basel III's capital charges, liquidity requirements, and leverage ratios is well underway. Although countries continue to debate technical details and implementation schedules, all agree that buffering the reserves of banks ex ante, and limiting both the amount of debt and the amount of low quality reserve securities, will greatly reduce the likelihood of failure, both at the firm and system level.

Table 26.8 The world's 100 biggest banks: assets, liabilities, and capital ratios 2012

	Bank name	Country	Total assets ($billions)	Assets (% of total assets)				Liabilities (% of total assets)					Capital ratios (% of total assets)		
				Net loans	Interbank lending	Securities	Other assets	Deposits	Money market and short-term borrowing	Long-term borrowing	Derivatives and trading	Other liabilities	Equity/ total assets	Tangible common equity/ tangible assets	Market cap/total assets
1	Industrial & Commercial Bank of China	China	2,789	48.9	24.4	23.5	3.2	84.8	3.0	1.3	1.9	2.5	6.4	6.1	2.2
2	HSBC	United Kingdom	2,693	37.1	5.9	46.9	10.2	54.0	2.7	5.7	24.6	5.7	6.5	5.2	7.0
3	Deutsche Bank	Germany	2,655	19.7	5.9	65.3	9.0	28.7	9.5	8.5	41.2	8.8	2.7	1.9	1.5
4	BNP Paribas	France	2,517	32.9	1.9	52.1	13.0	33.4	17.1	6.4	24.9	13.1	4.5	3.7	2.8
5	Crédit Agricole S.A.	France	2,431	17.9	20.9	52.6	8.6	35.0	3.8	5.5	33.4	19.3	2.5	1.5	0.8
6	Mitsubishi UFJ Financial Group	Japan	2,410	40.5	0.3	49.5	9.8	59.9	16.7	7.4	6.8	3.3	5.8	5.3	3.5
7	JP Morgan Chase	United States	2,359	30.2	5.2	52.4	12.2	50.6	13.7	10.1	5.6	11.0	8.3	5.9	7.1
8	Barclays	United Kingdom	2,352	28.6	2.8	61.3	7.4	31.2	20.3	10.4	34.0	-0.1	3.8	3.2	2.2
9	China Construction Bank Corp.	China	2,222	52.3	24.5	20.6	2.6	88.2	1.6	1.2	0.3	1.9	6.8	6.5	8.7
10	Bank of America Corp.	United States	2,210	40.9	0.8	38.3	20.0	50.0	14.7	12.1	5.4	6.7	9.9	5.8	5.7
11	Agricultural Bank of China	China	2,106	46.5	28.8	21.6	3.1	87.9	1.5	1.1	1.2	2.5	5.7	5.1	0.7
12	Royal Bank of Scotland Group	United Kingdom	2,071	32.8	2.2	54.8	10.2	37.4	11.6	7.4	35.6	2.3	5.0	3.8	1.5
13	Bank of China	China	2,016	52.9	24.3	17.8	4.9	84.6	3.5	1.5	0.3	3.0	6.8	6.6	1.9
14	Citigroup	United States	1,865	33.8	5.5	41.4	19.3	49.9	14.1	12.3	6.2	6.7	10.1	7.0	6.2
15	Mizuho Financial Group	Japan	1,841	39.4	0.3	50.8	9.5	52.2	26.7	7.4	7.0	2.3	4.2	3.9	2.8
16	Sumitomo Mitsui Financial Group	Japan	1,791	42.8	2.9	34.8	19.4	60.5	9.0	6.9	3.9	14.8	5.0	4.8	2.6

#	Bank	Country													
17	Banco Santander S.A.	Spain	1,675	55.2	3.8	25.4	15.6	49.8	12.7	16.2	10.4	3.9	6.6	3.2	5.1
18	Société Générale	France	1,650	28.5	3.4	55.4	12.7	31.9	9.9	11.4	29.1	13.3	3.8	2.9	1.8
19	ING	Netherlands	1,542	48.2	3.3	28.7	19.7	42.6	5.4	8.0	9.8	28.5	4.7	4.4	2.3
20	Lloyds Banking Group	United Kingdom	1,459	55.9	3.2	12.3	28.5	47.3	7.0	18.3	9.2	13.4	4.8	3.6	3.6
21	Wells Fargo	United States	1,423	58.3	7.2	25.9	8.6	70.5	5.1	7.5	0.8	4.6	10.3	7.2	12.6
22	UBS	Switzerland	1,374	22.2	1.7	67.8	8.3	31.4	16.7	8.3	34.1	5.5	3.6	2.7	4.3
23	UniCredit	Italy	1,223	59.0	5.2	25.5	10.3	50.1	6.7	18.1	13.0	4.5	7.2	5.6	2.3
24	Credit Suisse Group	Switzerland	1,008	23.5	2.9	51.6	21.9	36.7	19.6	15.3	10.0	12.9	4.2	3.1	3.2
25	Goldman Sachs	United States	939	0.0	5.3	73.1	21.6	0.0	35.4	17.8	13.5	25.2	7.4	6.9	6.4
26	Nordea Bank	Sweden	894	47.3	1.5	35.4	15.8	37.8	11.9	16.2	17.1	12.5	4.1	3.6	4.3
27	Intesa Sanpaolo	Italy	889	55.9	4.2	31.8	8.1	42.0	1.2	27.4	9.6	12.0	7.5	5.4	3.0
28	Banco Bilbao Vizcaya Argentaria S.A.	Spain	842	55.3	3.1	28.7	12.8	49.7	14.6	13.3	9.2	5.8	6.9	4.9	5.9
29	Commerzbank	Germany	839	38.5	5.1	51.9	4.6	50.4	11.6	11.6	20.3	1.6	3.9	3.2	1.3
30	Bank of China	China	838	54.6	25.0	16.8	3.6	84.2	5.0	1.3	0.2	2.1	7.2	7.0	3.1
31	Metlife	United States	837	9.7	0.9	49.7	39.7	0.8	3.7	3.1	0.0	85.0	7.4	6.3	4.6
32	Royal Bank of Canada	Canada	825	45.8	1.2	44.3	8.6	47.8	12.7	14.7	11.7	7.4	5.0	3.8	10.0
33	Toronto-Dominion Bank	Canada	811	50.4	2.7	41.3	5.6	60.1	8.9	4.6	15.9	4.1	5.6	3.9	9.2
34	National Australia Bank	Australia	798	64.8	6.2	16.5	12.4	48.2	11.5	16.5	6.7	11.1	5.1	4.2	7.7
35	Morgan Stanley	United States	781	3.7	7.3	74.6	14.3	0.0	38.9	17.9	15.4	18.3	8.7	7.5	4.8
36	Commonwealth Bank of Australia	Australia	732	74.5	1.5	16.2	7.7	55.9	13.9	14.2	5.8	3.7	5.7	4.3	11.8
37	Westpac Banking Corp.	Australia	706	76.2	1.5	15.9	6.4	52.6	11.4	18.4	7.2	2.9	6.8	5.1	11.3
38	Natixis	France	697	18.8	10.4	56.0	14.8	31.3	19.7	6.9	24.3	13.9	3.6	1.1	1.5
39	Australia and New Zealand Banking Group	Australia	672	66.6	1.6	18.8	13.0	55.3	11.3	11.1	8.2	6.9	6.3	5.1	10.5

(Continued)

Table 26.8 (Continued)

	Bank name	Country	Total assets ($billions)	Assets (% of total assets)				Liabilities (% of total assets)					Capital ratios (% of total assets)		
				Net loans	Interbank lending	Securities	Other assets	Deposits	Money market and short-term borrowing	Long-term borrowing	Derivatives and trading	Other liabilities	Equity/ total assets	Tangible common equity/ tangible assets	Market cap/total assets
40	Bank of Nova Scotia	Canada	668	54.6	7.4	30.5	7.5	69.4	11.3	1.5	5.3	6.1	5.5	4.2	9.6
41	Standard Chartered	United Kingdom	637	44.6	10.7	27.8	16.9	67.1	0.0	12.1	8.1	4.9	7.0	5.8	9.4
42	Danske Bank	Denmark	616	54.4	3.3	28.9	13.4	29.5	10.3	28.1	15.3	11.6	4.0	3.4	2.8
43	Banco do Brasil S.A.	Brazil	563	43.8	9.8	32.7	13.7	41.0	24.5	12.6	0.3	15.6	5.7	4.2	6.4
44	China Merchants Bank	China	547	54.2	27.6	15.1	3.0	81.2	8.2	1.9	0.3	1.8	5.8	5.4	1.6
45	Bank of Montreal	Canada	526	47.3	1.2	42.0	9.5	61.6	12.0	0.8	9.3	10.5	5.3	4.0	7.3
46	Industrial Bank	China	521	36.7	47.5	12.2	3.6	82.6	7.8	1.9	0.1	1.5	5.2	5.1	9.7
47	China Minsheng Banking Corp.	China	515	41.7	45.1	7.5	5.6	82.2	7.6	2.3	0.0	1.6	5.2	4.8	5.4
48	Shanghai Pudong Development Bank	China	505	47.5	34.2	15.5	2.8	84.5	3.7	2.2	0.1	3.1	5.7	5.5	5.9
49	Sberbank of Russia	Russia	494	70.0	0.8	13.6	15.6	71.8	8.8	4.6	0.3	1.7	10.8	10.4	13.4
50	China CITIC Bank Corp.	China	475	54.5	29.4	12.3	3.8	87.9	1.3	1.6	0.1	1.4	6.8	6.6	1.8
51	Dexia	Belgium	471	42.0	13.1	20.4	24.5	21.4	6.2	30.9	17.9	22.7	0.9	0.9	0.0
52	Itau Unibanco Holdings	Brazil	467	35.8	2.5	43.7	18.1	25.5	28.0	17.7	1.2	19.9	8.0	5.0	8.0
53	Caixa Bank	Spain	460	61.3	1.4	28.0	9.3	44.5	4.9	26.3	6.1	11.3	5.9	4.3	3.3
54	Resona Holdings	Japan	458	61.0	0.4	26.4	12.2	82.8	4.2	3.2	0.8	2.8	3.1	2.7	2.9
55	DnB ASA	Norway	407	57.2	1.6	23.3	17.8	46.8	10.8	21.2	2.8	12.4	5.6	5.4	5.1
56	Nomura Holdings	Japan	403	4.1	0.0	86.0	9.9	2.8	42.6	20.0	22.4	6.1	6.1	5.8	5.8
57	Sumitomo Mitsui Trust Holdings	Japan	395	61.6	1.4	21.2	15.8	62.5	21.9	5.8	0.6	2.9	6.0	5.3	5.0

58	Canadian Imperial Bank of Commerce	Canada	394	61.6	0.5	31.1	6.7	63.0	5.4	14.6	6.9	5.4	3.9	3.3	8.1
59	State Bank of India	India	392	64.7	2.6	24.1	8.6	75.6	9.5	0.0	0.0	9.0	6.0	6.1	6.5
60	Banco Bradesco S.A.	Brazil	391	33.7	3.0	46.9	16.3	54.0	3.8	7.0	0.5	26.0	8.9	6.3	8.4
61	Skandinaviska Enskilda Banken	Sweden	377	47.3	4.6	24.7	23.4	40.9	9.4	19.3	9.7	15.8	4.5	3.8	4.9
62	Bankia S.A.	Spain	373	47.5	2.5	40.4	9.5	38.0	13.5	30.5	12.9	3.5	-2.1	-5.1	0.3
63	Svenska Handelsbanken	Sweden	367	69.0	1.7	15.1	14.3	35.7	17.7	31.6	5.1	5.0	4.3	4.1	6.0
64	China Everbright Bank	China	366	43.4	30.1	20.9	5.6	85.0	4.2	2.3	0.1	2.5	5.0	4.8	2.5
65	Bank of New York Mellon Corp.	United States	359	12.9	37.3	36.3	13.4	68.6	7.0	5.0	5.1	3.7	10.1	4.0	8.4
66	US Bancorp	United States	354	64.1	0.0	21.1	14.8	70.4	7.4	7.1	0.0	3.6	10.0	6.9	17.0
67	KBC	Belgium	339	49.8	4.4	38.1	7.7	55.5	3.4	7.6	16.5	10.7	4.8	3.8	4.0
68	Shinkin Central Bank	Japan	323	17.9	2.1	68.9	11.1	74.3	5.4	14.3	0.5	1.2	4.1	4.1	0.4
69	Capital One Financial Corp.	United States	313	64.2	2.4	20.4	12.9	67.9	6.8	8.0	0.0	3.2	12.9	8.0	10.8
70	PNC Financial Services Group	United States	305	60.8	1.3	24.9	13.0	69.9	3.9	9.4	0.0	3.0	12.5	9.0	10.1
71	Woori Finance Holdings	Korea, Rep.	304	69.4	1.7	21.3	7.7	62.3	10.3	8.6	3.4	8.4	6.9	6.7	2.9
72	DBS Group Holdings	Singapore	289	59.5	8.1	22.9	9.4	75.1	3.4	3.0	5.5	2.6	9.0	7.7	10.3
73	Banca Monte dei Paschi di Siena	Italy	289	64.9	4.8	23.2	7.1	48.3	8.7	23.9	12.4	2.8	2.9	2.3	1.2
74	Swedbank	Sweden	284	64.5	3.8	17.0	14.8	36.3	12.6	31.0	6.0	8.1	5.6	4.9	6.5
75	Erste Group Bank	Austria	282	58.1	4.2	28.4	9.2	67.7	1.2	14.3	5.9	2.5	7.6	6.3	4.4
76	Shinhan Financial Group	Korea, Rep.	281	64.9	1.5	22.3	11.3	56.1	6.7	12.9	2.7	12.0	9.3	8.0	6.1
77	Hana Financial Group	Korea, Rep.	265	59.8	1.1	24.7	14.3	63.6	7.0	11.4	2.9	7.9	7.1	6.5	3.0

(Continued)

Table 26.8 (Continued)

	Bank name	Country	Assets (% of total assets)						Liabilities (% of total assets)				Capital ratios (% of total assets)		
			Total assets ($billions)	Net loans	Interbank lending	Securities	Other assets	Deposits	Money market and short-term borrowing	Long-term borrowing	Derivatives and trading	Other liabilities	Equity/total assets	Tangible common equity/tangible assets	Market cap/total assets
78	Ping An Bank	China	258	29.8	22.6	15.5	32.0	58.9	4.3	0.6	0.0	0.8	4.4	6.2	4.2
79	VTB Bank	Russia	243	63.0	4.0	15.7	17.3	59.5	12.7	15.0	1.1	2.0	9.5	7.3	7.6
80	Oversea-Chinese Banking Corp.	Singapore	242	48.0	10.4	14.8	26.8	63.7	1.6	2.9	2.1	19.9	8.0	6.8	11.4
81	Huaxia Bank Co.	China	239	46.6	38.7	12.2	2.5	84.2	7.9	0.3	0.0	1.4	5.0	4.8	3.4
82	State Street Corporation	United States	223	5.5	22.8	59.6	12.1	73.8	5.6	2.8	0.0	7.7	9.2	5.5	9.8
83	Banco de Sabadell SA	Spain	213	65.0	2.3	21.0	11.7	70.8	1.1	16.4	1.5	4.4	5.2	1.6	3.6
84	Banco Popular Espanol S.A.	Spain	208	69.0	3.0	16.9	11.1	61.7	13.6	13.8	2.2	2.4	5.9	2.3	3.1
85	United Overseas Bank	Singapore	207	60.4	4.7	17.6	17.3	79.2	3.2	3.7	2.2	1.7	9.1	7.5	12.3
86	Daiwa Securities Group	Japan	203	1.9	0.0	84.6	13.4	9.4	47.6	9.7	26.1	1.6	5.7	5.3	6.0
87	Bank of Ireland	Ireland	196	62.5	3.3	23.4	10.9	52.2	13.0	13.2	3.6	12.0	4.6	3.3	2.3
88	Cathay Financial Holdings	Taiwan	187	28.0	1.9	42.9	27.2	27.9	0.9	1.7	0.2	64.8	4.6	4.1	6.3
89	BB&T Corp.	United States	184	63.3	0.9	21.4	14.4	72.4	1.6	10.4	0.0	4.1	10.4	6.6	11.1
90	Standard Bank Group	South Africa	182	52.4	0.0	39.8	7.9	59.3	0.0	2.0	14.7	15.3	8.1	7.2	12.3
91	Raiffeisen Bank International	Austria	180	57.2	16.3	18.1	8.5	57.4	13.4	12.3	6.8	1.6	6.2	4.9	4.5

92	Bank of Beijing	China	180	42.8	32.5	22.2	2.5	84.5	6.2	0.9	0.0	1.1	6.3	6.2	6.0
93	Industrial Bank of Korea	Korea, Rep.	179	72.5	1.6	21.4	4.5	40.9	11.6	36.7	1.9	4.7	6.7	6.4	3.4
94	National Bank of Canada	Canada	178	46.5	1.8	43.7	8.0	52.4	21.2	1.4	3.1	17.2	4.2	3.2	7.0
95	UBI Banca	Italy	175	69.7	3.0	19.4	7.9	48.5	3.5	34.0	3.0	2.9	8.0	5.9	2.4
96	Banco Popolare	Italy	174	69.3	2.8	19.4	8.4	43.4	7.5	33.8	4.8	3.2	6.8	5.1	1.7
97	SunTrust Bank	United States	173	70.7	0.0	16.8	12.5	76.3	3.2	5.4	0.7	2.4	11.7	7.8	8.8
98	Malayan Banking Berhad	Malaysia	162	62.9	2.4	19.9	14.8	76.9	0.0	4.9	0.5	7.5	8.9	7.6	15.7
99	Allied Irish Banks plc	Ireland	162	59.5	2.3	30.0	8.2	52.4	22.8	9.7	2.7	3.3	9.1	6.0	21.1
100	Macquarie Group	Australia	157	33.5	0.3	42.1	24.1	32.3	7.0	28.1	10.8	13.5	7.9	6.7	8.4

Sources: BankScope and authors' calculation.

Note: Deposit includes customer deposits (current, savings, and term deposits) and deposits from banks. Data for certain compositions are assumed to be zero if the data for that composition is not available.

Table 26.9 Insolvency framework in countries

Country	Is there a separate bank insolvency framework that is distinct from that of non-financial firms?	Is the insolvency framework the same for bank holding companies and banks?	Which authority has the powers to perform the following problem bank resolution activities? (BS = Bank Supervisor, C = Court, DIA = Deposit Insurance Agency, BR/AMC = Bank Restructuring or Asset Management Agency)					Can the bank shareholders appeal to the court against a resolution decision of the banking supervisor?
			a. Declare insolvency	b. Supersede shareholders' rights	c. Remove and replace bank senior management and directors	d. Undertake bank resolution mechanisms	e. Appoint and oversee a bank liquidator/ receiver	
Argentina	Yes	No	BS	BS	BS	BS	C	Yes
Australia	No	Yes	BS & bank	C	BS	BS	BS	Yes
Brazil	Yes	No	BS	BS	BS	BS	BS	Yes
Canada	Yes	No	C	BS	BS	BS	C	Yes
China	No	Yes	C	BS	BS	BS	C	Yes
France	Yes	No	C	C	BS & C	C	C	No
Germany	No	Yes	C	BS	BS	BS & C	BS & C	Yes
India	Yes	No	C	C	BS	BS	C	Yes
Indonesia	Yes	Yes	BS	DIA	BS	BS	C	Yes
Italy	Yes	No	C	BS	BS	BS	DIA	Yes
Japan	n.a.	n.a.	n.a.	n.a.	n.a.	n.a.	n.a.	n.a.
Mexico	No	Yes	DIA	DIA	DIA	DIA	DIA	No
Russia	Yes	No	C	BS	BS	BS	DIA	Yes
Saudi Arabia	n.a.	n.a.	n.a.	n.a.	n.a.	n.a.	C, BS & Creditors	n.a.
South Africa	No	Yes	C	C	BS	BS	Minister of Finance	Yes

			Is court approval required for the following bank resolution activities?					
	C	C	BS	C / DIA	BS	BS		
	BS	DIA		DIA		DIA		
South Korea	No	Yes	BS	DIA	BS	DIA	BS	Yes
Turkey	Yes	No	---	---	---	---	DIA	Yes
United Kingdom	Yes	No	---	---	---	---	---	No
United States	Yes	No	BS	DIA	BS	BS	BS	Yes
European Union Total	"Yes": 15 "No": 10 "---": 2 n.a.: 2	"Yes": 12 "No": 13 "---": 0 n.a.: 2	"Yes": 19 "No": 6 "---": 0 n.a.: 2	"Yes": 9 "No": 15 "---": 1 n.a.: 2	"Yes": 0 "No": 24 "---": 1 n.a.: 2	"Yes": 4 "No": 20 "---": 1 n.a.: 2	"Yes": 16 "No": 8 "---": 1 n.a.: 2	"Yes": 22 "No": 3 "---": 0 n.a.: 2
Rest of the world	"Yes": 64 "No": 28 "---": 5	"Yes": 55 "No": 31 "---": 11	"Yes": 47 "No": 49 "---": 1	"Yes": 34 "No": 59 "---": 4	"Yes": 6 "No": 88 "---": 3	"Yes": 9 "No": 83 "---": 5	"Yes": 43 "No": 50 "---": 4	"Yes": 86 "No": 10 "---": 1

Note: Japan, Saudi Arabia, Czech Republic and Sweden did not complete this particular survey. "---" denotes no answer for this question.

Sources: World Bank Survey IV; Barth, Caprio and Levine (2013).

Table 26.10 Existing and new approaches to resolving problem banks prior to closure and liquidation

| Country | Which mechanisms are provided in existing legislation to resolve a problem bank prior to its closure and liquidation? | | | | Have you introduced significant changes to the bank resolution framework in your country as a result of the global financial crisis? | |
	a. Open bank assistance	b. Purchase and assumption transaction (with or without government support)	c. Government intervention (e.g. via conservatorship or nationalization)	d. Bridge bank	a. Introduce a separate bank insolvency framework	b. Implement coordination arrangements among domestic authorities
Argentina	No	Yes	No	Yes	No	No
Australia	No	Yes	No	No	No	Yes
Brazil	Yes	Yes	No	No	No	No
Canada	No	Yes	No	Yes	No	No
China	Yes	Yes	Yes	No	Yes	Yes
France	Yes	Yes	Yes	No	No	Yes
Germany	No	Yes	No	Yes	No	No
India	No	No	Yes	No	No	No
Indonesia	Yes	Yes	Yes	Yes	No	Yes
Italy	Yes	Yes	No	No	No	Yes
Japan	n.a.	n.a.	n.a.	n.a.	n.a.	n.a.
Mexico	Yes	Yes	Yes	Yes	Yes	No
Russia	Yes	Yes	Yes	No	No	No
Saudi Arabia	n.a.	n.a.	n.a.	n.a.	n.a.	n.a.

	(1)	(2)	(3)	(4)	(5)	(6)
South Africa	No	Yes	No	No	No	No
South Korea	Yes	Yes	Yes	No	No	Yes
Turkey	No	Yes	Yes	No	No	Yes
United Kingdom	No	Yes	Yes	Yes	Yes	Yes
United States	Yes	Yes	Yes	Yes	No	No
European Union **Total**	"Yes": 15 "No": 9 "--": 1 n.a.: 2	"Yes": 21 "No": 4 "--": 0 n.a.: 2	"Yes": 17 "No": 8 "--": 0 n.a.: 2	"Yes": 9 "No": 16 "--": 0 n.a.: 2	"Yes": 1 "No": 24 n.a.: 2	"Yes": 15 "No": 18 n.a.: 2
Rest of the world	"Yes": 61 "No": 31 "--": 5	"Yes": 57 "No": 32 "--": 8	"Yes": 50 "No": 38 "--": 9	"Yes": 33 "No": 52 "--": 12	"Yes": 5 "No": 92	"Yes": 16 "No": 81

Sources: World Bank Survey IV; Barth, Caprio and Levine (2013)

Note: Japan, Saudi Arabia, Czech Republic and Sweden did not complete this particular survey. "--" denotes no answer for this question.

Meanwhile, efforts to address the too-big-to-fail issue have been facilitated through not only the Basel Committee, but the FSB as well. Both institutions have worked towards better identifying both G-SIBs and G-SIFIs through the preparation of both standards and more prescriptive methodologies. These advances have also led to more proactive regulatory coordination in the face of cross-border systemic risks. In November 2011, the FSB promulgated its *Key Attributes of Effective Resolution Regimes for Financial Institutions* ("the Key Attributes") as a new international standard for resolution regimes. These attributes were drafted with G-SIFIs in mind, and include a range of intensified coordination efforts for national financial regulatory authorities. Included in the package of reform are: (1) requirements for cross-border crisis management groups (CMGs), in which key regulators and financial authorities are to meet and share information on systemically important activities within their jurisdictions, (2) institution-specific cross-border cooperation agreements (COAGs) aimed at meeting the risks of particular banks, (3) recovery and resolution plans (RRPs), and (4) resolvability assessments for all G-SIFIs.

None of these efforts constitutes, however, binding international law. They do not create obligations for governments in the way a peace accord or an international humanitarian accord might. As such, there is no ratification process of the type used for international treaties on issues like trade and investment. Instead, financial market regulators employ largely administrative processes to implement standards at home.

There is good reason for this departure from traditional international law. Formal agreements are often less than optimal instruments of financial coordination. Treaty-making often entails months, if not years, of negotiation between heads of state or their representatives, and local representatives.[25] And once it is created, they are hard to change, increasing the risk that rules generated through treaties fall out of step with practice.[26]

Soft law, by contrast, provides a decisively cheaper means of agreement-making.[27] It carries what can be thought of as low bargaining costs due to its informal status. Perhaps most important, it does not require extensive participation by heads of state or lengthy ratification procedures. Instead, agreements can be entered into between administrative agencies and technocrats, with relatively little interference by outsiders. As a result, fewer interests need be accounted for and the universe of interests becomes more finite, easing negotiation. Parties can also amend accords relatively easily, because of the flexibility afforded by soft law, so long as a basic agreement among parties exists.

From the standpoint of lawyers, regulators, and diplomats, soft law additionally involves far fewer "sovereignty costs," or constraints, that may limit the ability of a state to follow its own national prerogatives when circumstances dictate. It is not a formal obligation, so backtracking will not generate the same kinds of reputational costs as a treaty, at least with regard to whether or not it complies with its legal obligations. Furthermore, hard law is from time to time coupled with or enables various forms of retaliation by aggrieved states, which soft law standards to do not usually directly facilitate or bless. As such, soft law also helps facilitate agreement by lowering the risk of uncertainty that frequently pervades policy issue

---

[25] Consequently, hard law tends to be popular in areas like trade where the objects of regulation are comparatively less subject to change as financial markets. See Brummer (2012).

[26] See Levit (2005), noting that customary international law norms remain vague by design to ensure that they envelop enough "state practice" to constitute international law.

[27] See Gersen and Posner (2008) for a discussion of "cheap talk" theories.

areas. Frequently, there is considerable skepticism or angst concerning the adoption of any particular approach in part, as Abbott and Snidal (2000, p. 441) explain, because "[t]he underlying problems may not be well understood, so states cannot anticipate all possible consequences of a legalized arrangement." Abbott and Snidal also note that, by avoiding formal legality, parties to agreements are able to see the impact of rules in practice in order to better assess their benefits, while at the same time retaining the flexibility to avoid any unpleasant surprises the rules may hold.

Yet in spite of all of its advantages, international financial regulation is not without its own serious structural flaws and shortcomings. Brummer (2011) explains that though technically a non-binding area of international law, international financial regulation has been largely envisioned to carry both reputational consequences for countries that ignored best practices, as well as potentially higher funding costs for firms in noncompliant jurisdictions. Monitoring of compliance with international standards, has, however, traditionally been less than robust. Traditionally, the IMF and World Bank are the primary actors tasked with the lion's share of surveillance responsibilities with regards to compliance with international regulatory standards. However, prior to the crisis, only those countries that are recipients of loans from the World Bank and IMF face the prospect of surveillance by the two institutions. Furthermore, the information gained by surveillance was published only with the permission of the inspected country. Thus, as Clark and Drage (2000) point out, whether information regarding a given country's compliance is shared with market participants, and even regulators in other countries, remains at the discretion of the given country.

In the wake of the 2008 financial crisis, commitments made under the auspices of the FSB became institutionalized under the Articles of Agreement of the IMF, and the surveillance became both mandatory and more public. Furthermore, FSB members espoused as part of their membership obligations compliance with key coordination and cooperation measures. Although the international standard setting bodies have become increasingly active in investigating members' compliance through various "peer review processes," perhaps the most noteworthy regime aimed at assessing members' compliance with their commitments is the "thematic peer reviews" undertaken by the FSB. These reviews are designed to gauge countries' compliance with international financial standards and with policies that the FSB itself prioritizes, or that take stock of existing practices in particular policy areas. This work has been coupled with and complements individual "country" peer reviews focusing on the progress made by a given FSB member in implementing regulatory and supervisory recommendations. The idea is that by beefing up surveillance of country-level behavior, detection of a regulator's avoidance of international best practices would be easier. Additionally, the costs of defecting from or backtracking from commitments could be heightened. Not only might regulators be interested in this kind of review and information, but so might private market participants. For example, a bank headquartered in Basel III-compliant country X, and lending to a bank in non-Basel III compliant (or under-compliant) country Y, may well conclude that the country Y bank is for that reason riskier. Under those circumstances, country X bank is likely to charge a premium for lending to country Y bank. Indeed, a range of studies covering securities markets to banking markets suggest that choice of law can impact the cost of capital.

It is likely that some areas of SIFI regulation might be more prone to cross-border regulation than others. Relative to other financial services industries, (most) bank activities are (somewhat) more straightforward and hence (somewhat) more amenable to effective

Table 26.11 Progress on the implementation of Basel III.

	As of October 2012			As of end–March 2013		
	Basel II	Basel 2.5	Basel III	Basel II	Basel 2.5	Basel III
Number of countries which have issued final rules and implemented them	22	20	0	24	22	11
Number of countries which have issued final rules, but have not yet implemented them	1	0	6	1	0	3
Number of countries which are at various stages of finalization of rules	4	4	19	2	3	13
Number of countries which have not initiated any significant action to put in place the rules	0	3	2	0	2	0
Total	27	27	27	27	27	27

Source: BCBS (2013b).

regulatory "policing." Under those circumstances, countries have acted to varying degrees to begin to implement at least the core Basel capital standards, as illustrated in Table 26.11.

Relative to the implementation of Basel capital standards, progress on cross-border financial resolution has been considerably less impressive. This point was emphasized in a major thematic review on resolution procedures among FSB members, the results of which were published by the FSB in April 2013.[28] The study noted that while some FSB jurisdictions have undertaken major reforms to their resolution regimes since the crisis, and several others are in the process of adopting reforms to further strengthen their regimes and align them to the *Key Attributes*, overall the implementation of the *Key Attributes* is still at an early stage, and legislative action is necessary to fully align resolution regimes in FSB jurisdictions to that standard. The April thematic review identified several important obstacles. In many instances, authorities that have been tasked with resolution do not possess the capacity or ability to carry out their international mandates. In some countries, financial authorities do not have the power to convert a failing bank's debt into equity or prevent parties from exercising their rights under financial contracts they have with the firm. Most authorities also lack the power to assume managerial control of a failing financial institution or to resolve non-banks that though technically may have non-financial businesses may nonetheless pose systemic risks if they fail. Finally, even after the promulgation of the *Key Attributes* many jurisdictions lack a statutory resolution planning requirement or the power to require financial firms to reform their operations in ways to improve their resolvability.

At this point, even more problematic than bringing national resolution regimes up to the standards in the *Key Attributes* is the issue of coordinating resolution regimes across borders. To date, basic attempts to institutionalize coordination across borders remain

[28] See FSB (2013).

lackluster. Many jurisdictions lack formal procedures for giving effect to foreign resolution actions. Information sharing is also, broadly speaking, low, despite the exhortations of the *Key Attributes*. Furthermore, there have been only limited regulatory and legislative initiatives to create automatic triggers or cooperative actions where resolution or insolvency provisions are commenced abroad. Meanwhile, most jurisdictions are not even required to consider the impact of their own actions on the financial stability of others.

26.5 Summary and Concluding Observations

This chapter began by noting that, although financial system policymakers around the world continue to respond vigorously to the problems in financial markets, financial institutions, and financial system regulation and supervision brought into high relief by the global financial crisis, the overall understanding of what those responses are remains rather vague and limited. Our chapter contributes to improving the state of knowledge by focusing on one particularly relevant issue, the regulation and supervision of SIBs. The heart of our contribution is the presentation of information heretofore obscure, or new, or both. Our approach is to develop two complementary perspectives. The first is what we have characterized as "the global view." That discussion begins by noting that the G20 and the FSB are the architects of the most significant agenda in the world to reform the global financial system, including in particular as that system operates through SIFIs. We explain what the G20 and the FSB are, how they came to occupy the driver's seat so to speak, and the evolution of their major financial system reform initiatives since the darkest days of the global financial crisis. That discussion highlights SIFIs initiatives, emphasizing in particular those pertaining to G-SIFIs and G-SIBs.

Our second perspective is a country-specific one. It starts by making the important observation that while most of the largest banks around the world have not been designated as "globally" systemically important, they are nevertheless systemically important when considered in a national or "domestic" context. Under those circumstances it is therefore fortunate that, due to recent World Bank efforts, a large set of information exists about the regulation and supervision of SIBs. The study summarizes and highlights the new data collected by the World Bank on the post-crisis regulation and supervision of SIBs by 135 countries around the world. Broadly, that analysis shows that countries are more similar than different in the measures they have adopted for regulating and supervising SIBs. We conclude our study by suggesting that, although that fact should aid countries in coordinating policies internationally, there is a very long way to go in that respect.

References

Abbott, K. W. and Snidal, D. (2000). Hard and Soft Law in International Governance, *International Organization* 54(3), 421–441.

Barth, J. R., Caprio Jr., G. and Levine, R. (2012). *Guardians of Finance*. Cambridge: MIT Press.

Barth, J. R., Caprio Jr., G. and Levine, R. (2013). Bank Regulation and Supervision in 180 Countries from 1999 to 2011, *Journal of Financial Economic Policy* 5(2), 111–219.

BCBS (Basel Committee on Banking Supervision) (2013a). Global Systemically Important Banks: Updated Assessment Methodology and the Higher Loss Absorbency Requirement, July.

BCBS (Basel Committee on Banking Supervision) (2013b). Report to G20 Finance Ministers and Central Bank Governors on Monitoring Implementation of Basel III Regulatory Reform, April.

Brummer, C. (2011). How International Financial Law Works (And How It Doesn't), *The Georgetown Law Journal* 99, 257–327.

Brummer, C. (2012). *Soft Law and the Global Financial System: Rule Making in the 21st Century.* New York: Cambridge University Press.

Clark, A. and Drage, J. (2000). International Standards and Codes, *Financial Stability Review* 9, 162–166.

Financial Stability Board (FSB) (2013). Thematic Review on Resolution Regimes, April 11.

Gersen, J. E. and Posner, E. A. (2008). Soft Law: Lessons from Congressional Practice, *Stanford Law Review* 61(3), 573–589.

IMF (International Monetary Fund) (2013). Factsheet: The Financial Sector Assessment Program (FSAP), <http://www.imf.org/external/np/exr/facts/fsap.htm.>.

ISDA (International Swaps and Derivatives Association) (2012). Netting and Offsetting: Reporting Derivatives under US GAAP and under IFRS, May.

Lane, P. R. (2012a). Financial Globalisation and the Crisis, BIS Working Papers No. 397.

Lane, P. R. (2012b). The European Sovereign Debt Crisis, *Journal of Economic Literature* 26, 49–68.

Levit, J. K. (2005). A Bottom-Up Approach to International Lawmaking: The Tale of Three Trade Finance Instruments, *Yale Journal of International Law* 30(2), 125–171.

Nolle, D. E. (2011). US Domestic and International Financial Reform Policy: Are G20 Commitments and the Dodd-Frank Act in Sync?, Board of Governors of the Federal Reserve System International Finance Discussion Papers No. 1024, July.

Nolle, D. E. (2012). Global Financial System Reform: The Dodd-Frank Act and the G20 Agenda, *Journal of Financial Economic Policy* 4(2), 160–197.

Nolle, D. E. (2013). Who's in Charge of Fixing the World's Financial System? The Under Appreciated Lead Role of the G20 and the FSB. Office of the Comptroller of the Currency Economics Working Paper.

PART IV

MACROECONOMIC

PERSPECTIVES

CHAPTER 27

....

SYSTEMIC RISK IN BANKING AFTER THE GREAT FINANCIAL CRISIS*

....

OLIVIER DE BANDT, PHILIPP HARTMANN, AND JOSÉ-LUIS PEYDRÓ ALCALDE

The Fed will work closely and actively with the Treasury and other authorities to minimize systemic risk.

Ben Bernanke, Chairman of the Federal Reserve (Oct. 2008)[1]

The failure of Lehman Brothers in September triggered an unprecedented deterioration in the degree of confidence in the banking sector which ran the risk of undermining its fundamental function of financial intermediation.

Jean-Claude Trichet, President of the European Central Bank (Dec. 2008)[2]

27.1 INTRODUCTION

....

FINANCIAL instability and crises are a recurrent, albeit infrequent, phenomenon in history (Kindleberger, 1978; Reinhart and Rogoff, 2009). The crisis that broke out in August 2007 reached systemic dimensions in September 2008, with the demise of Lehmann Brothers

* This chapter builds on and updates de Bandt and Hartmann (2000, 2002) and de Bandt, Hartmann and Peydró (2010). Any views expressed in this chapter are the authors' own and do not necessarily reflect those of the European Central Bank, the Autorité de Contrôle Prudentiel et de Résolution or the Eurosystem. Additional references to the earlier literature is available in these papers. We thank Francesc R. Tous for his excellent research assistance.

[1] "Stabilizing the Financial Markets and the Economy," address at the Economic Club of New York <http://www.america.gov/st/texttransenglish/2008/October/20081016110841eaifas9.330386e-02.html>.

[2] Address to the European Parliament <http://www.ecb.int/press/key/date/2008/html/sp081208_2. en.html>. Lehman Brothers' failure became the largest bankruptcy in US history, listing liabilities of $613 billion in its filing.

in conjunction with a number of other events. This was one of the clearest illustrations in history of the fact that financial systems are subject to "systemic risk," in which banks and credit play a particularly important role. Other examples include the banking crises of the Great Depression during the 1930s and of Japan and the Nordic countries during the 1990s. While the earlier and the present episodes both share some common features and are characterized by specific factors, systemic risk is now widely accepted as a fundamental underlying concept for the study of such severe financial instabilities, with strong real effects for the economy at large, and possible public policy responses.

The two chapter epigraphs, observations which were made at the height of the crisis by the leaders of the two most important central banks in the world, illustrate the policy relevance of systemic risk. In fact, one widely shared lesson of the crisis is that financial supervision and regulation need to become much more "macroprudential" (rather than remaining "microprudential"), that is, they should be geared towards containing systemic risks (rather than the risks of individual intermediaries or markets).[3] To this effect many countries have created new bodies that should exercise such macroprudential policies. In Europe the European Systemic Risk Board has been created and, through the Single Supervisory Mechanism, the European Central Bank will have macroprudential competencies (Council of the European Union, 2013). In the United States the Financial Stability Oversight Council has been established.

In this chapter we provide a comprehensive analysis of systemic risk in banking, as the primary ingredient in understanding financial crises that cause severe negative effects for the real sector, and as a main rationale for banking regulation, prudential supervision, and crisis management. First, we bring together the most important analytical elements of systemic risk and integrate them into a coherent working concept, which can be used as a baseline for policies for ensuring the stability of financial systems, and distinguish three sources of systemic risk: contagion effects, aggregate shocks (exogenous to the financial system), and that emerging from the endogenous buildup and unraveling of widespread financial imbalances (ECB, 2009). We then analyse ex ante (preventive) and ex post (crisis management) public policy to contain systemic risk and crises (including macroprudential policy). Second, we also review the existing theoretical and empirical literature about systemic risk in light of the previously developed general concept. This could also help in identifying areas in which future research is needed. Finally, we offer some concluding remarks.

27.2 THE CONCEPT OF SYSTEMIC RISK

Systemic risk in a very general sense is by no means a phenomenon limited to economics or the financial system. Maybe the most natural illustration of the concept is in the area of health and epidemic diseases. For example, widespread contamination as a result of disease

---

[3] Extensive further discussions, reports, and papers on the current crisis are, for example, Ferguson et al. (2007); Ashcraft and Schuermann (2008); Evanoff, Hartmann, and Kaufman (2009); Federal Reserve Bank of Kansas City (2008); Financial Stability Forum (2008); Greenlaw et al. (2008), Institute of International Finance (2008); Senior Supervisors Group (2008); and many financial stability reports of central banks.

could wipe out a significant portion of a population. In the area of economics, it has been argued that systemic risk is a special feature of financial systems, in particular the banking system. While contamination effects may also occur in other sectors of the economy, they are often regarded as more likely and severe in financial systems, partly because of the adverse effects they may have on the economy at large. One comprehensive definition of systemic risk in an economy is then the risk that financial instability becomes so widespread that it impairs the functioning of a financial system to the point where economic growth and welfare suffer materially (ECB, 2009). A "systemic crisis" is the materialization of this risk.

This section first provides a framework for the economic analysis of systemic risk that is based on both the research literature and practical experience. Second, it explains the reasons why financial systems can be regarded as being more vulnerable to systemic risk than other parts of economic systems. Third, we discuss to which extent some systemic events may be regarded as "efficient" and others as "inefficient." Fourth, the relevance of systemic risk in banking for public policy is briefly examined.

27.2.1 Systemic Events and Crises[4]

Starting from the above definition one can first distinguish "horizontal" from "vertical" systemic risk. The "horizontal" perspective is limited to understanding what makes instability widespread *within* the financial system. The "vertical" perspective also takes into account the two-way interaction between the financial system and the macroeconomy which would be needed to assess growth and welfare effects. Until recently, standard macroeconomic models did not possess well-developed financial sectors, let alone characterisations of financial stability, so that the research literature did not cover the "vertical" perspective very well. This is why most of this survey focuses on the "horizontal" perspective of systemic risk, although we now also include some first macro models with financial instability and some empirical evidence on the importance of financial shocks for the real economy.[5]

A key question is what makes financial instability widespread, that is, making an instability event widespread in the banking system or the whole financial system. This can happen in three ways. First, instability can be transmitted in a sequential way from one financial intermediary to another (or from one financial market to another, often in the form of an externality), even though the instability of these intermediaries (or markets) has no common origin. We denote this form of systemic risk as contagion risk if certain further conditions are fulfilled such as that the transmission is particularly violent, leading, for example, to bank defaults (or market crashes), or is in other ways different from the regular transmission of shocks (it differs from simple interdependence across institutions in normal times, as opposed to crisis periods, and it cannot be explained by economic fundamentals: see Hartmann, Straetmans, and de Vries, 2006). Second, the system can be hit by a severe exogenous aggregate shock, which adversely affects a wide range of banks (markets) simultaneously and potentially leading to their default (crash). Third, widespread financial imbalances that have built up endogenously over time may unravel. For example, when a credit

---

[4] This subsection builds on de Bandt and Hartmann (2000 and 2002); de Bandt, Hartmann, and Peydró (2010); and ECB (2009 and 2010).

[5] For a specific overview of this novel line of research, see Hartmann, Hubrich, and Kremer (2013).

boom breaks down a number banks might collapse at the same time. Although these three "forms" of systemic risk are theoretically distinct, they are not unrelated and, in practice, generally happen in conjunction with each other. For example, in the 2007–08 crisis both the endogenous build-up of a strong credit and leverage boom in conjunction with contagion effects through financial linkages, fire sales, market and funding liquidity problems were key.

Since systemic risk refers to the risk of very severe problems and not regular financial or business cycles, it is useful to also distinguish "strong" from "weak" systemic events. The former mean events that lead to bank failures, although the banks have been fundamentally solvent ex ante, or at least to losses that are so severe that they cause drastic transmissions in the financial system or to the real economy. A systemic event can range between a few banks—accounting for a significant share of banking assets or deposits—and all banks of a financial system. A "systemic crisis" usually affects a considerable number of banks covering a large and significant share of banking assets/liabilities in a "strong" sense.

27.2.2 The "Financial Fragility Hypothesis"

Why is it then that systemic risk is of special concern in the financial system? Many of the traditional market imperfections play a role, notably externalities and asymmetric or imperfect information, incomplete markets and financial contracts, the public good character of financial stability and multiple equilibria. But many of these market imperfections are also present in other sectors of the economy. Therefore, they alone do not seem to be sufficient for justifying the special "fragility" of financial systems. The "financial fragility hypothesis" becomes supported when three interrelated features are also taken into account.

(1) First, the structure of banks' balance sheets matters, in particular the conjunction of maturity/liquidity mismatches, the highly (short-term dispersed) leverage, and the opacity of banking assets/liabilities. As a result of liquidity and maturity transformation activities, traditional commercial banks have short-term dispersed liabilities that are liquid and long-term assets that are illiquid. Moreover, banks tend to be highly leveraged in that a large share of their liabilities is in the form of debt.

For example, the fact that commercial banks take fixed value deposits that can be withdrawn (unconditionally and at fixed value) at very short notice even though loans can usually not be sold at short notice exposes them to the risk of bank runs (Bryant, 1980; and Diamond and Dybvig, 1983). In addition, bank loans are difficult to value, more generally banking assets are opaque, potentially contributing to asymmetric information between creditors and bank managers. In fact, the present credit-market crisis illustrates that the valuation of bank assets remains a challenge and that the expansion of securitization activity in the preceding years may have masked this fact. Therefore, the health of a bank depends not only on its success in picking profitable projects for lending and investment but also on the "confidence" of (retail and wholesale) depositors in the value of the loan and asset book and, importantly, in their confidence that "other" depositors will not run on the bank (Chari and Jaghannathan, 1988). In fact, such coordination problems among depositors may sometimes cause solvent but illiquid banks to fail (Goldstein and Pauzner, 2005).[6]

This "special" character of banks does not apply to many other financial intermediaries, such as insurance companies, securities houses, and the like. However, if banks and other intermediaries belong to the same financial entity, or the former are exposed to the latter, non-bank intermediaries' problems might still become a source of bank fragility. Something like this happened with special purposes vehicles to which banks had transferred some of their structured credit business before the crisis. Their design was not "balance-sheet remote" and many banks decided to repatriate them on their balance sheets rather than to liquidate them when they got in trouble. Moreover, the phenomenon of "shadow banking" is of concern. For a variety of reasons, including regulatory arbitrage, some of banks' business has migrated to other intermediaries, such as broker dealers, money market funds,[7] hedge funds or even some insurance companies. While legally not being banks ("credit institutions"), these entities have still acquired a significant role in the process of credit creation or some of them have balance-sheet structures very similar to banks (e.g., collateralized loans in the assets and short-term commercial paper in the liability), making them relevant for systemic risk assessments.[8] Despite the fact that they look like banks, they are not subject to regulation and deposit insurance and until recently to liquidity support, thus they can be more fragile than banks.

Another important feature of the financial crisis that began in 2007 is the role that short-term wholesale funding structures played. Most major investments banks, for example, acquired a large share of their high leverage through such funding structures, and as some main assets and hedging instruments became illiquid or turned out to be much less liquid than previously thought, effectively faced substantial maturity and liquidity mismatches. As market stresses deepened, wholesale financiers became unwilling to roll over the short-term debt, in ways reminiscent of depositor runs. This affected not only investment banks, but also other banks with undiversified funding structures and off-balance-sheet vehicles used for funding structured finance investments.[9] The deleveraging process during a crisis usually requires fire sales of assets, pushing instability through the system and thereby deepening the crisis (Adrian and Shin, 2008). Market illiquidity and funding

---

[6] Obviously, the more depositors are protected through some deposit insurance scheme the less likely it is that confidence crises occur through retail deposits. In fact, during the current global financial crisis, the deposit insurance thresholds were increased worldwide to contain runs on banks and some wholesale markets were also supported.

[7] US Money Market Mutual Funds experienced runs during the September 2008 crisis (Krainer, 2012).

[8] It is beyond the scope of this chapter to cover "shadow banking" in detail. See, e.g., Adrian and Ashcraft (2012) for further discussion and a literature survey.

[9] Many banks used off-balance-sheet vehicles to invest during the growth period of securitization in structured finance products. Funding was short term, as banks issued commercial paper backed by their (long-term) assets. Once valuations of structured products were in doubt, investors were no longer inclined to roll over this short-term debt and the vehicles had to be taken back on banks' balance sheets to avoid their failure. It is expected that these off-balance-sheet vehicles will lose importance after the crisis or even disappear.

illiquidity reinforce each other and cause negative externalities to financial intermediaries (Brunnermeier and Pedersen, 2009).

Finally, pervasive incentives and behavioral biases may explain systemic risk. Because banks and other intermediaries are highly leveraged financial institutions which can also pass on their losses to taxpayers (in bailouts, for example), they take excessive correlated risk-taking in the financial system from these wrong incentives, the so-called moral hazard problem as, for instance, in Acharya and Yorulmazer (2007, 2008b) and Farhi and Tirole (2012). Moreover, behavioral biases as for example neglecting tail risk as in Gennaioli, Shleifer and Vishny (2013) may also lead to systemic risk in financial markets.

(2) Financial intermediaries and markets are highly interconnected among each other and with the real economy. Thinking of the "horizontal" perspective of systemic risk, there is a complex network of exposures among banks (and other financial intermediaries), for example, through exposures in interbank money markets, derivative markets and large-value (wholesale) payment and security settlement systems. As the current financial crisis has again illustrated, malfunctioning wholesale markets have immediately systemic effects due to the extensive participation of most major banks in them.[10] Policy and market initiatives over the last two decades have significantly improved the safety of wholesale and retail payment and settlement systems, so that they played no specific role in the present crisis. Badly designed payment and settlement systems, however, imply substantial systemic risk. However, in the last crisis, the dense network of financial claims among banks (and other intermediaries) played an important role.

Concerning the "vertical" perspective of systemic risk, the financial sector constitutes a central component of a modern economy. All other sectors tend to be strongly connected to it, either as net borrower (e.g., the government and corporate sectors) or as net lender (e.g., the household sector). When the financial system malfunctions, then savings cannot be efficiently allocated to private or public investment and the borrowing sectors suffer. For example, a banking crisis can create strong negative results for the economy at large through a reduction of the supply of credit (a credit crunch).[11]

(3) The third feature is the information and control intensity of financial contracts, which rely on promises and expectations about future payments (e.g., Stiglitz, 1993). For example, the willingness of agents to extend credit depends on their confidence that borrowers reimburse them in the future. When asymmetric information emerges, uncertainty increases, or the credibility of a financial commitment starts to be questioned, market expectations may shift substantially and, in an "individually rational" way, in short periods of time leading to equally volatile investment and disinvestment decisions. For example, after the failure of Lehman Brothers and other negative events in September 2008, a general loss of confidence emerged in which many banks preferred to hoard liquidity rather than lend them out. Or, in the summer of 2007, significant doubts emerged about the viability of structured

---

[10] Northern Rock, for example, relied to 75% on wholesale deposits and therefore collapsed in autumn 2007, when the money market became dysfunctional.

[11] See Jiménez et al. (2012).

finance products, so that investors—who could not distinguish good from bad products—in general stopped rolling over asset-backed commercial paper financing the investments of off-balance-sheet vehicles.[12] These actions, in spite of being rational from an individual financial intermediary point of view, are very negative for the financial system as a whole as they cause severe negative externalities.

The combination of traditional market imperfections and these three special features in an environment of incomplete financial markets and contracts make financial systems subject to systemic risk, because it can give rise to particularly violent adjustments of behavior, powerful feedback, and amplification mechanisms that make financial problems spread widely and in non-linear ways.

27.2.3 "Efficient" versus "Self-Fulfilling" Systemic Events

Some bank failures are efficient, whereas many can be inefficient. General uncertainty and agents' awareness of potential asymmetries of information highlight the role that expectations can play in systemic events. In fact, systemic events driven by expectations can be individually rational but not socially optimal.

If the information about bank losses is released in full, and the bank is insolvent, it is individually rational for depositors to withdraw their funds and force those banks into liquidation. If instead the information about bank losses is not revealed in full but depositors receive only a bad "noisy" common signal, it might still be rational for them to withdraw their funds early and thereby force the default of those banks. Whether the signal has been "right" or "wrong" would determine, ceteris paribus, whether this outcome is "efficient" ex post or not. As it is triggered by imperfect information on fundamentals, this type of event could be denoted as "information-based."

Signals can also coordinate depositors in their strategies to run or not in one or multiple banks. If the signals are not related to the health of banks and are common, as in the sunspot mechanism à la Cass and Shell (1983), multiple equilibria—bank failures stemming from sunspots—are inefficient. On the other hand, private signals to depositors that convey information about *general* bank fundamentals help them to predict how good the health of a bank is, and also what other depositors might predict about the health of the bank (see Goldstein and Pauzner, 2005). Depending on the noise structure, the unique equilibrium could be that depositors run if the private signal regarding bank fundamentals is below a threshold. In particular, if the bank is close to insolvency but still solvent there will be failure as a consequence of the combination of uncertainty in fundamentals and strategic uncertainty among depositors about their behavior—illiquidity due to bad fundamentals causes insolvency. This implies an ex post inefficiency that should be contrasted with the ex ante disciplining incentives provided by short-term debt such as deposits (Calomiris and Kahn, 1991; Diamond and Rajan, 2001; and Rochet and Vives, 2004).

---

[12] See Dang, Gorton, and Holmström (2012).

The presence of asymmetric information also illustrates how banking problems can build up over an extended period of time before an "efficient" or "inefficient" crisis occurs. That is, the systemic event is only the manifestation of a fundamental underlying financial imbalance (e.g., reckless lending) that was hidden from investors or policymakers for some time or remained unaddressed by either of them. The general repricing of risk that triggered the crisis started only around summer 2007, although, it is widely believed nowadays that mortgage-lending and complex forms of securitizations had been on an unsustainable path for some years and imbalances built up undetected for a while.[13]

27.2.4 Systemic Risk and Public Policy

Given the market failures involving systemic risk and the potentially high costs of systemic crises,[14] there are public policies designed to contain systemic risk and crises—notably macroprudential policy. These policies can be divided into ex ante (pre-emptive—trying to contain systemic risks before they materialize as instability), and ex post (reactive—crisis management policies trying to stem instability that has broken out).[15]

The ex ante policies against systemic risk mean that banks (and other parts of the financial system) need to be supervised to identify emerging systemic risks early and regulated so as to contain systemic risks or create buffers against it. One of the widely shared policy conclusions from the recent financial crisis was that this branch of financial supervision and regulation needed to be developed properly. Before the crisis most supervision and regulation was *microprudential* in nature. The main difference is that macroprudential policies have the objective to contain *systemic* risk, whereas microprudential policies have the objective to contain the risks of *individual* banks or markets (Borio, 2003). While at present both policies continue to draw on a similar set of regulatory instruments (with an important role for various capital and liquidity requirements), and long-term objectives are aligned, it is important to recognize that their short-run objectives may sometimes differ, for example in the case of a downturn.[16] In this case, microprudential policy would aim that banks increase their capital and liquidity buffers, whereas this may be very negative for systemic risk, and therefore, contrary to macroprudential policy.

---

[13] See, e.g., Keys et al. (2010).

[14] See Slovin, Sushka, and Polonchek (1993, 1999) for the social costs incurred by the stakeholders of the initially failing bank, and Iyer and Peydró (2011) for the social costs induced by contagion on the stakeholders of the banks that are financially linked to the initial failed bank.

[15] For estimations of the macroeconomic costs of crises, see, e.g., Bordo et al. (2001); Hoggarth, Reis and Saporta (2002); Barkbu, Eichengreen, and Mody (2012); Schularick and Taylor (2012). The relationship between the performance of the real and financial sectors can go in both directions. This raises the issue of causality. Dell'Ariccia, Detragiache, and Rajan (2008) argue that if banking crises reduce real activity, then sectors more dependent on external finance should perform relatively worse during such crises. Financial crises can, however, also be the expression of an economy taking greater risks in financing real investment, which could be part of a long-term growth strategy. See Ranciére, Tornell, and Westermann (2008) for evidence that financial crises may lead to higher economic growth.

[16] Notice that from a macroprudential perspective the socially optimal probability of individual bank failures is *not* zero. For a socially optimal outcome, the probability of "pure" contagion (a self-fulfilling systemic event) and certain cases of "information-based" contagion *are* zero..

The ex post policies against systemic instability are often denoted as crisis management. On the macroprudential front, lower capital and liquidity requirements in a crisis can help banks, but crisis management also typically involves central banks, bank supervisors and fiscal authorities. Through its role as lender of last resort (LOLR) central banks often play a crucial role in crisis management. In principle, central banks can provide emergency liquidity assistance (ELA) to individual banks, provide liquidity to the banking system as a whole ("lending to the market") or more generally conduct an expansionary monetary policy to help stabilizing the financial system, thereby supporting the economy as a whole.

ELA may be justified if an individual bank is in trouble and is so large or interconnected that its failure could cause significant contagion effects. But it is only a temporary policy until the bank is either recapitalized or liquidated. Individual emergency loans can be sterilized through opposite transactions vis-à-vis the market as a whole, so that they do not interfere with the implementation of monetary policy. "Lending to the market" is, by definition, not sterilized, but any surplus liquidity could normally be taken out of the banking system at a later stage, when the crisis is over. For various reasons, the literature about the LOLR has shown much more controversy regarding ELA than regarding "lending to the market" (see Goodfriend and King, 1988; and Goodhart and Huang, 1999 for two opposite views).[17] Central banks could also relax standard monetary policy—lower short-term interest rates—in order to counter the effects of a crisis on the banking system and the economy at large. This, however, raises the issue of conflicts of objectives, in particular whether this could endanger the goal of price stability. Since most severe financial crises are associated with economic downturns and downward risks to price stability, standard monetary policy may, however, often go in the same direction as financial stability policies, so that a conflict may not materialize. Recently, central banks have also adopted a wide range of non-standard monetary policies, either to compensate for the fact that short-term interest rates reached the zero lower bound or in order to repair a malfunctioning transmission of monetary policy in times of severe financial instability. In a crisis the difference between LOLR activities and non-standard monetary policies tends to blur. In order to stabilize the macroeconomy in a systemic crisis, fiscal policy could also help. In the present crisis both accommodative monetary policy and substantial fiscal stimuli have happened in many countries. In fact, given the risks and long-term maturity involved in some non-standard monetary policy actions, monetary policy has a key fiscal component aspect.

Another policy with fiscal implications is a public bailout of financial intermediaries, in particular large and complex banks. This also serves to avoid the destabilizing contagion or confidence effects that may emanate from their failure. In order to preserve the financial health and monetary policy independence of central banks, their LOLR activity tends to be limited to various forms of liquidity support. As soon as solvency support is required to ensure systemic stability, fiscal authorities need to be involved. Since, however, the fiscal costs of such bailouts can be enormous, sometimes even endangering the solvency of the sovereign (as highlighted in the Eurozone sovereign crisis), efforts are underway to limit them as much as possible. These efforts not only include more effective macroprudential regulations but also resolution policies as bail-ins and ex ante insurance mechanisms.

---

[17] Holmström and Tirole (1998) derive an even broader role for the state to provide liquidity to the economy more generally when financial frictions become severe.

It is now widely recognized that public and private safety nets, whether they take the form of public bailouts, LOLR facilities or deposit insurance, bear the risk of creating moral hazard. For example, if deposit insurance premiums do not reflect the banks' relative portfolio risks, then the protection may incite banks to take on higher risks (Merton, 1978). Moreover, market expectations could be created that systemically large banks, with substantial market, clearing, and settlement links, are too-big-to-fail (TBTF) or "too complex to fail."[18] Such effects may be countered by very effective financial regulation and prudential supervision, as, for example, suggested by Kareken and Wallace (1978), Buser, Chen, and Kane (1981) and Furlong and Keeley (1989) for the case of deposit insurance. They also create a case for "constructive ambiguity" vis-à-vis the potential use of public emergency lending (see Rochet and Vives, 2004). In a fragile situation, however, "constructive ambiguity" could also have destabilizing effects if markets lose confidence that public authorities will act decisively when needed.[19] If the measures to control moral hazard are not successful, then the insured institutions could take on more excessive ex ante risk. This could contribute to the accumulation of ex ante endogenous imbalances enhancing the likelihood of financial instability in the future. Also too expansionary macro-policies can fuel credit supply booms triggering asset price bubbles and excessive risk-taking and, thereby, contribute to the emergence of financial imbalances.[20] This latter scenario would imply a higher level of systemic risk through inadequate safety net provisions.

The complications in making ex ante policies effective and in containing unintended side effects of ex post policies has increased interest in ensuring market discipline and the resolvability of banks. Two approaches are prominent. First, living wills and "structural regulation" (such as the Volcker, Vickers or Liikanen rules) are intended to ensure that banks are not too complex to be resolved and that excessive risk-taking in investment is not subsidized with deposit insurance and other public (potential) subsidies. Second, the inclusion of "bail-in" provisions in resolution mechanisms are intended to give investors greater incentives to impose discipline on bank management ex ante and relieve public budgets from heavy bailout costs through cost sharing. However, bail-ins may have ex post costs in terms of contagion, as clearly shown in the weeks after September 15, 2008.

---

[18] The takeover of Bear Stearns by JP Morgan Chase at a very low price supported by the US Fed in March 2008 is widely interpreted as an example of the "too complex to fail" case.

[19] Some observers wonder whether the decision by the US Fed and Treasury to let Lehman Brothers fail in September 2008 was an application of "constructive ambiguity." The loss of confidence following this episode could suggest that such an approach also involves risks. Fed chairman Bernanke, however, argued that the two US authorities did not have the authority to absorb the large expected losses, which was necessary to facilitate the acquisition of Lehman by another firm <http://www.america.gov/st/texttransenglish/2008/October/20081016110841eaifas9.330386e-02.html>. Caballero and Krishnamurthy (2008) challenge "constructive ambiguity" policies in the case of aggregate "Knightian" uncertainty (where agents even have no information about the probability distribution of asset returns). They argue that competent policy authorities should instead announce that they stand ready to provide liquidity in case of a crisis in order to avoid that investors show "flight to quality" behavior. This would amount to a "constructive clarity" approach.

[20] A new literature on the so-called risk-taking channel of monetary policy (Jiménez et al. 2014 and Ioannidou, Ongena, and Peydró, 2013) finds empirical evidence that expansionary monetary policy encourages bank credit risk-taking in the medium term.

27.3 THEORETICAL MODELS OF SYSTEMIC RISK IN BANKING

We now consider in greater detail the forms that systemic risk may take in banking. The theoretical literature in this area is surveyed in the light of the concept discussed in Section 27.2. The summary of theoretical (and, in Section 27.4, empirical) papers is not exhaustive and the reader should go into de Bandt and Hartmann (2000) and our 2010 chapter to get more extensive explanations of some papers (see de Bandt, Hartmann, and Peydró, 2010). We start in the next subsection with the bank contagion literature, and then, systemic banking risk as a consequence of macroeconomic shocks and lending booms.

27.3.1 Contagion

The banking literature in the last 20 years has developed sophisticated models of *single* banks' fragility starting from their balance sheet structure (see Section 27.2.2). However, regarding systemic risk this is only part of the story. One should distinguish between a "run" which involves only a single bank and a "banking panic" where more than one bank is affected (Calomiris and Gorton, 1991; and Bhattacharya and Thakor, 1993). One can distinguish two main channels through which contagion in banking markets can work: the "real" or exposure channel and the informational channel. In principle, these two fundamental channels can work in conjunction as well as quite independently.

27.3.1.1 Interactions of Retail Depositors across Banks

Chen (1999) combines an extension of the bank run models to multiple banks with the rational herding approach. There are two externalities in this model that cause contagious bank runs: a payoff externality through the first-come-first-served rule for servicing withdrawing depositors, and an information externality through the Bayesian updating of beliefs about the macroeconomic situation as a function of observed bank failures. There is a critical number of early failures above which a run on the remaining banks in the system will always be triggered. Finally, Chen shows that there also exists a deposit insurance scheme that could eliminate any contagious bank runs in this model.

27.3.1.2 Interbank Markets

A further important step is provided by theories of crises transmitted through the interbank market. Rochet and Tirole (1996) present a model of the interbank market, where peer monitoring among banks in this market solves the "moral hazard" problem between bank debtholders and bank shareholder-managers, but also induces contagion risk. The authors show that for certain parameter values of the model, a small increase in the size of the liquidity shock hitting any of the banks can lead to the closing down of the entire banking system, a particularly severe case of contagion.

A substantial part of this literature explains contagion by the structure of the banking network. Allen and Gale's (2000) model focus on the "physical exposures" of banks in different regions and on the "real" linkages between regions, as represented by the correlation of liquidity needs of the respective depositors. In their model, both depositors and banks choose deposits to insure against liquidity shocks. Liquidity shocks across regions fluctuate randomly, with aggregate liquidity staying constant with no bank failures. However, in an unexpected state of the world, to which all agents assign a probability of zero ex ante, one bank faces additional withdrawals, so that aggregate liquidity is not sufficient to serve all depositors. The authors show that contagion can occur in this situation. Whether and how much propagation of failures emerges depends on the structure of the banking system: with more "complete" markets (each bank has lending relationships with all the other regions) the system is likely to be more stable. In a related paper, Freixas, Parigi, and Rochet (2000) also show inefficient and contagious bank runs for fear of insufficient reserves in the system.

Following the above, there is a literature that uses "network theory" to model the different possible sources of connections between financial institutions, stemming from both the asset and the liability side of their balance sheet. By providing means to model the specifics of interbank linkages, network analysis is well designed to explain interbank linkages and contagion through the interbank system. In this type of models, narrow shocks can lead to strong and widespread systemic events (see, e.g., Babus, 2007).

Leitner (2005) studies the tradeoff between risk sharing and the potential for contagion in a network model. More interbank linkages imply better risk sharing among banks but also a higher potential for contagion with the possibility of multiple bank failures (systemic event). In the model, the return of a bank depends on the investments of other banks it is linked to. Banks, therefore, may be willing to bail out other banks, in order to prevent the collapse of the whole network. Conversely, Acharya, Gromb, and Yorulmazer (2012) suggest that surplus banks in the interbank market may strategically under-provide lending to cash stricken banks and, thereby, induce inefficient sales of assets that transmit a crisis. This provides a rationale for the provision of emergency liquidity assistance to individual banks by the central bank (see also Section 27.3.1.4).

Brusco and Castiglionesi (2007) extend Allen and Gale (2000) by modeling contagion in the interbank deposit market as an endogenous phenomenon, and introducing moral hazard problems in banks. Banks establish interbank links to insure against liquidity problems and accept the risk of contagion only when the risk is not too large. The main implication is that contagion is a rare phenomenon, since otherwise the banks would avoid establishing financial linkages. In addition, in their model, the extent of contagion is the greater the larger the number of interbank deposit cross-holdings since more banks will get affected by the initial failure. In consequence, the more interbank links banks have, the higher the potential for contagion.

Battiston et al. (2012a, 2012b) as well as Haldane and May (2011) also challenge the usual view that increasing interconnection is always beneficial to financial stability. The argument raised by Haldane is derived from a parallelism with life sciences and in particular food cycles: complexity of species may imply more fragility. As a consequence, and completing the Allen and Gale's (2000) result, the negative relationship between interconnection and systemic risk may appear to be non-monotonic and rather hump-shaped, depending on various factors (the initial situation of the banking system, the size of the shock, the nature of the links between banks). Weaker banks that are more interconnected may create more contagion.

Mishkin (1991) and Davis (1994, 1995) argued that "adverse selection" play an important role in the transmission of financial crises. Flannery (1996) sketched a model of interbank market crises due to asymmetric information among competing banks. Banks receive imperfect signals about the quality of prospective borrowers. Following a large shock in the financial system, banks may become more uncertain about their rivals' screening ability. As they feel less able to distinguish between banks exposed to more or less risky borrowers, lenders raise interest rates across the board. If the loan rate becomes too high, "good" banks might not be able to repay their interbank loans any more, so that illiquid but solvent banks may go bankrupt. Ferguson et al. (2007) and Cassola et al. (2008) argue that adverse selection problems also played an important role in the transmission of the subprime crisis. Heider, Hoerova, and Holthausen (2009) develop a theoretical model on this idea and show the possible breakdown of the (unsecured) interbank market.

There are some applications of global games theory to interbank contagion. The advantage of using this technique is to analyze at the same time coordination problems among depositors (panics) with depositor disciplining based on the health of the banking system (see Rochet and Vives, 2004). In fact, the level of (rational) panics depends in equilibrium on the level of banks' fundamentals and the equilibrium is unique. Dasgupta (2004) analyzes crossholding of deposits among banks as a source of contagious breakdowns. He shows that failure in one bank reduces the value of creditor banks thereby increasing its probability of failure. In Iyer and Peydró's (2007) model, depositors may start running when there are bank shocks forcing banks to unwind their positions in the interbank market to pay back the depositors thus generating a strong systemic event.

Fecht, Grüner, and Hartmann (2007) discuss the relationships between financial integration and systemic risk. They compare segmentation with three forms of inter-regional risk sharing: (1) integration through the secured interbank market; (2) integration through the unsecured interbank market; and (3) integration of retail markets. The secured interbank market is an optimal risk sharing device when banks report liquidity needs truthfully. It allows diversification without the risk of cross-regional bank contagion. However, free-riding on the liquidity provision in this market restrains the achievable risk sharing as the number of integrated regions increases. This can make that the moral hazard problem becomes so severe that either unsecured interbank lending implies contagion risk or, ultimately, the penetration of retail markets is preferable. Financial integration can also promote specialization in lending (and therefore production), which enhances risk sharing but also increases cross-border contagion risk even though this may be optimal from a welfare perspective (Fecht, Grüner, and Hartmann, 2012).

27.3.1.3 *Payment and Settlement Systems*

By providing the technical infrastructure through which wholesale bank market transactions are settled, large-value payment systems determine the physical exposures among financial institutions. Beyond the explicit interbank lending, one needs to take into account the implicit lending that may arise in payment system. In a way, looking at payment systems is like looking at the network of interbank exposures with a magnifying glass. Hence, depending on their internal organization they also influence how shocks may propagate through the financial system, in particular how severe bank contagion can be. There are three main types of interbank payment systems: net settlement systems, gross settlement systems, and correspondent banking. We just note here that the risks of netting systems explain the spreading of real-time gross settlement (RTGS) systems across the world (Bech and Hobijn, 2007). Most real-life systems have specific additional institutional features in order to reduce systemic risk or liquidity costs (and "gridlock" risk) in both net and gross systems, so that the two types that are very different in theory can become quite similar in practice ("hybrid" systems).

27.3.1.4 *"Fire Sales", Liquidity Problems, and Endogenous Risk*

Diamond and Rajan (2005) argue that banks are characterized by specific knowledge about borrowers, which make their assets particularly illiquid. So, if a bank fails, the common pool of liquidity shrinks creating or exacerbating aggregate liquidity shortages, which in turn may cause further failures. Carletti, Hartmann, and Spagnolo (2007) link individual bank and aggregate interbank market liquidity with competition in the loan market. When interbank markets are relatively efficient, bank concentration can exacerbate aggregate liquidity fluctuations. If a central bank does not offset them through liquidity provision, then system-wide liquidity shortages can become more severe and frequent. Unfortunately, liquidity and solvency problems interact and can cause each other, making it hard to determine the cause of a crisis. In Acharya and Yorulmazer (2008a), as the number of bank failures increases, the set of assets available for acquisition by the surviving banks expands but the total amount of available liquidity within the surviving banks falls. Since financiers not belonging to the banking system do not have the specific knowledge characterizing banks the previous results imply "cash-in-the-market" pricing (below the "fair value") for liquidation of banking assets.

Fecht (2004) asks whether an individual bank run has more severe systemic consequences in bank—or market-oriented financial systems. He finds that a bank run on a single bank causes contagion via the financial market only in moderately bank-dominated financial systems where "fire sales" of long-term financial claims by a distressed bank cause a sudden drop in asset prices, which hurts other banks. Cifuentes, Shin, and Ferrucci (2005) present a model where financial institutions are connected via common portfolio holdings. Contagion is mainly driven here by changes in asset prices through forced sales of assets by some banks that depress the market price inducing further distress to other banks. In Allen and Carletti (2008), asset prices in some markets may reflect the amount of liquidity available in the market rather than the future earning power of the asset. Mark-to-market accounting is not a desirable way to assess the solvency of a financial institution in such circumstances since it can lead to contagion where none would occur with historic cost accounting.[21]

27.3.2 Macroeconomic Fluctuations, Aggregate Shocks, and Lending Booms

Systemic risk may be associated with large exogenous macroeconomic shocks or the widespread accumulation of endogenous financial imbalances, such as credit booms. The former

---

[21] See also Allen and Gale (2005).

is an ex post argument in the sense that many banks may get into trouble at the same time when economic downturns or widespread financial market crashes occur. The latter is an ex ante argument in the sense that there are mechanisms in financial systems that encourage similar forms of risk-taking being pursued by many banks at the same time. So, widespread imbalances can accumulate over time, which may unravel violently only much later, be it through a macroeconomic shock or other events. Given their different nature we discuss the two sources of systemic risk in separate subsections.

27.3.2.1 Aggregate Shocks to the Banking Sector

It has been observed that many banking crises have occurred in conjunction with cyclical downturns or other aggregate shocks, such as interest rate increases, stock market crashes, or exchange rate devaluations (see, e.g., Gorton, 1988). Why is it that banks simultaneously get in trouble in those events (included in the concept of systemic risk in the "broad" sense according to the terminology given above), even in the absence of direct interbank contagion, and why are prudent banks not better protected than imprudent ones? One answer could be given on the basis of the individual bank run models. News about a cyclical downturn, for example, could provide the negative signal about banks' loans to all or a subset of depositors. Allen and Gale (1998) take issue with the interpretation of bank runs as random phenomena, because of their historical association with severe "business cycle fluctuations." They argue that in this framework if depositors make their withdrawal decisions based on a leading indicator for business cycles, the first-best outcome can occur in spite of the non-contingent character of the deposit contract. However, the result breaks down when early withdrawals are costly, so that a public intervention is necessary to restore the first-best outcome.[22]

Another source of systematic shocks to the banking sector can be "financial market crashes" or "market liquidity crises"—in particular when they concern any of the major markets and when they are contagious across markets (see, e.g., Morgenstern, 1959; King and Wadhwani, 1990; and Hartmann, Straetmans, and de Vries, 2004). Commercial and universal banks have become more involved in financial market trading (as opposed to traditional lending). Moreover, as part of the securitization trend over the last decade and more active credit risk management, banks have invested a lot in asset-backed securities and structured credit products, using also credit derivatives very actively. As a consequence, their trading books have grown significantly, exposing them more to shocks originating in financial markets. This implies that the structurally higher systemic risk in banking markets will be more dependent on market risk, (supposedly) tradable credit risk and liquidity in those markets than has previously been the case.

Various negative events in financial markets may increase uncertainty and the ability and willingness to trade in these markets. Imperfect information about asset valuations can lead to significant credit spreads even at shorter maturities or even credit rationing (Duffie and Lando, 2001; Tirole, 2008a, 2008b). Market makers might increase bid-ask spreads to reduce

[22] Of course, there can also be the reverse causality. Restrictions in bank lending due to financial fragility may affect the business cycle, thereby creating adverse acceleration or feedback effects. See, in particular, Mishkin (1991); and Bernanke, Gertler, and Gilchrist (1999). In the current global financial crisis this direction of causality was the more relevant one.

the likelihood of being hit by a transaction ("price rationing") or even "refuse" to trade at all ("quantity rationing"). Such a liquidity "freeze" could involve a systematic shock on all those banks and non-bank financial institutions whose risk management strategies depend on the ability to trade in these markets. In the ongoing credit market crisis valuation uncertainties for credit products had these effects and led to illiquidity in structured product and major money markets (Cassola et al. 2008).

One key question is how banks deal with aggregate shocks to the banking sector. Allen and Gale (2004, 2007) develop a general equilibrium framework for analyzing the normative aspects of financial crises with a more significant emphasis on the relationships between asset prices and banking crisis. They consider the interaction of banks and markets and focus on fundamental shocks (as opposed to coordination problems among depositors) as the driver of financial crises. Financial intermediaries provide liquidity insurance to consumers against idiosyncratic liquidity shocks. Markets allow financial intermediaries and their depositors to share aggregate liquidity and return shocks. The authors show that, when markets are incomplete, asset prices must be volatile to provide incentives for liquidity provision (otherwise, agents would not find liquidity holdings valuable). This asset price volatility can lead to costly and inefficient crises. There is a market failure that potentially provides a justification for regulation and other kinds of intervention to improve the allocation of resources.[23]

27.3.2.2 Credit Booms and Unraveling of Imbalances

Two different types of contributions need to be mentioned. First, the literature on credit booms, then the integration of fragility in macroeconomic models, the shift from "tranquil" to crisis period and their aggregate effect.

First, an issue related to the real macroeconomic shocks discussed above is why banks expand so much credit, implying risks that can bring many of them into trouble at turning points, even though they know they cannot pass on the risk to depositors. The lending boom literature has addressed this question. Minsky (1977, 1982) believed that the post-World War II free-market economy has a natural tendency toward financial instability at the aggregate level. In good times agents consume and invest, generating more income. As "euphoria" and "gregarious behavior" pick up, more speculative or even "Ponzi" finance is undertaken, as opposed to safer "hedging" finance.[24] The boom is fed by an overexpansion of bank credit until some exogenous outside shock to the macroeconomic systems ("displacement") brings it to an end. Kindleberger ([1978]1996) shares the basic idea, although perhaps being more moderate in pointing out that the market system "occasionally" faces such bubbles leading to financial crises. These early writers emphasized the role of uncertainty (of the "Knightian" type as opposed to risk) and the inability of banks to take the appropriate decisions in some circumstances. For example, Guttentag and Herring (1984) develop a simple model of credit expansion and discuss the consequences of "Knightian" uncertainty about catastrophic shocks on investment returns and default risk premiums. On the

---

[23] Allen and Carletti (2006) develop a model in which credit risk transfer can lead to contagion. In fact, they argue that credit risk transfer can be detrimental to welfare.

[24] Some observers may regard the Madoff scandal that became known during the present crisis as an example of the greater scope for Ponzi schemes during boom times.

basis of results from psychology they also argue that the subjective probabilities attached to catastrophic events will decline as time elapses after the realisation of such an event. This "disaster myopia" will lead to a widespread underestimation of the likelihood of extreme events that could question the health of banks.[25] Related explanations for lending booms are found in the more recent rational expectations literature on "herding" in investment and loan decisions. For example, Banerjee (1992) or Bikhchandani, Hirshleifer, and Welsh (1992) introduce formal models of information externalities that can lead to herding. Each agent only observes the actions of other agents and uses Bayesian updating to derive his or her own subjective probabilities of future returns on his investment decisions. Scharfstein and Stein (1990) model managers' incentives to mimic others in investment or loan decisions, when their own evaluation and reputation depends on their performance relative to the rest of the market.[26] The stance of "monetary policy" may also affect bank risk-taking and, in general, asset prices. The development of microeconomic banking models with such monetary channels is at an early stage. Allen and Gale (1998, 2000, and 2007) and Diamond and Rajan (2006), among others, have made steps in this direction. In Diamond and Rajan (2006) banks take higher liquidity risk when monetary policy is expansive. In their model, which provides "a liquidity version of the lending channel" of the monetary policy transmission mechanism, banks finance illiquid long-term projects with very liquid demand deposits. This mismatch makes banks reluctant to grant loans in times of liquidity shortages. Depending on the aggregate real liquidity conditions, monetary intervention can play a useful role by limiting the depositors' incentives to withdraw. Banks will respond by continuing, rather than curtailing, risky credit.[27] In line with such arguments, Dell'Ariccia and Marquez (2006) develop a model in which banks' incentives to screen borrowers diminish as interest rates become lower.[28] In sum, too lose monetary policy may contribute to the emergence of credit booms.

A further branch of the literature explains excessive or too-risky lending by banks with "moral hazard" (see also above). These writings refer to features of banking markets that normally do not exist for other industries. For example, Merton (1977, 1978) develops a model showing how fixed rate deposit insurance premiums that are insensitive to banks' portfolio risks (as observed in many countries) may lead them to increase risk-taking in order to maximize the put option value on the insurance corporation's funds. Boot and Thakor (1993) further argue that such deposit insurance can lead to an inefficiently low level of monitoring. Applying modern corporate finance models of firms' capital structures to the case of banks, Dewatripont and Tirole (1994) argue that banks' excessive reliance on debt financing (partly related to their provision of retail payment services to a large number of small and relatively uninformed depositors) can also lead to more risk-taking in lending. Owing to the existence of explicit or implicit government guarantees for financial

[25] See also Caballero and Krishnamurthy (2008).

[26] They quote Gwynne's (1986) description of a typical credit analyst's behavior in lending decisions to less developed countries: "His job would never be measured how correct his country risk analysis was. At the very least, Herrick was simply doing what hundreds of other large international banks had already done, and any ultimate blame for poor forecasting would be shared by tens of thousands of bankers around the globe; this was one of the curious benefits of following the herd."

[27] See also Rajan (2006).

[28] See also Ruckes (2004).

institutions, the issue of moral hazard has also been raised in the context of the US savings and loans crisis (Kane, 1989) or regarding the lending boom that partly led to the East Asian crisis (Krugman, 1998). Goodhart and Huang (1999), however, show that a positive level of moral hazard resulting from safety net provisions, such as lending of last resort, might be unavoidable or even optimal to contain the systemic costs or monetary disturbances associated with financial crises.

This credit boom literature addresses the issue of systemic risk in an indirect way. Banks' (or other financial intermediaries') herding and credit over-expansion leads to the (potentially slow) buildup of imbalances that imply vulnerabilities for a large number of banks (or even other firms and households), which increase the likelihood as well as the severity of systemic events. Once a negative aggregate shock or other event makes the non-sustainability of the boom apparent many banks may face similar problems simultaneously. According to Minsky, Kindleberger, and others, such financial cycles emerge endogenously as an inherent part of a market economy with relatively unregulated financial markets. The modern expression for this phenomenon is the strong "procyclicality" of financial systems. Many argue that the financial crisis that started in the summer of 2007 is also a reflection of it.

The second important dimension is the characterization of regime shifts in theoretical macroeconomic models. One important step in the characterisation of financial instability in these models was the introduction of occasionally binding credit constraints of agents that give rise to a non-linearity and amplification of economic fluctuations after a bad shock (e.g., Mendoza, 2002, 2010; Lorenzoni, 2008; Bianchi, 2011; or Korinek, 2011).

However, financial instability in the (static) general equilibrium model of Boissay (2011) does not rely on occasionally binding constraints but on the scope for freezes of (runs on) banks' wholesale funding markets. Banks differ in their ability to assess the investment projects they fund, but their financiers cannot observe their proficiency. As a consequence there may be multiple equilibria; a crisis equilibrium in which wholesale funding markets freeze—because financiers loose trust in banks' investment choices—and economic activity collapses and another in which high bank leverage is financed without a crisis and economic activity is high. The shift from one equilibrium to the other implies a major non-linearity and is not predictable. Boissay, Collard, and Smets (2013) introduce the possibility of wholesale bank funding market freezes in a dynamic stochastic general equilibrium model, showing how long credit booms can be followed by such liquidity crises (and without multiple equilibria). Illustrating the form of systemic risk characterized by the buildup and unraveling of widespread financial imbalances, they illustrate that crises can happen entirely endogenously, without any exogenous shocks, and that agents form expectations about them (anticipating likelihoods for such crises). Gertler and Kiyotaki (2013) incorporate self-fulfilling retail depositor runs in a dynamic stochastic general equilibrium model. The shift from the no-run to the run equilibrium also creates a major non-linearity, but in tranquil times the possibility of a bank run is unanticipated. Aoki and Nikolov (2012) capture two types of non-linearities; one through the leverage constraint of banks hit by a negative shock and another through switches between multiple equilibria. The multiple equilibria, originates from the incentives to not only lend to firms but also to invest in assets whose values may deviate from fundamentals in a self-fulfilling manner. When trust in the valuation of these assets erodes the equilibrium materialises in which banks make losses, they deleverage and the economy collapses.

27.4   EMPIRICAL EVIDENCE ON SYSTEMIC RISK IN BANKING

In this section we survey some of the existing empirical evidence on systemic events and systemic bank crises, as made available in the quantitative economic and finance literature.

27.4.1   Evidence on Bank Contagion

Testing for bank contagion amounts to testing whether "bad news" about the failure of a specific bank (or group of banks) adversely affects the health of other banks. The first branch of the bank contagion literature is a test for autocorrelation in bank failures. Provided that all macroeconomic shocks are effectively covered by the control variables, a positive and significant autocorrelation coefficient indicates that bank failures and periods of tranquillity cluster over time, which is consistent with the contagion hypothesis. These tests have to be undertaken for historical periods in countries without strong (public) safety nets.

Another test of contagion measures the reaction of depositors (wholesale and retail) to "bad news." If, in response to problems revealed about bank i (or a group of banks), depositors also withdraw funds from bank j, then there is evidence of a contagious bank run. Calomiris and Mason (1997) examine the June 1932 Chicago bank panic and conclude that only weaker banks ex ante actually failed during the panic, which is consistent with the hypothesis that "pure" contagious failures, or "strong" systemic events (in the "narrow" sense), did not occur. They explain this finding with the existence of private cooperative arrangements among banks. In Calomiris and Mason (2003) they argue that the regional 1930 bank panic was associated with greater deposit withdrawals than could have been predicted from bank level micro data, and regional and national fundamentals, but they question the notion that uniform withdrawals, unexplained by fundamentals, have happened at the national level before 1933. Iyer and Peydró (2011) test whether interbank lending exposures can explain contagious deposit withdrawals, as predicted, for example in Allen and Gale (2000), using a detailed micro dataset for a large idiosyncratic Indian bank failure. Banks with higher interbank exposure to the failed bank experience higher deposit withdrawals. This relationship is non-linear and is stronger for banks whose fundamentals are weaker. In addition, more exposed banks suffer further as other banks do not renew their interbank loans. Finally, both households and firms suffer from the relationship in terms of reduced deposits and loans, respectively.

Theoretical models of contagion suggest that banking contagion may also happen directly through interbank exposures. Kaufman (1994) reports that, shortly before the failure of Continental Illinois, 65 financial institutions had uninsured exposures to the bank in excess of their capital. However, Continental's actual losses finally reached 5%, which was below the 60% threshold that would have triggered insolvency of exposed banks.

The most popular approach to test for contagion effects are event studies of bank stock price reactions in response to "bad news," such as the announcement of an unexpected increase in loan-loss reserves or the failure of a commercial bank. The presence of contagion

is usually tested by measuring "abnormal" bank stock returns (measured by the deviation from a standard capital asset pricing model (CAPM) on historical data) following the
announcement of "bad news" for other banks. Aharony and Swary (1983) were the forerun-
ners of this approach, who looked at the effects of the three largest bank failures in the US
before 1980.

Related to but methodologically distinct from the above event studies are analyses of bank
stock price spillovers to measure bank contagion. In this approach, if a large negative return
of bank i (or a group of banks) is associated with a large negative return of bank j, then this
is taken as evidence of bank contagion. Hartmann, Straetmans, and de Vries (2006) apply
for the first time extreme-value theory (EVT) to the banking sector. They develop a measure
of multivariate extreme spillovers between bank stocks, which is based on the conditional
probability of any set of banks facing a dramatic decline in its stock price given a dramatic
decline of the stock prices of any set of other banks. The results for large and complex banking organizations (LCBOs) between 1992 and 2004 suggest that multivariate extreme bank
spillover risk in the US is both economically and statistically higher than in the Eurozone.
This measure of banking system risk has gradually increased during the second half of the
1990s, although only to a very limited extent in Europe, and stayed at the more elevated
levels until the end of the sample period. Hartmann, Straetmans, and de Vries (2006) also
apply the tail-beta method (i.e., an extreme-value equivalent of the beta in the CAPM, which
measures how very extreme downturns by the market factor affect the propensity of bank
stocks to crash as well) to Euro area and US LBCOs during the 1990s and early 2000s. The
results suggest that this extreme systematic bank risk is of significant and similar magnitude
on both sides of the Atlantic and that in both economies it increased over the sample period.

Generalizing this approach, several indicators have been proposed to measure the contribution of individual firms to trigger extreme events ("systemic importance") or their sensi-
tiveness to extreme events ("systemic fragility"). On the one hand, Adrian and Brunnermeier
(2011) rely on the usual risk measure Value at Risk (VaR) through the so-called Contagion
Value at Risk (CoVaR). The contribution of an institution is measured as the 5%-quantile
of loss of the whole financial system, that is the usual VaR, conditional on the fact that the
specific institution is already at its 5%-VaR. On the other hand, Acharya et al. (2011) have
extended the concept of expected shortfall to define the marginal expected shortfall (MES).
Here the indicator measures the "systemic fragility" of an institution. The systemic risk generated by one institution (its marginal contribution) is measured as the average net equity
return on the 5% lowest daily market returns. Conditioning on these returns restricts the
analysis to a situation of general distress. The risk measure aims at capturing the need for
capital of an institution in the case of a crisis. Taking a simplified view of banks' balance
sheet, the MES, combined with the leverage ratio, constitutes a leading indicator to predict
an institution's systemic expected shortfall (SES) that captures, according to the authors, the
propensity to be undercapitalized when the system as a whole is in that case.

Controlling for balance sheet composition, the MES is turned into systemic risk (SRISK)
by Brownlees and Engle (2013) who also include a very refined dynamic model on returns.
The SRISK is the expected capital shortage of a financial institution, conditional on a substantial market decline (e.g. a 40% fall over six months) and taking leverage and size into
account. However several criticisms have been raised: the channels of spillover are not identified; deviations of market efficiency as asset price bubbles and lack of market discipline
(due to, e.g., potential bailouts) strongly limit market-based measures of systemic risk, as

the previous ones. The use of measures based on fundamentals such as credit supply growth is therefore crucial (as in, e.g., Jiménez et al., 2012 and 2014).

Taking a broader perspective than solely banking markets, Hollo, Kremer, and Lo Duca (2012) construct the ECB's CISS (Composite Indicator of Systemic Stress) to assess contemporaneous stress. Using mostly market data, they first compute a financial stress sub-index for five sub-markets: financial intermediaries sector, money markets, equity markets, bond markets and foreign exchange markets. These sub-indicators are then aggregated using basic portfolio theory. The index takes a higher value in situations when stress prevails in several market segments at the same time, a standard feature of a systemic event.

All these measures should be assessed on the basis of out-of-sample prediction. Unfortunately, as shown by Giglio et al. (2013), very few measures survive the tests based on many historical recessions and financial crises. In fact, an aggregate measure that encompasses several of these systemic risk measures performs substantially better.

Greenwood, Landier, and Thesmar (2012) model the transmission channel of "fire sales" in an accounting model of the value of banks' portfolio, taken as given exposures and price reactions to asset sell-offs depending on the liquidity in the secondary market. The model is notably calibrated on banks' sovereign exposures as published during EBA's 2011 stress tests for 90 banks in the EU 27 countries to account for the deleveraging that took place in 2010–11. They thus appealingly distinguish between, on the one hand, a bank's contribution to financial sector fragility and, on the other hand, the impact on a bank's equity of a shock through deleveraging, hence its vulnerability to systemic risk. In that sense the paper features two of the three dimensions of systemic risk as it shows how the unraveling of imbalances through deleveraging interacts with contagion, through fire sale effects.

There is also a central bank research literature using confidential and often incomplete data on interbank exposures to assess the risk of contagion using counterfactual simulations. Single or multiple banks are assumed to fail and the simulations derive which other banks would fail as a consequence of this, everything else equal. Some of these studies suggest that contagion effects are relatively limited in most scenarios. For example, Furfine (2003) finds this for Fed Funds transactions by US commercial banks settled through the Fedwire real-time gross settlement system in 1998. He also shows that the degree of systemic risk depends dramatically on the recovery rate that is assumed for bank failures.[29] Elsinger, Lehar, and Summer (2006a, 2006b) combine information about interbank exposures with that on macroeconomic fluctuations for Austria and the UK. It turns out that contagion risk is generally quite low and dominated by risks from correlated assets. Other papers analyze Belgium (Degryse and Nguyen, 2007), Italy (Mistrulli, 2011), Netherlands (Van Lelyveld and Liedorp, 2006) and Germany (Upper and Worms, 2004).[30]

More recent papers provide information on banking networks on the basis of actual exposures. This is the case of Cont and Santos (2010) on Brazil and Alves et al. (2013) for the network of the 53 largest EU banks. Work for deriving systemic risk indicators from these measures is currently undertaken (Battiston et al. 2012a). Karas and Schoors (2012) introduce the K-coreness, defined by a recursive algorithm borrowed from physics that sequentially weights the nodes of the network with respect to their connectivity. It is presented as a robust

---

[29] In addition, Furfine (2003) studies the federal funds market during the LTCM and Russian crises, finding that risk premiums on overnight lending were largely unaffected and lending volumes increased.
[30] Further studies following the simulation approach are surveyed by Upper (2007).

and reliable predictor of an individual bank's potential to spread contagion. This indicator indeed clearly outperforms others when tested on the Russian interbank market leading to a promising way to identify too-interconnected-to-fail banks.

Alves et al. (2013) conclude that solvency shocks are rather innocuous and do not trigger contagion, while liquidity shocks may create more risks, through changes in funding behavior (banks stop lending to problem banks). While a full treatment of liquidity risk is not provided, this is a first step in the direction of dynamic and endogenous network formation, and hence to our understanding of systemic risk arising from interbank networks. Indeed, the experience of the ongoing financial crisis seems to be that endogenous responses by market participants can be very important and amplify risks considerably

27.4.2 Banking Crises, Aggregate Fluctuations, and Lending Booms

As explained earlier in section 27.3.2, financial intermediaries take excessive ex ante risks, increasing collectively the systemic risk in the financial system. But what are the specific factors and decisions that will cause excessive risks? The main channel is excessive credit and leverage. In fact, these variables show the strongest ex ante correlation with the incidence of financial crises as shown in the empirical literature analyzing large historical and cross-country episodes of systemic financial crises. Credit (debt and leverage) acceleration notably increases the likelihood of financial crises, and conditionally on a crisis occurring, it increases its systemic nature and the negative effects on the real economy associated with the crisis.

Because there is a great time gap between systemically important financial crises such as the one that started in 2007–08 and the Great Depression (i.e., financial crises are rare events at least in developed economies, and thus sample sizes are small), providing an econometric analysis implies expanding datasets across years and countries. [31] Reinhart and Rogoff (2008, 2009, 2011) and Schularick and Taylor (2012) analyze long historical time series about private and government debt. This set of papers shows the strong correlation between accelerations in aggregate debt (credit, leverage) and subsequent banking crises. Both papers identify accelerations in debt as the key antecedent to banking crises, with Reinhart and Rogoff focusing on public and private debt and Schularick and Taylor on bank credit.[32] Moreover, conditionally on a crisis, the ex ante acceleration of debt makes the ex post systemic costs higher (i.e., worse economic recessions).

[31] We follow Gorton and Metrick (2012).
[32] Reinhart and Rogoff define a banking crisis by the occurrence of one of the following events: "(1) bank runs that lead to the closure, merging, or takeover by the public sector of one or more financial institutions; or (2) if there are no runs, the closure, merging, takeover, or large-scale government assistance of an important financial institution (or group of institutions), that marks the start of a string of similar outcomes for other financial institutions." Using this definition, and given their dataset, the historical incidence of banking crises is about the same for advanced economies as for emerging markets, and the incidence varies strongly over time, with a marked reduction between the end of World War II and the late 1970s, which was a period of strong financial regulation after the 1930s systemic crisis.
The dataset used in Schularick and Taylor (2012) covers 14 advanced economies over the years 1870–2008 at annual frequency. The countries included are the United States, Canada, Australia, Denmark,

Jorda, Schularick, and Taylor (2011) study the role of credit in the business cycle, with a focus on private credit overhang. Based on a study of the universe of over 200 recession episodes, they document two key regularities of modern business cycles: financial-crisis recessions are more costly than normal recessions in terms of lost output; and for both types of recessions, more *ex ante* credit-intensive expansions tend to be followed by deeper recessions and slower recoveries. They indeed show that "credit bites back."

The historical evidence on the relationship between ex ante credit booms and financial crises is available for a relatively short panel of countries; however, using a sample of 57 emerging market economies and 22 advanced economies over the 1973-2010 period, Gourinchas and Obstfeld (2012) find also that the rapid buildup of leverage is important for the likelihood of financial crisis. In particular, using a discrete-choice panel analysis they find that domestic credit expansion and real currency appreciation have been the most robust and significant predictors of financial crises, regardless of whether a country is emerging or advanced. For emerging economies, moreover, higher foreign exchange reserves predict a sharply reduced probability of a subsequent crisis.

Credit booms are therefore a crucial ex ante correlate of financial crises. Yet, all of these empirical analyses condition on the occurrence of a crisis and asks what its determinants are. But, do all credit booms end up in a crisis? The IMF (2012) analyzes credit booms for 170 countries over the last 40 years of data. It shows that two-thirds of credit booms did not end up in a financial crisis. That is, credit booms due to strong economic fundamentals (demand) do not automatically translate into systemic risk, and therefore, policy should be cautious. However, there are ways that can help policymakers better understand the extent to which credit supply side factors generate aggregate fluctuations in credit. This requires that the regulator has access to a timely and comprehensive credit registry with information on every loan given out by the banking sector (see Khwaja and Mian, 2008; Jiménez et al. 2012, 2014; Jiménez et al. 2013).

There is an emerging literature on the effects of securitization on bank lending and risk-taking, hence on the generation of boom–bust credit cycles. For example, Keys et al. (2010) empirically examine this issue using a unique dataset on securitized subprime mortgage loan contracts in the United States. They exploit a specific rule of thumb in the lending market to generate exogenous variation in the ease of securitization and compare the composition and performance of lenders' portfolios around the ad hoc threshold. Conditionally on being securitized, the portfolio that is more likely to be securitized defaults by around 10–25% more than a similar risk profile group with a lower probability of securitization. Their results are confined to loans where intermediaries' screening effort may be relevant and soft information about borrowers determines their creditworthiness. Their findings suggest that existing securitization practices did adversely affect the screening incentives of lenders. Securitization has therefore been associated with lax lending and excessive credit creation in mortgage markets during the 2000s (Mian and Sufi, 2009), and in business loans (Maddaloni and Peydró, 2011; Jiménez et al. 2013).

Claessens et al. (2010) analyze the financial crisis of 2007–2008 by studying 58 advanced countries and emerging markets. Their main conclusion is that the crisis may be explained

France, Germany, Italy, Japan, the Netherlands, Norway, Spain, Sweden, Switzerland, and the United Kingdom. The share of global GDP accounted for by these countries was around 50% in the year 2000.

by a number of factors, some common to previous financial crises, but others (somewhat) new. Their analysis shows a differential impact of old and new factors. Factors common to other crises, like credit booms, asset price bubbles, and current account deficits, help to explain cross-country differences in the severity of economic impacts. New factors, such as increased financial integration and dependence on wholesale funding, help to account for the amplification and global spreading of the crisis.[33]

Within financial crises, there are important negative externalities from the excessive buildup of leverage in the boom, both from balance sheet, debt overhang and bank lending channels. For example, Jiménez et al. (2012) analyze the credit crunch in the 2007–10 crisis in Spain using a dataset consisting of loan applications. To achieve identification they focus on the set of loan applications made in the same month by the same borrower or for the same loan to different banks of varying balance-sheet strengths (by including in the specifications firm-month or alternatively loan fixed effects). Within this set of loan applications, for which the quality of potential borrowers is constant, they study how economic conditions affect the granting of loans depending on bank capital and liquidity. Moreover, they analyze whether firms that get rejected in their initial loan application can undo the resultant reduction in credit availability by successfully applying to other banks. They find that lower GDP growth reduces the probability that a loan application is granted, particularly during crisis times. The negative effect on loan granting is statistically stronger for banks with low capital. They also find that firms that get rejected in their initial loan application cannot undo the resultant reduction in credit availability by applying to other banks, especially in periods of tighter economic conditions.

González-Hermosillo, Pazarbaşioglu, and Billings (1997) and González-Hermosillo (1999) study the determinants of bank "distress" in various episodes in the US. It turns out that market and liquidity risk factors played a role in explaining "distress," whereas the role of credit risk and moral hazard is more case specific. However, the introduction of aggregate variables, such as macroeconomic fundamentals and regional variables, significantly improved the predictive power of the models tested, providing evidence in favor of the macro explanation of systemic bank difficulties in the "broad" sense.

Demirgüç-Kunt and Detragiache (1998) study the macroeconomic and structural determinants of banking crises in 45–60 developing and industrial countries between 1980 and 1994. Consistently with the business cycle hypothesis for bank crises, in all specifications, GDP growth, real interest rates, and inflation are highly significant. However, private sector credit growth has only explanatory power in some specifications, providing mixed evidence in favor of the lending-boom hypothesis. In contrast, the evidence in favor of the moral-hazard hypothesis regarding explicit deposit insurance schemes is stronger. Since data for crises and non-crises times are pooled, this study can claim to isolate the factors causing full-scale banking crises from those only causing a gradual increase in financial fragility or single bank failures.

Gourinchas, Valdés, and Landerretche (2001) examine more narrowly the properties of lending booms in a sample of 91 industrial and developing countries between 1960 and 1996

---

[33] Other studies have also investigated whether initial conditions can explain the differential impact of the 2008 crisis across countries. For example, in two related papers, Rose and Spiegel (2009, 2010) find that these initial conditions generally do a poor job in explaining the economic performance of countries during the crisis period, and conclude that global factors played a dominant role.

and link them to the likelihood of banking and currency crises. In fact, the unconditional probability of banking crises directly *after* lending boom periods is higher than during tranquil periods. Somewhat contrary to conventional wisdom, they also find that the buildup and ending phases of booms are fairly symmetric, so that on average abrupt and crash-type ends are not consistent with their data.

Dell'Ariccia, Igan, and Laeven (2012) link the current subprime mortgage crisis to a decline in lending standards associated with the rapid expansion of this market. They show that lending standards declined more in areas that experienced larger credit booms and house price increases. In addition, lending standards declined more in areas with higher mortgage securitization rates. This final finding has also been found by Mian and Sufi (2009).

An important issue is also how monetary policy relates to banking system risk. Jiménez, et al. (2014) and Ioannidou, Ongena, and Peydró (2013) find empirical evidence that lower levels of short-term interest rates increases the credit risk-appetite of banks (implying banks granting loans with higher default probability). Controlling for the macroecomic environment, bank, borrower, and loan characteristics, they find that lower short-term interest rates imply that banks give more loans to either borrowers with bad credit histories or to borrowers with no credit histories, or to borrowers with subprime ratings. More importantly, the new loans have a higher hazard rate. They also find that lower interest rates or higher in inflation reduce the default risk of outstanding loans, which implies that in the short-run expansive monetary policy reduces credit risk. Ioannidou, Ongena, and Peydró (2013), using the credit register of Bolivia, where the banking system is almost completely "dollarized," find that not only do banks take on higher credit risk when short-term rates (federal funds rates) are lower, but also loan spreads are reduced, especially for the banks with worse monitoring, thereby suggesting higher bank risk-taking.[34]

27.5 CONCLUSION

In this chapter we have discussed the various elements of systemic risk in banking, which are essential for the understanding of financial crises. The overall concept developed can be used as a baseline for financial and monetary policies when attempting to maintain stable banking systems. At the heart of systemic risk (in the narrow sense) is the notion of contagion—often a strong form of externality—working from one institution or system to another. In a broad sense, the concept also includes the unraveling of imbalances that have built up over time and the consequences of wide systematic shocks which adversely affect many banks at the same time. In this sense, systemic risk goes much beyond the vulnerability of single banks to runs in a fractional reserve system.

We have reviewed the quantitative literature in the light of our concept of systemic risk. Some important new theoretical contributions have appeared in this literature over the last decade. First of all, a considerable number of theoretical studies have now directly addressed the issue of contagion through interbank markets and the relative stability

[34] See also Rajan (2006); and Calomiris (2008).

associated with different lending patterns in them. Second, many models stress the interactions between banks and asset prices in crisis periods, emphasizing cumulative disruptions induced by forced asset sales. Finally, some progress has been made in better understanding the role of liquidity for banking system stability. Macroeconomic models now include some dimensions of "vertical" systemic risk. Available empirical research still continues to focus more on the assessment of bank contagion phenomena than on the macroeconomic causes for banking system instability. Interesting new developments include the use of actual interbank exposures for counterfactual simulations of contagion risk, the application of extreme-value theory to banking system risk, and a starting focus on factors that lead to the buildup of imbalances in financial systems. Further progress could still be made in controling for aggregate factors in contagion analyses. The difficulty to distinguish between macroeconomic causes of banking problems and contagion does not allow general answers to the relative merits of different crisis management policies, such as liquidity support to the market as a whole or macroeconomic stabilization policies versus emergency liquidity assistance to individual banks. Studies of systemic risks in payment and settlement systems remain relatively rare. Even though the practical and unambiguous identification of concrete contagion cases continue to be a challenge, the overall understanding of bank contagion risks has increased significantly over the last decade.

The ongoing financial crisis has highlighted the relevance of systemic banking stability. The available literature illustrates a number of mechanisms that played important roles in it. But, although substantial work has already been achieved (ECB, 2012), other important factors related inter alia to the use of macroprudential instruments or regarding bank business models should be better understood than is the case and will be of great value to the efforts launched recently to strengthen macroprudential supervision and regulation.

References

Acharya, V. V., Gromb, D., and Yorulmazer, T. (2012). Imperfect Competition in the Interbank Market as a Rationale for Central Banking, *American Economic Journal: Macroeconomics* 4, 184–217.

Acharya, V. V., Pedersen L., Philippon T., and Richardson, M. (2011). Measuring Systemic Risk. AFA 2011 Denver Meetings Paper.

Acharya, V. V. and Yorulmazer, V. (2007). Too Many to Fail: An Analysis of Time-inconsistency in Bank Closure Policies, *Journal of Financial Intermediation* 16, 1–31.

Acharya, V. V. and Yorulmazer, V. (2008a). Cash-in-the-Market Pricing and Optimal Resolution of Bank Failures, *Review of Financial Studies* 21, 2705–2742.

Acharya, V. V. and Yorulmazer, V. (2008b). Information Contagion and Bank Herding, *Journal of Money, Credit and Banking* 40, 215–231.

Adrian, T. and Ashcraft, A. B. (2012). Shadow Banking: A Review of the Literature, Federal Reserve Bank of New York Staff Reports No. 580, October.

Adrian, T. and Brunnermeier, M. (2011). CoVar, Federal Reserve Bank of New York Staff Reports No. 348.

Adrian, T. and Shin, H. (2008). Financial Intermediary Leverage and Value at Risk, Federal Reserve Bank of New York Staff Reports No. 338.

Aharony, J. and Swary, V. (1983). Contagion Effects of Bank Failures: Evidence from Capital Markets, *Journal of Business* 56, 305–317.

Allen, F. and Carletti, V. (2006). Credit Risk Transfer and Contagion, *Journal of Monetary Economics* 53, 89–111.

Allen, F. and Carletti, V. (2008). Mark-to-Market Accounting and Liquidity Pricing, *Journal of Accounting and Economics* 45, 358–378.

Allen, F. and Gale, D. (1998). Optimal Financial Crises, *Journal of Finance* 53, 1245–1284.

Allen, F. and Gale, D. (2000). Financial Contagion, *Journal of Political Economy* 108(1), 1–33.

Allen, F. and Gale, D. (2004). Financial Fragility, Liquidity and Asset Prices, *Journal of the European Economic Association* 2, 1015–1048.

Allen, F. and Gale, D. (2005). From Cash-in-the-Market Pricing to Financial Fragility, *Journal of the European Economic Association* 3, 535–546.

Allen, F. and Gale, D. (2007). *Understanding Financial Crises*. Oxford: Oxford University Press.

Alves, I., Ferrari, S., Franchini, P., Héam, J. C., Jurca, P., Langfield, S., Laviola, S., Liedorp, F., Sanchez, A., Tavolaro, S., and Vuillemey, G. (2013). Structure and Resilience of the European Interbank Market, European Systemic Board Occasional Paper No. 3.

Aoki, K. and Nikolov, K. (2012). Bubbles, Banks and Financial Stability, ECB Working Paper No. 1495, November.

Ashcraft, A. B. and Schuermann, T. (2008). Understanding the Securitization of Subprime Mortgage Credit, Federal Reserve Bank of New York Staff Report No. 318, March.

Babus, A. (2007). The Formation of Financial Networks, Fondazione Eni Enrico Mattei Working Paper No. 69.

Banerjee, A. V. (1992). A Simple Model of Herd Behaviour, *Quarterly Journal of Economics* 107, 797–811.

Barkbu, B., Eichengreen, B., and Mody, A. (2012). Financial Crises and the Multilateral Response: What the Historical Record Shows, *Journal of International Economics* 88, 422–435.

Battiston, S., Delli Gatti, D., Gallegati, M., Greenwald, B., and Stiglitz, J. E. (2012a). Default Cascades: When Does Risk Diversification Increase Stability?, *Journal of Financial Stability* 8, 138–149.

Battiston, S., Delli Gatti, D., Gallegati, M., Greenwald, B., and Stiglitz, J. E. (2012b). Liaisons Dangereuses: Increasing Connectivity, Risk Sharing and Systemic Risk, *Journal of Economic Dynamics and Control*, 36(8).

Bech, M. and Hobijn, B. (2007). Technology Diffusion within Central Banking: The Case of RTGS, *International Journal of Central Banking* 3, 147–181.

Bernanke, B., Gertler, M., and Gilchrist, S. (1999). The Financial Accelerator in a Quantitative Business Cycle Framework. In: J. B. Taylor and M. Woodford (Eds.), *Handbook of Macroeconomics*, 1. Amsterdam: Elsevier.

Bhattacharya, S. and Thakor, A. (1993). Contemporary Banking Theory, *Journal of Financial Intermediation* 3, 2–50.

Bianchi, J. (2011). Overborrowing and Systemic Externalities in the Business Cycle, *American Economic Review* 101, 3400–3426.

Bikhchandani, S., Hirshleifer, V., and Welsh, V. (1992). A Theory of Fads, Fashions, Customs and Cultural Changes as Informational Cascade, *Journal of Political Economy* 100, 992–1026.

Boissay, F. (2011). Financial Imbalances and Financial Fragility, ECB Working Paper No. 1317, April.

Boissay, F., Collard, F., and Smets, F. (2013). Booms and Systemic Banking Crises, ECB Working Paper No. 1514, February.

Boot, A. and Thakor, A. (1993). Bank Regulation, Reputation and Rents: Theory and Policy. In: C. Mayer and X. Vives, (Eds.), *Capital Markets and Financial Intermediation*, Cambridge: Cambridge University Press.

Borio, C. E. V. (2003). Towards a Macroprudential Framework for Financial Regulation and Supervision, Bank for International Settlements Working Paper No. 128, February.

Bordo, M., Eichengreen, B., Klingebiel, D., and Soledad-Martinez, M. (2001). Is the Crisis Problem Growing More Severe?, *Economic Policy* 16, 51–82.

Brownlees, C. and Engle, R. (2013). Volatility, Correlation and Tails for Systemic Risk Measurement. Mimeo.

Brunnermeir, M. and Pedersen, L. (2009). Market Liquidity and Funding Liquidity, *Review of Financial Studies* 22(6), 2201–2238.

Brusco, S. and Castiglionesi, F. (2007). Liquidity Coinsurance, Moral Hazard, and Financial Contagion, *Journal of Finance* 62, 2275–2302.

Bryant, J. (1980). A Model of Reserves, Bank Runs, and Deposit Insurance, *Journal of Banking & Finance* 4, 335–344.

Buser, S. A., Chen, A. H., and Kane, E. J. (1981). Federal Deposit Insurance, Regulatory Policy, and Optimal Bank Capital, *Journal of Finance* 35, 51–60.

Caballero, J. and Krishnamurthy, A. (2008). Collective Risk Management in a Flight to Quality Episode, *Journal of Finance* 63, 2195–2230.

Calomiris, C. W. (2008). The Subprime Turmoil: What's Old, What's New, What's Next? Paper Presented at the Jacques Polak Conference (IMF).

Calomiris, C. W. and Kahn, C. (1991). The Role of Demandable Debt in Structuring Optimal Banking Arrangements, *American Economic Review* 81, 497–513.

Calomiris, C. W. and Gorton, G. (1991). The Origins of Banking Panics: Models, Facts, and Bank Regulation. In: G. Hubbard (Ed.), *Financial Markets and Financial Crises*, Chicago, IL: The University of Chicago Press.

Calomiris, C. W. and Mason, J. (1997). Contagion and Bank Failures during the Great Depression: The June 1932 Chicago Banking Panic, *American Economic Review* 87, 863–883.

Calomiris, C. W. and Mason, J. (2003). Fundamentals, Panics and Bank Distress during the Depression, *American Economic Review* 93, 1615–1647.

Carletti, E., Hartmann, P., and Spagnolo, G. (2007). Bank Mergers, Competition and Liquidity, *Journal of Money, Credit and Banking* 39, 1067–1105.

Cass, D. and Shell, K. (1983). Do Sunspots Matter?, *Journal of Political Economy* 91, 193–227.

Cassola, N., Drehmann, M., Hartmann, P., Lo Duca, M., and Scheicher, M. (2008). Research Perspective on the Propagation of the Credit Market Turmoil, *European Central Bank Research Bulletin* 7.

Chari, V. and Jagannathan, R. (1988). Banking Panics, Information, and Rational Expectations Equilibrium, *Journal of Finance* 43, 749–760.

Chen, Y. (1999). Banking Panics: The Role of the First-Come, First-Served Rule and Information Externalities, *Journal of Political Economy* 107, 946–968.

Cifuentes, R., Shin, V., and Ferrucci, V. (2005). Liquidity Risk and Contagion, *Journal of the European Economic Association* 3, 556–566.

Claessens, S., Dell'Ariccia, G., Igan, D., and Laeven, L. (2010). Lessons and Policy Implications from the Global Financial Crisis, IMF Working Paper No. 10/44.

Cont, R. and Santos, E. B. (2010). The Brazilian Interbank Network Structure and Systemic Risk. Central Bank of Brazil Working Paper No. 210.

Council of the European Union (2013). Proposal for a Council Regulation Conferring Specific Tasks on the European Central Bank Concerning Policies Relating to the Prudential

Supervision of Credit Institutions No. 1024/2013 of 15 October 2013, *Official Journal of the European Union* October 29.

Dang, T. V., Gorton, G., and Holmström, B. (2012). Ignorance, Debt and Financial Crises. Working Paper.

Dasgupta, A. (2004). Financial Contagion through Capital Connections: A Model of the Origin and Spread of Bank Panics, *Journal of the European Economic Association* 6, 1049–1084.

Davis, E. P. (1994). Market Liquidity Risk. In: D. Fair, (Ed.), *The Competitiveness of Financial Institutions and Centres in Europe*, Dordrecht: Kluwer Academic

Davis, E. P. (1995). *Debt, Financial Fragility and Systemic Risk*. 2nd edition. Oxford: Clarendon Press.

de Bandt, O. and Hartmann, P. (2000). Systemic Risk: A Survey, ECB Working Paper No. 35, November.

de Bandt, O. and Hartmann, P. (2002). Systemic Risk in Banking: A Survey. In: C. Goodhart and G. Illing (Eds.), *Financial Crises, Contagion and the Lender of Last Resort: A Reader*, 249–298. Oxford: Oxford University Press.

de Bandt, O., Hartmann, P., and Peydró, J.-L. (2010). Systemic Risk in Banking: An Update. In: A. Berger, P. Molyneux, and J. Wilson (Eds.), *Oxford Handbook of Banking*, 633–672. Oxford: Oxford University Press.

Degryse, H. and Nguyen, G. (2007). Interbank Exposures: An Empirical Examination of Contagion Risk in the Belgian Banking System, *International Journal of Central Banking* 3, 123–171.

Dell'Ariccia, G., Detragiache, E., and Rajan, R. (2008). The Real Effect of Banking Crises, *Journal of Financial Intermediation* 17, 89–112.

Dell'Ariccia, G., Igan, D., and Laeven, L. (2012). Credit Booms and Lending Standards: Evidence from the Subprime Mortgage Market, *Journal of Money, Credit and Banking* 44, 367–384.

Dell'Ariccia, G. and Marquez, R. (2006). Lending Booms and Lending Standards, *Journal of Finance* 61(5), 2511–2546.

Demirgüç-Kunt, A. and Detragiache, E. (1998). The Determinants of Banking Crises in Developing and Developed Countries, IMF Staff Papers 45, 81–109.

Dewatripont, M. and Tirole, J. (1994). *The Prudential Regulation of Banks*. Cambridge: MIT Press.

Diamond, D. V. and Dybvig, P. (1983). Bank Runs, Deposit Insurance, and Liquidity, *Journal of Political Economy* 91, 401–419.

Diamond, D. V. and Rajan, R. (2001). Banks, Short-Term Debt and Financial Crises: Theory, Policy Implications and Applications, *Carnegie-Rochester Conference Series on Public Policy* 54(1), 37–71.

Diamond, D. V. and Rajan, R. (2005). Liquidity Shortages and Banking Crises, *Journal of Finance* 60, 615–647.

Diamond, D. V. and Rajan, R. (2006). Money in a Theory of Banking, *American Economic Review* 96, 30–53.

Duffie, D. and Lando, D. (2001). Term Structure of Credit Spreads with Incomplete Accounting Information, *Econometrica* 69, 633–664.

Elsinger, H., Lehar, A., and Summer, M. (2006a). Risk Assessment for Banking Systems, *Management Science* 52, 1301–1314.

Elsinger, H., Lehar, A., and Summer, M. (2006b). Using Market Information for Banking System Risk Assessment, *International Journal of Central Banking* 2, 137–166.

ECB (European Central Bank) (2009). The Concept of Systemic Risk, *Financial Stability Review* December, 134–142.

ECB (European Central Bank) (2010). Analytical Models and Tools for the Identification and Assessment of Systemic Risks, *Financial Stability Review* June, 138–146.

ECB (European Central Bank) (2012). Report on the First Two Years of the Macroprudential Research Network, Frankfurt, October.

Evanoff, D., Hartmann, P., and Kaufman, G. (Eds.). (2009). *The First Credit Market Turmoil of the 21st Century*. Hackensack, NJ: World Scientific Publishers.

Farhi, E. and Tirole, J. (2012). Collective Moral Hazard, Maturity Mismatch, and Systemic Bailouts, *American Economic Review* 102(1), 60–93.

Fecht, F. (2004). On the Stability of Different Financial Systems, *Journal of the European Economic Association* 2, 969–1014.

Fecht, F., Grüner, H. P., and Hartmann, P. (2007). Welfare Effects of Financial Integration, Center for Economic Policy Research Discussion Paper No. 6311, May.

Fecht, F., Grüner, H. P., and Hartmann, P. (2012). Financial Integration, Specialization and Systemic Risk, *Journal of International Economics* 88, 150–161.

Federal Reserve Bank of Kansas City (2008). *Maintaining Stability in a Changing Financial System.* Proceedings of the Jackson Hole, WY Conference. Kansas City: Kansas Federal Reserve Bank.

Ferguson, R., Hartmann, P., Panetta, F., and Portes, R. (2007). International Financial Stability, *Geneva Report on the World Economy*, 9, 17–41.

Financial Stability Forum (2008). Enhancing Market and Institutional Resilience, Basel, April 7.

Flannery, M. (1996). Financial Crises, Payment System Problems, and Discount Window Lending, *Journal of Money, Credit, and Banking* 28, 804–824.

Freixas, X, Parigi, B. M, Rochet, J.-C. (2000). Systemic Risk, Interbank Relations, and Liquidity Provision by the Central Bank, *Journal of Money, Credit and Banking* 32, 611–638.

Furfine, C. H. (2003). Interbank Exposures: Quantifying the Risk of Contagion, *Journal of Money, Credit and Banking* 35, 111–128.

Furlong, F. T. and Keeley, M. C. (1989). Capital Regulation and Bank Risk-Taking: A Note, *Journal of Banking & Finance* 13, 883–891.

Gennaioli, N., Shleifer, A., and Vishny, R. (2013). A Model of Shadow Banking, *Journal of Finance* 68, 1331–1363.

Gertler, M. and Kiyotaki, N. (2013). Banking, Liquidity and Bank Runs in an Infinite-Horizon Economy, NBER Working Paper No. 19129.

Giglio, S., Kelly, B., Pruitt, S., and Qiao, X. (2013). Systemic Risk and the Macroeconomy: An Empirical Evaluation, Chicago Booth Research Paper No. 12–49.

Goldstein, I. and Pauzner, A. (2005). Demand Deposit Contracts and the Probability of Bank Runs, *Journal of Finance* 60, 1293–1328.

González-Hermosillo, B. (1999). Determinants of Ex Ante Banking System Distress: A Macro-Micro Empirical Exploration of Some Recent Episodes, IMF Working Paper No. WP/99/33.

González-Hermosillo, B., Pazarbaşioglu, C., and Billings, R. (1997). Banking System Fragility: Likelihood Versus Timing of Failure: An Application to the Mexican Financial Crisis, IMF Staff Papers 44, 295–314.

Goodfriend, M. and King, R. (1988). Financial Deregulation, Monetary Policy, and Central Banking, *Restructuring Banking and Financial Services in America, American Enterprize Institute Studies* 481, 216–253.

Goodhart, C. A. E. and Huang, H. (1999). A Model of the Lender of Last Resort, LSE Financial Markets Group Discussion Paper No. 313.

Gorton, G. (1988). Banking Panics and Business Cycles, *Oxford Economic Papers* 40, 751–781.

Gorton, G. and Metrick, A. (2012). Getting Up to Speed on the Financial Crisis: A One-Weekend-Reader's Guide, *Journal of Economic Literature* 50(1), 128–150.

Gourinchas, P.-O. and Obstfeld, M. (2012). Stories of the Twentieth Century for the Twenty-First, *American Economic Journal: Macroeconomics* 4, 226–265.

Gourinchas, P.-O., Valdés, R., and Landerretche, O. (2001). Lending Booms: Latin America and the World, *Economia* 1, 2.

Greenlaw, D., Hatzius, J., Kashyap A., and Shin, H. S. (2008). Leveraged Losses: Lessons from the Mortgage Market Meltdown, US Monetary Policy Forum Report No. 2.

Greenwood, R., Landier, A., and Thesmar, D. (2012). *Vulnerable Banks*, NBER Working Paper No. 18537.

Guttentag, J. M. and Herring, R. J. (1984). Credit Rationing and Financial Disorder, *Journal of Finance* 39, 1359–1382.

Gwynne S. C. (1986). *Selling Money*. New York: Weidenfeld and Nicholson.

Haldane, A. G. and May, R. M. (2011). Systemic Risk in Banking Ecosystems, *Nature* 469, 351–355

Hartmann, P., Hubrich, K., and Kremer, M. (2013). Integrating Systemic Financial Instability into Macroeconomics: How to Meet the Challenge?, *ECB Research Bulletin* Autumn 19, 2–8.

Hartmann, P., Straetmans, S., and de Vries, C. (2004). Asset Market Linkages in Crisis Periods, *Review of Economics and Statistics* 86, 313–326.

Hartmann, P., Straetmans, S., and de Vries, C. (2006). Banking System Stability: A Cross-Atlantic Perspective. In: M. Carey and R. Stulz (Eds.), *The Risks of Financial Institutions*, 133–188. Chicago, IL: Chicago University Press and National Bureau of Economic Research.

Heider, F., Hoerova, M., and Holthausen, C. (2009). Liquidity Hoarding and Interbank Market Spreads: The Role of Counterparty Risk, ECB Working Paper No. 1126.

Hoggarth, G., Reis, R., and Saporta, V. (2002). Costs of Banking System Instability: Some Empirical Evidence, *Journal of Banking and Finance* 26, 825–855.

Holmström, B. and Tirole, J. (1998). Private and Public Provision of Liquidity, *Journal of Political Economy* 106, 1–40.

Hollo, D., Kremer, M., and Lo Duca, M. (2012). CISS—A Composite Indicator of Systemic Stress in the Financial System, European Central Bank Working Paper No. 527.

Institute of International Finance (2008). Final Report of the IIF Committee on Market Best Practice: Principles of Conduct and Best Practice Recommendations, Washington, July.

IMF (International Monetary Fund) (2012). Policies for Macrofinancial Stability: How to Deal with Credit Booms, IMF Staff Discussion Note No. 12/06.

Ioannidou V., Ongena, S., and Peydró, J. L. (2013). Monetary Policy, Risk-Taking and Pricing: Evidence from a Natural Experiment. Working Paper.

Iyer, R. and Peydró, J. L. (2007). How does a Shock Propagate? A Model of Contagion in the Interbank Market due to Financial Linkages. University of Amsterdam Working Paper.

Iyer, R. and Peydró, J. L. (2011). Interbank Contagion at Work: Evidence from a Natural Experiment, *The Review of Financial Studies* 24, 1337–1377.

Jiménez, G., Ongena, S., Peydró, J.-L., and Saurina, J. (2012). Credit Supply and Monetary Policy: Identifying the Bank Balance-Sheet Channel with Loan Applications, *American Economic Review* 102, 2301–2326.

Jiménez, G., Ongena, S., Peydró, J.-L., and Saurina, J. (2014). Hazardous Times for Monetary Policy: What do Twenty-Three Million Bank Loans Say about the Effects of Monetary Policy on Credit Risk-Taking?, *Econometrica* 82, 463–505.

Jorda, O., Schularick, M., and Taylor, A. (2011). When Credit Bites Back: Leverage, Business Cycles, and Crises, NBER Working Paper No. 17621.

Kane, E. (1989). *The S and L Insurance Mess: How Did it Happen?* Washington, DC: Urban Institute Press.

Karas, A. and Schoors, K. (2012). Bank Networks, Interbank Liquidity Runs and the Identification of Banks that are Too Interconnected to Fail. Mimeo.

Kareken, J. H. and Wallace, N. (1978). Deposit Insurance and Bank Regulation: A Partial-Equilibrium Exposition, *Journal of Business* 51, 413–438.

Kaufman, G. G. (1994). Bank Contagion: A Review of the Theory and Evidence, *Journal of Financial Services Research* 7, 123–150.

Keys, B., Mukherjee, T., Seru, A., and Vig, V. (2010). Did Securitization Lead to Lax Screening? Evidence from Subprime Loans, *Quarterly Journal of Economics* 125, 307–362.

Khwaja, A. and Mian, A. (2008). Tracing the Impact of Bank Liquidity Shocks: Evidence from an Emerging Market, *American Economic Review* 98, 1413–1442.

Kindleberger, C. P. (1978/1996). *Manias, Panics and Crashes. A History of Financial Crises.* 3rd edition. London: Macmillan.

King, M. and Wadhwani, S. (1990). Transmission of Volatility between Stock Markets, *Review of Financial Studies* 3, 5–35.

Korinek, A. (2011). Systemic Risk-Taking: Amplification Effects, Externalities, and Regulatory Responses, ECB Working Paper No. 1345.

Krainer, R. (2012). Regulating Wall Street: The Dodd Frank Act and the New Architecture of Global Finance, *Journal of Financial Stability* 8, 121–133.

Krugman, P. (1998). What Happened to Asia?. Massachusetts Institute of Technology: Mimeo.

Leitner, Y. (2005). Financial Network: Contagion, Commitment and Private Sector Bailouts, *Journal of Finance* 60, 2925–2953.

Lorenzoni, G. (2008). Inefficient Credit Booms, *Review of Economic Studies* 75, 809–833.

Maddaloni, A. and Peydró, J. (2011). Bank Risk-Taking, Securitization, Supervision, and Low Interest Rates: Evidence from the Euro Area and US Lending Standards, *Review of Financial Studies* 24, 2121–2165.

Mendoza, E. (2002). Credit, Prices and Crashes: Business Cycles with a Sudden Stop. In: S. Edwards and J. Frankel (Eds.), *Preventing Currency Crises in Emerging Markets*, 335–392. Chicago: University of Chicago Press.

Mendoza, E. (2010). Sudden Stops, Financial Crises and Leverage, *American Economic Review* 100, 1941–1966.

Merton, R. C. (1977). An Analytical Derivation of the Cost of Deposit Insurance and Loan Guarantees: An Application of Modern Option Pricing Theory, *Journal of Banking and Finance* 1, 3–11.

Merton, R. C. (1978). On the Cost of Deposit Insurance When There Are Surveillance Costs, *Journal Of Business* 51, 439–452.

Mian, A. and Sufi, A. (2009). The Consequences of Mortgage Credit Expansion: Evidence from the 2007 Mortgage Default Crisis, *The Quarterly Journal of Economics* 124, 1449–1496.

Minsky, H. P. (1977). A Theory of Systemic Fragility. In: E. I. Altman and A. W. Sametz, (Eds.), *Financial Crises*, 138–152. New York, NY: Wiley.

Minsky, H. P. (1982). The Financial-Instability Hypothesis: Capitalist Processes and the Behaviour of the Economy. In: C. P. Kindleberger and J.-P. Laffargue (Eds.), *Financial Crises: Theory, History, and Policy*, 13–39. Cambridge, UK: Cambridge University Press.

Mishkin, F. S. (1991). Asymmetric Information and Financial Crises: A Historical Perspective. In: G. Hubbard (Ed.), *Financial Markets and Financial Crises*, 69–108. Chicago: University of Chicago Press.

Mistrulli, P. E. (2011). Assessing Financial Contagion in the Interbank Market: Maximum Entropy versus Observed Interbank Linkages, *Journal of Banking & Finance* 35, 1114–1127.

Morgenstern, O. (1959). *International Financial Transactions and the Business Cycle*. National Bureau of Economic Research Studies in Business Cycles, Princeton, NJ: Princeton University Press.

Rajan, R. (2006). Has Finance Made the World Riskier?, *European Financial Management* 12, 499–533.

Ranciére, R., Tornell, A., and Westermann, F. (2008). Systemic Crises and Growth, *Quarterly Journal of Economics* 123, 359–406.

Reinhart, C. and Rogoff, K. (2008). Is the 2007 US Sub-prime Financial Crisis So Different? An International Historical Comparison, *American Economic Review* 98, 339–344.

Reinhart, C. and Rogoff, K. (2009). *This Time Is Different: Eight Centuries of Financial Folly*. Princeton, NJ: Princeton University Press.

Reinhart, C. and Rogoff, K. (2011). From Financial Crash to Debt Crisis, *American Economic Review* 101, 1676–1706.

Rochet, J.-C. and Tirole, J. (1996). Interbank Lending and Systemic Risk, *Journal of Money, Credit, and Banking* 28, 733–762.

Rochet, J.-C. and Vives, X. (2004). Coordination Failures and the Lender of Last Resort: Was Bagehot Right After All?, *Journal of the European Economic Association* 2, 1116–1147.

Rose, A. and Spiegel, M. (2009). Cross-country Causes and Consequences of the 2008 Crisis: Early Warnings, Federal Reserve Bank of San Francisco Working Paper No. 2009–17.

Rose, A. and Spiegel, M. (2010). Cross-country Causes and Consequences of the 2008 Crisis: International Linkages and American Exposure, *Pacific Economic Review*, 15, 340–363.

Ruckes, M. (2004). Bank Competition and Credit Standards, *Review of Financial Studies* 17, 1073–1112.

Scharfstein, D. S. and Stein, J. C. (1990). Herd Behaviour and Investment, *American Economic Review* 80, 465–479.

Schularick, M. and Taylor, A. M. (2012). Credit Booms Gone Bust: Monetary Policy, Leverage Cycles and Financial Crises, 1870-2008, *American Economic Review* 102, 1029–1061.

Senior Supervisors Group (2008). Observations on Risk Management Practices during the Recent Market Turbulence, March 6.

Slovin, M. B., Sushka, M. E., and Polonchek, J. A. (1993). The Value of Bank Durability: Borrowers as Bank Stakeholders, *Journal of Finance* 48, 247–266.

Slovin, M. B., Sushka, M. E., and Polonchek, J. A. (1999). An Analysis of Contagion and Competitive Effects at Commercial Banks, *Journal of Financial Economics* 54, 197–225.

Stiglitz, J. E. (1993). The Role of the State in Financial Markets. Paper Presented to the Annual World Bank Conference on Development Economics.

Tirole, J. (2008a). Liquidity Shortages: Theoretical Underpinnings, Special Issue on Liquidity, *Banque de France Financial Stability Review* 11, 53–63.

Tirole, J. (2008b). Lecons d'une crise. Toulouse Sciences Economiques Notes.

Upper, C. (2007). Using Counterfactual Simulations to Assess the Danger of Contagion in Interbank Markets, Bank for International Settlements Working Paper No. 234.

Upper, C. and Worms, A. (2004), Estimating Bilateral Exposures in the German Interbank Market: Is There a Danger of Contagion?, *European Economic Review* 48, 827–849.

Van Lelyveld, I. and Liedorp, F. (2006). Interbank Contagion in the Dutch Banking Sector, *International Journal of Central Banking* 2(2), 99–133.

CHAPTER 28

....

BANKING CRISES
*Those Hardy Perennials**

....

GERARD CAPRIO JR. AND PATRICK HONOHAN

28.1 INTRODUCTION

THE great international banking crisis that broke out in August 2007 and the ensuing euro crisis from 2010 are only the latest episodes in a lengthy history of recurrent banking crises around the world. Failures of banks have often been sudden—with depositors and other creditors scrambling to withdraw their funds or refusing to renew their maturing deposits. They have been costly, both in direct cash costs to bank creditors or to the governments who have bailed them out, and in the associated spillover effects on economic activity including that caused by reduced access to credit. Some financial crises have had their focus elsewhere, as in government debt, exchange rate, and stock market crises, but banks have typically played a central or important supporting role.

Although bank solvency is often the victim of adverse shocks arising elsewhere in the economy, and while panic can result in unnecessarily large and damaging depositor withdrawals, this chapter argues that the most damaging of systemic banking crises—including but not limited to the current one—have ultimately involved or were significantly exacerbated by what we call bad banking and bad policies—those that permitted or encouraged excessive risk-taking and even "looting" of other people's money. With each crisis there is an inevitable chorus of calls for more official prudential regulation and supervision to prevent a

* We would like to thank Thorsten Beck, Roger Bolton, Stijn Claessens, Asli Demirgüç-Kunt, James Hanson, Luc Laeven, Philip Lane, Millard Long, Peter Montiel, Steven Nafziger, Sergio Schmukler, and Andrew Sheng for comments. Nonetheless, the responsibility for any errors and omissions lies with the authors. And we owe the subtitle to Charles Kindleberger, from the title of Chapter 1 of his classic, *Manias, Panics, and Crashes: A History of Financial Crises*, originally published in 1978 (Wiley and Sons) and now in its 6th edition (with Robert Aliber, Palgrave Macmillan).

recurrence. However, cross-country empirical evidence suggests that policy is best directed toward ensuring a dynamic approach to regulation focusing on the information that is being disclosed to market participants, the degree of market discipline on the behavior of bankers, and the incentives in the financial system, including those for regulators.

Section 28.2 briefly sketches the historical background, noting the "boom in busts" of the post-Bretton Woods period following a 30-year lull. Not all crises are the same, and Section 28.3 highlights the distinct role of mismanagement, government interference, and macro-economic shocks. Section 28.4 reviews the aspects of crises which have received attention from economic theoreticians seeking to understand their recurrence and severity. Section 28.5 discusses the costs of crises. The size of these explains the importance of prevention and corrective policy and these are discussed in Section 28.6, while Section 28.7 looks as the extent to which recent crises are new phenomena. In conclusion, Section 28.8 suggests that, despite an inevitable overhaul of regulation in the coming years, crises will recur periodically, and the goal should be to minimize their frequency and cost without sacrificing the benefit to economic growth and income equality that a well-functioning financial system can deliver.

28.2 EARLY HISTORY

It is no exaggeration to say that banking crises—for now, the widespread insolvency of banks leading to closures, mergers, takeovers, or injections of government resources—are virtually as old as banking. When modern banking emerged as a development of money-changing in thirteenth-century Europe, bankers faced information problems more severe than in the least developed countries today. Clients' trade was subjected to a variety of shocks—wars, plague, shortage of coins, losses in trade (e.g., ships sinking or being plundered), defalcation by borrowers—that made lending hazardous. And depositors faced the risk that their bankers would not survive these shocks, or would themselves abscond with funds. Repeated failures led to some drastic remedies: a Barcelonan banker was executed in front of his failed bank in 1360—a far cry from the limited liability that protected bank owners in later times (Kohn, forthcoming: ch. 8). Sovereigns were less likely to impose such extreme sanctions when they were the source of the problem, and bankers often succumbed to the temptation or were required (literally for their survival) to lend to the monarch. Such famous early Italian banking houses as the Riccardi of Lucca, the Bardi, the Peruzzi, and even the illustrious Medici of Florence, owed their banking downfall in whole or large part to kings and princes that would not or could not repay. Financing the loser in a war was a sure route to failure, but even winners reneged, leading to a higher interest rate spread on loans to kings and princes than to the more business-minded town governments (Homer and Sylla, 1996, p. 94).

That bank failures have come in waves is suggested by the list assembled by Kindleberger and Aliber (2011) covering mostly the more advanced economies since the seventeenth century, and which displays, for example, the rather regular ten-yearly recurrence of crises through most of the nineteenth century and through to World War II. Emerging economies experienced a higher frequency of crises in the interwar period (Bordo, et al. 2001). The post-World War II era saw a period of exceptional quiescence that lasted through the early

1970s. Against the background of a relatively benign macroeconomic environment, regulations that restricted banking competition and product innovation, including cross-border
activities, probably contributed to this stability. Gradually, however, these regulations
became unsustainable as communications technology and financial innovation (including
the emergence of nearbank competitors) led to evasion.

The liberalization of banking and of capital flows, together with increasingly volatile
macroeconomic conditions (themselves associated with weakened fiscal discipline, the
abandonment of the Bretton Woods exchange rate pegs and surges in inflation rates)
were followed by a return to banking crises at a frequency comparable to what had been
experienced before. Already by 1997, over three out of every five member states of the
IMF had experienced banking problems severe enough to be regarded as systemic or
at least borderline systemic (Lindgren, Garcia, and Saal, 1996; and Caprio, Klingebiel
et al. 2005); the incidence of crises remains unchanged as of early 2013, as many of those
affected in recent years previously had at least borderline crises. But the etiology of crises
has varied.

28.3 DIVERSE ORIGINS: MANAGEMENT, GOVERNMENT, AND MACROECONOMICS IN RECENT CRISES

Many of the most spectacular systemic banking crises of recent decades have been inextricably linked with macroeconomic crises in a way that makes the direction of causality hard
to unravel. However, it is important not to neglect the role of fraud and mismanagement, on
the one hand, and government interference, on the other. Indeed, one or the other of these
two—bad banking and bad policies[1]—has been at the root of quite a number of systemic
banking crises, not only in the developing world (Honohan, 1997; and Caprio and Honohan,
2005) but also in the latest great international crisis that emerged in the US and Europe.

28.3.1 Management and Fraud

Two very large individual bank failures in the Caribbean area can be taken as classic
examples where *fraud or mismanagement* were at the root of the problem—namely, that
in Venezuela (1994) and the Dominican Republic (2003). Both appear to be cases of the
diverted deposits fraud, in which some of the deposits accepted by the bank are not recorded

---

[1] We use "bad banking" to embrace a range of management practice, from fraud to miscalculations
of risk to deliberate exploitation of the put option inherent in deposit insurance, that heightens the
likelihood of bank failure. Of course, all banking involves risk, not least because of the ever-present
information problems of adverse selection and moral hazard, but these are managed and adequately
priced in normal banking operation. Pressure of circumstances can turn good bankers into bad bankers,
as is graphically characterized by de Juan (2002).

as liabilities and the corresponding resources are looted by insiders even though the bank still appears solvent on paper and even though its recorded assets may be properly performing. In each of these cases, the bank involved was of systemic importance and the sums were so large that the loans, that eventually were made by the central bank to enable the bank to make the depositors whole, destabilized the macroeconomy.[2] And, in Venezuela, high deposit rates in the "rogue" bank forced up rates, and risk-taking, at other banks. Another very large failure in which the diverted deposits fraud appears to have been present was that of the international group BCCI. This group, headquartered in Luxembourg and London, was operating in about 70 countries and its failure was of systemic importance in some African countries where it had attained a sizable market share (cf. Herring, 2005). The diverted deposits fraud typically involves the acquiescence of audit professionals; the official supervisor can then be hard-pressed to detect such frauds because of the complexity of the false accounting structures that are created.

Inadequate management of "rogue" traders has caused several sizable bank failures, most famously that of Barings Bank in 1995, but, although the losses involved in some of these cases have run into ten figures (in dollars), no known cases have been of systemic importance. In January 2008, Société Générale reported the largest single bank loss (over $7 billion) ever attributed to fraud by a lone "rogue" trader. As with the even larger Ponzi scheme uncovered in Bernard Madoff's investment firm in late 2008, typically fraud is discovered in a period of asset market decline following a long run of overoptimism. Other forms of mismanagement weakness can be cited, none more apparent than the case of Crédit Lyonnais in the 1990s, where grandiosity and exaggerated ambition in lending policy broke the record for the largest single bank loss in the industrial world: without the French government's bailout, Crédit Lyonnais would have proved insolvent. Lack of management capacity on the part of new controlling insiders also brought insolvency in 1995 to the long-established Meridien BIAO bank in Western and Central Africa—although that bank had already been severely weakened by the effects of government intervention.

While the Mexican Tequila crisis (1994–1995) crystallized around a currency collapse, which hit the banks because of speculative derivative contracts that gave them a de facto long position on local currency, the underlying weakness of the Mexican banks was subsequently traced to insider lending and a long period of evasion of minimum capitalization requirements dating back to their privatization. With little shareholder equity at stake, banks were free to move out on the risk frontier and lend to the few sectors with the highest return, as confirmed by Caprio and Wilson (2000), Wilson, Saunders, and Caprio (2000), and Haber (2005).

Significant regime changes in the economy often devalue both the financial and skills portfolio of banks, sharply increasing the risk of a banking crisis. The introduction of new instruments or opportunities for risk-taking often leads some to take on new risks without adequate attention to their downside potential. Likewise, the liberalization of economic policies has definitely been associated with a surge of bank failures in countries

---

[2] The payments system can create a strong short-term interdependency of banks, so that the failure of one major bank could disrupt the entire system of payments and short-term credit on which much of day-to-day economic activity depends. For this reason, some banks of systemic importance are perceived as being too-big-to-fail (TBTF), requiring official support for their continued operation even if they are insolvent.

with weaker information and governance institutions (Demirgüç-Kunt and Detragiache, 1999). Liberalization of entry into banking increased competitive pressures for banks, liberalization of interest rates heightened repayment and market risks, and liberalization of other aspects of economic policy impacted on the creditworthiness of borrowers in ways that were not always easy to perceive, often entailing large changes in relative prices. And, to the extent that pre-liberalization portfolios were controlled, the lifting of controls often led banks to expand simultaneously. However, simultaneous portfolio shifts by the banking sector can move asset prices, making the shift look like a safe proposition, as in the case of the Malaysian property boom of the late 1970s and early 1980s, which led to a mid-1980s crisis. In addition to a skewed portfolio, liberalized banks inherit a staff that is short on banking skills, unfortunately precisely when they are greatly needed, just as the government begins with bank supervisors skilled only in checking that banks are complying with various government commands and not at all trained in modern risk-based bank supervision. Although even the best bankers and supervisors would be challenged during liberalization, those with weak skills are even more likely to fail.

In particular, the process of economic transition from socialist or planned economies proved fertile for banking crises, many of which can be attributed to inexperienced or reckless management. Although the first wave of post-transition inflation wiped out much of the real value of their pre-existing deposits, and reduced the debt burden of their borrowers, many transition economy banks—especially in Eastern Europe—misjudged the difficulty of credit appraisal especially in the fluid conditions of the transition. As a result, many made a new round of poor or self-serving loans, which soon fell into non-performing status.

Even where Transition was managed without a surge of high inflation, as in China and Vietnam, large banking losses were socialized. Indeed, in China, cumulative injections of government funds into the four main government-owned banks alone from 1998 to 2006 amounted to over $350 billion, or about 30% of 2001 GDP, with further injections still considered necessary to restore full capitalization on a realistic evaluation of the recoverability of the loan portfolio (see Barth and Caprio, 2007; and Honohan, 2008). This massive bailout was accomplished without loss of depositor confidence, reflecting the ability and undisputed willingness of the State to ensure that depositors at its banks would not suffer. Indeed, expressed as a percentage of GDP, bank deposits in China have been higher than almost anywhere else in the developing world, aside from offshore financial centers. These growing funds were effectively applied up to the mid-1990s as a transitional and partial substitute for the former budgetary allocations made under the planned system to key unprofitable state-owned enterprises (Lardy, 1998). Made as loans, these could never have been fully serviced, as was gradually recognized through the various bank restructuring measures adopted from 1998 on. The Chinese case, then, provides a conspicuous example of how government policy—specifically government-directed lending policy—has led to loan losses large enough to erode the banks' capital many times over.

28.3.2 Government Policies

Many of the poorest developing-country economies that were not subject to a centrally planned regime also experienced explicit or implicit government policies of directed credit. When these were enforced by statist regimes without regard to the viability of the lending banks, the result was losses, erosion of capital, and a weakening of financial autonomy and motivation of bank managers, often resulting in insolvency. The true financial condition of state-owned or heavily controlled banks of this sort was often acknowledged only at a time of regime change or a sizable policy reform. Even in non-socialist economies, government influence has often had similar effects. A good example comes from francophone West Africa where the banks in several countries made what proved to be unrecoverable loans to parastatals and government suppliers, unwisely taking comfort in the fact that these loans were being rediscounted by the regional central banks. A similar problem arises with provincial governments relying on the national authorities to bail out failing provincial banks, as was seen in Brazil.

Banks have always been dependent to a degree on the willingness of the state to allow them to function profitably. Calomiris and Haber (2013) argue that, in autocracies and in populist democracies, this inherent dependency on the government has made them fragile, and that it is only in a handful of liberal democracies that they have remained free of systemic crises. Even where directed credit is not an issue, quasi-fiscal impositions such as unremunerated reserve requirements have weakened bank profitability. Arbitrary exchange rate and exchange-control regulations also have a tax-like effect. The most dramatic example of this was the forced conversion to local currency of foreign currency deposits and loans at Argentine banks in late 2001. Because the conversion was not at market rates and furthermore was asymmetric, with a much larger effective write-down of bank loans than of bank deposits, this arbitrary measure created systemic bank insolvency at a stroke.

Banks have also needed the state to enforce contracts, a role that can often conflict with government's interest in maintaining political support. Calomiris and Haber (2013) argue that politics is a key deep determinant of crises. In their framework, there is a "game of bank bargains" among the various political constituencies that determines the availability of credit and the degree of instability, with the latter emerging in part as a result of attempts to use subsidies to cement political support.

28.3.3 Macro Boom and Bust

Although the roles of management and government are never irrelevant in a banking crisis, what has dominated many of the larger episodes of systemic crisis is a dynamic instability in widely held expectations about macroeconomic and business prospects generally. A wave of *overoptimism* about economic growth, often manifested in a real estate price boom, results in expansion of credit by most banks, especially to the sectors specifically favored by the optimism. The resulting increase in leverage often is fueled in part by capital inflows—as in Mexico and East Asia in the 1990s, but also in the recent mortgage finance booms in the US, Ireland, and elsewhere. Because of the optimism, loan-loss provisioning is lower than will prove necessary, and this for a time is justified by low delinquencies as the overall economic boom financed by credit expansion makes it easy for borrowers to service their debt. This could explain by itself why rapid credit expansion is a predictor of crises. In addition, of course, rapid credit expansion places stresses on credit appraisal capacity and results in errors even conditional on the overall optimism. Various forms of contagion or herd effect come into play. Even banks whose managers do not share the optimism feel pressure to relax credit approval standards for fear of losing market share. The formation of banker expectations can be influenced by peer observation, magnifying and generalizing emerging overconfidence. As a latecomer to the South Sea Bubble (John Martin, of Martin's Bank) said, "when the rest of the world are mad we must imitate them in some measure" (Dale, 2004, p. 113), words that were echoed in July 2007 (shortly before he lost his job) by the CEO of Citigroup, Chuck Prince, who told the *Financial Times* that "As long as the music is playing, you've got to get up and dance."

Whereas experienced bankers are normally alert to isolated indications of unsound practices among their peers, in contrast, during the euphoria of the boom phase, they are unlikely to detect even fatal weaknesses. These waves of overoptimism are sufficiently rare in any one country for learning to be imperfect. Disaster myopia prevails, with decision-makers disregarding the relevance of historical experience at home and abroad (Guttentag and Herring, 1986). Eventually, however, the unsustainability of the fundamentals on which the credit expansion was predicated becomes evident and the process goes into reverse. Sharp falls in property prices reveal the unrecoverability of property-related loans and erode the value of collateral, currency depreciation creates insolvency among unhedged borrowers, asset sales by distressed borrowers seeking liquidity drive down the prices of other securities too, and the resulting economic disruption also undermines the solvency of borrowers in unrelated sectors.

Previous examples of the boom-and-bust syndrome are provided by the correlated crises in Scandinavia around 1990, as well as the East Asian crisis of 1997–1998, in which extensive failure of banking systems especially in Thailand, Indonesia, and Korea were associated with currency collapse and a sharp—albeit transitory—contraction of economic activity following a long period of rapid growth and capital inflows. The sudden withdrawal of what had previously been readily available foreign funds was an aggravating factor in several other crises, notably Chile in 1982. Exchange rate collapse, too, has been a feature in many episodes; indeed, anticipations of currency movements during crises can result in sizable depositor withdrawals exacerbating bank liquidity problems. In all these cases, connected lending and excessive risk-taking were important parts of the story, as they often are in large crises (Harvey and Roper, 1999; World Bank, 2001).

Although some features of the international crisis that began in 2007, such as the role of derivative securities, seemed new, this crisis in fact displays many familiar features (below, and cf. Reinhart and Rogoff, 2008). In particular, it exhibits a wave of overoptimism leading to extreme leverage, and unsound management and regulatory responses to financial innovation.

Even after the existence of a bank solvency crisis has been publicly acknowledged, the scale of the crisis is rarely evident at first. Bank insiders have many reasons to conceal weaknesses as long as possible. Almost all recent systemic crises have involved several waves of intervention, generally spread over a period of months or even years.

28.4 PANIC AND CONTAGION: EXPLAINING SUDDEN AND FAST-MOVING BANKING CRISES

A sudden and irresistible depositor run, the classic form in which systemic crises have been seen as crystalizing, which was certainly present in September and October of 2008, and which dominates the theoretical literature, has actually only featured in a minority of the cases in recent years. Even in Argentina, 1995, the response of depositors to fears of a spillover from Mexico's 1994 Tequila event, aggregate depositor withdrawals from the system were little more than 20%, spread over several months. In this case, when depositor concerns shifted from the health of specific banks to the prospects for the currency peg, they exited the system altogether. This pattern was repeated in 2001, only then depositors were justified, in that the government did subsequently abandon the currency peg.

But, even if depositor runs are not as common as a reading of textbooks would suggest, the sudden onset of correlated bank failures that have characterized some systemic banking crises with widespread consequences for economic activity raises the question of what is special about banks that might make banking systems prone to such dramatic collapses.

Five distinctive and interrelated features of banking stand out as contributing factors to this vulnerability. First, the highly leveraged nature of modern banks; second, the degree of maturity transformation (or liquidity creation) with which they are associated; third, the demandable or very short-term nature of the bulk of their liabilities; fourth, the opaque nature of bank assets; and fifth, the fact that the bulk of their assets and liabilities are denominated in fiat currency. Of course, each of these features represents a key contribution of banking to the economy, which is probably part of the explanation as to why authorities have not adopted proposals for "narrow" banking—few are disposed to give up these benefits. Efforts to prohibit banks from taking risk can backfire—as those holding cash in times of inflation, or of government obligations when those default, have learned well throughout history. Moreover, to the extent that narrow banking forces risk-taking and funds into a less regulated non-bank financial sector, the likelihood of a subsequent clamor for the government to extend the scope of bailouts beyond narrow banking cannot be ignored.

That high leverage has a role in crises seems obvious: it is why much policy effort now focuses on limiting leverage through capital adequacy regulation (even though the risk-reducing goal of such regulation can often be nullified by bankers' offsetting assumption of higher risks in unregulated dimensions). Opacity also matters: just as banks are at an informational disadvantage vis-à-vis borrowers, so too are depositors and other creditors (as well as supervisors) in relation to banks. Much recent theory has developed around the second and third of these features (Allen and Gale, 2006). It is not only the liquidity problems that can arise if depositors wish to withdraw more than expected from a bank that has committed its resources to loans that can be liquidated early only at a loss. There is the consideration that even depositors who have no immediate need to withdraw might do so if they foresee a bank failure. The possibility of self-fulfilling depositor panics, not based on any fundamental change in the bank's asset portfolio or any special liquidity shock to its depositors, has been known to theoreticians for decades, though the real-world relevance of self-fulfilling panics unwarranted by weak fundamentals has been much debated. From this theoretical perspective, there is no difference between the visible retail depositor run and the "silent run" of the bank's wholesale creditors, including other banks through the interbank market. Indeed, in practice it is often the better-informed wholesale market that undermines a failing bank's liquidity and, as in the case of Northern Rock in 2007, leads to a run in the retail market. Better-informed wholesale market participants might realize that the bank's problem is less one of liquidity than of solvency. In theory, liquidity runs can lead to insolvency by forcing a "fire sale" of assets at unfavorable prices, but in practice it is difficult to distinguish this case from insolvency due to excessive risk-taking.

One structural feature of banking implicated in panics is the demandable nature of deposit liabilities, which has the effect of encouraging early withdrawals (Calomiris and Kahn, 1991). It is "first come, first served" for bank depositors (known as "sequential service" in the theoretical literature). Until an insolvent bank closes its doors, early withdrawing depositors will receive their full deposit, paid out of the bank's liquid assets; while those that arrive too late will bear between them the full capital deficiency. Even a small overall initial deficiency could result in the remaining depositors suffering severe losses if enough others have withdrawn before the bank is closed. Awareness of this risk makes astute depositors alert to signs of trouble and indeed serves to ensure that there will be an incentive for large depositors to monitor the performance of the bank managers. As is confirmed by well-documented cases such as that of Continental Illinois bank (Stern and Feldman, 2004), as well as from less precise information from the changing size distribution of deposits in crises in developing countries (Schmukler and Halac, 2004), it is wholesale depositors and interbank lenders who have been the first to withdraw.

Some system-wide bank failures may be simply due to numerous banks being hit by a common shock external to the banking system. But the speed with which several very large systemic crises have emerged without apparent warning and the depth of the ensuing financial and economic crisis has suggested a contagious transmission and amplification of the problems of one bank to others. Furthermore, even if the failure of a number of banks is attributable to an exogenous macroeconomic shock, the consequences of that failure on aggregate credit availability and on the value of asset prices may in turn amplify the macroeconomic downturn feeding back again into the banking system.

Models of contagion focus on different aspects. Contagion can occur through depositor panic, as the failure of one bank causes a reassessment by depositors of the default risks associated with other banks, and the loss of liquidity from one bank failure may cause depositors to withdraw from other banks in the system. At the broader national level, both such factors seem to have been at work in the international crises of 1997–1998 and in the liquidity and "credit crunch" of 2007–2009. Information and fears can be transmitted through several distinct channels including the prices of bank equity, credit default swaps, and the secondary market in bank debt, as well as ratings announcements. Regulations introduced during 2008 to suspend short-selling of bank equities reflect official suspicion of market manipulation in some of these markets at times of panic.

On the asset side too, bank distress can be transmitted through the system. If a bank forecloses on some of its borrowers or is unable to extend credit, its distress will be spread to the customers of those borrowers in turn worsening the loan-loss experience of other banks. The weakening of asset portfolios will become general if there is a scramble for liquidity in asset markets, which drives down prices including of assets used as collateral. Pure informational cascades, where pessimistic opinions of the part of some bankers or investors become generalized, have also been studied as channels of contagion. The use by banks of identical or similar formulaic risk assessment technologies could have the unfortunate effect of coordinating banks' responses to shocks, thereby amplifying their effect (IMF, 2007). Indeed, the depth of the "credit crunch" in 2007–2009 reflects the correlated realization by leading bankers that the risk management paradigm that they all shared had failed.

Models of such feedback can exhibit multiple equilibria: a good equilibrium in which investors' confidence is validated by high asset prices boosting the creditworthiness of borrowers with productive and profitable investments, and a bad equilibrium where investors' skepticism is justified by low asset prices, a lack of creditworthiness, weak aggregate demand, and business and bank insolvency. The equilibrium value of the nominal or real exchange rate is at the heart of several of these models, reflecting the central role of currency collapses in some of the largest crises. If there are multiple equilibria, the occurrence of a crisis can be considered a coordination failure (Diamond and Dybvig, 1983; and Allen and Gale, 2006).

28.5 Costs of Crises

Even if it is hard to get a precise estimate, it is clear that the aggregate costs of banking crises around the world have been very substantial indeed. Total fiscal costs of crises in developing countries alone since the 1970s exceeds US$1 trillion—a sum far in excess of all development aid provided by the advanced economies. The economic costs of crises have been felt across the income spectrum with sharp increases in the fraction of the population below the poverty line (World Bank, 2001; and Honohan, 2005).

Two main approaches have been adopted to calculate the cost of banking crises. The first approach focuses narrowly on the revealed capital deficiency of the banks and specifically on the fiscal and quasi-fiscal costs incurred by efforts to indemnify depositors of failing institutions. The other approach has sought to calculate system-wide economic costs of the failure, as in efforts to add up the cumulative loss of output in the wake of the crisis of 2007–2009. The two approaches have generated rather different figures for specific events, though on average across countries they come up with roughly similar total costs, expressed as a percentage of GDP. Thus, taking 39 systemic crises (from the last quarter of the twentieth century) for which both economic costs and fiscal costs have been calculated, the fiscal costs—ranging up to 55% of GDP (Argentina, 1982)—averaged 12.5%, whereas the estimated economic costs averaged 14.6%. The correlation between the two sets of costs was only 0.43, however (Hoggarth, Reis, and Saporta, 2002; and Hoggarth and Klingebiel, 2003). (In view of the fact that some of the large government guarantees and central bank asset purchases that have been undertaken are still outstanding, and the rapidly changing estimates of GDP declines in recent years and the prospective recovery, it is still too soon to hazard an overall estimate for the fiscal or economic costs of the wave of interrelated crises that began in 2007, though it seems clear that the experience of Cyprus, Iceland and Ireland will enter the rankings close to the top end of the historic range; cf. Laeven and Valencia, 2012.)

Neither approach to measuring costs is wholly satisfactory. The fiscal costs approach refers to what in principle is a concrete concept, though changing prices, exchange rates, and asset values in the months and years following the crisis greatly complicate the calculation. For example, favorable property price movements in Norway and Sweden allowed the authorities to recover most if not all of the outlays they had initially made in respect of failing banks. To the extent that the sums expended by the authorities are to fill resource gaps resulting from loss-making economic activity by borrowers, the fiscal costs can be considered as an estimate of true economic costs. But, since some of the fiscal outlays simply go to compensate depositors for resources that were diverted to others, and as such represent a transfer, this would overstate true economic costs.

On the other hand, the distortions created by poor banking practice will have affected decision making more widely, resulting in losses and missed opportunities that are not captured in the fiscal costs.[3]

Attempts to measure true economic costs from analysis of a dip in growth rates around the time of the crisis lack credibility to the extent that the economic downturn (which exposed the bank insolvencies) may have been triggered by unrelated factors. To attribute all of the downturn to the banking problems probably overstates the costs. On the other hand, some episodes have not been followed by an economic downturn. These include cases where the impact on economic growth was spread over a long number of years. Thus, the calculations are sensitive to the conjectural nature of the counterfactual macroeconomic growth path against which the actual is compared. Many crises are preceded by an economic boom, part of which was attributed to the excess optimism in banking and in other sectors. Since some part of the boom might have had sound foundations, backing out the sustainable path is no simple exercise.

Notwithstanding the heavy costs incurred in banking crises, some countries—Chile and Korea, for example—have seen their financial system recover nicely from even large crises. Unfortunately other countries, notably Argentina, have had numerous crises in the last 150 years, pointing to a sizable, even critical, benefit from the application of good policies of prevention, containment, and resolution.

28.6 CRISIS RESPONSE AND PREVENTION

28.6.1 An Ounce of Prevention

The design of regulatory policy and practice that could most effectively reduce the risk of banking crises is controversial. The Basel Committee on Bank Supervision, established in 1974, has emerged as a standard setter for bank regulation and supervision. In Basel II and Basel III (the latest variant, adopted in 2010–2011 and to be implemented by 2019 and beyond in many countries), the Committee's approach to prudential regulation involves three pillars: capital, supervision, and disclosure. The first pillar defines a minimum amount of capital (and now also liquidity) to be held by banks in relation to the risks that they have assumed; the second pillar is a supervisory regime to ensure compliance with this capital minimum and generally discourage excessive risk-taking; the third pillar mandates disclosure of relevant accounting information.

Unfortunately, Basel's approach to setting required capital is highly controversial (Keating, et al. 2001), not only because of the difficulty of measuring the underlying risks, but because reliance on the mandated approaches could exacerbate herding to the extent that banks adopt similar approaches to modeling risk. Indeed, such herding seemed to play

---

[3] Reinhart and Rogoff (2009) stress the damaging indirect effects on long-term economic growth that may result from the accumulation by fiscal authorities of sharp increases in debt as a result of banking costs through socialization of unpayable banking debts and through the automatic stabilizers associated with the accompanying macroeconomic downturn. Although their estimates of the scale of such an effect can be challenged, it would be unwise to neglect this possible channel of causation.

an important role in the crisis of 2007–2009, the epicenter of which was in the countries that had been supposed to be the models for bank regulation and supervision. Furthermore, cross-country empirical evidence casts considerable doubt on the merits of relying on discretionary action by official supervisors to limit banking failure. Specifically, Barth, Caprio, and Levine (2006) show that this approach does *not* seem to help prevent banking crises. Using their database on bank regulation and supervision around the world, this study compiled indexes that represented the extent of capital regulation, supervisory powers, market monitoring (effectively, the three pillars of Basel II) and other regulatory variables, and related them to the development, efficiency, vulnerability, integrity (lack of corruption), and governance of the banking system, after controlling for other determinants of the latter variables and also dealing with concerns about endogeneity. On vulnerability, they found that none of the three pillars explained the probability of a banking crisis (though private monitoring helped explain the other endogenous variables of interest). Instead, this research indicates that authorities concerned with reducing the likelihood of a crisis should either not adopt or greatly circumscribe deposit insurance, and should encourage banks to diversify both their activities and their geographic and sectoral exposure. Lack of such diversification helps explain the large number of failures in the US (roughly 15,000 bank failures in the period 1920–1933), compared with Canada (just 1 in the period). This research also suggests that an approach to regulation that in effect tries to work with market forces, rather than supplant them, would work better.

Although devising appropriate rules is difficult enough, finding a way to encourage regulators to implement them in a timely fashion is more difficult still. Barth, Caprio, and Levine (2012) argue that regulators had many tools to address the buildup of risk prior to 2007, and yet, despite many clear warning signs, failed to take obvious actions (e.g., to reign in overly rapid credit expansion at banks in Iceland and Ireland, or to respond to evidence in 2004 of widespread fraud in US mortgage markets). Previous crises, such as that of the Savings and Loans institutions in the US, were characterized by similar failures of implementation, yet regulatory changes enacted in the wake of that crisis to require "prompt, corrective actions" were not effective.

Prevention would be easier if the onset of crises could be predicted, but models are better at showing fragility than predicting timing (Demirgüç-Kunt and Detragiache, 2005). With no effective forecasting system, good containment and resolution policies are also needed to deal with the next crisis when it comes. Understandably, efforts focused on detecting underlying misalignments are more promising; as noted, in many crises the warning signs of excessive leverage are usually evident.

28.6.2 A Pound of Cure

When a crisis hits, the public authorities can act as lender of last resort (LOLR) and as organizer or participant in the restructuring of troubled entities. The threat of contagion among banks has led many policymakers to intervene to stop a run before healthy banks and borrowers are impaired. Central banks have accepted the role as LOLR since the early nineteenth century, though not uniformly or without contention (Wood, 2003). The advice from Bagehot, that the LOLR should lend freely but at a penalty rate and only to solvent institutions with good collateral, has become conventional wisdom, if not always followed, and his additional lessons—lend quickly before a run takes off, and only use the LOLR rarely to avoid moral hazard—also are regularly quoted by central bankers. This seemingly straightforward advice is notoriously difficult to apply in practice, as it involves judgments on collateral, solvency, and speed.[4] As noted below, in the wake of the most recent crisis, the role of the LOLR has become more controversial.

Longer-term restructuring and rehabilitation of banks raise issues that go beyond the scope of this chapter (World Bank, 2001; and Honohan and Laeven, 2005). In the spirit of Bagehot, it is worth noting that once authorities decide to intervene, it is important that their intervention be comprehensive, dealing with all potential problem banks especially where depositors fear that they will suffer from bank closures. The failure of the initial 1997 bank restructuring package in Indonesia (according to the announcement of which only 16 banks would be closed—both a much smaller number than had been expected by public opinion and than subsequently proved necessary) has been attributed to its less than comprehensive nature. Soon, all the private banks were run, with depositors putting their funds in what they assumed were safe public banks. The central bank then extended liquidity support to the private banks, who appear to have used the funds to buy foreign exchange, exacerbating the decline of the currency (for a chronology of the events, see Enoch, et al. 2001). In several crises in Argentina, the public would run to public sector and foreign banks, from the domestic private banks.

In almost all crises, a sizable fraction of the banking system has survived, remaining solvent and liquid (Caprio and Honohan, 2005). An exception: all but one of the seven banks in Guinea, accounting for 98% of the banking assets in the country were deemed insolvent and closed following massive frauds. Interestingly, the one bank left open failed several years later. Another exception is Iceland, where all three of the main banks failed in 2008; in this case there was no adequately resourced LOLR because the banks had expanded into international business, denominated in foreign exchange, and had gross liabilities of the order of ten times Iceland's GDP. In Ireland too, all the major banks lost all or most of their equity capital, but most were recapitalized by their foreign shareholders or by the Irish Government.

Although luck can play a part in survival, that in each case some banks typically survive points to the potential for well-managed banks to cope with severe shocks, and to the importance of maintaining an incentive structure that encourages safe-and-sound banking. But, the survivors may not be easily able or willing to expand to fill the gap that would be created if the failed banks are removed from the system and often become more conservative in

---

[4]   LOLR actions need an effective communications strategy if they are to be successful in restoring depositors' confidence. When the UK mid-sized mortgage lender Northern Rock in 2007 had difficulty in refinancing its mortgage portfolio in the wholesale markets and was given exceptional liquidity support by the Bank of England (eventually amounting to the equivalent of about US$50 billion, larger than any previous such loan in history), the tone of the accompanying statements seems to have triggered a retail depositor run so unnerving that the authorities issued a temporary open-ended depositor guarantee. It is too soon to know if Northern Rock was solvent at the time of its first request. If it was, the authorities' initial hesitation to assist may have been inconsistent with Bagehot's rule; if not, it demonstrates the difficulty for the LOLR when insolvent banks are not promptly closed before a run begins. This recent case also illustrates the importance of encouraging banks to manage carefully their risks, including liquidity positions, which frequent LOLR support will undermine.

their lending decisions. Indeed, post-crisis "credit crunches" are significant contributors to the macroeconomic dips noted earlier, which was one of the reasons for the exhortations of Bagehot.

28.7 The Crisis of 2007 and the Euro Crisis: Some Things Old and New

Was the crisis of 2007 or for that matter the euro crisis very different? At the center of the former were the growing market in US-originated mortgage-backed securities and the boom in housing prices in many industrial countries. Provided by Basel I with a clear incentive to reduce required capital by shifting loans off their balance sheet, and notwithstanding the well-understood adverse selection problem that historically had limited loan sales, banks in the US (to a much less extent in other countries) had increasingly turned to an "originate and distribute" model, in which standardized loans, mostly mortgages, could be bundled and sold as securities without recourse to the originating bank, thereby leaving that institution free to reuse its capital elsewhere.[5] Non-depository financial intermediaries jumped into the same business, given the ability to earn fees and yet not retain credit risk. By careful structuring of these securities and in particular their priority in receiving cash flow from the servicing of the original portfolios, favorable credit ratings were obtained for most of the securities sold, seemingly overcoming the adverse selection problem that had hitherto prevented such loan sales (buyers' assumption that sellers would only part with their worst loans). However, knowing that the loans they originated would be sold to others reduced the incentive to make careful credit assessment. Indeed, US banks and finance companies originated a large number of high-risk mortgages (e.g., "no money down," interest only or less as the initial payment, with no documentation on borrowers' capacity to pay and initial "teaser" interest rates that would adjust upwards even if market rates remained constant).

Rating agencies seemed to become the partners of those doing the securitization, rather than serving as unbiased arbiters of credit quality. The initial ratings they had attached to the securities proved overoptimistic and most had to be downgraded sharply. As the US housing market cooled and rates adjusted (from teaser levels, and then with the tightening of monetary policy), defaults spread leading to sizable loan losses for most of the world's leading international banks, and inducing them to raise additional capital to strengthen their balance sheets. Thanks to securitization, US banks had retained only part of the mortgage risk, passing much of it to European and other banks and investment funds. Indeed, the first bank failures from the US subprime mortgages were two German banks, which had taken unwarranted risks in this market.

Banks were not really able to assess the risk of the increasingly complex securities that were being created. This very complexity destroyed information and made resolution and workout of distressed debt enormously more difficult and uncertain. The dramatic decline

---

[5] According to the Basel system, various loans and other assets were assigned different risk weights, thereby leading to the incentive to shed assets with a higher risk charge.

in the market value of these securities both illustrated and precipitated a growing revulsion for complex and risky lending, and a retreat to liquidity leading to a global "credit crunch." Yet, possibly sedated by being paid so well, almost all involved—including the purchasers of these securities in many countries—played along despite the warning signs the sedation coming from the fact that, at each stage of the securitization process, large bonuses were taken from the fees, even by the ratings agencies. The bonus boom, in turn, was most pronounced in the US and Europe, where a bank merger boom was encouraging growth at any costs. Thus, in banks such as Lehman Brothers and UBS, audits found that bonuses were rewarding return, with insufficient attention to risk, and indeed with conscious manipulation or evasion by some agents of risk management mechanisms (Valukas, 2011; see also Barth, Caprio, and Levine, 2012, ch. 3).

But the crisis of 2007 was much more than a US story. As reports in Iceland, Ireland, and the United Kingdom show, their crises were entirely homegrown, meaning that they would have occurred regardless of the American crisis (Barth, Caprio, and Levine, 2012, ch. 5). Lending in these three countries was growing at astonishing rates (all three cases), with clear violations of lending criteria (Anglo-Irish Bank), currency mismatches (Iceland), and excessive reliance on short-term funding (Northern Rock), yet without regulatory intervention. While the global boom in finance may have suppressed banker and regulatory skepticism in the face of what was thought to have been an astonishing record of profitable growth, the timing of these crises, but not their inevitability, was influenced by that of the US. Thus while portions of the US side of the crisis seems new, with the reliance on securitized finance, in Europe securitization played a distinctly minor role. And although the plethora of new instruments appeared to disguise the American crisis, some facts were plainly visible to all: the boom in leverage, the availability of loans with no requirements for information, soaring compensation in the sector, and the financial alchemy of manufacturing safe securities from doubtful loans. As with the South Sea Bubble and many similar events, many were gulled into playing along and, at least with more modern crises, regulators did not do their jobs.

Two elements of the crisis seem new. First, it spread with even greater speed than previous international crises, with markets drying up or disappearing, thus preventing the valuation of erstwhile assets. This speed was linked with the growth of a number of internationally active banks. Perhaps more significantly, securitization not only led to over half of US mortgage debt being held abroad but also far greater complexity. With the ability to offload their own loans and buy securities with hundreds or thousands of loans and other obligations, often held off a bank's balance sheet, it became more difficult to know which institutions were safe and which were not. Consequently, as news of defaults in US mortgage markets rose, the response was to a generalized run and a drying up of financing.

Second, and perhaps even more notable, was the appearance of "too big to save," the problem that banking systems in some countries had grown so large relative to GDP that a rescue of the banks either was not possible (Iceland, Cyprus) or at a crippling budgetary cost (other countries led by Ireland). The potential mismatch between the scale of some banking systems in Europe relative to the fiscal capacity of the host governments, combined with lack of national control over monetary policy and the exchange rate had been recognized conceptually in advance. To be sure, offshore financial systems have operated with banks that were much larger together than the local economy, but as most of their business was offshore, few thought local governments were standing behind them, nor would many have placed much value on such support. More cases of "too big to save" became apparent in recent years in light of exceptionally rapid financial deepening. Also, increased government indebtedness puts a premium on a parsimonious use of guarantees, so, without any available central resources from a European fund, it was inevitable that the banking crisis that crystallized in Cyprus in 2013 (associated with large prospective losses of the two main banks on their Cyprus and Greek loan portfolio, as well as losses incurred by them in the Greek debt exchanges of 2011–2012) resulted in large losses for uninsured depositors and other creditors. "Too big to save" and "too indebted to save anyone" likely will lead to a decreased willingness to protect the uninsured and perhaps even to more expensive or less generous deposit insurance. The vicious circle linking bank failure, government solvency stress and macroeconomic instability, already evident not least from historic episodes in Argentina, Brazil and Chile, was highlighted most vividly in the euro crisis that got under way in 2010.

The euro crisis from 2010 was the result of interrelated banking and fiscal and competitiveness weaknesses in many euro area countries. Cross-border banking claims threatened to transmit weakness from the most stressed countries such as Greece, Portugal and Ireland, to banks elsewhere in the monetary union. High indebtedness of countries such as Italy no longer seemed as easily supportable as had previously appeared. And even stronger countries experienced sizable banking losses. At certain moments, the combination of problems seemed to market participants to threaten the very sustainability of the institutional arrangements supporting the common currency. Accelerated balance sheet repair associated with aggregate macroeconomic demand weakness aggravated the situation (Lane, 2012; Shambaugh, 2012). As unique as the Eurozone crisis may seem, that part pertaining to banking—excessive loans to governments—is as old as modern banking. The euro crisis also revealed clearly the problems occurring absent a common approach to bank regulation and to resolution (so that banks headquartered in one location do not become the fiscal obligation of that locale Véron and Wolff, 2013)—the "too big to save" issue just mentioned. In the US prior to the 1930s, even modest unit banks became too expensive for states to save, and the failure most state-run deposit insurance schemes led those states' representatives to propose about 150 bills for federal deposit insurance before the Great Depression eroded the opposition to this policy (Calomiris and White, 1994).

Crisis management during 2007–2009 evolved slowly. Despite numerous indications that should have triggered alarm, a degree of complacency with regard to the likely scale and likely incidence of losses embedded in what was a very opaque set of banking portfolios and with regard to the market's likely resilience meant that government intervention in insolvent banks and loss allocation were slow to start, reactive on a case-by-case basis, and piecemeal. At first, the main efforts were devoted to addressing the illiquidity that suddenly emerged in the interbank and other short-term money markets from August 2007. Progressively over the following 18 months, central banks bought, or accepted as collateral, an increasingly large and varied range of assets. A few banks were rescued by public authorities during the early months, but they were treated as poorly managed outliers, which had become excessively exposed to the mispriced securities backed by badly underwritten mortgages, rather than as symptomatic of a wider solvency problem. Even with the failure in March 2008 of the important US investment bank Bear Stearns, policy remained on a case-by-case basis. But after three major ad hoc actions in September: (1) the guarantees provided to the large US government-sponsored wholesale mortgage banks Fannie Mae and Freddie Mac; (2) the decision to allow another US investment bank Lehman Brothers go into bankruptcy; and (3) the rescue of the large insurance company AIG which had underwritten credit default swap contracts on a systemic scale; market expectations were destabilized. Confidence was not helped by the initial Congressional reaction to the US Treasury's sketchy proposal to use vast budgetary resources to buy from the banks the most opaque securities. The following weeks were marked by sharp declines in stock market values, a widening of credit spreads and sharp curtailment of credit, including international trade credit, and the failure or near-failure of several large banks in Europe and the US. The prospect of a generalized freezing of the global banking system triggered coordinated international decisions in mid-October 2008 to make public funds available systematically and on a large scale to recapitalize the main banks. This action, which led, for example, to the UK government assuming a majority and large minority stake in two of its four largest banks, Royal Bank of Scotland and Lloyds, reassured markets of governments' intention to rescue any other large banks getting into difficulties—as indeed was confirmed by a package announced by the US authorities in late November 2008 for Citigroup.

The delay in recognizing the scale of the solvency issues and the piecemeal official response probably exacerbated the growth in risk aversion in and around banks during 2008. By the end of that year credit remained extremely tight (with interbank rates well above the equivalent swap rates). The "credit crunch" had begun to depress economic activity worldwide, even in countries whose banks had not been implicated in the excesses and errors of US and European markets. This deepening global turndown began in turn to have a feedback effect on bank loan losses.

The fallout from these two crises continued into 2013, with the experience of Cyprus showing that, even after almost six years of crisis, no fixed template had emerged for dealing with each new situation, and instead a sequence of novel policy responses were taken. Partly as a result of the associated persistence of market uncertainty, macroeconomic recovery in high income economies has been much weaker than in previous recessions, with greater fiscal tightening (notwithstanding greater easing early in the US) and more reliance on monetary easing. Impairment of the market for securitized finance, which had become a central element in the way in which advanced country banking systems delivered credit to the economy, seemed likely to persist. The main reason for weak recovery, though, was probably the fallout from the amplitude of the boom, which implied the need for sizable deleveraging, and the fact that it had been associated mainly with a housing price and construction boom. As was shown by Claessens, Kose, and Terrones (2011), credit crises coupled with housing price collapses tend to be more severe and longer than credit downturns on their own. Indeed, Japan has been dealing for almost a quarter century with the consequences of a credit, real estate, and housing price collapse; after two decades of weak growth and with the highest government debt/GDP ratio in the OECD area, Japan embarked in 2013 on a newly vigorous policy of monetary expansion to end the persistence of negative inflation, aiming for a 2% inflation target as the basis for monetary policy. Extrapolating from Japan's experience, it may be that the adverse growth impact of the banking crisis in the advanced economies could be very long-lasting.

The hallmarks of these recent crises have been their large fiscal cost and, for many, their occurrence at all, as they occurred in countries where the state of regulation and supervision was thought to be most advanced. In addition to changes both in regulation and how regulators are held to account (below), governments, particularly those with especially heavy bills coming due from demographic changes, should consider how to reduce the generosity of guarantees and to make sure that their fiscal position is sufficiently strong to sustain the guarantees that they are offering.

28.8 TOWARD DYNAMIC REGULATION

In the years leading up to the current crisis, the regulatory approach in industrial countries, as embodied by the work of the Basel Committee on Bank Supervision, was taken as a model for others. Quantitative risk management was on the rise, and the Basel Committee reflected this by moving away from crude, arbitrary risk weights decided by regulators (Basel I) to an approach that placed reliance either on weights derived from the judgments of credit rating organizations (CROs) or the risk models of the banks themselves. Yet the locus of failures in the current crisis prominently featured some wildly overoptimistic ratings by the CROs and the utter failure of risk management modeling to protect the banking system—indeed, over-confidence in the effectiveness of these systems contributed to management complacency and common-sense being overridden. Similarly, prompt corrective action, the key regulatory change in the wake of the US S&L crisis, was too often dormant—neither prompt, nor corrective. Modern financial instruments, which were supposed to parcel out risk to those who could best bear it, were pushed beyond their capacity by users who ignored the danger that variances and correlations might not be stationary over time, and indeed that they might be endogenous to the common behavior of bankers. As a result, these tools instead contributed to a reduction in information and in the incentive to monitor risk.

It is striking how many of the features stressed by Minsky (1986) as being typical of previous banking crises have been present in recent events. Low interest rates made many debtors look good, and their subsequent rise regularly revealed "surprises." Financial safety nets, not limited to the boom in deposit insurance since the 1980s, increased risk-taking. And large current account imbalances contain their own risks, as they are sooner or later eroded by a slowdown in the dynamism of the surplus party (whether that be a UK or China) or a revision of opinion as to the creditworthiness of the borrower (an Argentina or the US).

Since finance itself is dynamic, easily adjusting to changes in the real economy and regulation, financial regulation and supervision necessarily must be dynamic as well; any notion that it is possible to come up with a static set of rules to govern the sector and then leave the system to operate on automatic pilot should be dismissed. Such an approach can too easily be blindsided by some distinctively new and unexpected features, such as the hidden weaknesses of risk management for highly engineered financial instruments. Finance cannot return to the highly controlled and segmented world of the 1930s. Regulatory arbitrage needs to be acknowledged as a fact of life, one made infinitely easier thanks to inexpensive communications and computing.

In making regulation more dynamic, it should be geared to revealing information, not sequestering it in the files of the supervisor, and to be revealing, especially in boom times, the risks that are being taken and the compensation of the risk takers. By publication or by regulatory consequences, financial firms need to be dissuaded from paying out huge rewards out of current profits. Those managing other people's money need to face the

consequences of their decisions rather than be protected by their fulfillment of requirements that they hold highly rated paper. And, those with deeper pockets who lend to intermediaries need to experience losses when they have made poor decisions. In other words,
crises focus attention on incentives, and the less regulation is incentive-based, the larger will
be the losses to society. If regulators are to have the discretion to respond, some ways (such
as that proposed by Barth, Caprio, and Levine (2012) must be found to hold them more
accountable. Hitherto, responses to the latest crises have focused on changing the rules, not
on what it takes to get them enforced and to have regulators respond to new risks. At some
point, this focus might change.

REFERENCES

Allen, F. and Gale, D. (2006). *Understanding Financial Crises*. New York: Oxford University
Press.
Barth, J. and Caprio Jr., G. (2007). China's Changing Financial System: Can It Catch Up With,
or Even Drive Growth? *Milken Review* 9(3), 1–52.
Barth, J., Caprio Jr., G., and Levine, R. (2004). Bank Regulation and Supervision: What Works
Best, *Journal of Financial Intermediation* 12, 205–248.
Barth, J., Caprio Jr., G., and Levine, R. (2006). *Rethinking Bank Regulation: Till Angels Govern*.
New York: Cambridge University Press.
Barth, J., Caprio Jr., G., and Levine, R. (2007). Changing Bank Regulation: For Better or for Worse?,
http://econ.worldbank.org/WBSITE/EXTERNAL/EXTDEC/EXTRESEARCH/0,,contentM
DK:20345037~pagePK:64214825~piPK:64214943~theSitePK:469382,00.html>., July.
Barth, J., Caprio Jr., G., and Levine, R. (2012). *Guardians of Finance: Making Regulators Work for
Us*. Cambridge, MA: MIT Press.
Bordo, M., Eichengreen, B., Klingebiel, D., and Martinez-Peria, M. (2001). Is the Crisis Problem
Growing More Severe? *Economic Policy* 32, 51–82.
Calomiris, C. W. and Haber, S. (2013). *Fragile by Design: Banking Panics, Scarce Credit and
Political Bargains*. Princeton, NJ: Princeton University Press.
Calomiris, C. W. and Kahn, C. (1991). The Role of Demandable Debt in Structuring Optimal
Banking Arrangements, *American Economic Review* 81(3), 497–513.
Calomiris, C. W. and White, E. (1994). The Origins of Federal Deposit Insurance. In: C. Goldin
and G. Libecap (Eds.), *The Regulated Economy: A Historical Approach to Political Economy*,
145–188. Cambridge: National Bureau of Economic Research.
Caprio Jr., G. and Honohan, P. (2005). Starting Over Safely: Rebuilding Banking Systems.
In: G. Caprio Jr., J. A. Hanson, and R. E. Litan (Eds.), *Financial Crises: Lessons from the Past,
Preparation for the Future*, 217–256. Washington, DC: Brookings Institution Press.
Caprio Jr., G., Klingebiel, D., Laeven, L., and Noguera, G. (2005). Banking Crisis Database. In: P.
Honohan and L. Laeven (Eds.), *Systemic Financial Crises*, 307–340. Cambridge: Cambridge
University Press.
Caprio Jr., G. and Wilson, B. (2000). Financial Fragility and Mexico's 1994 Peso Crisis: An
Event-Window Analysis of Market Valuation Effects, *Journal of Money, Credit, and Banking*
32(2), 450–468.
Claessens, S., Kose, A. M., and Terrones, M. E. (2011). Financial Cycles: What? How? When?,
The International Monetary Fund IMF Working Paper No. WP/11/76, April.

Dale, R. (2004). *The First Crash: Lessons from the South Sea Bubble*. Princeton, NJ: Princeton University Press.

de Juan, A. (2002). From Good Bankers to Bad Bankers. In: G. Caprio, P. Honohan, and D. Vittas (Eds.), *Financial Sector Policy for Developing Countries: A Reader*, 19–30. Washington, DC: The World Bank.

Demirgüç-Kunt, A. and Detragiache, E. (1999). Financial Liberalization and Financial Fragility. In: B. Pleskovic and J. E. Stiglitz (Eds.), *Proceedings of the 1998 World Bank Conference on Development Economics*, 1–54. Washington, DC: World Bank.

Demirgüç-Kunt, A. and Detragiache, E. (2005). Cross-Country Empirical Studies of Systemic Bank Distress: A Survey, *National Institute Economic Review* 192, 60–83.

Diamond, D. and Dybvig, P. (1983). Bank Runs, Deposit Insurance, and Liquidity, *Journal of Political Economy* 91, 401–419.

Enoch, C., Baldwin, B., Frecaut, O., and Kovanen, A. (2001). Indonesia: Anatomy of a Banking Crisis: Two Years of Living Dangerously 1997–99, IMF Working Paper No. 01/52.

Guttentag, J. M. and Herring, R. J. (1986). Disaster Myopia in International Banking, *Princeton Essays in International Finance*, 164, 1–29.

Haber, S. (2005). Mexico's Experiments with Bank Privatization and Liberalization, 1991–2003, *Journal of Banking & Finance* 29, 2325–2353.

Harvey, C. and Roper, A. (1999). The Asian Bet. In: A. Harwood, R. E. Litan, and M. Pomerleano (Eds.), *The Crises in Emerging Financial Markets*. Washington, DC: Brookings Institution Press.

Herring, R. J. (2005). BCCI and Barings: Bank Resolutions Complicated by Fraud and Global Corporate Structure. In: D. Evanoff and G. Kaufman (Eds.), *Bank Resolutions and Financial Stability*. Cambridge, MA: MIT Press.

Hoggarth, G., Reis, R., and Saporta, V. (2002). Costs of Banking System Instability: Some Empirical Evidence, *Journal of Banking & Finance* 26, 857–860.

Homer, S. and Sylla, R. (1996). *A History of Interest Rates*. New Brunswick, NJ: Rutgers University Press.

Honohan, P. (1997). Banking System Failures in Developing and Transition Countries: Diagnosis and Prediction, Bank for International Settlements Working Paper No. 39, January, <http://www.bis.org/publ/work39.htm>.

Honohan, P. (2005). Banking Sector Crises and Inequality, World Bank Policy Research Working Paper No. WPS 3659.

Honohan, P. (2008). Protecting Depositors in China: Experience and Evolving Policy. In: A. Demirgüç-Kunt, E. Kane, and L. Laeven (Eds.), *Deposit Insurance*. Cambridge, MA: MIT Press.

Honohan, P. and Klingebiel, D. (2003). Controlling the Fiscal Costs of Banking Crises, *Journal of Banking & Finance* 27, 1539–1560.

Honohan, P. and Laeven, L. (2005). *Systemic Financial Distress: Containment and Resolution*. New York: Cambridge University Press.

IMF (International Monetary Fund) (2007). *The Global Financial Stability Review*. Washington, DC: The International Monetary Fund.

Keating, C., Shin, H. S., Goodhart, C., and Danielsson, J. (2001). An Academic Response to Basel II, London School of Economics Financial Markets Group Special Paper No. 130.

Kindleberger, C. P. and Aliber, R. (2011). *Manias, Panics, and Crashes: A History of Financial Crises*. Basingstoke and New York: Palgrave Macmillan.

Kohn, M. (Various). The Origins of Western Economic Success: Commerce, Finance, and Government in Pre-Industrial Europe, <http://www.dartmouth.edu/~mkohn/>./.

Laeven, L. and Valencia, F. (2012). Systemic Banking Crises Database: An Update, IMF Working Paper No. WP/12/163.

Lane, P. (2012). The European Sovereign Debt Crisis, *Journal of Economic Perspectives* 26(3), 49–68.

Lardy, N. R. (1998). *China's Unfinished Economic Revolution*. Washington, DC: Brookings Institution Press.

Lindgren, C. J., Garcia, G., and Saal, M. (1996). *Bank Soundness and Macroeconomic Policy*. Washington, DC: International Monetary Fund.

Minsky, H. P. (1986). *Stabilizing an Unstable Economy*. New Haven: Yale University Press.

Reinhart, C. M. and Rogoff, K. S. (2008). Is the 2007 US Subprime Financial Crisis So Different? An International Historical Comparison, *American Economic Review* 98, 339–344.

Reinhart, C. M. and Rogoff, K. S. (2009). *This Time Is Different: Eight Centuries of Financial Folly*. Princeton, NJ: Princeton University Press.

Schmukler, S. and Halac, M. (2004). Distributional Effects of Crises: The Financial Channel, *Economia* 5(1), 1–67.

Shambaugh, J. (2012). The Euro's Three Crises. Brookings Papers on Economic Activity 44(1), 157–211.

Stern, G. H. and Feldman, R. J. (2004). *Too Big to Fail: The Hazards of Bank Bailouts*. Washington, DC: Brookings Institution Press.

Valukas, A. R. (2011). Lehman Brothers Holdings Inc. Chapter 11 Proceedings Examiner Report, New York, United States Bankruptcy Court Southern District of New York, <http://jenner.com/lehman/>.

Véron, N. and Wolff, G. (2013). From Supervision to Resolution: Next Steps on the Road to European Banking Union, *Bruegel Policy Contribution* 2013/04, 1–7.

Wilson, B., Saunders, A., and Caprio Jr., G. (2000). Mexico's Financial Sector Crisis: Propagative Links to Devaluation, *Economic Journal* 110, 292–308.

Wood, J. H. (2003). Bagehot's Lender of Last Resort: A Hollow Hallowed Tradition, *The Independent Review* 7, 343–351.

World Bank (2001). *Finance for Growth: Policy Choices in a Volatile World*. Washington, DC and New York: The World Bank and Oxford University Press.

CHAPTER 29

....

BANK FAILURES, THE GREAT DEPRESSION, AND OTHER "CONTAGIOUS" EVENTS*

....

CHARLES W. CALOMIRIS

29.1 INTRODUCTION

....

CONCERNS about the susceptibility of banks to unwarranted withdrawals of deposits during panics, the possibility of bank failures, and contractions of bank credit resulting from unwarranted withdrawals of deposits (which is sometimes described as the result of "contagious" weakness among banks) and the attendant adverse macroeconomic consequences of bank disappearance or bank balance sheet contraction have motivated much of public policy toward banks. The global financial crisis of 2007–2009 was the most recent illustration of this phenomenon (Calomiris, 2008; Litan, 2012; for a broader review of international experience in systemic banking crises, see Claessens et al. 2013). In reaction to initial bank losses (e.g., on subprime mortgage-related exposures), a scramble for liquidity ensued in which banks reduced their lending and scrambled to shore up their liquidity and reduce their leverage. Interest rate spreads on risky assets skyrocketed, and money market instruments (commercial paper, interbank deposits, and repurchase agreements) contracted sharply, adding to the "liquidity crunch."

Several policies have come into existence to deal with such shocks, including assistance mechanisms intended to protect banks from unwarranted withdrawals of deposits (central bank lending during crises, deposit insurance, and government-sponsored bank bailouts), and a host of prudential regulatory policies (intended to promote banking system stability, and especially to prevent banks from taking advantage of government protection by increasing their riskiness—the so-called "moral-hazard" problem of protection). This chapter reviews the theory and historical evidence related to the prevalence of banking contagion and the effects of the policies designed to mitigate it.

29.2 "Contagion" vs. Fundamentals as Causes of Bank Failures

Theoretical models have been devised in which banking crises result from systemic "contagion," when banks that are intrinsically solvent are subjected to large unwarranted withdrawals, and may fail as a consequence of this withdrawal pressure. Advocates of the view that banking systems are inherently vulnerable to such contagion often emphasize that the structure of banks—the financing of illiquid assets with demandable debts, and the "sequential service constraint" (which mandates that depositors who are first in line receive all of their deposits)—tends to aggravate the tendency for unwarranted withdrawals (see Diamond and Dybvig 1983; Allen and Gale, 2000; and Diamond and Rajan, 2002).

Unwarranted withdrawals (that is, those unrelated to the solvency of the bank) can occur, in theory, for a number of reasons. Diamond and Dybvig (1983) develop a banking model with multiple equilibria, where one of the equilibria is a systemic bank run, which occurs simply because depositors believe that others will run. More generally, observers of historical panics sometimes document depositors imitating each other's withdrawal behavior; depositors may line up to withdraw their funds simply because others are doing so, particularly in light of the incentives implied by the sequential service constraint. It is important to recognize, however, that evidence about mimetic withdrawals does not generally confirm the all-or-nothing runs by all depositors imagined by some theoretical models; rather, mimesis may be partial and gradual (see Ó Gráda and White, 2003; and Bruner and Carr, 2007).

A second possibility, which is particularly relevant for understanding pre-World War I banking panics in the US (e.g., the nationwide US Panics of 1857, 1873, 1884, 1890, 1893, 1907, and some events during the Great Depression, including the Chicago banking panic of June 1932) is that a signal is received by depositors, which contains noisy information about the health of the various banks. Depositors have reason to believe that something has occurred that might cause a bank to suffer a significant loss or even become insolvent, but they cannot observe which bank has suffered the loss. In that circumstance, depositors may withdraw large amounts of funds from all banks, including those that are (unobservably) financially strong, simply because they would rather not risk leaving their money in a bank that turns out to be weak or insolvent.

For fundamental shocks to precipitate withdrawals they need not lead depositors or other holders of similar short-term "money market" debts (such as commercial paper or repurchase agreements) to believe that insolvency risk has risen substantially. Indeed, one of the key insights of recent models of banking is that depositors may have reason to be risk-intolerant, not only risk averse—meaning that even a small increase in the risk of default may lead to significant withdrawals (for recent evidence, see Calomiris, Himmelberg, and Wachtel, 1995; Gorton and Metrick, 2011). In theory, this can be a consequence either of concerns about changes in behavior by weakened banks (Calomiris and Kahn, 1991; Calomiris, Heider, and Hoerova, 2013), or the reduced liquidity of bank deposits when they become risky (Gorton and Pennacchi, 1990; Dang, Gorton, and Holmstrom, 2012).

Third, exogenous shocks to depositors' liquidity preferences, or to the supply of reserves in the banking system, unrelated to banks' asset condition, may cause an excess demand for cash on the part of depositors relative to existing reserves, which can lead banks to a scramble for reserves, which can produce systemic runs (a banking version of the game "musical chairs"). Liquidity demand and supply shocks may be related to government policies affecting the reserve market, or to foreign exchange risks that lead depositors to want to convert to cash. This mechanism may have had a role in some banking system crises (notably, the nationwide US Panics of 1837 and 1933).

Withdrawal pressures can be associated with warranted concerns traceable to fundamentals or unwarranted withdrawals that result from "panic." Withdrawal pressures can accumulate over time or can take the extreme form of a sudden bank run (when depositors decide en masse to remove deposits). During the Great Depression, deposit withdrawals, bank closures, and even the threat of withdrawal, induced substantial contraction of bank credit as banks disappeared or sought to shore up their liquidity and reduce their fundamental risk to increase their chances of surviving. Such contractions in credit supply can have important macroeconomic consequences, which can amplify business cycle downturns and spread financial distress from banks to the whole economy (Bernanke, 1983; Calomiris and Mason, 2003b; Calomiris and Wilson, 2004; Carlson and Rose, 2011). Part of the reason that bank distress during the Depression caused such a significant decline in bank credit was that many banks were forced to exit the market, not only because their losses were large, but because few banks were healthy enough to acquire those that were failing (Carlson, 2010; Carlson and Rose, 2011). Other episodes of banking panics outside the Great Depression have also been identified as times of severe withdrawal pressure on banks, especially in the US during the nineteenth and early twentieth centuries, although the adverse consequences for bank credit seem to have been less severe.

Differences in opinion about the sources of shocks that cause bank failures can have important implications for policy. While it is true that both concerns about panic and concerns about fundamental loss can motivate public policies to prevent runs, bank closures and credit crunches, the emphasis on panics provides special motives for public policies to protect banks from withdrawal risk. The fundamentalist view, in contrast, sees banks as generally inherently stable—that is, neither victims of unwarranted withdrawals, nor a major source of macroeconomic shocks. According to the fundamentalist view, market discipline of banks is not random, and indeed, helps preserve efficiency in the banking system. It may be desirable to limit or even avoid government protection of banks to preserve market discipline in banking (making banks more vulnerable to the risk of depositor withdrawal). Preserving market discipline encourages good risk management by banks (Calomiris, Heider, and Hoerova, 2013), even though bank deposit and credit contractions attendant to adverse economic shocks to bank borrowers may aggravate business cycles. Indeed, some empirical studies have argued that policies that insulate banks from market discipline tend to produce worse magnifications of downturns, due to excessive bank risk-taking in response to protection (e.g., Barth, Caprio, and Levine, 2006).

These two views of the sources of bank distress (the panic view that banks are fragile and highly subject to panic, or, alternatively, the fundamentalist view that banks are stable and generally not subject to unwarranted large-scale withdrawals) do not define the universe of possibilities. One or the other extreme view may do a better job explaining different historical crises, and both fundamentals and unwarranted withdrawals may play a role during some banking crises. The recent empirical literature on banking crises has tried to come to grips with the causes and effects of systemic bank failures in different places and times, to ascertain the dominant causal connections relating banking distress and macroeconomic decline, and to try to draw inferences about the appropriate public policy posture toward banks. The remainder of this chapter selectively reviews the empirical literature on the causes of bank failures during systemic banking crises. This review begins with a lengthy discussion of the Great Depression in the US, which is followed by a discussion of US bank distress prior to the Depression, historical bank distress outsides the US, and contemporary banking system distress (which is discussed more fully in Chapter 28 of this volume, by Caprio and Honohan).

29.3 US Bank Distress during the Great Depression

The list of fundamental shocks that may have weakened banks during the Great Depression is a long and varied one. It includes declines in the value of bank loan portfolios produced by waves of rising default risk in the wake of regional, sectoral, or national macroeconomic shocks to bank borrowers, as well as monetary policy-induced declines in the prices of the bonds held by banks. There is no doubt that adverse fundamental shocks relevant to bank solvency were contributors to bank distress; the controversy is over the size of these fundamental shocks—that is, whether banks experiencing distress suffered increased insolvency risk or were simply illiquid.

Friedman and Schwartz (1963) are the most prominent advocates of the view that many bank failures resulted from unwarranted "panic" and that failing banks were in large measure illiquid rather than insolvent. Friedman and Schwartz's emphasis on contagion imagined that bank failures mainly reflected a problem of illiquidity rather than insolvency. Illiquid but solvent financial institutions, in their view, failed purely as the result of withdrawal demands by depositors, particularly during sudden moments of panic. In contrast, an insolvent institution fails to repay depositors as the result of fundamental losses in asset value, rather than the suddenness of depositor withdrawals.

Friedman and Schwartz attach great importance to the banking crisis of late 1930, which they attribute to a "contagion of fear" that resulted from the failure of a large New York bank, the Bank of US, which they regard as itself a victim of panic. They also identify two other banking crises in 1931—from March to August 1931, and from Britain's departure from the gold standard (21 September 1931) to the end of the year. The fourth and final banking crisis they identify occurred at the end of 1932 and the beginning of 1933, culminating in the nationwide suspension of banks in March 1933. The 1933 crisis and suspension was the beginning of the end of the Depression, but the 1930 and 1931 crises (because they did not result in suspension) were, in Friedman and Schwartz's judgment, important sources of shock to the real economy that turned a recession in 1929 into the Great Depression of 1929–1933.

The Friedman and Schwartz argument is based upon the suddenness of banking distress during the panics that they identify, and the absence of collapses in relevant macroeconomic time series prior to those banking crises (see charts 27–30 in Friedman and

Schwartz, 1963, p. 309). But there are reasons to question Friedman and Schwartz's view of the exogenous origins of the banking crises of the Depression. As Temin (1976) and many others have noted, the bank failures during the Depression marked a continuation of the severe banking sector distress that had gripped agricultural regions throughout the 1920s. Of the nearly 15,000 bank disappearances that occurred between 1920 and 1933, roughly half predate 1930. And massive numbers of bank failures occurred during the Depression era outside the crisis windows identified by Friedman and Schwartz (notably, in 1932). Wicker (1996, p. 1) estimates that "[b]etween 1930 and 1932 of the more than 5,000 banks that closed only 38% suspended during the first three banking crisis episodes." Recent studies of the condition of the Bank of US indicate that it too may have been insolvent, not just illiquid, in December 1930 (Joseph Lucia, 1985; and Wicker, 1996). So there is some prima facie evidence that the banking distress of the Depression era was more than a problem of panic-inspired depositor flight.

How can one attribute bank failures during the Depression mainly to fundamentals when Friedman and Schwartz's time series evidence indicates no prior changes in macroeconomic fundamentals? Friedman and Schwartz omitted important aggregate measures of the state of the economy relevant for bank solvency—for example, measures of commercial distress and construction activity may be useful indicators of fundamental shocks. Second, aggregation of fundamentals masks important sectoral, local, and regional shocks that buffeted banks with particular credit or market risks. The empirical relevance of these factors has been demonstrated in the work of Wicker (1980; 1996) and Calomiris and Mason (1997, 2003a).

Using a narrative approach similar to that of Friedman and Schwartz, but relying on data disaggregated to the level of the Federal Reserve districts and on local newspaper accounts of banking distress, Wicker argues that it is incorrect to identify the banking crisis of 1930 and the first banking crisis of 1931 as national panics comparable to those of the pre-Fed era. According to Wicker, the proper way to understand the process of banking failure during the Depression is to disaggregate, both by region and by bank, because heterogeneity was very important in determining the incidence of bank failures.

Once one disaggregates, Wicker argues, it becomes apparent that at least the first two of the three banking crises of 1930–1931 identified by Friedman and Schwartz were largely regional affairs. Wicker (1980, 1996) argues that the failures of November 1930 reflected regional shocks and the specific risk exposures of a small subset of banks, linked to Nashville-based Caldwell and Co., the largest investment bank in the South at the time of its failure. Temin (1989: 50) reaches a similar conclusion. He argues that the "panic" of 1930 was not really a panic, and that the failure of Caldwell and Co. and the Bank of US reflected fundamental weakness in those institutions.

Wicker's analysis of the third banking crisis (beginning in September 1931) also shows that bank suspensions were concentrated in a very few locales, although he regards the nationwide increase in the tendency to convert deposits into cash as evidence of a possible nationwide banking crisis in September and October 1931. Wicker agrees with Friedman and Schwartz that the final banking crisis (of 1933), which resulted in universal suspension of bank operations, was nationwide in scope. The banking crisis that culminated in the bank holidays of February-March 1933 resulted in the suspension of at least some bank operations (bank "holidays") for nearly all banks in the country by March 6.

From the regionally disaggregated perspective of Wicker's findings, the inability to explain the timing of bank failures using aggregate time series data (which underlay the Friedman–Schwartz view that banking failures were an unwarranted and autonomous source of shock) would not be surprising even if bank failures were entirely due to fundamental insolvency. Failures of banks were local phenomena in 1930 and 1931, and so may have had little to do with national shocks to income, the price level, interest rates, and asset prices.

The unique industrial organization of the American banking industry historically plays a central role in both the Wicker view of the process of bank failure during the Depression, and in the ability to detect that process empirically. Banks in the US (unlike banks in other countries) did not operate throughout the country. They were smaller, regionally isolated institutions. In the US, therefore, large region-specific shocks might produce a sudden wave of bank failures in specific regions even though no evidence of a shock was visible in aggregate macroeconomic time series (see the cross-country evidence in Bernanke and James, 1991; and Grossman, 1994). The regional isolation of banks in the US, due to prohibitions on nationwide branching or even statewide branching in most states, also makes it possible to identify regional shocks empirically through their observed effects on banks located exclusively in particular regions.

Microeconomic studies of banking distress have provided some useful evidence on the reactions of individual banks to economic distress. White (1984) shows that the failures of banks in 1930 are best explained as a continuation of the agricultural distress of the 1920s, and are traceable to fundamental disturbances in agricultural markets.

Calomiris and Mason (1997) study the Chicago banking panic of June 1932 (a locally isolated phenomenon). They find that the panic resulted in a temporary contraction of deposits that affected both solvent and insolvent banks, and, in that sense, unwarranted deposit contraction did occur. Fundamentals, however, determined which banks survived. Apparently, no solvent banks failed during that panic. Banks that failed during the panic were observably weaker ex ante, judging from their balance sheet and income statements, and from the default risk premiums they paid on their debts. Furthermore, the rate of deposit contraction was not identical across banks; deposits declined more in failing weak banks than in surviving banks.

Calomiris and Wilson (2004) study the behavior of New York City banks during the interwar period, and, in particular, analyze the contraction of their lending during the 1930s. They find that banking distress was an informed market response to observable weaknesses in particular banks, traceable to ex ante bank characteristics. It resulted in bank balance sheet contraction, but this varied greatly across banks; banks with higher default risk were disciplined more by the market (that is, experienced greater deposit withdrawals), which encouraged them to target a low risk of default.

Calomiris and Mason (2003a) construct a survival duration model of Fed member banks throughout the country from 1929 to 1933. This model combines aggregate data at the national, state, and county level with bank-specific data on balance sheets and income statements to identify the key contributors to bank failure risk and to gauge the relative importance of fundamentals and panics as explanations of bank failure. Calomiris and Mason find that a fundamentals-based model can explain most of the failure experience of banks in the US prior to 1933. They identify a significant, but small, national panic effect around September of 1931, and some isolated regional effects that may have been panics, but, prior to 1933, banking panics were not very important contributors to bank failures compared with fundamentals.

The fact that a consistent model based on fundamentals can explain the vast majority of US bank failures prior to 1933 has interesting implications. First, it indicates that the influence of banking panics as an independent source of shock to the economy was not important early in the Depression. Only in 1933, at the trough of the Depression, did failure risk become importantly delinked from local, regional, and national economic conditions and from fundamentals relating to individual bank structure and performance. Second, the timing of this observed rise in risk unrelated to indicators of credit risk is itself interesting. In late 1932 and early 1933, currency risk became increasingly important; depositors had reason to fear that President Roosevelt would leave the gold standard, which gave them a special reason to want to convert their deposits into (high-valued) dollars before devaluation of the dollar (Wigmore, 1987). Currency risk, of course, is also a fundamental.

It is also interesting to connect this account of bank distress during the Depression—which emphasizes fundamental shocks, rather than simply illiquidity, as the source of bank distress—with the history of lender of last resort (LOLR) assistance to banks during the Depression. Many commentators have faulted the Federal Reserve for failing to prevent bank failures with more aggressive discount window lending. While it is certainly true that expansionary monetary policy, particularly in 1929–1931, could have made an enormous difference in preventing bank distress (through its effects on macroeconomic fundamentals), that is not the same as saying that more generous terms at the discount window (holding constant the overall monetary policy stance) would have made much of a difference. Discount window lending only helps preserve banks that are suffering from illiquidity, which was not the problem for most banks in the 1930s that were experiencing large depositor withdrawals.

At the same time, recent work on the Depression has shown that under some circumstances, timely liquidity assistance can be useful in preventing crises from becoming more severe. For example, Carlson, Mitchener, and Richardson (2011) show that aggressive action by the Federal Reserve Bank of Atlanta to provide liquidity to banks in Florida in 1929 arrested a panic and prevented many banks from failing. Similarly, Richardson and Troost (2009) show that the Atlanta Fed's relatively aggressive approach to liquidity assistance reduced bank failure rates in the early 1930s.

Nevertheless, the impact of liquidity assistance was limited. In 1932, President Hoover created the Reconstruction Finance Corporation (RFC), to enlarge the potential availability of liquidity, but this additional source of liquidity assistance seems to have made no difference in helping borrowing banks avoid failure (Mason, 2003; Calomiris, Mason et al. 2013). Commentators at the time noted that, because the collateralized RFC and Fed loans were senior to deposits, and because depositor withdrawals from weak banks reflected real concerns about bank insolvency, loans from the Fed and the RFC to banks experiencing withdrawals did nothing to help, and actually often did harm to banks, since those senior loans from the Fed and the RFC reduced the amount of high quality assets available to back deposits, which actually increased the riskiness of deposits and created new incentives for deposit withdrawals.

In 1933, however, once the RFC was permitted to purchase preferred stock of financial institutions (which was junior to depositors), RFC assistance to troubled banks was effective in reducing the risk of failure and increasing the supply of lending (Mason, 2003; Calomiris, Mason, et al. 2013). Finland enjoyed similar success with its use of preferred stock in the early

1990s. Preferred stock injections were not so successful in resolving Japanese bank distress in 1999 and 2000, which reflected the magnitude of the Japanese banks' problems, problems in the implementation of the program, and the limitations of preferred stock injections for helping resolve problems of deep bank insolvency (Calomiris and Mason, 2004; Calomiris, 2009). Preferred stock injections had limited beneficial effects on large global banks during the 2007–2009 crisis, perhaps for similar reasons.

29.4 MICROECONOMIC STUDIES OF LOCAL CONTAGION

As part of their bank-level analysis of survival duration during the Depression, Calomiris and Mason (2003a) also consider whether, outside the windows of "panics" identified by Friedman and Schwartz, the occurrence of bank failures in close proximity to a bank affects the probability of survival of the bank, after taking into account the various fundamental determinants of failure. This measure of "contagious failure" is an upper bound, since in part it measures unobserved cross-sectional heterogeneity common to banks located in the same area, in addition to true contagion. Calomiris and Mason (2003a) find small, but statistically significant, effects associated with this measure. The omission of this variable from the analysis raises forecasted survival duration by an average of 0.2%. They also consider other regional dummy variables associated with Wicker's (1996) instances of identified regional panics, and again find effects on bank failure risk that are small in national importance.

Ó Gráda and White (2003) provide a detailed account of depositor behavior based on individual account data during the 1850s for a single bank, the Emigrant Savings Bank of New York, which offers a unique perspective on depositor contagion during banking panics. In 1854, Emigrant experienced an unwarranted run that can be traced to mimetic behavior among inexperienced, uninformed depositors. This run, however, was easily handled by the bank, which was able to pay off depositors and restore confidence. In contrast, the run in 1857 was an imitative response to the behavior of informed, sophisticated depositors who were running for a reason, and that run resulted in suspension of convertibility. Furthermore, in both of these episodes, mimesis was not sudden: "In neither 1854 nor 1857 did depositors respond to a single signal that led them to crowd into banks all at once. Instead, panics lasted a few weeks, building and sometimes ebbing in intensity, and only a fraction of all accounts were closed" (Ó Gráda and White, 2003, p. 215). Ó Gráda and White show that contagion can be a real contributor to bank distress, but they also show that runs based on random beliefs tend to dissipate with little effect, while runs based on legitimate signals tend to grow in importance over time. The fact that runs are not sudden, and that many depositors do not participate in them at all, is important, since it implies the ability of events to unfold over time; that is, for a form of collective learning among depositors to take place during panics.

A similar account of mimetic withdrawals based on a random rumor can be found in an article by Nicholas in *Moody's Magazine* in 1907. A bank in Tarpen Springs, Florida, experienced an unwarranted outflow of deposits based on a false rumor that was spread through the local Greek-American community, which included many of the bank's depositors. The bank quickly wired to have cash sent from its correspondent bank, which arrived in time to prevent any suspension of convertibility, and brought the run to an end. Nicholas noted that, if the bank had really been in trouble, not only would the correspondent not have provided the funds, but it and other banks would have probably withdrawn any funds it had on deposit at the bank long before the public was aware of the problem (a so-called "silent run"; see the related discussions in Stern and Feldman, 2003; and Halac and Schmukler, 2004).

29.5 US Bank Distress in the Pre-Depression Era

As many scholars have recognized for many years, for structural reasons, US banks were unusually vulnerable to systemic banking crises that saw large numbers of bank failures before the Depression, compared to banks in other countries (for reviews, see Bordo, 1985; Calomiris, 2000; Calomiris and Haber, 2014). Calomiris and Gorton (1991) identify six episodes of particularly severe banking panics in the US between the Civil War and World War I, and prior to the Civil War, there were other nationwide banking crises in 1819, 1837, 1839 and 1857. In the 1920s, the US experienced waves of bank failures in agricultural states, which have always been identified with fundamental shocks to banks, rather than national or regional panics. Other countries, including the US's northern neighbor, Canada, however, did not suffer banking crises during these episodes of systemic US banking system distress. The key difference between the US and other countries historically was the structure of the US banking system. The US system was mainly based on unit banking—geographically isolated single-office banks; no other country in the world imitated that approach to banking, and no other country experienced the US pattern of periodic banking panics prior to World War I, or the waves of agricultural bank failures that gripped the US in the 1920s.

Canada's early decision to permit branch banking throughout the country ensured that banks were geographically diversified and thus resilient to large sectoral shocks (such as shocks to agriculture in the 1920s and 1930s), able to compete through the establishment of branches in rural areas (because of low overhead costs of establishing additional branches), and able to coordinate the banking system's response in moments of confusion to avoid depositor runs (the number of banks was small, and assets were highly concentrated in several nationwide institutions). Coordination among banks facilitated systemic stability by allowing banks to manage incipient panic episodes to prevent widespread bank runs. In Canada, the Bank of Montreal occasionally would coordinate actions by the large Canadian banks to stop crises before the public was even aware of a possible threat.

The US was unable to mimic this behavior on a national or regional scale (Calomiris and Schweikart, 1991; Calomiris, 2000; Calomiris and Haber, 2014). US law prohibited nationwide branching, and most states prohibited or limited within-state branching. US banks, in contrast to banks elsewhere, were numerous (e.g., numbering more than 29,000 in 1920), undiversified, insulated from competition, and geographically isolated from one another, thus were unable to diversify adequately or to coordinate their response to panics (US banks did establish clearing houses in cities, which facilitated local responses to panics beginning in the 1850s, as emphasized by Gorton, 1985).

The structure of US banking explains why the US uniquely suffered banking panics despite the fact that the vast majority of banks were healthy and were able to avoid ultimate failure. Empirical studies show that the major US banking panics of 1857, 1873, 1884, 1890, 1893, 1896, and 1907 were moments of heightened asymmetric information about bank risk. Banking necessarily entails the delegation of decision making to bankers, who specialize in screening and monitoring borrowers and making non-transparent investments. Bankers consequently have private information about the attendant risks. During normal times, the risk premium banks pay in capital markets and money markets contains a small "opacity" premium—part of the risk depositors and bank stockholders face and charge for comes from not being able to observe the value of bank assets moment to moment—that is, not being able to mark bank portfolios to market. During the US panics, the normally small opacity premium became very large, as people became aware that risks had increased and as they also were aware of what they *didn't* know—namely, the incidence among banks of the probable losses that accompanied the observable increased risk.

Calomiris and Gorton (1991) show that banking panics were uniquely predictable events that happened at business cycle peaks. In the pre-World War I period (1875–1913), every quarter in which the liabilities of failed businesses rose by more than 50% (seasonally adjusted) and the stock market fell by more than 8%, a panic happened in the following quarter. This happened five times, and the Panic of 1907 was the last of those times. Significant national panics (i.e., events that gave rise to a collective response by the New York Clearing House) never happened otherwise during this period.

Bank failure rates, even during these panic episodes, were small, and the losses to depositors associated with them were also small. In 1893, the panic with the highest failure rate and highest depositor loss rate, depositor losses were less than 0.1% of GDP. *Expected* depositor losses during the panics also appear to have been small. Oliver Sprague (1910, pp. 57–58, 423–424) reports that the discount applied to bankers' cashier checks of New York City banks at the height of the Panic of 1873 did not exceed 3.5% and, with the exception of an initial ten-day period, remained below 1%, and a similar pattern was visible in the Panic of 1893. A 1% premium would be consistent with depositors in a New York City bank estimating a 10% chance of a bank's failing with a 10% depositor loss if it failed. Clearly, banking panics during this era were traceable to real shocks, but those shocks had small consequences for bank failures in the aggregate and even at the height of the crisis those consequences were expected to be small. Historical US panics teach us that even a small expected loss can lead depositors to demand their funds, so that they can sit on the sidelines until the incidence of loss within the banking system has been revealed (usually a process that took a matter of weeks).

Bank failure rates in the 1830s and the 1920s were much higher than those of the other pre-Depression systemic US banking crisis episodes. The 1830s saw a major macroeconomic contraction that caused many banks to fail, which historians trace to large fundamental problems that had their sources in government-induced shocks to the money supply (Rousseau, 2002), unprofitable bank-financed infrastructure investments that went sour and international balance of payments shocks (Temin, 1969). The 1920s agricultural bank failures were also closely linked to fundamental problems—in this case, the collapses of agricultural prices at the end of World War I, which were manifested in local bank failures in the absence of regional or national bank portfolio diversification (Calomiris, 1992; and Alston, Grove, and Wheelock, 1994).

29.6 Other Historical Experiences with Bank Failures

Although the US was unique in its propensity for panics, it was not the only economy to experience occasional waves of bank failures historically. Losses (i.e., the negative net worth of failed banks), however, were generally modest and bank failure rates were much lower outside the US. The most severe cases of banking distress during this era, Argentina in 1890 and Australia in 1893, were the exceptional cases; they suffered banking system losses of roughly 10% of GDP in the wake of real estate market collapses in those countries. Only three other countries experienced severe insolvency crises during the pre-World War I period: Brazil in 1892, Italy in 1893, and Norway in 1900.

Loss rates tended to be low because banks structured themselves to limit their risk of loss by maintaining adequate equity-to-assets ratios, sufficiently low asset risk, and adequate liquidity. Market discipline (the potential for depositors fearful of bank default to withdraw their funds) provided incentives for banks to behave prudently (Calomiris and Kahn, 1991; Calomiris, Heider and Hoerova, 2013). The picture of small depositors lining up around the block to withdraw funds has received much attention by journalists and banking theorists, but perhaps the more important source of market discipline was the threat of an informed ("silent") run by large depositors (often other banks). Banks maintained relationships with each other through interbank deposits and the clearing of deposits, notes, and bankers' bills. Banks often belonged to clearing houses that set regulations and monitored members' behavior. A bank that lost the trust of its fellow bankers could not long survive.

29.7 Bank Failures in the Late Twentieth Century

Recent research on systemic bank failures has emphasized the destabilizing effects of bank safety nets. This has been informed by the experience of the US Savings and Loan industry debacle of the 1980s, the banking collapses in Japan and Scandinavia during the 1990s, and similar banking system debacles occurring in scores of countries in the last two decades of the twentieth century (data are from Caprio and Klingebiel, 1996, updated by Laeven and Valencia, 2013).

Empirical studies of these unprecedented losses concluded that deposit insurance and other policies that protect banks from market discipline, intended as a cure for instability, have instead become the single greatest source of banking instability. The theory behind the problem of destabilizing protection has been well known for over a century, and was the basis for Franklin Roosevelt's opposition to deposit insurance in 1933 (an opposition shared by many). Ironically, federal deposit insurance is one of the major legacies of the Roosevelt presidency, despite the fact that President Roosevelt, the Federal Reserve, the Treasury, and Senator Carter Glass—the primary authorities on banking policy of the time—all were opposed to it on principle. Deposit insurance was seen by them and others as undesirable special-interest legislation designed to benefit small banks. They acquiesced in its passage for practical reasons—to get other legislation passed—not because they wanted deposit insurance to pass per se. Numerous attempts, dating from the 1880s, to introduce federal deposit-insurance legislation failed to attract support in the Congress (Calomiris and White, 1994). Opponents understood the theoretical arguments against deposit insurance espoused today—that deposit insurance removes depositors' incentives to monitor and discipline banks, and frees bankers to take imprudent risks (especially when they have little or no remaining equity at stake, and see an advantage in "resurrection risk-taking"); and that the absence of discipline also promotes banker incompetence, which leads to unwitting risk-taking.

Research on the banking collapses of the last two decades of the twentieth century have produced new empirical findings indicating that the greater the protection offered by a country's bank safety net, the greater the risk of a banking collapse (see, e.g., Caprio and Klingebiel, 1996; Demirgüç-Kunt and Detragiache, 2002; Barth, Caprio, and Levine, 2006; Demirgüç-Kunt, Kane, and Laeven, 2008). Empirical research on prudential bank regulation similarly emphasizes the importance of subjecting some bank liabilities to the risk of loss to promote discipline and limit risk-taking (Shadow Financial Regulatory Committee 2000; Mishkin, 2001; Barth, Caprio and Levine, 2006).

Studies of historical deposit insurance reinforce these conclusions (Calomiris, 1990). Opposition to deposit insurance in the 1930s reflected the disastrous experience with insurance in several US states in the early twentieth century, which resulted in banking collapses in all the states that adopted insurance. Government protection of banks played a similarly destabilizing role in Argentina in the 1880s (leading to the 1890 collapse) and in Italy (leading to its 1893 crisis). In retrospect, the successful period of US deposit insurance, from 1933 through the 1960s, was an aberration, reflecting limited insurance during those years (insurance limits were subsequently increased), and the unusual macroeconomic stability of the era.

29.8 CONCLUSION

Banking failures, in theory, can be a consequence either of fundamental, exogenous shocks to banks, or, alternatively, unwarranted withdrawals by depositors associated with contagions of fear, or panics. Interestingly, although many economists associate contagions of fear with the banking distress of the Great Depression, empirical research indicates that panics played a small role in Depression-era distress, which was mainly confined to regional episodes (e.g., June 1932 in Chicago) or to the banking collapse of 1933.

More importantly, empirical research on banking distress clearly shows that panics are neither random events nor inherent to the function of banks or the structure of bank balance sheets. Panics in the US were generally not associated with massive bank failures, but rather were times of temporary confusion about the incidence of shocks within the banking system. This asymmetric-information problem was particularly severe in the US. For the late nineteenth and early twentieth centuries, system-wide banking panics like those that the US experienced in that period did not occur elsewhere. The uniquely panic-ridden experience of the US, particularly during the pre-World War I era, reflected the unit bank-ing structure of the US system. Panics were generally avoided by other countries in the pre-World War I era because their banking systems were composed of a much smaller num-ber of banks operated on a national basis, who consequently enjoyed greater portfolio diver-sification ex ante, and a greater ability to coordinate their actions to stem panics ex post. The US also experienced waves of bank failures unrelated to panics (most notably in the 1920s), which reflected the vulnerability to sector-specific shocks (e.g., agricultural price declines) in an undiversified banking system.

More recent banking system experience worldwide indicates unprecedented costs of banking system distress—an unprecedented high frequency of banking crises, many bank failures, and large losses by failing banks, sometimes with disastrous costs to taxpayers who end up footing the bill of bank loss. This new phenomenon has been traced empirically to the expanded role of the government safety net. Government protection removes the effect of market discipline. It thereby encourages excessive risk-taking by banks, and also creates greater tolerance for incompetent risk management (as distinct from purposeful increases in risk). Ironically, the government safety net, which was designed to forestall the (overesti-mated) risks of contagion, seems to have become the primary source of systemic instability in banking.

References

Allen, F. and Gale, D, (2000). Financial Contagion, *Journal of Political Economy* 108, 1–33.

Alston, L. J., Grove, W. A., and Wheelock, D. C. (1994). Why Do Banks Fail? Evidence from the 1920s, *Explorations in Economic History* 30, 409–431.

Barth, J. R., Caprio Jr., G. and Levine, R. (2006). *Rethinking Bank Regulation: Till Angels Govern.* Cambridge: Cambridge University Press.

Bernanke, B. S. (1983). Nonmonetary Effects of the Financial Crisis in the Propagation of the Great Depression, *American Economic Review* 73, 257–276.

Bernanke, B. S. and James, H. (1991). The Gold Standard, Deflation, and Financial Crisis in the Great Depression: An International Comparison. In: R. Glenn Hubbard (Ed.), *Financial Markets and Financial Crises*, 33–68. Chicago: University of Chicago Press.

Bordo, M. (1985). The Impact and International Transmission of Financial Crises: Some Historical Evidence, 1870–1933, *Revista di Storia Economica* 2, 41–78.

Bruner, R. F. and Carr, S. D. (2007). *The Panic of 1907: Lessons Learned from the Market's Perfect Storm.* Chichester: Wiley.

Calomiris, C. W. (1990). Is Deposit Insurance Necessary? A Historical Perspective, *Journal of Economic History* 50, 283–295.

Calomiris, C. W. (1992). Do Vulnerable Economies Need Deposit Insurance? Lessons from US Agriculture in the 1920s. In: P. L. Brock (Ed.), *If Texas Were Chile: A Primer on Bank Regulation*, 237–349, 450–458. San Francisco: The Sequoia Institute.

Calomiris, C. W. (2000). *US Bank Deregulation in Historical Perspective.* Cambridge: Cambridge University Press.

Calomiris, C. W. (2008). The Subprime Turmoil: What's Old, What's New, and What's Next. Maintaining Stability in a Changing Financial System, *Federal Reserve Bank of Kansas City's Jackson Hole Symposium* August, 21–22.

Calomiris, C. W. (2009). Helping Wall Street—And Main Street, January 21, <http://www.forbes.com.>.

Calomiris, C. W. and Gorton, G. (1991). The Origins of Banking Panics: Models, Facts, and Bank Regulation. In: R. Glenn Hubbard (Ed.), *Financial Markets and Financial Crises*, 107–173. Chicago: University of Chicago.

Calomiris, C. W. and Haber, S. (2014). *Fragile By Design: The Political Origins of Banking Crises and Scarce Credit*. Princeton, NJ: Princeton University Press.

Calomiris, C. W., Heider, F., and Hoerova, M. (2013). A Theory of Bank Liquidity Requirements. Columbia University: Mimeo.

Calomiris, C. W., Himmelberg, C., and Wachtel, P. (1995). Commercial Paper, Corporate Finance, and the Business Cycle: A Microeconomic Approach, *Carnegie-Rochester Series on Public Policy* 42, 203–250.

Calomiris, C. W. and Kahn, C. M. (1991). The Role of Demandable Debt in Structuring Optimal Banking Arrangements, *American Economic Review* 81, 497–513.

Calomiris, C. W. and Mason, J. R. (1997). Contagion and Bank Failures during the Great Depression: The June 1932 Chicago Banking Panic, *American Economic Review* 87, 863–883.

Calomiris, C. W. and Mason, J. R. (2003a). Fundamentals, Panics and Bank Distress during the Depression, *American Economic Review* 93, 1615–1647.

Calomiris, C. W. and Mason, J. R. (2003b). Consequences of Bank Distress during the Great Depression, *American Economic Review* 93, 937–947.

Calomiris, C. W. and Mason, J. R. (2004). How to Restructure Failed Banking Systems: Lessons from the US in the 1930s and Japan in the 1990s. In: T. Ito and A. Krueger (Eds.), *Governance, Regulation, and Privatization in the Asia-Pacific Region*, 375–420. Chicago: University of Chicago Press.

Calomiris, C. W., Mason, J. R., Weidenmier, M., and Bobroff, K. (2013). The Effects of Reconstruction Finance Corporation Assistance on Michigan Banks' Survival in the 1930s, *Explorations in Economic History* 50, 526–547.

Calomiris, C. W. and Schweikart, L. (1991). The Panic of 1857: Origins, Transmission, and Containment, *Journal of Economic History* 51, 807–834.

Calomiris, C. W. and White, E. N. (1994). The Origins of Federal Deposit Insurance. In: C. Goldin and G. Libecap (Eds.), *The Regulated Economy: A Historical Approach to Political Economy*, 145–188. Chicago: University of Chicago.

Calomiris, C. W. and Wilson, B. (2004). Bank Capital and Portfolio Management: The 1930s "Capital Crunch" and Scramble to Shed Risk, *Journal of Business* 77, 421–455.

Caprio, G. and Klingebiel, D. (1996). Bank Insolvencies: Cross Country Experience, The World Bank Working Paper No. 1620.

Carlson, M. (2010). Alternatives for Distressed Banks during the Depression, *Journal of Money, Credit and Banking* 42, 421–441.

Carlson, M., Mitchener, C., and Richardson, G. (2011). Arresting Banking Panics: Federal Reserve Liquidity Provision and the Forgotten Panic of 1929, *Journal of Political Economy* 119, 889–924.

Carlson, M. and Rose, J. (2011). Credit Availability and the Collapse of the Banking Sector in the 1930s. Federal Reserve Board of Governors: Mimeo.

Claessens, S., Kose, A., Laeven, L., and Valencia, F. (2013). *Financial Crises: Causes, Consequences, and Policy Responses*. Washington, DC: IMF.

Dang, T. V., Gorton, G., and Holmstrom, B. (2012). *Ignorance, Debt and Financial Crises*. New Haven, CT: Yale School of Management.

Demirgüç-Kunt, A. and Detragiache, E. (2002). Does Deposit Insurance Increase Banking System Stability? An Empirical Investigation, *Journal of Monetary Economics* 49, 1373–1406.

Demirgüç-Kunt, A., Kane, E., and Laeven, L. (Eds.) (2008). *Deposit Insurance around the World*. Cambridge: MIT Press.

Diamond, D. and Dybvig, P. (1983). Bank Runs, Deposit Insurance, and Liquidity, *Journal of Political Economy* 91, 401–419.

Diamond, D. and Rajan, R. (2002). Liquidity Shortage and Banking Crises, National Bureau of Economic Research Working Paper No. 8937, May.

Friedman, M. and Schwartz, A. J. (1963). *A Monetary History of the United States, 1867–1960*. Princeton, NJ: Princeton University Press.

Gorton, G. (1985). Clearing Houses and the Origin of Central Banking in the United States, *Journal of Economic History* 45, 277–283.

Gorton, G. and Metrick, A. (2011). Securitized Banking and the Run on Repo, *Journal of Financial Economics* 104, 425–451.

Gorton, G. and Pennacchi, G. (1990). Financial Intermediaries and Liquidity Creation, *Journal of Finance* 45, 49–71.

Grossman, R. S. (1994). The Shoe That Didn't Drop: Explaining Banking Stability during the Great Depression, *Journal of Economic History* 54, 654–682.

Halac, M. and Schmukler, S. (2004). Distributional Effects of Crises: The Financial Channel, *Economia* 5, 1–67.

Laeven, L. and Valencia, F. (2013). Systemic Banking Crises Database, *IMF Economic Review* 61, 225–270.

Litan, R. E. (Ed.). (2012). *The World in Crisis: Insights from Six Shadow Financial Regulatory Committees*. Philadelphia: Wharton Financial Institutions Center.

Lucia, J. L. (1985). The Failure of the Bank of United States: A Reappraisal, *Explorations in Economic History* 22, 402–416.

Mason, J. R. (2003). Do Lender of Last Resort Policies Matter? The Effects of Reconstruction Finance Corporation Assistance to Banks during the Great Depression, *Journal of Financial Services Research* 20, 77–95.

Mishkin, F. S. (Ed.) (2001). *Prudential Supervision: What Works and What Doesn't*. Chicago: University of Chicago Press.

Nicholas, H. C. (1907). Runs on Banks, *Moody's Magazine* December, 23–26.

Ó Gráda, C. and White, E. N. (2003). The Panics of 1854 and 1857: A View from the Emigrant Industrial Savings Bank, *Journal of Economic History* 63, 213–240.

Richardson, G. and Troost, W. (2009). Monetary Intervention Mitigated Banking Panics during the Great Depression: Quasi-Experimental Evidence from a Federal Reserve District Border, 1929-1933, *Journal of Political Economy* 117, 1031–1073.

Rousseau, P. (2002). Jacksonian Monetary Policy, Specie Flows, and the Panic of 1837, *Journal of Economic History* 62, 457–488.

Shadow Financial Regulatory Committee (2000). *Reforming Bank Capital Regulation*. Washington, DC: American Enterprise Institute.

Sprague, O. M. W. (1910). *History of Crises under the National Banking System*. Washington, DC: National Monetary Commission.

Stern, G. H. and Feldman, R. J. (2003). *Too Big to Fail: The Hazards of Bank Bailouts*. Washington, DC: Brookings Institution Press.

Temin, P. (1969). *The Jacksonian Economy*. New York: W. W. Norton.

Temin, P. (1976). *Did Monetary Forces Cause the Great Depression?*. New York: W. W. Norton.

Temin, P. (1989). *Lessons from the Great Depression*. Cambridge, MA: MIT Press.

White, E. N. (1984). A Reinterpretation of the Banking Crisis of 1930, *Journal of Economic History* 44, 119–138.

Wicker, E. (1980). A Reconsideration of the Causes of the Banking Panic of 1930, *Journal of Economic History* 40, 571–583.

Wicker, E. (1996). *The Banking Panics of the Great Depression.* Cambridge: Cambridge University Press.

Wigmore, B. A. (1987). Was the Bank Holiday of 1933 a Run on the Dollar Rather than the Banks?, *Journal of Economic History* 47, 739–756.

CHAPTER 30

··

SOVEREIGN DEBT CRISES*

··

RICARDO CORREA AND HORACIO SAPRIZA

30.1 INTRODUCTION

SOVEREIGN debt crises have occurred frequently over the past two centuries (Reinhart and Rogoff, 2009). The earlier crises were mostly associated with large and costly endeavors such as wars, and with fluctuations in commodity prices. More recently, sovereign debt crises have been increasingly linked to the banking sector. As noted in Reinhart and Rogoff (2011), banking crises typically precede or coincide with sovereign debt crises. Although "twin" sovereign debt and banking crises are not as frequent as episodes that include a currency crisis (Laeven and Valencia, 2012), the recent European sovereign turmoil has shown that the economic impact of this type of "twin" crisis can be deep and prolonged.

Figure 30.1 provides a schematic characterization of the link between sovereigns and banks. Problems in the banking sector, which could lead to a full fledged crisis, can have a notable effect on the sovereign's condition (the left arrow in the figure). There are two main channels through which this transmission can take place. First, a more encompassing banking "safety net" increases the contingent liability associated with banking failures for the sovereign. In a banking crisis, the government may assume a sizeable portion of banks' liabilities, affecting its own solvency. Second, the transmission of banking shocks to the sovereign can also take place indirectly. The role of banks as the primary financial intermediaries in a country implies that problems at these institutions may affect aggregate macroeconomic conditions and subsequently lead to a deterioration in the fiscal position of the sovereign.

* The authors are, respectively, Chief and Economist in the Division of International Finance at the Board of Governors of the Federal Reserve System. We would like to thank Lesley Baseman and Michael Donnelly for excellent research assistance. The views expressed in this chapter are solely the responsibility of the authors and should not be interpreted as reflecting the views of the Board of Governors of the Federal Reserve System or of any other person associated with the Federal Reserve System.

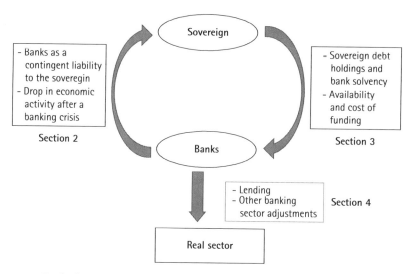

FIGURE 30.1 Links between the sovereign, banks, and the real sector.

The connection between sovereigns and banks can also flow in the opposite direction (the right arrow in Figure 30.1). Doubts about the fiscal soundness of the sovereign, unrelated to the banking system, can also affect banks' performance. In the extreme case of a sovereign default, losses incurred by banks due to their holdings of government issued securities could threaten their solvency. Similarly, as sovereign stress leads to an increase in debt yields, funding costs for banks will likely rise and impact bank profitability. In some cases, the effect of sovereign stress on funding costs may be larger for those banks that are deemed to be "too-big-to-fail" (TBTF) by the market. As the ability of the government to support these banks is questioned by investors, funding costs can increase relative to those of other banks.

Although these linkages between sovereigns and banks may act separately and with a causal direction, it is also possible that they devolve rapidly into a "feedback loop." Problems in one of the two sectors can be amplified by the interconnections noted above. Under these circumstances, the outcome of this type of "twin" crisis can have significant implications for aggregate economic activity (the bottom arrow in Figure 30.1).

The deep linkages between banks and sovereigns are, in some cases, exacerbated by banking regulation and the prevalence of a bank "safety net." To weaken the "feedback loop" between sovereigns and banks, there has to be a reassessment of these policies. The focus should be on reducing the contingent liability to the sovereign that represents its connection to the banking sector. Policy actions, such as establishing a clear and transparent resolution framework for banks of all sizes, should contribute to break this loop. Similarly, policies that enhance market discipline and the accurate assessment of sovereign risk should lead to more resilient bank balance sheets that can absorb a wider array of shocks arising from sovereign distress.

Section 30.2 provides a historical overview of sovereign debt crises. It also describes the causal connection from banking crises to sovereign stress. Conversely, sovereign crises can impact the solvency and funding conditions of banks, and the channels that explain this connection are reviewed in Section 30.3. The "feedback loop" between sovereigns and banks can amplify shocks affecting one of the two sectors, and then impact the real economy, a topic that is covered in Section 30.4. Lastly, Section 30.5 discusses some adjustments to the financial "safety net" that could break the link between sovereigns and banks.

30.2 TRANSMISSION FROM BANKING SECTOR STRESS TO THE SOVEREIGN

30.2.1 An Overview of Sovereign Debt Crises

Sovereign debt crises are a recurring feature in the international financial landscape. For example, Reinhart, Rogoff, and Savastano (2003) report that France defaulted on its sovereign debt eight times between 1500 and 1800, while Spain defaulted 13 times between 1500 and 1900. Tomz and Wright (2007) document 250 sovereign defaults by 106 countries between 1820 and 2004.

From a legal perspective, a default episode is an event in which a scheduled debt service is not paid beyond a grace period specified in the debt contract. Sovereign defaults do not necessarily imply a total repudiation of the outstanding debt, and any sovereign restructuring offer containing less favorable terms than the original debt contract is considered a "technical" default by credit rating agencies. Most sovereign default episodes are followed by a settlement between creditors and the debtor government. The settlement may take the form of a debt exchange or debt restructuring, and the new stream of payments promised by the government generally involves some combination of lower principal, lower interest payments, and longer maturities (Cruces and Trebesch, 2013). Credit rating agencies define the duration of a default episode as the time between the default event and when the debt is restructured, even if there are holdout creditors.

Default episodes have occurred in clusters, often following lending booms and large capital inflows. Subsequent normal periods typically reflect both more cautious behavior of borrowers and the loss of capital market access for riskier borrowers. The wave of defaults associated with the Great Depression and World War II marked the last period of default in Western Europe during the twentieth century. Developing countries defaulted in even greater numbers during that period, and they did not access capital markets for several years thereafter. Lending to developing countries resurged in the 1970s in the form of syndicated bank loans, in contrast to previous periods, when bond issuance had been the main borrowing vehicle. A spate of sovereign defaults followed in developing economies, beginning in the 1980s. The amount of sovereign debt in default peaked at more than $335 billion in 1990. This debt was issued by 55 countries (Beers and Chambers, 2006). Soon after the Russian sovereign debt crisis in 1998, several emerging markets experienced sovereign debt episodes. These emerging market episodes and the European sovereign debt crisis of 2009–12 invigorated the study of sovereign defaults and motivated several policy initiatives intended to improve the international financial architecture, including the effectiveness of crisis resolution.

A variety of circumstances can lead to a sovereign debt crisis. Political factors can be important determinants of sovereign debt events, as evidenced by the recent European crisis. There is a large literature discussing the links between political risk and sovereign defaults (Bilson, Brailsford, and Hooper, 2002; Cuadra and Sapriza, 2008; Hatchondo, Martinez, and Sapriza, 2009). Empirical studies have also highlighted the importance of external factors in raising the borrowing cost of countries, and thus increasing the likelihood of a sovereign default. For instance, Arora and Cerisola (2001) and Uribe and Yue (2006) find that the interest rates paid by sovereigns in emerging markets have tended to move in the same direction as US interest rates.

The empirical evidence also indicates that a sovereign tends to default in periods of low available resources. Government resources are low during cyclical downturns. Tomz and Wright (2007) report that 62% of defaults over the last 200 years occurred in years when the output level in the defaulting country was below its long run trend. At the same time, several emerging economies strongly rely on commodity taxation as a source of public revenues and depend largely on imported intermediate goods that have no close substitutes. Some authors find that terms of trade fluctuations (ratio of the price of exports to the price of imports) are a significant predictor of sovereign default and interest rate spreads in emerging economies (Caballero, 2003; Cuadra and Sapriza, 2006). Events adversely affecting a country's productivity, such as wars or civil conflicts, can also lead to sovereign defaults (Sturzenegger and Zettelmeyer, 2006).

Defaults may also be triggered by a devaluation of the local currency when a relatively large fraction of the sovereign's debt is denominated in foreign currency and its revenues rely heavily on the taxation of nontradable goods. The magnitude of crises triggered by a devaluation of the local currency can be amplified by currency mismatches of households, the non-financial corporate sector, or the banking sector. The next section discusses in more depth how stress in the banking sector may lead to a sovereign debt crisis.

30.2.2 Sovereign Debt Crisis as a Result of Banking Crises

Banking crises are very frequently followed by, or are concurrent to, sovereign debt crises, as documented by Reinhart and Rogoff (2011). Banks lie at the heart of the payments system, so a downturn in this sector can readily spread through the rest of the economy, with far reaching consequences for both the private and public sectors. As a result, governments have very strong incentives to avoid disruptions in the banking system. The recent European crisis offers the latest evidence as to the large extent to which governments may go to rescue their banks, making it clear that financial sector problems tend to become fiscal sector problems. In that way, banking crises commonly set the stage for sovereign debt crises. Banking crisis episodes like those in Ireland in 2008 and in Spain in 2012 showcase how the liquidity and solvency troubles of the banking sector can radically turn into a fiscal burden large enough to lead into a sovereign debt crisis that requires external assistance for its containment.

Banking crises may translate into sovereign debt crises through two types of risk transmission channels. A first set of channels is associated with the role of the government as the provider of a "safety net" to the financial system, and the resulting presence of government contingent liabilities. A second set of channels relates to the existing domestic structural macroeconomic conditions at the time of the crisis.

The government plays the role of a "safety net" to the banking system via three mechanisms: first, a government's commitment to provide support to the banking sector through explicit or implicit bank liability guarantees can saddle the government with substantial debt from private banks, and thus leave it financially vulnerable. For instance, the 27 member countries of the European Union (EU) approved government guarantees on bank liabilities totaling about 30% of 2011 EU GDP from the first quarter of 2008 to the third quarter of 2012. There is an important dispersion in the value of guarantees across these countries, with Ireland providing the most guarantees at about 250% of 2011 GDP. As Acharya, Drechsler, and Schnabl (2013) highlight, Ireland's provision of blanket guarantees on deposits of six of its largest banks on September 30, 2008 was immediately followed by a sharp decline in the credit default swap (CDS) premiums for banks, and an equally marked increase in the government's CDS premium, which over the next month more than quadrupled to over 100 basis points and increased further to about 400 basis points within six months. The sharp increase and opposite move in the sovereign CDS premium in Ireland strongly suggests that the provision of guarantees by the government to the banking sector resulted in an important risk transfer from the banking sector to the government. The interest rate spread of Irish sovereign bonds over comparable German debt instruments rose to historically high levels, and Ireland eventually needed a bailout in 2010. Acharya, Drechsler, and Schnabl (2013) also point out that this episode is not isolated to Ireland.

Second, sovereign bailouts are a major source of concern for fiscal sustainability. The extent to which the liabilities of the banking sector are socialized and the costs are transferred to taxpayers depends significantly on the resolution regime adopted for the stressed banks (Laeven and Valencia, 2010). Moreover, the lack of schemes to resolve insolvent institutions can result in a large contingent liability for the sovereign. Hence, governments often contemplate a wide range of measures to aid the banking sector, including recapitalizations, asset relief interventions, and liquidity measures other than guarantees. For example, according to the European Commission, all the different forms of state aid approved by European Union member countries from the first quarter of 2008 to the third quarter of 2012 add up to about 5 trillion euros, or about 40% of 2011 EU GDP.

Third, balance sheet holdings of sovereign securities by the banking sector can represent a substantial fraction of total bank assets in many economies, and can amplify bailout costs for the government by reinforcing adverse asset price dynamics during banking crises. A bailout of the banking sector lowers government debt prices, and further deterioration of the balance sheets of those banks holding public debt can induce a broader, more costly, public bailout or even a sovereign debt default (Bolton and Jeanne, 2011).

A second set of channels that help explain how banking crises can affect sovereign debt sustainability relates to the macroeconomic conditions in the crisis country: first, as discussed in Kaminsky and Reinhart (1999), banking crises commonly precede currency crises. As a result, a large sovereign or banking sector exposure to foreign currency liabilities weakens the ability of the government to act as a "safety net" for the banking sector, and increases the likelihood that banking problems lead to a sovereign debt crisis.

Second, banking crises tend to induce severe economic downturns that weaken the fiscal position of the government. A crisis in the banking sector translates into credit rationing and higher borrowing costs for firms. For instance, non-financial firms may have to switch their source of funding and tap bond markets, an option that may not be available to medium and smaller firms, especially during a crisis. Similarly, companies will likely have to rely more heavily on more expensive working capital financing from other non-financial firms. The collapse in tax revenues and the increase in public expenses from automatic stabilizers are generally accompanied by a surge in public debt, sovereign credit rating downgrades and, on occasion, sovereign debt defaults. Laeven and Valencia (2012) and Gennaioli, Martin, and Rossi (2014) show and explain that the output losses and the increases in public debt tend to be larger in advanced economies in part because deeper financial systems lead to more disruptive banking crises. Interestingly, fiscal costs relative to GDP, or to the financial system assets, are larger in developing economies, but while the fiscal outlays in developing countries are largely associated with bailouts, in advanced economies they represent a small fraction of the increase in public debt, with discretionary fiscal policy and automatic fiscal stabilizers constituting the largest component.

30.3 TRANSMISSION FROM SOVEREIGN STRESS TO BANKS

Section 30.2 discussed the effect of banking crises on the sovereign's solvency. Sovereign stress can also have significant effects on banks' solvency and their access to funding. This section outlines some channels through which sovereign troubles can affect banks.

30.3.1 Sovereign Debt Holdings and Bank Solvency

The most direct channel for the transmission of sovereign stress to the banking sector is through the banks' holdings of sovereign debt. Banks maintain a portion of their assets in sovereign debt for different reasons. In several countries, sovereign securities are the most liquid asset available, and banks can use them to store their liquid reserves to satisfy deposit redemptions (Gennaioli, Martin, and Rossi, 2014). Banks also hold sovereign debt for investment purposes. Traditionally, bank regulators have considered sovereign debt less risky than corporate debt, allowing banks to fund a lower proportion of their sovereign debt holdings with capital (Hannoun, 2011).[1] As we discuss later in Section 30.3.2, banks also use sovereign debt for secured funding transactions like repurchase agreements. Similarly, government debt may also be pledged as collateral in derivatives transactions. Some banks also

---

[1] Prior to the introduction of the Basel III capital requirements, supervisors followed the guidelines on risk weights for sovereign exposures proposed under the Basel II capital accord (BCBS, 2006). Under these guidelines, debt securities issued by an AA– rating or above would receive a 0% risk weight, while securities rated between A– and A+ would receive a 20% risk weight. However, the guidelines also stated that "at national discretion, a lower risk weight may be applied to banks' exposures to their sovereign (or central bank) of incorporation denominated in domestic currency and funded in that currency." Some countries relied on this statement to deviate from the proposed guideline and assign different risk weights to sovereign exposures. For example, European Union regulators transposed this requirement into European regulation in the Capital Requirements Directive (CRD), which assigned a 0% risk weight on sovereign debt issued by a member state and denominated and funded in domestic currency (Directive 2006/48/EC of the European Parliament and of the Council).

maintain sovereign bonds in their balance sheet as part of their market-making role in the sovereign debt market.

Exposures to sovereign debt can lead to losses for the banks if the domestic or foreign government that issued the debt becomes distressed. This type of bank loss has been common in sovereign debt crises in both emerging and advanced economies. The most recent example is the crisis that affected several Eurozone countries starting in 2010. Before and during the crisis, banks amassed large holdings of sovereign debt, some of it issued by countries with weak fundamentals and large sovereign debt outstanding (Bolton and Jeanne, 2011; Acharya and Steffen, 2013). As the crisis deepened, countries like Greece restructured their sovereign debt, triggering material losses on those banks with this type of claims on their balance sheets.

In episodes of sovereign default, the solvency of the banking sector is greatly affected due to its sovereign holdings. However, the empirical evidence on the effect that sovereign holdings have on banks during periods of sovereign stress, excluding defaults or restructurings, is mixed. Some studies find that there is a significant correlation between sovereign holdings and banks' stock prices and CDS premiums in periods of heightened sovereign stress (Angeloni and Wolff, 2012), while others find that the effect of sovereign holdings on stock returns is weaker when focusing on sovereign rating events. Using a sample of banks that participated in the 2011 EU-wide stress test, Correa et al. (2013) test whether the stock returns of banks with more own-sovereign debt holdings had a significant reaction after the rating of their own-sovereign debt changed, or was placed on watch for a future change. For this sample of banks, the authors do not find that the stock returns of banks with larger sovereign exposures react significantly to negative rating changes in a window of one day prior and after the ratings announcement.

These mixed results are not surprising, as sovereign debt can be used in most circumstances as collateral in transactions with domestic central banks, the lenders of last resort (Bank for International Settlements, 2013). Thus, in periods of broad liquidity stress, banks can substitute private market funds for central bank financing using their sovereign debt holdings as collateral, and remain viable institutions (Drechsler et al. 2013). However, as noted in Section 30.3.2, stress at the sovereign level may affect bank financing through some additional channels.

30.3.2 Cost and Availability of Funding

The link between banks and sovereigns is not limited to the potential losses that banks may face in the event of a sovereign's default. Banks' funding costs may increase even in cases when sovereign debt holdings do not lead to losses in their balance sheets. There are at least three channels through which sovereign stress can affect banks' funding costs: the collateral channel, the ratings channel, and the government support channel.

The collateral channel describes changes in banks' funding conditions that are explained by the quality of collateral held by banks. An important portion of banks' financing is done through secured transactions, such as repurchase agreements, or repos for short (CGFS, 2011). And one of the main securities used for these collateralized transactions is sovereign debt (International Capital Markets Association, 2013). In a repo transaction, the amount of funds a bank can borrow against a portfolio of securities will depend on the credit and liquidity risk of that collateral. The "buyer" of these securities may impose a haircut (the difference between the market value and the purchase price of the asset at the start of the repo) to this collateral to take into account such risks. In normal times, sovereign securities are considered to have very low risk, thus, the haircuts applied to these securities are relatively small. However, in periods of sovereign stress, banks that are reliant on sovereign collateral to conduct their secured financing transactions may face notable funding constraints. The deterioration in the value of sovereign collateral is more likely to affect banks domiciled in countries where the sovereign is in distress, but it could also impact banks with holdings of sovereign debt issued by a foreign government in distress, transmitting the funding shock across borders.

The second channel explains the changes in the cost and access to bank funding that are triggered by the decision of rating agencies to downgrade (or upgrade) the debt issued by the bank's home sovereign. Rating agencies typically revise the ratings assigned to corporate issuers after a review of the home-sovereign's own rating (Borensztein, Cowan, and Valenzuela, 2007; Moody's Investors Service, 2012). Some rating agencies assign ratings ceilings to countries ("country ceiling") which determine the maximum rating that they can assign to a bank's foreign currency denominated liabilities (Fitch Ratings, 2008). This ceiling is closely linked to the sovereign's own foreign currency debt rating and takes into account the risk of exchange controls being introduced or the risk of other interventions by the sovereign that may impair the functioning of the private sector.

As noted by the CGFS (2011), sovereign rating changes are closely followed by bank ratings changes. In turn, bank rating changes have been shown to have an effect on equity prices, affecting banks' funding costs (Gropp and Richards, 2001). The effect of sovereign rating changes on banks may also arise from movements in sovereign yields that later affect aggregate bank borrowing costs (Kaminsky and Schmukler, 2002; Gande and Parsley, 2005). Black et al. (2013) show that a Eurozone sovereign risk premium (the spread between Italian and Spanish sovereign debt yields and comparable German sovereign yields) explains a significant share of the increase in European banks' contribution to systemic risk during the recent Eurozone sovereign crisis. This is evidence that a sovereign risk premium is priced into banks' funding costs. It is empirically difficult to disentangle the changes in bank funding costs that are directly explained by sovereign ratings from those explained by actual changes in sovereign yields, but it is clear that sovereign rating events have an important effect on bank funding costs.

This leads to the last transmission channel between sovereign risk and bank funding cost: the government support channel. Several studies have identified a pattern of financing cost advantages for institutions that are deemed to be supported by their domestic sovereign (the so-called TBTF subsidy).[2] This implicit government support allows "protected" banks to raise funds in capital markets at lower rates than comparable financial institutions not benefitting from this implicit guarantee (Schich and Lindh, 2012; Acharya, Anginer, and Warburton, 2013). Moreover, implicit government support typically translates into explicit support during a banking crisis (Brandao-Marques, Correa, Sapriza, 2013). Both implicit and explicit support of the banking sector depend on three factors: the willingness of the

---

[2] The concept that some banks are TBTF has been discussed in the academic literature since the 1980s. Morgan and Stiroh (2005) and Flannery (2010) summarize several of the studies that have tried to assess the impact of implicit government guarantees on banks.

government to support the banks, its ability or fiscal capacity to provide this support, and the size of banks and the banking sector (Demirgüç-Kunt and Huizinga, 2013). Both the willingness and the structure of the banking sector are factors that remain fixed in the short to medium term. Thus, the link between government support and bank financing in the short run is mostly influenced by changes in the ability of the government to provide support to the banks.

Figure 30.2 shows a measure of government support extracted from bank ratings assigned by Moody's Investor Services, one of the three largest global rating agencies. The "ratings uplift" captures the willingness and ability of a government to provide systemic support to a bank. It is calculated as the difference, in ratings notches, between a bank's foreign (domestic) currency deposits rating and the bank financial strength rating (BFSR). We follow Brandao-Marques, Correa, and Sapriza (2013) and calculate the "ratings uplift" for a sample of roughly 300 banks in 54 countries between 1996 and 2013. This sample excludes subsidiaries of global banks, as most of the "ratings uplift" for these institutions is accounted by the support provided by their parent organizations. In addition, we calculate banks' probability of receiving support from the government based on the same ratings information. The probability of support is defined as $p=1-td/d$, where d is the default frequency implied by the BFSR of a bank and td the default frequency based on the deposit rating. We map the BFSR rating of a bank and its deposit rating to the historical one-year-ahead default frequencies collected by Moody's Investor Service (2011) to calculate the probability of support.

In Figure 30.2, we show the median "ratings uplift" as well as the implicit probability of government support for this sample of banks. These measures clearly show an increase in expected government support tied to systemic banking crises like the Asian and Japanese

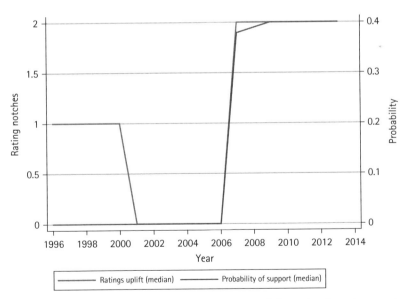

FIGURE 30.2 Measure of government support extracted from bank ratings assigned by Moody's Investor Services. The "ratings uplift" and probability of support are measures of expected government support of banks calculated based on Moody's Investors Service ratings information.

crises in the late 1990s and the more recent financial crisis in the late 2000s. Although not captured in the graph, the recent sovereign European crisis, which strained several countries in peripheral Europe, led to a reduction in rating agencies' expectations of government support for banks in the most deeply affected countries (e.g., Greece and Ireland). The reduction in expected support did not arise as a result of the governments' unwillingness to provide support to the banks, but it is largely explained by the lack of fiscal capacity to provide such support.

Events in which the sovereign's creditworthiness is in doubt will reduce the markets expectation that the government would be able to support the banks and increase banks' funding costs. This link is not limited to the cost of bank-issued debt, as it affects all components of the capital structure including the cost of equity (Correa et al., 2014). The impact also varies across banks within a country. Financial institutions that are perceived to enjoy more government support will experience larger increases in funding costs. These institutions are typically large banks or banks that are partially or fully owned by the government. As their funding costs increase, banks will adjust their balance sheets to cope with the increased financing costs.

It is difficult to empirically identify the contribution of each of these channels to banks' funding conditions during periods of sovereign stress. However, the European Central Bank (ECB), as part of its "Eurozone bank lending survey," has collected information on the banks' views on the impact of the Eurozone sovereign debt crisis on their funding conditions since the first quarter of 2012.[3] There are three factors that may affect banks' funding conditions for which the banks are asked to provide an opinion and that are related to the channels described above, namely: the direct exposure of banks to the sovereign; the value of sovereign collateral available for wholesale funding transactions; and other factors, which include "automatic ratings downgrades affecting your bank following a sovereign downgrade or changes in the value of the domestic government's implicit guarantee." Although this information is available for a short period of time and geographical location, it can provide some insights into the interplay between sovereign risks and bank funding.

Figure 30.3 presents the Eurozone banks' responses to the questions related to the link between sovereign risk and bank funding. The lines in the figure show the difference, in percentage points, between the shares of banks reporting that a factor contributed to a deterioration of the banks' funding conditions and those that reported that it contributed to an easing of funding conditions. The answers are weighted based on the share of loans outstanding of each country in total Eurozone lending. As shown in the figure, the three factors were significant contributors to banks' funding conditions in early 2012, a period of heightened sovereign stress in the Eurozone. After that episode, the importance of these factors has decreased substantially, with the exception of mid-2012 when Greece restructured its debt. One important pattern to note is that the "other effects," which are related to bank ratings changes linked to sovereign rating events or changes in a government's implicit guarantee of banks, have remained a drag on banks' funding conditions, underlining that these factors are materially important.

---

[3] Results of "the Eurozone bank lending survey" can be found at: <http://www.ecb.europa.eu/stats/money/surveys/lend/html/index.en.html.>.

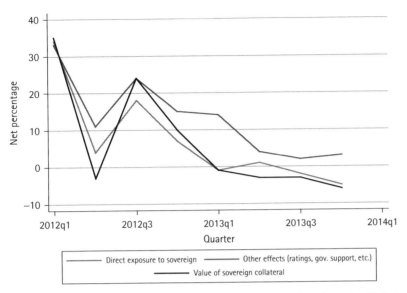

FIGURE 30.3 Eurozone banks' responses to the questions related to the link between sovereign risk and bank funding. The figure shows the difference, in percentage points, between the shares of banks reporting that a factor contributed to a deterioration of the banks' funding conditions and those that reported that it contributed to an easing of funding conditions. The answers are weighted based on the share of loans outstanding of each country in total Eurozone lending.

The close relationship between sovereigns and banks increases the fragility of the system, as it amplifies shocks that either one of these sectors may suffer independently. As a result, broad domestic economic conditions may suffer and spillovers may affect other countries. The effect of the sovereign bank negative "feedback loop" on real outcomes will be explored in Section 30.4.

30.4 SOVEREIGN STRESS AND ITS EFFECT ON BANKING ACTIVITY

Sovereign debt crises have significant effects on economic activity (Furceri and Zdzienicka, 2011). The impact is larger when sovereign stress is accompanied by problems in the banking sector (De Paoli, Hoggarth, and Saporta, 2009). However, there are very few studies that document the direct contribution of the banking sector in these types of episodes. This is understandable, as crises are broad events in which it becomes difficult to identify the impact of individual contributors. The recent Eurozone sovereign debt crisis, with its prolonged duration and heterogeneous effects across countries, has proven to be fertile ground for analyzing the behavior of banks in periods of sovereign stress. We rely on a set of new studies focusing on this period to analyze the real economic impact of sovereign and banking crises.

30.4.1 Lending

A close relationship between a bank and its domestic sovereign may affect its lending activity during periods of sovereign stress. As noted before, there are several channels through which deteriorating conditions for the sovereign may affect banks' level of capitalization and their access to external financing. In turn, these shocks to banks' balance sheets also affect their lending activity. However, it is very difficult to empirically isolate the direct and causal effect of sovereign stress on banks' supply of credit. Sovereign crises are typically accompanied by recessions that may affect borrowers' demand for credit, and such recessions may be triggered by problems in the banking sector. These confounding effects make it difficult to identify the amplification mechanism provided by banks during a sovereign event.

Despite these identification problems, some studies have attempted to test the impact of sovereign distress on bank lending. Focusing on a cross-country sample of sovereign default episodes, Gennaioli, Martin, and Rossi (2014) find that aggregate private credit falls more in those countries where the banking system is more exposed to sovereign debt securities. These results are consistent with their theoretical model, in which banks optimally hold public bonds as an instrument to store liquidity. As the government defaults, domestic banks' liquidity decreases and this affects their ability to lend. In their empirical analysis, their identification strategy focuses on the cross-section. The authors collect information on 110 defaults for 81 countries between 1980 and 2005. The main estimation of the paper tests whether banking sectors with larger net claims on the government reduce their private credit to GDP more severely during sovereign default episodes. The results are economically significant, as a one standard deviation increase in a banking sector's exposure to a defaulting sovereign implies a larger reduction in private credit to GDP of about 2.5%.

These results are also significant at the bank level. In a subsequent paper, Gennaioli, Martin, and Rossi (2013) use a sample of roughly 4,000 banks in 140 countries to analyze the effect of individual banks' exposures to government debt on lending during 12 sovereign defaults between 1998 and 2012. The authors find that banks with larger exposures to government debt, in an episode when their own-sovereign defaults, decrease lending by more relative to their total assets. This result is mostly explained by banks' "permanent" holdings of government debt, as opposed to "transitory" increases in government debt holdings during these crises.

As shown by these studies, sovereign debt crises have a significant effect on domestic credit. This negative shock is compounded by the marked effect that sovereign crises also have on firms' access to foreign sources of credit. Arteta and Hale (2008) find that countries enduring a debt crisis have limited access to international debt markets. The impact is stronger for non-financial private firms that do not export their goods and services.

As a whole, these results provide some direct evidence on the effect of sovereign defaults on domestic and cross-border bank lending, which could translate into aggregate macroeconomic outcomes. However, there is still some room for causality going in the opposite direction, as the macroeconomic conditions that led to the default or debt crisis are perhaps correlated with the characteristics of borrowers from banks that are more exposed to the sovereigns in distress.

The European sovereign debt crisis of the early 2010s has provided some empirical evidence to support the hypothesis that banks amplify the impact of sovereign distress on the economy through their lending behavior. Using micro-level data for Italy, Bofondi, Carpinelli, and Sette (2013) find that lending by Italian banks grew by less than the credit provided by foreign banks in Italy during the recent sovereign episode. In addition, the authors show that the interest rate charged by these domestic banks also increased as conditions deteriorated. These results demonstrate that, even without default, banks can amplify sovereign stress by adjusting their lending behavior.

Sovereign financial stress can also be transmitted to other countries through global banks. As banks with large international operations face capital shortfalls due to losses on domestic (or foreign) sovereign exposures, they may pare down their participation in cross-border lending arrangements in the form of syndicated loans. Popov and Van Horen (2013) show that European banks with notable exposures to sovereign securities during the recent European debt crisis increased their global syndicated lending at a significantly lower pace than counterparts with smaller exposures to these countries.

Liquidity pressures are another source for the transmission of sovereign risk. Global banks with foreign operations (e.g., branches), particularly those funded with wholesale financing, may lose access to local funding as their domestic sovereign becomes stressed. The ensuing liquidity shock forces the global bank to replace that local funding with financing sourced at the parent. If the new inflow from the parent is not enough to finance new or existing lending, the foreign office of the bank will have to adjust its lending. Correa, Sapriza, and Zlate (2013) show that this mechanism was also important during the European sovereign debt crisis. US branches of European banks faced rapid withdrawals from US wholesale investors, mostly US money market funds, triggered by broad fears about the European sovereign crisis. The parents of the branches replaced some of the outflows with their own funds, but these resources were not enough to compensate for the reduction in financing from non-related sources. As a result, branches had to decrease their lending, which is mostly done through syndicated arrangements. Firms with links to the affected branches endured real adjustments, as they invested less compared to similar firms that had lending relationships with unaffected branches.

Transmission of sovereign shocks can also take place indirectly through interbank lending. As shown in Schnabl (2012), a sovereign in stress may lead global banks with exposures to that country to pull back on their lending to banks in other countries. In turn, the domestic banks affected by limited access to international debt markets will cut on their lending and their borrowers will reduce their economic activity. This type of contagion risk grew rapidly prior to the financial crisis of the late 2000s, as global banks became more interconnected and increased their involvement in international capital markets.

In sum, sovereign distress can be amplified through the banking sector contributing to the poor macroeconomic outcomes observed after debt crises episodes. Moreover, sovereign debt problems can also be transmitted to third countries through global banks that are directly or indirectly exposed to the sovereign in distress. But lending is not the only activity that banks adjust during debt crises. That will be the subject of the next section.

30.4.2 Sovereign Stress and Risk-Taking

As we outlined before, banks adjust their lending activities during periods of sovereign distress. However, sovereign debt crises may also alter other activities conducted by financial institutions. In some cases, the outcome of this adjustment can lead to a higher level of risk in the system with additional macroeconomic implications.

Bank assets are traditionally composed of loans and securities. These securities are further decomposed between those issued by the private sectors and those issued by the sovereign or local governments. In periods of sovereign stress, banks may have an incentive to shift the composition of their securities' holdings. As noted before, under normal circumstances banks will hold sovereign securities as a means to maintain liquidity and repay withdrawals from depositors or other creditors (Gennaioli, Martin, and Rossi, 2013, 2014). In contrast, in periods of sovereign stress, banks may find it desirable to increase their holdings of "risky" sovereign securities to increase their returns (Acharya and Steffen, 2013). This risk-taking behavior may enhance the adjustment that banks will have to perform in the event of a sovereign default.

There are several factors that explain the banks' decision to increase their sovereign debt holdings in periods of stress. First, sovereign securities are perhaps the safest asset for domestic banks, as private sector borrowers may become riskier under weak macroeconomic conditions. However, as shown by Acharya and Steffen (2013), banks without this constraint may also increase their holdings of "risky" sovereign securities. This was the case for some European banks, which purchased debt from foreign sovereigns in distress during the recent European sovereign crisis.

Second, banks may have the incentive to arbitrage regulatory rules. As noted before, risk-weights on sovereign debt securities are zero in most cases. If the bank is faced with the option of making a loan or holding a sovereign security, regulatory requirements may tip the balance toward the latter. Consistent with this claim, banks with lower regulatory capital levels were also found to increase their "risky" sovereign holdings in the European sovereign crisis.

Third, securities issued by sovereigns are one of the main types of collateral used by central banks in their liquidity operations with banks. As such, banks will have an incentive to hold more of these securities to be able to access the funding provided by the lender of last resort during a crisis. However, banks could take advantage of this arrangement by purchasing and pledging increasingly riskier sovereign debt as collateral in central bank operations. Using micro-level data for Eurozone banks, Drechsler et al. (2013) find that both mechanisms are at play in periods of financial and sovereign stress. Banks hold more sovereign debt to be able to access liquidity from the lender of last resort, but they also shift some of their holdings to "riskier" sovereign securities.

Banks' lending activity is not the only dimension that banks can adjust in periods of sovereign stress. They can also adjust their risk-taking by arbitraging regulatory rules and the role of the lender of last resort. The main consequence of this action is an increase in systemic risk which could deepen a sovereign crisis. The question that arises from these findings is whether policy makers can adjust the system to take into account the negative structural feature embedded in the relationship between sovereigns and banks. That will be the subject of the next section.

30.5 Breaking the Sovereign-Bank "Feedback Loop"

The close connection between banks and sovereigns leads to financial instability by amplifying any shocks that affect either sector. A country's fiscal position typically becomes strained as it intervenes to support the banking sector during periods of financial turmoil. This in turn leads to worsening conditions for the banks due to an increase in financing costs and a deterioration of balance sheets. This "feedback loop" between the sovereign and the banks exacerbates any shock that in isolation would have resulted in smaller macroeconomic effects.

Sovereign distress can be the product of a broad spectrum of problems, both structural and cyclical. The factors that impact a government's finances span from demographic changes to fluctuations in commodity prices that affect the exporting sector in a small open economy. The focus of our analysis will be on just one of those factors, the impact of the financial "safety net" on the sovereign "feedback loop." The "safety net" is defined as the system of explicit and implicit guarantees provided by the government to protect a country's financial infrastructure from systemic events (Kane, 2004). The most common component of this "safety net" is the deposit insurance scheme, which is intended to provide a guarantee to depositors in case of a bank's insolvency. Other guarantees are implicit or implemented during periods of systemic stress. In the event of broad bank insolvencies, these guarantees are likely to become explicit, and lead to a deterioration in the fiscal position of the sovereign (Laeven and Valencia, 2012). Given the features of the current financial "safety net" and its impact on the sovereign, the following question arises: how can a country minimize the macroeconomic impact of a banking crisis, while reducing the fiscal cost to the sovereign?

It is unrealistic to assume that banking crises can be resolved without any macroeconomic effects. However, some aspects of the "safety net," if not well designed, may exacerbate these crises through their impact on the sovereign. There are at least three adjustments to the "safety net" that can be implemented to minimize the effect of the sovereign-bank feedback loop: a well-established and transparent bank resolution regime, a deposit insurance scheme that is optimally priced, and capital requirements that reduce the probability of failure of a bank.

The European Union has adopted some of these measures to deal with the sovereign stresses affecting some countries of the Eurozone since 2010. A proposed EU "banking union" would include a single supervisor, a well-defined resolution regime, and a consistent structure of deposit insurance schemes across the region. Although progress has been made (Beck, 2013), and this in turn has reduced banks' funding pressures, there are still several adjustments to the "safety net" that would have to be implemented to break the sovereign feedback loop.

The first desirable adjustment to the "safety net" is to implement a bank resolution regime that minimizes the cost to taxpayers from banking failures, especially of large banks. Some countries have already moved in this direction by establishing rules that would make it easier to resolve such large financial institutions (FDIC and BoE, 2012). A well-defined resolution regime, which would likely include provisions for the bail-in of subordinated, and in some cases, senior creditors, also has the additional benefit of enhancing market discipline. As governments rely more on this tool to resolve banking crises, rather than bailing out banks through capital injections or other means, investors will price the debt of banks taking into account the credit risk posed by each institution, reducing the so-called TBTF subsidy (Acharya, Anginer, and Warburton, 2013).

Deposit insurance schemes are a common feature of the "safety net." However, a poorly designed scheme may lead to financial instability and significant costs to the sovereign in the event of large or multiple bank failures. Banks operating in an environment with this type of guarantee are prone to increase the riskiness of their assets due to moral hazard, which in turn may increase the likelihood of a banking crisis (Demirgüç-Kunt and Detragiache, 2002). To limit the cost to the sovereign in the event of a crisis, the deposit insurance scheme should be explicit and clearly define the financial institutions and depositors covered (Financial Stability Board, 2012). In addition, to limit banks' risk-taking incentives, the pricing of deposit insurance premiums should be sensitive to each financial institution's own risk, as well as its contribution to systemic risk (Acharya, Santos, Yorulmazer, 2010). These conditions are necessary, yet not sufficient, to reduce the effect of deposit losses on the sovereign's finances.

Lastly, increasing the resilience of banks to shocks is probably the best alternative to insulate the sovereigns from problems arising in the financial sector. A tool available to bank regulators is the imposition of capital requirements for banks. The establishment of high capital requirements can be thought of as a mechanism to internalize the externality posed by the systemic consequences of large bank failures. Increasing the reliance on capital to finance bank assets may be costly (Jiménez et al. 2013), but these costs are outweighed by the social benefits of fewer bank failures and better bank performance during banking crises (Berger and Bouwman, 2013). Additionally, capital regulation should incentivize banks to accurately reflect the risk embedded in sovereign debt. Allowing risk-weights to be sensitive to sovereign creditworthiness may prevent banks from holding large and concentrated exposures to government-issued debt. In general, a banking sector with more capital financing will decrease the cost to taxpayers of resolving banks that are still deemed systemically important.

References

Acharya, V. V., Anginer, D., and Warburton, J. (2013). The End of Market Discipline? Investors Expectations of Implicit State Guarantees, <http://ssrn.com/abstract=1961656.>.

Acharya, V. V., Drechsler, I., and Schnabl, P. (2013). A Pyrrhic Victory? Bank Bailouts and Sovereign Credit Risk, *Journal of Finance* (Forthcoming).

Acharya, V. V., Santos, J. A. C., and Yorulmazer, T. (2010). Systemic Risk and Deposit Insurance Premiums, *FRBNY Economic Policy Review* August, 89–99.

Acharya, V. V. and Steffen, S. (2013). The Greatest Carry Trade Ever? Understanding Eurozone Bank Risks, NBER Working Paper No. 19039.

Angeloni, C. and Wolff, G. B. (2012). Are Banks Affected by their Holdings of Government Debt?. Bruegel Working Paper, July.

Arora, V. and Cerisola, M. (2001). How Does US Monetary Policy Influence Sovereign Spreads in Emerging Markets? IMF Staff Papers 48(3), 474–498.

Arteta, C. and Hale, G. (2008). Sovereign Debt Crises and Credit to the Private Sector, *Journal of International Economics* 74(1), 53–69.

Bank for International Settlements (2013). Central Bank Collateral Framework and Practices, Markets Committee Publications No. 6.

BCBS (Basel Committee on Banking Supervision) (2006). Basel II: International Convergence of Capital Measurement and Capital Standards: A Revised Framework.

Beck, T. (2013). Banking Union for Europe—Where Do We Stand?, <http://www.voxeu.org/article/banking-union-europe-where-do-we-stand.>.

Beers, D. and Chambers, J. (2006). Sovereign Defaults at 26-Year Low, To Show Little Change in 2007, *Standard & Poor's Commentary*, September 18.

Berger, A. N. and Bouwman, C. H. S. (2013). How Does Capital Affect Bank Performance during Financial Crises?, *Journal of Financial Economics* 109(1), 146–176.

Bilson, C., Brailsford, T., and Hooper, V. (2002). The Explanatory Power of Political Risk in Emerging Markets, *International Review of Financial Analysis* 11(1), 1–27.

Bofondi, M., Carpinelli, L., and Sette, E. (2013). Credit Supply during a Sovereign Debt Crisis, Banca D'Italia Working Paper No. 909.

Bolton, P. and Jeanne, O. (2011). Sovereign Default Risk and Bank Fragility in Financially Integrated Economies, *IMF Economic Review* 59, 162–194.

Borensztein, E., Cowan, K., and Valenzuela, P. (2007). Sovereign Ceilings "Lite"? The Impact of Sovereign Ratings on Corporate Ratings in Emerging Market Economies, IMF Working Paper No. 07/75.

Black, L., Correa, R., Huang, X., and Zhou, H. (2013). The Systemic Risk of European Banks during the Financial and Sovereign Debt Crises, International Finance Discussion Papers No. 1083.

Brandao-Marques, L., Correa, R., and Sapriza, H. (2013). International Evidence on Government Support and Risk-Taking in the Banking Sector, International Finance Discussion Papers No. 1086.

Caballero, R. J. (2003). The Future of the IMF, *The American Economic Review, Papers and Proceedings* 93(2), 31–38.

CGFS (Committee on the Global Financial System) (2011). The Impact of Sovereign Credit Risk on Bank Funding Conditions, CGFS Papers No. 43.

Correa, R., Lee, K.-H., Sapriza, H., and Suarez, G. (2014). Sovereign Credit Risk, Banks' Government Support, and Bank Stock Returns around the World, *Journal of Money, Credit and Banking* 46, 93–121.

Correa, R., Sapriza, H., and Zlate, A. (2013). Liquidity Shocks, Dollar Funding Costs, and the Bank Lending Channel during the European Sovereign Crisis, International Finance Discussion Papers No. 1059.

Cuadra, G. and Sapriza, H. (2006). Sovereign Default, Terms of Trade, and Interest Rates in Emerging Markets, Banco de México Working Paper No. 2006-01.

Cuadra, G. and Sapriza, H. (2008). Sovereign Default, Interest Rates and Political Uncertainty in Emerging Markets, *Journal of International Economics* 76(1), 78–88.

Cruces, J. J. and Trebesch, C. (2013). Sovereign Defaults: The Price of Haircuts, *American Economic Journal: Macroeconomics* 5(3), 85–117.

De Paoli, B., Hoggarth, G., and Saporta, V. (2009). Output Costs of Sovereign Crises: Some Empirical Estimates, Bank of England Working Paper No. 362.

Demirgüç-Kunt, A. and Detragiache, E. (2002). Does Deposit Insurance Increase Banking System Stability? An Empirical Investigation, *Journal of Monetary Economics* 49(7), 1373–1406.

Demirgüç-Kunt, A. and Huizinga, H. (2013). Are Banks Too Big to Fail or Too Big to Save? International Evidence from Equity Prices and CDS Spreads, *Journal of Banking and Finance* 37(3), 875–894.

Drechsler, I., Drechsel, T., Marques-Ibanez, D., and Schnabl, P. (2013). Who Borrows from the Lender of Last Resort? Unpublished Manuscript.

FDIC and BoE (Federal Deposit Insurance Corporation and the Bank of England) (2012). Resolving Globally Active, Systemically Important, Financial Institutions. Unpublished Manuscript.

Financial Stability Board (2012). Thematic Review of Deposit Insurance Systems. Peer Review Report.

Fitch Ratings (2008). *Country Ceilings*. New York: Fitch Group.

Flannery, M. J. (2010). What To Do About TBTF? Unpublished Manuscript.

Furceri, D. and Zdzienicka, A. (2011). How Costly Are Debt Crises?, IMF Working Paper No. 11/280.

Gande, A. and Parsley, D. C. (2005). News Spillovers in the Sovereign Debt Market, *Journal of Financial Economics* 75(3), 691–734.

Gennaioli, N., Martin, A., and Rossi, S. (2013). Banks, Government Bonds, and Default: What do the Data Say? Unpublished Manuscript.

Gennaioli, N., Martin, A., and Rossi, S. (2014). Sovereign Default, Domestic Banks, and Financial Institutions, *Journal of Finance* 69, 819–866.

Gropp, R. and Richards, A. J. (2001). Rating Agency Actions and The Pricing Of Debt and Equity of European Banks: What can we Infer about Private Sector Monitoring of Bank Soundness?, ECB Working Paper Series No. 0076.

Hannoun, H. (2011). Sovereign Risk in Bank Regulation and Supervision: Where do we Stand?. Speech at the Financial Stability Institute High-Level Meeting, Abu Dhabi, UAE, October 26.

Hatchondo, J. C., Martinez L., and Sapriza, H. (2009). Heterogeneous Borrowers in Quantitative Models of Sovereign Default, *International Economic Review* 50(4), 1129–1151.

International Capital Market Association (2013). European Repo Market Survey, No. 25, June.

Jiménez, G., Ongena, S., Peydró, J.-L., and Saurina, J. (2013). Macroprudential Policy, Counter-cyclical Bank Capital Buffers, and Credit Supply: Evidence from the Spanish Dynamic Provisioning Experiments, European Banking Center Discussion Paper No. 2012–2011.

Kaminsky, G. and Reinhart, C. M. (1999). The Twin Crises: The Causes of Banking and Balance-of-Payments Problems, *The American Economic Review* 89(3), 473–500.

Kaminsky, G. and Schmukler, S. L. (2002). Emerging Market Instability: Do Sovereign Ratings Affect Country Risk and Stock Returns?, *World Bank Economic Review* 16(2), 171–195.

Kane, E. J. (2004). Financial Regulation and Bank Safety Nets: An International Comparison. Unpublished Manuscript.

Laeven, L. and Valencia, F. (2010). Resolution of Banking Crises: The Good, the Bad, and the Ugly, IMF Working Paper No. 10/146.

Laeven, L. and Valencia, F. (2012). Systemic Banking Crises Database: An Update, IMF Working Paper No. 12/163.

Moody's Investors Service (2011). *Corporate Default and Recovery Rates, 1920-2010*. New York: Moody's.

Moody's Investors Service (2012). *How Sovereign Credit Quality May Affect Other Ratings*. New York: Moody's.

Morgan, D. P. and Stiroh, K. (2005). Too Big to Fail After All These Years, Federal Reserve Bank of New York Staff Report No. 22.

Popov, A. and Van Horen, N. (2013). The Impact of Sovereign Debt Exposure on Bank Lending: Evidence from the European Debt Crisis, DNB Working Paper No. 382.

Reinhart, C. and Rogoff, K. S. (2009). *This Time is Different: Eight Centuries of Financial Folly*. Princeton and Oxford: Princeton University Press.

Reinhart, C. and Rogoff, K. S. (2011). From Financial Crash to Debt Crisis, *American Economic Review* 101(5), 1676–1706.

Reinhart, C., Rogoff, K. S., and Savastano, M. A. (2003). Debt Intolerance, *Brookings Papers on Economic Activity* 1, 1–74.

Schich, S. and Lindh, S. (2012). Implicit Guarantees for Bank Debt: Where Do We Stand?, *OECD Journal: Financial Market Trends* 1, 1–22, <http://www.oecd.org/dataoecd/16/25/50586138.pdf.>.

Schnabl, P. (2012). The International Transmission of Bank Liquidity Shocks: Evidence from an Emerging Market, *Journal of Finance* 67(3), 897–932.

Sturzenegger, F. and Zettelmeyer, J. (2006). *Debt Defaults and Lessons from a Decade of Crises*. Cambridge, MA: MIT Press.

Tomz, M. and Wright, M. L. J. (2007). Do Countries Default in "Bad Times"?, *Journal of the European Economic Association* 5(2–3), 352–360.

Uribe, M. and Yue, V. (2006). Country Spreads and Emerging Countries: Who Drives Whom?, *Journal of International Economics* 69(1), 6–36.

CHAPTER 31

....

BANKING GLOBALIZATION

International Consolidation and
*Acquisitions in Banking**

....

CLAUDIA M. BUCH AND GAYLE L. DELONG

31.1 INTRODUCTION

....

ONCE rare animals, cross-border bank acquisitions grew in number and prevalence until the international financial crisis in 2008. In 2007, nearly 40% of acquisitions involving at least one commercial bank included firms headquartered in two different countries. This trend reversed during the course of the crisis. In 2009 alone, the number of domestic bank acquisitions worldwide increased by over 55%, from 717 in 2007 to 1117, according to data provided by *Thomson Financial*. However, the number of cross-border bank acquisitions *fell* by over 40% from 432 in 2007, to 247 in 2009. This decline in mergers activity is one facet of the increasing fragmentation of financial markets that could be observed during the crisis. It shows that, as of to date, many implicit and explicit barriers to the integration of markets continue to exist. Uncertainties that crises inevitably create magnify these barriers.[1] Politicians and regulators erect barriers, because government officials typically consider the banking industry to be strategically important for the real economy and for financial stability. Non-political obstacles such as cultural barriers might be influencing bank acquisitions as well. These barriers, in turn, could affect the risk and efficiency effects of bank acquisitions.

In this chapter, we provide an overview of research on the causes and effects of international bank acquisitions. Considering the vast number of issues at stake, we naturally have

---

* Sabrina Keller has provided excellent research assistance. All errors and inaccuracies are solely our own responsibility.
[1] See European Central Bank (2012) for more insights on how uncertainties influence merger activity.

to be selective. Berger, Demsetz, and Strahan (1999) and Berger et al. (2000) review earlier literature on the consolidation and globalization of financial institutions. We largely abstract from the rich literature on the impact of financial integration on macroeconomic stability and on the effects of cross-border banking for the transmission of shocks across countries. We also do not attempt to review the growing literature on systemic risk in banking and on the implications of concentration in banking markets for financial stability. Instead, our focus is on three main questions. First, what are the determinants and driving forces of cross-border bank acquisitions? Second, what are the effects of cross-border bank acquisitions on the efficiency and competitiveness of financial institutions and the financial system? Third, what are the implications of bank acquisitions for risks in banking? Our focus is on empirical studies of the commercial banking industry. We begin with a brief review of the stylized facts on international bank acquisitions.

31.2 INTERNATIONAL M&AS IN BANKING: NO LONGER THE RARE ANIMAL

Starting in the mid-1990s, cross-border bank acquisitions became more and more common. Yet a careful examination of the numbers suggests that international acquisitions of financial institutions are relatively recent phenomena and tend to occur mainly in and between certain countries.

Figures 31.1 and 31.2 show how domestic and international bank acquisitions have evolved over time. We examine cross-border acquisitions that were announced and completed between 1985 and 2012 where at least one of the partners was a commercial bank and the other partner was any type of firm. Usually, the other partner was in financial services, that is, commercial banking, securities, or insurance. We define a cross-border acquisition as any acquisition whereby the headquarters of the target are not located in the same country as the ultimate parent of the acquirer. We obtain the names of acquirers and targets from Thomson Financial Securities Data. Up to 1992, the database includes all deals with values of at least $1 million. After 1992, deals of any value are covered. Also included are transactions with undisclosed values as well as public and private transactions. Thomson Financial Securities Data identifies 6,120 acquisitions that meet our criteria.

We present the number and relative significance of cross-border acquisitions. Figure 31.1 shows that the number of international bank acquisition acquisitions mirrors worldwide macroeconomic conditions. When the world economy is prospering, the number of cross-border acquisitions goes up; when the world experiences economic turmoil, the number falls. The number of cross-border acquisitions increased steadily between 1985 and 2000, but dipped between 2001 and 2003, when the internet bubble burst. The number peaked at 432 in 2007, but fell steadily from 2008. Figure 31.2 shows that the percentage of bank acquisitions that are cross-border grew rather steadily from essentially zero in 1985 to peak at 37% in 2007. The percentage fell precipitously in 2008 to roughly 20% and has remained at that level since.

Table 31.1 looks further into the regional structure of cross-border M&As in banking and reveals three phases of development. All regions experienced a growth in the number of

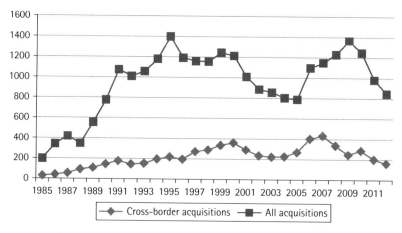

FIGURE 31.1 Bank acquisitions (by year) 1985–2012.

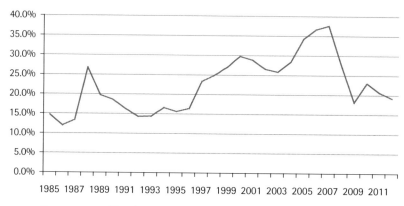

FIGURE 31.2 Percentage of bank acquisitions that are cross-border (by year) 1985–2012.

cross-border acquisitions in the years 1996 to 2007 compared with the years 1985 to 1995. Almost all regions doubled and sometimes more than tripled the number of cross-border acquisitions. Growth in domestic acquisition activity also accompanied these increases, but, despite the domestic growth, Europe, the Americas, and Africa/Middle East experienced a significant growth in the share of cross-border bank acquisitions between the time periods. Asia was the only region to experience a significant fall in the percentage of bank acquisitions represented by cross-border transactions between those time periods, albeit from a small base. The trend ended abruptly in 2008, and both the number and percentage of cross-border acquisitions have fallen to pre-1996 levels.

Table 31.1 also shows a pattern regarding acquisitions between continents. Comparing the earliest phase (1985–1995) to the middle phase (1996–2007), cross-border acquisitions increasingly occurred *between* continents. Comparing the middle phase to the most recent phase (2008–2012), banks appear to have retreated to acquisitions closer to home. Data through 2007 suggest that as banks polish the skills needed for cross-border acquisitions, they venture farther from their homes. Since 2008, however, the percentage of acquisitions

Table 31.1 Cross–border bank acquisitions by continent, 1985–2012.

	Europe	America	Africa/ Middle East	Asia	Australasia	Worldwide
Panel A: 1985 to 2012						
Number of bank acquisitions	11,808	13,309	977	2,721	523	27,628
Cross-border as a % of total	38.0%	14.1%	53.1%	44.1%	53.9%	22.9%
Intra-continental as a % of total	86.7%	90.2%	64.0%	71.9%	61.0%	91.0%
Panel B: 1985 to 1995						
Number of bank acquisitions	3,069	5,117	138	430	154	8,401
Cross-border as a % of total	32.7%	8.6%	45.7%	49.8%	57.8%	16.2%
Intra-continental as a % of total	87.3%	93.1%	58.7%	65.8%	57.1%	94.0%
Panel C: 1996 to 2007						
Number of bank acquisitions	5,722	6,245	556	1,644	270	13,553
Cross-border as a % of total	45.9%	17.9%	54.1%	44.8%	51.9%	27.5%
Intra-continental as a % of total	84.6%	88.6%	62.4%	72.0%	65.6%	89.1%
Panel D: 2008 to 2012						
Number of bank acquisitions	3,018	1,945	283	646	99	5,672
Cross-border as a % of total	28.5%	16.5%	54.8%	38.9%	53.5%	21.8%
Intra-continental as a % of total	90.0%	87.6%	69.6%	75.9%	80.8%	91.5%
Differences between panels B and C						
Cross-border as a % of total	13.2***	9.2***	8.5*	−5.0*	−5.9	11.3***
(z-statistic)	(12.3)	(14.8)	(1.8)	(−1.8)	(−1.2)	(20.4)
Intra-continential as a % of total	−2.8***	−4.5***	3.7	6.1**	8.4*	−4.9***
(z-statistic)	(−3.6)	(−8.4)	(0.8)	(2.4)	(1.7)	(−13.1)
Differences between panels C and D						
Cross-border as a % of total	−17.4***	−1.4	0.6	−5.9**	1.7	−5.7***
(z-statistic)	(−16.5)	(−1.5)	(0.2)	(−2.6)	(0.3)	(−8.6)
Intra-continential as a % of total	5.5***	−1.0	7.2**	3.9*	15.3***	2.4***
(z-statistic)	(7.5)	(−1.1)	(2.1)	(1.9)	(3.1)	(5.1)

* Totals are less then the sum of the continents due to acquisitions between banks headquartered in two nations that are located on the same continent.

** (pq/N + pq/N) ^.5

between continents returned to pre-1996 levels, suggesting that economic uncertainty negatively influences the desire to venture to far off lands.

Evidence from the UNCTAD's World Investment Report[2] supports the finding that banks from advanced market economies dominate the global banking industry. Ranking the top

[2] See <http://www.unctad.org/sections/dite_dir/docs/wir2006top50_spreadindex_en.pdf.>

50 multinational firms in the financial services sector by an index based on the number and the location of their foreign affiliates shows that 10 out of 50 firms were headquartered in the United States in 2004. Only a handful of firms were headquartered outside the European Union (EU) or the United States. The uneven degree of internationalization of banks from different continents is also supported by a study of Schoenmaker and van Laecke (2007). Interestingly, they find that economic integration does not only stimulate integration within the region but also beyond.

The crisis that struck international financial markets beginning in 2007 had a major impact on the incentives for banks to merge and to form alliances, both across-borders and domestically. Defaults on subprime loans in the United States forced investors to question the value of all their assets, which triggered a downward spiral of revaluations and declines in asset prices across the globe. Banks have been forced to sell parts of their assets and to raise new capital. (See Hellwig, 2008 for a detailed account of the causes and potential consequences of the crisis.) In Europe, for instance, the governments of Belgium, Luxembourg, and the Netherlands have initiated the divesture of *Fortis* and the sale of its assets to other financial institutions in Europe. The British mortgage lender Bradford & Bingley sold its deposits and branches to the Spanish bank Santander. Part of the resolution of the crisis have thus been acquisitions of domestic banks, be it through market forces, moral suasion of the supervisors, or outright interventions of policymakers. While the share of cross-border acquisitions decreased worldwide, the percentage of intra-continental acquisition increased. This suggests banks made fewer forays into foreign lands, and when they did, the foreign land was not far from home.

In many countries, rescue packages that governments have put into place to recapitalize the banking systems foresee provisions to restructure and to merge financial institutions. As expected, the number of bank acquisitions increased. One reason for the decline in cross-border acquisitions could be that acquisitions that officials believe are not urgently needed to rescue a failing bank have been curtailed; in other words, the main motive for acquisitions during such economic turmoil is macroeconomic necessity. At the same time, banks seem to have tried to join forces domestically. As a result, the number of domestic acquisitions has increased while international acquisitions have become almost as rare as they were in the mid-1980s.

As a result of the international financial crisis that began in 2007, regulators are subjecting banks to more scrutiny, requiring more justification for acquisitions, especially cross-border acquisitions. Beltratti and Paladino (2013) show that the stock market noticed the increased scrutiny and was indifferent to the announcements of bank acquisitions between 2007 and 2012. After acquirers passed regulatory hurdles and completed a takeover, the market rewarded them. This increased scrutiny, however, could increase the riskiness of a bank. In this sense, the analysis of this chapter will provide some broad guidelines and assessments about what to expect based on an analysis of cross-border acquisitions.

More specifically, we will focus on an explanation of the relatively modest increase in cross-border acquisition activity in the past, the regional concentration, and the dominance of a few large countries. We will also address the implications of cross-border bank acquisitions for efficiency and risks in banking.

31.3 Determinants of Cross-Border Bank Acquisitions[3]

Why should a bank acquire an institution in a different country? The theoretical literature on the determinants of international banking has taken a relatively eclectic approach to answer this question. Traditionally, this literature distinguishes between location—and ownership-specific factors (Sagari 1992; Williams 1997). There has been relatively little formal theoretical work providing an encompassing model of the international banking firm. (See textbooks covering banking theory such as Allen and Gale, 2000 or Freixas and Rochet, 1998.) Typically, theoretical work focuses on specific aspects of international banking such as regulatory consequences (Repullo 2000; Dalen and Olsen 2003; Harr and Ronde, 2005) or the determinants of entry into markets in Eastern Europe (Claeys and Hainz, 2007). Gray and Gray (1981) and Berger et al. (2004) thus suggest borrowing from the literature on cross-border foreign investment of non-financial firms to explain cross-border banking activity. Goldberg (2004) also discusses whether researchers can treat multinational activities of banks and of non-financial firms in the same matter. While she identifies parallels in the two literatures, she also notes differences between foreign direct investment (FDI) in financial services and manufacturing, especially with respect to the implications for local institution building and business cycles.

In the remainder of this section, we review the empirical literature on the determinants of cross-border bank acquisitions more carefully. We structure the discussion around the main determinants—information costs, regulations, bank-specific variables, and other mostly macroeconomic factors. From a policy perspective, the distinction between efficiency barriers caused by regulations and by information costs is important. While the former can eventually be removed, the latter will remain even in (legally) integrated markets.

Most of the studies we review make use of a gravity-type model, which essentially relates bilateral economic activities between two countries to the size of markets and geographic distance. Studies using bank-level data additionally take into account the entry decision by estimating limited dependent variable models of banks' foreign expansions.

31.3.1 Information Costs

Operating a financial institution in a foreign country raises a number of performance challenges for financial institution managers (Berger et al., 2004). Managers have to grapple with differences in languages, laws, social practices, regulations, and customer expectations, as well as the sheer geographic distance between the home and host countries. These cross-border managerial challenges add to the usual difficulties of operating an acquired institution during the post-acquisition transition period. Hence, Berger, DeYoung, and Udell (2001) argue that

---

[3] This section partly draws on Buch and DeLong (2004) and Berger et al. (2004).

"efficiency" barriers such as distance as well as differences in language, culture, currency, and regulatory or supervisory structures could inhibit cross-border bank acquisitions.

One important impediment to cross-border bank acquisitions could thus be information costs. These can be proxied by geographical distance, a common language, or a common legal system. The motivation for the use of the distance variable is related to a strand of the literature that applies gravity-type models to international investment decisions. In this literature, researchers typically consider distance to capture transportation costs. In contrast, international finance literature interprets distance in terms of information costs. Empirical applications by Ahearne, Griever, and Warnock (2004), Buch (2003, 2005), Portes and Rey (2005), or Buch and Lipponer (2006, 2007) show that distance influences banks' international capital flows and investment decisions of banks just as it influences international trade. Besides geographic proximity, sharing a common language is likely to lower the costs of melding two corporate cultures. Company employees need only one language in which to communicate information. More indirectly, sharing a common language can be a proxy for common cultural links. Furthermore, the presence of a common legal system should have a positive impact on cross-border acquisitions. For more recent evidence applying a gravity model to banks, see Niepmann (2011) or Brüggemann, Kleinert, and Prieto (2012).

Buch and DeLong (2004) use bilateral data on the number of bank acquisitions between countries and find that information costs and regulations in fact impede cross-border acquisitions. At the same time, large, efficient banks located in countries with developed banking markets can overcome these barriers and tend to be the banks that expand abroad. Alibux (2007) uses more recent data (1995–2005) and confirms the importance of information costs and regulations as impediments to cross-border acquisitions. Focarelli and Pozzolo (2005) look at where banks expand their cross-border shareholdings and find the most important determinants are potential profit opportunities as well as regulatory environments. The paper uses bank-level data on foreign investment for a representative sample of 260 large banks from the OECD countries. Cross-border shareholdings in their analysis include both acquisitions and greenfield investment.

Another barrier may be preferences for domestically owned institutions due to the "concierge" services that they can provide in terms of knowledge of the local conditions and information about local nonfinancial suppliers and customers. Berger et al. (2003) find that foreign affiliates of multinational corporations operating in European countries usually choose domestically-owned banks for cash management services, consistent with the "concierge" effect.

31.3.2 Regulations[4]

While information costs measure indirect, implicit barriers to the integration of banking markets, regulations of banking activities can erect direct, explicit barriers. The empirical

---

[4] A detailed database on banking regulations around the world can be found at. <http://econ. worldbank.org/WBSITE/EXTERNAL/EXTDEC/EXTGLOBALFINREPORT/o, contentMDK:23267421 ~pagePK:64168182~piPK:64168060~theSitePK:8816097,00.html>. See Barth, Caprio, and Levine (2001) for a description of these data. Also see Cihák et al. (2012) and Barth, Caprio, and Levine (2008).

literature on the determinants of bank acquisitions generally supports the hypothesis that deregulation has a substantial impact on acquisition decisions. Jayartne and Strahan (1998) and Saunders (1999) discuss the influence of deregulation in a domestic setting. Obviously, the presence of an international financial center in the target country makes countries more attractive destinations for international acquisitions (Choi, Tschoegl, and Yu, 1986; Ter Wengel, 1995). In addition, foreign banks have often found it easy to make inroads into domestic banking systems that have undergone major privatization programs. Guillén and Tschoegl (2000) show that privatization has paved the way for many Spanish banks into Latin America, and Bonin and Abel (2000) show that privatization has been one of the reasons for the high market shares of foreign banks in the transition economies of Central and Eastern Europe. Generally, evidence on the experience with foreign banks in transition economies can be found in de Haas and Lelyveld (2006), de Haas and Naaborg (2006), or Haselmann (2006). Claeys and Hainz (2007) study the effects of different modes of entry for lending rates. Berger (2007) supports this finding and adds net comparative advantages for foreign banks, coupled with low government entry barriers, as explanations for high ratios of foreign bank ownership in some emerging markets.

Buch and DeLong (2004) provide evidence for the importance of the regulatory environments for cross-border bank acquisitions. They find that national banking regulations affect the probability of being an acquirer or target in cross-border bank mergers. Looking at changes in acquisition characteristics over time, they find that regulatory changes made to encourage regional integration produced mixed results. The number of cross-border bank acquisitions within the European Union following its Single Market Program in 1992 did not increase significantly, but the number of cross-border bank acquisitions among Canada, Mexico, and the United States did increase after the implementation of the North American Free Trade Agreement in 1994.

The integration of banking markets in Europe indeed provides an interesting case study for the effects of regulations (see also Berglöf et al. 2008). While governments have largely abolished official restrictions to the cross-border entry of banks, implicit barriers through the "misuse of supervisory power" (European Commission, 2005: p. 4) remain prevalent. According to a survey by the European Commission (2005), savings of fixed costs resulting from cross-border acquisitions are relatively small compared to those that can be achieved through domestic acquisitions, and in particular smaller financial institutions find it difficult to sell the same product in different markets. Hence, political factors, differences in institutions and cultures, the use of different payment and settlement systems, and remaining differences in capital markets, taxes, and regulations across countries may all serve to deter cross-border consolidation (Giddy, Saunders, and Walter, 1996; Lannoo and Gros, 1998; Boot, 1999; Blandon, 2000; Goddard, Molyneux, and Wilson, 2001).

Fecht and Grüner (2008) provide an alternative explanation for a relative limited degree of pan-European bank acquisitions. In a theoretical model, they argue that the allocation of liquidity shocks may constitute a natural limit to the merger of banks. In their model, benefits from diversification and the costs of contagion may be traded off optimally when banks from some but not all regions merge. Carletti, Hartmann, and Spagnolo (2007) propose a theoretical model discussing the liquidity effects of bank mergers focusing on the tradeoff between an internalization and a diversification effect.

Besides directly encouraging acquisitions, the regulatory process can influence the probability of acquisition in a more subtle way. Köhler (2009) finds that the lack of transparency in the target country's merger process inhibits foreign acquirers in the banking industry. The lack of transparency reduces the probability of a foreign firm taking over a large bank in particular, suggesting that political maneuvering may be influencing the takeover market of large institutions.

The search for capital to meet regulatory standards could spur cross-border bank acquisitions. Valkanov and Kleimeier (2007) find evidence to support the excess regulatory capital hypothesis: acquiring banks that want to avoid regulatory scrutiny will strategically raise their capital levels by taking over banks that hold capital beyond the amount mandated by regulators. The stock market recognizes and rewards this strategy.

31.3.3 Bank-Specific Factors

Bank-specific characteristics that increase the likelihood of entering into an acquisition include efficiency, experience in a competitive environment, economies of scale and scope, and domestic clients that have international operations. Using various measures of efficiency and profitability, studies find that stronger banks take over weaker ones in that acquirers tend to be more cost efficient (Berger and Humphrey, 1992), more profitable (Peristiani, 1993), or better capitalized (Wheelock and Wilson, 2000) than their targets. For European banks, Vander Vennet (1998) confirms that acquiring banks tend to be larger and more efficient than their targets. Correa (2009) finds that foreign banks tend to take over bad performing banks in small countries with concentrated banking systems. Acquirers in cross-border consolidations are generally large institutions from countries with developed financial markets (Focarelli and Pozzolo 2001, 2005).

31.3.4 Macroeconomic Factors

Macroeconomic factors such as a high growth potential of host countries (so-called pull-factors) or lagging growth in the home country (push factors) affect cross-border capital flows and foreign direct investments of banks. Also, the demand for differentiated financial services tends to increase with the level of economic development. The heightened demand increases the incentives for banks to form cross-border alliances and to jointly provide financial services. A high gross domestic product (GDP) per capita and large market size could also generate economies of scale and hence create motives for international acquisitions (Berger, Hunter, and Timme, 1993; Benston, Hunter, and Wall, 1995; Berger et al. 2000). Consistent with these hypotheses, empirical literature finds a positive effect of market size and GDP per capita on cross-border bank acquisitions (Buch and DeLong, 2004; Focarelli and Pozzolo, 2005).

In addition to standard push and pull factors, literature on international banking has also borrowed possible determinants of the foreign expansion of banks from the theory of multinational firms (Goldberg, 2004). One implication of these theories is that, as two countries become more similar in size, relative factor endowments, and technical efficiency, foreign direct investment will increase relative to trade between the two countries (Markusen and Venables, 1995). Moreover, trade literature predicts that in industries such as banking, for which intangible, firm-specific, and knowledge-based assets are important, international firms are more likely to export their management expertise via foreign direct investment rather than exporting the goods and services themselves. Thus, trade theory would predict significant cross-border financial institution M&As primarily between country pairs with similar national characteristics.

Berger et al. (2004) test the relevance of the new trade theory and the traditional theory of comparative advantage for explaining the geographic patterns of international M&As of financial institutions between 1985 and 2000. Their data provide statistically significant support for both theories. They also find evidence that the United States has idiosyncratic comparative advantages at both exporting and importing financial institutions management. Claessens and van Horen (2007) use data on foreign direct investments of banks and confirm the importance of comparative advantages and institutional familiarity.

In Section 31.3.3, we reviewed the literature that stresses the importance of relative efficiency at the *bank*-level for the probability of becoming an acquirer in an international bank consolidation. Literature also shows the importance of profitability at the *country*-level. Focarelli and Pozzolo (2001) study the pattern of cross-border acquisitions in the banking industry relative to the non-financial sector. Using data on almost 2,500 banks from 29 OECD countries, they find that banks tend to expand into countries where banking systems are inefficient.

A large literature on FDI in banking has dealt with the question of whether or not trade and finance are linked. According to this literature, banking organizations engage in a "follow-your-customer" strategy of setting up offices in countries where their home country customers have foreign affiliates (Goldberg and Saunders, 1981; Brealey and Kaplanis, 1996). However, other researchers point out that foreign-owned banks lend mostly to borrowers other than customers from the home country, which suggests that follow-your-customer may not be the dominant motivation behind cross-border acquisitions (Stanley, Roger, and Mcmanis, 1993; Seth, Nolle, and Mohanty, 1998). Focarelli and Pozzolo (2005) support the "follow-your-customer" hypothesis, especially for branches. However, they also find that other factors such as institutions and profit opportunities are relatively more important. Ultimately, however, firm- or bank-level evidence would be necessary to disentangle causality between the foreign expansions of banks and non-financial firms and thus to ultimately resolve the "follow-your-customer" hypothesis.

31.3.5 Summary

The determinants of international bank acquisitions and cross-border banking in general are one of the most intensively researched areas in the context of international bank acquisitions. A number of stylized facts stand out. At the bank level, the probability of becoming an acquirer in an international deal is positively linked to size and profitability. At the country level, acquisitions are more frequent between large and developed market economies and countries with similar cultural background. In addition, regulatory entry barriers deter entry. The fact that implicit regulatory and cultural entry barriers into foreign markets still prevail is likely to have implications for the efficiency and risk effects of bank acquisitions. This is an issue to which we turn next.

31.4 EFFECTS OF CROSS-BORDER BANK ACQUISITIONS: EFFICIENCY AND COMPETITION

Cross-border bank acquisitions can affect the efficiency of banks through a number of channels. The merged entity could be able to exploit economies of scale and scope, or management and corporate governance practices could be improved. At the same time, however, managing an increasingly large and complex organization operating in several countries may also lead to managerial inefficiencies and lower performance—the largest multinational banks operate affiliates in up to 70 host countries, according to data collected by the United Nations Conference on Trade and Development. The debate about which of the two effects dominates has been the subject of a large body of empirical literature.

Studies on the efficiency effects of cross-border bank acquisitions fall into two main groups. A first set of studies uses event studies to address the impact of acquisitions on banking performance. A second set of studies compares the efficiency of domestic versus foreign-owned banks. Since foreign ownership is often the result of acquisitions, these studies provide indirect evidence on efficiency effects of acquisitions. These studies also incorporate insights into the effects of foreign entry on competition in banking, thus addressing the potential tradeoff between higher efficiency in the banks involved in cross-border acquisitions and the competitive structure of the banking system. Boot and Marinc (2009) present a theoretical study of the tradeoff between competition, efficiency, and the effectiveness of bank regulation.

31.4.1 Event Studies

Research on cross-border acquisitions of financial institutions in developed countries suggests, at best, mediocre post-acquisition financial performance. A study of cross-border acquisitions in Europe found that the associated combined bidder and target value changes were generally zero or negative, compared with domestic acquisitions, where combined values were positive on average (Beitel and Schiereck, 2001). Similarly, a study of US domestic deals found that acquisitions that combine two firms from different geographic areas create less shareholder value, consistent with fewer benefits from cross-border acquisitions (DeLong, 2001). Cybo-Ottone and Murgia (2000) found that for 54 inter-European bank acquisitions between 1988 and 1997, the acquirers' abnormal returns were insignificantly different from zero.

DeLong (2003) goes one step further and compares market reactions to US bank acquisitions and to cross-border acquisitions. She examines abnormal returns of publicly traded partners upon the announcement of 41 non-US bank acquisitions and compares the returns with a US control group. She finds acquirers of domestic banks outside the United States earn more on average than acquirers of domestic banks in the United States. Moreover, non-US targets tend to earn less than their US counterparts. However, for the subset of acquisitions in countries with relatively well developed stock markets, she finds that partners both inside and outside the United States earn similar returns. Kiymaz (2004) also finds that macroeconomic factors are important in market returns to cross-border merger partners. When he examines cross-border mergers of financial institutions that involve a US partner, he finds there is an inverse relationship between US bidder returns and target country economic conditions. Conversely, he finds that returns to US targets are higher when US economic conditions are better than conditions in the bidder's country.

Ayadi and Pujals (2005) study bank M&As in Europe. They find that domestic acquisitions help cut costs but fail to achieve revenue synergies. Cross-border acquisitions, in contrast, generate revenue synergies, possibly due to improved geographical diversification.

Carletti, Hartmann, and Ongena (2007) analyze the impact of regulations on the effects of acquisitions. Using a new and unique dataset, they identify events that strengthen competition policy for 19 countries and for the years 1987–2004. They find two positive effects of a more competition-oriented regime for acquisition control. First, the stock price increases for banks but not for non-financial firms. Second, the targets of bank acquisitions become larger and more profitable.

31.4.2 Comparisons of Bank Efficiency

Whereas event studies of cross-border consolidations analyze the stock market reaction to bidders and targets upon the announcement of a foreign acquisition, several studies compare the efficiency of domestic and foreign-owned banks (see Berger, 2007 for an encompassing survey). Since acquisitions are a key channel for banks to enter foreign markets, these studies provide indirect evidence on the efficiency effects of bank acquisitions. In terms of the *host* country effects of acquisitions, we focus on competition and efficiency effects in the following. Other aspects such as the impact on lending to small and mid-sized firms are addressed, inter alia, in Berger, Klapper, and Udell (2001) and Berger et al. (2004), or Goldberg, Dages, and Kinney (2000). Herrero and Simón (2003) survey the determinants and impact of financial sector FDI for the home economy.

Most of the efficiency studies of foreign-owned versus domestically owned banks within a developed country found the foreign-owned banks to be less efficient with the possible exception of US banks operating abroad (DeYoung and Nolle, 1996; Chang, Hasan, and Hunter, 1998; Berger et al. 2000). However, a few studies found that foreign institutions have about the same efficiency on average as domestic institutions (Vander Vennet, 1996). Peek, Rosengren, and Kasirye (1999) argue that the poor performance of foreign bank subsidiaries is mainly due to pre-existing conditions. At the same time, foreign owners are also unable to turn around the banks they acquire.

Many of the alleged benefits of cross-border bank acquisitions are more prevalent for developing countries than for advanced market economies. Through foreign entry, emerging host countries can benefit from technology transfer, competition, and demonstration effects (BIS, 2004). Research on foreign banks in developing countries in fact finds results different from those in developed countries. For example, one study of foreign banks in over 80 countries found that foreign-owned banks in emerging markets have a relatively high profitability (Claessens, Demirgüç-Kunt, and Huizinga, 2001). This is consistent with disadvantages in financial institution management for local banks in these countries. Evidence in Demirgüç-Kunt and Huizinga (1999) supports the finding that foreign banks in emerging markets tend to outperform domestic banks.

Bank acquisitions that have a positive effect on efficiency at the bank-level may have a negative effect on the competitive structure of the banking system. To assess the overall welfare implications of bank acquisitions, we must examine the impact of acquisitions on market power as well.

Huizinga, Nelissen, and vander Vennet (2001) show that the tradeoff between efficiency and competition need not be steep. Using a sample of 52 horizontal bank acquisitions in Europe and studying the pre-euro period, they find evidence for unexploited scale economies and X-inefficiencies in European banking. To some extent, cross-border acquisitions reduce these inefficiencies. However, the authors do not find evidence for a greater market power of the merged banks.

31.4.3 Summary

The influence of foreign banks on a country's banking system is not well established. Theoretically, the added competition should increase efficiency and lower costs. Empirically, researchers have found foreign-owned banks to be less efficient than domestic banks in developed countries, suggesting they do not add much competition. In contrast to these general findings, banks from developed countries expanding into developing countries tend to be more efficient than their domestic counterparts. While operating in a developing country may add to a bank's risk, there may be benefits both to the bank and to the host banking system. We now look at aspects of that risk.

31.5 EFFECTS OF CROSS-BORDER BANK ACQUISITIONS: RISK[5]

A large set of studies looks at the determinants of risks in banking, but only a handful of these addresses the impact of the internationalization of banks (De Nicolò, 2001; González, 2005; Nier and Baumann, 2006). Yet, there is a growing awareness that cross-border banking activities could affect the risk and thus the stability of the domestic banking system.

A common argument in banking is that cross-border (geographic) acquisitions have the potential to reduce bank (and thus regulators') risk of insolvency (Segal, 1974; Vander Vennet, 1996; Berger, 2000). This conventional wisdom is based on the notion that it is better for a bank not to put all its "eggs in one basket" and thus geographic diversification is a naturally risk reducing activity.

However, offsetting these perceived benefits are at least two potential costs that may well enhance the risk of bank insolvency and ultimately the risk exposure of bank regulators. The first risk increasing effect comes from the incentives banks have to shift risk when the regulatory "safety net" and its associated implicit and explicit guarantees are underpriced. As discussed by John, John, and Senbet (1991) and John, Saunders, and Senbet (2000), banks

---

[5] This section draws partly on Amihud, DeLong, and Saunders (2002).

have incentives to increase their risk exposure beyond the level that would be privately opti-mal in a world in which there are no safety net guarantees or the safety net—deposit insur-ance, capital requirements, and implicitly, bank closure—is fairly priced. One way for a bank to exploit the safety net might be to acquire other (risky) banks by cross-border expansion. If the risky investment pays off, then the acquiring bank has the potential to keep any upside returns. If the acquisition of the foreign target fails and the domestic bank's (acquirer's) solvency is threatened, then the acquiring bank may be bailed out either by its own home regulator or perhaps by the host regulator (the regulator of the target bank). As a result, cross-border acquisitions may increase the insolvency risk exposure of either one or both the domestic (acquirer) and host (target) bank regulators.

A second reason why cross-border acquisitions may increase an acquirer's risk concerns "who is watching the eggs in the basket" (Winton, 1999). Specifically, by extending its opera-tions into new overseas markets, the (domestic) bank is confronted with potentially new and risk increasing monitoring problems related to the loan customer base, the operating cost structure, etc., of the target bank. If monitoring costs are high, these problems may also increase the insolvency risk of the domestic acquiring bank and implicitly the risk of domestic (and foreign) regulators.

The question is whether and to whom cross-border acquisitions are net beneficial. For example, if cross-border acquisitions do not raise the risk of acquiring banks rela-tive to other domestic (home country) banks, or indeed, reduce their risk, then domestic regulators may encourage domestic banks to expand abroad. By contrast, if cross-border acquisitions increase the relative domestic riskiness of the acquiring bank, then domes-tic regulators may wish to scrutinize such acquisitions more carefully and may even seek to restrict them in an effort to reduce safety net subsidies and to reduce risk-shifting behavior.

To gain insight into these issues, Amihud, DeLong, and Saunders (2002) examine risk effects of cross-border bank acquisitions. They analyze the change in total risk of an acquir-ing bank as a result of a cross-border banking deal, changes in the systematic risk of acquir-ing banks relative to home, foreign, and world market bank indexes, and the reaction of stock prices to news about the acquisition and examine the relationship between this stock price reaction and changes in risk brought about by cross-border bank acquisitions. They find that, on average, cross-border bank acquisitions do not change the risk of acquiring banks in any significant way. This finding has important regulatory policy implications in that the effect of an overseas acquisition is highly bank dependent or idiosyncratic. On aver-age the risk decreasing effects of cross-border bank acquisitions are offset by risk increasing effects, and the nature of the merging partners' operation changes in a way so as to leave the acquirer's risk unchanged. In a follow-up study, Buch and DeLong (2008) look further into the determinants of risk following bank acquisitions. They find that strong bank supervision is associated with banks reducing risk after acquisitions. The results suggest banks subject to strong supervision use cross-border acquisitions to diversify risk rather than to shift risk to banks in countries with weaker supervision.

Whereas the focus in Amihud, DeLong, and Saunders (2002) is on the exposure of banks to market risks, recent research has also addressed the exposure of banks to macroeconomic risks. Méon and Weill (2005) study the impact of acquisitions among large banks in Europe on the banks' exposure to macroeconomic risk. They find that loan portfolios of European banks provide a sub-optimal risk-return tradeoff. Hence, there are potential gains in risk diversification from cross-border acquisitions even within the European Union due to imperfect correlations of business cycles.

A quite comprehensive theoretical literature also deals with the risk and regulatory consequences of international bank acquisitions. Repullo (2001), for instance, has a theoretical model in which a foreign bank becomes a branch of the domestic banks. Each bank is initially supervised by the domestic supervisory agency. Under home country control, the takeover moves responsibility to the domestic agency. The model shows that while cross-border bank acquisitions may reduce risk due to diversification, they also shift responsibility for supervision and deposit insurance to the domestic regulatory agency. Harr and Ronde (2005) study the regulatory implications of banks' organizational choice between branch and subsidiary, which fall under home and country supervision, respectively. Their results do not show incentives for regulators to engage in a "race to the bottom" by relaxing banking regulations. Karolyi and Taboada (2012) substantiate the result and find targets engage in less risk-taking after banks from countries with stronger regulatory regimes acquire them. Stricter regulations in the acquirer's home country are also associated with higher stock market returns to the target upon the announcement of an acquisition. Dalen and Olsen (2003) show that the link between multinational banking and risk-taking is not clear-cut. On the one hand, a lack of international coordination of supervisory towards subsidiaries of foreign banks tends to lower capital requirements. On the other hand, regulators respond by increasing incentives to improve asset quality.

Questions of supervisory responsibility are becoming more urgent as banks form more complex cross-border acquisitions. Dermine (2006), for instance, details the regulatory treatment and challenges presented by the Scandinavian bank Nordea, which was formed by banks from four different Nordic countries. Nordea adopted the Societas Europaea, a corporate structure that is governed by EU law. The structure allows banks in the European Union to branch across national borders. Nordea is incorporated in Sweden, and Swedish supervisors are responsible for the supervision and deposit insurance of the entire entity. The result is that a branch operating in Finland, Denmark, or Norway has different supervisory and deposit insurance systems than host country banks with which they are competing.

31.6 CONCLUSIONS

In this chapter, we have reviewed the empirical literature on the determinants and effects of cross-border acquisitions in banking. We summarize our results as follows.

First, researchers understand relatively well the determinants of international banking activities. Implicit and explicit barriers to the integration of markets can hold back cross-border acquisition activity. Implicit barriers include information costs as well as regulations impeding the market access of foreign banks. As policymakers have lowered explicit, direct barriers to the integration of markets significantly in developed market economies, these indirect barriers have gained in relative importance. Furthermore, bank acquisitions tend to take place mostly between large and developed countries, between countries in close regional proximity, and between countries that share a common cultural background. Considering the bank-level determinants of cross-border bank acquisitions, there is clear evidence for larger and more profitable banks to be the acquirers.

Second, several studies have looked into the effects of international bank acquisitions in terms of competition and efficiency. One common finding of this literature is that foreign-owned banks—which are often the result of acquisitions—outperform domestically owned banks in developing countries. The comparative advantages of foreign banks in developed countries are less evident.

Third, despite the growing recognition that international banking can have an important impact on (international) financial stability, relatively few studies analyze the risk effects of bank acquisitions. At the bank level, studies find little evidence for a systematic change in risk following bank acquisitions.

In terms of future research in the field, we see three main gaps in the literature.

First, testing the determinants of acquisitions in banking based on a full-fledged model of the international bank would be desirable. Applying the literature on multinational firms to international banking while taking into account that "banks are special" seems a potentially fruitful avenue for future theoretical work. One avenue that consider particularly useful is research modeling bank heterogeneity and the implications for cross-border banking (e.g., De Blas and Russ, 2013). The empirical banking literature provides ample evidence on the stylized facts that such a theoretical model should be able to match.

Second, improving our understanding of the risk-return-tradeoffs in international bank acquisitions requires the more extensive use of bank-level data. Looking into the portfolio structures of internationally active banks and assessing the impact of foreign activities on risks and returns could provide important insights into the effects of cross-border acquisitions.

Third, in the theoretical literature, there are a number of papers that analyze the regulatory consequences of multinational banking. At the bank level, these papers focus on the organizational choice between branched and subsidiaries; at the supervisory level, the focus is on the costs and benefits between home and host country control. To the best of our knowledge though, few of these papers have been put to an empirical test. This would be the natural next step.

Ultimately, linking empirical and theoretical work on international bank acquisitions more closely together and making use of new bank-level datasets is not only of academic interest. It will also pay in terms of improved information for policymakers. The increase in cross-border financial institutions raises some important policy issues, such as the transmission of systemic risk across-borders, the governance and supervision of multinational financial institutions, and the extent to which foreign-owned institutions will provide sufficient services in times of local crises. Reacting to these challenges in an appropriate way is particularly important for developing countries. These countries enjoy relatively great benefits of foreign bank entry in terms of efficiency but they may also encounter potentially greater risks. Policymakers must react via adjustments in the supervisory framework, information sharing among supervisors, developing supervisory skills.

References

Ahearne, A., Griever, W., and Warnock, F. (2004). Information Costs and Home Bias: An Analysis of US Holdings of Foreign Equities, *Journal of International Economics* 62, 313–336.

Alibux, A. N. R. N. (2007). Cross-Border Mergers and Acquisitions in the European Banking Sector. Erasmus University of Rotterdam Dissertation.

Allen, F. and Gale, D. (2000). *Comparing Financial Systems*. Cambridge, MA: MIT Press.

Amihud, Y., DeLong, G., and Saunders, A. (2002). The Effects of Cross-Border Bank Mergers on Bank Risk and Value, *Journal of International Money and Finance* 21(6), 857–877.

Ayadi, R. and Pujals, G. (2005). Banking Mergers and Acquisitions in the EU: Overview, Assessment and Prospects, Société Universitaire Européenne de Recherches Financiéres (SUERF) Study No. 3.

Barth, J. R., Caprio Jr., G., and Levine, R. (2001). The Regulation and Supervision of Banks Around the World: A New Database. In: R. E. Litan and R. Herring (Eds.), *Integrating Emerging Market Countries into the Global Financial System*, Washington, DC: Brookings Institution Press.

Barth, J. R., Caprio Jr., G., and Levine, R. (2008). Bank Regulations Are Changing: For Better or Worse?, *Comparative Economic Studies* 50, 537–563.

Beitel, P. and Schiereck, D. (2001). Value Creation at the Ongoing Consolidation of the European Banking Market. Institute for Mergers and Acquisitions Working Paper.

Beltratti, A. and Paladino, G. (2013). Is M&A Different During a Crisis? Evidence from the European Banking Sector, *Journal of Banking and Finance* (Forthcoming).

Benston, G., Hunter, C., and Wall, L. (1995). Motivations for Bank Mergers and Acquisitions: Enhancing the Deposit Insurance Put Option Versus Earnings Diversification, *Journal of Money, Credit and Banking* 27, 777–788.

Berger, A. N. (2000). The Big Picture of Bank Diversification. *Federal Reserve of Chicago Proceedings* May, 162–174.

Berger, A. N. (2007). Obstacles to a Global Banking System: "Old Europe" versus "New Europe," *Journal of Banking and Finance* (31) 7, 1955–1973.

Berger, A. N., Buch, C. M., DeLong, G., and DeYoung, R. (2004). Exporting Financial Institutions Management via Foreign Direct Investment Mergers and Acquisitions, *Journal of International Money and Finance* 23, 333–366.

Berger, A. N., Dai, Q., Ongena, S., and Smith, D. C. (2003). To What Extent Will the Banking Industry be Globalized? A Study of Bank Nationality and Reach in 20 European Nations, *Journal of Banking and Finance* 27 (3), 383–415.

Berger, A. N., Demsetz, R. S., and Strahan, P. E. (1999). The Consolidation of the Financial Services Industry: Causes, Consequences, and Implications for the Future, *Journal of Banking and Finance* 23 (2–4), 135–194.

Berger, A. N., DeYoung, R., Genay, H., and Udell, G. F. (2000). The Globalization of Financial Institutions: Evidence from Cross-Border Banking Performance, *Brookings-Wharton Papers on Financial Services* 3, 23–158.

Berger, A. N., DeYoung, R., and Udell, G. F. (2001). Efficiency Barriers to the Consolidation of the European Financial Services Industry, *European Financial Management* 7, 117–130.

Berger, A. N. and Humphrey, D. B. (1992). Megamergers in Banking and the Use of Cost Efficiency as an Antitrust Defense, *Antitrust Bulletin* 37, 541–600.

Berger, A. N., Hunter, W. C., and Timme, S. G. (1993). The Efficiency of Financial Institutions: A Review and Preview of Research Past, Present, and Future, *Journal of Banking and Finance* 17, 389–405.

Berger, A. N., Klapper, L. F., and Udell, G. F. (2001). The Ability of Banks to Lend to Informationally Opaque Small Businesses, *Journal of Banking and Finance* 25 (12), 2127–2167.

Berglöf, E., Burkart, M., Friebel, G., and Paltseva, E. (2008). Widening and Deepening—Reforming the European Union, *American Economic Review* 93 (5), 1824–1829.

BIS (Bank for International Settlements) (2004). *Foreign Direct Investment in the Financial Sector of Emerging Market Economies*, Basel: CGFS Publications No. 22.

Blandon, J. G. (2000). Cross-Border Banking in Europe: An Empirical Investigation, Universitat Pompeu Fabra Economics Working Paper No. 509.

Bonin, J. P. and Abel, I. (2000). Retail Banking in Hungary: A Foreign Affair? Wesleyan University Economics Department Middletown Working Paper.

Boot, A.W.A. (1999). European Lessons on Consolidation in Banking, *Journal of Banking and Finance* 23(2–4), 609–613.

Boot, A. W. A. and Marinc, M. (2009). Competition and Entry in Banking: Implications for Capital Regulation. University of Amsterdam and CEPR: Mimeo.

Brealey, R. A. and Kaplanis, E. C. (1996). The Determination of Foreign Banking Location, *Journal of International Money and Finance* 15 (4), 577–597.

Brüggemann, B., Kleinert, J., and Prieto, E. (2012). A Gravity Equation for Bank Loans. Universities of Graz and Tuebingen: Mimeo.

Buch, C. M. (2003). Information Versus Regulation: What Drives the International Activities of Commercial Banks?, *Journal of Money, Credit, and Banking* 35(6), 851–869.

Buch, C. M. (2005). Distance and International Banking, *Review of International Economics* 13(4), 787–804.

Buch, C. M. and DeLong, G. L. (2004). Cross-Border Bank Mergers: What Lures the Rare Animal?, *Journal of Banking and Finance* 28(9), 2077–2102.

Buch, C. M. and DeLong, G. L. (2008). Do Weak Supervisory Systems Encourage Bank Risk-Taking?, *Journal of Financial Stability* 4(1), 23–39.

Buch, C. M. and Lipponer, A. (2006). Clustering or Competition? The Foreign Investment Behaviour of German Banks, *International Journal of Central Banking* 5, 135–168.

Buch, C. M. and Lipponer, A. (2007). FDI versus Exports: Evidence from German Banks, *Journal of Banking and Finance* 31(3), 805–826.

Carletti, E., Hartmann, P., and Ongena, S. (2007). The Economic Impact of Merger Control: What Is Special About Banking?, European Central Bank Working Paper Series No. 786.

Carletti, E., Hartmann, P., and Spagnolo, G. (2007). Bank Mergers, Competition and Liquidity, *Journal of Money, Credit and Banking* 39(5), 1067–1105.

Chang, C. E., Hasan, I., and Hunter, W. C. (1998). Efficiency of Multinational Banks: An Empirical Investigation, *Applied Financial Economics* 8(6), 1–8.

Choi, S.-R., Tschoegl, A. E., and Yu, E-M. (1986). Banks and the World's Major Financial Centers, 1970-1980, *Weltwirtschaftliches Archiv* 122, 48–64.

Cihák, M., Demirgüç-Kunt, A., Soledad Martínez Pería, M., and Mohseni-Cheraghlou, A. (2012). Banking Regulation and Supervision Around the World: A Crisis Update. World Bank, Washington, DC, Policy Research Working Paper.

Claessens, S., Demirgüç-Kunt, A., and Huizinga, H. (2001). How Does Foreign Entry Affect Domestic Banking Markets?, *Journal of Banking and Finance* 25, 891–911.

Claessens, S. and van Horen, N. (2007). Location Decisions of Foreign Banks and Competitive Advantage, International Monetary Fund, World Bank Policy Research Working Paper Series No. 4113.

Claeys, S. and Hainz, C. (2007). Acquisition versus Greenfield: The Impact of the Mode of Foreign Bank Entry on Information and Bank Lending Rates, Sveriges Riksbank, Stockholm, Working Paper Series No. 210.

Correa, R. (2009). Cross-Border Bank Acquisitions: Is There a Performance Effect?, *Journal of Financial Services Research* 36(2–3), 169–197

Cybo-Ottone, A. and Murgia, M. (2000). Mergers and Shareholder Wealth in European Banking, *Journal of Banking and Finance* 24(6), 831–859.

Dalen, D. M. and Olsen, T. E. (2003). Regulatory Competition and Multinational Banking, Munich, CESifo Working Paper Series No. 971.

De Blas, B. and Russ, K. (2013). All Banks Great, Small, and Global: Loan Pricing and Foreign Competition, *International Review of Economics and Finance* 26, 4–24.

de Haas, R. and Naaborg, I. (2006). Foreign Banks in Transition Countries: To Whom Do They Lend and How are They Financed?, *Financial Markets, Institutions and Instruments* 15(4), 159–199.

de Haas, R. and van Lelyveld, I. (2006). Foreign Banks and Credit Stability in Central and Eastern Europe: A Panel Data Analysis, *Journal of Banking and Finance* 30(7), 1927–1952.

DeLong, G. L. (2001). Stockholder Gains from Focusing versus Diversifying Bank Mergers, *Journal of Financial Economics* 59 (2), 221–252.

DeLong, G. L. (2003). Does Long-Term Performance of Mergers Match Market Expectations? Evidence from the US Banking Industry, *Financial Management* 32(2), 5–26.

Demirgüç-Kunt, A. and Huizinga, H. (1999). Determinants of Commercial Bank Interest Margins and Profitability: Some International Evidence, *World Bank Economic Review* 13, 379–408.

Dermine, J. (2006). European Banking Integration: Don't Put the Cart before the Horse, *Financial Markets, Institutions and Instruments* 15(2), 57–106.

De Nicolò, G. (2001). Size, Charter Value and Risk in Banking: An International Perspective. In: *The Financial Safety Net: Costs, Benefits and Implications for Regulation*, 197–215. Proceedings of the 37th Annual Conference on Bank Structure and Competition, Federal Reserve of Chicago.

DeYoung, R. and Nolle, D. E. (1996). Foreign-Owned Banks in the US: Earning Market Share or Buying It?, *Journal of Money, Credit, and Banking* 28(4), 622–636.

European Central Bank (2012). Financial Integration in Europe, <http://www.ecb.europa.eu/pub/pdf/other/financialintegrationineurope201204en.pdf>.

European Communities (2005). Cross-Border Consolidation in the EU Financial Sector, Commission Staff Document, Brussels, SEC (2005) No. 1398.

Fecht, F. and Grüner, H. P. (2008). Limits to International Banking Consolidation, *Open Economies Review* 19(5), 651–666.

Focarelli, D. and Pozzolo, A. F. (2001). The Patterns of Cross-Border Bank Mergers and Shareholdings in OECD Countries, *Journal of Banking and Finance* 25, 2305–2337.

Focarelli, D. and Pozzolo, A. F. (2005). Where Do Banks Expand Abroad?, *Journal of Business* 78(6), 2435–2462.

Freixas, X. and Rochet, J.-C. (1998). *Microeconomics of Banking*. Cambridge: MIT Press.

Giddy, I., Saunders, A., and Walter, I. (1996). Alternative Models for Clearance and Settlement: The Case of the Single European Capital Market, *Journal of Money, Credit and Banking* 28(4), 986–1000.

Goddard, J., Molyneux, P., and Wilson, J. O. S. (2001). *European Banking: Efficiency, Technology and Growth*. Chichester, UK: John Wiley and Sons.

Goldberg, L. (2004). Financial-Sector FDI and Host Countries: New and Old Lessons, Cambridge, MA, NBER Working Paper No. 10441.

Goldberg, L., Dages, B. G., and Kinney, D. (2000). Foreign and Domestic Bank Participation in Emerging Markets: Lessons from Mexico and Argentina, *Federal Reserve Bank of New York Economic Policy Review* 6(3), 17–36.

Goldberg, L. G. and Saunders, A. (1981). The Determinants of Foreign Banking Activity in the United States, *Journal of Banking and Finance* 5(1), 17–32.

Gonzáles, F. (2005). Bank Regulation and Risk-Taking Incentives: An International Comparison of Bank Risk, *Journal of Banking and Finance* 29, 1153–1184.

Gray, J. M. and Gray, H. P. (1981). The Multinational Bank: A Financial MNC?, *Journal of Banking and Finance* 5(1), 1–153.

Guillén, M. and Tschoegl, A. E. (2000). The Internationalization of Retail Banking: The Case of the Spanish Banks in Latin America, *Transnational Corporations* 9, 63–97.

Harr, T. and Ronde, T. (2005). Branch or Subsidiary? Capital Regulation of Multinational Banks. University of Copenhagen and CEPR: Mimeo.

Haselmann, R. (2006). *Performance and Strategies of Banks in Transition Economies*. Marburg: Metropolis Verlag.

Hellwig, M. (2008). The Causes of the Financial Crisis, *CESifo Forum, Ifo Institute for Economic Research at the University of Munich* 9(4), 12–21.

Herrero, A. G. and Simón, D. N. (2003). Determinants and Impact of Financial Sector FDI to Emerging Economies: A Home Country's Perspective, Madrid, Documentos ocasionales— Banco de España No. 8.

Huizinga, H. P., Nelissen, J. H. M., and Vander Vennet, R. (2001). Efficiency Effects of Bank Mergers and Acquisitions in Europe, Tinbergen Institute, Rotterdam, Discussion Paper No. 088/3.

Jayaratne, J. and Strahan, P. (1998). Entry Restrictions, Industry Evolution, and Dynamic Efficiency: Evidence from Commercial Banking, *Journal of Law and Economics* 41, 239–273.

John, K., John, T., and Senbet, L. (1991). Risk Shifting Incentives of Depository Institutions: A New Perspective on Federal Deposit Insurance Reform, *Journal of Banking and Finance* 15(45), 895–915.

John, K., Saunders, A., and Senbet, L. (2000). A Theory of Bank Compensation and Management Regulation, *Review of Financial Studies* 3(1), 95–126.

Karolyi, G. A. and Taboada, A. G. (2012). The Role of Regulation in Cross-Border Bank Acquisitions: It is Really a "Race to the Bottom"? Cornell University Working Paper.

Kiymaz, H. (2004). Cross-border Acquisitions of US Financial Institutions: Impact of Macroeconomic Factors, *Journal of Banking & Finance* 28, 1413–1439.

Köhler, M. (2009). Transparency of Regulation and Cross-Border Bank Mergers, *International Journal of Central Banking* 5, 39–73.

Lannoo, K. and Gros, D. (1998). Capital Markets and EMU: Report of a CEPS Working Party. Centre for European Policy Studies.

Markusen, J. R. and Venables, A. J. (1995). The Increased Importance of Multinationals in North American Economic Relationships: A Convergence Hypothesis. In: M. W. Canzoneri, W. J. Ethier, and V. Grilli (Eds.), *The New Transatlantic Economy*, 169–188. London: Cambridge University Press.

Méon, P. G. and Weill, L. (2005). Can Mergers in Europe Help Banks Hedge Against Macroeconomic Risk?, *Applied Financial Economics* 15(5), 315–326.

Niepmann, F. (2011). Banking Across-borders, Netherlands Central Bank, Research Department, Amsterdam, DNB Working Papers No. 325.

Nier, E. and Baumann, U. (2006). Market Discipline, Disclosure and Moral Hazard in Banking, *Journal of Financial Intermediation* 15, 332–361.

Peek, J., Rosengren, E. S., and Kasirye, F. (1999). The Poor Performance of Foreign Bank Subsidiaries: Were the Problems Acquired or Created?, *Journal of Banking and Finance* 23, 579–604.

Peristiani, S. (1993). The Effects of Mergers on Bank Performance. In: *Studies on Excess Capacity in the Financial Sector*.WP93-13. New York: Federal Reserve Bank of New York.

Portes, R. and Rey, H. (2005). The Determinants of Cross-Border Equity Flows, *Journal of International Economics* 65 (2), 269–296.

Repullo, R. (2001). A Model of Takeovers of Foreign Banks, *Spanish Economic Review* 3, 1–21.

Sagari, S. B. (1992). United States Foreign Direct Investment in the Banking Industry, *Transnational Corporations* 3, 93–123.

Saunders, A. (1999). Consolidation and Universal Banking, *Journal of Banking and Finance* 23, 693–695.

Schoenmaker, D. and van Laecke, C. (2007). Determinants of International Banking: Evidence from the World's Largest Banks. Government of the Netherlands Ministry of Finance: Mimeo.

Segal, Z. (1974). Market and Industry Factors Affecting Commercial Bank Stocks: An Analysis of the Price Behavior of Bank Stock Prices. New York University, Unpublished Doctoral Dissertation.

Seth, R., Nolle, D. E., and Mohanty, S. K. (1998). Do Banks Follow Their Customers Abroad?, *Financial Markets, Institutions, and Instruments* 7(4), 1–25.

Stanley, T. O., Roger, C., and McManis, B. (1993). The Effects of Foreign Ownership of US Banks on the Availability of Loanable Funds to Small Business, *Journal of Small Business Management* 31(1), 51–66.

Ter Wengel, J. (1995). International Trade in Banking Services, *Journal of International Money and Finance* 14, 47–64.

Valkanov, E. and Kleimeier, S. (2007). The Role of Regulatory Capital in International Bank Mergers and Acquisitions, *Research in International Business and Finance* 2 (1), 50–68.

Vander Vennet, R. (1996). The Effect of Mergers and Acquisitions on the Efficiency and Profitability of EC Credit Institutions, *Journal of Banking and Finance* 20(9), 1531–1558.

Vander Vennet, R. (1998). Causes and Consequences of EU Bank Takeovers. In: S. Eijffinger, K. Koedijk, M. Pagano, and R. Portes (Eds.), *The Changing European Landscape*, 45–61. Brussels: Centre for Economic Policy Research.

Wheelock, D. C. and Wilson, P. W. (2000). Why Do Banks Disappear? The Determinants of US Bank Failures and Acquisitions, *Review of Economics and Statistics* 82(1), 127–138.

Williams, B. (1997). Positive Theories of Multinational Banking: Eclectic Theory versus Internalisation Theory, *Journal of Economic Surveys* 11, 71–100.

Winton, A. (1999). Don't Put All Your Eggs in One Basket? Diversification and Specialization in Lending. University of Minnesota Working Paper.

CHAPTER 32

REVISITING THE STATE'S ROLE IN FINANCE AND DEVELOPMENT*

ASLI DEMIRGÜÇ-KUNT AND MARTIN ČIHÁK

Abstract:
Financial systems underpin economic development. This chapter reviews the role of the state in finance and economic development, based on evidence from both before and during the global financial crisis. The crisis has given greater credence to the idea that active state involvement in the financial sector can help maintain economic stability, drive growth, and create jobs. There is evidence that some interventions may have had an impact in the short run. But there is also strong evidence on longer-term negative effects. This suggests a need to adjust the role of the state from direct interventions to less direct involvement. But the state still has a very important role, especially in supervision, competition, and financial infrastructure. The challenge of financial sector policies is to better align private incentives with public interest without taxing or subsidizing private risk-taking.

Keywords:
financial systems, economic development, state role, state-owned banks, financial supervision, competition policy, financial infrastructure

32.1 INTRODUCTION

ECONOMISTS hold very different views on the role of the financial sector in economic development. One group believes that the operation of the financial sector merely responds to

* The authors are grateful to Meghana Ayyagari, Thorsten Beck, Bob Cull, Patrick Honohan, Vojislav Maksimovic, and Sole Martinez for helpful comments on an earlier version of this text. This chapter's findings, interpretations, and conclusions are entirely those of the authors and do not necessarily represent the views of the World Bank, its Executive Directors, or the countries they represent. They also do not necessarily represent those of the International Monetary Fund (IMF) or IMF policy.

economic development, adjusting to changing demands from the real sector (Robinson, 1952; and Lucas, 1988). Other researchers believe that financial systems play a crucial role in alleviating market frictions and hence influencing savings rates, investment decisions, technological innovation, and therefore long-run growth rates (Schumpeter, 1912; Gurley and Shaw, 1955; Goldsmith, 1969; McKinnon, 1973; and Miller, 1998).[1]

The recent global financial crisis has moved the potentially disastrous consequences of weak financial sector policies back into the forefront of policy debate. At its best, finance works quietly in the background, contributing to growth and poverty reduction; but when things go wrong, financial sector failures are painfully visible. Both success and failure have their origins largely in the policy environment; hence, getting the important policy decisions right has always been and continues to be one of the central development challenges.

Despite their inherent fragility, financial institutions underpin economic prosperity. Financial markets and institutions arise to mitigate the effects of information and transaction costs that prevent direct pooling and investment of society's savings. While some theoretical models stress the importance of the different institutional forms financial systems can take, more important are the underlying functions that these systems perform (Levine, 1997; Levine, 2000; and Merton and Bodie, 2004). Financial systems help to mobilize and pool savings, provide payments services that facilitate the exchange of goods and services, produce and process information about investors and investment projects to enable efficient allocation of funds, monitor investments and exert corporate governance after these funds are allocated, and help diversify, transform, and manage risk.

While still far from being conclusive, the bulk of the empirical literature on finance and development suggests that well-developed financial systems play an independent and causal role in promoting long-run economic growth. More recent evidence also points to the role of the sector in facilitating disproportionately rapid growth in the incomes of the poor, suggesting that financial development helps the poor catch up with the rest of the economy as it grows. These research findings have been instrumental in persuading developing countries to sharpen their policy focus on the financial sector. If finance is important for development, why do some countries have growth-promoting financial systems while others do not? And, importantly, what can a state do to develop the national financial system?[2]

This chapter addresses these questions. Section 32.2 reviews the extensive empirical literature on finance and economic development and summarizes the main findings. Section 32.3 discusses the state's role in building effective and inclusive financial systems. Section 32.4 concludes with a discussion of the implications of the global financial crisis on financial sector policies going forward.

---

[1] Two well-known quotes by Robinson and Schumpeter illustrate these different views. Joan Robinson (1952) argued: "Where enterprise leads finance follows," whereas Joseph Schumpeter (1950) observed: "The banker, therefore, is not so much primarily a middleman... He authorizes people in the name of society... (to innovate)."

[2] The state is defined here as including not only the government but also other public sector agencies, such as the central bank, the prudential regulatory agency, and the competition agency.

32.2 FINANCE AND ECONOMIC DEVELOPMENT: EVIDENCE

An ever-expanding body of evidence suggests that countries with better developed financial systems experience faster economic growth (Levine, 1997; and Levine, 2005). Recent evidence also suggests that financial development not only promotes growth, but also improves the distribution of income. This section provides a review of the literature and its findings, discussing also the main criticisms.

32.2.1 Finance and Growth

A significant part of the differences in long-run economic growth across countries can be explained by differences in financial development (King and Levine, 1993; and Levine and Zervos, 1998). The finding that better-developed banks and markets are associated with faster growth is confirmed by panel and time series estimation techniques (Levine, Loayza, and Beck, 2000; Christopoulos and Tsionas, 2004; and Rousseau and Sylla, 1999). This research also indicates that financial sector development helps economic growth through more-efficient resource allocation and productivity growth rather than through the scale of investment or savings mobilization (Beck, Levine, and Loayza, 2000; Levine, Loayza, and Beck, 2000). Furthermore, cross-country time series studies also show that financial liberalization boosts economic growth by improving allocation of resources and the investment rate (Bekaert, Harvey, and Lundblad, 2005).

Nonetheless, addressing *identification issues* is difficult with aggregate data. Problems include heterogeneity of effects across countries, measurement errors, omitting relevant explanatory variables, and endogeneity, all of which tend to bias the estimated effect of the included variables. Although the studies cited above have made plausible efforts to deal with these concerns relying on instruments and making use of dynamic panel estimation methodologies, questions still remain. Hence, researchers used micro data and tried to exploit firm-level and sectoral differences. These studies address causality issues by trying to identify firms or sectors that are more likely to suffer from limited access to finance and see how the growth of these firms and sectors is affected in countries with differing levels of financial development. Demirgüç-Kunt and Maksimovic (1998) and Rajan and Zingales (1998) are two early examples of this approach.

Both studies start by observing that if financial underdevelopment prevents firms (or industries) from investing in profitable growth opportunities, it will not constrain all firms (or industries) equally. Firms that can finance themselves from retained earnings, or industries that technologically depend less on external finance will be minimally affected, whereas firms or industries whose financing needs exceed their internal resources may be severely constrained. Looking for evidence of a specific mechanism by which finance affects growth—that is, ability to raise external finance—allows both papers to provide a stronger test of causality.

Specifically, Demirgüç-Kunt and Maksimovic (1998) use firm-level data from 8,500 large firms in 30 countries and a financial planning model to predict how fast those firms would have grown if they had no access to external finance. They find that in each country the proportion of firms that grew faster than this rate was higher, the higher the country's financial development and quality of legal enforcement.

Rajan and Zingales (1998) instead use industry-level data across 36 sectors and 41 countries, showing that industries that are naturally heavy users of external finance benefit disproportionately more from greater financial development compared with other industries. Natural use of external finance is measured by the finance-intensity of US industries since the US financial system is relatively free of frictions, so each industry's use of external finance in the US is assumed to be a good proxy for its demand.

The additional information obtained by working with cross-country firm or industry-level data may not be adequate to satisfy the skeptics, however. For example, although the measure of external financing employed by Demirgüç-Kunt and Maksimovic does not require the assumption that external capital requirements in each industry are the same across countries as that of Rajan and Zingales, it is also more endogenous since it relies on firm characteristics. And although Rajan and Zingales' analysis looks at within-country, between-industry differences and is therefore less subject to criticism due to omitted variables, the main underlying assumption that industry external dependence is determined by technological differences may not be accurate. After all, two firms with the same capital-intensive technology may have very different financing needs, since their ability to generate internal cash flow would depend on the market power they have or the demand they face. Moreover, the level of competition faced by the firm may itself depend on the development of the financial system, introducing more endogeneity.

Beck et al. (2006) use Rajan and Zingales' (1998) approach to highlight a distributional effect. They find that industries that are naturally composed of small firms grow faster in financially developed economies, a result that provides additional evidence that financial development disproportionately promotes the growth of smaller firms. Beck, Demirgüç-Kunt, and Maksimovic (2008) also highlight the size effect, but using firm-survey data: they show that financial development eases the obstacles that firms face to growing faster, and that this effect is stronger particularly for smaller firms. More recent survey evidence also suggests that access to finance is associated with faster rates of innovation and firm dynamism consistent with the cross-country finding that finance promotes growth through productivity increases (Ayyagari et al., 2011).

Dropping the cross-country dimension and focusing on an individual country often increases the confidence in the results by reducing potential biases due to measurement error and reducing concerns about omitted variables and endogeneity. In a study of individual regions of Italy, Guiso et al. (2004) use a household dataset and examine the effect of differences in local financial development on economic activity across different regions. They find that local financial development enhances the probability that an individual starts a business, increases industrial competition, and promotes growth of firms. And these results are stronger for smaller firms which cannot easily raise funds outside the local area. Another example is Haber's (1997) historical comparison of industrial and capital-market development in Brazil, Mexico, and the US between 1830 and 1930. Haber uses firm-level data to illustrate that international differences in financial development significantly affected the rate of industrial expansion.

Perhaps one of the cleanest ways of dealing with identification problems is to focus on a particular policy change in a specific country and evaluate its impact. One example of this approach is Jayaratne and Strahan's (1996) investigation of the impact of bank branch reform in individual states of the US. Since the early 1970s, US states started relaxing impediments on their intrastate branching. Using a difference-in-difference methodology, Jayaratne and

Strahan estimate the change in economic growth rates after branch reform relative to a control group of states that did not reform. They show that bank branch reform boosted bank lending quality and accelerated real per capita growth rates. In another study, Bertrand et al. (2007) provide firm-level evidence from France that shows the impact of 1985 deregulation eliminating government intervention in bank lending decisions fostered greater competition in the credit market, inducing an increase in allocative efficiency across firms. Of course, focusing on individual country cases often raises the question how applicable the results are in different country settings. Nevertheless, these careful country-level analyses boost our confidence in the link between financial development and growth that is suggested by the cross-country studies.

Unfortunately, many potential causal factors of development interest do not vary much within a country, and exogenous policy changes do not occur often enough. For example, besides debates concerning the role of finance in economic development, economists have for a long time debated the relative importance of bank-based and market-based financial systems (Goldsmith, 1969; Boot and Thakor, 1997; Allen and Gale, 2000; and Demirgüç-Kunt and Levine, 2001). Research findings in this area have established that the debate matters much less than was previously thought, and that it is the financial services themselves that matter more than the form of their delivery. Financial structure *does* change during development, with financial systems becoming more market-based as the countries develop (Demirgüç-Kunt and Levine, 1996). But, controlling for overall financial development, differences in financial structure per se do not help explain growth rates. Nevertheless, these studies do not necessarily imply that institutional structure is unimportant for growth, rather that there is not one optimal institutional structure suitable for all countries at all times. A growth-promoting mixture of markets and intermediaries is likely to be determined by the legal, regulatory, political, policy and other factors that have not been adequately incorporated into the analysis or the indicators used in the literature may not sufficiently capture the comparative roles of banks and markets.

Financial development has also been shown to play an important role in dampening the impact of external shocks on the domestic economy (Beck, Lundberg, and Majnoni, 2006; and Raddatz, 2006), although financial crises do occur in developed and developing countries alike (Demirgüç-Kunt and Detragiache, 1998; Demirgüç-Kunt and Detragiache, 1999; and Kaminsky and Reinhart, 1999). Indeed, deeper financial systems without the necessary institutional development has been shown to lead to a poor handling or even magnification of risk rather than its mitigation. For example, when banking systems grow too quickly, booms are inevitably followed by busts, in which case size and depth may actually reflect policy distortions rather than development, as in numerous country case studies discussed in Demirgüç-Kunt and Detragiache (2005).

Besides issues of identification, problems associated with *measurement* and *non-linearities* also plague the literature. For example, below a certain level of development, small differences in financial development do not seem to help growth (Rioja and Valev, 2004). Distinguishing between the short-run and long-run effects of financial development is also important. Loayza and Rancière (2006) estimate both effects using a pooled mean-group estimator. While they confirm a positive long-run effect, they also identify a negative short-run effect, where short-term surges in bank lending can actually signal the onset of financial crisis as discussed above. Further, financial development may boost income and allow developing countries to catch up, but not lead to an increase in the long-run growth rate. Aghion et al. (2005) develop a model that predicts that low-income countries with low financial development will continue to fall behind the rest, whereas those reaching the higher level of financial development will converge. Their empirical results confirm that financial development helps an economy converge faster, but that there is no effect on steady-state growth.

32.2.2 Finance, Income Distribution, and Poverty

If finance promotes growth, over the long term financial development should also help to reduce poverty by lifting the welfare of most households. But do poor households benefit proportionately from financial development? Could there be a widening of income inequalities with the deepening of financial systems? And how important is direct access to financial services in this process?

Theory provides conflicting predictions in this area.[3] Some theories argue that financial development should have a disproportionately beneficial impact on the poor since informational asymmetries produce credit constraints that are particularly binding on the poor. Poor people find it particularly difficult to become entrepreneurs and fund their own investments, or invest in their education internally or externally since they lack resources, collateral, and political connections to access finance (see, e.g., Banerjee and Newman, 1993; Galor and Zeira, 1993; and Aghion and Bolton, 1997). More generally, some political economy theories also suggest that better-functioning financial systems make financial services available to a wider segment of the population, rather than restricting them to politically connected incumbents (Rajan and Zingales, 2003; and Morck et al., 2005). Yet others argue that financial access, especially to credit, only benefits the rich and the connected, particularly at early stages of economic development, and therefore, while financial development may promote growth, its impact on income distribution is not clear (Lamoreaux, 1994; and Haber, 2005).

Finally, if access to credit improves with aggregate economic growth and more people can afford to join the formal financial system, the relationship between financial development and income distribution may be non-linear, with adverse effects at early stages, but a positive impact after a certain point (Greenwood and Jovanovic, 1990). Hence, at the outset, expanding access to finance may actually increase inequality, as new entrepreneurs who manage to finance their investments will experience a surge in their incomes. Only after labor and product market effects start becoming significant, increasing employment opportunities and wages of the poor, we would see a reduction in income inequality. This is, indeed, what Gine and Townsend (2004) find when they build a general equilibrium model of Thai growth and use household data over the 1976–1996 period to estimate some of the model's parameters and calibrate others. Their simulations suggest net welfare benefits of financial development to be substantial, though they are initially disproportionately concentrated on a small group of talented, low-income individuals who were unable to become entrepreneurs without access to credit. But, eventually, the greatest impact of financial deepening on income inequality and poverty comes through indirect effects, as more people enter the labor market and the wages increase. Although these calibrated theoretical models illuminate important aspects of the financial development process, their results need to be interpreted with care since, despite their complexity, it is very difficult to model all relevant aspects of the growth and inequality processes.

There is also considerable empirical work on the impact of access to finance on the poor from the microfinance literature (see Armendariz de Aghion and Morduch, 2005). Although

---

[3] See Demirgüç-Kunt and Levine (2007) for an extensive review of the theoretical literature in this area.

success stories of microfinance are well documented in the practitioner literature, a rigorous evaluation requires careful distinction between those changes that can clearly be attributed to financial access from those that might have happened anyway or are due to other changes in the environment in which microfinance clients operate. In other words, identification issues again complicate the analysis. The debate surrounding the most famous microfinance institution, Bangladesh's Grameen Bank, illustrates how difficult this task has been. While Pitt and Khandker (1998) found a significant effect of use of finance on household welfare, more careful analyses and greater attention to identification issues by Morduch (1998) and Khandker (2003) found insignificant or much smaller effects. There is quite a bit of ongoing research in this area, and research using randomized experiments to address identification issues will probably shed more light on the issue of impact (World Bank, 2007). However, it is fair to say that, at present, the large body of empirical research evidence on the benefits of microfinance is not conclusive (Cull, Demirgüç-Kunt, and Morduch, 2008).

But to evaluate the impact of finance on poverty and income distribution one needs to look beyond the direct impact on the households, since the theoretical models discussed above suggest the spillover effects of financial development through labor and product markets are likely to be significant. Given that these effects cannot be analyzed through micro studies, a more macro approach helps to complete the picture.

For example, in cross-country regressions, Beck, Demirgüç-Kunt, and Levine (2007) investigate the relationship between financial depth and changes in both income distribution and absolute poverty. Looking at the 1960–2005 period, they find that not only does a deeper financial system accelerate national growth but it is associated with a faster increase in the income share of the poorest group. They also find a negative relationship between financial development and the growth rate of the Gini coefficient, suggesting that finance reduces income inequality.[4] These findings are not only robust to controlling for other country characteristics associated with economic growth and changes in income inequality, but the authors make an attempt to control for potential reverse causality using instrumental variables, as well as using panel techniques that control for omitted variable and endogeneity bias.

Although they are able to capture spillover effects, these results obtained in cross-country regressions are subject to caveats given the difficulty of resolving identification issues as discussed above. But, these results are also consistent with the findings of the general equilibrium models which suggest that, in the long run, financial development is associated with reductions in income inequality.

If financial development promotes growth and improves income inequality, it should also reduce poverty. Beck, Demirgüç-Kunt, and Levine (2007) also estimate the change in the share of each country's population below international poverty lines resulting from financial deepening. Again, they find a positive effect of finance on poverty reduction. Countries with higher levels of financial development experience faster reductions in the share of population living on less than a dollar a day over the 1980s and 1990s. Investigating levels rather than growth rates, Honohan (2004) also shows that even at the same average income, economies with deeper financial systems have fewer poor people.

As in the case of finance and growth literature, here, too, further evidence comes from case studies that investigate the impact of specific policy changes better to deal with identification issues. Following the Jayaratne and Strahan (1996) approach discussed above, Beck,

---

[4] Examining levels, rather than growth rates, Clarke, Xu, and Zhou (2003) provide further evidence that financial development is associated with lower levels of inequality.

Levine, and Levkov (2007) exploit the same policy change to assess the effect of US branch deregulation, this time on income inequality. They find that states see their Gini coefficient decrease by a small but statistically significant amount in the years after deregulation relative to other states, and relative to before the deregulation. They also find that the main decrease on income inequality comes not from enhancing entrepreneurship, but rather through indirect effects of higher labor demand and higher wages.

Another study looks at the branching restrictions policy imposed by the Indian government between 1977 and 1990, which allowed new branching in a district that already had bank presence, only if the bank opened four branches in districts without bank presence. This led to the opening of 30,000 new rural branches over this period. Burgess and Pande (2005) find that this branch expansion during the policy period accounted for 60% of rural poverty reduction, largely through an increase in non-agricultural activities and especially through an increase in unregistered or informal manufacturing activities. Although the poverty impact is striking, there were also large losses incurred by the banks due to subsidized interest rates and high loan losses, suggesting significant long-term costs.

Although a large body of evidence suggests that financial development reduces income inequality and poverty, the channels through which this effect operates are still not fully understood. For example, how important is direct provision of finance to the poor? Is it more important to improve the functioning of the financial system so that it expands access to existing firms and households or it is more important to broaden access to the underserved (including the non-poor who are often excluded in many developing countries)? Of course, efficiency and access dimensions of finance are also likely to be linked; in many countries improving efficiency would have to entail broader access beyond concentrated incumbents. Much more empirical research using micro datasets and different methodologies will be necessary to better understand the mechanisms through which finance affects income distribution and poverty.

Qualifications and caveats notwithstanding, taken as a whole, the empirical evidence reviewed in this section suggests that countries with better-developed financial systems grow faster and that this growth disproportionately benefits the poorer segments of the society. Hence, for policymakers, making financial development a priority makes good sense. Yet financial system development differs widely across countries. What makes some countries develop growth-promoting financial systems, while others cannot? If finance is crucial for economic development, what can governments do to ensure well-functioning financial systems? These questions are examined in the next section.

32.3 POLICY CHOICES IN FINANCE: THE STATE'S ROLE IN MAKING FINANCE WORK

The global financial crisis has prompted many people to reassess state interventions in financial systems, from regulation and supervision of financial institutions and markets, to competition policy, to state guarantees and state ownership of banks, and to enhancements in financial infrastructure. But the crisis does not necessarily negate the considerable body of evidence accumulated over the past few decades. It is important to use the crisis experience to examine what went wrong and how to fix it. Which lessons about the connections between finance and economic development should shape policies in coming decades?

There are sound economic reasons for the state to play an active role in financial systems, but there are also practical reasons to be wary of the state playing too active a role in financial systems. The tensions between these two sets of reasons highlight the complexity of financial policies. Though economics advertises the social welfare advantages of certain state interventions, practical experience suggests that the state often does not intervene successfully. Furthermore, since economies and the state's capacity differ across countries and over time, the appropriate involvement of the state in the financial system also varies case by case. Nonetheless, with appropriate caution, it is possible to tease out broad lessons for policymakers from a variety of experiences and analyses.

32.3.1 Political and Macroeconomic Environment

Even if historical factors are favorable to financial development, political turmoil may lead to macroeconomic instability and deterioration in business conditions.[5] Civil strife and war destroys capital and infrastructure, and expropriations may follow military takeovers. Corruption and crime thrive in such environments, increasing cost of doing business and creating uncertainty about property rights. Detragiache, Gupta, and Tressel (2005) show that for low-income countries political instability and corruption have a detrimental effect on financial development.

Given a stable political system, well-functioning financial systems also require fiscal discipline and stable macroeconomic policies on the part of governments. Monetary and fiscal policies affect the taxation of financial intermediaries and provision of financial services (Bencivenga and Smith, 1992; and Roubini and Salai-Martin, 1995). Often, large financing requirements of governments crowd out private investment by increasing the required returns on government securities and absorbing the bulk of the savings mobilized by the financial system. Bank profitability does not necessarily suffer given the high yields on these securities, but the ability of the financial system to allocate resources efficiently is severely curtailed. Empirical studies have also shown that countries with lower and more-stable inflation rates experience higher levels of banking and stock market development (Boyd, Levine, and Smith, 2001) and high inflation and real interest rates are associated with higher probability of systemic banking crises (Demirgüç-Kunt and Detragiache, 1998; and Demirgüç-Kunt and Detragiache, 2005).

32.3.2 Legal and Information Infrastructure

Financial systems require developed legal and information infrastructures to function well. Firms' ability to raise external finance in the formal financial system is quite limited if the

---

[5] There is also a large literature that discusses the historical determinants of financial development—such as legal origin, religion and culture, ethnic diversity, and initial geographic endowments. See Ayyagari, Demirgüç-Kunt, and Maksimovic (2008b, 2013) for a discussion and evaluation of these theories.

rights of outside investors are not protected. Outside investors are reluctant to invest in companies if they will not be able to exert corporate governance and protect their investment from controlling shareholders/owners or the management of the companies. Thus, protection of property rights and effective enforcement of contracts are critical elements in financial system development.

The global financial crisis has highlighted the importance of a resilient financial infrastructure for financial stability. It also has led to a discussion about the role of the state, particularly in promoting the provision of high-quality credit information and in ensuring stable systems for large-value financial transactions.

Transparent exchange of credit information reduces information asymmetries between borrowers and lenders and is an essential requisite of a well-functioning credit market. However, the financial crisis has shown that there is much room for improvement in this area, especially in the use of existing credit reporting systems for prudential oversight and regulation.

Evidence shows that it is easier for firms to access external finance in countries where legal enforcement is stronger (La Porta et al., 1997; Demirgüç-Kunt and Maksimovic, 1998; and Beck, Demirgüç-Kunt, and Maksimovic, 2005), and that better creditor protection increases credit to the private sector (Djankov, McLiesh, and Shleifer, 2007). More effective legal systems allow more flexible and adaptable conflict resolution, increasing firms' access to finance (Djankov et al., 2007; and Beck, Demirgüç-Kunt, and Levine, 2005). In countries where legal systems are more effective, financial systems have lower interest rate spreads and are more efficient (Demirgüç-Kunt, Laeven, and Levine, 2004).

Timely availability of good quality information is equally important, since this helps reduce information asymmetries between borrowers and lenders. The collection, processing, and use of borrowing history and other information relevant to household and small business lending—credit registries—have been rapidly growing in both the public and private sectors (see Miller, 2003, for an overview). Computer technology has greatly improved the amount of information that can be analyzed (for example, by credit scoring techniques) to assess creditworthiness. Governments can play an important role in this process, and while establishment of public credit registries may discourage private entry, in several cases it has actually encouraged private registries to enter in order to provide a wider and deeper range of services. Governments are also important in creating and supporting the legal system needed for conflict resolution and contract enforcement, and strengthening accounting infrastructures to enable financial development.

The volume of bank credit is significantly higher in countries with more information sharing (Jappelli and Pagano, 2002; and Djankov, McLiesh, and Shleifer, 2007). Furthermore, firms report lower financing obstacles with better credit information (Love and Mylenko, 2004). Detragiache, Gupta, and Tressel (2005) find that better access to information and speedier enforcement of contracts are associated with deeper financial systems even in low-income countries. Indeed, compared with high-income countries, in lower-income countries it is credit information more than legal enforcement that matters (Djankov, McLiesh, and Shleifer, 2007).

Information sharing in credit markets acts as a public good that improves credit market efficiency, access to finance, and financial stability. Nonetheless, for an individual commercial bank, proprietary credit information is valuable, so it has incentives to collect the information and keep it away from others. Information sharing among private lenders thus may not arise naturally, especially where banking systems are concentrated (Bruhn, Farazi, and Kanz, 2013). This creates an important rationale for state involvement. In addition, information sharing in credit markets has increasing returns to scale: the benefits of credit reporting for financial access and stability are greatest when participation is as wide as possible and includes banks as well as non-bank financial institutions. Therefore, another important role for the state is to create a level playing field for the provision and exchange of credit information, and to facilitate the inclusion of nonregulated lenders into existing credit reporting systems. In many emerging markets, such as China and South Africa, major initiatives are underway to integrate the rapidly growing microfinance and consumer loan markets into the existing credit reporting infrastructure.

32.3.3 Regulation and Supervision

The global financial crisis that intensified with the collapse of Lehman Brothers in September 2008 presented a major test of the international architecture developed over many years to safeguard the stability of the global financial system. Although the causes of the crisis are still being debated, there is agreement that the crisis revealed major shortcomings in market discipline as well as regulation and supervision (Demirgüç-Kunt and Servén 2009; Caprio, Demirgüç-Kunt, and Kane, 2010). The financial crisis has reopened important policy debates on financial regulation.

Regulation and supervision represent one area in which the important role of the state is not in dispute. For as long as there have been banks, there have also been governments regulating them. The crucial role of the state is acknowledged by virtually all involved in global finance and policy and is well established in the economic and financial literature. Hence, the debate is not about whether the state should regulate and supervise the financial sector, but about how best to go about ensuring that regulation and supervision supports sound financial development. While most economists agree that there is a role for the state in the regulation and supervision of financial systems, the extent of this involvement is an issue of active debate (Barth, Caprio, and Levine, 2006). One extreme view is the laissez-faire or invisible-hand approach, where there is no role for the state in the financial system, and markets are expected to monitor and discipline financial institutions. This approach has been criticized for ignoring market failures, as depositors, particularly small depositors, often find it too costly to be effective monitors.

At the other extreme is the complete interventionist approach, where the state's regulation is seen as the solution to market failures (Stigler, 1971). According to this view, powerful supervisors are expected to ensure stability of the financial system and guide banks in their business decisions through regulation and supervision. To the extent that officials generally have limited knowledge and expertise in making business decisions and can be subject to political and regulatory capture, this approach may not be effective (Becker and Stigler, 1974; and Haber, Maurer, and Razo, 2003).

Between the two extremes lies the private empowerment view of financial regulation. This view simultaneously recognizes the potential importance of market failures which motivate state intervention, and political/regulatory failures, which suggest that supervisory agencies do not necessarily have incentives to ease market failures. The focus is on enabling markets, where there is an important role for states in enhancing the ability and incentives of private agents to overcome information and transaction costs, so that private investors can exert effective governance over banks. Consequently, the private empowerment view seeks to provide supervisors with the responsibility and authority to induce banks to disclose accurate information to the public, so that private agents can more effectively monitor banks (Barth, Caprio, and Levine, 2006).

Empirical evidence overwhelmingly supports the private empowerment view. While there is little evidence that empowering regulators enhances bank stability, there is evidence that regulations and supervisory practices that force accurate information disclosure and promote private sector monitoring boost the overall level of banking sector and stock market development (Barth, Caprio, and Levine, 2006).

Beck, Demirgüç-Kunt, and Levine (2006) show that bank supervisory practices that force accurate information disclosure ease external financing constraints of firms, while countries that empower their official supervisors actually make external financing constraints more severe by increasing the degree of corruption in bank lending. Consistent with these findings, Demirgüç-Kunt, Detragiache, and Tressel (2008) investigate compliance with Basel Core Principles of regulation and supervision and show that only information disclosure rules have a significant impact on bank soundness. Finally, Detragiache, Gupta, and Tressel (2005) find little significant impact of regulatory and supervisory practices on financial development of low-income countries. Where there is significance, greater supervisory powers seem to be negatively associated with financial depth.

To find out what works in financial regulation and what does not, much can be learned from a recently updated World Bank survey of regulation and supervision around the world. This is the fourth round of the survey, and the first one that provides comprehensive information on the state of banking regulation and supervision after the onset of the crisis. Juxtaposing the findings from this survey with a dataset on banking sector performance during the crisis shows that countries that were directly hit by the global financial crisis had weaker regulation and supervisory practices compared with the rest. Specifically, they had less stringent definitions of capital, less stringent provisioning requirements, and greater reliance on banks' own risk assessment. Moreover, while the quality of publicly available financial information was roughly comparable in crisis and non-crisis countries, the former were characterized by much less scope for incentives to actually use that information and monitor financial institutions (for example, they had more generous deposit insurance coverage). These findings are confirmed also by more in-depth statistical analysis (Čihák et al., 2012).

Tracking changes during the crisis (and comparing the latest bank regulation survey with the pre-crisis surveys) confirms that countries have stepped up efforts in the area of macroprudential policy, as well as on issues such as resolution regimes and consumer protection. However, it is not clear whether incentives for market discipline have improved. Some elements of disclosure and quality of information have improved, but deposit insurance coverage has increased during the crisis. This increased coverage, together with other aspects—such as generous support for weak banks—did not improve incentives for monitoring. The survey suggests that there is further scope for improving disclosures and monitoring incentives (Čihák et al., 2012).

Despite the progress made on regulatory reform, there are still important areas of disagreement and discussion. Hence, there are numerous reform proposals that call for further reform. One area of criticism relates to greater emphasis on simplicity and transparency. This criticism warns against the trend toward growing complexity of regulation, which may reduce transparency and accountability, increase regulatory arbitrage opportunities, and significantly strain regulatory resources and capacity.

In implementing supervisory best practices, emerging markets and developing economies should focus on establishing a basic robust supervisory framework that reflects local financial systems' characteristics, and refrain from incorporating unnecessary (and in several cases inapplicable) complex elements. For example, the complicated rules and procedures for determining bank capital adequacy under the advanced forms of the Basel rules presuppose expertise and governance conditions which simply do not exist in most low-income countries. Caprio, Demirgüç-Kunt, and Kane (2010) point out the flaws in the Basel approached exposed by the recent financial crisis, and argue that true reform of regulation and supervision must go beyond improving transparency but address incentive conflicts and increase accountability in government and industry alike.

Following up on these reasons, several proposals suggest regulatory approaches that are more focused on proactively identifying and addressing incentive problems and making regulations incentive-compatible to end the continuous need to eliminate deficiencies and close loopholes that are inevitably present in ever more complex sets of regulations. In particular, Čihák, Demirgüç-Kunt, and Johnston (2013) propose "incentive audits" as a tool that could help in pinpointing incentive misalignments in the financial sector and identifying reforms that are incentive-robust (as discussed also by Calomiris, 2011). Other proposals address the incentives that the regulators face and propose adjustments in the institutional structures for regulation and supervision (Barth, Caprio, and Levine, 2001; Masciandaro, Pansini, and Quintyn, 2011).

Research has also questioned safety net design, particularly adoption of deposit insurance in developing countries by highlighting the potential costs of explicit schemes-lower market discipline, higher financial fragility, and lower financial development—in countries where complementary institutions are not strong enough to keep these costs under control (Demirgüç-Kunt and Kane, 2002; Demirgüç-Kunt and Detragiache, 2002; Demirgüç-Kunt and Huizinga, 2004; and Cull, Senbet, and Sorge, 2005). These findings are particularly important for lower-income countries with underdeveloped institutions. For example, Detragiache, Gupta, and Tressel (2005) also find that presence of an explicit deposit insurance system does not lead to more deposit mobilization in low-income countries; to the contrary, it is associated with lower levels of deposits. Demirgüç-Kunt, Kane, and Laeven (2008) summarize the cross-country evidence on the impact of deposit insurance.

Overall, there is broad agreement that it is important to address the "basics" first (; Rajan, 2010; Squam Lake Group, 2010; World Bank, 2012). That means having in place a coherent institutional and legal framework that establishes market discipline complemented by strong, timely, and anticipatory supervisory action. In many developing economies, this also means that building up supervisory capacity needs to be a top priority. Among the important lessons of the global financial crisis are renewed focus on systemic risk and the need to pay greater attention to incentives in the design of regulation and supervision.

32.3.4 Contestability and Efficiency

Policymakers around the world frequently express concern about whether their countries' bank competition policies are appropriately designed to produce well-functioning and stable banks. Globalization and the resulting consolidation in banking have further spurred interest in this issue, leading to an active public policy debate. Competition policies in banking may involve difficult tradeoffs. While greater competition may enhance the efficiency of banks with positive implications for economic growth, greater competition may also destabilize banks with costly repercussions for the economy.

Recent research has shown that contrary to conventional wisdom, the tradeoffs are exaggerated when it comes to bank competition. Greater competition—as captured by lower entry barriers, fewer regulatory restrictions on bank activities, greater banking freedom, and better overall institutional development—is good for efficiency, good for stability, and good for firms' access to finance (Berger et al., 2004). Indeed, regulations that interfere with competition make banks less efficient, more fragile, and reduce firms' access to finance. Thus, it seems to be a good idea for the state to encourage competition in banking by reducing the unnecessary impediments to entry and activity restrictions. Similarly, improving the institutional environment and allowing greater freedoms in banking and economy in general would lead to desirable outcomes.

The global financial crisis also reignited the interest of policymakers and academics in assessing the impact of bank competition and rethinking the role of the state in shaping competition policies. While the benefits of bank competition for efficiency and for access to finance are relatively well established, the relationship between competition and stability has been subject to active debate (Claessens and Klingebiel, 2001; Allen and Gale, 2004; Claessens, 2009; Casu and Girardone, 2009; Schaeck, Čihák, and Wolfe, 2009; Hakenes and Schnabel, 2010; Gropp, Hakenes, and Schnabel, 2011; Vives, 2011; and Delis, 2012). The debate has intensified with the crisis. While some believe that increasing financial innovation and competition in certain markets, such as subprime mortgage lending, contributed to the global financial turmoil, and are calling for policies to restrict competition. Others worry that, as a result of the crisis and the actions of governments in support of the largest banks, concentration in banking increased, reducing the competitiveness of the sector and access to finance, and potentially also contributing to future instability as a result of moral hazard problems associated with "too-big-to-fail" institutions. The design of competition policy is challenging because it involves a possible tradeoff between efficiency and growth on one hand and stability concerns on the other hand. Another reason why it is important to rethink competition policies is the changing mandate of central banks and bank regulatory agencies: survey data reveal that the majority now have explicit responsibilities in the areas of competition policy (Čihák, et al., 2012).

Research suggests that bank competition brings about improvements in efficiency across banks and enhances access to financial services, without necessarily undermining systemic stability. A review of trends in average systemic risk and bank market power indicates that greater market power (that is, less competition) is associated with more systemic risk. This observation is confirmed also by more in-depth panel data analysis (Anginer, Demirgüç-Kunt, and Zhu, 2012). The evidence of a real tradeoff is thus weak, at best.

This analysis suggests that policies to address the causes of the recent crisis should not unduly restrict competition. The appropriate public policy is (1) to establish a regulatory framework that does not subsidize risk-taking through poorly designed exit policies and too-big-to-fail subsidies and (2) to remove barriers to entry of "fit and proper" bankers with well-capitalized financial institutions.

For competition to improve access to finance, the state has an important role to play in enabling a market-friendly informational and institutional environment. Policies that guarantee market contestability, timely flow of adequate credit information, and contract enforceability will enhance competition among banks and improve access. For instance, evidence across business line data in Brazil (Urdapilleta and Stephanou, 2009) shows that competition in the corporate segment is higher than that in the retail segment. This reflects the existence of a larger pool of credit providers and easier access to information for large corporations. Competition in the retail sector can be fostered by promoting portability of bank accounts, expanding credit information sharing, and increasing payment system interconnection.

Governments should also be aware that their direct interventions during crises—such as blanket guarantees, liquidity support, recapitalizations, and nationalizations—distort risk-taking incentives. For example, Calderon and Schaeck (2013), using data for banks in 124 countries, find that liquidity support, recapitalizations, and nationalizations reduce traditional proxies for competition, such as Lerner indices and net interest margins. However, this effect is problematic, because it coincides with an increased market share of economically unviable ("zombie") banks. State interventions during crises may thus constitute a barrier to exit that permits insolvent and inefficient banks to survive, while generating unhealthy competition.

32.3.5 Government Ownership of Financial Institutions

Policymakers in many countries have felt the need to retain public ownership of some banks. However, research suggests that government ownership of banks everywhere, and especially in developing countries, is associated with lower levels of financial development, more concentrated lending, lower economic growth, and greater systemic fragility (La Porta et al., 1997; Lopez-De-Silanes and Shleifer, 2002). The inefficient allocation of credit by state-owned banks to politically favored and commercially unviable projects frequently necessitates costly recapitalizations (Dinc, 2005; and Cole, 2009a). Evidence also suggests that bank customers face higher barriers to credit in banking systems which are predominantly government-owned (Beck, Demirgüç-Kunt, and Martínez Pería, 2008). Overall, a large body of empirical evidence suggests that the ownership of financial firms is an area where the public sector tends not to have a comparative advantage; such ownership weakens the financial system and the economy.

Nevertheless, privatization also entails risks and needs careful design. Studies of privatization processes suggest the preferred strategy is moving slowly but deliberately with bank privatization, while preparing state banks for sale and addressing weaknesses in the overall incentive environment. On average, bank privatization tends to improve performance over continued state ownership, there are advantages to full rather than partial privatizations, and in weak institutional environments selling to a strategic investor and inviting foreign interests to participate in the process increase the benefits (see Clarke, Cull, and Shirley, 2005, for an overview). Privatization, however, is not a panacea, and privatizing banks without addressing weaknesses in the underlying incentive environment and market structure will not lead to a deeper and more efficient financial system.

During the global financial crisis, countries pursued a variety of strategies to restart their financial and real sectors. As the balance sheets of private banks deteriorated and they curtailed their lending activities, many countries used state-owned banks to step up their financing to the private sector. Most countries relied heavily on the use of credit guarantee programs. Others adopted a number of unconventional monetary and fiscal measures to prop up credit markets.

Historically, many state-owned banks were created to fulfill long-term development roles by filling market gaps in long-term credit, infrastructure, and agriculture finance, and to promote access to finance to underserved segments of the economy—notably, small and medium enterprises. In practice, however, there is widespread evidence that state banks have generally been very inefficient in allocating credit, more often than not serving political interests. Nevertheless, the global financial crisis underscored the potential countercyclical role of state-owned banks in offsetting the contraction of credit from private banks, leading to arguments that this is an important function that can perhaps better justify their existence. Indeed, during the recent crisis, a number of major countries used their public bank infrastructure to prop up financial conditions (World Bank, 2012).

Hence, the crisis and the actions adopted by different countries reignited the age-old debate on whether there is a need for direct government intervention in the financial sector (Altunbas, Evans, and Molyneux, 2001; La Porta, López-de-Silanes, and Shleifer, 2002; Sapienza, 2004; Micco and Panizza, 2006; Micco, Panizza, and Yañez, 2007; Andrianova, Demetriades, and Shortland, 2008; Beck, 2008). Supporters of state-owned banks now argue that these financial institutions provide the state with an additional tool for crisis management and, relative to central banks, may be more capable of providing a safe haven for retail and interbank deposits, creating a fire break in contagion, and stabilizing aggregate credit. On the other hand, those opposing state bank ownership point out that agency problems and politically motivated lending render state-owned banks inefficient and prone to cronyism. Furthermore, past experiences of numerous countries suggest that cronyism in lending may build up large fiscal liabilities and threaten public sector solvency and financial stability, as well as misallocate resources and retard development in the long run.

A review of the historical and new research evidence suggests that lending by state-owned banks tends to be less procyclical than that of their private counterparts (Bertay, Demirgüç-Kunt, and Huizinga, 2012; Cull and Martínez Pería, 2012). During the global financial crisis, some state-owned banks have indeed played a countercyclical role by expanding their lending portfolio and restoring conditions in key markets. World Bank (2012) documents that the expansion of the lending portfolio of state-owned commercial banks (such as PKO Bank Polski in Poland) and state-owned development banks (such as BNDES in Brazil) did mitigate the effects from the global credit crunch and fill the gap of lower credit from the private sector. Also, Mexican development banks supported the credit channel through the extension of credit guarantees and lending to private financial intermediaries.

However, because in many cases lending growth continued even after economic recovery was under way, and loans were not directed to the most constrained borrowers, it is not clear that the recent crisis illustrates that state-owned banks can effectively play a countercyclical role. Furthermore, the evidence from previous crises on this issue is also mixed. Importantly, efforts to stabilize aggregate credit by state-owned banks may come at a cost: particularly through the deterioration of the quality of intermediation and resource misallocation. In other words, a temporary boom in state bank lending has long-term adverse effects by creating a portfolio of bad loans in crises that take a long time to sort out.

Ideally, focusing on the governance of these institutions may help policymakers address the inefficiencies associated with state-owned banks. They need to design a clear mandate, work to complement (rather than substitute for) the private banks, and adopt risk management practices that allow them to guarantee a financially sustainable business (Scott, 2007, Gutiérrez, et al. 2011). However, these governance reforms are particularly challenging in weak institutional environments, further emphasizing that the tradeoff is a serious one for policymakers.

Credit guarantee schemes have also been a popular intervention tool during the recent crisis. However, given their limited scale, they are used not to stabilize aggregate credit but to alleviate the impact of the credit crunch on segments that are most severely affected, such as small and medium enterprises. Unfortunately, rigorous evaluations of these schemes are very few, and existing studies suggest that the benefits of these programs tend to be rather modest, particularly in institutionally underdeveloped settings, and they tend to incur fiscal and economic costs. Nevertheless, best practices can be identified. These include leaving credit assessments and decision making to the private sector; capping coverage ratios and delaying the payout of the guarantee until recovery actions are taken by the lender so as to minimize moral hazard problems; having pricing guarantees that take into account the need for financial sustainability and risk minimization; and encouraging the use of risk management tools. Success again hinges on overcoming the challenges of getting the design right, particularly in underdeveloped institutional and legal settings.

32.3.6 Financial Liberalization, Financial Development, and the Sequencing of Reforms

Many countries have liberalized their financial systems in the 1980s and 1990s with mixed results. Liberalization, including deregulation of interest rates and more-relaxed entry policies, often led to significant financial development, particularly in countries where there was significant repression, but the enthusiasm with which financial liberalization was adopted in some countries in the absence of or slow implementation of institutional development also left many financial systems vulnerable to systemic crises (Demirgüç-Kunt and Detragiache, 1999). Poor sequencing of financial liberalization in a poorly prepared contractual and supervisory environment contributed to bank insolvencies as banks protected by implicit and explicit state guarantees aggressively took advantage of new opportunities to increase risk, without the necessary lending skills. Banking crises in Argentina, Chile, Mexico, and Turkey in the 1980s and 1990s have been attributed to these factors (Demirgüç-Kunt and Detragiache, 2005).

On the other hand, many Sub-Saharan African countries that have also liberalized their interest rates and credit allocation and privatized their institutions by allowing entry of reputable foreign banks did not suffer instability but from lower intermediation and in some cases lower access to financial services. Some of this was due to the absence of an effective contractual and informational framework (Honohan and Beck, 2007).

This has also resulted in claims of failed liberalizations in these countries and calls for greater state intervention in the financial sector. Both of these experiences with financial liberalization underline the importance of sequencing liberalization and institutional improvements.

32.3.7 Impact of Foreign Entry

With financial liberalization, more and more developing economies also allow entry of foreign financial institutions. While governments have worried about whether allowing foreign banks to take a large ownership share in the banking system could damage financial and economic performance, the bulk of the empirical research in this area, particularly drawing on the experience of Latin American and Eastern European countries, suggests that facilitating entry of reputable foreign institutions to the local market should be welcomed. Arrival or expansion of foreign banks can also be disruptive as the Indian experience shows evidence of cream-skimming by foreign banks (Gormley, 2004). Even there, however, in the years following entry, foreign banks have started expanding their clientele base. Overall, a large body of evidence suggests that over time foreign bank entry brings competition, improves efficiency, lifts the quality of the financial infrastructure, and expands access (Claessens, Demirgüç-Kunt, and Huizinga, 2001; and Clarke, Cull, and Martínez Pería, 2001).

However, as the African experience discussed above illustrates, foreign bank entry cannot guarantee rapid financial development in the absence of sound contractual and informational weaknesses. Such weaknesses can prevent low-income countries from reaping full benefits of opening their markets to foreign providers of financial services, and can potentially explain the finding that greater foreign bank penetration is associated with lower levels of financial development (Detragiache, Tressel, and Gupta, 2008). For example, while in some countries (such as Pakistan), foreign banks have been shown to lend less to smaller, more opaque borrowers, because they rely on hard information (Mian, 2006), evidence from Eastern Europe has shown that foreign banks eventually go down-market, increasing small business lending (De Haas and Naaborg, 2005). Overall, addressing institutional weaknesses is likely to allow foreign banks to act as an important catalyst for the sort of financial development that promotes growth.

32.3.8 Facilitating Access

Access to financial services has increasingly been receiving greater emphasis over the recent years, becoming a focal part of the overall development agenda. One reason is that modern development theory sees the lack of access to finance as a critical mechanism for generating persistent income inequality, as well as slower growth. Another is the observation that small enterprises and poor households face much greater obstacles in their ability to access finance all around the world, but particularly in developing countries.

What does access to finance mean? Broad access to financial services implies an absence of price and non-price barriers. It is difficult to define and measure because there are many dimensions of access, including availability, cost, and range and quality of services being offered. While there is much data on financial sector development more broadly, until recently there was very little data on usage and access to finance, for both households and firms. Hence, there is also very limited analysis on the impact of access to finance on economic development. Research using firm-level survey data suggests that financing obstacles are the most constraining among different barriers to growth (Ayyagari, Demirgüç-Kunt, and Maksimovic, 2008a). Financing obstacles are also found to be highest and most constraining for the growth of smaller firms (Beck, Demirgüç-Kunt, and Maksimovic, 2005). At the household level, lack of access to credit is shown to perpetuate poverty because poor households reduce their children's education (Jacoby and Skoufias, 1997). Similarly, Beegle, Dehejia, and Gatti (2007) show that transitory income shocks to greater increases in child labor in countries with poorly functioning financial systems. A better understanding of what the chief obstacles to improving access are will be possible with better data and analysis in this area (see World Bank, 2007 for a discussion). Some of the data obstacles have recently been removed with the release of the Global Findex, a major dataset capturing the use of financial services around the world (Demirgüç-Kunt and Klapper, 2012).

There are many different reasons why the poor do not have access to finance—loans, savings accounts, insurance services. Social and physical distance from the formal financial system may matter. The poor may not have anyone in their social network who knows the various services that are available to them. Lack of education may make it difficult for them to overcome problems with filling out loan applications, and the small number of transactions they are likely to undertake may make the loan officers think it is not worthwhile to help them. As financial institutions are likely to be in richer neighborhoods, physical distance may also matter: banks simply may not be near the poor. Specifically for access to credit services, there are two important problems. First, the poor have no collateral, and cannot borrow against their future income because they tend not to have steady jobs or income streams to keep track of. Second, dealing with small transactions is costly for the financial institutions. Ceilings on the rates financial institutions can charge backfire and limit access to the poor even more.

Microfinance—specialized institutions that serve the poor—tries to overcome these problems in innovative ways. Loan officers come from similar social status as the borrowers and go to the poor instead of waiting for the poor to come to them. Microcredit also involves education as much as it provides credit. Group lending schemes not only improve repayment incentives and monitoring through peer pressure, but they are also a way of building support networks and educating borrowers.

Has microfinance fulfilled its promise? Microfinance allows poor people to have more direct access, but development of microfinance around the world has been non-uniform, with significant penetration rates only in a few countries such as Bangladesh, Indonesia, and Thailand (Honohan, 2004). Group lending is very costly since the labor cost per dollar of transactions needs to be high by design. The most controversial aspect of microfinance, however, has been the extent of subsidy required to provide this access. Overall, the microfinance sector remains heavily grant- and subsidy-dependent. Skeptics question whether microfinance is the best way to provide those subsidies and point out that development of mainstream finance is a more promising way to reach the poor and alleviate poverty in significant ways.

There are also good political economy reasons why we should not focus on the poor and ask how we can make microfinance more viable, but instead ask how financial services can be made available for all (Rajan, 2006). The poor lack the political clout to demand better services, and subsidies may spoil the "credit culture." By defining the issue more broadly to include the middle class, who often also lack access, would make it more likely that promotion of financial access will be made a priority.

What can governments do to promote access? Many of the policies recommended above to enhance the overall development of the financial sector will also help increase access. However, the overlap is not perfect, and explicit prioritization of access is therefore important. For example, certain regulations aimed at financial stability or "combating terrorism" can restrict access of small firms and poor households. Or focusing on development of offshore financial centers to export wholesale financial services may lead to the neglect of onshore financial infrastructures necessary for access of small firms and individuals. Also, it is important to set realistic goals; not all potential borrowers are creditworthy, and many banking crises were precipitated by overly relaxed credit policies, including the latest crisis of structured securitization. These tensions between improving access without increasing vulnerabilities are discussed in World Bank (2007).

First and foremost, governments can further access by making and encouraging infrastructure improvements. However, prioritizing different reform efforts is important and recent research also suggests that in low-income countries improving information infrastructures seems to yield more immediate access benefits than legal reforms (Djankov, McLiesh, and Shleifer, 2007). But legal reforms are also important, and among those there is evidence that while protection of property rights against the state is more important for financial development generally, other aspects of contract enforcement (such as institutions relating to collateral) may be more important for access (Haselmann, Pistor, and Vig, 2010).

Institutional reform is a long-term process and specific policy actions can help boost access sooner. There are a wide range of such measures, ranging from specific legislation to underpin non-blank intermediation, including leasing and factoring; technologies based on the Internet and mobile phones; development of credit registries; protection against money laundering and "anti-terrorist" financing, without jeopardizing household access and others.

For example, at the household level, giving each individual a national identification number and creating credit registries where lenders share information about their clients' repayment records would help since all borrowers could then borrow using their future access to credit as collateral (Rajan, 2006). Reducing costs of registering and repossessing collateral is also crucial. In Brazil, for example, inability to repossess property has contributed to the cost of the housing—finance program, keeping the mortgage rates too high to be affordable for the poor. Governments can also be instrumental in facilitating innovative technologies to improve access. For example in Mexico, a program developed by Nafin, a government development bank, allows many small suppliers to use their receivables from large creditworthy buyers to receive working capital financing (Klapper, 2006). This type of trade finance is called "reverse factoring" and effectively allows small firms to borrow based on the creditworthiness of their buyers, allowing them to borrow more at cheaper rates.

Regulation can also help. Removal of interest ceilings, or usury laws, would allow institutions to charge the rates that they need to be profitable and improve access. These regulations end up hurting the very poor they are trying to protect as the supply of these services completely dry up. Anti-predatory lending or truth-in-lending requirements are also very important since households may also be forced into overborrowing by unscrupulous lenders, as the latest subprime mortgage crisis amply illustrates. Anti-discrimination policies may also help against cases of active or passive discrimination against the poor or different ethnic groups.

It is important to ensure that other complex regulations—such as Basel II regulations that are intended to help banks minimize costly bank failures—do not inadvertently penalize small borrowers and hurt access by failing to make full allowance for the potential for a portfolio of small and medium-size enterprise (SME) loans to achieve risk pooling. Financial regulations can also prevent the emergence of institutions better suited to the needs of lower-income households or smaller firms. Rigid chartering rules, high capital adequacy requirements, or very strict accounting requirements may reduce the ability of institutions to serve the poorer segments of the society. As many households are interested in savings services but not in credit services, considering and regulating savings mobilization separately from credit services may be helpful (Claessens, 2006). For example, in South Africa, extension of bank regulation and supervision to microfinance institutions reduced their capacity to offer their services profitably.

Governments can also opt to stimulate access more directly. In the United States, the Treasury's electronic transfer accounts to increase use of bank accounts and the Community Reinvestment Act are two examples of measures to improve access to credit services, and there are similar legal measures from the UK, France, Sweden, Ireland, and many others. However, there is little consensus on the success of those schemes (Claessens, 2006) and whether they can be replicated in developing countries. The experiences with credit extensions, especially to improve the maturity structure of debt and reach the SMEs, are extensive in both developed and developing countries. However, both the rationale for and effectiveness of those interventions are much more doubtful (see Caprio and Demirgüç-Kunt, 1997; and Beck and Demirgüç-Kunt, 2006). As already discussed above, interventions through ownership of government institutions have also not been successful, overall.

Last, but perhaps most importantly, governments can improve access by increasing competition in the financial sector. As financial institutions find their traditional business coming under competition they seek out new lines of profitable opportunities, including lending to the SMEs and the poor. Given the right incentives, the private sector can develop and make use of new technologies—like credit scoring—to reach the underserved segments. As already discussed above, foreign banks' role in improving the competition environment and improving access is important. Accumulating evidence suggests that, over time, foreign banks can enhance access. Indeed, multinational banks have been leading the way in expanding access all around the world.

32.4 CONCLUSIONS

In an effort to contain the global financial crisis, many country authorities have taken unprecedented steps that have included extensive provision of liquidity, issuing blanket guarantees and other assurances to bank depositors and creditors, taking large ownership stakes in financial institutions, and boosting credit by state-owned financial institutions.

These policy responses to the crisis have shaken the confidence of developed and developing countries alike in the very blueprint of financial sector policies that underlie Western capitalist systems. However, as pointed out for example by Demirgüç-Kunt and Servén

(2009), based on a large body of econometric evidence and country experience, policies employed to contain a crisis—often in a haste to re-establish confidence and with inadequate consideration of long-term costs—should not be interpreted as permanent deviations from well-established policy positions. The fact that governments may end up providing blanket guarantees or owning large stakes in the financial sector in an effort to contain and deal with the crisis does not negate the fact that generous guarantees over the long term are likely to backfire or that government officials make poor bankers. For the most part, the confusion arises from not being able to recognize incentive conflicts and tradeoffs inherent in short-term and long-term responses to a systemic crisis.

The overall message from the research is thus a cautionary one. The global financial crisis has given greater credence to the idea that active state involvement in the financial sector can help maintain economic stability, drive growth, and create jobs. There is evidence that some interventions may have had an impact, at least in the short run. But there is also evidence on longer-term negative effects. The evidence suggests that, as the crisis subsides, there may be a need to adjust the role of the state from direct interventions to less direct involvement. This does not mean that the state should withdraw from overseeing finance. To the contrary, the state has a very important role, especially in providing supervision, ensuring healthy competition, and strengthening financial infrastructure.

Incentives are crucial in the financial sector. The main challenge of financial sector policies is to better align private incentives with public interest without taxing or subsidizing private risk-taking. Design of public policy needs to strike the right balance—promoting development, yet in a sustainable way. This approach leads to challenges and tradeoffs.

In regulation and supervision, one of the crisis lessons is the importance of getting the "basics" right first. That means solid and transparent institutional frameworks to promote financial stability. Specifically, it means strong, timely, and anticipatory supervisory action, complemented with market discipline. In many developing economies, that combination of basic ingredients implies a priority on building up supervisory capacity. Here, less can mean more: less complex regulations, for instance, can mean more effective enforcement by supervisors and better monitoring by stakeholders.

The evidence also suggests that the state needs to encourage contestability through healthy entry of well-capitalized institutions and timely exit of insolvent ones. The crisis fueled criticisms of "too much competition" in the financial sector, leading to instability. However, research presented in this report suggests that, for the most part, factors such as poor regulatory environment and distorted risk-taking incentives are what promote instability, rather than competition itself. With good regulation and supervision, bank competition can help improve efficiency and enhance access to financial services, without necessarily undermining systemic stability. Hence, what is needed is to address the distorted incentives and improve the flow of information as well as the contractual environment, rather than to restrict competition.

Lending by state-owned banks can play a positive role in stabilizing aggregate credit in a downturn, but it also can lead to resource misallocation and deterioration of the quality of intermediation. The report presents some evidence that lending by state-owned banks tends to be less procyclical and that some state-owned banks even played a countercyclical role during the global financial crisis. However, the track record of state banks in credit allocation remains generally unimpressive, undermining the benefits of using state banks as a countercyclical tool. Policymakers can limit the inefficiencies associated with state bank credit by paying special attention to the governance of these institutions and schemes and ensuring that adequate risk management processes are in place. However, this oversight is challenging, particularly in weak institutional environments.

Experience points to a useful role for the state in promoting transparency of information and reducing counterparty risk. For example, the state can facilitate the inclusion of a broader set of lenders in credit reporting systems and promote the provision of high-quality credit information, particularly when there are significant monopoly rents that discourage information sharing. Additionally, to reduce the risk of freeze-ups in interbank markets, the state can create the conditions for the evolution of markets in collateralized liabilities.

The general recommendations outlined in this chapter apply rather broadly, but the directions in which the financial sector needs improvement in different countries will be based on their initial conditions (World Bank, 2001; World Bank, 2007). Furthermore, policy implementation requires complementing the research results with practitioner experience, tailoring this chapter's advice to individual country circumstances. In general, reforms are likely to be most challenging for low-income countries, where the legacy of financial repression and state ownership has generally hampered the development of a private financial system, where the underlying legal and information infrastructure is weak, and achieving minimum efficient scale will be difficult.

Despite their inherent fragility, financial systems underpin economic development. The challenge of financial sector policies is to align private incentives with public interest without taxing or subsidizing private risk-taking. The task is becoming increasingly complex for all countries in an ever more integrated and globalized financial system.

References

Aghion, P. and Bolton, P. (1997). A Trickle-Down Theory of Growth and Development with Debt Overhang, *Review of Economic Studies* 64, 151–172.

Aghion, P., Howitt, P., and Mayer-Foulkes, D. (2005). The Effect of Financial Development on Convergence: Theory and Evidence, *Quarterly Journal of Economics* 120, 173–222.

Allen, F. and Gale, D. (2000). *Comparing Financial Systems*. Cambridge, MA: MIT Press.

Allen, F. and Gale, D. (2004). Competition and Financial Stability, *Journal of Money, Credit and Banking* 36(32), 453–480.

Altunbas, Y., Evans, Y., and Molyneux, P. (2001). Bank Ownership and Efficiency, *Journal of Money, Credit and Banking* 33(4), 926–954.

Andrianova, S., Demetriades, P., and Shortland, A. (2008). Government Ownership of Banks, Institutions, and Financial Development, *Journal of Development Economics* 85, 218–252.

Anginer, D., Demirgüç-Kunt, A., and Zhu, M. (2012). How Does Bank Competition Affect Systemic Stability?, World Bank Policy Research Working Paper No. 5981.

Armendariz de Aghion, B. and Morduch, J. (2005). *The Economics of Microfinance*. Cambridge, MA: MIT Press.

Ayyagari, M., Demirgüç-Kunt, A., and Maksimovic, M. (2008a). How Important Are Financing Constraints? The Role of Finance in the Business Environment, *World Bank Economic Review* 22(3), 483–516.

Ayyagari, M., Demirgüç-Kunt, A., and Maksimovic, M. (2008b). How Well Do Institutional Theories Explain Firms' Perceptions of Property Rights?, *The Review of Financial Studies* 21, 1833–1871.

Ayyagari, M., Demirgüç-Kunt, A., and Maksimovic, M. (2011). Firm Innovation in Emerging Markets: Role of Finance, *Journal of Financial and Quantitative Analysis* 46(6), 1545–1580.

Ayyagari, M., Demirgüç-Kunt, A., and Maksimovic, M. (2013). What Determines Protection of Property Rights? An Analysis of Direct and Indirect Effects, *Journal of Financial Econometrics* 11(4), 610–649.

Banerjee, A. and Newman, A. (1993). Occupational Choice and the Process of Development, *Journal of Political Economy* 101, 274–298.

Barth, J. R., Caprio Jr., G., and Levine, R. (2001). The Regulation and Supervision of Banks Around the World: A New Database, University of Minnesota Financial Studies Working Paper No. 0006; World Bank Policy Research Working Paper No. 2588, <http://ssrn.com/abstract=262317>.

Barth, J., Caprio Jr., G., and Levine, R. (2006). *Rethinking Bank Regulation: Till Angels Govern.* New York: Cambridge University Press.

Beck, T. (2008). Bank Competition and Financial Stability: Friends or Foes?, World Bank Policy Research Working Paper No. 4656.

Beck, T. and Demirgüç-Kunt, A. (2006). Small and Medium-Sized Enterprises: Access to Finance as a Growth Constraint, *Journal of Banking & Finance* 30, 2931–2943.

Beck, T., Demirgüç-Kunt, A., Laeven, L., and Levine, R. (2004). Finance, Firm Size, and Growth, World Bank Policy Research Working Paper No. 3485.

Beck, T., Demirgüç-Kunt, A., and Levine, R. (2003). Law, Endowments, and Finance, *Journal of Financial Economics* 70, 137–181.

Beck, T., Demirgüç-Kunt, A., and Levine, R. (2005). Law and Firms' Access to Finance, *American Law and Economics Review* 7, 211–252.

Beck, T., Demirgüç-Kunt, A., and Levine, R. (2006). Bank Supervision and Corruption in Lending, *Journal of Monetary Economics* 53, 2131–2163.

Beck, T., Demirgüç-Kunt, A., and Levine, R. (2007). Finance, Inequality and the Poor, *Journal of Economic Growth* 12, 27–49.

Beck, T., Demirgüç-Kunt, A., and Levine, R. (2012). *Guardians of Finance: Making Regulators Work for Us.* Cambridge, MA: MIT Press.

Beck, T., Demirgüç-Kunt, A., and Maksimovic, V. (2005). Financial and Legal Constraints to Firm Growth: Does Size Matter?, *Journal of Finance* 60, 137–177.

Beck, T., Demirgüç-Kunt, A., and Maksimovic, V. (2008). Financing Patterns around the World: Are Small Firms Different?, *Journal of Financial Economics* 89(3), 467–487.

Beck, T., Demirgüç-Kunt, A., and Martínez Pería, M. S. (2008). Banking Services for Everyone? Barriers to Bank Access and Use around the World, *World Bank Economic Review* 22(3), 397–430.

Beck, T., Levine, R., and Levkov, A. (2007). Big Bad Banks? The Impact of US Branch Deregulation on Income Distribution, National Bureau of Economic Research Working Paper No. 13299.

Beck, T., Levine, R., and Loayza, N. (2000). Finance and the Sources of Growth, *Journal of Financial Economics* 58, 261–300.

Beck, T., Lundberg, M., and Majnoni, G. (2006). Financial Intermediary Development and Growth Volatility: Do Intermediaries Dampen or Magnify Shocks?, *Journal of International Money and Finance* 25, 1146–1167.

Becker, G. and Stigler, G. (1974). Law Enforcement, Malfeasance, and the Compensation of Enforcers, *Journal of Legal Studies* 3, 1–18.

Bertay, A., Demirgüç-Kunt, A., and Huizinga, H. (2012). Bank Ownership and Credit over the Business Cycle: Is Lending by State Banks Less Procyclical?, World Bank Policy Research Working Paper No. 6110.

Beegle, K., Dehejia, R., and Gatti, R. (2007). Child Labor and Agricultural Shocks, *Journal of Development Economics* 81, 80–96.

Bekaert, G., Harvey, C. R., and Lundblad, C. (2005). Does Financial Liberalization Spur Growth?, *Journal of Financial Economics* 77, 3–55.

Bencivenga, V. R. and Smith, B. D. (1992). Deficits, Inflation and the Banking System in Developing Countries: The Optimal Degree of Financial Repression, *Oxford Economic Papers* 44, 767–790.

Berger, A., Demirgüç-Kunt, A., Haubrich, J., and Levine, R. (2004). Introduction: Bank Concentration and Competition: An Evolution in the Making, *Journal of Money, Credit, and Banking* 36, 433–453.

Bertrand, M., Schoar, A. S., and Thesmar, D. (2007). Banking Deregulation and Industry Structure: Evidence from the French Banking Reforms of 1985, *The Journal of Finance* 62(2), 597–628.

Boot, A. W. A. and Thakor, A. (1997). Financial System Architecture, *Review of Financial Studies* 10, 693–733.

Boyd, J. H., Levine, R., and Smith, B. D. (2001). The Impact of Inflation on Financial Sector Performance, *Journal of Monetary Economics* 47, 221–248.

Burgess, R. and Pande, R. (2005). Can Rural Banks Reduce Poverty? Evidence from the Indian Social Banking Experiment, *American Economic Review* 95, 780–795.

Bruhn, M., Farazi, S., and Kanz, M. (2013). Bank Concentration and Credit Reporting, World Bank Policy Research Working Paper No. 6442.

Calderon, C. and Schaeck, K. (2013). Bank Bailouts, Competition, and the Disparate Effects for Borrower and Depositor Welfare, World Bank Policy Research Working Paper No. 6410.

Calomiris, C. (2011). An Incentive-Robust Programme for Financial Reform, *Manchester School* 79, 39–72.

Caprio, G. and Demirgüç-Kunt, A. (1997). The Role of Long-Term Finance: Theory and Evidence, *World Bank Economic Review* 10, 291–321.

Caprio, G., Demirgüç-Kunt, A., and Kane, E. (2010). The 2007 Meltdown in Structured Securitization: Searching for Lessons not Scapegoats, *World Bank Research Observer* 25(1), 125–155

Casu, B. and Girardone. C. (2009). Testing the Relationship between Competition and Efficiency in Banking: A Panel Data Analysis, *Economic Letters* 105, 134–137.

Christopoulos, D. K. and Tsionas, E. G. (2004). Financial Development and Economic Growth: Evidence from Panel Unit Root and Cointegration Tests, *Journal of Development Economics* 73, 55–74.

Čihák, M., Demirgüç-Kunt, A., Feyen, E., and Levine, R. (2012). Benchmarking Financial Development around the World, World Bank Policy Research Working Paper No. 6175.

Čihák, M., Demirgüç-Kunt, A., and Johnston, R. (2013). Incentive Audits: A New Approach to Financial Regulation, World Bank Policy Research Working Paper No. 6308.

Čihák, M., Demirgüç-Kunt, A., Martínez Pería, M. S., and Mohseni-Cheraghlou, A. (2012). Bank Regulation and Supervision around the World: A Crisis Update, World Bank Policy Research Working Paper No. 6286.

Claessens, S. (2006). Access to Financial Services: A Review of the Issues and Public Policy Objectives, *World Bank Research Observer* 21(2), 207–240.

Claessens, S. (2009). Competition in the Financial Sector: Overview of Competition Policies, *World Bank Research Observer* 24(1), 83–118.

Clacssens, S., Demirgüç-Kunt, A., and Huizinga, H. (2001). How Does Foreign Entry Affect Domestic Banking Markets?, *Journal of Banking & Finance* 25, 891–911.

Claessens, S. and Klingebiel, D. (2001). Competition and Scope for Financial Services, *World Bank Research Observer* 16(1), 18–40.

Clarke, G., Cull, R., and Martínez Pería, M. S. (2001). Does Foreign Bank Penetration Reduce Access to Credit in Developing Countries: Evidence from Asking Borrowers, World Bank Policy Research Working Paper No. 2716.

Clarke, G., Cull, R., and Shirley, M. (2005). Bank Privatization in Developing Countries: A Summary of Lessons and Findings, *Journal of Banking & Finance* 29, 1905–1930.

Clarke, G., Xu, L. C., and Zhou, H. (2003). Finance and Income Inequality: Test of Alternative Theories, World Bank Policy Research Working Paper No. 2984.

Cole, S. (2009a). Fixing Market Failures or Fixing Elections? Agricultural Credit in India, *American Economic Journal: Applied Economics* 1(1), 219–250.

Cole, S. (2009b). Financial Development, Bank Ownership, and Growth: or, Does Quantity Imply Quality?, *Review of Economics and Statistics* 91(1), 33–51.

Cull, R., Demirgüç-Kunt, A., and Morduch, J. (2008). Microfinance: The Next Capitalist Revolution?, *Journal of Economic Perspectives* 23, 167–192.

Cull, R. and Martínez Pería, M. S. (2012). Bank Ownership and Lending Patterns during the 2008–2009 Financial Crisis: Evidence from Eastern Europe and Latin America, World Bank Policy Research Paper No. 6195.

Cull, R., Senbet, L., and Sorge, M. (2005). Deposit Insurance and Financial Development, *Journal of Money, Credit, and Banking* 37, 43–82.

De Haas, R. and Naaborg, I. (2005). Does Foreign Bank Entry Reduce Small Firms' Access to Credit? Evidence from European Transition Economies?, Dutch National Bank Working Paper No. 50.

Delis, M. (2012). Bank Competition, Financial Reform, and Institutions: The Importance of Being Developed, *Journal of Development Economics* 97(2), 450–465.

De Luna-Martínez, J. and Vicente, C. (2012). Global Survey of Development Banks, World Bank Policy Research Working Paper 5969.

Demirgüç-Kunt, A. and Detragiache, E. (1998). The Determinants of Banking Crises: Evidence from Developing and Developed Countries, IMF Staff Papers No. 45, 81–109.

Demirgüç-Kunt, A. and Detragiache, E. (1999). Financial Liberalization and Financial Fragility. In: B. Pleskovic and J. Stiglitz (Eds.), *Proceedings of the Annual World Bank Conference on Development Economics*, 332–334. Washington, DC: The World Bank.

Demirgüç-Kunt, A. and Detragiache, E. (2002). Does Deposit Insurance Increase Banking System Stability? An Empirical Investigation, *Journal of Monetary Economics* 49, 1373–1406.

Demirgüç-Kunt, A. and Detragiache, E. (2005). Cross-Country Empirical Studies of Systemic Bank Distress: A Survey, *National Institute Economic Review* 192, 68–83.

Demirgüç-Kunt, A., Detragiache, E., and Merrouche, O. (2010). Bank Capital: Lessons from the Financial Crisis, World Bank Policy Research Working Paper No. 5473.

Demirgüç-Kunt, A., Detragiache, E., and Tressel, T. (2008). Banking on the Principles: Compliance with Basel Core Principles and Bank Soundness, *Journal of Financial Intermediation* 17, 511–542.

Demirgüç-Kunt, A. and Huizinga, H. (2004). Market Discipline and Deposit Insurance, *Journal of Monetary Economics* 51, 375–399.

Demirgüç-Kunt, A. and Kane, E. (2002). Deposit Insurance around the Globe: Where Does it Work?, *Journal of Economic Perspectives* 16, 175–196.

Demirgüç-Kunt, A., Kane, E., and Laeven, L. (2008). *Deposit Insurance around the World: Issues of Design and Implementation.* Cambridge, MA: MIT Press.

Demirgüç-Kunt, A. and Klapper, L. (2012). Measuring Financial Inclusion: The Global Findex, World Bank Policy Research Working Paper No. 6025.

Demirgüç-Kunt, A., Laeven, L., and Levine, R. (2004). Regulations, Market Structure, Institutions, and the Cost of Financial Intermediation, *Journal of Money, Credit, and Banking* 36, 593–622.

Demirgüç-Kunt, A. and Levine, R. (1996). Stock Market Development and Financial Intermediaries: Stylized Facts, *World Bank Economic Review* 10, 291–322.

Demirgüç-Kunt, A. and Levine, R. (2001). *Financial Structure and Economic Growth: A Cross-Country Comparison of Banks, Markets, and Development.* Cambridge, MA: MIT Press.

Demirgüç-Kunt, A. and Levine, R. (2007). Finance and Economic Opportunity. World Bank Working Paper.

Demirgüç-Kunt, A. and Maksimovic, V. (1998). Law, Finance, and Firm Growth, *Journal of Finance* 53, 2107–2137.

Demirgüç-Kunt, A. and Servén, L. (2009). Are All the Sacred Cows Dead? Implications of the Financial Crisis for Macro and Financial Policies, World Bank Policy Research Working Paper No. 4807.

Detragiache, E., Gupta, P., and Tressel, T. (2005). Finance in Lower-Income Countries: An Empirical Exploration, International Monetary Fund Working Paper No. 05/167.

Detragiache, E., Tressel, T., and Gupta, P. (2008). Foreign Banks in Poor Countries: Theory and Evidence, *Journal of Finance* 63, 2123–2160.

Dinc, S. (2005). Politicians and Banks: Political Influences on Government-Owned Banks in Emerging Markets, *Journal of Financial Economics* 77, 453–479.

Djankov, S., McLiesh, C., and Shleifer, A. (2007). Private Credit in 129 Countries, *Journal of Financial Economics* 84, 299–329.

Galor, O. and Zeira, J. (1993). Income Distribution and Macroeconomics, *Review of Economic Studies* 60, 35–52.

Gine, X. and Townsend, R. (2004). Evaluation of Financial Liberalization: A General Equilibrium Model with Constrained Occupation Choice, *Journal of Development Economics* 74, 269–307.

Goldsmith, R. W. (1969). *Financial Structure and Development.* New Haven, CT: Yale University Press.

Gormley, T. A. (2004). Banking Competition in Developing Countries: Does Foreign Bank Entry Improve Credit Access? John M. Olin School of Business, St. Louis, Washington University Working Paper.

Greenwood, J. and Jovanovic, B. (1990). Financial Development, Growth, and the Distribution of Income, *Journal of Political Economy* 98, 1076–9107.

Gropp, R., Hakenes, H., and Schnabel, I. (2011). Competition, Risk-Shifting, and Public Bail-Out Policies, *Review of Financial Studies* 24(6), 2084–2120.

Guiso, L., Sapienza, P., and Zingales, L. (2004). Does Local Financial Development Matter?, *Quarterly Journal of Economics* 119(3), 929–969.

Gutiérrez, E., Rudolph, H., Homa, T., and Beneit, E. (2011). Development Banks: Role and Mechanisms to Increase Their Efficiency, World Bank Policy Research Working Paper No. 5729.

Haber, S. H. (1997). Financial Markets and Industrial Development: A Comparative Study of Governmental Regulation, Financial Innovation and Industrial Structure in Brazil and Mexico, 1840–1940. In: S. Haber (Ed.), *How Latin America Fell Behind?*, 146–178. Stanford, CA: Stanford University Press.

Haber, S. H. (2005). Mexico's Experiments with Bank Privatization and Liberalization, 1991–2003, *Journal of Banking & Finance* 29, 2325–2350.

Haber, S. H., Maurer, N., and Razo, A. (2003). *The Politics of Property Rights: Political Instability, Credible Commitments, and Economic Growth in Mexico, 1876–1929.* New York: Cambridge University Press.

Hakenes, H. and Schnabel, I. (2010). Banks Without Parachutes: Competitive Effects of Government Bail-Out Policies, *Journal of Financial Stability* 6, 156–168.

Haselmann, R. F. H., Pistor K., and Vig, V. (2010). How Law Affects Lending, *Review of Financial Studies* 23(2), 549–580.

Honohan, P. (2004). Financial Development, Growth, and Poverty: How Close are the Links? In: C. Goodhart (Ed.), *Financial Development and Economic Growth: Explaining the Links*, 1–37. London: Palgrave.

Honohan, P. and Beck, T. (2007). *Making Finance Work for Africa.* Washington, DC: World Bank.

Jacoby, H. G. and Skoufias, E. (1997). Risk, Financial Markets, and Human Capital in a Developing Country, *The Review of Economic Studies* 643, 311–335.

Jappelli, T. and Pagano, M. (2002). Information Sharing, Lending and Defaults: Cross-Country Evidence, *Journal of Banking & Finance* 26, 2017–2045.

Jayaratne, J. and Strahan, P. E. (1996). The Finance-Growth Nexus: Evidence from Bank Branch Deregulation, *Quarterly Journal of Economics* 111, 639–670.

Kaminsky, G. and Reinhart, C. M. (1999). The Twin Crises: The Causes of Banking and Balance of Payments Problems, *American Economic Review* 89, 473–500.

Kaminsky, G. and Schmukler, S. (2003). Short-Term Pain, Long-Term Gain: The Effect of Financial Liberalization, National Bureau of Economic Research Working Paper No. 9787.

Khandker, S. R. (2003). Microfinance and Poverty: Evidence Using Panel Data from Bangladesh, World Bank Policy Research Working Paper No. 2945.

King, R. G. and Levine, R. (1993). Finance and Growth: Schumpeter Might Be Right, *Quarterly Journal of Economics* 108, 717–738.

Klapper, L. (2006). The Role of Factoring for Financing Small and Medium Enterprises, *Journal of Banking & Finance* 30, 3111–3130.

Laeven, L. and Valencia, F. (2012). Systemic Banking Crisis Database: An Update, International Monetary Fund Working Paper No. 08/224.

Lamoreaux, N. (1994). *Insider Lending: Banks, Personal Connections, and Economic Development in Industrial New England.* New York: Cambridge University Press.

La Porta, R., Lopez-De-Silanes, F., and Shleifer, A. (2002). Government Ownership of Commercial Banks, *Journal of Finance* 57, 265–301.

La Porta, R., Lopez-De-Silanes, F., Shleifer, A, and Vishny, R. W. (1997). Legal Determinants of External Finance, *Journal of Finance* 52, 1131–1150.

Levine, R. (1997). Financial Development and Economic Growth: Views and Agenda, *Journal of Economic Literature* 35, 688–726.

Levine, R. (2005). Finance and Growth: Theory and Evidence. In: P. Aghion and S. Durlaff (Eds.), *Handbook of Economic Growth*, 866–934. The Netherlands: Elsevier Science.

Levine, R., Loayza, N., and Beck, T. (2000). Financial Intermediation and Growth: Causality and Causes, *Journal of Monetary Economics* 46, 31–77.

Levine, R. and Zervos, S. (1998). Stock Markets, Banks, and Economic Growth, *American Economic Review* 88, 537–558.

Loayza, N. and Ranciere, R. (2006). Financial Development, Financial Fragility, and Growth, *Journal of Money, Credit and Banking* 38(4), 1051–1076.

Love, I. and Mylenko, N. (2004). Credit Reporting and Financing Constraints, World Bank Policy Research Working Paper No. 3142.

Lucas, R. E. (1988). On the Mechanics of Economic Development, *Journal of Monetary Economics* 22, 3–42.

Masciandaro, D., Pansini, R. V., and Quintyn, M. (2011). The Economic Crisis: Did Financial Supervision Matter?, International Monetary Fund Working Paper No. 11/261.

Merton, R. C. and Bodie, Z. (2004). The Design of Financial Systems: Towards a Synthesis of Function and Structure, *Journal of Investment Management* 3(1), 6.

Mian, A. (2006). Distance Constraints: The Limits of Foreign Lending in Poor Economies, *Journal of Finance* 61, 1465–1505.

Micco, A. and Panizza, U. (2006). Bank Ownership and Lending Behavior, *Economics Letters* 93, 248–254.

Micco, A., Panizza, U., and Yañez, M. (2007). Bank Ownership and Performance. Does Politics Matter?, *Journal of Banking and Finance* 31, 219–241.

Miller, M. (2003). *Credit Reporting Systems and the International Economy.* Cambridge, MA: MIT Press.

Morck, R., Wolfenzon, D., and Yeung, B. (2005). Corporate Governance, Economic Entrenchment, and Growth, *Journal of Economic Literature* 43, 655–720.

Morduch, J. (1998). Does Microfinance Really Help the Poor? New Evidence from Flagship Programs in Bangladesh, Princeton University Working Paper No. 198.

Pitt, M. M. and Khandker, S. R. (1998). The Impact of Group-Based Credit Programs on Poor Households in Bangladesh: Does the Gender of Participants Matter?, *Journal of Political Economy* 106, 958–996.

Raddatz, C. (2006). Liquidity Needs and Vulnerability to Financial Underdevelopment, *Journal of Financial Economics* 80, 677–722.

Rajan, R. (2006). Separate and Unequal, *Finance and Development* 43, 56–57.

Rajan, R. (2010). *Fault Lines: How Hidden Fractures Still Threaten the World Economy.* Princeton, NJ: Princeton University Press.

Rajan, R. and Zingales, L. (1998). Financial Dependence and Growth, *American Economic Review* 88, 559–586.

Rajan, R. and Zingales, L. (2003). *Saving Capitalism from the Capitalists.* New York: Random House.

Rioja, F. and Valev, N. (2004). Does One Size Fit All? A Reexamination of the Finance and Growth Relationship, *Journal of Development Economics* 74, 429–447.

Robinson, J. (1952). *The Rate of Interest and Other Essays.* London: Macmillan

Roubini, N. and Sala-I-Martin, X. (1995). A Growth Model of Inflation, Tax Evasion, and Financial Repression, *Journal of Monetary Economics* 35, 275–301.

Rousseau, P. L. and Sylla, R. (1999). Emerging Financial Markets and Early US Growth, National Bureau of Economic Research Working Paper No. 7448.

Sapienza, P. (2004). The Effects of Government Ownership on Bank Lending, *Journal of Financial Economics* 72, 357–384.

Schaeck, K., Čihák, M., Maechler, A., and Stolz, S. (2011). Who Disciplines Bank Managers?, *Review of Finance* 16, 197–243.

Schaeck, K., Čihák, M., and Wolfe, S. (2009). Are Competitive Banking Systems More Stable?, *Journal of Money, Credit, and Banking* 41(4), 711–734.

Scott, D. (2007). Strengthening the Governance and Performance of State-Owned Financial Institutions, World Bank Policy Research Working Paper No. 4321.

Squam Lake Group. (2010). *The Squam Lake Report: Fixing the Financial System*. Princeton, NJ: Princeton University Press.

Stigler, G. (1971). The Theory of Economic Regulation, *Bell Journal of Economics and Management Science* 2, 3–21.

Urdapilleta, E., and Stephanou, C. (2009). Banking in Brazil: Structure, Performance, Drivers, and Policy Implications, World Bank Policy Research Working Paper No. 4809.

Vives, X. (2011). Competition Policy in Banking, *Oxford Review of Economic Policy* 27(3), 479–497.

World Bank (2001). *Finance for Growth: Policy Choices in a Volatile World. A World Bank Policy Research Report*. Washington, DC: World Bank.

World Bank (2007). *Finance for All: Policies and Pitfalls in Expanding Access. A World Bank Policy Research Report*. Washington, DC: World Bank.

World Bank (2012). *Global Financial Development Report 2013: Rethinking the Role of the State in Finance*. Washington, DC: World Bank.

CHAPTER 33

BANKING AND REAL ECONOMIC ACTIVITY

NICOLA CETORELLI

33.1 INTRODUCTION

ON 12 December AD 56, Lucius Caecilius Jucundus recorded a transaction related to a loan for 11,039 sesterces, which he had extended for the completion of an auction sale that took place in the city of Pompeii.[1] Wax tablets recording this and 16 other similar loan contracts were found, charred but still legible, in an archeological excavation of his house, partially destroyed after the Vesuvius eruption on August 24–5 AD 79.

L. Caecilius Jucundus was a very wealthy banker in Pompeii, the son of a freedman, who had become a banker himself. They were bankers in the basic definition of the term, in that they would accept deposits from clients and extend loans using part of the received deposits. The standard terms for such loan contracts implied a commission plus an interest rate that was normally about 2% a month, with a typical duration of up to one year but normally no more than a few months.

Their main role, and the one documented in the above-mentioned tablet, was to provide credit at auctions for the sale of property, harvests, and slaves. In many cases they would arrange the sale of the very same collateral that had been pledged on past due loans that could not be repaid. They would also act as assayers of coins, provide foreign exchange services, extend types of loans other than those related to auction transactions, and engage in activities resembling what would currently be defined as trust management (Andreau, 1999, p. 36).

---

[1] As a term of reference, in that same period, a laborer's wage was 2–4 sesterces per day, and the average price for the purchase of a slave was 2,000 sesterces (Stambaugh, 1988).

While there is significant written evidence of banking activity in the first and second centuries AD in Rome, professional bankers were already in operation in Athens in the fifth century BC and were found at about the same time in Egypt and Palestine (Andreau, 1999, pp. 30–32).

Banks have thus been present even in the earliest instances of pre-modern, pre-capitalist societies, their role so pervasive and ingrained in the basic functioning of markets and economies that one almost wonders about the need to discuss the importance of banking institutions for the real economy. However, a debate on the basic determinants of the process of economic development has been alive and kicking at least throughout the entire twentieth century. Within this debate, the role of banks, and the financial sector in general, has been either readily dismissed (see, e.g., Robinson, 1952; and Lucas, 1988) or alternatively recognized as "too obvious for serious discussion" (Miller, 1998, p. 14). The start of the modern analysis of this issue is normally associated with the work of Joseph Schumpeter, who synthesized the idea that credit, especially bank credit, does create real value, in his *Theory of Economic Development* (1911). In fact, Schumpeter himself drew on an even older debate when he challenged, for instance, the view of Ricardo that "banking operations cannot increase a country's wealth" (Schumpeter, 1911, p. 98). This chapter first illustrates the reasons why the debate went on for so long, and goes on to make the claim that perhaps scholars have finally reached a consensus. Second, it presents the most current directions of research on this topic.

33.2 THE CAUSALITY DEBATE

Perhaps the main reason for the persistence of this debate is that it has been very difficult to pin down the issue of causality.[2] Anecdotal evidence from historical case studies, or even broader informal observations from cross-country data, will normally show a strong, positive correlation between any standard measure of real economic activity—per capita output growth, per capita capital growth, and productivity growth—with standard measures of development of financial markets. For instance, in what is widely recognized as the first contribution to reignite the most current interest in this debate, King and Levine (1993) drew on data from 77 countries from 1960 to 1989 to show that a basic measure of the "depth" of the financial system—the aggregate value of currency demand and interest-bearing liabilities of banks and non-bank intermediaries—had a positive and economically very significant association with real economic activity.

The underlying idea behind this and related measures of the size of the financial sector is that a broader, deeper financial sector increasingly facilitates firms' access to capital. This is the basic "financial engine" of growth. More precisely, King and Levine show that if a country could increase the size of its financial sector from the bottom quartile to the top quartile of the distribution, the resulting superior access to capital would be reflected in an increase in per capita income growth by almost 1% per year. Given that the difference in income growth between countries in the top and the bottom quartile of the distribution for

---

[2] For a good illustration of the econometrics of the finance and growth literature, see Beck (2008).

the countries in this dataset over this sample period was about 5%, the change in financial depth would contribute to an impressive 20% reduction of such a gap (King and Levine, 1993, Table 7).

In subsequent work, a more specific link between just *bank* credit and real economic activity was also confirmed using similar data and empirical methodology. Levine and Zervos (1998) show with a dataset for 42 countries between 1976 and 1993 that an increase in bank credit by one standard deviation results in an increase in real per capita income growth of 0.7% points per year (Levine and Zervos, 1998: Table 3). The basic message of such studies is that the economic magnitude of increasing the overall scale of the banking industry is potentially very significant. However, despite the robustness and the strength of such results, skeptics in the underlying debate have always maintained that while this empirical evidence clearly indicates an important correlation between finance and real activity, it cannot address the fundamental issue at stake—namely, whether banking activity—and by extension activity of the financial sector—is somewhat exogenously determined and, if it is, whether it exerts an independent impulse on real economic sectors. Critics of the role of finance in real economic activity have always argued that characteristics of financial markets are *endogenously* determined—that is, the existence and the development of anything financial is simply a reflection of real economic activity. The empirical evidence mentioned above cannot disprove the argument that financial markets simply develop simultaneously to accommodate the expanding needs of a growing economy, or even that measures to deepen financial activity could be undertaken in anticipation of predicted future economic growth.

Much subsequent work, most of it by Levine and coauthors, has addressed specifically this issue of endogeneity and causality. It has done so by departing from basic cross-sectional analysis and embracing the more sophisticated econometric tools of dynamic panel estimation techniques (see, e.g., Beck, Levine, and Loayza, 2000; and Levine, Loayza, and Beck, 2000) and instrumental variables (Levine, 1998; Levine, 1999; and Levine, Loayza, and Beck, 2000). In essence, the basic strategy involves trying to identify an exogenous component of financial development. This is achieved assuming that the level of development of the financial sector in a country is very much a reflection of the quality of the basic institutional setting that has developed in that country over time. In turn, such institutional setting (reflected in the degree of protection of property rights, in the quality of the legal enforcement system, in the overall level of trust, in the degree of corruption, etc.) is found to be highly determined by the legal origin of that country (see La Porta, et al., 1998). More specifically, the nature and quality of basic institutions appear to be highly correlated with whether the legal system of a country has roots in the British, German, French, or Scandinavian traditions of rule of law. Since the basic activity of financial markets relies on the possibility of writing well-defined contracts describing transactions based on promises of future payments, financial markets will be more or less developed to the extent to which the legal system allows protection and enforcement of such contracts. And, since the establishment of a given legal system in a country is to a large extent the result of past events, such as experiences of colonization, it is plausible to consider this feature as exogenously determined.

Thus, by either augmenting basic cross-sectional studies with instrumental variable analysis, or by using instrumental variables in dynamic panel models, the studies mentioned above came to conclusions that were remarkably similar to the earlier ones that relied on simpler identification techniques. That is (the exogenous component of) financial development has a substantial economic impact on the real economy.

While this represented an important step in addressing the causality issue, questions could still be raised regarding the quality of the instruments and, perhaps most important, the fact that both the quality of the financial sector and that of other important institutions could all be determined by still other omitted factors. Hence, the doubt remains, following this approach, that an observed positive effect of financial sector variables could in fact be the reflection of something else affecting simultaneously the financial and the real side (see Zingales, 2003).

No less important, however, is the interpretation that we can give to studies that have used the measures of depth illustrated earlier to capture the importance of financial markets for the real economy. Depth, or size, is really an *outcome* measure, meaning that whatever it is that is done or could be done to improve the financial industry is then reflected in its relative size, which is what is observed. Yet, by focusing on this end-result variable, we are at least one step removed from addressing causality in that we do not directly investigate *how* banks or other parts of the financial industry generate an independent impact on real economic activity. This leaves unanswered the above-mentioned criticisms that financial markets evolve hand in hand with other economic variables and that those are the ones actually responsible for real sector growth. What is more, by maintaining the focus on the depth variables, the analysis is also much constrained in terms of the quality of its normative content: if it is probably the case that, going from the bottom to the top quartile in the banking size, distribution is associated with considerably higher income growth, these studies are not able to prescribe exactly how deepening can be achieved.

33.3 BANKS MATTER

Both the issue of causality and of normative content were directly addressed in another highly influential study, Jayaratne and Strahan (1996), which represented another significant leap forward in the quest for the ultimate word on the role of banking for the real sector. The authors narrowed the focus of analysis down from a cross-country perspective to a country-specific case study, that of the US. While the choice may seem deficient with respect to the broader cross-country variability of previous studies, it actually comes with a tremendous payoff for a study on the role of banking: as a result of decades of regulatory restrictions preventing or limiting bank expansion within and/or across states, until the mid-1970s the US featured what was in effect 50 separate banking markets (Morgan, Rime, and Strahan, 2004), with state lines demarcating the boundaries of each individual market. Hence, studies limited to US banking alone still allows substantial cross-sectional variation. At the same time, the narrower focus on one country also reduces potentially important sources of unobservable heterogeneity that are more likely to plague multi-country data. Moreover, and most importantly, the end of the 1970s marks the beginning of an intense process of deregulation, in which individual states—*at different points in time*—removed regulatory barriers that had prevented bank entry. By the mid-1990s the process had concluded, allowing banks originally headquartered anywhere from that point on to expand potentially anywhere else without restriction.

As a result of this process of deregulation, banking markets have become increasingly more competitive and efficient. This should in turn translate into more credit availability, a clear and direct effect on the real economy. This is exactly what Jayaratne and Strahan (1996)

test. The simultaneous existence of cross-sectional and over-time variation concerning individual states' timing of deregulation represents a unique opportunity to conduct analysis in
conditions that approximate those of a "natural experiment," a scenario notoriously hard
to achieve in social science inquiry. More precisely, it is possible to measure the impact of
bank deregulation—and the associated changes in competition and efficiency—comparing
state-specific real economic variables *before and after* deregulation. In the language of natural experiment analysis, the control group is represented by observations in a state before
deregulation, including observations in other states that have not deregulated yet, while the
treatment group is represented by all observations in years following deregulation. Because
deregulation is not implemented at the same time in all states, unobserved state-specific
omitted factors and time-specific events common across states that could explain the
dependent variable can be absorbed by state and time indicator variables, still leaving sufficient variation to identify the specific effect of deregulation.

This identification strategy makes an important step forward in dealing with causality for
at least two reasons: first, it does not capture developments in the financial sector, banking
in particular, by looking at an ex post outcome performance such as credit size, capturing
instead the effect of a specific event, bank deregulation, that is supposed to generate developments in the sector. And, because theory would suggest that the resulting improvement in
competition and efficiency should be associated with more and better allocated capital, the
causal link is now much more direct. Second, the event in question can be plausibly considered to be exogenous and occurring independently of current or expected developments in
the real economy. For example, studies have indicated that small banks had been very influential in establishing tight restrictions to expansion as early as the 1930s and that their influence remained strong through the early 1980s (Economides, Hubbard, and Palia, 1996; and
White, 1998). Also, the extensive failure of thrifts in the 1980s has been considered another
cause of deregulation, as large, better-diversified banks were allowed to acquire the failing
banks (Kane, 1996). Finally, Kroszner and Strahan (1999) find that technological changes in
both deposit and lending activity were among the leading factors behind deregulation.

With these premises, Jayaratne and Strahan (1996) were able to find evidence confirming
a causal link between banking deregulation and state income growth. In particular, using a
panel from 1972 to 1992, they find that income growth in a state was more than half a percentage point higher, per year, after deregulation of its banking industry. Their contribution
should be recognized both methodologically, for the important tightening in the strategy
to address causality, but also because it focused on a specific characteristic of the banking
industry, thereby bringing the data closer to theory and at the same time enhancing the normative content of the analysis. Their evidence represents, in my opinion, the closest to a nail
in the coffin of the causality debate.[3] After this paper, it has become very difficult to counter
Schumpeter's assertion that "bank credit does create value," or at the very least the burden of
proof has shifted squarely to the other side of the debate.[4]

---

[3] In a related paper, Morgan, Rime, and Strahan (2004) focused on the impact of bank deregulation
for macroeconomic stability, testing the response of state-specific measures of business cycle volatility
to the deregulation events. They find that volatility drops substantially, between 30 and 40%, after
deregulation.

[4] A parallel paper that should also be considered as a turning point, although focusing on the broader
relationship between overall financial development and economic growth, is Rajan and Zingales (1998).
Their contribution is described in detail in the previous chapter.

33.4 How Do Banks Matter?

From this point on, the research frontier advances forward. No longer is it necessary to expend effort making the point that banks are important for the real economy. Taking that as a given, scholars have focused on the perhaps richer and more satisfying quest of fully understanding the *mechanisms* through which banks can affect the real economy. The operative questions at stake are what specific characteristics of banks and of the banking industry are likely to matter the most for real output variables, such as income or productivity growth? And, similarly, from the other end, what specific elements or features of the real sectors of the economy are really affected by banks' activity, so that ultimately such activity is reflected in an impact on real output? Delving deeper into the *micro* details governing the banking-real-economy relationship, it is now possible really to put to the test specific theories of banking. Moreover, and as mentioned earlier, the normative value of the newest studies of banking and the real economy increases tangibly. As economists fine tune what works the most, policymakers are increasingly able to navigate the sometimes turbulent waters of banking regulatory activity.

33.5 The Role of Bank Competition

In the decade following Jayaratne and Strahan (1996), research work in this field evolved in multiple directions, in which emphasis was directed at the explicit features and characteristics of the banking industry. A relatively large amount of work, in particular, has been— and continues to be—dedicated to studying the role played by bank *competition* for the real economy. The reasons for the attention paid to this characteristic of the industry are twofold. First, in contrast to most industries, where the default is that market structure and competitive conduct evolve endogenously, the banking industry has historically been heavily regulated, and for the most varying reasons, both in the US and in other countries. Hence, it is plausible to make the case that this is an exogenously determined characteristic of the industry when studying the impact on the real economy. Second, and not less important, there is a fascinating contrast of theoretical conjectures that can be formulated about the effects of bank competition.[5] Petersen and Rajan (1995) expressed very clearly the essence of this contrast. The authors challenged the conventional view that enhancing bank competition necessarily leads to better loan terms and better access to credit. The theoretical argument is that in fact banks need at least some degree of market power to have the right incentives to undertake the proper investments in screening and monitoring necessary to resolve uncertainty about the quality of new entrepreneurs. The intuition is that in the absence of some ability to "capture" the client firm over time, a bank anticipates that an entrepreneur that

---

[5] The basic ideas behind the Petersen and Rajan contribution were already present in Schumpeter, 1911 and formulated in Mayer, 1988. For additional theoretical work see, e.g., Rajan (1992), Pagano (1993), Shaffer (1998), Manove, Padilla, and Pagano (2001), Marquez (2002), Dell'Ariccia and Marquez (2004), Boot and Thakor (2000), Boyd and De Nicolo (2005), and Hauswald and Marquez (2006).

turns out to be successful has the possibility to seek better terms from competing banks that would not need to incur any additional cost of screening and monitoring (or would spend just a fraction of what the original bank had to).

Hence, in a highly competitive banking environment, banks would be required to charge loan terms reflecting the high intrinsic risk of the entrepreneurs. A bank with market power could instead offer better initial terms knowing that any upfront cost in starting such a lending relationship could be recuperated at later stages. The unconventional prediction that follows is that firms, especially young ones, might have better access to credit if they operate in more concentrated banking markets.

This tension between incentives to screen and competition was formalized in a full-fledged, general equilibrium dynamic model of capital accumulation in Cetorelli and Peretto (2012). They show that because of this tension, the banking market structure that maximizes long term economic growth is in fact neither perfect competition nor monopoly. Moreover, the "optimal" market structure itself varies at different stages of economic developments, and too much competition may also lead to the emergence of development traps in economies that otherwise would be characterized by unique equilibria.

Another paper to focus on the role of bank competition for the real economy is Cetorelli and Gambera, 2001. This paper explored the empirical relevance of the market structure of the banking sector for industrial growth. The authors took the basic cross-sectional work initiated by King and Levine (1993) and then asked: if it is agreed that the size of the banking industry is important to capital accumulation, does it matter whether the underlying industry structure is unconcentrated, thus approximating perfectly competitive conditions, or whether instead market power is concentrated among few banking institutions? From a theoretical standpoint, Cetorelli and Gambera played with the same antagonism of conjectures presented in Petersen and Rajan (1995). Their methodological approach built on the contribution of Rajan and Zingales (1998), in that they used a cross-country dataset but looked at the differential impact of bank concentration in a country *across* industrial sectors that for their own idiosyncratic reasons display varying degree of dependence on external sources of finance for capital investment. The identification strategy is then based upon the intuition that if bank competition has a role, it should matter more for firms in sectors that are highly dependent on external finance availability. As in Rajan and Zingales (1998), by seeking such a differential effect, the identification strategy considerably raises the bar for potential objections on ground of endogeneity, omitted variable biases, and reverse causality. The findings suggest a non-trivial impact of bank concentration on industrial growth and in fact simultaneous support for both sides of the theoretical controversy. First, there is evidence that bank concentration has a first-order negative effect on growth. This finding is consistent with the theoretical prediction that higher bank concentration results in a lower amount of credit available in the economy *as a whole*. Regardless of their external financial dependence, this effect is common to all industrial sectors. However, the paper also finds evidence that bank concentration has a *heterogeneous* effect across industries. In particular, sectors where young firms are more dependent on external finance enjoy a beneficial effect from a concentrated banking sector, which could actually more than compensate the first-order, negative effect. This finding supports the basic argument in Petersen and Rajan (1995) predicting that concentration of market power in banking facilitates the development of lending relationships, which have in turn an enhancing effect on firms' growth.

33.6 BANKS AND INDUSTRY DYNAMICS IN PRODUCT MARKETS

As the research agenda on bank competition and the real economy picked up momentum, it also became more ambitious. Much current work has been done, for example, on understanding how bank competition can actually affect the lifecycle dynamics of industrial sectors of production. For instance, does more bank competition mean more entry in non-financial industries? And what is the related impact for *incumbent* firms? Would changes in bank competition lead to *structural* changes in other industries, such as affecting average firm size, or the whole firm size distribution?

The framework proposed by Petersen and Rajan (1995) described above offers key insights to develop conjectures regarding the role of bank concentration on industry concentration. In their reasoning, banks with market power have stronger incentives to fund unknown young firms. This would then suggest that entry should be enhanced when credit markets are less competitive, and consequently industry competition should be fostered by market power in the credit sector. At the same time, the same setting could also produce opposite predictions: the bank with market power facilitates entry of young firms with the expectations of rent extractions at later stages in their lifecycle. This rent extraction ability will be enhanced if those young firms maintain their own profitability at later stages, but that may imply in fact that banks with market power, once lending relationships are established, will have incentives to preserve those relationships to firms that have become industry incumbents and constrain access to credit to newer entrants. As recognized in Petersen and Rajan (1995), market power gives banks an implicit equity stake in the firms they are already financing, and this implicit equity stake distorts their incentive to lend across firms in product markets. Using this alternative argument then banking market power should lead to industry concentration.

These alternative conjectures have been brought to the data. A first example is represented by Black and Strahan (2002).[6] Regulatory action that removes entry barriers and leads to a more efficient and competitive banking industry should be reflected in a direct effect on entrepreneurship. More precisely, the entry rates of business entrepreneurships should be higher if the kind of deregulation illustrated above is followed. Using data on new business incorporations between 1976 and 1996, Black and Strahan compare the number of new incorporations, and the growth rate of new incorporations before and after deregulation, using the same identification methodology in Jayaratne and Strahan (1996). The authors

---

[6] Studies in economic history had previously addressed the relationship between banking and industry concentration, usuall finding a positive link. Examples are the study of Italian industrialization in the late nineteenth century by Cohen (1967), Capie and Rodrik-Bali (1982) on British banking in the early 1890s, Haber (1991) on Mexico between 1830 and 1930, and Cameron (1967), summarizing that "competition in banking is related to the question of competition in industry. In general the two flourish—and decline—together. Whether this phenomenon is a joint by-product of other circumstances, or whether it results from the decline or restriction of competition among banks, is a matter worthy of further research. It is a striking coincidence, in any case, that industrial structure— competitive, oligopolistic, or monopolistic—tends to mirror financial structure" (Cameron, 1967, p. 313).

find that after deregulation that first allowed banks freely to branch within a state, the number of new businesses increased by almost 10%, and its growth rate between 3% and 4%. Subsequent to deregulation that also allowed banks to expand across state lines, the number of new businesses increased further by about 6%, while there was no significant effect on the growth rate. The economic impact on new business creation of opening up banking markets is therefore very large. Moreover, allowing more businesses to be in operation may be reflected in increasing output accumulation. Hence, analyzing the relationship between banking deregulation and business formation puts substance in the original goal of understanding the mechanism through which banking activity can affect real economic activity and ultimately long-term economic growth.

At the same time, going back to the theoretical conjectures outlined in Sections 33.1 and 33.2, while it is certainly consistent with theory that bank competition enhances business entry, it may not be inconsistent to speculate that banks may also have, as noted earlier, diminished incentives to screen and monitor entrepreneurs. Consequently, more entry may also be associated with higher mortality of young firms. A first take on this issue was presented in Cetorelli (2003). The author used a public version of the US Bureau of the Census dataset on business establishments that contains information on age categories to test—among other things—the impact of banking deregulation on entry, but also on the persistence rates of young businesses, as measured by rates of job destruction. The evidence was consistent with that presented by Black and Strahan (2002) on entry. Moreover, it suggested that the persistence of younger businesses was actually higher after deregulation (hence, lower job destruction). In contrast, using the more detailed, confidential version of the census data, Kerr and Nanda (2008) find that the failure rates (complete business shutdown) of enterprises three years and younger are actually higher after deregulation. Since the authors also find evidence consistent with more entry, they interpret the combination of results as suggesting that improvements in bank competition favor a "democratization" of the entry process. That is, potential entrepreneurs have a greater chance to start a business but they do not necessarily have a greater chance of surviving and remaining in business.

More work has been conducted related to the effects of bank competition on lifecycle dynamics. In the above-mentioned paper, Cetorelli (2003) also looks at the growth rates of incumbent enterprises and at their own persistence rates. The evidence there suggests that *less* bank competition meant *delayed exit* of incumbent firms, a finding consistent with the idea exposed before that monopolistic banks may have distorted incentives in favoring their older clients, thus preventing a healthier process of creative destruction.

Still with a focus on lifecycle dynamics, Cetorelli and Strahan (2006) attempted a broad analysis of the impact of more bank competition on a complete set of metrics of the market structure of non-financial industries. The authors use US Census data between 1977 and 1994 on the number of business establishments and their size—measured by employment level—located in the different states and operating in any of the 20, two-digit Standard Industrial Classification (SIC) manufacturing sectors. Consistent with previous findings, they show evidence that more vigorous competition leads to more firms in operation. In addition, they also find that the average firm size decreases as banks become more competitive. Lower average firm size is consistent with the finding of more firms in operation, and both add strength to the idea that more bank competition favors entry and allows entry at a smaller scale.

Moreover, they find that the whole firm size distribution is shifted, with an increase in mass toward smaller-size firms. The additional evidence on the size distribution adds content to the conjecture that the impact of improved competition may be felt differently by different firms—young or old, small or large—and in different sectors. More firms in operation and smaller average size could reflect entry by very small establishments. If that were simply the case, one would expect an increase in mass at the smallest end of the size distribution and declines in mass elsewhere in the distribution. If better bank competition also helps the existing small firms to grow (due to an overall increased supply of financial resources), then we ought to see a greater proportion not only of the smallest but also of medium-sized establishments as well. Moreover, testing for shifts in the whole size distribution allows us to compare how the shares of small and medium-sized (presumably bank-dependent) establishments behave relative to another sort of control group— namely, the share of the very largest establishments. These establishments (those with 1,000 or more employees) should not be affected by banking conditions because very large firms have access to nationwide (and competitive) securities markets. Thus, their fortunes should not vary with local credit conditions (Cetorelli and Strahan, 2006: 455).

Finally, Cetorelli (2014) investigates whether the process of banking deregulation could be so important as to render firms after deregulation intrinsically different from those that started their operations prior to deregulation. This idea, commonly referred to in corporate demography as "imprinting" effect, posits that in a time when external capital was relatively harder to obtain, prospective firms needed a set of organizational and managerial characteristics that would increase their chance not only to obtain (scarcer) financing, but also to survive in the event of constraints to obtaining additional credit. Conversely, after deregulation, and the removal of important frictions to credit supply, new firms may not need to develop that set of characteristics that were previously required, thus resulting in a group of intrinsically more fragile units. Cetorelli finds evidence consistent with this conjecture. Firms born prior to deregulation seem to have a "thicker skin" than firms with similar characteristics born after deregulation.

The material reviewed in this chapter has been developed using datasets drawn almost exclusively from US banks and US sectors of production. A legitimate criticism could be made about whether these conclusions have broader, international validity. Recent work based on specific country studies or cross-sections of non-US countries seems to confirm the findings examined so far. A very ingenious paper drawing extensively on the comparison of many decades of economic history is Haber (1991). The author essentially presents a horse race between Mexico, Brazil, and the US starting from the earliest stages of industrialization and then following the evolution of industrial structure in response to developments in capital markets. Haber focuses his attention on the evolution of the textile industry between approximately the 1840s and the 1930s. The reason to focus on such an industry is that, aside from the fact that it had a much higher relevance in the past, it also had specific characteristics (including low entry barriers, divisibility of capital, and scale efficiencies exhausted at small size) such that the industry was not naturally prone to encourage concentration. The only substantial barrier to entry was the ability to access external capital. Focusing on such industry represents a good case study to understand the finance–real economy relationship, because any change in the financial sector that may have occurred in the three countries could convincingly be argued not to be endogenously determined by events in the textile industry.

Haber documents very persuasively the relationship between efficiency, regulatory reforms—or lack thereof—in the financial sector, and the structure of the textile industry. Specifically, he shows that the US adopted important reforms of both the banking industry and capital markets early on. In particular, the National Banking Act of 1863 produced important entry in the banking industry that facilitated access to credit in the production sector. As Haber remarks, "by the end of World War I the textile industry was awash in finance and many companies took advantage of the swollen credit markets to float numerous securities issue" (Haber, 1991, p. 564).

The experience of Mexico was just the opposite. The textile industries, and production in general, had no access either to bank finance or to capital markets throughout a large part of the nineteenth century. When banks eventually emerged, they actually developed as institutions tightly connected to a limited number of entrepreneurs, who were themselves connected to government officials. Hence, external finance remained severely limited and differentially available in the market. The result was a textile industry that evolved as highly concentrated. Brazil had a very similar experience and developmental trajectory as Mexico, at least initially. Financial markets were extremely underdeveloped, but in 1890 important reforms sowed the seeds for significant expansions of the banking sector and capital markets. As a result, the structure of the textile industry in Brazil in the first decades of the twentieth century looked a lot more like that of the US than that of Mexico.

Another example of a non-US country study is the experience of France in response to the reform of the banking industry of 1985, analyzed by Bertrand, Schoar, and Thesmar (2007). The French reform reduced significantly government intervention in banks' lending activity. This reform led naturally to a boost in efficiency in private banks and enhanced competition in the credit market. The reforms to the banking industry, the authors document, generated important changes in the microeconomic behavior of firms and had a related strong impact on the structure of industries. In relation to the topics analyzed in this chapter, the authors show that the regulatory reform of the banking sector in France had a positive effect on firm entry and exit rates and a negative effect on product market concentration.

Still in the field of banking reforms, but with a focus on Europe, Cetorelli (2004) investigated the effect of the implementation of the Second Banking Directive of the European Union—a regulatory reform that essentially created the conditions for an integrated European banking market—on industrial structure. Cetorelli used a panel of manufacturing industries in 29 Organisation for Economic Co-operation and Development (OECD) countries, both European Union and non-European Union members. The evidence showed that enhanced competition in European Union banking markets lead to markets in non-financial sectors characterized by lower average firm size. This conclusion is consistent with the findings in Cetorelli and Strahan (2006) and points at a beneficial effect of bank competition on credit access to young firms.

Finally, Beck, Demirgüç-Kunt, and Maksimovic (2004) use data from a World Bank survey of firms in a large cross-section of countries. One of the questions the survey asked was whether firms had difficulty in obtaining credit. Matching this and other information with the specific market structure of the banking sector where those firms were located, the authors found that higher bank concentration was associated with more financing obstacles, especially for smaller firms.

Two important points can be made regarding the role of bank competition in enhancing real economic activity. First, there does not seem to be a Pareto-dominant policy regarding the optimal banking market structure: competition in banking does not necessarily dominate monopoly, and vice versa. Second, regulation of the financial industry is intimately related to industrial policy. Depending on the level of concentration of the banking industry, *ceteris paribus*, individual sectors will grow at different speeds. Therefore, banking market structure plays an important role in shaping the cross-industry size distribution within a country.

33.7 UNINTENDED CONSEQUENCES OF THE GREAT RECESSION

Both the extent and the geographic scope of economic destruction measured in the aftermath of the financial crisis of 2007–2009 was only second to that experienced during the Great Depression. The event led to the reawakening of debates in the economic profession that had laid dormant for quite some time. Interestingly, it also led to a significant expansion in interest over the role of banks in the real economy.[7] Perhaps most notably, this increase in popularity is found in the well-established literature that has attempted to account for and calibrate the impact of financial frictions in macroeconomic models.

This literature goes at least as far back as Bernanke and Gertler (1989), Kiyotaki and Moore (1997), and Bernanke, Gertler and Gilchrist (1999). The common theme is the attempt to recognize explicitly the importance of financial market frictions as drivers of significant cyclical behavior in real variables. However, these models feature financial frictions as resulting from constraints on borrowers, with little focus, if any, on the roles played by financial intermediaries. This limitation was explicitly recognized in Gertler and Kiyotaki's own words: "[this] literature with financial frictions emphasized credit market constraints on non-financial borrowers and *treated intermediaries largely as a veil*" (Gertler and Kiyotaki, 2010, emphasis added).

Gertler and Kiyotaki itself is one of the first attempts in this literature to model financial intermediaries, and derive business cycle effects directly from the solution of intermediaries' optimization problem. The contribution of Gertler and Kiyotaki is to recognize explicitly the balance sheet of financial intermediaries and characterize intermediaries' behavior in relation to explicit asset and liabilities constraints. In particular, in their model intermediaries raise both equity and debt, but their leverage (the amount of debt over equity that they can raise) is constrained by the existence of agency problems between the intermediaries and households supplying debt. Hence, in the event of shocks leading to equity depletion, the intermediary would be forced to execute substantial delevering, and this shrinking of their balance sheet would then amplify the impact of the original shock and its macroeconomic consequences. The importance of this leverage constraint is also the core element of a number of other post-crisis contributions, such as Gertler and Karadi (2011) and Iacoviello (2013). Brunnermeier and Sannikov (2014) use a similar framework but they also model as

---

[7] And also to some suggestions that "too much" banking in fact may not be good for the real economy (see, e.g. Cecchetti and Kharroubi, 2012).

an additional channel of amplification the feedback effect associated with the impact on asset prices from the delevering attempt of the intermediaries (an example of fire sale effect).

These papers have contributed to bridging the gap between macroeconomics and banking and they are testimony of a stronger and broader recognition of the role of financial intermediation activity for the real economy. And yet banking, and intermediation activity more broadly, are in continuous evolution. Analyses of the financial crisis have indicated the rising importance of a model of intermediation based on a complex system of interconnected markets and entities operating to a large extent outside the perimeter of the banking regulator (what became popularly known as shadow banking).[8] The next step in the research agenda will require allowing for the endogenous emergence and evolution of financial intermediaries, and evolution of their roles for real economic activity.[9]

33.8 CONCLUSIONS

It is not by chance that Lucius Caecilius Jucundus established himself and prospered in the city of Pompeii. Pompeii was a well-developed center with close proximity to the sea and where markets were held on a regular basis. It is well recognized that bankers like him were instrumental in facilitating and developing commercial activity. And, while the contours of entrepreneurship in ancient Rome may not fit a modern profile, it is clear that Jucundus and others still played a role in assisting productive activity (Andreau, 1999, pp. 145–152).

The tale of Lucius Caecilius Jucundus serves as a good example to illustrate the crux of the debate around the role of banks for the real economy. It is certainly the case that banks—and financial activity—follow where real activity goes. The direction of causality from economics to finance, in other words, has never been seriously questioned. Much harder to prove is that banking can develop independently of what goes on in the real economy and that developments in the banking industry can in fact alter economic activity.

The impulse to map these dynamics has inspired a lively body of literature, one that reflects both the intrinsic intellectual interest on the issues at stake but also their vast policy implications. After all, the pervasive nature of policy control of the banking industry rests on certain assumptions about banks' fundamental role in the real economy. After more than a decade of rigorous research we are now in a position to assert with a significant degree of confidence that banking does matter for real economic activity. We have not only learned that banking activity has a large impact on various measures of output growth but have also made important progress in understanding exactly how that happens. Developments in the way banks operate bring with them far-reaching implications for economic activity. Pushing

---

[8] See, e.g., Adrian, Ashcraft, and Cetorelli, "Shadow Banking Monitoring," Chapter 16 in this volume.

[9] Woodford (2010) recognizes this explicitly: "Neither standard macroeconomic models that abstract from financial intermediation nor traditional models of the "bank lending channel" are adequate as a basis for understanding the recent crisis. Instead we need models in which intermediation plays a crucial role, but in which intermediation is modeled in a way that better conforms to current institutional realities. In particular, we need models that recognize that a market-based financial system—one in which intermediaries fund themselves by selling securities in competitive markets, rather than collecting deposits subject to reserve requirements—is not the same as a frictionless system."

research further in this direction is expected to continue to yield significant results with no diminishing returns in sight yet.

REFERENCES

Andreau, J. (1999). *Banking and Business in the Roman World (Key Themes in Ancient History)*, trans. J. Lloyd, Cambridge: Cambridge University Press.

Beck, T. (2008). Econometrics of Finance and Growth. In: T. Mills and K. Patterson (Eds.), *Palgrave Handbook of Econometrics*, 1180–1212. Basingstoke: Palgrave.

Beck, T., Demirgüç-Kunt, A., and Maksimovic, V. (2004). Bank Competition and Access to Finance: International Evidence, *Journal of Money, Credit, and Banking* 36, 627–648.

Beck, T., Levine, R., and Loayza, N. (2000). Finance and the Sources of Growth, *Journal of Financial Economics* 58, 261–300.

Bernanke, B. and Gertler, M. (1989). Agency Costs, Net Worth and Business Fluctuations, *American Economic Review* 79, 14–31.

Bernanke, B., Gertler, M., and Gilchrist, S. (1999). The Financial Accelerator in a Quantitative Business Cycle Framework. In: J. Taylor and M. Woodford (Eds.), *Handbook of Macroeconomics*, 1341–1393. Amsterdam: Elsevier.

Bertrand, M., Schoar, A., and Thesmar, D. (2007). Banking Deregulation and Industry Structure: Evidence from the French Banking Reforms of 1985, *The Journal of Finance* 62, 597–628.

Black, S. E. and Strahan, P. E. (2002). Entrepreneurship and Bank Credit Availability, *Journal of Finance* 57, 2807–2833.

Boot, A. W. A. and Thakor, A. V. (2000). Can Relationship Banking Survive Competition?, *Journal of Finance* 55, 679–713.

Boyd, J. and De Nicolo, G. (2005). The Theory of Bank Risk-Taking and Competition Revisited, *Journal of Finance* 60, 1329–1343.

Brunnermeier, M. and Sannikov, Y. (2014). A Macroeconomic Model with a Financial Sector, *American Economic Review*, 104(2): 379–421.

Cameron, R. (1967). *Banking in the Early Stages of Industrialization*. New York, NY: Oxford University Press.

Capie, F. and Rodrik-Bali, G. (1982). Concentration in British Banking, 1870–1920, *Business History* 24, 280–292.

Cecchetti, S. G. and Kharroubi, E. (2012). Re-assessing the Impact of Finance on Growth, Bank of International Settlements Working Paper No. 382.

Cetorelli, N. (2003). Life-Cycle Dynamics in Industrial Sectors. The Role of Banking Market Structure, *Federal Reserve Bank of St. Louis Review* 85, 135–147.

Cetorelli, N. (2004). Real Effects of Bank Competition, *Journal of Money, Credit and Banking* 36, 543–558.

Cetorelli, N. (2014). Surviving Credit Market Competition, *Economic Inquiry* 52, 320–340.

Cetorelli, N. and Gambera, M. (2001). Banking Market Structure, Financial Dependence and Growth: International Evidence from Industry Data, *Journal of Finance* 56, 617–648.

Cetorelli, N. and Peretto, P. F. (2012). Credit Quantity and Credit Quality: Bank Competition and Capital Accumulation, *Journal of Economic Theory* 147, 967–988.

Cetorelli, N. and Strahan, P. (2006). Finance as a Barrier to Entry: Bank Competition and Industry Structure in Local US Markets, *Journal of Finance* 61, 437–461.

Cohen, J. (1967). Financing Industrialization in Italy, 1894–1914, *Journal of Economic History* 27, 363–382.

Dell'Ariccia, G. and Marquez, R. (2004). Information and Bank Credit Allocation, *Journal of Financial Economics* 72, 185–214.

Economides, N., Hubbard, G. R., and Palia, D. (1996). The Political Economy of Branching Restrictions and Deposit Insurance: A Model of Monopolistic Competition among Small and Large Banks, *Journal of Law & Economics* 39, 667–704.

Gertler, M. and Karadi, P. (2011). A Model of Unconventional Monetary Policy, *Journal of Monetary Economics* 58, 17–34.

Gertler, M. and Kiyotaki, N. (2010). Financial Intermediation and Credit Policy in Business Cycle Analysis, *Handbook of Monetary Policy* 3, 547–599.

Haber, S. (1991). Industrial Concentration and the Capital Markets: A Comparative Study of Brazil, Mexico, and the United States, 1830–1930, *Journal of Economic History* 51, 559–580.

Hauswald, R. and Marquez, R. (2006). Competition and Strategic Information Acquisition in Credit Markets, *Review of Financial Studies* 19, 967–1000.

Iacoviello, M. (2013). Financial Business Cycles. Federal Reserve Board Working Paper.

Jayaratne, J. and Strahan, P. E. (1996). The Finance-Growth Nexus: Evidence from Bank Branch Deregulation, *Quarterly Journal of Economics* 111, 639–670.

Kane, E. J. (1996). De Jure Interstate Banking: Why Only Now?, *Journal of Money, Credit, and Banking* 28, 141–161.

Kerr, W. and Nanda, C. (2008). Democratizing Entry: Banking Deregulation, Financing Constraints and Entrepreneurship, *Journal of Financial Economics* 94, 124–149.

King, R. G. and Levine, R. (1993). Finance and Growth: Schumpeter Might Be Right, *Quarterly Journal of Economics* 108, 717–737.

Kiyotaki, N. and Moore, J. (1997). Credit Cycles, *Journal of Political Economy* 105, 211–248.

Kroszner, R. S. and Strahan, P. E. (1999). What Drives Deregulation? Economics and Politics of the Relaxation of Bank Branching Restrictions, *Quarterly Journal of Economics* 114, 1437–1467.

La Porta, R., Lopez-de-Silanes, F., Shleifer, A., Vishny, R., (1998). Law and Finance, *Journal of Political Economy* 106, 1113–1155.

Levine, R. (1998). The Legal Environment, Banks, and Long Run Economic Growth, *Journal of Money, Credit, and Banking* 30, 596–613.

Levine, R. (1999). Law, Finance and Economic Growth, *Journal of Financial Intermediation* 8, 8–35.

Levine, R., Loayza, N., and Beck, T. (2000). Financial Intermediation and Growth: Causality and Causes, *Journal of Monetary Economics* 46, 31–77.

Levine, R. and Zervos, S. (1998). Stock Markets, Banks, and Economic Growth, *American Economic Review* 88, 537–558.

Lucas, R. (1988). On the Mechanics of Economic Development, *Journal of Monetary Economics* 22, 3–42.

Manove, M., Padilla, J., and Pagano, M. (2001). Collateral vs. Project Screening: A Model of Lazy Banks, *RAND Journal of Economics* 32, 726–744.

Marquez, R. (2002). Competition, Adverse Selection, and Information Dispersion in the Banking Industry, *Review of Financial Studies* 15, 901–926.

Mayer, C. (1988). New Issues in Corporate Finance, *European Economic Review* 32, 1167–1183.

Miller, M. H. (1998). Financial Markets and Economic Growth, *Journal of Applied Corporate Finance* 11, 8–14.

Morgan, D. P., Rime, B., and Strahan, P. E. (2004). Bank Integration and State Business Cycle, *Quarterly Journal of Economics* 119, 1555–1585.

Pagano, M. (1993). Financial Markets and Growth. An Overview, *European Economic Review* 37, 613–622.

Petersen, M. A. and Rajan, R. G. (1995). The Effect of Credit Market Competition on Lending Relationships, *Quarterly Journal of Economics* 110, 407–443.

Rajan, R. G. (1992). Insiders and Outsiders: The Choice between Informed and Arm's-Length Debt, *Journal of Finance* 47, 1367–1400.

Rajan, R. G. and Zingales, L. (1998). Financial Dependence and Growth, *American Economic Review* 88, 559–586.

Robinson, J. (1952). *The Rate of Interest and Other Essays*. London: Macmillan.

Shaffer, S. (1998). The Winner's Curse in Banking, *Journal of Financial Intermediation* 7, 359–392.

Schumpeter, J. (1911). *The Theory of Economic Development: An Inquiry into Profits, Capital, Interest, and the Business Cycle*, trans. Redverse Opie, Brunswick, NJ: Transaction Books, 1983.

Stambaugh, J. E. (1988). *The Ancient Roman City*. Baltimore, MD: Johns Hopkins University Press.

White, E. (1998). The Legacy of Deposit Insurance: The Growth, Spread, and Cost of Insuring Financial Intermediaries. In: M. Bordo, C. Goldin, and E. N. White (Eds.), *The Defining Moment: The Great Depression and the American Economy in the Twentieth Century*, 87–124. Chicago: University of Chicago Press.

Woodford, M. (2010). Financial Intermediation and Macroeconomic Analysis, *Journal of Economic Perspectives* 24(4), 21–44.

Zingales, L. (2003). Commentaries to More on Finance and Growth: More Finance More Growth? by Ross Levine, *Federal Reserve Bank of St. Louis Review* 85, 31–46.

PART V

BANKING SYSTEMS AROUND THE WORLD

CHAPTER 34

....

BANKING IN THE UNITED STATES

....

ROBERT DEYOUNG

34.1 INTRODUCTION

....

IN the United States, the concept of "banking" has meant different things at different times. For most of the twentieth century, banking services were produced and delivered by a pot-pourri of financial institutions in separate industry segments—for example, commercial banks, investment banks, insurance companies—each of which specialized in different types of financial services, as determined by rigid financial regulations. Commercial banking was traditionally the largest sector and firms in this sector offered the greatest array of financial services. As shown in Table 34.1, depository institutions (mainly commercial banks) held about one-half of all US financial assets in 1980, compared with just 18% for pension companies, the next largest segment. While commercial banks today no longer occupy such a clearly dominant position, they continue to be the largest overall provider of financial services for US businesses and households. For this reason, we will use commercial banking as a prism through which to view the larger US "banking" industry.

We will also view the industry through another revealing prism: change. Over the past quarter century, no sector of the US economy has absorbed a more penetrating set of changes and shocks than has the US banking industry. We have witnessed historic episodes of both bank deregulation and re-regulation, wholesale transformations of banking production technologies and business strategies, greatly intensified banking market competition, and a deep (and largely self-inflicted) macroeconomic downturn that did its greatest damage by way of the banking sector. Now that most of the dust has cleared from these changes and shocks, commercial banks and other depository institutions now hold only about one-quarter of all US financial assets. Where did banks' lost market share end up? The big winners were mortgage finance companies, investment pools and funds (which more than doubled their market share), securities firms (market share quintupled) and mutual funds (market share grew six times larger). These shifts reveal the increasing importance of market-based financial intermediation in Western economies relative to more traditional

Table 34.1 Distribution of assets at US financial intermediaries in 1980 and 2012

	1980	2012
Depository institutions (banks, thrifts, credit unions)	50.6	24.5
Pension funds (public and private)	18.0	18.5
Insurance companies	14.8	11.5
Mortgage finance companies and funds *	7.1	16.3
Finance companies	4.9	2.5
Mutual funds (stock, bond, money market)	3.3	19.9
Securities firms (brokers, dealers, funding corporations)**	1.4	6.9
Total	100.0%	100.0%

* Includes government-sponsored enterprises (GSEs) and pools they sponsor, private mortgage securitizers and pools they sponsor, mortgage banks, and real estate investment trusts (REITs).

** Includes assets held by investment banks.

Source: Federal Reserve System Flow of Funds Accounts.

bank-based systems. Moreover, as commercial banks' asset shares diminished over the past 25 years, banks' cash flows grew more volatile as well. With the potential for wide swings in profitability, the US commercial banking sector hardly resembles the stable and strictly regulated sector of just a generation ago.

34.2 THE EVOLUTION OF THE US BANKING INDUSTRY

It is difficult to understand the US banking industry today without first becoming familiar with the massive shocks that the industry has absorbed over the past several decades. The production technologies that today's banks use to produce financial services, and the regulatory frameworks that govern those activities, would be barely recognizable to a banker from the 1980s.

34.2.1 Restrictive Government Regulations

For the better part of the twentieth century, US banks were insulated from geographic competition, product competition, and price competition. The McFadden Act of 1927 protected banks from competitors outside their home states by prohibiting interstate branch banking, and most states imposed at least some restrictions on intrastate branching. By prohibiting commercial banks from engaging in insurance, underwriting and brokerage activities, the Glass–Steagall Act of 1933 effectively prevented competition between commercial banks and non-depository institutions (insurance companies, investment banks, brokerage firms). Furthermore, depository institutions that made residential mortgage loans (thrifts, credit unions) were not permitted to make commercial loans. And the Federal Reserve's Regulation Q imposed interest-rate ceilings on most deposit accounts, effectively prohibiting price competition among these various institutions for deposit accounts.

In this highly protected environment, the number of commercial banks in the US remained relatively unchanged throughout the 1960s, 1970s, and early 1980s (see Figure 34.1). During this time period, so-called "community banks" with less than $1 billion of assets (2006 dollars) held about one-third of the industry's total assets and accounted for well over 95% of all commercial bank charters. Protected from competition by interstate banking and intrastate branching regulations, community banks established competitive advantages in local lending, local deposit-taking, and payments services. At the time, most payments in the US were made with checks. This paper-based payments system required both payors and payees to have deposit accounts upon which to write checks and deposit checks, and also required depository institutions to have convenient physical locations for processing those checks. In a world before electronic payments (e.g., automated teller machines, credit card networks, Internet banking), community banks provided much of the physical bricks-and-mortar infrastructure necessary for this system to work.

Because mutual funds were not yet well established, small household investors simply held their funds in various forms of savings and time deposit accounts at banks. Similarly, banks combined with thrift institutions to dominate residential mortgage markets. In 1983 (the first year these data were available from the Federal Reserve's Survey of Consumer Finance), US households allocated approximately 23% of their assets to depository institutions, and obtained approximately 60% of their mortgage and consumer debt from depository institutions. Of the five basic financial needs of a typical household—credit, investments, transactions, safekeeping, and insurance—commercial banks were the dominant providers of all

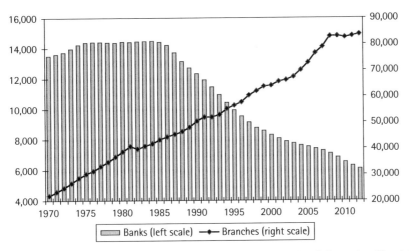

FIGURE 34.1 Number of commercial banks and commercial bank branch offices[*] in the US between 1970 and 2012.

Source: Federal Deposit Insurance Corporation.

[*] Excludes the main bank office.

but insurance products. (Insurance and pension products, as well as securities underwriting and brokerage services, were provided by specialized, non-depository institutions that comprised relatively small portions of the overall financial services market.)

As the name implies, commercial banks were also the main supplier of loans to US businesses. Large commercial banks made loans to businesses of all sizes: they were the major source of both long-term and short-term financing to large businesses, and they also made long-term loans to small businesses for purchasing fixed assets such as equipment and real estate (Carey et al., 1993). Community banks made loans to small businesses: commercial and industrial (C&I) loans accounted for between 20 and 30% of small bank loan portfolios during the 1970s and 1980s (DeYoung, Hunter, and Udell, 2004).

34.2.2 Innovation and Technological Change

In the 1970s, a parade of innovation and technological change began to erode the competitive advantages of US commercial banks and forced banks to drastically alter the ways that they produced financial services. By the 1990s, deregulation became necessary for banks to remain competitive with non-banking financial services firms.

The earliest of these innovations was the money market mutual fund (MMMF). MMMFs transformed large-denomination money market instruments (i.e., commercial paper, negotiable CDs, Treasury securities) into smaller denomination investments that were affordable to the average household, allowed investors limited check-writing privileges, and were not subject to Regulation Q. Household funds flowed out of bank deposit accounts and into MMMFs—a process known as "disintermediation"—during the late 1970s when tight Federal Reserve monetary policy pushed money market interest rates as much as 10% points above the Regulation Q ceiling on deposit interest rates.

The automated teller machine (ATM), also introduced during the 1970s, had an equally powerful impact on retail banking. Besides providing greater convenience for retail deposit customers, the ATM made bank branches more efficient: ATMs were a cheap substitute for human tellers and they enabled banks to charge customers of other banks a fee for access to cash. DeYoung, Hunter, and Udell (2004) show that the average commercial bank branch in the US became markedly more productive during the 1980s—with assets, operating income, and number transactions per banking office all increasing—which helps explain why the number of bank branches has increased even while the overall number of banks has consolidated (see Figure 34.1).

Following close after the ATM, electronic payments technologies also increased customer convenience and reduced banks' costs of production. During the 1990s, the number of checks paid in the US declined by about 3% annually, while payments made with credit cards and debit cards increased by 7.3% and 35.6% per year, respectively (Gerdes and Walton, 2002; Humphrey, 2002). The volume of automated clearinghouse (ACH) transactions (e.g., automatic bill payment, direct deposits of paychecks) handled by the Federal Reserve increased at a 14.2% annual rate between 1990 and 2000 (Berger, 2003). Because electronic payments are more timely and predictable than check-based payments, precautionary balances in bank deposit accounts shrank: the proportion of household financial assets held in transactions accounts fell from 7.3% in 1983 to 4.6% in 2001 (Federal Reserve Survey of Consumer Finance, 2004).

Like the ATM and electronic payments, Internet banking has further reduced banks' cost of production. The variable cost of producing a basic Internet banking transaction is a small fraction of the cost to do so in-person; moreover, there is evidence that having an Internet banking presence enhances the profitability of small banks (DeYoung, 2005; DeYoung, Lang, and Nolle, 2007). The predominant Internet banking strategy is the "click-and-mortar" model that combines a transactional Internet site with networks of traditional brick-and-mortar offices and ATMs; less than two dozen US banks offer their services exclusively over the Internet. The rapid growth of on-line banking (via the Internet or mobile devices) during the 2010s is the most likely reason that the annual increases in the number of US bank branches have finally halted (see Figure 34.1).

Securitized lending has perhaps left the biggest imprint on the structure and performance of the US banking industry. This lending technology—in which banks originate loans but do not finance them—has yielded large production and financing efficiencies for banks that use it, and has increased access to credit for millions of households and small businesses. But the failings of this lending technology are closely tied to the global financial crisis of 2008–09.

A loan securitization is a free-standing financial vehicle or trust that issues "asset-backed securities" (ABSs) and uses the proceeds to purchase existing loans from lenders. The most common loan securitization issues mortgage-backed securities (MBSs) and purchases residential mortgage loans from banks, thrifts or non-bank mortgage brokers. The MBSs yield returns based on the performance of the mortgage loans held in the trust. This process allows banks to sell their otherwise illiquid loans, using the proceeds to fund additional loan originations or other investments. The loan securitization production process exhibits large scale economies; these efficiencies are generated largely by the use of credit scoring, a statistical process that transforms quantitative information about individual borrowers (e.g., income, employment, payment history) into a single numerical "credit score" (Mester, 1997). Lenders use credit scores to quickly screen large numbers of loan applications; investment banks use credit scores to construct pools of loans to be securitized; and bond-rating companies use credit scores to assign risk ratings to ABSs. Most large retail banks in the US have used this technology to transform their retail credit operations (home mortgages, credit card loans, auto loans) from the traditional "originate-and-hold" model to the "originate-to-sell" model. In this new model, banks rely less on the interest income generated by the loans, and rely more on the fee income generated from loan origination, loan securitization and loan servicing. The large scale efficiencies associated with this new lending model created incentives for lenders to increase the supply of securitizable mortgages and other types of retail credit (Frame, Srinivasan, and Woosley, 2001; Berger, Frame, and Miller, 2005). In hindsight, we now know that these incentives helped to inflate the US housing bubble and subsequent global financial crisis.

Financial innovation also allowed US commercial banks to remain competitive in providing credit to large businesses. The growth of the corporate bond and commercial paper markets during the 1980s and 1990s provided large business firms access to low cost long-run (bonds) and short-term (commercial paper) funding directly from market investors, thus bypassing banks. In response, banks innovated by creating the syndicated loan (Berlin, 2007). These large loan facilities—which typically combine a term loan with a revolving line of credit—are funded jointly by a syndicate of multiple banks. Splitting up these credits across multiple banks provides diversification benefits for the lenders, and because the borrowing firms are large and well known to investors, syndicated loans trade in over-the-counter secondary markets, which provides liquidity benefits for the lenders.

34.2.3 Deregulation

By the 1980s, financial innovation and high nominal interest rates had made the old regulatory regime untenable. Fifty years of restrictive bank regulations were dismantled in three movements: price controls on bank deposit rates were removed, geographic barriers to bank expansion were lifted, and constraints on bank product powers were relaxed. These changes helped to accelerate the adoption of new financial processes and information technologies by US banks.

The Depository Institutions Deregulation and Monetary Control Act of 1980 began a six-year process of removing the ceilings on bank interest rates contained in the Federal Reserve's Regulation Q. The Garn–St. Germain Depository Institutions Act of 1982 authorized banks and thrifts to offer money market deposit accounts (MMDAs). (The Act also permitted thrift institutions to make commercial loans and thus compete more directly with small commercial banks.) These two pieces of legislation staunched the disintermediation out of bank deposits by allowing banks to compete directly on price with MMMFs.

Between 1980 and 1994, 32 states liberalized geographic restrictions on banking and branching within and across their borders; by the end of the 1980s, all but six states allowed some sort of interstate banking. In 1994 the US Congress passed the Riegle–Neal Interstate Banking and Branching Efficiency Act, which effectively repealed federal geographic banking restrictions (the McFadden Act) and harmonized the patchwork of state-by-state banking and branching rules. Interstate expansion of commercial banking companies remained limited in just one way: should a bank's share of the national deposit market exceed 10%, its further growth via acquisition of other banks would be prohibited. These deregulatory changes set off an historic wave of commercial bank mergers and acquisitions. There were approximately 3,500 mergers and acquisitions of healthy banks in the US during the 1980s, nearly 5,000 more during the 1990s, and over 2,000 more between 2000 and 2006. These combinations increased the size and geographic footprints of US commercial banks of all sizes, and for the first time ever the US had large, multi-state banking companies.

In 1987 the Federal Reserve began permitting bank holding companies to underwrite limited amounts of corporate securities in "Section 20" subsidiaries, and gradually expanded this new product power in the decade that followed. In 1999 Congress passed the Graham–Leach–Bliley Financial Services Modernization Act, which granted broad-based securities and insurance powers to commercial banking companies and effectively repealed the Glass–Steagall Act. Large multi-state banks were quicker than community banks to adopt new financial and information technologies—for example, credit-scoring and loan securitization, various forms of electronic payments, and financial derivatives and other off-balance-sheet activities. But the declining costs of delivering these technologies, and aggressive competition among third-party technology vendors, in some cases allowed smaller banks to catch up after a few years lag (Frame and White, 2004). For example, imaging technology allows banks of all sizes to transmit checks as electronic images, saving the substantial transportation and handling expenses associated with paper checks; the Check

Clearing for the 21st Century Act of 2003 (Check 21) facilitated these efficiencies by recognizing an electronic image as a legal substitute for a paper check.

These deregulatory acts would later be criticized for facilitating (if not causing) the large bubble in US real estate asset prices that preceded the global financial crisis of 2008–09. On the surface, this theory fits the facts: new product powers allowed banks to dabble, or even concentrate, in relatively riskier financial services; geographic deregulation allowed banks to achieve the size needed to exploit the production scale economies in these new services; and unfettered pricing of deposits allowed banks to attract the deposit funding necessary to finance this growth. But the actual story is far more complex. A comprehensive explanation requires that we first understand how innovation and deregulation transformed the strategic map of the US banking industry.

34.3 A Stylized View of Banking Strategies

The combination of deregulation and technological change created a strategic crossroads for US commercial banks. Figure 34.2 is highly a stylized version of that new strategic landscape (DeYoung 2000). Bank size, and the scale economies that result from increased bank size, are measured along the two vertical axes. Banks' investment in customer information,

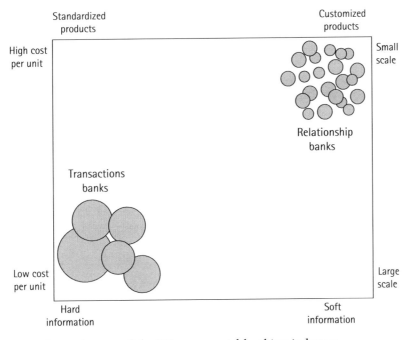

FIGURE 34.2 Strategic map of the US commercial banking industry.

Source: DeYoung (2000).

and the style of financial service provision made possible by that information, are measured along the two horizontal axes. A bank could choose to locate anywhere on this strategic map—large or small, personalized or standardized—but economic logic, casual observation, and empirical evidence (see below) suggest that just two competitive strategies will dominate all others.

Bank size and economies of scale are key to the analysis—along with the realization that a bank need not be completely scale-efficient to be profitable. A bank with around $500 million in assets is very small bank by today's standards, and operates at a large unit cost disadvantage compared to the largest US banks. But $500 million is large enough for a bank to profitably operate using the traditional "originate-and-hold" banking model (DeYoung, 2013). These banks could access additional scale savings by growing larger, but unit cost reductions come more slowly beyond this point. More importantly, growing larger could eventually jeopardize their ability to practice originate-and-hold banking. By remaining relatively small, these "community banks" can interact in-person with local customers and potential customers; over time, this results in a valuable store of soft (non-quantifiable) information about the credit quality and financial needs of their customers (Scott, 2004). This relationship-based approach to banking gives small banks comparative advantages in lending to small firms that are unable to access public capital markets (Berger, Miller, et al. 2005) and serving households that want or need in-person financial attention. Relationship banks sacrifice high sales volume and lower unit costs in exchange for local economic focus and high service quality. Their customers are willing to pay higher prices for personalized products and services (e.g., small business loans, financial planning), which offset the unit cost disadvantages of these banks.

While the small bank model is built upon close customer relationships, the large bank model is based upon high volumes of transactions. While community bank assets are typically measured in hundreds of millions of dollars, large bank assets are measured in hundreds of billions of dollars. This huge scale of operation is necessary to fully exploit the potential scale economies associated with the "originate-to-sell" business model (Hughes et al., 1996; Rossi, 1998), which thrives on the collection and use of hard (quantifiable) information about borrower creditworthiness. Personal credit scores allow large banks to automate the accept/reject decision for thousands of consumer loan (credit cards, auto loans, mortgages) applications, and afterwards provide the credit quality information necessary to market the loan securitizations into which the banks sell these loans (Stein, 2002). The retail deposit delivery channels favored by large banks (e.g., ATM networks, electronic payments, Internet banking) are also high-volume and impersonal. Customers are treated as transactions and the products they buy are essentially financial commodities. Because all large banks have access to the same hard information (supplied by credit bureaus) and the same production technologies, they face intense price competition. Transaction banks sacrifice personalized service and high prices in exchange for high sales volume, standardized products, and low unit costs.

A key implication of the model is that the banking industry will naturally settle into a dichotomous structural equilibrium (as shown in Figure 34.2) in which numerous small banks cluster separately from a smaller cluster of large banks. Goddard et al. (2014) analyzed the size distribution of US commercial banking companies between 1980 and 2010; they find that US banks do cluster in this way, and moreover, that the number of very large banks clustered in upper tail of the size distribution has grown more exclusive over time. A more

Table 34.2 Selected financial ratios (mean values) for 490 US commercial banks in 2006*

	"small" banks	"large" banks
Number of banks	434	56
Asset range	$500 million to $2 billion	over $10 billion
Small business loans (% of loans)	8.55%	4.46%
Securitized loans (% of consumer loans)	0.14%	15.59%
Core deposits (% of assets)	63.07%	50.70%
Purchased federal funds (% of assets)	3.01%	7.85%
Net interest income (% of assets)	3.63%	2.82%
Interest income (% of assets)	6.18%	5.33%
Interest expense (% of assets)	2.54%	2.51%
Standby financial letters of credit (% of assets)	0.59%	3.98%
Non-interest income (% of operating income)	20.28%	38.66%
Deposit service charges (% of operating income)	7.94%	8.39%
Fiduciary income (% of operating income)	1.71%	8.58%
Trading income (% of operating income)	0.02%	2.03%
Investment banking income (% of operating income)	0.60%	2.02%
Insurance income (% of operating income)	0.73%	1.29%
Loan servicing income (% of operating income)	0.01%	0.88%
Fees from mutual fund sales (% of operating income)	0.54%	1.16%
Other non-interest income (% of operating income)	8.19%	13.15%
Return on assets	1.12%	1.23%
Return on equity	12.81%	13.70%

*Each of the banks in this analysis operated with either a state or a federal commercial banking charter. If a bank was affiliated with bank holding company, it was included only if it was the largest bank (i.e., the "lead bank") in their organization. Banks less than 10 years old were excluded to insure that all banks in the analysis were financially mature (DeYoung and Hasan 1998). Banks investing more than 10% of their assets in either agricultural loans or credit card loans were also excluded, as these banks tend to face idiosyncratic market conditions and/or use more specialized production functions.

Source: Federal Deposit Insurance Corporation.

important implication of the model is that banks in both the small bank cluster and the large bank cluster can be profitable. It is straightforward to produce evidence consistent with the latter implication. Table 34.2 displays various financial ratios for small and large US commercial banks in 2006, just prior to the disruptions caused by the financial crisis. The small bank group is comprised of the 434 banks with $500 million and $2 billion in assets, while the large bank group consists of the 56 banks with at least $10 billion in assets. The data indicate two fundamentally different approaches to banking.

The average large bank sold or securitized roughly a dollar of consumer loans (automobile, home mortgage, home equity, or credit card) for every eight dollars of consumer loans on its balance sheet (15.61%), while the average small bank held nearly all of its consumer loans as portfolio investments (0.14%). Consistent with this transactions-based approach, the average large bank invested only half as many of its assets (4.46%) in small business loans—the quintessential relationship banking product—compared to the average small bank (8.55%). Differences in funding structures also support the strategic dichotomy. At the small banks, 63% of assets were funded with "core deposits" (stable deposit balances with long expected durations, including transactions deposits, small savings deposits, and certificates of deposit less than $100,000) compared with only about 51% at the large banks. Consistent with this relationship-based funding approach, small banks relied on interbank markets to finance their assets (3.01%) far less than did large banks.

Revenues and profits reflect the differences in lending and deposit funding. Net interest margins averaged only 2.82% for the large banks, substantially less than the 3.63% average for the smaller banks; moreover, this 81 basis point difference was driven completely by higher interest income at the smaller banks, not by any advantage in interest expense. This remarkable finding is consistent with the differences in returns to hard information lending and soft information lending. But large banks make up for their low interest margins by generating higher amounts of non-interest income (e.g., deposit service charges, investment banking, brokerage, insurance activities). On average, non-interest income accounts for nearly 40% of operating income (net interest income plus non-interest income) at the large banks, or roughly twice the amount generated by the small banks. Overall, the large banks earned both higher returns of assets (1.23% versus 1.12%) and higher returns on equity (13.70% versus 12.81%) than the smaller banks. But these returns are not adjusted for risk, and (as shown in Section 34.4) large banks need to generate higher equity returns to reward their owners for the higher riskiness of their banking model.

To be sure, the above analysis oversimplifies the array of strategic choices available to commercial banks. Large banks do offer customized, relationship-based services to some of their clients, such as corporate investment banking clients and high net worth private banking customers. And most small banks do rely on hard information when they write business loans, such as pledged collateral and audited financial statements. Moreover, the strategic map in Figure 34.2 is static, but both large and small banks are constantly attempting to migrate toward the lower right-hand corner of the map, where they might benefit from both high prices and low unit costs. For example, as large banks sell standardized deposit and loan products, they also attempt to differentiate these products in the minds of their customers with image-based advertising campaigns, in attempts to support prices. And as small banks trumpet the value of in-person relationship banking, they also encourage their customers to use ATMs, online banking and other impersonal delivery channels in attempts to drive down operating expenses.

34.4 INDUSTRY STRUCTURE

The structure of the US commercial banking industry has been in flux for the past three decades and shows little sign of stabilizing soon. Until the mid-1980s, regulation had stifled competition and this resulted in a very stable industry structure. But when state and federal lawmakers began to permit interstate competition, banks moved quickly to expand across state borders, and the fastest way to do this was to acquire existing banks in other

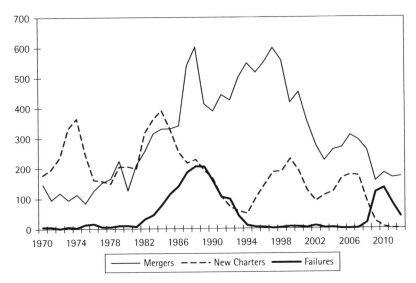

FIGURE 34.3 Changes in the number of commercial bank charters in the US from 1970 to 2012 due to mergers, failures, and new entry.

Source: Federal Deposit Insurance Corporation.

states. On average, about 350 commercial banks were acquired each year during the 1980s, about 500 each year during the 1990s, and about 300 each year during the 2000s—in all, over 10,000 bank charters were merged out of existence since 1980 (see Figure 34.3). These acquisitions substantially altered the structure of the US banking industry and continue to do so today. The number of US commercial banks has been cut in half, from a plateau of approximately 14,000 banks that had remained remarkably stable since the 1950s, to only about 6,000 banks by 2012 (see Figure 34.1). Berger, Kashyap, and Scalise (1995) provide an excellent overview of the first 15 years of this transformation; FDIC (2012) provides a largely graphical analysis of structural change in the US commercial banking industry from 1984 through 2011.

Two separate waves of bank failures also reduced the population of US commercial banks. Between 1982 and 1993, the FDIC shut down over 1,400 insolvent banks—roughly 10% of the industry—the most bank failures in the US since the Great Depression. The primary causes of these insolvencies were real estate-related. When interest rates dramatically and unexpectedly increased in the early 1980s, interest margins turned negative at banks that financed long-term fixed rate loans (mainly mortgages) with short-term deposits. (Similarly, interest rate risk exposure led to a one-third reduction in the population of federally chartered savings institutions, from about 3,600 in 1986 to about 2,400 in 1992.) And when real estate values declined in New England and also in Southwest oil producing states, the credit quality of both business and retail loans banks substantially declined at banks in those regions. The more recent wave of bank failures during the "Great Recession" was also related to declines in real estate values—this time, banks suffered large losses in MBSs when the nationwide housing bubble collapsed. Despite the severe depth of this recession, only about 400 commercial banks, or about 6% of the industry, failed between 2008 and 2012. The regulatory and supervisory responses to the earlier bank failure wave—in particular, the Federal Deposit Insurance Corporation Improvement Act of 1991—had something to do with this. US banks went into the financial crisis holding historically high levels of equity capital, were being examined a more frequent schedule than in the past, and were subject to earlier supervisory interventions when their capital levels declined.

Over 7,000 new commercial banking charters have been granted in the US since 1970, partially offsetting the reduction in bank numbers due to failures and mergers. While "de novo" banks occur rarely outside the US, the presence of 51 separate chartering authorities (the federal government plus all 50 state governments) makes the creation of new banks relatively easy in the US. New banks are more likely to start up in local markets soon after established local banks are acquired in mergers (Keeton 2000; Berger et al. 2004). When a small, locally focused bank is acquired by a larger and non-local banking company, some portion of the local depositors, borrowers, and bank employees inevitably become unhappy with post-acquisition changes and will want to change banks. Combining these three essential banking inputs—deposits, loans, and skilled banking employees—with a relatively small amount of investment capital is a simple recipe for a new bank. (In most cases, US banking authorities require less than $20 million in startup capital.)

The size of the typical US bank has also changed over time. As clearly implied by Figure 34.4, most of the banks that disappeared via failure or acquisition between 1980 and 2011 held less than $500 million of assets. Moreover, other banks with assets less than $500 grew up and out of this size class by acquiring other small banks. In sharp contrast, the number of banks with more than $1 billion in assets remained relatively stable between 300 and 500 between 1980 and 2006, as has the number of banks with between $500 million and $1 billion in assets. Interpreting these three time series as a "survivor

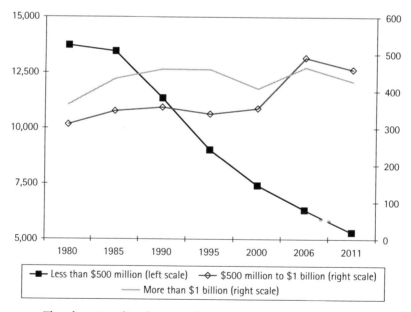

FIGURE 34.4 The changing distribution of US commercial banks by size (measured in 2005 dollars) between 1980 and 2011.

Source: Federal Deposit Insurance Corporation.

analysis" (Stigler, 1958), one could infer that the most meaningful scale economies exist for banks with less than $500 million in assets, and that reductions in unit costs slow down as banks continue to grow larger beyond this point. Consistent with this implication, DeYoung and Rice (2004) and DeYoung (2013) show that small banks can unambiguously improve their risk-return positions (i.e., expected returns will increase and the variability of these returns will decrease) by growing their assets up to $500 million, but substantial increases in bank size beyond $500 million require banks to accept higher risk for higher returns.

This is not to say that production or cost scale economies cease to exist for banks with more than $500 million of assets. Recent studies argue that cost scale economies exist for even the very largest US commercial banking companies (Wheelock and Wilson, 2012; Hughes and Mester, 2013). However, nationwide banks use business models different from those of local banks (e.g., transactions banking versus relationship banking) that rely on different production technologies (e.g., higher capital-to-labor ratios) and generate different risk-return tradeoffs. For example, Rossi (1998) showed that mortgage banking companies exhibited larger economies of scale than traditional mortgage lenders, and DeYoung (2005) found that Internet-only banks exhibit larger scale economies than banks that use branches; both mortgage banks and Internet banks use pure transactions banking strategies. But while unit costs may indeed be falling as large banks get larger, and those scale savings may also be supporting higher profit margins, those higher earnings may be necessary to offset the riskier cash flows associated with the business models used by large banks. To the extent that the largest US banks enjoy too-big-to-fail (TBTF) status, cost scale economies may simply reflect lower interest rates paid by these banks to issue bonds that have zero probability of default (Davies and Tracy, 2014).

Whether in pursuit of scale economies, strategic advantage or simply earnings growth, the largest banks in the US have grown at staggering speeds since industry deregulation. In 1988 only one US-owned banking company had more than $100 billion in assets (Citibank); today four US-owned banks exceed $1 trillion in assets (JPMorgan Chase, Bank of America, Citigroup and Wells Fargo). As shown in Table 34.3, a number of storied US banking franchises disappeared over the past two decades, such as Chemical Bank, Bankers Trust and Wachovia, their assets purchased by surviving companies higher up on the lists. However, much of the bank growth in the US has come via geographic expansion, as banks in one city, state, or region acquired banks in other cities, states, or regions. As a result, the rapid expansion of US banking companies has not resulted in increased concentration and pricing power in local banking markets; when a local bank is acquired by a bank from outside the local market, its ownership changes but its local market share is unaffected. Indeed, competitive rivalry appears to be jump-started: at the typical small bank, cost efficiency tends to improve after one of its local peers is acquired by a large out-of-market bank (DeYoung, Hasan, and Kirchhoff, 1998; Evanoff and Ors, 2008).

By definition, geographic expansion increases the distances between banking offices, which can create managerial challenges at far-flung banking companies. Berger and DeYoung (2001, 2006) found that the operational efficiency of bank holding company affiliates declined as they were located further away from their headquarters banks. While advances in communications and information technologies have helped mitigate these long-distance management problems, the very existence of these inefficiencies indicates a competitive advantage (at the margin) for small, locally focused banks. Distances between

Table 34.3 Ten largest US-owned banking companies, ranked by millions of dollars of same year assets, in 1988, 1997, 2007, and 2012

	June 1988		December 1997	
1	Citicorp	$194,600	Chase Manhattan Corp.	$365,531
2	Chase Manhattan Corp.	$98,860	Citicorp	$262,159
3	BankAmerica	$96,923	NationsBank Corp.	$260,159
4	Chemical Banking Company	$78,410	J.P. Morgan & Co.	$157,274
5	J.P. Morgan & Co.	$74,681	Bankamerica Corp.	$140,102
6	Maunfacturers Hanover Corp	$73,826	First Union Corp.	$116,182
7	Security Pacific Corp.	$64,714	Bankers Trust New York Corp.	$140,102
8	Bankers Trust New York Corp.	$54,700	Banc One Corp.	$116,182
9	First Interstate Bancorp	$51,790	First Chicago NBD Corp.	$114,096
10	Wells Fargo & Co.	$44,721	Wells Fargo & Co.	$97,456
	June 2007		**December 2012**	
1	Citigroup Inc.	$2,220,866	JPMorgan Chase & Co.	$2,359,141
2	Bank of America Corp.	$1,535,684	Bank of America Corp.	$2,212,004
3	JPMorgan Chase & Co.	$1,458,042	Citigroup, Inc.	$1,864,660
4	Wachovia Corp.	$719,922	Wells Fargo & Co.	$1,422,968
5	Wells Fargo & Co.	$539,865	Goldman Sachs	$938,770
6	Washington Mutual Inc.	$349,140	Morgan Stanley	$780,960
7	US Bancorp	$222,530	General Electric Capital Corp.	$548,771
8	SunTrust Banks Inc.	$180,314	Bank of New York Mellon	$359,301
9	Capital One Financial Corp.	$145,938	US Bancorp	$353,855
10	National City Corp.	$140,648	Capital One Financial Corp.	$313,040

Source: American Banker.

US banks and their loan clientele have also increased over time, due largely to advances in financial and information technologies. Automated, credit-scored lending models allow banks to make consumer, mortgage, credit card, and small business loans to borrowers they have never met in person; asset securitization and credit derivatives can help banks manage the risk associated with this type of lending (Petersen and Rajan, 2002; DeYoung, Glennon, and Nigro, 2008; DeYoung et al., 2011).

The geographic expansion of US banking companies has not been limited to domestic markets. As shown in Table 34.4, five of the largest 30 banking companies in the world in 2011 were US-owned and operated: JP Morgan Chase (ranked 9th in terms of assets), Bank of America (10th), Citigroup (14th), Wells Fargo (23rd) and the investment banking company Goldman Sachs (28th). And although they are slightly smaller than their European and Japanese peers in terms of assets, US banking companies dominate non-US banks in securities underwriting. As shown in Table 34.5, US banks now hold the first, second and third positions—and five of the ten top spots—in worldwide bond underwriting, equities underwriting, and syndicated loan underwriting.

Securities underwriting is largely a fee-based activity: unlike deposit-taking and lending, underwriting new equity and credit issues typically generates neither interest income nor interest expense for the bank, and bank balance sheets display little if any evidence that

Table 34.4 Largest banking companies in the world, ranked by millions of dollars of assets, in December 2011 US-owned banks are in bold

1	Deutsche Bank	$2,799,977
2	HSBC	$2,555,579
3	BNP Paribas	$2,542,738
4	Industrial and Commercial Bank of China	$2,456,287
5	Mitsubishi UFJ Financial Group	$2,447,950
6	Crédit Agricole	$2,431,796
7	Barclays Group	$2,417,327
8	Royal Bank of Scotland	$2,329,726
9	**JPMorgan Chase**	**$2,265,792**
10	**Bank of America**	**$2,129,046**
14	**Citigroup**	**$1,873,878**
23	**Wells Fargo**	**$1,313,867**
28	**Goldman Sachs**	**$942,140**

Source: Global Finance (www.gfmag.com).

the bank is engaged in these activities.[1] Non-interest income from securities underwriting and other fee-based financial services (e.g., loan securitization and servicing, securities brokerage, insurance sales and underwriting, investment banking, service charges on deposit accounts, private banking and investment advice) more than doubled in importance at US commercial banks between 1980 and 2000, as illustrated in Figure 34.5.

The increased reliance on non-interest income altered the dynamics of bank earnings, expenses and risk in unexpected ways. DeYoung and Roland (2001) showed that noninterest revenue tends to be more volatile over time than interest revenue; moreover, this top-line volatility (revenues) translated into even greater bottom-line volatility (earnings) because the techniques for producing fee-based financial services tend to exhibit high operating (e.g., fixed and quasi-fixed labor inputs) and financial leverage. During the 1980s and 1990s, US banks earned higher profits by shifting from interest-based to non-interest-based sources of income, but these earnings were also less stable. Clark et al. (2007) come to similar conclusions using more recent data, while Demirgüç-Kunt and Huizinga (2010) find similar evidence for a set of international banks. DeYoung and Torna (2013) find that some fee-based activities (e.g., venture capital, investment banking, asset securitization) were positively associated with distressed bank failure during the recent financial crisis, while other activities (e.g., securities brokerage, insurance sales) helped banks to recover from financial distress.

The wholesale change in industry structure, competition, and risk in US banking markets has increased the pressure under which US bank supervisors must operate. When viewed from the outside, the US bank regulatory system appears complicated. A commercial bank

---

[1] There are some exceptions. In a "full commitment" underwriting contract, the portion of the new issue that the bank cannot immediately sell will for a short time remain on its balance sheet. And the lead bank in a loan syndication will retain a portion of the credit on its books.

Table 34.5 Ten largest debt underwriters, equity underwriters, and loan syndicators in the world in 2012, by proceeds in billions of dollars.

US companies are in bold

Corporate Bond Underwriting

1	JP Morgan	$268
2	Citi	$213
3	Bank of America Merrill Lynch	$197
4	Deutsche Bank AG	$185
5	Morgan Stanley	$172
6	Barclays	$171
7	Goldman Sachs & Co	$171
8	HSBC Bank PLC	$161
9	UBS	$117
10	Credit Suisse	$113

Global Equity Underwriting

1	Morgan Stanley	$51
2	Goldman Sachs & Co	$51
3	JP Morgan	$50
4	Citi	$50
5	Bank of America Merrill Lynch	$46
6	Deutsche Bank AG	$40
7	Credit Suisse	$37
8	UBS	$35
9	Barclays	$31
10	Banque Saudi Fransi	$13

Syndicated Loans

1	JP Morgan	$267
2	Bank of America Merrill Lynch	$235
3	Citi	$148
4	Wells Fargo & Co	$135
5	Barclays	$86
6	Credit Suisse	$51
7	Morgan Stanley	$49
8	RBS	$44
9	Goldman Sachs & Co	$43
10	Deutsche Bank AG	$42

Source. Bloomberg.

can choose to operate with a national bank charter or a state bank charter. The Office of the Comptroller of the Currency (OCC), a bureau of the US Treasury Department, has legal authority to grant national bank charters, while each of the 50 state governments has the legal authority to grant state banking charters. In the past, national banks had somewhat greater geographic range and somewhat broader product powers than state banks, but today state banks have essentially the same powers as national banks. Each of the 51 chartering authorities is primarily responsible for supervising its own banks, but they share their supervisory

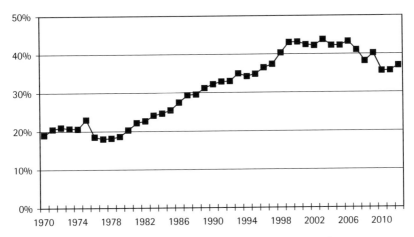

FIGURE 34.5 Aggregate non-interest income as a percentage of aggregate operating income of US commercial banks, 1970 to 2012.[*]

Source: Federal Deposit Insurance Corporation.

[*] Operating income is equal to net interest income plus non-interest income.

responsibilities—usually alternating annual bank examinations—with the Federal Deposit Insurance Corporation (FDIC) or the Federal Reserve (the Fed).

The FDIC has two important non-supervisory responsibilities: it insures the deposits of both national banks and state banks (up to $250,000 per deposit account) and it is responsible for resolving national banks, state banks, thrift institutions, and financial holding companies if they become insolvent. The Fed is the monetary authority (central bank) but also has some key bank supervision responsibilities: it is the primary supervisor of bank holding companies (BHCs), financial holding companies (FHCs) and any commercial banking company designated as a systemically important financial institution (SIFI). The federal banking authorities—the FDIC, the Fed and the OCC/Treasury Department—cooperate closely in a number of efforts, such as serving jointly with other federal authorities on the Financial Stability Oversight Council (FSOC), which is charged with limiting the existence and consequences of systemic risk in banking, financial and real economic markets.

34.5 THE FINANCIAL CRISIS IN THE US

Despite having to absorb 20 years of continually shifting industry structure, rapid innovation in the production of banking services, and intensified competition, the US commercial banking industry appeared to be healthy, safe and sound in the mid-2000s. As illustrated in Figure 34.6, banks were earning historically high profits and were flush with equity capital. Berger et al. (2008) show the largest US banking companies were targeting equity capital ratios well in excess of the minimum levels set by bank regulators, and were retaining large percentages of their record earnings rather than increasing payouts to shareholders. If bank earnings were about to suffer a large setback, these large reservoirs of equity capital were thought to be more than adequate to cushion the blow. This was a mistaken notion.

In mid-2007, US home prices began a steep decline and unusually large numbers of home owners began defaulting on their mortgage loans. Most of these bad mortgages were sub-prime loans—that is, loans to households with poor credit histories, little collateral, and questionable long-run abilities to service the loans—produced using the originate-to-sell transactions lending model that powered the growth of large retail and investment banks in the US during the 1990s and 2000s. Trillions of dollars of securities backed by these subprime loans (private MBS) declined in value, imposing large losses on the portfolios of commercial banks, investment banks, and other institutional investors that held them. These losses precipitated a wave of bank failures (see Figure 34.3) as well as three credit crunches: investors refused to roll over the short term commercial paper and repo financing that had been keeping large investment banks afloat; funding for nonconventional mort-gages and private MBS collapsed; and commercial banks rationed credit to small businesses (DeYoung 2013). Overall industry earnings plunged to around zero in both 2008 and 2009 (see Figure 34.6). While mortgage defaults and losses in MBS investments were the headline cause of this banking slump, the recession also revealed the underlying instability of nonin-terest income, which tumbled 17% from 2006 to 2010 (see Figure 34.5). The collateral mac-roeconomic damage to the US economy was enormous—real GDP growth was negative in both 2008 and 2009 and the official US unemployment rate hit 10% in October 2009—and spread quickly to European economies in which financial institutions had invested heavily in securities backed by US real estate loans.

US bank regulators took a series of unprecedented policy actions to prevent a systemic collapse of the financial sector. The Federal Reserve (among other actions too numerous to detail here) opened new lending facilities in order to make liquidity freely available to all types of financial institutions; temporarily guaranteed all investments in MMMFs against losses; pledged to purchase up to $600 billion in agency (GSE) MBSs from financial

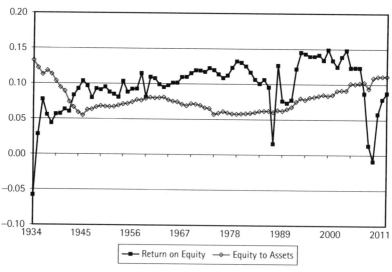

FIGURE 34.6 Aggregate return-on-equity and equity-to-assets ratios for the US com-mercial banking industry, 1934 to 2012.

Source: Federal Deposit Insurance Corporation

institutions; and for the first time since the Great Depression began lending directly to non-financial firms by purchasing their newly issued commercial paper. The Fed also set into motion a chain of events that marked the end of the large independent investment banking model in the US. The Fed subsidized JP Morgan Chase's acquisition of the insolvent Bear Stearns; a few weeks later denied assistance to Lehman Brothers, which required the firm to file for bankruptcy; and a week after that converted Goldman Sachs and Morgan Stanley to bank holding company charters—in essence, these two firms accepted stricter regulations and supervisory scrutiny in exchange for access to the Federal Reserve's discount window and the ability to issue inexpensive insured deposits. Kroszner and Melick (2009) provide a detailed overview of the policy actions taken by the Federal Reserve during the crisis.

The US Treasury nationalized Fannie Mae and Freddie Mac (as discussed above); provided $150 billion in loans and other support to prop up and eventually nationalize American International Group, the largest insurance company in the US; and gained authority under the Troubled Assets Relief Program (TARP) to inject up to $700 billion into commercial banks via equity injections and purchases of mortgage-backed securities, which it began doing in October 2008. The FDIC increased deposit insurance coverage from $100,000 to $250,000 per account; provided billions of dollars of open bank assistance to prevent the insolvency of Citigroup, at the time the largest banking company in the world; and used a variety of innovative structures and techniques to resolve insolvent banks and thrifts, including the largest depository failure in US history (to date) in Washington Mutual.

While the financial crisis had largely ended by 2010, neither the US economy nor the US banking system had yet fully recovered as of mid-2013. The economic wealth of US households (comprised largely of owner-occupied housing and retirement savings) declined massively during the financial crisis, while the debt owed by US households (comprised largely of initial mortgage debt and home equity loans) had increased to record levels prior to the financial crisis. In order to work off the resulting spike in their debt-to-assets ratios, US households have reduced spending and increased savings, and as a result the post-crisis recovery has been very slow. With consumer spending (which accounts for about two-thirds of US GDP) growing slowly, home construction running at about half its pre-crisis level, and little reason for businesses to expand, the demand for bank lending has been weak. US commercial banks have the capacity to make new loans—they are holding nearly 10% of their assets in cash compared to only about 4% pre-crisis, and have equity-to-assets ratios around 11% compared to around 10% pre-crisis—but little reason to do so. The aggregate industry ratio of loans-to-deposits ratio, which had plateaued just above 90% in 2004 through 2007, sits at just above 70% as of mid-2013.

To what extent were US banking companies culpable for the financial crisis? The initial impetus for the housing bubble was provided by a change in federal government housing policy, namely, efforts to make home ownership more universally possible across US households. During the Clinton administration, Fannie Mae, and Freddie Mac were mandated to make multi-trillion dollar investments in affordable mortgage loans to low income households. The Bush administration followed with its "ownership society" policy aimed at increasing household ownership of both their homes and their retirement savings. Indeed, the rate of home ownership increased from around 64% in the early 1990s to a peak of 69% just prior to the financial crisis. But expanding home ownership would not have been possible without substantial increases in the amount of available home mortgage finance, and this was made possible by two of the fundamental phenomena discussed above. First, the originate-to-sell lending model was introduced and perfected by mortgage banking insti-tutions—some of the more prominent examples were American Home Mortgage, New Century Financial, Countrywide Financial and Washington Mutual, all of which failed rela-tively early during the financial crisis—and also adopted by large and super-regional com-mercial banks to augment their existing operations. Second, deregulation (the Riegle–Neal Act of 1994 and the Gramm–Leach–Bliley Act of 1999) allowed banks to achieve the scale of operations necessary to fully exploit the efficiencies of transactions banking technologies, and provided banks the investment banking powers necessary to fully integrate the transac-tions banking in-house.

It must be stressed that commercial banking companies did not have to participate in the financing of the housing bubble. Indeed, the fee-based transactions banking model exposes a financial institution to a different (and likely greater) set of risks than the tra-ditional interest-based banking model, and as such senior bank managers may have been reticent to adopt this new approach. DeYoung, Peng, and Yan (2013) provide evidence that commercial banking companies gave contractual incentives to their managers to take these risks. At large publically traded US commercial banking companies, they show that the risk-taking incentives in CEO compensation packages increased with the passage of the Gramm–Leach–Bliley Act, that CEOs responded to these incentives by shifting their busi-ness mix toward transactions banking activities, and that the actual market risk profiles of these banks increased as a result.

34.6 OUTLOOK FOR THE US BANKING INDUSTRY

In the decade to come, it is highly likely that the US banking industry will continue to consolidate. It is a near certainty that the number of small banks (i.e., those with less than $500 million in assets) will continue to decline, as dictated by increasing competitive pres-sures and the economics of bank production processes. At the other end of the industry, it is not at all clear whether the very largest banks will continue to grow, will shrink in size, or perhaps even cease to exist entirely. Amid populist dislike of large banking companies—both in general as well as for their culpability in the financial crisis—combined with real uncertainty among experts about the feasibility of ending the TBTF doctrine, a movement has developed to simply break up the largest banking companies into several smaller firms. Strong advocates of this policy include FDIC Vice Chairman Thomas Hoenig; Independent Community Bankers of America (ICBA) president Camden Fine, and US Senators Sherrod Brown and David Vitter who have introduced legislation to this effect. The most likely out-come is the status quo, with the very largest US banking companies remaining large but steering a careful strategic (and political) course.

There is likely to be some strategic retrenchment away from the transactions banking business model back toward more traditional banking models. An increased percentage of home mortgages and other retail loans will likely be funded by bank deposits rather than ABSs, and as a result less credit will likely be available for marginal and subprime borrowers. But technology does not disappear. Although the securitization of subprime mortgage loans essentially ceased at the end of 2008 and has not yet rebounded in any substantial volume, the loan-to-sell credit channel generates far too much financial and informational efficiency to be abandoned. Moreover, important lessons are learned from the application of any new technology, and it is safe to say that subprime loan securitization will be employed again in the future, albeit with more prudence by lenders, more diligence by investors, and greater regulatory oversight.

Having approved over $1 trillion of taxpayer funds to "bail out" or otherwise subsidize US financial institutions during the crisis, the US Congress took immediate action to more strictly regulate those institutions by passing the Dodd–Frank Wall Street Reform and Consumer Protection Act of 2010. This far-reaching legislation sets new and tighter parameters under which US banks must operate going forward, and will reshape the industry in a number of important ways. For example, the Dodd–Frank Act places strict limits on proprietary trading at commercial banking companies, requires banks to purchase and sell most derivatives contracts through central clearinghouses, and creates a Consumer Financial Protection Bureau (CFBP) with broad powers to delineate the types and terms of retail financial products that banks can sell. But by far, the most important regulatory reform contained in the Dodd–Frank Act is the "orderly liquidation authority" (OLA) granted to the FDIC.

OLA extends the existing legal authority of the FDIC, enabling it to seize and resolve insolvent SIFIs without bailing them out. The FDIC has proposed a "single point of entry" approach in which it will: (1) seize the insolvent holding company, (2) fire senior management, (3) impose a 100% loss on stockholders, (4) impose further losses on bondholders and other creditors, and (5) place the assets and remaining liabilities of the holding company into a temporary "bridge bank" structure. The bridge institution has a three-year charter (extendable to five years) which will receive additional funding as needed from the FDIC to finance its bank, thrift, investment bank, brokerage or insurance affiliates. The FDIC will interfere as little as possible with the day-to-day operations of these affiliated firms, other than to make sure that insured bank deposits suffer no losses. New managers will run the bridge holding company and its large affiliates, and these temporary managers will use the information contained in so-called "living wills" (resolution plans kept on file by all SIFIs) to wind down financial contracts and otherwise stabilize the holding company and its affiliated firms. Once stabilized, management will sell off the holding company, as a whole or in parts, to healthy financial institutions without any further expense to the FDIC.

Critics of OLA argue that it legislates TBTF regulatory practices, and thus guarantees the existence of TBTF financial institutions into the future. If the OLA approach works as described above, then this argument will be moot, as neither SIFI owners, SIFI uninsured creditors, nor SIFI senior managers will have been bailed out. Most importantly, with the credibility of the resolution authorities established, and TBTF subsidies (e.g., lower cost of debt finance for TBTF banks) eliminated, becoming TBTF will no longer be an incentive for banks to grow large. However, if the OLA approach does not work, or if it is not fully implemented by regulatory authorities during a crisis, then no such credibility will be established and TBTF incentives will remain. This is a real concern, because the Dodd–Frank Act requires that the Treasury Department, the Federal Reserve, and the FDIC must mutually agree to implement OLA on an insolvent bank holding company; if one or more of these three agencies feels that a bailout is the preferable course of action, then an OLA resolution will not occur. This eventuality is most plausible during a severe financial crisis when the fear of short-run disruptions from multiple large bank insolvencies is considered more costly than the long-run damage caused by allowing TBTF incentives (DeYoung, Kowalik, and Reidhill, 2013).

REFERENCES

Berger, A. N. (2003). The Economic Effects of Technological Progress: Evidence from the Banking Industry, *Journal of Money, Credit, and Banking* 35, 141–176.

Berger, A. N., Bonime, S. D., Goldberg, L. G., and White, L. J. (2004). The Dynamics of Market Entry: The Effects of Mergers and Acquisitions on De Novo Entry and Small Business Lending in the Banking Industry, *Journal of Business* 77, 797–834.

Berger, A. N. and DeYoung, R. (2001). The Effects of Geographic Expansion on Bank Efficiency, *Journal of Financial Services Research* 19, 163–184.

Berger, A. N. and DeYoung, R. (2006). Technological Progress and the Geographic Expansion of the Banking Industry, *Journal of Money, Credit, and Banking* 38, 1483–1513.

Berger, A. N., DeYoung, R., Flannery, M. J., Lee, D., and Öztekin, Ö. (2008). Why Do Large Banking Organizations Hold So Much Capital? *Journal of Financial Services Research* 34, 123–149.

Berger, A. N., Frame, W. S., and Miller, N. H. (2005). Credit Scoring and the Availability, Price, and Risk of Small Business Credit, *Journal of Money, Credit, and Banking* 37, 191–222.

Berger, A. N., Kashyap, A. K., and Scalise, J. M. (1995). The Transformation of the US Banking Industry: What a Long, Strange Trip It's Been, *Brookings Papers on Economic Activity* 2, 55–218.

Berger A. N., Miller, N. H., Petersen, M. A., Rajan, R. G., and Stein, J. C. (2005). Does Function Follow Organizational Form: Evidence from the Lending Practices of Large and Small Banks, *Journal of Financial Economics* 76, 237–269.

Berlin, M. (2007). Dancing with Wolves: Syndicated Loans and the Economics of Multiple Lenders, *Federal Reserve Bank of Philadelphia Business Review* Third Quarter, 1–8.

Carey, M., Prowse S., Rea, J., and Udell, G. F. (1993). The Economics of Private Placements: A New Look, *Financial Markets, Institutions, and Instruments* 2, 1–66.

Clark, T., Dick, A., Hirtle, B., Stiroh, K., and Williams, R. (2007). The Role of Retail Banking in the US Banking Industry: Risk, Return, and Industry Structure, *Federal Reserve Bank of New York Economic Policy Review* 13, 39–56.

Davies, R. and Tracey, B. (2014). Too Big to be Efficient? The Impact of Implicit Funding Subsidies on Scale Economies in Banking, *Journal of Money, Credit and Banking* 46, 219–253.

Demirgüç-Kunt, A. and Huizinga, H. (2010). Bank Activity and Funding Strategies: The Impact on Risk and Returns, *Journal of Financial Economics* 98, 626–650.

DeYoung, R. (2000). Mergers and the Changing Landscape of Commercial Banking (Part II), Federal Reserve Bank of Chicago Fed Letter No. 150.

DeYoung, R. (2005). The Performance of Internet-based Business Models: Evidence from the Banking Industry, *Journal of Business* 78, 893–947.

DeYoung, R. (2013). Economies of Scale in Banking. In: F. Pasiouras (Ed.), *Efficiency and Productivity Growth: Modelling in the Financial Services Industry*, 49–76. Chichester: John Wiley.

DeYoung, R., Frame, W. S., Glennon, D., and Nigro, P. (2011). The Information Revolution and Small Business Lending: The Missing Evidence, *Journal of Financial Services Research* 39, 19–33.

DeYoung, R., Glennon, D., and Nigro, P. (2008). Borrower-lender Distance, Credit Scoring, and the Performance of Small Business Loans, *Journal of Financial Intermediation* 17, 113–143.

DeYoung, R., Gron, A., Torna, G., and Winton, A. (2013). Risk Overhang and Loan Portfolio Decisions: Small Business Loan Supply Before and During the Financial Crisis, <http://papers.ssrn.com/sol3/papers.cfm?abstract_id=2140952>.

DeYoung, R. and Hasan, I. (1998). The Performance of De Novo Commercial Banks: A Profit Efficiency Approach, *Journal of Banking and Finance* 22, 565–587.

DeYoung, R., Hasan, I., and Kirchhoff, B. (1998). The Impact of Out-of-state Entry on the Efficiency of Local Commercial Banks, *Journal of Economics and Business* 50, 191–203.

DeYoung, R., Hunter, W. C., and Udell, G. F. (2004). The Past, Present, and Probable Future for Community Banks, *Journal of Financial Services Research* 25, 85–133.

DeYoung, R., Kowalik, M., and Reidhill, J. (2013). A Theory of Bank Resolution: Technological Change and Political Economics, *Journal of Financial Stability* 9, 612627.

DeYoung, R., Lang, W. W., and Nolle, D. L. (2007). How the Internet Affects Output and Performance at Community Banks, *Journal of Banking and Finance* 31, 1033–1060.

DeYoung, R., Peng, E., and Yan, M. (2013). Executive Compensation and Business Policy Choices at US Commercial Banks, *Journal of Financial and Quantitative Analysis* 48, 165–196.

DeYoung, R. and Rice, T. (2004). How do Banks Make Money? A Variety of Business Strategies, *Federal Reserve Bank of Chicago Economic Perspectives* 28, 52–67.

DeYoung, R. and Roland, K. P. (2001). Product Mix and Earnings Volatility at Commercial Banks: Evidence from a Degree of Total Leverage Model, *Journal of Financial Intermediation* 10, 54–84.

DeYoung, R. and Torna, G. (2013). Nontraditional Banking Activities and Bank Failures during the Financial Crisis, *Journal of Financial Intermediation* 22, 397–421.

Evanoff, D. and Ors, E. (2008). Local Market Consolidation and Bank Productive Efficiency, *Journal of Money, Credit and Banking* 40, 897–928.

FDIC (Federal Deposit Insurance Corporation) (2012). *FDIC Community Banking Study*. Washington: Federal Deposit Insurance Corporation.

Federal Reserve Board (2004). *Survey of Consumer Finances*. Washington, DC: Federal Reserve Board.

Frame, W. S., Srinivasan, A., and Woosley, L. (2001). The Effect of Credit Scoring on Small Business Lending, *Journal of Money, Credit, and Banking* 33, 813–825.

Frame, W. S. and White, L. J. (2004). Empirical Studies of Financial Innovation: Lots of Talk, Little Action? *Journal of Economic Literature* 42, 116–144.

Gerdes, G. R. and Walton, J. K. (2002). The Use of Checks and Other Retail Noncash Payments in the United States, *Federal Reserve Bulletin* August, 360–374.

Goddard, J., Liu, H., McKillop, D., and Wilson, J. O. S. (2014). The Size Distribution of US Banks and Credit Unions, *International Journal of the Economics of Business* 21, 139–156.

Hughes, J. P., Lang, W. W., Mester, L. J., and Moon, G. (1996). Efficient Banking under Interstate Branching, *Journal of Money, Credit, and Banking* 28, 1045–1071.

Hughes, J. and Mester, L. (2013). Who Said Banks Don't Experience Scale Economies? Evidence from a Risk-Return-Driven Cost Function, *Journal of Financial Intermediation*, 22, 559–585.

Humphrey, D. (2002). US Cash and Card Payments Over 25 Years. Florida State University Unpublished Manuscript, <http://www.phil.frb.org/research-and-data/events/2002/financial-services-and-payments/papers/Humphrey.pdf.>.

Keeton, W. (2000). Are Mergers Responsible for the Surge in New Bank Charters? *Federal Reserve Bank of Kansas City Economic Review* First Quarter, 21–41.

Kroszner, R. S. and Melick, W. (2009). The Response of the Federal Reserve to the Recent Banking and Financial Crisis. University of Chicago Booth School of Buinsess, December.

Mester, L. J. (1997). What's the Point of Credit Scoring?, *Federal Reserve Bank of Philadelphia Business Review* September/October, 3–16.

Petersen, M. A. and Rajan, R. G. (2002). Does Distance Still Matter? The Information Revolution and Small Business Lending, *Journal of Finance* 57, 2533–2570.

Rossi, C. V. (1998). Mortgage Banking Cost Structure: Resolving an Enigma, *Journal of Economics and Business* 50, 219–234.

Scott, J. A. (2004). Small Business and the Value of Community Financial Institutions, *Journal of Financial Services Research* 25, 207–230.

Stein, J. C. (2002). Information Production and Capital Allocation: Decentralized versus Hierarchical Firms, *Journal of Finance* 57, 1891–1921.

Stigler, G. J. (1958). The Economies of Scale, *Journal of Law and Economics* 1, 54–71.

Wheelock, D. and Wilson, P. (2012). Do Large Banks Have Lower Costs? New Estimates of Returns to Scale for US Banks, *Journal of Money, Credit and Banking* 44, 171–200.

CHAPTER 35

BANKING IN THE EUROPEAN UNION

*Deregulation, Crisis, and Renewal**

JOHN GODDARD, PHILIP MOLYNEUX, AND
JOHN O. S. WILSON

35.1 INTRODUCTION

THE European banking industry has been subject to major shocks since the mid-2000s, including the turmoil following the US subprime crisis in 2007–08, and the more recent European sovereign debt crisis. The former led to large losses and the failure and closure of many banks, and forced large-scale interventions by central banks and governments on an unprecedented scale (Goddard, Molyneux, and Wilson, 2009). Government action has included four types of intervention: guarantees for bank liabilities; recapitalizations; asset support (measures to provide relief for troubled assets); and increased deposit insurance coverage. Between 1 October 2008 and 1 October 2011 the European Union's (EU) European Commission approved €4.5 trillion (approximately 37% of EU gross domestic product (GDP)) in government support to the banking sector (Koopman, 2011). In 2008 alone, €3.5 trillion (28% of EU GDP) was approved, mainly in the form of guarantees, after the main emphasis of state support shifted towards recapitalization and impaired asset relief. Most of the changes to deposit insurance were made in 2008.

EU member states did not take up their full quota of approved aid. The amount of state support actually deployed between 2008 and 2010 stood at €1.6 trillion (just over 13% of

* The authors would like to thank Barbara Casu and José Liñares-Zegarra for useful comments and suggestions. We would also like to thank Yalman Onaran of Bloomberg for supplying data on bank write-downs. The usual disclaimer applies.

EU GDP, the equivalent of 2% of EU banking sector assets) (Petrovic and Tutsch, 2009; Pisani-Ferry and Sapir, 2010; Stolz and Wedow, 2010). Around €1.2 trillion took the form of guarantees and other liquidity measures, and the remainder, around €410 billion, took the form of recapitalizations and support for banks with impaired assets. Between October 2008 and October 2011, around 250 decisions were taken regarding state support to the banking industry. The only European countries in which no support was provided were Bulgaria, Czech Republic, Estonia, Malta, and Romania. The large-scale injection of state funds, coupled with an array of regulatory reforms aimed at bolstering capital and liquidity and curtailing excessive risk, was successful in averting a collapse of the banking system.[1]

During 2010 and 2011, the financial crisis evolved into a European sovereign debt crisis. Since the introduction of the euro in 1999, the financial sector had been subject to rapid expansion, both within the Eurozone and beyond in countries such as Switzerland and the UK. During the 2000s several southern European economies, such as Greece, Italy, Portugal, and Spain, ran large current account deficits, offset by surpluses in Germany and some other northern European countries (Arnold, 2012; Lane, 2012; Correa and Sapriza, Chapter 30, this volume). Credit flows channeled through the rapidly expanding financial sector in the core of the Eurozone fuelled property market bubbles in countries such as Ireland and Spain. Spiraling government deficits and debt, exacerbated by the bailouts of troubled banks following the crisis, triggered a crisis of confidence, reflected in widening differences between bond yields and credit default swap spreads of deficit and surplus countries. The euro crisis has been described as a continuation of the financial crisis by alternative means. On the one hand, the perception that bank balance sheets remain contaminated to a significant extent by hidden or undeclared delinquent lending raises concerns over the implications for fiscal sustainability of the future need for further bank bailouts. On the other hand, the banks themselves are major investors in government debt, and recognition of the possibility that a euro member country might default on its debt and withdraw from the single currency has heightened the prospects of additional bank failures. Proposals for a European banking union, which would entail pooling responsibility for the rescue of ailing banks, seek to break this symbiotic relationship that has developed between distressed banks and distressed sovereigns.

In May 2010, the Eurozone authorities and the International Monetary Fund (IMF) agreed a €110 billion loan for Greece, conditional on the implementation of tough austerity measures. Later in the same month, the European Financial Stability Facility (comprising of a broad rescue package amounting to $1 trillion) was established with the aim of ensuring financial stability in the Eurozone. Following the Greek bailout, further support programs were approved for Ireland (€85 billion in November 2010) and Portugal (€78 billion in May 2011), benefitting European banks that were large holders of sovereign debt. In many countries, however, banks have still been forced to raise large amounts of new capital, and many have struggled to achieve returns in excess of their cost of capital. In March 2013, Cyprus was awarded a €10 billion bailout to stabilize its financial system and finance its fiscal deficit. The largest and most internationally diversified banks are also subject to increased capital and liquidity requirements under Basel III (EBA 2012; ECB, 2012). At the time of writing of this chapter, large banks throughout Europe were continuing efforts to improve their

---

[1] Marquez, Correa, and Sapriza (2013) in a large cross-country study find that more government support is linked to greater bank risk-taking particularly between 2009 and 2010.

capitalization, by reducing risk-adjusted assets. This was achieved mainly by reducing lending and scaling down investment banking business (Vause et al. 2012; Dermine, 2013; Feyen and Gonzalez del Mazo, 2013).

It is against this background, that this chapter discusses the evolution of the European banking industry, along with recent regulatory developments including the plans for a European banking union. The remainder of the chapter is structured as follows. Section 35.2 provides an overview of the structure and performance of the European banking industry. Section 35.3 provides a brief discussion of credit crises. Section 35.4 outlines proposed structural reforms set out in the UK's Vickers Report of 2011, and the EU's Liikanen Report of 2012, and describes the proposed banking union. Section 35.5 concludes.

35.2 Structural and Performance Features of European Banking

35.2.1 Deregulation and Integration

European banking has changed dramatically since the passing of the First Banking Directive in 1977. In response to developments such as financial deregulation, the creation of the single market in financial services and the introduction of the euro, banks have increased the range of products and services to customers, blurring the distinction between banks, insurance companies and other financial firms. Entry by foreign-owned banks has led to increased competition in some market segments. This has placed additional pressure on banks to reduce costs, and find ways of increasing revenues from the sale of new types of products and services.

Since the passing of the First Banking Directive in 1977, EU legislation has been directed consistently towards reducing barriers to cross-border bank ownership and activity. Deregulation of financial markets at the national level has also eroded the lines of demarcation between banks and non-bank financial firms, facilitating both domestic as well as cross-border competition. Despite these developments, however, by the end of the 2000s there were still significant barriers to full-scale European financial integration. While wholesale banking had become highly integrated throughout Europe, retail banking and small business lending in Western Europe remained primarily nationally oriented, with only limited cross-border ownership or activity. In Eastern Europe, by contrast, there was extensive foreign ownership of retail banking. Bond and equity markets also remain largely fragmented along national lines. In regard to banking, the financial crisis constituted a major setback to the project of European financial integration (Sapir and Wolff, 2013). The scaling back of interbank lending sharply reduced the level of activity in the area where integration had been furthest advanced. The fragmentation of bank resolution authorities along national lines engendered divergence and, in some cases, home country bias in the arrangements for assistance to distressed banks that were implemented during the crisis.

During the 1990s and 2000s, many European banks expanded the scale of their operations, in some cases through merger and acquisition (M&A). Consolidation was motivated by the objectives of realizing scale and scope economies, reducing labor and other variable costs, cutting operational inefficiencies, and spreading risk through product or geo-graphic diversification. Rapid growth in the loans portfolios of some banks was financed via the securitization of prospective cash flows from sources such as mortgages and credit card debt, which commonly took place off-balance sheet. Growth in European banks' non-interest income reflected the growing use of securities-based financing by private sec-tor companies, increased demand by the household sector for insurance and personal pen-sions, and investment in mutual funds.

Changes embodied in the European Company Statute allowed banks to form sin-gle legal entities that operate freely across the EU, and enabled the conversion of subsidi-aries to branches. However, subsidiaries have remained predominantly the preferred cross-border organizational form (ECB, 2007a), suggesting that the benefits associated with risk spreading between different legal entities within a banking group are of strategic importance. The introduction of the Financial Services Action Plan between 1999 and 2004 provided momentum towards increased integration of the banking system, and increased cross-border inter connections between financial institutions. Technological advance also impacted on bank behaviour, through the proliferation of internet banking and the emer-gence of new payments media. Technology revolutionized delivery systems, and led to the adoption of different business models by small and large banks (Goddard, Molyneux, and Wilson, 2001, 2010; Goddard et al., 2007). The growing emphasis on performance and shareholder value also encouraged many banks to reappraise their asset and liability man-agement strategies.

In the two decades preceding the financial and sovereign debt crises, European banking was transformed by an array of developments including: globalization, deregulation, tech-nological change, as well as integration resulting from legislative moves to create a European single banking market (Goddard, Molyneux, and Wilson, 2010). These forces impacted on the industrial structure of European banking. Table 35.1 reports structural indicators for the banking industries of EU15 countries. Between 1985 and 2011 the total number of banks declined substantially in all major countries. Over the same period, the combined nominal total assets of French, German, Italian, Spanish, and UK banks increased by around 400%.

In France, Greece, Italy, Spain, and Portugal, the number of bank branches increased sub-stantially between 1985 and 2011, owing to the lifting of branching restrictions. The number of branches declined in Belgium and the UK, where banks sought to increase efficiency by rationalizing branch networks. EU15 banking sector employment increased by more than 13% over the same period, reaching 2.65 million by 2011. Germany has the largest number of staff employed in banking (664,000), followed by the UK (454,000) and France (430,000). Typically, employment in the banking industry accounts for around two-thirds of total financial sector employment. A general trend since the 1970s has been the increased pres-ence of female and part-time employees. In the UK, for example, the top ten banks employed 288,100 staff in 2012, of which 60% were female. Around 37% of female employees, but only 4% of male employees, were part-time (British Bankers Association, 2012).

Table 35.1 indicates that banking industry concentration has increased in the majority of countries. Domestic consolidation has been a prominent feature of this trend. M&A within national borders presents more straightforward opportunities for realizing efficiency gains than cross-border M&A, and perhaps fewer complications if the corporate cultures of the merger partners are homogeneous (Buch and DeLong, Chapter 31, this volume). Having said this, cross-border consolidation has become more common, which suggests there has

Table 35.1 Structural indicators for EU 15 banking sectors.

Country	Number of banks				Assets (billion euros)				Number of branches				Employees ('000s)				Concentration (Assets CR5)			
	1985	1995	2005	2011	1985	1995	2005	2011	1985	1995	2005	2011	1985	1995	2005	2011	1985	1995	2005	2011
Austria	1406	1041	880	783	–	396.8	720.5	1010.4	–	4856	4300	4431	–	74	75	78	–	39.0	45.0	35.9
Belgium	120	143	100	122	285.9	589.4	1055.3	1198.4	8207	7668	4564	3881	71	77	69	61	48.1	54.0	85.2	70.8
Denmark	259	202	197	164	96.3	125.5	722.1	1144.9	3411	2215	2114	1557	52	47	48	47	61.2	72.1	66.3	66.3
Finland	498	381	363	358	–	196.3	234.5	642.4	–	1612	1616	1422	–	31	25	23	–	70.6	83.1	80.9
France	1952	1895	1577	1147	1348.8	2513.7	5090.1	8391.5	25782	26606	27075	38323	449	408	430	379	46.0	41.3	53.5	48.3
Germany	4739	3785	2089	1956	1495.1	3584.1	6826.6	8393.5	39925	44012	44044	37853	591	724	705	664	–	16.7	21.6	33.5
Greece	41	53	62	79	69.2	94.0	281.1	476.9	1815	2417	3576	3845	27	54	61	60	80.6	75.7	65.6	72.0
Ireland	42	56	78	590	21.0	45.8	941.9	1312.8	–	808	910	1099	–	38	38	36	47.5	44.4	46.0	53.2
Italy	1101	970	792	785	546.8	1070.5	2509.4	4065.0	13033	20839	31498	33561	319	337	336	316	–	32.4	26.7	39.5
Luxembourg	177	220	155	554	169.8	445.5	792.4	1101.5	120	224	155	227	10	19	23	27	26.8	21.2	30.7	31.2
Netherlands	178	102	401	297	226.7	650.0	1697.7	2428.7	6868	6729	3748	2653	92	111	117	105	72.9	76.1	84.8	83.6
Portugal	226	233	186	159	38.0	116.3	360.2	573.8	1494	3401	5427	6403	59	60	58	61	61.0	74.0	68.8	70.8
Spain	364	506	348	415	311.3	696.3	2150.7	3643.0	32503	36405	41979	40103	244	249	253	246	35.1	47.3	42.0	48.1
Sweden	598	249	200	205	–	146.9	653.2	1140.4	–	2731	1910	2083	–	44	46	50	–	59.3	57.3	57.8
UK	772	564	400	405	1293.6	1999.5	8320.2	9708.2	22224	17522	13694	11686	375	445	483	454	–	28.3	36.3	44.1

Note: The large increase in the number of Irish banks in 2011 was due to a reclassification of credit unions as banks.

Sources: Central Bank Reports (various); ECB (2006), ECB (2007b), ECB (2010) and also from ECB Consolidated Banking Data (online resource).

been a reduction of several barriers that have inhibited international expansion in the past. Such barriers include difficulties in selling generic products across borders; differences in competition, employment, regulatory and supervisory policy; political interference; and a lack of consumer trust in foreign banks. In the past, there has been an inclination for the competition authorities in some countries to disqualify mergers between banks that already dominate their domestic retail markets. This approach may have had the unintended consequence of promoting cross-border M&A. For example, in the past the UK's Competition Commission has indicated that mergers between the four largest retail banks (HSBC, Barclays, Lloyds TSB, and RBS) would be discouraged. Accordingly, these banks often looked beyond the UK for feasible acquisition targets. The fateful bidding war between Barclays and a consortium including RBS to acquire the Dutch bank ABN AMRO in 2007 was a case in point. However, a number of European governments, unwilling to sanction the foreign acquisition of important domestic banks, present an obstacle to cross-border consolidation in certain cases.

35.2.2 Profitability and Efficiency

Europe has a diverse and dynamic banking sector, highlighted by the Final Report of the High-level Expert Group on Reforming the Structure of the EU Banking Sector (the so-called Liikanen Report):

> The EU banking sector is diverse, which is valuable. Banking sectors differ substantially across Member States, in terms of size, market concentration, foreign ownership, asset and liability structure, supervision, credit cycle, and public involvement. Diversity strengthens the resilience of the banking system as it mitigates vulnerability to systemic interconnections and promotes effective competition. Diversity is explicitly protected by the EU treaty. (Liikanen, 2012, p. 32)

Commercial banks traditionally depended upon interest margins as the main driver of profits. Profitability depended on banks' ability to maintain a sizeable gap between interest income and interest cost, while attempting to maximize operational efficiency. As banking systems were liberalized, competition in loan and deposit markets intensified. This was an observable trend from the early 1980s to the early 2000s in many European countries. Reductions in margins encouraged banks to supplement their income (where possible) by diversifying into non-interest income, or non-traditional areas such as insurance and securities underwriting. Following the EU Second Banking Directive of 1989, for example, non-interest income as a proportion of total income increased from 26% in 1989 to 41% by 1998 (ECB, 2000), and has since remained at a similar level.[2]

The shift towards non-interest income did not necessarily feed through to enhanced profitability. Shifts into non-traditional banking activities such as trading do not necessarily boost profits and can increase volatility. Furthermore, diversification does little to reduce risk if banks are merely selling different products to the same group of customers. An extensive literature suggests that banks do not benefit from diversification (Laeven and Levine,

---

[2] According to ECB (2013) Consolidated Banking Data for 2012 the non-interest income as a % of total income amounted to 41% See <http://www.ecb.int/stats/money/consolidated/html/index.en.html>.

2007; Stiroh, Chapter 9, this volume). Mercieca, Schaeck, and Wolfe (2007) examine a sample of small European banks from 1997 and 2003, and find no evidence of direct diversification benefits, while Baele, De Jonghe, and Vander Vennet (2007) find that diversification appears to destroy value for a sample of large European banks. For the period 1996–2002, Lepetit et al. (2008) report that European banks that earned higher commissions and fee income had lower interest margins, suggesting that loans were underpriced in order to boost fee-based services. By diversifying into non-interest income business, banks may lose focus in traditional lending business, and managers become less conservative in their lending. During the securitization boom, credit growth expanded rapidly with weak monitoring and risk transferred to investors through the sale of mortgage-backed and other asset-backed securities. Brunnermeier, Dong, and Palia (2012) suggest that banks with a high proportion of non-interest income from securities trading, venture capital and investment banking typically contribute more to systemic risk than those that focus on traditional commercial banking.

The general recognition that a reliance on non-interest revenue, particularly securities trading and investment banking, creates risk for financial stability informs proposals in the UK to "ring-fence" retail banking from investment banking and proposals in the EU to separate high-risk activities from low-risk deposit-taking within each banking group.

While the contribution of non-interest revenue to total revenue has risen, technological innovation has substantially reduced the costs associated with the collection, storage, processing and transmission of data, and transformed the means whereby customers gain access to banking services and products. Front-office innovation is reflected in the growth in number and usage of automated teller machines (ATMs), electronic funds transfer at the point of sale (EFTPOS), Internet banking and e-money services. Back-office operations have been transformed by the adoption of new internal systems, such as customer relationship management and business management technologies, core processing technologies and various support and integration technologies. Many of these innovations involve large setup costs relative to marginal costs, and the impact is not always cost saving. Even if technology reduces costs, revenues might adversely be affected (customers might be unhappy with a new technology, and demand less service). The cost-to-income ratio provides a crude measure of cost efficiency. In the 1980s and 1990s, a cost-to-income ratio of around 70% was considered excessive, and indicative of a bank that was badly managed. By the mid-2000s, a ratio below 60% was considered respectable. While bankers and analysts often focus on this efficiency metric, academics have used more sophisticated modeling techniques to compute efficiency scores for banks. These more technical measures can be obtained via parametric or non-parametric statistical methods, allowing controls for variations in the mix of inputs, and of outputs. Berger and Humphrey (1997) review 133 efficiency studies. In general, large banks are more efficient than their smaller counterparts, and there is greater potential for realizing cost savings by emulating best practice than by increasing size (scale economies) or product diversification (scope economies).

Weill (2009) reports evidence that European intergration has coincided with convergence in bank efficiency across countries. Using both parametric and non-parametric modeling approaches, Casu and Girardone (2010) report that bank efficiency has generally improved as a result of European integration. Related to this work is the literature investigating European bank productivity. Altunbas, Goddard, and Molyneux (1999), for example, report that technical change reduced EU banks' average costs during the 1990s, whereas Battese, Heshmati, and Hjalmarsson (2000) in a study of Swedish banks find that the cost-saving effects of technical change became exhausted, as "average" banks caught up with the industry best practice. Casu, Girardone, and Molyneux (2004) report that banks in some European countries benefited from productivity growth during the 1990s, but the pattern was varied. Several studies suggest deregulation often had a negative impact on bank productivity (Lozano-Vivas, 1998; Canhoto and Dermine, 2003). This is somewhat surprising, as studies for countries outside the US and Europe typically find that liberalization boosts productivity. Fiorentino et al. (2009) report evidence that consolidation and privatization fostered productivity growth among Italian and German banks during the period 1994–2004. Conflicting productivity results may derive from variations in assumptions relating to the structure of common production frontiers across countries and banks, as well as uniform operating environments. Casu et al. (2013) investigate the total factor productivity growth of commercial banks in nine Eurozone countries between 1992 and 2009, allowing for heterogeneous technology and the presence of "technology gaps" between countries. The analysis suggests that while technical improvements have occurred, there is variation between countries in the benefits to each banking industry. There are signs that all banking industries are converging towards use of the best available technology. The speed of convergence accelerated after the introduction of the single currency, but decelerated following the 2007–08 sub prime crisis.

As perhaps one might expect, substantial variations in European bank profitability persist. Table 35.2, for example, highlights the relatively low profitability of German banks during the early and mid-2000s, when banks in Belgium, Sweden, and UK enjoyed relatively high profits. Differences in profitability between countries have been attributed to a variety of factors including: variation in accounting and tax systems; structural factors such as the intensity of competition in specific product segments; the extent of product and geographic diversification; and business cycle effects (Llewellyn, 2005; Carbó and Rodriguez, 2007; Goddard et al. 2007). Goddard et al. (2013) investigate competitive behavior in European banking before and after the introduction of the euro and the implementation of the Financial Services Action Plan (FSAP), by examining the persistence of bank profitability. Comparisons between the periods 1992–98 and 1999–2007, before and after the introduction of the euro and the implementation of the FSAP, suggest that the persistence of profit fell in most countries, indicating an increase in the intensity of competition.[3]

35.2.3 Competition and Risk

Since the banking crisis there has been much discussion in both policy and academic circles as to which type of business model will yield the safest and most profitable banking system. According to Liikanen (2012), while the adverse effects of the crisis were universal, those banks that were "less resilient" typically relied heavily on short-term wholesale funding, excessive leverage and trading activity, and were characterized by excessive lending and weak corporate governance. The impact of the crisis, together with state support for

---

[3] Weill (2013) computes Lerner and Rosse-Panzar H—Indices in order to explore the evolution of competition in European banking. Integration appears to have led to a convergence in the level of competition across countries. However, there is no significant increase in competition.

Table 35.2 Average profitability (% return on equity) of EU 15 national banking sectors, 1990 to 2011.

Country	1990–94	1995–99	2000	2001	2002	2003	2004	2005	2006	2007	2008	2009	2010	2011
Austria	8.13	9.17	11.33	7.85	7.83	9.50	10.49	10.91	16.31	7.81	1.60	1.63	6.41	1.47
Belgium	9.57	14.54	20.48	15.90	11.76	16.07	14.03	17.11	19.46	9.94	-1.74	6.89	10.48	1.36
Denmark	-2.77	15.70	15.24	10.23	11.26	15.75	16.46	12.06	16.84	9.00	-12.36	-6.90	2.39	0.60
Finland	-21.57	8.05	22.07	22.79	8.40	18.11	12.12	7.36	10.92	6.71	1.23	7.92	6.96	8.11
France	6.18	7.36	12.08	10.94	9.38	9.85	13.43	9.54	14.77	9.47	5.80	8.36	8.35	5.59
Germany	12.97	12.48	7.86	0.84	-1.71	-2.70	2.26	8.33	11.02	4.79	2.87	3.57	15.2	2.16
Greece	24.60	21.16	19.21	11.80	7.71	14.01	11.54	10.86	13.93	11.44	2.86	-1.95	-4.73	5.88
Ireland	n/a	19.80	17.88	10.77	11.90	14.50	18.30	12.46	17.84	7.07	-0.16	-49.97	-65.22	-11.12
Italy	11.14	9.29	17.58	8.42	6.44	7.59	11.45	8.17	10.50	8.74	6.75	3.47	3.68	-12.99
Luxembourg	12.73	21.87	20.51	12.89	10.62	13.73	9.88	12.79	19.22	10.99	2.10	8.24	8.47	6.17
Netherlands	13.99	15.92	17.19	12.39	9.75	14.73	19.50	14.14	16.96	18.63	11.43	9.41	7.54	6.16
Portugal	10.07	7.78	8.84	13.43	12.30	13.44	11.40	8.04	13.40	18.63	11.43	9.41	7.54	6.16
Spain	9.73	10.40	10.37	12.30	12.65	13.35	14.60	8.94	15.22	11.53	8.65	1.74	8.04	0.09
Sweden	17.09	18.42	19.50	18.85	13.39	15.34	18.45	11.07	15.70	9.60	3.56	9.98	10.18	10.65
UK	15.40	27.88	21.49	13.47	11.59	14.43	19.90	9.84	16.10	12.59	10.38	4.37	4.37	4.24
EU-15 Mean	8.48	14.65	16.11	12.19	9.55	12.51	13.59	10.77	15.21	10.46	3.62	1.08	1.98	2.30
EU-15 Median	10.61	14.54	17.58	12.30	10.62	14.01	13.43	10.86	15.70	9.60	2.87	4.37	7.54	4.24

Source: Constructed from Bankscop and ECB Consolidated Banking Data.

ailing banks, on competition in banking has been debated widely. Until the 1980s there was a general consensus that competition between banks was damaging for financial stability (Carletti, 2010). Competition encouraged excessive risk-taking on the assets (loans) side of banks' balance sheets, increasing the likelihood of individual bank failure. More recently it has been suggested that competition may be helpful in reducing risk. According to theory, the allocation of bank assets is determined by solving a portfolio problem, emphasizing the liabilities side of the balance sheet. Upon confronting increased competition on the deposits side, banks tend increase their offered rates to attract depositors. When paying higher deposit rates, neglecting the effects of competition in the loans market, earnings decline. In an attempt to recapture lost profits, banks tend to accept more risky investments. By contrast, when competition is restrained, banks exercise market power by paying lower deposit rates, and can thereby increase their profits. Banks that are subject to limited competition are less willing to invest in high return—high-risk projects, reducing the likelihiood of failure.

The counter-argument that competition lowers risk is developed by Koskela and Stenbacka (2000) and Boyd and De Nicolo (2005), who develop a theoretical model of competition on both the deposits and loans sides of the balance sheet. Project risk is determined by the interest rates charged to borrowers. The portfolio problem is transformed into a contracting problem that is subject to moral hazard. Banks with market power charge lower rates on deposits and higher rates on loans. In this context, portfolio theory suggests that banks with market power have little incentive to take on risk, because they can earn monopoly profits without doing so. However, the contracting problem reverses this logic. Higher loan rates force bank borrowers to seek out more risky projects, increasing portfolio risk for (monopoly) banks. By contrast, banks subject to competitive pressure offer lower loans rates in order to reduce moral hazard, and face reduced risk because their borrowers are less likely to pursue risky investments. Martinez-Miera and Repullo (2010) suggest the relationship between competition and stability may be non-linear. Liu, Molyneux, and Wilson (2013) construct measures of competition and economic activity using regional data for ten European countries over the period 2000-08. There is an inverted U-shaped relationship between bank competition at regional level, and stability. Either "too little" or "too much" competition is associated with high risk. Regional economic conditions play a significant role in determining stability.

Following the financial and sovereign debt crises, moral hazard issues concerning large banks too-big-, too-interconnected—or too-systemically-important-to-fail have been debated extensively in academic and policy circles. Large banks obtain implicit (or explicit) subsidies via government safety nets, which encourage excessive risk-taking (O'Hara and Shaw, 1990; Stern and Feldman, 2004, 2009; Herring and Carmassi, 2010; Brown and Dinç, 2011; and Demirgüç-Kunt and Huizinga, 2013). Empirical evidence on the competition-fragility and competition-stability hypotheses is mixed (Turk-Ariss, 2010; Beck, De Jonghe, and Schepens, 2013; Jiménez, López, and Saurina, 2013). Using data for EU-25 countries, Uhde and Heimeshoff (2009) show that national banking market concentration has a negative impact on banking sector stability. Berger, Klapper, and Turk-Ariss (2009) examine market power and risk issues for a sample of more than 8,000 banks in 23 developed countries for the period 1999–2005. Banks with more market power have lower risk exposure. The results provide some support for both the competition-fragility and competition-stability hypotheses: market power increases credit risk, but banks with more market power are less exposed to other types of risk. Overall, both the theoretical and the empirical evidence concerning the nature of the relationship between competition and risk in banking are inconclusive.

There is, at least, anecdotal evidence that the intensity of competition in European banking has increased in recent years. As noted earlier, barriers to product and geographic diversification have been reduced or eliminated. Banks have diversified into non-traditional lines of business such as insurance and mutual funds, private banking and asset management. Prior to the credit crisis of 2007 and 2008 the securitization of European banks' loans portfolios had been proceeding rapidly. Securitization issues amounted to €496 billion in 2007, of which over 50% related to residential mortgages (European Securitisation Forum, 2008). Meanwhile insurance companies and investment and pension funds encroached into territory previously occupied by banks, as household savings were siphoned towards alternative savings and investment products. By the end of the 2000s, non-bank institutions such as supermarkets and telecommunications firms competed in financial services markets.

Table 35.3 reports estimates of the performance of large, complex banking groups in the Eurozone for the period 2005–10. Large losses were recorded in 2008, followed by a modest recovery. Tier 1 capital and solvency ratios increased in 2009 and 2010. Stress tests conducted by the European Banking Authority (EBA), published in July 2011 and covering 90 banks operating in 21 European countries provide a useful snapshot of the performance of large European banks. For this exercise the EBA allowed specific capital increases during the first four months of 2011 to be included in their calculations, providing an incentive for banks to boost solvency prior to the tests. The main results were as follows:

- By December 2010 some 20 banks would not have achieved the benchmark 5% Tier 1 capital ratio over the 2010–12 time horizon of the exercise, amounting to a capital shortfall of €26.8 billion.
- The 90 banks raised an additional €50 billion between January and April 2011.
- 16 banks achieved a Tier 1 ratio of between 5% and 6%.

On the basis of these findings the EBA issued a recommendation to national supervisory authorities that banks with Tier 1 capital below the 5% threshold should remedy the

Table 35.3 Performance of large and complex banking groups in the Eurozone

Year	Return on Equity (%) Median	Average	Impaired Loans/ Total Assets (%) Median	Average	Cost-Income Ratio (%) Median	Average	Tier 1 Ratio (%) Median	Average	Solvency Ratio (%) Median	Average
2005	10.04	11.93	0.08	0.11	60.69	58.87	7.89	8.20	11.05	11.23
2006	14.81	14.61	0.07	0.11	5595	56.40	7.75	8.07	11.01	11.16
2007	11.97	11.65	0.05	0.10	63.00	62.95	7.40	7.72	10.60	10.72
2008	2.26	-14.65	0.27	0.31	73.36	160.96	8.59	8.58	11.70	11.37
2009	2.97	0.34	0.45	0.55	60.35	62.47	10.15	10.33	13.60	13.37
2010	7.68	6.76	0.24	0.32	60.40	62.01	11.20	11.38	14.10	14.38

Source: Adapted from ECB, Financial Stability Review, June 2011, Table S5, page S30-S31.

situation as soon as possible. In addition the EBA also recommended that national supervisory authorities request all banks whose Tier 1 ratio is above but close to 5% (and that have sizeable exposures to sovereigns under stress), to take specific steps to strengthen their solvency, including (where necessary), restrictions on dividends, deleveraging, issuance of fresh capital or conversion of lower-quality instruments into Core Tier 1 capital.

The impact of the sovereign debt crisis on bank funding costs is an ongoing concern (see BIS 2011, and IMF 2011). An increase in sovereign risk leads to a higher spread vis-à-vis the typical risk-free asset in Europe, the German Bund, and an increased cost of servicing liabilities (especially since bonds comprise a substantial proportion of bank balance sheets). The aforementioned stress tests showed that in December 2010, the 90 banks had €8.2 trillion of short-term wholesale/interbank funding. Replacing this funding is a major challenge for the sector. The ECB's Financial Stability Reviews (ECB 2011, 2012) sound a note of caution about the risks.

35.3 CRISIS IN EUROPEAN BANKING

The impact of the financial crisis on European banking began in the summer of 2007, with the failure of a structured investment vehicle (known as Rhineland) of IKB Deutsche Industriebank, a small German lender. This event prompted a state-led rescue. Liquidity within the banking system evaporated, and overnight interest rates increased dramatically. An injection of liquidity into the Eurozone banking system was effective in averting any major bank failure. The outlook deteriorated dramatically in September 2008, however, following the collapse of the US investment bank Lehman Brothers (DeYoung, Chapter 34, this volume). These events created a crisis of confidence that brought the US and European banking systems perilously close to the brink of collapse in September and October 2008 (European Economy, 2009; Goddard, Molyneux, and Wilson, 2009).

Between 2007 and 2010, the largest European banks reported huge credit losses. Several major UK and Swiss banks were among the largest casualties. Since October 2008 the capitalization of many of Europe's largest banks has been bolstered through injections of public funding, predominantly in the form of government purchase of preference shares and other quasi equity instruments (see Table 35.4). In response to the crisis, most European governments announced a combination of loan guarantee schemes, bank rescue plans and fiscal stimulus packages (Stolz and Wedow, 2010; Pisani-Ferry and Sapir, 2010; ECB, 2011).

Since this wave of government-backed bank bailouts, recapitalization plans, liquidity injections, and credit guarantee schemes, there has been widespread concern over the business models of European banks. Large-scale banking rescues have raised serious worries about the social and economic costs of "too-big-to-fail" (TBTF) or "too systemically important to fail." Such concerns are not confined to the largest banks: for example, the UK's Northern Rock was bailed out with public funds because it was perceived to be of systemic importance. An important question for policy makers is whether limits should be placed on bank size, growth or concentration, to minimize the moral hazard concerns raised by banks having achieved TBTF or related status. Besides the actions of national governments, the European Commission has issued several communications concerning aspects of the crisis: the application of state aid rules to the banking sector; the treatment of banks' impaired

Table 35.4 European bank write-downs and capital raised to December 2010

Rank	Name	Country	Write down and losses $bn	Capital $bn
1	Royal Bank of Scotland Group Plc	UK	75.9	97.8
2	UBS AG	Switzerland	58.4	51.1
3	HSBC Holdings Plc	UK	56	28.8
4	Barclays Plc	UK	44.8	31.6
5	Banco Santander SA	Spain	30.2	29.4
6	HBOS Plc	UK	29.5	25.7
7	UniCredit SpA	Italy	27.9	15.9
8	Credit Suisse Group AG	Switzerland	27.4	22.3
9	Deutsche Bank AG	Germany	24.5	28.9
10	BNP Paribas	France	24	13.6
11	ING Groep N.V.	Netherlands	19.8	24.6
12	Societe Generale	France	19.5	17.8
13	Bayerische Landesbank	Germany	19.3	21.4
14	Commerzbank AG	Germany	17.1	26.3
15	KBC Groep NV	Belgium	15	7.9
16	IKB Deutsche Industriebank AG	Germany	14.8	11
17	Allied Irish Banks Plc	Ireland	13	18
18	Banco Bilbao Vizcaya Argentaria	Spain	12.7	0
19	Danske Bank A/S	Denmark	10.8	0
20	Credit Agricole S.A.	France	9.9	12.9
21	Intesa Sanpaolo	Italy	9.7	5.8
22	Fortis	Belgium	9.4	23.2
23	Natixis	France	9	8.3
24	Landesbank Baden-Wurttemberg	Germany	8	7.2
25	DZ Bank AG	Germany	7.8	0
26	Anglo Irish Bank Corp	Ireland	7.6	4.4
27	Hypo Real Estate Holding AG	Germany	7.2	11.2
28	Dexia SA	Belgium	7	9.2
29	Erste Group Bank	Austria	6.1	3
30	Dresdner Bank AG	Germany	5.2	0
31	Banco Popolare	Italy	4.5	0
32	HSH Nordbank AG	Germany	4.2	1.8
33	National Bank of Greece SA	Greece	4.1	0.8
34	Bank of Ireland	Ireland	4.1	11.7
35	WestLB AG	Germany	4	7.2
36	EFG Eurobank	Greece	3.9	0
37	Lloyds Banking Group Plc	UK	3.6	51.2
38	Banco Popular Espanol SA	Spain	3.6	1.7
39	Rabobank	Netherlands	3.5	1.5
40	Northern Rock PLC	UK	3.3	5.6
41	Alliance & Leicester Plc	UK	2.6	0
42	Landesbank Sachsen AG	Germany	2.5	0
43	Deutsche Postbank AG	Germany	2.5	1.4
44	ABN AMRO Holding NV	Netherlands	2.3	0
45	Alpha Bank	Greece	2.1	0
46	Bradford & Bingley PLC	UK	2.1	3.1
47	Piraeus Bank	Greece	2	0
48	Groupe Caisse d'Epargne	France	1.2	5.2
49	Landesbank Hessen-Thueringen	Germany	0.8	0
50	HVB Group	Germany	0.7	0

Source: Bloomberg. Data beyond 2010 is no longer being collected.

assets; the recapitalization of financial institutions; and the provision of restructuring aid to banks. Many of the regulatory or supervisory frameworks for dealing with problems in the financial system at an EU level were found to be deficient in key respects (Fonteyne et al., 2010). National approaches to crisis management and depositor protection were inadequate, and sometimes produced adverse spillover effects on banking systems in other EU member states. There was a lack of cooperation and agreement over arrangements for sharing the burden of fiscal costs arising from the crisis. Effective regulation has also been constrained by a lack of transparency concerning banks' business models. While the crisis has forced banks to provide detailed information on their exposures, disclosure of practices concerning risk management and valuation remains limited. Likewise, the restoration of confidence in over the counter (OTC) markets for securitized assets and credit derivatives requires greater transparency, reduced complexity and improved oversight.

35.4 New Regulatory Architecture and Banking Union

There is a general recognition that before the crisis European banks focused too heavily on high risk non-interest revenue generation, particularly through securities trading and investment banking activity. In response, a series of major structural proposals and legislation has aimed to reduce bank risk and minimise the likelihood of further taxpayer-financed bank bailouts. In the UK, the Independent Commission on Banking (or Vickers Commission after its Chair Sir John Vickers) was tasked with considering structural and non-structural reforms to the UK banking industry, to promote competition and financial stability. The recommendations of the Commission's Final Report, published in September 2011, included the following:

- Retail banking activity should be "ring-fenced" from wholesale and investment banking.
- Systemically important banks with large retail banking activities should have a minimum 10% equity-to-assets ratio.
- Contingent capital and debt should be available to improve absorb future losses.
- Risk management should become a self-contained, less complex business for retail banking, but remain complex for wholesale and investment banking.

At the time of writing, the recommendations of the Report are being incorporated into a planned Banking Act. The annual cost of these reforms to the UK economy are estimated to range between £1 billion and £3 billion, which compares favorably with an estimated annual cost of £40 billion in lost output following the financial crisis. If adopted, the proposed reforms should be implemented by 2019.

   The recommendations made by the EU High-level Expert Group on Reforming the Structure of the EU Banking Sector chaired by Erkki Liikanen (the Liikanen Report, published in October 2012) suggests proprietary trading and other significant trading activities should be assigned to a separate legal entity if the activities to be separated amount to a significant share of a bank's business. Banks should draw up and maintain effective and realistic recovery and resolution plans, as proposed by the Recovery and Resolution Directive. The resolution authority should be able to request wider separation than the mandatory level described above, if deemed necessary. Banks should build up a sufficiently large layer of bail-in debt, and such debt should be held outside the banking system. More robust risk weightings should be used in the determination of minimum capital standards, and risk should be treated more consistently in internal models. Finally, reform of corporate governance should be extended to: strengthen boards and management; promote the risk management function; amend compensation for bank management and staff; improve risk disclosure; and strengthen sanctioning powers. At the time of writing, reform is still work in progress. Comparing Vickers, Liikanen and the US Dodd–Frank Act, all three recommend or require the imposition of restrictions on investment banking, and the decoupling of deposit banking from investment banking, albeit with variations in the detail of the mechanisms employed. In the US all insured banks must separate deposit banking from investment banking. The Liikanen Report recommends separation only if the activities form a major share of the bank's activities, or pose a systemic threat to stability. The White Paper following the Vickers Commission Final Report states that ring-fencing should occur only for banks with retail deposits greater than £25 billion. Trading and investment banking activity can be undertaken by a company in the same corporate group as the deposit bank, provided it does not pose resolution problems (in the case of Vickers and Liikanen). Under the Volcker Rule in the US, propriety trading in any group that contains a deposit bank is prohibited, and the bank's parent must be a financial holding company if it is involved in any investment banking or trading activity. Deposit banks are also prohibited from an array of securities activity in the US—for example, deposit-taking banks are precluded from investing in most securities, and entirely from securities dealing (including market-making) and underwriting. Under Dodd–Frank they must withdraw from some derivatives and credit default swap (CDS) trading that, at present, can be undertaken by deposit-taking banks. In the proposed UK legislation, there is a long list of prohibited securities trading activity (including propriety trading, securities lending, trading, origination, securitization originated outside the ring-fence); but these are permitted if they are regarded as "ancillary" to the main business. Liikanen takes a similar approach, prohibiting banks from conducting proprietary trading and investing in hedge funds (albeit other subsidiaries in the same banking group can still conduct these businesses).

The legislation is tougher and more restrictive in the US on the (legal) relationships between deposit banks and investment banks in the same corporate entity. The legislation goes far beyond large intra-group exposure rules, owing to US concerns over practices such as tunneling (appropriation of company resources by insiders). Liikanen and Vickers are somewhat vague on these issues. The UK has some tentative proposals for reducing intra-group guarantees. The UK and EC proposals (the latter linked to other legislation) both include detailed bank resolution regimes, whereas Dodd–Frank asks banks to develop their own resolution plans (living wills). While the use of bail-in debt is proposed for the UK and EC, Dodd–Frank merely encourages the Federal Reserve to ask the biggest US banks to hold more contingent capital. On capital requirements, EC (and therefore UK) banks are subject to the Capital Requirements Directive 4 (CRD IV) and Capital Requirements Regulation (of 2011). Liikanen recommends that more capital should be held against trading book exposures and real estate lending; for the UK it is proposed that more Tier 1 capital should be held by systemically important banks; and the US also has capital buffers for systemically important financial institution (SIFIs).

Although the broad features of the aforementioned legislation and reform proposals are similar, they differ in detail and the legal position on many issues is unclear. This situation creates further difficulties for international banks, some of which have claimed that they may need to create three separate legal entities (or silos/divisions) to ensure compliance with different regulatory regimes. At the time of writing, few of the proposed changes had been implemented, with progress having been somewhat faster in the US than in Europe. In particular, the prospects for effective reform at the EU level are uncertain, with legislation likely to be delayed by disagreements over the European banking union.

35.4.1 European Banking Union

In June 2012 the European Council outlined proposals to create a European banking union as part of a program aimed towards strengthening the resilience of the European financial system (European Council, 2012; Véron, 2013; Véron and Wolff, 2013). By addressing the entanglement of non-performing bank debt with sovereign debt, the proposals for banking union are designed to tackle a fundamental cause of the ongoing European financial and sovereign debt crises. Almost all commentators concur that an effective banking union will consist of three pillars. First, responsibility for bank supervision should be at the European level. Second, common mechanisms should be established for the resolution of ailing banks. Third, common arrangements should be created for insurance of customer deposits. Proposals for banking union have evolved swiftly, as outlined in Table 35.5. However, the extent and pace of implementation remain highly uncertain, owing to disagreements over several key issues of principle and detail.

The first pillar of banking union will involve a transfer of supervisory responsibilities for around 150 banks deemed to be "significant," from national supervisors to a Single Supervisory Mechanism (SSM) operated by the European Central Bank (ECB). The objective is to implement a single harmonized supervisory rulebook based on Basel III, rather than divergent national arrangements. Differences in standards applied at national level lead to differences between countries in the availability and cost of credit, inhibiting the emergence of an integrated market in financial services. National supervision inhibits or distorts cross-border capital flows: in a crisis, banks with subsidiaries abroad are encouraged by their home-country supervisors to repatriate capital or liquidity; while subsidiaries of foreign banks are encouraged by their host-country supervisors not to repatriate funds to their parent banks abroad (Gros, 2012).

The criteria for a bank to qualify for direct ECB supervision are one or more of the following: assets above €30 billion; assets above €5 billion and 20% of GDP in the EU member state in which the bank is located; one of the top three banks in the state in which the bank is located; significant cross-border activity; or recipient of bailout assistance. The role of the European Banking Authority (EBA) will be adapted to the new regulatory arrangements, and new rules on capital regulation (the EU Capital Requirements Regulation and the Fourth Capital Requirements Directive CRD IV) will take effect. Prior to the establishment of the SSM in 2014, the ECB is scheduled to undertake an asset quality review (AQR) of the banks that will fall under its jurisdiction. The AQR will be crucial in establishing the ECB's

Table 35.5 European banking union: timeline of developments

June 2012: Publication of the Recovery and Resolution Directive proposals.

June 2012: Publication of the Van Rompuy report *Towards a Genuine Economic and Monetary Union.*

June 2012: Meeting of the European Council and Eurozone Member States. Four Presidents asked to develop "a specific and time-bound road map for the achievement of a Genuine Economic and Monetary Union."

September 2012: Publication of the Single Supervisory Mechanism legislative proposals, including a proposed ECB Regulation, a proposed EBA Amending Regulation, and the Commission Communication *A roadmap towards a Banking Union.*

September 2012: Publication of the Van Rompuy *Issues Paper on Completing the Economic and Monetary Union.*

October 2012: Publication of the Van Rompuy *Towards a Genuine Economic and Monetary Union: Interim Report.*

October 2012: Meeting of the European Council. It was proposed to produce a legislative framework for the proposals on a Single Supervisory Mechanism by the end of 2012, with implementation to follow in 2013.

December 2012: Target deadline for agreement of the legislative framework of the Single Supervisory Mechanism and the Recovery and Resolution Directive, as well as the two existing proposed elements of the "single rulebook," the Capital Requirements Directive and Regulation (CRD IV) and the recast Deposit Guarantee Schemes Directive.

December 2012: Publication of the Van Rompuy *Towards a Genuine Economic and Monetary Union: Final Report.*

December 2012: Meeting of the European Council.

2013: Proposed date for implementation of the Single Supervisory Mechanism. Prospective date for publication of further steps towards banking union, including a common resolution scheme, and, possibly, a single deposit insurance scheme.
Date to be confirmed: Possibility of the ESM engaging in direct recapitalisation of Eurozone banks.

Source: House of Lords (2012, p. 9).

supervisory credibility, and in dealing with legacy issues of undeclared non-performing assets, which may constitute a major barrier to the implementation of pan-European resolution and deposit insurance arrangements. Doubts over the rigor of the AQR exercise are heightened by past embarrassments arising from the subsequent failure of banks that had previously been given clean bills of health in prior EBA "stress tests." Further concern centers on the ECB's lack of financial resources to recapitalize banks whose balance sheets are revealed to contain gaps, and the lack of legal authority to enforce either recapitalization by other means, or resolution.

Questions have been raised as to whether the ECB can attract sufficient qualified supervisory staff to take on the SSM role. Further, the interface between the ECB and national supervisors—in both euro and non-euro member countries—remains unclear. To act as an effective supervisor, the ECB requires detailed current knowledge of all banks within its remit. Information filtered through national supervisors may fail to meet this requirement, owing to a tendency for regulatory forbearance on the part of national supervisors that are either concerned over the high potential fiscal costs of intervention, or too close to bankers or politicians to exercise independent judgment. Furthermore, the proposal to limit European-level supervision to the largest banks may tend to undermine stability. If the ECB does not exercise supervisory responsibility over small banks, it is also debarred from providing liquidity or emergency support. However, small bank failure is a significant source of systemic risk, evidenced by the role of the Spanish savings banks, or the small German lender Hypo Real, in the financial and sovereign debt crises (Beck, 2012; Wyplosz, 2012). Finally, potential tensions may emerge between the ECB's dual responsibilities for price stability through monetary policy on the one hand, and financial stability through supervision of the banking system on the other. With respect to the latter, Schoenmaker (2013) advocates a separation of the functions of macroprudential (systemic) and microprudential (individual bank) supervision within the ECB.

The UK authorities, along with Sweden, have declined to participate in the SSM. The arrangements are designed primarily to bolster financial stability within the Eurozone and address the tensions that threaten the survival of the single currency. Non-euro members are invited to enter into "close cooperation arrangements." A UK House of Lords (2012) study of the banking union suggests that the SSM seeks to establish a set of supervisory rules for euro members, at the expense of efforts by the EBA to create a single rulebook for all EU members. Similar arguments over differential treatment have arisen over the role of the European Systemic Risk Board, as well as the BIS-based Financial Stability Board (chaired by the Governor of the Bank of England) concerning its role in harmonizing regulatory standards across countries.

The second pillar, a pan-European resolution scheme to be mainly funded by the banks, aims to provide a mechanism for the orderly shutdown of non-viable banks, so minimizing the likelihood of taxpayer-funded bank bailouts. Features of the proposed resolution scheme are incorporated into the 2012 Recovery and Resolution Directive, which is applicable to all credit institutions and most investment firms including financial groups. The Directive requires firms to make "living wills"; affords supervisors early intervention powers; specifies minimum harmonized resolution tools (including the power to sell businesses to third-parties, to transfer a business to a state-owned bridge institution or "bad" assets to a publicly owned asset management firm); requires institutions to issue bail-in debt that can convert to equity; requires EU member states to set up pre-funded resolution funds; and configures national deposit guarantee schemes for resolution funding purposes.

In Europe, existing insolvency frameworks are fragmented along national lines, and major reform would be required for a single resolution scheme to be established along the lines of prompt corrective action (PCA) in the US.[4] Banking systems in Europe, as noted above (see Table 35.1), are highly concentrated, and TBTF moral hazard is pervasive. Sapir and Wolff (2013) argue that broader steps in the direction of European financial integration will be required. The fragmentation of retail banking along national lines raises barriers to the creation of an effective pan-European resolution scheme, because it increases the

---

[4] PCA has provided extensive experience of bank resolution; but a recent report by the US Government Accountability Office suggests that PCA did not always operate effectively during the financial crisis, and recommends that additional early warning triggers (related to asset quality and asset concentration) be adopted (US Government Accountability Office, 2011)).

exposure of banks to shocks at national level, and limits the options for cross-border merger as a means of achieving resolution. The national orientation of most European banks also translates into a bias towards lending to their own governments, or providing funds for state-sponsored projects that are not financially or commercially viable. In exchange, implicit or explicit guarantees offered to banks by national governments effectively subsidise the banks' funding costs. All of this strengthens the dangerous ties between banks and sovereigns, to the detriment of the prospects for financial stability and resolution of the debt crisis. Acharya (2012) identifies the need to curb excessive sovereign borrowing from home-country banks as a further prerequisite (and as a natural counterpart to banking union) for addressing the crisis. Realistic (rather than zero) risk weightings should be applied to sovereign debt on banks' balance sheets, and sovereign credit risk should be recognized in the application of liquidity requirements in bank regulation. Limits on individual bank lending to a single sovereign borrower could be imposed.

The cases of countries such as Ireland and Spain during the financial and sovereign debt crises demonstrate that existing national deposit insurance and resolution funds can rapidly be depleted, creating a need for government support which, in turn, pushes sovereigns in the direction of insolvency. The third pillar of the banking union is the creation of a European deposit insurance scheme that would operate, along with the resolution fund, under a common resolution authority. This pillar, however, is hugely controversial because it implies a form of debt mutualization, whereby deposit protection, say, funded by a member with an orderly banking system would be used to protect depositors in a country with a failing banking system. The German authorities, in particular, are skeptical over the feasibility or desirability of such a scheme:

> *Ambassador Boomgaarden made clear Germany's opposition to a single deposit insurance scheme with "centralised credit lines between national intervention funds." He stressed that further integration was necessary before a centralised scheme could be considered. More recently, in comments delivered to a German mutual banking event in Frankfurt, the ECB President Mario Draghi indicated that plans for a common deposit scheme may not be revived.* (House of Lords, 2012, p. 36)

The question whether an effective banking union can be achieved in a piecemeal fashion, with implementation of the first pillar and partial implementation of the second preceding implementation of the third, or with the third deferred indefinitely, has been debated widely in the context of current EU proposals that envisage a gradual transition of this kind. For example, Pisani-Ferry and Wolff (2012) argue that the importance of deposit insurance has been overstated in the debate. Whether deposit insurance is organized at a national or European level, it is only designed to safeguard depositors against the risk of failure of a single financial institution, and not against the risk of a systemic crisis. Therefore banking union could proceed while deposit insurance continues to operate at national level. Schoenmaker (2012) argues to the contrary that depositor confidence can be maintained only if the supervisory, resolution and deposit insurance functions are integrated at the European level, backed up by a fiscal backstop supplied by the ESM. Separation of the supervisory function from resolution and deposit insurance would lead to conflict and confusion, with a tendency on the part of the ECB to advocate early restructuring or closure in order to defend systemic stability, while the national authorities seek to delay or avert drastic action so as to minimise the financial burden on the insurance fund or the treasury. The balance of expert opinion appears to favor the latter view, that all three pillars are integral to the formation of an effective banking union. There is concern that the current piecemeal approach places financial stability and the entire project of European financial integration in considerable jeopardy.

35.5 SUMMING UP AND GOING FORWARD

Since the onset of the financial crisis in 2007–2008, European banking has remained in a fragile state, and is subject to ongoing major reform. Basel III and the related EU (Fourth) Capital Requirements Directive have forced all banks, especially the largest, to increase substantially their regulatory capital. Banks have moved towards compliance by shrinking their risk assets, curtailing lending and selling off non-core activities. There is similar pressure to boost liquidity. Investors are demanding the same, and the objectives of regulators and the market appear broadly aligned. Coupled with the above are major structural reforms proposed in the UK's Vickers and EU's Liikanen Reports, including restrictions on banks' trading activities, various forms of ring-fencing or separation of investment banking from retail banking, and new resolution procedures.

The proposed European banking union consists of three pillars: a single supervisory mechanism, a pan-European resolution, and deposit insurance schemes. Implementation remains a major challenge, however, in view of ongoing disagreements over core principles and technical details. Ultimately, the need for the creation of a banking union that disentangles the dangerous link between indebted banks and enfeebled sovereigns appears paramount, if Europe is to move forward from the ongoing financial and sovereign debt crises. Resolution of the vexed question of "who pays?" in the event of either a systemic crisis or the failure of a single financial institution is an inescapable prerequisite for banking union. It remains to be seen how events will unfold, but in our view the barriers to the formation of an effective banking union in the short term remain daunting.

REFERENCES

Acharya, V. (2012). Banking Union in Europe and Other Reforms. In: Beck, T. (Ed.), *Banking Union for Europe: Risks and Challenges*, 43–52. London: Centre for Economic Policy Research.

Altunbas, Y., Goddard, J., and Molyneux, P. (1999). Technical Change in Banking, *Economics Letters* 64, 215–221.

Arnold, I. J. M. (2012). Sovereign Debt Exposures and Banking Risk in the Current EU Financial Crisis, *Journal of Policy Modelling* 34, 906–920.

Baele, L., De Jonghe, O., and Vander Vennet, R. (2007). Does the Stock Market Value Bank Diversification?, *Journal of Banking and Finance* 31, 1999–2023.

Battese, G. E., Heshmati, A., and Hjalmarsson, L., (2000). Efficiency of Labour Use in the Swedish Banking Industry: A Stochastic Frontier Approach. *Empirical Economics* 25, 623–640.

Beck, T. (2012). Why the Rush? Short-term Crisis Resolution and Long-term Bank Stability. In: T. Beck (Ed.), *Banking Union for Europe: Risks and Challenges*, 35–42. London: Centre for Economic Policy Research.

Beck, T., De Jonghe, O. G., and Schepens, G. (2013). Bank Competition and Stability: Cross-country Heterogeneity, *Journal of Financial Intermediation* 22, 218–244.

Berger, A. N. and Humphrey, D. B. (1997). Efficiency of Financial Institutions: International Survey and Directions for Further Research, *European Journal of Operational Research* 98, 175–212.

Berger, A. N., Klapper, L. F., and Turk-Ariss, R. (2009). Bank Competition and Financial Stability, *Journal of Financial Services Research* 35, 99–118.

BIS (Bank for International Settlements) (2011). The Impact of Sovereign Credit Risk on Bank Funding Conditions. Committee on the Global Financial System, Basel, July.

Boyd, J. H. and De Nicolo, G. (2005). The Theory of Bank Risk Taking and Competition Revisited, *Journal of Finance* 60, 1329–1343.

British Bankers Association (2012). *Annual Abstract of Statistics*, 29. London: British Bankers Association.

Brown, C. O. and Dinç, I. S. (2011). Too Many to Fail? Evidence of Regulatory Forbearance When the Banking Sector is Weak, *Review of Financial Studies* 24, 1378–1405.

Brunnermeier, M., Dong, G., and Palia, D. (2012). Banks' Non-interest Income and Systemic Risk. Working Paper, January.

Canhoto, A. and Dermine, J. (2003). A Note on Banking Efficiency in Portugal, New vs. Old Banks, *Journal of Banking & Finance* 27, 2087–2098.

Carbó, S. and Rodriguez, F. (2007). The Determinants of Bank Margins in European Banking, *Journal of Banking & Finance* 31, 2043–2063.

Carletti, E. (2010). Competition, Concentration and Stability in the Banking Sector, Istituto Luigi Einaudi per gli Studi Bancari Finanziari e Assicurativi (IstEin), Rome, ISTEIN, Working Paper No. 8.

Casu, B. and Girardone, C. (2010). Integration and Efficiency Convergence in EU Banking Markets, *Omega* 38, 260–267.

Casu, B., Girardone, C., Ferrari, A., and Wilson, J. O. S. (2013). Integration, Productivity and Technological Spillovers: Evidence for Eurozone Banking Industries, <http://ssrn.com/abstract=1879963>.

Casu, B., Girardone, C., and Molyneux, P. (2004). Productivity Change in European Banking: A Comparison of Parametric and Non-Parametric Approaches, *Journal of Banking & Finance* 28, 2521–2540.

Demirgüç-Kunt, A. and Huizinga, H. (2013). Are Banks Too-Big-Too-Fail or Too-Big-To-Save? International Evidence from Equity Prices and CDS Spreads, *Journal of Banking & Finance* 37, 975–894.

Dermine, J. (2013). Banking Regulations after the Global Financial Crisis, Good Intentions and Unintended Evil, *European Financial Management* 19, 658–674.

EBA (European Banking Authority) (2012). *Report on Risks and Vulnerabilities of the European Banking System*, July. London: European Banking Authority.

ECB (European Central Bank) (2000). *EU Banks' Income Structure, Banking Supervision Committee*, April. Frankfurt: ECB.

ECB (European Central Bank) (2006). *EU Banking Structures*, September. Frankfurt: European Central Bank.

ECB (European Central Bank) (2007a). *Financial Integration in Europe*. Frankfurt: European Central Bank.

ECB (European Central Bank) (2007b). *EU Banking Structure*, September. Frankfurt: European Central Bank.

ECB (European Central Bank) (2010). *EU Banking Structures*, September. Frankfurt: European Central Bank.

ECB (European Central Bank) (2011). *Financial Stability Review*, June. Frankfurt: European Central Bank.

ECB (European Central Bank) (2012). *Financial Stability Review*, June. Frankfurt: European Central Bank.

ECB (European Central Bank) (2013). *Consolidated Banking Data for 2012*. Frankfurt: European Central Bank.

European Council (2012). Report by the President of the European Council, Herman Van Rompuy, Towards a Genuine Economic and Monetary Union, June, <http://ec.europa.eu/economy_finance/focuson/crisis/documents/131201_en.pdf>.

European Economy (2009). *Economic Crisis in Europe: Causes, Consequences and Responses*, European Economy, 2. Brussels: European Commission.

European Securitisation Forum (2008). *ESF Securitisation Data Report*, Winter. London: European Securitisation Forum.

Feyen, E. and Gonzalez del Mazo, I. (2013). European Bank De-leveraging and Global Credit Conditions, World Bank Research Policy Paper No. 6388.

Fiorentino, E., De Vincenzo, A., Heid, F., Karmann A., and Koetter M. (2009). The Effects of Privatization and Consolidation on Bank Productivity: Comparative Evidence from Italy and Germany, Deutsche Bundesbank Discussion Paper, Series 2 Banking and Financial Studies No. 03/2009.

Fonteyne, W., Bossu, W., Cortavarria-Checkley, L., Giustiniani, A., Gullo, A., Hardy, D., and Kerr, S. (2010). Crisis Management and Resolution for a European Banking System, IMF Working Papers No. WP/10/70.

Goddard, J., Liu, H., Molyneux, P., and Wilson, J. O. S. (2013). Do Bank Profits Converge?, *European Financial Management* 19, 345–365.

Goddard, J., Molyneux, P., and Wilson, J. O. S. (2001). *European Banking: Efficiency, Technology and Growth*. Chichester: John Wiley and Sons.

Goddard, J., Molyneux, P., and Wilson, J. O. S. (2009). The Financial Crisis in Europe: Evolution, Policy Responses and Lessons for the Future, *Journal of Financial Regulation and Compliance* 17, 362–380.

Goddard, J., Molyneux, P., and Wilson, J. O. S. (2010). Banking in the European Union. In: A. N. Berger, P. Molyneux, and J. O. S Wilson, *Oxford Handbook of Banking*, 777–806. Oxford: Oxford University Press.

Goddard, J., Molyneux, P., Wilson, J. O. S., and Tavakoli, M. (2007). European Banking: An Overview, *Journal of Banking & Finance* 31, 1911–1936.

Gros, D. (2012). The Single European Market in Banking in Decline—ECB to the Rescue?. In: T. Beck (Ed.), *Banking Union for Europe: Risks and Challenges*, 49–54. London: Centre for Economic Policy Research.

Herring, R. J. and Carmassi, J. (2010). The Corporate Structure of International Financial Conglomerates: Complexity and its Implications for Safety and Soundness. In: A. N. Berger, P. Molyneux, and J. O. S Wilson, *Oxford Handbook of Banking*, 195–232. Oxford: Oxford University Press.

House of Lords (2012). European Banking Union: Key Issues and Challenges, Report House of Lords (HL) Paper No. 88, December 12.

IMF (International Monetary Fund) (2011). *Global Financial Stability Report*, April. Washington DC: IMF.

Jiménez, G., López, J. A., and Saurina, J. (2013). How Does Competition Impact Bank Risk Taking?, *Journal of Financial Stability* 9, 185–195.

Koopman, G-J. (2011). Stability and Competition in EU Banking during the Financial Crisis: The Role of State Aid Control, *Competition Policy International* 7, 8–21.

Koskela, E. and Stenbacka, R. (2000). Is There a Tradeoff between Bank Competition and Financial Fragility?, *Journal of Banking & Finance* 24, 1853–1873.

Laeven, L. and Levine, R. (2007). Is There a Diversification Discount in Financial Conglomerates?, *Journal of Financial Economics* 85, 331–367.

Lane, P. (2012). The European Sovereign Debt Crisis, *Journal of Economic Perspectives* 26, 49–68.

Lepetit, L., Nys, E., Rous, P., and Tarazi, A. (2008). The Expansion of Services in European Banking: Implications for Loan Pricing and Interest Margins, *Journal of Banking and Finance* 32, 2325–2335.

Liikanen, E. (2012). High-level Expert Group on Reforming the Structure of the EU Banking Sector, Brussels, October 2, <http://ec.europa.eu/internal_market/bank/docs/high-level_expert_group/report_en.pdf>.

Liu H., Molyneux, P., and Wilson, J. O. S. (2013). Competition and Stability in European Banking: A Regional Analysis, *Manchester School* 81, 176–201.

Llewellyn, D. T. (2005). Competition and Profitability in European Banking: Why are UK Banks so Profitable?, *Economic Notes* 34, 279–311.

Lozano-Vivas, A. (1998). Efficiency and Technical Change for Spanish Banks, *Applied Financial Economics* 8, 289–300.

Marquez, L. B., Correa, R., and Sapriza, H. (2013). International Evidence on Government Support and Risk Taking in the Banking Sector, International Monetary Fund Working Paper No. WP/13/94.

Martinez-Miera, D. and Repullo, R. (2010). Does Competition Reduce the Risk of Bank Failure?, *Review of Financial Studies* 23, 3638–3664.

Mercieca, S., Schaeck, K., and Wolfe, S. (2007). Small European Banks: Benefits from Diversification and the Regulatory Environment, *Journal of Banking & Finance* 31, 1975–1998.

O'Hara, M. and Shaw, W. (1990). Deposit Insurance and Wealth Effects: The Value of Being "Too Big to Fail," *Journal of Finance* 45, 1587–1600.

Petrovic, A. and Tutsch, R. (2009). National Rescue Measures in Response to the Current Financial Crisis, European Central Bank, Frankfurt, Legal Working Paper Series No. 8, July.

Pisani-Ferry, J. and Sapir, A. (2010). Banking Crisis Management in the EU: an Early Assessment, *Economic Policy* 62, xx–xxx.

Pisani-Ferry, J. and Wolff, G. (2012). The Fiscal Implications of a Banking Union. Bruegel Policy Brief Issue, September.

Sapir, A. and Wolff, G. (2013). The Neglected Side of Banking Union: Reshaping Europe's Financial System. Note Presented at the Informal ECOFIN, Vilnius, September.

Schoenmaker, D. (2012). Banking Union: Where We're Going Wrong. In: T. Beck (Ed.), *Banking Union for Europe: Risks and Challenges*, 95–102. London: Centre for Economic Policy Research.

Schoenmaker, D. (2013). An Integrated Financial Framework for the Banking Union: Don't Forget Macro-Prudential Supervision, European Economy Economic Papers No. 495, April.

Stern, G. H. and Feldman, R. (2004). *Too Big To Fail: The Hazards of Bank Bailouts*. Washington: Brookings Institution Press.

Stern, G. H. and Feldman, R. (2009). Addressing TBTF by Shrinking Financial Institutions: An Initial Assessment, *The Region*, June, 8–13.

Stolz, S. H. and Wedow, M. (2010). Extraordinary Measures in Extraordinary Times—Public Measures in Support of the Financial Sector in the EU and the United States, European Central Bank Occasional Paper Series No. 117, July.

Turk-Ariss, R. (2010). On the Implications of Market Power in Banking: Evidence from Developing Countries, *Journal of Banking & Finance* 34, 765–775.

Uhde, A. and Heimeshoff, U. (2009). Consolidation in Banking and Financial Stability in Europe: Empirical Evidence, *Journal of Banking & Finance* 33, 1299–1311.

US Government Accountability Office (2011). *Modified Prompt Corrective Action Framework Would Improve Effectiveness.* Washington: Government Accountability Office.

Vause, N., Von Peter, G., Drehmann, M., and Sushko, V. (2012). European Bank Funding and De-leveraging, *Bank of International Settlements Quarterly Review*, March, 1–12.

Véron, N. (2013). A Realistic Bridge Toward European Banking Union, Bruegel Policy Contribution No. 9.

Véron, N. and Wolff, G. B. (2013). From Supervision to Resolution: Next Steps on the Road to European Banking Union, Bruegel Policy Contribution No. 4.

Vickers, J. (2011). *Independent Commission on Banking, Final Report.* London: HMSO.

Weill, L. (2009). Convergence in Banking Efficiency across European Countries, *Journal of International Financial Institutions, Markets & Money* 19, 818–833.

Weill, L. (2013). Bank Competition in the EU: How Has It Evolved?, *Journal of International Financial Institutions, Markets & Money* 26, 100–112.

Wyplosz, C. (2012). Banking Union as a Crisis-management Tool. In: T. Beck (Ed.), *Banking Union for Europe: Risks and Challenges*, 17–22. London: Centre for Economic Policy Research.

CHAPTER 36

....

BANKING IN JAPAN*

....

HIROFUMI UCHIDA AND GREGORY F. UDELL

36.1 INTRODUCTION

....

THIS chapter focuses on the Japanese banking industry. We examine its structure, its performance, and some of its defining characteristics. There are a number of reasons why an analysis of the banking industry in Japan may be of particular interest. First, it is an essential part of one of world's largest economies—an economy that is one of the world's largest in terms of the size of its gross domestic product (GDP). Second, like some other developed economies such as Germany, Japan has historically been a banking-oriented financial system. Third, the banking industry has some very interesting idiosyncratic features related to the nature of the Japanese corporate environment such as its "main banking system." Fourth, like other countries, the Japanese banking system has been in a period of significant transition, some of which is idiosyncratic to Japan, such as the banking crisis of the 1990s.

In Section 36.2 we provide an overview of the Japanese banking system. Then in Section 36.3 we turn to some specific topics on banking in Japan including the Japanese main banking system, lending technologies in Japan, and the Japanese banking crisis. Section 36.4 concludes.[1]

* The authors would like to thank Allen Berger, Phil Molyneux, John Wilson, Kozo Harimaya, Hikaru Fukanuma, Hiroshi Fujiki, Takeo Hoshi, Tae Okada, Arito Ono, Kenji Fujii, Wako Watanabe, and Yoshiaki Ogura for their helpful comments.

[1] For a more comprehensive analysis of corporate finance and the Japanese banking industry we suggest that the reader refer to Hoshi and Patrick (2000) and Hoshi and Kashyap (2001). For an analysis of the Japanese economy we refer the reader to Flath (2000). And for a comprehensive evaluation of economic policies related to the recent recession we refer the reader to Ito, Patrick, and Weinstein (2005).

36.2 OVERVIEW OF THE JAPANESE
BANKING SYSTEM

In this section we provide an overview of the banking industry in Japan including discussions of its market structure, efficiency, permissible activities, and regulation.

36.2.1 The Importance of Banking and Intermediated Finance in Japan

The importance of banking and intermediated finance in Japan can be seen in Table 36.1. This breakdown of Japanese financial assets shows that of the 6,200 trillion yen of financial assets, 47% are held by Japanese financial institutions. Depository financial institutions are by far the largest component, holding 26% of the country's financial assets, virtually all of which can be loosely classified as "banks"—the main focus of this chapter. The largest segment of the banking industry is domestically licensed banks (58% of banking assets). The remainder consists of foreign banks (2%), "financial" (banking) institutions for agriculture, forestry and fisheries (14%), and "financial" (banking) institutions for small businesses (26%).

We can also see the importance of the banking system in terms of the dependency of the Japanese corporate, government, and household sectors. Table 36.2 shows the composition of financial assets and claims by financial instruments for each of these sectors. In the corporate sector, loans by private financial institutions and shareholders' equity (i.e., "shares") are the largest categories of claims. They comprise respectively 23.2% and 25.1% of firms' total financing. Other forms of relatively less important debt include commercial paper (0.5%) and corporate bonds (i.e., "industrial securities") (4.8%). By way of comparison, in the US domestic bank loans comprise 4.3% of corporate liabilities with commercial paper providing 1.0% and corporate bonds providing 42.2% (Q1 2013 US Flow of Funds Accounts).

As is often the case in developed economies, the government sector is the largest debtor sector in Japan. Not surprisingly this sector is heavily dependent on bonds and bills for its financing ("financing bills", "central government securities and FILP bonds", and "local government securities": 81.5%). Many of these bonds and bills are held by the banking sectors, and only a relatively some amount of this is owned directly by the public (i.e., "households") (29 out of 874 trillion yen).

On the consumer side, of the 1,517 trillion yen of financial assets held by households, 51.1% is invested in demand ("transferable") and time and savings deposits. The next biggest category of consumer assets is insurance and pension assets (27.9%) followed by equity investments ("shares and other equity") (7.0%). The biggest component of consumer debt is housing loans from either private or public financial institutions (52.6%). Overall, these data indicate that Japan is very much a bank-intermediated financial system compared to market-oriented systems such as the UK and the US

Table 36.1 Financial assets in Japan by holder

Financial institutions	29,175,887 (47%)		
Central bank		1,485,559 (2%)	
Depository corporations		15,965,890 (26%)	
Banks			15,885,248 (26%)
Domestically licensed banks			9,188,269 (58% among "Banks")
Foreign banks in Japan			277,793 (2% among "Banks")
Financial institutions for agriculture, forestry, and fisheries			2,261,014 (14% among "Banks")
Financial institutions for small businesses			4,158,172 (26% among "Banks")
Collectively managed trusts		80,642 (0%)	
Insurance and pension funds		3,928,129 (6%)	
Insurance	5,158,326 (8%)		
Life insurance			3,095,224
Nonlife insurance			347,667
Mutual aid insurance			485,238
Pension funds		1,230,197 (2%)	
Other financial intermediaries	6,452,619 (10%)		
Securities investment trusts		954,346 (2%)	
Nonbanks		781,198 (1%)	
Finance companies			523,358
Structured-financing special purpose companies and trusts			257,840

(Continued)

Table 36.1 (Continued)

Financial institutions	29,175,887 (47%)	
Public financial institutions		
Fiscal Loan Fund	3,342,984 (5%)	
Government financial institutions		1,596,539
Financial dealers and brokers		1,746,445
Financial auxiliaries (financial institutions other than intermediaries)	113,493 (0%)	
Nonfinancial corporations	8,605,487 (14%)	
General government	4,845,633 (8%)	
Households	15,166,016 (24%)	
Private nonprofit institutions serving households	459,392 (1%)	
Overseas	3,662,810 (6%)	
Total	**61,915,225 (100%)**	

Source: Flow of Funds Account (the Bank of Japan) (100 million yen, March 31, 2012)

Table 36.2 Assets and liabilities of the Japanese corporate, government, and household sectors

	Private nonfinancial corporations		General Government		Households	
	Assets	Liabilities	Assets	Liabilities	Assets	Liabilities
Currency and deposits	2,123,610 (26.2%)	—	409,456 (8.5%)	—	8,330,680 (54.9%)	—
Currency	224,561 (2.8%)	—	23 (0.0%)	—	523,977 (3.5%)	—
Government deposits	—	—	18,324 (0.4%)	—	—	—
Transferable deposits	1,261,165 (15.5%)	—	187,625 (3.9%)	—	3,106,529 (20.5%)	—
Time and savings deposits	440,476 (5.4%)	—	98,424 (2.0%)	—	4,642,127 (30.6%)	—
Certificates of deposits	146,191 (1.8%)	—	90,294 (1.9%)	—	179 (0.0%)	—
Foreign currency deposits	51,217 (0.6%)	—	14,766 (0.3%)	—	57,868 (0.4%)	—
Deposits with the Fiscal Loan Fund	—	—	—	—	—	—
Loans	383,573 (4.7%)	3,345,350 (31.5%)	415,409 (8.6%)	1,603,725 (15.0%)	33 (0.0%)	2,977,963 (81.8%)
Call loans and money	30,270 (0.4%)	—	317,457 (6.6%)	—	—	—
Loans by private financial institutions	—	2,464,740 (23.2%)	1,408 (0.0%)	521,540 (4.9%)	—	2,486,008 (68.3%)
Housing loans	—	—	—	—	—	1,641,908 (45.1%)
Consumer credit	—	—	—	—	—	226,608 (6.2%)
Loans to companies and governments	—	2,464,740 (23.2%)	—	521,540 (4.9%)	—	617,492 (17.0%)
Loans by public financial institutions	—	348,947 (3.3%)	—	1,040,037 (9.7%)	—	431,213 (11.8%)
Of which: housing loans	—	—	—	—	—	273,336 (7.5%)
Loans by the nonfinancial sector	322,126 (4.0%)	369,978 (3.5%)	207,692 (4.3%)	38,605 (0.4%)	33 (0.0%)	58,245 (1.6%)

(Continued)

Table 36.2 (Continued)

	Private nonfinancial corporations				General Government				Households			
	Assets		Liabilities		Assets		Liabilities		Assets		Liabilities	
Installment credit (not included in consumer credit)	—		—		—		—		—		2,497	(0.1%)
Repurchase agreements and securities lending transactions	31,177	(0.4%)	42	(0.0%)	108,357	(2.2%)	3,543	(0.0%)	—		—	
Securities other than shares	372,424	(4.6%)	671,047	(6.3%)	1,145,711	(23.6%)	8,739,018	(81.6%)	942,665	(6.2%)	—	
Financing bills	—		—		120,027	(2.5%)	1,586,794	(14.8%)	—		—	
Central government securities and FILP bonds	113,568	(1.4%)	—		714,336	(14.7%)	6,454,028	(60.2%)	276,729	(1.8%)	—	
Local government securities	19,236	(0.2%)	—		83,913	(1.7%)	694,736	(6.5%)	12,550	(0.1%)	—	
Public corporation securities	32,253	(0.4%)	2,267	(0.0%)	114,453	(2.4%)	1,536	(0.0%)	6,032	(0.0%)	—	
Bank debentures	6,080	(0.1%)	—		13,464	(0.3%)	—		7,208	(0.0%)	—	
Industrial securities	20,761	(0.3%)	509,097	(4.8%)	93,944	(1.9%)	—		25,470	(0.2%)	—	
External securities issued by residents	—		70,917	(0.7%)	15	(0.0%)	1,924	(0.0%)	—		—	
Commercial paper	15,104	(0.2%)	52,972	(0.5%)	16	(0.0%)	—		—		—	
Investment trust beneficiary certificates	26,554	(0.3%)	35,794	(0.3%)	1,302	(0.0%)	—		593,000	(3.9%)	—	
Trust beneficiary rights	20,023	(0.2%)	—		4,066	(0.1%)	—		21,676	(0.1%)	—	
Structured-financing instruments	118,845	(1.5%)	—		175	(0.0%)	—		—		—	
Shares and other equities	1,414,959	(17.4%)	3,813,962	(36.0%)	968,158	(20.0%)	151,336	(1.4%)	1,062,432	(7.0%)	—	

Of which: shares	692,907 (8.5%)	2,665,126 (25.1%)	195,024 (4.0%)	— (—)	628,294 (4.1%)	— (—)
Financial derivatives	11,033 (0.1%)	48,401 (0.5%)	— (—)	576 (0.0%)	2,909 (0.0%)	4,716 (0.1%)
Insurance and pension reserves	— (—)	— (—)	— (—)	— (—)	4,225,527 (27.9%)	— (—)
Insurance reserves	— (—)	— (—)	— (—)	— (—)	2,234,613 (14.7%)	— (—)
Pension reserves	— (—)	— (—)	— (—)	— (—)	1,990,914 (13.1%)	— (—)
Deposits money	308,565 (3.8%)	352,660 (3.3%)	32,026 (0.7%)	42,776 (0.4%)	108,984 (0.7%)	559,548 (15.4%)
Trade credits and foreign trade credits	2,240,510 (27.6%)	1,740,337 (16.4%)	6,310 (0.1%)	— (—)	— (—)	— (—)
Accounts receivable/payable	84,853 (1.0%)	386,356 (3.6%)	169,182 (3.5%)	68,224 (0.6%)	317,738 (2.1%)	50,681 (1.4%)
Outward direct investment	451,680 (5.6%)	— (—)	— (—)	— (—)	— (—)	— (—)
Outward investment in securities	485,984 (6.0%)	— (—)	1,257,733 (26.0%)	— (—)	88,782 (0.6%)	— (—)
Other external claims and debts	94,188 (1.2%)	20,394 (0.2%)	84,983 (1.8%)	18,390 (0.2%)	— (—)	— (—)
Others	140,508 (1.7%)	227,822 (2.1%)	39,208 (0.8%)	89,985 (0.8%)	86,266 (0.6%)	47,616 (1.3%)
Total	8,111,887 (100.0%)	10,606,329 (100.0%) (debtor)	4,845,633 (100.0%)	10,714,030 (100.0%) (debtor)	15,166,016 (100.0%)	3,640,524 (100.0%) (creditor)
(Difference between financial assets and liabilities)		−2,494,442		−5,868,397		11,525,492

Source: Flow of Funds Account (the Bank of Japan) (100 million yen, March 31, 2012).

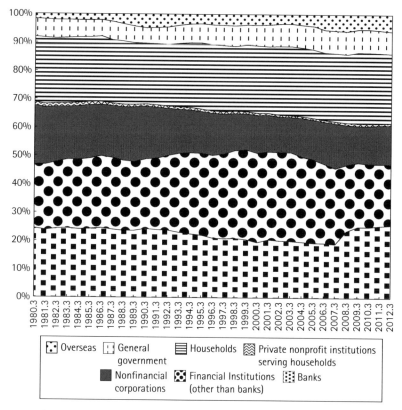

FIGURE 36.1 Composition of financial assets in Japan by holder.

It has been suggested that high growth in the post-war period may have been facilitated by the banking-oriented nature of Japan's financial system, and some have further argued that this type of financial system with its emphasis on financial intermediation may be a good model for developing economies (Aoki and Patrick, 1994). However, it should also be noted that Japan suffered a banking crisis that began in the 1990s, the cause of which has been linked to the banking system. The dependence on banking appears to have diminished. Specifically, the proportion of financial assets held in banks has been on a general downward trend throughout the 1990s and the 2000s (see Figure 36.1), although the decline might have ended after the late 2000s.[2]

36.2.2 Segmentation in the Japanese Banking Market

The Japanese banking sector can best be described as segmented. In particular, since World War II the Japanese financial industry had been segmented by the nature of the services that each type of financial institution (discussed later in this section) could provide. The origin of

---

[2] Note that the spike in 2008 is due to the inclusion of Japan Post Bank in "Banks."

this regulatory segmentation dates back to the crisis-mode wartime system. Its purpose was to limit competition in order to promote banking profitability, thereby enhancing the safety and soundness of the financial system. Although financial liberalization in the 1980s and 1990s blurred the divide between different types of financial institutions, there still remain some boundaries (see Hoshi and Kashyap, 2001, ch. 4).

In Japan today commercial banks and commercial banking are defined under the 1981 Banking Law. The Law defines banking as either the simultaneous provision of lending- and deposit-taking, or just the provision of payments/settlements services. Among financial institutions regulated under the Law, ordinary banks (*futsuu ginko*) are the most common, although there are other financial institutions and public banks that engage in the business of banking

The Banking Law also permits banks to engage in other activities including investing in bonds and stocks—in Japan banks are allowed to own equity in non-financial corporations.[3] As we will see in Section 36.3.1, bank equity ownership gives banks an important role in corporate governance not only as a creditor but also as a stockholder. In the case of certain activities such as factoring and leasing, banks must engage in them indirectly through affiliates. With this background in mind we now turn to a description of the various types of bank in Japan.[4]

36.2.2.1 *City Banks*

City banks are a type of ordinary bank. Although there are now only four city banks in Japan (Mitsui-Sumitomo, Mitsubishi-Tokyo-UFJ, Mizuho, and Resona), they are the largest single category (see Table 36.3). City banks grew quite rapidly in absolute and relative importance during the 1980s (see Figure 36.2). All four city banks are universal banks, all offer nationwide branch banking and three city banks have extensive foreign bank networks (Mitsui-Sumitomo, Mitsubishi-Tokyo-UFJ, and Mizuho). Because of their large size, city banks are sometimes called mega banks.

36.2.2.2 *Regional Banks and Second Regional Banks*

Regional banks are medium-sized banks whose banking operations are regionally focused. There are 64 of these banks in Japan, and while they are individually substantially smaller than the city banks, they collectively comprise the second largest category (Table 36.3). Like the regional banks, the second (-tier) regional banks also operate regionally but they tend to be smaller in size. Historically these banks were established as mutual (*Sogo*) banks whose purpose was to provide financing to small and medium enterprises (SMEs). While they are no longer restricted to this sector of the economy they still tend to focus on SMEs. As a group the second regional banks are considerably smaller than city banks and regional

[3] There are now two key restrictions on this ownership. Banks cannot hold more than 5% of one company's equity to prevent predominating influence and they cannot own equity in aggregate that exceeds their own capital to enhance their safety and soundness.

[4] Liu and Wilson (2010, 2012) respectively compare banks' profitability and risk, and examine their determinants across bank types (city banks, regional banks, second-regional banks, Shinkin banks, and credit cooperatives).

Table 36.3 Descriptive statistics for different bank types in Japan

		# of banks	Assets	Loans	Deposits	Loans / assets	Loans / Deposits	supervisory authority
Private banks	City banks	4	4,527,792	1,798,636	2,758,508	0.40	0.65	FSA (Financial Services Agency)
	Regional banks	64	2,535,602	1,616,955	2,207,560	0.64	0.73	FSA
	Second regional banks	41	656,557	446,643	596,704	0.68	0.75	FSA
	Trust banks	16	667,073 *	349,022 *	364,226 *	0.52	0.96	FSA
	Foreign banks	57	313,210	42,364	59,475	0.14	0.71	FSA
	Japan Post Bank	1	1,958,199	41,345	1,756,354	0.02	0.02	FSA
	Other banks under the Banking Act	15	390,164 #	163,445 #	312,790 #	0.42	0.52	FSA
	Shinkin banks+	270	1,319,587	637,886	1,225,883	0.48	0.52	FSA
	Credit cooperatives	157	190,598	94,760	177,766	0.50	0.53	FSA
	Agricultural cooperatives	714	1,064,117	235,244	880,635	0.22	0.27	(Ministry of Agruculture, Forestry and Fishery)
Government financial institutions	Japan Housing Finance Agency	1	336,065	213,555	0	0.64	NA	Ministry of Land, Infrastructure and Transport
	Development Bank of Japan	1	155,633	137,050	0	0.88	NA	(Ministry of Finance)
	Shoko Chukin Bank	1	122,728	96,270	38,308	0.78	2.51	(Ministry of Economy, Trade, and Industry)

Japan Finance Corporation	Micro Business and Individual Unit (formerly National Life Finance Corporation)	1	70,970	70,656	0	1.00	NA	Ministry of Health, Labour and Welfare and MoF
	Agriculture, Forestry, Fisheries and Food Business Unit (formerly Agriculture Forestry and Fisheries Finance Corporation)	1	26,275	25,445	0	0.97	NA	MAFF
	Small and Medium Enterprise (SME) Unit (formerly Japan Finance Corporation for Small and Medium Enterprises)	1	61,655	62,848	0	1.02	NA	METI
	Japan Bank for International Cooperation	1	126,932	81,104	0	0.64	NA	MoF

Notes: Deposits do not include CDs (certificates of deposits) and financial bonds issued by some banks (similar to time-deposits).

* These figures for trust banks are for 6 banks that are full members of the Japanese Bankers Association. # These figures for Other banks under the Banking Law are for 14 banks (Aozora Bank, AEON Bank, Shinhan Bank Japan, Citibank Japan, Jibun Bank, Japan Net Bank, Shinginko Tokyo, Shinsei Bank, SBI Sumishin Net Bank, Seven Bank, Sony Bank, Daiwa Next Bank, Rakuten Bank, and Saitama Resona Bank). The Resolution and Collection Bank is excluded because it is not a commercial bank in an usual sense.

Sources and dates: [# of banks for private banks]: FSA (other than agricultural cooperatives: as of July 1, 2013) and Norinchukin Research Institute (for agricultural cooperatives: as of March 2012). [Balance sheet figures]: The Bank of Japan (for city, regional, second regional, and foreign banks), the Japanese Bankers Association (for trust banks), National Shinkin Banks Financial Statements (Kin-yu Tosho Consultant Inc.: for Shinkin banks), National Central Society of Credit Cooperatives (credit cooperatives), Norinchukin Research Institute (for agricultural cooperatives), and respective banks (for Other banks under the Banking Act and the government financial institutions), as of March 31, 2012. [Unit (for assets, loans, and deposits)]: 100 million yen.

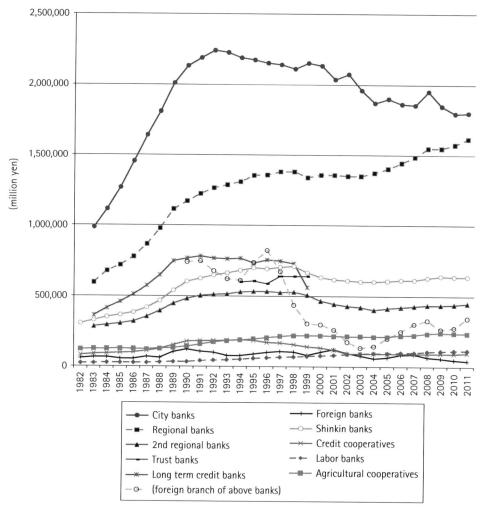

FIGURE 36.2 Loans outstanding of private banks.

banks but they still play an important role in providing SME financing. Economists have often grouped regional and second regional banks together because both categories tend to focus on local and retail banking.

36.2.2.3 Trust Banks

Under the 1943 Act on Provision of Trust Business by Financial Institutions a special type of bank called trust banks are allowed to offer trust services. They are, nevertheless, commercial banks under the Banking Law with respect to their provision of normal banking services (deposits, loans and payments/settlements). These banks offer money trusts (*kinsen shintaku*) to their customers which are essentially a form of medium- to long-term time deposit. These money trusts enable the banks to make long-term commercial loans and investments in bonds and equities. That is, from an asset-liability perspective these banks specialize in long-term lending funded by long-term liabilities. As a result, the trust banks have played an important role in providing long-term funding to Japanese corporate borrowers. This role is especially important given that the domestic post-war Japanese corporate bond market had been undeveloped.

36.2.2.4 Long-term Credit Banks

Historically long-term credit banks also played an important role in providing long-term corporate funding in the post-war Japanese financial system. Until the banking crisis of the 1990s they operated under the 1952 Long-term Credit Banking Law. They no longer exist in their original form, however. They were initially designed to complement ordinary banks which were (supposed to be) restricted to short-term lending based on the asset-liability management principle that commercial banks whose funding comes from short-term demand deposits should be prohibited from investing in long-term loans. Long-term credit banks could issue bonds that were historically more attractive to investors than time deposits because of deposit rate ceilings and other attributes.

In the mid-1990s there were only three long-term credit banks. During the banking crisis the Industrial Bank of Japan was merged with two city banks and consolidated together to become the Mizuho Bank and the Mizuho Corporate Bank (they further merged and became Mizuho bank). The other two, the Long-Term Credit Bank of Japan and the Nippon Credit Bank, both went into bankruptcy in 1998, marking a key event in Japan's banking crisis. After being temporarily nationalized, these two banks now operate under the Banking Law under different names, the Shinsei Bank and the Aozora Bank, respectively. The disappearance of the long-term credit banks and the long-term debt financing that they provided to large Japanese corporations is partly a consequence of the emergence of a domestic corporate bond market in Japan and increased access by Japanese corporations to the Eurobond and other international bond markets.

36.2.2.5 Foreign Banks

There are a large number of foreign banks that have branch offices or agencies in Japan. These branches require a banking license, and are regulated in the same manner as domestic banks under the Banking Law. Overall, focusing primarily on providing foreign exchange-related services, they play only a minor role in Japanese financial intermediation as indicated in Table 36.3, and Figure 36.2.

36.2.2.6 Shinkin Banks and Credit Cooperatives

Shinkin banks (*Shin-you Kinko*) and credit cooperatives (*Shin-you Kumiai*) are both cooperative banks that specialize in providing commercial banking services to member SMEs and individuals. Although they are not legally "banks" because they operate under a special set of laws, they engage in the same activities as banks do under the Banking Law—that is, lending, deposit-taking, and payments/settlements. However, with respect to lending, they are restricted to lending to their member firms. Shinkin banks can offer deposits to non-members, but credit cooperatives can offer deposits to members only. Firms that are members of a Shinkin bank must have fewer than 300 employees or a capitalization less than

900 million yen, while members of credit cooperatives must have fewer than 300 employees or a capitalization less than 300 million yen. These banks are also restricted geographically typically to an area no larger than a single prefecture. Since financial deregulation in the 1980s, both types of banks have been permitted to expand their business scope to activities that include, for example, offering loans to nonmembers and offering mutual funds.

36.2.2.7 *Other Financial Institutions providing Commercial Banking Services*

As shown in Table 36.3, there are also a number of other financial institutions that provide commercial banking services. Other banks under the Bank Law include two former long-term credit banks (see Section 36.2.2.4), Internet banks, a resolution bank to manage, collect, and dispose of assets of failed financial institutions, and, recently established banks which do not fit into the classification above.

There are also cooperative banks that operate for the benefit of their members: labor banks, agricultural cooperatives, fishery cooperatives, and forestry cooperatives. Among these, the agricultural cooperatives (commonly called collectively as JA Bank (Japan Agriculture Bank)) are relatively large in number (see Table 36.3). Like Shinkin banks and credit cooperatives, some of the restrictions on these cooperatives have been lifted to allow, for example, the provision of services to non-members and sales of mutual funds. Thus, to a certain degree these banks are becoming similar to banks that operate under the Banking Law.

36.2.2.8 *Public Banks*

As in some other countries, postal savings have played a historically important role in Japan. Postal savings had long been provided by the government (the Ministry of Posts and Telecommunications). Funds collected through postal savings flowed to the Ministry of Finance that, in turn, allocated the funds to government financial institutions and other official accounts through the Fiscal Investment Loan Program (FILP) (see, e.g., Cargill and Yoshino, 2000).

The program has been restructured. In January 2001 the Postal Services Agency assumed the operation of the three postal businesses (postal savings as well as postal insurance and postal mail services), and in April 2001 stopped sending its funds to the Ministry of Finance and started to allocate the funds at its own discretion. In 2003 the three businesses were further transferred to Japan Post, a state-owned company. Finally, in October 2007 the operation of postal saving business was succeeded by a newly established private bank, Japan Post Bank. All the equity of the Japan Post Bank is owned by a government holding company (the Japan Post Holdings). The equity is supposed to be sold in the market in a stepwise manner, and the completion of the privatization process is scheduled for 2017, but, at the time of writing this chapter, whether and how to privatize the Japan Post Bank is still a contentious political issue (see Sawada, 2013).

Although in the past they had tax and institutional advantages, postal savings today are almost the same as deposits provided by other private banks, and Japan Post Bank is effectively the single largest depository institution in Japan (see Table 36.3). Due to historical inertia, most of the assets of the Japan Post Bank are now invested in very low-risk instruments, making it effectively similar to a narrow (100% reserve) bank, although there is some interest in expanding its asset composition into such categories as housing and corporate loans.

There are also a number of other government financial institutions, some of whom are not, technically, banks (Table 36.3). They had been users of the FILP funds raised through postal savings (and related sources). Now, however, they raise funds themselves by issuing special government guaranteed bonds. They have also been in the process of being privatized and consolidated. The Japan Housing Finance Agency (formerly the Government Housing Loan Corporation) had historically provided housing loans, although it has now ceased investing in these loans, focusing instead on securitizing housing loans by private banks. The Development Bank of Japan is a public bank that has been providing long-term funds to corporations. It played an important role in the post-war development of Japan. There are also some institutions that focus on SME lending: the Shoko Chukin Bank and the Japan Finance Corporation (JFC). The latter was established in 2008 as a successor to the National Life Finance Corporation and the Japan Finance Corporation for Small and Medium Enterprises (formerly the Japan Finance Corporation for Small Business) (for the role of these government financial institutions for SMEs, see Fukanuma, Nemoto, and Watanabe, 2006). The JFC also absorbed the Agriculture Forestry and Fisheries Finance Corporation and temporarily absorbed the Japan Bank for International Cooperation (JBIC). However, the JBIC which provides support for the Japanese government's foreign economic policy initiatives and economic cooperation programs, was again made an independent institution on April 1, 2012.

36.2.3 Market Structure and Competition of the Japanese Banking Industry

The segmentation explained above makes it difficult to describe the market structure of the Japanese banking industry. Regarding the deposit market, it does not appear to be segmented by bank type because no product differentiation is likely to exist, even between bank deposits and postal savings. However, the lending market is more complicated. On the one hand, financial deregulation has likely promoted integration (overlap) of the markets of different bank types. On the other hand, different types of bank are likely to have different comparative advantages with respect to different types of borrower. Moreover, geographical segmentation may still be important, particularly for certain types of lending such as relationship loans that likely have a spatial dimension. Thus, two types of segmentation are likely to exist: spatial segmentation and bank-type segmentation. Defining the scope of lending markets in Japan is an important empirical question.

Very few empirical studies have investigated market segmentation in Japan. A rare exception is Kano and Tsutsui (2003), who investigate segmentation by prefecture (i.e., spatial segmentation). They find that the lending market for Shinkin banks is segmented by prefecture (probably due to geographical restrictions on their operating areas), whereas prefectural segmentation is only weakly confirmed for regional banks. However, they do not investigate segmentation by bank type. Instead they implicitly *assume* that lending markets for Shinkin banks and for regional banks are segmented. Thus, bank-type segmentation remains untested. Segmentation by prefecture was also found by Ishikawa and Tsutsui (2013).

Whether or not markets are segmented by type or by region, banks can compete via branching. However, there had been strict regulation on branching in Japan. To open a new bank branch office, banks had to satisfy regulatory criteria and obtain approval by the Ministry of Finance, the bank regulatory authority at that time. The criteria were relaxed in a stepwise manner from the 1980s through the 1990s, and banks are now virtually unconstrained in opening branch offices, following a 2002 amendment to the Banking Law. Also, banks are now able to provide banking services through their agents, such as other banks, insurance companies, securities companies, and non-financial companies.

Table 36.4 shows the number of branch offices of the four major types of banks. City banks have many branches in their nationwide operations (except for Mizuho Corporate which focused on big businesses).[5] Typically, there are one or two regional banks and one or two second regional banks in a prefecture (there are 47 prefectures in Japan). These banks typically have branch offices in and around their own prefecture and in large cities such as Tokyo and Osaka. Regional banks have a larger number of branch offices than second regional banks.

How competitive is the Japanese banking market? Again there is a scarcity of research. Pooling city and regional banks, Molyneux, Thornton, and Lloyd-Williams (1996) report that Japanese banks were uncompetitive in 1986 and 1988. Another study, using a sample of city and regional banks from 1974 to 2000, estimates the degree of competition by bank type using a marginal price (Lerner index) approach (Uchida and Tsutsui, 2005). They find that competition had improved throughout the sample period, especially in the 1970s and in the first half of the 1980s when financial deregulation began. They also find that city banks had been facing more competitive pressure than regional banks.

36.2.4 The Efficiency of Japanese Banks

Most of the studies on the efficiency of Japanese banks focus on ordinary banks (plus long-term credit banks and trust banks).[6] On balance, they find evidence of economies of scale, at least for the average bank. Some studies found evidence of scale economies until the early 1990s regardless of bank size (Fukuyama 1993; and McKillop, Glass, and Morikawa, 1996), although one study found evidence of diseconomies (Tadesse, 2006). Fukuyama (1993) finds that regional banks are scale inefficient, second regional banks are more efficient than regional banks, and city banks are close to efficient, exhibiting constant returns to scale.

However, subsequent studies do not uniformly find evidence of scale economies in later periods. Altunbas et al. (2000) find during the 1993–96 period scale economies for smallest banks only (1–2 trillion yen of assets or less), but find scale diseconomies for large banks. They also find that when bank asset quality and liquidity risk are not controlled for, the optimal bank size is much larger. However, their proxy for asset quality, a non-performing

---

[5] There are five city banks in this table due to the merger of Mizuho with Mizuho-Corporate on July 2013.

[6] Fukuyama (1996) examines the efficiency of Shinkin banks, and Fukuyama, Guerra, and Weber (1999) investigates the efficiency of credit cooperatives.

Table 36.4 Four main types of bank in Japan

	# of branches			# of
	Total	Domestic	Foreign	employees
5 City banks total	**2,378**	**2,259**	**119**	**89,773**
Mizuho Bank	459	459	–	20,052
Bank of Tokyo-Mitsubishi UFJ	818	757	61	30,243
Sumitomo Mitsui Banking Corporation	679	654	25	24,602
Resona Bank	347	347	–	9,698
Mizuho Corporate Bank	75	42	33	5,178
64 Regional banks total	**7,504**	**7,489**	**15**	**132,888**
Hokkaido Bank	139	139	–	2,385
Aomori Bank	105	105	–	1,465
Michinoku Bank	102	102	–	1,315
Akita Bank	99	99	–	1,527
Hokuto Bank	82	82	–	923
Shonai Bank	80	80	–	827
Yamagata Bank	79	79	–	1,355
Bank of Iwate	109	109	–	1,511
Tohoku Bank	58	58	–	628
77 Bank	141	141	–	2,898
Toho Bank	113	113	–	1,995
Gunma Bank	149	148	1	3,325
Ashikaga Bank	150	150	–	2,788
Joyo Bank	176	176	–	3,762
Tsukuba Bank	146	146	–	1,915

	# of branches			# of
	Total	Domestic	Foreign	employees
42 Second regional banks total	**3,129**	**3,128**	**1**	**47,395**
North Pacific Bank	189	189	–	3,833
Shokusan Bank	117	117	–	981
Kita-Nippon Bank	81	81	–	979
Sendai Bank	72	72	–	760
Fukushima Bank	53	53	–	523
Daito Bank	62	62	–	634
Towa Bank	94	94	–	1,535
Tochigi Bank	95	95	–	1,821
Keiyo Bank	120	120	–	2,025
Higashi-Nippon Bank	77	77	–	1,397
Tokyo Star Bank	31	31	–	1,181
Kanagawa Bank	34	34	–	475
Taiko Bank	70	70	–	992
Nagano Bank	55	55	–	775
First Bank of Toyama	67	67	–	773
Fukuho Bank	39	39	–	545
Shizuoka Chuo Bank	43	43	–	537
Gifu Bank	49	49	–	605
Aichi Bank	105	105	–	1,741
Bank of Nagoya	112	111	1	2,119
Chukyo Bank	93	93	–	1,319
Daisan Bank	98	98	–	1,568

(Continued)

Table 36.4 (Continued)

	# of branches			# of
	Total	Domestic	Foreign	employees
Musashino Bank	93	93	—	2,187
Chiba Bank	177	174	3	4,308
Chiba Kogyo Bank	72	72	—	1,280
Tokyo Tomin Bank	77	77	—	1,738
Bank of Yokohama	205	204	1	4,614
Daishi Bank	121	121	—	2,385
Hokuetsu Bank	89	89	—	1,394
Yamanashi Chuo Bank	91	91	—	1,704
Hachijuni Bank	156	155	1	3,355
Hokuriku Bank	188	188	—	2,755
Toyama Bank	35	35	—	357
Hokkoku Bank	117	117	—	1,951
Fukui Bank	97	97	—	1,282
Shizuoka Bank	195	192	3	3,122
Suruga Bank	127	127	—	1,696
Shimizu Bank	80	80	—	1,055
Ogaki Kyoritsu Bank	147	147	—	2,885
Juroku Bank	147	147	—	2,971
Mie Bank	75	75	—	1,247
Hyakugo Bank	132	132	—	2,465
Shiga Bank	129	128	1	2,358
Bank of Kyoto	162	162	—	3,286
Kinki Osaka Bank	128	128	—	2,342
Senshu Ikeda Bank	141	141	—	2,956
Kansai Urban Banking Corporation	159	159	—	2,733
Taisho Bank	27	27	—	339
Minato Bank	107	107	—	2,167
Shimane Bank	34	34	—	436
Tomato Bank	60	60	—	848
Momiji Bank	118	118	—	1,848
Saikyo Bank	63	63	—	710
Tokushima Bank	77	77	—	934
Kagawa Bank	85	85	—	1,116
Ehime Bank	102	102	—	1,517
Bank of Kochi	71	71	—	945
Fukuoka Chuo Bank	41	41	—	522
Saga Kyoei Bank	35	35	—	398
Bank of Nagasaki	30	30	—	341
Kumamoto Family Bank	70	70	—	1,082
Howa Bank	42	42	—	519
Miyazaki Taiyo Bank	53	53	—	670
Minami-Nippon Bank	63	63	—	714
Okinawa Kaiho Bank	52	52	—	631
Yachiyo Bank	84	84	—	1,757
6 Trust banks total	**282**	**273**	**9**	**21,548**
Mitsubishi UFJ Trust and Banking	69	64	5	7,033
Mizuho Trust & Banking	50	50	—	3,741

Bank			
Nanto Bank	130	130	—	2,803
Kiyo Bank	107	107	—	2,383
Tajima Bank	75	75	—	702
Tottori Bank	71	71	—	723
San-in Godo Bank	144	144	—	2,017
Chugoku Bank	162	161	1	3,259
Hiroshima Bank	167	167	—	3,399
Yamaguchi Bank	141	138	3	2,024
Awa Bank	98	98	—	1,392
Hyakujushi Bank	122	122	—	2,194
Iyo Bank	151	150	1	2,752
Shikoku Bank	114	114	—	1,539
Bank of Fukuoka	166	166	—	3,832
Chikuho Bank	43	43	—	642
Bank of Saga	100	100	—	1,443
Eighteenth Bank	100	100	—	1,479
Shinwa Bank	88	88	—	1,473
Higo Bank	122	122	—	2,276
Oita Bank	103	103	—	1,715
Miyazaki Bank	95	95	—	1,516
Kagoshima Bank	126	126	—	2,527
Bank of the Ryukyus	71	71	—	1,216
Bank of Okinawa	65	65	—	1,099
Nishi-Nippon City Bank	206	206	—	3,782
Kitakyushu Bank	28	28	—	389
The Chuo Mitsui Trust and Banking	92	92	—	4,373
Sumitomo Trust & Banking	66	62	4	5,273
Nomura Trust and Banking	2	2	—	361
Chuo Mitsui Asset Trust and Banking	3	3	—	767
Other banks	**194**	**194**	**—**	**6,524**
Shinsei Bank	42	42	—	1,895
Aozora Bank	20	20	—	1,543
Saitama Resona Bank	132	132	—	3,086
Total	**13,487**	**13,343**	**144**	**298,128**
Cf) Japan Post Bank	24,249	24,249	—	12,796

Note: Only the full members of the Japanese Bankers Association are included.

Source: Japanese Bankers Association and Japan Post Bank homepage (As of March 31, 2012).

loan ratio, might be problematic during the period 1993–96 due to imprecise disclosure. Drake and Hall (2003) find similar results in 1996, but the optimal bank size in their study is larger: 6–10 trillion yen in terms of loans outstanding. Further, whether the disappearance of universal scale economies after the 1990s in empirical studies is due to an underlying environmental change or due to methodological improvements is an open question.

Drake and Hall (2003) also find that in comparing bank types ordinary banks are scale inefficient, whereas long-term credit banks and trust banks are scale efficient. However, the efficiency results for long-term credit banks and trust banks found in this and other studies may be due to the lack of appropriate controls for the difference between these banks and ordinary banks with respect to their asset/liability structure.

Studies based on data envelopment analysis investigate pure technical inefficiency, or adequate/excessive use of inputs. Fukuyama (1993) finds pure technical inefficiency for ordinary banks with the magnitude being the greatest for regional banks. Drake and Hall (2003) find that the magnitude of pure technical inefficiency is greater than that of scale inefficiency— that is, banks can reduce cost more by adopting a technology requiring fewer inputs than by increasing the scale of their operation. Drake and Hall (2003) also show that in terms of pure technical inefficiency, regional banks, and next second regional banks are inefficient, while city banks are almost efficient and trust and long-term credit banks are efficient. They also report that the larger the bank size, the smaller the pure technical inefficiency becomes.[7]

Only a few studies investigated scope economies in Japanese banks, and their results are not consistent with each other.[8] Tachibanaki, Mitsui, and Kitagawa (1991) find cost complementarity between lending and securities investment in 1987 for city, regional, long-term credit, and trust banks. However, McKillop, Glass, and Morikawa (1996) find for five city banks from 1978 to 1991 no global economy of scope among lending, liquid asset holdings, and securities investments. Rather, they find cost anti-complementarity between lending and holding liquid assets and between lending and securities investment, and cost complementarity between holding liquid assets and securities investment.

Harimaya (2008), using the sample of regional banks from 1994 to 2003, finds that there is cost anti-complementarity between lending and securities investment, and between lending and trust businesses, but cost complementarity between securities investment and trust businesses. He also reports that although scale economies are observed on average, product-specific scale diseconomies are found for banks' trust business, which casts doubt on the prospect of banks increasing their profitability by focusing on fee businesses. On balance, it is still unclear whether there are scope economies in banking.

Interestingly, a recent study revealed that efficiency results might vary depending on modeling methodologies (Drake, Hall, and Simper, 2009). Using bank data from 1995–2002, they show that the efficiency ranking of different types of Japanese banks considerably vary across modeling approaches casting some doubt on earlier studies.[9]

---

[7] Glass et al. (2014) investigates the efficiency of Shinkin banks and credit cooperatives. See also for references to other recent studies.

[8] As Berger, Hunter, and Timme (1993) point out the measurement of the economy of scope is methodologically challenging.

[9] Assaf, Barros, and Matousek (2011) analyze the productivity and efficiency of Shinkin banks from 2000 to 2006 using the bootstrap and Bayesian approaches.

36.2.5 Commercial vs. Universal Banking in Japan

Historically Japan's regulation of universal banking has mirrored regulation in the US (with the exception of equity ownership). Like the Glass–Steagall Act in the US, Article 65 of the 1948 Securities and Exchange Law in Japan separated investment banking from commercial banking. As in the US there was a sequential dismantling of this separation beginning significantly in the 1980s when city, long-term, trust, and regional banks were allowed to underwrite and deal in public bonds. In addition to the banking activities discussed above, corporate underwriting was allowed in affiliates beginning in 1993, and in 1998 banks could form financial holding companies. These measures were part of a "big bang" financial system liberalization similar to that in the UK and the US (see Horiuchi, 2000 and Royama, 2000). Investment banking and trust activities, however, must still be conducted in affiliate organizations that are separate from the banking entity. As of July 1, 2013, there were 17 bank financial holding companies in Japan including those of the four city banks and the Japan Post Bank.

There have been some studies that have examined issues related to universal banking in Japan, including the conflict of interest issue and relationship-building across commercial and investment banking services. The results are mixed. Hamao and Hoshi (2000) show that the new-issue corporate bond yield spread does not depend on whether the underwriter is a bank subsidiary or not. However, Takaoka and McKenzie (2004) find that underwriting commissions are smaller when the lead underwriter is a bank-owned securities company. They also find that, after the entry of bank-affiliated securities companies, underwriting commissions and yield spreads decreased. Takaoka and McKenzie (2004) further find that commissions and spreads do not vary depending on the strength of the bank-issuer relationship, but Yasuda (2007), using a more elaborate methodology, find that the bank-issuer relationship does have a beneficial effect.[10]

36.2.6 Regulation of the Japanese Banking System

Before the banking crisis in Japan, from the mid-1990s, the Ministry of Finance (MoF) played a dominant role in prudential supervision of most of the banking system. In 1998 bank regulatory responsibility was shifted to the new Financial Supervisory Agency, which was reorganized as the Financial Services Agency (FSA) in 2000. As can be seen in Table 36.3, the FSA supervises and charters most of the banking system including, most importantly, the ordinary banks and financial holding companies. Some of the other private banking institutions are supervised by various ministries of the government as are all of the government financial institutions.[11]

As the central bank, the Bank of Japan also has the ability to monitor its customer banks (so-called "on-site examinations") in order to discharge its responsibilities in determining and executing monetary policy and in providing liquidity to the banking system including

---

[10] Other studies on the commercial and investment banking services include Kang and Liu (2007), Kutsuna, Smith, and Smith (2007), and Suzuki and Yamada (2012).

[11] For a more extensive discussion of the FSA and bank regulation including financial stability, see IMF (2012).

its role as lender of last resort. The deposit insurance system in Japan was established in 1971 and is provided by the Deposit Insurance Corporation.

36.3 SELECTED TOPICS IN JAPANESE BANKING

36.3.1 The Main Bank System and Relationship Banking

The main bank system in Japan can be more precisely defined as a "system of corporate financing and governance involving an informal set of practices, institutional arrangements, and behaviours among industrial and commercial firms, banks of various types, other financial institutions, and the regulatory authorities. At its core there is the relationship between the main bank and the firm" (Aoki, Patrick, and Sheard, 1994, p. 3). Originally set up in war-time Japan based on zaibatsus to help coordinate wartime production, these industrial groups allegedly became a driver of economic growth during the post-war period when they became known as *keiretsu* (see Hoshi and Kashyap, 2001; and Teranishi, 1994).

This relationship has many dimensions including reciprocal shareholdings, the supply of management resources and directors, and the provision of various financial services (including loans, guarantees, trustee administration, operation of settlement accounts, foreign exchange dealings, securities underwriting, and investment banking advisory services). Also important is the relationship between the main bank and the firm's other financiers (see Sheard, 1994b) and the relationships among the regulatory authorities and all of these actors. The financial institutions and firms tied together under this system are referred to as the "financial keiretsu" (horizontal keiretsu). This can be distinguished from the concept of a "corporate keiretsu" (vertical keiretsu) that mainly focuses on ties through vertical relationships among suppliers and sellers (see Aoki and Patrick, 1994 for more on the main bank system).

Before the empirical studies in the mid-1990s on relationship banking in the US (e.g., Petersen and Rajan, 1994; Berger and Udell, 1995) and later in Europe (e.g., Angelini, DiSalvo, and Ferri, 1998), the practitioner and academic analysis of banking and commercial lending in Japan had focused primarily on the role of Japan's main bank system. As we shall see in Section 36.3.1.1, these earlier main bank-focused studies share much of their theoretical foundation with the newer literature on relationship-lending.

However, two distinctions need to be made between the newer literature on relationship lending and the study of the role of the main bank in the financial keiretsu. First, the main bank literature has a corporate governance component which is lacking in the newer relationship lending literature. Second, the main bank literature focuses, for the most part, on large companies while most of the newer relationship lending literature focuses on SMEs. These distinctions are important because corporate governance issues are much less relevant in the SME sector where there is usually no separation of ownership and management. It is important to note that there have been some studies on SME lending in Japan conducted in the spirit of the newer literature on relationship-lending that focus on the relationship between SMEs and their main banks.

36.3.1.1 *Traditional Main Bank Studies*

Numerous academic studies since the 1980s have examined the role of main banks in financial keiretsus. The early focus of these studies was on risk-sharing among keiretsu members (e.g., Nakatani, 1984; Osano and Tsutsui, 1985). The literature then gradually shifted to the role of banks as providers of corporate governance (see Aoki, 1994). Some studies emphasize a special corporate governance role of the main bank in periods of firm distress (Sheard, 1994a; Osano, 1998). Other studies emphasize a contingent governance role for the main bank: the main bank plays a minimal role in *normal* times but in financial distress the bank assumes managerial control (e.g., Berglöf and Perotti, 1994). To a certain extent the Japanese main banking system in terms of corporate governance can be viewed as similar to Germany's historical *Hausbank* system, each standing in contrast to markets-oriented economies such as the UK and the US where the market for corporate control and shareholder activism play a more important role (Prowse, 1995).

Empirically, the issue of the very definition of "the main bank" is challenging. A common approach is to use the information provided by the data source, such as (1) keiretsu affiliation in *Keiretsu no Kenkyu* (Studies on Keiretsu) data, (2) a first-listed bank in *Quarterly Corporate Report* (Japan Company Handbook), (3) an affiliation in *Dodwell Marketing Consultants' Industrial Groupings in Japan*. Alternatively, the main bank is defined as a bank that (4) has a director on the borrower's board, (5) is the largest lender, (6) is the largest shareholder, or (7) is both (5) and (6) (plus other characteristics).

Empirical studies here can also be broadly classified based on their focus on the role of the main bank. Some emphasize the role of the main bank in mitigating liquidity constraints (e.g., Hoshi, Kashyap, and Scharfstein 1990a, 1990b, 1991; Ogawa and Suzuki, 2000).[12] Others investigate managerial intervention by main banks. Kaplan and Minton (1994), Kang and Shivdasani (1995, 1997), and Morck and Nakamura (1999) find that during the late 1980s banks assigned new board members in a timely and effective manner. Shin and Korali (2004) found that main banks played a unique role in information production specific to the 1995–97 period during the banking crisis.[13]

However, to some extent the tone of the research on main banks may reflect the timing of the studies themselves and the changing view of the Japanese economy from the more positive pre-crisis perspective to the more critical post-crisis perspective. Other later studies find that firms with a main bank exhibit weaker performance (e.g., Weinstein and Yafeh, 1998; Hanazaki and Horiuchi, 2000; Wu and Xu, 2005), suggesting that main banks extract excessive rents from their borrowers. Kang and Shivdasani (1999) and Kang and Stultz (2000) find similar results for bank (though not necessarily main bank-) dependent firms. Some authors even argue that the main bank system and the importance of keiretsus is a "myth" and that many of the empirical results in this literature cannot be reproduced (Miwa and Ramseyer 2002, 2005).

[12] Although the methodology in the Hoshi, Kashyap and Scharfstein papers has been criticized (Kaplan and Zingales, 1997; Hayashi, 2000), similar findings have been reported in a subsequent study using an improved methodology (Hori, Saito, and Ando, 2006).
[13] See Gao (2008), Inoue, Kato, and Bremer (2008), and Kang et al. (2011) for more recent empirical studies on the role of main banks.

One interpretation of these seemingly conflicting results is that the benefits from the main bank system (e.g., liquidity provision) may come at the cost of extracted rents. Interestingly, Weinstein and Yafeh (1998) find (in effect) evidence of a tradeoff where a main bank relationship may mitigate financing constraints even though it reduces firm performance. Moreover, the possibility of such a tradeoff between the benefits and costs of a main bank relationship had already been noted in a much earlier study (Nakatani, 1984).

It is important to add here that recently there has been a fundamental change in corporate governance in Japan—a change that has been associated with a dismantling of keiretsu ties (Aoki, Jackson, and Miyajima, 2007). This suggests that for large businesses the main bank relationship may be significantly less important in the future. However, it seems unlikely that this trend has altered the importance of the main bank relationship for SMEs. This recent trend also suggests the possibility that if access to capital markets had not been constrained in post-war Japan, the role of the keiretsus and the main bank would not have been as prominent.[14]

36.3.1.2 SME Relationship Lending

Relatively recently there has been growing interest in research that examines relationship lending in the context of Japanese SMEs. A recent increase in the availability of SME data in Japan has spawned new empirical work that has investigated financing constraints in the SME sector including the impact of bank–borrower relationships and the extent to which these relationships benefit borrowers through the production of soft information.[15] This coincides with increased practitioner and policy interest in SME financing and the FSA's adoption of measures that are intended to promote relationship banking between SMEs and smaller banks (the Action Program concerning Enhancement of Relationship Banking Functions (2003 and 2004), and its successor program Ensuring Further Promotion of Regionally-based Relationship Banking (2005 and 2006)).

Findings in the academic literature on SME lending practices in Japan are interesting from an international perspective. Kano et al. (2011) find that the lower loan interest rate and enhanced credit availability that are associated with long-term banking relationships occur only when hard information is unavailable for the borrower and the bank is small and faces stiff competition. However, the lending relationship in this sample is quite long (32.2 years on average) compared with that in other countries. Uchida, Udell, and Watanabe (2008) find that the *mode* of relationship building in Japan is somewhat different from that in the US as reported in Berger et al. (2005). Findings in Uchida, Udell, and Yamori (2012) also suggest that the role of the loan officer in Japan may be different than in the US.

36.3.2 Lending Technologies in Japan

Recently, the literature on business lending, especially small business lending, classifies types of lending as different lending technologies with relationship-lending (discussed

---

[14] Kobayashi and Osano (2011) and Wu and Yao (2012) provide a more current theoretical assessment of the main bank system.
[15] See, for example, Boot (2000) for a summary of the theoretical and empirical work on relationship-lending.

above) being one of the technologies (Berger and Udell 2002, 2006). There are some interesting aspects of Japanese business lending from the lending technology viewpoint.[16] In this subsection, we will discuss three of these: the role of collateral, business credit scoring, and government credit guarantee programs.

36.3.2.1 *The Role of Collateral in Business Lending in Japan*

Collateral is one of the most powerful contracting tools used by bankers to mitigate information-based problems associated with business lending and is a vital component of many SME lending technologies. Lending against real estate, for example, is quite common globally in SME lending. Japan is no exception (see Ono et al., 2010). In fact, the role of collateral historically appears to have been of particular importance in Japan where banks practiced the so-called "collateral principle" under which they routinely underwrote business loans based almost entirely on real estate—either real estate owned by the business and/or the entrepreneur. Interestingly, however, analyses from the post crisis period (mid 2000s) suggests that the collateral principle is no longer a dominate SME loan underwriting technology (see Uchida, Udell and Yamori, 2008; Uchida, 2011).

Whether or not the use of collateral is associated with borrower risk has been extensively studied in the literature, particularly in the US (see John, Lynch, and Puri, 2003). Evidence from one study on Japan suggests that there is a positive association, and that collateral's use mitigates ex post moral hazard (Ono, Sakai, and Uesugi, 2012), but another study shows that ex ante borrower risk does not change the likelihood of a collateral use (Ono and Uesugi, 2009). Another interesting finding in Japan (perhaps related to the collateral principle) is that stronger banking relations appear to be associated with an increased likelihood of pledging collateral (e.g., Ono and Uesugi, 2009; Kano et al. 2011).

Relatively recently the requisite legal and commercial infrastructure to allow lending against movable assets (i.e., account receivables and inventory) was introduced in Japan (see Ono et al. 2010, sec. 4.1). As a result, commercial banks in Japan have begun offering an SME lending technology known as asset-based lending (ABL), a type of collateral lending against receivables and inventory associated with intense monitoring. ABL had been confined almost entirely to common law countries such as Australia, Canada, New Zealand, the UK, and the US and is generally associated with a riskier class of borrowers (Carey, Post, and Sharpe, 1998; Udell, 2004). Some research suggests that ABL is still in the development stage in Japan (Kinjo, 2013).

36.3.2.2 *Small Business Credit Scoring in Japan*

Japanese banks have also adopted another lending technology originally introduced in the US in the mid-1990s—small business credit scoring (SBCS). Bank of Japan (2007) describes that large banks, and subsequently regional banks, started to adopt SBCS in SME lending in the early 2000s. Volume rapidly increased to more than 2 trillion yen by 2005 (Bank of Japan, 2007). Its introduction was facilitated by a government policy initiative mentioned earlier to promote relationship banking by smaller banks (the Action Program Concerning

---

[16] See Uchida (2011) for different use of various lending technologies by banks in Japan.

Enhancement of Relationship Banking Functions 2003 and 2004). This is a broad initiative to encourage SME lending that is not limited to relationship lending, and SBCS is promoted as a form of lending that does not depend on collateral.

However, due to the huge loan losses in SBCS loans, particularly those extended by Shinginko Tokyo (a bank established by the Tokyo Metropolitan Government to focus on SME lending), banks decreased the volume of their SBCS lending in the late 2000s (Hasumi and Hirata, 2010). Even before these losses had materialized, the Bank of Japan (2007) had already identified the poor performance of SBCS loans partially attributing this to the inadequacy of the informational infrastructure in Japan—for example, the inability to link the corporate financial data with the owners' personal credit history data. In addition, the Bank of Japan identified problems with the scoring model as it was applied to relatively large borrowers where the fit was generically poor. Hasumi and Hirata (2010) conclude that adverse selection problems exacerbated by financial statement window-dressing (from which SBCS inputs were drawn) were the main causes of the huge losses.[17]

36.3.2.3 Government Guarantee Programs in Japanese Business Lending

There is widespread evidence that SME financing is characterized by a "funding gap" in which SMEs are systematically financially constrained. As a result, governments in both developed and developing economies have directly or indirectly provided substantial amounts of funding to SMEs (e.g., Cressy 2000, 2002). There is also evidence that this funding gap is exacerbated by macro shocks that affect the banking system (e.g., Jimenez et al. 2012; Popov and Udell, 2012).

In addition to direct lending by government financial institutions (see Section 36.2.2.8), Japan has long implemented massive government loan guarantee programs for small business. Multiple credit guarantee corporations (CGRs) around the country, which are public institutions established based on the Credit Guarantee Corporation Law, provide guarantees on loans to SMEs, and the Japan Finance Corporation's Small and Medium Enterprise Unit provides insurance on the guaranteed liabilities associated with the loans. The outstanding amount of liabilities guaranteed by the credit guarantee corporations is 34.4 trillion yen at the end of March 2012.[18]

Historically, the most important feature of these guarantee programs was the assumption of all risk (by CGRs) stemming from a 100% guarantee. To mitigate the screening and monitoring problems that arose from the 100% guarantee, a "Responsibility-Sharing System" was implemented in 2007 that reduced in principle the guarantee coverage to 80%. However, there have been some significant exceptions in the form of "special" 100% guarantee programs, including guarantee programs to respond to the global financial crisis (the "Emergency (Safety-Net) Credit Guarantee Program," from 2008), and to the Great Tohoku Earthquake (the "Great East Japan Earthquake Recovery Emergency Guarantee," from 2011).

Collectively, the credit guarantee programs in Japan provide a unique opportunity to study this type of government intervention and whether or not their benefits are outweighed

---

[17] Hasumi, Hirata, and Ono (2011) investigates the ex post performance of SBCS borrowers with special attention to relationship versus non-relationship lenders.

[18] For more information about the credit guarantee system in Japan, see National Federation of Credit Guarantee Corporations (2012).

by the potential adverse selection problems they might invite. Some evidence on the "Special Credit Guarantee Program for Financial Stability" implemented in 1998–2001 suggests that the benefits were significant and that many firms—specifically low risk firms—actually became more efficient (Uesugi, Sakai and Yamashiro, 2010). Other evidence on the same program suggests that it might have had a bigger effect on the supply of funds to non-users of the program (Wilcox and Yasuda, 2008). Yet another study focusing on the "Emergency (Safety-Net) Credit Guarantee Program" calls for a more nuanced view. Ono, Uesugi, and Yasuda (2013) find that while the relevant program improved credit availability for borrowing firms, it also encouraged a portfolio substitution by the borrower's main banks away from non-guaranteed loans to guaranteed loans. They also find deteriorating ex post performance of firms obtaining guaranteed loans from their main bank as compared with those obtaining non-guaranteed loans.

36.3.3 The Japanese Banking Crisis

The banking crisis in Japan rose to the surface as a public policy issue in the middle of the 1990s, escalated dramatically shortly thereafter, and then continued perhaps as late as the mid-2000s. [19] Given our space limitation, we offer a brief overview of the crisis, its causes and its effects on bank behavior. We also provide some account for the banks in Japan during the Global Financial Crisis.

36.3.3.1 Brief Review of the Crisis

The visible beginning of the crisis is associated with the failures of two credit cooperatives in 1994. Ultimately there were 171 bank failures in Japan from 1994 through 2003 involving one city bank, two long-term credit banks, one regional bank, 12 second regional banks, 23 Shinkin banks, and 132 credit cooperatives (Nikkin, 2005). The enormity of the banking crisis was revealed in stages that progressed from the early 1990s through the early 2000s. [20] The regulatory response to the crises can best be described as one of catching up with rapidly unfolding events. In particular, the regulatory policies and infrastructure in place at the beginning of the crisis were simply not capable of handling a crisis of this magnitude. New policies and infrastructure were created to address the problem—but these were implemented with a significant lag.

A limited number of bank failures prior to 1994 were resolved in a conventional manner using arranged mergers. However, the crisis moved to a more visibly serious stage in late 1994 with failures of Tokyo Kyowa and Anzen, the two urban credit cooperatives. They were too large to be resolved by an arranged merger, and the deposit insurance fund was insufficient to cover the unprecedented losses. Concern about contagion effects persuaded regulators to avoid a payoff resolution in which depositors would take a haircut. The ultimate "hand-made" (Nakaso, 2001, p. 7) nature of the resolution of these two failures involved

---

[19] Our reading of the literature suggests that there is no agreement on exactly when the crisis began and when it ended. As described below, the first bank failures, though small, began occurring in the early 1990s but then escalated dramatically later in the decade. Bank capital and non-performing loans, however, did not appear to stabilize until the mid-2000s.

[20] The following discussion of the stages of the banking crisis is based on Nakaso (2001).

the establishment of a new successor bank capitalized by funds from the deposit insurance agency, the Bank of Japan, and private financial institutions including those that had no relationship with the two cooperatives.

In the following year a number of other banks failed including a much larger urban cooperative. In addition, a group of real estate finance companies known as the *jusen* failed. The jusen were initially founded by commercial banks to augment their residential mortgage lending, but by the time that they failed, they had shifted their focus to financing real estate developers. Because of the collective size of these institutions, the resolution could not be handled without the use of taxpayer funding. Additional emergency measures were also undertaken at this time including the creation of the Resolution and Collection Bank, and the temporary implementation of a 100% deposit insurance guarantee.[21]

Following several other bank failures the financial crisis escalated in 1997 as it became apparent that problem loans were threatening the viability of Japan's largest banks. Nippon Credit Bank, one of the three long-term credit banks, was bailed out, two securities firms failed, and major bank failures began occurring on a regular basis in the fall, including that of Hokkaido Takushoku Bank (a city bank) and some second regional banks. Belatedly in 1997 the government implemented emergency and permanent measures to cope with the crisis. These measures resulted in capital injections into 21 large banks in 1998.

Nevertheless, problems in the banking system continued to mount in 1998 including the failure of two of the long-term credit banks—the Nippon Credit Bank (bailed out earlier) and the Long Term Credit Bank of Japan, each being resolved by temporary nationalization. Early in 1998 legislation was passed that provided for further injection of $230 billion of public funds, part of which was allocated to the Deposit Insurance Corporation and the remainder was allocated to direct capital injections. Later in 1998 the Diet (Parliament) passed two pieces of legislation that significantly expanded the regulatory infrastructure to handle the disposition of failed banks and to inject capital into viable banks. Also available funds were doubled from the original $230 billion. Additionally, in June 1998 responsibility for prudential supervision of banks was shifted from the Ministry of Finance to the Financial Supervisory Agency, which was later reorganized as Financial Services Agency in 2000.

On October 2002, the Financial Services Agency officially announced the Program for Financial Revival: Revival of the Japanese Economy through Resolving Non-Performing Loans Problems of Major Banks. Therein, the agency declared that by taking necessary measures, they strived to reduce the NPL ratio of major banks by around 50%. Following the various measures actually taken, including sporadic capital injections as described above and made thereafter, the crisis subsided. Consistent with the Program's goals, the non-performing loans ratio of major banks decreased by more than half, from 8.4% as of March 2002 to 2.9% as of March 2005 (from FSA's webpage: Status of Non-Performing Loans).[22] No major bank failure has occurred since the failure and nationalization of Ashikaga Bank (a regional bank) in 2003.

---

[21] Even before this temporary measure, deposits had been implicitly 100% guaranteed under the convoy system (Hoshi, 2002). See Hoshi (2002) for a discussion of the "convoy" system in use until the early stages of the crisis in which the MoF protected and kept alive all financial institutions, including the most inefficient.

[22] As for the resolution of the non-performing loans problems for smaller banks, the FSA acknowledged the difficulty in taking a drastic approach in a short period of time as they did for major banks. To solve the problem by revitalizing SMEs and by activating regional economies, the FSA adopted

In hindsight, the resolution of the crisis saw the government and bank regulators deploy a variety of tools that had been used (or would be used) elsewhere in the world. These included establishing a bridge bank for segregating non-performing loans, and temporarily nationalizing large banks. Ultimately these measures were associated with the injection of massive amounts of government funding to back up the 100% deposit insurance coverage.[23]

36.3.3.2 Causes of the Crisis

Cargill (2000) argues that there were five underlying causes of the crisis: a rigid financial regime, the failure of the Bank of Japan's monetary policy, a slow and indecisive regulatory response to emerging problems, a lack of public support to deal with troubled financial institutions with public funds (and a lack of a political will to do so), and the intransigence of financial institutions in accepting criticism of management policies. Hoshi (2001) and Hoshi and Kashyap (2001) make a related argument that a fundamental cause of the banking crisis was the slow and incomplete deregulation of the financial system in the 1980s, which brought about the flight of good borrowers from the bank loan market (disintermediation), forcing banks to lend to borrowers with whom they were unfamiliar.

Ueda (2000) points out that excessive lending to real estate and related industries might have contributed to the accumulation of non-performing loans.[24] This factor is essentially a consequence of the financial deregulation. As discussed above, disintermediation encouraged banks to lend to unfamiliar borrowers particularly those in the real estate industry (Hoshi and Kashyap, 2001). Banks lent aggressively to this industry both directly and indirectly through affiliates.

Ueda (2000) speculates that rising land prices decreased the perceived risk in real estate lending, prompting more lending ex ante. He also finds evidence that the big drop in land prices ex post was an important determinant of deteriorating non-performing loans. The "collateral principle" discussed above might also have exacerbated this pathology. Ogawa et al. (1996) and Ogawa and Suzuki (2000) found that large firms with more real estate were less financially constrained than those with less real estate.

Anecdotal evidence indicates that euphoric lending practices driven by the formation of the asset price bubble ultimately led to problem loans in the banking system. This is partly consistent with the lazy bank hypothesis (Manove, Padilla, and Pagano, 2001). Irrational herding behavior may also have occurred (Uchida and Nakagawa, 2007; Nakagawa and Uchida, 2011).[25] [26] Kashyap (2002), however, argues that the loan problems that were

the Action Program concerning Enhancement of Relationship Banking Functions (2003 and 2004), and its successor program Ensuring Further Promotion of Regionally-based Relationship Banking (2005 and 2006) to promote relationship banking (see Section 36.3.1.2). Although the causality is unclear, it turned out that the non-performing loans ratio of regional banks actually decreased from 8.0% as of March 2002 to 5.5% as of March 2005, and then to less than 4% from 2007 on (from FSA's webpage, Status of Non-Performing Loans).

[23] Studies on policy responses to the crisis include Hoshi and Patrick (2000), Hoshi and Kashyap (2001), Spiegel and Yamori (2003), and Montgomery and Shimizutani (2009).

[24] He also finds evidence of inefficient (lax) bank management and the safety net-driven moral hazard problem as factors driving poor loan performance.

[25] "Reckless lending" more broadly defined could include the practice of evergreening (the behavior of banks to keep zombie firms alive) as we will discuss in Section 36.3.3.3.

[26] A practice in Japan, known as *amakudari*—hiring retired government officials as board

ultimately revealed in the later stages of the crisis were simply too large to be entirely attributable to euphoric or reckless lending during the formation of the bubble. Further, Ono
et al. (2014) find that the increase in the amount of loans was far smaller than the increase
in land prices, which is at least quantitatively inconsistent with the euphoric or herding scenarios. These arguments notwithstanding, the evidence seems clear that the initial cause of
problems in the banking sector was a pricing bubble in real estate that burst around 1990
(Hoshi and Kashyap, 2010).

36.3.3.3 The Effects of the Crisis

Did the banking crisis lead to a credit crunch? It is clear that the policymakers at the Bank
of Japan concluded that the country was suffering from a credit crunch, noting in the minutes of their Monetary Policy Meeting (January 16, 1998) that the "prospects for a more
restrictive lending attitude of financial institutions and its possible effects were discussed in
detail." Also, a quarterly survey on business expectations conducted by the Bank of Japan,
the TANKAN survey, showed a significant shift in the perception of credit tightening by
corporate Japan beginning in late 1997.[27]

A number of research papers have shown that bank capital deterioration and the decline
in the health of the banking industry reduced bank lending (Ito and Sasaki, 2002), firm
capital expenditures, and firm performance (Gibson, 1997; Fukuda, Kasuya, and Nakajima,
2005; Hosono and Masuda, 2005; Miyajima and Yafeh, 2007), and increased likelihood of
bankruptcy of borrowers (Fukuda, Kasuya, and Akashi 2009).[28] Woo (2003) and Watanabe
(2007) find that the negative impact of the capital crunch was the greatest in fiscal year 1997,
when the MoF became stricter on bank asset valuation.[29]

The view that the credit crunch had significant real effects, however, is not universal.
Hayashi and Prescott (2002) provide evidence showing that the stagnation of the Japanese
economy in the 1990s was not due to a breakdown of the financial system, but rather due
to low productivity growth (measured as total factor productivity (TFP)) in the real economy. Motonishi and Yoshikawa (1999) also report that, at least as far as large firms are
concerned, tighter lending attitudes in banks did not constrain corporate investments
although they also found that small firms were constrained by tighter lending behavior.

Nevertheless, some studies claim that the low TFP was a consequence of banking sector problems. Peek and Rosengren (2005) found that the practice of "evergreening" (where
banks roll over or renew problem loans to make them appear performing), contributed to

---

members—may also have been a factor that leads to non-performing loans. Horiuchi and Shimizu
(2001) find that for regional banks from 1979 through 1991 that more amakudari was associated with
lower bank capital asset ratios and higher non-performing loan ratios. However, another study using a
more elaborated methodology did not find this association (Konishi and Yasuda, 2004).

[27] For a more detailed discussion of the minutes of the Bank of Japan meeting in January 1998 and the
TANKAN survey see Hoshi and Kashyap (2008).

[28] Also, there are studies on the impact of bank failures on borrower performances, e.g., Yamori and
Murakami (1999), Brewer et al. (2003), Hori (2005); Fukuda and Koibuchi (2006), and Minamihashi
(2011). Giannetti and Simonov (2013) examine the effect of bank bailout on the banks' supply of credit
and the performance of their borrowers.

[29] Some studies also found that the introduction of Basel capital standards may have reduced bank
lending (Hall, 1993; Konishi and Yasuda, 2004).

a decrease in TFP. The practice of evergreening facilitates the perpetuation of economically unviable firms ("zombies") who should otherwise be liquidated.[30] The evidence indicates that the perpetuation of these zombies caused real economic distortion and led to lower productivity (Caballero, Hoshi and Kashyap, 2008). There is also some evidence suggesting that the Darwinian natural selection process by which good firms survive and bad firms disappear was inoperative during the crisis (e.g., Nishimura, Nakajima, and Kiyota, 2005).

It should be noted that the capital crunch story and the evergreening story have the opposite predictions on lending. The former predicts a decrease in lending, while the latter predicts an increase. Further research on which effect dominated would be helpful: the issue of real vs. financial stagnation and the causality problem between economic stagnation and the banking crisis has not been fully investigated.[31]

36.3.3.4 *Japanese Banks and the Global Financial Crisis*

Soon after the persistent adverse effect from the banking crisis subsided in Japan, the turmoil in the US subprime residential mortgage market beginning in early 2007 triggered an unprecedented worldwide financial crisis. The effect of the global financial crisis spread to the Japanese economy after the failure of Lehman Brothers in September 2008. For the most part, however, the effect was minimal and Japan was not significantly affected by the global financial crisis in ways that were comparable to Europe and the US (see IMF, 2012, p. 7). As shown in Table 36.5, which shows the profits and losses for major banks and regional banks, the adverse effect was only short-lived.

There were several reasons for this. First, residential mortgages underwritten in Japan are all prime mortgages. Second, securitization is relatively undeveloped in Japan. Table 36.6 shows the amount of residential mortgages (housing loans) underwritten and the amount of RMBS issued in each year. Even at the peak in fiscal 2006, the volume of RMBS issued is one fourth of the volume of residential mortgages underwritten. Third, Japan did not experience a real estate bubble during this period, and Japanese banks did not purchase significant amounts of US subprime mortgage-backed securities.[32] Finally, the crisis was not propagated through capital-impaired foreign banks as in Europe (e.g., Popov and Udell, 2012) because Japanese banking is dominated by domestic banks.

However, banks in Japan attracted wide attention during the global financial crisis, not as victims of the crisis but as a negative example to draw lessons from. There are a number of parallels between the Japanese crisis in the 1990s and the financial crisis in the US including the root cause—the bursting of a real estate bubble. Other similarities include the failure of investment banks and other non-banking financial institutions and the "hand made"/ad hoc

---

[30] Watanabe (2010) finds evidence suggesting that a large loss of bank capital in 2007 due to the regulators' toughened stance lead to the banks' evergreening.

[31] A study that is related and suggestive in this regard is Ishikawa and Tsutsui (2013), which uses prefectural panel data to try to identify whether the credit contraction in the 1990s was supply- or demand-driven.

[32] The Bank of Japan's Financial System Report (Bank of Japan 2008, p. 2) notes that "(w)hile Japanese banks' losses stemming from the US subprime mortgage problem increased as the problem became more serious, such losses seem to have been contained within their current profit levels and capital strength, since Japanese banks' related exposures were mainly in the form of investments in structured credit products."

Table 36.5 Recent profits and losses for major banks and regional banks

(Bank type)	(period)	Credit related expenses[+] (billion yen)	Losses on sales and depreciation losses for equity and bond holdings (billion yen)	Net profits (billion yen)
Major Banks *	Fiscal 2006	272.9	99.7	2,575.0
	Fiscal 2007	411.0	-41.3	1,452.7
	Fiscal 2008	1,911.4	-1,561.3	-1,606.9
	Fiscal 2009	965.5	62.2	1,159.4
	Fiscal 2010	392.2	-299.7	1,850.4
	Fiscal 2011	170.1	-209.7	1,748.6
	Fiscal 2012	163.4	-231.2	2,215.2
Regional and Second Regional Banks **	Fiscal 2006	773.0	189.1	805.6
	Fiscal 2007	712.8	97.0	640.1
	Fiscal 2008	1,183.4	-413.2	-413.8
	Fiscal 2009	720.6	-33.8	643.7
	Fiscal 2010	614.5	-107.0	652.7
	Fiscal 2011	291.2	-123.0	727.2
	Fiscal 2012	365.0	-81.1	815.7

+ Before fiscal 2009, labled as "Disposal of bad loans".

* Mizuho Bank, Mizuho Corporate Bank, Mizuho Trust Bank, Bank of Mitsubishi-Tokyo UFJ, Mitsubishi UFJ Trust Bank, Mitsui Sumitomo Bank, Resona Bank, Sumitomo Mitsui Trust Bank (before Fiscal 2011, Chuo Mitsui Bank and Sumitomo Trust Bank), Shinsei Bank, and Aozora Bank.

** Regional banks (64 banks), Second regional banks (from 45 (fiscal 2006) to 41 banks (for fiscal 2012)), and Saitama Resona Bank.

Source: Financial Services Agency (based on disclosure information by individual banks).

Table 36.6 Residential mortgages underwritten and RMBs issued

	(A) Residential mortgages underwritten	(B) RMBS issued	(B) / (A)
Fiscal 2004	227,203.0	24,517.4	(10.8%)
Fiscal 2005	236,955.0	49,245.6	(20.8%)
Fiscal 2006	211,917.0	51,214.5	(24.2%)
Fiscal 2007	195,830.5	32,628.1	(16.7%)
Fiscal 2008	107,537.7	19,690.9	(10.0%)
Fiscal 2009	193,211.3	19,603.4	(10.1%)
Fiscal 2010	194,490.7	19,473.5	(10.0%)
Fiscal 2011	197,911.8	25,805.6	(13.0%)

Source: Japan Housing Finance Agency (for (A)) and Japan Securities Dealers Association (for (B)).

Unit: 100 million yen.

nature of the regulatory response.[33] For a more complete comparison of the Japanese bank-ing crisis and the current financial crisis in the US, see Udell (2009), Hoshi and Kashyap (2010) and Allen, Chakraborty, and Watanabe (2011).

36.4 CONCLUSION

In this chapter we have examined the structure, the performance, and some of the defin-ing characteristics of the Japanese banking industry. In addition to this overview, we have reviewed the literature on three interesting topics related to the Japanese banking sys-tem: the Japanese main bank system, lending technologies in Japan, and the Japanese bank-ing crisis in the 1990s.

We conclude this chapter by pointing out the scarcity of research on Japanese banking. Even on the selected topics discussed above there remain many open questions. For exam-ple, how and to what extent are banking markets in Japan segmented? Are there economies of scale or scope in banks in Japan, and to what extent? What were, and what are, the pros and cons of the main bank system? Did the banking crisis cause the prolonged stagnation in the Japanese economy, or vice versa? What is the future of the Japanese banking industry and the keiretsu-driven ties between firms and their main banks?

The banking-oriented Japanese financial system has been a critical component of the country's economy—an economy that has grown to one of the largest in the world. Despite the idiosyncratic nature of Japanese banking, its seems quite likely that there is much we can learn from the Japanese experience that will inform us more generally about the role of banks in the global financial system architecture. More research on the banking industry in Japan is clearly called for.

REFERENCES

Allen, L, Chakraborty, S., and Watanabe, W. (2011). Foreign Direct Investment and Regulatory Remedies for Banking Crises: Lessons from Japan, *Journal of International Business Studies* 42, 875–893.

Altunbas, Y., Liu, M.-H., Molyneux, P., and Seth, R. (2000). Efficiency and Risk in Japanese Banking, *Journal of Banking and Finance* 24, 1605–1628.

Angelini, P., DiSalvo, R., and Ferri, G. (1998). Availability and Cost of Credit for Small Businesses: Customer Relationships and Credit Cooperatives, *Journal of Banking and Finance* 22, 925–954.

Aoki, M. (1994). Monitoring Characteristics of the Main Bank System: An Analytical and Developmental View. In: M. Aoki and H. T. Patrick, (Eds.), *The Japanese Main Bank System*, 109–141. New York: Oxford University Press.

Aoki, M., Jackson, G., and Miyajima, H. (2007). *Corporate Governance in Japan.* Oxford: Oxford University Press.

---

[33] Imai (2009) find evidence suggesting that the political pressure mattered on the declaration of insolvency of regional financial institutions.

Aoki, M. and Patrick, H. T. (1994). *The Japanese Main Bank System: Its Relevance for Developing and Transforming Economies.* New York: Oxford University Press.

Aoki, M., Patrick, H. T., and Sheard, P. (1994). The Japanese Main Bank System: An Introductory Overview. In: M. Aoki, and H. T. Patrick, (Eds.), *The Japanese Main Bank System,* 1–50. New York: Oxford University Press.

Assaf, A. G., Barros, C. P., and Matousek, R. (2011). Productivity and Efficiency Analysis of Shinkin Banks: Evidence from Bootstrap and Bayesian Approaches, *Journal of Banking and Finance* 35, 331–342.

Bank of Japan (2007). Financial System Report, September 2007.

Bank of Japan (2008). Financial System Report, September 2008.

Berger, A. N., Hunter, W. C., and Timme, S. G. (1993). The Efficiency of Financial Institutions: A Review and Preview of Research Past, Present and Future, *Journal of Banking and Finance* 17, 221–249.

Berger, A. N., Miller, N. H., Petersen, M. A., Rajan, P. G., and Stein, J. C. (2005). Does Function Follow Organizational Form? Evidence from the Lending Practices of Large and Small Banks, *Journal of Financial Economics* 76, 237–269.

Berger, A. N. and Udell, G. F. (1995). Relationship Lending and Lines of Credit in Small Firm Finance, *Journal of Business* 68, 351–381.

Berger, A. N. and Udell, G. F. (2002). Small Business Credit Availability and Relationship Lending: The Importance of Bank Organizational Structure, *Economic Journal* 112, F32–F53.

Berger, A. N. and Udell, G. F. (2006). A More Complete Conceptual Framework for SME Finance, *Journal of Banking and Finance* 30, 2945–2966.

Berglöf, E. and Perotti, E. (1994). The Governance Structure of the Japanese Financial Keiretsu, *Journal of Financial Economics* 36, 259–284.

Boot, A. W. A. (2000). Relationship Banking: What Do We Know? *Journal of Financial Intermediation* 9, 7–25.

Brewer, E., Genay, H., Hunter, W. C., and Kaufman, G. G. (2003). The Value of Banking Relationships during a Financial Crisis: Evidence from Failures of Japanese Banks, *Journal of the Japanese International Economies* 17, 233–262.

Caballero, R. J., Hoshi, T., and Kashyap, A. K. (2008). Zombie Lending and Depressed Restructuring in Japan, *American Economic Review* 98, 1943–1977.

Carey, M., Post, M., and Sharpe, S. A. (1998). Does Corporate Lending by Banks and Finance Companies Differ? Evidence on Specialization in Private Debt Contracting, *Journal of Finance* 53, 845–878.

Cargill, T. F. (2000). What Caused Japan's Banking Crisis? In: T. Hoshi and H. T. Patrick (Eds.), *Crisis and Change in the Japanese Financial System,* 37–58. Amsterdam: Kluwer Academic.

Cargill, T. F. and Yoshino, N. (2000). The Postal Savings System, Fiscal Investment and Loan Program, and Modernization of Japan's Financial System. In: T. Hoshi and H. T. Patrick (Eds.), *Crisis and Change in the Japanese Financial System,* 201–230. Amsterdam: Kluwer Academic.

Cressy, R. C. (2000). European Loan Guarantee Schemes: Who Has Them, Who Pays, and Who Gains? In: B. Green (Ed.), *Risk Behaviour and Risk Management in Business Life,* 235–246. Amsterdam: Kluwer Academic.

Cressy, R. C. (2002). Funding Gaps: A Symposium, *Economic Journal* 112, F1–F16.

Drake, L. and Hall, M. J. B. (2003). Efficiency in Japanese Banking: An Empirical Analysis, *Journal of Banking and Finance* 27, 891–917.

Drake, L., Hall, M. J. B., and Simper, R. (2009). Bank Modeling Methodologies: A Comparative Non-Parametric Analysis of Efficiency in the Japanese Banking Sector, *Journal of International Financial Markets, Institutions and Money* 19, 1–15.

Flath, D. (2000). *The Japanese Economy*.Oxford: Oxford University Press.

Fukanuma, H., Nemoto, T., and Watanabe, W. (2006). Do Governmental Financial Institutions Help Startups Grow? Evidence from Japan. Keio University: Mimeo.

Fukuda, S., Kasuya, M., and Akashi, K. (2009). Impaired Bank Health and Default Risk, *Pacific-Basin Finance Journal* 17, 145–162.

Fukuda, S., Kasuya, M., and Nakajima, J. (2005). Bank Health and Investment: An Analysis of Unlisted Companies in Japan, Bank of Japan Working Paper Series No. 05-E-5.

Fukuda, S. and Koibuchi, S. (2006). The Impacts of "Shock Therapy" under a Banking Crisis: Experiences from Three Large Bank Failures in Japan, *Japanese Economic Review* 57, 232–256.

Fukuyama, H. (1993). Technical and Scale Efficiency of Japanese Commercial Banks: A Non-Parametric Approach, *Applied Economics* 25, 1101–1112.

Fukuyama, H. (1996). Returns to Scale and Efficiency of Credit Associations in Japan: A Nonparametric Frontier Approach, *Japan and the World Economy* 8, 259–277.

Fukuyama, H., Guerra, R., and Weber, W. L. (1999). Efficiency and Ownership: Evidence from Japanese Credit Cooperatives, *Journal of Economics and Business* 51, 473–487.

Gao, W. (2008). Banks as Lenders and Shareholders: Evidence from Japan, *Pacific-Basin Finance Journal* 16, 389–410.

Giannetti, M. and Simonov, A. (2013). On the Real Effects of Bank Bailouts: Micro Evidence from Japan, *American Economic Journal: Macroeconomics* 5, 135–167.

Gibson, M. S. (1997). More Evidence on the Link between Bank Health and Investment in Japan, *Journal of the Japanese and International Economies* 11, 296–310.

Glass, J. C., McKillop, D. G., Quinn, B., and Wilson, J. O. S. (2014). Cooperative Bank Efficiency in Japan: A Parametric Distance Function Analysis, *European Journal of Finance* 20, 291–317.

Hall, B. J. (1993). How has the Basle Accord Affected Bank Portfolios?, *Journal of the Japanese and International Economies* 7, 408–440.

Hamao, Y. and Hoshi, T. (2000). Bank-owned Security Subsidiaries in Japan: Evidence after the 1993 Financial System Reform. In: M. Aoki and G. R. Saxonhouse (Eds.), *Finance, Governance, and Competitiveness in Japan*, 105–117. Oxford: Oxford University Press.

Hanazaki, M. and Horiuchi, A. (2000). Is Japan's Financial System Efficient?, *Oxford Review of Economic Policy* 16, 61–73.

Harimaya, K. (2008). Impact of Nontraditional Activities on Scale and Scope Economies: A Case Study of Japanese Regional Banks, *Japan and the World Economy* 20, 175–193.

Hasumi, R. and Hirata, H. (2010). *Small Business Credit Scoring: Evidence from Japan*, RIETI Discussion Paper Series No. 10-E-029.

Hasumi, R., Hirata, H., and Ono, A. (2011). Differentiated Use of Small Business Credit Scoring by Relationship Lenders and Transactional Lenders: Evidence from Firm-Bank Matched Data in Japan, RIETI Discussion Paper Series No. 11-E-070.

Hayashi, F. (2000). The Main Bank System and Corporate Investment: An Empirical Reassessment. In: M. Aoki and G. R. Saxonhouse (Eds.), *Finance, Governance, and Competitiveness in Japan*, 81–98. Oxford: Oxford University Press.

Hayashi, F. and Prescott, E. C. (2002). The 1990s in Japan: A Lost Decade, *Review of Economic Dynamics* 5, 206–235.

Hori, K., Saito, M., and Ando, K. (2006). What Caused Fixed Investment to Stagnate during the 1990s in Japan? Evidence from Panel Data of Listed Companies, *Japanese Economic Review* 57, 283–306.

Hori, M. (2005). Does Bank Liquidation Affect Client Firm Performance? Evidence from a Bank Failure in Japan, *Economics Letters* 88, 415–420.

Horiuchi, A. (2000). The Big Bang: Idea and Reality. In: T. Hoshi and H. T. Patrick (Eds.), *Crisis and Change in the Japanese Financial System*, 233–252. Amsterdam: Kluwer Academic.

Horiuchi, A. and Shimizu, K. (2001). Did Amakudari Undermine the Effectiveness of Regulator Monitoring in Japan?, *Journal of Banking and Finance* 25, 573–596.

Hoshi, T. (2001). What Happened to Japanese Banks?, *Bank of Japan Monetary and Economic Studies* 19, 1–30.

Hoshi, T. (2002). The Convoy System for Insolvent Banks: How it Originally Worked and Why it Failed in the 1990s, *Japan and the World Economy* 14, 155–180.

Hoshi, T. and Kashyap, A. (2001). *Corporate Financing and Corporate Governance in Japan*. Cambridge, MA: MIT Press.

Hoshi, T. and Kashyap, A. (2008). Will the US Bank Recapitalization Succeed? Lessons from Japan. Paper Presented at 2008 American Economic Association Meeting.

Hoshi, T. and Kashyap, A. K. (2010). Will the US Bank Recapitalization Succeed? Eight Lessons from Japan, *Journal of Financial Economics* 97, 398–417.

Hoshi, T., Kashyap, A., and Scharfstein, D. (1990a). Bank Monitoring and Investment: Evidence from the Changing Structure of Japanese Corporate Banking Relationships. In: R. G. Hubbard (Ed.), *Asymmetric Information, Corporate Finance, and Investment*, 105–126. Chicago: University of Chicago Press.

Hoshi, T., Kashyap, A., and Scharfstein, D. (1990b). The Role of Banks in Reducing the Costs of Financial Distress in Japan, *Journal of Financial Economics* 27, 67–88.

Hoshi, T., Kashyap, A., and Scharfstein, D. (1991). Corporate Structure, Liquidity, and Investment: Evidence from Japanese Industrial Groups, *Quarterly Journal of Economics* 106, 33–60.

Hoshi, T. and Patrick, H. T. (2000). The Japanese Financial System: An Introductory Overview. In: T. Hoshi and H. T. Patrick (Eds.), *Crisis and Change in the Japanese Financial System*, 1–36. Amsterdam: Kluwer Academic.

Hosono, K. and Masuda, A. (2005). Bank Health and Small Business Investment: Evidence from Japan, RIETI Discussion Paper Series No. 05-E-030.

Imai, M. (2009). Political Influence and Declarations of Bank Insolvency in Japan, *Journal of Money, Credit, and Banking* 41, 131–158.

IMF (2012). Japan: Financial Sector Stability Assessment Update, IMF Country Report No. 12/10, August.

Inoue, K., Kato, H. K., and Bremer, M. (2008). Corporate Restructuring in Japan: Who Monitors the Monitor?, *Journal of Banking and Finance* 32, 2628–2635.

Ishikawa, D. and Tsutsui, Y. (2013). Credit Crunch and its Spatial Differences in Japan's Lost Decade: What Can We Learn From It?, *Japan and the World Economy* 28, 41–52.

Ito, T., Patrick, H. T., and Weinstein, D. E. (2005). *Reviving Japan's Economy: Problems and Prescriptions*. Cambridge, MA: MIT Press.

Ito, T. and Sasaki, Y. N. (2002). Impacts of the Basle Capital Standard on Japanese Banks' Behavior, *Journal of the Japanese and International Economies* 16, 372–397.

Jimenez, G., Ongena, S., Peydro, J., and Saurina, J. (2012). Credit Supply and Monetary Policy: Identifying the Bank-Balance Sheet Channel with Loan Applications, *American Economic Review* 102, 2121–2165.

John, K., Lynch, A. W., and Puri, M. (2003). Credit Ratings, Collateral and Loan Characteristics: Implications for Yield, *Journal of Business* 76, 371–409.

Kang, J. K., Kim, K. A., Kitsabunnarat-Chatjuthamard, P., and Nishikawa, T. (2011). The Effects of Bank Relations on Stock Repurchases: Evidence from Japan, *Journal of Financial Intermediation* 20, 94–116.

Kang, J. K. and Liu, W. L. (2007). Is Universal Banking Justified? Evidence from Bank Underwriting of Corporate Bonds in Japan, *Journal of Financial Economics* 84, 142–186.

Kang, J.-K. and Shivdasani, A. (1995). Firm Performance, Corporate Governance, and Top Executive Turnover in Japan, *Journal of Financial Economics* 38, 29–58.

Kang, J.-K. and Shivdasani, A. (1997). Corporate Restructuring during Performance Declines in Japan, *Journal of Financial Economics* 46, 29–65.

Kang, J.-K. and Shivdasani, A. (1999). Alternative Mechanisms for Corporate Governance in Japan: An Analysis of Independent and Bank-Affiliated Firms, *Pacific-Basin Finance Journal* 7, 1–22.

Kang, J.-K. and Stulz, R. (2000). Do Banking Shocks Affect Borrowing Firm Performance? An Analysis of the Japanese Experience, *Journal of Business* 73, 1–23.

Kano, M. and Tsutsui, Y. (2003). Geographical Segmentation in Japanese Bank Loan Markets, *Regional Science and Urban Economics* 33, 157–174.

Kano, M., Uchida, H., Udell, G. F., and Watanabe, W. (2011). Information Verifiability, Bank Organization, Bank Competition and Bank-Borrower Relationships, *Journal of Banking and Finance* 35, 935–954.

Kaplan, S. N. and Minton, B. (1994). Appointments of Outsiders to Japanese Boards: Determinants and Implications for Managers, *Journal of Financial Economics* 36, 225–257.

Kaplan, S. N. and Zingales, L. (1997). Do Investment-Cash Flow Sensitivities Provide Useful Measures of Financing Constraints?, *Quarterly Journal of Economics* 112, 169–215.

Kashyap, A. (2002). Sorting out Japan's Financial Crisis, *Federal Reserve Bank of Chicago Economic Perspectives* 26 42–55.

Kinjo, A. (2013). Function of Collateral When Asset Class is Accounts Receivables and Inventory: A Comparative Analysis of Japanese and US Bank Inspection Manuals, Presented at the Japan Society of Monetary Economics 2013 Spring Annual Meeting.

Kobayashi, M. and Osano, H. (2011). The New Main Bank System, *Journal of the Japanese and International Economies* 25, 336–354.

Konishi, M. and Yasuda, Y. (2004). Factors Affecting Bank Risk Taking: Evidence from Japan, *Journal of Banking and Finance* 28 215–232.

Kutsuna, K., Smith, J. K., and Smith, R. L. (2007). Banking Relationships and Access to Equity Capital Markets: Evidence from Japan's Main Bank System, *Journal of Banking and Finance* 31, 335–360.

Liu, H. and Wilson, J. O. S. (2010). The Profitability of Banks in Japan, *Applied Financial Economics* 20, 1851–1866.

Liu, H. and Wilson, J. O. S. (2012). Competition and Risk in Japanese Banking, *European Journal of Finance* 19, 1–18.

Manove, M., Padilla, A. J., and Pagano, M. (2001). Collateral versus Project Screening: A Model of Lazy Banks, *Rand Journal of Economics* 32, 726–744.

McKillop, D. G., Glass, J. C., and Morikawa, Y. (1996). The Composite Cost Function and Efficiency in Giant Japanese Banks, *Journal of Banking and Finance* 20, 1651–1671.

Minamihashi, N. (2011). Credit Crunch Caused by Bank Failures and Self-Selection Behavior in Lending Markets, *Journal of Money, Credit, and Banking* 43, 133–161.

Miwa, Y. and Ramseyer, J. M. (2002). The Fable of the Keiretsu, *Journal of Economics & Management Strategy* 11, 169–224.

Miwa, Y. and Ramseyer, J. M. (2005). Does Relationship Banking Matter? The Myth of the Japanese Main Bank, *Journal of Empirical Legal Studies* 2, 261–302.

Miyajima, H. and Yafeh, Y. (2007). Japan's Banking Crisis: An Event-Study Perspective, *Journal of Banking and Finance* 31, 2866–2885.

Molyneux, P., J., Thornton, P., and Lloyd-Williams, D. M. (1996). Competition and Market Contestability in Japanese Commercial Banking, *Journal of Economics and Business* 48, 33–45.

Montgomery, H. and Shimizutani, S. (2009). The Effectiveness of Bank Recapitalization Policies in Japan, *Japan and the World Economy* 21, 1–25.

Morck, R. and Nakamura, M. (1999). Banks and Corporate Control in Japan, *Journal of Finance* 54, 319–339.

Motonishi, T. and Yoshikawa, H. (1999). Causes of the Long Stagnation of Japan during the 1990's: Financial or Real?, *Journal of the Japanese International Economies* 13, 181–200.

Nakagawa, R. and Uchida, H. (2011). Herd Behaviour by Japanese Banks after Financial Deregulation, *Economica* 78, 618–636.

Nakaso, H. (2001). The Financial Crisis in Japan during the 1990s: How the Bank of Japan Responded and the Lessons Learnt, BIS Papers No. 6.

Nakatani, I. (1984). The Economic Role of Financial Corporate Grouping. In: M. Aoki (Ed.), *The Economic Analysis of the Japanese Firm*, 227–258. Amsterdam: Elsevier.

National Federation of Credit Guarantee Corporations (2012). Credit Guarantee System in Japan 2012.

Nikkin (2005). Nikkin Data Annual (in Japanese).

Nishimura, K. G., Nakajima, T., and Kiyota, K. (2005). Does the Natural Selection Mechanism Still Work in Severe Recessions? Examination of the Japanese Economy in the 1990s, *Journal of Economic Behavior and Organization* 58, 53–78.

Ogawa, K., Kitasaka, S.-I., Yamaoka, H., and Iwata, Y. (1996). Borrowing Constraints and the Role of Land Asset in Japanese Corporate Investment Decision, *Journal of the Japanese and International Economies* 10, 122–149.

Ogawa, K. and Suzuki, K. (2000). Demand for Bank Loans and Investment under Borrowing Constraints: A Panel Study of Japanese Firm Data, *Journal of the Japanese and International Economies* 14, 1–21.

Ono, A., Sakai, K., and Uesugi, I. (2012). The Effects of Collateral on Firm Performance, *Journal of the Japanese and International Economies* 26, 84–109.

Ono, A., Uchida, H., Kozuka S., Hazama, M., and Uesugi, I. (2010). Current Status of Firm-Bank Relationships and the Use of Collateral in Japan: An Overview of the Teikoku Databank Data, Institute of Economic Research, Hitotsubashi University Research Center for Interfirm Network Discussion Paper Series No. 4.

Ono, A., Uchida, H., Udell, G. F., and Uesugi, I. (2014). Lending Pro-Cyclicality and Macro-Prudential Policy: Evidence from Japanese LTV Ratios. Mizuho Research Institute, Kobe University, Indiana University, and Hitotsubashi University.

Ono, A. and Uesugi, I. (2009). Role of Collateral and Personal Guarantees in Relationship Lending: Evidence from Japan's SME Loan Market, *Journal of Money, Credit, and Banking* 41, 935–960.

Ono, A., Uesugi, I., and Yasuda, Y. (2013). Are Lending Relationships Beneficial or Harmful for Public Credit Guarantees? Evidence from Japan's Emergency Credit Guarantee Program, *Journal of Financial Stability* 9, 151–167.

Osano, H. (1998). Default and Renegotiation in Financial Distress in the Multiple Bank Model: An Analysis of the Main Bank System, *Japanese Economic Review* 49, 138–157.

Osano, H. and Tsutsui, Y. (1985). Implicit Contracts in the Japanese Bank Loan Market, *Journal of Financial and Quantitative Analysis* 20, 211–230.

Peek, J. and Rosengren, E. S. (2005). Unnatural Selection: Perverse Incentives and the Misallocation of Credit in Japan, *American Economic Review* 95, 1144–1166.

Petersen, M. A. and Rajan, R. G. (1994). The Benefits of Lending Relationships: Evidence from Small Business Data, *Journal of Finance* 49, 3–37.

Popov, A. and Udell, G. F. (2012). Cross-Border Banking, Credit Access, and the Financial Crisis, *Journal of International Economics* 87, 147–161.

Prowse, S. (1995). Corporate Governance in an International Perspective: A Survey of Corporate Control Mechanisms among Large Firms in the USA, UK, Japan and Germany, *Financial Markets, Institutions and Instruments* 4, 1–63.

Royama, S. (2000). The Big Bang in Japanese Securities Markets. In: T. Hoshi and H. T. Patrick (Eds.), *Crisis and Change in the Japanese Financial System*, 253–276. Amsterdam: Kluwer Academic.

Sawada, M. (2013). Measuring the Effect of Postal Saving Privatization on the Japanese Banking Industry: Evidence from the 2005 General Election, *Pacific-Basin Finance Journal* 21, 967–983.

Sheard, P. (1994a). Main Banks and the Governance of Financial Distress. In: M. Aoki and H. T. Patrick (Eds.), *The Japanese Main Bank System*, 188–230. New York: Oxford University Press.

Sheard, P. (1994b). Reciprocal Delegated Monitoring in the Japanese Main Bank System, *Journal of the Japanese and International Economies* 8, 1–21.

Shin, G. H. and Kolari, J. W. (2004). Do Some Lenders have Information Advantages? Evidence from Japanese Credit Market Data, *Journal of Banking and Finance* 28, 2331–2351.

Spiegel, M. M. and Yamori, N. (2003). The Impact of Japan's Financial Stabilization Laws on Bank Equity Values, *Journal of the Japanese and International Economies* 17, 263–282.

Suzuki, K. and Yamada, K. (2012). Do the Use of Proceeds Disclosure and Bank Characteristics Affect Bank Underwriters' Certification Roles?, *Journal of Business Finance & Accounting* 39, 1102–1130.

Tachibanaki, T., Mitsui, K., and Kitagawa, H. (1991). Economies of Scope and Shareholding of Banks in Japan, *Journal of the Japanese and International Economies* 5, 261–281.

Tadesse, S. (2006). Consolidation, Scale Economies and Technological Change in Japanese Banking, *Journal of International Financial Markets, Institutions and Money* 16, 425–445.

Takaoka, S. and McKenzie, C. R. (2004). The Impact of Bank Entry in the Japanese Corporate Bond Underwriting Market, *Journal of Banking and Finance* 30, 59–83.

Teranishi, J. (1994). Loan Syndication in War-time Japanese and the Origins of the Main Bank System. In: M. Aoki and H. T. Patrick (Eds.), *The Japanese Main Bank System*, 51–88. New York: Oxford University Press.

Uchida, H. (2011). What Do Banks Evaluate When They Screen Borrowers? Soft Information, Hard Information and Collateral, *Journal of Financial Services Research* 40, 29–48.

Uchida, H. and Nakagawa, R. (2007). Herd Behavior in the Japanese Loan Market: Evidence from Bank Panel Data, *Journal of Financial Intermediation* 16, 555–583.

Uchida, H. and Tsutsui, Y. (2005). Has Competition in the Japanese Banking Sector Improved?, *Journal of Banking and Finance* 29, 419–439.

Uchida, H., Udell, G. F., and Watanabe, W. (2008). Bank Size and Lending Relationships in Japan, *Journal of the Japanese and International Economies* 22, 242–267.

Uchida, H., Udell, G. F., and Yamori, N. (2008). How Do Japanese Banks Discipline Small—and Medium-Sized Borrowers?: An Investigation of the Deployment of Lending Technologies, *International Finance Review* 9, 57–80.

Uchida, H., Udell, G. F. and Yamori, N. (2012). Loan Officers and Relationship Lending, *Journal of Financial Intermediation* 21, 97–122.

Udell, G. F. (2004). *Asset Based Finance*. New York: Commercial Finance Association.

Udell, G. F. (2009). Wall Street, Main Street, and a Credit Crunch: Thoughts on the Current Financial Crisis, *Business Horizons* 52, 117–125.

Ueda, K. (2000). Causes of Japan's Banking Problems in the 1990s. In: T. Hoshi and H. T. Patrick (Eds.), *Crisis and Change in the Japanese Financial System*, 59–84. Amsterdam: Kluwer Academic.

Uesugi, I., Sakai, K., and Yamashiro, G. M. (2010). The Effectiveness of Public Credit Guarantees in the Japanese Loan Market, *Journal of the Japanese and International Economies* 24, 457–480.

Watanabe, W. (2007). Prudential Regulation and the "Credit Crunch": Evidence from Japan, *Journal of Money, Credit and Banking* 39, 639–665.

Watanabe, W. (2010). Does a Large Loss of Bank Capital Cause Evergreening? Evidence from Japan, *Journal of the Japanese and International Economies* 24, 116–136.

Weinstein, D. E. and Yafeh, Y. (1998). On the Costs of a Bank-Centered Financial System: Evidence from the Changing Main Bank Relations in Japan, *Journal of Finance* LIII, 635–672.

Wilcox, J. A. and Yasuda, Y. (2008). Do Government Loan Guarantees Lower, or Raise, Banks' Non-Guaranteed Lending? Evidence from Japanese Banks. World Bank Workshop.

Woo, D. (2003). In Search of "Capital Crunch": Supply Factors Behind the Credit Slowdown in Japan, *Journal of Money, Credit, and Banking* 35, 1019–1038.

Wu, W. and Xu, L. L. (2005). The Value Information of Financing Decisions and Corporate Governance during and After the Japanese Deregulation, *Journal of Business* 78, 243–280.

Wu, X. and Yao, J. (2012). Understanding the Rise and Decline of the Japanese Main Bank System: The Changing Effects of Bank Rent Extraction, *Journal of Banking and Finance* 36, 36–50.

Yamori, N. and Murakami, A. (1999). Does Bank Relationship have an Economic Value?: The Effect of Main Bank Failure on Client Firms, *Economics Letters* 65, 115–120.

Yasuda, A. (2007). Bank Relationships and Underwriter Competition: Evidence from Japan, *Journal of Financial Economics* 86, 369–404.

CHAPTER 37

....

BANKING IN AFRICA*

....

THORSTEN BECK AND ROBERT CULL

37.1 INTRODUCTION

....

BANKING in Africa has undergone dramatic changes over the past 20 years. While the continent was dominated by government-owned banks in the 1980s and subject to restrictive regulation—including interest rate ceilings and credit quotas—financial liberalization, institutional and regulatory upgrades and globalization have changed the face of financial systems across the region. Today, most countries have deeper and more stable financial systems, although challenges of concentration and limited competition, high costs, short maturities, and limited inclusion persist.

This chapter takes stock of the current state of banking systems across Sub-Saharan Africa and discusses recent developments including innovations that could help Africa leapfrog more traditional banking models. We use an array of different data sources to document different dimensions of the development of African banking systems, highlighting variation within the region and changes over time. We compare Africa's banking systems to those of comparable low- and lower-middle income countries outside the region, and gauge whether there is an "Africa-specific" element to banking development. We also discuss progress in policies and institutions underpinning financial deepening and the results of specific innovations, including innovative branch expansion programs, mobile banking, and new financial products to reach out to previously unbanked population segments. Overall, we will show a picture of achievements and challenges, with progress along some fronts but other challenges persisting and new ones arising.

* We would like to thank Blaine Stephens, Scott Gaul, and the MIX for access to the microfinance data and Ippei Nishida for excellent research assistance. This paper's findings, interpretations, and conclusions are entirely those of the authors and do not necessarily represent the views of the World Bank, its Executive Directors, or the countries they represent.

When talking about financial systems in Africa, one has to take into account the enormous variation within the region.[1] On the one hand, South Africa and Mauritius have relatively developed banking systems and capital markets. On the other hand, smaller and poorer countries, such as the Central African Republic or South Sudan, have shallow banking systems offering only the most rudimentary financial services, with few if any non-bank financial institutions or capital markets. In spite of the variation within the region, however, there are four specific characteristics that make banking in Africa more difficult than in other regions of the developing world, and most of those apply to many, if not all, African economies (see Honohan and Beck, 2007; and Beck et al., 2011).

First, the small size of many economies does not allow financial service providers to reap the benefits of scale economies. The limited demand for savings, insurance, credit, or even simple payment transactions means that large parts of the population of African economies are not commercially viable customers. The dispersion of population in many African countries means that financial service provision outside urban centers is not cost-effective. Second, large parts of the economy and a large share of all economic agents operate in the informal sector and do not have the necessary formal documentation that facilitates financial transactions, such as enterprise registration, land titles, or even formal addresses. This increases the costs and risks for financial institutions and excludes large segments of the population from formal financial services. Third, volatility increases costs and undermines risk management. At the individual level, volatility is related to informality and the consequent fluctuations in the income streams of many microenterprises and households. This means these agents are less attractive for financial institutions. At the aggregate level, volatility refers to the dependence of many African economies on commodity exports, which makes economies vulnerable to the large price swings characteristic of commodities, as well as to political and social unrest, from which Africa has suffered over the past 50 years of independence. Finally, governance problems continue to plague many private and government institutions throughout the continent and undermine not only the market-based provision of financial services, but also reform attempts and government interventions aimed at fixing market failures.

These characteristics make banking in Africa more challenging and increase the need for innovative solutions. Technology can reduce transaction costs and risks, thus enabling the processing of smaller transactions, turning more households and enterprises into commercially viable clients. Innovative products and delivery channels can address the constraints discussed above. Critically, these interventions and policy reforms have to work both on the supply and demand side. In what follows we will discuss several examples of such innovative approaches to financial inclusion.

The recent crisis in the developed world has shed doubt on the positive impact that the development of the banking system can have on economic development, in contrast to an extensive literature illustrating a positive finance-growth relationship (Levine, 2005). Consumer credit booms in the US and several European countries, fueled by a combination of the liquidity glut linked to the global macroeconomic imbalances, regulatory neglect and the feeling that "this time is different" have ended in the global financial crisis. If there is a lesson to be learnt for Africa's banking systems from the crisis, it seems that the growth

---

[1] Please note that in the following, we will use the expressions Africa and Sub-Saharan African interchangeably. We do not include North African countries in our analysis.

benefits of financial deepening can only be reaped in a stable macroeconomic environment and with the appropriate safeguards framework, both in terms of external regulation and supervision and internal bank governance. Notwithstanding the recent negative experience in countries with the deepest financial sectors, banking systems in Africa can and must play a critical role in the economic development process of the region.

The remainder of this chapter is structured as follows. Section 37.2 documents financial development across different dimensions, in international comparison, but also illustrating variation within the region and over time. Section 37.3 discusses recent evidence on policies and interventions that can help deepen and broaden financial systems in Africa. Section 37.4 concludes with a discussion of policy challenges for the region going forward.

37.2 Stock-Taking: Where does Africa Stand?

Earlier stock-taking exercises of banking and finance in Africa suffered from a lack of data for a broad cross-section of countries in the region (Honohan and Beck, 2007). Most cross-country studies on financial development included only a few larger African financial markets and their focus was on other developing and emerging regions of the world. This situation has changed over the past five years, with data available for a large part of the region and several segments of the financial system. Global data collection efforts on the depth, outreach, stability and efficiency of financial systems have been much more successful in collecting data on African financial systems.[2] Aggregate data have been complemented with a number of enterprise surveys, and surveys for some countries now have a panel dimension (i.e., firms being surveyed at several points in time). Similarly, household surveys specialized on financial services, such as the Finscope and Finaccess surveys in several African countries, have provided important insights into individual and household access to and use of formal and informal financial services. In the following, we will therefore use an array of databases and other sources to document the development and structure of banking systems across the region.

37.2.1 Aggregate Financial Development in Africa in International Comparison

Africa's banking systems are small, costly, and focused on the short-term end of the yield curve as we will illustrate in the following. However, we will also document the progress Africa's banking systems have made over the past decade.

To compare banking systems in Africa to a proper benchmark, we limit our sample to low- and lower-middle income countries in Sub-Saharan Africa and compare the median

---

[2] Beck, Demirgüç-Kunt, and Levine (2000, 2010), Demirgüç-Kunt and Klapper (2012), Laeven and Valencia (2012).

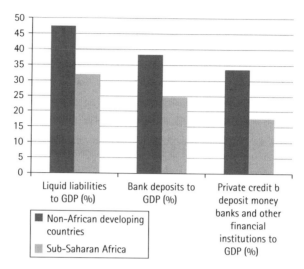

FIGURE 37.1 Aggregate financial development in international comparison.

Source: Global Financial Development Indicators, World Bank

for this group to the median country across a sample of low- and lower-middle income countries outside Africa. We thus explicitly drop several upper-middle income African countries in our statistical comparison, although we will include them in the discussion on infra-regional variation below.[3]

Figure 37.1 shows that the median African country has a significantly shallower financial system than the median non-African country. We present three standard indicators of financial development: Liquid Liabilities to GDP, Bank Deposits to GDP and Private Credit to GDP, using data for 2011. While the median non-African developing country has Liquid Liabilities of 47% of GDP, the median African country has only 32%. Similarly, the median deposit to GDP ratio outside Africa is 38%, compared to 25% in Africa, while the median Private Credit to GDP ratio is 34% outside Africa, but only 18% inside Africa. Comparing the African gap between deposit and credit data also shows that African banks are less effective in intermediating society's savings, a topic we will return to below.

It is important to note that behind the median there is wide variation across Africa. Even excluding the most financially developed African economies, such as Mauritius and South Africa, there is a wide range in Private Credit to GDP across the low- and lower-middle income countries of the region, from 5% in Chad to 61% in Cape Verde. This compares with 141% in South Africa and 87% in Mauritius.

While Africa's financial systems are shallow in international comparison, there have been marked improvements over the past decade, as documented in Figure 37.2. All three standard indicators of financial development have substantially improved over the period 2000 to 2011.[4] The median value for Liquid Liabilities to GDP increased from 20 to 31%, while

---

[3] The countries not included in the statistical comparison are: Botswana, Gabon, Mauritius, Namibia, Seychelles, and South Africa.

[4] The median is computed over a balanced sample of 28 African countries, for which data were available over all 12 years.

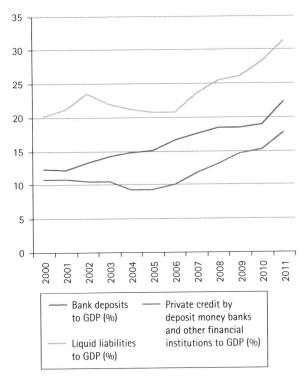

FIGURE 37.2 Financial deepening in Africa over the past decade.
Source: Global Financial Development Indicators, World Bank

that for Deposits to GDP increased from 12 to 22%. Median Private Credit to GDP increased from 11% to 18%. And this improvement has been broad based. If one considers the 25th, 50th, and 75th percentiles of private credit to GDP over the same period, it is evident that countries at different points of the distribution have all witnessed improvements.

Africa's banking systems are not only shallower than banking systems in non-African developing countries, they are also less inclusive (Figure 37.3). Here we present four indicators of access to and use of financial services. First, we present two aggregate indicators: bank accounts per 10,000 adults and bank branches per 100,000 adults. Both indicators are substantially lower in the median African country than in the median non-African developing country. Specifically, there are only 15 bank accounts for every 100 adults in the median African country, while there are 42 outside Africa. There are 3.1 branches per 100,000 adults in Africa, while there are 9.6 outside Africa. Second, the more limited outreach of Africa's banking systems is also reflected in indicators of use of formal finance by enterprises and households. While in the median African country, only 21% of firms indicate that they have a line of credit or loan from a formal financial institution, this share is 43% outside Africa.[5]

---

[5] Unlike the previous comparisons, which are all for 2011, data for Enterprise Surveys were averaged over 2009 to 2011.

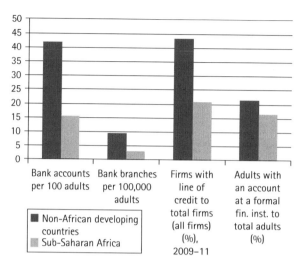

FIGURE 37.3 Access to and use of financial services in international comparison.

Source: Global Financial Development Indicators, World Bank

Similarly, 16.5% of adults in the median African country indicate that they have an account with a formal financial institution, while this share is 21% outside Africa.

Africa's banks are, on average, less efficient, but more profitable and operate in less competitive environments. Net interest margins in the median African country stood at 5.9% in 2011, while they stood at 4.7% outside Africa. Similarly, the interest rate spread between lending and deposit rate was 10.3% in Africa and 8.2% outside. While there are many reasons that spreads and margins are higher in Africa, one important reason is higher operating costs. Specifically, overhead costs in the median African financial system stood at 5.5% of total assets, while they were 3.4% outside Africa. On the other hand, African banks are also more profitable than banks outside Africa. The return on assets (ROA) stood at 2.1% in the median African country, while it was 1.5% outside Africa. We will revisit this issue below with bank-level data.

The higher interest rate spreads go hand in hand with greater concentration and lower competitiveness in African banking markets. While the share of the five largest banks was 81% in the median African country in 2011, it was 64% outside Africa. While there are countries in Africa where aggregate data point to five banks making up the whole or almost the whole banking system (Cape Verde, Gambia, Lesotho, Swaziland, and Togo), there are only a few such countries among the much larger group of non-African developing countries. Greater concentration can also partly explain the lower degree of competition within African banking system. The median Lerner index, which is the markup between marginal revenue and costs, is 30% in the median African country, while it is 25% outside Africa. It is important to note that the correlation between concentration and the Lerner index of market power is relatively low within Africa, at only 11%, suggesting that market structure is only one, and maybe not the most important, determinant of the lack of competition within Africa, consistent with cross-country evidence (Claessens and Laeven, 2004).

Africa's banking systems focus mostly on the short-end of the yield curve, as illustrated by the maturity structure on both the asset and liability sides of African banks' balance sheets

(Beck et al. 2011). More than 80% of deposits are sight deposits or deposits with a maturity of less than one year and less than 2% of deposits have a maturity of more than ten years. There is a similar, though not as extreme, bias towards the short-end on the lending side. Almost 60% of loans are for less than one year, and less than 2% of loans are for more than ten years. This maturity distribution is consistent with the dearth of non-bank long-term financial instruments, including the limited development of contractual savings institutions, such as insurance companies, pension funds, and mutual funds. Fewer than half of the countries in the region have stock exchanges and few of them are liquid. Another indication for the short-term nature of African banking is the dearth of mortgage finance. While mortgage depth to GDP in the median African country was below 1%, it was above 2% outside Africa (Badev et al., 2013). These aggregate numbers match with anecdotal evidence that mortgage systems in many smaller African countries comprise just a few hundred mortgages, concentrated among wealthy individuals.

While shallow, Africa's banking systems have also proven stable and resilient over the past years. The shallowness of Africa's banking systems appears to have helped them weather the global financial crisis of 2008 better than some other regions of the world, with the impact of the crisis on Africa mostly working through real sector channels, such as lower demand for export goods, or through lower foreign direct investment. Given the limited integration with global financial markets and exposure to "toxic" assets, financial institutions across the region largely evaded the direct impact of the global financial crisis.

Greater stability is also illustrated in the aggregate balance sheet indicators of African banks. In 2011, the capital to risk-weighted asset ratio was 19% in the median African country, compared to 17% outside Africa. On the systemic level, Africa has suffered few banking crises since the bout of systemic fragility in the 1980s and 1990s (Laeven and Valencia, 2012). Notwithstanding these positive headline indicators, pockets of (hidden) fragility continue to exist, often related to political crisis and/or governance deficiencies.

The shallowness of African financial markets is not surprising given the region's low levels of economic development and the four characteristics—small size, informality, volatility, and governance. However, many of the non-African low and lower-middle income countries suffer from similar problems. Is there an Africa-specific element to financial underdevelopment? We address this issue next, before documenting in more detail specific dimensions of African banking, including the structure and efficiency of banking system, enterprise and household access to financial services, and the development of the microfinance sector.

37.2.2 Benchmarking Africa's Banking Systems

The level of financial development in Africa is low compared to other parts of the developing world, but it is also low relative to what would be predicted based on underlying factors that drive financial development. Allen et al. (2012b) use cross-country regressions to benchmark African financial development based on its correlates in other developing countries, revealing a substantial gap between predicted and actual levels of African financial development. In addition, both country-level and firm-level tests indicate that the determinants of banking development in Africa differ from the rest of the world. For example, measures of the quality of macroeconomic management (inflation and the current account balance) are not correlated with African financial development as they are in other developing countries. Measures of institutional development (such as adherence to rule of law) are positively linked to African financial development, though substantially less strongly than in other parts of the developing world.

Perhaps the most striking difference is that population density is more strongly linked to financial development in Africa than elsewhere. Population density is also more closely linked to bank branch penetration in Africa than in other developing economies, and both are more strongly linked to firm-level access to external finance in Africa than elsewhere (Allen et al., 2012b). Presumably, bank branch penetration figures remain low in Africa because of difficulties in achieving minimum viable scale in sparsely populated, low-income areas, though below we discuss financial institutions, strategies, and technological innovations that are rising to meet that challenge.

Those benchmarking exercises show that predicted 2001–06 levels of private credit/GDP based on the correlates of financial development from developing countries outside of Africa tended to be 10–15% points higher for African countries than their actual levels. Only rarely did actual levels of financial development exceed predicted levels, and then only for countries that are not particularly reflective of Sub-Saharan Africa such as Cape Verde and Mauritius. The same set of authors recently re-did that benchmarking exercise for 2007-2011 (Figure 37.4), which shows some improvement over the past handful of years in achieving predicted private credit levels for countries such as Nigeria ("NGA" in Figure 37.4), Kenya (KEN), and Namibia (NAM). Cape Verde (CPV) and Mauritius (MUS) continue to exceed predicted financial development levels as does South Africa (ZAF), which was not part of the 2001–06 analysis. Most African countries, however, continue to fall short of predicted development levels though the gap has narrowed a bit.

Moreover, demand-side evidence from the Global Financial Inclusion Index (Global Findex) indicates that the credit extended by financial institutions is not spread evenly across the population. The predicted share of Findex respondents that had a loan from a financial institution (again based on regression models from other developing countries) exceeds the actual share in almost all cases (including South Africa), and by a noticeably wider margin than for Private Credit to GDP in many cases. Though crude tools, the benchmarking regressions indicate that private credit provision in Africa, though improving somewhat, lags behind what fundamentals would predict, and that the allocation of what credit there is does not extend deeply into the population. To a lesser extent, there are also development gaps on the savings side. Predicted liquid liabilities/GDP levels exceed actual levels for most countries, though the gap has narrowed since 2001–06, and the share of individuals age fifteen or over with an account at a formal institution actually exceeds predicted levels in many countries (Allen et al., 2013). Indeed, most African countries are near predicted levels on that metric, and about the same number fall above and below the prediction line.

37.2.3 Drilling Deeper—Bank-Level Evidence

While the aggregate data already give us some indication of the shallowness of African banking systems, bank-level data provide more detailed insights. Comparing a sample of 307 banks from low and lower-middle income countries in Africa and 720 banks from

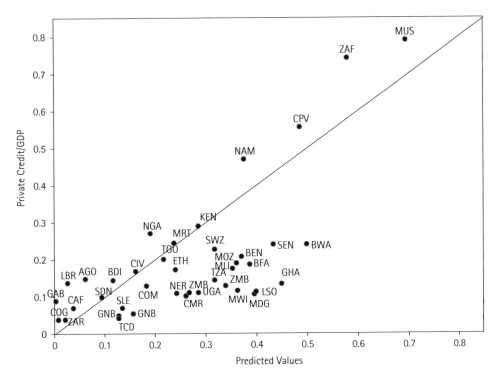

FIGURE 37.4 Private credit/GDP in African countries 2007–11, actual vs. predicted values. Predicted values of banking sector development, measured by credit to the private sector extended by deposit money banks/GDP, come from OLS regressions that control for a set of country-level variables including endowment (population and resources), macroeconomics, institutions, banking structure and other variables. Note that negative predicted values are replaced by zero. *Source*: Allen et al., 2013.

non-African developing countries shows significantly higher liquidity ratios for African banks. Specifically, the ratio of liquid assets to short-term funding and deposits is 42.9% for African banks, as compared with 29.3% for non-African banks. Similarly, African banks are better capitalized, with an equity-asset ratio of 14.3%, compared with 13.3% for non-African banks. These comparisons give a picture of African banks that are well capitalized, over-liquid and provide only limited lending to the real economy, as highlighted previously by Honohan and Beck (2007) and Beck et al. (2011).

As discussed above, African banks are less efficient than banks in other developing regions of the world and financial services are therefore more expensive. A lot of discussion in this context has focused on interest rate spreads and margins, i.e. the difference between lending and deposit interest rates. But what drives high interest rate spreads in Africa? There are two different ways to analyze spreads and margins; one is a decomposition of spreads into the different components, while the other analyzes the relevant underlying bank-, industry-, and country-level traits.

Table 37.1 presents a decomposition of interest rate spreads for Uganda and shows that high operating costs are one important factor, while loan loss provisions reflecting loan

Table 37.1 Decomposition of interest rate spreads in Uganda in 2008

	All Banks	Domestic	Foreign
Average Lending Rate	16.72	18.44	15.24
Average Deposit Rate	1.97	2.31	1.90
Spread	14.75	16.13	13.34
Overhead Costs	4.66	2.74	6.22
Loan-loss Provisions	0.72	0.38	1.01
Reserve Requirements	0.22	0.26	0.21
Taxes	2.51	3.34	1.64
Profit Margin	6.65	9.42	4.26

Source: Cull and Trandafir (2010).

losses and reserve requirements are rather minor components of the interest rate spread. The highest component of interest rate spreads, however, is the high profit margin, consistent with limited competition, but also a high risk premium. Comparing domestically and foreign-owned banks, we see that domestic banks show much higher spreads, due to higher lending rates, which most likely reflect a riskier loan portfolio. The spread decompositions indicate that domestic banks generate high profit margins from a group of borrowers that repay their loans at a higher rate than clients of foreign banks. The relatively high overhead costs and low profit margins for the foreign banks could be consistent with the idea that they deal with a set of "blue-chip" clients whose projects are more costly to evaluate and maintain. In addition, higher wages might add to their costs, though, higher costs could also result from foreign banks' propensity to invest more, including in IT and technology to develop new products.[6]

Table 37.2 uses regression analysis to relate bank-level variation in overhead costs to bank- and country-level characteristics and compares banks in Africa with banks in non-African developing countries. As overhead costs is one of the major components of interest rate spreads, we regress overhead costs in 2011 for a cross-country sample of banks on (1) the share of non-interest income, (2) the equity-asset ratio, (3) the liquidity ratio, (4) loan growth over previous year, (5) the log of total assets, (6) inflation rate, and (7) the Kaufman, Kraay and Mastruzzi indicator of Rule of Law. The results in Table 37.2 indicate the extent to which these different factors contribute to substantially higher overhead costs of banks in Africa (6.05%) than in banks outside Africa (4.51%). Relatively high reliance by African banks on non-interest income and their smaller size can explain 93 and 18 basis points, respectively, of the difference in overhead costs. Higher inflation in African countries and less efficient contractual frameworks can explain 11 and 12 basis points, respectively. Even after accounting for these bank and country characteristics, there is still an unexplained Africa residual of 18 basis points.

As discussed earlier, the ownership structure of Africa's banking systems has undergone significant changes over the past decades, with a larger number of countries dominated by foreign banks and only few banking systems with mainly government-owned banks, a

---

[6] For a more detailed discussion, see Cull and Trandafir (2010) and Beck et al. (2011).

Table 37.2 Explaining overhead costs in Africa

	Overhead costs
African banks	605
Rest of World banks	451
Difference	**154**
Of which: Contractual framework	12
Non-interest income	93
Bank size	18
Equity-asset ratio	5
Other bank characteristics	-3
Inflation	11
Africa residual	18

Source: Authors' calculations using data from Bankscope.

result of the privatization wave in Africa in the 1980s and 1990s. While foreign bank penetration has increased from already high levels over the past decade, the composition of the foreign bank population has changed substantially. Long dominated by European banks, banks from emerging markets and—critically—from inside Africa have gained importance over the past years. After the end of Apartheid, several South African banks, most notably Standard Bank and ABSA, started expanding through the continent. More recently, two West African banks—Ecobank and Bank of Africa—have begun expanding throughout Sub-Saharan Africa. Similarly, Moroccan banks have started to expand southwards. Finally, and as consequence of the recent consolidation wave in Nigeria, Nigerian banks started expanding throughout West Africa, but increasingly also throughout the rest of the continent.

What has been the effect of the increase in foreign bank ownership on the development, efficiency, stability, and outreach of African banking?[7] Foreign bank entry seems to have several advantages that are specific to Africa: international banks can help foster governance; they can bring in much-needed technology and experience that should translate into increased efficiency in financial intermediation; and they can help exploit scale economies in small host countries. Nonetheless, especially in Africa, with its many small, risky, and opaque enterprises, the dark side of foreign bank entry can become obvious, even more so in countries in which foreign banks have captured almost 100% of the banking market. Specifically, the greater reliance of foreign banks on hard information about borrowers as opposed to soft information can have negative repercussions for riskier and more opaque borrowers if foreign banks crowd out domestic banks. The absence of a sound contractual and informational framework reduces the feasibility of small business lending further and thus the positive effect of foreign bank entry (Claessens and van Horen, 2014). Finally, the small size of many financial markets in Sub-Saharan Africa may make foreign banks reluctant to incur the fixed costs of introducing new products and technologies.

---

[7] For a general overview of the literature on the effects of foreign bank entry, see Cull and Martínez Pería (2012).

While there is limited quantitative evidence across the region, country-specific analysis points to an overall positive effect of private bank ownership and foreign bank entry. Beck, Cull, and Jerome (2005) show for Nigeria that the privatization of state-owned banks led to performance improvements, although those authors also found that maintaining a substantial minority government ownership share was detrimental to privatized banks' performance. In Uganda, UCB, the largest government-owned bank—and also the largest bank in the system—was successfully privatized in the second attempt to the South African Standard Bank. Although an agreement not to close any branches was in place for two years following sale of UCB, Standard Bank kept all branches in place and opened even new ones. It also introduced new products and increased agricultural lending (Clarke, Cull, and Fuchs, 2009). In Tanzania, the National Bank of Commerce was privatized after splitting it into a commercial bank that assumed most of the original bank's assets and liabilities, and the National Microfinance Bank, which assumed most of the branch network and the mandate to foster access to financial services. The new National Bank of Commerce's profitability and portfolio quality improved although credit growth was initially slow. Although finding a buyer for the National Microfinance Bank proved difficult, profitability eventually improved and lending grew, while the share of non-performing loans remained low (Cull and Spreng, 2011).

37.2.4 Enterprise Access to Finance in International Comparison

As documented above, access to formal financial services is lower in the median African country than in the median non-African developing country (Figure 37.5). These aggregate indicators are based on Enterprise Surveys conducted across countries. The Enterprise Survey data, however, also allow us to dig deeper and distinguish between firms of different

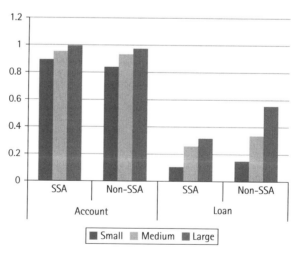

FIGURE 37.5 Use of formal account and loan services across firm size groups in international comparison.

Source: authors' calculations based on Enterprise Surveys (http://www.enterprisesurveys.org>.)

sizes. Figure 37.5 shows that there is only a small gap across firms of different sizes in the use of formal account services in both African and non-African developing countries. On the loan side, on the other hand, there is a stark difference across small, medium-sized and large enterprises, though the size gap is actually smaller within than outside Africa. However, across all three size groups, enterprises within Africa are less likely to have a loan than outside Africa, with large firms in Africa as likely to have a loan as mid-sized firms outside Africa.

Enterprise survey data also allow an exploration of the reasons why enterprises do not have loans with formal financial institutions. Specifically, enterprises are asked for the reason that they did not apply for a loan with a formal financial institution over the past year. The share of enterprises that quote lack of demand is significantly lower in Africa (43%) than in other developing countries (62%), suggesting that lack of demand is a less important factor in Africa than elsewhere. High interest rates were also mentioned as a reason for not applying for loans (14% in Africa vs. 10% in other developing countries), which could indicate that the return on investment projects is too low. On the other hand, and as noted by many observers of African finance, the high cost of credit might impede the use of bank finance. Interest rate spreads and thus lending rates are significantly higher in Africa than in non-African developing countries. Those high costs of credit can be explained not only by the lack of competition noted above, but also by monetary and socio-political instability resulting in high risk premia. The importance of monetary and socio-political stability can be appreciated when considering that the share of non-applicants due to high interest rates is especially high in DRC and Zimbabwe. Even more striking is the difference in the share of respondents indicating that application procedures are the reason for not applying: 16% of non-applicant enterprises in Africa as opposed to 7% in other developing countries. Collateral requirements also seem to be a greater impediment in Africa than in other regions of the developing world (9% vs. 4%), as is the need for bribes (4% vs. 2%). These data point to a large array of barriers both on the macroeconomic but also the bank-specific levels for enterprises in Africa to access formal sources of external finance.

The financing of small and medium-sized enterprises thus continues to pose a significant challenge, and not only for African financial systems. However, it is important to distinguish between segments within this group of enterprises that have different financing needs and profiles. A large share of the enterprises in Africa is informal microenterprises whose establishment often stems from the lack of alternative economic opportunities. Not being able to produce formal financial accounts or formal guarantees, it is hard to see this segment of the enterprise population becoming bankable over the medium to long term, at least not for credit services. They seem a natural target group for microcredit institutions and rely more heavily than other enterprises on informal finance providers. A second segment is medium-sized enterprises, often well established and export-oriented companies. In most cases they have access to bank finance, but struggle to get access to equity finance, including through financial markets. Finally, there are small formal enterprises, some of which might have high growth potential. These firms—often also referred to as the missing middle—are usually too big for microfinance institutions, but not formal or established enough for banks. It is especially this last segment that seems to be affected by shallow financial markets. This is also illustrated in Figure 37.5, where there is only a small difference in the use of formal loans between mid-sized and large enterprises (26% vs. 32%), with a much smaller share of small enterprises using such loans (11%).

37.2.5   Household Access to Finance in International Comparison

As discussed above, the share of households with a formal bank account is lower in Africa than in developing countries outside Africa. Behind this low median, however, there is substantial variation within the region. While in Kenya 42% of households use a formal account, this share is below 5% in DRC, Guinea, the Central African Republic and Niger. The share is even greater in upper middle-income countries, such as South Africa (54%) and Mauritius (80%).

The Global Findex survey not only allows an aggregate picture of the share of households using formal financial services, but also a more detailed look into who uses what kind of financial services. One striking finding is that the gender gap in the use of formal financial services is larger in Africa than outside Africa. While men are more likely to use a formal financial account than women across the developing world, the gap is significantly larger inside Africa than outside. It is important to note, however, that these are unconditional comparisons. Using more detailed financial sector surveys for a number of Eastern and Southern African countries, Aterido, Beck, and Iacovone (2013) show that when key observable characteristics of individuals are taken into account the gender gap disappears. The lower use of formal financial services by women can be explained by gender gaps in other dimensions related to the use of financial services, such as their lower level of income and education, and by their household and employment status.

Household data on the use of financial services reconfirm the importance of leap-frogging with the help of technology. While the share of households with a formal account is larger outside than inside Africa, the share of households that have used mobile phones for payment services is larger inside than outside Africa. Specifically, 5% of population in the median African country reported using mobile phones for payment services, compared to 3.8% in non-African developing countries.

Similar to the case of enterprise data, the Global Findex data also allow us to explore the reasons why households do not have accounts with formal financial institutions. In the median African country, 68% of the population cites lack of money as a reason for not having an account, while only 52% in non-African countries do. Twenty-five percent of the population in the median African country cites high costs or lack of the necessary documentation, while 22% point to geographic barriers. Outside Africa, 18% of the population in the median developing country point to prohibitive costs, 13% to geographic barriers and 11% to lack of necessary documentation. Almost the same share of population cites lack of trust for not having an account (12% in Africa, 11% outside), while religious reasons are less prevalent in Africa (2%) than outside (4%). Finally, a smaller share of the population cites no need for an account in Africa (5%) than outside (9%). Overall, this points to similar barriers in Africa and other developing countries, though some of these barriers seem stronger in Sub-Saharan Africa.

37.2.6   The Role of Microfinance in Africa

Like other developing regions, microfinance has grown rapidly in Sub-Saharan Africa. The number of borrowers served by the African microfinance institutions (MFIs) that report to the Microfinance Information eXchange (the MIX) increased from 1.6 million in 2003 to 8.5 million in 2009.[8] A part of this increase is attributable to the MIX's efforts to expand the number of MFIs that report to them, but even among the 48 African MFIs that reported information to the MIX in all years between 2005 and 2009, the number of active borrowers increased from 2.3 million to 4.8 million.

The institutional presentation is quite similar in Africa and the rest of the developing world. For example, as of 2009, MFIs organized as banks represented 7% of the institutions in Africa and elsewhere. In Africa, banks hold 42.1% of microfinance assets compared with 48.6% in the rest of the developing world (Table 37.3). NGOs actually comprise a smaller share of the institutions in Africa than outside Africa (26 vs. 35%), though the African NGOs hold a larger share of total microfinance assets (20.4 vs. 11.6%). Non-bank financial institutions (NBFIs) appear to play a somewhat more important role outside Africa, while credit unions and cooperatives play a larger role in Africa. In all, the range of institutions in Africa appears to be about as diverse as elsewhere, and the reliance on more commercially oriented forms of microfinance similar. That conclusion is further supported in that group liability loans typically favored by less commercialized institutions represented only 15% of microfinance assets and 26% of loans in Africa in 2009 based on the MIX data, compared with 15% of assets and 20% of total loans in the rest of the developing world. Beck et al. (2011) also note that African MFIs shifted away from the group liability lending mechanisms made famous in Bangladesh under Muhammad Yunus early in their development. In West Africa, they argue that only individual liability mechanisms were used.

The growth in borrowers coincided with a declining trend in the financial performance of African MFIs as measured by the MIX's Operational Self-Sufficiency (OSS) index, a trend that was more pronounced than in other developing regions (Figure 37.6, panel B).[9] In part, this reflects the arrival to the MIX of new African MFIs that were less profitable than existing ones, but even the 50 African MFIs that reported profitability figures to the MIX in all years from 2005 to 2009 displayed a leveling off in terms of OSS (Figure 37.6, panel A). At the same time, the average loan size (relative to GDP per capita) increased more for African MFIs than others, for both the balanced panel that reported consistently to the MIX

Table 37.3 Share of microfinance assets, by institutional type, 2009

| | % of Assets, by MFI Type | | | |
| | Africa | | Non-Africa | |
	# of institutions	% of Assets	# of institutions	% of Assets
Bank	12	42.06%	59	48.57%
Coops/Credit unions	39	23.71%	109	8.39%
NGO	44	20.42%	297	11.60%
NBFI	70	13.46%	320	29.68%
Rural bank	3	0.33%	55	1.65%

[8] We are very grateful to Blaine Stephens of the MIX and Scott Gaul (formerly of the MIX) for help in obtaining the data and advice on its use.

[9] The operational sustainability ratio is financial revenue divided by the sum of financial expenses, net loan loss provision expenses, and operating expenses.

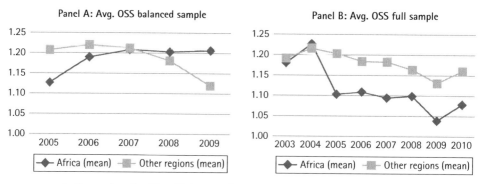

FIGURE37.6 Operational self-sufficiency of MFIs over time.

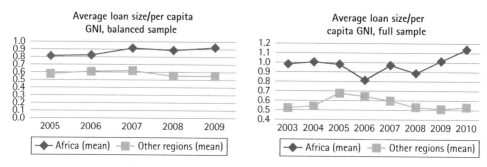

FIGURE 37.7 Average loan size of MFIs over time.

and the full sample (Figure 37.7). Similarly, but not shown, the share of women borrowers declined steadily among the consistent African reporters to the MIX. Within the full sample of African MFIs (panel B), the average share of lending to women was relatively stable, suggesting that new African entrants focused more on lending to women while better established MFIs were moving away from that market segment.

It seems plausible that the reach of MFIs in Africa will continue to expand, extending to much larger numbers of customers. At the same time, the figures presented here suggest that continued expansion could coincide with greater competitive pressure on MFI profitability and, perhaps, somewhat less focus on reaching the poorest. At the least, the explosive growth of microfinance in Africa since 2000 makes it a sub-sector that bears monitoring over the coming years.

37.3 OVERCOMING BARRIERS TO FINANCIAL INCLUSION: BRANCH EXPANSION, FIELD EXPERIMENTS, AND TECHNOLOGY

Africa has made substantial progress over the past years, not only in financial depth and inclusion, but also in the underlying macroeconomic stability, with few countries presenting double-digit inflation rates. Similarly, there has been some underlying institutional progress, including in creditor rights, contract enforcement and credit information sharing. Specifically, the average cost of property registration dropped from 13 to 9% of property value between 2004 and 2012, while creditor rights increased from an average of 4.2 to an average of 5.6 (out of a maximum of 10) over the same period. While in 2004, fewer than half of the countries had a public or private credit registry, in 2012 70% of countries in the region had one. On the other hand, the average cost of contract enforcement has remained high, barely decreasing from 56% of the average claim in 2004 to 54% in 2012.[10]

While macroeconomic management and institutional development have thus shown a certain degree of improvement, the benchmarking exercise discussed in Section 2.2 suggests that these are necessary and not sufficient conditions for financial deepening in Sub-Saharan Africa and that other barriers, including geographic disadvantages, hold back the further deepening of African banking systems. As also alluded to in the previous section, however, financial innovation, i.e. new delivery channels, new players and new products, can help overcome these barriers, especially geographic barriers. Africa has seen a lot of such innovation over the past years, as reported by Beck et al. (2011). Much of it comes from different financial institutions, banks, NGO, and MFIs, both domestic and foreign-owned, often with support from donors. In many countries, regulators have reacted flexibly, opening space for innovation within existing regulatory frameworks or adjusting them where necessary.

In this section, we report on different forms of financial innovation, summarizing research findings on the recent branch expansion by some banks into more sparsely populated areas and the potential for banks to use agent networks to further extend their reach. Agents are typically owners of small retail businesses that are trained by a formal financial institution (most often a bank) to collect deposits and process payments, including payments on small-scale loans. We also summarize results from recent field experiments in Africa that are beginning to shed light on the types of financial services that could benefit underserved market segments and overcome impediments to their uptake. Finally, we explore the role that technological innovation could play in bridging some of the geographic and informational divides that currently characterize the African financial landscape.

37.3.1 Bank Branching

In Kenya, the total number of bank branches increased from 576 in 2006 to 970 in 2009, while the share of the adult Kenyan population that had a bank account increased from 14% to 23%. While many Kenyan banks, including some state- and foreign-owned, expanded their branch footprints during this period, the expansion strategy of one private domestic bank in particular, Equity Bank, stood out for its potential impact on outreach to underserved market segments. As part of its expansion strategy, Equity Bank emphasized that local languages be spoken in its branches, an important consideration since 30–40% of the people in central Kenya do not speak English or Swahili.

Allen et al. (2012a, 2012b) exploit the fact that Equity Bank's branching policy in Kenya favored minority-speaking districts more than other banks, and use instrumental variables

[10] These numbers are based on data from the Doing Business database (http://www.doingbusiness.org>.).

and difference-in-differences techniques to identify the impact of Equity Bank's branch penetration on households' access to banking services. They find that the presence of Equity Bank branches has a positive and significant impact on households' use of bank accounts and bank credit. [11] Across estimation techniques, Equity's presence was associated with a 4% to 9% point increase in the probability of having a bank account. Similar regressions confirm that Equity's presence was associated with an increase in borrowing, although loan use increased less dramatically, from 2.9% of respondents in 2006 to 4.4% in 2009.

As noted above, another potential method for promoting financial inclusion in sparsely populated areas is agent banking. [12] However, to our knowledge, there have been no rigorous studies of the effects of agent banking, and certainly none for Africa. However, a review of the Latin American experience suggests that agents have been effective in reaching the unbanked (Alliance for Financial Inclusion, 2012). In Kenya, Equity Bank has also moved forcefully into agent banking, expanding its number of agents from under 1,000 in early 2011 to over 6,000 by the end of 2012. These agents now account for over 30% of Equity Bank's total transactions.

In all, Equity Bank's experience in Kenya and those of a handful of banks in other developing countries suggest that it might be possible to generate sustainable profits with a business model focused on the provision of financial services to population segments that are typically ignored by commercial banks. At the same time, the number of studies is small (and most are not from African countries) making it hard to identify the factors that lead to successful adaptation of those strategies.

37.3.2 Assessing Tailored Interventions with Randomized Field Experiments

Although the number of field experiments based on randomized controlled trials (RCTs) in Africa involving financial services is low, patterns are beginning to emerge that point to key impediments to broader financial inclusion. On the savings side, commitment devices that enable users to guard accumulated funds from outside demands (often from relatives and friends) have led to increased investment and more rapid growth of firms. For example, Dupas and Robinson (2013) show that female shopkeepers in Kenya were much more likely to take up non-interest-bearing bank accounts that were subject to high withdrawal fees (and thus less attractive than standard interest bearing accounts) than male business owners, and investment in those female-owned businesses was nearly double that of female business owners in the control group. Brune et al. (2011) document changes in the production methods of tobacco farmers in Malawi who were offered a "commitment" savings

---

[11] For similar studies, see Bruhn and Love (2014) on the extension of Banco Azteca in Mexicos, Burgess and Pande (2005) on an exogenous change in branching restrictions in India to identify the effects of increased branch penetration on poverty reduction, and Brown, Guinn, and Kirshenmann (2013) documenting substantial gains in financial inclusion associated with the expansion of a major microfinance provider (ProCredit) in Albania, Bulgaria, Macedonia, and Serbia.

[12] Anecdotal evidence suggests that agency banking allows overcoming not only geographic but also socio-cultural barriers that might prevent low-income population segments from entering formal bank offices.

account that allowed the account holders to freeze their funds until a specified date (typically just prior to the planting season, thus preserving funds for purchases of farm inputs). Deposit and withdrawal activity spiked just prior to the planting season, land under cultivation increased by 9.8%, agricultural input use in that planting by 26.2%, crop output in the subsequent harvest by 22%, and household expenditures in the months immediately after harvest by 17.4% (all relative to the mean for the control group). Another study from western Kenya shows how a commitment savings device enabled farmers to increase their use of fertilizer (Duflo, Kremer, and Robinson, 2011).

There is less evidence from experiments involving African credit products than for savings products. But the evidence from micro-credit experiments in other parts of the developing world suggests that effects are harder to identify than for savings. For example, one of the best-known studies of micro-credit finds no significant impact on income and consumption among poor households in Hyderabad, India (Banerjee et al., 2013), though multiple studies show modest impact on investment.[13] Critically, recent research has identified differential effects across different borrower groups, with entrepreneurial types increasing their investment when gaining access to external finance while non-entrepreneurial types increase consumption.

A key impediment to broader extension of credit in Africa is the lack of reliable methods for personal identification. Individuals who lack collateral and credit histories, which characterizes a large share of the African population, struggle to overcome informational asymmetries that make it almost impossible to access credit from formal sources. Establishing collateral and credit registries could help, but these can only function if people can be accurately identified. A field experiment among paprika farmers in Malawi tested whether biometric identification methods can improve the functioning of credit markets in a country where identity theft is common (Giné et al., 2013). Applicants for agricultural input loans from a state-owned bank were randomly assigned to a treatment group in which a fingerprint was collected from each member as part of the loan application, or to a control group in which no fingerprint was taken. Both treatment and control groups attended a training session on the importance of a credit history in ensuring future access to credit. For the subgroup of farmers identified as having high ex-ante default risk, fingerprinting led to a 40% increase in repayment rates.[14]

As in other parts of the developing world, micro-insurance products could offer benefits in Africa, especially in agricultural areas. For example, rainfall insurance, which pays a set amount when rainfall falls below (or surpasses) a predetermined threshold could be useful to African farmers.[15] Yet, empirical studies of micro-insurance are rare. In Ghana, Karlan et al. (2013) find that rainfall insurance counters farmers' risk aversion and improves

---

[13] See Roodman (2012) and Bauchet et al. (2011) for summaries of evidence from randomized evaluations of microfinance. In their review of microfinance studies in Africa, Van Rooyen, Stewart, and De Wet (2012) find that micro-credit and micro-savings interventions have mixed effects on household income and accumulation of assets. In part, this could stem from the uneven quality of the studies they review.

[14] Moreover, a rough cost–benefit analysis suggests that the benefits from improved repayment greatly outweighed the cost of equipment and fingerprint collection.

[15] Because farmers' behavior does not influence payments, rainfall insurance eliminates moral hazard problems and could therefore be a viable product for financial services providers.

decision making, though effects were largest when insurance was combined with subsidized capital. Farmers that received both increased their spending on agricultural chemical inputs by 47%, expanded their land under cultivation by 22%, and were less likely to report that their households suffered from hunger. But in another experiment in Malawi, Giné and Yang (2007) find that take-up rates for an agricultural loan product were somewhat *lower* when the loan was coupled with an insurance policy (priced at an actuarially fair rate) that paid off in the event of poor rainfall. In part, the reluctance to purchase the insurance product may have stemmed from farmers' belief that they only faced limited liability for their loans in the event of severe weather problems (and thus they already had a form of implicit insurance). In both experiments, the take-up rate for insurance products was puzzlingly low, suggesting a weak match between the insurance products and farmers' needs and/or farmers not fully understanding how these products could benefit them. More research in the insurance area is clearly warranted.

37.3.3 Technological Innovation

Mobile money transfer ("m-transfer") systems facilitate financial transactions via mobile phones, allowing users to deposit and withdraw cash from an account that is accessible by mobile handset. Users can store value in the account and transfer value between users via text messages, menu commands, and personal identification numbers (Aker and Mbiti, 2010). M-transfer arrangements therefore enable users to make payments and transfer funds at relatively low cost across much wider geographic areas than is possible using localized informal payment solutions. Aker et al. (2011) report that, since 2005, m-transfer systems have been established in 80 developing countries in Africa, Asia, and Latin America.

M-Pesa, the mobile payments wallet launched in 2007 by Kenyan mobile network operator Safaricom, had 15 million registered users by early 2012, a network of 35,000 cash-in/ cash-out agents, and a transaction volume of US$665 million per month (Mark, 2012; Rotman, Ferrand, and Rasmussen, 2012). M-Pesa use has brought about a substantial decline in the costs of sending transfers and a substantial increase in their volume (especially remittances), a greater likelihood of being formally banked, and decreased use of informal savings mechanisms (Jack and Suri, 2011; Mbiti and Weill, 2011). At the same time, M-Pesa was rarely used for storing value for any significant period (most transactions were of the cash-in, immediate cash-out variety) and the vast majority of M-Pesa transactions was undertaken by relatively affluent Kenyans, though there were some indications of less intensive use by poorer population segments.[16]

The extent to which mobile payment services can facilitate spatial risk sharing within an economy is illustrated by Blumenstock, Eagle, and Fafchamps (2011) who show that the Lake Kivu earthquake in 2008 in Rwanda caused individuals living outside the affected area to transfer a large and significant volume of airtime to people living close to the earthquake's epicenter. They also show that the transfers were consistent with reciprocal risk sharing rather than charity or altruistic motivations, suggesting that mobile payment services

---

[16] One potential explanation for limited time savings is that balances stored in an M-Pesa account accrued no interest (though that could change as M-Pesa teams up with banking partners to link M-Pesa accounts to mainstream bank accounts).

facilitate informal inter-personal insurance mechanisms, although it seems again that wealthier segments of the population benefitted most.

Another example comes from Niger, where an m-transfer system is providing a more cost-effective means of implementing a cash transfer program. While Bold, Porteous, and Rotman (2012) argue that electronic payment methods for social cash transfers work best when piggy-backing upon existing payments infrastructure, the experience in Niger suggests that electronic cash transfer via an m-system could also work where more traditional payments infrastructure is lacking.[17]

An experiment comparing traditional cash transfers with transfers via an m-system called Zap was undertaken in 96 "food-deficit" villages in Niger, meaning they had produced less than half of their consumption needs during the 2009 harvest (Aker et al. 2011). One-third of villages received traditional assistance in cash; another third received mobile phones and electronic transfers via Zap; while recipients in the remaining villages received a mobile phone, but continued to receive assistance in cash. Inclusion of the third group was designed to isolate the effects of mobile phone usage on financial and other outcomes from the effects of e-transfer. Zap substantially reduced the cost of distributing and obtaining the cash transfers, and households used their transfers to purchase a more diverse set of goods, increased the diversity of their diets, depleted fewer assets, and grew a wider variety of crops (including marginal crops typically grown by women). The authors speculate that lower costs, in particular the time savings to recipients of electronic transfers, and greater privacy in receiving those transfers (reducing obligations to share money within social networks) is driving the changes in household outcomes associated with Zap usage.

Though preliminary, the experimental results thus far suggest that financial products that can reach the poor at low cost (both to providers and to the poor themselves), and that incorporate elements that enable borrower/savers to protect funds to meet financial goals, hold promise for expanding financial inclusion in Africa.

37.4 CONCLUSIONS AND LOOKING FORWARD

While we have documented achievements in deepening and broadening African financial systems, challenges remain. In this concluding section, we point to five areas where future research could support policy formulation. The first of these challenges refers to the short-term nature of finance across the region, as illustrated not only in the balance sheet structures of banks, but also in the limited development of contractual savings institutions and financial markets. While financial inclusion has dominated the recent policy debate and research agenda, the need for long-term finance by households, enterprises and government is enormous. The cost of addressing Africa's physical infrastructure needs is estimated at US$93 billion per year, some 15% of Africa's gross domestic product (GDP) (Foster and Briceño-Garmendia, 2010). Demand for housing, especially in urban areas, continues to rise across the continent as Africa rapidly urbanizes. And firms continue to lack the necessary resources for long-term investment.

---

[17] In Niger, there is less than one bank per 100,000 residents.

The long-term finance agenda is thus an extensive one, both for researchers and policy makers. First, there is still a dearth of data on long-term financing arrangements, including on corporate bond market structures and costs, insurance markets and private equity funds. Second, identifying positive examples and gauging interventions and policies will be critical, as will be expanding to Africa the small literature on equity funds and their effect on enterprises that exists for US and Europe and (increasingly) for emerging markets. One important constraint mentioned in the context of long-term finance is the lack of risk mitigation tools. Partial credit guarantees can play an important role, but their design and actual impact has not been studied sufficiently yet.

A second challenge relates to small enterprises. Research on financial inclusion has identified policy levers to improve access to and use of financial services by households and microenterprises; looking forward, this research has to move beyond micro to small enterprises, both in terms of supply- and demand-side constraints. The emphasis stems from the realization that job-intensive and transformational growth is more likely to come through formal than informal enterprises. While there is a large literature gauging financing constraints of firms of different size, there is less evidence on specific policies and interventions that have differential effects across firms of different sizes. While access to formal finance might be less of a (testable) challenge for small enterprises, the quality of access is important, including maturity, choice of currency and collateral requirements. Assessing different lending techniques, delivery channels and organizational structures conducive to small business lending is important, as is assessing the interaction of firms' financing constraints with other constraints, including lack of managerial ability and financial literacy.

A third important agenda refers to regulatory reform. While global discussions and reform processes are driven and dominated by the recent global financial crisis and the fragility concerns of economies with developed if not sophisticated financial markets, Africa's fragility concerns are different and its reform capacity lower. Some of the suggested or implemented reforms seem irrelevant for almost all African countries (such as centralizing over-the-counter trades) or might have substantially worse effects in the context of shallow financial markets than in sophisticated markets increasingly dominated by high frequency trading (such as securities trading taxes). This is not to argue that payments and clearing systems are less important in Africa than elsewhere, but that payment systems needs in Africa may be more basic. It also is somewhat surprising that research to date has focused on mobile payments in Africa rather than on broadening payments options (for direct deposit, direct debit for payments of consumer bills, business-to-business transactions, and other forms of e-commerce) using automated clearing house (ACH) solutions.

Kasakende, Bagyenda, and Brownbridge (2012) esteem the proposed Basel III reforms as not sufficient in the African context, and call for additional regulatory tools, including the possibility to impose restrictions on banks' asset exposures and regulations on loan concentration and foreign exchange exposure. In the context of regulatory reform, an approach of best fit would be more appropriate than a best practice approach that blindly adopts international standards. Prioritizing regulatory reforms according to risks and opportunity costs for financial deepening and inclusion is therefore critical.

In the context of regulatory reform, a fourth topic worth highlighting is globalization and cross-border bank regulation, partly informed by the experience of the global financial crisis, partly driven by the increasing financial integration of Africa with emerging and developed countries but also intra-regionally. Identifying cross-border linkages between countries is critical, and the dataset collected by Claessens and van Horen (2014) represents an important first step. Understanding the channels through which cross-border banking can help deepen financial systems and foster real integration, and the channels through which cross-border banks can threaten financial stability, is critical. In this context, the optimal design of cross-border cooperation between regulators and supervisors to minimize risks from cross-border banking while maximizing its benefits is important (Beck and Wagner, 2013).

A final important area, which we have not touched upon, is the political economy of financial sector reform. Politicians primarily maximize private interests, whether the interests of their voters or special interest groups. Short-term election cycles undermine the focus on long-term financial development objectives; objectives that maintain the dominant position of elites undermine the incentives of these elites to undertake reforms that can open up financial systems and, thus, dilute the dominant position of the elites. Path dependence in political structures and the underlying socioeconomic distribution of resources and power make the adoption of growth-enhancing policies, such as financial sector policies, difficult or impossible if the policies threaten to reduce the relative dominance of the incumbent elites. On the other hand, the financial sector is critical for an open, competitive, and contestable economy because it provides the necessary resources for new entrants and can thus support economic transformation. Better understanding the political constraints in financial sector reforms and identifying windows of opportunity are therefore important. Focusing on the creation of broader groups with a stake in further financial deepening can help develop a dynamic process of financial sector reforms.

Research in these five areas will have to be supported by an array of new data and a variety of methodological approaches. Increased data availability has helped spur a rich research agenda on African finance over the past decade. Further advances will require expanding this data availability towards non-bank providers, such as equity funds, but also exploiting existing data sources better, including credit registry and central bank datasets. In addition to exploiting more extensive micro-level datasets, a variety of methodological approaches is called for. First, randomized experiments involving both households and micro- and small enterprises will shed light on specific technologies and products that can help overcome the barriers to financial inclusion in Africa. One of the challenges to overcome will be to include spillover effects and thus move beyond partial equilibrium results to aggregate results. Second, further studies evaluating the effect of specific policy interventions can give insights into which policy reforms are most effective in enhancing sustainable financial deepening and positive real sector outcomes.

References

Aker, J. C., Boumnijel, R., McClelland, A., and Tierney, N. (2011). Zap It to Me: The Short-Term Impacts of a Mobile Cash Transfer Program, Center for Global Development Working Paper No. 268.

Aker, J. C. and Mbiti, I. M. (2010). Mobile Phones and Economic Development in Africa, *Journal of Economic Perspectives* 24(3), 207–232.

Allen, F., Carletti, E., Cull, R., Qian, J., Senbet, L., and Valenzuela, P. (2012a). Improving Access to Banking: Evidence from Kenya. Paper Presented at the 2012 Summer Research Conference on "Recent Advances in Corporate Finance," at the Centre for Analytical Finance, Indian School of Business in Hyderabad.

Allen, F., Carletti, E., Cull, R., Qian, J., Senbet, L., and Valenzuela, P (2012b). Resolving the African Financial Development Gap: Cross-country Comparisons and a Within-country Study of Kenya, National Bureau of Economic Research, Cambridge, MA, Working Paper No. 18013, <http://www.nber.org/papers/w18013>.

Allen, F., Carletti, E., Cull, R., Qian, J., Senbet, L., and Valenzuela, P. (2013). The African Financial Development and Financial Inclusion Gaps, *Journal of African Economies* (Forthcoming).

Alliance for Financial Inclusion (2012). Agent Banking in Latin America. AFI Discussion Paper, March.

Aterido, R., Beck, T., and Iacovone, L. (2013). Access to Finance in sub-Saharan Africa: Is There a Gender Gap?, *World Development* 47, 102–120.

Badev, A., Beck, T., Vado, L., and Walley, S. (2013). Housing Finance across Countries: New Data and Analysis. World Bank: Mimeo.

Banerjee, A., Duflo, E., Glennerster, R., and Kinnan, C. (2013). The Miracle of Microfinance? Evidence from a Randomized Evaluation. Cambridge, MA, MIT Working Paper.

Bauchet, J., Marshall, C., Starita, L., Thomas, J., and Yalouris, A. (2011). Latest Findings from Randomized Evaluations of Microfinance, Access to Finance FORUM, CGAP and Its Partners Reports No. 2.

Beck, T., Cull, R., and Jerome, A. (2005). Bank Privatization and Performance: Empirical Evidence from Nigeria, *Journal of Banking and Finance* 29, 2355–2379.

Beck, T., Demirgüç-Kunt, A., and Levine, R. (2000). A New Database on Financial Development and Structure, *World Bank Economic Review* 14, 597–605.

Beck, T., Demirgüç-Kunt, A., and Levine, R. (2010). Financial Institutions and Markets Across Countries and Over Time: The Updated Financial Development and Structure Database, *World Bank Economic Review* 24, 77–92.

Beck, T., Munzele Maimbo, S., Faye, I., and Triki, T. (2011). *Financing Africa: Through the Crisis and Beyond*. Washington, DC: The World Bank.

Beck, T. and Wagner, W. (2013). Supranational Supervision: How Much and for Whom?, CEPR Discussion Paper No. 9546.

Bold, C., Porteous, D., and Rotman, S. (2012). Social Cash Transfers and Financial Inclusion: Evidence from Four Countries, CGAP Focus Note No. 77.

Blumenstock, J., Eagle, N., and Fafchanps, M. (2011.) Risk and Reciprocity Over the Mobile Phone Network: Evidence from Rwanda, CSAE Working Paper No. 2011-19.

Brown, M., Guinn, B., and Kirshenmann, K. (2013). Microfinance Banks and Household Access to Finance. University of St. Gallen: Mimeo.

Bruhn, M. and Love, I. (2013). The Economic Impact of Expanding Access to Finance in Mexico. In: R. Cull, A. Demirgüç-Kunt, and J. Morduch, (Eds.), *Banking the World: Empirical Foundations of Financial Inclusion*, 137–156. Cambridge, MA: MIT Press.

Bruhn, M. and Love, I. (2014). The Economic Impact of Banking the Unbanked: Evidence from Mexico, *Journal of Finance* (Forthcoming).

Brune, L., Giné, X., Goldberg, J., and Yang, D. (2011). Commitments to Save: A Field Experiment in Rural Malawi, World Bank Policy Research Working Paper No. 5748.

Burgess, R. and Pande, R. (2005). Can Rural Banks Reduce Poverty? Evidence from the Indian Social Banking Experiment, *American Economic Review* 95(3), 780–795.

Clarke, G. R. G., Cull, R., and Fuchs, M. (2009). Bank Privatization in sub-Saharan Africa: The Case of Uganda Commercial Bank, *World Development* 37(9), 1506–1521.

Claessens, S. and Laeven, L. (2004). What Drives Bank Competition? Some International Evidence, *Journal of Money, Credit, and Banking* 36, 563–583.

Claessens, S. and van Horen, N. (2014). Foreign Banks: Trends and Impact, *Journal of Money, Credit and Banking* (Forthcoming).

Cull, R. and Martínez Pería, M. S. (2012). Foreign Bank Participation in Developing Countries: What do we Know about the Drivers and Consequences of this Phenomenon? In: J. Caprio (Ed.), *Encyclopedia of Financial Globalization*. Amsterdam: Elsevier.

Cull, R. and Spreng, C. P. (2011). Pursuing Efficiency While Maintaining Outreach: Bank Privatization in Tanzania, *Journal of Development Economics* 94(2) 254–261.

Cull, R. and Trandafir, M. (2010). Credit Market Segmentation in Uganda. World Bank: Mimeo.

Demirgüç-Kunt, A. and Klapper, L. (2012). Measuring Financial Inclusion: The Global Financial Inclusion Index, World Bank Policy Research Working Paper No. 6025.

Duflo, E., Kremer, M., and Robinson, J. (2011). Nudging Farmers to Use Fertilizer: Theory and Experimental Evidence from Kenya, *American Economic Review* 101(6), 2350–2390.

Dupas, P. and Robinson, J. (2013). Savings Constraints and Microenterprise Development: Evidence from a Field Experiment in Kenya, *American Economic Journal: Applied Economics* 5, 163–192.

Foster, V. and Briceño-Garmendia, C. (2010). *Africa's Infrastructure: A Time for Transformation.* Washington, DC: World Bank.

Gine, X. and Yang, D. (2007). *Insurance, Credit, and Technology Adoption: Field Experimental Evidence from Malawi*, World Bank Policy Research Working Paper No. 4425.

Giné, X., Goldberg, J., Sankaranarayanan, S., Sheerin, P., and Yang, D. (2013). Use of Biometric Technology in Developing Countries. In: R. Cull, A. Demirgüç-Kunt, and J. Morduch (Eds.), *Banking the World: Empirical Foundations of Financial Inclusion*, 429–446. Cambridge, MA: MIT Press.

Honohan, P. and Beck, T. (2007). Making Finance Work for Africa, World Bank Working Paper No. 6626.

Jack, W. and Suri, T. (2011). The Economics of M-PESA. MIT Sloan Working Paper.

Karlan, D., Osei, R., Osei-Akoto, I., and Udry, C. (2013). Agricultural Decisions after Relaxing Credit and Risk Constraints, *Quarterly Journal of Economics* (Forthcoming).

Kasakende, Louis, Justine Bagyenda and Martin Brownbridge, 2012, "Basel III and the global reform of financial regulation: how should Africa respond? a bank regulator's perspective," Bank of Uganda mimeo.

Laeven, L. and Valencia, F. (2012). *Systemic Banking Crises Database: An Update*, IMF Working Paper No. 12/163.

Levine, R. (2005). Finance and Growth: Theory and Evidence. In: P. Aghion and S. N. Durlauf (Eds.), *Handbook of Economic Growth*, 865–934. Amsterdam: Elsevier.

Mark, O. (2012). M-Pesa Drives Safaricom as Profit Declines to Sh12.8bn, *Business Daily* May 10.

Mbiti, I. and Weil, D. (2011). Mobile Banking: The Impact of M-Pesa in Kenya, NBER Working Paper No. 17129.

Roodman, D. (2012). Latest Impact Research: Inching Toward Generalization, CGAP Blog, April 11, <http://microfinance.cgap.org/2012/04/11/latest-impact-research-inching-toward-generalization/>.

Rotman, S., Ferrand D., and Rasmussen, S. (2012). "The Jipange KuSave Experiment in Kenya." *CGAP Brief*, October, Washington DC.

van Rooyen, C., Stewart, R., and de Wet, T. (2012). The Impact of Microfinance in sub-Saharan Africa: A Systematic Review of the Evidence, *World Development* 40, 2249–2262.

CHAPTER 38

....

BANKING IN THE DEVELOPING NATIONS OF ASIA

Changes in Ownership Structure and Lending over the Financial Crisis*

....

LEORA KLAPPER, MARIA SOLEDAD
MARTINEZ PERIA, AND BILAL ZIA

38.1 INTRODUCTION

....

DEVELOPING economies in East and South Asia have seen their banking sectors go through important transformations. Throughout the last decade, pressures brought on by the 1997 East Asian crisis and by the global trend toward increasing financial integration have resulted in significant reforms and structural changes. In particular, countries in East and South Asia have embarked in efforts to clean up their banking systems, reduce state ownership, and allow greater foreign participation. However, progress has not been even and some economies have made strides in these areas more quickly than others. While countries such as Pakistan and Korea have been relatively aggressive in their reform agendas, others, including India and China, have proceeded more slowly. In particular, the banking sectors in India and China remain dominated by government-owned banks and are still relatively closed to foreign interests. Also, relative to other regions such as Latin America and Eastern Europe, reform in East and South Asia—in particular privatization and foreign entry—has been less comprehensive and far-reaching in China and India.

* We thank Ariel BenYishay, Christian Salas, Soledad Lopez, Subika Farazi, and Trang Tran for excellent research assistance.

After presenting some basic statistics on the banking sectors of East and South Asia, this chapter focuses on characterizing the regions' banking sector ownership structure, discussing the recent reforms and changes that have given way to the current structure, and summarizing the evidence available so far on the effects of the reform process. In light of the recent global financial turmoil, the chapter also discusses the impact of the crisis on the banking sectors in Asia and empirically analyzes the behavior of foreign bank lending in the region during the crisis. The chapter is organized as follows. Section 38.2 presents some basic statistics on the size, depth, efficiency, and outreach of banking sectors in East and South Asia. In the case of East Asia, we focus on China, Indonesia, Korea, Malaysia, Philippines, and Thailand, while for South Asia we center our description on Bangladesh, India, and Pakistan. Section 38.3 illustrates the degree of public and foreign ownership across East and South Asian economies and compares it to the experience of developing countries in other regions. Section 38.4 describes the recent reforms and transformations that have led to the current banking structure. Section 38.5 reviews the existing evidence on the implications from the recent ownership changes. Section 38.6 discusses the consequences of the global financial crisis of 2008–09 on developing countries in Asia. Section 38.7 empirically analyzes the impact of foreign bank ownership on bank lending during the crisis. Section 38.8 concludes.

38.2 CHARACTERIZING BANKING SECTORS IN ASIA

Banking sectors in East and South Asia have many similarities, but are also quite different from each other in a number of respects, and within each of these regions there are also important differences across countries. For example, in terms of size, relative to gross domestic product (GDP), the banking sector is twice as large in East Asia as it is in South Asia (see Table 38.1). On average, in East Asia, bank assets accounted for roughly 80% to 90% of GDP, between 2007 and 2009, while they represented around 50% of GDP in South Asia. But within East Asia there is significant variation. While the share of bank assets in China, Malaysia, and Thailand exceeds 100% of GDP, Indonesia (30%–32%) and the Philippines (35%–44%) have significantly smaller banking sectors than other countries in the region and, in fact, are more similar in size to the banking sectors of Bangladesh (52%–55%), India (58–64%), and Pakistan (37%–39%). Relative to other regions, banking sectors in East Asia are much larger than those of all other regions, while the size of South Asian banking sectors is comparable to that of other regions such as Eastern Europe (46%–52%), Latin America (40%–42%), the Middle East and Northern Africa (58%–65%), and Sub-Saharan Africa (48%–57%).

A similar pattern to that described for the banking sector size holds for a commonly used measure of banking sector depth, the share of bank credit to the private sector relative to GDP. At 71% to 79% of GDP in 2007–2009, banking sector depth in East Asia is more than twice that for South Asia, where it averages close to 35%, and also far exceeds that for other regions like Eastern Europe, Latin America, Middle East, North and Sub-Saharan Africa. Again, Indonesia and Philippines are an exception, where the

Table 38.1 Banking sector statistics in developing countries of Asia

	Bank assets to GDP (%)		Private credit to GDP (%)		Overhead cost to assets (%)		Net interest margins to assets (%)		Branches (per 100,000 people)		ATMs (per 100,000 people)		ATMs (per 1000 square km)	
	2007	2009	2007	2009	2007	2009	2007	2009	2007	2009	2007	2009	2007	2009
China	109.5	122.5	99.7	112.5	1.5	1.1	3.7	2.3	n.a.	n.a.	n.a.	n.a.	n.a.	n.a.
Indonesia	31.5	30.4	22.7	23.9	3.8	3.8	6.5	6.6	5.9	7.5	11.3	13.9	10.4	13.2
Korea, Rep.	99.5	111.3	93.1	104.7	1.2	1.4	1.9	2.1	18.4	18.3	235.4	248.6	967.1	1045.7
Malaysia	102.9	120.7	97.0	107.6	1.4	1.4	3.2	2.8	10.7	10.4	39.4	53.1	22.2	31.3
Philippines	35.0	43.6	22.4	28.7	3.6	3.0	4.2	3.9	7.7	7.7	12.7	14.4	24.0	28.4
Thailand	100.9	108.0	89.6	95.9	2.4	2.2	3.6	3.3	9.6	10.7	46.9	72.6	48.7	77.2
East Asia Pacific	79.9	89.4	70.7	78.9	2.3	2.2	3.8	3.5	10.5	10.9	69.1	80.5	214.5	239.2
Bangladesh	51.8	55.5	34.6	37.7	3.4	2.7	2.5	4.2	7.0	7.3	0.5	1.3	3.7	9.7
India	57.7	63.6	41.1	44.6	2.1	1.9	3.1	3.1	9.0	9.6	3.4	5.2	9.1	14.7
Pakistan	38.8	36.6	27.2	23.8	2.5	2.8	5.1	5.2	7.9	8.3	2.7	3.9	3.6	5.5
South Asia	49.4	51.9	34.3	35.4	2.7	2.5	3.6	4.2	8.0	8.4	2.2	3.5	5.5	9.9
Eastern Europe & Central Asia	51.8	45.6	41.7	44.9	4.9	2.5	3.9	3.5	25.6	26.9	42.3	55.1	33.1	39
Latin America	42.2	40.5	21.7	24.6	4.5	4.6	5.6	5.2	21.1	22.3	50.7	55.6	10.5	11.8
Middle East & North Africa	58.6	65.1	38.6	42.2	1.7	1.5	2.9	2.6	7.3	9.8	7.8	10.5	3.4	4.7
Sub-Saharan Africa	47.6	57.1	39.1	47.2	4.6	6.9	5.3	5.9	4.9	6.7	13.3	23.7	4.8	9.6

Source: World Bank-World Development Indicators (World Bank, 2012); BankScope (2012); Financial Access Survey Database (IMF, 2012).

share of bank credit to the private sector—at less than 30% of GDP—approaches banking sector depth measures for South Asia. In turn, banking sector depth measures for South Asia are smaller than those observed for Eastern Europe, Middle East, North and Sub-Saharan Africa.

When it comes to measures of efficiency, the averages for East and South Asia are similar to each other and are in general better than those observed in other regions except the Middle East and North Africa. Average overhead costs stand at 2.2% in East Asia and 2.5% in South Asia, while they exceed 4% in Eastern Europe and Latin America and average close to 6% in Sub-Saharan Africa. Within East Asia, banks in Indonesia and the Philippines seem relatively less efficient than those in other countries. Overhead costs are generally more than 3% in Indonesia and the Philippines, while they stand at close to 1% for China, Korea, and Malaysia. In South Asia, the share of overhead costs to bank assets decreased to less than 2% for India, while averaging closer to 3% for Bangladesh and Pakistan.

The cost of financial intermediation is similar in East and South Asia and is also lower than that observed for all regions except for the Middle East and Northern Africa. Net interest margins average close to 5%–6% in in Latin America, and Sub-Saharan Africa. Cross-country analyses of the determinants of net interest margins indicate that margins in Latin America and Sub-Saharan Africa tend to be higher primarily because of higher overhead costs (see Gelos, 2006; and Honohan and Beck, 2007). Within East Asia, net interest margins are lowest in Korea (2.1% in 2009) and Malaysia (2.8%) and highest in Indonesia (6.6%). Net interest margins are 4.2% in Bangladesh, 3.1% in India, and 5.2% in Pakistan in 2011.

Countries in East and South Asia rank below those in Eastern Europe and Latin America in terms of one measure of banking outreach: the number of branches per person.[1]

Across East and South Asia, per capita branch penetration averages around 11 and 8 branches per 100,000 people, respectively. In contrast, there are on average around 20 branches per 100,000 people in Eastern Europe in Latin America in 2011. However, when measured by the number of ATMs both by population and by area, East Asia far exceed other regions in outreach (note that the averages for East Asia do not include China due to missing data). South Asia, on the other hand, lags behind most other regions in terms of these two outreach measures.

Another area where East and South Asia seem to be lagging behind other regions is in the degree of private and foreign ownership in the banking sector. Because this is an area where important changes are taking place, the rest of the chapter is devoted to describing these changes and exploring the evidence on their implications.

---

[1] The following countries are included in the regional averages: in East Europe, we consider the Czech Republic, Hungary, Poland, and Russia; in Latin America, we include Argentina, Brazil, Mexico, and Venezuela; in the Middle East, we include Algeria, Egypt, and Morocco; and in Sub-Saharan Africa, we include Kenya, Nigeria, and South Africa.

Indicators of financial outreach—the extent to which the population has access to financial services—are hard to come by. Beck, Demirgüç-Kunt, and Martinez Peria (2007) collected information on the number of branches, ATMs, loans, and deposits across a number of countries. However, for the purpose of comparison across regions and countries, information on branches is the most comprehensive.

38.3 BANKING SECTOR STRUCTURE IN ASIA: EVOLUTION AND COMPARISON WITH OTHER REGIONS

Since the mid-2000s, developing countries in Asia have witnessed noticeable changes in their banking sectors' structure. In general, as shown in Figure 38.1, the trend has been toward less government ownership of banks and increased foreign participation in the sector. However, there are significant differences across countries in the extent to which reforms have taken place. In South Asia, Pakistan has led the way in reducing government participation in the banking sector. Between 1997 and 2009, government ownership fell from 68% to 21%. On the other hand, though some progress was made by Bangladesh and less so by India, in both countries, but especially in India, government banks still play a dominant role. Over this period, Bangladesh reduced the share of assets held by government banks from 70% to 35%, while in India government participation declined only from 80% to 72%. In terms of foreign bank participation, progress in South Asia has been slow. While India had practically no foreign presence in 1997, as of 2009 foreign banks account for close to 8% of the system. In Bangladesh, the share of bank assets held by foreign banks barely increased from 6% to 7% over the period 1997–2009.

In East Asia, government ownership has declined across the board but continues to be significant in Indonesia and especially in China. Although since 2001 the Chinese government

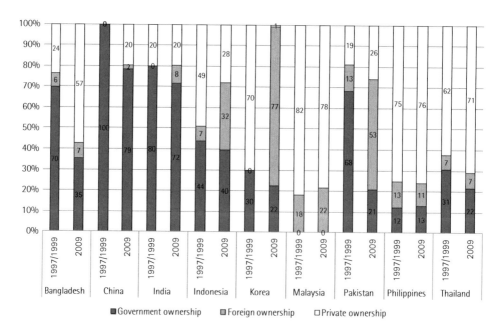

FIGURE 38.1 Changes in bank ownership structure in East and South Asia.

Source: Barth, Caprio, and Levine Supervision and Regulation Database (2012).

has introduced important banking sector reforms, which have resulted in an increase in private ownership of banks, government banks still account for 79% of the sector in 2009. In Indonesia, the share of government-owned banks fell only from 44% to 40% between 1997 and 2009. Korea and Thailand also witnessed a decline in government ownership, but the baseline levels of government participation were much lower in these countries. In both economies, government banks controlled roughly 30% of banking sector assets in 1997. By 2009, the shares of government participation declined to 22% in both Korea and Thailand. In the Philippines, government participation has remained roughly unchanged at 12%–13% of banking sector assets.

With the exception of China, where foreign ownership has only recently been allowed and accounts for close to 2% of bank assets in 2009, foreign bank participation in East Asia is much higher than that observed in South Asia and the changes have been more significant. In Indonesia, for example, the share of assets held by foreign banks increased from 7% to 32% in 2009. Korea experienced an even more significant increase in foreign bank participation. The share of assets held by foreign banks in this country rose from close to zero to almost 77%. Malaysia and Philippines also underwent an increase in foreign bank presence, but the changes in these countries were much less pronounced. In Malaysia, the share of assets held by foreign banks rose from 18% to 22%. Finally, Thailand experienced almost no change in foreign participation, which stayed at close to 7%.

Despite recent changes toward more private and foreign ownership in the banking sectors of South and East Asia, even excluding China, government ownership in Asia is still higher than that in most other regions of the world (see Figure 38.2). While on average 28% of assets are held by government banks in Asia, government bank participation is on average 10% in Sub-Saharan Africa, 17% in Latin America, and 23% in Eastern Europe. Only

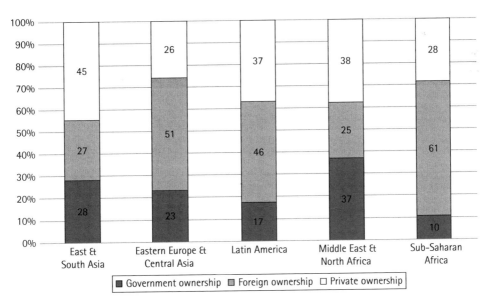

FIG. 38.2 Bank ownership structure across regions.

Note: China is excluded from the East & South Asia average due to missing data.

Source: Barth, Caprio, and Levine Supervision and Regulation Database (2012).

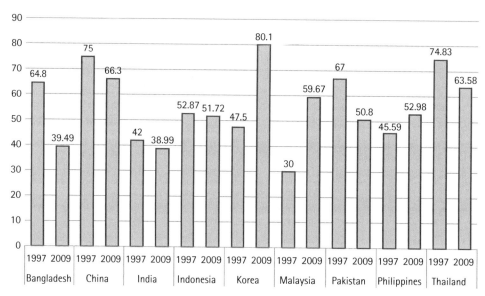

FIGURE 38.3 Banking sector concentration in East and South Asia (% share of assets held by the top largest 5 banks).

Source: Barth, Caprio, and Levine Supervision and Regulation Database (2012).

countries in North Africa and the Middle East exhibit higher levels of government ownership (37% of assets). In terms of foreign ownership, Asia also ranks below all other regions except the Middle East and Northern Africa. On average, 27% of assets are held by foreign banks in Asia vis-à-vis 61% in Sub-Saharan Africa, 51% in Eastern Europe and 46% in Latin America.

While the Asian economies have undergone significant changes in banking sector ownership structure, there is less evidence of noticeable shifts in the degree of concentration (see Figure 38.3). With the exception of Korea and Malaysia—where the share of assets held by the top five banks rose from 48% to 80% and from 30% to near 60%, respectively—in the other countries concentration levels remained constant or declined slightly. Concentration levels in Bangladesh and Pakistan in particular decreased by 16% from 1997 to 2009.

38.4 EXPLAINING THE RECENT CHANGES IN ASIA'S BANKING SECTOR STRUCTURE

While, as described above, most banking sectors in Asia have witnessed a decline in government participation and an increase in foreign bank presence, there are significant differences in the ways and speed in which these changes are being implemented. In addition, the development of the banking sector in the region is rooted in historical events, both political and economic. For instance, the legacy of bank nationalizations in India followed populist socialist movements, the state ownership of banks in China was established under the communist regime, and the reorganization and domestic and foreign sales of banks in East Asia was in response to the economic crisis. This section discusses the reform process in the main economies in East and South Asia.

38.4.1 China

China's entry into the World Trade Organization (WTO) in 2001 brought pressure to reform the largely government-owned and almost completely closed Chinese banking sector. During the 1990s, foreign banks were prohibited from conducting consumer banking in local currency with Chinese residents and, by the end of 1999, only 25 foreign banks had permission to conduct local currency business with Chinese enterprises. Following accession to the WTO, China allowed foreign banks to provide foreign currency services for Chinese residents and enterprises and in 2004 China opened its local currency market and allowed foreign banks to provide local currency services to Chinese enterprises in selected cities and areas. The retail market was supposed to be opened for foreign banks in December 2006; however, in late 2006, the Chinese government imposed the additional requirement that banks had to incorporate locally in order to cater to Chinese residents, delaying foreign banks' access to consumers. This notwithstanding, in April 2007, four foreign banks (Citigroup, HSBC, Standard Chartered, and Bank of East Asia) received approval from Chinese regulators and began accepting deposits in renminbi (RMB) from Chinese residents (Berger, Hasan, and Zhou, 2009).

Chinese regulators have also relaxed the rules concerning foreign acquisition of domestic banks. Since 2003, foreigners can collectively own up to 25% of any domestic bank but individual investors are limited to between 5% and 20% ownership, subject to regulatory approval. Following these changes, foreign strategic investors have acquired stakes in four of the top five banks in China, as well as in other smaller banks. In August 2004, the Hong Kong Shanghai Banking Corporation (HSBC) acquired a 19.9% stake of Bank of Communications. On June 17, 2005, Bank of America reached a deal to buy a 9% stake in China Construction Bank. Also in 2005, Royal Bank of Scotland and Temasek each acquired a 10% stake in Bank of China, while in 2006, Goldman Sachs, Allianz AG, and American Express agreed to buy a total 10% stake in the Industrial and Commercial Bank of China.

In an effort to improve the management and governance of Chinese banks, regulators have also recently allowed banks to list on stock exchanges. Between 2005 and 2006, Bank of Communications, Bank of China, China Construction Bank, and the Industrial and Commercial Bank of China had successful initial public offerings in the Hong Kong and Shanghai stock markets, raising over $40 billion in total.

38.4.2 The Rest of East Asia

The East Asian crisis began in Thailand in mid-1997, when an ailing financial sector, an export slowdown, and large increases in Central Bank credit to weak financial institutions triggered a run on the local banks. The crisis quickly spread to Indonesia and Korea, as common vulnerabilities and changes in international sentiment resulted in large capital outflows. East Asian governments were initially slow to address the growing distress in the banking sector (Kho and Stulz, 2000). At first, the governments tried to keep insolvent institutions afloat by injecting liquidity. This strategy, however, incurred large (and unpopular) fiscal costs. The governments' delayed and sometimes partial responses to the crisis caused financial turbulence and runs on financial institutions. The governments responded to the crisis in public confidence (in Indonesia and Thailand) and foreign currency outflows (in Korea) by issuing unlimited guarantees on their financial systems' liabilities. These guarantees stemmed the confidence crisis, but weakened governments' need to act comprehensively (Djankov, Jindra, and Klapper, 2005).

Responses and progress on financial restructuring varied considerably across the three crisis countries. Korea moved aggressively to strengthen its banking system through recapitalizations, nationalizations, removal of bad debt, and mergers. Although Korean officials closed over 100 non-bank financial institutions, no banks were shut down. Instead, 11 banks were merged with other domestic banks and four banks were nationalized (Delhaise, 1999).

Thailand adopted a market-based approach, allowing banks to raise capital over a longer time period. The Thai authorities closed down two-thirds of the finance companies but allowed banks a transitional period to raise capital through phased-in tighter loan provisioning requirements. At the same time, the government offered to inject Tier-1 capital, subject to the condition that any bank accepting public money would have to satisfy certain stringent conditions—for example, meeting strict loan-loss provisioning and making management changes. As a result, the Thai government was only required to shut down one bank. In addition, three banks were merged with other domestic banks and four banks were nationalized.

Of the three crisis countries, Indonesia has made the least progress in reforming its banking sector. By October 1999, 64 small banks were closed down, 12 banks were nationalized, and nine of the large banks were recapitalized. However, most financial institutions remained insolvent or undercapitalized. In response, the government guaranteed deposits of all Indonesian banks and nominated the Central Bank to act as a paying agent for depositors of the closed banks.

In addition, all three crisis countries reformed existing bank regulations to permit foreign banks to purchase domestic banks shortly following the crisis. The expected benefits of this measure were to infuse foreign capital and bring banking expertise.

However, as discussed above and in previous chapters, foreign bank participation in these countries is still low, relative to other developing regions.

38.4.3 India

Following independence in 1945, the Reserve Bank of India (RBI) was formed as the central bank and high priority was given to increasing credit to rural areas and small businesses. In 1955, the government took over the largest bank, the Imperial Bank of India, to form the State Bank of India (SBI). The State Bank of India Act in 1959 directed SBI to take over regional banks that were associated with local governments and make them subsidiaries of SBI, which were later named "associates." SBI is now the largest commercial banking organization in the country—and one of the largest in the world. SBI and its seven regional associates have a substantial rural branching footprint—of about 14,000 branches of these banks, 74% are located in rural and semi-urban areas (India Banks' Association, 2003).

Given continued pressure to extend bank credit to the agricultural and small business sectors, the Indian government nationalized 14 large banks in 1969 and another six in 1980 to redirect credit to "underserved" sectors and populations. Unlike SBI, nationalized banks remained corporate entities and retained most of their management and staff. Although their boards of directors were replaced by the state, appointees included representatives from both the government and private industry (Banerjee, Cole, and Duflo, 2005). RBI continued to fix interest rates on loans, and a significant portion of nationalized banks' deposit bases were redirected to support government expenditures through statutory measures that required banks to maintain specified fractions of their total deposits as cash balances with RBI and additional fractions in government and quasi-government securities. These lending restrictions and other RBI regulations affected the extension of credit by Indian banks (Bhaumik and Piesse, 2005). However, the nationalized banks continue to the present day to maintain relationships with large firms that begun prior to nationalization.

Banking sector liberalization and deregulation in India started in the early 1990s as part of a comprehensive reform agenda. This included permission to establish de novo banks and the entry of foreign banks, the deregulation of branch expansion, and the privatization of some state-owned banks. Interest rates were also liberalized and banks were permitted to invest in equity. However, commercial banks are still required to make loans to "priority sectors" at below market rates. These sectors consist largely of agriculture, exporters, and small businesses.[2]

Most foreign banks began operating in the 1990s under a license to open branches and are permitted to take deposits and provide credit in accordance with local banking laws and RBI regulations.[3] As of 2005, 33 foreign banks operated in India, but accounted for fewer than 0.5% of bank branches, 5% of deposits, and less than 7% of assets (Federal Reserve Bank of San Francisco, 2005; and *Hindu Times*, 2007, respectively). Foreign banks have generally not purchased shares of local Indian banks, since, prior to 2006, foreign banks were restricted to a ceiling of 10% of voting rights, even though foreign banks could legally own up to 74% of equity. Foreign banks have typically focused their operations in the top 25 cities in the country, probably due in part to restrictions on branch expansion;[4] they also generally use more modern equipment, pay higher salaries, and attract better-trained employees (IndiaMart, 2007).

In 2005, the government announced reforms to foreign banking laws that will be gradually implemented between 2005 and 2009 and will allow foreign banks to establish or convert existing operations into wholly owned subsidiaries. In addition, the RBI raised the limit of foreign direct investment in private banks to 74% from 49% and announced "roadmap" plans to amend the Banking Regulation Act to allow for the voting rights of foreign banks to reflect their ownership level, eliminating the current 10% cap. In June 2009, RBI announced

---

[2] Reforms in 2007 permit banks to hold securitized portfolios of priority loans, but this still effectively directs credit away from private commercial lending.

[3] A few foreign banks, such as Standard Chartered, have had limited operations in India for decades.

[4] Foreign banks currently operate only on a branch-license basis under which they are required to keep locally US $25 million in capital for the first three branches. Further expansion does not require additional capital, but requires RBI approval, which is often difficult to receive.

that permission for foreign banks to acquire any private bank will be delayed because of the global financial crisis. At that point, wholly owned subsidiaries will be allowed to list or dilute their stake to 74% through an IPO or offer for sale. Regardless of the decline in Indian markets and bank stock prices in 2008, there remains popular support for reform. For example, the Raghuram Rajan 2008 Committee on Financial Sector Reform strongly endorses the abolition of branch licensing and more liberal permission for bank takeovers and mergers.

Private banks are primarily de novo entrants that were granted banking licenses during the financial liberalization in the early 1990s. A total of 25 de novo private banks began operations between 1994 and 2000. There are also a small number of incumbent private banks that existed before 1990 and some state-owned institutions that have been successfully privatized. An example of the latter is ICICI, which was formed in 1955 as a state-owned institution at the initiative of the Government of India and the World Bank to create a development financial institution for providing medium- and long-term project financing to Indian businesses. During the 1990s, ICICI was privatized and evolved into a private, full-service bank and is now India's second largest bank, offering a wide range of services to retail and corporate customers.

To summarize, although there are numerous foreign banks in India, they have relatively few branches and accounts and also have fewer deposits and assets than the other types. Nationalized banks are the largest type, as measured by number of branches, accounts, deposits, and assets. The state-owned banks combined—SBI plus the nationalized banks—dominate the banking sector with about 80% of deposits and assets.

38.4.4 Pakistan

In 1974, the banking industry in Pakistan—which was predominately owned by the private sector—was nationalized following political pressure to break up the large and powerful ownership holdings (in both the industrial and banking sectors) held by a few business groups. For more than 27 years the banking sector remained closed to the private sector. In addition, the foreign exchange market was highly regulated through a system of direct exchange control over suppliers and users of foreign exchange.

In late 1996, the banking system was on the verge of a crisis. A World Bank report summarized the problems that plague many state-dominated banking systems:

In late 1996, Pakistan's banking system was on the verge of a crisis. Political interference vitiated the financial intermediation function of the banking system and borrowers expected not to repay loans they took, especially from the state-owned banks. Overstaffing and over-branching and undue interference by labor unions in bank personnel and operations resulted in large operating losses. Poor disclosure standards abetted corruption by window-dressing the true picture of banks (World Bank, 2000).

In 2000, the government of Pakistan began a process of banking reform. The objective of the reform package was to increase competition among financial institutions and markets, revise banking laws to strengthen bank governance and supervision, and adopt a market-based indirect system of monetary, exchange, and credit management for better allocation of financial resources (Husain, 2003). This sector, which had been fully dominated by nationalized commercial banks, was opened up to the private sector: 14 new domestic private commercial banks and 16 private investment banks were established, and 19 foreign commercial banks began operating in the country. In addition, four out of the five nationalized commercial banks were privatized. Following the privatization of Habib Bank—the largest Pakistani bank—in 2004, the market share of public sector banks was reduced to 20%, with the remaining 80% of banking assets in the hands of private banks. This is a remarkable accomplishment for a country which only a decade ago had almost 90% of banking assets under government ownership and control and, as previously discussed, few countries in the region have accomplished such a feat.

38.5 EVIDENCE ON THE IMPLICATIONS OF RECENT BANKING SECTOR STRUCTURE CHANGES IN ASIA

While changes in the ownership structure of the Asian banking sectors are still underway, it is interesting to survey the evidence available so far. For the most part, studies have tested for differences in performance among bank ownership types and evaluated the implications of recent ownership changes for bank efficiency and bank credit availability.

Cross-country studies on the performance of banks in Asia have generally found a positive association between foreign bank ownership and bank performance, though some empirical issues remain. Using data on commercial banks in Hong Kong, Indonesia, Korea, Malaysia, the Philippines, Singapore, and Thailand between 1994 and 2004, Laeven (2005) finds that foreign-owned banks exhibited significantly stronger performance than state-owned banks in terms of their operating income relative to total assets. In fact, Laeven finds that even after controlling for a variety of country-level policies and bank-level diversification measures, there exists a roughly one-to-one correspondence between increases in foreign ownership and increases in bank performance. A caveat to Laeven's measure of bank performance is that it assumes that all banks are profit maximizers, and that higher operating income relative to assets means better performance. State-owned banks, however, may have certain social objectives that are not tied to operating income, such as lending to certain developing sectors. Nonetheless, Laeven does find that, based on the same measure of performance, privately owned banks did not outperform state-owned ones in terms of their operating income relative to total assets. Moreover, this work builds on additional evidence provided by Laeven (2005) that foreign-owned banks not only enjoyed stronger profit efficiency in East Asia, but they did so while maintaining portfolios with less risk. Using data-envelopment analysis for a sample of commercial banks in Indonesia, Korea, Malaysia, the Philippines, and Thailand between 1992 and 1996, Laeven (1999) shows that those banks whose portfolios reflected larger risks—primarily domestic banks—were also more likely to be restructured at the time of the Asian financial crisis.

Focusing on profit efficiency as their measure of performance, Williams and Nguyen (2005) study a similar cross-country set of banks between 1990 and 2003, finding that foreign banks did enjoy stronger overall performance, but with significant lags before these performance gains were realized. In addition, the authors temper their results by point-ing out that banks selected for foreign acquisition had the greatest profit efficiencies prior to acquisition, hence highlighting a selection bias. Bank privatization, on the other hand, did yield some efficiency gains that were realized much sooner than was the case with foreign acquisitions. While there is similar evidence that governments did privatize their best-performing banks, these banks increased their profit efficiency in the period after their privatization significantly more than non-privatized banks.

While cross-country studies have shown a somewhat consistent relationship between bank ownership and bank performance, the evidence from within-country studies in Asia is very mixed. This is especially the case when measuring the impact of banking sector deregu-lation, where even studies within the same country have shown contradictory results.

Studies of the Chinese banking sector have mostly focused on comparing the perfor-mance of the "Big Four" banks—the Agricultural Bank of China, the Bank of China, the China Construction Bank, and the Industrial and Commercial Bank of China—relative to majority state-owned, majority foreign-owned, and other joint-equity banks. Studies focus-ing on the cost efficiency of banks (Chen, Skully, and Brown, 2005; Fu and Heffernan, 2007; and Kumbhakar and Wang, 2007) have yielded mixed evidence: Chen, Skully, and Brown (2005) find that the Big Four banks outperformed medium-sized joint-equity banks in terms of cost efficiency, while others (Fu and Heffernan 2007; and Kumbhakar and Wang, 2007) find that the Big Four are less cost efficient than the joint-equity banks over a similar time-period. These cost-efficiency studies also identify contradictory results on the effects of in financial deregulation the mid-1990s. Chen, Skully, and Brown (2005) find that dereg-ulation had positive efficiency implications, while Kumbhakar and Wang (2007) find no sig-nificant improvements in efficiency due to the deregulation.

Moving away from cost-efficiency measures, papers such as Berger et al. (2005) and Yao and Jiang (2007) focus instead on profit efficiency, arguing that this measure cap-tures both cost and revenue performance. Analyzing a panel of 38 Chinese banks over the 1994–2003 period, Berger, Hasan, and Zhou (2009) find significant differences in profit efficiency due to the identity of banks' majority owners. Banks with majority foreign own-ership were the most efficient, followed in order by private domestically owned banks, non-Big Four majority state-owned banks, and the Big Four. The identity of minority owners yields even more dramatic effects on profit efficiency—for example, the presence of a minority foreign stake in non-Big Four state-owned banks is associated with an effi-ciency level almost 20% points higher than enjoyed by other non-Big Four state-owned banks. To address selection issues, Berger et al. (2008) use a difference-in-difference approach to examine the change in efficiency after minority foreign investments are made, finding significant efficiency improvements for both private domestic banks and non-Big Four state-owned banks. Specifically, they compare the four-year pre-and post-average efficiency change for banks with and without foreign ownership. Hence, they are able to control for any industry-wide efficiency improvements that affected all banks during their sample period. Nonetheless, as in other studies, the possibility of selection due to foreign investors' expectations of future efficiency improvements by these banks remains a poten-tial source of upward bias.

Yao and Jiang (2007) offer complementary findings in studying Chinese commercial banks between 1995 and 2005, noting that state-owned banks continue to lag behind in terms of efficiency, despite overall improvements in banking efficiency. Moreover, Yao and

Jiang find that foreign acquisition is associated with long-term efficiency improvements, but find no such evidence for banks that undergo an IPO.

In the Philippines, Unite and Sullivan (2003) find that while the relaxation of entry regulations for foreign banks generated cost-efficiency gains (reductions in operating expenses), the relaxation of limits on foreign ownership stakes did not produce significant benefits. Studying Thailand's banking system between 1990 and 1997, Williams and Intarachote (2002) find that, following liberalization, entry by foreign banks did increase, but, over the entire period, the efficiency of the entire banking system actually regressed. This is particularly striking because Williams and Intarachote examine alternative profit efficiency,[5] and not only the cost side. While it appears that Japanese-owned banks fared somewhat better in terms of their profit efficiency, there is little evidence that foreign-owned banks more generally enjoyed any efficiency advantages over domestic banks. Looking at foreign bank efficiency after the Thai reforms of foreign entry regulations in 1997, Rajan and Montreevat (2001) do offer some casual albeit unsystematic evidence that greater entry by foreign banks did involve the introduction of new technologies and lower operating costs. However, none of these within-country studies can entirely distinguish whether the contemporaneous improvements in efficiency among domestic banks were related to increased competition from foreign banks or other facets of the reform process.

In India, Sanyal and Shankar (2005) offer evidence that the expansion of private ownership in India's banking sector has not been causally connected to greater bank efficiency. They find that following the mid-1990s' deregulations, state-owned banks gained as much as private banks in most measures of productivity and performance. In contrast, other research on the impact of deregulation in India has yielded some evidence of a positive relationship between foreign or private ownership and bank performance. Sahoo, Sengupta, and Mandal (2007) examine the productivity performance trends of Indian commercial banks between 1997 and 2005 using data envelopment analysis, finding that private banks enjoy greater cost efficiency than nationalized banks. In addition, the authors find that foreign banks outperform nationalized banks in both cost-based and price-based measures of performance. Similar results are offered by Reddy (2005), who finds that foreign and newly formed private banks enjoyed advantages in overall technical efficiency between 1996 and 2002. Ghosh, Harding, and Phani (2006), meanwhile, look at changes in stock market prices of shares of both private and public sector banks around the Indian Government's removal of limits on foreign ownership in commercial banks. Since they condition these stock market prices on the actual assets and income of the banks, Ghosh, Harding, and Phani can assess the extent to which valuation gains were due to expectations over each bank's improvement under foreign ownership (i.e., a 'takeover premium'). Their results show that the benefits of foreign takeover were indeed concentrated among inefficient, poorly managed banks with lower existing market valuations. Ataullah, Cockerill, and Le (2004), meanwhile, also use data envelopment analysis in studying commercial banks in both India and Pakistan between 1988 and 1998, finding that India's financial liberalization led to efficiency improvements for both public sector and private sector banks. In Pakistan, however, public sector banks did not improve their pure technical efficiency following liberalization. Finally, Casu, Ferrari,

---

[5] Alternative profit efficiency captures the profit rather than simply the cost-based efficiency story, but it can be estimated even when certain conditions required for standard profit efficiency estimation are not met.

and Zhao (2013) study the impact of regulatory reform on Total Factor Productivity growth in Indian banks and find that the banking industry experienced sustained productivity growth due to technological progress in the late 1990s and early 2000s.

More specific studies of the relationship between banks and firms in Asia have produced intriguing evidence that foreign-owned and private domestic banks operate quite differently from state-owned banks. For example, Berger et al. (2008) study the role of bank ownership type in shaping relationships among firms and banks in India, finding that firms which maintain relationships with foreign banks differ from those with ties to state-owned banks in a number of ways: they are more likely to maintain multiple relationships, interact with a larger number of banks, and diversify their relationships across bank ownership types. Further, papers such as Mian (2006) in Pakistan and Gormley (2010) in India show that foreign banks can be limited in how far they can lend to local firms. Mian (2006) shows evidence that foreign banks have a tougher time lending to informationally opaque firms and are less likely to lend based on "soft" information. This characteristic, in turn, makes it difficult for foreign banks to renegotiate and recover bad loans, a process that requires strong soft information skills.

In a similar vein, Gormley (2010) finds evidence that foreign bank entry in India yielded a reallocation of loans toward the most profitable firms. He finds that following the deregulation of foreign entry in 1994, the entry of a foreign bank in a particular location was associated with a significant reduction in the likelihood that the average firm in that location obtained a long-term loan. This was particularly true among firms associated with business groups for which moral hazard related to tunneling and informational asymmetries may be most pronounced, and thus those for which foreign banks may be at a particular disadvantage in serving. Based on this evidence, Gormley points out that the growth in foreign bank ownership in India may generate further market segmentation and may not be sufficient for—and in fact may counteract—the expansion of access to credit.

Apart from studying the general and specific effects of bank ownership type on performance, a number of studies in Asia have examined the differential response of foreign banks to the Asian financial crisis. The bulk of the evidence suggests that these banks increased the stability of the banking system rather than weakened it. Looking at 26 domestic banks and 59 foreign banks operating in Korea between 1994 and 1999, Jeon and Miller (2005) find that while the returns on assets and equity of Korean banks deteriorated dramatically in 1998, foreign-owned banks experienced no such drop-off (with a statistically significant difference in their performance). Extending this sample through 2005, Jeon, Miller, and Yi (2007) use a generalized Bennet dynamic decomposition to assess the extent to which aggregate bank performance was due to adjustments within banks, reallocations between banks, and entry or exit of banks. The authors confirm that foreign banks enjoyed a higher return on equity both before and during the crisis, although domestic Korean banks experienced an advantage after the crisis. Nonetheless, there is not much evidence that restructuring among either foreign or domestic banks played a significant role in driving aggregate performance, which instead mostly reflected within-bank changes. In a similar vein, Detragiache and Gupta (2004) study 39 Malaysian banking institutions between 1996 and 2000 and find no evidence that foreign banks scaled down their operations faster than domestic banks during the crisis, contradictory to concerns that foreign banks are likely to flee volatile emerging markets during crises. The authors do find that while the foreign-owned banks mainly active in Asia performed similarly to domestic banks during the crisis, non-Asia-oriented foreign banks enjoyed profits that were significantly higher than domestic banks. On the other hand, evidence on the entry decisions of foreign banks suggests that Asian banks do in fact enjoy an advantage over non-Asian banks when operating in or entering other countries in the region. For example, Leung, Digby, and Young (2003) use survival analysis to study the entry decisions of banks into China between 1985 and 1996, finding that Asian banks were much more likely to establish a branch in China than non-Asian banks (and to do so earlier).

In conclusion, research on the effects of bank ownership in Asia has produced mixed findings. Foreign and private ownership in general is associated with stronger bank performance, particularly in the context of cross-country samples. However, the effects on financial access are less clear, with many studies in the region identifying limited positive effects, and some even identifying significant negative effects on access. It is worth noting that although much of the research on the effects of foreign and private ownership in banking has focused on efficiency gains, the contribution of such ownership types can often happen by changing the nature of services being offered, not only by providing existing services more efficiently. He and Fan (2004), for example, point out that foreign entry into China's banking sector has introduced the use of credit card services, financial derivatives, and cross-selling of investment and insurance products, among other features. However, further study of the effects of these new product lines for Asian banks remains warranted.

38.6 EVIDENCE ON THE IMPACT OF THE GLOBAL FINANCIAL CRISIS ON ASIA ECONOMIES

The recent global financial crisis had a far-reaching impact on the world economy, though its effects on Asian markets were relatively muted compared to other regions.[6] Part of the reason was that the banking sectors in many Asian countries, even in large economies such as India, were not significantly exposed to US derivatives and subprime mortgages. In Thailand, for example, a 2009 paper by the Bank of International Settlements reports that bank balance sheets had less than 1% exposure to US-based collateralized debt obligations (CDOs) (BIS, 2009). Likewise, even banks in other countries such as Singapore, which had greater exposure to CDOs, additionally held safe assets as insurance and, hence, were significantly less leveraged than their counterparts in the United States and Europe.

---

[6] Of the estimated US $300 billion total write-downs and credit losses worldwide, write-downs in Asia are expected to be less than 6% (estimates by Crisil consulting firm, an S & P subsidiary, reported by *United News of India*, May 9, 2008).

This is not to say that Asia has not suffered some of the repercussions of the global credit crunch. Interbank lending rates have risen, stock markets have experienced severe drops in value, foreign exchange reserves have fallen, and Asian central banks have been required to pump liquidity into their financial systems. Pakistan has been among the hardest hit countries and has been forced to enter into a Stand-By Arrangement with the IMF for US $7.6 billion.

Nevertheless, Asian financial sectors were not entirely insulated from the aftermath of the crisis and eventually suffered from a general loss of consumer confidence, dwindling demand from developed economies, and reduced capital inflows. Goldstein and Xie (2009) present evidence on growth declines in emerging markets in Asia as a result of the crisis, but also highlight that these declines were not as severe as those experienced during the earlier Asian financial crisis of 1997–1998. The authors argue that while Asian economies suffered declines in exports and equity prices as well as spikes in indices of financial stress, governments in the region did not have to commit as much resources and financial support to bail out troubled financial institutions as in the US and other large advanced economies.[7] Further, international reserves, exchange rates, and domestic credit flows were relatively less affected.

The public sector was also quick to intervene in Asian economies, with several central banks cutting their reserve requirement ratios, with the largest cuts made in Sri Lanka, Vietnam and India, followed by China, Korea, Indonesia, Taipei, and Thailand (Kawai, 2009). In order to mitigate the risk of the crisis spilling over to their local financial systems, several Asian economies, Korea and Singapore in particular, tapped the US Federal Reserve's US$30 billion line of credit to shore up their foreign exchange reserves in advance. These steps led to a notable decline in money market rates. Finally, many countries instituted broad protection measures for bank deposits to forestall runs on banks, and some even guaranteed bank loans (Kawai, Mayes, and Morgan, 2012). The Reserve Bank of India, for example, established refinancing facilities for loans for housing, export credit, and SMEs (Sinha, 2012); the Korean government set up a debt stabilization fund to provide liquidity to non-bank financial institutions and SMEs (BIS, 2009); and Hong Kong, Korea, and Japan established facilities for additional capital to locally incorporated licensed banks (Kawai, 2009).

While the literature on the impact of the global financial crisis on Asian economies summarizes the general impact and preventative measures undertaken by governments, rigorous evidence on differential impacts, for example by bank type or size, is surprisingly sparse. Ree (2011) is an exception, and uses Bankscope data from ten low-income and emerging market economies in Asia to analyze the impacts of the financial crisis on the Asian banking sector. He finds that although the average impacts were muted, cross border interbank capital flows of the largest Asian banks were significantly affected by the crisis, which led to a large decline in loan growth relative to deposit growth.

In the next section of this chapter, we take a similar approach and present a new analysis of the differential response of Asian banks by ownership type, specifically differentiating between foreign and domestic banks. This analysis is important especially since the academic literature on banking suggests that foreign bank lending tends to play an important role in crisis contagion (Cetorelli and Goldberg, 2011; de Haas et al., 2012). Xu (2012) also contributes to addressing this question and uses Bankscope data to differentiate the impacts of the financial crisis between foreign banks in Asia with ownership originating in the US and Europe, and regional foreign banks with ownership in other parts of Asia. Xu's

---

[7] G3 economies represent 60% of final demand for Asian exports. The IMF World Economic Outlook Update (2008) predicts that growth in developing Asia will drop from 10% in 2007 to 8.3% in 2008, and 7.1% in 2009. The Asian Development Bank predicts an even slower growth rate for 2008 and 2009: 7.5% and 7.2%, respectively (ADB, Asian Development Outlook Update, 2008).

analysis shows that growth and momentum among regional foreign banks in Asia remained strong during and after the crisis, whereas loan growth among global foreign banks reduced sharply.

We now turn to an analysis of loan growth between foreign and domestic banks in Asia.

38.7 EMPIRICAL ANALYSIS OF BANK LENDING IN ASIA DURING THE GLOBAL CRISIS

To examine the behavior of bank loans in Asia before and during the global crisis and to contrast loan growth by foreign banks vis-à-vis domestic banks, we follow Cull and Martinez-Peria's (2012) analysis for Eastern Europe and Latin America and estimate a model to explain the annual growth of total gross loans (expressed in dollars). Our main variables of interest indicate foreign ownership 2008 and 2009, which capture the impact of foreign bank ownership on loan growth during the recent crisis, relative to the lending behavior of domestic banks throughout this episode. We also control for other bank characteristics that can also impact loan growth (such as size, capital, liquidity, and funding structure).[8]

We find that while there was no significant decline in bank lending at the start of the global crisis in 2008, bank loan growth fell by almost 50% points during 2009. Relative to domestic banks, foreign banks' loan growth in Asia fell by more than 13% points. These results are robust to the exclusion of China and India, which account for a third of the observations in our baseline estimations. We also estimate the sample of only the largest economies in Asia (those we focus on in Table 38.1, that is, Bangladesh, China, India, Indonesia, Korea, Malaysia, Pakistan, Philippines, Thailand) and find results consistent with our earlier findings. Overall, we find that lending declined in Asia during the crisis and that foreign banks experienced a greater decline in loan growth relative to domestic banks. These results mirror those found for Eastern Europe and to some extent Latin America (Cull and Martinez-Peria, 2012; and de Haas et al., 2012), as well as in a large number of other developed and developing countries (Claessens and van Horen, 2012).

---

[8] Bank level data on total assets, bank equity, liquid assets and deposits to total liabilities come from Bankscope, a commercial dataset provided by Bureau van Dijk. Ownership information was gathered from a variety of sources including Bankscope, Fitch Research, the Bankers' Almanac, bank websites, Central Bank publications, parent company's reports and banking regulation agencies. To minimize the influence of outliers, we exclude observations in the top and bottom 1% of lending growth. Similarly, we exclude from our analysis observations for bank equity, liquidity and funding structure that fall in the same 1% range. Our final database includes 1988 observations covering 567 banks operating in 14 countries in Asia.

In additional analysis, we include bank fixed effects and country × year fixed effects to control for country characteristics (e.g., macroeconomic growth, exchange rate changes, etc.) that might have changed over time and affected loan growth.

38.8 CONCLUSIONS

This chapter has described the recent changes in bank ownership structure in Asia, and has offered a detailed account of the reform process in the main economies in the region, evaluating the evidence on the implications of these changes before and during the global financial crisis.

Important changes in the structure of the banking sector structure have recently taken place in Asia. Across the board, we have witnessed a trend toward less government ownership of banks and greater foreign bank presence. However, the largest countries in the region, such as China, India, and Indonesia, still have a way to go in terms of fostering private and foreign bank ownership and offering a level playing field for all types of banking institutions.

The existing literature analyzing the implications of recent ownership changes in Asia produces missed findings when it comes to performance improvements and quite negative in terms of the effects of foreign ownership on access to finance. These findings stand in contrast to the evidence from Eastern Europe and Latin America, where many studies have documented the benefits from private and foreign ownership, especially in terms of performance and efficiency improvements (see Chapters 33 and 34, this volume; and Cull and Martinez-Peria, 2007). What explains these differences across regions? This is an important question beyond the scope of this chapter. However, we offer two potential explanations. First, while reforms promoting foreign and private ownership were implemented in the early to mid-1990s in Latin America and Eastern Europe, these changes are very new to Asia. It may take time for economies in Asia to see the benefits that the other two regions have already experienced. Furthermore, in practical terms, more data might be needed for empirical studies to detect whatever benefits these changes might bring. Second, the extent of reforms (i.e., how far they have gone in producing ownership changes) has been quite different in Asia relative to Latin America and Eastern Europe. While these regions drastically altered the structure of their banking sectors, promoting majority private and foreign ownership, Asia so far has taken a more piecemeal approach. We hope that future research will establish the merit of these proposed explanations and shed light on the question of why foreign and private ownership seemed to have had different effects in Asia relative to other regions.

What has been the impact of the crisis on Asia? The existing evidence indicates that though Asian economies were affected by the recent global crisis the impact was less deep than that of the 1997 Asian crisis and also than the impact in other regions of the world. Nonetheless, our analysis of bank lending suggests that bank lending growth declined in Asia during the crisis and that foreign bank loan growth declined significantly more than domestic bank lending.

TECHNICAL APPENDIX

EMPIRICAL ANALYSIS OF BANK LENDING IN ASIA DURING THE GLOBAL CRISIS

To examine the behavior of bank loans in Asia before and during the global crisis and to contrast loan growth by foreign banks vis-à-vis domestic banks, we follow Cull and Martinez Peria's (2012) analysis for Eastern Europe and Latin America and estimate equation (1) below over the period 2005-2009:

$$\Delta L_{i,t,j} = Foreign_{i,t,j} + Crisis\_2008_t + Crisis\_2009_t + Crisis\_2008_t \times Foreign_{i,t,j}$$
$$+ Crisis\_2009_t \times Foreign_{i,t,j} + X_{i,t-1,j} + Crisis\_2008_t \times X_{i,t-1,j} + Crisis\_2009_t$$
$$\times X_{i,t-1,j} + \alpha_j + u_{i,t,j}$$

where $\Delta Li,t,j$ is the annual growth of total gross loans (expressed in dollars) for bank i at time t in country j. *Foreign* is a dummy that takes the value of one for foreign-owned banks, respectively. *Crisis_2008* and *Crisis_2009* are dummies that equal one during 2008 and 2009, respectively. Both dummies are zero in all other periods. The interaction of the foreign dummy with the crisis dummies capture the impact foreign bank ownership on loan growth during the crisis, relative to the lending behavior of domestic banks throughout this episode. $Xi,t-1,j$ is a matrix of bank characteristics that can also impact loan growth (such as size, capital, liquidity, and funding structure). These variables are lagged one period to avoid endogeneity concerns. We also include the interaction of this matrix and the crisis dummies to allow the impact of bank characteristics on loan growth to change during the crisis period. α_j are country fixed effects. In additional analysis, we include bank fixed effects and country×year fixed effects to control for country characteristics (e.g., macroeconomic growth, exchange rate changes, etc.) that might have changed over time and affected loan growth.

Bank level data on total assets, bank equity, liquid assets and deposits to total liabilities come from Bankscope, a commercial dataset provided by Bureau van Dijk. Ownership information was gathered from a variety of sources including Bankscope, Fitch Research, The Bankers' Almanac, bank web-sites, Central Bank publications, parent company's reports and banking regulation agencies.

To minimize the influence of outliers, we exclude observations in the top and bottom 1% of lending growth. Similarly, we exclude from our analysis observations for bank equity, liquidity and funding structure that fall in the same 1% range. Our final database includes 1988 observations covering 567 banks operating in 14 countries in Asia: Bangladesh, Cambodia, China, India, Indonesia, Korea, Malaysia, Mongolia, Nepal, Pakistan, Philippines, Sri Lanka, Thailand, and Vietnam.

Table A.1 shows our baseline results. Table A.2 presents results for the largest economies in Asia (those we focus on in Table 38.1, i.e., Bangladesh, China, India, Indonesia, Korea, Malaysia, Pakistan, Philippines, Thailand).

Table A.1 Baseline estimations for bank loan growth in Asia during 2005–2009

Variables	(1)	(2)	(3)
Foreign	-0.0336	-0.0278	
	(0.0268)	(0.0273)	
Crisis_2008	0.0385		
	(0.192)		
Crisis_2009	-0.506***		
	(0.166)		
Foreign × Crisis_2008	0.0182	0.000925	0.00634
	(0.0396)	(0.0374)	(0.0335)
Foreign × Crisis_2009	-0.130***	-0.140***	-0.138***
	(0.0380)	(0.0386)	(0.0349)
Equity ratio (equity to assets) at t-1	0.00287	0.00263	-0.000429
	(0.00197)	(0.00213)	(0.00371)
Log of assets at t-1	-0.0126**	-0.0150**	-0.233***
	(0.00594)	(0.00689)	(0.0532)
Liquid to total assets at t-1	0.00137	0.00146	0.00691***
	(0.00101)	(0.00114)	(0.00116)
Customer deposits to total liabilities at t-1	-0.000213	-6.51e-05	-0.000399
	(0.000589)	(0.000593)	(0.000951)
Equity ratio at t-1 × Crisis_2008	-0.00324	-0.00145	0.00239
	(0.00336)	(0.00366)	(0.00326)
Equity ratio at t-1 × Crisis_ 2009	0.00247	0.00256	0.00598*
	(0.00268)	(0.00288)	(0.00325)
Log of assets at t-1 × Crisis_2008	-0.0169*	0.00253	0.00691
	(0.00912)	(0.0101)	(0.00814)
Log of assets at t-1 × Crisis_2009	0.0187**	0.0102	0.0117
	(0.00763)	(0.00885)	(0.00812)
Liquid to total assets × Crisis_2008	0.000782	-0.000885	0.000693
	(0.00152)	(0.00195)	(0.00192)
Liquid to total assets × Crisis_2009	0.000269	0.000680	0.00245
	(0.00151)	(0.00173)	(0.00206)
Customer deposits to total liabilities Crisis_2008	0.00102	0.000852	0.000398
	(0.000852)	(0.000851)	(0.000891)
Customer deposits to total liabilities Crisis_2009	0.00218**	0.00199**	0.00215***
	(0.000869)	(0.000878)	(0.000829)
Constant	0.303***	0.182	3.186***
	(0.112)	(0.132)	(0.832)
Country FE	Yes		
Country*year FE		Yes	Yes
Bank FE			Yes
Observations	1988	1988	1964
R-squared	0.181	0.260	0.362
Number of banks			567

Table A.2 Estimations for bank loan growth in the largest economies of Asia

Variables	(1)	(2)	(3)
Foreign	-0.00813	-0.00856	
	(0.0289)	(0.0294)	
Crisis_2008	0.185		
	(0.226)		
Crisis_2009	-0.362*		
	(0.198)		
Foreign × Crisis_2008	-0.0134	-0.0153	-0.00634
	(0.0441)	(0.0411)	(0.0340)
Foreign × Crisis_2009	-0.130***	-0.133***	-0.133***
	(0.0412)	(0.0402)	(0.0359)
Equity ratio (equity to assets) at t-1	0.00313	0.00280	-0.00170
	(0.00234)	(0.00247)	(0.00394)
Log of assets at t-1	-0.00681	-0.00941	-0.209***
	(0.00622)	(0.00678)	(0.0582)
Liquid to total assets at t-1	0.000605	0.00127	0.00619***
	(0.00118)	(0.00133)	(0.00122)
Customer deposits to total liabilities at t-1	0.000172	8.23e-05	-0.000393
	(0.000662)	(0.000668)	(0.000953)
Equity ratio at t-1 × Crisis_2008	-0.00462	-0.00213	0.00213
	(0.00381)	(0.00399)	(0.00285)
Equity ratio at t-1 × Crisis_2009	0.00105	0.00160	0.00468
	(0.00330)	(0.00340)	(0.00340)
Log of assets at t-1 × Crisis_2008	-0.0222**	-7.85e-05	0.00298
	(0.0109)	(0.0103)	(0.00775)
Log of assets at t-1 × Crisis_2009	0.0101	0.00614	0.00704
	(0.00884)	(0.00922)	(0.00834)
Liquid to total assets at t-1 × Crisis_2008	0.00138	-0.00168	0.000913
	(0.00170)	(0.00208)	(0.00184)
Liquid to total assets at t-1 × Crisis_ 2009	0.000842	0.000716	0.00306
	(0.00176)	(0.00197)	(0.00225)
Customer deposits to total liabilities at t-1 × Crisis_2008	0.000381	0.000719	-0.000204
	(0.000983)	(0.000968)	(0.000904)
Customer deposits to total liabilities at t-1 × Crisis_2009	0.00219**	0.00251**	0.00204**
	(0.00100)	(0.00102)	(0.000903)
Constant	0.196	0.0912	2.993***
	(0.124)	(0.138)	(0.905)
Country FE	Yes		
Country*year FE		Yes	Yes
Bank FE			Yes
Observations	1673	1673	1655
R-squared	0.148	0.214	0.313
Overall R2			0.0274
Number of banks			474

REFERENCES

Asian Development Bank (2008). *Asian Development Outlook Update*. Manila, Philippines: Asian Development Bank.

Ataullah, A., Cockerill, T., and Le, H. (2004). Financial Liberalization and Bank Efficiency: A Comparative Analysis of India and Pakistan, *Applied Economics* 36, 1915–1924.

Banerjee, A., Cole, S., and Duflo, E. (2005). *Banking Reform in India*, National Council for Applied Economic Research (NCAER), New Delhi and Brookings Institution, Washington, DC, India Policy Forum No. 1.

Barth, J. R.; Caprio Jr., G., and Levine, R. (2012). The Evolution and Impact of Bank Regulations, World Bank Policy Research Working Paper No. 6288.

Beck, T., Demirguc-Kunt, A., and Martinez-Peria, M. S. (2007). Reaching Out: Access to and Use of Banking Services across Countries, *Journal of Financial Economics* 85, 234–266.

Beck, T. and Honohan, P. (2007). *Making Finance Work for Africa*. Washington DC: World Bank.

Berger, A. N., Clarke, G., Cull, R., and Klapper, L. (2005). Corporate Governance and Bank Performance: A Joint Analysis of the Static, Selection, and Dynamic Effects of Domestic, Foreign and State Ownership, *Journal of Banking & Finance* 29, 2179–2221.

Berger, A. N., Hasan, I., and Zhou, M. (2009). Bank Ownership and Efficiency in China. What will Happen in the World's Largest Nation?, *Journal of Banking & Finance* 33, 113–130.

Berger, A. N., Klapper, L., Martinez-Peria, M. S., and Zaidi, R. (2008). Bank Ownership Type and Banking Relationship, *Journal of Financial Intermediation* 17, 37–6.

Bhaumik, S. K. and Piesse, J. (2005). The Risk Aversion of Banks in Emerging Credit Markets: Evidence from India, William Davidson Institute Working Paper No. 774.

BIS (Bank for International Settlements) (2009). The International Financial Crisis: Timeline, Impact and Policy Responses in Asia and the Pacific. BIS Representative Office for Asia and Pacific.

Bureau van Dijk (2012). *BankScope*. London: Bureau van Dijk.

Casu, B., Ferrari, A., and Zhao, T. (2013). Regulatory Reform and Productivity Changes in Indian Banking, *Review of Economics and Statistics* 95(3), 1066–1077.

Cetorelli, N. and Goldberg, L. (2011). Global Banks and International Shock Transmission: Evidence from the Crisis, *IMF Economic Review* 59, 41–76.

Chen, X., Skully, M., and Brown, M. (2005). Banking Efficiency in China: Application of DEA to Pre-and Post-Deregulations Era: 1993–2000, *China Economic Review* 16, 229–245.

Claessens, S. and van Horen, N. (2012). Foreign Banks, Trends, Impact and Financial Stability, IMF Working Paper No. 12/10.

Cull, R. and Martinez-Peria, M. S. (2007). Crises as Catalysts for Foreign Bank Activity in Emerging Markets. In: J. Robertson (Ed.), *Power and Politics After Financial Crises: Rethinking Foreign Opportunism in Emerging Markets*, 52–81, New York: Palgrave Macmillan.

Cull, R. and Martinez-Peria, M. S. (2012). Bank Ownership and Lending Patterns during the 2008-2009 Financial Crisis: Evidence from Latin America and Eastern Europe, World Bank Policy Research Working Paper No. 6195.

de Haas, R., Kominyenko, Y., Loukianova, E., and Pivorarsky, A. (2012). Foreign Banks and the Vienna Initiative: Turning Sinners into Saints?, EBRD Working Paper No. 143.

Delhaise, P. (1999). *Asia in Crisis: The Implosion of the Banking and Finance Systems*. 1st edition. New Jersey: John Wiley & Sons.

Detragiache, E. and Gupta, P. (2004). Foreign Banks in Emerging Market Crises: Evidence from Malaysia, IMF Working Paper No. 04/129.

Djankov, S., Jindra, J., and Klapper, L. (2005). Corporate Valuation and the Resolution of Bank Insolvency in East Asia, *Journal of Banking & Finance* 29, 2095–2118.

Federal Reserve Bank of San Francisco (2005). Indian Banking Reforms: A Changing Landscape for State-Owned and Foreign Banks, *Asia Focus* May.

Fu, X. and Heffernan, M. S. (2007). Cost X-Efficiency in China's Banking Sector, *China Economic Review* 18, 35–53.

Gelos, G. (2006). Bank Spreads in Latin America, IMF Working Paper No. 06/44.

Ghosh, A., Harding, J., and Phani, B. V. (2006). The Effect of Liberalization of Foreign Direct Investment (FDI) Limits on Domestic Stocks: Evidence from the Indian Banking Sector. Mimeo.

Goldstein, M. and Xie, D. (2009). The Impact of the Financial Crisis on Emerging Asia, Peterson Institute for International Economics Working Paper Series No. WP09-11.

Gormley, T. (2010). Banking Competition in Developing Countries: Does Foreign Bank Entry Improve Credit Access?, *Journal of Financial Intermediation* 19, 26–51.

He, L. and Fan, X. (2004). Foreign Banks in Post-WTO China: An Intermediate Assessment, *China and the World Economy* 12, 3–16.

Hindu Times (2007). Banking Reform: A Balancing Act, March 7.

Husain, I. (2003). Reforms of Public Sector Banks: Case Study of Pakistan. World Bank Conference on Transforming Public Sector Banks, Washington, DC, April 9.

Honohan, P. and Beck, T. (2007). Making Finance Work for Africa, World Bank Working Paper Number No. 6626.

Indian Banks' Association (2003). *Indian Banking Yearbook 2003*. Mumbai: Indian Banks' Association.

IndiaMart (2007). India Finance and Investment Guide, October 23.

IMF (International Monetary Fund) (2008). *World Economic Outlook Update*. Washington, DC: International Monetary Fund.

IMF (International Monetary Fund) (2012). *Financial Access Survey Data*. Washington, DC: International Monetary Fund.

Jeon, Y. and Miller, S. (2005). Performance of Domestic and Foreign Banks: The Case of Korea and the Asian Financial Crisis, *Global Economic Review* 34, 145–165.

Jeon, Y., Miller, S., and Yi, I. (2007). Performance Comparisons and the Role of Restructuring for Foreign and Domestic Banks. Mimeo.

Kawai, M. (2009). The Impact of the Global Financial Crisis on Asia and Asia's Response, Kiel, July 7, AEEF Conference Paper.

Kawai, M., Mayes, D., and Morgan, P. (2012). Implications of the Global Financial Crisis for Financial Reform and Regulation in Asia. Asian Development Bank Institute.

Kho, B. C. and Stulz, R. (2000). Banks, the IMF, and the Asian Crisis, *Pacific-Basin Finance Journal* 8, 177–216.

Kumbhakar, S. C. and Wang, D. (2007). Economic Reforms, Efficiency, and Productivity in Chinese Banking, *Journal of Regulatory Economics* 32, 105–129.

Laeven, L. (1999). Risk and Efficiency in East Asian Banks, World Bank Policy Research Working Paper No. 2255.

Laeven, L. (2005). Banking Sector Performance in East Asian Countries: The Effects of Competition, Diversification, and Ownership. Mimeo.

Leung, M., Digby, D., and Young, T. (2003). Entry of Foreign Banks in the People's Republic of China: A Survival Analysis, *Applied Economics* 35, 21–31.

Mian, A. (2006). Distance Constraints: The Limit of Foreign Lending in Poor Economies, *Journal of Finance* 61, 1465–1505.

Rajan, R. and Montreevat, S. (2001). Financial Crisis, Bank Restructuring, and Foreign Bank Entry: An Analytic Case Study of Thailand, Adelaide University Centre for International Economic Studies Working Paper No. 131.

Reddy, A. (2005). Technical Efficiency and Its Decomposition in Indian Banks in Post Liberalization. Indian Institute of Capital Markets Paper.

Ree, J. (2011). Impact of the Global Crisis on Banking Sector Soundness in Asian Low-Income Countries, IMF Working Paper No. 11/115.

Sahoo, B., Sengupta, J., and Mandal, A. (2007). Productive Performance Evaluation of the Banking Sector in India Using Data Envelopment Analysis, *International Journal of Operations Research*, 4, 63–79.

Sanyal, P. and Shankar, R. (2005). Financial Sector Reforms and Bank Efficiency in Developing Countries: Lessons from India. Brandeis University Working Paper.

Sinha, A. (2012). Impact of the International Banking Crisis on the Indian Financial System. Bank for International Settlements Working Paper.

Unite, A. and Sullivan, M. (2003). The Effect of Foreign Entry and Ownership Structure on the Philippine Domestic Banking Market, *Journal of Banking & Finance* 27, 2323–2345.

Williams, J. and Intarachote, T. (2002). Financial Liberalization and Profit Efficiency in the Thai Banking System, 1990–1997: The Case of Domestic and Foreign Banks. Mimeo.

Williams, J. and Nguyen, N. (2005). Financial Liberalization, Crisis, and Restructuring: A Comparative Study of Bank Performance and Bank Governance in South East Asia, *Journal of Banking & Finance* 29, 2119–2154.

World Bank (2000). Financial Sector Update, Washington, DC, May 31.

World Bank (2012). World Development Indicators, Washington DC, December.

Xu, Y. (2012). Foreign Bank Lending and Shock Transmission: The Case of Asia. Australian National University Working Paper.

Yao, S. and Jiang, C. (2007). The Effects of Governance Changes on Bank Efficiency in China: A Stochastic Distance Function Approach, University of Nottingham Research Paper No. 2007/19.

CHAPTER 39

BANKING IN TRANSITION COUNTRIES*

JOHN P. BONIN, IFTEKHAR HASAN, AND
PAUL WACHTEL

39.1 INTRODUCTION

BANKING in the transition countries is particularly interesting because banks played no economic role in planned Soviet-style economies while the financial sectors in most transition countries are now dominated by banks rather than equity markets. The first phase of transition banking is the emergence of banking sectors from the planned economies in the late 1980s and early 1990s. The birthing process—Section 39.2 of this chapter—was hardly smooth; it took place amidst massive macroeconomic collapse and considerable economic uncertainty. Not surprisingly, these nascent banking sectors experienced crises ranging from serious bad loan problems to total collapse. The next section deals with the emergence of modern banking systems, particularly the responses to the bad loan problem and the process of bank privatization. Section 39.4 characterizes the second phase of transition banking, the remarkably rapid emergence in the late 1990s and early 2000s of more mature banking sectors with a dominant role played by foreign banks. By the late 2000s, banking sectors in many transition economies looked little different from their counterparts elsewhere except for the distinctive high percentage of foreign ownership. The third phase of transition banking coincides with the financial crisis and global recession starting in 2008. The crisis tested the resilience of new institutions and regulatory structures and brought the issue of foreign ownership to the fore. The advantages of foreign ownership as a conduit for good banking

* The authors are grateful to Stephan Barisitz, Ralph De Haas, Rainer Haselmann, and Tomislav Presecan for helpful suggestions.

practice is actively being weighed against the disadvantages associated with the international transmission of financial shocks. All in all, these banking sectors are not immune to problems and do not always provide sufficient impetus for economic development, which is problematic because most transition economies have bank-dominated financial sectors. Our last section (39.6) considers the problems of, and prospects for, banks fulfilling this role in the transition countries.

To illustrate the commonalities and differences in the transition experience, we have selected 14 representative countries from Central Eastern Europe (CEE), South Eastern Europe (SEE), and the former Soviet Union (FSU). We group the countries as follows: CEE consists of the Czech Republic, Hungary, Poland, and Slovakia; SEE consists of Bulgaria, Croatia, Romania, Serbia, and Slovenia; and the FSU consists of Russia, Estonia, Latvia, Lithuania, and Ukraine. Banking and macroeconomic data for these countries at five year intervals from 1995 to 2010 are presented in the tables, and the examples used in the text are drawn from these country experiences.[1]

39.2 THE EMERGENCE OF BANKING INSTITUTIONS

Banking sectors in the European transition economies were relatively underdeveloped compared with the real economies in these countries due mainly to the legacies of the pre-transition centrally planned economy. As examples of real sector development, Czechoslovakia had a relatively modern automobile industry, Hungary produced buses, and Bulgaria made computers and software for use within the Soviet bloc. However, in the planning framework, financial intermediation between savers and borrowers was internalized wholly within the state banking apparatus. Capital was allocated through a system of directed credits to state-owned enterprises (SOEs) for both investment needs and budget allocations for the working capital necessary to meet the output plan. Credit evaluation and risk management played no role in lending decisions. The national monobank served only as an accounting clearinghouse for inter-enterprise transactions. Cash issuances by enterprises were based on planned wage bills that were calibrated to the expected aggregate value of consumer goods sold to households at administered prices. Money was entirely passive in that it was used solely as a unit of account in enterprise transactions and as a medium of exchange between households and the state distribution sector. Household savings, oftentimes the result of forced accumulation of monetary balances due to the unavailability of desirable consumer goods to purchase, were collected by a state savings bank that operated an extensive branch network throughout the country.

---

[1] Data on transition banking are sometimes unreliable or subject to revision. The data in the tables are from European Banking for Reconstruction and Development sources, both online data files (*Structural Change Indicators*) and annual *Transition Reports*. Additional sources for data in the tables and the text are Barisitz (2007), Raiffeisen *CEE Banking Sector Reports* available online, and the online World Bank dataset.

Pre-transition banking sectors typically included a foreign trade bank that handled all foreign currency transactions to isolate these from the domestic financial system and often contained separate specialty banks to oversee the financing of the agricultural and construction sectors. In this environment, banking was segmented along functional lines and credit allocation was entirely subservient to the plan. Hence, structural segmentation, state control of banking activities, and high concentration ratios are the major legacies inherited from the planning period by the banking sectors in the transition economies. Despite these commonalities, important differences among the experiences of countries both prior to and during the transition period yield unique characteristics. As an example, we begin with a brief discussion of banking in the SEE transition countries that were former republics of Yugoslavia because their sectors inherited somewhat special legacies. We continue with a consideration of the initial developments in banking during the first half decade of the transition followed by a more detailed look at several transition countries. This section concludes with a discussion of foreign bank participation in the early transition years.

In the 1950s, Yugoslavia established a two-tier banking system with a traditional central bank located in Belgrade, the National Bank of Yugoslavia (NBY), and republic-level commercial banks. Banks were owned collectively, as were all enterprises under the Yugoslavian system of self-management. Because Yugoslavia was a small, open economy, commercial banks made a significant number of loans denominated in foreign currency throughout the 1980s. However, these republic-level banks were required to remit most of their foreign exchange deposits to the NBY in exchange for credits in dinars. Hence, the balance sheets of republic-level banks exhibited a serious currency mismatch between assets and liabilities by the late 1980s. Upon the secession of Croatia and Slovenia in 1991, the NBY froze the forex deposits of the republic banks in these two countries, creating large gaps in their balance sheets. Although many private banks, often company-owned, dated back to the 1970s in these countries, high concentration, weak capitalization and a substantial accumulation of problem loans were important legacies from the Yugoslavian past. Government rehabilitation policies that were designed to deal with bank insolvency led to the nationalization of most banks; hence, state-owned banks were created at the beginning of the transition in Slovenia and Croatia (Bonin 2004).

The first step in banking sector reform for most transition economies involved the creation of a two-tier system with commercial activities carved out of the portfolio of the national monobank. The top tier consists of a traditional central bank that is charged with pursuing monetary policy, including exchange rate policy, and is given responsibility for supervising and monitoring the nascent banking sector. The second tier consists of the newly created state-owned commercial banks (SOCBs), the state-owned specialty banks, which themselves morphed into SOCBs, any operating foreign and joint-venture banks, and all private domestic banks, including those that entered after the political transition. As a rule, lax entry requirements led to the creation of many new private banks, some of which were of dubious quality, or even fraudulent, and virtually all of which were severely undercapitalized. Hence, the seeds for a banking crisis were planted at the beginning of the transition, or even before, in virtually all transition countries due partly to the adoption of lax entry requirements with the intent of fostering competition for state-owned banks in highly segmented banking sectors. Moreover, the nascent regulatory systems were overwhelmed by the mismatch between their capabilities, which were severely restricted by a lack of human capital, and their mandates provided by quickly adopted standard financial rules and regulations, especially given the inherited loan portfolios of the SOCBs.

Although each country's financial restructuring program involved hiving off the commercial bank portfolio of the national bank to establish the two-tier system, different approaches were taken toward the creation of SOCBs, all of which were established initially as wholly state-owned joint-stock entities. In Hungary, the commercial portfolio was divided along sectoral lines—for example, industry, agriculture, and infrastructure plus the nascent small business sector, to create three SOCBs. In Poland, the commercial portfolio was divided along regional lines to create nine SOCBs from regional offices of the national monobank. The commercial portfolio of the Czechoslovak national monobank was separated into two parts regionally to create two SOCBs, a Czech and a Slovak one. After the Velvet Divorce, each new country had a single large SOCB. Similarly, in Romania, only one SOCB was created from the entire commercial portfolio of the national monobank. All CEE countries and Russia had specialty banks that obtained universal banking licenses and, thus, became SOCBs after the transition.

At the opposite extreme, full separation of all commercial activities from the Bulgarian national bank's balance sheet occurred in 1990 when each of its 145 branch offices was granted a universal banking license that allowed it to pursue commercial business either as an individual entity or in combination with other branches. Again, the intent of this policy was to foster competition. As a result, 59 SOCBs were formed and, in 1992, the Bank Consolidation Company was established to oversee and orchestrate the eventual consolidation of the Bulgarian banking sector by the government. By 1995, 41 banks were operating in Bulgaria and the two largest SOCBs were the former state foreign trade bank and the former state savings bank.

In Russia, then the Soviet Union, the two-tier banking system was established in 1987 with the separation of all commercial bank functions from the national monobank and the creation of sectoral banks by enterprises or former branch ministries. As in Bulgaria, branches of the national bank became independent entities and then regrouped into larger banks. In addition, new entry into Russian banking was dramatic. By 1995, about 2,300 banks were licensed and operating in Russia. Most of the newly created banks were small and poorly capitalized. Some of them were merely internal or house banks owned by industrial enterprises. However, by 1996, six of the de novo domestic private banks had grown sufficiently to be among the ten largest banks in Russia, a group that included the former state foreign trade bank and the former state savings bank as the two largest SOCBs. However, as noted below, the Russian private banking sector retracted due to numerous bank failures during the 1998 ruble crisis.

In the first transition phase, policies toward foreign bank participation, both in establishing subsidiaries and in purchasing equity stakes in SOCBs, differed considerably across the region. In some countries, policies that invited entry, such as providing tax holidays, encouraged Greenfield foreign operations. In others, licensing was restrictive and foreign banks were limited to taking minority stakes in SOCBs or to participating in the resuscitation of ailing smaller domestic banks. Claeys and Hainz (2014) show that the mode of foreign bank entry—Greenfield or acquisition—has important implications. Greenfield banks, as new entrants, charge lower interest rates and the pressures of competition affect the domestic banks as well. Foreign participation in the banking sector was viewed initially by most governments as a vehicle for importing banking expertise and training to augment the scarce domestic human capital in the sector. Even before the political change, the Hungarian government pursued a liberal licensing policy toward foreign financial institutions. The Central European International Bank Ltd., was founded as an offshore joint-venture bank by six foreign banks and the Hungarian National Bank in 1979; in 1986, Citibank Budapest Ltd. began operations as a foreign-majority-owned, joint-venture bank. By 1995, foreign-owned financial institutions held over one-third of banking assets in Hungary due in large part to the privatization of two SOCBS to foreign owners.

In the first decade of transition, the majority of Greenfield operations in the region were banks from Austria (Raiffeisen, Creditanstalt, Bank Austria, and Hypo-Alde-Adria) and the Netherlands (ING and ABN-Amro). Several German banks (BNP-Dresdner, Commerzbank, and HypoVereinsbank) also established a presence. The early privatizers acquiring stakes in formerly state-owned banks during the latter part of the decade were the two Dutch banks already mentioned above, Erste (Austria), Société Générale (France), KBC Bank (Belgium), Allied Irish Banks (Ireland), Bayerische Landesbank (Germany), Citibank, and GE Capital (United States). Swedbank AB accounted for the majority of foreign bank presence in the Baltic countries.

As Table 39.1 indicates for the early transition period, about one-third of bank assets were owned by foreign financial institutions in Hungary, Slovakia, and Latvia in 1995 while the figures were smaller in the Czech Republic and Poland and foreign ownership was minuscule elsewhere in the region. The relatively high figure for Slovaka is due to Czech-owned banking assets being considered as foreign while ownership was being unwound in Slovakia after the Velvet Divorce. In the Czech Republic, state-owned banks were included in the voucher privatization program, thus restricting foreign ownership. In Poland, the nine SOCBs were slated early on for privatization as part of a program supported by US Treasury. However, the eclectic privatization plans with two-tier tenders and employee participation inhibited foreign entry. These governments followed a more protectionist strategy, taking an infant industry approach according to which domestic banks are nurtured to become strong enough to fend off foreign competition when it arrives

For the most part, governments in transition countries succeeded in establishing the foundations for building commercial banking sectors early in the transition period. However, developing efficient banking sectors required the completion of three interrelated tasks namely, the resolution of non-performing loans, the privatization of the SOCBs, and the establishment of effective regulatory institutions. We discuss the progress made on these fronts during the first decade of transition in Section 39.3. With the development of modern banking sectors, foreign ownership spread rapidly. As Table 39.1 indicates for the mid-transition period, the foreign asset share in most of the CEE and SEE as well as in the Baltic States exceeded 50%, and was often substantially more by 2000. The other FSU countries, Russia and Ukraine, were the notable exceptions along with Slovenia which did not allow foreign ownership until KBC took a stake in Nova Ljubljanska Banka in 2002 and Serbia which was still politically unstable.

39.3 THE DEVELOPMENT OF MODERN BANKING SECTORS

As described in the previous section, the typical banking sector in a transition economy consisted initially of state-owned banks that were carved out of the planned economy

Table 39.1 Banking in the first decade of transition: selected data

	Number of banks (foreign owned)	Asset share of foreign banks (%)	Domestic credit to GDP ratio (%)	Net Interest margin (%)	Non-performing loans % of total	EBRD Bank Transition Index
			Early Transition—1995			
CEE						
Czech Rep.	55(23)	15.5	62.5	3.44	31.5	3
Hungary	43(21)	36.8	22.7	5.99	12.1	3
Poland	81(18)	4.4	16.7	8.84	23.9	3
Slovakia	33(18)	32.7	26.3	3.93	41.3	2.7
SEE						
Bulgaria	41 (3)	<1	39.4	2.17	12.5	2
Croatia	54 (1)	<1	33.4	5.73	12.9	2.7
Romania	24 (8)	<1	7.8	8.27	37.9	3
Serbia	103(3)	<1	9.2	3.62	12.0	1
Slovenia	39 (6)	4.8	27.3	4.48	9.3	3
FSU						
Estonia	19 (5)	1.8	14.4	9.26	2.4	3
Latvia	41 (17)	34.6	7.5	10.29	18.9	3
Lithuania	15 (0)	0	15.2	10.87	17.3	3
Russia	2297 (21)	3	8.7	8.89	4.6	2
Ukraine	230 (1)	<1	1.5	5.43	--	2
			Mid-Transition—2000			
CEE						
Czech Rep.	40 (26)	65.4	44	2.03	33.8	3.3
Hungary	42 (33)	67.4	29.9	4.01	3.1	4
Poland	73 (46)	72.6	26.9	4.36	16.8	3.3
Slovakia	23 (13)	42.7	43.7	2.69	26.2	3
SEE						
Bulgaria	35 (25)	75.3	12.5	5.52	10.9	3
Croatia	45 (21)	84.1	39.9	4.89	22.6	3.3
Romania	33 (21)	46.7	7.2	7.57	5.3	2.7
Serbia	81 (3)	0.5	63.6	3.31	27.8	1
Slovenia	28 (6)	15.3	36.7	3.75	9.3	3.3
FSU						
Estonia	7 (4)	97.4	23.3	3.55	1.3	3.7
Latvia	22 (12)	74.4	19.5	3.38	4.5	3
Lithuania	13 (6)	54.7	11.3	3.78	10.8	3
Russia	1311 (33)	9.5	13.3	5.26	9.6	1.7
Ukraine	154 (14)	11.1	11.2	6.35	12.5	2

Notes: Data are from country tables in EBRD *Transition Report*, various issues and the EBRD on line "Structural and Institutional Change" indicators. Some additional data for 1995 are from Barisitz (2007) and for various years from the World Bank online database. EBRD Index takes values between 1.0 and 4.0+. In case of a missing number in 2010, we use the value from the previous available year. CEE—Central and Eastern Europe; SEE—Southeastern Europe; FSU—Former Soviet Union; − indicates data not available.

structure along with newly established small private domestic banks. Some countries began to privatize the large SOCBs quickly and also opened up to foreign bank entry early in the transition. However, the creation of market-based legislation and institutions did not lead automatically to good banking practices. On the contrary, the SOCBs and the newly created banks often did not behave like proper commercial banks due to distorted incentives.

First, the SOCBs continued to maintain banking relationships with their large clients, the state owned enterprises (SOEs). Such lending was either politically mandated or simply the result of long-standing relationships between clients having little experience in choosing viable projects and banks unable to evaluate the risk of loans. Second, in many countries, de novo banks were created without adequate regulatory oversight. As a result, some de novo banks were used to channel loans improperly to their owners, many of which were enterprises so that these banks acted as pocket banks for their owners. Entry requirements for de novo domestic banks were initially very lenient because policy was based on the mistaken notion that competition would be enhanced by easy entry. The proliferation of new, often undercapitalized, banks placed an added burden on an underdeveloped regulatory structure. Although most countries adopted modern banking and regulatory legislation immediately, effective supervision did not follow automatically due partially to the scarcity of knowledgeable staff.

Not surprisingly, bad loans were a serious problem for all transition economies due partly to the inherited legacies but also to continuing lending practices. As Table 39.1 indicates, the ratio of non-performing loans to total loans in 1995 averaged 27% in the four CEE countries. The reported ratio in 1995 was smaller for the SEE and FSU countries with the notable exception of Romania. However, information about the performance of borrowers in a rapidly changing environment is revealed only slowly under the best of circumstances so that these measures are only illustrative of the serious overall problem of bad loans that would only be revealed later on. Most governments responded to failing banks with efforts to save them from closure by recapitalization and the removal of bad loans from their balance sheets. For small insolvent banks, mergers with state-owned banks were commonly resorted to. Repeated problems were inevitable because recapitalizations addressed only the stock of existing bad loans.

In the absence of independent market-oriented banking institutions, the flow of new bad loans continued to accumulate. Regulators did not have proper incentives, the requisite expertise, or sufficient independence to cope with this problem. To some extent the bad loan problem was unavoidable because transition recessions and the dissolution of trading relationships within the Soviet bloc generated severe real sector shocks that were mirrored on the balance sheets of the banks. Nonetheless, even though the roots of this problem were difficult to resolve, the average ratios of non-performing loans to total loans fell sharply; by 2005 Poland was the only country in our data with a ratio greater than 10%. To examine the resolution of the bad loans problem in more detail, we consider several country experiences.

The Hungarian government began to clean up the portfolios of its banks in the early 1990s when it enacted strong bankruptcy laws, new accounting regulations, and a new banking law. At the time, the Hungarian government provided guarantees to cover a portion of the debts of SOEs as firms continued to accumulate debts in arrears. The government replaced non-performing loans on bank balance sheets with government securities and transferred these assets to a government collection agency. Repeated recapitalizations introduced an element of moral hazard into banking. The situation only changed when the authorities began to pursue an aggressive strategy of selling controlling stakes of the large SOCBs to foreign investors, signaling a credible commitment to no further bailouts. However, such a privatization strategy was not without difficulties as exemplified by an early transaction. The sale of a controlling stake in Budapest Bank, the third largest SOCB in Hungary, to GE Capital in 1995 was controversial because the buyer was given the right to off load bad loans that were uncovered after the sale. Nonetheless, the banking expertise and discipline imposed by foreign owners of the three major SOCBs in Hungary led to rapid improvements in the banking environment. By the end of the 1990s, the Hungarian banking sector was well capitalized, loan quality had improved, claims on the state were a declining share of bank assets, bank staffing declined, bank margins narrowed and, incidentally, bank regulation improved markedly (Hasan and Marton, 2003).

The government in the Czech Republic developed an explicit and detailed plan for privatization of most state-owned institutions, including SOCBs, using vouchers rather than direct sales. Initially in 1991, bad loans were removed from bank balance sheets and replaced with government bonds while the bad assets were taken over by a newly established hospital bank, Konsolidacni Bank. These recapitalized SOCBs were privatized by placing a minority stake of bank stock in the voucher program. As a result, non-state ownership of these partially privatized banks was dispersed with the largest stakes held by bank-related investment funds. Furthermore, the bank-related funds held ownership interests in their unrestructured industrial clients so that the large banks continued to lend to SOEs, which resulted in more bad loans. The key problems in the Czech Republic were interconnectedness between banks and their clients resulting from voucher privatization and the lack of independence of bank governance from a government which continued to hold controlling stakes in the banks. As a result, the resolution of bad loans required several rounds of recapitalization by the government, which increased the state's stake further and necessitated a second round of privatization. In this final round, foreign investors were allowed to take majority stakes in the large Czech banks and bank behavior changed accordingly. The continuing efforts to restructure the Czech banks over the first decade of transition were expensive with total costs amounting to more than 25% of 1998 gross domestic product (GDP) (Bonin and Wachtel, 2005).

In Poland, the first bank privatizations utilized a combination of domestic initial public offerings (IPOs) and tenders to sell non-majority stakes to a strategic foreign investor. The Polish stock market was not very large; trading was not very extensive and bank stocks were the largest issues traded. Thus, bank IPOs were difficult to price and accusations of market manipulation lead to the political defeat of one of the early governments. The new government developed a bank consolidation program as an alternative approach to privatization and attempted to force mergers and acquisitions of banks, but not without controversy. In one case, the attempt to include an already partially privatized bank (BPH) in the program caused a public uproar. Delays in privatization followed; over 20% of Polish bank assets remained in state hands as late as 2005 including the largest bank, the zloty savings bank PKO which had not participated in either consolidation or privatization programs.

In other countries, banking crises reached systemic proportions and severely impeded the overall transition to a market economy. In Bulgaria, weak bank governance and poor regulation of the many small SOCBs created from the commercial portfolio of the original mono bank resulted in considerable asset stripping and insider lending. Repeated rounds of recapitalization of banks resulted in a total cost to the government at 42% of 1998 GDP, which made the Bulgarian banking crises one of the most costly of all transition countries. A currency board introduced in 1997 restored macroeconomic stability in Bulgaria and the banking system was rationalized quickly thereafter. In Romania, the dominant SOCBs accumulated large portfolios of bad loans and also required massive capital injections from the government. Non-performing loans peaked at 58% in 1998. In both of these SEE countries, severe macroeconomic shocks led to serious banking crises, and sustainable economic growth resumed only after these crises were resolved. Most of the later bank privatization programs in Romania, Bulgaria, Croatia, and the Czech Republic involved negotiated deals between the government and a single foreign bank, sometimes after a tender.

After a decade and a half of transition, privatization of SOCBs with extensive foreign ownership was largely completed in CEE, SEE and the Baltics, although the situation was different in many other countries of the former Soviet Union. Both the method—attracting a strategic foreign investor—and the timing of privatization matter to bank performance. Even after considering selection effects, Bonin, Hasan, and Wachtel (2005b) conclude that voucher-privatized and late-privatized banks lagged in performance and efficiency relative to non-voucher and early-privatized banks

The surprising aspect of banking in the transition countries is not the depth of the crises after the end of communism but the speed with which financial restructuring took place subsequently. The rapid changes in the last decade can be attributed to two related phenomenon. First, the desire of European transition countries to qualify for EU membership was a strong force for reform, not only in the eight original transition accession countries but also in the later joiners and in countries still hoping to join. Thus, improvements in bank regulation and investments in the banking sector took place rapidly. Second, the prospect of EU membership (and ultimately the adoption of the euro) made these under-served banking markets attractive to European banks once macroeconomic stability was attained and a reasonably effective regulatory structure was in place. However, the governments in many transition countries were reluctant to allow foreign ownership for all the common arguments that attempt to show that foreign direct investment (FDI) in banking, unlike all other FDI, is dangerous. The usual claims that foreign-owned banks would facilitate capital flight and fail to provide credit for local economic development were made. As noted earlier, Hungary was the exception in that foreign banks were allowed to operate even before the transition and SOCBs were sold to foreign investors early in the transition. However, other transition governments took longer to realize that privatization to foreign buyers is not only a source of revenue but also a means of improving bank performance.

The proportion of assets in foreign-owned banks rose from virtually zero in the early 1990s to more than half in most countries a decade later. As Table 39.2 indicates for the later transition period, the average share of assets in foreign-owned banks was 85% in the CEE countries and 63% in the SEE counties by 2005. In most cases, privatization by itself was not sufficient to improve bank performance; rather joint ownership with foreign strategic investors was the crucial determinant in behavioral change (Bonin, Hasan, and Wachtel, 2005a). The FSU countries are an exception; foreign banks were not a major factor in Russia or in any other former Soviet republic except for the Baltic countries although this is changing slowly. Kazakhstan, with large capital inflows related to the energy industry, has allowed foreign bank entry since 2005; the foreign bank share of assets peaked before the financial crisis at almost 20%. Corruption in the banking industry continues to be a problem in Kazakhstan where some foreign banks require their employees to take regular polygraph tests. Many

Table 39.2 Banking in the second decade of transition: selected data

	Number of banks (foreign owned)	Asset share of foreign banks (%)	Domestic credit to GDP ratio (%)	Net Interest margin (%)	Non-performing loans % of total	EBRD Bank Transition Index
Later Transition—2005						
CEE						
Czech Rep.	36 (27)	84.4	35.8	2.39	4	4
Hungary	38 (27)	82.6	49.9	4.46	3.1	4
Poland	61 (50)	74.3	33.4	2.96	11.6	3.7
Slovakia	23 (16)	97.3	35.1	2.08	5.5	3.7
SEE						
Bulgaria	34 (23)	74.5	41	3.96	3.8	3.7
Croatia	34 (13)	91.3	56.4	3.50	6.2	4
Romania	33 (24)	59.2	19.9	4.23	1.7	3
Serbia	40 (17)	66	30.7	5.69	–	2.7
Slovenia	25 (9)	22.6	56.3	2.19	6.4	3.3
FSU						
Estonia	13 (10)	99.4	56.6	3.01	0.2	4
Latvia	23 (9)	57.9	67.8	2.93	0.7	3.7
Lithuania	12 (6)	91.7	40.9	2.02	3.4	3.7
Russia	1253 (52)	8.3	25.7	5.57	2.7	2.3
Ukraine	165 (23)	21.3	32.2	3.96	2.2	2.7
Post-crisis—2010						
CEE						
Czech Rep.	37(15)	84.8	75.3	2.68	2.8	4
Hungary	38 (23)	81.3	66.5	3.82	6.7	3.7
Poland	67 (57)	72.3	55.2	3.18	8	3.7
Slovakia	26 (13)	91.6	51.1	2.77	5.2	3.7
SEE						
Bulgaria	30 (22)	84	75.3	3.59	6.7	3.7
Croatia	32 (15)	91	69.6	2.95	7.8	4
Romania	31 (25)	84.3	40.7	4.35	8.5	3.3
Serbia	33 (--)	72.5	45	4.54	16.9	3
Slovenia	25 (11)	29.5	92.7	2.36	6	3.3
FSU						
Estonia	17 (14)	98.3	98.8	3.21	5.3	4
Latvia	27 (18)	69.3	103.3	1.57	16.4	3.7
Lithuania	17 (0)	91.6	69.8	1.44	20.8	3.7
Russia	1058 (108)	18.3	44.4	5.08	9.7	2.7
Ukraine	182 (51)	50.8	73.3	4.66	47.9	3

Notes: Data are from country tables in EBRD Transition Report, various issues and the EBRD on line "Structural and Institutional Change" indicators. Some additional data for various years from the World Bank online database. EBRD Index takes values between 1.0 and 4.0+. In case of a missing number in 2010, we use the value from the previous available year. CEE—Central and Eastern Europe; SEE—Southeastern Europe; FSU—Former Soviet Union; – indicates data not available.

FSU countries have banking regulations that inhibit foreign entry and there is a continuing reluctance on the part of many governments to accept foreign dominance of the banking sector. For example, although Russia has relaxed its limits on the overall size of the foreign banking sector, it sets minima for the number of Russian employees and board members in foreign banks. In addition, unstable supervisory environments and weak legal protection have deterred foreign interest in such investments.

The characteristics of banking in Russia differ considerably from patterns found in CEE and SEE. In addition to three dominant SOCBs, Russia has a large number of very small private commercial banks and many pocket banks having industrial owners. Some of these banks were involved in speculative activity and many were insolvent when the Russian government defaulted on its debt in 1998. At that time, weak bankruptcy laws and poor regulation made it difficult to close institutions so that the managers or owners were able to strip banks of any remaining good assets. The 1998 banking crisis did not have a very large impact on the real economy because the credit to GDP ratio was considerably lower in Russia than such ratios in the CEE transition countries and cash was used widely for transactions throughout the FSU. Exacerbating the economic crisis in 1998 was uncertainty about the economic and legal environment.

The Russian banking sector has shown signs of improvement since 1998. Although about 1,100 banks still operate, this number is roughly half of the total in 1995 due to consolidations and closures. In addition, the influence of foreign banks is increasing as three foreign-controlled banks are among the 15 largest banks in Russia. Moreover, financial intermediation has increased as the bank asset to GDP ratio is double its level before 1998, though still lower than in the European transition countries. Nonetheless, some of the private banks still operate as private financial services institutions for their energy-sector owners and provide little overall intermediation. The banking system is still fragmented with many small and poorly capitalized institutions characterized by poor governance, inadequate risk management, and high operating costs. Although deposits have increased, household savings are still largely held in the state savings bank, Sberbank, or in cash (Steinherr, 2006). Sberbank and Vneshtorgbank, the former foreign trade bank, have begun to provide credit to the private sector. Sberbank remains the dominant bank in Russia, holding 27% of all banking assets in 2012.[2] The next two largest banks in Russia are also SOCBs; Vneshtorgbank has about a 6% market share and Gazprombank has a 3% market share. Interestingly, there are no known plans for privatization; moreover, state-owned Sberbank and Vneshtorgbank are "foreign owners" of banks in other countries in the region.

In all countries, successful restructuring and privatization in the financial sector depends on the establishment of an effective institutional and legislative framework for regulation as well as bankruptcy laws and appropriate accounting standards. An arms-length relationship between banks and regulators, and the state generally, is required in order to change the behavior of economic agents who are accustomed to operating in a non-market environment. Moreover, training of bank supervisors and other types of professional human capital development are needed to promote effective implementation of the legislation. Although the basic legal framework for modern banking was established early in the transition,

---

[2] Data for assets shares of banks come from Raiffeisen *CEE Banking Sector Reports* available online.

additional related elements that are crucial for its effective functioning took more time to develop. In particular, a modern banking sector needs a functioning credit information system, which includes a credit registry and ratings agencies, and a reliably functioning court system to mediate contract disputes.

Hungary took the lead among the transition countries in promoting such institutional development with a legislative shock therapy program in 1992. In January, the government promulgated new, modern banking legislation, instituted international accounting standards, and revised its bankruptcy law to include a draconian trigger that resulted in a large number of company insolvencies. In addition, Poland developed a computer-supported system of bank oversight at the beginning of the transition and had in place rather stringent bankruptcy legislation for private firms even before the political change. Other countries took considerably longer to address these problems and, as a consequence, bank restructuring and privatization took longer to complete.

39.4 The Maturation of Transition Banking Sectors

The distinctive characteristic of the banking sectors in virtually all transition countries was the rapid emergence of foreign-dominated ownership. As Table 39.2 indicates in the post-crisis period, foreign banks dominated the banking sectors in all countries in our sample by 2010 except for Slovenia and Russia where foreign participation was 30%, and 18%, respectively. The asset shares of foreign-owned banks in CEE and SEE countries are now among the highest of any banking sectors in the world. Serbian banking experienced a remarkable transformation over the last decade; foreign ownership increased from a negligible amount in 2000 to 72.5% in 2010 (see Table 39.2).

In most transition countries, state ownership of banks basically disappeared over a ten-year period centered on the turn of the century. The only countries in our sample with state ownership as a percentage of assets in double digits in 2005 were Poland (20%), Slovenia (18%), Serbia (24%), and Russia (34%).

After 1995 the EBRD index of banking reform increased (denoting an improvement), gradually in all the countries in our sample with just a few reversals. As Table 39.2 reports, four countries in our sample had attained a rating of 4.0 by 2005 on a scale from 1.0 to 4+ where the highest score reflects full convergence to performance norms and regulation standards of advanced industrial economies. These four were the Czech Republic, Hungary, Croatia, and Estonia. However, Serbia and Romania had lower scores in 2005 than five years earlier and Hungary's rating was downgraded during the crisis. By 2010, Serbia, Romania, Slovenia, Russia and Ukraine were the only countries in our sample with scores lower than 3.7. Hence, banking sectors in most transition countries have reached, or are rapidly approaching, their counterparts in developed market economies with one major difference, namely, an extremely high foreign bank presence.

Based on the origins of the bank and exacerbated by consolidation programs, banking concentration is high in most transition countries. Using banking assets, the three-firm concentration ratios were above 30% in all the countries in our sample in 2012; they were above

Table 39.3 Average interest rate spread and inflation rate in transition

	Interest Rate Spread				Inflation Rate			
	1991-95	1996-00	2001-05	2006-10	1991-95	1996-00	2001-05	2006-10
CEE								
Czech Rep.	6.5	4.7	5.6	4.7	20.1	6.4	2.2	1.7
Hungary	7.2	4.4	2.3	2.4	24.9	14.0	5.4	5.5
Poland	5.6	6.7	7.0	4.1	38.7	11.7	2.2	3.1
Slovakia	5.7	5.8	5.7	3.6	22.3	8.0	5.6	3.0
SEE								
Bulgaria	29.4	61.9	6.5	5.9	127.4	181.6	5.0	6.6
Croatia	489.2	10.5.	8.7	7.6	467.6	4.9	2.8	2.9
Romania	23.1	19.5	15.9	6.7	161.4	68.9	16.0	6.1
Serbia	86.4	72.2	15.7	7.9	12.4	52.5	18.6	8.5
Slovenia	13.5	6.0	4.7	3.5	78.3	8.2	5.2	3.0
FSU								
Estonia	7.9	4.0	4.3	4.4	272.8	7.9	3.8	5.1
Latvia	25.5	8.6	3.2	5.8	261.1	5.6	4.5	12.5
Lithuania	28.6	6.4	3.7	2.4	355.1	5.9	1.8	5.2
Russia	155.3	25.8	9.1	6.0.	767.8	34.8	14.2	10.4
Ukraine	43.0	31.1	13.4	6.6	2725.6	23.0	7.3	14.4

Note: Spreads are computed as the difference between lending rates and deposit rates from the country tables in EBRD *Transition Report*, various issues. Maturities are always less than one year but they differ across countries. In case of a missing number in Transition Report, we have taken available numbers from the World Bank's World Development Indicator (WDI) data. If it is missing in WDI, we used forecasted numbers in the EBRD report "annual indicators and projections." Inflation rate is the average of year end changes in the Consumer Price Index. Same data sources as for spreads. Missing values followed the same procedure as mentioned above. In case of a missing number in a given year, we have taken the value from the previous available year. CEE—Central and Eastern Europe; SEE—Southeastern Europe; FSU—Former Soviet Union.

50% in Croatia, Slovakia and a few very small countries.[3] The concentration ratios declined in the six years to 2012 in Czech Republic (to 49.5%), Hungary (to 38.2%), and Poland (to 31.6%) but they rose in Russia (to 48.4%) and Ukraine (to 30.7%). Although high, these concentration ratios are similar to those found in countries of a similar size and having similar financial deepening. Moreover, relatively high concentration ratios have not prevented competition from developing in many of these banking sectors.

As Table 39.3 reports, interest rate spreads declined considerably since the beginning of the transition, which may be attributable as much to improvements in the macroeconomic environment as to increased banking competition. Very high spreads between lending and deposit rates, often in excess of 10%, in the early transition years were due to instability and high inflation. However, considerable differences among the transition

---

[3] We use the data for assets shares of banks from Raiffeisen *CEE Banking Sector Reports* (available on line) to compute all concentration ratios.

countries persist. Throughout the decade of the 2000s, spreads were lowest in Hungary, generally less than 2.5%. Spreads in the Czech Republic and Poland were often two or more percentage points higher. There are still many countries, notably Croatia, Romania and Russia, with spreads above 5% which we take to be the threshold to indicate a relatively competitive banking sector. Interestingly, the inflation rate since 2000 has been higher in Hungary than in the neighboring countries, Czech Republic, Croatia, and Poland, with higher spreads. Overall, the experiences of the transition countries indicate that neither high foreign participation in the banking sector nor low inflation is a sufficient condition for competitive interest rate spreads.

Financial depth, the ratio of domestic credit to the private sector to GDP, is a common measure of financial sector development and the extent of intermediation in the economy. There were considerable differences among the transition countries in 1995 as well as wide variation in the growth of the ratio subsequently. The data in Tables 39.1 and 39.2 show that the Czech Republic had the deepest financial markets in 1995; its financial depth ratio was 62% and grew to 75% in 2010. Stabilization of the banking sectors led to financial deepening throughout the region in the decade to 2005. The credit to GDP ratios were over 30% in 2005 in all the shown countries except Romania and Russia. Ratios around 50% are higher than those found in under-banked developing countries with little intermediary activity and are similar to those found in many emerging markets.

The financial depth ratio can also be an indicator of financial fragility because it often increases dramatically when there is a credit boom. It is sometimes hard to distinguish between improvements in the financial sector and potentially dangerous increase in credit. For example, as reported in Table 39.2, financial depth increased in the decade beginning in 2000 in Bulgaria from 12% to 75%, in Hungary from 30% to 67% and in Croatia from 40% to 70%. It is difficult to say which of these might represent increased public confidence in the banking system (perhaps Bulgaria) and which reflect the excessive expansion of lending. By 2010, the credit to GDP ratios were between 40% and 80% in most of our transition countries though figures were higher in a few small countries with credit booms (Slovenia and the Baltics). The range is consistent with other middle income countries around the world. However, credit depth in 2010 in the most advanced transition countries, the new member states, was well below the EU average which was 86% in 2005. Even the four leading transition countries are well below the EU average in providing credit to the private sector.

A discussion of financial depth in the 2006 EBRD *Transition Report* notes that financial deepening in CEE and SEE countries was often due to sharp increase in loans to households, particularly mortgage lending. Household credit, in particular mortgage lending, depends on well-defined property rights over collateral and an effective legislative infrastructure to facilitate the collection of collateral in case of default. Hence, the dramatic growth of both types of lending in many transition countries reflects significant improvements in supportive institutions. Nevertheless, rapid growth in such lending can also signal an asset price boom, usually in real estate, and the potential vulnerability of the financial sector. The explosion of retail credit in some transition countries contributed to instability in the banking sector when the global financial crisis occurred.

Retail credit accounted for well over half of all loans in Croatia and around half of the total in the Czech Republic and Poland in 2005. Mortgage lending as a percentage of GDP in 2005 was highest in Croatia and Hungary, somewhat smaller in Bulgaria and Poland and virtually non-existent in Romania and Russia.

At the start of transition, many argued against foreign ownership of banks and for maintaining the national identity of the financial system. However, by the end of the 1990s, it was widely acknowledged that foreign ownership promotes efficient banking and has spillover effects on the domestic banking system. Privatization to foreign owners was both a source of revenue and a means of improving bank performance.

In conclusion, the second phase of transition banking successfully created mature and stable banking systems throughout the region. By the mid-2000s, banking systems in the more advanced transition countries were little different from their counterparts in other middle income and emerging market countries. The global financial crisis starting in 2008, which was quickly followed by a European sovereign debt crisis, put this conclusion to test. The resilience of transition banking in the face of major shocks is the third phase in the development of transition banking.

39.5 TRANSITION BANKING IN THE FINANCIAL CRISIS

The global financial crisis starting in 2008 put to the test the progress in transition banking from the previous decade. First, foreign ownership of banks which had been an important source of managerial and technological improvements in the industry also serves to link the financial systems of the home and host countries. Second, many transition countries experienced retail credit booms in the years leading up to the crisis which tested the regulatory and supervisory capabilities of these still relatively new financial systems. In several instances transition economies were able to put timely policy responses to the credit boom in place which made them appear prescient when the crisis hit. Although the impact of the financial crisis on the region was severe, systemic problems were rare and many banks in the region generally outperformed their counterparts in more developed countries. The two important characteristics of the banking systems in this era—foreign ownership and credit booms—were related. The EBRD *Transition Report* (2009) indicates that prior to the crisis abundant foreign financing often intermediated by foreign banks contributed to booms in retail credit. In many countries much of it is denominated in foreign currency which exposes domestic borrowers to foreign exchange risks.

When foreign banks entered the region, the flow of resources and capital was from the developed home countries to the transition hosts. The expertise, technology and know-how, as well as the equity investments in banks and the spillover effects on the domestic industry were important elements in the transformation of transition banking. In the credit boom of the 2000s, capital also flowed from the home countries to the transition hosts. No one discussed the possibility of resource flows in the opposite direction as weakened international banks transmitted the crisis shock to the transition economies. The crisis introduced the possibility that foreign ownership could amplify the effect of a home country shock on host countries (De Haas, 2014).

Between 2004 and 2013 eleven transition countries joined the EU which spurred further consolidations and mergers in the banking system so that foreign ownership was concentrated in a handful of banks with extensive interests in many countries. Six large West

European banking groups (the Big 6)—Unicredit (Austria),[4] Erste, Raiffeisen, Société Générale, KBC, and Intesa—accounted for more that two-thirds of foreign banking assets in the region in 2010. In addition Swedbank dominates the banking sectors of the Baltic countries. The roots of this foreign takeover are found to a considerable degree in the early participation of foreign banks in the region and subsequent mergers and acquisitions. Unicredit through takeovers and mergers acquired the Greenfield operations of several Austrian banks (Bank Austria and Creditanstalt) and a former German bank (HypoVerinsbank) that had operated in the region since the beginning of the transition. Erste's strategy involved establishing a small Greenfield operation and subsequently acquiring state-owned savings banks in five countries to focus on retail banking activities having a solid in-country deposit base. Raiffeisen's business strategy involved growing its Greenfield operations that it had in the region since the beginning of the transition with a focus on corporate lending. Societe Generale purchased previously state-owned banks with mixed deposit bases in three countries. KBC participated by taking over banks in three of the early EU entrants and taking a minority stake in the largest bank in Slovenia, which it subsequently sold in 2013. Intesa is a relative latecomer to the region, having purchased the largest bank in Serbia and the second largest bank in both Slovakia and Croatia. Taken together in 2010, the Big 6 account for the five largest banks in the Czech Republic and Slovakia, the four largest banks in Croatia, four of the five largest banks in Serbia, and three of the five largest banks in Romania, Hungary, and Slovenia. For each bank, the region became what Epstein (2014) calls "a second home market" to which these Big 6 banks remained committed during the crisis.

The advantages of foreign bank ownership quickly came into question when the crisis started. It was feared that foreign-owned banks, particularly if they relied on funding and liquidity from their parent, would transmit the crisis shock to the region. Poor conditions in the home country might lead the parent banks to reduce funding or even try to withdraw capital. If parent banks attempted to limit their losses by reducing foreign exposures they could trigger systemic crises in banking systems dominated by foreign ownership.

These concerns led to a joint action plan, the Vienna Initiative (VI) which was adopted in January 2009. Both the International Financial Institutions (IFIs) such as the EBRD, IMF, and the EIB and private institutions (i.e., the parent banks in the region) participated in the VI. The banks agreed to maintain their exposures to the transition countries and recapitalize banks as necessary while the IFIs offered support of 33 billion euros to maintain stability in the region. Five of the Big 6 multinational banks signed letters of commitment to host countries as part of this program (the sixth, KBC was restricted by the terms of a support package it received from its home country, Belgium). An expanded plan, VI 2.0, was adopted in 2012 in response to the European sovereign debt crisis.

According to De Hass et al. (2012), the contraction in credit by foreign bank subsidiaries in 30 transition countries occurred earlier and was deeper than that of domestic banks during the crisis years of 2008 and 2009. However, these authors find that banks that participated in the Vienna Initiative were less likely to contract credit in the region than banks that did not participate. Popov and Udell (2012) show that transition country firms' access to credit during the crisis was affected by the balance sheet conditions of foreign parent

---

[4] Although Unicredit is a banking conglomerate with its head office in Italy, the subset of banks in the group active in the region are members of the Austrian division of Unicredit.

banks. Ongena, Peydro and van Horen, 2013) indicate that banks in the transition countries that borrow internationally or are foreign-owned reduced their lending more during the crisis than banks that depend on domestic sources of funds. Thus, there is evidence of the international transmission of the crisis shock to the transition countries. Nonetheless, Epstein (2014) argues that it was the business models of the banks themselves rather than the intervention of the IFIs that kept the Big 6 committed to their longer-term objectives of maintaining market share and reputation in their "second-home" markets. In fact, the Big 6 themselves originated the idea of a coordinated approach in a letter expressing concern for the financial stability of the region sent to the European Commission in November 2008, which led to the VI. The Big 6 remained committed to the region and maintained a relatively stable credit situation in the European transition countries.

Credit growth throughout the region slowed as the international financial crisis affected economies, particularly those that were closely integrated with the Eurozone (Hungary and the Baltics) or vulnerable to swings in energy prices (Russia and Kazakhstan). The worldwide credit crunch reduced volume in international bond and syndicated loan markets. Further, countries with macroeconomic imbalances were particularly vulnerable to contagion effects when the European sovereign debt crisis spread across the periphery of Europe.

Hungary was among the first emerging market countries to suffer the fallout of the global credit crunch. It was vulnerable because of a large fiscal deficit, its reliance on external financing and the extent of domestic, particularly household, borrowing in foreign currency. The credit crunch led to pressure on the forint and an increase in the country risk premium. In October 2008, the IMF, the World Bank and the EU joined forces to provide a $25 billion support program. Importantly, the program included provisions for preemptive additions to bank capital and guarantees for the interbank market. That is, macroeconomic issues and financial sector stability are inseparable problems. As the Hungarian currency depreciated, the country faced a serious problem since the vast majority of loans in its large mortgage market were denominated in Swiss francs. The regulatory authorities and the government intervened by allowing repayment of these mortgages at a preferential exchange rate. However, the program was of limited success because the holder of the mortgage had to have sufficient funds to buy out the entire mortgage at the preferential exchange rate. Although the recession in Hungary deepened and credit contracted, Hungary avoided a systemic banking crisis like that which occurred in the first phase of transition.

Croatia also faced a rapid expansion of household borrowing in the years prior to the crisis. Unlike other countries around the world, it imposed prudential constraints on lending activity through a series of innovative central bank actions which enabled it to mitigate the effects of the boom. In retrospect these steps could well have been emulated by more advanced countries.

Croatia suffered from a common combination of problems. First, the growth of credit outstripped GDP growth; it was fueled by improvements in the banking sector capabilities and low external borrowing costs. Second, the resultant capital inflows created a large external imbalance. Third, over two-thirds of mortgages in Croatia were denominated in euros. Even if the deposit base of the banks is also in euros, foreign exchange risk is not eliminated by this matching because a domestic slowdown or exchange rate shock would affect the ability of domestic borrowers to repay in euros (as was the case in Hungary).

The first measure introduced by the Croatian National Bank for a short period of time starting in 2003 was a ceiling on credit growth above 16%. Further measures included compulsory bank purchases of central bank notes, required holdings of liquid foreign currency assets to balance their domestic currency exposures and marginal reserve requirements on external borrowing by the banks. Starting in 2006, the central bank increased the risk weights on foreign currency loans to domestic customers with the expressed purpose of discouraging such loans. The variety of programs and the frequent changes in their application introduced some uncertainty into the banking environment. Nevertheless, Croatia was able to maintain the stability of its banking sector throughout the crisis period.

Credit expanded rapidly in Poland as well; the credit to GDP ratio almost doubled between 2004 and 2008 and much new lending was denominated in foreign currency. This might appear to be a recipe for financial instability except that the bank regulators leaned on the banks to increase capital buffers and maintain the quality of loan portfolios. Although more formal tightening of regulatory standards did not occur until much later, Poland did not suffer any systemic instability during the global crisis.

The Russian banking system encountered serious liquidity problems before the crisis, in 2004, and again late in 2008. A lack of trust paralyzed the interbank market for a short period in 2004 though this did not have much effect since deposits were concentrated in the large state owned banks. In the decade after 1998, the ratio of bank credit to GDP doubled. Thus, the problems were more serious in 2008 when oil prices fell and the Ruble depreciated while many institutions borrowed abroad in foreign currencies. This time the closure of the Russian interbank market threatened a significant systemic crisis. Deposits were switched into foreign currency and total deposits declined. Nonperforming loans increased, loans outstanding fell and there were some bank closures. However, unlike the crisis a decade earlier, there were no major bank runs. Furthermore, there was a rapid and comprehensive policy response. The central bank eased its refinancing terms and extended deposit insurance coverage and the government offered support to enterprises in trouble. The Russian banking system is much stronger than it was before the 1998 crisis but it is still vulnerable to large macroeconomic shocks.

These episodes suggest that transition banking in its most recent or third stage of development is still vulnerable to both external and internal shocks. Despite the international transmission of crisis shocks, foreign ownership continues to bolster the ability of transition country banking systems to absorb shocks. Further, the ability of, central bankers in many transition countries to react in a timely fashion served as an additional shock absorber. Romania, among others, introduced formal Financial Stability Reports to monitor systemic risks and introduce macroprudential policy responses. Although the transition banking sectors are fragile, they exhibited surprising resilience in the face of the global financial crisis.

39.6 Retrospective on Transition and Prospects for the Future

While banks in the transition countries have made rapid strides in improving performance and services since the early 1990s, the banking sectors in the transition economies still do not posses the financial depth of their EU counterparts nor are banking services as well developed in these countries. Nonetheless, with few exceptions, the transition in banking is complete. State mono banking structures have been replaced by privately owned, market-oriented, well-capitalized banking institutions that are independent from the government and from state-owned clients. The legal environment has improved with respect to bankruptcy laws, collateral laws, and confidence in the application of the law. Furthermore, banking regulatory and supervisory capabilities have developed considerably. Thus, any evaluation of the structure of banking in transition countries must be positive. However, banking conduct is a somewhat different matter; any evaluation of what banks are doing and how they are contributing to economic performance in the transition economies must be more nuanced.

For the transition countries, the financial depth ratio is well below industrial country levels, although the numbers are not unusual for countries having similar GDP levels. In some CEE countries, this ratio has fallen as bad loans have been removed from balance sheets while GDP has grown. Deepening has occurred in the major FSU countries with the achievement of financial stability and the resulting return of public confidence in banks. Financial deepening or increasing intermediation has been shown to be associated with more rapid economic growth in cross-country studies (Wachtel, 2001). Thus, the increased credit ratios should be viewed as a positive development even though there is reason for concern that credit deepening has come in the form of rapid growth in mortgage lending and other forms of consumer credit. As the crisis suggested, such rapid credit increases might have been more a sign of excessive risk taking and financial vulnerability than a precursor of financial deepening and long term growth.

Lending to households has grown rapidly in many countries. The expansion of household lending in transition countries may be related to the dominance of foreign-owned banks. Once the legal environment is in place, lending to households is a commodity business that can be entered easily through the application of banking technology from abroad and is therefore particularly attractive for foreign owned banks. Yet ratios of household credit to GDP are still not large by developed country standards. However, the ratio of household credit to the financial wealth of the consumer sector is high in Croatia and elsewhere suggesting that the credit expansion increased the vulnerability of consumers to economic shocks.

In contrast, lending to enterprises requires developing client relationships and having the ability to evaluate unique situations, both of which require expertise that is generally lacking in foreign banks although acquired banks may bring such local knowledge. Using the first EBRD Banking Environment and Performance Survey, Haselmann and Wachtel (2010) show that banks in many transition economies have shifted their asset portfolios out of government securities towards mortgages and consumer credit. Foreign banks in particular have increased consumer lending and only maintained the existing level of lending to enterprises The EBRD/World Bank surveys of enterprises in transition countries indicate that many firms are financially constrained in the sense that they are unable to obtain bank lending. Based on these surveys, the EBRD concludes that "despite some regional variation, bank loans still play a limited role in enterprise financing" (EBRD *Transition Report*, 2006, p. 47). Since lending to enterprises is important to support economic growth, this finding has important implications for any evaluation of the conduct of banking in transition countries.

The EBRD surveys indicate that improvements in the legal environment for banking have been associated with greater risk taking and more credit extended to small and medium enterprises (EBRD *Transition Report*, 2006; Haselmann and Wachtel, 2007). However such lending remains small; survey respondents often indicate that a lack of creditworthy borrowers and difficulty in evaluating risks were the main reasons for slow loan growth. In their lending activity, banks in transition countries tend to favor large firms and foreign affiliates. However, improvements in the legal and regulatory environment, such as good bankruptcy laws, efficient ownership structures, reliable court systems for their application, credit registries, and defined legal rights to collateral should lead to more lending to firms and more support of local entrepreneurs (De Haas and Lelyveld, 2006).

The largest enterprises in the transition countries, particularly those that are part of the EU, face fewer problems in obtaining financing because of the growth in cross border financings. Such firms have access to the European syndicated loan market as well as direct access to banks and capital markets in Frankfurt and London. Further such activity introduces competition into some of the highly concentrated domestic markets. However, cross border activity ceased during the financial crisis, particularly syndicated loans which had been growing rapidly and has been slow to recover.

The relationship between parent banks and their local partners is a mixed blessing. In some cases, a parent bank provided assistance for a troubled local institution. For example, prior to its own crisis difficulties, KBC from Belgium supported its troubled Polish subsidiary, Kredytbank. However, parent bank support can not be taken for granted—the Bayerische Landesbank walked away from its Croatian subsidiary, Rijecka Banka, when fraud was uncovered. In addition, ownership changes in the parent bank can affect the structure of banking in the host country. When HypoVerinsbank joined the Unicredito banking group in late 2005, several Polish subsidiaries were merged to create the second largest bank in Poland despite objections from the Polish authorities.

Banking regulation in the European Union follows the home country principle in that the home country regulators supervise the consolidated balance sheet of multinational banks. At the same time, the host country regulators have responsibility over the local subsidiaries. Hence, a potential for conflict arises if a home country regulator does not have sufficient influence over a foreign subsidiary that is a small part of a multinational bank but an important player in the financial sector of the host country. The lack of explicit coordination of bank regulation across borders is a problem that is finally getting attention through the ongoing discussions regarding a European Banking Union which would include the new member states.

In summary, virtually all of the European transition countries have developed mature banking sectors and considerable strides in this direction have been made by banks in the other transition countries. The FSU countries now have models to emulate; hence, their progress toward achieving mature and effective banking institutions warrants careful watching to see if the relevant lessons have been learned. Further, banks around the world have lessons to learn from the recent experiences of the transition countries regarding the role of foreign banks in the transmission of shocks and the ability of central banks to respond to credit booms. Banks in the transition economies have become part of the competitive global financial industry.

REFERENCES

Barisitz, S. (2007). *Banking in Central and Eastern Europe 1980–2006: A Comprehensive Analysis of Banking Sector Transformation in the Former Soviet Union, Czechoslovakia, East Germany, Yugoslavia, Belarus, Bulgaria, Croatia, the Czech Republic, Hungary, Kazakhstan, Poland, Romania, the Russian Federation, Serbia and Montenegro, Slovakia, Ukraine, and Uzbekistan.* New York and London: Routledge.

Bonin, J.P. (2004). Banking in the Balkans, the Structure of Banking Sectors in Southeast Europe, *Economic Systems* 28, 141–153.

Bonin, J. P., Hasan, I., and Wachtel, P. (2005a). Bank Performance, Efficiency and Ownership in Transition Countries, *Journal of Banking and Finance* 29, 31–53.

Bonin, J. P., Hasan, I., and Wachtel, P. (2005b). Privatization Matters: Bank Efficiency in Transition Countries, *Journal of Banking and Finance* 29, 2155–2178.

Bonin, J. P. and Wachtel, P. (2005). Dealing with Financial Fragility in Transition Economies. In: D. Evanoff and G. Kaufman (Eds.), *Systemic Financial Crises: Resolving Large Bank Insolvencies*, 141–159. Singapore: World Scientific Publishing.

Claeys, S. and Hainz, C. (2014). Modes of Foreign Bank Entry and Effects on Lending Rates: Theory and Evidence, *Journal of Comparative Economics* 42, 160–177.

De Haas, R. (2014). The Dark and Bright Side of Global Banking: A (Somewhat) Cautionary Tale from Emerging Europe, *Comparative Economic Studies* 56, 271–282.

De Haas, R., Korniyenko, Y., Loukoianova, E., and Pivovarsky, A. (2012). Foreign Banks and the Vienna Initiative: Turning Sinners into Saints, EBRD Working Paper No. 143, March.

De Haas, R. and Lelyveld, I. V. (2006). Foreign Banks and Credit Stability in Central and Eastern Europe: A Panel Data Analysis, *Journal of Banking and Finance* 30, 1927–1952.

EBRD (2006, 2009). *Transition Report*. London: European Bank for Reconstruction and Development.

Epstein, R. (2014). When do Foreign Banks "Cut and Run"? Evidence from West European Bailouts and East European Markets, *Review of International Political Economy* 21, 847–877.

Hasan, I. and Marton, K. (2003). Banking in Transition Economy: Hungarian Evidence, *Journal of Banking and Finance* 27, 2249–2271.

Haselmann, R. and Wachtel, P. (2007). Risk Taking by Banks in the Transition Countries, *Comparative Economic Studies* 49, 411–429.

Haselmann, R. and Wachtel, P. (2010). Bankers Perception of the Legal Environment and the Composition of Bank Lending, *Journal of Money, Credit and Banking* 42, 965–984.

Ongena, S., Peydro, J. L., and van Horen, N. (2013). Shocks Abroad, Pain at Home? Bank-Firm Level Evidence on the International Transmission of Foreign Shocks, *Tilburg University Center for Economic Research* Discussion Paper No. 2013–040.

Popov, A. and Udell, G. (2012). Cross-border Banking, Credit Access and the Financial Crisis, *Journal of International Economics* 87 147–161.

Steinherr, A. (2006). Russian Banking since the Crisis of 1998, *Economic Change and Restructuring* 39, 235–259.

Wachtel, P. (2001). Growth and Finance—What Do We Know and How Do We Know It?, *International Finance* 4, 335–362.

CHAPTER 40

....

BANKING IN LATIN AMERICA

....

FERNANDO J. CARDIM DE CARVALHO,
LUIZ FERNANDO DE PAULA, AND
JONATHAN WILLIAMS

40.1 INTRODUCTION

WHEN the first version of this chapter was prepared, in 2008, it was still unclear how deep the unfolding financial crisis was, how strongly it would impact the non-financial sector of the various economies, and how long its effects would be felt. The worst world economic crisis known since the 1930s Great Depression had not yet showed how destructive it would be for domestic financial systems and for public finance in a large number of countries, particularly in the United States and Western Europe. The protracted sovereign debt crisis in the European Union was still two years in the future, international trade had not yet become a channel for contagion of the crisis to emerging and developing economies. Despite the immediate shock caused by the failure of Lehman Brothers, in September 2008, Latin American economies saw what then-President Lula da Silva of Brazil classified as a little wave in contrast to the tsunami described by former Federal Reserve Chairman Alan Greenspan.

In fact, banking systems in Latin America suffered relatively little damage from the crisis. For this reason, not many fundamental changes can be observed in domestic banking markets in the region since 2008. The continuing deleterious impact of financial instability in the United States and Western Europe was felt mostly through macroeconomic channels instead of financial instability, whilst the contraction of demand for imports in industrialized economies was compensated by the increasing role of China as importer (especially of raw materials) for most Latin American countries. Besides, as we will show, the decades immediately before the crisis had witnessed a strong movement of structural change in banking systems across Latin America. During the 1980s and, even more notably, the 1990s, banking systems in Latin America were deeply transformed. Liberal reforms were widely adopted in the region. Common features of these reforms were the liberalization of interest rates, the attenuation of barriers to entry in the provision of banking services, large-scale privatization of state-owned banks and the facilitation of entry for foreign banks (see Singh et al, 2005; Stallings and Studart, 2006). In parallel, but in a largely independent process, liberalization of the capital account of the balance of payments also influenced the evolution of domestic financial systems, since it opened new opportunities of investment for resident wealth-holders at the same time in which it made possible for non-residents to buy assets and offer financial services to residents. The downside of such a process, of course, was the increasing exposure of these economies to the volatility of international financial markets.

The joint impact of all these changes was to transform deeply the ways financial systems work in Latin America. In fact, the transformation process is still unfolding, although nowadays in the shape of a sharp expansion of securities markets and also of a fast increasing supply of bank credit to private borrowers, even though it has generally started from very low levels in the region. Among the most visible changes already achieved is the strong process of bank consolidation that has taken place in the period. Of particular interest are the effects of consolidation on competition and efficiency in banking sectors.

In the post-subprime crisis period, the most important changes occurred, as one would expect, in the area of financial regulation, particularly prudential regulation. Not only did Latin American countries share the perception that financial regulation and supervision had failed in their role to ensure financial stability, particularly in the banking sector, but geopolitical changes (particularly the rise of the G20 group of countries) had strengthened the voice of these countries, or at least some of them, in the international fora where regulation is debated and formulated, such as the Financial Stability Board and the Basel Committee on Bank Supervision. In the other topics of interest, changes were more gradual and incremental in contrast to the reforms of the 1980s and 1990s.

This chapter is structured in the following way. After this Introduction, Section 40.2 provides an overview of the recent consolidation of banking sectors in Latin America. In Section 40.3 we consider the evolution of financial policy and how it has contributed towards the recent consolidation process. Section 40.4 investigates the effects consolidation has had on banking sectors. Besides updating the preceding sections, this chapter now includes a new section (40.5) on the post-crisis period changes in bank regulation and supervision which were implemented as a response to the financial crisis. Some concluding notes are then developed in Section 40.6.

40.2 BANKING CONSOLIDATION IN LATIN AMERICA: A QUICK OVERVIEW

Banking crises, financial deregulation and the globalization of financial services has led to a significant increase in foreign bank penetration of emerging market banking sectors over the second half of the 1990s. The effects of these developments have been summarized as follows: "global market and technology developments, macroeconomic pressures and banking crises in the 1990s have forced the banking industry and the regulators to change the old way of doing business, and to deregulate the banking industry at the national level and open up financial markets to foreign competition. (. . .) These changes have significantly increased competitive pressures on banks in the emerging economies and have led to deep changes in the structure of the banking industry" (Hawkins and Mihaljek, 2001, p. 3).

Whilst the process of bank consolidation in industrialized and emerging markets has been shaped by the above forces, some specific features have characterized consolidation in emerging markets (IMF, 2007; Gelos and Roldós, 2004). First, cross-border mergers and acquisitions (M&A) have been an important source of consolidation in emerging markets yet the exception in industrialized markets. Second, consolidation was used to restructure emerging market banking sectors after financial crises rather than to eliminate excess capacity or improve bank efficiency as in industrialized markets. Finally, emerging market governments actively participated in the process of consolidation, whereas consolidation tended to be "market-driven" in industrialized markets since it represented financial institutions' response to policies of financial deregulation that were implemented in the 1970s and 1980s.

Bank consolidation has been more advanced in Latin America compared to other emerging markets. National governments actively participated in bank restructuring and implemented substantial bank privatization programs, although in countries such as Argentina and Brazil some large banks remain under state ownership. Since the end of the 1990s, the consolidation process—especially in Brazil and Mexico—has become increasingly market-driven (as in industrialized markets). Generally, the desire to enhance competition and efficiency and, in some cases, to restructure public finances formed the background to almost all privatization programs in the region. The role played by foreign banks in the restructuring and consolidation of domestic banking sectors should not be underestimated. The mid-1990s banking sector crises offered foreign banks "a one time set of opportunities to invest in financial institutions and to expand business. . . A standard response to crises by EME (emerging market economies) government, encouraged by the international financial institutions, was to accelerate financial liberalization and to recapitalize banks with the help of foreign investors" (CGFS, 2004, p. 6). This has happened in Argentina, Brazil and Mexico. Foreign banks' shares of banking sector assets did increase substantially in Latin America, and although foreign bank penetration was not as extensive as in Central and Eastern Europe it was higher than in Asia (Domanski, 2005). Notwithstanding, the level of foreign bank penetration is lower in 2010 compared to a decade earlier, which reflects difficulties foreign banks faced in some countries in the region, the expansion of private-owned banks, and use of state-owned banks to provide credit during the recent crisis (see Table 40.1).

In the 1990s, Latin America received record levels of foreign direct investment (FDI). In 1998 alone, the region received an inflow of US$76.7 billion which was equivalent to 41% of total FDI to developing countries (ECLAC, 2000, pp. 35–36). The majority of investments were made in banking sectors. Between 1991 and 2005, a total of US$121 billion was expended on cross-border M&A involving the acquisition of banks in emerging markets (Domanski, 2005). Of the total, 48% was spent in Latin America, with Asia and Central and Eastern Europe receiving 36% and 17%, respectively. The main source of investment in Latin America came from Spanish banks (46.6% of the value of acquisitions made by foreign banks of domestic banks in the region) followed by US (26.5%), UK (10.0%), Dutch (6.4%), and Canadian banks (3.6%).

Bank restructuring has increased the level of concentration in regional banking sectors. Whilst banks numbers have fallen—considerably in some countries—the accompanying increases in concentration were not as sharp. Table 40.2 shows the three-firm asset vs.

Table 40.1 Share of banking sector assets: by ownership, %

	Argentina	Brazil	Chile	Mexico	Venezuela
State-owned banks					
1990	69.65	53.65	22.79	98.44	11.75
2000	26.56	32.16	14.03	0.87	3.60
2010	44.82	34.14	18.69	0.29	53.75
Foreign-owned banks					
1990	0.00	3.03	41.98	0.29	0.00
2000	55.18	27.89	38.32	49.88	59.88
2010	29.76	17.38	23.96	73.90	0.73
Private-owned banks					
1990	30.35	43.26	72.94	1.27	82.33
2000	18.26	39.87	42.14	49.25	33.95
2010	22.13	48.48	47.11	25.80	14.48

Source: Authors' calculations from BankScope.

Table 40.2 Banking sector concentration; CR3 ratio, %

Country	2000	2005	2010
Argentina	32.3	46.4	34.0
Bolivia	47.4	50.3	57.1
Brazil	38.7	46.1	61.7
Chile[1]	38.4	55.1	52.1
Colombia	32.1	43.4	50.1
Ecuador	54.4	49.7	54.5
Mexico	57.4	60.4	53.3
Peru	61.9	76.9	74.2
Paraguay	45.4	47.8	49.5
Uruguay	34.9	57.7	61.6
Venezuela	44.7	36.4	68.7
Japan	35.0	40.0	44.2
UK	30.4	49.4	56.0
US	21.4	29.8	31.6

Notes: CR3 is the share of the three largest banks in total assets.

[1] For Chile, the ratio shown in the column 2010 is for 2007.

Source: World Bank Financial Structure database.

ratios (CR3) for banking sectors in the region plus comparative data for Japan, the UK, and US. In all countries (bar Ecuador and Venezuela) the three largest banks gain market share between 2000 and 2005. Concentration levels continue to rise in several countries between 2005 and 2010 including the largest economy, Brazil, where CR3 is nearly 1.6 times larger than in 2000 which demonstrates the extent of the consolidation process in that country.

Other significant increases in concentration occur in Colombia, Uruguay, and Chile. In Venezuela, the marked rise in CR3 between 2005 and 2010 is indicative of banking sector duress and ongoing bank restructuring.

In countries such as Mexico and Argentina, the rise in the level of consolidation was closely tied to foreign bank penetration. In Mexico, foreign banks had unrestricted access to all sectors of the banking market and became market leaders. Whilst foreign banks came to dominate domestic banks in Argentina—as they increased their market share from 16.1% of total bank deposits in November 1994 to 51.8% in December 2001 (Fanelli, 2003, p. 52)— their presence partially wavered after the 2001–2002 financial crisis as their market share declined whilst the market shares of private and mainly public-owned banks increased. Domestic private and public banks are market leaders in Brazil. Indeed, private-owned banks responded proactively to foreign bank penetration and became active in domestic M&A (Paula and Alves, 2007). The consolidation process in Chile proceeded more gradually: it has increased because of M&A in Spain (the home country of the parent banks of the two largest banks in Chile); technically, the enlarged Spanish parent has operated its Chilean subsidiaries as individual entities (Ahumada and Marshall, 2001).

Bank restructuring and privatization ushered in a new wave of cross-border (and domestic) M&A activity. Cross-border bank M&A partially reflects country-specific factors: positively related to shared language (Spanish bank entry, Sebastián and Hernansanz, 2000) and geographical proximity (North American bank entry; Buch and DeLong, 2001); and the availability of access to large, relatively poor countries with widely spaced populations and underdeveloped financial sectors (Buch and DeLong, 2001; Focarelli and Pozzolo, 2001). M&A can be analyzed in terms of the financial condition of buyers and targets. An application to Brazil differentiates between M&A involving domestic-owned and foreign-owned banks. The results suggest that domestic and foreign buyers acquired target banks that had alternative profiles: domestic buyers have tended to buy underperforming banks whilst foreign buyers tended to acquire large, slow growing institutions; the implication is that foreign banks have used M&A as the vehicle to increase bank size and market share (Cardias Williams and Williams, 2008).

One important development in Brazil, after, and as a result, of the crisis was the mergers between Itaú and Unibanco. It was rather an acquisition of Unibanco that was weakened by its exposure to the more serious threat created by the Lehman Brothers shock wave that caused the Brazilian currency (Real) to depreciate when many large firms had bet that the Real would continue to appreciate and suffered heavy losses.

40.3 THE EVOLUTION OF FINANCIAL POLICY IN LATIN AMERICA

Although the process of transformation of Latin American banking systems has exhibited basically the same features, and took place in roughly the same period, its causes diverged from country to country. Post-1945, Latin American financial systems were typically repressed, and governments across the region attempted from the late 1940s, with varying success, to accelerate economic growth and transform national social and economic structures. The key to become a developed country was thought to be becoming industrial-ized as quickly as possible. Inspired by the experiences of Central European countries (cf. Gerschenkron, 1962), Latin American governments, particularly in the largest countries (Brazil, Mexico, Argentina, and Chile) saw in the banking system a powerful instrument to centralize and direct the necessary resources to finance the growth of manufacturing pro-duction. Unwilling to rely on the eventual ability of freely operating financial markets to support an accelerated growth process, governments in those countries imposed financial repression (Fry, 1995), which consisted in this case mostly of creating, or enlarging the func-tions of existing, state-owned banks, setting maximum interest rates to be charged on loans by private banks (frequently adopted in the context of usury laws), and directing the credit supplied by these banks to sectors considered strategic to enhance economic growth.

This is not the place to assess how successful these initiatives were in promoting growth.[1] The region suffered heavily with the oil shocks of the 1970s. The attempts to deal with the effects of those shocks by increasing short-term foreign debt led to the debt crisis of the early 1980s that brought the most important economies of the region to a stand still that lasted so long it became known as the "lost decade of economic growth." As part of the negotiated resolution package for that crisis, almost all countries in Latin America accepted to pro-mote liberalizing reforms, including in the financial sector and thereby ending the financial repression experiment.

Chile was the pioneer in this process (see Foxley, 1983; Stallings and Studart, 2006). Liberal reforms in the banking markets, including privatization of state-owned financial institutions began right after the 1973 military coup that ousted then-President Salvador Allende. The root cause of financial liberalization in the case of Chile was the radically con-servative nature of the military regime led by General Pinochet, which aimed at erasing all and any trace of the policies adopted before. As it has happened in similar experiences, strong liberalization policies created new profitable opportunities for banks which raised their competitiveness. However, financial regulation and bank supervision were deficient either because regulators lacked experience with open markets or because the state was assumed to be an inefficient player in the economic game so no investment in upgrading the skills of regulators and supervisors was made. Inevitably, as has been the general experi-ence, this first wave of liberalization ended up generating a profound banking crisis in the early 1980s. To resolve the crisis, the government intervened heavily in the banking system. On the one hand, banks were allowed to sell to the government their non-performing assets under the obligation of buying them back over time, when the crisis was expected to be over. In addition, tougher bank regulation was adopted to prevent the disorderly expansion of the past from repeating itself.

In the case of Mexico, banking reforms were inspired by less dramatic events (see Singh et al. 2005; Avalos and Trillo, 2006; Stallings and Studart, 2006). Mexico had also followed the general pattern set by the largest economies of Latin America in the post-war period of creating strong state-owned banks to stimulate economic development. Room for pri-vate banks was very limited and foreign banks were all but banned from operating in the domestic markets. As late as in the early 1980s, foreign banks were still prevented from

---

[1] Higher growth rates were in fact achieved although at the cost of the emergence of some important disequilibria.

controlling more than 7% of the net worth of the largest banks. The 1982 debt crisis, the ensuing period of economic stagnation, and the conditionality clauses included in the rescue packages negotiated by the Mexican government with creditor banks and multilateral institutions led the Mexican authorities to a change of heart. The government endeavored to promote liberal reforms in the economy, of which banking reform was an important element (see de Vries, 1987). Later, this drive was strengthened by Mexico's adhesion to NAFTA which led to a gradual but steady reduction of barriers to entry to American and Canadian banks.[2] The defining act of Mexico's reforms, however, was the bungled privatization process of 1991, which took place when there were still strong restrictions against foreign participation in the domestic banking sector. Banks were acquired by businessmen inexperienced in the banking business, at prices widely considered to be excessive. The rush to recover their investments and to obtain profits led to a credit boom unrestrained by any kind of proper regulation. Credit was expanded without any attention being given to credit risks. The fast expansion ultimately caused the 1994 crisis, when bank assets were virtually renationalized. In fact, the Mexican government, first in 1995, and again in 1996, bought the huge amount of non-performing assets in banks' balance sheets through a crisis resolution entity created to manage the problem (Fobaproa).[3] Contrary to what was done in Chile, however, those assets were not to be reabsorbed by the banking system; rather, taxpayers' money paid for the losses of banks, since Fobaproa's liabilities were transformed into public debt. The weakness of the banking system led the Mexican government to change the law to allow an increasing participation of foreign banks in domestic markets, including the acquisition of local problem banks. Consequently, the market share of foreign banks in Mexico was over 80% in 2000 (Hernandez-Murillo, 2007, p. 416).

In Brazil and Argentina, the causes of the liberalization process were somewhat more complex, due to persistently high inflation. In both cases, most (but not all) reforms were adopted as elements of price stabilization strategies. Until the 1970s, the Brazilian banking system was highly repressed (Carvalho, 1998). Although the presence of private banks was strong, the system was dominated by state-owned institutions. Foreign banks were confined to attending mostly foreign companies, and as in other countries, prevented from reaching domestic clients (Carvalho, 2000). In the mid-1960s, the structure of the Brazilian financial system had been changed, and a segmented market model, similar to the one set by the Glass–Steagall Act in the US, was imposed. Commercial banks would provide short-term credit and payment services, investment banks should help develop an incipient securities market, specialized institutions would finance the acquisition of durable consumption goods and public institutions would give financial support to productive investments in manufacturing, agriculture and construction.

Thanks to loopholes in the legislation, financial conglomerates, with interests in virtually all segments of the financial system, and in non financial sectors as well, emerged in

---

[2] In 1995 a modification increased the limits of foreign participation established under the NAFTA agreement (initially foreign banks could not buy domestic banks whose market share exceeded 1.5%). In December 1998 the Mexican Congress approved a further modification allowing foreign investment in domestic banks to reach 100%. Subsequently, the largest banking institutions (Bancomer, Banamex and Serfin) were acquired by foreign banks (Maudos and Solis, 2011).

[3] The ratio of non-performing loans-to-total loans is estimated to have reached 52.6% by December 1996 (Hernandez-Murillo, 2007, p. 421).

the 1970s and early 1980s. In parallel, the acceleration of inflation after the oil shocks of the 1970s steadily reduced the access of private borrowers to credit markets. Banks were increasingly devoting the resources they controlled to buying public debt issued by the federal government, unable as the latter was to control its fiscal deficits. Market segments other than deposit-taking and public-debt-buying, and the institutions supposed to operate them, gradually faded and disappeared. Under these circumstances, in 1988, the Central Bank of Brazil passed a resolution adopting the German-type universal banking model in the place of the aforementioned segmented model.[4] In the same resolution, interest rate controls were lifted. Financial liberalization in Brazil, therefore, began as the result of the acknowledgement that past regulations had become obsolete rather than being the first step of a well-defined strategy (Paula, 2011).

In Argentina, developments that were to some extent similar took place in the same period.[5] Accelerating inflation, as in Brazil, was the most important problem faced by policymakers at the time. In the late 1980s, the arsenal of instruments to control inflation was fast being depleted, after many failed attempts at price stabilization. Moreover, foreign creditors were demanding implementation of financial liberalization policies as a conditionality clause in the resolution package for the debt crisis of 1982. The Argentine government had little choice but to begin a liberalization process, by freeing interest rates and moving toward a universal bank model, leaving to each financial institution the choice of sectors where to operate.

After 1991, with the adoption of the Convertibility Plan (also known as the Cavallo Plan, named after then Finance Minister Domingo Cavallo), in contrast to the more pragmatic Brazilian experience, a radical liberalization strategy was put in place. A central element of this strategy was the opening of the domestic banking market to foreign banks. As a result, foreign penetration of the Argentinean banking system increased dramatically as it was deliberately promoted by a restructuring and concentration policy, which had been implemented after the contagion of Mexico's Tequila crisis that severely tested both the Convertibility system and the financial sector. Among the ten largest banks in Argentina in December 2000, seven banks were foreign-owned, two were public-owned—the market leaders, Banco de la Nación (Federal) and Banco de la Provincia de Buenos Ayres (provincial)—and only one bank was domestic, private-owned (Paula and Alves, 2007, p. 97).

The process of privatization of state-owned banks in Argentina illustrated an important change of views that had already taken place in countries such as Chile and Uruguay. In these cases, privatization was seen not only as a temporary convenience or an unavoidable evil. Liberalization was adopted as a *strategy*, rather than as an expedient. Bank privatization was conducted as an element, no matter how important, of an overall liberalization process that was expected to help the region to overcome its long-term inefficiencies. The deep crisis of the early 2000s led Argentina to partially repudiate this view. It is still dominant in Chile and Uruguay, even after center-left administrations were elected in the latter countries at the beginning of the new century.

[4] Universal banks are called *multiple* banks in Brazil.
[5] Decisions concerning financial liberalization in Argentina since the late 1980s are listed (in Portuguese) in Studart and Hermann (n.d.) and are reproduced and discussed in Carvalho (2008). For an overview of the process, see O'Connell (2005).

In Brazil, in contrast, this path was explored with caution. In fact, the end of inflation in 1994 caused severe stress in a large number of banks that earned their profits mostly from securing deposits to finance the purchase of public debt, the yield of which was indexed to the rate of inflation. When inflation fell precipitously, after the implementation of the Real Plan in 1994, many banks were revealed to be practically bankrupt. The Brazilian government, to avoid panic, took measures to allow splitting problem banks in two parts: a "sane" one, with healthy assets and its corresponding share of liabilities; and the failed one, with the non-recoverable assets. The sane part was to be sold to other banks; the failed part would be liquidated by the Central Bank.

The same scheme, actually inspired by rules used in the US to deal with the Continental Illinois Bank in the mid-1980s, was adopted in Argentina (De la Torre, 2000). In Argentina and Brazil, panic was avoided, at the cost of pushing bank consolidation forward. In Brazil, the Central Bank decided to invite foreign banks to buy domestic banks that were either being privatized or facing difficulties that would probably lead them to fail. The decision to allow foreign banks in was made to prevent excess concentration, which was expected to ensue should the leading domestic banks be allowed to buy problem banks. Although, the Brazilian government never lifted the legal restrictions banning the entry of new foreign banks in the domestic system, it allowed "exceptions" to take place while they were needed. Once the economy was stabilized and the stock of problem banks was sold, practically no new foreign bank was authorized into the country. Mexico was the last large country in Latin America to open its market to foreign banks. However, it is also the country where foreign banks were granted the most unrestrained access to domestic markets, leading to an almost complete disappearance of domestic private banks, let alone state-owned banks.

The 2008 financial crisis changed the appreciation of the role of state-owned banks in some countries. In the case of Brazil, the three largest federally owned banks (the National Development Bank, BNDES, Bank of Brazil and the National Savings Bank, CEF) served as instruments for the implementation of anticyclical policies, supplying credit when private banks retreated in the face of increased uncertainty. As a result, the market share of federally owned banks increased during the crisis and the lead was maintained even after private banks felt the need to expand to recover at least part of their lost market share. More recently, state-owned banks have also been used to push bank spreads down by reducing their lending interest rates thereby forcing private banks to follow their lead. State-owned banks have been likewise employed as instruments of anticyclical policy in Argentina lately (BCRA, 2012). In fact, the role of the Argentine Central Bank was widened in April 2012 to make it responsible for promoting growth, full employment and income distribution, besides maintaining the purchasing power of the peso. As a result, many programs were created to spur growth of credit to non-financial firms.

The trend towards consolidation is not new to the region. Previously, waves of bank consolidation had taken place in some countries, mostly induced by domestic policies. In Brazil, for instance, in the early 1970s, a strong consolidation process was promoted by the federal government under the expectation that taking advantage of supposedly strong economies of scale would allow the reduction of interest rates necessary to keep the economy growing as rapidly as it was. Financial repression was still in force, and no increase of foreign participation was envisaged. Increasing efficiency via scale economies should lighten the burden of interest rate control on banks, attenuating the incentives to evade these controls. In any case, Latin American economies are still relatively small. If to the small dimension of these economies one also adds the generally high degree of income concentration, markets for banking services would be even smaller. If scale economies exist in banking, one would expect to find a relatively high degree of concentration in the region anyway.

In the 1980s, and more so, in the 1990s, the push for consolidation came from many sources. Political and ideological factors were very important in the case of Chile in the mid-1970s, to allow banks to decide their own policies, including larger and stronger banks to absorb smaller ones. After the early 1980s crisis, the push for consolidation was strengthened by the assumption that larger banks, especially foreign ones, are capable of managing risk more efficiently, specially if prudential regulation was improved, thereby making the system more stable.

Concerns with systemic stability help to explain consolidation, in one way or another, in nearly all of the region's recent experiences. Many of the regulatory initiatives adopted to strengthen the stability of banking systems contributed to push consolidation forward. The introduction of modern payments systems, the increasing use of ATMs, Internet banking and so forth, also lead to increased consolidation if individual banks have to provide their own equipment and other facilities. Even privatization initiatives were frequently defended with systemic safety arguments, on the notion that state-owned financial institutions increase the risk of feeding dangerous forms of crony capitalism. Consequently, at the turn of the millennium, the most important banking systems in Latin America came to exhibit a relatively similar ownership structure.

40.3.1 Financial Penetration in Latin America

Latin American financial systems are characterized by similar features: financial depth is limited; financial sectors are bank-based since stockmarkets are mostly small and illiquid and corporate debt markets even more so; intermediation margins are high by international standards; banking sector concentration has increased; and bank lending is low relative to overall economic activity. Indeed, the limited access to bank credit and uncertainty about financial stability are factors that have contributed to economic volatility in the region (Singh et al. 2005, Ch. 1).

Whereas Latin American financial systems are deeper than they were a decade ago (Rojas Suarez, 2007, p. 3), the level of financial depth is low compared with industrialized countries and also some other emerging market regions such as East Asia. Nevertheless, Table 40.3 suggests that the combined share of the banking sector and stock market in GDP increased in all countries in the region between 1990 and 2010 with only limited exceptions. However, the table also shows there is considerable heterogeneity in financial depth in Latin America: in 2010 financial penetration is significantly deeper in Chile followed by Brazil, Peru, and Colombia. Between 1990 and 2010 the financial sectors in these three countries deepened considerably albeit from a relatively low base. In Argentina and Bolivia the financial sector's share of GDP rapidly increased between 1990 and 2000. Whereas financial depth was lower in 2010, nevertheless it exceeded the level of 1990. Only in Uruguay and Venezuela does the financial sector account for a lower share of GDP in 2010 compared to 1990. Chile is the only country to have achieved a level of deepening comparable with industrialized countries (Betancour, De Gregorio, and Jara, 2006; Rojas Suarez, 2007). Furthermore, households' access to financial services in Chile is closest to

Table 40.3 **Financial sector share of GDP, %**

	GDP $m	Financial sector, % of GDP			Intermediation, %		
	2010	1990	2000	2010	1990	2000	2010
Argentina	434,406	22.59	116.24	40.71	167.37	74.48	47.92
Bolivia	12,240	41.32	96.82	77.66	101.72	114.44	52.21
Brazil	919,487	50.95	111.93	131.41	121.88	68.17	71.19
Chile	110,042	190.05	182.93	208.60	116.14	142.76	87.18
Colombia	149,691	56.92	53.34	99.07	100.75	85.96	83.34
Ecuador	24,996	39.16	42.22	40.02	74.68	150.97	83.89
Mexico	692,479	45.33	62.25	68.96	84.98	59.80	60.14
Paraguay	10,463	33.22	41.46	40.69	70.10	95.29	79.38
Peru	92,507	28.57	94.87	90.14	34.06	80.63	68.04
Uruguay	30,534	75.60	56.44	39.73	61.67	106.00	52.59
Venezuela	159,405	69.16	34.04	31.69	47.62	50.57	56.84
Japan	5,094,423	358.05	347.80	295.13	90.78	80.63	45.99
UK	1,744,580	275.68	330.91	304.94	123.25	118.83	115.22
US	11,547,905	214.06	268.47	196.87	75.31	70.85	67.37

Note: GDP is at 2000 prices; we measure the size of the financial sector by the sum of liquid liabilities and stockmarket capitalization; Intermediation is the ratio of banking sector credit to the private sector-to-liquid liabilities.

Source: World Bank Development Indicators; World Bank Financial Structure database.

levels observed in industrialized countries; over 90% of households have access to financial services in Western industrialized countries compared with 60–80% in Chile, 40–60% in Brazil and Colombia, and 20–40% in Argentina and Mexico (Honohan, 2007). Table 40.3 traces developments in banking sector intermediation. Generally speaking, the level of intermediation increased in most countries between 1990 and 2000 (notable exceptions include the larger economies of Argentina, Brazil, and Mexico). The data for 2010 suggest the 2008 financial crisis substantially and adversely affected the provision of credit to the private sector in nearly all countries. However, intermediation in 2010 was higher than a decade earlier in Brazil, Mexico and Venezuela.

Table 40.4 offers a closer inspection of the depth of banking sectors in terms of deposits (liquid liabilities) and credit as shares of GDP over a longer time frame from 1980 to 2010. Generally speaking, the low levels of depth observed in 1980, during the period of financial repression, are considerably below the levels achieved in 2010 (for deposits). Significant enhancements have occurred in Bolivia, Brazil, Chile, and Paraguay. Whilst a similar pattern emerges for credit, the data for 2010 imply that one effect of the subprime crisis seems to have been to reduce the rate of financial deepening between 2000 and 2010 for several countries, namely Argentina, Bolivia, Ecuador, Peru, and Uruguay. On the contrary, credit markets deepened in Brazil, Chile, Colombia, Paraguay and Venezuela. Chile and Brazil host the deepest credit and deposit markets in 2010.

If financial depth and access to financial services are to increase, the institutional environment which conditions the effective operation of financial intermediaries and financial markets must be developed further. The World Bank Governance Indicators show an improved

Table 40.4 Financial depth of banking sectors; credit and deposit markets

	Liquid liabilities-to-GDP, %				Credit-to-GDP, %			
	1980	1990	2000	2010	1980	1990	2000	2010
Argentina	21.45	7.64	31.83	25.65	16.01	12.79	23.70	12.29
Bolivia	16.12	19.58	52.19	62.19	14.38	19.92	59.73	32.47
Brazil	12.57	25.26	43.30	64.34	24.20	30.79	29.51	45.80
Chile	22.69	35.45	41.76	79.05	30.72	41.17	59.62	68.92
Colombia	24.20	26.50	25.90	36.00	25.18	26.70	22.26	30.00
Ecuador	21.77	17.31	22.99	31.81	17.20	12.93	34.71	26.69
Mexico	27.48	17.10	27.87	29.48	16.69	14.53	16.66	17.73
Peru	16.10	9.66	32.48	33.38	5.55	3.29	26.18	22.71
Paraguay	22.43	18.82	28.02	40.69	17.87	13.19	26.70	32.30
Uruguay	31.38	40.44	41.49	39.36	29.05	24.94	43.98	20.70
Venezuela	43.98	32.31	18.68	30.15	22.10	15.38	9.45	17.14
Japan	137.94	182.04	238.89	224.86	115.71	165.26	192.63	103.41
UK	30.56	88.01	100.60	175.48	26.00	108.47	119.55	202.18
US	69.01	73.33	68.68	84.87	55.94	55.22	48.66	57.17

Source: World Bank Financial Structure database.

level of governance in Brazil, Chile, and Mexico (between 1996 and 2004), but only Chile achieved a level comparable with industrialized countries (Rojas Suarez, 2007, p. 25).

The effectiveness of financial liberalization in Latin America may be gauged from the evolution of interest rate spreads. Weaknesses in the institutional environment are offered as a partial explanation for the relatively high, by international standards, spreads observed and the dispersion of spreads across the region (Gelos, 2006). Across Latin America, credit is not only scarce but costly too. The IADB (2005) show that between the mid-1990s and early 2000s, interest margins in Latin America (at 8.5%) exceeded those in East Asia and the Pacific (5.1%) and the developed countries (2.9%), although slightly lower than Eastern Europe and Central Asia (8.8%).

In the first edition of this book, we highlighted a narrowing of bank interest spreads in Latin America from 1993 to the mid-2000s, though spreads were high by international standards and varied across countries. The convergence of spreads continues to the present. Spreads are correlated more with loan rates than deposit rates (especially in Argentina and Peru) meaning that a shock that causes spreads to widen will raise lending rates rather than decrease deposit rates. Whilst Brazilian spreads remain highest they are currently (2012) around 15 percentage points below the 2003 level; spreads are particularly affected by risk variables (risk premium, interest rate volatility), output growth and the level of short-term interest rate (Oreiro and Paula, 2010). Since 2008, Brazilian spreads have narrowed by around five percentage points as the authorities loosened monetary policy as part of the strategy to combat the effects of the subprime crisis. Whereas spreads in Paraguay and Peru exceed most other countries in the region, after 2008 spreads in Argentina, Chile, and Mexico have narrowed and are below 5%.

The relationship between market concentration and interest rate margins is scarcely analyzed in Latin America. Recent evidence suggests market share exerts little or no influence on interest rate margins; indeed, lower spreads result from more competitive markets and improvements in efficiency (Chortareas, Garza- García, and Girardone, 2012). Such findings, however, do not generalize across the region: in Mexico, for instance, the recent growth in banking system profitability is attributed to monopolistic competition (Maudos and Solis, 2011).

Besides the generally low but deepening levels of credit identified in Table 40.4, the pattern of credit growth in Latin America has been marked by boom and bust cycles, particularly in economies with the lowest amounts of bank credit-to-GDP. Credit had expanded sharply across the region in the early 1990s, in part due to increased capital inflows, but it collapsed in many cases after the mid-1990s banking crises and remained subdued for many years. Only after 2004, has credit begun to recover, due to stronger economic growth, easier global monetary conditions, and progress in bank restructuring. Credit growth has been particularly strong in Argentina and Brazil (Jeanneau, 2007, pp. 6–7). Yet, in most Latin American countries, the unstable macroeconomic environment has been a critical factor in holding back financial system development and generating a high volatility of credit growth. For example, high short-term interest rates used to combat inflation or defend the exchange rate has added to banks' funding costs and increased loan-default rates (Singh et al. 2005, pp. 70–71).

There are legitimate concerns that the composition of bank portfolios probably led to some crowding out of private sector credit. This was because of banks' tendencies to hold high proportions of government securities in their portfolios, which possibly reflected historical patterns of behavior associated with hyper inflation. In the latter 1990s, banks replaced nonperforming loans with sizable portfolios of government securities in Argentina, Mexico and Venezuela. More recently, and due to fiscal consolidation (in Argentina, Mexico, and also Brazil), the amount of government securities in banks' portfolios has declined.

Table 40.5 shows the allocation of domestic credit by banking sectors as a share of GDP between 1980 and 2010. It provides a breakdown of bank credit allocated to the private and state sectors. The Table demonstrates the relatively low level of credit allocation in Latin America compared to industrialized countries which persists across time. What is particularly notable in the larger economies of Brazil and Mexico, and Argentina in 2010, is the relatively even distribution of bank credit between the private and public sectors. In most other countries, the private sector receives the bulk of domestic credit.

40.3.2 Banking Sector Heterogeneity and Dollarization

The observed heterogeneity across Latin America's financial systems results from a variety of different historical and institutional features. Financial sector penetration (depth) of the economy is highly variable but unrelated to country size and per capita incomes. The relatively large economies of Argentina and Mexico have smaller banking sectors than what is implied by their levels of economic development, which can be attributed to long lasting effects of financial crises. As a result of the 1990s Tequila crisis, the ratio of Mexican bank assets-to-GDP fell from an historical high of almost 70% in 1994 to between 32% and 35% over 2000 to 2005 (Sidaoui, 2006, p. 287). Estimates imply that private sector credit should be around 50% of GDP given the economic size of Argentina, rather than the observed 1990s average of 20% (IADB, 2005, p. 6). Uruguay has one of the most internationalized and open financial systems in the region with the banking sector performing the role of regional offshore financial center. Due to its longer track record of greater macroeconomic stability,

Table 40.5 Allocation of domestic credit by banking sector: % of GDP

	1980	1990	2000	2010		1980	1990	2000	2010
Argentina	32.96	32.42	34.45	29.18	Paraguay	16.83	14.92	31.34	32.48
To private sector	25.40	15.60	23.89	14.62	To private sector	18.37	15.80	29.76	37.81
To state sector	7.56	16.82	10.56	14.56	To state sector	-1.54	-0.88	1.59	-5.33
Bolivia	28.80	22.97	62.03	49.37	Peru	20.66	20.21	25.97	18.09
To private sector	17.09	24.03	58.72	40.34	To private sector	12.89	11.80	25.96	24.32
To state sector	11.71	-1.06	3.31	9.03	To state sector	7.77	8.41	0.01	-6.23
Brazil	43.04	87.63	71.86	95.22	Uruguay	39.85	46.67	50.23	32.13
To private sector	42.48	42.08	31.66	55.14	To private sector	37.24	32.44	45.09	22.78
To state sector	0.57	45.54	40.20	40.07	To state sector	2.61	14.23	5.13	9.35
Chile	46.96	70.18	82.40	88.85	Venezuela	45.98	38.64	14.91	22.51
To private sector	46.85	45.31	73.62	84.85	To private sector	49.86	26.21	12.47	18.83
To state sector	0.10	24.88	8.77	4.00	To state sector	-3.88	12.43	2.44	3.68
Colombia	30.84	36.45	30.24	65.59	Japan	185.66	255.34	304.74	325.99
To private sector	30.46	30.78	20.85	43.44	To private sector	129.36	191.94	219.28	169.66
To state sector	0.38	5.67	9.39	22.15	To state sector	56.30	63.40	85.46	156.33
Ecuador	21.28	15.49	35.16	26.44	UK	36.20	118.23	130.15	222.61
To private sector	22.53	13.64	29.94	30.85	To private sector	27.33	113.15	129.34	202.86
To state sector	-1.24	1.86	5.22	-4.40	To state sector	8.87	5.09	0.82	19.75
Mexico	43.76	37.34	34.10	45.06	US	120.22	151.00	198.41	232.85
To private sector	19.37	17.45	18.31	24.67	To private sector	97.42	119.03	168.41	202.64
To state sector	24.39	19.89	15.79	20.39	To state sector	22.81	31.97	30.00	30.22

Note: The WBDI record the allocation of domestic credit on a gross basis, except credit to central government which is net. We calculate credit to the state sector as the difference between domestic credit-to-GDP and private sector credit-to-GDP for indicative purposes. It is possible that private sector credit might include some loans to public enterprises.

Source: World Bank Development Indicators

sustained economic growth, and earlier financial sector reform, Chile has achieved a more even pattern of credit growth.

Latin American financial systems are characterized by varying degrees of dollarization. In several countries, relatively large shares of bank deposits and loans have been denominated in US dollars: the average dollarization ratio across 1998 to 2004 shows that over 75% of total banking sector deposits were foreign currency denominated in Bolivia, Peru and Uruguay whilst the ratio was approximately 60% for Paraguay (see Table 40.6). In these countries, informal dollarization has been developed partially as a response to the hyperinflation of the 1980s (in Bolivia and Peru), when confidence in the value of domestic currencies was severely undermined.

Table 40.6 Dollarization ratio* in selected countries in Latin America (percentage)

Countries	1998	2000	2001	2004
Argentina	58.4	66.6	2.9	11.0
Bolivia	93.1	93.8	92.1	90.5
Brazil	0.0	0.0	0.0	0.0
Chile	6.2	0.0	11.5	13.0
Colombia	0.0	0.0	0.0	0.0
Costa Rica	44.4	44.9	48.0	48.0
Ecuador	–	–	100.0	100.0
Mexico	8.0	5.6	4.7	3.4
Panama	100.0	100.0	100.0	100.0
Paraguay	47.5	61.6	68.5	61.9
Peru	76.5	76.9	73.2	68.9
Uruguay	90.6	91.6	93.6	90.0
Venezuela	0.0	0.1	0.2	0.1
South America	**21.4**	**23.2**	**27.5**	**27.0**

* Total foreign currency deposits in the domestic banking system/total deposits in the domestic banking system.

Source: BIS (2007, p. 68).

In Peru dollarization started with the inflationary process of the mid-1970s and peaked during the hyperinflation of 1988–1990, despite efforts to de-dollarize the financial system in 1985, when Peruvian government forced the conversion of foreign currency deposits to domestic currency, resulting in capital flight and financial disintermediation. When the restriction on foreign currency deposits (mainly in US dollars) was lifted, re-dollarization process was rapidly retaken, and, consequently about 80% of deposits were denominated in foreign currency by the end of the 1990s (Table 40.6). In particular, after the implementation of the inflation target regime in early 2000s, Peru has experienced a gradual and sustained market-driven financial de-dollarization: dollarization of credit declined from around 80% at the end of the 1990s to below 55% by end-2009 (Garcia-Escribano, 2010). It should be added that prudential measures, such as the introduction of asymmetric reserve requirements (higher to deposits in foreign currencies) and provisions for currency-induced credit risk, have affected banks' incentives to borrow and lend in domestic currency (soles).

In Ecuador, full dollarization was implemented for price stability purposes in 1999. Elsewhere, economic policies that stimulated the dollarization of the domestic economy were adopted. In 1991, Argentina implemented its currency board regime that guaranteed the full convertibility of dollars and pesos; financial intermediation increasingly became dollar-denominated until the regime collapsed in 2002. In contrast, other countries (Brazil, Chile, Colombia, Mexico, and Venezuela) have avoided dollarization, by either prohibiting most holdings of foreign currency deposits, or imposing prudential constraints on such holdings. Prohibition has had the adverse effect of shifting deposits and loans offshore; consequently, financial system vulnerability increased because of greater liquidity and solvency risks (Jeanneau, 2007, pp. 7–8).

40.4 The Effects of Banking Consolidation

40.4.1 Market Structure, Privatization, Foreign Bank Penetration, and Bank Performance

Bank privatization of state-owned banks dramatically altered the market structure of domestic banking sectors. Privatization has transformed the governance structure of domestic banks as new, private owners (domestic and foreign) assumed control of banks. Generally speaking and across the region, state-owned banks had served political and social purposes and they shared certain characteristics: weak loan quality, underperformance, and poor cost control. Indeed, privatization was deemed to be a cheaper option than restructuring and recapitalization. The outcomes of bank privatization have varied across countries. For Argentina and Brazil, the evidence suggests that privatized bank performance improved post-privatization (Berger et al., 2005 for Argentina; Nakane and Weintraub, 2005 for Brazil). In stark contrast, the 1991 privatization program in Mexico failed in the mid-1990s with the onset of the Tequila crisis. The crisis revealed deep-seated problems in the banking sector which had been masked by weak property rights and ineffective bank regulation that failed to prevent imprudent behavior by newly privatized banks. Bank privatization failed to the tune of a bailout costing an estimated $65 billion (Haber, 2005). Yet, unlike in Argentina and Brazil, the 1991 Mexican program disbarred foreign banks from entering the auctions. Beginning in February 1995, a post-Tequila second round of restructuring and privatization liberalized the treatment of foreign ownership of domestic banks and was completed in 1996 (with effect from 1997). This led to a large-scale transfer of bank ownership from domestic to foreign hands: foreign banks held 5% of banking sector assets in 1995 that leapt to 82% by 2003 (Haber, 2005). In 2007, two of the three largest Mexican banks are owned by foreign banks.

One must be cautious when interpreting the apparent positive outcome of bank privatization. The observed post-privatization improvements in bank performance may reflect selection bias. In order to raise the viability of state-owned banks to prospective buyers, bank balance sheets were sanitized and healthy banks were privatized whilst bad banks were funded using public funds (Clarke and Cull, 2000). Certainly, statistically significant differences in the balance sheet structures of privatized and non-privatized state-banks are reported for Argentina (Berger et al., 2005). Similar transfers were carried out in Brazil. The utilization of the bad bank model can be expected to have influenced post-privatization bank performance.

Bank privatization assisted foreign bank penetration in Latin America as foreign banks acquired large, domestic banks. For policymakers, foreign bank entry was expected to raise competition leading to efficiency gains and banking sector recapitalization. Foreign bank entry increased banking sector capitalization in Mexico between 1997 and 2004 by more than US$8.8 billion—equivalent to 42% of total banking sector capital in 2004 (Schulz, 2006). Country-level evidence suggests bank efficiencies improved at the same time as foreign bank penetration increased. Arguably, this is too general a claim since there are caveats to consider. First, one should distinguish between the performance of existing foreign banks and domestic banks acquired by foreign banks—mainly large banks purchased via cross-border bank M&A. We refer to the latter as foreign bank acquisitions. Second, it is difficult to disentangle the effects of foreign bank entry from other liberalization effects that could have affected bank efficiency. Finally, many studies use proxy measures of efficiency like the ratio of overhead costs-to-assets; there is limited evidence where econometric estimates of bank efficiency were employed (Berger, 2007).

One exception reports there were intercountry differences in bank cost efficiencies with very small and very large banks more inefficient than large banks. Cost inefficient banks tended to be small, undercapitalized, relatively unprofitable, less risk averse, facing unstable deposit bases and intermediating less. Country-level factors also determined bank-level cost efficiencies: countries with higher rates of economic growth, denser demand for banking services, and lower levels of market power achieved better cost efficiency performance (Carvallo and Kasman, 2005).

It is very difficult to identify the separate effects of bank privatization and foreign bank entry on bank condition and performance. One study reported little difference in the performances of private-owned domestic banks and foreign-owned banks, though the former did outperform state-owned banks (Crystal, Dages, and Goldberg, 2002). Foreign banks achieved higher average loan growth than domestic banks (in Argentina, Chile and Colombia) with loan growth stronger at existing foreign banks compared to acquired foreign banks. It is suggested that management at foreign bank acquisitions focused on restructuring the former domestic banks and integrating operations with the parent (foreign) bank. This implies that foreign bank acquisitions adopted a defensive strategy towards market share and growth until the integration process was completed. The cautious nature of foreign bank strategies explains why foreign banks, and foreign bank acquisitions in particular, had better loan quality than domestic-owned banks, although stronger provisioning and higher loan recovery rates translated into weaker profitability at foreign banks. Foreign banks were relatively more liquid, have relied less on deposit financing, and realized stronger loan growth during episodes of financial difficulty than domestic banks. The available evidence suggests that foreign banks have achieved a greater efficiency in intermediation because they were better able to evaluate credit risks and allocate resources at a faster pace than their domestic-owned competitors (Crystal, Dages, and Goldberg, 2002).

In Argentina, foreign banks typically entered the market via cross-border M&A rather than de novo entry. The targets of foreign banks tended to be the larger and more profitable domestic banks. On average, foreign banks achieved better loan quality and were more highly capitalized and profitable than domestic banks (Clarke, Crivelli, and Cull, 2005). The effects of the governance changes on bank performance are summarized by Berger et al. (2005): state-owned banks under performed against domestic and foreign banks due partly to poor loan quality associated with directed lending and subsidized credit. The privatization of provincial banks realized efficiency gains as the amount of non-performing loans fell and profit efficiencies increased. However, the improvement in profit efficiency may simply reflect selection bias since cost efficiencies were consistent before and after privatization. M&A activity involving domestic banks and foreign bank entry were reported to have had little effect on bank performance (Berger et al., 2005).

These findings do not apply to Brazil. Foreign banks in Brazil have faced difficulties in adapting to the peculiarities of the Brazilian banking sector, which is dominated by private domestic banks (Paula, 2002). Incidentally, the empirical record offers no support for the hypothesis that foreign banks are either more or less efficient than domestic banks (Guimarães, 2002; Paula, 2002; Vasconcelos and Fucidji, 2002), although more recent evidence shows foreign banks realized a good performance in terms of cost and profit efficiency by either establishing new affiliates or acquiring domestic banks (Tecles and Tabak, 2010). This is unsurprising in the light of evidence that the operational characteristics and balance sheets of domestic and foreign banks are similar (Carvalho, 2002). Hence, the expected benefits of foreign bank entry have yet to materialize in Brazil, because foreign banks have witnessed and graduated towards similar operational characteristics of the large private domestic banks (Paula and Alves, 2007).

40.4.2 Market Concentration and Competition Effects

The ongoing consolidation process has increased concentration in Latin American banking sectors. Whereas the expectation of policymakers has been that higher concentration would lead to more competition and efficiency improvements, there was the possibility that competitive gains would not materialize, and instead bank market power would increase. The latter implies that the evolution of highly concentrated market structures could limit the deepening of financial intermediation and the development of more efficient banking sectors (Rojas Suarez, 2007). Since a non-competitive market structure often produces oligopolistic behavior by banks, the suggestion is that further consolidation could incentivize banks to exploit market power rather than become more efficient.

It is an empirical matter to determine if bank consolidation (more concentration) has raised competition and banking sector efficiency, or instead realized market power gains for banks. Some degree of market power can check bank risk-taking, and there are tradeoffs between increased competition and financial stability. One difficulty when considering the relationship between consolidation and competitive conditions is the measurement of competition. The literature commonly employs the H statistic showing the sum of the elasticities of bank revenue with respect to input prices (Panzar and Rosse, 1987). Using this approach, banks in Latin America were found to operate under monopolistic conditions, consistent with results from industrialized countries and other emerging markets.

Some studies focus on the relationship between market concentration and bank efficiency (measured by parametric or non-parametric techniques) in Latin America in a test of the so-called "quiet life" hypothesis. This posits a negative relationship between bank efficiency and market power, as greater concentration due to M&A can allow banks to exploit market power and behave less competitively. It contrasts against the "efficiency structure hypothesis," which proposes the expected relationship is positive (due, among other factors, to the possibility for large banks to exploit scale economies). The literature indicates that the quiet life hypothesis is rejected in Latin American banking sectors and that bank restructuring has promoted competition and yielded efficiency gains at banks under conditions of monopolistic competition (Williams, 2012). Efficiency gains, particularly in terms of scale efficiencies, appear to have a significant impact on banking profitability, supporting the efficiency structure hypothesis in some Latin American countries (Chortereas, Garza-García, and Girardone, 2010). However, when considering how concentration influences cost and profit efficiency, that profit inefficiency is higher than cost inefficiency suggests that the bulk of inefficiency comes from the revenue side, and possibly results from a certain level of market power (Tabak, Fazio, and Cajueiro, 2011).

Importantly, the recent increase in consolidation has not weakened competitive conditions (Gelos and Roldós, 2004; Yeyati and Micco, 2007; Yildirim and Philippatos, 2007). Despite this general finding, there are country level features of note and some inconsistencies between studies. For instance, there is agreement that banking sector competition increased in Argentina and remained constant in Mexico from the mid-1990s to the 2000s. On the other hand, competitive conditions in Brazil and Chile are reported to have changed little (Gelos and Roldós, 2004) or weakened (Yildirim and Philippatos, 2007).

In general, the literature rejects the notion of collusion between banks, but evidence from Brazil suggests that banks possessed some degree of market power (Nakane, 2001; Nakane, Alencar, and Kanczuk, 2006). Other Brazilian evidence has illustrated the complexities associated with identifying competition effects. Whereas the banking sector has operated under conditions of monopolistic competition, this finding cannot be generalized across bank ownership and size. Whilst small banks and state-owned banks operated under the above banking sector conditions, large banks and foreign banks behaved competitively. This implication is of markedly different competitive conditions in local markets and the national market (Belaisch, 2003). In local markets, private-owned banks were more pro-competitive than state-owned banks, although the latter entered markets which the former did not service (Coelho, de Mello, and Rezende, 2007). Small and large banks have also faced different competitive conditions in Argentina and Chile (Yildirim and Philippatos, 2007). Evidence from Colombia finds more competition reduced banks' market power (Barajas, Steiner, and Salazar, 1998). Differently from Brazil and Colombia, the overall view of the efficiency and profitability of the banking sector in Mexico infers that efficiency gains may have translated into extraordinary profits for banks due to the decrease in competitive rivalry in banking markets. Banks have used a cross subsidization strategy, granting loans with very small margins and recuperating this loss by setting higher margins on deposits, that has proven to be very profitable to banks (Maudos and Solis, 2011).

Table 40.7 shows indicators of banking sector financial stability, profitability, and efficiency. The five-year interval data show the most stable banking sectors are in Chile, Mexico, and Brazil. For Brazil and Chile, profitability improved between 2000 and 2005; between 2005 and 2010, a modest reversal occurs in Brazil whilst a greater reduction occurs in Chile. The data suggest that the maintenance of stability is due to a strengthening of bank capital positions. Nevertheless, the profitability of Latin American banking sectors exceeds that the industrialized countries where stability would also appear to reflect (supported) capital levels. It is clear from the data that banking sectors across the region have become more efficient over time by realizing lower cost income ratios although Uruguay and Venezuela show signs for concern. At 2010, the efficiency of several Latin American banking sectors compare favorably with the US banking sector, which was not the case in 2000.

At first sight, greater competition brought about by the changes in the banking industry in the 1990s has not weakened bank safety. Table 40.8 shows capitalization ratios for Latin American and other emerging market banking sectors. From 2006 the level of capitalization in Latin America has been consistent and relatively high compared with other regions, although sectors in South East Asia, Russia, and Turkey are also well capitalized. Surprisingly, Chile is the least capitalized sector in Latin America at a level comparable with China.

Table 40.7 Banking sector stability and performance indicators

	Stability (Z score)			Profitability (Return on Assets)			Efficiency (Cost-income ratio)		
	2000	2005	2010	2000	2005	2010	2000	2005	2010
Argentina	3.8	4.5	5.3	0.50	0.65	2.47	67.0	69.3	54.0
Bolivia	9.0	12.4	10.1	-0.87	0.63	1.40	65.5	82.8	62.2
Brazil	17.5	18.4	17.4	0.95	1.67	1.28	78.1	59.4	52.0
Chile[1]	18.6	19.3	20.1	1.42	1.79	0.61	57.5	55.0	56.3
Colombia	4.9	8.2	8.5	-1.94	8.19	2.21	81.6	57.6	48.1
Ecuador	-6.7	-4.7	2.1	-18.00	-5.08	1.37	165.9	94.2	65.7
Mexico	24.1	29.8	20.3	1.10	0.21	0.67	70.5	73.5	58.2
Peru	11.1	12.5	13.3	0.34	2.17	2.41	67.9	55.5	42.4
Paraguay	12.6	11.8	12.2	1.29	1.95	2.87	101.0	81.1	57.8
Uruguay	2.5	2.0	2.8	1.02	0.94	0.90	67.6	68.3	79.1
Venezuela	10.7	16.6	9.1	2.46	3.00	9.14	74.6	62.1	95.7
Japan	10.5	12.7	11.7	-0.07	0.50	0.25	58.3	53.8	55.2
UK	14.8	8.2	7.8	1.16	0.78	-0.02	50.6	54.6	68.7
US	20.7	24.3	25.3	1.16	1.30	0.66	61.2	58.8	54.0

Note: ([1]) For Chile the Z score for 2010 is at 2009 and cost-income ratio 2008.

Source: World Bank Financial Structure database.

One should read these data with some care, though. It is true that the 1990s and the 2000s witnessed a widespread effort at modernization of regulatory and supervisory methods and institutions everywhere in the region. Nevertheless, in part the data may be hiding one important source of fragility which is the dependence of the banking industry, at least in some of the largest economies, on the supply of credit to the government. Public debt securities tend to benefit from zero risk-weighting (and thus do not require any capital to cover credit risk) adding one more incentive to banks to accumulate them, instead of private credit. As a result, in countries such as Argentina, Brazil, or Mexico, high capitalization may not necessarily translate into higher defences against insolvency, but in fact, to higher dependency on Treasury policies.

In the discussion so far, no attempt has been made to disentangle the impact of foreign bank entry on competition. A priori greater foreign bank penetration was expected to increase competition and to offset the potential rise in domestic bank market power resulting from higher concentration. Consistent with expectations, there is cross-country evidence that suggests the increased foreign bank penetration raised the level of competition (Yildirim and Philippatos, 2007). An alternative view claims that increased concentration had little effects on competition and financial stability. Rather, foreign bank entry caused competitive conditions to weaken (Yeyati and Micco, 2007). The intuition for this claim is that foreign banks typically acquired domestic banks that were under duress and consequently operating with relatively high interest margins. For new foreign owners, the franchise value of high margins and the time needed to transform the fortunes of their acquisitions can explain why increased foreign bank penetration was associated with weaker, rather than stronger competition. Whilst this apparent feature was inconsistent

Table 40.8 Bank capital-to-assets ratios (%); 2003–2012

Country	2003	2006	2007	2008	2009	2010	2011	2012
Latin America								
Argentina	11.90	13.60	13.10	12.90	13.30	11.90	11.60	12.10
Bolivia	12.10	10.00	9.00	9.30	8.70	8.40	8.40	8.30
Brazil	9.60	10.80	11.30	10.70	11.30	11.00	10.50	10.40
Chile	7.30	6.80	7.10	6.90	7.40	7.10	7.00	6.90
Colombia	11.60	13.30	12.90	12.60	14.20	10.30	14.30	14.80
Ecuador	8.80	8.20	8.10	8.90	9.40	8.90	8.60	
Mexico	11.40	9.50	9.60	9.20	10.70	10.40	9.90	10.10
Paraguay	9.50	8.50	9.70	10.20	9.50	9.40	9.00	10.30
Peru	9.30	9.50	8.80	8.30	10.20	9.50	10.10	9.80
Uruguay	7.20	9.40	10.50	8.90	9.80	9.50	8.50	8.50
Venezuela	14.30	9.80	9.40	9.40	8.60	9.80	10.40	10.30
Other emerging markets								
China	3.80	5.10	5.70	6.00	5.60	6.10	6.40	6.30
India	5.70	6.60	6.40	7.30	7.00	7.10	7.10	6.90
Russian Federation	14.60	12.10	13.30	10.80	13.10	12.90	11.80	12.40
South Africa	8.00	7.90	8.00	5.60	6.70	7.10	7.30	7.30
Turkey	13.70	11.90	12.80	12.10	12.50	12.30	11.70	12.00
Eastern Europe								
Czech Republic	5.70	6.00	5.70	5.50	6.10	6.50	6.50	6.80
Poland	8.30	7.80	8.00	7.50	8.10	7.80	7.70	8.60
Slovak Republic	8.90	7.00	8.00	8.20	9.60	9.70	10.80	11.00
South East Asia								
Indonesia	10.40	10.10	9.20	9.10	10.10	10.70	11.00	11.90
Malaysia	8.50	7.60	7.40	8.10	9.00	9.40	8.90	9.00
Philippines	13.10	11.70	11.70	10.60	9.50	10.20	11.10	13.10
Thailand	7.40	9.20	9.80	10.10	11.00	11.30	9.40	10.50

Source: World Bank Development Indicators.

with policymakers' objectives, the franchise value of the high margins disciplined banks' risk-taking because of fears that the increased bank profitability of the period could be dissipated. In short, although foreign bank entry may have weakened competition it appears to have had a beneficial effect on banking sector stability (Yeyati and Micco, 2007).

Foreign bank entry raises the threat of increased competition which conditions the behavior of domestic banks and reduces their market power (Claessens, Demirgüç-Kunt, and Huizinga, 2001). The evidence suggests this has happened in Latin America: greater foreign bank penetration has caused lower interest margins and profits at domestic banks (Yildirim and Philippatos, 2007). Individual country studies offer a richer interpretation of events. Evidence from Colombia suggests that foreign bank and domestic bank behavior began to evolve differently following the announcement (in 1990) that financial liberalization policies were to be implemented (Barajas, Steiner, and Salazar, 2000). This study was able to control for other liberalizing reforms that affected bank behavior; for instance, it differentiated between foreign bank entry and the entry of new domestic institutions, and it controlled for the opening of the capital account as well as improvements made to bank reg-ulation and supervision. Whereas foreign bank entry did condition domestic bank behavior by reducing excess intermediation spreads over marginal costs, the effect of new domestic entrants on bank behavior was greater, reducing non-financial costs and interest spreads. The Colombian evidence implies bank behavior reflected the degree of market power of banking groups; since foreign banks had relatively little market power they were more able to adapt to changes in competitive conditions (Barajas, Steiner, and Salazar, 2000).

In Mexico, the lower administrative costs of foreign banks released downward pres-sure on administrative costs across all banks, which improved bank efficiency (Haber and Musacchio, 2005). Others have suggested that the impact of foreign bank entry on bank efficiency was limited because the low level of competitive intensity in the banking sector abated pressures for banks to improve operational efficiency (Schulz, 2006). Evidence from Argentina and Brazil has reported there was no significant difference in the behavior of for-eign and domestic banks; both types of bank reacted similarly to the macro-institutional environments (Paula and Alves, 2007).

40.4.3 Consolidation and the Allocation of Credit

The governance changes resulting from bank privatization and foreign bank penetration raised concerns in relation to the supply of bank credit. Three concerns were voiced: first, that increased foreign bank penetration would affect the stability of bank lending; second, foreign bank entry and/or new private ownership of banks might lead to a reallocation of credit towards certain geographic or product market segments; and third, given the govern-ance changes, would bank credit be responsive to market signals.

Foreign bank penetration has raised foreign banks' share of total banking sector loans in Latin America. Foreign bank lending has tended to concentrate in specific market seg-ments, mostly the commercial loans markets (including government and interbank sectors) in Argentina, Colombia, and Mexico (Barajas, Steiner, and Salazar, 2000; Dages, Goldberg, and Kinney 2002; Paula and Alves, 2007). In these countries foreign banks limited their exposure to the household and mortgage sectors. In Chile, household credit has domi-nated foreign banks' loan portfolio increasing from 18.4% to 27% of total foreign bank loans between 1990–1999 and 2000–2005 (Betancour, De Gregorio, and Jara, 2006). In Argentina and Brazil, foreign and domestic banks competed in loans markets and shared loan portfo-lio characteristics (Dages, Goldberg, and Kinney, 2002; Paula and Alves, 2007). However, foreign banks in Argentina weighted the loan portfolio towards relatively less risky loans (Dages, Goldberg, and Kinney, 2002), which was not the case in Brazil where no distinction was found between interest rates charged by foreign banks and domestic banks. This gave rise to claims that variations in pricing occurred within the foreign bank and domestic bank sectors rather than between the two sectors (Carvalho, 2002).

Interestingly, the negative impact of the 2008 financial crisis on foreign banks' lending to Latin America has been cushioned by the specific nature of foreign banks' operations in the region. This is one of the reasons why the retrenchment of foreign banks' credit to the region was significantly less severe compared to other emerging markets. Indeed, the expansion of foreign bank activities in Latin America in the last years has largely taken the form of increased domestic currency lending by their local affiliates rather than direct cross-border lending in foreign currencies from headquarters. Furthermore, local affiliates' funding mostly came from an expanding domestic deposit base rather than from parent banks or offshore wholesale markets, which provided a more stable source of funding during the crisis. Consequently, domestic financial systems tended to be more resilient to external financial shocks (Kamil and Rai, 2010).

Foreign banks have become an important source of finance for specific customer segments. Indeed, they have achieved higher loan growth (better quality and less volatile) than domestic banks (especially vis-à-vis state-owned banks) (Dages, Goldberg, and Kinney, 2002). Foreign banks—and also private domestic banks—are responsive to market signals: in particular, lending is procyclical and sensitive to movements in GDP and interest rates, which is indicative of transactions-based activities. The finding of higher loan growth and lower volatility at foreign banks—even during crisis periods—implies they were important stabilizers of bank credit (Dages, Goldberg, and Kinney, 2002).

After being granted unrestricted access in 1997, foreign banks came to dominate the Mexican banking sector quicker than they had done in other countries: in 1997, foreign banks supplied 11% of bank credit which grew to 83% in 2004 (Haber and Musacchio, 2005). During this time, a credit crunch occurred and private sector lending fell by 23% in real terms between December 1997 and December 2003 (Haber, 2005). It appeared foreign bank penetration had altered bank lending strategies, but this was not the case because the acquired foreign banks had begun to reduce private lending before acquisition. Prior to the 1991 bank privatizations, the ratio of commercial bank loans-to-GDP was 24% and rose to 26% in 1996; subsequently, it declined to 14% in 2003 (Haber, 2005). Furthermore, the behavior of foreign bank acquisitions, pre and post M&A, differed little from domestic banks. In brief, the credit crunch was driven by factors affecting all banks and unrelated to foreign bank entry.

In Argentina, bank privatization and foreign bank entry raised fears of a reallocation of bank lending. Initially, fears arose because the acquirers of the privatized provincial banks tended to be small, wholesale banks based in Buenos Aires who were expected to raise deposits in the provinces and allocate resources more in the centre (Clarke, Crivelli, and Cull, 2005). State-owned bank lending had been geographically diversified though concentrated more in the public sector with fewer manufacturing loans. Other concerns were that the volume of bank credit would decrease post privatization because the transfer of non-performing loans to bad banks meant the size of the privatized provincial banks was smaller than pre-privatization (Berger et al., 2005). Since foreign banks had mainly located in Buenos Aires and tended to finance large-scale manufacturing and utilities firms in that province, commentators questioned foreign banks' commitment to diversify lending to the provinces (Berger et al., 2005).

Temporarily, privatization and foreign bank entry disrupted credit in the 1990s. Disruptions were most pronounced in provinces that had privatized banks; credit levels fell but quickly returned to pre-privatization levels once privatized banks increased in size. Privatization did not affect the lending of private domestic or foreign banks. For foreign bank acquisitions, lending increased in importance and as a ratio of total assets, with loans growth allocated more towards consumers than manufacturing (Berger et al., 2005). Fears that foreign banks would concentrate their lending in Buenos Aires did not materialize. Foreign banks entered provincial markets, aggressively in provinces which had privatized their banks. In contrast, the newly privatized banks decreased lending relative to total assets to control risk through more prudent lending (Berger et al., 2005). In summary, foreign bank penetration caused an increase in provincial lending because foreign banks offset changes in lending of domestic banks (Clarke, Crivelli, and Cull, 2005).

40.4.4 Consolidation and Interest Rate Spreads

Finally, we review the effects that foreign bank penetration and market concentration have had on the evolution of bank interest rate spreads and on the process of financial intermediation. The effects were determined by comparing the spreads charged by foreign banks and domestic banks and the evidence comes from several countries (Argentina, Chile, Colombia, Mexico, and Peru). Generally speaking, foreign banks have operated with lower spreads compared with domestic banks (especially de novo foreign banks), but the main impact of foreign bank penetration has been the inducement for all banks to reduce costs rather than a marked decline in spreads. Concentration, on the other hand, could offset the apparent benefit of foreign bank penetration since higher concentration could raise operational costs and thereby widen spreads especially for domestic banks (Martinez Peria and Mody, 2004).

40.5 THE INTERNATIONAL FINANCIAL CRISIS OF 2008 AND BEYOND

In September 2008, Latin American economies were hit by the shock waves generated by the closure of Lehman Brothers. Losses suffered by foreign investors in their markets of origin led them to repatriate their investments, depreciating local currencies (and/or depleting international reserves to the extent that some local authorities tried to limit currency depreciation). Almost all Latin American countries have suffered, at some point in their recent history, serious balance of payments crises so capital flow reversals led to a deterioration of expectations that amplified the impact of the initial shock.

The economies and financial systems of Latin America were, however, better placed to withstand the effects of such exogenous shocks than at any other time in the recent past. Since 2003, Latin America has enjoyed "an unprecedented cycle of economic growth with macroeconomic stability. . . while inflation has fallen and fiscal positions have improved. . . This period of economic growth was supported by an exceptionally favorable external financing environment" (BIS, 2008b, p. 2). In many regional economies, current account surpluses have replaced deficits, which together with increasing foreign direct investment and growth in remittances have allowed a substantial accumulation of international reserves. Consequently, external borrowing and debt have fallen aided by important changes in financial structure—for instance, the development of local currency bond markets.

The current global financial crisis initiated with the collapse of the subprime mortgage market in the United States, in 2007, did not have a strong immediate impact on banking markets in the main economies in the region. Although there had been fast-paced growth in securitization in Latin America, the market was relatively nascent, although issuance of domestic asset-backed securities (ABSs) increased fivefold from 2003 to 2006. In 2006, the value of issues of domestic ABSs in Latin America was US$13.6 billion with activity concentrated in Brazil and Mexico (40% and 32% of total) followed by Argentina (18%). Mortgage backed securitization accounted for 21% of market activity in 2006 (BIS, 2008a). There were no subprime mortgage securities markets however in the region. Housing finance for lower income groups were in many cases provided by state banks or benefited from state subsidies. On the other hand, Latin American banks were not significantly exposed to the US subprime mortgage market as such, contrary to what happened in Europe. As a result, they were spared the credit and market value losses that plagued banking systems in the US, Europe and, to some extent, Asia.

After the initial impact, therefore, no significant after-shock financial turbulence created difficulties in the area that could be compared to developments in the United States and Western Europe. In fact, the most important crisis transmission channel from the eye of the storm became the contractionary impact on trade that resulted from the transmutation of the financial crisis into a full-blown economic crisis in 2009. Even then, however, the negative impact on the region was relatively more benign than in other emerging economies. Several factors contributed to this result.

First, as already mentioned, Latin American banks never held significant positions in subprime mortgage securities, either because of domestic controls on foreign financial investment, or for lack of access to these markets or, in some cases, notably the case of Brazil, because there was no point of investing in securities that would return a yield lower than what could be obtained by investing in domestic public debt, a much safer investment.

One possible source of transmission of the crisis into Latin American financial markets could be through a retrenchment of claims on the region by international banks. However, the 2008 capital flow reversal was itself reversed in 2009, when capital inflows to the region were resumed. Market analysts and wealth managers, apparently under the increasing perception that the financial crisis in industrialized economies would be deeper, and more durable, than initially expected, elected emerging economies as their investment of choice. Later, the adoption of "quantitative easing" monetary policies increased even further the world supply of liquidity stimulating even more strongly financial investments in the region. In fact, capital inflows became so great that some countries had to take measures to restrain foreign financial investment, reviving capital controls that had been abandoned in the 1990s.

Loss of steam or downright contraction of international trade could represent a bigger risk to the region. In fact, countries like Mexico, closely dependent on the level of activity in the United States, did exhibit a worse macroeconomic performance than other comparably large Latin American economies. Contracting trade with the United States and Western Europe were, however, more than compensated by the rapid growth of trade with China. Countries such as Chile and Peru, but also Argentina and Brazil, increased their exports to China, particularly of raw materials. Thus, both current accounts and capital accounts were improved as the crisis in the industrialized countries progressed, at least until the end of 2012, when the Chinese economy itself began to lose steam.

The absence of harder balance of payments constraints and the expansion of exports to China and other emerging economies allowed Latin American governments to attenuate the residual impacts of the international crisis by deploying anticyclical monetary and fiscal policies to support output and employment, a relatively new experience for most of those countries. In this process, many countries, most notably Brazil and Argentina used public banks to increase credit supply to firms and households to support aggregate demand.

The combined effect of all these factors was the quick and relatively painless way through which Latin American countries (again with the exception of Mexico) overcame the difficulties created by the first wave of contagion in late 2008. But one final element that was left out of the preceding narrative should now be added because it represents an important structural development for banking markets in the region.

Financial regulation had been in process of modernization at least since the early 1990s in all the most important among Latin American economies, all of which had adhered to the Basel Agreement of 1988 and its additional guidelines. By 2008, when the crisis became international, many of these countries were in process of implementation of Basel II. The new rules had been widely criticized because of their complexity, their procyclical nature, and their demands on banks and on supervisors. The crisis, however, added to these criticisms another one: risk-based capital coefficients as prescribed by Basel II did not ensure the safety of the banking system. A new effort was to begin to write more efficacious rules to build safer banking systems. It was also decided that this effort should involve a larger number of countries than it did before. The Basel Committee on Banking Supervision was directed to increase their membership to include the G20 members, instead of the original G10. The same happened with the Financial Stability Forum, transformed into the Financial Stability Board. The widened membership of these entities now included three Latin American countries, members of the G20, Argentina, Brazil, and Mexico.

As members of these entities, the three Latin American countries saw themselves as morally obligated to follow their decisions. Accordingly, they committed to implement Basel III, the set of toughened capital coefficients defined to deal not only with the risks already defined in Basel II and Basel 2.5, but also to comply with the new rules included in Basel III, such as the liquidity provisions and the leverage ratio. Thus, at least with respect to Argentina, Brazil, and Mexico the effort to strengthen banking regulation that had contributed to make their banking systems more resilient against crises is to continue at the same pace (sometimes even more quickly) that is followed by developed economies. The Basel Committee (BCBS, 2013) reported in April 2013 that Mexico already put in place Basel III in what refers to capital rules, while Argentina and Brazil had already published the rules to be adopted by the end of 2013. It is interesting to note that the report shows the three countries ahead of the United States and of the European Union in the speed of implementation of Basel III.

The latest data on risk-weighted capital coefficients provided by the World Bank strengthen the notion that banks in Latin America suffered generally little from the international financial crisis (see also Table 40.8 above). They show that banks from nine Latin American countries maintained capital-to-total asset ratios of close to (and in many times over) 10%[6]. The exceptions were Ecuador and, surprisingly, Chile from 2003 to 2012. According to the World Bank, Chile in fact exhibited the lowest ratios of all ten countries, followed by Ecuador and Uruguay. In Argentina, the ratio was 11.9% in 2003 and 12.1% in 2012, while in Brazil it increased from 9.6% to 10.4%, from 2003 to 2012. The series are not particularly volatile and there is no visible break in the years around 2008.

---

[6] Argentina, Bolivia, Brazil, Chile, Colombia, Ecuador, Mexico, Peru, and Uruguay.

The same source also publishes data on non-performing loans as a share of gross loans. All ten countries exhibited low rates of non-performing credits, except in the beginning of the decade when some countries, particularly Argentina and Uruguay, suffered domestic financial crises that resulted in high rates of problem loans. Rates have fallen since then for the countries that began the decade with credit problems and remained stable for the others. While non-performing loans/total loans ratios reached 17.7% in Argentina and 14.3% in Uruguay in 2003, they fell to 1.5% in each of those two countries by 2012. In fact, in 2012, the ratio varied from a low of 1.5% in Argentina and Uruguay to 3.6% in Brazil, while in the US it was 3.9%. Again, the international financial crisis seems to have had no impact on the domestic performance of these institutions and the data suggests the hypothesis that loan management improved in the whole region in the period, either by bank managers or by bank supervisors or both.

Table 40.9 shows an asset quality indicator by countries and across regions from 2003 to 2012. A general picture emerges across different regions namely an inter-temporal

Table 40.9 Asset quality (non–performing loans-to-gross loans, %)								
Country	2003	2006	2007	2008	2009	2010	2011	2012
Latin America								
Argentina	17.7	3.4	2.7	2.7	3.0	1.8	1.2	1.5
Bolivia	16.7	8.7	5.6	4.3	3.5	2.2	1.7	1.7
Brazil	4.1	3.5	3.0	3.1	4.2	3.1	3.5	3.6
Chile	1.6	0.8	0.8	1.0	2.9	2.7	2.4	2.4
Colombia	6.8	2.7	3.2	3.9	4.0	2.9	2.5	3.0
Ecuador	7.9	4.1	3.7	3.4	4.1	3.5	3.2	
El Salvador	2.8	1.9	2.1	2.8	3.7	3.9	3.6	3.4
Mexico	3.2	1.8	2.4	3.0	2.8	2.0	2.1	2.2
Paraguay	20.6	3.3	1.3	1.1	1.6	1.3	1.7	2.4
Peru	14.8	4.1	2.7	2.2	2.7	3.0	2.9	3.1
Uruguay	14.3	3.7	1.1	1.0	1.2	1.0	1.3	1.5
Venezuela	7.7	1.1	1.2	1.9	3.0	3.4	1.4	1.2
Other emerging markets								
China	20.4	7.1	6.2	2.4	1.6	1.1	1.0	0.9
India	8.8	3.3	2.7	2.4	2.4	2.5	2.3	3.0
Russian Federation	5.0	2.4	2.5	3.8	9.5	8.2	6.6	6.7
South Africa	2.4	1.1	1.4	3.9	5.9	5.8	4.7	4.6
Turkey	11.5	3.9	3.3	3.4	5.0	3.5	2.6	2.5
Eastern Europe								
Czech Republic	4.9	3.6	2.4	2.8	4.6	5.4	5.2	5.1
Poland	21.2	7.4	5.2	4.4	7.9	8.8	8.2	8.4
Slovak Republic	3.7	3.2	2.5	3.2	5.3	5.8	5.6	5.3
South East Asia								
Indonesia	6.8	6.1	4.0	3.2	3.3	2.5	2.1	2.1
Korea	2.6	0.8	0.7	1.1	1.2	1.9	1.4	1.5
Malaysia	13.9	8.5	6.5	4.8	3.6	3.4	2.7	2.2
Philippines	16.1	7.5	5.8	4.5	3.5	3.4	2.6	2.4
Thailand	13.5	8.1	7.9	5.7	5.3	3.9	2.9	2.7

Source: World Bank Development Indicators.

Table 40.10 Capital coefficients

Country	Latest Data Available	Regulatory capital-to-risk weighted assets	Regulatory tier 1 capital-to-risk weighted assets
Argentina	12 Q3	16.6	12.9
Brazil	12 Q4	16.7	11.9
Mexico	13 Feb	16.7	14.8
China	12	13.3	10.6
India	12 Q4	13.1	9.3
Russia	12 Q4	13.7	10.6
USA	12 Q4	14.5	12.7
Germany	12 Q4	17.9	14.2
UK	11 Q4	15.7	13.3
Japan	12 Q3	14.2	11.7

improvement in asset quality since the early 2000s. The data suggest that the reform processes in Latin American countries, including bank privatization and foreign bank acquisitions, have arrested the formerly high proportions of non-performing loans and significantly reduced them in several countries to levels which are better than those found in other emerging market banking sectors. Nevertheless, and contrary to the trend, the subprime crisis adversely affected asset quality in 2008 and 2009, although Latin America appears to have been less scathed compared with other regions. Indeed, Latin American banking sectors managed to shake off the impact of the crisis quicker than other emerging markets.

Table 40.10, built with IMF data, shows that data from the beginning of 2013 puts risk-weighted capital coefficients in the three largest economies of Latin America among the highest found in G20 countries. In sum, the international financial crisis has not, so far, threatened in significant ways the stability of banking systems in Latin America. The resilience shown by banks in the region is a result of the success in maintaining overall macroeconomic stability in the face of adverse shocks coming mostly from the United States first, and then from Europe. But it is also a measure of the success of these countries in modernizing their financial stability supervisory systems. Presently, the process of modernization is even more advanced in some Latin American countries than in some industrialized economies, at least if it is measured in terms of implementation of Basel III rules.

40.6 CONCLUSION

The last two decades have witnessed deep changes in the operation of the banking sector everywhere, but without a doubt these changes have been particularly strong in Latin America. In these 20 years financial repression was eliminated or drastically attenuated from Mexico to the Southern Cone. The role of state-owned banks was streamlined either

by privatization or by increasing specialization in the provision of financial support to special groups of borrowers, such as, medium and small firms, as in the case of Mexico. In a few
countries, however, and most notably in Argentina and Brazil, a large sector of state-owned
banks survived the financial liberalization process and went on to become leaders in their
domestic banking sectors.

A common feature of the financial liberalization process in the whole region has been the
increasing presence of foreign banks in domestic markets. Led by US and Spanish banks,
foreign institutions have aggressively taken advantage of the relaxation of restrictions on the
operation of foreign banks in virtually the whole continent.

Liberalization, privatization, and foreign bank entry combined with larger macroeconomic policy changes and strategies to generate a process of consolidation in the banking
sector of all countries in the region. Consolidation was actively supported by local government policies aiming at taking advantage of possible economies of scale and scope in the
production of banking services. Nevertheless, the results of these efforts are still to appear
more clearly, although there is some evidence of efficiency improvements in bank operations in the region.

In the major countries of Latin America, banks faced important difficulties in adapting
to the new context of financial deregulation and liberalization. Serious banking sector crises took place in Chile, which pioneered the liberalization process, Argentina, also in the
early stages of liberalization, and Mexico. In Brazil, banks suffered strong pressures resulting
from the joint impact of deregulation and price stabilization processes in the mid-1990s,
forcing the government to create a special crisis-resolution program. Argentina suffered
another banking crisis in 2001, connected to the balance of payments crisis that put an end
to the Convertibility Plan.

In sum, practically all the changes in the book have been implemented in the region since
the late 1980s. Interest rates are currently market-determined everywhere but Venezuela,
where controls still subsist. Privatization advanced strongly everywhere, except Brazil,
where the leading banks were kept in the hands of the federal government. Directed credit
was reduced or eliminated across the region, again with the partial exception of Brazil,
where a federal development bank (BNDES) is almost the only provider of long-term
credit. Monetary policy in all parts of Latin America is implemented through open market
operations.

The results of the process have been relatively disappointing, given the high expectations that surrounded the liberalization process in the late 1980s. The jury is still out, of
course, given the relatively short time during which these changes have been in place and
the turbulence that characterized some periods in the 1990s. There is some evidence of
improvement in many cases, but still not enough to generate enthusiasm. Banking crises
and stresses, however, have not led to reversals in the financial liberalization process so
far. On the contrary, most countries in the area have been investing in building regulatory
and supervisory institutions while adhering to modern regulatory paradigms, such as the
Basle accords. If the assumptions underlying the process of financial liberalization are in
fact true, better results should begin to show in the short term in the form of lower cost of
capital, wider access to finance, better allocation of resources while, of course, maintaining
a reasonable degree of financial stability. It is a tall order, but financial liberalization promises no less.

References

Ahumada, A. and Marshall, J. (2001). The Banking Industry in Chile: Competition, Consolidation and Systemic Stability, BIS Papers No. 4, August.

Avalos, M. and Trillo, F. (2006). Competencia Bancaria en Mexico, UN CEPAL, August.

Barajas, A., Steiner, R., and Salazar, N. (1998). Interest Spreads in Banking: Costs, Financial Taxation, Market Power, and Loan Quality in the Colombian Case 1974-96, IMF Working Paper No. WP/98/110.

Barajas, A., Steiner, R., and Salazar, N. (2000). The Impact of Liberalization and Foreign Investment in Colombia's Financial Sector, *Journal of Development Economics* 63, 157–196.

BCBS (Basel Committee on Banking Supervision) (2013). Report to G 20 Finance Ministers and Central Bank Governors on Monitoring Implementation of Basel III Regulatory Reform, April.

BCRA (Banco Central de la República Argentina) (2012). Financial Stability Report, October.

Belaisch, A. (2003). Do Brazilian Banks Compete?, IMF Working Paper No. WP/03/113.

Berger, A. N. (2007). International Comparisons of Bank Efficiency, *New York University Salomon Center, Financial Markets, Institutions and Instruments* 16(3), 119–144.

Berger, A. N., Clarke, G. R. G., Cull, R., Klapper, L., and Udell, G. F. (2005). Corporate Governance and Bank Performance: A Joint Analysis of the Static, Selection, and Dynamic Effects of Domestic, Foreign, and State Ownership, *Journal of Banking and Finance* 29, 2179–2221.

Betancour, C., De Gregorio, J., and Jara, A. (2006). Improving the Banking System: The Chilean Experience, BIS Papers No. 28, August.

BIS (Bank for International Settlements) (2007). Annex Tables, BIS Papers No. 33, February.

BIS (Bank for International Settlements) (2008a). New Financing Trends in Latin America: A Bumpy Road Towards Stability, BIS Papers No. 36, February.

BIS (Bank for International Settlements) (2008b). Monetary and Financial Stability Implications of Capital Flows in Latin America and the Caribbean, BIS Papers No. 43, November.

BIS (Bank for International Settlements) (2008c). International Banking and Financial Market Developments, *BIS Quarterly Review* December, 1–91.

Buch, C. M. and DeLong, G. L. (2001). Cross-border Bank Mergers: What Lures the Rare Animal?, Kiel Institute of World Economics Working Paper No. 1070.

Cardias Williams, F. and Williams, J. (2008). Does Ownership Explain Bank M&A? The Case of Domestic Banks and Foreign Banks in Brazil. In: P. Arestis and L. F. Paula (Eds.), *Financial Liberalization and Economic Performance in Emerging Countries*, 194–215. Basingstoke: Palgrave Macmillan.

Carvalho, F. C. (1998). The Real Stabilization Plan and the Banking Sector in Brazil, *Banca Nazionale del Lavoro Quarterly Review* 206, 291–236.

Carvalho, F. C. (2000). New Competitive Strategies of Foreign Banks in Large Emerging Economies: The Case of Brazil. *Banca Nazionale del Lavoro Quarterly Review* 213, 135–170.

Carvalho, F. C. (2002). The Recent Expansion of Foreign Banks in Brazil: First Results, *Latin American Business Review* 3(4), 93–119.

Carvalho, F. C. (2008). Financial Liberalization in Brazil and Argentina. In: P. Arestis and L. F. Paula (Eds.), *Financial Liberalization and Economic Performance in Emerging Countries*, 121–141. Basingstoke: Palgrave Macmillan.

Carvallo, O. and Kasman, A. (2005). Cost Efficiency in the Latin American and Caribbean Banking Systems, *Journal of International Financial Markets, Institutions and Money* 15, 55–72.

CGFS (Committee on the Global Financial System) (2004). Foreign Direct Investment in the Financial Sector of Emerging Market Economies. Report Submitted by a Working Group Established by the CGFS, Basel, BIS, March.

Chortareas, G., Garza-García, J. G., and Girardone, C. (2012). Competition, Efficiency and Interest Rate Margins in Latin American Banking, *International Review of Financial Analysis* 24, 93–103.

Claessens, S., Demirgüç-Kunt, A., and Huizinga, H. (2001). How Does Foreign Bank Entry Affect Domestic Banking Markets?, *Journal of Banking and Finance* 25, 891–911.

Clarke, G. R. G. and Cull, R. (2000). Why Privatize? The Case of Argentina's Public Provincial Banks, *World Development* 27, 865–886.

Clarke, G. R. G., Crivelli, J. M., and Cull, R. (2005). The Direct and Indirect Impact of Bank Privatization and Foreign Entry on Access to Credit in Argentina's Provinces, *Journal of Banking and Finance* 29, 5–29.

Coelho, C. A., de Mello, J. M. P., and Rezende, L. (2007). Are Public Banks Pro-competitive? Evidence from Concentrated Local Markets in Brazil, Pontifícia Universidade Católica do Rio de Janeiro Texto para Discussão No. 551.

Crystal, J. S., Dages, B. G., and Goldberg, L. (2002). Has Foreign Bank Entry Led to Sounder Banks in Latin America?, *Current Issues in Economics and Finance* 8(1), 1–6.

Dages, B. G., Goldberg, L., and Kinney, D. (2002). Foreign and Domestic Bank Participation in Emerging Markets: Lessons from Mexico and Argentina, *FRBNY Economic Policy Review* September, 17–36.

De la Torre, A. (2000). Resolving Bank Failures in Argentina: Recent Developments and Issues, World Bank Policy Research Working Paper Series No. 2295.

De Vries, M. G. (1987). *Balance of Payments Adjustment, 1945 to 1986: The IMF Experience.* Washington, DC: IMF.

Domanski, D. (2005). Foreign Banks in Emerging Market Economies: Changing Players, Changing Issues, *BIS Quarterly Review* December, 69–81.

ECLAC (Economic Commission for Latin American and Caribbean) (2000). *Foreign Investment in Latin America and the Caribbean—1999 Report.* Santiago: ECLAC.

Fanelli, J. M. (2003). *Estrategias para la Reconstrucción Monetaria y Financiera de la Argentina.* Buenos Aires: Siglo XXI.

Focarelli, D. and Pozzolo, A. F. (2001). The Patterns of Cross-border Bank Mergers and Shareholdings in OECD Countries, *Journal of Banking and Finance* 25, 2305–2337.

Foxley, A. (1983). *Latin American Experiments with Neo-Conservative Economics.* Berkeley: University of California Press.

Fry, M. (1995). *Money, Interest, and Banking in Economic Development.* 2nd edition. Baltimore, MD: The Johns Hopkins University Press.

Garcia-Escribano, M. (2010). Peru: Drivers of De-dollarization, Banco Central de Reserva del Perú Working Papers Series No. 2010-11, July.

Gelos, R. G. (2006). Banking Spreads in Latin America, IMF Working Paper No. WP06/44.

Gelos, R. G. and Roldós, J. (2004). Consolidation and Market Structure in Emerging Market Banking Systems, *Emerging Markets Review* 5, 39–59.

Gerschenkron, A. (1962). *Economic Backwardness in Historical Perspective.* Cambridge, MA: The Belknap Press of Harvard University Press.

Guimarães, P. (2002). How Does Foreign Entry Affect Domestic Banking Market? The Brazilian Case, *Latin American Business Review* 3(4), 121–140.

Haber, S. (2005). Mexico's Experiments with Bank Privatization and Liberalization, 1991-2003, *Journal of Banking and Finance* 29, 2325–2353.

Haber, S. and Musacchio, A. (2005). Foreign Banks and the Mexican Economy, 1997–2004. Stanford Center for International Development Working Paper.

Hawkins, J. and Mihaljek, D. (2001). The Banking Industry in the Emerging Markets Economies: Competition, Consolidation and Systemic Stability, BIS Papers No. 4, August.

Hernandez-Murillo, R. (2007). Experiments in Financial Liberalization: The Mexican Banking Sector, *Federal Reserve Bank of St Louis Review* 89(5), 415–432.

Honohan, P. (2007). Cross-country Variation in Household Access to Financial Services. Paper Prepared for World Bank Conference on Access to Finance, March 15-16.

IADB (Inter-American Development Bank) (2005). *Unlocking Credit: The Quest for Deep and Stable Bank Lending*. Washington, DC: IADB.

IMF (2007). *Global Financial Stability Report*. Washington, DC: IMF.

Jeanneau, S. (2007). Banking Systems: Characteristics and Structural Changes, BIS Papers No. 33, 3–16, February.

Kamil, H. and Rai, K. (2010). The Global Credit Crunch and Foreign Banks' Lending to Emerging Markets: Why Did Latin American Fare Better?, IMF Working Paper No. WP/10/102, April.

Martinez Peria, M. S. and Mody, A. (2004). How Foreign Participation and Market Concentration Impact Bank Spreads: Evidence from Latin America, *Journal of Money, Credit and Banking* 36(3), 511–537.

Maudos, J. and Solis, L. (2011). Deregulation, Liberalization and Consolidation of the Mexican Banking System: Effects on Competition, *Journal of International Money and Finance* 302, 337–353.

Nakane, M. I. (2001). A Test of Competition in Brazilian Banking, Banco Central do Brasil Working Paper Series No. 12.

Nakane, M. I., Alencar, L. S., and Kanczuk, F. (2006). Demand for Bank Services and Market Power in Brazilian Banking, Banco Central do Brasil Working Paper Series No. 107, June.

Nakane, M. I. and Weintraub, D. B. (2005). Bank Privatization and Productivity: Evidence for Brazil, *Journal of Banking and Finance* 29, 2259–2289.

O'Connell, A. (2005). The Recent Crisis—and Recovery—of the Argentine Economy: Some Elements and Background. In: G. Epstein (Ed.), *Financialization and the World Economy*. Cheltenham: Edward Elgar.

Oreiro, J. L. and Paula, L. F. (2010). Macroeconomic Determinants of Bank Spread in Latin America: A Recent Analysis with Special Focus on Brazil, *International Review of Applied Economics* 24(5), 573–590.

Panzar, J. C. and Rosse, J. N. (1987). Testing for Monopoly Equilibrium, *Journal of Industrial Economics* 35, 443–456.

Paula, L. F. (2002). Expansion Strategies of European Banks to Brazil and Their Impacts on the Brazilian Banking Sector, *Latin American Business Review* 3(4), 59–91.

Paula, L. F. (2011). *Financial Liberalization and Economic Performance: Brazil at the Crossroads*. London and New York: Routledge.

Paula, L. F. and Alves Jr., A. J. V. V. (2007). The Determinants and Effects of Foreign Bank Entry in Argentina and Brazil: A Comparative Analysis, *Investigación Económica* 66(259), 63–102.

Rojas Suarez, L. (2007). The Provision of Banking Services in Latin America: Obstacles and Recommendations, Center for Global Development Working Paper No. 124, June.

Schulz, H. (2006). *Foreign Banks in Mexico: New Conquistadors or Agents of Change?*. Pennsylvania: University of Pennsylvania.

Sebastián, M. and Hernansanz, C. (2000). The Spanish Banks Strategy in Latin America, SUERF Working Paper No. 9.

Sidaoui, J. (2006). The Mexican Financial System: Reforms and Evolution 1995-2005, BIS Papers No. 28, August.

Singh, A., Belaisch, A., Collyns, C., de Masi, P., Krieger, R., Meredith, G., and Rennhack, R. (2005). Stabilization and Reform in Latin America: A Macroeconomic Perspective on the Experience Since the Early 1990s, IMF Occasional Paper No. 238.

Stallings, B. and Studart, R. (2006). *Finance for Development: Latin America in Comparative Perspective*. Washington, DC: The Brookings Institution.

Studart, R. and Hermann, J. (n.d.). Sistemas Financeiros Argentino e Brasileiro, manuscript.

Tabak, B. M., Fazio, D. M., and Cajueiro, D. O. (2011). Profit, Cost and Scale Efficiency for Latin American Banks: Concentration-performance Relationship, Banco Central do Brasil Working Paper Series No. 244, May.

Tecles, P. and Tabak, B. (2010). Determinants of Bank Efficiency: The Case of Brazil, Banco Central do Brasil Working Paper Series No. 210, May.

Vasconcelos, M. R. and Fucidji, J. R. (2002). *Foreign Entry and Efficiency: Evidence from the Brazilian Banking Industry*. Brazil: State University of Maringá.

Williams, J. (2012). Efficiency and Market Power in Latin American Banking, *Journal of Financial Stability* 8, 263–276.

Yeyati, E. L. and Micco, A. (2007). Concentration and Foreign Penetration in Latin American Banking Sectors: Impact on Competition and Risk, *Journal of Banking and Finance* 31, 1633–1647.

Yildirim, H. S. and Philippatos, G. C. (2007). Restructuring, Consolidation and Competition in Latin American Banking Markets, *Journal of Banking and Finance* 31, 629–639.

INDEX

CDO *see* collateralized debt obligations
CDSs *see* credit default swaps
CEE *see* Central Eastern Europe
Central African Republic 914
central banks 431–51
  as 'bankers' banks 431, 432–40
  centralization of payments 432–50
  current threats 449–51
  daylight credit 421, 424
  emergence of 433–6
  emergency liquidity assistance 675
  impact of GFC 446–7
  key intervention rates (2007– 12) 492 Fig. 20.2
  law of reflux 433–5
  as LOLR 61–2, 437–40, 451, 489, 491–3,
    675, 711
  and LOLR liquidity injections 494–8, 497
    Tab. 20.1
  and monetary policy 440–9
  as multilateral clearing systems 435
  nominal anchor 440, 448, 450
  regulation of payment systems 436–7
  role as crisis managers 479
  role of 431–2
  rules of 432–3
  total liabilities (2008– 9) 491 Fig. 20.1
  see also discount windows
Central Eastern Europe (CEE) 964, 966, 967,
    969, 971, 973, 974, 976, 980
Central European International Bank,
    Ltd 966–7
centralization of payment systems 432–40
Cetorelli, Nicola 13–14, 18, 378–404, 807–20
CFTC *see* Commodity Futures Trading
    Commission
Chad 916
charter value 265
Chase Manhattan Corporation 93, 119
Check Clearing for the 21st Century Act
    (2003), US 830–1
checks (cheques) 410, 411–12, 413, 827, 828
Chemical Bank 93, 837
Chicago banking panic (1932) 685, 722, 726
Chicago Board of Trade (CBOT) 169
Chicago Mercantile Exchange (CME) 169
Chile 988, 989, 991, 993–4, 995, 997, 1002,
    1005, 1009
  financial crisis (1982) 706

China 938, 939, 941, 942–3, 945, 953, 954,
    955, 956, 984, 1002, 1008
  bailouts 704
  bank performance 950–1
  credit intermediation 403–4
  diversification 233
  shadow banking 381, 403–4
China Construction Bank 950
CHIPS *see* Clearinghouse Interbank
    Payments System
Chrysler 534
Čihák, Martin 18, 777–999
Citibank 162, 837, 967
Citibank Budapest Ltd 967
Citicorp merger with Travellers (1998) 124
Citigroup 83, 84, 438, 584, 706, 716, 837, 838,
    843, 945
City of London 442
Clearinghouse Interbank Payments System
    (CHIPS), US 418, 419–20, 422–3,
    483–4
click-and-mortar model 829
Clinton, President Bill 843
CLOs *see* collateralized loan obligations 369
close-out netting 98
CLTV *see* combined loan-to-value
CME *see* Chicago Mercantile Exchange
CMOs *see* collateralized mortgage obligations
collateral, criteria for 437
collateralized debt obligations (CDOs) 209,
    359–61, 382, 953
collateralized loan obligations (CLOs) 363–4,
    369, 389
collateralized mortgage obligations
    (CMOs) 161
Collins Amendment, US 104
Colombia 1004–5
combined loan-to-value (CLTV) ratios 276
commercial bank charters, US 835 Fig. 34.3,
    836
commercial bank clearing houses (CBCs), as
    lenders of last resort 482–3
commercial paper (CP) 198, 199, 209, 829
Commerzbank 129, 967
Commodity Futures Trading Commission
    (CFTC) 168
community banks 231, 233, 278, 293, 296,
    302, 601, 827, 828, 832

Printed and bound by CPI Group (UK) Ltd, Croydon, CR0 4YY